THE HOLOCA

D0263382

MARTIN GILBERT was born in London in 1936. Since 1962 he has been a Fellow of Merton College, Oxford, and since 1968 the official biographer of Sir Winston Churchill. In 1988 he completed the eighth and final volume of the Churchill biography, and in 1991 published a single-volume *Churchill, A Life*.

Among his books on the Holocaust period are *Auschwitz and the Allies* (1981) and an *Atlas of the Holocaust* (1982). He has also published a study of the struggle of the emergence of Jewish Statehood, *Exile and Return* (1978), a study of the plight of Soviet Jewry, *The Jews of Hope* (1984) and a biography *Shcharansky: Hero of Our Time* (1986), written while Shcharansky was still in captivity. Martin Gilbert lives in London, with his wife and two sons; he also has a daughter who teaches and writes.

PLEASE READ THIS BOOK
EVERY PAGE
EVERY DETAIL
NEVER FORGET

MIKE MWORO
25/4/19

ALSO BY MARTIN GILBERT

THE CHURCHILL BIOGRAPHY

Volume III *The Challenge of War 1914–1916*
Volume III (documents; in two parts)
Volume IV *The Stricken World 1917–1922*
Volume V (documents; in three parts)
Volume V *The Prophet of Truth 1922–1939*
Volume V *The Exchequer Years 1923–1929* (documents)
Volume V *The Wilderness Years 1929–1935* (documents)
Volume V *The Coming of War 1936–1939* (documents)
Volume VI *Finest Hour 1939–1941*
Volume VI *At the Admiralty 1939–1940* (documents)
Volume VI *Never Surrender 1940* (documents)
Volume VII *Road to Victory 1942–1945*
Volume VIII *'Never Despair' 1945–1965*

OTHER BOOKS

The Appeasers (with Richard Gott)
The European Powers 1900–1945
The Roots of Appeasement
Britain and Germany Between the Wars (documents)
Plough My Own Furrow: the Life of Lord Allen of Hurtwood (documents)
Servant of India: Diaries of the Viceroy's Private Secretary (documents)
Sir Horace Rumbold: Portrait of a Diplomat
Churchill: a Photographic Portrait
Churchill's Political Philosophy
Auschwitz and the Allies
Exile and Return: the Struggle for Jewish Statehood
The Jews of Hope: the Plight of Soviet Jewry Today
Jerusalem: Rebirth of a City 1838–1898
Final Journey: the Fate of the Jews in Nazi Europe
Shcharansky: Hero of Our Time
First World War
Second World War
Churchill, A Life
In Search of Churchill
Empires in Conflict: A History of the 20th Century 1900–1933
Descent into Barbarism: A History of the 20th Century 1933–1951
Challenge to Civilization: A History of the 20th Century 1952–1999

ATLASES

Recent History Atlas 1860–1960
British History Atlas
American History Atlas
Jewish History Atlas
First World War Atlas
Russian History Atlas
The Arab-Israeli Conflict: Its History in Maps
The Jews of Russia: Their History in Maps and Photographs
Jerusalem Illustrated Atlas
Children's Illustrated Bible Atlas
The Jews of Arab Lands: Their History in Maps and Photographs
Atlas of the Holocaust

THE HOLOCAUST

The Jewish Tragedy

MARTIN GILBERT

FontanaPress
An Imprint of HarperCollins*Publishers*

Fontana Press
An Imprint of HarperCollins*Publishers*
77–85 Fulham Palace Road,
Hammersmith, London W6 8JB

www.fireandwater.com

Published by Fontana Press 1987
13 15 16 14

First published in Great Britain by
Collins 1986

ISBN 0 00 637194 9

Set in Sabon

Printed in Great Britain by
Clays Ltd, St Ives plc

Dedicated to Professor Alexander Lerner,
two of whose daughters, aged five and three,
were killed by the Nazis in 1941

CONTENTS

LIST OF MAPS

LIST OF ILLUSTRATIONS

ACKNOWLEDGEMENTS

Many people have helped me with advice and encouragement since I began collecting material for this book in 1979. Special thanks are due to a number of survivors who guided me in my researches, spoke to me about their own experiences, or gave me contemporary documents connected with their own fate and that of their families.

I was particularly helped during my researches by Rabbi Hugo Gryn, who not only told me of his own experiences, but introduced me to many other survivors, and was always ready with thoughtful advice and guidance. For more than a decade, he has encouraged me to seek out, and to set down, the facts of what is, inevitably, a painful story.

Two other survivors to whom I am grateful are Ben Helfgott, who read the book in typescript, and Dr Shmuel Krakowski, who has always been most generous with his time and expert advice, derived from many years of historical research, first in Warsaw and then in Jerusalem. Other survivors who have spoken to me about their experiences, answered my queries, and given me historical material, and to whom I wish to express my most sincere thanks are Maja Abramowitch (now living in Johannesburg), Harry Balsam (London), Raya Barnea (Hadera), Arieh L. Bauminger (Jerusalem), Judge Moshe Bejski (Jerusalem), Leo Bretholz (Baltimore), Reuven Dafni (Jerusalem), Dr Szymon Datner (Warsaw), Jack Eisner (New York), Vera Elyashiv (London), Michael Etkind (London), Rebecca Fink (Ramat Aviv), Violette Fintz (Cape Town), Leslie Frankel (Johannesburg), Solomon Gisser (Montreal), Roman Halter (London), Kitty Hart (Birmingham), Rabbi Harry M. Jacobi (Zurich), Jack Kagan (London), Lilli Kopecky (Ramat Gan), Dr Luba Krugman Gurdus (New York), Erich Kulka (Jerusalem), Naphtali Lavie (New York), Lea Leibowitz (Johannesburg), Don Levin (Jerusalem), Jakub Lichterman (Cape Town), Eric Lucas (Herzliya), Helena Manaster (Haifa), Czeslaw Mordowicz (Tel Aviv), Maria Osovskaya (Beersheba), Alexander Pechersky (Rostov-on-Don), Leon Pommers (New York), Cantor Martin Rosenblum (Toronto), Dana Schwartz (Los Angeles), Helen Shabbes (Allentown), Bertha Shachovskaya (Moscow), Levi Shalit (Johannesburg), Henry Slamovich (San Francisco), Rudolf Vrba (Vancouver), Jaffa and Norris

Wallach (Haifa), Harold Werner (Miami), Freda Wineman (London), and Jack Young (London).

A special note of thanks is due to my friends in Moscow and Leningrad, among them Yakov Gorodetsky, Boris Kelman, Vladimir Lembrikov and Aba Taratuta, for providing me with historical material relating to the fate of the Jews on Soviet soil during the years of German occupation. I also received important material from Soviet printed sources from Dr Anatol Khazanov, then of Moscow, now of Jerusalem.

In the course of my researches, many other people have patiently answered my queries, and have sent me documentary material. I should like to thank, in this regard, Ora Alcalay (Head Librarian, Yad Vashem, Jerusalem), Flavio Andreis (Istituto Italiano di Cultura, London), Dr Jean Angel, Dr Yitzhak Arad (Chairman, Yad Vashem, Jerusalem), J. M. Aspden (Library Secretary, the Royal College of Surgeons of England), Baruch Bandet, Arieh Barnea, Professor Yehuda Bauer, Dr Konstantin Bazarov, Solomon Berger, Professor Yehuda Blum, Tom Bower, David Brauner (*Jerusalem Post* Archives), Teresa Ceglowska (Panstwowe Muzeum w Oswiecimiu), Deena Cohen, Peter Coombs, Francis Cuss, Lonnie Darwin (The Holocaust Library and Research Center, San Francisco), Barbara Distel (KZ-Gedenkstätte, Dachau), Dr Lucjan Dobroszycki (YIVO Institute for Jewish Research, New York), Adina Drechsler, Meira Edelstein, Dr Liliana Picciottc Fargion (Centro di Documentazione Ebraica Contemporanea, Milan), Eitan Finkelstein, Joseph Finkelstone, Clement Freud, Henning Gehrs (Nationalmuseet, Copenhagen), Sam Goldsmith, Whitney Harris, Alfred Herzka, Dr Zygmunt Hoffman (Zydowski Instytut Historyczny w Polsce, Warsaw), Celia Hurst (Archivist, Sigmund Freud Copyrights Ltd), Professor Henry R. Huttenbach, Professor Louis de Jong (Rijksinstituut voor Oorlogsdocumentatie, Amsterdam), Ida Kadane, Dr Rivka Kauli, Dr Donald Kenrick, Dr J. Kermish, Serge Klarsfeld, Stanislaw Krajewski, Dr Shmuel Krakowski (Archivist, Yad Vashem), Professor Konrad Kwiet, Dr Vera Laska, Naomi Layish, Sinai Leichter, Jack Lennard, Dr M. Lubetzky, Hadassa Modlinger (Custodian of Testimonies, Yad Vashem), Miriam Novitch (Ghetto Fighters' House, Kibbutz Lohamei Ha-gettaot), Professor Czeslaw Pilichowski (Glowna Komisja Badania Zbrodni Hitlerowskich w Polsce, Warsaw), Matthew Rinaldi, Eli M. Rosenbaum (United States Department of Justice, Washington, DC), Rafi Ruppin, Moshe Sakkis, Gustav Schildkraut, Freddie Shaw, Neal M. Sher (United States Department of Justice, Washington, DC), Dr M. R. Sheridan, R. Silbert (Librarian, *Jewish Chronicle*), Professor

Kazimierz Smolen (Panstwowe Muzeum w Oswiecimiu), Dr Shmuel Spector, Rebecca and Edith Spivack, Rabbi Charles W. Steckel, Solomon H. Stekoll, Professor J. P. Stern, Jennie Tarabulus, Ida Taratuta, Mike Tregenza, Major N. P. Uniake (Central Army Records Office, Australian Army, Melbourne), Victor West, Yigal Zafoni, K. Zeilinger (Director, Service Social Juif, Brussels), Dr Ludmila Zeldowicz and Alexander Zvielli (Archivist, *Jerusalem Post*).

Any book that deals with Jewish resistance must mention the pioneering work by Reuben Ainsztein. It was my privilege to have known him, and to have been able to discuss with him many aspects of his researches.

For their help in translating testimonies, I am grateful to Alexandra Finkelstein, Nan Greifer, Richard Grunberger, Mira Marody, Richard Sakwa, Taffy Sassoon, Michael Sherborne, and the late Halina Willets.

Important suggestions as to form and content were made by Erica Hunningher. The burden of the typing and retyping was borne by Sue Rampton, assisted in the last stages of the work by Helen Gardiner. The photographic prints were prepared, often from faded or damaged originals, by Zev Radovan, Gerry Moeran and Jean Hunt. The maps were designed specially for this volume by Terry Bicknell. The first section of photographs are from the archive of the Wiener Library, London; the second and third sections from the photographic archive of Yad Vashem.

Particular thanks are due to Professor Yehuda Bauer for his scrutiny of the text in its final stage, and for his many valuable comments and suggestions.

I am also grateful to my publishers, Helen Fraser of Fontana Paperbacks, Philip Ziegler and Carol O'Brien of Collins Publishers, and Richard Seaver of Holt, Rinehart and Winston, for their encouragement at every stage of the work.

Special thanks must go my wife Susie, who for many years has helped me to tell the story in all its aspects: the suffering, the heroism, the relentless oppression, the struggle for human dignity and – in many ways the most painful of all the tragedies of the Holocaust – the fate of the children. No one can read about those terrible years without being moved, and at times overwhelmed, by the ruthless, diabolical destruction of young life, from the tiniest baby to the teenager on the verge of what ought to have been the years of opportunity and fulfilment.

Merton College, Oxford   MARTIN GILBERT
4 September 1985

PREFACE

In the late summer of 1959, accompanied by a Polish friend, a non-Jew, I travelled by car to the River Bug near Malkinia junction, on the Warsaw–Leningrad railway. We had intended, my friend and I, both of us students, to cross the river by the road bridge marked on my pre-war map. But on reaching the river, we found that the bridge was gone: destroyed in the fighting of fifteen years before, when the Red Army had driven the Wehrmacht from eastern Poland.

It was late afternoon. From the river bank, my friend called to a peasant on the far side, who was loading wood into a small, barge-like boat. Eventually, the peasant rowed over to our side of the river, and took us back with him. We explained our purpose, and he took us to his village, half a mile away. Then he found a cart filled with logs, harnessed his horse to it, and drove us over the rough road, southwards towards the village of Treblinka.

From Treblinka village we proceeded for another mile or two, along the line of an abandoned railway through a forest of tall trees. Finally we reached an enormous clearing, bounded on all sides by dense woodland. Darkness was falling, and with it, the chill of night and a cold dew. I stepped down from the cart on to the sandy soil: a soil that was grey rather than brown. Driven by I know not what impulse, I ran my hand through that soil, again and again. The earth beneath my feet was coarse and sharp: filled with the fragments of human bone.

Twenty-two years later I returned to Treblinka. The bridge over the Bug had long been rebuilt. At the entrance to the camp was a museum, placards and explanations. Further on was the clearing, filled now with small stone monuments, each stone inscribed with the name of a town or village whose Jews had been murdered there. The sites of the railway siding and the gas chamber had been identified and marked. The railway itself had been re-created symbolically, with concrete sleepers.

I could not bend down again to disturb the soil. In the years that had passed I had learned too much of what had happened there, and of what torments had been inflicted on my fellow Jews.

The systematic attempt to destroy all European Jewry – an attempt now known as the Holocaust – began in the last week of June 1941, within hours of the German invasion of the Soviet Union. This onslaught upon Jewish life in Europe continued without respite for nearly four years. At its most intense moments, during the autumn of 1941, and again during the summer and autumn of 1942, many thousands of Jews were killed every day. By the time Nazi Germany had been defeated, as many as six million of Europe's eight million Jews had been slaughtered: if the killing had run its course, the horrific figure would have been even higher.

Jews perished in extermination camps, execution sites, ghettos, slave labour camps, and on the death marches. The testimony of those who survived constitutes the main record of what was done to the Jews during those years. The murderers also kept records, often copious ones. But the victims, the six million who were done to death, could leave no record. A few fragments of diaries, letters and scribbled messages do survive. But in the main, others must bear witness to what was done to the millions who could never tell their own story.

This book is an attempt to draw on the nearest of the witnesses, those closest to the destruction, and through their testimony to tell something of the suffering of those who perished, and are forever silent.

The preparations for mass murder were made possible by Germany's military successes in the months following the invasion of Poland in 1939. But from the moment that Adolf Hitler had come to power in Germany in 1933, the devastating process had begun. It was a process which depended upon the rousing of historic hatreds and ancient prejudice, and upon the cooperation or acquiescence of many different forces: of industry, science and medicine, of the Civil Service and bureaucracy, and of the most modern mechanisms and channels of communication. It depended also upon collaborators from countries far beyond the German border; and it depended most of all, one survivor has remarked, 'upon the indifference of bystanders in every land'.[1]

I

First steps to iniquity

FOR MANY CENTURIES, primitive Christian Europe had regarded the Jew as the 'Christ-killer': an enemy and a threat to be converted and so be 'saved', or to be killed; to be expelled, or to be put to death with sword and fire. In 1543, Martin Luther set out his 'honest advice' as to how Jews should be treated. 'First,' he wrote, 'their synagogues should be set on fire, and whatever does not burn up should be covered or spread over with dirt so that no one may ever be able to see a cinder or stone of it.' Jewish homes, he urged, should likewise be 'broken down or destroyed'. Jews should then be 'put under one roof, or in a stable, like Gypsies, in order that they may realize that they are not masters in our land.' They should be put to work, to earn their living 'by the sweat of their noses', or, if regarded even then as too dangerous, these 'poisonous bitter worms' should be stripped of their belongings 'which they have extorted usuriously from us' and driven out of the country 'for all time'.[1]

Luther's advice was typical of the anti-Jewish venom of his time. Mass expulsion was a commonplace of medieval policy. Indeed, Jews had already been driven out of almost every European country including England, France, Spain, Portugal and Bohemia. Further expulsions were to follow: in Italy Jews were to be confined to a special part of the towns, the ghetto, and, in Tsarist Russia, to a special region of the country, the 'Pale'. Expulsion and oppression continued until the nineteenth century. Even when Jews were allowed growing participation in national life, however, no decade passed without Jews in one European state or another being accused of murdering Christian children, in order to use their blood in the baking of Passover bread. This 'blood libel', coming as it did with outbursts of popular violence against Jews, reflected deep prejudices which no amount of modernity or liberal education seemed able to overcome. Jew-hatred, with its two-thousand-year-old history, could arise both as a spontaneous outburst of popular instincts, and as a deliberately fanned instrument of scapegoat politics.

The Jews of Europe reacted in different ways to such moments of hatred and peril. Some sought complete assimilation. Some fought to be accepted as Jews by local communities and national structures. Others struggled to maintain an entirely separate Jewish style of life and observance, with their own communities and religious practice.

The nineteenth century seemed to offer the Jews a change for the better: emancipation spread throughout Western Europe, Jews entered politics and parliaments, and became integrated into the cultural, scientific and medical life of every land. Aristocratic Jews moved freely among the aristocracy; middle-class Jews were active in every profession; and Jewish workers lived with their fellow workers in extreme poverty, struggling for better conditions. But in Eastern Europe, and especially in the Polish and, even more, the Ukrainian provinces of the Tsarist Europe, anti-Jewish violence often burst out into physical conflict, popular persecution, and murderous pogrom. Here, in the poorest regions of Tsarist Russia, church and state both found it expedient, from their different standpoints, to set the Jew aside in the popular mind as an enemy of Christianity and an intruder in the life of the citizen. Jealousies were fermented. Jewish 'characteristics' were mocked and turned into caricatures. The Jew, who sought only to lead a quiet, productive and if possible a reasonably comfortable life, was seen as a leech on society, even when his own struggle to survive was made more difficult by that society's rules and prejudices.

These eastern lands where prejudice was most deeply rooted spread from the Baltic to the Black Sea. Their most densely populated regions were White Russia, the Volhynia, Podolia and the Ukraine. In these regions there had existed throughout the nineteenth century and into the twentieth a four-tiered social structure, from which was to emerge the most savage of all wartime hatreds. At the top of this structure was the Pole: the 'Pan', the landowner, Roman Catholic, Polish-speaking. Next was the Ukrainian peasant: the 'Chlop', adherent to the Russian Orthodox faith, Ukrainian-speaking. Next was the *Volksdeutsch*, or Ethnic German:

descendant of German settlers who had been brought to these regions in the eighteenth century, farmer, Protestant, German-speaking. Fourth, and, in the eyes of each of the other three, last, was the Jew: resident in those regions for just as long, if not longer, eking out an existence as a pedlar or merchant, Jewish by religion, and with Yiddish as his own language, 'Jewish' also by speech.

No social mobility existed across these four divides. By profession, by language and by religion, the gulfs were unbridgeable. Pole, Ukrainian and Ethnic German had one particular advantage: each could look to something beyond the imperial and political confines of Tsarist Russia in order to assert his own ascendancy, and could call upon outside powers and forces to seek redress of wrongs and indignities. The Jew had no such avenue of redress, no expectation of an outside champion. Unable to seek help from the emerging Polish or Ukrainian nationalisms, or from German irridentism, he lacked entirely the possibility each of the other three had, that war, revolution and political change might bring about better times.

The four-tier structure of Pole, Ukrainian, Ethnic German and Jew ensured that the conditions of assimilation and emancipation which came into being in Western Europe after the French Revolution did not exist, and could not exist, east of the River Bug; that the ideals and opinions which benefited Jew and non-Jew alike throughout Western Europe in the hundred years following the destruction of the remnants of the medieval ghetto system, and much more, by Napoleon, failed to penetrate those regions in which by far the largest number of Jews were living in the hundred years between Napoleon's defeat at Waterloo and the First World War.

In the war which came to Europe in August 1914, Jews served in every army: and on opposite sides of the trenches and the wire. German Jews fought and died as German patriots, shooting at British Jews who served and fell as British patriots. Of the 615,000 German Jews in 1914, more than 100,000 served in the German army, although before 1914 Jews could enter the military academies only with difficulty, and certain regiments almost entirely excluded Jews. Man for man, the Jewish and non-Jewish war casualties were in an almost exact ratio of the respective populations. Jews and non-Jews alike fought as Germans: for duty and for the Fatherland.

The first member of the German parliament to be killed in action was a Jew, Dr Ludwig Haas, member for Mannheim: one of twelve thousand German Jews to fall on the battlefield in German uniform.[2] Jews in the Austro-Hungarian army fought Jews in the Russian, Serbian and Italian armies. When the war ended in November 1918, Jewish soldiers, sailors and airmen had filled the Rolls of Honour, the field hospitals and the military cemeteries, side by side with their compatriots under a dozen national flags.

After 1918, within the new frontiers of post-war Europe, Jews found themselves under new flags and new national allegiances. The largest single Jewish community was in the new Polish state. Here lived more than three million Jews, born in the three empires destroyed in the war: the Russian, the Austro-Hungarian and the German. In the new Hungarian kingdom lived 473,000 Jews. A similar number lived in the enlarged Rumania, and only slightly more, perhaps 490,000, in Germany. Czech Jewry numbered 350,000; French Jewry, 250,000. Other communities were smaller.

The security of the new borders depended upon alliances, treaties, and the effectiveness of the newly created League of Nations, whose covenant not only outlawed war between states, but also guaranteed the rights of minorities. In each state, old or new, the Jews looked to the local laws for protection as a minority: for equal rights in education and the professions; and for full participation in economic life.

Even as the First World War ended on the western front, more than fifty Jews were killed by local Ukrainians in the eastern Polish city of Lvov. In the then independent Ukrainian town of Proskurov, seventeen hundred Jews were murdered on 15 February 1919 by followers of the Ukrainian nationalist leader, Simon Petlura, and by the end of the year, Petlura's gangs had killed at least sixty thousand Jews. These Jews were victims of local hatreds reminiscent of Tsarist days, but on a scale unheard of in the previous century. In the city of Vilna, the 'Jerusalem of Lithuania', eighty Jews were murdered during April 1919; in Galicia, five hundred perished.[3] 'Terrible news is reaching us from Poland,' the Zionist leader Chaim Weizmann wrote to a friend on 29 November 1918. 'The newly liberated Poles there are trying to get rid of the Jews by the old and familiar method which they learnt from the Russians. Heart-rending cries are reaching us. We are doing all we can, but we are so weak!'[4]

On 18 December 1919 a British diplomat wrote an account of one such episode, during which Poles had killed a number of Jews suspected of Communist sympathies, and arrested many others. The Jewish women who had been arrested, but who had been exempted from execution, he noted, 'were kept in prison without trial and enquiry. They were stripped naked and flogged. After the flogging they were made to pass naked down a passage full of Polish soldiers. Then, on the following day, they were led to the cemetery where those executed were buried, and made to dig their own graves, then, at the last moment, they were told they were reprieved; in fact, the gendarmerie regularly tormented the survivors.' The victims, added the diplomat, 'were respectable lower middle-class people, schoolteachers and such like'.[5]

In Germany, in the immediate aftermath of the First World War, Jews were among those active in rebuilding the broken nation. Hugo Preuss, Minister of Interior of the new government, prepared the draft of the Weimar Constitution, one of the most democratic in post-war Europe. Another Jew, Walther Rathenau, served as Weimar's Minister of Reconstruction, and then as Foreign Minister.

But in the turmoil of defeat, voices were raised blaming 'the Jews' for Germany's humiliation. In Berlin, the nation's capital, there were clashes between Jews and anti-Semites: 'Indications of growing anti-Semitism', the Berlin correspondent of *The Times* reported on 14 August 1919, 'are becoming frequent.'[6]

A manifestation of this anti-Semitism was shown by one of Germany's new and tiny political parties, the National Socialist German Workers' Party, the NSDAP, soon better known as the 'Nazi' Party, after the first two syllables of 'National' – *Nazional*. The party's twenty-five-point programme was published in Munich on 25 February 1920, at a time when it had only sixty members. The essence of its programme was nationalistic, the creation of a 'Great Germany', and the return of Germany's colonies, which had been lost at the time of Germany's defeat. Point Four was a racialist one: 'None but members of the Nation', it read, 'may be citizens of the State. None but those of German blood, whatever their creed, may be members of the Nation. No Jew, therefore, may be a member of the Nation.'[7] Another point demanded that all Jews who had come to Germany since 1914 should be forced to leave: a demand which would effect more than eighteen thousand Jews, most of them born in the Polish provinces of Tsarist Russia.

The anti-Jewish sections of the Nazi Party's programme had been drafted by three members. One of them, Adolf Hitler, was number seven in the party's hierarchy. A former soldier on the western front, he had been wounded and gassed in October 1918, less than a month before the war's end. On 13 August 1920, Hitler spoke for two hours in a Munich beer cellar on the theme, 'Why we are against the Jews'. During his speech, he promised his listeners that his party, and his party alone, 'will free you from the power of the Jew!' There must, he said, be a new slogan, and one not only for Germany – 'Anti-Semites of the World, Unite! People of Europe, Free Yourselves!' – and he demanded what he called a 'thorough solution', in brief, 'the removal of the Jews from the midst of our people'.[8]

A year later, on 3 August 1921, Hitler set up a group within the Nazi Party whereby he would control his own members and harass his opponents. This *Sturmabteilung*, or 'Storm Section' of the party, was quickly to be known as the SA; its members as Stormtroops. These Stormtroops were intended, according to their first regulations, not merely to be 'a means of defence' for the new movement, but, 'above all, a training school for the coming struggle for liberty'. Stormtroops were to defend party meetings from attack, and, as further regulations expressed it a year later, to enable the movement itself 'to take the offensive at any given moment'.[9] Brown uniforms were designed; their wearers soon becoming known as Brownshirts. Parades and marches were organized. The party symbol became the *Hakenkreuz*, or swastika, an ancient Sanskrit term and symbol for fertility, used in India interchangeably with the Star of David, or *Magen David*, whose double triangle had long signified for the Jewish people a protective shield, and had become since 1897 a symbol of Jewish national aspirations.

From the Nazis' earliest days, the swastika was held aloft on flags and banners, and worn as an insignia on lapels and armbands.

By the time of the establishment of the Stormtroops, membership of the Nazi Party had risen to three thousand. Hatred of the Jews, which permeated all Hitler's speeches to his members, was echoed in the actions of his followers. Individual Jews were attacked in the street, and at public meetings and street-corner rallies Jews were blamed, often in the crudest language, for every facet of Germany's problems including the military defeat of 1918, the subsequent economic hardship, and sudden, spiralling inflation.

Hitler's party had no monopoly on anti-Jewish sentiment. Several other extremist groups likewise sought popularity by attacking the Jews. One target of their verbal abuse was Walther Rathenau, who, as Foreign Minister, had negotiated a treaty with the Soviet Union. Street demonstrators sang, 'Knock off Walther Rathenau, the dirty, God-damned Jewish sow.' These were only words, but words with the power to inspire active hatred, and on 24 June 1922, Rathenau was assassinated.

Following Rathenau's murder, Hitler expressed his pleasure at what had been done. He was sentenced to four weeks in prison. 'The Jewish people', he announced on 28 July 1922, immediately on his release, 'stands against us as our deadly foe, and will so stand against us always, and for all time.'[10] In 1923, a Nuremberg Nazi, Julius Streicher, launched *Der Sturmer*, a newspaper devoted to the portrayal of the Jews as an evil force. Its banner headline was the slogan: 'The Jews are Our Misfortune'.

On 30 October 1923 Arthur Ruppin, a German Jew who had earlier settled in Palestine, noted in his diary, while on a visit to Munich, how 'the anti-Semitic administration in Bavaria expelled about seventy of the 350 East European Jews from Bavaria during the past two weeks, and it is said that the rest will also be expelled before too long.'[11]

On 9 November 1923 Hitler tried, and failed, to seize power in Munich. Briefly, he had managed to proclaim a 'National Republic'. He was arrested, tried for high treason, and on 1 April 1924 sentenced to five years in detention.

After less than eight months in prison, Hitler was released on parole. During those eight months he had begun a lengthy account of his life and thought. Entitled *Mein Kampf*, My Struggle, the first volume was published on 18 July 1925. In it, the full fury of Hitler's anti-Jewish hatred was made clear: he explained that he was drawing upon his personal experiences as a young man in Vienna before the First World War.[12] He had come to Vienna in February 1908, shortly before his nineteenth birthday, and had remained there until May 1913.[13]

Every page of Hitler's recollections contained references to the

Jews of Vienna and their evil influence. 'The part which the Jews played in the social phenomenon of prostitution,' he wrote, 'and more especially in the white slave traffic, could be studied here better than in any other West European city,' with the possible exception, he added, of 'certain ports' in southern France: 'a cold shiver ran down my spine when I first ascertained that it was the same kind of cold-blooded, thick-skinned and shameless Jew who showed his consummate skill in conducting that revolting exploitation of the dregs of the big city. Then I became filled with wrath.'[14]

There were, Hitler argued, two perils threatening 'the existence of the German people', Marxism and Judaism.[15] It was in Vienna, he wrote, that he had discovered the truth about the Jewish conspiracy to destroy the world of the 'Aryan', by means of political infiltration and corruption, using as its tool the Social Democratic Party, and as its victim, the working class. This word 'Aryan' was a linguistic term, originally referring to the Indo-European group of languages. Since before the end of the nineteenth century it had already been distorted as a concept by a number of writers, among them Houston Stewart Chamberlain, who gave it racial connotations, and used it to denote superiority over the 'Semitic' races. Yet the term 'Semitic' itself was originally not a racial but a linguistic term, relating, not to Jews and non-Jews, but to a language group which includes Hebrew and Arabic. None of these refinements troubled the new racialism. For Hitler, 'Aryan' was synonymous with 'pure', while 'Semitic' was synonymous with 'Jew', and hence 'impure'.

Considering the 'satanic skill' displayed by Jewish 'evil councillors', Hitler wrote, 'how could their unfortunate victims be blamed?' The Jewish politicians were masters of 'dialectical perfidy', their very mouths 'distorted the truth'. Marxism was a Jewish device, a Jewish trap. 'The more I came to know the Jew, the easier it was to excuse the workers.'[16]

Hitler presented himself as the man who had seen, and who would prevent, not only the destruction of German life, but the destruction of life on earth, by 'the Jew'. The dangers, as he saw them, concerned the racial integrity of the German people, and a deliberate assault on that integrity. As he told his readers:

> The black-haired Jewish youth lies in wait for hours on end, satanically glaring at and spying on the unsuspicious girl whom

he plans to seduce, adulterating her blood and removing her from the bosom of her own people.

The Jew uses every possible means to undermine the racial foundations of a subjugated people. In his systematic efforts to ruin girls and women he strives to break down the last barriers of discrimination between him and other peoples.

The Jews were responsible for bringing negroes into the Rhineland, with the ultimate idea of bastardizing the white race which they hate and thus lowering its cultural and political level so that the Jew might dominate.

For as long as a people remain racially pure and are conscious of the treasure of their blood, they can never be overcome by the Jew. Never in this world can the Jew become master of any people except a bastardized people.

For this reason, Hitler added, 'the Jew systematically endeavours to lower the racial quality of a people by permanently adulterating the blood of the individuals who make up that people.'[17]

In *Mein Kampf* Hitler outlined his mission: to expose, and then to destroy the threat posed by a worldwide Jewish effort to destroy the foundations of 'Aryan' life. 'Was there any shady undertaking,' he asked, 'any form of foulness, especially in cultural life, in which at least one Jew did not participate?' and he went on to answer his own question in these words: 'On putting the probing knife carefully to that kind of abscess one immediately discovered, like a maggot in a putrescent body, a little Jew who was often blinded by the sudden light.'[18]

Germany could only become a great nation again, Hitler argued, if it saw, and repelled, the Jewish danger. Germany's defeat in 1918 could have been prevented, but for 'the will of a few Jews': traitors inside the German Reich.[19] 'There is no such thing', Hitler concluded, 'as coming to an understanding with the Jews. It must be the hard-and-fast "Either-Or".'[20]

In his book, Hitler described the mission that inspired him, telling his readers:

> Should the Jew, with the aid of his Marxist creed, triumph over the people of this world, his Crown will be the funeral wreath of mankind, and this planet will once again follow its

orbit through ether, without any human life on its surface, as it did millions of years ago.

And so I believe today that my conduct is in accordance with the will of the Almighty creator. In standing guard against the Jew I am defending the handiwork of the Lord.[21]

There was little reason for anyone to heed such hate-mongering in the summer of 1925. The Weimar republic was scarcely halfway through its first decade, slowly establishing a democratic, parliamentary regime. The twin economic pressures of reconstruction and the payment of reparations to the Allies were being lessened year by year. The crisis of whirlwind inflation had passed. Employment was slowly rising. International conferences offered Germany, for the first time since her defeat, equal participation in European diplomacy. On 16 October 1925, three months after the publication of Hitler's first, bitter, obscure volume, Germany signed the Locarno Agreement, guaranteeing, as an equal partner with Britain, France, Belgium and Italy, the frontiers of Western Europe.

Under Article Two of Locarno, Germany and France, as well as Germany and Belgium, mutually undertook 'that they will in no case attack or invade each other or resort to war against each other'.[22] These undertakings offered the prospect of security for the war-weary masses of all the signatory states, which included Poland and Czechoslovakia.

For the eight million Jews of Europe, Locarno seemed to offer the prospect of a quiet life. Several years had passed since the Ukrainian massacres of 1918 and 1919. But in at least one Jew's mind, vengeance was called for. His name was Shalom Schwarzbard – his Hebrew first name meaning 'Peace'. On 25 May 1926, in Paris, he killed the exiled Ukrainian leader, Simon Petlura. 'I am performing a duty for our poor people,' he had written to his wife a few hours earlier. 'I am going to avenge all the pogroms, the blood. . . .'[23]

On 10 December 1926 Hitler published the second volume of *Mein Kampf*. Once again, anti-Jewish venom permeated its pages. 'At the beginning of the war,' Hitler wrote, 'or even during the war, if twelve or fifteen thousand of these Jews who were corrupting the nation had been forced to submit to poison gas, just as hundreds of thousands of our best German workers from every social stratum and from every trade and calling had to face it in the field, then the millions of sacrifices made at the front would not have been in vain.' On the contrary, Hitler continued, 'if twelve thousand of these malefactors had been eliminated in proper time, probably the lives of a million decent men, who would be of value to Germany in the future, would have been saved.'[24]

These were still the writings of an extremist with no prospect of political influence, let alone power. In 1926 his party's member-ship stood at seventeen thousand, among them the black-uniformed *Schutzstaffeln*, 'Protection Squad', or SS, set up a year earlier to provide Hitler and the Nazi leadership with personal protection: a personal security service. It was all on a small, if noisy, scale.

On 4 July 1926 a youth movement had been inaugurated for young Nazis: the Hitler Youth. In 1927 the Nazi membership rose to forty thousand. The uniformed Stormtroops were active on the streets: brutal thugs, with a political party to give them respect-ability.

In May 1928, the Nazi Party participated in the German national elections, securing twelve seats in the Reichstag.

European democracy did not seem to be endangered by such apparently minor developments. Germany, disarmed, by the Treaty of Versailles, posed no military threat to its neighbours. The Locarno Agreement, signed with such high hopes, continued to serve as an apparent guarantee of stability. Germany's remain-ing reparations payments were being rapidly reduced by negotia-tions.

Suddenly events began to favour Hitler and his followers. Inflation began to rise again. Unemployment grew to unprecedented levels. The growth of German Communist support triggered a reaction on the right. Extremism replaced the Weimar democratic ideal.

The internal problems which had given the Nazis their first few seats continued to worsen. Unemployment rose yet again, reaching three million by the end of 1929. Both workers and employers were its victims. Small businessmen suffered equally with those on the factory floor. As the economic distress grew, the Nazis denounced Jewish 'wealth' and 'conspiracy'. In Berlin on 1 January 1930, brown-uniformed Stormtroops killed eight Jews: the first Jewish victims of the Nazi era. For the next nine months, Jews were molested in cafés and theatres, and synagogue services were constantly interrupted by these uniformed hooligans, already dignified by the title 'Party Members'.[25]

An election was called for mid-September 1930. During the campaign, the Stormtroops were again active in terrorizing Jews as well as Communist voters and other political opponents. In the course of the campaign, seventy-eight Jews were among those wounded by SA thugs. The election itself was held on 14 September 1930. To the amazement of election-watchers in Germany and abroad, the number of Nazi seats rose from 12 to 107. With more than six million votes, the Nazi Party was now the second largest party in the state.[26] On the day the Reichstag opened, several Jews were attacked in Berlin, and the windows of Jewish-owned department stores were broken. As the Nazi deputies walked to the Reichstag, their supporters in the crowd chanted one of the party's popular slogans, '*Deutschland erwache, Juda verrecke!*', 'Germany awake, death to Judah!'

On 15 March 1931 Nazi Party officials were told: 'The natural hostility of the peasant against the Jews, and his hostility against the Freemason as a servant of the Jew, must be worked up to a frenzy.'[27] Six months later, on the eve of the Jewish New Year, squads of young Stormtroops attacked Jews returning from synagogue. An eye-witness recorded how, in one incident, 'while three youths beat an elderly gentleman with their fists and rubber truncheons, five other young men stood around to protect them.'[28]

The strong helping the strong to attack the weak; this was to become a hallmark of Nazi action. So too was the deliberate choice of a Holy Day in the Jewish calendar and of a religious target. In 1931 alone, fifty synagogues were desecrated, and several thousand tombstones defiled in more than a hundred Jewish cemeteries.[29]

Frequent though they were, it was not these anti-Jewish actions, but the spectre of unemployment that made daily headlines throughout Germany, providing the Nazis with a massive source of discontent, recruits and votes. In the election for President in June 1932, which the incumbent President, Field Marshal Hindenburg, won with 53 per cent of the ballot, the former corporal, Adolf Hitler, came second, winning over 36 per cent of the votes cast. The Communist candidate, Ernst Thälmann, received only one in ten of the votes. Of the two extremes, Nazism had proved the more attractive. It was also the more effectively organized: in 1931 the SS, organized and enlarged by Heinrich Himmler, established its own Intelligence Service, the *Sicherheitsdienst*, or SD, headed by Reinhard Heydrich, to keep a close watch on dissent within the party.

In further national elections on 31 July 1932, the Nazi Party won 230 seats in the Reichstag. Hitler had now established enough power to form a government in coalition with others. But he declined to accept second place, refusing to agree to a coalition unless he were Chancellor. At further elections three months later, on 6 November 1932, Nazi votes and seats both fell. Hitler's opponents declared that the Nazi movement was on the wane: that its chances of power were ended.

With 196 seats, a loss of 34, Hitler was outnumbered by the combined forces of the Socialists and Communists. But his opponents on the left lacked sufficient unity, or sense of danger, to combine. A prolonged political crisis led to negotiations, and negotiations led to a compromise. The parties of the centre and the right agreed to accept Hitler as Chancellor, at the head of the coalition in which they would share Cabinet seats and power. Hitler agreed, and on 30 January 1933 was appointed Chancellor. He was forty-three years old.

'I had been skating that day,' a ten-year-old Jewish boy, Leslie Frankel, who lived in the village of Biblis, near Worms, later recalled. 'When I got home,' Frankel added, 'we heard that Hitler had become Chancellor. Everybody shook. As kids of ten we shook.'[30]

2

1933:
the shadow of the swastika

HITLER MOVED RAPIDLY to establish his dictatorship. An Emergency Decree, passed by the Reichstag on 5 February 1933, expropriated all Communist Party buildings and printing presses, and closed down all pacifist organizations. In the following week, the Stormtroops, now buoyed up by the enthusiasm of the constitutional victory, attacked trade union buildings, and beat up political opponents in the streets.

Three weeks after the passing of the Emergency Decree, Hitler found the opportunity to take a second step towards dictatorship, when on February 27, fire broke out in the Reichstag building. Even before the blaze had been extinguished, and long before any guilt could be established, the Nazis had demanded new rules concerning 'protective custody', and these rules, legalizing arbitrary imprisonment without warrant or trial, came into effect on February 28, followed immediately by mass arrests, and a settling of accounts with political opponents. One of those arrested, a Berliner by the name of Bernstein, was given fifty lashes because he was a Communist, and then a further fifty lashes because he was 'also a Jew'.[1]

On March 9 the Stormtroops were active throughout Berlin. Many Jews were beaten, the *Manchester Guardian* reported, 'until the blood streamed down their heads and faces, and their backs and shoulders were bruised. Many fainted and were left lying on the streets. . . .' The Stormtroops worked in groups of between five and thirty men, 'the whole gang often assaulting one person'.[2]

The terror in the streets was witnessed by foreign diplomats and journalists from the world press. But from March 9, terror found a hidden base behind barbed wire. For, beginning on that day, the SS sent thousands of critics of the regime, including many Jews, to a so-called 'concentration camp', at Dachau, near Munich. The camp, 'empty huts in a gravel pit', was run by the local Dachau SS, which had already become notorious as 'one of the most savage and brutal SS platoons in Bavaria'.[3]

During March 1933 Dachau was enlarged to enable five thousand prisoners to be kept there. Meanwhile, the terror in the streets continued. On March 11, Jewish-owned department stores in Braunschweig were looted. On March 13, all Jewish lawyers and judges were expelled from court in Breslau. On March 15, in Berlin, three Jews were arrested by Stormtroops in the Café New York, taken to a local Stormtroop headquarters, robbed of all their money, 'beaten bloody with rubber truncheons, and then turned out in the streets in a semi-conscious state'.[4]

All over Germany, Jews, as well as non-Jewish critics of the regime, were attacked and beaten. Against the Jews, these so-called Einzeloperationen, or 'individual operations', were carried out against shopkeepers, rabbis and communal leaders. 'A considerable number of people were arrested without any reason at all,' a Berlin lawyer, Benno Cohn, later recalled, 'and among them were a considerable number of Jews.'[5] One of these Jews was a baker's apprentice, Siegbert Kindermann. Before Hitler's coming to power, Kindermann, a member of the Bar Kochba Jewish Sports Society, had been attacked by Nazi thugs. His attackers had been brought to court, and convicted. Now the thugs took their revenge. On March 18 Kindermann was taken to a Stormtroop barracks in Berlin and beaten to death. His body was then thrown out of a window into the street. Those who found his body discovered that a large swastika had been cut into his chest.[6]

An imminent boycott of Jewish shops, publicized outside Germany, led to considerable protest. On March 27 a mass rally in New York's Madison Square Garden threatened a counter-boycott of all German-made goods, until the anti-Jewish boycott was called off.[7] The Nazi leaders therefore limited themselves to a one-day, Sabbath, boycott of all Jewish-owned shops, cafés and businesses. 'The Jews of the whole world are trying to destroy Germany,' posters declared in every German city. 'German people, defend yourselves! Don't buy from the Jews!'[8]

The boycott began at ten in the morning of Saturday, April 1. Stormtroops, standing outside Jewish-owned shops, carried placards urging 'Germans' not to enter. The Star of David was painted

GERMANY 1933

in yellow on black across the doors and windows of thousands of shops, and, in crude lettering, the single word *Jude*, 'Jew', the sign of the swastika, and the slogans, 'Perish Judah!', 'Jews, Out!', 'Go to Palestine!' and 'Go to Jerusalem!'

'On every Jew shop', wrote Lady Rumbold, the wife of the British Ambassador in Berlin, 'was plastered a large notice warning people not to buy in Jewish shops. In many cases special notices were put up saying that sweated labour was employed in that particular shop, and often you saw caricatures of Jewish noses.' It was, she added, 'utterly cruel and Hunnish the whole thing, just doing down a heap of defenceless people.' 'To see people pilloried in this fashion,' she wrote three days later, 'a very large number of them quite harmless, hardworking people, was altogether revolting, and left a very nasty taste in the mouth. I shall never forget it.'[9]

German Jews were stunned by this organized, absurd, cruel display, which Hitler's Minister of Propaganda, Dr Joseph Goebbels, described in his diary as 'an imposing spectacle'.[10] During the course of the day of the boycott, one Jew was killed, a lawyer by the name of Schumm, who had been arrested at Kiel after an altercation with a Stormtrooper, taken to Stormtroop headquarters, and shot. This 'lynching', as it was described, was headline news in almost every British newspaper on the following Monday morning.[11] 'As a matter of fact,' Hitler declared in his first speech after the boycott, 'the Jews in Germany had not had a hair of their heads rumpled.'[12]

The Jews of Germany had been among Europe's most assimilated, most cultured, most active contributors to the national life of the state in which they lived. Hundreds of thousands of them had become an integral part of German society. They had made significant contributions to German medicine, literature, science, music and industry. 'They could not possibly believe', Benno Cohn later recalled, 'that this cultured German nation, the one which was the most cultured of the peoples of the world since time immemorial, would resort to such iniquitous things.'[13]

The impact of the one-day boycott was considerable. 'Many Jews on this Saturday were depressed,' wrote the editor of the German-language *Judische Rundschau*, Robert Weltsch, in his editorial on April 4. They had been 'forced to admit their Jewishness', not for 'an inner conviction, not for loyalty to their people, not for their pride in a magnificent history and in noblest human achievement', but by 'the affixing of a red placard or a yellow badge', and by the sticking of placards to their windows, and the daubing of their window-panes.

During these boycott activities, the Stormtroops had painted the Star of David on the windows of Jewish-owned shops. 'They meant to dishonour us,' Weltsch noted, and went on to declare: 'Jews, take it upon yourselves, that Star of David, and honour it anew.'

In his editorial, Weltsch expressed his hope that the Nazi movement, 'which took such pride, as a pioneer, in raising the pride of the

German nation, will not find work to be done in the degradation of others.' But if it were to do so, 'we, the Jewish people, will be able to defend our pride.'[14]

On April 7 the concept of a racial difference between German Jews and all other Germans was given legal status when the German government ordered the dismissal – called in the Order 'retirement' – of all civil servants 'who are not of Aryan descent'.[15] By giving German non-Jews the status of 'Aryan', this imaginary concept, based upon nonsensical and discredited theories of 'purity of race', Hitler formally divided German citizens into two groups. 'The greatest achievements in intellectual life', Hitler told the German Doctors' Union, 'can never be produced by those of an alien race, but only by those who are inspired by the Aryan and German spirit.'[16]

German cities competed in zealous pursuit of the new 'Aryan' ideal. In Frankfurt, on the day of this first 'Aryan law', German Jewish teachers were forbidden to teach in the universities, German Jewish actors to perform on the stage, and German Jewish musicians to play in concerts. The very concept of 'German Jewish' was being denied and denounced: one could either be a German, or one could be a Jew.

To terrorize political opponents, churchmen, Communists, homosexuals and Jews, the new government set up concentration camps at Esterwegen and Sachsenhausen, in addition to Dachau. In each of these camps, daily beatings and harsh treatment quickly became the rule. By the beginning of April 1933, at Dachau, there were less than a hundred Jews among the thousand German citizens being held without warrant, or trial. News of conditions in the concentration camps circulated both inside and outside Germany. 'This Nazi revolution', wrote the British Ambassador in Berlin, Sir Horace Rumbold, to a diplomatic colleague, 'has brought out some of the worst characteristics in the German character, namely, a mean spirit of revenge, brutality amounting in many cases to bestiality, and complete ruthlessness.'[17]

Rumbold's letter was dated 11 April 1933. On the following day, in Dachau, four Jews died as a result of deliberate sadism. An eye-witness account of their deaths was smuggled to Britain by a prisoner who was later released. 'A few days ago', he wrote, 'we were going out as usual to work. All of a sudden the Jewish prisoners – Goldmann and Erwin Kahn, merchants, Benario, a lawyer from Nuremberg, and a medical student, Artur Kahn – were ordered to fall out of the ranks. Without even a word, some Stormtroop men shot at them; they had not made any attempt to escape. All were killed on the spot. All had bullet wounds in their foreheads.' The four Jews were buried openly, the SS being present. 'Then a meeting was called, and a Stormtroop leader made a speech in which he told us that it was a good thing these four Jewish sows were dead. They had been hostile elements who had no right to live in Germany; they had received their due punishment.'[18]

German Jews acted as best they could to ameliorate their situation. On April 13 a group of Jewish bankers, community leaders and Zionists established in Berlin a Central Bureau for Relief and Rehabilitation. But on that same day, at Berlin University, notices appeared on the campus: 'Against the un-German spirit'. 'Our most dangerous opponent', these notices declared, 'is the Jew. The Jew can only think Jewish. If he writes German, he is lying. The German who writes German and thinks Jewish is a traitor.'

The first Jews had reached German soil in Roman times. Jews had lived in Germany for more than a thousand years. The Jewish contribution to Germany's sacrifices in the Great War had been a source of pride to the German Jewish community. Jews had been among the leading rebuilders of Germany after the defeat of 1918, and among those who suffered most severely from the post-war economic turmoils. All this was now to be forgotten, or denied. 'We mean to treat the Jew as a foreigner,' the Berlin University placards stated.[19] Twelve days later, the German government passed an Act 'against the excessive number of students of foreign race in German schools and universities'. Under the Act, German Jews were to be considered 'of foreign race'.[20]

Throughout Germany, Jews were singled out for violent assault. On April 22 a press report from Wiesbaden stated blandly that a Jewish merchant, Salomon Rosenstrauch, was 'shot in his flat'.[21] On the following day, at Worms, another Jewish merchant, Mathau Frank, was hanged, six days after his sixty-sixth birthday.[22]

On April 26 the *Geheime Staatspolizei*, or Secret State Police, was taken over by the Nazis. Known as the Gestapo, it was given powers to shadow, arrest, interrogate and intern, without reference to any other state authority. The apparatus of dictatorship was now complete: the SS security service; its SD intelligence arm; the Gestapo secret police; and the concentration camps to which their victims could be consigned. Law courts, and due process of law, defence lawyers, and appeal courts, became things of the past.

Expulsion of Jews from the universities was rapid and total. On learning that the Nobel Prize-winning chemist, Fritz Haber, had been deprived of his professorship, *The Times* commented on the 'irony' that Germany's ability to carry on fighting for four years in the First World War 'was in all probability due to him more than to any other man'.[23] Another distinguished professor, Martin Wolff, the leading German authority on civil law, was driven out of his lecture room by swastika-wearing students. Albert Einstein was forced into exile. 'We do not want to be the land of Goethe and Einstein,' declared Berlin's Nazi newspaper, linking Goethe's cultural genius with Einstein's Jewishness.[24] Within two weeks it had been announced that no Jewish painter, no Jewish sculptor, and no engineer was to be represented at the annual Academy Exhibition: 'Even Jewish artists who were at the front', it was reported, 'have been excluded from exhibitions.'[25]

'When I hear the word culture, I get my Browning pistol ready': hundreds of theatre audiences cheered at these lines, spoken by the hero in a play by Hans Johst. On May 10, in front of the Berlin Opera House, and opposite the main entrance to Berlin University, thousands of books were burned in a massive bonfire: books judged degenerate by the Nazis. Many of these were by Jewish authors.

The burning of books, and the killing of individuals, went on side by side. On the day before the book-burning, Dr Meyer, a Jewish dentist in Wuppertal, was mutilated by Stormtroops, and then drowned.[26] In Dachau, in the last two weeks of May, four Jews were murdered: Dr Alfred Strauss, a lawyer, on May 15; Louis Schloss, a businessman, on May 25; Karl Lehburger, a businessman, on May 27; and Willi Aron, a lawyer, two days later.[27]

Jews reacted in different ways to the renewed violence. A few, in despair, committed suicide. Thousands left Germany as exiles, abandoning their possessions, friends and lifetime links and associations. More than five thousand emigrated to Palestine. Most German Jews waited, however, hoping that the storm would pass.

In Upper Silesia, the Jews found a legal means of protection. This pre-war region of Germany had been incorporated in post-war

Germany as a result of a League of Nations plebiscite, and would remain under the legal protection of the League until 1937. A Jewish office worker there, Franz Bernheim, who had been dismissed as a result of the new German racial laws, appealed to the League for redress. His appeal was discussed by the League Council on May 30, and again five days later. 'It was no easy matter', the historian Nathan Feinberg has noted, 'for a persecuted people without a country to compete against the might of such a major power as Germany.'[28]

Bernheim's petition was upheld, and a Mixed Commission of the League, headed by a Swiss diplomat, Felix Calonder, ensured that the Jews of Upper Silesia could practise law and medicine, as well as receive official funds for education, at least until the expiry of the Geneva Convention four years later.

The Nazis did not like to defer to the League in Upper Silesia. But Nazi Germany, for all its internal anger, was still disarmed, still looking for international approval, still seeking to match dictatorship at home with respectability abroad. The Nazi press made no secret, however, of the national goal. 'We must build up our state without Jews,' the party newspaper declared on 26 June 1933. 'They can never be anything but stateless aliens, and they can never have any legal or constitutional status. Only by this means can Ahasuerus be forced once again to take up his wanderer's staff.'[29]

Jews outside Germany watched Nazi Germany's words and actions with alarm. Most fearful were the three million Jews of Poland, Germany's eastern neighbour, and themselves often the victims of popular anti-Semitic incidents. In Warsaw, a young Jewish historian, Emanuel Ringelblum, was so distressed by events in Germany that he decided, as he wrote on June 2, to begin 'the intensive collection of materials relating to the Hitler decrees' – photographs, letters, documents, posters – as well as material on 'Jewish countermeasures'.[30] On July 14, in the Polish city of Vilna, on the day on which, in Berlin, the Nazi Party was declared the only legal party in Germany, Dr Jacob Wigodsky wrote in a Vilna newspaper: 'We must continue to fight against the Hitler pogroms. We are fighting for the equal rights of all, everywhere in the world, but first and foremost, equal rights for us.'[31] In Warsaw, during the summer of 1933, Polish Jews boycotted German-made goods, and

Jewish students threw stink bombs in cinemas showing German films.[32]

On July 30 the editor of *Der Sturmer*, Julius Streicher, newly appointed Reich Commissar for Franconia, gave orders that 250 Jewish tradesmen in Nuremberg, Franconia's capital, should be arrested, 'and set to plucking the grass out of a field with their teeth'.[33]

By the end of July, more than twenty-six thousand Germans had been taken in to the 'protective custody' of concentration camps or Gestapo prisons. Many of those arrested were Jews who had been members of the Social Democratic and Communist parties. Others were lawyers who, in the days of the Weimar Republic, had defended individual workers or trade union organizations. Many Jewish businessmen and shopkeepers were also arrested. In a single town, Regensburg, where the Jewish community numbered 427 members, more than a hundred Jews had been taken into 'protective custody' by the beginning of August 1933, while others, endangered by street violence, 'had requested to be arrested in order to assure their personal safety'.[34]

Among those Jews killed in August were Felix Fechenbach, a Jewish editor from Detmold, who was killed at Dachau on August 7, and Julius Rosemann, Area Secretary of the Miners' Union in Hamm, shot dead on August 22. Throughout the month, Jews continued to be expelled from public and private organizations: in the third week of August the Central Association for German Deaf excluded all Jewish members. In Berlin, thirty-two deaf Jews were expelled from the local deaf relief organization, among them an old woman who had been a member of the organization for fifty-seven years, since 1876. At the same time, all elderly deaf members lost the monthly financial relief to which they were entitled as a result of payment of their subscriptions over many years.[35]

In October 1933, a new disciplinary and punishment code was introduced at Dachau, intended to make the camp a 'Model Concentration Camp', in which absolute compliance with orders would be assured by the strictest of penalties. 'Agitators', the new regulations stated, 'are to be hanged by virtue of the Law of the Revolution.'[36]

News of individual Jewish deaths in Dachau continued to reach the West. On October 10 Dr Theo Katz who had worked in the camp hospital was killed. Also in October, Dr Albert Rosenfelder, a Jewish lawyer, disappeared while in his cell, and was never heard of again.[37]

By the end of October 1933, placards had appeared on thousands of cafés, sports stadiums, shops, and roads leading to towns and villages: 'Jews not wanted'. In some villages, the names of the Jewish war dead were erased from the war memorials.

As 1933 came to an end, the half million Jews of Germany could look back over a year in which thirty-six Jews had been murdered, six killed in the course of 'mob outrages', and three others killed 'while trying to escape'.[38] It had also been a year of mass emigration. The Nazi aim was to eliminate Jewish influence from every facet of German life. They had no objection to emigration. In 1933, 5,392 German Jews sought entry, and were admitted, to Palestine.[39] A further thirty thousand German Jews left for elsewhere in Western Europe, for Britain, and for the United States.

In the last week of October 1933, in reaction to the growth in Jewish immigrants to Palestine, Arab rioters attacked public buildings in Nablus, Jaffa and Jerusalem. The British drove back the rioters, leaving twenty-six Arabs dead. Nazi propaganda broadcasts, beamed to Palestine, Syria and Egypt, helped ensure Arab hostility towards the Jewish immigrants would be kept as high as possible. In its turn, this Arab hostility ensured that the British Mandate authorities would be forced to look again, in due course, at their immigration laws, and to restrict Jewish entry into the Jewish National Home proclaimed in 1917 at the very moment when such entry had become a matter of urgent need.

3

Towards disinheritance

EARLY IN 1934, the campaign to create 'Jew-free' villages gathered momentum. A typical episode took place that February, when Stormtroops entered the village of Arnswalde, in Pomerania, and at a given signal hurled stones at all Jewish houses, shops and meeting halls. Breaking into the synagogue, and into the house of the rabbi, the Stormtroops destroyed the furnishings, tore up and trampled on the Torah, and extinguished the Eternal Lamp. Throughout the night, Jewish homes were attacked, and Jews, if caught, beaten up in the street. On the following morning, most of the Jews left the village. That same morning, German children on their way to school helped themselves to toothpaste, soap and sponges lying in the wreckage of a Jewish chemist's shop, 'while parents and teachers looked on'.[1]

A month later, on Palm Sunday, a member of Julius Streicher's personal bodyguard, Kurt Baer, marched at the head of a squad of Stormtroops into Gunzenhausen, his parents' home village, and also the home of nineteen Jewish families, small shopkeepers, craftsmen and innkeepers. Baer ordered these Jews to be dragged from their homes, and from the cellars in which they had hidden. He himself dragged one Jewish woman through the streets by her hair. Throughout the night, the Jews were beaten, whipped and cursed: and on the following morning two Jews were found dead, a seventy-five-year-old man, Rosenfelder, his chest torn open with knife wounds, and a thirty-year-old man, Rosenau, hung on a garden fence.[2]

The fanning of popular resentment and physical attack was not only against wealthy Jews, or those who had supported the democratic parties, or the Communists. It was an assault upon every Jew in Germany: an attempt to turn all German Jewry into an outcast, fit only for persecution, harassment and expulsion. The Jew would be driven from every profession, and then from the life of the nation. On 1 May 1934 *Der Sturmer* gave vent to this all-embracing hatred in a special fourteen-page issue by reviving the medieval 'blood libel' accusation against the Jews of using Christian blood in the baking of their Passover bread, and in other 'Judaic' rituals.

This 'ritual murder' issue, of which 130,000 copies were printed and sold, and which was displayed on public noticeboards, reproduced an old engraving showing four rabbis sucking the blood of a Christian child through straws. There was also a photograph of a dead child, with the caption 'Slaughtered on 17 March, 1929, near Manau, shortly before the Jewish Passover'. Eleven columns listed alleged ritual murders from 169 BC until 1929.

This issue of *Der Sturmer* also portrayed the Christian Holy Communion as yet another example of a Jew, Jesus, drinking Christian blood in the Communion ceremony. Two weeks after it was published, and following protests from the Christian churches about this particular portrayal, Hitler ordered the issue banned, 'owing', it was explained, 'to an attack on Christ's Holy Communion'. But copies of the issue were still widely available throughout that summer.[3] Nor was there any lessening of the demand for 'Jew-free' villages. On May 26, a German newspaper described how, at Hersbruck in Franconia, Streicher's province, 'on Thursday at 5 p.m. the swastika flag was hoisted on the property of the last Jew to leave Hersbruck. The Hersbruck district is now definitely purged of Jews. With pride and satisfaction the population takes cognizance of this fact. . . .' The newspaper was convinced that other districts 'will soon follow suit and that the day is not now far off when the whole of Franconia will be rid of Jews, just as one day that day must dawn when throughout the whole of Germany there will no longer be one single Jew.'[4]

On June 3 the Jewish community of Worms celebrated the nine hundredth anniversary of the foundation of its Old Synagogue. No single city official or non-Jew participated in the ceremony. According to legend, in Roman times the Jews of Worms had declined to participate in the Sanhedrin elections in Jerusalem, claiming to have built their own 'new' Jerusalem on the banks of the Rhine. Now, in common with every German Jewish community, the Jews of Worms had to decide whether to ride out a storm which would pass, or to leave. In 1933, sixty Jews had left Worms for France, forty-three for Palestine, and thirty-two for Poland. The idea that the storm might travel to France or Poland did not arise: no man could foresee the unforeseeable. In 1934 the exodus from Worms continued, twenty-nine Jews going to the United States and twenty-six to Palestine. By the end of 1934 a total of 264 Jews, nearly a quarter of the Worms community, had left Germany.[5]

The pressures to leave were continuous. On 14 June 1934 a special court at Nuremberg sentenced the non-Jewish wife of a Jew to four months in prison as a 'race-defiling female'.[6]

In the Nazi perspective, the rule of law went parallel with the rule of fear and the rule of the gun. On 15 July 1934 Kurt Baer shot dead two Jews, Simon Straus and his son, who had given evidence against him after he had been accused of the killing of the two other Jews in Gunzenhausen in March. At the trial, the court had found that the two murdered Jews had 'definitely committed suicide', while Baer was found guilty only of 'a breach of the peace'. Baer's vengeance against Straus and his son, bringing the number of Jews whom he had murdered to four, went unpunished.[7]

Success for the continuing Nazi broadcasts to the Arab world, through Radio-Berlin and Radio-Stuttgart, came on August 3, with the beginning of three days of anti-Jewish riots in the Algerian city of Constantine. In three days, twenty-three Jews were killed, and thirty-eight wounded.[8] But Arab unrest could not staunch the flow of German refugees, either to Palestine or elsewhere. In 1934 a total of 6,941 German Jews were admitted to Palestine.[9]

By the end of 1934, more than fifty thousand German Jews had left Germany. About four hundred and fifty thousand remained. Ten years later, two Jewish historians, Arieh Tartakower and Kurt Grossman, experts on the refugee question, wrote, of 1933 and 1934: 'During this first period, the refugee movement had a rather tentative character. To many it seemed that the anti-Jewish excesses would pass, to be followed by a new Jewish policy, embodying moderate restrictions and disabilities.' It was hoped by many German Jews, the authors added, 'that there would be only a limited exodus, and that the bulk of the Jewish population would remain in Germany'. There were even cases of Jews, who, 'unable to adjust themselves abroad', returned to Germany.[10]

The first months of 1935 seemed to bear out the hopes of those, both inside and outside Germany, who felt that the extremes of Nazism would pass. In March 1935 a young German journalist, Bella Fromm, noted a much less violent incident in her diary. She was dining at a Berlin restaurant, when she saw a page boy go up to a young couple at the next table, and discreetly place a teacup, with a slip of paper in it, in front of them. The couple seemed about to rise from their seats. 'May I take the liberty?' Bella Fromm asked them, taking the slip of paper from the teacup. On it was written: 'We do not serve Jews.'[11]

In Dachau, the number of prisoners had fallen sharply, and almost all the Jews interned there in 1933 had been released. After thirteen known Jewish deaths in the camp in 1933, only one Jew, Erich Gans, was known to have been killed there in 1934, on July 1. For ten months no further Jewish deaths were reported, until 22 May 1935, when Max Hans Kohn, a student, died in the camp.[12]

On 1 March 1935, following a result of a plebiscite held under the auspices of the League of Nations, the Saar had become an integral part of Hitler's Germany. All five thousand Jews chose French or Belgian citizenship, and left for France and Belgium. Inside Germany, some twenty thousand Jews had left the towns and villages which did not want them, and sought sanctuary in Berlin.[13] Riding out the storm seemed one possibility. Another possibility was emigration. But here the problem was not only that of severing the links of a lifetime and of generations. It was also financial. On June 14, while on a visit to New York, two leading German Jews, Otto Hirsch and Max Kreutzberger, pleaded for further financial help to be made available for future refugees, only to be told that no campaign for further fund-raising on German Jewry's behalf was contemplated for 1936.[14] Later that year, however, a special fund-raising effort was made.

On July 15, in further anti-Jewish riots in Berlin, several Jews were severely beaten. Twelve days later an article entitled 'Finish up with the Jews' urged 'German' girls to wake up and 'not go with Jews any longer'. 'German woman,' the article declared, 'if you buy from Jews, and German girl if you carry on with Jews, then both of you betray your German Volk and its Führer, Adolf Hitler, and commit a sin against your German Volk and its future!'[15]

A newspaper campaign now began, demanding legislation to prevent sexual relations between Jews and non-Jews. On August 1 a Mannheim newspaper began a series of fourteen separate articles in eight weeks, devoted to this theme, which was promoted by newspapers throughout Germany. 'A Heidelberg Jew as Race Defiler' read the headline on the first article; 'Race Defilers in Protective Custody' read the headline on August 26, followed two days later, after the arrest of a Jew called Moch, by the headline: 'Race Defiler Moch in Protective Custody'.[16]

Tens of thousands of German Jews were not Jews at all, in their own eyes. Some were the children of Jewish converts to Christianity. Others had grandparents who had converted. But Hitler had redefined 'Jew' as a question of race, of 'purity' of blood: declaring that the mere 'taint' of a Jewish ancestor made it impossible for a person ever to be a 'true' German, a member of the 'Volk'. These primitive concepts had become the slogans of a nation, and the obsession of its rulers.

Near Worms, in the village of Biblis, a thirty-seven-year-old Jew, Richard Frankel, awaited arrest. Frankel was a former First World War soldier and invalid, a recipient of the Iron Cross, First Class. In 1932, before Hitler had come to power, he had openly challenged the local Nazis in their beer cellar. His son, then twelve years old, later recalled his father's mood, as he awaited the Nazi revenge. 'I remember him sharpening his knife and saying, "If they take me, six will go with me," and then brandishing his knife in a circle.' The Nazis came, and Frankel was taken to a nearby concentration camp at Osthofen. 'We knew', his son Leslie recalled, 'that if one was taken there, he came back in a coffin – in a sealed coffin you were forbidden to open.'

Richard Frankel was fortunate to return from Osthofen alive. A year later, he and his son left for South Africa. None of their relatives who remained in Germany was to survive the war.[17]

Those German Jews who, like Richard Frankel, were under pressure, left Germany: more than seventy-five thousand German Jews had emigrated or fled by the end of August 1935. Of these, several thousand were Jewish only according to Nazi concepts, and were known, in Nazi terminology, as 'Christian non-Aryans'. It was the definition 'non-Aryan' that condemned them. In their own minds, and behaviour, they were Christians: baptized, Church-going, and believers in the divinity of Jesus.

Of the seventy-five thousand Jewish refugees of 1933, 1934 and 1935, the largest single group, thirty thousand in all, had gone to Palestine. Nine thousand had gone to the United States. Several thousand had gone to Britain, others to South Africa, Canada and Australia. Many thousands more had found a haven in France, Holland and Belgium, in Austria, and in Czechoslovakia.

Inside Germany, at least a quarter of the Jews who remained had been deprived of their professional livelihood by boycott, decree, or local pressure. More than ten thousand public health and social workers had been driven out of their posts, four thousand lawyers were without the right to practise, two thousand doctors had been expelled from hospitals and clinics, two thousand actors, singers and musicians had been driven from their orchestras, clubs and cafes. A further twelve hundred editors and journalists had been dismissed, as had eight hundred university professors and lecturers, and eight hundred elementary and secondary school-teachers.[18]

The search for Jews, and for converted Jews, to be driven out of their jobs was continuous. On 5 September 1935 the SS newspaper published the names of eight half-Jews and converted Jews, all of the Evangelical-Lutheran faith, who had been 'dismissed without notice' and deprived of any further opportunity 'of acting as organists in Christian churches'. From these dismissals, the newspaper commented, 'It can be seen that the Reich Chamber of Music is taking steps to protect the church from pernicious influence.'[19]

For more than two and a half years, the Jews of Germany had faced terror, hostility and discrimination. Yet each act against them could be seen, by an optimist, if not as the last, then at least as the worst. Nasty, irrational and humiliating as it was, the dismissal of eight organists was not the end of the world. But ten days after this 'minor' episode, comprehensive new laws were announced which elevated random discrimination into a system: the Nuremberg Laws of 15 September 1935.

Two laws, both signed by Hitler personally, defined 'Reich Citizenship' and set out the rules for 'the Protection of German Blood and German Honour'. Under the first law, Citizenship could only belong to 'a national of German or kindred blood'.[20] Under the second law, all Jews were defined as being not of German blood. Marriages between Jews and German 'nationals' were forbidden; all marriages conducted 'in defiance of this law' were invalid. Sexual relations outside marriage were forbidden between Jews and Germans. Jews were forbidden to fly the German flag.[21]

Under the headline 'The Shame of Nuremberg', the *New York Herald Tribune* described the two laws as 'a signal victory for the violent anti-Jewish wing of the Nazi Party, led by Julius Streicher' and as the realization 'of nearly the whole anti-Semitic portion of the Nazi programme'.[22] In London, *The Times* declared: 'Nothing like the complete disinheritance and segregation of Jewish citizens, now announced, has been heard since medieval times.'[23]

The Nuremberg Laws made it clear that the Jews were to be allowed no further part in German life: no equality under the law; no further citizenship; no chance of slipping back into the mainstream of German life in which for several generations they had been an integral part, but from which, for two and a half years, they had been gradually cut off.

Following Nuremberg, each move against the Jews could be made with the backing of legal segregation; and such moves began at once. Only a week after the Nuremberg Laws were announced, news reached the outside world that Jews had been forbidden access to any holiday resort in Bavaria.[24]

On 6 October 1935 two Englishmen, Eric Mills, the Commissioner for Migration and Statistics in Palestine, and Frank Foley, Passport Control Officer in Berlin, met members of the German Economics Ministry in Berlin, to discuss the financial aspects of emigration of German Jews to Palestine. What they heard gave them an insight into the current mood and intentions. 'German policy', they wrote in their report to the Foreign Office in London, 'is clearly to eliminate the Jew from German life, and the Nazis do not mind how this is accomplished. Mortality and emigration provide the means.'[25]

'While before I went to Germany', Mills wrote in a private letter after the meeting, 'I knew that the Jewish situation was bad, I had not realized as I now do that the fate of German Jews is a tragedy, for which cold, intelligent planning by those in authority takes rank with that of those who are out of sympathy with the Bolshevik regime, in Russia; or with the elimination of Armenians from the Turkish Empire.' Mills added: 'The Jew is to be eliminated and the state has no regard for the manner of his elimination.'[26]

4

After the Nuremberg Laws

A MONTH AFTER THE PROMULGATION of the Nuremberg Laws on 15 September 1935, one German newspaper reported that the transfer of private Jewish businesses 'into Aryan hands' was proceeding 'on a considerable scale'.[1] As Wilhelm Frick, the Minister of the Interior, explained in a speech at Saarbrucken on October 14, attention would also be given, in codifying the Laws, 'to the imposition of legal restrictions on Jews taking part in trade and industry'.[2]

The net of expropriation and punishment was cast more and more widely. In mid-October all Jewish cinema proprietors were ordered to sell their cinemas within two months, and all Jewish film producers lost their licences to operate. On October 20 several Western newspapers reported the case of a Jewish doctor, Hans Serelman, who had been sent to a concentration camp for seven months for having given a blood transfusion of his own blood to a non-Jew, in order to save the non-Jew's life. The charge against him had been 'race defilement'.[3]

Not only in the press, but in every German school, these racial concepts were being taught from day to day. 'It will be generations', Bella Fromm wrote despondently in her diary on October 20, 'before the Germans can find their way back to an ethical code of life. The evil Nazi doctrine, with its abject conceptions, is deeply planted in the minds of adults, youths, and children.'[4]

Academic thesis writers promulgated the new doctrines. In 1936 Hans Puvogel, a twenty-five-year-old doctoral student in Saxony, successfully explained to his examiners that an individual's worth to the community 'is measured by his or her racial personality. Only a racially valuable person has a right to exist in the community. A racially inferior or harmful individual must be eliminated.'[5]

The year 1936 saw outbreaks of anti-Jewish activity in several states beyond the borders of Germany. In Rumania, in the city of Timisoara, members of the Iron Guard organization attacked the audience at a Jewish theatre: a bomb was thrown, and two Jews were killed. Elsewhere in Rumania, anti-Jewish riots broke out, including in Kishinev, scene of one of the worst of the pogroms in Tsarist times, and in Bucharest, the Rumanian capital. In Lithuania, in an attempt to establish restrictions on the percentage of Jewish students, not a single Jewish medical student was given a place in the medical faculty of Kovno University.

The Nazis had sent emissaries to several countries to explain the need for anti-Jewish legislation. On 4 February 1936, one of these emissaries, Wilhelm Gustloff, who was Hitler's personal representative in Switzerland, was assassinated by a twenty-five-year-old Jewish medical student, David Frankfurter. Having shot Gustloff, Frankfurter went at once to the police, reported what he had done, and explained his motives. He wanted, he said, to draw world attention to the Nazi treatment of the Jews in Germany, which he had witnessed at first hand while a medical student there. Frankfurter, the son of a rabbi in a small community in Yugoslavia, was sentenced to eighteen years' imprisonment.[6]

Six days after Gustloff's assassination, with the unification of the police and the SS, the Gestapo became the supreme police agency of Nazi Germany. Henceforth, the Gestapo could make arrests anywhere in Germany without reference to the courts of law.

Several thousand German Jews had already fled to Poland. There, however, the Jewish community looked with alarm at growing anti-Jewish activity. One incident caused particular concern: the 'Przytyk pogrom'. To the south of Warsaw, on Saturday, March 7 the Jews in the village of Przytyk learned that a group of peasants had gathered to attack them. 'My mother gave me two bottles of benzine, and matches to throw,' the nine-and-a-half-year-old Shalom Lindenbaum later recalled, 'but nothing happened.' Then, on Monday, March 9, market day, 'with sticks and stones they came'.[7]

The peasants who attacked the Jews that day broke into the village square, entering Jewish houses, smashing the windows, and breaking the furniture. Two Jews, a shoemaker Josef Minkowski and his wife Chaya, were tortured to death. Their children, who were discovered hiding under the bed, were savagely beaten.

Gathering in the village square, the Jews decided to resist. One of them, Shalom Lasko, aged twenty, a religious Jew, fired a revolver, killing one of the peasants in the attacking gang.[8]

News of the Przytyk pogrom horrified Polish Jewry. The successful self-defence was forgotten in the spectre of the two deaths, and in the implications for the future of Polish Jewry.[9] Tens of thousands of Polish Jews sought safety in emigration. By the end of 1936, a record annual influx of Polish Jews – 11,596 men, women and children – had been admitted to Palestine.[10] But even at the rate at which Britain was granting Palestine certificates, such emigration could never be anything but a minor amelioration for three million Polish Jews; and Arab hostility inside Palestine to Jewish immigration was already leading to violent Arab protests and to the decision by the British authorities to seek a drastic reduction in the number of future certificates.

On 15 April 1936, just over five weeks after the Przytyk pogrom, the Palestinian Arabs began a General Strike in protest against Jewish immigration. Violent acts against Jewish property and against individuals culminated in the killing of two Jews in Tulkarm on the first day of the strike. On April 19 nine Jews were killed in Jaffa, and on April 20 a further five. Meeting in Jerusalem on May 7, the Arab leaders demanded an end to Jewish immigration.

Within a month, twenty-one Jews had been killed in Arab attacks. Six Arabs had been killed by the British police. No Arabs had been killed by Jews.[11]

The news of the killing of Jews in Palestine had a disturbing impact on the emigration from Germany. On June 12, two Berlin Jews, Wilfrid Israel and Lola Hahn Warburg, telegraphed to Jerusalem for funds to strengthen the defences of the children's village of Ben Shemen, between Tel Aviv and Jerusalem, as many German Jewish parents were now worried about sending their children to Palestine, despite a comprehensive youth programme of training and settlement.[12]

In Germany, Hitler moved steadily to consolidate his power. Secret rearmament, begun by his predecessors, increased in scale and speed. On 7 March 1936 Hitler sent German troops into those parts the Rhineland Province which, although within the borders of postwar Germany, had been demilitarized since 1918 under the Treaty of Versailles.

Hitler's action flouted a solemn Treaty. But it went unchallenged by Britain and France. Hitler had achieved his first success in breaching international law. Inside Germany, the creation of 'Jew free' villages continued. Hundreds of thousands of Jews, driven out of their professions, found themselves with no means of livelihood. Placards inscribed 'Jews not wanted here' appeared on more and more buildings. Jewish schoolchildren were forbidden to sit on the same benches as non-Jews, and were subjected to abuse from teachers and pupils alike. In every sphere of daily life, the segregation enjoined by the Nuremberg Laws was being enforced.

In the summer of 1936 a German Jew, Stefan Lux, one of over two thousand Jewish film producers who had been forced to give up their professional work, decided to make a public protest against the continuing persecutions. The place he chose for his protest was the assembly room of the League of Nations building in Geneva. There, on 3 July 1936, surrounded by journalists in the Press Gallery, he committed suicide. He was forty-eight years old.

Stefan Lux left a letter to Anthony Eden, the British Cabinet Minister responsible for League affairs. In this letter, Lux said that he had killed himself in order to draw attention to the persecutions in Germany. 'I do not find any other way to reach the hearts of men,' he wrote, adding that the persecutions had failed to pierce the 'inhuman indifferences' of the world.[13]

In August 1936 the Polish Ministry of Commerce, in Warsaw, ordered all shops throughout Poland to include, as part of the shop sign, the name of the owner as it appeared on his birth certificate.[14] This made the fact that the owner was Jewish obvious to every Pole, and provided instant incitement for the anti-Semite.

Jews fled from Poland, as from Germany, and fled in vast numbers. Between 1921 and 1937, 395,223 Polish Jews emigrated.[15] Yet this enormous figure was little more than ten per cent of Polish Jews. Half of Germany's Jews were able to find refuge, and many of them safety, in emigration. Polish Jewry was so large as to be without prospect of safety through flight.

In Hitler's phraseology and in the Nazi propaganda, the Jews were an evil disease, poisoning the blood of decent humanity, a conscious plague-bacillus infecting the pure, innocent 'Aryan'. But it was the virus of anti-Semitism which was much in evidence in 1936, spreading across national borders as if those borders did not exist. 'The virus spread', a young Polish Jew, Ben Helfgott, later recalled, as he remembered – he was then seven years old – signs daubed on Jewish-owned shops in his home town of Piotrkow: 'Don't buy at Jewish shops', 'Jews out', and the equally Nazi-echoing slogan: 'Get out to Palestine'.[16]

The power of Nazi Germany was still confined to the borders of the Reich, and it was in Germany that the dangers seemed greatest, the pressures most severe. On September 7, a twenty-five-per-cent tax was imposed on all Jewish wealth, substantially reducing the power of the Jewish community to help those who were now jobless. Denunciation of Jews and Jewish values continued: on November 29 the Minister of Agriculture, Walther Darre, declared that liberalism and democracy were 'Jewish conceptions', and that all democratic governments were 'essentially Jewish'.[17]

Throughout 1937 the German government increased its military and air strength. 'We seem to be moving,' Winston Churchill told the House of Commons on April 14, 'drifting steadily, against our will, against the will of every race and every people and every class, towards some hideous catastrophe.'[18] In Poland, on May 13, Polish anti-Semites attacked the Jews of Brest-Litovsk, under the slogan 'We owe our troubles to the Jews'. In Germany, a young Jew of twenty, Helmut Hirsch, in despair at the unyielding pressures against his people, had been caught with a revolver and a suitcase of bombs. He was charged with intending to assassinate Streicher. Hirsch was then tried, and sentenced to death. As Hirsch was technically an American citizen, although he had never been to America, the American Ambassador, William Dodd, appealed to Hitler to commute the death sentence. But Hitler's reply, Dodd told the American journalist William Shirer, 'was a flat negative'. Dodd then sought a personal interview with Hitler to plead the case; he was 'rebuffed'.[19]

At dawn on June 4, Helmut Hirsch was executed with an axe. Eight days later, a number of Jews accused of 'race defilement' were sent to Dachau concentration camp, where some three hundred Jews were being held.

The German government lost no opportunity to extend its racial laws. On July 15, the Geneva Convention in respect of Upper Silesia expired. German Jews in Upper Silesia now faced the full rigour of those laws: expulsion from their jobs, loss of the rights of citizenship, segregation from the community around them. The application of the Nuremberg Laws to Upper Silesia had been promulgated two weeks before the expiry of the Geneva Convention.[20]

The desperate search for safety continued: in 1937 a further 3,601 German Jews reached Palestine, as did 3,636 Jews from Poland.[21] But these figures, so much lower than those for 1936, reflected new restrictions imposed by the British Mandate authorities as the Arab revolt against Jewish immigration continued.[22] For the Jews of Germany, this was an ominous development, reflected in Palestine itself by the deaths, between April 1936 and the end of 1937, of 113 Jews, and by the first Arab deaths, fifteen in all, in Jewish reprisal raids, despite the condemnation of such reprisals by the Jewish National Council in Palestine.[23]

In Germany, the Jews registered one small success in the late autumn of 1937. David Glick, a Pittsburgh lawyer, and the unofficial representative of the American Jewish Joint Distribution Committee – the 'Joint' – negotiated with the Gestapo the release of 120 of the three hundred Jews then being held in Dachau. The Gestapo agreed to release them on condition that the 120 Jews emigrated immediately to a country beyond Europe. At Glick's urging, the British Consul General in Munich, Consul Carvell, agreed to issue Palestine visas on condition that £5,000 was paid into a bank outside Germany to assist the settlement of the released men in Palestine. The Joint agreed, and paid the money. The Jews were released.

Glick's experiment was later repeated on a larger scale. Its second success was when three thousand German Jews were sent with a similar payment to Bolivia, financed by Don Mauricio Hochschild, a Jewish tin-mine millionaire in Peru.[24]

At the same moment that the Germans were agreeing to Jewish emigration, anti-Jewish propaganda was intensifying. On 8 November 1937 an exhibition opened in Nuremberg, 'The Eternal Jew', portraying the Jew as a taskmaster for international Bolshevism, aimed at enslaving Germany within the Soviet system.[25]

In 1937, as in 1936, anti-Jewish actions had again spread throughout Eastern Europe. In Poland, 350 physical assaults against Jews were recorded in the single month of August. In the Rumanian town of Piatra Neamt, twenty-six out of the town's twenty-eight Jewish barristers were dismissed, and there were anti-Jewish riots in several towns throughout the year. On 21 January 1938, in a law which abrogated the minority rights of Jews – established in 1918 – many Jews who had lived in Rumania since 1918 were deprived of their citizenship.[26] Four months later, on May 29, the Hungarian government published its first Law specifically restricting, to twenty per cent, the number of Jews allowed to hold jobs in commerce, industry, the liberal professions, and the administration.[27]

In four years, the German government had turned Jews into less than second-class citizens. Now other governments, and other peoples, especially those in Eastern Europe, looked with envy at the Nazi achievements, and allowed their own anti-Jewish prejudices to flourish.

Not every nation in Europe on the eve of the Second World War was so sophisticated as to be able to resist the pressures of more than six years of Nazi propaganda. This propaganda, in the press and on radio, in books and films, in schools and universities, stirred up deep jealousies and hatreds, casting the Jew as the scapegoat for all existing ills and dangers, great and alleged. To an ill-educated person, to a poor person, to a person whose secure world was under apparent threat from outside, international forces, the Nazi cry 'the Jews in our misfortune' rang like a clarion call.

In some countries, such as Italy, anti-Jewish hatred was hard to fan. In others, like Rumania, it was substantially fanned among large numbers. In Poland, it succeeded even more widely. The emancipations of mind and judgement which had been set in train by the French Revolution in 1789, and had so marked the progress of the nineteenth century, was far from universal. The concept of the Jew as an alien and outsider remained a convincing one in many lands. jealousy of the Jew who had succeeded, contempt for the Jew who had failed, willingness to believe in sinister changes and evil design, were still capable of being stirred up into physical violence over large parts of Europe, and especially Eastern Europe.

5

'Hunted like rats'

ON 30 JANUARY 1938, Hitler celebrated the fifth anniversary of his coming to power. For five years he had rearmed Germany, and given repeated notice to the world that he considered himself responsible for German-speaking people wherever they lived, whether in his birthplace, Austria, in the Sudeten mountain border-lands of Czechoslovakia, in the Free City of Danzig, or even in the western provinces of Poland. As yet his growing armies had crossed no frontier. The Rhineland province of Germany had been remili-tarized and the Saar had been reincorporated to Germany by the overwhelming vote of its population. Neither action had led to the death of a single foreign soldier.

Even Hitler's anti-Jewish record over five years was open to positive interpretation. German Jews had been allowed to leave, and to leave in their tens of thousands. No more than two hundred had been killed, most of them in the first fourteen months of his rule.[1] The number of Jews, as well as of political opponents, liberals and churchmen, held in concentration camps, had continually dropped. The negotiated release of the 120 Jews from Dachau had been a prelude to further negotiations and further releases.

But for those actually involved, the signs were terrifying. German Jews had been deprived of the rights of citizenship. The fate of the three hundred Jews still inside Dachau was not known until early in 1939, with the publication in Paris of an account by a former prisoner. He described his arrival in the camp on 4 February 1938:

> The Jewish prisoners worked in special detachments and received the hardest tasks. They were beaten at every oppor-tunity – for instance, if the space between the barrows with which they had to walk or even run over loose flints was not correctly kept. They were overwhelmed with abusive epithets

such as 'Sow Jew', 'Filth Jew' and 'Stink Jew'. During the working period the non-Jewish prisoners were issued with one piece of bread at breakfast – the Jews with nothing. But the Jews were always paraded with the others to see the bread ration issued.

This former prisoner's account continued:

> In February, March and April there were a number of 'suicides' and shootings 'during attempted escape'. The Jew Lowenberg was horribly beaten during a works' task, and committed suicide that night. In March two men were 'shot while attempting escape'. The Jew Lowy was shot dead for approaching closer than the regulation six metres to a sentry who had called him up. Another was ordered by a sentry again and again to approach until he stepped on the forbidden 'neutral zone' outside the barbed wire, whereupon he was shot dead.

'When, during great heat,' the former prisoner added, 'it was allowed to fetch water for the working detachments, it sometimes happened that the Jews were forbidden to drink.'[2]

On February 15, eleven days after this eye-witness had been sent to Dachau, an ominous event took place in Austria. Local Nazis, confident that Austria would soon become a part of Germany, began to make preparations for the taking over of every Jewish office, shop and factory, with 'managing commissars', often someone employed by the enterprise, designated for each.[3]

On March 12 the German army entered Vienna. Independent Austria was no more: absorbed into a new entity, Greater Germany. The 183,000 Jews of Austria, most of them living in the capital, suddenly became a part of the Nazi hegemony. Numerically, they constituted an addition of outcasts and pariahs greater than the total number of German Jews who had managed to leave Germany in the previous five years.

The process of isolation and abuse had been a gradual one in Germany. More than two months had passed between Hitler coming to power and the April boycott. Two and a half years had intervened between the April boycott and the Nuremberg Laws. But for the Jews of Vienna, the torments and the discrimination were immediate. During the very first days, all Jewish enterprises were branded with enormous red inscriptions such as 'Jew', 'Jewish shop' or 'Jewish coffee house'. Any non-Jew daring to enter such an establishment was at once caught by Stormtroops or SS men, and made to wear a placard around his or her neck: 'I, Aryan swine, have bought in a Jewish shop'.[4]

Overnight, the Jews of Vienna, one sixth of the city's population, were deprived of all civil rights: the right to own property, large or small, the right to be employed or to give employment, the right to exercise their profession, any profession, the right to enter restaurants or cáfes, public baths or public parks. Instead they experienced physical assault: the looting of shops, the breaking of heads, the tormenting of passers-by. A British journalist, G. E. R. Gedye, wrote, after the suicide of a young Jewish doctor and his mother in his own block of flats, 'From my window I could watch for many days how they would arrest Jewish passers-by – generally doctors, lawyers or merchants, for they preferred their victims to belong to the better educated classes – and force them to scrub, polish and beat carpets in the flat where the tragedy had taken place, while insisting that the doctor's non-Jewish maid should sit at ease in a chair and look on.'

Gedye also saw the Nazis 'gloating over the daily suicide lists'.[5]

Among those who committed suicide were Dr Kurt Sonnenfeld, a well-known Viennese author and journalist; the distinguished lawyer, Dr Moritz Sternberg; and one of Austria's leading playwrights and historians, the sixty-year-old Egon Friedell, whose important *Cultural History of the Modern Age* had been published six years earlier. Friedell's suicide was the result of a tragic misapprehension. Unknown to Friedell, his maid was having an affair with a Stormtrooper. One evening, this man and another Stormtrooper, both in uniform, came to the block of flats. Friedell, seeing them outside, and then hearing them knocking, believed that they had come for him, and threw himself from his third-floor window.[6]

Under the Treaty of St Germain in 1919, Austrian Jews had been guaranteed minority rights. These rights had now been swept away, and in their place the Jews suffered all the humiliations of a puerile and sadistic imagination. 'I was given a bucket of boiling water,' Moritz Fleischmann, a senior representative of the Jewish Community of Vienna, later recalled, 'and I was told to clean the steps. I lay down on my stomach and began to clean the pavement. It turned

out that the bucket was half-full of acid and this burned my hands.'
Fleischmann added that while he was lying down on his stomach
cleaning the pavement, 'the SS sentries threw out the Chief Rabbi,
Dr Taglicht, a man of seventy, and he, like myself, was ordered to
brush these pavements. In order that he should feel the full force of
the degradation and the humility of it, he was thrown out wearing
his gown, and with his prayer shawl on.'[7]

Such cruel pastimes gave pleasure to the perpetrators. Dozens of
passers-by also watched these scenes of humiliation, laughing and
mocking as Jews, having been forced to put their sacred prayer
bands on their arms, were then made to clean unflushed lavatory
bowls.[8]

Inside the main Vienna synagogue, while SS men lolled about
smoking pipes and cigarettes, Jews were forced to perform physical
jerks, knees bending and stretching, holding a chair in each hand.
The older and feebler ones, who stumbled or collapsed, were
brutally kicked and beaten by their Nazi taskmasters. Outside the
synagogue, G. E. R. Gedye watched as 'here and there a victim
would be flung out, grey-faced, with trembling limbs, eyes staring
with horror and mouths they could not keep still'.[9]

Within a month, more than five hundred Jews had committed
suicide in Austria. 'A family of six Jews', a British dental student
wrote to London on 18 March 1938, 'have just shot themselves, a
few houses down the street. They are well out of it.'[10]

These scenes received wide publicity in the British, American and
Western European press and radio, and in the newsreels, where they
were seen with shock and disgust. But some of those who followed
events in Austria were encouraged to imitate the Nazi course. In
Poland, beginning on April 5, anti-Jewish riots spread from city to
city, including Vilna and Warsaw. Nor was the torment ended for
the Jews of Vienna. Saturday April 23, was the Jewish Sabbath, a
day which the Nazis were beginning to choose for these indignities.
On that Sabbath, groups of Stormtroops, patrolling the streets of
Vienna, seized as many Jews as they could find, put them into
lorries, and drove them out to the Prater, Vienna's amusement park.
There, the Jews were thrown to the ground and ordered to 'eat
grass'. As they ate, Stormtroops trampled on their hands, or forced
them roughly to climb up into the lower branches of the trees and to
'twitter and croak and gibber like birds'.[11]

At a command, men and women, including even pregnant women, were forced to run in circles, and to continue running until they fainted or collapsed. Those whom the Stormtroops felt had only pretended to faint in order to escape the order were beaten until they got up and ran again. Other Jews were strapped into the carriages of the Prater's scenic railway, and then driven at top speed until they lost consciousness. Hundreds of elderly Jews suffered heart attacks during these activities – activities which were dubbed by the Nazis as 'pleasure hours' – and several Jews died.[12]

On Easter Sunday, in the Austrian province of the Burgenland, fifty-one Jews, stripped of all their possessions, were taken from their homes, put into boats, and pushed out into the Danube. All night they lay stranded on a sandbank in mid-river. Their cries for help were heard across the river, in Czechoslovakia, whose government gave them asylum.[13]

In the Austrian provinces, where small numbers of Jews had lived in more than seven hundred towns and villages, almost every one of the seven hundred raised a white flag to tell the world that no Jews remained.[14] Thousands of Jews flocked to Vienna, homeless, and deprived of their possessions. Thousands more crossed the borders into Czechoslovakia, Hungary and Poland. This new wave of refugees roused worldwide fears of an endless flow of the dispossessed. One by one, the countries which for more than five years had accepted German Jews almost without restrictions now imposed new rules and regulations.

The pressures on Jews to leave Germany and Austria were intensifying. On May 28, scarcely a month after the day of indignities in the Prater, the Jews of Frankfurt were subjected to a similar day of intimidation. Their plight was witnessed by the British Consul-General in Frankfurt, R. T. Smallbones, who saw boycott scenes similar to those in Berlin in April 1933. 'On the windows of Jews' shops,' he reported to London, 'various caricatures of Jews were painted, such as Jews hanging from gibbets, with insulting inscriptions.' Jewish families were visited by gangs who told them 'to leave Germany quickly as, next time, quite different measures would be taken against them'.

For some time, Smallbones pointed out, it had been 'impossible' for Jews to go to the theatre or to have a meal in a restaurant. The Jew had become an outcast. 'A young Jew of my acquaintance', he wrote, 'has had since infancy an Aryan friend.' Recently, this friend has been 'reported' to the Nazi Party officials, but had explained that he had known the Jew for fifteen years, liked and admired him, and could see 'no reason why he should terminate this friendship'. The party official then explained to him, as Smallbones reported, 'that segregation of the Jews was such a paramount duty that it had to override any sentiment of friendship or comradeship or gratitude'. The party official then instanced the case 'of Jews who may have lain in the same trenches with Nazis during the war and shared the agonies and perils of those days'. Even if a Jew had saved the life of a Nazi 'at whatever risk and at whatever sacrifice', Smallbones commented, that Jew 'is now to be looked upon as an accursed outcast with whom he who was rescued may have no truck'.[15]

Following the German annexation of Austria in March 1938, and the beginning of mass arrests in June, more than fifteen hundred Jews were sent to Dachau, and to a newly opened concentration camp at Buchenwald. The cruelties of these camps had not abated. As a former prisoner at Dachau recalled a few months later, 'In June a Jew was brought here under suspicion of "race pollution". He was so ill that we had to wheel him into camp on a wheelbarrow, and to wheel him to morning and evening roll-call, as the doctor would not put him on the sick list. In a week he was dead.'[16]

Among those taken from Vienna to Buchenwald was the Jewish opera librettist and satirist Fritz Beda, whose first volume of collected satires had been published in 1908 when he was twenty-five years old. In Buchenwald, Beda composed a song which ended with the words:

> Whatever our fate,
> We still say 'yes' to life.[17]

Beda remained in Buchenwald for more than three years. While in the camp he organized, as best he could, cultural activities and competitions. On 17 October 1942 he was deported from Buchenwald to his death.[18]

Emigration still offered a way out for those Jews of Germany and Austria who were at liberty. More than ninety-eight thousand Jews, nearly half of the Jews of Austria, left for other lands. They were, indeed, encouraged to do so by the Nazis, and a special emigration office, the Central Office for Jewish Emigration, was set up in

Vienna for them, headed by a thirty-two-year-old SS officer, Adolf Eichmann. At the same time, twelve thousand Jewish families were evicted from their homes, almost eight thousand Jewish businesses were 'Aryanized', and more than thirty thousand Jews were thrown out of their jobs.

On 9 June 1938 a new type of Nazi 'action' took place: the burning down of a synagogue. The synagogue was the main one in Munich. The burning was followed by the arrest of more than two thousand Jews throughout Germany. These Jews, Wilfrid Israel reported from Berlin, 'are now suffering the tortures of hell in one of the new concentration camps, the so-called quarries of death. They are mostly made to slave for fourteen to sixteen hours a day by hauling or carrying stones. Their supervisors use their whips only too willingly under this or that pretext. Discipline is enforced by lashing old and young to tree trunks and beating them while others are made to be eye-witnesses of their misery.'

Wilfrid Israel also reported that for many of those inside these camps 'the only way of escaping this torture is to run into wire entanglements loaded with high-tension electricity'. Deaths, he added, 'are frequent, for this and other reasons'.[19]

On the day that Wilfrid Israel sent this report to London, Bella Fromm witnessed, in Berlin, renewed scenes of looting and violence against the now impoverished Jewish community. The Stormtroops had created havoc, she wrote in her diary. 'Everywhere were revolting and bloodthirsty pictures of Jews beheaded, hanged, tortured, and maimed, accompanied by obscene inscriptions.'

Bella Fromm went to see an elderly couple, both of whose sons had been killed in action in the First World War. 'Killed for Germany!' she wrote. 'We went to find out whether they had suffered. Their shop was in ruins. Their goods, paper and stationery, trampled into the gutter. Three SA men, roaring with obscene laughter, forced the trembling old man to pick up the broken glass with his hands that were covered with blood.'

On the following day Bella Fromm returned with food for her two friends, hoping to comfort them. 'We found two coffins, surrounded by silent neighbours. The faces of the old couple seemed peaceful and serene amid the broken glass and destruction. As we put down our basket and stood there wretchedly, a young woman spoke to me. "It is better for them. They took poison last night." '[20]

In his official report from Berlin for June 1938, Captain Foley summed up the events of the month. In Berlin, as well as elsewhere in Germany, there had, he wrote, been 'systematic house-to-house searches for, and arrests of, Jews'; cafés had been raided and cinema halls emptied of Jews 'so that they could be arrested in concentration camps'. In Berlin, the 'methods of persecution' had been particularly severe. It was 'no exaggeration', Foley concluded, 'to say that Jews have been hunted like rats in their homes, and for fear of arrest many of them sleep at a different address overnight'.[21]

The Germans who carried out the atrocities and cruelties had already become corrupted by their tasks; laughing when inflicting pain, and drawing in passers-by to laugh with them. Gradually entire populations became immune to feelings of outrage, and learned to shun compassion.

On 6 July 1938 an international conference opened at Evian, a French resort town on the shores of Lake Geneva, with the purpose of discussing the future reception of refugees. More than 150,000 Jews had already been taken in from the torments of Germany, and now of Austria. Of these 8,000 had been admitted to Britain, 40,000 into Palestine, 55,000 into the United States, 8,000 into Brazil, 15,000 into France, 2,000 into Belgium, at least 14,000 into Switzerland, several thousand into Bolivia, 1,000 into Sweden, 845 into Denmark and 150 into Norway.[22]

Not all the delegates at Evian were sympathetic to the Jewish plight. 'It will no doubt be appreciated', the Australian delegate, T. W. White, told the conference, 'that as we have no racial problem, we are not desirous of importing one.' The conference agreed to set up an intergovernmental agency to examine what could be done. But, as the number of Jews seeking to leave grew, the restrictions against them also grew: Britain, Palestine and the United States each tightened their rules of admission. Four South American countries, Argentine, Chile, Uruguay and Mexico, adopted laws severely restricting the number of Jews who could enter; in the case of Mexico to a hundred a year.

The situation inside Germany made the search for escape even more urgent. Every day, more Jews sought the escape of suicide. On July 29, in Worms, Dr Friedrich Gernsheim, a sixty-six-year-old physician, committed suicide together with his wife Rosa.[23]

In Nuremberg, on August 10, the synagogue was destroyed by fire, two months after the synagogue in Munich had been burnt down. Hitler, without having made war on any of his neighbours, and having avoided war with the European powers, seemed oblivious to outside indignation and protest. The six months which had passed since he celebrated his first five years in power had seen an acceleration of violence against the Jews, but no ill-effects abroad as far as German national interests were concerned. For five years his anti-Jewish actions, although always severe, had been tempered with moments of caution. Since the annexation of Austria, and the Evian conference, he seemed to have thrown caution to the winds.

The international community, which at Evian had been presented with an opportunity to keep open the gates of refuge, chose that moment, so desperate for the Jews already under Nazi rule, to signal its own hesitations and reluctance. It was a neutral stance, not a hostile one, but this neutral stance was to cost a multitude of lives.

The hardening response of the European powers towards Jewish refugees was typified on August 13, when the Cabinet in Finland held a secret discussion about 'the arrival visas' of Austrian refugees. An official in the Finnish Embassy in Vienna had apparently been giving entry visas to Austrian Jews 'without requesting permission from Finland first'. It was decided that all future visa applications should be submitted for approval, not only to the Finnish Foreign Ministry, but also to the German Foreign Ministry. Four days later, on August 17, fifty-three Austrian Jews reached Helsinki by sea. They were refused permission to disembark, and the boat which had brought them was ordered to Germany. Several of the passengers had the necessary papers to enter the United States, and sought only transit rights through Finland. But no exceptions were made to the new policy. A pregnant Jewess, who was about to have her baby, was allowed to leave the ship and go to a hospital, but after the birth, the mother and child had to rejoin the other passengers. On the way back to Germany, as the ship was sailing past the Porkkala peninsula, three of the rejected refugees threw themselves overboard and were drowned.[24]

6

'The seeds of a terrible vengeance'

THROUGHOUT THE SUMMER OF 1938, Hitler dominated European diplomatic activity by his demand for the cession of the Sudetenland to Germany. This German-speaking region of Czechoslovakia had never been a part of Germany, but, before 1914, had been within the Austro-Hungarian Empire. Austria having itself become part of Germany in March 1938, Hitler now argued that the Sudetenland should also be annexed to the Reich. His demands were backed by the reiterated threat of military force.

On the last day of September 1938, at Munich, the British, French and Italian leaders bowed to Hitler's demands: the Sudetenland would become a part of Greater Germany on 10 October 1938, and Czechoslovakia would lose its natural mountain defences. More than twenty thousand Jews lived in the Sudetenland. They fled, most of them to the Czechoslovakian provinces of Bohemia and Moravia, which Hitler had allowed to retain their independence.

On October 27, less than three weeks after annexing the Sudetenland, Hitler moved again. He struck this time against the Jews alone, expelling from Germany eighteen thousand Jews who, although living in Germany since 1918, had been born in the former Polish provinces of the Russian Empire. The expulsion, eastward, to the Polish border, was a swift and brutal act, but it was in keeping with what the world now understood to be the Nazi method. Two days before the expulsions, a British diplomat, Sir George Ogilvie-Forbes, wrote from Berlin that the treatment of Jews and political opponents in concentration camps made the Germans 'unfit for decent international society'. A senior colleague in the Foreign Office in London agreed. The Germans, he minuted, 'are out to eliminate the Jews at any cost to the latter and nothing we can do or say will stop them'.[1]

One of the eighteen thousand Jews expelled from Germany, Zindel Grynszpan, had been born in the town of Radomsko, in Russian Poland, in 1886. Since 1911 he had lived in Hanover. His eldest son, Hirsch Grynszpan, had gone to Paris, as a student, in 1936. The rest of the family, Zindel, his wife, his daughter and second son, remained in Hanover. As Zindel Grynszpan later recalled:

On the 27th October 1938 – it was Thursday night at eight o'clock – a policeman came and told us to come to Region II. He said, 'You are going to come back immediately; you shouldn't take anything with you. Take with you your passports.'

When I reached the Region, I saw a large number of people; some people were sitting, some standing. People were crying; they were shouting, 'Sign, sign, sign.' I had to sign, as all of them did. One of us did not, and his name, I believe, was Gershon Silber, and he had to stand in the corner for twenty-four hours.

They took us to the concert hall on the banks of the Leine and there, there were people from all the areas, about six hundred people. There we stayed until Friday night; about twenty-four hours; then they took us in police trucks, in prisoners' lorries, about twenty men in each truck, and they took us to the railway station. The streets were black with people shouting, 'The Jews out to Palestine.'

After that, when we got to the train, they took us by train to Neubenschen on the German-Polish border. It was Shabbat morning; Saturday morning. When we reached Neubenschen at 6 a.m. there came trains from all sorts of places, Leipzig, Cologne, Dusseldorf, Essen, Bielefeld, Bremen. Together we were about twelve thousand people.

When we reached the border, we were searched to see if anybody had any money, and anybody who had more than ten marks, the balance was taken from him. This was the German law. No more than ten marks could be taken out of Germany. The Germans said, 'You didn't bring any more into Germany and you can't take any more out.'

The SS were giving us, as it were, protective custody, and we walked two kilometres on foot to the Polish border. They told us to go – the SS men were whipping us, those who lingered they hit, and blood was flowing on the road. They tore away their little baggage from them, they treated us in a most barbaric fashion – this was the first time that I'd ever seen the wild barbarism of the Germans.

They shouted at us: 'Run! Run!' I myself received a blow and I fell in the ditch. My son helped me, and he said: 'Run, run, dad – otherwise you'll die!' When we got to the open border – we reached what was called the green border, the Polish border – first of all, the women went in.

Then a Polish general and some officers arrived, and they examined the papers and saw that we were Polish citizens, that we had special passports. It was decided to let us enter Poland. They took us to a village of about six thousand people, and we were twelve thousand. The rain was driving hard, people were fainting – some suffered heart attacks; on all sides one saw old men and women. Our suffering was great – there was no food – since Thursday we had not wanted to eat any German bread.[2]

'I found thousands crowded together in pigsties,' a British woman sent to help those who had been expelled later recalled. 'The old, the sick and children herded together in the most inhuman conditions.' Conditions were so bad, she added, 'that some actually tried to escape *back* to Germany and were shot'.[3]

Another of those who had gone to the Polish frontier, to the frontier town of Zbaszyn, was the thirty-nine-year-old Polish historian Emanuel Ringelblum, who not only directed relief work on behalf of the American Jewish Joint Distribution Committee, but also collected testimonies from many of the deportees, and used the opportunity to gather information on recent events in Nazi Germany.[4]

While at Zbaszyn, Zindel Grynszpan later recalled, the Jews were put in stables still dirty with horse dung. At last a lorry with bread arrived from Poznan, but at first there was not enough bread to go round.[5]

Zindel Grynszpan decided to send a postcard to his son Hirsch, in Paris, describing his family's travails. The young man, enraged by what he read, went to the German Embassy in Paris, and, on 6 November 1938, shot the first German official who received him, Ernst vom Rath.

As vom Rath lay wounded, Hitler and the Nazis denounced the deed as part of a Jewish-inspired world conspiracy against Germany. On November 8 Wilfrid Israel called at the British Embassy in Berlin to repudiate Grynszpan's act, and to warn of imminent reprisals.[6] By the following day, November 9, vom Rath was dead. From the moment that news of his death reached Hitler in Munich, an unprecedented wave of violence broke over Germany's remaining three hundred thousand Jews.

One young boy, Paul Oestereicher, later recalled how he was walking with his mother in one of the main shopping streets of Berlin, excitedly window-shopping after several months in hiding, when, in seconds the dream was over. 'What seemed like hundreds of men, swinging great truncheons, jumped from lorries and began to smash up the shops all around us.'[7]

Among those who witnessed this outburst of destruction was a twenty-five-year-old Jew from Holland, Wim van Leer. Walking in a Leipzig street, he saw a truck draw up a few houses down the road from him, and 'some twenty louts jumped down'.

Van Leer watched as Stormtroops rang the door bells, smashed the glass windows in the doors if there was no reply, and entered the Jewish houses. 'Suddenly,' he later recalled, 'third-floor balcony doors were flung open, and Stormtroops appeared, shouting to their mates below. One yelled something about all blessings coming from above, and, in expectation, that part of the pavement beneath the balcony was cleared. Next they wheeled an upright piano on to the balcony and, smashing the balustrade with one mighty heave – there must have been eight of them – they pushed the piano over the edge. It nose-dived on to the street below with a sickening crash as the wooden casing broke away, leaving what looked like a harp standing in the middle of the debris . . .'.[8]

Bonfires were lit in every neighbourhood where Jews lived. On them were thrown prayer books, Torah scrolls, and countless volumes of philosophy, history and poetry. In thousands of streets, Jews were chased, reviled and beaten up.

In twenty-four hours of street violence, ninety-one Jews were killed. More than thirty thousand – one in ten of those who remained – were arrested and sent to concentration camps. Before most of them were released two to three months later, as many as a thousand had been murdered, 244 of them in Buchenwald. A further eight thousand Jews were evicted from Berlin: children from orphanages, patients from hospitals, old people from old peoples' homes. There were many suicides, ten at least in Nuremberg; but it was forbidden to publish death notices in the press.[9]

It was not by the killing, however, nor by the arrests or the suicides, that the night of November 9 was to be remembered. During the night, as well as breaking into tens of thousands of shops and homes, the Stormtroops set fire to one hundred and ninety-one synagogues; or, if it was thought that fire might endanger nearby buildings, smashed the synagogues as thoroughly as possible with hammers and axes.

The destruction of the synagogues led the Nazis to call that night the *Kristallnacht*, or 'night of broken glass': words chosen deliberately to mock and belittle. From Leipzig, the United States Consul, David H. Buffum, reported that the three main synagogues, set on fire simultaneously, 'were irreparably gutted by flames'. At the Jewish cemetery in Leipzig the Nazis practised 'tactics which approached the ghoulish', uprooting tombstones and violating graves. In the city itself, Buffum reported, 'Having demolished dwellings and hurled most of the effects to the streets, the insatiably sadistic perpetrators threw many of the trembling inmates into a small stream that flows through the Zoological Park, commanding horrified spectators to spit at them, defile them with mud and jeer at their plight.'[10]

Among the witnesses to these events was Dr Arthur Flehinger from Baden-Baden. Later he recalled how all Jewish men in the town were ordered to assemble on the morning of November 10. Towards noon they were marched through the streets to the synagogue. Many non-Jews resented the round-up. 'I saw people crying while watching from behind their curtains,' Dr Flehinger later wrote, and he added: 'One of the many decent citizens is reported to have said, "What I saw was not one Christ, but a whole column of Christ figures, who were marching along with heads high and unbowed by any feeling of guilt." '

While being marched up the steps to the synagogue, several Jews fell, only to be beaten until they could pick themselves up. Once inside the synagogue, the Jews were confronted by exuberant Nazi officers and SS men. Dr Flehinger himself was ordered to read out passages from *Mein Kampf* to his fellow Jews. 'I read the passage quietly, indeed so quietly that the SS man posted behind me repeatedly hit me in the neck,' Dr Flehinger later recalled. 'Those who had to read other passages after me were treated in the same manner. After these "readings" there was a pause. Those Jews who wanted to relieve themselves were forced to do so against the synagogue walls, not in the toilets, and they were physically abused while doing so.'

The Jews were led away. Within an hour, the synagogue was in flames. 'If it had been my decision,' one of the SS men remarked, 'you would have perished in that fire.'[11]

No village in which Jews still lived was immune from the destruction. In Hoengen, a small village near Aachen, the tiny Jewish community had built its synagogue in 1926: now, twelve years later, Michael Lucas, a butcher by trade, whose house was opposite the meadow, watched from his window as Stormtroops stood on guard. His nephew Eric later recalled:

After a while, the Stormtroops were joined by people who were not in uniform; and suddenly, with one loud cry of, 'Down with the Jews', the gathering outside produced axes and heavy sledgehammers. They advanced towards the little synagogue which stood in Michael's own meadow, opposite his house. They burst the door open, and the whole crowd, by now shouting and laughing, stormed into the little House of God.

Michael, standing behind the tightly drawn curtains, saw how the crowd tore the Holy Ark wide open; and three men who had smashed the ark, threw the Scrolls of the Law of Moses out. He threw them – these Scrolls, which had stood in their quiet dignity, draped in blue or wine-red velvet, with their little crowns of silver covering the tops of the shafts by which the Scroll was held during the service – to the screaming and shouting mass of people which had filled the little synagogue.

The people caught the Scrolls as if they were amusing themselves with a ball-game – tossing them up into the air again, while other people flung them further back until they reached the street outside. Women tore away the red and blue velvet and everybody tried to snatch some of the silver adorning the Scrolls.

Naked and open, the Scrolls lay in the muddy autumn lane; children stepped on them and others tore pieces from the fine parchment on which the Law was written – the same Law which the people who tore it apart had, in vain, tried to absorb for over a thousand years.

When the first Scroll was thrown out of the synagogue, Michael made a dash for the door. His heart beat violently and his senses became blurred and hazy. Unknown fury built up within him, and his clenched fists pressed against his temples. Michael forgot that to take one step outside the house amongst the crowds would mean his death.

The Stormtroopers, who still stood outside the house watching with stern faces over the tumultuous crowd which obeyed their commands without really knowing it, would have shot the man, quietly, in an almost matter of fact way. Michael's wife, sensing the deadly danger, ran after her husband, and clung to him, imploring him and begging him not to go outside. Michael tried to fling her aside, but only her tenacious resistance brought him back to his senses.

He stood there, in the small hall behind the front door, looking around him for a second, as if he did not know where he was. Suddenly he leaned against the wall, tears streaming from his eyes, like those of a little child.

After a while, he heard the sound of many heavy hammers outside. With trembling legs he got up from his chair and looked outside once more. Men had climbed on to the roof of the synagogue, and were hurling the tiles down, others were cutting the cross beams as soon as they were bare of cover. It did not take long before the first heavy grey stones came tumbling down, and the children of the village amused themselves as they flung stones into the many-coloured windows.

When the first rays of a cold and pale November sun penetrated the heavy dark clouds, the little synagogue was but a heap of stone, broken glass and smashed-up woodwork.

Where the two well cared for flowerbeds had flanked both sides of the gravel path leading to the door of the synagogue, the children had lit a bonfire and the parchment of the Scrolls gave enough food for the flames to eat up the smashed-up benches and doors, and the wood, which only the day before had been the Holy Ark for the Scrolls of the Law of Moses.[12]

Similar scenes were repeated throughout the Reich. In Worms, Herta Mansbacher, the assistant principal of the Jewish school, was among those who managed to put out the fire in the synagogue, but a gang of louts soon arrived to light it again. In a gesture of defiance, Herta Mansbacher barred the entrance. 'As much as they sought to put a Jewish house of worship to the torch,' the historian of Worms Jewry has written, 'she was equally willing to stop them, even at the risk of her life.'[13]

Herta Mansbacher was eventually pushed aside, and the synagogue burned to the ground. She survived, until the deportation from Worms of 20 March 1942.

In the aftermath of the Kristallnacht, German Jewry was 'fined' for the damage done. The fine, a thousand million marks, was levied by the compulsory confiscation of twenty per cent of the property of every German Jew.[14] This confiscation was promulgated by government decree on 12 November 1938. Three days later, following more than five years of being pilloried and discriminated against in the classroom, German Jewish children were finally barred from German schools.

Not every German watched these events unmoved, or unprepared to challenge them. On 16 November 1938, a week after the Kristallnacht, Pastor J. von Jan preached to his congregation in Swabia: 'Houses of worship, sacred to others, have been burned down with impunity – men who have locally served our nation and conscientiously done their duty, have been thrown into concentration camps simply because they belong to a different race. Our nation's infamy is bound to bring about Divine punishment.'

Dragged out of his Bible class by a Nazi mob, Pastor Jan was brutally beaten, then thrown on to the roof of a shed. The mob then smashed his vicarage, just as, a week earlier, so many Jewish houses had been smashed. Pastor Jan was imprisoned.[15]

The 'opportunity offered by Grynszpan's criminal act', Sir George Ogilvie-Forbes wrote to London from Berlin on that same day, November 16, 'has let loose forces of medieval barbarism'. The position of the German Jews was, he commented, 'indeed tragic', and he added: 'They dwell in the grip and at the mercy of a brutal oligarchy, which fiercely resents all humanitarian foreign intervention. Misery and despair are already there and when their resources are either denied to them or exhausted, their end will be starvation.' The Jews of Germany, he feared, were 'not a national but a world problem which if neglected contains the seeds of a terrible vengeance'.[16] On November 19 the burning spread to the Free City of Memel, many of whose Jews fled eastward into Lithuania.

The Jews who had been seized during the Kristallnacht, and sent to concentration camps, experienced a foretaste of what that vengeance might be. On November 23 the *News Chronicle*, a London newspaper, reported the arrival of sixty-two Jews, including two rabbis, at Sachsenhausen concentration camp, north of Berlin. The arrested men had reached the camp gates under police escort from Berlin. At the gates, the police were made to hand them over to an SS unit. The sixty-two Jews were then forced to run a gauntlet of spades, clubs and whips. According to an eye-witness, the police, 'unable to bear their cries, turned their backs'. As the Jews were beaten, they fell. As they fell they were beaten further. This 'orgy' of beating lasted half an hour. When it was over, 'twelve of the sixty-two were dead, their skulls smashed. The others were all unconscious. The eyes of some had been knocked out, their faces flattened and shapeless.'[17]

In New York, on November 23, a mass demonstration organized by the Joint Boycott Council protested against the renewed violence. Two days later, in Chicago, protesters burned swastika flags.[18] Elsewhere, however, the Nazi excesses only fanned the flames of hatred. In the Slovak province of the now truncated Czechoslovakia, the anti-Jewish party having gained the ascendancy, attacks on Jews not only increased, but went unchallenged by the police. The writer Dr Geza Fischer was attacked in the street. 'He was an inoffensive man', one of Fischer's colleagues later recalled, 'of definite Jewish appearance. He was brought into a doorway and his head was knocked against the wall. He was brought to the hospital half dead, and he died within a few hours. His wife committed suicide.'[19]

The search for refuge had become desperate. From Berlin, Captain Foley sent a strongly worded telegram to Jerusalem, asking for extra Palestine certificates, including one thousand for young Jews who might thereby be allowed in without their parents. As Benno Cohn recalled, Foley 'did everything in his power to enable us to bring over as many Jews as possible. He helped all the categories, and one can say that he rescued thousands of Jews from the jaws of death.'[20]

Among those who saw Captain Foley at work in the British Passport Control Office in Berlin was the young Dutchman, Wim van Leer. Forty-six years later he recalled Foley's 'genuine compassion for the throngs that day in, day out besieged his office with their applications, requests and enquiries as to the progress of their case'. Van Leer added: 'The winter of 1938 was a harsh one, and elderly men and women waited from six in the morning, queuing up in the snow and biting wind. Captain Foley saw to it that a uniformed commissionaire trundled a tea-urn on a trolley along the line of frozen misery, and all this despite the clientele, neurotic with frustration and cold, doing little to lighten his task.'[21]

On December 2 the first train bound for Harwich with German Jewish children on board arrived from the Hook of Holland: two hundred children, all of them orphans, who had left Germany at twenty-four hours' notice, each with two bags of clothing.[22] In Britain they found sanctuary, as had more than fifty thousand German and Austrian refugees. But while tens of thousands found sanctuary, there were neither permits nor funds for the hundreds of thousands. 'The first effort', noted the provincial Council for German Jewry in Hull, 'will be to save the children.'[23]

The persecutions in Germany continued. The only possibility of bringing pressure to bear on the German Government, wrote one British official, Roger Makins, 'is by retaliation, expulsion of German citizens, and by a clear indication that until persecution or spoliation of Jews ceases, the policy of appeasement is at an end'.[24] But the policy of appeasement was not at an end. Nor were the gates of immigration to be opened by any country to the extent required. On December 14, the British Cabinet, headed by the Prime Minister, Neville Chamberlain, decided to allow ten thousand German Jewish children to enter Britain, provided the refugee organizations would guarantee to maintain them; but it rejected an appeal from the Jewish Agency for Palestine for an additional twenty-one thousand Palestine certificates.[25]

Several thousand Jews, travelling by boat from German ports to Shanghai, were able to enter Shanghai without visas. Despite Foreign Office hesitation in London, Captain Foley supported this method of emigration: 'It might be considered humane on our part not to interfere officially to prevent the Jews from choosing their own graveyards. They would rather die as free men in Shanghai than as slaves in Dachau.' Speaking in Berlin on 30 January 1939, Hitler declared that in the event of war: 'The result will not be the bolshevization of the earth, and thus the victory of Jewry, but the annihilation of the Jewish race in Europe.'[26]

Six days before Hitler's speech, Field Marshal Goering had instructed General Heydrich to 'solve' the so-called Jewish problem 'by emigration and evacuation'.[27] In England, a disused army camp at Richborough in Kent was opened in February for future arrivals; it could hold three thousand people at a time. Individual visas were not required by those who arrived: only a block permit. Within twelve months, eight thousand Jews had passed through this camp to homes in Britain, most of them young men who had been sent to Dachau, Sachsenhausen and other concentration camps after the Kristallnacht, and had later been released.[28]

Among those German Jews who now found haven in Britain was Eric Lucas, whose Uncle Michael had watched the destruction of the small Hoengen synagogue on 9 November 1938. 'It was a cold, dark February morning,' Lucas later recalled. 'The train which was to carry me to safety waited on the platform. I had hoped that in a few days, that train would carry my sister, and perhaps in a few months, my parents, to safety.' His account continued:

> The town where we lived was the border-control point, as beyond it stretched the still free towns of Belgium and Holland. In just over an hour the train would speed through the fertile lowlands of Belgium, and would take me right to the Channel Port of Ostend.
>
> I was the only passenger who boarded the train at that station. To travel abroad, to leave the country, was only granted to emigrants and those who had a special reason connected with the interest of the state. The travellers were few, but the customs officials and the guarding soldiers were many. The men on whose whim hung one's final leaving were the sinister tall figures in new black uniforms.
>
> When I was at last allowed to board the train, I rushed to the window to look for my parents, whom I could not see until I had left the customs shed. They stood there, in the distance, but they did not come to the train. I waved timidly, and yet full of fear, after the control I had just passed; but even that was too

much. A man in a black uniform rushed towards me, 'You Jewish swine — one more sign or word from you and we shall keep you here. You have passed the customs.'

And so I stood at the window of the train. In the distance stood a silent and aging couple, to whom I dared neither speak nor wave a last farewell; but I could see their faces very distinctly in the light of the oncoming morning.

A few hours previously, first my father and then my mother had laid their hands gently on my bowed head to bless me, asking God to let me be like Ephraim and Menashe.

'Let it be well with you. Do your work and duty, and if God wills it we shall see you again. Never forget that you are a Jew, do not forget your people, and do not forget us.' Thus my father had said and his eyes had grown soft and dim.

'My boy — it may be that we can come after you, but you will never be away from me — from your mother.' Tears streamed down her infinitely kind and sad face. With a last effort she continued in the old, so familiar Hebrew words, 'Go now, in life and peace.'

Standing at the window of the train, I was suddenly overcome with a maiming certainty that I would never see my father and mother again. There they stood, lonely, and with the sadness of death. Cruel hands kept us apart in that last intimate moment. A passionate, rebellious cry stuck in my throat against all that senseless brutality and inhuman cruelty. Why, O God, had it all to be like that?

There stood my father and my mother. An old man, leaning heavily on his stick and holding his wife's hand. It was the first and the last time in my life that I had seen them both weep. Now and then my mother would stretch her hand out, as if to grasp mine — but the hand fell back, knowing it could never reach.

Can the world ever justify the pain that burned in my father's eyes? My father's eyes were gentle and soft, but filled with tears of loneliness and fear. They were the eyes of a child that seeks the kindness of its mother's face, and the protection of its father.

As the train pulled out of the station to wheel me to safety, I leant my face against the cold glass of the window, and wept bitterly.

Those who have crossed the Channel, escaping from fear of death to safety, can understand what it means to wait for those who are still beyond it, longing to cross it, but who will never reach these white cliffs, towering over the water.[29]

In March 1939, Eric Lucas was still trying to find a foreign embassy in London willing to give his parents a visa:

'Have you sufficient money for your parents to live there without working?'

'A small sum could be got together'.

'Have your parents a valid passport?'

'No, because they can only apply for a passport to leave the country if they have a visa and permission to proceed to the country to which they want to go'.

'Yes, I see, but they cannot get a visa until they have a valid passport'.

'Months passed,' Lucas added, 'and hope vanished.'[30]

Eric Lucas was one of more than fifty thousand German Jews who found safety in Britain. His parents, unable to obtain the necessary papers and permits, perished three years later.

The persecutions which in November 1938 had aroused so much sympathy were now arousing fear, and even hostility. In February 1939 the Baldwin Fund, set up to help Jewish refugees, was said by a Foreign Office official to 'feel that they are being blackmailed by the threat that if they do not take over this or that individual, he will be beaten to death in a camp'.[31]

Immigration regulations were far more stringent in the United States than in Britain. More than ten thousand German Jewish children were admitted to Britain in 1938 and 1939, but less than five hundred to the United States.

On March 15 German forces occupied the Bohemian and Moravian provinces of Czechoslovakia. Slovakia declared its independence. Bohemia and Moravia became a German Protectorate. In the capital, Prague, lived fifty-six thousand Jews, of whom twenty-five thousand were refugees from Germany and Austria. Eight days later, German forces occupied the autonomous city of Memel, on the Baltic coast, and nine thousand more Jews came within the Nazi orbit. Most of them were able to flee, to neighbouring Lithuania. Some of Prague's Jews were able to flee northwards to Poland, or southwards to Hungary. Others went to France, a few to Britain. But those who sought to enter Britain, by air, without permits, were put on the next plane back to Europe.

Now even Britain was hesitating, afraid, as one minister, Lord Winterton, told a deputation of German Jews on May 18, that there were limits, occasioned by 'anti-Semitism and anti-alienism' beyond which 'it was dangerous to go'.[32]

As Nazi rule was imposed on Bohemia and Moravia, the Hungarian government took a further step towards isolating its own five hundred thousand Jews, and those tens of thousands of Jews brought within its borders by the annexation of southern Slovakia and Ruthenia, both formerly parts of post-1918 Czechoslovakia. On May 3 a second 'Jewish Law', issued in Budapest, forbade any Hungarian Jew from becoming a judge, a lawyer, a schoolteacher or a member of the Hungarian parliament.

On May 17, two weeks after this new Hungarian law, the British government issued a Palestine White Paper fixing an upper limit of seventy-five thousand Jews to be admitted to Palestine over the next five years. Of these, twenty-five thousand could be refugees. There were still over two hundred thousand Jews trapped in Germany, at least fifty-five thousand in what had formerly been Austria, and tens of thousands more seeking refuge from the Protectorate and from the newly independent, viciously anti-Semitic Slovakia, as well as Polish Jews seeking to leave for Palestine at a rate of more than thirty thousand a year.

To enforce its new immigration restrictions, the British government began to put diplomatic pressure on the governments of Yugoslavia, Rumania, Turkey and Greece, not to allow boats with 'illegal' immigrants on board to proceed towards Palestine. On May 26 an inter-departmental conference in London discussed the possibility of paying the Rumanian government fifteen days' worth of food for each 'illegal' refugee, in order to encourage the Rumanians to detain these Jewish emigrants and then send them back to Poland, central Europe and Germany.[33]

Despite the growing restrictions and pressures, Jews still sought escape to Palestine; those who set out without valid certificates travelled down the Danube, and crossed the Black Sea in small boats, often hardly seaworthy. Among these 'illegals' in the summer of 1939 was the seventeen-year-old Julius Lowenthal, from Vienna.

Earlier, he had managed to cross the border from Germany into Holland, hoping to find refuge in England. But he had been arrested by the Dutch police in Amsterdam, and deported back across the German border. From Germany he then made his way, by train and boat, through central Europe to Rumania, and down to the Black Sea coast. From there, he travelled on board a cattle boat, the *Liesel*, whose several hundred other 'illegal' refugees reached the Palestine shore on May 29. Intercepted by a British warship, they were nevertheless allowed to land.[34]

While Lowenthal's cattle boat was approaching the shores of Palestine, an ocean liner, the *St Louis*, was anchored off the coast of Cuba, with 1128 German Jewish refugees on board. More than seven hundred of these refugees held United States immigration quota numbers, permitting them entry, but in three years' time. Despite long negotiations with Cuba, the United States, Colombia, Chile, Paraguay and the Argentine, only twenty-two of the refugees were allowed to land at Havana. In mid-June 1939, the rest were forced back across the Atlantic, their voyage on the *St Louis* followed by the world's press and newsreel cameras: 288 found haven in Britain, while 619 were admitted by Holland, Belgium and France. Few of those refugees who returned on the *St Louis* to continental Europe were to survive the war years. But in June 1939, as they found new homes in Paris, Brussels and Amsterdam, no one in those three capitals, whether refugees or inhabitants, had any reason to fear for their freedom. France, Belgium and Holland were, after all, independent states. The immediate threat to the Jews seemed primarily an internal German one, spread chiefly to those countries which Germany had already annexed: the newly designated 'province' of Austria, with Vienna as its principal city; the so-called 'Protectorate' of Bohemia and Moravia, with its capital in Prague; and Memel.

From the first days of the German occupation of Prague, thousands of Czech Jews had appealed for asylum in Western Europe, Britain and the United States. Most of them realized that the permitted places were so few that, if fortunate, they might gain admittance only for their children. One such parent was Charles Wessely, Secretary of the Prague Produce Exchange, and a Judge at the Arbitration Court. He was forty-three years old, his wife, thirty-eight, their son Rudolf, fourteen. Charles Wessely's appeal was sent from Prague to Britain on 11 March 1939. His son was found a home in Britain, arriving in London on July 1. But despite the offers of the Judge and his wife 'to do any work' even domestic posts, inconsiderable of our former social standing', no places could be found for them.[35]

The fate of the Jews trapped in central Europe had become a matter of controversy. Those who had to determine the British government's policy towards Jewish refugees who had reached Poland from the Protectorate were not convinced that these refugees were in any real danger. 'A great many of these', wrote one official, Patrick Reilly, on July 24, 'are not in any sense political refugees, but Jews who panicked unnecessarily and need not have left.' Many of them, he added, 'are quite unsuitable as emigrants and would be a very difficult problem if brought here'.[36] Six days later, on July 30, the British Prime Minister, Neville Chamberlain, commented in a private letter on the persecution of German Jews: 'I believe the persecution arose out of two motives: a desire to rob the Jews of their money and a jealousy of their superior cleverness.' Chamberlain continued: 'No doubt Jews aren't a lovable people; I don't care about them myself; but that is not sufficient to explain the Pogrom.'[37]

Shortly before a meeting of the British Cabinet on August 4, the Colonial Secretary, Malcolm MacDonald, who was responsible for policy towards Jewish immigration to Palestine, had asked that the question of 'illegal' immigration be put on the agenda. Then he reported that the High Commissioner in Palestine had been authorized to announce that 'no immigration quota would be issued for the next six-monthly period October 1939–March 1940'. The second step to stop illegal traffic was the Foreign Office's 'strong representations' to certain governments 'against their laxity' in the 'discouragement of this traffic'. MacDonald added:

> Very strong representations had been made in particular to Rumania, Poland and Greece, and the first results of this action had been good. Rumania and Greece had taken action which should secure much stricter surveillance, and while the good effect of our representations might not last, since the power of Jewish money was great, for the present at any rate the results were good.[38]

MacDonald's reference to what he called 'the power of Jewish money' was ill-chosen; in reality, the funds of the Jewish charitable institutions were nearly exhausted. Two weeks later, on August 17, news of just how desperate the Jewish situation was in Europe reached the Foreign Office from Slovakia. The report, on the fate of the eighty-five thousand Jews of Slovakia, was distressing. Non-Jews, encouraged by the Germans, 'do all they can to rob and plunder Jewish property and persecute the Jewish people'. Other Slovaks, 'unable to show their hatred of the Germans, so vent their wrath instead upon the Jews'. 'Jew-baiting' had become a frequent occurrence. All but a small proportion of Jews had been excluded since the previous March from the professions and the universities. Many Jewish shops and businesses had been forced to close.

Many Slovak Jews were joining the 'illegal' movement to Palestine. 'Their nerves can stand no more,' the report explained. 'Fear of the unknown in other countries is more pleasant to them than present persecution and feeling that they are trapped.' Several thousand had already fled, and some had even succeeded in reaching Palestine. 'This made the others more reckless,' the reported added, 'especially as conditions in Slovakia grew worse.'[39]

On 23 August 1939 the world learned of the signature of a non-aggression pact between Nazi Germany and the Soviet Union. Suddenly it became clear that if Hitler were to invade Poland, the Soviet Union would stand aside. This pact was ominous news for the 3,250,000 Jews of Poland.

Since 1921, more than four hundred thousand Polish Jews had emigrated, many to France and Belgium, others to Palestine. One of these emigrants, Ze'ev Sherpski, from the Polish village of Szrensk, arrived in Palestine, as a tourist, together with his daughter, at the very moment of the signature of the Nazi-Soviet Pact. Sherpski's wife Hanna, and their son, were to have followed in a few months' time. But time had run out.[40]

On the evening of August 31, as German radio poured out a stream of venom against the Polish Republic, sixty German Jewish children were travelling with their adult escort in a train crowded with German soldiers from Cologne to Cleve, the only point on the Dutch frontier to which trains were still running. Crossing the frontier, the train proceeded to the Hook of Holland. Overnight, the children crossed the North Sea to the British port of Harwich.

There, at dawn on September 1, they learned that Germany had invaded Poland.[41]

Ze'ev Sherpski was safe in Palestine. The sixty German Jewish children were safe in Britain. But, as German forces broke through the Polish frontier, and German bombs fell on Warsaw, more than three million Polish Jews, the largest single mass of European Jewry, were trapped in a front line of uncertainty and hatred. Among them were Hanna Sherpski and her son. No one had yet determined what their exact future would be; but neither was to survive the war.

7

September 1939:
the trapping of Polish Jewry

THE GERMAN FORCES crossed into Poland in the early hours of Friday, 1 September 1939. For six and a half years Poland's Jews had watched with alarm the violent anti-Semitism imposed by Nazi Germany first upon German, then upon Austrian and finally upon Czech Jewry. They knew, at first hand, from Polish anti-Semites, what mob hatred could do. But Polish Jewry had its own means of defence, its own press, its own institutions, and its own representation in the Polish parliament. With the German invasion, these protective shields were torn away. On the railway carriages bringing German troops into the war zone, were painted crude pictures of Jews with hooked noses, and the slogan: 'We're off to Poland – to thrash the Jews'.[1]

On that first day of the German invasion, 393,950 Jews lived in Warsaw, the Polish capital. This was a third of Warsaw's population; a greater number of Jews than were left in Germany. Only in New York, where two million Jews lived, were there more Jews in a single city. In the whole of Palestine there were only a few thousand more Jews than in Warsaw alone.

At nightfall on September 1, tens of thousands of Warsaw Jews flocked to synagogue to welcome the Sabbath, among them eighteen-year-old Alexander Wojcikiewicz, who worked as a proofreader at his father's printing press. Forty years later, he recalled how, that Friday night, 'the Jews of Warsaw prayed as never before. The synagogue at Tlomackie Street was full to overflowing and large crowds stood and prayed outside. People cried to the Almighty to have pity on them and their children. They begged for mercy for themselves and all those who might die on the battlefield.'

'Long after midnight,' Wojcikiewicz added, 'my father took me to the press once more. There he hid some of our valuables under one of the linotype machines, deeply cemented in a large hole. I have never found out what happened to those gold coins, patiently saved over the years. Today another building, on another street bearing the same name, stands where our press once stood. The lost treasure was but a tiny speck of the wealth Polish Jewry had gathered for centuries to lose, irretrievably within a single day.'[2]

From the first day of the German advance into Poland, Jewish soldiers fought alongside Polish soldiers in the battles for the frontier, and, later, in the battles around Warsaw. Inside Warsaw, more than three thousand Jews were among some ten thousand citizens killed during more than a week of intense aerial bombardment.

In western Poland, Saturday, September 2, saw the heavy air bombardment of several cities. In Piotrkow, home of fifteen thousand Jews, Romek Zaks was killed that day, 'the first Jewish victim'.[3]

On Sunday, 3 September 1939, Britain and France declared war on Germany. They could do nothing to halt, or even to slow down, the pace of the German advance across Poland. As the German forces advanced, and within hours of their occupation of a town or village, Jews were singled out for abuse and massacre by special SS 'operational groups', acting in the rear of the German fighting forces. That same Sunday, September 3, a few hours after German troops had entered the frontier town of Wieruszow, one of these SS groups seized twenty Jews, among them several prominent citizens, took them to the market place, and lined them up for execution. Among these Jews was Israel Lewi, a man of sixty-four. When his daughter, Liebe Lewi, ran up to her father to say farewell, a German ordered her to open her mouth for her 'impudence', and then fired a bullet into it. Liebe Lewi fell dead on the spot. The twenty men were then executed: among them Abraham Lefkowitz, Moshe Mozes and Usiel Baumatz.[4]

The air bombardment continued to take a heavy toll. On September 4, more than a thousand Jews who had managed to flee from Piotrkow to the nearby village of Sulejow, believing that they would be safe in this remoter corner, were killed as German bombers twice attacked the village, and fighters strafed those who sought to flee. Among the people killed in Sulejow was one of Piotrkow's leading rabbis, Jacob Glazer, his daughter and his grandchild. The

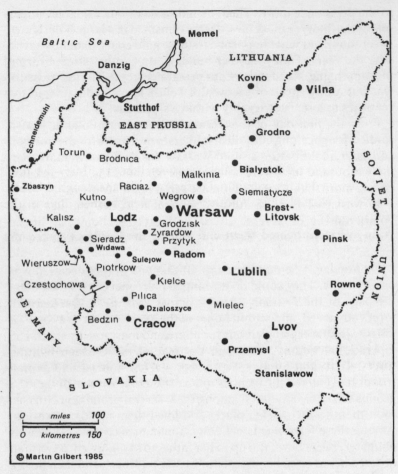

Baltic Sea · **Memel**
Danzig
LITHUANIA
Kovno
Vilna
Stutthof
EAST PRUSSIA
Schneidemuhl
Grodno
Torun · **Brodnica**
Bialystok
Zbaszyn · **Raciaz** · **Malkinia**
Kutno · **Wegrow** · **Siemiatycze**
Kalisz · **Lodz** · **Warsaw** · **Brest-Litovsk**
Grodzisk
Zyrardow
Sieradz · **Przytyk** · **Pinsk**
Widawa
Wieruszow · **Sulejow** · **Radom**
Piotrkow
Czestochowa · **Kielce** · **Lublin**
Pilica · **Rowne**
Dzialoszyce · **Mielec**
GERMANY
Bedzin · **Cracow**
Lvov
SOVIET UNION
Przemysl
Stanislawow
SLOVAKIA

O   miles   100
O   kilometres   150
© Martin Gilbert 1985

POLAND

Goldblum family was wiped out in its entirety. Entering Piotrkow
itself on September 5, the Germans tried to set fire to the predominantly Jewish section of the city, shooting dead those Jews who ran
from the burning buildings. After the fires had died down, German
soldiers entered a house which had escaped the flames, took out six
Jews, and ordered them to run. As the Jews ran, they were shot. Five
died violently; the sixth, Reb Bunem Lebel, died later of his
wounds.[5]

In the first ten days of the German advance, such onslaughts against unarmed, defenceless civilians were carried out in more than a hundred towns and villages. In the city of Czestochowa, home of thirty thousand Jews, 180 Jews were shot on September 4, 'Bloody Monday'.[6] At the village of Widawa, home of one hundred Jewish families, the Germans ordered the rabbi, Abraham Mordechai Morocco, to burn the Holy books. He refused, whereupon they burned him, with the Scrolls of the Law in his hands.[7] On September 8, in the city of Bedzin, where more than twenty thousand Jews lived, two hundred were driven into the synagogue, which was then locked, and set on fire.[8] At Mielec, on September 13, thirty-five Jews were arrested in the communal baths, taken to the slaughterhouse, and then burned alive. Another twenty were burned alive in the synagogue.[9]

In every conquered town and village, the Germans forced the Jews to clear rubble, to carry heavy loads, to hand over any gold, silver or jewellery, to scrub floors and lavatories with their prayer shawls, and to dance in front of their captors. Elderly Jews had their beards cut off with scissors, or ripped from their chins. Young religious Jews had their sidelocks cut, or torn from their faces, amid much laughter and ribaldry.

On September 10, General Halder, of the German General Staff, noted in his diary that some SS men, having ordered fifty Jews to work all day repairing a bridge, had then flung them into a synagogue and shot them. Light sentences had been imposed on the killers. But even these light sentences were later overruled, by Himmler personally, on the grounds that they came under a general amnesty. At the trial of one of the killers, the Judge Advocate had pleaded that, 'as an SS man, he was particularly sensitive to the sight of Jews. He had therefore acted quite thoughtlessly, in a spirit of adventure.'[10]

In the first fifty-five days of the German conquest and occupation of western and central Poland five thousand Jews were murdered behind the lines: dragged from their homes, and from their hiding places.[11] 'On the first day', Eda Lichtmann has recalled, of the occupation of Pilica, 'the Germans took people, especially men, to work, and forced them to clean and collect the dust with their hands: Jewish men. They were ordered to undress, and behind each Jewish man there was a German soldier with a fixed bayonet who ordered him to run. If the Jew stopped, he would be hit in the back with a bayonet. Almost all the Jewish men returned home bleeding and amongst them – my father.' Then, a few days later, on September 12, 'large trucks appeared all of a sudden', soldiers jumped off the trucks, then went from house to house, seizing men, irrespective of their age.

Thirty-two Jews were seized that day in Pilica, as well as four Poles. First they were photographed, and their names recorded. Then they were marched into the market place and forced to call out, in German: 'We are traitors of the people.' Then they were taken away in trucks. Eda Lichtmann ran after the trucks, with a friend whose father had also been seized. 'We ran after them until a small forest. All the Jews taken were already dead on the ground. My father as well, shot in many parts of his body.' Jews and Poles: all were dead. 'I kissed my father; he was as cold as ice.'[12]

In 1939 the Jewish New Year began on Thursday, September 14. That day, German forces entered the Polish city of Przemysl, where seventeen thousand citizens, one third of the population, were Jews. Forty-three leading Jewish citizens were arrested, taken to forced labour, savagely beaten, and then shot.[13] Among the forty-three was Asscher Gitter, whose son had emigrated to the United States in 1938, hoping that one day his father would join him. In Sieradz, on New Year's Day, five Jews and two Poles were shot.[14] That same day in Czestochowa, Order No. 7 of the German Civilian Administration transferred all Jewish industrial and commercial enterprises to 'Aryan' hands, such enterprises to be taken over 'without distinction whether the owner fled or remained'.[15]

At Piotrkow, a decree issued on the eve of the New Year forbade Jews to be outside their homes after five o'clock in the afternoon. The twenty-seven-year-old Getzel Frenkel, coming home five minutes late, was shot dead for his breach of this decree.[16]

Even while these outbursts of confiscation and killing were taking place throughout western Poland, a conference was held in Berlin on September 21 at which the long-term future of Polish Jewry was discussed. The host of the conference was Reinhard Heydrich, Chief of the Reich Central Security Office. Those present included the commanders of several of the SS operational groups in Poland.

Those who could not be present were sent a secret note of the discussion.

Opening the meeting, Heydrich stressed, as the secret note recorded, that what he called the 'planned overall measures (i.e., the ultimate aim)' were to be kept 'strictly secret'. He also insisted that a 'distinction' must be made between what he called 'the ultimate aim, which requires a prolonged period of time' and the 'stages' leading to the fulfilment of this ultimate aim.

Heydrich told the conference that, as a prerequisite of the 'ultimate aim', Polish Jews were to be concentrated in the larger cities. If possible, large areas of western Poland 'should be cleared completely of Jews', or should at least have in them 'as few concentration centres as possible'. Elsewhere in Poland, Jews should be concentrated only in cities situated at railway junctions, or along a railway, 'so that future measures may be accomplished more easily'.

To ensure that all instructions for the movement of Jews were carried out on time, Heydrich added, a Council of Jewish Elders was to be set up in each city. In case of 'sabotage of such instructions', these Jewish Councils were to be threatened with 'the severest measures'.

This 'concentration of Jews in cities' meant the creation of ghettos, such as had not existed in Europe since the Middle Ages. To facilitate this 'concentration', Heydrich noted, orders would probably have to be given 'forbidding Jews to enter certain districts of that city altogether'. At the same time, farmland belonging to Jews should be taken away from them: 'entrusted to the care' of neighbouring German 'or even Polish' peasants.[17]

On September 23, two days after Heydrich's conference, the Jews celebrated the holiest day in their calendar, the Day of Atonement, a time of repentance, solemnity, and hope for the year to come. For the Nazis, it was a time for cruel indignities, as it was to be for the next five years. At Siemiatycze, a town whose Jewish population of five thousand was already much enlarged by two thousand refugees from western Poland, SS men broke into the synagogue in the middle of the opening prayer, and sang their own hymn in its place: then, on the following day of prayer, they again entered the synagogue, already crowded. 'A great panic', writes the historian of the Jews of Siemiatycze, 'broke out among the worshipping Jews. Many jumped out of the windows. In the synagogue on

Drogoczyner Street, Yosl the turner was shot while trying to escape, and remained hanging on the window-sill.'[18]

At Wegrow, the rabbi was ordered to sweep the streets. Then he was ordered to collect the refuse in his fur hat. While he was bending over to carry out this order, he was bayoneted three times. 'He continued working,' it was later learned in Warsaw, 'and died at work.'[19]

At Kielce, home of more than eighteen thousand Jews, hundreds were seized, that Day of Atonement morning, from some of the smaller houses of prayer in the city, and dragged to the market place. There, Maria Feferman-Wasoff has recalled, 'their beards were sliced off. Bareheaded, and in their fringed prayer shawls, they were forced to dig ditches.' In the midst of those digging she had caught sight of her own uncle, Abish Kopf, a small, fragile man, and a scholar. 'Now the sweat was rolling down his face,' she recalled, 'and the white prayer shawl was soiled, drenched and twisted on his back. Uncle Abish's daughters, Andzia, Mania and Dorka, pleaded with the amused guards. "Please," they cried, "let our father go, can't you see he is collapsing?" All they received was loud laughter. Someone standing close by remarked with bitterness, "If there is a God, let Him strike these Nazis dead." Late that night the Jews were set free.'[20]

At the small town of Raciaz, on that same sacred day, all old and weak Jews were ordered to shave off their beards. They were then harnessed to dustcarts, 'and made to drag the carts from place to place', as one eye-witness, Abraham Altus, later recalled, while other Jews had to load refuse on the carts. 'Since the Nazis were drunk with spirits and liquor,' Altus continued 'they cruelly thrashed the old men, while some stood photographing these scenes of horror and hell. Between the beating and the photographing they made us dance and jump, and hit us with sticks and mistreated us.' These torments continued throughout the Day of Atonement, until, bleeding and abased to the very earth', Abraham Altus wrote, 'desolate and broken and confused, we were no longer capable of standing or praying. Our spirits were numbed and our eyes were closed against tears. So we simply lay on the floor at home.'

'After we had rested a while', Altus added, 'and our spirits returned to us, then we burst out weeping, weeping without a break like forsaken children.'[21]

In Piotrkow, the Day of Atonement was marked by another aspect of the new 'Nazi order'. The Germans forced several thousand Polish prisoners-of-war, many of them Jews, into the hall of the Jewish Religious School, and, forbidding access to lavatories, forced these thousands of men to relieve themselves in the school hall. They were then given prayer shawls, Holy books, the curtains of the Holy Ark and the beautifully embroidered covers of the Scrolls of the Law, and ordered to clean up the excrement with these fine and sacred objects.[22]

Almost all of western Poland was now under German control. In Poland's eastern regions, Soviet forces were advancing, according to one of the secret clauses of the Nazi-Soviet Pact: cutting off the Polish army from any possible regrouping in the Vilna or Lvov regions. Warsaw, on that Day of Atonement, was still holding out, a city besieged. But during the day there was an intense German artillery and air bombardment, striking with particular ferocity on the main Jewish district. 'In the midst of this bombardment,' a fifteen-year-old Warsaw schoolgirl, Mary Berg, recorded, 'a strange meteorological phenomenon took place: heavy snow mixed with hail began to fall in the middle of a bright sunny day. For a while the bombing was interrupted, and the Jews interpreted the snow as a special act of heavenly intervention: even the oldest among them were unable to recall a similar occurrence.' But later in the day, when the snowstorm was over, the Germans 'made up for lost time with renewed fury'.[23]

In the fighting now nearly ended, six thousand Jews had been killed in action with the Polish forces. A further sixty-one thousand had been among the six hundred thousand Polish soldiers taken prisoners-of-war by the Germans. From the first days of their captivity, the Jewish soldiers were subjected to particularly harsh treatment. One prisoner-of-war, Joseph Berger, later recalled how, on the Day of Atonement, he and other Jewish prisoners-of-war were forced to clean the lavatories with their bare hands, as a special indignity.[24] Another Jewish prisoner-of-war described how, marching with a group of Polish prisoners-of-war, he hurt his foot, and was unable to keep up with the rest:

> The transport leader noticed this and told me to sit on one of the carts which accompanied us. I mounted the wagon, sat

down and took my shoes off to ease the pain in my feet, which were covered in blood. Unfortunately, the German who had given out the bread saw this. He made me get off the cart, aimed his rifle at me and bellowed: 'Du kannst laufen, Jude.' 'You can run, Jew.' He began pushing me towards those at the front, who were about five hundred metres ahead. By making a supreme effort I managed to avoid his bayonet and, given no alternative, began to run. For more than ten kilometres my 'guard' gave me no peace, constantly threatening to shoot me, cutting my coat with his bayonet. When the German cavalry passed us he pushed me among the horses so that they should trample me. In this fashion, under incessant threat of death, I reached Wegrowiec. I was a broken man, I wanted to cry from pain.

At Wagrowiec, this eye-witness later recalled, whenever the Germans discovered a Jewish prisoner-of-war, 'they made him stand in a ditch full of water for more than half an hour'.[25]

On September 28, before the Polish army had been finally defeated, and two days before German forces entered Warsaw, Soviet and German forces reached their pre-arranged line, east of Warsaw, and Poland was partitioned. Tens of thousands of Polish soldiers, among them several thousand Jews, gave themselves up to the Red Army as it occupied the eastern Polish cities of Vilna, Grodno, Bialystok, Brest-Litovsk, Pinsk, Rowne and Lvov. In certain areas, German troops withdrew to make way for their Soviet counterparts. Among the towns thus transferred from German to Soviet control were Przemysl, where Asscher Gitter had been among the forty-three leading citizens murdered by the Nazis, and Siemiatycze, where Yosl the turner had been shot.

As soon as the fighting stopped, but before the new border had been patrolled and closed, a mass movement of Polish Jews began, eastward, to the Polish territory which had so suddenly and unexpectedly come under Soviet control. In the six years between 1933 and 1939, three hundred thousand German Jews had left Germany as refugees; now, in the six weeks between the end of September and mid-November 1939, more than a quarter of a million Polish Jews were able to flee eastwards, crossing the rivers Narew, Bug and San, to the Soviet zone, and to the Soviet Union.

'We only knew that we must get to the Bug,' an eighteen-year-old

Jewish girl, Vitka Kempner, later recalled. 'The Jews in the little towns on the Bug, they did a wonderful job,' rescuing Jews, sheltering them, and helping them to cross the river. Vitka Kempner had come from the western Polish city of Kalisz: on the night after the Germans had locked many Jews in the city church, she had managed to jump from one of the windows, and to begin her journey eastward.[26]

While some Jews were now shot in flight, others were ordered by the Germans to flee. From Pultusk more than eight thousand Jews, nearly half of the town's population, were driven out of the town to the river Narew and forced to cross to the Soviet zone. The Jews of Pultusk could trace their residence in the town back to 1486. A Jewish festival, Succoth, was chosen for their deportation. The week of Succoth began on the evening of 28 September 1939, the day of the establishment of the Nazi-Soviet partition line.[27]

Several large towns close to the new border were the scenes of sudden, mass expulsion. In each of them the Jews were expelled without time even to bundle up their essential needs. At Tarnobrzeg, some four thousand Jews were assembled in the market place, robbed of everything they carried, and then driven eastwards across the San, many being murdered on the way.[28]

At the bank of the San, several thousand Jews, driven out of Rozwadow, Lezajsk and Lancut, were forced over the river. An eye-witness of these events recalled, immediately after the war:

> We arrived at the river San on the third day of our exile. What happened there is difficult to describe. On the bank of the river Gestapo-men were waiting and driving people into a boat, or rather raft of two unbalanced boards, from which women and children fell into the river. We saw floating corpses everywhere; near the bank women stood in the water, holding their children above their heads and crying for help, to which the Gestapo-men answered by shooting. Blood, masses of floating corpses. It is impossible to describe the despair, shouts and helplessness of people in such a situation.[29]

Hardly had the expulsion of Jews eastward been completed, than a new policy, emanating from Berlin, led to the expulsion into German-occupied Poland of thousands of Jews from the eastern towns of Greater Germany. On October 17, more than a thousand

Jews from the former Czechoslovak city of Moravska Ostrava were deported by train to the Lublin region of Poland, and there forced to build a labour camp for themselves. In the Nazi terminology of deception, the camp was given the name 'Central Office for Jewish Resettlement'.

As one of their number, Max Burger, later recalled, the Jews deported from Moravska Ostrava were put into railway coaches – passenger coaches – on October 17. The coaches were placed under SS guard, locked and sealed. On October 18 the train began to move. No water was available, and when, at Cracow station, those in the train pleaded for water, and Poles on the platform wished to help them, Stormtroops chased away the Poles 'with rifle blows'. On reaching Nisko station, in the Lublin region, all engineers, builders and doctors among the deported Jews were ordered to leave the train. Because the doors of the train were sealed, they had to clamber out through the windows. Then, surrounded by SS guards, they found themselves among other Jews who had been deported from Prague and Vienna.

A German officer then addressed them. He was Adolf Eichmann, now in charge of 'Jewish resettlement', as he had earlier been in charge of emigration. 'About seven or eight kilometres from here,' Eichmann told them, 'across the river San, the "Führer" of the Jews has promised a new homeland. There are no apartments and no houses – if you will build your homes you will have a roof over your head.' There was 'no water', Eichmann added. 'The wells are full of epidemics, there's cholera, dysentery and typhus. If you dig for water, you'll have water.'

The deported Jews were then sent across a pontoon bridge to the 'resettlement' region. Once there, such luggage as they had been able to bring was opened, and German soldiers 'just took whatever they wanted'.[30] Thousands of other Jews soon arrived: elderly Jews from Vienna, Jews who had been captured trying to escape from Moravska Ostrava to Prague, Jews caught on the outbreak of war at Hamburg docks, waiting to board ship for the United States, and Jews from the port city of Stettin.

The conditions in the Lublin region, and in the city of Lublin, were harrowing: in December 1939 the Commander-in-Chief of the German Army Group South, Field Marshal Blaskowitz, who served briefly as Military Governor of Poland, reported that many Jewish children arrived in the transport trains frozen to death, and that those who survived the journey then died of starvation in the villages in which they were 'resettled'.[31]

Also sent to Lublin were several thousand Jewish prisoners-of-war. They were put in a special camp in the city itself, at 7 Lipowa Street, and allowed to write short letters to their families. Almost none of the letters was posted. Five years later, at the time of the liberation of Lublin, they were found in the Nazi archives in Lublin. Their 'senders' had subsequently been killed after more than four years of torment in the Lipowa Street camp.[32]

From the first week of the invasion of Poland, the Germans had established a euthanasia programme for 'mental defectives': not only Poles and Jews, but also Germans. The site to which mental patients were sent, and then killed, was in a forest near the village of Piasnica, not far from Danzig. Here, from the middle of October 1939 until the end of the year, several thousand 'defectives' were killed: twelve hundred of them being Germans who were sent there from psychiatric institutions inside Germany. Kurt Eimann, the SS officer in charge of the executions, was later accused – at Hanover in 1968 – of having personally shot the first victim in the back of the head, as an example for the rest of his men.[33]

One victim of this programme was Adolf Lipschitz, a psychiatric patient in a hospital near Poznan, and a Jew. One day in November 1939, Lipschitz's father, who lived in Warsaw, was summoned to Gestapo headquarters, where he was presented with a bill for his son's treatment starting on 1 September 1939, the day of the German occupation of the hospital, and ending on October 19. When asked why the bill was only up to October 19, he was told that on that day his son, together with all the other mentally ill, had been shot. The bill covered the cost of his son's maintenance up to the day of his execution. The father was then presented with a receipt, and with a death certificate signed by a doctor.[34]

On October 21, while the deportations continued of Jews to the Lublin region, and of mentally ill to Piasnica, in Warsaw four citizens were executed for 'possession of firearms and ammunition in violation of the regulations'. One of them was listed in the official German announcement as 'A Jew, Samson Lutsenburg'.[35] Four days later, in Cracow, Hans Frank, Governor of a newly created administrative area, the 'General Government', covering central

Poland, including Warsaw and Cracow, announced, in the first issue of his official General Government gazette, that 'as of now' all Jews living in the newly created region 'are obliged to work', and that they would, 'with this aim in mind', be formed into forced labour teams.[36] Henceforth, all Polish Jewish males between the ages of fourteen and sixty had to register for work, and were rapidly taken off to a growing number of forced labour camps, of which there were twenty-eight in the Lublin region, twenty-one in the Kielce region, fourteen in the Warsaw region, twelve in the Cracow region and ten in the Rzeszow region by the end of 1939.

In order to end the random and cruel abduction of Jews seized on the streets and taken to forced labour, a Jewish Council, which had already been set up in Warsaw in conformity with Heydrich's directive of September 21, offered to organize a daily quota of Jewish workers, provided that the abductions stopped. The Germans accepted this suggestion, and in October set a quota for 'work brigades' which averaged 381 men a day. Providing this quota thus became the responsibility of the Jewish Council, and of its Chairman, Adam Czerniakow.

The abductions ceased, and the brigades were created by voluntary enlistment, made up mostly of Jewish refugees in the city, and of poor Jews for whom the pittance paid was their sole income.[37]

The process of confining the Jews according to Heydrich's directive of September 21 began just over a month later, on October 8, with the order to establish a ghetto in Piotrkow by the end of the month. All Jews who lived outside the ghetto-designated area were forced to leave their homes and to move into the ghetto. The only Jews who were later allowed to live outside the ghetto were Dr Shanster, who had converted to Christianity sixty years earlier, Jacob Witorz, who held Turkish citizenship, his wife and two sons Beniek and Shimek, and a Jew who was an Egyptian citizen, Kem, with his wife and twelve-year-old son Jerzyk.[38]

Before the end of the year, a second ghetto had been set up in nearby Radomsko, while plans were also being made for a ghetto to be established in Lodz, the home of Poland's second largest Jewish community.[39]

In Lodz, where 233,000 Jews made up a third of the city's population, daily incidents characterized the fate of Polish Jewry. Mary Berg, who had gone from Warsaw to Lodz, and had begun to keep a diary, recorded how, on November 2, she looked out of her window:

> A man with markedly Semitic features was standing quietly on the sidewalk near the curb. A uniformed German approached him and apparently gave him an unreasonable order, for I could see that the poor fellow tried to explain something with an embarrassed expression. Then a few other uniformed Germans came upon the scene and began to beat their victim with rubber truncheons. They called a cab and tried to push him into it, but he resisted vigorously. The Germans then tied his legs together with a rope, attached the end of the rope to the cab from behind, and ordered the driver to start. The unfortunate man's face struck the sharp stones of the pavement, dyeing them red with blood. Then the cab vanished down the street.[40]

The Germans who carried out such atrocities had been exposed for more than six years to the full venom of anti-Jewish propaganda: at school, in the newspapers, in their place of work, in the streets, and in their military indoctrination. 'Behind all the enemies of Germany's ascendancy', a Berlin anti-Communist magazine declared on November 2, 'stand those who demand our encirclement – the oldest enemies of the German people and of all healthy, rising nations – the Jews.'[41]

On November 7 the Germans began the expulsion of Jews from western Poland. Three regions were each to be 'cleared' of Jews: the former Polish corridor, now part of Danzig-West Prussia; the Poznan region, now the Warthegau; and the Plonsk region north of Warsaw, now part of Greater East Prussia. From these three regions, forty thousand Jews were driven out; each family forced overnight, or at most in a few days, to abandon its home, its livelihood and its possessions, and move into one of the towns of the newly established General Government region of Poland.

As an added indignity, the Jews of Sierpc, one of the towns in the newly declared Greater East Prussia, were ordered to wear a distinctive mark on their coats. 'Yes,' wrote Chaim Kaplan, a leading Warsaw educationalist, 'with my own eyes I saw the "badge of shame" which the conqueror awarded the exiled Jews of Sierpc. It is a yellow patch on which is written "Jude", sewn to one of the coat lapels.' Kaplan added that all the officials of the American Jewish Joint Distribution Committee in Warsaw saw it too, 'and their faces were filled with shame'. Kaplan advised the Jew to add, next to the word 'Jude', the words 'Mein Stolz', 'my pride'. 'But the Jew answered as one who knows, that the conqueror calls such things "sabotage" and condemns the guilty one to death.'[42]

Six days after Kaplan had seen and been so shocked by this yellow badge, Hans Frank announced from Cracow that 'all Jews and Jewesses over the age of nine throughout the General Government must wear a four-inch armband in white, marked with 'the star of Zion on the right sleeve of their inner and outer clothing'. In Warsaw, the star had to be blue. 'Transgressors', Frank warned, would be punished with imprisonment.[43]

Behaviour which in normal times was of no particular significance had become, in the Nazi perspective, a crime, and crimes, by their nature, have to be punished. Step by step, and by means of 'rules', 'regulations', 'laws' – the terminology of civilized life – the conqueror, with the full power of enforcement, created a logical corridor into a bizarre world of cruelty and injustice.

With the coming of war between Britain and Germany, tens of thousands of Jews, would-be refugees from Germany, Austria and Czechoslovakia, now had no chance of leaving. Overnight the mass of applications and requests to leave became mere scraps of paper. 'We have waited in vain', Eric Lucas's mother wrote, from near Aachen, to her son, now safe in Britain. 'We shall never see you again,' and she added: 'Was there no space in the whole wide world for us two, old people?' Her letter continued: 'I know we shall not live very long, now there is nothing left to hope for. We are so lonely and forsaken now, was there nobody who could have helped?'

Sophie Lucas could write no more. Her husband Isaac took up the pen. 'Perhaps there will still be a chance of going to our relations in Denmark,' he wrote. 'Write to them, and we shall try the same. We are thinking of you. With the help of God we shall manage.'[44]

Neither Sophie nor Isaac Lucas was to survive the war. Their place of death, place of execution, some time in 1942 or 1943, was to be recorded only as 'unknown' and 'the East'.[45]

8

'Blood of innocents'

THE MASS KILLINGS of September and October 1939 in German-occupied Poland left five thousand Jewish dead. As German rule was consolidated throughout the General Government, these killings continued, but on a smaller scale, in the form of almost daily punitive actions against Jew and non-Jew alike for every attempt at protest. These reprisal actions were arbitrary and relentless. Among six men and three boys seized at the village of Zielonka, near Warsaw, on 11 November, taken to the nearby woods and shot, were two Jews, Aron Kaufman, the village butcher, and Edward Szweryn, proprietor of the village café.¹ That same day, in Zdunska Wola, after the killing of a policeman, Jews and Poles were taken as hostages, and several were shot.²

On 12 November 1939 another stage in Heydrich's September directive was put into effect, less than two months after the Berlin meeting. This was the order for the removal of all Jews, as well as some Poles, from the newly constituted Warthegau province, formerly part of western Poland, and now incorporated into Greater Germany. The areas 'south of Warsaw and Lublin' were designated as 'the quarters for those removed'.³ But even in the areas in which Jews could live, restrictions were soon imposed. From mid-November Jews were forbidden to work in any government offices, to buy or sell to 'Aryans', to travel by train, to bake bread, to go to an 'Aryan' doctor or to have an 'Aryan' patient. In the first days of the German occupation of Warsaw, Dr Adam Zamenhof, the fifty-two-year-old manager of the Jewish hospital on Czyste Street, was arrested 'and never seen again'.⁴ Zamenhof, the son of the inventor of Esperanto, was himself the inventor of a device for checking blind spots in the field of vision.

Wherever Jews were allowed to live, their homes were liable to search and looting. David Wdowinski, the chief of the psychiatric department of the Czyste Street hospital, has recalled how, outside an apartment block in Warsaw, in the first weeks of the occupation, a truck arrived with three German officers and two civilians, who then entered one of the apartments:

> There they demanded money, jewels, goods and food. They shut the women up in one room and the men in another. They stole everything they could lay their hands on and ordered the men to load it on to the trucks, to the accompaniment of kicks and beatings. The women were searched individually for anything that they might have hidden. But they were still unsatisfied with their loot. At the point of guns they forced the women and young girls to undress and they performed gynaecological examinations on each one of them. And even this was not enough. They forced the women and girls to get up on the tables and jump to the floor with legs straddled. 'Maybe something will fall out. One never knows how deep the Jewish swindlers can hide their jewels.'[5]

Such raids happened every day. Often, a German would arrive in a truck, enter an apartment, demand certain items of furniture, and then force the Jewish owner to carry the furniture down to the truck, 'under pain of beatings with whips and sticks'.

David Wdowinski has recalled how a Jewish refugee family, who had fled to Warsaw from Polish Silesia, was 'visited' one November evening in 1939 by three German officers:

> They demanded money and jewellery and threatened the woman at the point of a gun that she give them everything. She gave them all she had. Suddenly one of the officers noticed a small medallion hanging around the neck of the little boy. This child had been ill from birth. He had petit-mal, a form of epilepsy, which forced on as many as forty and sixty seizures a day, lasting one or two seconds. The child was mentally retarded. He could express himself only in inarticulate sounds. The only thing which gave this child any comfort was this very medallion. In the presence of the officers the child was taken with a seizure and the mother pleaded that the medallion be left for her child. One of the officers watching the child said: 'I see

that the child is ill. I am a doctor, but a Jew-kid is not a human being,' and he tore the medallion off the neck of the little boy.[6]

Not only pillaging, accompanied by physical and mental violence, but also executions, continued almost daily. On November 16, among seven Poles executed in Warsaw was one Jew, Leib Michel Hochman, killed, according to the official German notification, 'for refusal to perform a job' and 'for flight'.[7] Three days later, among fifteen Poles executed in Warsaw, the German notification of the execution included, curtly, 'Knecht, Majer, Jew, born Zelechow, 1890, resident Warsaw, 29 Franciszkanska Street'.[8]

In the exultation of their military victory, the Nazi conquerors acted without restraint. Hundreds of synagogues were destroyed during the first months of the occupation. 'The synagogue on Kosciuszko Alley went up in flames yesterday morning,' the official German newspaper in Lodz reported on November 16, adding that 'the first and third fire brigades prevented the flames from spreading to adjoining buildings'.[9] The destruction of the books in the Talmudic Academy in Lublin gave so much pleasure to the conquerors that it was recalled with glee more than a year later. 'For us', a German eye-witness later reported, 'it was a matter of special pride to destroy the Talmudic Academy, which was known as the greatest in Poland', and he went on to describe how:

> We threw the huge Talmudic library out of the building and carried the books to the market place, where we set fire to them. The fire lasted twenty hours. The Lublin Jews assembled around and wept bitterly, almost silencing us with their cries. We summoned the military band, and with joyful shouts the soldiers drowned out the sounds of the Jewish cries.[10]

Throughout November 1939, the Germans continued to demand Jewish labour and to receive a daily quota of work brigades. One task assigned to Jews was the clearing of rubble in towns which had been the scene of fighting or bombardment. Conditions were deliberately made severe. 'Truly we are cattle in the eyes of the Nazis,' Chaim Kaplan wrote in his diary on November 18. 'When they supervise Jewish workers they hold a whip in their hands. All are beaten unmercifully.' The details of Nazi cruelty, Kaplan added, 'are enough to drive you crazy. Sometimes we are ashamed to look at one another. And worse than this, we have begun to look upon ourselves as "inferior beings", lacking God's image.'

Poland had been conquered. Britain and France, at war with Germany, had as yet taken no offensive action. The United States remained staunchly neutral. And yet, Kaplan wrote, the defeat of the Nazis 'will surely come. We have only one doubt, whether we shall live to see that day. And I say: Yes, we will live; we will reach that day! No power endures for ever.'[11]

On 13 November 1939, a twenty-year-old former convict, Pinkus Zylberryng, a Jew, had shot and killed a Polish policeman at 9 Nalewki Street, in the centre of Warsaw's Jewish district. Although Zylberryng was identified, the Germans arrested all fifty-three male inhabitants of no. 9. On November 22, all fifty-three were executed.[12] But before announcing the execution, the Germans demanded 300,000 zlotys from the Jewish Council. 'The levy was to be a ransom for the lives of the men under arrest,' a member of the Council, Ludwik Landau, noted, 'but when the representatives of the Council arrived, the money was taken from them, but they were told that the prisoners had already been shot.'[13]

Among those shot in this reprisal action was one of Warsaw's leading gynaecologists, the forty-five-year-old Samuel Zamkowy.[14] 'This was the first mass arrest and murder,' David Wdowinski later recalled, 'and it threw the Jewish population into panic.'[15]

On November 28 Hans Frank formally ordered the setting up of Jewish Councils in every Jewish community in the General Government. The Councils were to have twenty-four members in communities of over ten thousand Jews, and twelve members in smaller communities. It was the German intention, as Heydrich had laid down in September, to issue all orders to the Jews through these Councils. It would then be the responsibility of Council members to ensure that these orders were obeyed. But the Germans retained the power of arbitrary action, in matters large and small. Walking through a Warsaw street in December 1939, David Wdowinski 'saw a German officer take a fur coat off the back of a Jewish woman and give it to his female companion'.[16] In Lodz, Mary Berg noted in her diary how their German neighbours, railway workers, were constantly calling on them. 'Every time they come, they ask for something, but their requests are really orders. Last week, for instance, they asked for pillows, pretending they had nothing to sleep on.'[17] Against such pilferings there was no redress.

Typical of the work which the Jewish Councils were forced to do, and part of the Nazi plan to isolate and impoverish the Jewish communities of Poland, on the morning of November 29 the German Civil Commissar in Piotrkow, Hans Drexel, presented the Council with a decree, signed by Hans Frank, for the delivery of 350,000 zlotys 'to my office by 11 a.m. today'. If this request were not complied with, Drexel added, 'punitive measures will be taken as ordered by the Governor-General'.

This enormous sum had somehow to be paid. While the Jews searched for the money, the Germans held three hostages. As the search for the money continued, the hostages were so savagely beaten that one of them, Leib Dessau, died.

As soon as the sum of money was collected, it was taken in a sack to the German Commissar. Later the Germans demanded more money, as well as 12,000 eggs, 500 sacks of flour, 300 kilogrammes of butter and 100 sacks of sugar. The payment of these sums and commodities bankrupted Piotrkow's Jews, as it was intended to do. All over Poland, the wealth accumulated by generations of hard work and enterprise was seized by the conqueror, leaving the Jews with none of the basic strengths that money can so often provide.[18]

On the German-Soviet demarcation line, the border had now been effectively sealed, halting further escapes eastward. The expulsion of Jews across the border was also ending. One last deportation was announced on December 1, in the city of Hrubieszow. There, all men between the ages of fifty and sixty, together with men from the nearby city of Chelm, were ordered to assemble in the central square on the following day. The Jews were told that they would be going out to work. Many women and children tried to join their menfolk, not wishing to be separated from them, but were ordered to return home. Craftsmen, shoemakers and carpenters were ordered to lead the march.

'We started marching,' recalled Hirsch Pachter. 'One girl succeeded in following the marchers, shouting "Father" all the way. At the first village, they took this girl away. We do not know what happened to her, but we heard a shot.'

The marchers were divided into about ten groups of two hundred men each. At the end of the first day's march, on the evening of December 2, twenty Jews were taken out of Hirsch Pachter's group: two rabbis, two synagogue beadles, 'and other people with long beards'. They were never seen again. From the other groups, a further two hundred men were taken away.

Early on December 3 the march resumed. At the first village, three bearded Jews were led away: Shmuel Topocostok, Benjamin Rosenberg and a man by the name of Loewenberg. As Loewenberg was led away, Pachter later recalled, 'his son jumped up and said, "Leave my father alone, I will take his place. Take me," and they said, "You come along too," and they took both of them and the other two.' Pachter added: 'They were all shot in the back of their heads and the bullets came out of their foreheads.'

The third day of the march, December 4, saw further shootings, the Germans competing as to the number of Jews they could kill in a specific time. 'They would lay a hand on a man. He would lie down – whoever did not want to lie down would be hit on the head with a rifle butt and the blood ran. But most people were so tired that they could not resist. We were only shadows after all this marching. The slaughter on that day was horrible.'

Of the eighteen hundred Jews who had set off from Hrubieszow, more than fourteen hundred were murdered on that day. The surviving marchers had been given nothing to eat but a small bread roll each. Seeing a fifteen-year-old boy without any food at all, a fellow marcher threw him a piece of his own roll. When the boy bent down to pick it up, he was shot, by the commander of the march himself. 'He shot him,' Pachter recalled, 'but he did not kill him, and he ordered another man to finish the job. The other one apologized in a way – as if to say that the boy had jumped out of the line, and if he had not done that he would not have been shot.'

Two hundred marchers reached the Soviet border on the morning of December 9, starving and in pain from their torn and bleeding feet. 'The sun was rising,' Pachter recalled. 'We were told to sing. Whoever would not sit down and sing would be shot. We started singing Jewish melodies.' All day the marchers sat, and sang. That night they were taken to a bridge across the River Bug, which marked the border, and ordered to march across it, hands held high, shouting, 'Long live Stalin'.[19]

In Warsaw, the reprisal actions continued. On December 8, six

Jews and twenty-five Poles were shot for 'complicity in acts of sabotage'.[20] 'There is no strength left to cry,' Chaim Kaplan noted in his diary: 'steady and continued weeping leads finally to silence. At first there is screaming; then wailing; and at last a bottomless sigh that does not leave even an echo.'[21]

On December 11, all Jews living within the borders of the General Government were officially made liable to two years' forced labour, with a possible extension 'if its educational purpose is not considered fulfilled'.[22] Further tasks were now devised for the Jews deported to labour sites: clearing swamps, paving roads, and building fortifications. Two days later, a secret instruction from SS headquarters in Poznan stated that any Jews still living in the western regions of Poland annexed to Germany 'in disregard of the removal order', even if they had gone to another province of the annexed areas, 'are to be shot under martial law'. This ruling, the order added, 'is to be passed on orally to the leaders of the Jewish communities, insofar as they still exist'.[23]

The Jews expelled from western Poland went mostly to Warsaw and Lodz, whose combined Jewish populations rose to well over one million. The indignities continued. In his diary on December 16, Chaim Kaplan gave two examples which had just reached him from Lodz. The first concerned some Jewish girls, seized for forced labour:

> These girls were compelled to clean a latrine – to remove the excrement and clean it. But they received no utensils. To their question: 'With what?' the Nazis replied: 'With your blouses.' The girls removed their blouses and cleaned the excrement with them. When the job was done they received their reward: the Nazis wrapped their faces in the blouses, filthy with the remains of excrement, and laughed uproariously. And all this because 'Jewish England' is fighting against the Fuhrer with the help of the *Juden*.

The second incident recorded by Kaplan was of a rabbi in Lodz who was forced to spit on a Scroll of the Law:

> In fear of his life, he complied and desecrated that which is holy to him and to his people. After a short while he had no more saliva, his mouth was dry. To the Nazi's question, why did he stop spitting, the rabbi replied that his mouth was dry.

Then the son of the 'superior race' began to spit into the rabbi's open mouth, and the rabbi continued to spit on the Torah.[24]

Mary Berg also recorded in her diary various Nazi 'entertainments' in Lodz, when five or ten Jewish couples would be brought to a room, ordered to strip, and then made to dance together naked to the accompaniment of a gramophone record. Two of her schoolmates had experienced this in their own home, when, as Mary Berg noted:

> Several Nazis entered their apartment and, after a thorough search of all the rooms, forced the two girls into the parlour, where there was a piano. When their parents tried to accompany them, the Nazis struck them over the head with clubs. Then the Nazis locked the parlour door and ordered the girls to strip. They ordered the older one to play a Viennese waltz and the younger one to dance. But the sounds of the piano merged with the cries of the parents in the adjoining room. When the younger girl fainted in the midst of the dancing, the other sister began to cry for help at the window. This was too much for the Nazis, and they left. My schoolmates showed me the black and blue marks left on their bodies after their struggles with their tormentors.[25]

To those in authority, such obscenities and torments were a gratifying game. But they did not provide the answer to the future of Polish Jewry. 'The Jews represent for us', Hans Frank noted in his diary on December 19, 'extraordinarily malignant gluttons. We have now approximately 2,500,000 of them in the General Government and counting half-Jews, perhaps 3,500,000.' Frank could see no solution. 'We cannot shoot 2,500,000 Jews,' he wrote, 'neither can we poison them. We shall have to take steps, however, designed to extirpate them in some way – and this will be done.'[26]

On December 27, as a reprisal for the death of two German policemen, shot in a tavern at Wawer, outside Warsaw, the Germans shot 114 residents of the suburb. Almost all those executed were Poles: but eight at least were Jews.[27] 'The screams of those suffocated and killed do not reach us,' Chaim Kaplan noted in his diary two days later, 'only the voice of the Nazi is heard in the newspapers. He publishes lies upon lies, spreads falsehoods upon falsehoods every day, casts filthy epithets upon Jew and Pole alike.'[28] The conqueror, Kaplan added a few days later, 'preys upon and devours guiltless people, free of crime, and dips himself in the blood of innocents, even in the blood of children who have never known sin.'[29]

The Jewish refugees in Warsaw lived in conditions of growing hardship. 'Some move in with a relative, a friend, or a distant acquaintance,' Kaplan noted on December 30. 'The poor ones fill the synagogues, which have become refugee centres. One cannot describe the crowded conditions, the congestion and filth in these centres.' Sometimes, Kaplan noted, 'you see a provincial Polish Jew, who truly presents an exotic appearance in a European city. Even his brethren, fellow Jews of Warsaw, are not accustomed to him, and in Gentile eyes he is the object of ridicule and mockery.' Some of the newly arrived refugees, Kaplan added, 'go out with their yellow patches in the shape of a Star of David. In such cases they are rebuked and forced to change them for the blue and white patch – symbol of the Jewishness of the Jews of Warsaw.'[30]

By the end of 1939, only a few Jews were able to find a means of escape from Greater Germany. A few still managed, however, to make their way southward, to Yugoslavia or Rumania, usually along the Danube, hoping to be able to proceed across the Black Sea by ship to Palestine. But it was not only the Germans who sought to close these escape routes. On December 30 a river boat, *Uranus*, reached the Iron Gates. On board were 1,210 Jews who had left Vienna and Prague in November, as an 'illegal' transport bound for Palestine, organized by a young Viennese Jew, Ehud Uberall.[31] At the Iron Gates, the Danube began to freeze over. The refugees were taken for shelter to the nearest Yugoslav port, Kladovo, to await the warmer weather, when they could continue their journey down the lower Danube. As a result of repeated British diplomatic protests, however, urging the Yugoslav government not to allow boats to proceed, lest they made for Palestine, the refugees were interned in Yugoslavia, for nine months, first at Kladovo and then at Sabac.[32] There, early in 1940, 207 teenagers received Palestine certificates, and were allowed to proceed to Palestine by train. The remaining 1,003 were massacred at Sabac in October 1941, within six months of the German conquest of Yugoslavia.[33]

In spite of the Palestine White Paper of 17 May 1939, restricting

CENTRAL POLAND

the number of Jews to be allowed into Palestine to twenty thousand a year, the British authorities in Palestine had allowed more Jews into Palestine during 1939 than in the previous two years: 27,561 immigrants for 1939 alone. This brought the total Jewish immigration to Palestine since 1936 to more than eighty thousand. But now the gates both of emigration and of immigration were being closed.

In Warsaw, a book had been published in Yiddish that year, describing some of the worst moments in Jewish history: the Crusader massacre of Jews in the twelfth century, the Chmielnicki killings in the Ukraine in the seventeenth century, and the Ukrainian pogroms of 1918 and 1919. 'But it did not occur to us', Yitzhak Zuckerman, then a young Zionist in Warsaw, later wrote, 'that the poison cup was not yet empty, and that we would have to drain it to its last dregs.'[34]

9

1940: 'a wave of evil'

STARVATION HAD BEGUN to haunt the Jews of Warsaw; during the first week of January 1940 Emanuel Ringelblum noted 'fifty to seventy deaths daily', as against normal pre-war mortality of ten. The random killings also continued. 'Tonight,' Ringelblum wrote on January 1, 'Dr Cooperman was shot for being out after eight o'clock. He had a pass.' In Praga, a suburb of Warsaw across the Vistula, 'A Jewish worker who belonged to the labour battalion was killed.'[1] On January 2, a General Government ordinance forbade the posting of obituary notices.[2] On January 5, Jews were forbidden both to be in the streets between nine at night and five in the morning, and to do any trading outside the predominantly Jewish section of Warsaw.[3]

As the deportations from western Poland continued, the pressures inside Warsaw increased. Elderly refugees died from the exhaustion of their journeys. Fuel was so hard to obtain that on January 6 Ringelblum noted that books from the library of the Socialist-Zionist movement Hashomer Hatzair 'are being used by the refugees to stoke ovens at 6 Leszno Street'.[4] 'The Jews joke that they no longer have to travel to Carlsbad,' Chaim Kaplan wrote in his diary that same day, 'for the Spa has come to them. Their weight has dropped, and their drawn, thin faces show poverty and privation.'[5]

Another hazard was the activity of those whom Mary Berg, who had returned to Warsaw from Lodz, described as Polish 'hoodlums': young men 'who beat and rob every Jewish passer-by', and who led the Nazis to the apartments of well-to-do Jews, and participated in the looting. Some Poles 'not blessed with Nordic features' had also been beaten up by these same roving gangs. For many days, Mary Berg noted, 'a middle-aged Polish woman, wrapped in a long black shawl and holding a stick in her hand, has been the terror of Marszalkowska Street. She has not let a single Jew by without beating him, and she specializes in women and children.' The Germans, Mary Berg added, 'look on and laugh'.[6]

Away from the sight of passers-by, Jewish or non-Jewish, a death march similar in its cruelties to the death march from Hrubieszow at the beginning of December was taking place in the Lublin region. On January 14 a group of former soldiers in the Polish army, 880 Jews in all, were taken from the prisoner-of-war camp in Lublin and told that they were to be marched to the Soviet border where, as Jews born east of the new Nazi-Soviet demarcation line, they would be transferred to Soviet authority.

The 880 prisoners were escorted on the march by SS men armed with rifles and machine guns. Just before the town of Lubartow, the SS men opened fire, and more than a hundred of the prisoners-of-war were killed. 'The invalids were the first to be shot at,' one of the prisoners-of-war, Avraham Buchman, later recalled, 'because they were too weak to walk. There was one man who was shot in the lung.'[7]

The prisoners-of-war thought seriously of rebelling; there were only thirteen guards, albeit armed. But, as Ringelblum later learned, the guards told them that if any tried to escape 'that would be a great catastrophe for all the Jews of Poland'. Some twenty prisoners-of-war did manage to escape. But the retaliation was immediate: three men were killed 'with one bullet', while the cruellest of the guards 'wantonly killed people walking along the road'.[8]

That night the prisoners-of-war were locked in an abandoned stable, and in the local synagogue. On the following day, between Lubartow and Parczew, a second massacre took place: only 400 of the 880 reached the outskirts of Parczew alive. There, Arieh Helfgot, one of the survivors, later recalled, 'a delegation of Jews came out to meet us in order to conduct negotiations with our murderers. We were astonished at their courage, as they could quite easily have died together with us.'

These local Jews gave the SS men money, in return for permission to provide the prisoners-of-war with food. That night the prisoners-of-war were again locked in the local synagogue. But during the night, with the help of the same local Jews who had come so bravely to intercede for them, forty of the prisoners managed to escape.

The local Jews then found them civilian clothes, and hiding places.

On the following morning the remaining 360 prisoners-of-war were again marched off, and once more subjected to bursts of machine-gun fire; less than two hundred survived, to be imprisoned in another prisoner-of-war camp, at Biala Podlaska. The transfer to Soviet territory never took place. At Biala Podlaska, refused medical attention, most of the survivors of the march died of typhus.[9]

There were other Jewish prisoners-of-war murdered that winter, among them 320 who had been captured by the Germans in central Poland, but who had also been born east of the new demarcation line. They were sent in sealed, unheated cattle trucks towards the border town of Wlodawa. They too were told that they would be sent across the border. During the train journey, with frequent halts at sidings, more than two hundred died of starvation, or froze to death. In the forest between Wlodawa and the village of Sobibor, the train was stopped and the survivors were ordered to remove the corpses. After they had done this, the men were led into the forest, where the SS guards opened fire with automatic weapons. The prisoners-of-war tried to run away, but only a few succeeded; 120 were killed. Some days later, in return for payment, the Wlodawa Jewish Council obtained the permission of the Germans to remove the wounded and to bury the dead in the Jewish cemetery of Wlodawa.[10]

News of the Parczew and Wlodawa killings did not reach Warsaw for several months. There, it was the publication on January 13 of the forced labour decree of December 11 that had created a sudden panic. 'This decree', Chaim Kaplan wrote in his diary, 'will uproot all of Polish Jewry and bring utter destruction upon it.'[11] Two days later Kaplan wrote again:

> The forced labour decree gnaws away at our people. Because of the extent of the catastrophe, the Jews do not believe that it will come to pass. Even though they know the nature of the conqueror very, very well, and his tyrannical attitude toward them has already been felt on their backs; even though they know he has no pity or human feeling in relation to the Jews – in spite of all this, their attitude toward the terrible decree he has published is one of frivolity. I do not join them in this. Thousands and perhaps tens of thousands will become slave labourers – that is, if the tyrant's defeat does not intervene.[12]

Not the tyrant's defeat, however, but his capacity for killing, dominated the talk and experience of Warsaw Jewry. Early in January, the Germans had arrested Andrzej Kott, the leader of a secret youth association, the Polish People's Independent Action, dedicated to action against the occupying power. Kott was of Jewish origin: his family had converted to Catholicism some time in the past. Using his Jewish origin as their reason, the Gestapo arrested 255 Jews at random, including many professional people: industrialists, engineers, furriers, businessmen, lawyers, hatters, doctors and teachers, tailors, tie-makers, book-keepers, chemists and musicians. Beginning on January 18, and continuing for seven days, all those arrested were taken in groups to the Palmiry woods, outside Warsaw, and shot. Among those murdered were the dental surgeon Franz Sturm, the lawyer Ludwik Dyzenhaus, and the photographer Pinkus Topaz.[13]

'Every house is filled with sadness and a spirit of depression,' Kaplan noted in his diary on January 24, before news of the executions had become known. 'The Kott affair brought misfortune to a number of families among the intelligentsia, whose husbands or sons were arrested for no legal reason. And those who had not yet been arrested live in mortal fear. Every echo of footsteps on the stairs in the dark of night drives mute panic into their hearts.'[14]

That same week, the Germans ordered all synagogues and houses of prayer in Warsaw to close.

Following the publication of the forced labour decree, thousands of Jews were taken from the main Polish cities. Plans were also made to deport Jews from Slovakia for forced labour. On January 30, in Berlin, Heydrich announced the setting up of a special government bureau, IV-D-4, for handling all deportation details, including the continuing removal of Jews from the annexed regions of western Poland.

Labour camps were set up near the Soviet frontier, in the expectation, as Zygmunt Klukowski, a Polish doctor in the Lublin region, noted in his diary, 'that there will be some heavy fighting in our area'. Klukowski listed several towns and villages near which 'very solid trenches were being built', among them Frampol, Zamosc and Belzec, all in the border zone.[15]

Jews were sent to work at each of these labour sites. But 'from the outset', Chaim Kaplan noted in his diary on February 4, 'the People of Hope did not believe that the decree of forced labour would be put into effect. As is the way with Jews, they didn't understand the decree in its simple sense', trying to find in it instead 'some hint for an enormous financial contribution'.[16] But Kaplan himself was fully aware of what the decree meant. He wrote, the next day, of a Jew who had been 'caught for forced labour' in Warsaw:

> The work consisted of transferring cakes of ice from one place to another. The terrible cold pierces the flesh. Who could endure the icy chill? But there was no choice. It was the Nazis' order and, as such, could not be avoided. The Jew did his job with gloves, but the Nazi overseer forced him to do the work barehanded. The Jew was forced to fulfil the wishes of the oppressor, and with terrible suffering he moved the ice cakes barehanded, in below-zero cold. The Jew fell under the agony of this torture. His palms were so frozen that they are beyond help and his hands will have to be amputated.[17]

Each day, new rules made the life of Warsaw Jewry more difficult. On February 7 Ringelblum noted that 'Jews may not visit the public libraries which were built through Jewish philanthropy', and the Jews could only travel by train on presentation of a 'delousing certificate', each certificate being valid for only ten days.[18] Four days later he recorded incidents where Jews who had been taken off to work in a garage 'are ordered to beat one another with their galoshes'. A Jew who had been seized while at prayer wearing his phylacteries 'was forced to work all day in them'. Workers were divided into groups and made to fight each other: 'I have seen people badly injured in these games.' On another occasion, a rabbi 'was ordered to shit in his pants'.[19]

The cruelties and indignities recorded by Ringelblum and Kaplan in Warsaw were repeated in every Polish city under Nazi rule. In Piotrkow, on February 18, two German sergeants seized two Jewish girls, the eighteen-year-old Miss Nachmanowicz and the seventeen-year-old Miss Satanowska, forced them at gunpoint to the Jewish cemetery, and raped them. The Nuremberg Laws against 'race defilement' had proved no protection.[20]

On February 19 a report from Warsaw, sent through Copenhagen, was published in England, in the *Manchester Guardian*. 'The humiliations and tortures inflicted upon the Jewish workmen,' the report declared, 'who are compelled by their Nazi overseers to dance and sing and undress during their work, and are even forced to belabour each other with blows, show no signs of abating.'[21]

In his diary, Ringelblum recorded mounting indignities. On February 21 he recorded how Germans, whom he called 'the Others' or 'the lords and masters', threw a woman out of a moving tram. Large numbers of Jewish women had been seized from various cafés, and taken away, 'no one knows where to; it is said that about a hundred came back a few days later, some of them infected'. He had heard about a ten-year-old boy, beaten on the head, who 'went mad', and of a place where 'during the work registration those Jews who said they were sickly were killed'.[22]

On March 6, Ringelblum recorded how, at a house in the Jewish district, 'three lords and masters ravished some women; screams resounded through the house'. The Gestapo, Ringelblum added, 'were concerned over the racial degradation' involved, 'but are afraid to report it'.[23]

Every morning, several hundred Jews, collected by the Jewish Council, were assembled for forced labour: in early March their task was the clearing of snow from the centre of Warsaw. 'You can recognize them,' Chaim Kaplan noted, 'not only by the "Jewish insignia" on their sleeves, but by their gestures, by the sorrow implanted in their faces. They receive no pay for this,' Kaplan added, 'not even food. The Gentiles too are required to work, but they are paid.'[24]

The Lublin region deportations had been abandoned: but six weeks later, on 22 April 1940, SS General Odilo Globocnik, the most senior SS officer in the Lublin district, proposed a substantial extension of the labour-camp system throughout the Lublin region to make use of a much larger number of Jews, isolating men from women. These camps were set up at once: in July 1940 there were more than thirty, employing ten thousand Jews; the number of forced labourers doubled by the end of the year.[25] From Piotrkow, Jews were taken to two nearby swamps, where they were forced to dig canals and ditches. Some of those who were taken off for this work were only twelve years old. Many were forced to work naked and barefoot, standing in the water up to their waists. Many died of pneumonia or tuberculosis.[26]

The purpose of these labour camps was actual physical work, albeit in cruel conditions. But from the first days of the German conquest of Poland, two other types of camp had been created, both near the Free City of Danzig, annexed to the Reich on the outbreak of war. The first was in the woods near the village of Piasnica, twenty-five miles north-west of Danzig, to which mental defectives had been sent since October 1939. 'It is said', Ringelblum had noted on 7 February 1940, 'that many hundreds of madmen had been killed,' although he did not know where.[27] The second camp was in the village of Stutthof, twenty miles east of Danzig. Several hundred Danzig Jews had been deported to Stutthof in the third week of September, among them the writer and journalist Jacob Lange, and the cantor of the Danzig synagogue, Leopold Shufftan. Within a few weeks, most of them had died.[28] A Polish Socialist leader, who was imprisoned at Stutthof for fifteen months, later described a 'mass slaughter' of Jews at Stutthof during the Passover of 1940. This festival of Jewish liberation from bondage began, in 1940, on the evening of April 23:

> All the Jews were assembled in the courtyard; they were ordered to run, to drop down and to stand up again. Anybody who was slow in obeying the order was beaten to death by the overseer with the butt of his rifle.
>
> Afterwards Jews were ordered to jump right into the cesspit of the latrines, which were being built; this was full of urine. The taller Jews got out again since the level reached their chin, but the shorter ones went down. The young ones tried to help the old folk, and as a punishment the overseers ordered the latter to beat the young. When they refused to obey they were cruelly beaten themselves. Two or three died on the spot and the survivors were ordered to bury them.

The surviving Jews were then sent to a smaller camp at Gransdorf where discipline, the Polish Socialist reported, 'was even more severe'. His account continued:

> One single Jew, a sculptor, was left in Stutthof. The SS men took all his works, put him to a carriage loaded with sand, and forced him to run while flogging him with a lash. When he fell down they turned the carriage over on him; and when he nevertheless succeeded in creeping out of the sand they poured

water on him and hung him; but the rope was too thin and gave way. They then brought a young Jewess, the only one in the camp, and with scornful laughter they hanged both on one rope.

Women also were detained at Stutthof, the Polish Socialist recalled. 'The beautiful ones had to clean the houses of the overseers and officers; most of them were pregnant, and were released from the camp. The young Jewess above mentioned was also pregnant, but instead of being released she was hanged.'[29]

On February 8 the Germans had ordered the setting up of a ghetto in Lodz, and chose as the site of the ghetto two of the most neglected districts of the city. Of a total of 31,721 apartments in this ghetto area, most of them with a single room, only 725 had running water. The use of electricity in the ghetto was forbidden between eight in the evening and six in the morning.[30] More than 160,000 Jews were moved inside the ghetto, which was 'closed' on May 1, from which day the German police were ordered to shoot without warning any Jew who might approach the barbed-wire fence which now surrounded it.[31]

The evacuations from Germany to the Lublin region continued. On 12 March 1940, all 160 Jews from the Baltic port of Schneidemuhl were taken in sealed freight cars to Lublin. They were allowed to take with them only the clothes they wore: no other possessions, not even suitcases, bedding, food or dishes. In the bitter weather, some deportees had their coats taken away from them. From Lublin, these 160 men, women and children were marched in the freezing weather, along rough roads covered in snow, to three small villages more than twenty kilometres away. There they found the survivors of twelve hundred deportees from Stettin who, in their fourteen-hour march from Lublin, had left seventy-two Jews dead at the roadside.[32]

The Jews of Lublin decided to protest to Berlin. In their letter, which was forwarded to Himmler, they described how:

Among others, a mother who was carrying a three-year-old child in her arms, trying to protect him from the cold with her own clothes, was found dead, frozen in this position. The half-frozen body of a five-year-old girl was found wearing around her neck a cardboard sign with words, 'Renate Alexander, from Hemmerstein, Pomerania'. This child was visiting relatives in Stettin and was included in the deportation; her mother and father stayed in Germany. Her hands and feet had to be amputated at the Lublin Hospital.[33]

On March 22, after Hans Frank had protested to Berlin about the 'dumping' of Jews in the General Government, Hermann Goering ordered a halt to the expulsions to the Lublin region.

Inside the Gestapo there were a few Germans who sought to warn the Jews of what was impending. Heinrich Grüber, a Protestant pastor in Berlin, who was later imprisoned for helping Jews, recalled one such German at Gestapo offices in Berlin. The Gestapo always sought to employ those who might have some pathological or personal animus against the Jews. For this reason, they had taken on the father of the murdered German diplomat, Ernst vom Rath. Vom Rath senior was given an official position because, as Grüber later recalled, it was thought 'he would certainly like to get his own back on Jews and would be particularly severe with regard to Jews'. But this, Grüber added, 'was certainly not the case. Our relationship was rather friendly, and I must say that this man helped us clandestinely on many occasions.' Vom Rath senior would, for example, leave out on his desk the latest orders and decrees so that Grüber could see them, and report them to those who might then still have time to take measures to avoid them.[34]

With the Soviet Union still neutral, a number of Polish Jews who had fled eastward in Soviet-occupied Poland and Lithuania were able to escape from Europe altogether, as a result of a curious diplomatic arrangement. In Kovno, the representative of the Dutch firm of Phillips was prepared to issue certificates to the effect that travellers wishing to enter the island of Curacao, in the Dutch West Indies, did not need an entry permit or visa.

Armed with this document, Jews persuaded the Japanese Vice-Consul in Kovno, Sempo Sugihara, to issue them a transit visa through Japan, ostensibly to the Dutch West Indies. Travelling to Moscow on this transit visa, the Jews then received permission to leave the Soviet Union through the Far Eastern port of Vladivostok. Once in Tokyo, many of the Jews went to the Polish Ambassador there – the Ambassador of the Polish government in London – who gave them documents to enable them, as Polish citizens in exile, to travel to Canada. By such stratagems, several thousand Polish Jews reached safety in the summer and autumn of 1940. Among them was Leon Pommers, a twenty-six-year-old music student from Warsaw, who, more than a year after leaving Kovno, having travelled through Japan to Shanghai, Hong Kong and Australia, finally reached San Francisco in February 1942.[35]

In Shanghai were twenty thousand Jews, two thousand refugees from Communist Russia, who had found a haven there before 1933, the majority refugees from Germany, who, since 1933, had been able to take advantage of the fact that, alone of all states or cities, Shanghai since 1933 had not required a prior visa or permit to enable a Jew to live there.[36]

The Japanese government also took in several hundred Jewish refugees who had managed to cross the Soviet Union during this period of Soviet neutrality. One small Jewish community in Japan, that of Kobe, gave the Japanese authorities a guarantee that refugees would not become a financial burden on Japan. Following this guarantee, refugees who landed at the port of Tsuruga from Vladivostok were admitted to Japan without question, welcomed at Tsuruga by members of the Jewish community, and brought to Kobe by train. In this way, 'many hundreds' were housed and cared for, a German Jewish refugee, Kurt Marcus, later recalled. But the task of financing the refugees was beyond the resources of the Kobe Jewish community; they therefore sought, and received, help from the American Jewish Joint Distribution Committee. Recalling his nine years as a refugee in Japan, Marcus added: 'At no time did I experience even the slightest hint of anti-Semitism.'[37]

While Nazi terror in Poland tightened its grip, Britain and France, at war with Germany since September 1939, had made no military move against Hitler's Reich. These were the months of the Phoney War. In Warsaw, Chaim Kaplan noted in his diary on 7 March 1940, 'Those who understand the military and political situation well are going about like mourners. There is no ground for hope that the decisive action will come this spring, and lack of a decision means that our terrible distress will last a long time.'[38]

10

War in the West: terror in the East

IN APRIL 1940, German forces occupied Norway, forestalling a British move, and defeating the British, French and Polish exile forces sent against them at Narvik. 'Misery over the defeat in Norway,' Ringelblum noted. 'Our spirits have fallen.'[1] In Norway, seventeen hundred Jews, of whom three hundred were refugees from Germany, came under German rule. In Denmark, which German forces occupied as part of their Norwegian campaign, seven thousand four hundred more Jews were now within the Nazi orbit, fourteen hundred of them refugees from Germany, Austria and Czechoslovakia. But neither the Norwegian nor the Danish Jews were molested, at the insistence of the Danish and Norwegian authorities, who retained certain minimal powers of internal administration.

In German-occupied Poland there was no relaxation in the restrictions, the persecutions, or the hunger imposed on the Jews. On May 9 Ringelblum recorded how, in a centre for Jewish refugees from outside the city, 'an eight-year-old child went mad. Screamed, "I want to steal, I want to rob, I want to eat, I want to be a German." In his hunger he hated being Jewish.'[2]

A day later, on May 10, German forces struck at Belgium, Holland and France. The speed and scale of the German advance, accompanied by air bombardment, soon overwhelmed the Belgian and Dutch forces. In north-eastern France, a large British army, trapped at Dunkirk, was forced to evacuate, leaving much of its equipment behind. The Germans then turned towards Paris.

Confident of a German victory, on May 25 Himmler sent Hitler 'some thoughts' on the post-war treatment of non-Germans in the East. 'I hope', he wrote, in his only reference to the Jews, 'that, through the possibility of large-scale emigration of all Jews to

Africa or some other colony, the concept of Jew will have completely disappeared from Europe.'[3]

As the German armies drove through Holland on May 15, a further 140,000 Jews, among them several thousand refugees from pre-war Germany, Austria and Czechoslovakia, had been trapped behind the German lines. A few thousand managed to escape southwards through France, travelling on roads crowded by other refugees and constantly strafed by German aircraft: several hundred reached the distant safety of the Pyrenees, and of neutral Spain and Portugal. Others reached sanctuary in Switzerland.

In Amsterdam, a non-Jewish woman, Geertruida Wijsmuller-Meijer, who had been in charge of Jewish refugees from Germany, decided, as German troops approached Amsterdam, to make one last rescue bid. Assembling half a dozen coaches, she quickly gathered two hundred Jewish refugees, among them eighty children. One of the children, the fourteen-year-old Harry Jacobi, later recalled the drive from Amsterdam to the port of Ijmuiden, where British troops were still landing in a last-minute attempt to bolster the Dutch defences. At Ijmuiden, Geertruida Wijsmuller persuaded the captain of a Dutch freighter to take the Jews on board, and to set sail across the North Sea for England. 'At 7 p.m. we sailed,' Harry Jacobi later recalled. 'Far away from the shore we looked back and saw a huge column of black smoke from the oil storage tanks that had been set on fire to prevent the Germans having them. At 9 p.m. news came through, picked up by the ship's radio. The Dutch had capitulated.'

Harry Jacobi and the two hundred other Jewish refugees reached Britain and safety. Neither his parents, who were still in Berlin, nor his grandparents, then in Holland, were to survive the war. There had been no room for his grandparents on the crowded coaches.

Geertruida Wijsmuller-Meijer remained in Holland, where she continued to seek to smuggle Jews into neutral Spain and Switzerland.[4] Another non-Jew who helped save Jews was Captain Foley, the former Passport Control Officer in Berlin, now, briefly, at Bordeaux, with thousands of retreating soldiers and civilians. But the swiftness of the German advance usually made escape impossible. The German military victories, wrote Chaim Kaplan in distant Warsaw, 'beat upon our heads like hailstones':

Today it is Copenhagen, in which there is a Jewish community; the next day it is Amsterdam, The Hague, and Rotterdam, full of Jews who until now dwelt quietly and peacefully in their homeland. Just now the news has reached us that Brussels too has opened its gates to the Nazis. All the military activities of the past nine days prove that the earth trembles under the feet of the Nazis. It seems that these are not chance victories, but rather that the balance of power is such as to make these victories inevitable. Anyone with any perception can clearly see that the Western Powers are incapable of withstanding the military force of the Nazis. This is a gigantic military power in whose path there is no obstacle. And so the day after tomorrow Paris, too, will fall into their hands. And what then?[5]

On 14 June 1940 German forces entered Paris. Tens of thousands of French Jews were trapped: and with them, several thousand refugees from pre-war Germany and central Europe. Among these refugees was Ernst Weiss, the Austrian novelist, pupil of Freud, friend of Kafka, medical officer in the 1914–17 war in the Austro-Hungarian army, and master of the psychological novel. In March 1938 he had fled Vienna for Prague. In March 1939 he had fled Prague for Paris. As German troops marched down the Champs Elysées, he committed suicide. He was fifty-six years old.[6]

In Poland, the Germans had decided to set up a new concentration camp, organized by SS men with previous experience of similar camps in Germany. The camp was intended to serve as a place of punishment for Polish political prisoners. The site chosen was in East Upper Silesia, a region annexed by Germany: the town, Oswiecim, was known in German as Auschwitz.

The Commandant of the new camp, Rudolf Hoess, had arrived on April 29 with five other SS men. On May 30, thirty more Germans, almost all of them convicted criminals, had been sent from the concentration camp at Sachsenhausen, north of Berlin, to serve as barrack chiefs, or Kapos. Then, in the first two weeks of June, three hundred Jews from the town of Auschwitz were brought in to clean the site, a former Austro-Hungarian artillery barracks of the First World War. The Jews, having worked under the supervision of fifteen SS cavalrymen, were then sent back to Auschwitz town, whose six thousand Jews were later dispersed to other towns in the region.[7]

The first deportation to Auschwitz concentration camp came from the city of Tarnow. It consisted of 708 Poles, then held in Tarnow prison. Some were in prison because they had been caught trying to escape southwards into Slovakia. Others had been arrested because they were community leaders: priests and schoolteachers. About twenty Jews were also deported to Auschwitz in this first deportation among them Maximilian Rosenbusz, the director of the local Hebrew school, and two lawyers, Emil Wieder and Isaac Holzer.[8]

As the passenger train in which the deportees were being taken to Auschwitz passed through Cracow station, the deportees heard an excited station announcer trumpet the fall of Paris. On arrival in Auschwitz, the prisoners were put to work digging ditches and moving earth. Of the first 728 deportees, only 137 survived the war. The Jews among them perished.[9]

The fall of France, Holland, Belgium, Denmark and Norway, recalled Mania Feferman, then living in the Polish town of Kielce, 'did not inspire much hope for a quick end to the war. Father would say, "If these nations cannot withstand the Nazis, what could we possibly do, without any weapons in such a hostile country?"'[10]

Throughout Poland, the number of forced labour camps was growing. On July 17, Dr Zygmunt Klukowski noted in his diary that 'about five hundred Jews' had been taken from Szczebrzeszyn to various work camps.[11] On the following day it was announced that all Jews between the ages of sixteen and fifty must report daily to the Jewish Council. No Jew was allowed outside the town without a pass. Able-bodied Jews were sent to work camps. Conditions in these camps, Klukowski wrote on July 23, were 'extremely hard', and he added:

The worst consists of digging ditches to drain the marshes. They have to work standing in water. They are really badly fed because their families can rarely afford to send them food. They sleep in terrible barracks amidst filth – with a complete lack of space. The barracks are several kilometres from the places of work, and they have to walk this distance every day, and are continuously beaten. They are plagued with lice. Some of their clothing looks as if it has been sprinkled with poppy seeds. I was able to see it for myself as there was an epidemic of typhus and all the sick from the work camps were sent to me.[12]

To defend their frontier with the Soviet Union, the Germans were constructing a fortified line, the 'Otto Line', in south-eastern Poland. Tens of thousands of Jews were sent to the construction sites: to dig anti-tank ditches and artillery dugouts. Of two thousand young men and women sent from Radom to work in the Zamosc region, 'almost all of them perished'.[13] Of a thousand young men between the ages of eighteen and twenty-five sent from Czestochowa in August 1940, 'almost none survived'.[14] Thousands more were brought from independent Slovakia, a state delighted to comply with the German request for labour-deportees.[15]

The fall of France did not lead, as Hitler expected, to a negotiated peace with Britain. He therefore launched a 'blitz' on London, and many other British cities. At sea, German submarines sought to destroy Britain's trans-Atlantic lifeline. With Britain under virtual siege, and the United States still neutral, the Germans continued to pursue their anti-Jewish policies, unhampered by the outside world. On 1 August 1940 the first expulsion began from Cracow, with its eighty thousand Jewish inhabitants and refugees. In the first two weeks of August, a third of the Jews of Cracow were driven out to Warsaw and to other Polish towns. By the end of October, fifty thousand had been deported.[16]

Anti-Jewish laws were now introduced in three of the countries under German rule, control or influence. On August 10 the Rumanian government passed racial laws, as did Vichy France on October 3, and the German authorities in Belgium on October 28. In Rumania, the introduction of these laws coincided with an outburst of anti-Jewish violence, as Chaim Barlas, a Jewish Agency representative, reported from neutral Turkey on August 13: 'Every day Jews are being thrown out of railway carriages.' It was true, Barlas added, that the Rumanian newspapers, acting under government instructions, 'tell the people not to molest the minorities, but in regard to the Jews this appeal has no effect whatever'.[17]

In France, the end of August saw both personal and community tragedies. On August 26 the German Jewish philosopher and literary critic, Walter Benjamin, a refugee in France since Hitler had come to power in Germany, was crossing into Spain with a group of refugees, in search of yet another place of refuge. At Port Bou, the first town on the Spanish side of the border, the local police chief threatened to send the refugees back. In despair, Benjamin committed suicide. He was forty-eight years old.[18]

On the day after Benjamin's suicide, another Jew, Israel Karp, was shot by the German military authorities in Bordeaux. His had been an individual act of resistance, one of the first of the war in occupied France. Karp had attacked a detachment of German soldiers marching in goose-step through the town.[19]

Also on August 27, the government of Marshal Pétain abrogated the pre-war French decree of 21 March 1939 which forbade all incitement to race hatred.[20] In Luxembourg, just over a week later, on September 5, the German occupation authorities introduced the Nuremberg Laws of 1935, and at the same time seized all 355 Jewish-owned businesses and handed them over to 'Aryans'. In addition to Luxembourg's pre-1933 Jewish community of 1,171 Jews, a further three thousand Jews from Germany had, between 1933 and 1940, found refuge in the Duchy. Hundreds now sought escape, through France, to Spain or Switzerland. Altogether, seven hundred were able to escape to safety.[21]

On September 1, in Kovno, the Soviet authorities ordered the Japanese Consul, Sempo Sugihara, to leave the city. Up to that moment he had issued, it was later calculated, about 3,400 visas for Jews in Kovno to travel eastward, through Moscow and Siberia, to Japan and beyond. Even on September 1, on his way to the railway station with his family, Sugihara continued to stamp the precious transit visas. He did so, it was later reported, 'in the street and at the station, even through the window of the train compartment, until the train actually began to pull away from the platform.'[22]

In Poland, the isolation of Jews from the rest of the population was being accelerated by regulations forcing Jews to live only in one section of the town. Some of these specially created ghettos were marked by signs on the streets at which they began, and known as 'open' ghettos. Others were surrounded by wooden fences, or barbed wire, or by high walls built for the purpose. Many ghettos were on the outskirts of the town, usually in the dirtiest and poorest suburbs, or in some deserted, or even ruined factory area.[23]

Week by week during 1940, the number of enforced ghettos

grew: the Czestochowa ghetto was one of three established in March; the Lodz ghetto was one of two ghettos closed in May. In each ghetto, the German authorities ordered the Jewish Council to carry out its demands, whether for money, forced labour or the reduction in size of the ghettos themselves. In the Lodz ghetto, these responsibilities were carried out by the Chairman of the Council, Chaim Rumkowski, known as the 'Eldest of the Jews', who quickly became a controversial figure. On September 6, in Warsaw, Ringelblum noted in his diary:

> Today, the 6th of September, there arrived from Lodz, Chaim, or, as he is called, 'King Chaim', Rumkowski, an old man of seventy, extraordinarily ambitious and pretty nutty. He recited the marvels of his ghetto. He has a Jewish kingdom there, with four hundred policemen, three gaols. He has a Foreign Ministry, and all the other ministries, too. When asked why, if things were so good there, the mortality is so high, he did not answer. He considers himself God's annointed.[24]

As yet, Warsaw had no ghetto. 'People's spirits have improved,' Ringelblum noted on September 9. 'The Jewish populace believes the war will end in two or three months, because of the recent bombardments.'[25] These 'bombardments' were the first British air raids on Berlin, beginning on the night of August 25, when eighty British bombers struck at the German capital. In Berlin itself, the Jews of the city were to suffer more than non-Jews in these air raids, which continued with growing intensity. On September 24, William Shirer, one of several American newspaper correspondents in Berlin, noted in his diary:

> If Hitler has the best air-raid cellar in Berlin, the Jews have the worst. In many cases they have none at all. Where facilities permit, the Jews have their own special *Luftschutzkeller*, usually a small basement room next to the main part of the cellar, where the 'Aryans' gather. But in many Berlin cellars there is only one room. It is for the 'Aryans'. The Jews must take refuge on the ground floor, usually in the hall leading from the floor of the flat to the elevator or stairs. This is fairly safe if a bomb hits the roof, since the chances are that it will not penetrate to the ground floor. But experience so far has shown that it is the most dangerous place to be in the entire building if

a bomb lands in the street outside. Here where the Jews are hovering, the force of the explosion is felt most; here in the entryway where the Jews are, you get most of the bomb splinters.[26]

For non-Jews in Berlin, September 24 marked the first night of one of the most formidable propaganda films made in Nazi Germany, *Jew Suss*. A fictional story, it told of the life and death of an eighteenth-century court Jew, Suss Oppenheimer, Chief Minister of the Duke of Wurttemberg.

Suss Oppenheimer is shown in the film as a half-assimilated Jew who goes from ghetto to court within a few years. Through money and black magic he and his fellow Jews scheme to seize power by manipulationg the corrupt, drunken Duke of Wurttemberg whom they see as the archetype of the pliable non-Jew. The Jews who remain in the ghetto appear on the screen physically repulsive. But the message of the film is that they are less dangerous than Suss, who has acquired a veneer of court polish, and that no infamy was too great if it served the Jews in their quest for money and power.

A film suffused with hatred, *Jew Suss* was shown in cinemas throughout the Reich and occupied Europe, as well as at special sessions for the SS and the Hitler Youth.[27] Even the world of film and entertainment had been recruited to serve the cause of race hatred.

The second winter of the war was approaching; in labour camps throughout the Reich, Jews continued to suffer torment. Early in September, Ringelblum had noted, from reports reaching him in Warsaw, that 'worst of all' the labour camps in the General Government was the one near Belzec. 'There have been cases', he wrote, 'when weak people were shot to death. Happened to an old man of over sixty.' At another camp, in Jozefow, 'four hundred became sick with bleeding diarrhoea. They were dispatched while still sick.' When Jews in Otwock were seized for forced labour, and a large number escaped, 'more than ten paid with their lives'.[28]

Sometimes there were moments of reassurance. In Szczebrzeszyn, on October 1, Zygmunt Klukowski noted in his diary: 'Today the Jews had a happy day because almost all of them came back.' These were the young men sent for forced labour to Belzec. 'The Jews had paid 20,000 zloty for freeing them,' Klukowski added.[29] On

October 16, however, Klukowski noted that at the airfield at Klemensow, just outside Szczebrzeszyn, 'the workers are complaining that the Germans beat them with rubber truncheons for no reason, and they are beating Poles and Jews alike.'[30]

From Lodz, in October 1940, some two hundred and fifty young men were taken for work at Ruchocki Mlyn, in the Poznan region, straightening a river bank. One of these young men, Leo Laufer, then aged eighteen, later recalled the deaths of many of his fellow prisoners, forced to live like cattle in a barn: 'They were dying like flies, not so much from no food, because I believe there was almost sufficient food to sustain yourself. They died from the frost, and mainly they died from lack of hygiene. Never in my life do I recall seeing lice by the bushel.'[31]

Amid these torments, the Jewish spirit struggled to retain its strength, and sanity. On October 2 the Yiddish song-writer, Mordche Gebirtig, wrote a ballad bidding his fellow Jews to be merry: 'Jews, be gay, don't walk about in sadness, but be patient and have faith.' Gebirtig urged the Jews: 'Don't relinquish for a moment your weapon of laughter and gaiety, for it keeps you united.' His song ended:

> Drive us from our dwellings!
> Cut off our beards!
> Jews! Let's be gay.
> To hell with them![32]

Of the 400,000 Jews of Warsaw, more than 250,000 lived in the predominantly Jewish district. The remaining 150,000 lived throughout the city, some Jews in almost every street and suburb. On 3 October 1940, at the start of the Jewish New Year, the German Governor of Warsaw, Ludwig Fischer, announced that all Jews living outside the predominantly Jewish district would have to leave their homes and to move to the Jewish area. Whatever belongings could be moved by hand, or on carts, could go with them. The rest – the heavy furniture, the furnishings, the stock and equipment from shops and businesses – had to be abandoned.

Warsaw was to be divided into three 'quarters': one for Germans, one for Poles, and one for Jews. The Jews, who constituted a third of Warsaw's population, were to move into an area less than two and a

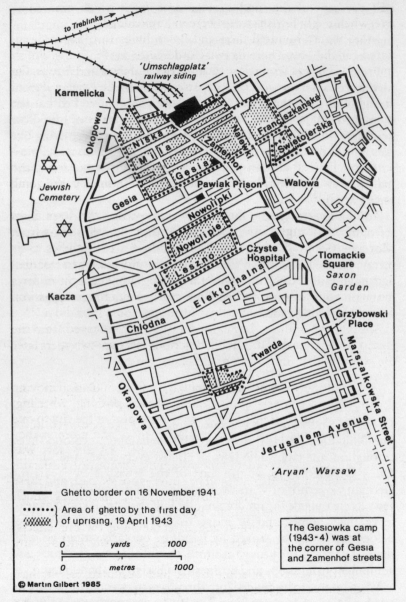

to Treblinka

'Umschlagplatz'
railway siding

Karmelicka

Okopowa

Niska

Mila

Zamenhof

Nalewki

Franciszkanska

Swietojerska

Jewish
Cemetery

Gesiek

Gesia

Pawiak Prison

Walowa

Nowolipki

Nowolipie

Kacza

Leszno

Czyste
Hospital

Tlomackie
Square

Saxon
Garden

Elektornalna

Chlodna

Grzybowski
Place

Twarda

Marszalkowska Street

Okopowa

Jerusalem Avenue

'Aryan' Warsaw

━━━━━ Ghetto border on 16 November 1941

••••••) Area of ghetto by the first day
〰〰〰) of uprising, 19 April 1943

0   yards   1000

0   metres   1000

© Martin Gilbert 1985

The Gesiowka camp
(1943-4) was at
the corner of Gesia
and Zamenhof streets

THE WARSAW GHETTO

half per cent of the total city: an area from which even some overwhelmingly Jewish streets were to be excluded.

More than a hundred thousand Poles, living in the area designated for the Jews, were likewise ordered to move, to the 'Polish quarter'. They too would lose their houses and their livelihoods. On October 12, the second Day of Atonement of the war, a day of fasting and of prayer, German loudspeakers announced that the move of Poles and Jews into their special quarters must be completed by the end of the month. 'Black melancholy reigned in our courtyard,' Ringelblum noted. 'The mistress of the house' – a Pole – 'had been living there some thirty-seven years, and now has to leave her furniture behind. Thousands of Christian businesses are going to be ruined.'[33]

The moving began at once. 'The removal of the Jews from the suburbs,' Ringelblum noted on October 13, 'as well as from poverty-stricken Praga' – across the Vistula – 'signifies their complete ruination; they will not even have the money to resettle.' Ringelblum added: 'Today was a terrifying day; the sight of Jews moving their old rags and bedding made a horrible impression. Though forbidden to remove their furniture, some Jews did it.'[34]

Another eye-witness, Toshia Bialer, who later escaped from the ghetto with her husband and son, described just over two years later the events of that third week of October:

> Try to picture one-third of a large city's population moving through the streets in an endless stream, pushing, wheeling, dragging all their belongings from every part of the city to one small section, crowding one another more and more as they converged. No cars, no horses, no help of any sort was available to us by order of the occupying authorities. Pushcarts were about the only method of conveyance we had, and these were piled high with household goods, furnishing much amusement to the German onlookers who delighted in overturning the carts and seeing us scrambling for our effects. Many of the goods were confiscated arbitrarily without any explanation. . . .
>
> In the ghetto, as some of us had begun to call it, half ironically and in jest, there was appalling chaos. Thousands of people were rushing around at the last minute trying to find a place to stay. Everything was already filled up but still they kept

coming and somehow more room was found.

The narrow, crooked streets of the most dilapidated section of Warsaw were crowded with pushcarts, their owners going from house to house asking the inevitable question: Have you room? The sidewalks were covered with their belongings. Children wandered, lost and crying, parents ran hither and yon seeking them, their cries drowned in the tremendous hubbub of half a million uprooted people.[35]

Both Poles and Jews obeyed the fierce decree. Both, Chaim Kaplan noted in his diary on October 22, 'curse the murderer with the wish that his world darken in his lifetime, just as he darkened their world by ordering them to do something against their will'.[36]

October 22 was also a day of woe elsewhere, for on that day a total of 6,500 German Jews from Baden, the Saar and the Palatinate were sent by train across France to internment camps in the French Pyrenees.[37] All the property of the deported Jews, their homes, businesses and belongings, was seized by the local German authorities. They came, these new deportees, from some of the oldest Jewish communities in Germany, two thousand of them from Mannheim, where the first synagogue was built in 1664, and thirty-four from Alt Briesach, where the first Jews settled in 1301. Some of the Jews sent to the camps in the Pyrenees, the largest of which was in the village of Gurs, had been born outside Germany, in Warsaw, Budapest and Zagreb. One deportee, Lieba Lust, had been born in 1875 in the then Austro-Hungarian frontier town of Auschwitz: she died at Gurs, six weeks after deportation, three weeks before her sixty-fifth birthday.[38]

'From this camp Gurs,' Pastor Heinrich Grüber later recalled, 'we had – in Berlin – very bad news, even worse news than reached us from Poland. They did not have any medicaments or any sanitary arrangements whatsoever.'[39] Grüber had tried to go to Gurs, to do what he could to ameliorate the situation, but instead he was arrested, and sent as a prisoner first to Sachsenhausen and then to Dachau.

In Warsaw, the creation of the ghetto continued, marked by scenes of chaos and fear as predominantly Jewish streets, into which Jews had moved from elsewhere, were suddenly and arbitrarily excluded. 'People are walking around crazy with anxiety,' Ringelblum noted, 'because they don't know where to move to. Not a single street is sure of being assigned to the ghetto.' There were some Jews, Ringelblum added, 'who said they'd rather be poisoned with gas than tortured so'.

Two lawyers, Ringelblum noted, Koral and Tykoczynski – Koral having been the legal counsel of the French Embassy before the war – 'have committed suicide because of the resettlement decree'. Ringelblum also learned that day that, nine months earlier, in Praga, a Jew called Friedman 'stood up for the rabbi when the latter was being impressed for work and beaten. Friedman was shot on the spot.'[40]

The main Jewish hospital in Warsaw, the Czyste hospital, was among one of many Jewish institutions forced to leave its buildings and move to the ghetto, although no suitable premises existed for it there.

On October 24, as the uprooting continued, the Jewish calendar reached the night of Simchat Torah, the Rejoicing of the Law. 'An additional doubt', wrote Chaim Kaplan, 'is gnawing at us: Will it be a closed ghetto?' There were signs, he noted, 'in both directions, and we hope for a miracle – which doesn't always happen in time of need. A closed ghetto means gradual death. An open ghetto is only a halfway catastrophe.'[41] The uncertainty was deliberate, its effect bewildering. 'Everyone bites his lip', Kaplan noted two weeks later, 'in anger born of helplessness. Everyone is choked up with his own anxieties. When friends meet, each one hastens to ask the standard question: what do you think? Will we be able to hold out?'[42]

On October 25, in a directive issued from the capital of the General Government, Cracow, any further granting of exit visas to Polish Jews was forbidden, on the grounds that Jewish emigration would lead to a 'renewal' of Jewry in the United States, its growth and concentration. If Eastern European Jews were to be allowed to go to America, J. A. Eckhardt explained in a General Government memorandum, it would enable American Jewry to fulfil its plan 'to create a new platform from which it contemplates to continue its battle most forcibly against Germany'.[43]

Outside German control, a new phase of the war began with the Italian invasion of Greece on 28 October 1940. Mussolini, too, was eager to extend his empire. But the Greek forces fought fiercely, and the Italian advance was halted. In the fighting, more than twelve thousand Greek Jews served with distinction: 613 Jews from Salonica were killed in action, and 1,412 became total invalids. Among the Jews who fought was the Greek national hero Mordechai Fraggi, who was killed in action.[44]

On 15 November 1940 the Warsaw ghetto was officially declared to be in existence. 'Jews are forbidden', noted Mary Berg, 'to move outside the boundaries formed by certain streets. There is considerable commotion.' Work had already begun on walls to encircle the ghetto area. These walls were three yards high. 'Jewish masons,' Mary Berg wrote, 'supervised by Nazi soldiers, are laying bricks upon bricks. Those who do not work fast enough are lashed by the overseers.'[45] With only twenty-seven thousand apartments available in the area of the ghetto, six or seven people were forced to live in each room.[46]

Writing in his diary four days later, Ringelblum noted that Jewish women in the ghetto were surprised to discover that the markets outside the ghetto were closed to them. Many items had suddenly disappeared from the ghetto shops. On the first day after the ghetto wall was completed, and the ghetto closed, 'many Christians brought bread for their Jewish acquaintances and friends'. This, Ringelblum added, 'was a mass phenomenon. Meanwhile, Christian friends are helping Jews bring produce into the ghetto.' But that day, November 19, a Christian was killed by the Germans, 'throwing a sack of bread over the wall'.

At one ghetto street corner, Ringelblum noted, German soldiers were tearing up paper into small pieces, scattering the pieces in the mud, ordering Jews to pick the pieces up, and then 'beating them as they stoop over'. On another street, a German soldier 'stopped to beat a Jewish pedestrian. Ordered him to lie down and kiss the pavement.' A 'wave of evil', Ringelblum commented, 'rolled over the whole city. . . .'[47]

The four hundred thousand Jews of Warsaw were in a trap, their means of contact with the outside world, and even with the rest of Warsaw, being systematically cut off. 'Extraordinary meetings are taking place in every house,' Mary Berg wrote in her diary. 'The tension is terrific. Some people demand that a protest be organized. This is the voice of the youth; our elders consider this is a dangerous idea. We are cut off from the world. There are no radios, no telephones, no newspapers.'[48]

With the closing of the Warsaw ghetto, another new feature of Nazi rule was introduced, the Jewish policeman: at German insistence, his was to be the responsibility for maintaining order in the ghetto. At first the Jewish policeman was a welcome, even a prized figure. As Chaim Kaplan wrote in his diary a few weeks later:

> The residents of the ghetto are beginning to think they are in Tel Aviv. Strong, bona fide policemen from among our brothers, to whom you can speak in Yiddish! First of all, it comes as a godsend to the street vendors. The fear of the Gentile police is gone from their faces. A Jewish policeman, a man of human sensibilities – one of our own brothers would not turn over their baskets or trample their wares. The other citizens of the ghetto are relieved too, because a Jewish shout is not the same as a Gentile one. The latter is coarse, crude, nasty; the former, while it may be threatening, contains a certain gentility, as if to say: 'Don't you understand?'[49]

For Mary Berg, there was a similar sense of relief, and indeed of pleasure, at the sight of policemen wearing a white armband with the blue Star of David. Their duties, she wrote, included guarding the gates of the ghetto with German and Polish policemen, directing traffic in the ghetto streets, guarding post offices, soup kitchens and community offices, detecting 'and suppressing' smugglers, and driving the growing number of beggars from street to street. 'I experience', she wrote, 'a strange and utterly illogical feeling of satisfaction when I see a Jewish policeman at a crossing – such policemen were completely unknown in pre-war Poland.' From time to time, she added, 'Gestapo cars rush by, paying no attention whatsoever to the Jewish policeman's directions. . . .'[50]

The four hundred thousand Jews of Warsaw, and the two million and more Jews under German rule in November 1940, had no means of escape. But Jewish refugees from central Europe who had reached Slovakia some months earlier had been able to go by ship down the Danube and, once at the Black Sea, to sail to Palestine. In the third week of November, as Warsaw Jewry contemplated the grim reality of the ghetto, 1,771 refugees, most of them from

Germany, Austria and Czechoslovakia, reached Haifa, on board two tramp steamers, the *Milos* and the *Pacific*. A few days later, a further 1,783 refugees arrived on board a third boat, the *Atlantic*.

None of these refugees had valid certificates for Palestine. The British authorities therefore ordered them to transfer to another boat, the *Patria*, for deportation to the Indian Ocean island of Mauritius. On November 25, as the refugees were being transferred, some of the Jews, determined to remain in Palestine, blew up the *Patria*. Their aim had been only to disable the ship, to prevent it from sailing, but it sank, and 250 of the refugees were drowned.[51]

On November 28, as Palestine Jewry mourned the *Patria* dead, a second anti-Jewish film was given its premiere in Berlin. *Der Ewige Jude*, 'The Eternal Jew', was to be shown in cinemas throughout Germany and German-occupied Europe. The film sought to explain the part played by the Jews in world history. Scenes of rats and Jews were juxtaposed. The Jews, like the rats, were carriers of diseases, 'money-mad bits of filth devoid of all higher values, corrupters of the world'.[52]

These images fanned the vicious racism of German propaganda, as they were designed to do. When German soldiers entered the Warsaw ghetto, they treated the Jews as vermin, entering houses at will to steal whatever they could find. 'A Jew does not dare make a sound of protest,' Chaim Kaplan noted on December 6. 'There have been cases when courageous Jews were shot in full view of their entire family, and the murderers were not held responsible, because their excuse was that the filthy Jew cursed the Führer and it was their duty to avenge his honour.'[53] Four days later Ringelblum recorded how, on December 9, 'a soldier sprang out of a passing automobile and hit a boy on the head with an iron bar. The boy died.'[54]

As 1940 drew to a close, Richard Lichtheim, the head of the Geneva office of the Jewish Agency for Palestine, reported to Palestine, London and New York what he had heard of the plight of the Jews of Europe. From Rumania, he wrote, there were reports of 'killings and lootings'. From the camp at Gurs came details of barracks with neither floors nor beds: 'The people are lying on the ground and many of them have not even blankets.' In Belgium and Holland the German authorities wanted 'to eliminate the Jews from public life'. In Switzerland there were six thousand Jewish refugees, 'of whom 2,600 are destitute'. In Poland, the situation of the Jews was 'even worse than in Germany itself'.

In his letter, Lichtheim wrote of the hundreds of thousands of European Jews 'who tried to escape but did not go fast or far enough': Jews who had earlier fled from Germany, Austria, Czechoslovakia and even Poland, who were now caught in France, Belgium, Holland, Norway and Denmark.[55] Others, while still in Europe, had found refuge in neutral countries, six thousand in Switzerland, ten thousand in Portugal, several thousand interned while trying to pass through Spain, several thousand finding havens in Sweden and Finland, others in Rumania, Hungary, Bulgaria and Italy.

From Varna, in Bulgaria, a tiny craft of some 130 tons, the *Salvador*, had set out in mid-November with more than three hundred and fifty Jewish refugees crammed on board. The British government, seeking to prevent their entry in Palestine, urged the Turkish and Greek governments not to allow the ship through the Dardanelles, or into the Aegean Sea. These urgings were unnecessary, however, for on December 12, while still in the Sea of Marmora, the *Salvador* sank: two hundred of the refugees were drowned, including seventy children. Five days later two British officials responsible for refugee policy for central Europe exchanged notes. 'If anything can deter these poor devils from setting out for Zion, that story should,' wrote one, to which the other replied: 'I agree. There could have been no more opportune disaster from the point of view of stopping this traffic. . . .'[56]

The 'traffic' did not stop. But with every passing month, escape became more difficult. Wherever German rule was established, the Jews were deprived of their passports and travel documents, or denied them, while in the streets and concentration camps they continued to be singled out for particular abuse. When the Berlin pastor, Heinrich Grüber, was sent to Sachsenhausen concentration camp on December 17, he was a witness to one such episode. As he later recalled, it was 'one of the first impressions' of his imprisonment:

> I myself on that night was on guard in our hut and heard cries all of a sudden. Two SS men – drunk – appeared; they were always at their worst when they were drunk, these SS men.

They demanded of the Jews, in the neighbouring hut – because there was a special hut for every kind of prisoner – that they should come out into the cold night, to the frost and ice; they were required and ordered to 'roll', as they would call it, in the snow; later, when the SS men themselves were too cold they ordered the Jews back to the unheated cold huts and ordered them to go back to bed under their thin blankets.

'Of course,' Gruber added, 'these people contracted pneumonia, and some of them died of pneumonia.'[57]

In Warsaw, German soldiers in a car were terrorizing the Jews of the ghetto. 'Today,' noted Emanuel Ringelblum on Christmas Eve, 1940, 'the car appeared at Karmelicka again; the soldiers got out and beat up all the Jews. Men, women and children. A woman was going down the street with her child; the child got so powerful a blow he fell unconscious in the middle of the street.'[58] Near Kalisz, a group of British soldiers captured in France in June 1940 were being held in a prisoner-of-war camp. One of them, Sergeant Donald Edgar, later recalled:

One morning as we were trudging through the snow to work we saw coming towards us a heavy cart being pulled by six . . . yes, as they came nearer we were sure . . . by six women. What is more, six young women, thin, emaciated and bent forward in their rope harness. They scarcely looked up as we passed.

As the cart, which was wheeled and not on sleds as most were at this time of the year, passed I saw that it was loaded with old tombstones and I recognised that they were inscribed with Hebrew characters. Beside the cart marched a black-uniformed SS guard, rifle on shoulder.

When they had gone I asked a guard whom I was on chatting terms with, who the girls were. 'Judische Madel,' 'Jewish girls,' he replied curtly, and started to shout at us to get a move on.[59]

Thus, for the Jews of German-occupied Europe, the year 1940 ended, and ended without hope of any improvement in their situation. But few imagined that worse brutality, worse sadism, and mass murder, were yet to come.

11

January–June 1941:
the spreading net

IN WARSAW, in a ghetto covered with deep snow, the Germans would allow the Jews no fuel for heating. 'Wherever I go,' Mary Berg noted on 4 January 1941, 'I find people wrapped up in blankets or huddling under feather beds, that is, if the Germans have not taken all these warm things for their own soldiers.' To relieve their boredom, some of the Nazi guards near the ghetto entrances arranged 'entertainments' for themselves, choosing a passer-by at random and ordering him to throw himself in the snow with his face down, 'and if he is a Jew who wears a beard, they tear it off together with the skin until the snow is red with blood'.

Even the Jewish policemen did not go unscathed. 'Yesterday', Mary Berg recorded, 'I myself saw a Nazi gendarme "exercise" a Jewish policeman near the passage from the Little to the Big Ghetto on Chlodna Street. The young man finally lost his breath, but the Nazi still forced him to fall and rise until he collapsed in a pool of blood. Then someone called for an ambulance, and the Jewish policeman was put on a stretcher and carried away on a hand truck.'[1]

The hunger in the ghetto was made worse by the cold. 'Walking down Leszno Street,' Emanuel Ringelblum noted on 5 January 1941, 'you come across people lying at the street corner, frozen, begging.' Recently, he added, 'streetwalking has become notable. Yesterday, a very respectable-looking woman detained me.' 'Necessity', he commented, 'drives people to anything.'[2]

It was the daily, and nightly, danger of Nazi 'actions' that was the scourge of the ghetto. On the evening of January 9, Mary Berg was at a meeting of her house committee when, at eleven o'clock, Nazi gendarmes broke into the room, searched the men, took away whatever money they found, and then ordered the women to strip. Her account continued:

> Our subtenant, Mrs R., who happened to be there, courageously protested, declaring that she would not undress in the presence of men. For this she received a resounding slap on the face and was searched even more harshly than the other women. The women were kept naked for more than two hours while the Nazis put their revolvers to their breasts and private parts and threatened to shoot them all if they did not disgorge dollars or diamonds.
>
> The beasts did not leave until 2.00 a.m., carrying a scanty loot of a few watches, some paltry rings, and a small sum in Polish zlotys. They did not find either diamonds or dollars.

Such attacks, Mary Berg added, took place nightly in the Warsaw ghetto.[3] They had become a commonplace of German actions throughout Poland, and the perpetrators were urged by their superiors not to flag. At a Nazi Party meeting in Lublin on January 22, Hans Frank spoke of the few 'humanitarian dreamers' who, out of 'sheer German good-nature', were in the habit, as he expressed it, 'of falling asleep over world history'. But he went on to warn that: 'We who for twenty years past have been fighting beside the Führer cannot be asked to have any consideration left for the Jews.' If, he added, 'the Jews in the world ask for pity today, this leaves us cold'.[4]

In the Lodz ghetto, a Chronicle of Events, begun on January 12, recorded the daily deaths. These, the chroniclers wrote, were 'the result of complete physical exhaustion brought on by hunger and cold': on January 20 there were three such deaths noted by name, the thirty-four-year-old Icek Brona, the fifty-seven-year-old Ita Kinster and the sixty-nine-year-old Abram Szmulewicz.[5] Several suicides were also recalled in the Lodz ghetto in that first week of systematic records, among them a twenty-one-year-old girl, Bluma Lichtensztajn, who jumped from a fourth-floor window on January 29. 'Her condition leaves no hope for recovery,' the Chronicle commented.[6] Also on January 29, in the Lodz ghetto, hunger led to the death of the seventy-nine-year-old painter Maurycy Trebacz, winner of a Gold Medal at the San Francisco World Exhibition of 1894.[7] Trebacz was one of five thousand Jews who died of starvation in the Lodz ghetto between January and June 1941.

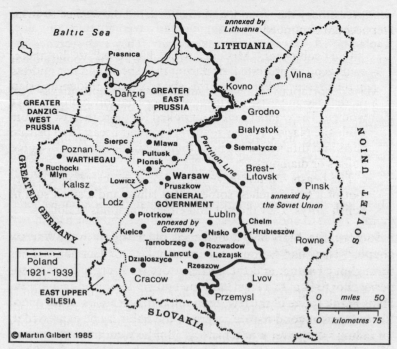

THE GENERAL GOVERNMENT

Having established the Warsaw ghetto, the Germans now began to uproot Jews from all the smaller towns and villages west of the city, and drive them into the ghetto. On January 31, three thousand such 'new exiles', as Chaim Kaplan described them, reached Warsaw, mostly from the nearby town of Pruszkow. Describing the morning of their deportation, Kaplan wrote:

> The exiles were driven out of their beds before dawn, and the Führer's minions did not let them take money, belongings, or food, threatening all the while to shoot them. Before they left on their exile, a search was made of their pockets and of all the hidden places in their clothes and bodies. Without a penny in their pockets or a covering for the women, children, old people, and invalids – sometimes without shoes on their feet or staffs in their hands – they were forced to leave their homes and possessions and the graves of their ancestors, and go – whither? And in terrible, fierce, unbearable cold!

On reaching the ghetto boundary, the deportees from Pruszkow were searched once more. If anyone had saved anything of value, Kaplan noted, 'it was quickly taken away. They even searched the invalids and the sick people in wheelchairs, and if they found a bit of food, it too was stolen.'[8]

Mass deportations followed from all the towns and villages west and south of Warsaw. Between the end of January and the end of March, more than seventy thousand Jews were brought into the ghetto, raising its population to nearly half a million. 'We ourselves', Zivia Lubetkin later recalled, 'lived twelve or fifteen people to a room.' Refugees, she added, were sent to special houses which had somehow been evacuated of their usual inhabitants. These were 'the worst conditions' of the ghetto. She remembered vividly a visit to one such house in search of a family she had known before the war, the husband a teacher, the wife a doctor, a well-off couple, with children:

> When I came to look for this family, I found them on the floor, one on top of the other. They were in a corner of a room. I could not come up to them because there was no room to put my foot to cross the room. In this house, there was no lavatory in the whole house and they had a lavatory in the yard and they were on the fourth floor. There was no water in the house. And people lived this way. They degenerated because there was no possibility of getting work, no employment. There was hunger. Sanitary conditions were below description, and of course, the typhoid epidemic began in those houses.

There was no possibility, Zivia Lubetkin added, of separating the sick from the healthy, 'and sometimes it was impossible to separate the dead from the living, those who died of starvation, children in the arms of their mothers'.

How well Zivia Lubetkin remembered, also, the evenings after curfew 'when silence would come to the ghetto and everyone would hide in his corner – and the voice of the small children, "a piece of bread, a piece of bread". But no one could give us that piece of bread, because very few of us had a piece of bread.'[9]

In Rumania, the anti-Jewish hatred of the Iron Guard burst out anew on 21 January 1941, when gangs of Legionnaires, some armed with guns, others with staves, hunted for Jews in the streets. Thousands of Jews were caught and beaten, hundreds of shops and houses were looted or burned, and twenty-five synagogues desecrated. After three days of these manhunts, 120 Jews had been killed.[10] As in German-occupied Europe, these killings were carried out in a repulsive manner: 'sadistic atrocities unsurpassed in horror', one of Churchill's Private Secretaries described them, 'taking hundreds of Jews to cattle slaughterhouses and killing them according to the Jews' own ritual practices in slaughtering animals'.[11] The bodies of many of those murdered were then hung on meat hooks in the slaughterhouse, with placards around them announcing 'Kosher meat'.[12]

In the Lodz ghetto, the Chairman of the Jewish Council, Chaim Rumkowski, negotiated with the Germans for the establishment of workshops in which more than ten thousand Jews had found work by February 1941: many of them as carpenters, tailors and shoemakers, producing goods for Germany. 'My main slogan', Rumkowski explained in a speech to Jewish Council officials on February 1, 'has been to give work to the greatest possible number of people.' In this way, he hoped, those in the ghetto, and those being deported to it, would be able to survive.[13]

Throughout Eastern Europe, the German authorities had begun to make considerable use of local German-speaking groups, the Ethnic Germans, or *Volksdeutsch*, to carry out their orders. The descendants of German settlers in the eighteenth and nineteenth centuries, the Ethnic Germans had long felt themselves a deprived minority, cut off from their original homeland, and isolated by language and tradition from the people among whom they lived. The coming of German rule seemed to offer many Ethnic Germans the opportunity to prosper; for some it was the opportunity for revenge. In areas where they were numerically large, they provided Berlin with valuable allies. In Lodz, a city with 350,000 Poles and 250,000 Jews, there were 75,000 Ethnic Germans living on the eve of war. By 1941 their number had doubled, as a result of the deliberate transfer by the German authorities of Ethnic Germans from the Volhynia to western Polish territory. For the Jews of the Lodz ghetto, the presence of so many Ethnic Germans was an added danger. It also meant that the Poles in Lodz and in its surrounding areas were less able to organize resistance and escape routes, Jew and Pole alike being confronted in the Ethnic Germans with a formidable barrier to resistance or escape.[14]

Deportations continued throughout February and March 1941, to Warsaw, Lodz and several other ghettos. One deportation, from Plock to Czestochowa, has been described by Moshe Shklarek:

> In the early hours of that morning the house shuddered from violent knocks on the door and from the savage cries of the Germans, 'Filthy Jews, outside!' Within a few moments we found ourselves huddled together in a crowd of the town's Jews on Sheroka Street.
>
> With the help of the Volksdeutsche and with cruel blows and many murders, they loaded the assembled ones on to trucks, crowding them tightly, and the long convoy drove out of town. We were not permitted to take anything with us, not even something else to wear other than what we had put on in our terrified haste.
>
> On the same day, after hours of difficult travelling, the trucks came to a stop in the midst of Dzialdowo camp, at the entrance to the town of Mlawa. Two rows of Germans, equipped with clubs and whips, stood in a line several tens of meters long, extending from the trucks to the camp gate.
>
> We were ordered to jump out of the trucks and run the gauntlet towards the gate. Before the first ones to jump had managed to set foot on the torture-pass, the clubs and whips flew and a torrent of blows rained down on the runners' heads. With difficulty and desperate haste, each one hurried to reach the camp gate, people falling and being trampled under their brothers' feet in their frantic race.
>
> Only an isolated few managed to get through the gate without being wounded by the blows and lashes of the Germans. In the aftermath of this act of terror, scores of slain bodies were left lying and were buried next to the single privy which was provided for the men and women who lived in the camp.
>
> The hundreds of wounded and injured lay without any medical care in the stables that were full of mud and dung, and into which we had been squeezed and packed without room

enough to free our aching limbs. In this camp we endured days of torment and distress, thirst and hunger.

It was in these conditions, Shklarek added, that one of the women went into labour 'and brought into the world a Jewish baby, destined for pain and destruction'.[15]

The deportees came not only from Polish towns, but from Austria. Beginning on February 15, and continuing at weekly intervals for five weeks, one thousand Jews a week, all men, were brought by train from Vienna to the ghettos of Kielce and Lublin, and from there to work in the labour camps on the Soviet border, building fortifications along the River Bug.[16]

There was also, in February, a deportation from Holland, where, as in Denmark and Norway, the Jews had been spared the fate of Polish Jewry. On February 19 a German patrol in Amsterdam entered a tavern run by a Jewish refugee from Germany, Ernst Cahn. In the tavern, a protective device which Cahn had installed, an ammonia flash, went off by accident, spraying the Germans with the irritant fluid. Cahn was at once arrested, and, three days later, as a reprisal for his act of 'resistance', the SS raided the Jewish quarter of Amsterdam, seized 425 Jews, most of them young men, subjected them to beatings and abuse, and then, on February 27, deported 389 of them to the concentration camp at Buchenwald.

One of the deportees later recalled how, on the journey from Amsterdam to Buchenwald, the German guards 'seemed to have a special prediliction for people with glasses, whom they would hit straight in the face'.[17]

During their time in Buchenwald, twenty-five of the deportees died, some from the brutal treatment, some shot while attempting to escape.

After two months at Buchenwald, all but three of the remaining 364 were deported to the concentration camp at Mauthausen. There, all of them were put to work in the punitive stone quarries, hauling massive blocks of stone up a steep incline. As they climbed the 148 steps, they were whipped and beaten.

On the third day after the arrival of the Dutch deportees at Mauthausen, the camp guards began machine-gunning the climbers on the steps. On the fourth day, some ten young Jews linked hands and jumped to voluntary death. The Germans referred to those who had jumped as 'parachutists'. In order to prevent a recurrence of this collective suicide, the remaining prisoners were placed under the charge of two particularly sadistic guards, one known as 'the blonde fraulein', the other as 'Hans the killer'. By the autumn, there were no survivors.[18]

Ernst Cahn, the man whose alleged resistance had led to this mass murder, was tortured at Gestapo headquarters in Amsterdam, but refused to reveal who had fixed the offensive ammonia bottle in his tavern. On 3 March 1941 he was shot by a German firing squad: the first person to be shot by firing squad in Holland since the German occupation ten months earlier.[19]

In the Warsaw ghetto, Emanuel Ringelblum had been recording in his notes the news that reached him from elsewhere in Poland, as well as events in the ghetto itself. Ringelblum was forty-one years old, a historian deprived of a university library, pupils or the possibility of publishing his work. But he continued writing and collecting material with a calm dedication, determined that this terrible episode of Jewish history would be recorded.

During February 1941, Ringelblum noted that in Plonsk a group of Jews had been locked up in the synagogue 'until they hacked the Holy Ark to bits'. The two Cracow rabbis, Kornitzer and Rappaport, who had been sent to the concentration camp at Auschwitz, 'are no longer alive'. Their 'only sin' had been that they had appealed against the continuing deportations from Cracow. The Auschwitz camp in which they died was the punishment camp, set up for Polish political prisoners in June 1940, and at that time seldom used to punish Jews.

In Warsaw, a ban had been imposed 'on selling of merchandise to Jews'. But Jewish cultural activity was flourishing: in more than a hundred of the 1,700 courtyards around which the apartments of the ghetto were built, Yiddish schools had been set up, whose pupils were celebrating the anniversary of the birth of Mendele Mocher Seforim, the 'father' of modern Hebrew and Yiddish literature. Libraries, also, were to be found in 'dozens of courtyards'.

Ringelblum wanted every facet of ghetto life to be recorded, however cruel. On Leszno Street, he wrote, 'the head of a Jewish smuggler is thrust through a hole in the basement of the gutted post office building. Six guards see him, call over two Jews, and order them to pull the man out. They do it, receiving a blow from the guards in the act. They order the smuggler to crawl back into his hole again, and, as he crawls, pierce his head with their bayonets. His screams ring through the quiet street.'[20]

In January 1941, two thousand Jews had died of starvation in the Warsaw ghetto. The February toll was just as high. 'Almost daily', Ringelblum noted on February 28, 'people are falling dead or unconscious in the middle of the street. It no longer makes so direct an impression.' The streets themselves were 'forever full of newly arrived refugees'. Scabies were widespread because of lack of soap. In the streets, hawkers plied their wares with the cry: 'If you must buy a rag, buy a clean one.'

As well as recording the information that reached him, Ringelblum sought out those from whom he could take testimony. 'Terrible case of a three-year-old refugee child,' he noted at the end of February. During the journey to Warsaw, 'the guard threw the child into the snow. Its mother jumped off the wagon and tried to save the child. The guard threatened her with a revolver. The mother insisted life was worthless for her without her child. Then the guard threatened to shoot all the Jews in the wagon. The mother arrived in Warsaw, and here went out of her mind.'

In every street of the ghetto, beggars. 'Child in arms, a mother begs – the child appears dead,' Ringelblum noted. Three- and four-year-old children were begging, 'and that is the most painful'.

Ringelblum was not alone in recording Jewish suffering under the Nazis. 'Even young people in labour camps do it,' he wrote. 'The manuscripts are discovered, torn up, and their authors beaten.'[21]

The number of labour camps in German-occupied Poland continued to grow. In March 1941, in the annexed region of East Upper Silesia, a special organization was created, under the control of General Albrecht Schmelt, for the employment of Jewish skilled labour, both men and women, in factories throughout the region. The factories paid normal wages for the work, but transferred half the wage to the Schmelt organization. These Jews were employed in mining, metallurgy and textiles.

From Lodz, two hundred Jews volunteered for work in Germany in return for a wage of nine marks a week, to be sent to their families in Lodz. They were sent to an autobahn-building camp, to work for sixteen hours a day, shovelling earth. 'You bloody Jews here,' the camp commander greeted them, 'you are going to sweat blood here,' whereupon, as one fourteen-year-old boy later recalled, 'he took a large stave and with one blow struck *two* chaps – who were killed.'[22]

Conditions in these camps quickly worsened. The share of the wage paid to the labourer was reduced almost to nothing. When the first workers came back 'most of the girls', as Frieda Mazia, of Sosnowiec, later recalled, 'were swollen with hunger, ill – sometimes with TB or rheumatoid arthritis; they told us how they had suffered, described the tortures, the prolonged roll calls, the meagre rations. . . .'

Frieda Mazia also witnessed, in Sosnowiec, a public execution. A Jewish mother had bought an egg from a Polish peasant so that her child would not die of hunger. Both mother and peasant were hanged: the bodies left hanging for two or three days, 'so one couldn't avoid seeing them – if we wanted to go out we had to pass them'.[23]

In Kielce, several thousand of the deportees from Vienna, and all sixteen thousand Jews of Kielce itself, were driven into a ghetto zone on 7 April 1941. The zone was at once declared a 'contagious' one: entry and exit were forbidden. To amuse himself, one German Governor of Kielce renamed the ghetto streets. Among the names he chose were Jerusalem Street, Moses Street, Zion Street, Palestine Street, Non-Kosher Street, Grynszpan Street – after the murderer of vom Rath in November 1938 – and Happy Street.[24] 'I will somehow manage to survive,' wrote Gertrude Zeisler, a fifty-two-year-old deportee from Vienna. 'Since the sun is shining, things do not seem so terrible any longer.'[25]

Hunger stalked all the ghettos: 'Two weeks ago', Ringelblum noted in Warsaw on March 18, 'some two hundred Jews died. Last week there were more than four hundred deaths. The corpses are laid in mass graves, separated by boards. Most of the bodies, brought to the graveyard from the hospital, are burned naked.'[26]

In Lodz the rate of starvation was almost as high as in Warsaw. 'Although the ghetto of Lodz was initiated as a mere trial,' a Cologne newspaper commented on April 5, 'as a mere prelude to the solution of the Jewish question, it has turned out to be the best and most perfect temporary solution. . . .'[27] A week later, the Germans announced publicly that any Jews leaving the Lodz ghetto would be shot on sight.[28]

Such shootings had already begun. On March 12, as the Lodz Ghetto Chronicle recorded, the thirteen-year-old Wolf Finkelstein 'was shot dead by a sentry. The boy received a fatal wound to his lungs and heart.' On March 19, the thirty-one-year-old Rafal Krzepicki 'was shot dead around midnight'. On March 23 the twenty-year-old Awigdor Lichtenstein 'was shot dead near the latrine . . .'.[29] 'Tonight', the Chronicle noted on March 26, 'forty-four-year-old Chana Lewkowicz was shot dead', while, in the House of Culture, 'there was a musical recital today. . . .'[30]

On Sunday, 6 April 1941, Palm Sunday, the Germans invaded Yugoslavia and Greece. There were many thousands of Jews serving in the Yugoslav and Greek armies. As both countries were overwhelmed by the force of the German onslaught, Jews fell alongside their fellow soldiers-in-arms. On April 13 German troops entered Belgrade. There, according to one account, the first civilian to be shot in cold blood was a Jewish tailor, who, as German troops marched by, spat at the column and shouted out, 'You will all perish.'[31]

There were more than seventy thousand Jews living in Yugoslavia in 1941, as well as several thousand refugees from Germany, Austria, Czechoslovakia and Poland. In Greece, seventy-five thousand Jews now came under joint German and Italian rule. For a while, the Greek Jews were unmolested. Mussolini's Italy did not share the fanatical anti-Semitism cultivated in Nazi Germany during the previous eight years. But in Yugoslavia, Hitler had an ideological and physical ally in the Croat Ustachi movement, and from April 1941, with the establishment of an independent Croat state, Jews were singled out for savage treatment; thousands were murdered in the first months of the new regime.

The rabbi of the Yugoslav town of Vinkovci, Mavro Frankfurter, was the father of David Frankfurter, who had shot Wilhelm Gustloff in Switzerland in 1936. Then, the father had condemned his son's action. Now, as German soldiers occupied the town, Rabbi Frankfurter was made to stand on a table while soldiers spat in his face, pulled out the hair from his long beard, and struck him with their rifle butts.[32]

On April 13, in Belgrade, German troops and local Germans ransacked Jewish shops and homes. On April 14, as Hungarian troops occupied parts of northern Yugoslavia, five hundred Jews and Serbs were seized, and shot. On April 16, German forces entered Sarajevo, and, with local Muslims, plundered and demolished the main synagogue.[33]

In Sarajevo, Mustafa Hardaga, a Muslim, the owner of a building in which a Jew, Josef Cavilio, had a factory manufacturing steel pipes, sheltered Cavilio and his family for ten days. Posters on the streets warned the locals not to give shelter to Communists and Jews. The Hardaga family defied the order. After six weeks in hiding, Josef Cavilio, his wife and children managed to escape over the mountains to Mostar, in the Italian zone.[34]

In Warsaw, Ringelblum noted on April 17 that the high cost of food, the fall of Yugoslavia, and the work camps were 'the awful trio that determines our situation in the ghetto'. It was the festival of Passover, of the flight of the Jews from their bondage under Pharaoh. But in Warsaw, the savagery of the German guards was unabated, even against Jewish policemen. Vicious reprisals were carried out for the merest acts of independence. In his notes for April 17, Ringelblum recorded how a German guard had taken a sack of potatoes away from a Jewish woman:

> Ginsberg, a Jewish policeman from Lodz, asked the guard to give the potatoes back to the poor woman. As punishment for Ginsberg's audacity, the guard knocked him to the ground, stabbed him with his bayonet, and shot him as he lay there. Weak from hunger, Ginsberg died in the hospital. Another Jewish policeman was wounded by a guard's bullet at the same place. The same evening a group of people who had been out late were shot at after nine o'clock and two of them were injured.

Ringelblum had two pieces of encouraging news to report. The first was from the towns of Bedzin and Sosnowiec, where no ghettos had been established, owing to the efforts of Moses Merin, the head of the Jewish Councils in East Upper Silesia, who had also success-fully resettled in Bedzin and Sosnowiec the six thousand Jews forced to leave the town of Auschwitz, while at the same time keeping the mortality in his two towns 'actually lower than it had been before the war'. On a recent visit to Warsaw, Ringelblum commented with some sarcasm, Merin had received 'a royal reception'.

The second piece of encouraging news was that seven Warsaw Jews had managed to smuggle themselves across the border to Slovakia, had reached Bratislava, on the Danube, and migrated from there to Palestine.[35]

These seven Jews had been *chalutzim*, young people who had trained before the war for work in Palestine. Another would-be Palestinian pioneer was the twenty-five-year-old Yitzhak Zuckerman, who in September 1939 had been in Soviet-occupied Poland, but had crossed back into German-occupied Poland in the spring of 1940, in order not to abandon his Jewish youth movement. On the last day of Passover, April 24, while at a Zionist 'collective' in the ghetto, Zuckerman was seized, together with a hundred other Jews in the collective, and taken to a camp in the Kampinos forest, to dig canals and drain swamps.

Ten Jews died each day at Kampinos, weakened by more than a year and a half of privation. Zuckerman later recalled seeing people talking one to the other and then, 'all of a sudden, out of a blue sky', one of them would fall down, 'and he was dead'.

After a few days in Kampinos, a visitor came looking for Zuckerman. This was Lonka Kozibrodska, a Jewish girl who had recently been among the deportees from Pruszkow to Warsaw, and was now acting as a courier, posing as a non-Jewish girl. The suspicion of the guards was roused, but 'Brodska', as she was known, managed to escape back to Warsaw. Zuckerman was at once summoned for interrogation:

> I was beaten. My head was cracked open. My hands were wounded. First of all they wanted to know whether this woman was a Jewess or not. Since I knew that she did not have the Jewish badge I said that no, she is not Jewish, and that we had gone to school together and she must have heard about my being in this camp and come. Then they accused me of shaming the race and they would execute me, they said.
>
> They said I was violating the Aryan race, if she is a Polish woman. I was not executed. I was put into a pit full of water. I can't remember too much of that night. I had fever. I shivered.

In the morning I was taken in front of the entire camp and the commander announced, these were his words more or less, 'This man knows when he was born but he does not know when he will die.' But here he promised us solemnly that three days and three nights my body will hang from the gallows. And I stood there and waited for the moment of death. But I was put back into this pit. I wanted it all to be over with. And I beat on the doors. I wanted to be executed.

I applied to the sentry. I said, 'Execute me.' But I don't know what happened, I don't know whether I heard correctly. I heard the commander at night. There were various authorities there, various commanders. I heard somebody saying in Polish, 'A pity on this boy.'

Zuckerman was released from the pit, and later from the camp: his colleagues in the collective had managed to raise enough money to bribe the camp authorities to release him. The camp commander had also decided to send back a hundred Jews 'who could not work any more, who were just a burden on the camp'. As Zuckerman recalled:

One day at sunrise the commander appeared and told me, 'Look here, it's your responsibility. People who will break the line and will have no strength left to reach the railroad train, they will die on the spot.'

I took that responsibility. I organized the younger men and we carried the others, but many died. Not because we left them behind. They died, scores of people, out of the slow starvation death, this frightening death.

All of a sudden, when we were near the train, and were almost saved, these people lay down. They would utter the last word and then they died. They were taken away, numbers were written on their arms. They were put on a cart and taken to the cemetery.[36]

Zuckerman returned to Warsaw, and began again to organize as best he could a resistance network. Among those active with him were Zivia Lubetkin and Lonka Kozibrodska.[37]

While at Kampinos, Zuckerman had noted the presence, and cruelty, of the Ukrainian guards. There were Ukrainian guards also at another camp near Warsaw, at Lowicz. In Warsaw, it became known early in May that ninety-one Jews had been murdered at Lowicz. The 'basic cause', Ringelblum noted, 'has been the terrible treatment of those in the camp by most of the Ukrainian camp guards', as well as the 'starvation' rations.[38] These Ukrainians had been brought by the Germans from south-eastern Poland, where many had lived before the war as a dissatisfied minority. Now they were taking their revenge, on Jews as well as on Poles. 'The seventeen corpses brought to Warsaw from work camp on May 7th', Ringelblum noted in his diary, 'made a dreadful impression: earless, arms and other limbs twisted, the tortures inflicted by the Ukrainian camp guards clearly discernible.'[39]

In Bedzin and Sosnowiec, each with a pre-war population of twenty-five thousand, Moses Merin was confident that he could govern, and protect, his people. Equally confident, in the Lodz ghetto, Chaim Rumkowski obtained German permission to open schools for five thousand Jewish children, the teaching to be in Yiddish and Hebrew. But in the Warsaw ghetto, the situation continued to deteriorate, with between five hundred and six hundred Jews dying of hunger every week. 'Death lies in every street,' noted Ringelblum on May 11. 'The children are no longer afraid of death. In one courtyard, the children played a game tickling a corpse.'[40]

In the Lodz ghetto, the deaths from starvation and the suicides had also mounted. On April 21 a mentally ill woman, the forty-one-year-old Cwajga Blum, who was often seen at the ghetto's edge, was ordered by a German sentry to dance in front of the barbed wire. She did as ordered. 'After she had performed a little dance,' the Ghetto Chronicle recorded, 'the sentry shot her dead at nearly point-blank range.'[41]

For almost a year, the Jews of France had been spared the cruelties and killings of German-occupied Poland. But as many as forty thousand foreign-born Jews had been interned in metropolitan France, and a further fourteen thousand in French North Africa: in these internment camps 'several thousand perished'.[42] Many Jews in France, especially those who had come from Poland before the war, in search of work, and a life free from anti-Semitism, were drawn into the growing resistance network.

On 10 May 1941, at Suresnes, the Germans executed the twenty-year-old Aron Beckermann, the first Jew to be shot for resistance in France.[43] Ten days later, the first measures designed to drive Jews out of French economic life were promulgated: no Jew was to be allowed to engage in the wholesale or retail trade, or to own a restaurant, a hotel or a bank. Restrictions on the number of Jews who could be lawyers, doctors, midwives or architects, however, were not introduced until later in the summer; even radios, forbidden to Polish Jews since the first months of the war, were not forbidden to French Jews until August 1941.

Several hundred Jews in France, with United States or Latin American passports, had managed to leave, legally, for Lisbon, and for the New World. But on 20 May 1941 the Central Office of Emigration in Berlin sent a circular letter to all German consulates, informing them that Goering had banned the emigration of Jews from all occupied territories, including France, in view of the 'doubtless imminent final solution'.[44] This was the first official reference to any such 'final' solution, or *Endlösung*. Within two weeks, on June 2, the threat of arbitrary arrest was embodied in a law authorizing the 'administrative internment' of all Jews in France, whether French-born, or foreign-born.[45]

The Jews of German-occupied Europe followed each phase of the war with close attention. 'The Jewish populace is in a depression these days,' noted Ringelblum on May 11, after German forces, having entered Athens, forced the British troops to evacuate Greece altogether, and to prepare for the defence of Palestine against possible German attack. A ghetto humourist coined the epigram: 'If the Germans win the war, 25 per cent of the Jews will die; if the English win, 75 per cent' – because it would take such a long time for a British victory.[46]

On May 11 Hitler's deputy, Rudolf Hess, flew to England where he insisted that peace was possible between Britain and Germany. His mission was quickly denounced by Hitler as the act of a lunatic. But in Warsaw, the thirty-five-year-old Alexander Donat later recalled, 'people went wild' as the news of Hess's mission broke on May 13. 'The war would now soon be over. Our suffering had not been in vain after all, and liberation was just around the corner.' Said one wisecrack: 'Mit Hess iz geshen a ness,' 'Hess has wrought a miracle.'[47]

Hess was denounced by Hitler, and Britain remained at war with

Germany. The United States and the Soviet Union were still neutral; Yugoslavia and Greece were now defeated. Britain was alone. But there were rumours of Russia's imminent entry into the war. When Stalin replaced Molotov as Chairman of the Council of People's Commissioners, becoming Soviet Premier, Warsaw Jews celebrated with 'Stalin Premier' bread.[48]

For twenty months, Poland up to the River Bug had been under German occupation. For twenty months, the Jews in occupied Poland had been cut off from the outside world, from world Jewry, and from the rights and protections afforded civilians in wartime. Jewish prisoners-of-war continued, after twenty months, to be deprived of the protection laid down for all prisoners-of-war by the Geneva conventions. On May 15 the Jewish prisoner-of-war camp at Biala Podlaska, near the Soviet border, was closed down, and the surviving prisoners taken by sealed train to Konskowola, further west. When the train was unloaded, it was discovered that four of the prisoners-of-war had managed to break their way out of the wagons during the journey. As a reprisal, twelve others were murdered on the spot.[49]

For several months, German reconnaissance aircraft had been flying over the border regions of western Russia, but the two million and more Jews on Soviet territory felt safe from danger. Despite the deportation of several thousand Jews to labour camps in April and May 1940, on Stalin's orders, for the mass of Soviet Jews there was no immediate threat to their existence. On June 21 Zalman Grinberg, a leading Jewish doctor in Kovno, noted in his diary: 'The peaceful life is running its usual course.'[50] That Saturday night, in the Soviet border town of Siemiatycze, there was a ball: attended, as had become usual for some days, by the German border patrol from the other side, and by many Jews. At four o'clock on the Sunday morning, the ball was still in progress. 'Suddenly,' the historian of Siemiatycze has recorded, 'bombs began to fall. The electricity in the hall was cut off. Panic-stricken and stumbling over each other in the darkness, everyone ran home.'[51] Unknown to the Jews of Siemiatycze, of Nazi-occupied Europe, or of the Soviet Union, the mass murder of Jews was about to begin: the killing, not of thousands, but of millions.

'It cannot happen!'

OPERATION BARBAROSSA, the German invasion of the Soviet Union launched on 22 June 1941, marked a tragic turning-point in German policy towards the Jews. In the twenty-one months before Barbarossa, as many as thirty thousand Jews had perished. Of these, ten thousand had been murdered in individual killings, in street massacres, in punitive reprisals, in outbreaks of savagery in the ghettos, and in the labour camps. Twenty thousand had died of starvation in the Warsaw and Lodz ghettos. But in no Jewish community had more than two or three per cent been murdered, while in Western Europe, the Jews had been virtually unmolested.

From the first hours of Barbarossa, however, throughout what had once been eastern Poland, Latvia, Lithuania and Estonia, as well as in the Ukraine, White Russia and the western regions of the Russian Republic, a new policy was carried out, the systematic destruction of entire Jewish communities. These were the regions in which the Jew had been most isolated and cursed for more than two centuries, the regions where Catholic, Russian Orthodox, Ethnic German and Jew had been most marked in their distinctive ways of life, in which language differences had been a barrier, social divisions a source of isolation, and religious contrasts a cause of hatred. The German invaders knew this well and exploited it to the full. In advance of the invasion of Russia, the SS leaders had prepared special killing squads, the *Einsatzgruppen*, which set about finding and organizing local collaborators, Lithuanians and Ukrainians, in murder gangs, and were confident that the anti-Jewish hatreds which existed in the East could be turned easily to mass murder. In this they were right.

In the first hours, many Jews in Western Europe, in Greater Germany, even in German-occupied Poland, saw the German invasion of the Soviet Union as a hopeful sign. 'The Jews somehow believed that the Russians would advance,' Zivia Lubetkin later recalled, 'beat the Germans, and perhaps this would mean the end of the war.'[1] At four o'clock on the afternoon of June 22, as a German announcer broadcast the news of the invasion of Russia over the loudspeakers in Grzybowski Place, another Warsaw resident noticed that the Jews in the square 'were trying unsuccessfully to hide their smiles'.[2] 'With Russia on our side,' Alexander Donat recalled, 'victory was certain and the end for Hitler was near.'[3]

The German forces advanced rapidly, however, and it soon became clear that the sudden upsurge of hope had been premature. 'What good will it do to me when I am dead,' one Warsaw ghetto-dweller said to another, 'if they come to my grave and say, "Mazel Tov, congratulations, you won the war"?'[4] But still some optimism survived. 'Don't worry,' a Red Army officer told the Jews of Nieswiez as his men withdrew eastwards, 'we'll be back.'[5]

In Kovno, the twenty-five-year-old Leon Bauminger, a refugee from Cracow, had a chance to hide as a non-Jew. But when he saw the Jews of Kovno being driven to a special ghetto area in the Slobodka suburb, house of a famous Talmudic academy, he decided to join them. 'What will be with all the Jews will be with me,' he told himself. It was rumoured that the Germans would send all the Jews to Madagascar. Bauminger later recalled: 'I said to myself: I will be the Robinson Crusoe on Madagascar.'[6]

Yet the slaughter in the East began from the first day of the German invasion of the Soviet Union. Helped by Lithuanian, Latvian and Ukrainian policemen and auxiliaries, the Einsatzgruppen moved rapidly forward behind the advancing German forces. An eye-witness later recalled how, at the frontier village of Virbalis, Jews 'were placed alive in anti-tank trenches about two kilometres long and killed by machine guns. Lime was thereupon sprayed upon them and a second row of Jews was made to lie down. They were similarly shot.' Six more times, a new line of Jews were driven into the trench. 'Only the children were not shot. They were caught by the legs, their heads hit against stones and they were thereupon buried alive.'[7]

Even before the German killing squads reached a region, the local population often attacked the Jews who had lived in their midst for centuries. These attacks were not pogroms to beat and wound, to

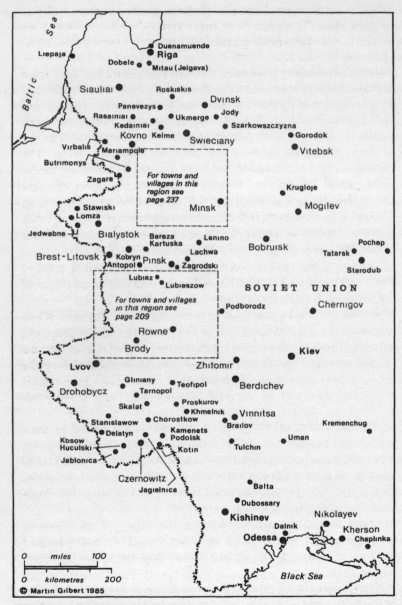

Sea

Baltic

Liepaja

Duenamuende
Riga
Dobele
Mitau (Jelgava)

Siauliai
Roskiskis
Dvinsk
Panevezys
Ukmerge   Jody
Rasainiai
Kedainiai   Szarkowszczyzna
Kovno Kelme
Swieciany
Virbalis Mariampole
Gorodok
Butrimonys
Vitebsk
Zagare

Krugloje

Stawiski
Mogilev
Lomza   Minsk
Jedwabne
Bialystok Bereza   Lenino
Kartuska
Pochep
Brest - Litovsk Kobryn Lachwa   Bobruisk
Antopol Pinsk   Tatarsk
Zagrodski   Starodub
Lubiaz
Lubieszow   **S O V I E T   U N I O N**

Podborodz   Chernigov
Rowne

Brody   **Kiev**
Lvov   Zhitomir
Gliniany Teofipol Berdichev
Drohobycz Tarnopol
Skalat   Proskurov
Khmelnik **Vinnitsa**
Stanislawow Chorostkow Brailov   Kremenchug
Delatyn Kamenets
Kbsow   Podolsk   Uman
Huculski   Kotin   Tulchin
Jablonica

Czernowitz
Jagielnica
Balta

Dubossary
Kishinev   Nikolayev
Dalnik
Odessa   Kherson
Chaplinka

For towns and
villages in this
region see
page 237

For towns and villages
in this region see
page 209

Black Sea

O   *miles*   100

O   *kilometres*   200

Ⓒ Martin Gilbert 1985

THE GERMAN INVASION OF RUSSIA

loot and burn, but attacks to kill: to destroy a whole community at one swift blow. The records of these attacks are scant. Few Jews survived to recount what happened. In hundreds of smaller villages, no Jew was left alive.

Wherever possible, Jews tried to resist the killers. But the forces against them were overwhelming. Sometimes the Jews succeeded, if only briefly, in halting the tide of killing. At Lubieszow, Jews armed themselves with axes, hammers, iron bars and pitchforks, to await the arrival of local Ukrainians intent upon murder as soon as the Red Army withdrew, and before the Germans had arrived. The Ukrainians came, and were beaten off. But then, retreating to the nearby village of Lubiaz, they fell immediately upon the few isolated Jewish families living there. When, the following morning, the Jews of Lubieszow's self-defence group reached Lubiaz, 'they found the bodies of twenty children, women and men without heads, bellies ripped open, legs and arms hacked off'.

Ten days later, on July 2, a German cavalry patrol entered Lubieszow. As its first task, it hunted down and destroyed the local Jews who had dared to resist their attackers.[8]

There were many examples of bravery, amid the slaughter. When German forces entered Luck on June 25 they found Dr Benjamin From in the hospital operating room, performing an operation on a Christian woman. The doctor was immediately ordered to stop the operation. He refused, was dragged out of the hospital, taken to his home, and killed with his entire family. He was forty-seven years old.[9]

In Kovno, on June 26, hundreds of Jews were seized in their homes, taken to one of the fortifications which surrounded the city, the Ninth Fort, and murdered. A Kovno Jewess whose father was among those seized that day, later wrote: 'We never saw him again, I suppose that his end was the same as the end of so many hundreds of thousands of European Jewry.'[10]

It was not always obvious, in those first days of the German occupation, what the future of the Jews would be. In the former Latvian city of Dvinsk, more than sixteen thousand Jews had been trapped by the rapid German advance. Hardly had German forces occupied the city, than all Jewish males between the ages of sixteen and sixty were ordered to report to the market place. The Jews were then divided into groups, each with a German or a Latvian overseer, and taken to different parts of the city to clear rubble. Jews who tried to hide from these labour tasks were rounded up by zealous Latvians, members of a pre-war Fascist organization.

Hundreds of Dvinsk Jews were taken to work, going off 'without suspicion or hesitation', Maja Zarch, whose father was among those taken, later recalled. Her recollection continued:

The first day the men were in good spirits although the thought had crossed the minds of some of them that it was strange that only Jews had been singled out for the task. Even more strange was the fact that after work the men were not allowed to return to their homes. This created suspicion and they were given various reasons why this was so. Some said that it was to save time and would eliminate the difficulties in rounding up the men each morning for work. On several occasions my mother, like all the other wives and mothers, went to investigate the whereabouts of my father. Mother would return from seeing Father with bits of bread, soap or whatever the men had salvaged from their cleaning operations.

As the days passed it became known that some of the wives could not find their husbands with the working commandos. Rumours started to circulate that these men had been shot. As the town was beginning to be restored to order fewer and fewer men were to be found in town. Many conflicting reports were heard. Some doubted the stories regarding the shooting and dismissed them as impossible. Why should they be shot? What crimes had they committed? They were probably being sent away to do other work out of town. But rumours of the shootings continued.

One day my mother returned from town in a very agitated state. She could not find my father. The men she had found would not tell what had happened to the others. Rumours of shooting persisted. Someone who lived not far from the prison had heard shooting right through the night. She went to the prison and found my father in a most terrible state. His eyes were swollen and tears were running down his face. He told her of the horrifying night they had spent. Uncle Isaac, together with a lot of men, were called out, made to dig their own graves and then shot. He was sure that the same fate would befall him and the rest of the men. Mother returned with this terrible news. My aunt, who had not accompanied her this time, fainted. We were all crying, mourning my uncle's death.

The next day, when she went to see my father in prison again, no one was there – the prison was empty. The men were gone. All enquiries were futile. In a state of confusion, she was returning home and on her way she encountered someone who told her that they had seen lorry-loads of men being transported from the prison the previous night. They had been taken in the direction of the outskirts of the town. She went there hoping to find Father but instead she came across the most horrifying sight: horse-drawn carts full of men's clothing were passing her. The ghastly truth dawned on her – he was no more.

She staggered into the house – there was no need to ask her what had happened. They are all gone, she whispered, murdered, in cold blood![11]

The ferocity of hatred was not directed only against Jews. Russian prisoners-of-war were also murdered in cold blood by the occupying forces. These Russians were likewise unarmed, defeated, and at the mercy of the conqueror. But the Germans showed them no mercy: by the end of the war, two and a half million Russian prisoners-of-war had been murdered.[12]

Towards the Soviet soldiers as prisoners, as towards the Jews as a people, the Nazis inculcated a sense of loathing, wishing for their total removal, and rejoicing at their destruction. Throughout the newly conquered areas, revolting tortures were perpetrated upon Russian prisoners-of-war, towards whom the Germans did not recognize the pre-war Geneva Conventions which served to protect hundreds of thousands of British and French prisoners-of-war. As in the creation of a spurious racial concept of 'the Jew', the Germans had stimulated a similar hatred of the Russian prisoner-of-war, portraying him as a 'degenerate Slav', a coward for whom the honour and dignity of the 'Aryan' soldier were of no relevance, and of no avail.[13]

A young Jew, Shalom Cholawski, has recalled how, on June 27, the day on which the Germans entered Nieswiez:

Groups of Russian prisoners-of-war were brought into the synagogue courtyard. They lay hungry and exhausted. The

Germans moved among them, kicking them with their heavy shoes.

One of the soldiers began beating a prisoner. He raised the man to his feet and cursed him with every punch. The prisoner, a short fellow with dull Mongolian features, did not know why the German had singled him out or what he was raving about. He stood there, not resisting the blows. Suddenly, he lifted his hand and, with a terrific sweep, slapped his attacker powerfully and squarely on the cheek. Blood trickled slowly down the German's face. For a moment they stared at each other. One man seething with anger, the other calm. Several Germans brusquely shoved the man to a place behind the fence. A volley of shots echoed in the air. I witnessed the scene from my window.

Jews stayed in their houses, Cholawski added, 'still waiting and hoping; maybe the others would return.' But with every hour, the Red Army was driven further eastward.[14]

In the early hours of June 27 the Germans entered Bialystok, a city which they had occupied briefly in September 1939, before handing it over to the Soviet Union under the terms of the Nazi-Soviet Pact. Since September 1939, as many as ten thousand Jewish refugees from German-occupied Poland had found refuge in the city, raising its Jewish population to more than fifty thousand. On the morning of their entry into the city, 'Red Friday' in the annals of the Jewish community of Bialystok, a large German motorized unit gathered at one end of the Jewish quarter and began drinking 'to death'. A few minutes later they besieged the Szulhojf quarter around the Great Synagogue. It was eight in the morning. The slaughter started at once. The Germans, in small units, armed with automatic pistols and hand grenades, started chasing Jews on the narrow, winding streets around the Great Synagogue.

'Dante-esque scenes', as the Bialystok historian Szymon Datner later wrote, 'took place on these streets. Jews were taken out of the houses, put against the walls, and shot. From everywhere, the unfortunate people were driven in the direction of the Great Synagogue, which was burning with a great fire, and from which horrible cries came out.' At least eight hundred Jews had been locked into the synagogue, before it had been set on fire.

The Germans then forced further victims to push one another

into the burning synagogue. Those who resisted, they shot; then they threw the dead bodies inside the burning building. 'Soon the whole quarter around the synagogue was burning. The soldiers were throwing hand grenades inside the houses, which being mostly wooden, burned easily. A sea of flames which embraced the whole Szulhojf overflowed into the neighbouring streets.'

Until late in the afternoon, Jews were driven into the burning synagogue, shot on the streets and in the houses. The noise of exploding grenades, Datner had written, 'mingled with the shots from the pistols, and with the drunken cries of the Germans, and the horrible cries of the murdered victims'. Among those who died in the burning synagogue were the well known Dr Kracowski, a pharmacist named Polak, a celebrated chess player, Zabludowski, and a popular comedian, Alter Sztajnberg.

At one moment, when the Germans were not watching, a Pole – his name is not known, he was the porter of the synagogue – opened a small window at the back of the synagogue, and several dozen Jews managed to escape. Among those saved was Pejsach Frajnd. By the end of that day of burning and shooting, two thousand Jews had been murdered.[15]

The last days of June 1941 also saw the first of the deportations from the Rumanian province of Bessarabia. Jews, uprooted from their towns and villages, were driven hundreds of miles eastwards, some on foot, some by train, in conditions of hardship and violence. On June 27 it was the Jews of Falesti who were the victims. Imprisoned in the Great Synagogue, where the women were assaulted by both German and Rumanian troops, they were then forced to walk eastward.[16] In nearby Dombroveni, a Jewish agricultural village whose rabbi and communal leaders had been deported to Siberia in 1940, the remaining Jews were taken to a schoolyard and robbed of all their money and valuables, before being sent on the eastward march.[17] Every day, Jews died on the march, or were killed by guards impatient with the slow pace of the sick or elderly.[18]

No day now passed without Jews being murdered. In Kovno, on Saturday, June 28, Lithuanian police joined with released convicts to hunt through the streets with iron bars, searching for Jews, and beating several hundred to death.[19] On June 29, in the Rumanian city of Jassy, Rumanian soldiers and police went on the rampage, watched by German SS men, killing at least two hundred and sixty Jews in their homes.[20] At the same time, five thousand Jews were arrested, marched through the streets while being beaten continuously by Rumanian and German police, shot if they fell, and, at the railway station, forced to lie on the ground while all their money, jewellery, rings and documents were taken from them. Eventually they were put into sealed cattle trucks, a hundred people and more in each, in two trains, without food or water. One of the survivors of those on the train that travelled southward later recalled:

> The heat and stench inside were fearful. Before our eyes our children fell, our parents and our friends. They might possibly have been saved if only we had had a few drops of water. There were some who drank their own urine or that of their friends. A little water was afterwards poured into the truck through its holes when the death train was halted at different stations. Meantime the heat in the truck became fearful, it was literally an inferno.
>
> The journey of the living together with the dead lasted for four days; and then the train halted at Tromat so that the corpses should be removed.
>
> On the way to Kalarash the train stopped at Mirteshet, near a pool of filthy water. The reckless victims or madmen, whichever we ought to call them, broke down the doors of the trucks and made for the pool. They paid no attention to the warnings of the trainmaster that they would be killed and refused to move away from the turbid water. Dozens of them were shot by the guards as they stood in the pool and drank the filthy mess.[21]

By the time the train had reached Mirteshet, more than six hundred Jews had perished. At Mirteshet, a further 327 had died, or were shot. At the next halt, Sabaoani, 172 bodies were taken out of the train, and at Roman, a further 53. While at Roman, the surviving Jews were taken out of the train, made to strip naked in order to enter a disinfectant bath in a sanitary train, and then forced to spend the night naked on the ground. Fortunately, a local Christian woman, Viorica Agarici, head of the region's Red Cross, insisted that measures be taken to lessen the torment of the journey, and some Jews were allowed out of the train altogether: but even of these, 143 died in the coming month.[22] At the next stop, Inotesti, forty bodies were taken out, and at Kalarash, the train's destination, a further twenty-five. The journey from Jassy had lasted eight days.

Sixty-nine of the Jews who reached Kalarash were so weak that they did not survive more than a few days in the Kalarash camp. From a second train sent from Jassy on the same day, but in a different direction, 1,194 died: bringing the number of those killed, according to the officially certified Rumanian police reports, to more than two and a half thousand.[23]

On 30 June 1941, eight days after their invasion of the Soviet Union, German forces entered the city of Lvov. In 1939 there had been 109,500 Jews in Lvov, a third of the city's population. After Warsaw and Lodz, it was the third largest Jewish community in inter-war Poland. The first Jews are believed to have reached Lvov in the Byzantine era. In 1340 there was an influx of Jewish refugees from Germany and Bohemia. A 'Holy Congregation outside the walls' was founded in 1352. Under Austrian rule from 1772 to 1914, Polish from 1919 to 1939, Lvov Jewry had made its contribution to every facet of Jewish and Polish life. With the German occupation of western Poland in September 1939, a further fifty thousand Jews had reached Lvov as refugees. Under Soviet rule, they sheltered under the protection of the Nazi-Soviet Pact, and the Red Army. Both were now swept away.

From the first hours of the German occupation, mobs of Ukrainian hoodlums, incited by German proclamations and pamphlets, combed the streets and houses, murdering Jews wherever they found them, or taking them off to the city's prisons, where thousands were tortured and shot. In an attempt to halt the slaughter, Yechezkel Lewin, editor-in-chief of the Jewish weekly newspaper *Opinja*, and rabbi of the Reform Synagogue in Lvov, went, in his rabbinical robes, to see the head of the Ukrainian Catholic Church, Metropolitan Sheptitsky, in his palace. 'You told me once, "I am a friend of Israel,"' Lewin declared. 'You have always emphasized your friendship to us, and we ask you now, at this time of terrible danger, to give proof of your friendship and to use your influence over the wild crowds rioting against us.'

Responding to Lewin's appeal, Sheptitsky issued a proclamation against the killings. But the mobs were on the rampage, the howls of the killers mingled with the screams of the victims, and the slaughter in the streets continued. Sheptitsky urged Lewin to remain in the palace until the violence had subsided. But Lewin told him: 'My mission is completed. I have come to make a request for the community, and shall return to the congregation, where my place is.'

Lewin walked back towards his home. On the way, several of his Christian friends urged him to go back to the Metropolitan's palace, but he refused to do so. At the threshold of his house he was seized by Ukrainian militiamen, and dragged to prison. There, still in his rabbinical robes, he was pushed and beaten with the rifle butts of German soldiers, before being shot down in the prison courtyard.

Several thousand Jews were murdered in these prison killings, among them Lewin's brother, Rabbi Aaron Lewin, a former deputy in the Polish parliament, and head of the rabbinical court of the city of Rzeszow.[24] A sixteen-year-old eye-witness of the slaughter in Lvov, Leon Weliczker, later recalled how, after he and his father had been arrested, they were taken to the yard of a police station, where more than five thousand Jews were assembled:

> Thousands of men were lying here in rows. They lay on their bellies, their faces buried in the sand. Around the perimeter of the field searchlights and machine guns had been set up. Among them I caught sight of German officers standing about. We were ordered to lie flat like the others. We were pushed and shoved brutally, this way and that. My father was separated from me, and I heard him calling out in despair: 'Let me stay with my son! I want to die with my son!' Nobody took any notice of him.
>
> Now that we were all lying still, there was a hush that lasted for a moment or two. Then the 'game' started. We could hear the sound of a man, clearly one of us, stumbling awkwardly around, chased and beaten by another as he went. At last the pursued collapsed out of sheer exhaustion. He was told to rise. Blows were rained down upon him until he dragged himself to his feet again and tried to run forward. He fell to the ground again and hadn't the strength to get up. When the pursuers were at last satisfied that the incessant blows had rendered him

unable to stir, let alone run, they called a halt and left him there. Now it was the turn of a second victim. He received the same treatment.

Now a third was hauled out. The Germans, in pursuit of their sport, tramped up and down over our backs as we lay there. No one dared to raise his head. The dread of being picked out for the next turn almost drove me crazy. Every few minutes I touched my neighbour to see if he was still there or if he had gone to face this merciless ordeal. Where could my father be? Was he already among those now lying stunned, with the ordeal behind them? And what of my brother Aaron? Had not he, too, been recruited for work?

Thoughts raced in disorder and confusion through my mind. I was so exhausted that I fell asleep. Not even the agonizing screams, the sound of savage blows, or the continual trampling on our bodies could prevent me any longer from sinking into oblivion. I dreamed of home – the whole family was there, sitting happily together. I dreamed that my brother has been sent home.

The welcome state of unconsciousness passed all too quickly. I came to, and was startled by a painful stab of dazzling light. Powerful searchlights were focused on us. We sat up, one beside the other, so close that we could not stir. Directly in front of me sat two men with shattered skulls. Through the mess of bone and hair I could see the very brains. We whispered to them. We nudged them. But they did not stir. They just sat there, propped up, bulging eyes staring ahead. They were quite dead.

'The sun rose slowly', Weliczker's account continued: 'The day promised to be heavy and oppressive. Thirst was already making itself felt among us. Ten at a time we were allowed to go to the toilets. The greater number, however, were so apathetic, still so full of numbing dread, that they declined to budge. An almost stupefying stench arose from the many battered bodies of the dead.'

Two days later, Weliczker was taken with 150 other Jews to unload artillery guns. By the end of the day, more than sixty of the Jews had been crushed to death under the wheels of the guns.[25]

While these Eastern slaughters continued day after day and town after town, elsewhere in German-occupied Europe the earlier patterns of destruction were being repeated. On June 30, the day of the German occupation of Lvov, three hundred more young men were rounded up in Amsterdam and deported to the stone quarries of Mauthausen. 'They followed the same thorny path,' one Dutch witness of their deportation later recalled. 'Nobody survived. . . .'[26]

In the East, throughout July, the first victims were carefully chosen so that the communities immediately lost their natural leadership. In Minsk, within hours of the German occupation, forty thousand men and boys between the ages of fifteen and forty-five were assembled for 'registration', under penalty of death: Jews, captured Soviet soldiers, and non-Jewish civilians. Taken to a field outside the city, each group was put into a separate section. For four days all were kept in the field, surrounded by machine guns and floodlights. Then, on the fifth day, all Jewish members of the intelligentsia – doctors, lawyers, writers – were ordered to step forward. Some two thousand did so, not knowing for what purpose they would be needed, perhaps as administrators, as functionaries, or in their professional capacities. Many non-professionals were among those who stepped forward, believing that this group was to be given some privileged work or position, and wanting to be a part of it. All two thousand were then marched off to a nearby wood, and machine-gunned.[27]

On the following day, in Bialystok, three hundred of the Jewish leaders and professional men were arrested, driven to a field outside the town, and murdered there. Among those murdered was Pejsach Frajnd, who had escaped the burning synagogue on June 27.[28]

News of the killings in Minsk and Bialystok was sent to the chief of the Gestapo, Heinrich Muller, in Berlin. Muller asked Adolf Eichmann to see him, Eichmann being the SS officer in charge of the department IV-D-4, responsible for deportations and emigration. Twenty years later, in a court in Jerusalem, on trial for his life, Eichmann recalled that Muller had said to him: 'In Minsk they're shooting Jews. I want you to report how it's going.' Eichmann went at once, first to Bialystok and then to Minsk. At his trial he recalled how, reaching the execution site in Minsk,

There were the piles of dead people. They were shooting into the pit – it was rather a large one, so I was told, perhaps four to five times the size of this room, perhaps even six or seven times. I didn't think much about it because I could hardly express any thoughts about it – I only saw it and that was quite enough – they were shooting into the pit and I saw a woman, her arms seemed to be at the back; and then my knees went weak and I went away.

From Minsk, Eichmann travelled by train to Lvov, the capital of Eastern Galicia during the reign of the Emperor Franz Josef, at the turn of the century:

I came to Lvov and saw for the first time a charming picture – the railway station which was built in honour of the sixtieth year of the reign of Franz Josef; and since I always find pleasure in that period, maybe because I heard so many nice things about it in my parents' home – the relatives of my stepmother were of a certain social standing. It was painted yellow and I remember it, I remember that the date was inscribed on the wall. This for the first time drove away these terrible thoughts which had never left me since Minsk, this was the first time I could forget.

I came to the state police, and even had an order – or maybe I did not have an order – I went there out of curiosity and visited the commander, because I was passing that way; and said: 'Yes, this is terrible, the things which are going on. We educate the young people to grow up as sadists.'

This, Eichmann insisted, was 'exactly' what he said to Muller, and, at a later time, 'to everyone I met', including his deputy, SS Major Rolf Gunther, and his colleague in the Race and Resettlement Main Office of the SS, Lieutenant-Colonel Friedrich Suhr. Eichmann added:

I told everyone who came my way – I said: 'How can you shoot a woman and children, how is this possible? It cannot be done – these people can go mad or become sadists, and they are our own people.' He said: 'This is true, and this is how it is done here. The shootings are carried out here, too – do you wish to see for yourself?' I said: 'No, I do not want to see.' And he said: 'We shall see whether you wish to or not, because it is on our way.' There was a trench, but the trench was already filled in; and there was a kind of spring of blood gushing from the earth – and this, too, I had never seen before. As far as I was concerned, I'd had enough, and went back to Berlin and told Gruppenführer Muller.

Eichmann was then asked, in court, if he had ever seen a 'written order' for such killings, for the 'physical extermination' of the Jews. He replied:

I never saw a written order. All I know is that Heydrich told me, 'the Führer ordered the physical extermination of the Jews.' He said this quite early and with certainty, the way I repeat it at this moment. And these were the first results. These were small things that I have just related.

I asked the Gruppenführer: 'Please do not send me there, send someone else, someone stronger than I am. You see I was never sent to the front, I was never a soldier; there are other men who can look upon such actions. I cannot. At night I cannot sleep, I dream. I cannot do it, Gruppenführer.'

His request, Eichmann added, 'was not granted'.[29] He continued to be sent to the mass murder sites, and the mass murder continued with unabated fury.

In Kovno, since the first days of the German occupation at the end of June, hundreds of Jews had continued to be taken to the Jewish cemetery and shot. Other Jews were seized in the streets, were dragged to a garage, where hoses 'were put into their mouths and opened', with the horrendous result that 'the Jews would burst'.[30] On July 4 Lithuanian militiamen, on German instructions, murdered 416 Jewish men and 47 Jewish women in Kovno's Seventh Fort; two days later, again on German instructions, a further 2,514 Jews were murdered in the fort; the figures precisely recorded by the commander of SS *Einsatzkommando* 3 in his report submitted to Berlin at the end of the year.[31]

The killing of Jews was continuous; in Vilna, where the pre-war Jewish population of some sixty thousand had been swollen to at least eighty thousand by the refugees of September 1939, it began on July 4, when fifty-four Jews were shot, followed by a further ninety-three on July 5, by members of an Einsatzkommando unit.[32] Also on July 5, in Lvov, Ukrainian gangs continued to drag Jews from their homes, and to kill them in the streets; those killed included one of the city's leading opthalmologists, the forty-nine-year-old Dr Kornelia Graf-Weisenberg, murdered together with her daughter, a medical student.[33] On the following day, all the surviving Jews in Lvov were ordered to wear the yellow star.[34]

In the town of Nowogrodek, in which Jews had lived since 1484, the Germans, who had entered the town on July 3, asked for fifty volunteers to serve as members of the Jewish Council. People 'pushed to join', Idel Kagan later recalled. Some were the natural leaders of the community, others were people for whom some sort of 'public office' had always been an aspiration. 'They were then arrested, and disappeared.' A further fifty Jews were then seized at random, on the spurious charge of having sheltered Soviet parachutists – of whom there had been none. These fifty were taken to the town square and shot, while a German band was playing. Jewish women were then forced to wash the blood from the stones.

Following the execution of the fifty, Jews were seized throughout Nowogrodek for various menial tasks. One of them, a twenty-two-year-old woman, Haya Dzienciolski, was forced to clean out a hall, while her friend was made to stand on a table and sing songs. Haya Dzienciolski decided not to accept any further humiliation. Finding a pistol, she left Nowogrodek for a nearby village. Her escape, Idel Kagan later recalled, 'was the first resistance'. After a short while in hiding, she went into the nearby village of Lida and took out with her a young man, Asael Belsky, with whom she was in love. Later she was able to smuggle her own parents out of the ghetto, followed by Belsky's sister and the sister's boyfriend. Slowly, there grew up in the countryside around Nowogrodek a group of young people determined not to be caught or forced into the ghetto. In this way, the forest communities began.

Inside Nowogrodek, Jews continued to be seized in the streets and taken out of the town. But those who saw them being led away had no idea that they were about to be shot. Local peasants, indeed, in order to make a little money, would tell the Jews in Nowogrodek that they had seen those who had been taken away working on the roads, and would offer to smuggle parcels and messages to them.[35]

No such work was in progress: but the parcels enriched the peasants, and the messages gave, to the Jews, a false hope and sense of normality.

On July 7, a special raiding party of Einsatzkommando 3, under the command of First Lieutenant Hamann, an SS officer, began the systematic slaughter of Jews throughout Lithuania. Their first action, that day, was to kill thirty-two Jews in Mariampole. Hamann conducted his operation with eight to ten 'trustworthy' men of the Einsatzkommando, 'in cooperation' with large numbers of Lithuanian militiamen.[36]

With every day of the German advance into Russia, tens of thousands of Jews found themselves trapped behind the German lines. So rapid was the advance that no one could outrun it. Local units, Lithuanian or Ukrainian, joined in the hunt for victims. Following the first furious slaughter in streets and homes, sites were chosen, such as the Ninth Fort in Kovno, or the empty fuel pits at Ponary, outside Vilna, beyond the view of witnesses.

The first Ponary executions took place on July 8. A hundred Jews at a time were brought from the city to Ponary, to a 'waiting zone'. Here, in what had once been a popular holiday resort for Vilna Jewry, they were ordered to undress and to hand over whatever money or valuables they had with them. They were then marched naked, single file, in groups of ten to twenty at a time, holding hands, to the edge of the fuel pits, and shot down by rifle fire. After they had fallen into the pit, no attempt was made to see if they were all dead. If anyone moved, another shot was fired. The bodies were then covered, from above, with a thin layer of sand, and the next group of naked prisoners led from the waiting area to the edge of the pit. From where they had waited, the people had heard the sound of rifle fire, but had seen nothing.

In the twelve days following July 8, as many as five thousand Vilna Jews were murdered in this way.[37] In the smaller towns and villages, whole communities could be killed in a single day. On July 10, in the village of Jedwabne, all sixteen hundred Jews were driven into the market place by the SS, tortured for several hours, then driven into a barn and burned alive.[38]

In Drohobycz, a member of the local Einsatzkommando, the thirty-five-year-old SS Sergeant Felix Landau, kept a diary. In 1934, Landau had been one of the instigators of the murder of the

Austrian Chancellor, Dr Engelbert Dollfuss. Landau noted, on July 14:

> Again I am roused from deep sleep. 'Get up for execution!' Alright, why not? Among the inmates are two women. One can admire them – they don't even want to take a glass of water from us. I will certainly guard them well; should anyone try escape, I shall shoot.
>
> We drive a few kilometres along the main road till we reach a wood. We go into the wood and look for a spot suitable for mass executions. We order the prisoners to dig their graves. Only two of them are crying, the others show courage. What can they all be thinking? I believe each still has the hope of not being shot. I don't feel the slightest stir of pity. That's how it is, and has got to be. My heart beats very faintly when I recall being in the same position once. In the Federal Chancellery on 25.7.1934, I was also in peril of my life. At that time I was younger and thought it was all over. Yet I had the firm conviction that my death won't be in vain. It happened differently, however. I stayed alive, and now I stand here and shoot others.
>
> Slowly the grave gets bigger and deeper. Two are crying without let-up. I let them dig more so they can't think. The work really calms them. Money, watches and valuables are collected. The two women go first to be shot; placed at the edge of the grave they face the soldiers. They get shot. When it's the men's turn, the soldiers aim at the shoulder. All our six men are allowed to shoot. Three prisoners have been shot in the heart.
>
> The shooting goes on. Two heads have been shot off. Nearly all fall into the grave unconscious only to suffer a long while. Our revolvers don't help either. The last group have to throw the corpses into the grave; they have to stand ready for their own execution. They all tumble into the grave.[39]

In Kishinev, the killings began on July 17, with the entry of German and Rumanian forces into the city. The German forces included an Einsatzkommando unit. Thirty-eight years earlier, in the notorious Kishinev pogrom, the deaths of forty-nine Jews had provoked worldwide protest, Christian as well as Jewish. The scale of that pogrom had shocked the civilized world. Now, killing had become commonplace. In a single week, five thousand of Kishinev's Jews had been murdered, yet even then the killings continued.[40] Among those killed in Kishinev was Judah Leib Zirelson, a member of the Rumanian parliament from 1922, a Rumanian Senator from 1926, Chief Rabbi of Bessarabia, and the leader of Orthodox Jewry in Rumania. He was eighty-one years old.[41]

The first news of these Eastern killings reached England on July 18, through intercepted German police messages which told of the mass shooting of 'Jews', 'Jewish plunderers', 'Jewish bolshevists' and 'Russian soldiers' in numbers ranging from under a hundred to several thousand at a time.[42] One such execution took place in Minsk on July 21, when a group of forty-five Jews were forced to dig pits, then roped together and thrown into the pits alive. The SS then ordered thirty White Russian prisoners to cover the live Jews with earth. But the White Russians refused. The SS then opened fire with machine guns on Jews and White Russians alike: all seventy-five were killed.[43]

To the anger of the Germans, the Jews in White Russia had managed to organize a 'signal service' between villages, to warn of the arrival of Einsatzkommando units. As a result of these warnings, one unit commander reported on July 23, the Jews 'escape into the surrounding forest and swamps'.[44] But the ability to flee, or to resist, was minimal. The Germans were armed, the Jews unarmed, while from among the local populace, especially in Lithuania and the Ukraine, hundreds could be found willing not only to round up Jews, but to kill them. With the German invasion of the Soviet Union the anti-Semitism of centuries had been given an unprecedented opportunity to be translated into brutal action.

The speed and scale of the slaughter gave no time for organized resistance. The Germans continued, in every town, to destroy the natural leaders. 'By now', reported one Einsatzgruppe on July 24, from the town of Lachowicze, 'the entire Jewish intelligensia has been liquidated (teachers, professors, lawyers etc . . .)'. Of the professional classes, only doctors had been spared, to remain alive with the survivors in a specially created ghetto. But the numbers killed exceeded by far the intelligentsia of the town: this particular Einsatzgruppe reported, with the usual precision, a total of 4,435 'liquidated' in Lachowicze.[45]

In Lvov, where several thousand Jews had been murdered at the beginning of July, there had been a pause in the killing. For the tens of thousands of surviving Jews there was no logical reason to believe that the killing would start again. But on July 25 the local Ukrainians launched the 'Petlura action', a three-day orgy of killing to 'avenge' the murder of Simon Petlura by Shalom Schwarzbard, fifteen years before. Thousands of men and women were seized, ostensibly for forced labour. Most were taken to a prison in the city, where they were beaten to death. Hundreds disappeared without trace. At least two thousand were killed.[46]

As the 'Petlura action' began in Lvov, in Belgrade a seventeen-year-old Jewish boy, Hayim Almoslino, in despair at the daily murder of Jews, threw a petrol bomb at a German car, hoping to set the car on fire. He failed, and fled. On the same day, there were four other such attacks on German vehicles, one by a sixteen-year-old Serbian girl who, the Germans reported, 'confessed that a Jew had incited her to the deed'.[47]

The Germans acted swiftly, determined to prevent any further acts of resistance, even those in which no Germans were killed. On July 27, 1,200 Jews were brought to the camp at Tasmajdan, just outside Belgrade. They were then divided into their professions. Every tenth person was declared a hostage, and 120 hostages taken to Jajinci and shot.[48]

In the east, with every week, German forces overran more Soviet cities: and in each city Russians and Russian Jews were massacred from the first hours of the occupation. One Einsatzgruppe report at the end of July listed those murdered in its region of operations: at Vinnitsa 146, at Berdichev 148, at Proskurov 146, at Zhitomir 41. These were only the first killings. Nor were these killings committed only by the Germans. At Chorostkow, in Eastern Galicia, where 30 Jews had been killed by the Einsatzkommando, its own report noted that a further 110 Jews had been 'slain by the population'.[49]

In the Eastern Galician town of Drohobycz, a second execution was in progress, recorded once again by SS Sergeant Felix Landau, in his diary entry for July 28:

> In the evening we drive into town. Here we experience things it is impossible to describe. We drive to the prison. The streets tell of murder. We would like to take a closer look at

everything, but it is impossible to enter the gas chambers and cellars of the prison without gas masks. In a side turning we notice some Jewish corpses covered with sand. We look at each other in surprise. One living Jew rises up from among the corpses. We dispatch him with a few shots.

Eight hundred Jews have been herded together; they are to be shot tomorrow. We drive further along the street. Hundreds of Jews with bloodstained faces, with bullet holes in the head, broken limbs and gouged-out eyes, run ahead of us. One of the Jews carries another one, who is bleeding to death.

We drive to the Citadel. Here we see things no one has ever seen on earth before. It is absolutely impossible to describe them. Two soldiers stand at the entrance to the citadel. Wielding sticks as thick as fists, they lash furiously at the crowd. Jews are being pushed out from inside. Covered with blood, they collapse on top of one another – they scream like pigs – we stand and look on.

Who gave the order to kill the Jews? No one! Somebody ordered them to be set free.

They were all murdered because we hate them.[50]

Throughout Eastern Galicia and the Volhynia, the Ukrainian population frequently provided an added dimension of danger for the local Jews. The Jewish historian Philip Friedman, who was in Lvov during these terrible months, and who subsequently carried out considerable historical research into the fate of the Jews of Eastern Galicia and the Volhynia, has recorded how, in Lvov, the Ukrainians themselves seized Jews and turned them over to the authorities. In Buczacz the pogrom was directed by the local Ukrainian intelligentsia. In Delatyn, the pogrom was largely the work of the music teacher Slawko Waszczuk; in Stanislawow, of Professor Lysiak, of the local teachers' seminary.

In Dubno, Friedman writes, the pogrom was carried out under the direction of several members of the new Ukrainian municipal administration. In Tarnopol, a Ukrainian pharmacist, a teacher, and several others participated with the Germans in planning the pogrom. In Kosow Huculski, the leading figures in the massacre of the Jews included a former Ukrainian schoolteacher who, before the war, had been the foremost agitator against the Jews. In Skalat, a Ukrainian priest and a Ukrainian judge were members of a delegation that presented an anti-Jewish petition to the Germans. In Jablonica, after the Ukrainian priest incited the local Eastern Carpathian mountaineers against the Jews, several Jews were dragged at night from their beds and drowned in the Czeremosz River. In Gliniany, the Ukrainian priest Hawryluk incited his parishioners against the Jews.

Also in Gliniany, the local Ukrainians staged a People's Court, 'on the Gestapo style', as Salomon Speiser later recalled. 'They condemned eleven people to die, took them to the woods and shot them all.' Among those shot was Drescher, the local Jewish teacher, Polack the carpenter, and the fourteen-year-old Aryeh Borer.[51]

The Germans encouraged these actions, offering the local peasantry rewards if they would deliver Jews to them. 'As a rule,' Philip Friedman has written, 'it was no more than some quarts of vodka, several pounds of sugar or salt, cigarettes, or, occasionally, small sums of money.'[52]

One of those who perished at Ukrainian hands in Lvov was the well-known Yiddish writer Alter Kacyzne, from Vilna, who had fled to Lvov as a refugee in 1940. There, during the year and a half of Soviet rule, he served as a spokesman for the many Jewish writers in the city, and was appointed by the Soviet authorities to be literary director of the Yiddish-language broadcast on Radio Lvov.[53] With the German invasion of Russia, Kacyzne fled from Lvov. But on the way to Tarnopol he was seized by Ukrainians, and beaten to death.[54]

Within five *weeks* of the German invasion of Russia on June 22, the number of Jews killed exceeded the total number killed in the previous eight *years* of Nazi rule. The invasion of Russia had provided the Germans with an opportunity hitherto lacking: a remote region, the cover of an advancing army, vast distances, local collaborators, and an intensified will to destroy. The first 'five-figure' massacre ended on July 31, in Kishinev, after fourteen days' uninterrupted slaughter, in which ten thousand Jews were murdered.[55] Similar mass executions were taking place in every city: in Zhitomir more than two and a half thousand had been murdered.[56]

It was in Zhitomir, at the end of July, that the regimental commander of the regular German troops in the city, Major Rosler, on hearing rifle volleys and pistol shots, decided to investigate.

Accompanied by two of his officers, he went in the direction of the shooting. As he drew nearer, he saw soldiers and civilians hurrying from all directions towards a railway embankment. The scene which confronted him when he reached the embankment was 'so brutally base', he wrote five months later, 'that those who approached unprepared were shaken and nauseated'.

Rosler was looking down into a ditch filled with corpses. Among them he saw an old man with a white beard and a cane on his arm. The man was still breathing. At the top of the embankment stood German policemen in bloodstained uniforms. German soldiers were congregating in groups. It was a hot day, and some of the soldiers were wearing bathing shorts. Civilians, too, were watching, together with their wives and children. 'I saw nothing like it,' Rosler wrote, 'either in the First World War or during the Civil War in Russia or during the Western Campaign. I have seen many unpleasant things, having been a member of the Free Corps in 1919, but I never saw anything like this.'

Five months after he had looked in the execution ditch in Zhitomir, Major Rosler was still determined to voice his sense of outrage. In an official report to his superiors, he wrote: 'I cannot begin to conceive the legal decisions on whose basis these executions were carried out. Everything that is happening here seems to be absolutely incompatible with our views on education and morality.'

'Right out in the open,' Rosler continued, 'as if on a stage, men murder other men. I must add that according to the accounts of the soldiers, who often see spectacles of this kind, hundreds of people are thus killed daily.'[57] Rosler, with his concern for 'education and morality', could not know that on July 31, Goering had instructed Heydrich 'to carry out all the necessary preparations with regard to organizational and financial matters for bringing about a complete solution of the Jewish question in the German sphere of influence in Europe'.[58] This was Goering's second reference, the first having been two months earlier, on May 20, to a 'complete' or 'final' solution of what the Germans chose to call 'the Jewish question'.

The 'preparations' to which Goering referred on July 31 were to involve a dozen countries, many of which, like Hungary and Italy, had not turned against their Jews in any murderous way; in others of which, like France, Belgium, Holland and Norway, the Jews, despite discrimination and some executions, were not being physically destroyed. Even in German-occupied Poland, where several thousand Jews were dying of hunger each month in Warsaw and Lodz, two million and more Jews were alive, struggling to maintain their morale until Germany should be defeated.

Goering's letter of July 31 made it clear that something drastic was in preparation, albeit at an early phase: a 'complete solution', unexplained, yet comprehensive. Meanwhile, in the East, there was to be no respite in the savage, daily slaughter. 'It may be safely assumed', Heydrich informed Himmler on August 1, 'that in the future there will be no more Jews in the annexed Eastern Territories. . . .'[59]

There was no pause in the daily killings and there was to be no pause. On July 29 forty mental patients were seized in Lodz, and deported: driven away in a covered truck to an unknown destination. They were in fact shot by the Nazis in a nearby forest. The Ghetto Chronicle noted, on July 31: 'The patients resisted in many cases.' But the chroniclers had no idea of the fate of the deportees once they had been taken out of the ghetto.[60]

Occasionally, a postcard from a Jew in German-occupied Poland reached the West. But any messages other than purely personal ones had to be skilfully disguised. On July 23 one such postcard was sent from a Jew in Radzymin to his brother in Brooklyn. Referring to three Jewish Holy days – the solemn fast day of Yom Kippur, the festival of Purim, when Jewish children dress up in colourful costumes, and the festival of Tabernacles, or Sukkot, during which Jews build a booth of trellis and greenery, the message read: 'We are eating as on Yom Kippur, clothed as at Purim, and dwelling as at Sukkot.'[61]

At Ponar, outside Vilna, the shootings had continued without respite. A Polish journalist, W. Sakowicz, who lived at Ponar, and who was himself killed during the last days of German rule in Vilna, noted in his diary:

1941. July 27, Sunday. Shooting is carried on nearly everyday. Will it go on for ever?

The executioners began selling the clothes of the killed. Other garments are crammed into sacks in a barn at the highway and taken to town.

People say that about five thousand persons have been killed in the course of this month. It is quite possible, for about two hundred to three hundred people are being driven up here nearly every day. And nobody ever returns. . . .

1942. July 30, Friday. About one hundred and fifty persons shot. Most of them were elderly people. The executioners complained of being very tired of their 'work', of having aching shoulders from shooting. That is the reason for not finishing the wounded off, so that they are buried half alive.

August 2, Monday. Shooting of big batches has started once again. Today about four thousand people were driven up. . . . shot by eighty executioners. All drunk. The fence was guarded by a hundred soldiers and policemen.

This time terrible tortures before shooting. Nobody buried the murdered. The people were driven straight into the pit, the corpses were trampled upon. Many a wounded writhed with pain. Nobody finished them off.[62]

Such executions were now a daily occurrence throughout German-occupied Russia. No town, no village, no hamlet was spared the search for Jews to be driven out of their houses, stripped, driven with guns and whips to the pits, and shot. In the Volhynian village of Misosz a German cameraman recorded the last moments of a group of women and children being led to their execution.[63]

On August 1, in Kishinev, more than a thousand Jews were shot. That same day, at Ukmerge, '254 Jews and 42 Jewesses' were among those murdered by Lieutenant Hamann's Einsatzkommando. On August 2, in Kovno, Hamann listed his victims as '170 Jewish men, 1 USA Jew, 1 USA Jewish woman, 33 Jewish women, 4 Lithuanian communists'.[64] On August 3, from Czernowitz, the local Einsatzgruppe reported the execution of 682 Jews, out of 1,200 arrested. They had been shot, the report added, 'in collaboration with the Rumanian police'. At Kotin, '150 Jews and Communists were liquidated'. At Mitau 'the 1,550 Jews who still remained' had been 'removed' from the population, 'without any exception'.[65] That same day, at Stanislawow, several hundred Jewish doctors, lawyers and other professionals were rounded up and shot, among them the forty-one-year-old Dr Boleslaw Fell, who had practised in Warsaw before the war; Ernestyna Fach, a graduate of the University of Nantes; and her sister, Dr Klara Fach.[66] On August 4, First Lieutenant Hamann's squad murdered 326 Jews, 41 Jewesses, 5 Russian and 4 Lithuanian Communists at Panevezys. On August 5, at Rasainiai, he noted the murder of '213 Jewish men and 66 Jewish women'.[67] That same day, in its summary of past executions, the Berlin 'Situation Report' noted the killings of 1,726 Jews in Lvov, 128 in Brest-Litovsk, and 941 in Bialystok.[68]

These random samples, for five consecutive days, show a total of some 7,800 Jews murdered. They do not include several dozen equally terrible episodes elsewhere in the East during those same five days, or the hundreds of Jews shot on each of those five days on the continuing death marches from Bessarabia towards the River Dniester, during which time Jews also died each day in the Bessarabian transit camp at Edineti.[69]

In Dvinsk, a ghetto had been set up at the end of July in the suburb of Griva. 'Thousands upon thousands of people,' Maja Zarch later recalled, 'with hardly any sanitary facilities, no food; with only one or two taps for water.' The overcrowding was almost unbearable, its horrors augmented by a summer heat wave. But in the first week of August relief was offered. According to a German announcement, all old and sick Jews would be taken to a less uncomfortable place. 'Within minutes', Maja Zarch recalled, 'there were so many volunteers that queues were being formed. Any place, they thought, could only be better than this.'

A few days later, a similar offer to be resettled elsewhere was made to all parents with small children. Once more, Maja Zarch witnessed the sequel:

> This time again, the flood of people who wanted to go was enormous. Even people who did not have children tried to get in. Everyone who wanted to go was taken. In a day or two, strange rumours started to filter through. Someone heard from non-Jews who lived out of town that for a day and a night shooting took place at a certain place where no one was allowed to go. Slowly the picture emerged – there were definitely fresh mass graves! But even then people would not believe it. It cannot happen! How could innocent children be shot? For what purpose?[70]

13

'A crime without a name'

As the Einsatzkommando units advanced, several hundred
Jewish communities, mostly those in villages and small towns, were
destroyed completely. At the same time, Jews in the larger towns
and cities were forced, after the initial killings, into closed ghettos.
Each ghetto was ordered to set up a Jewish Council, which received
from day to day the German demands, and which was made
responsible for the regulation and maintenance of daily life within
the ghetto.

To safeguard what could be safeguarded, the Jews needed the
best Jewish Councils, and the best Council Chairmen, they could
find. In Kovno, on 5 August 1941, no Jewish leader had been willing
to accept the position of Chairman: to be the vehicle of German
wishes, whims and cruelty. But someone was needed, and Dr
Elchanan Elkes, a doctor, and a leading Zionist, who had already
declined the position, was appealed to in these words:

> The Jewish community of Kovno stands on the brink of
> destruction. Our daughters are being raped, and our sons
> executed. Death appears at our windows. Fellow Jews! The
> German oppressor demands that we appoint an *Oberjude*, but
> what we need is a faithful community leader. In this historic
> hour, the most appropriate candidate among us is Dr Elkes.
> Therefore, we appeal to you, Dr Elkes: In the eyes of the
> German criminals you will fill the position of *Oberjude*, but to
> us you will be the community leader.

> We are aware of the fact that the position demands responsi-
> bility and is fraught with dangers never before encountered by
> Jews. Nevertheless, to stand at the helm of our community is
> both a great duty and a command of the Almighty Himself in
> this fateful hour. We shall be with you to the end, until the day
> of redemption when we leave this ghetto – which is in itself an

exile within an exile – and you lead us from slavery to freedom in our Holy Land.

And now, we beg you: Assume, without fear, the position as our leader, for those who perform a holy mission shall meet no evil thanks to the prayers of many. Amen.[1]

'If this be the situation,' Elkes replied, 'and you think that it is my duty to accept the post, then I shall do.' Three young lawyers then went up to Elkes and said to him: 'Dr Elkes, we shall help you in whatever way we can.' One of those three lawyers, Abraham Golub, later recalled Elkes's qualities: 'Never in the Kovno ghetto was a Jew handed over at the request of the Gestapo – such a thing was unheard of.'[2] Dr Elkes was also to give active help to Jews in the ghetto who wished to train in the use of arms, to escape to the partisans, and to provide the partisans with equipment.[3]

Members of the Jewish Councils throughout the newly conquered areas reacted in different ways to the German demands, and threats. In August 1941, in the village of Kamien Koszyrski, the Chairman of the Jewish Council, Shmuel Verble, was ordered to deliver a list of eighty names. He did so, unaware of the purpose of the list. But when, after handing it over, he learned that the Germans intended to kill all those on the list, he went at once to the local German police post and asked to be included. His request was accepted. He was shot last: the eighty-first victim.[4]

The Jewish Council in Gliniany, headed by Aaron Hochberg, 'defended our people', so Salomon Speiser recalled, 'to the very day when they themselves fell victim to the murderers'.[5] In the Volhynian town of Miedzyrzec, the Chairman of the Jewish Council, Abraham Shvetz, committed suicide after the Germans ordered him to deliver a hundred, or according to another version, two hundred and fifty young and healthy Jews, ostensibly for labour in Kiev.[6]

Following a similar order to deliver a large group of able-bodied Jews for forced labour outside Rowne, Jacob Sucharczuk appealed to his fellow Council members not to submit any lists at all. When he was overruled, he went home and committed suicide. Some time later, when the Chairman of the Jewish Council at Rowne, Dr Bergman, was ordered to deliver a number of Jews for resettlement, he said he would deliver only himself and his family. Shortly afterwards, he too committed suicide.[7]

German reports make it clear that the Jews were not without resources of their own. 'Jews continue to display hostile behaviour,' one Einsatzkommando reported on August 9. 'They sabotage German orders, especially where they are strong in numbers.' But the fire power of the Germans was overwhelming: against machine guns, rifles and grenades, unarmed men had no means of successful resistance, or of protecting their women and children. The Einsatzkommando report of August 9 listed 510 Jews killed most recently in Brest-Litovsk and 296 in Bialystok. It added that Ukrainian militia commandos 'have persons shot if they do not please them, as was done before'.[8]

As the Einsatzkommando units moved on to new towns and villages, the surviving Jews in the newly established ghettos were subject to the full rigour of segregation. On August 15 Hinrich Lohse, the Reich Commissar for the newly designated Eastern Territories of the Ostland region, covering what had earlier been Lithuania, Latvia, Estonia and White Russia, issued a directive ordering all Jews to be registered; to wear two yellow badges, one on the chest, one on the back; not to walk on the pavements, not to use public transport, not to visit parks, playgrounds, theatres, cinemas, libraries or museums; not to own cars or radio sets. All Jewish property outside the designated ghetto area was to be confiscated. The ghetto was to be cut off physically from the rest of the town, its food supplies to be restricted to food that was 'surplus' to local needs. All able-bodied Jews were to be subject to forced labour.[9]

By August 15, the day of Lohse's directive, the twenty-six thousand surviving Jews of Kovno had been forcibly removed from their homes throughout the city, to a small suburb, Viliampole, in which, henceforth, they were to be confined. Each person was allowed only three square feet of living space. Dr Grinberg later recalled:

Three square feet! But we ignore the lack of space, the dirt, and squalour and try to be content having our wives and children with us. We do not know how we are going to feed ourselves or our family, how we are going to clothe ourselves, how we are going to find warmth. We soon learn, though, to forget the future, to think about the present day only. We become hardhearted, for false illusions will only make us more bitter in the end. Our sole hope was that the most difficult part was now over, and that here in the ghetto we would be able to carry on some sort of existence. Around the ghetto a fence of barbed wire is built. A guard with fixed bayonets is stationed. We are imprisoned!

One now believes that the devil would be satisfied after you have thrown into his greedy throat silver, gold, wedding rings, furs, fabrics, and linen. It is calm one day, and perhaps the crisis has passed. Now that we were poor, they should leave us in peace. But, in keeping with Nazi policy, this was not the case. The new orders are: that our ten cows are to be delivered to the authorities, our children remaining without milk. That all valuables remaining should be delivered voluntarily. This is done, for we want to display our good will, we do not want to provoke the devil — we want to save our lives![10]

Another survivor of the Kovno ghetto, Aharon Peretz, has confirmed that the creation of the ghetto was seen at first as a security against further pogroms.[11]

The daily murder of Jews in hundreds of smaller localities continued, unaffected by the establishment of ghettos in the larger towns and cities. On August 15, the day of confinement and apparent safety for the twenty-six thousand Jews in Kovno, six hundred Jews in Stawiski, near Bialystok, were taken to the nearby woods, and shot.[12] Only sixty remained alive, as forced labourers. That same day, at Rokiskis, a two-day massacre began, in which 3,200 Jews were shot: men, women and children, together with '5 Lithuanian Communists, 1 Pole, 1 partisan'.[13] On the second day of the Rokiskis killings, an official report drawn up in Berlin dwelt upon the attitude of the Catholic Church in Lithuania. Bishop Brisgys, the report stated, 'has forbidden clergymen to help Jews in any form whatsoever. He rejected several Jewish delegations who, approaching him personally, asked for intervention with the German authorities. He will not admit any Jews at all in future.'[14]

On August 17, at Khmelnik in the Ukraine, three hundred of the 'most healthy' men were assembled. The pretext, Maria Rubinstein later recalled, 'was that there was a need for workers. All were killed. It was known almost at once, because some people heard shots. My father was among them.' So Grigory Rubinstein met his death, leaving in the ghetto his wife Polina, and seven sons and daughters, the youngest Dina, only a year old.[15]

The Einsatzkommando justified their murders by tales of growing Jewish resistance, including the activities of special 'destruction' battalions of the Red Army whose task was to carry out sabotage behind the German lines. A 'great number' of Jews had been found in these battalions, among them many Jewish women.[16] Even outside these battalions, another report stated, 'the insubordinations of the Jews increases', so much so that repair work had been stopped on the Kowel–Luck road. At Lida, the local brewery 'was burnt down by Jews'.[17]

To prevent any show of Jewish resistance, the Germans resorted to massive reprisals. After a single German policeman had been shot dead in an ambush near Pinsk, the Einsatzkommando unit in the area reported that, 'as a reprisal, 4,500 Jews were liquidated'.[18] Jewish acts of defiance, however hopeless, were continuous. An Einsatzkommando report of August 22 tells of Jews in a town on the line of the German advance towards Kiev, giving 'fire signals' to the Red Army 'even after the town had been occupied by German troops'. In this same town, one Jew had set fire to his house when he learned that it had been requisitioned by the German army, while another 'managed to tell a German soldier that a box containing gunpowder that had been found, was harmless and not inflammable. A soldier who joined them smoking a cigarette suffered severe burns.'[19]

Jewish defiance took many forms. At Kedainiai, on August 28, an Einsatzkommando unit drove more than two thousand Jews, among them 710 men, 767 women and 599 children, into a ditch. Suddenly, a Jewish butcher jumped up, seized one of the German soldiers, dragged him into the ditch, and sank his teeth into the German's throat with a fatal bite. All two thousand Jews, including the butcher, were then shot.

At nearby Kelme, where the Jews had been forced to dig the ditch in which they were to be shot, the local rabbi, Rabbi Daniel, asked the German commander for permission to speak to his congregation. Permission was granted, on condition that the rabbi would be brief. He spoke softly and unhurriedly, telling his congregation of the significance of the Jewish religious precept of *Kiddush Ha-Shem*, Hebrew for 'the sanctification of the Name of God', a term used in Jewish tradition for martyrdom. After a while, the German officer interrupted. The time had come to finish. 'Fellow Jews!' Rabbi Daniel called out. 'The moment has come when we have to fulfil the precept of sanctification of the Name which I just spoke about. I request only one thing of you: let us not panic; let us accept our fate willingly and lovingly.' Rabbi Daniel then turned to the German commander with the words: 'I have finished; you may begin now.'

When news of the destruction of the Jews of Kedainiai and Kelme reached the Jews of Kovno, Rabbi Shapiro of Kovno was asked by his troubled congregation which of the two reactions, that of Rabbi Daniel or that of the butcher, he thought to be more laudable. 'In my opinion', he replied, 'they were equally noble.' The farewell sermon of Rabbi Daniel 'was the most fitting form of behaviour for him; on the other hand, the Jew who bit the German's throat also fulfilled the precept of sanctification of the Name.' Rabbi Daniel had glorified God's name by spiritual devotion, the butcher by way of a physical act. 'I am certain', Rabbi Shapiro added, 'that under certain circumstances Rabbi Daniel could also have done the same as the butcher.'[20]

The smallest act of resistance provoked savage reprisals. In September 1941 a White Russian villager, in explaining to a Soviet partisan parachutist why his village was reluctant to take part in anti-German action behind the lines, told the parachutist this story:

> Horses pulled a cart into Lukoml, and inside the cart was an interpreter who had been shot dead and a German officer who was breathing his last. He was lying there, his face downwards with a knife sticking out of the nape of his neck. People say he just about managed to whisper: 'A *Jude*, a Jew, that is, killed me,' before kicking the bucket. So by the order of the Kommandant they collected the Jews of Lukoml, about one hundred and fifty families, and mowed them all down with machine-guns. One hundred and fifty families, just imagine! The children they buried alive. And you are telling us to attack them in our village![21]

Among the Jews who urged resistance to German rule was a former Polish senator, Dr Jacob Wigodsky, who for twenty years had been the leader of Vilna Jewry. He was arrested in Vilna on

August 24 and held in prison.[22] He was eighty-six years old. A week later, he was killed at Ponar.

With the United States still neutral, with Russian forces being driven eastward, and with Britain still on the defensive in North Africa, the German power to treat the Jews as it wished was unchallengeable. News of the killings, however, continued to reach the West, and was thought to be exclusively of Russian defenders in or behind the battle zone. As Hitler's armies advanced, Churchill broadcast to the British people on August 24, 'whole districts are being exterminated. Scores of thousands – literally scores of thousands – of executions in cold blood are being perpetrated by the German police-troops upon the Russian patriots who defend their native soil. Since the Mongol invasions of Europe in the sixteenth century, there has never been methodical, merciless butchery on such a scale, or approaching such a scale.'

Churchill made no specific reference to the Jews: had he done so, it would have indicated to the Germans that British Intelligence was listening to their most secret messages. But he did make it clear that the Germans were carrying out what he called 'the most frightful cruelties', and he added: 'We are in the presence of a crime without a name.'[23] The week following Churchill's broadcast, seventeen separate reports of the shooting of Jews and Russians, in groups of between 61 and 4,200, were sent to Berlin by secret radio code from the eastern front.[24]

Throughout August and September, the scale of killings increased. On August 25, at a conference in Vinnitsa, the German military and civilian authorities discussed the future of eleven thousand Jewish forced labourers who were then at Kamenets Podolsk. These were Hungarian Jews, mostly from the areas annexed by Hungary from Czechoslovakia in 1938 and 1939, who had been deported by the Hungarian government, in an act of mass expulsion. The Germans demanded that these Jews be taken back, as they 'could not cope' with them. The Hungarian government refused. A senior SS officer, Lieutenant-General Franz Jaeckeln, then assured the Vinnitsa conference that he would 'complete the liquidation of those Jews by September 1, 1941'.

Between August 27 and August 29, the eleven thousand Jews were marched out of Kamenets Podolsk, to a series of bomb craters ten miles outside the town. There, they were ordered to undress, and machine-gunned. Many were buried alive.[25] Franz Jaeckeln had kept his promise.[26]

One of those who was forced to dig what he believed to be anti-tank ditches at Kamenets Podolsk, Leslie Gordon, later recalled the deportation from Budapest to the east. On reaching a certain eastern town the Jews were forced out of the trucks and told: 'Go eastward. Don't come back. Don't even look back.' Some people left the group 'to do the hygienic things on the side, and they were shot right on the spot'. With Leslie Gordon had been his sixty-eight-year-old father, his forty-three-year-old mother, his four brothers aged twenty-two, sixteen, fourteen and five, and his younger sister, aged eight. Only he survived, and he survived only because he had been taken away for a special task:

> I was taken to a group of young men, about twenty-five or thirty young men. We were first given food and then we were given shovels and other tools and were taken about two or three kilometres out of the town beyond the hills.
>
> We had been taken up there and they told us to start digging ditches. We believed that this was for the tanks, that perhaps the Russians were coming back, and the size of the ditches had almost convinced us that this is what was going to be.
>
> We finished one of the trenches at about late evening, I don't know the time. The size of that trench was about twenty metres long on both sides and about five metres wide and about two to two-and-a-half metres deep. That night we were sent to our place to sleep. Before going to sleep they gave us some food.
>
> Next day we started to dig another trench until about late forenoon when we saw two cars coming to the place. Stepping out were very high ranking SS officers, about six or seven of them. They were talking to our commanders and to our guards. We could not hear what they were saying but they pointed to our trenches we had dug.
>
> Shortly after this we saw the people coming up also with shovels and different tools in their hands and they had been ordered to lay down their tools.
>
> These people they ordered to take off all their clothes, they were put in order, and then they were all naked. They were sent to these ditches and SS men, some of them drunk, some of them

sober, and some of them photographing, it seems, these people numbering about three hundred to four hundred, I don't know the exact number, were all executed and most of them only got hurt and got buried alive. Quicklime was brought there too, four or five trucks of quicklime.

Firstly, after the shooting we were ordered to put some earth back on the bodies, some of them were still crying for help. We put the earth back on the bodies and then the trucks were emptied of the quicklime.

I am talking about people who are all Jews, no exception. There were some Christians who were trying to hide some Jews and they were hanged.

Some of the SS men, Gordon later recalled, 'got almost hysterical', some were 'close to a nervous breakdown', while others 'were shooting and killing'. 'All in all,' he added, 'it was like a slaughterhouse.'[27]

Also on September 3, the Germans carried out their first 'action' against the Jews of Dubossary, a town on the banks of the River Dniester where for nearly two months they had tried and failed to find Jews willing to serve on the Jewish Council. Not a single Jew had agreed to do so. The three Barenboim brothers, Itskhok, Idel and Moshe, were among the Jews who, having refused to serve, were hanged in the centre of the town. Three others hanged for this same crime were Dr Fain, Peisakh Glimberg and Sara Shkolnik.

At the end of August 1941 a Jewish underground organization, led by Yakov Guzanyatskii, had begun to function in Dubossary. In the same square and on the very gallows where the six Jews had been hanged, the underground hanged a local man, Matveenko, who had helped the Germans carry out the six death sentences. The underground also blew up the bridge over the Dniester.

During the 'action' of September 3, six hundred elderly Jews were thrown out of their houses and driven into Dubossary's eight synagogues. Completely surrounded by Germans, the synagogues were then set on fire. All six hundred died an agonizing death. The very next day, Guzanyatskii's underground 'avengers' carried out the death sentence on the German Commander Kraft, while another underground group, led by Efim Boim, blew up a large store of German arms.

By the end of the year, five Jewish partisan groups had begun to operate in the environs of Dubossary, their ranks filled by Jews escaping from Dubossary itself, from Tulchin and Mogilev, and by Soviet prisoners of war escaping from captivity. Near Balta, one group of Jews was led by a former Red Air Force pilot, Lyuni Zaltsman. In the Vinnitsa region, another group was commanded by a sixteen-year-old former postal clerk, Zalman Bernshtein.[28]

On the Leningrad front, a partisan detachment led by Tevye Yakovlevich disrupted German communications in the region of Gdov. 'Only our "neighbours" are restless,' Yakovlevich wrote on one occasion to his son Zosenka. 'They keep looking for us. But, as you can see, it's not that easy. We do not worry. We won't give ourselves up so easily, and if we die, it won't be for nothing. . . .'

Tevye Yakovlevich was killed in action behind the German lines. In 1968 his son was present when a monument in his honour was unveiled in Gdov, amid much ceremonial.[29]

Even in the labour camps in German-occupied Poland, there was no security against random massacre. On August 30 Emanuel Ringelblum received information smuggled out of a labour camp at Osowa, near Chelm. 'There were a few cases of typhus. The SS men took over, ordered the Jewish workers (around fifty of them) to line up. Five men dug a trench-grave behind the line-up, another five were machine-gunned, then still another five dug and were machine-gunned etc. Finally only five or six men were left of the whole camp. . . .'[30]

The security suggested by the creation of ghetto walls and fences, like the security of labour camps, was an illusion. As Dr Aharon Peretz, from Kovno, later recalled:

> A few days after the closing of the ghetto, when we hoped that we would be left alone within the fences, within the hedges, then already during the first days the eldest of the community got an order to gather the intelligentsia (that was the Council of Elders) of the people in order to sort the archives in the town. They asked the people, the young, intelligent, highly educated, well-dressed; and of course it never occurred to us that this was only a trick.
>
> We collected the best in the ghetto. Some of them volunteered because they thought it would be an interesting job.

There were some 530 men. They left the ghetto, left families behind because most of them were young married people, and we waited for them to return – one day, two days, and then we learned they were taken behind Kovno, and all of them were shot down.

'We then realized', Peretz added, 'that the fence was no guard.' Nor was the murder of the 530 educated young Jews of Kovno the end of the agony. As Peretz explained:

We were being crammed all the time, more and more people into a small area. But within the fences there were gardens and there were potatoes in those gardens. Other vegetables too. People used to go into the gardens to dig for the potatoes and then they were shot from behind the fence by the guards. Especially after those shootings, I had to take care of the wounded. They were the 'dumdum bullets' which would split when they hit the body.

Such shots at the beginning were very frequent and there would always be a victim brought to the hospital. Once it would be a rabbi, who would not remove his hat when he met a German. Once it was a doctor, a friend of mine, who did not notice the SS man immediately and did not remove his hat. He was shot in his kidneys and died on the same day.

Of course, the shootings would threaten the people and scare them. Then the searches began, the organized plunder. And of course there were daily victims to keep on this rule of terror and force the Jews to hand over all their valuables. There were special orders regarding gold, money, jewels, as in all other ghettos.

The orders were to hand everything over. And in order to make the instructions effective, searches were conducted. People, women, were undressed. In their homes. To search for money in the intimate parts of their body. I received two such patients in hospitals, who were wounded by SS men with leather gloves. And I had to sew up their intimate parts as a result of those searches.[31]

In Minsk, as in Kovno, there was no security behind the ghetto walls. Three times in August, after the establishment of the ghetto, German soldiers broke into the ghetto, killing, looting and raping. On each raid, thousands were rounded up, and 'disappeared', the inhabitants of the ghetto did not know where.[32] Those seized were taken, not for work, but for execution, in nearby pits. On one occasion, Himmler himself, as SS General Karl Wolff later recalled, 'asked to see a shooting operation', and 'on an inspection of the SS Operations Centre at Minsk' had a hundred prisoners selected 'for a demonstration'. Wolff, who was then Himmler's Liaison Officer at Hitler's headquarters, was also present. His recollection continued:

> An open grave had been dug and they had to jump into this and lie face downwards. And sometimes when one or two rows had already been shot, they had to lie on top of the people who had already been shot and then they were shot from the edge of the grave. And Himmler had never seen dead people before and in his curiosity he stood right up at the edge of this open grave – a sort of triangular hole – and was looking in.
>
> While he was looking in, Himmler had the deserved bad luck that from one or other of the people who had been shot in the head he got a splash of brains on his coat, and I think it also splashed into his face, and he went very green and pale; he wasn't actually sick, but he was heaving and turned round and swayed and then I had to jump forward and hold him steady and then I led him away from the grave.
>
> After the shooting was over, Himmler gathered the shooting squad in a semi-circle around him and, standing up in his car, so that he would be a little higher and be able to see the whole unit, he made a speech. He had seen for himself how hard the task which they had to fulfil for Germany in the occupied areas was, but however terrible it all might be, even for him as a mere spectator, and how much worse it must be for them, the people who had to carry it out, he could not see any way round it.
>
> They must be hard and stand firm. He could not relieve them of this duty; he could not spare them. In the interests of the Reich, in this hopefully Thousand Year Reich, in its first decisive great war after the take-over of power, they must do their duty however hard it may seem. He appealed to their sense of patriotism and their readiness to make sacrifices. Well, yes – and then he drove off. And he left this – this police unit to sort out the future for themselves, to see if and how far they could come to terms with this – within themselves, because for some it was a shock which lasted their whole lives.[33]

To calm the Jews, to avert a mass revolt, deception was an essential part of the Nazi plan. After each raid, the Jews who had been left behind in the ghetto consoled themselves with the belief, fostered by the Germans, that those who had been taken away were in labour camps, under duress no doubt, but alive nevertheless. On August 31, in Vilna, before the ghetto had been established there, a young Jew, Abba Kovner, went to the Jewish Council building to try to find out about the whereabouts of some of his friends who had been taken away in the raids and abductions of the previous weeks. 'I still thought that part of these people, or most of them, would return,' he later recalled.

Early that afternoon, the predominantly Jewish section of Vilna was surrounded by an Einsatzkommando unit, together with several hundred armed Lithuanians. It was announced that any Jew who left his home would be killed, and that a search was in progress for those guilty of ambushing a German patrol. 'The streets were surrounded,' Abba Kovner recalled, 'but again a few hours went by, and nothing happened.' Then, when the sun set, the 'action' began:

> People were taken out of their flats, some carrying a few of their possessions, some without any possessions, out of all the courtyards, out of all the flats, they were driven out with cruel beatings. I don't know whether out of wisdom or instinct or momentary weakness I found myself in a stairway, in a dark recess there and I stood there. Out of a small window I saw what was happening in that narrow street.
>
> Until one o'clock a.m., past midnight, this operation was still in progress. During those hours, at midnight I saw from the other courtyard on the other side of the street, it was 39 Ostrashun Street, a woman was dragged by the hair by two soldiers, a woman who was holding something in her arms. One of them directed a beam of light into her face, the other one dragged her by her hair and threw her on the pavement.
>
> Then the infant fell out of her arms. One of the two, the one with the flashlight, I believe, took the infant, raised him into the air, grabbed him by the leg. The woman crawled on the earth, took hold of his boot and pleaded for mercy. But the soldier took the boy and hit him with his head against the wall, once, twice, smashed him against the wall.[34]

That night, 2,019 Jewish women, 864 men and 817 children were taken from Vilna in trucks to the pits at Ponar and murdered.[35] Their fate was unknown to those who remained behind.

Among those deported to Ponar on the night of August 31 were many Jews who were being held in prison, after having been arrested in the previous weeks, among them Dr Jacob Wigodsky and the young Jewish historian Pinkus Kohn. Others were murdered in the prison itself, among them the Yiddish grammarian Noah Prilutzki. Two months earlier, Prilutzki had been brought to the prison with his friend, the Yiddish writer A. I. Goldschmid. Each day the two scholars had been taken from prison to the famous Strashun Library, where they were made to prepare a list of the valuable collection of Yiddish manuscripts for a German specialist on Judaica, Dr Gotthart. After a month, Gotthart returned to Berlin. Prilutzki and Goldschmid were left in their cell, where a fellow prisoner, the librarian Haikel Lunsky, heard them discussing Maimonides. At the time of the 'Night of Provocation' of August 31, Prilutzki was seen lying almost naked on the floor of the prison, his shirt wrapped around his head soaked in blood, and near him lay Goldschmid; both were killed.[36]

At sunrise on the morning of September 1, there was another scene in Vilna which Abba Kovner has described:

In the deserted streets – no Jews were in the streets – all over the streets there were scattered their belongings. Diagonally across the street there was a column of armed Lithuanians; behind them and flanking them on their sides – a multitude of men and even more women, neighbours who came from all over the area, from the suburbs.

The smell of booty, of loot was in their nostrils. They saw an opportunity of gain. On the side, in polished boots and uniforms, stood the Germans.[37]

The fate of the deportees to Ponar was still unknown. But on September 3 a Jewish woman arrived in the city, bandaged, barefoot, and with dishevelled hair. Her name was Sonia. In the street she spoke to a Jewish doctor, Meir Mark Dvorjetsky. She had come, she said, from Ponar. No, it was not a labour camp. And then she told the doctor her story; how she and her two children had been among the Jews seized, imprisoned and then taken out of the city on

August 31; how they were brought to Ponar, how Jews were 'trying to reckon with their own consciences, how they were trying to confess their sins before death', how she heard shots and saw blood and fell. As the doctor later recounted it:

> She was among the corpses up to sunset and then she heard the wild shoutings of those who carried out the murder; she somehow or other managed to get out of the heap of corpses. She got to the barbed wire entanglements; she managed to cross them, and she found a common Polish peasant woman who bandaged her wounds, gave her flowers and said, 'Run away from here, but carry flowers as if you were a common peasant, so that they shouldn't recognize that you are a Jewess.'
>
> And then she came to me. She unwrapped the bandage and I saw the wound. I saw the hole from the bullet and in the hole there were ants creeping.

Dvorjetsky hurried to a gathering of Vilna Jews to tell them the story. 'This is not a labour camp where you're going to be sent to,' he said. 'This is something else.' But they could not believe him. 'You are also the one who is a panic-monger,' they replied. 'Instead of encouraging us, instead of consoling us, you are telling us cock-and-bull stories about extermination. How is it possible that the Jews will be simply taken and shot?'

As for Sonia, henceforth she refused to tell anybody about Ponar, for fear, as Dvorjetsky explained, 'that if the Germans might get wind of it, they would do away with her'.[38]

It was to be several months before an account of the massacres at Ponar reached the Jews of Warsaw. It too came from a woman who, like Sonia, had escaped from the pit on the morning of September 1. She was twenty-two years old. 'As it took such a long time to shoot such a large number of people,' she wrote, 'the murderers took a break, wolfed down a good meal, and then finished their bloody, fiendish work.'[39]

The work was finished only momentarily. Every day in September 1941 Jews were slaughtered by Einsatzkommando units. Even in Vilna, despite the establishment on September 6 of two ghettos, the 'large' and the 'small', the killers soon returned, taking to Ponar a further 3,434 Jews on September 12 and 1,267 five days later. Of those murdered, according to the careful statistics of the SS, 2,357 were women and 1,018 were children.[40] Even on the day of the setting up of the ghetto, a day on which it was intended to lull the Jews into some sense of security, killings had taken place. 'When I arrived at the ghetto', Avraham Sutzkever later recalled, 'I saw the following scene. Martin Weiss – a member of the District Commissar's staff – came in with a young Jewish girl. When we went in further he took out his revolver and shot her on the spot. The girl's name was Gitele Tarlo.' Gitele Tarlo was eleven years old.[41]

'The struggle against Bolshevism', General Keitel informed his commanders on September 12, 'demands ruthless and energetic measures, above all against the Jews, the main carriers of Bolshevism.'[42]

It was not only the Germans who spoke in this tone. Many Ukrainian nationalists used similar language and sought a similar solution. On September 1, Ulas Samchuk, the editor of the newspaper *Volhyn*, told his readers: 'The element that settled our cities, whether it is Jews or Poles who were brought here from outside the Ukraine, must disappear completely from our cities. The Jewish problem is already in the process of being solved, and it will be solved in the framework of a general reorganization of the "New Europe".' The vacuum that would be created by this reorganization was to be filled, Samchuk wrote, 'by the true proprietors of the land, the Ukrainian people'.[43]

On September 13, in the General Government city of Piotrkow, eleven Jews reached the end of a series of tortures which had begun more than two months earlier. All were members of the Jewish Council of Piotrkow. All had been arrested when the Germans discovered that they had been cooperating with the Jewish underground movement in the ghetto. One Council member, Jacob Berliner, who had avoided capture, gave himself up to the Gestapo 'out of loyalty to his comrades'. The underground link had spread to the ghetto in Tomaszow Mazowiecki, where the Gestapo arrested another senior member of the Jewish community, Kosherowski. After prolonged tortures, the twelve Jews were sent to a punitive camp. A few days later, their families received telegrams informing them of the deaths 'due to illness' of every one of the deportees. Their ashes were returned to the city.[44]

On September 17 several thousand Kovno Jews were seized in the streets, most of them women and children. 'They were taken to the synagogue for three days,' the twenty-four-year-old Leah Klompul later recalled. 'For three days graves were dug for them on the football field. Then they were taken there, and killed.' Among those murdered were Leah Klompul's mother Rachel, and her sister Gita. Her father had already been taken away six or seven weeks earlier with a number of other men, ostensibly for some labour task. 'They were all killed in the woods.'[45]

News of these Eastern massacres was carefully concealed. In Warsaw, only the war news was known. 'The Nazis are victorious,' Mary Berg noted in her diary on September 20. 'Kiev has fallen. Soon Hitler will be in Moscow. London is suffering severe bombardments.'[46] Unknown to the Jews of Warsaw, or of Western Europe, the Eastern massacres continued without respite.

An eye-witness of three of these massacres was a German army officer, Lieutenant Erwin Bingel. Four years later, while a prisoner-of-war, he set down his recollections. On September 15, he recalled, he was ordered to report to the commander of the town of Uman, in occupied Russia, and instructed to set up guards on all railways in the area, and around the airport. He did so, discovering, as he put his men in place, that ditches had just been dug in the square in front of the airport.

At dawn on September 16, Lieutenant Bingel's men were in place. They then saw a crowd of people brought to the ditches in front of the airfield, 'not only men but also women, and children of all ages'. His account continued:

When the people had crowded into the square in front of the airport, a few trucks drove up from the direction of the town. From these vehicles a troop of field gendarmes alighted, and were immediately led aside. A number of tables was then unloaded from one of the trucks and placed in a line at distances from each other. Meanwhile, a few more trucks with Ukrainian militiamen commanded by SS had arrived. These militiamen had work tools with them and one of their trucks also carried chloride of lime.

The truck now drove alongside these ditches and the men on it unloaded six to eight sacks of chloride of lime at intervals of fifteen to twenty metres.

In the meantime, a number of transport planes (Model 'Junker 52') had landed at the airport. Out of these stepped several units of SS soldiers who, having fallen in, marched up to the Field Gendarmerie unit, subsequently taking up positions alongside it. As could be discerned from the distance, the two units were obviously being sworn in. I was then informed by my interpreter, who was Jewish – which fact, however, was known only to me personally – that he had learned that the people had been brought together following upon an order which had been posted in the streets of Uman and which had been given the widest publicity throughout Uman sub-district by the Ukrainian militia.

The order was for all Jews 'in the town of Uman and its sub-district', Jews 'of all ages', to assemble for the purpose of preparing 'an exact census of the Jewish population'. Anyone not complying with this order would be punished 'most severely'. Lieutenant Bingel's account continued:

The result of this proclamation was, of course, that all persons concerned appeared as ordered. This relatively harmless summons, it was thought, could be connected in some way or other with the preparations we were observing.

It was because we took the matter so lightly that we were all the more horrified at what we witnessed during the next few hours.

One row of Jews was ordered to move forward and was then allocated to the different tables where they had to undress completely and hand over everything they wore and carried. Some still carried jewellery which they had to put on the table. Then, having taken off all their clothes, they were made to stand in line in front of the ditches, irrespective of their sex. The commandos then marched in behind the line and began to perform the inhuman acts, the horror of which is now known to the whole world.

With automatic pistols and 0.8 pistols these men mowed down the line with such zealous intent that one could have supposed this activity to have been their life-work.

Even women carrying children a fortnight to three weeks old, sucking at their breasts, were not spared this horrible ordeal.

198 · THE HOLOCAUST   1941

Nor were mothers spared the terrible sight of their children being gripped by their little legs and put to death with one stroke of the pistol-butt or club, thereafter to be thrown on the heap of human bodies in the ditch, some of which were not quite dead. Not before these mothers had been exposed to this worst of all tortures did they receive the bullet that released them from this sight.

The people in the first row thus having been killed in the most inhuman manner, those of the second row were now ordered to step forward. The men in this row were ordered to step out and were handed shovels with which to heap chloride of lime upon the still partly moving bodies in the ditch. Thereafter, they returned to the tables and undressed.

After that they had to set out on the same last walk as their murdered brethren, with one exception – this time the men of the alternative firing squad surpassed each other in cruelty, lest they lag behind their predecessors.

The air resounded with the cries of the children and the tortured. With senses numbed by what had happened, one could not help thinking of wives and children back home who believed they had good reason to be proud of their husbands and fathers, who, they thought, were fighting heroically in the ranks of the German army on behalf of the Fatherland, whilst the so-called Elite troop, always referred to as unique, perpetrated the most horrible acts of cruelty in the honourable uniform of a nation.

Two of Lieutenant Bingel's men suffered 'a complete nervous breakdown' as a result of what they had witnessed. Two others, arrested for having taken 'snapshots of the action', were sentenced to a year's imprisonment, and served their term in a military prison in Germany.

On September 22, Lieutenant Bingel and his men witnessed a second massacre, in Vinnitsa. This was followed by a third, also in Vinnitsa, carried out by Ukrainian militia who had been trained by the SS, and were commanded 'by a small group of SS officers and NCOs'. In the first two massacres, Bingel calculated, first twenty-four thousand and then twenty-eight thousand Jews were killed. In the third, Ukrainian militia killings, six thousand were murdered. As Lieutenant Bingel recalled:

In the morning at 10.15, wild shooting and terrible human cries reached our ears. At first, I failed to grasp what was taking place, but when I approached the window from which I had a broad view over the whole of the town park, the following spectacle unfolded before my eyes and those of my men who, alerted by the tumult, had meanwhile gathered in my room.

Ukrainian militia on horseback, armed with pistols, rifles and long, straight cavalry swords, were riding wildly inside and around the town park. As far as we could make out, they were driving people along before their horses – men, women, and children. A shower of bullets was then fired at this human mass. Those not hit outright were struck down with the swords. Like some ghostly apparition, this horde of Ukrainians, let loose and commanded by SS officers, trampled savagely over human bodies, ruthlessly killing innocent children, mothers and old people whose only crime was that they had escaped the great mass murder, so as eventually to be shot or beaten to death like wild animals.[47]

In a village several miles from Vinnitsa, six Jews were in hiding, among them two little girls, the five-year-old Ingar and the three-year-old Victoria. Their parents, Alexander and Judith Lerner, who lived in Moscow, had sent them for safety to Vinnitsa two months earlier, to Judith Lerner's parents. This couple, as the German armies approached, fled to the village, to the children's great grandparents. All six were betrayed by a neighbour, and killed.[48]

September 22 was the beginning of the Jewish New Year. The ten days that followed were the Days of Awe of the Jewish calendar, ending on that most solemn of days, the Day of Atonement. In 1941, the ten Days of Awe saw a greater intensity of killing than any previous ten-day period of the war. At Vinnitsa, twenty-eight thousand Jews were murdered on September 22. Two days later, in Wolkowysk, two thousand women and children were taken from the already established ghetto and murdered. At Kovno, on September 26, the SS recorded the shooting, in the Fourth Fort, of '412 Jewish men, 615 Jewish women, 581 Jewish children' described as 'sick people and carriers of epidemics'.[49]

From many towns, young Jews sought to break out of the

German and Lithuanian cordons, and make for the forests. On the night of September 26 several hundred young men managed to escape from Swieciany. 'This being the night before the expulsion,' one of them, Yitzhak Rudnicki, later recalled, 'Lithuanian police vigilantly patrolled the area. Nearby villages were informed that anyone who caught an escaping Jew and turned him over to the police would receive a reward.' Nor did the young men know where to go. 'The Germans were approaching Moscow,' Rudnicki explained, 'the front was far away, and we could not possibly get there.'

Some were captured, but some reached the comparative safety of the Naroch forest, fifty miles to the east. There, they joined other fugitives, and, with the arrival of Soviet partisans a year later, joined the partisan ranks. Others like Rudnicki, unable to see a way past the hostile villagers, returned to Swieciany, where he joined the ghetto underground, and, seven months later, escaped again, this time successfully, to become a partisan in the forests.[50]

On September 22 it was the turn of 4,000 Jews in Ejszyszki to face the ordeal. Alerted by the leaders of their community, nearly five hundred managed to escape, but most were hunted down by German and Lithuanian police. 'Bluma Michalowski and her sister were shot on the Lithuanian-Russian border not far from Radun,' recalled one of the escapees, Shalom Sonenson. 'They were given a Jewish burial. They were the lucky ones!'[51]

Sonenson, reaching Radun safely, later learned that on September 23 all those unable to escape had been locked into three buildings, including the synagogue, and kept without food or water. Then, all the following day and night, they were forced to stand in the cattle market, still denied food and water. This ordeal continued throughout the night. Then, on the morning of September 25, 250 of the healthiest men were marched away.[52]

To reassure those who remained, the Lithuanians read out a letter, alleged to be from Lev Milikowski to his wife, telling her: 'We are in a courtyard of a farmhouse, and we are preparing a ghetto for you. Don't be afraid!' ' It was a trick. Throughout that day, and September 26, in batches of 250, the Jews of Ejszyszki were led away to specially prepared pits, where they were shot.[53]

One survivor of this massacre was the sixteen-year-old Zvi Michalowski, who had fallen into the pit a fraction of a second before the volley of shots which killed those next to him, including his father. Later he had heard the chief executioner, the Lithuanian Ostrovakas, singing with his fellow executioners as they drank to their successful work.

Just beyond the Jewish cemetery were a number of Christian homes. Michalowski knew them all. Naked, covered with blood, he knocked on the first door. The door opened. A peasant, he later recalled, was holding a lamp which he had looted earlier in the day from a Jewish home. 'Please let me in,' Zvi pleaded. The peasant lifted the lamp and examined the boy closely. 'Jew, go back to the grave where you belong!' he shouted at Zvi and slammed the door in his face. Zvi knocked on other doors, but the response was the same.

Near the forest lived a widow whom Michalowski also knew. He decided to knock on her door. The old widow opened the door. She was holding in her hand a small, burning piece of wood. 'Let me in!' begged Michalowski. 'Jew, go back to the grave at the old cemetery!' She chased him away with the burning piece of wood as if exorcising an evil spirit.

Michalowski, desperate for shelter, returned. 'I am your Lord, Jesus Christ,' he said. 'I came down from the cross. Look at me – the blood, the pain, the suffering of the innocent. Let me in.' The widow crossed herself and fell at his bloodstained feet. 'Boze moj, Boze moj,' 'My God, my God,' she kept crossing herself and praying. The door was opened.

Michalowski walked in. He promised the widow that he would bless her children, her farm, and her, but only if she would keep his visit a secret for three days and three nights and not reveal it to a living soul, not even the priest. She gave Michalowski food and clothing and warm water to wash himself. Before leaving the house three days later, he once more reminded her that the Lord's visit must remain a secret, because of His special mission on earth.

Dressed in a farmer's clothing, with a supply of food for a few days, the young man made his way to the nearby forest. He was to survive the war in hiding, and as a partisan.[54]

Since the German occupation of Kiev on September 19, the Jews had waited, uncertain of their fate, noting, as the sixteen-year-old Konstantin Miroshnik later recalled, the 'joyful faces' of some of the

Ukrainians who stood watching the German troops arrive. On the second day of the occupation, Ukrainian policemen appeared on the streets, wearing armbands announcing that they belonged to the 'Organisation of Ukrainian Nationalists'. For nine days the Jews were unmolested. But both they and the Ukrainians had a sense that all was not well. Miroshnik later recalled how one of their Ukrainian neighbours said to his grandfather, 'Well, Leib, your Jewish power has come to an end, the new order will begin now, so keep in mind, you'll be reckoned with. . . .'[55]

On September 21, as Golda Glozman was told by one of her Jewish neighbours, her father Shlomo Glozman, one of the Jewish community leaders in Kiev, was murdered. As she later learned from neighbours:

> . . . the Nazis put him and nine other most honourable old Jews in a lorry, forced them to put on their prayer vestments, and drove them through the town until dinner-time. They repeated this procedure several days in succession. The people in the streets were laughing. On one of these days Nazis came to their house after the dinner and drove him in the direction of Konstantinovskaya Street. There, nearby the cinema, 'Udarnik', he was beaten badly and only just managed to reach his house afterwards. However, on the next day he was forced again, together with others, to stand on the 'chariot of disgrace'.

A few days later Shlomo Glozman left his house in order to visit his son. As he crossed Kiev, a drunken SS man attacked him in the street and beat him to death.[56]

At Kiev, on September 27 and 28, posters throughout the city demanded the assembly of Jews for 'resettlement'. More than thirty thousand reported. Because of 'our special talent of organisation', the commander of the Einsatzkommando reported two days later, 'the Jews still believed to the very last moment before being executed that indeed all that was happening was that they were being resettled.'[57]

The Jews of Kiev were brought to Babi Yar, a ravine just outside the city. There, they were shot down by machine-gun fire. Immediately after the war, a non-Jew, the watchman at the old Jewish cemetery, near Babi Yar, recalled how Ukrainian policemen:

... formed a corridor and drove the panic-stricken people towards the huge glade, where sticks, swearings, and dogs, who were tearing the people's bodies, forced the people to undress, to form columns in hundreds, and then to go in the columns in twos towards the mouth of the ravine.

At the mouth of the ravine, the watchman recalled:

... they found themselves on the narrow ground above the precipice, twenty to twenty-five metres in height, and on the opposite side there were the Germans' machine guns. The killed, wounded and half-alive people fell down and were smashed there. Then the next hundred were brought, and everything repeated again. The policemen took the children by the legs and threw them alive down into the Yar.

That day the watchman witnessed 'horrible scenes of human grief and despair'. In the evening, he noted, 'the Germans undermined the wall of ravine and buried the people under the thick layers of earth. But the earth was moving long after, because wounded and still alive Jews were still moving. One girl was crying: "Mammy, why do they pour the sand into my eyes?" '[58]

After the war, a Jewish doctor, David Rosen, was told of the fate of his Aunt Lisa, who had been so far advanced in pregnancy that she had been unable to leave Kiev in the last evacuation trains before the Germans arrived in the city. 'Aunt Lisa', Dr Rosen was told by a neighbour after the war, 'and her six-year-old son Tolik went to Babi Yar. She was so horrified and frightened that she began giving birth. Driven by the Germans and policemen to the ravine, together with her son and the newborn child in her arms, she fell down into Babi Yar and perished there in pangs.'[59]

The horrors of Babi Yar were endless and obscene. When the war was over, Victoria Shyapeltoh learned that when the Jews had been ordered to assemble, her neighbour, a Ukrainian woman who had lived in the same apartment with them for many years, had dragged her seventy-year-old father, Yakov-Pinhas Zindelivich, from the apartment into the street, and handed him over to the Germans. The old man was wearing his prayer shawl. Still wearing it, he was driven to Babi Yar, 'praying all the way'.[60]

One of the few Jews to escape from the pit at Babi Yar was Dina Pronicheva. After the war, she told her story to the Russian writer Anatoli Kuznetsov, who published it, first in Russia in 1966, and then, under the name A. Anatoli, in Britain in 1970. Dina Pronicheva, like hundreds of those who were shot during these massacres, was not in fact killed. But unlike most of those who fell into the pit alive, she managed to avoid being suffocated, and to escape undetected:

All around and beneath her she could hear strange submerged sounds, groaning, choking and sobbing: many of the people were not dead yet. The whole mass of bodies kept moving slightly as they settled down and were pressed tighter by the movements of the ones who were still living.

Some soldiers came out on to the ledge and flashed their torches down on the bodies, firing bullets from their revolvers into any which appeared to be still living. But someone not far from Dina went on groaning as loud as before.

Then she heard people walking near her, actually on the bodies. They were Germans who had climbed down and were bending over and taking things from the dead and occasionally firing at those which showed signs of life.

Among them was the policeman who had examined her papers and taken her bag: she recognized him by his voice.

One SS-man caught his foot against Dina and her appearance aroused his suspicions. He shone his torch on her, picked her up and struck her with his fist. But she hung limp and gave no signs of life. He kicked her in the breast with his heavy boot and trod on her right hand so that the bones cracked, but he didn't use his gun and went off, picking his way across the corpses.

A few minutes later she heard a voice calling from above:
'Demidenko! Come on, start shovelling!'

There was a clatter of spades and then heavy thuds as the earth and sand landed on the bodies, coming closer and closer until it started falling on Dina herself.

Her whole body was buried under the sand but she did not move until it began to cover her mouth. She was lying face upwards, breathed in some sand and started to choke, and then, scarcely realizing what she was doing, she started to struggle in a state of uncontrollable panic, quite prepared now to be shot rather than be buried alive.

With her left hand, the good one, she started scraping the sand off herself, scarcely daring to breathe lest she should start coughing; she used what strength she had left to hold the cough back. She began to feel a little easier. Finally she got herself out from under the earth.

The Ukrainian policemen up above were apparently tired after a hard day's work, too lazy to shovel the earth in properly, and once they had scattered a little in they dropped their shovels and went away. Dina's eyes were full of sand. It was pitch dark and there was the heavy smell of flesh from the mass of fresh corpses.

Dina could just make out the nearest side of the sandpit and started slowly and carefully making her way across to it; then she stood up and started making little foot-holds in it with her left hand. In that way, pressed close to the side of the pit, she made steps and so raised herself an inch at a time, likely at any moment to fall back into the pit.

There was a little bush at the top which she managed to get hold of. With a last desperate effort she pulled herself up and, as she scrambled over the ledge, she heard a whisper which nearly made her jump back.

'Don't be scared, lady! I'm alive too.'

It was a small boy in vest and pants who had crawled out as she had done. He was trembling and shivering all over.

'Quiet!' she hissed at him. 'Crawl along behind me.'

And they crawled away silently, without a sound.

Dina Pronicheva survived. The boy, Motyn, stayed with her, but as they sought to leave the area, he called that danger was near. 'Don't move, lady, there's Germans here!' – those were Motyn's words. Luckily for Dina Pronicheva, the Germans did not understand them. But hearing him speak, they killed him on the spot.[61]

The courage of Motyn was recorded only by chance: only because a Russian writer, a non-Jew, was in search of facts about the past. He recorded also an episode, in Kiev, of a Jewish girl 'running down the street, shooting from a revolver'. She killed two German officers, 'then shot herself'.[62] Her name is not known. Only her deed survives, and then, only by chance.

After two days of shooting, the Einsatzkommando unit recorded the murder of 33,771 Jews at Babi Yar. The unit's machine-gunners had been helped by Ukrainian militiamen. The same Einsatzkommando report also gave details of an even larger slaughter further south, 35,782 'Jews and Communists' killed in the Black Sea ports of Nikolayev and Kherson.[63]

On the Day of Atonement, October 2, it was the turn, among other places, of the village of Podborodz to face the fury of the killers. An eight-year-old girl, Hadassah Rosen, was hiding with her parents in the attic of the synagogue. From the attic, she later recalled, 'we squinted through the cracks in the boards and saw them shoving the Jews into wagons. Whoever was slow in getting into the wagon was clubbed to death.' It was very early in the morning: 'soon afterwards we heard volleys of shots. That was how they killed the Jews they took in wagons out of the ghetto of Podborodz.'[64]

Also on the Day of Atonement, an Einsatzgruppe report recorded how, at Zagare, as 633 men, 1,017 women and 496 children were being 'led away', 'a mutiny began which was put down immediately'. In the course of the mutiny, the report added, '150 Jews were shot right away.'[65] The rest, driven to the execution site, were then killed. At Butrimonys, where 976 Jews were murdered, the Germans organized a 'spectacle', placing benches at the execution site so that local Lithuanians could have a 'good view'.[66]

In Vilna, whose Jewish population had already been decimated by slaughter, the Day of Atonement was chosen for yet another raid into the ghetto, and for the deportation of more than three thousand Jews to Ponar, and to their deaths.[67] In their raids on the ghetto, the SS men, known to the Jews as 'hunters', worked with their dogs. 'These hunters dragged the Jews out of the cellars,' Abraham Sutzkever recalled immediately after the war, of the raid on the small ghetto on the Day of Atonement, 'and tried to drive them to Ponar. But the Jews fled into their cellars, trying to hide.'

The 'hunters' began to search with dogs for those who had fled, to drive them out with shots, and to shoot them in the street if they were still resisting. During one such a moment, Sutzkever recalled, an SS officer, Horst Schweinberger, began to shoot the Jews who had been discovered. But at that moment the dog at Schweinberger's side jumped at him and began to bite his throat 'like a mad dog'. Then Schweinberger killed his dog and told the Jews to bury it and cry over its grave. 'We really cried then,' Sutzkever recalled. 'We cried because it was not Schweinberger but his dog that had been buried.'[68]

At Ponar, men were shot first, then women. Even those who had not been killed outright, could not survive the whole day in the pit, lying there wounded as more and more bodies fell on top of them. Only towards evening, when the last of the women were being shot, did a few of those who were only wounded have some small chance of remaining alive until it was dark, and then of creeping away unseen: naked, bleeding, crushed, but alive.

From the end of June 1941 to the end of December, at least forty-eight thousand Jews were murdered at Ponar. After the killings of September 3, six are known to have crawled out of the pit alive, and survived. All of them were women.[69]

One of the survivors of the October killings, Sara Menkes, returned to Vilna, where she told Abba Kovner the story of a former pupil of his, Serna Morgenstern. At the edge of the pit, Sara Menkes reported:

> ... they were lined up; they were told to undress; they undressed and stood only in their undergarments and there was this line of the *Einsatzgruppen* men – and an officer came out, he looked at the row of women and he looked at this Serna Morgenstern; she had wonderful eyes, a tall girl, long-braided hair – he looked at her searchingly for a long time and then he smiled and said, 'Take a step forward.' She was dazed, as all of them were. No one wept any more, no one asked for anything; they must have been paralysed and she was so paralysed she did not step forward and he repeated the order and asked, 'Hey, don't you want to live? You are so beautiful. I tell you to take one step forward.'
>
> So she took that step forward and he told her, 'What a pity to bury such beauty under the earth. Go, but don't look backward. There is the street. You know that boulevard, you just follow that.' She hesitated for a moment and then she started marching, and the rest, Sara Menkes told me, 'We looked at her with our eyes – I don't know whether it was only terror or jealousy, envy too, as she walked slowly step by step and then the officer whipped out his revolver and shot her in the back.'

'Must I tell more?' Abba Kovner asked the court to which he told this story.[70]

Throughout October 1941 the Eastern killings continued. In the newly established ghettos of Kovno and Vilna, work passes were handed out, and those who did not receive them, women and children especially, were sent to the Ninth Fort, or to Ponar. On September 25 the Kovno Jewish Council had been ordered by the Germans to distribute five thousand work permits to workers and their families. Cruelly, the Germans thrust on the Council the burden of choice. The Council discussed refusing to distribute the permits, and even burning them. But after a long debate it decided that it had no moral right to condemn five thousand Jews to death by not distributing what then appeared to be 'life permits'.[71]

On October 4, the Kovno ghetto was raided, and fifteen hundred Jews who had no work permits were taken to the Ninth Fort and murdered. But from the hospital in Kovno, no one was taken away, even though none of them had work permits. Instead, the building was locked, and then set on fire. Patients, doctors and nurses were burned alive. 'Even now,' Zalman Grinberg recalled three and a half years later, 'I can see the blazing hospital. It seems like a bad dream, but, alas, it was true!'[72]

On October 6, two days after the slaughter in Kovno, a similar selection was made in the Dvinsk ghetto, where only those with work permits were spared. The rest, the majority of those in the ghetto, were led away, no one knew whither. The selection took two days. At the end of the first day, a woman, who had been among those led away, returned. 'She was hysterical and uncontrollable,' Maja Zarch later recalled. 'When she eventually quietened down, it transpired that she had been in a group that had been taken for slaughter. She described in detail what had happened. She had fallen into the mass grave and had been taken for dead but had escaped from among the corpses. . . .'

The selection in Dvinsk continued on October 7, when the woman who had escaped from the pit on the previous day was among those taken away, 'never to return'. Maja Zarch also recalled how a woman, returning from work, could not find her son. 'For days she walked around – a woman possessed, talking to her son's hat, clutching it, kissing it.'[73]

In Rowne, on October 7, more than seventeen thousand Jews were driven from their homes, marched towards the pits, and then ordered to undress. A Jewish eye-witness, Major Zalcman, later recalled that those who refused to undress had their eyes gouged out. Zalcman also recalled that as the Chief Rabbi of Rowne, Ma-Jafit, was telling his congregation that their deaths would not be in vain, he was shot dead by an SS man.[74] It was the second day of the Jewish harvest festival of Succoth.

On October 10, three days after the Rowne massacre, Field Marshal Walter von Reichenau, commander of the German Sixth Army, issued a directive in which he explained that 'the most essential aim of the campaign against the Jewish-Bolshevist system

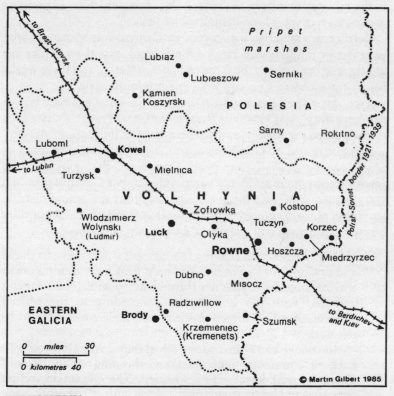

THE VOLHYNIA

is the complete crushing of its means of power, and the extermination of Asiatic influences in the European region'. His directive continued:

> This poses tasks for the troops that go beyond the one-sided routine of conventional soldiering. In the Eastern region, the soldier is not merely a fighter according to the rules of the art of war, but also the bearer of an inexorable national idea and the avenger of all bestialities inflicted upon the German people and its racial kin.
>
> Therefore the soldier must have full understanding for the necessity of a severe but just atonement on Jewish sub-humanity.

An 'additional aim in this', Reichenau went on to explain, 'is to nip in the bud any revolts in the rear of the army, which, as experience proves, have always been instigated by Jews'.[75]

Reichenau's directive was copied by General von Manstein, who issued it in the Crimean city of Simferopol nine days before the killing of 4,500 Jews at the Crimean port of Kerch, and three weeks before the murder of 14,300 Jews in Simferopol itself.[76]

Two days after Reichenau issued his directive against 'Jewish sub-humanity', was Hoshana Rabba, the Great Prayer, a day which is considered by many Jews to be a day of judgement. An eye-witness of that day, October 12, in the Eastern Galician town of Stanislawow, recalled four years later how, that morning, the Jewish streets 'were suddenly surrounded by the Gestapo men and Ukrainian militia', the latter summoned from the whole district, and how 'old and young, men and women, were driven out of their houses to the town hall squares'. His account continued:

> I felt quite certain that my labour card would serve to shield and save me. So I went out and even took a pregnant woman with me in order to pass her through as my wife. (Her husband had fled with the Red Army.) According to the official announcement all forced workers and their wives were to be released.
>
> No sooner had I entered the street than I was attacked by a gang of Ukrainian young ruffians shouting wildly, 'Look! There are still Jews!' They whistled. The Ukrainian militia appeared and began dragging me along with all the other Jews.

A blind old women aged 104 who lived in my courtyard was also dragged along, and no attention was paid to all her entreaties to be allowed to remain where she was.

I was ordered to carry the old woman on my back, while at my side strode two companions. One pushed me along with his rifle butt and shouted that I was going too slowly and idly; while the other kept on hitting me for being in such a hurry.

Beaten and bleeding, I dragged my way to the town hall square. Not a single Jew of all those I saw there was uninjured. They were wounded and bruised, and blood was running on all sides. From the square they were led off in separate groups. To begin with they were loaded on huge lorries which afterwards returned empty. Then the Germans and Ukrainians began to hurry up very much indeed and ordered them all to line up in three rows, each three men deep.

These rows began to drag along, covering a length of three kilometres and containing many thousand Jews. We were driven to the road behind the town, towards the new Jewish cemetery at Batory. When we approached we understood the full horror of the situation. The sound of shots reached us from the cemetery.

We were driven into the cemetery with cruel, brutal beatings. I saw that the Germans were driving the people standing on the one side towards the graves, while those standing on the other were being permitted merely to stand and watch. Then came an order, 'Hand over all valuables!' I used the tumult and hubbub, and crossed over to the side of the watchers.

The German stormtroops together with the Ukrainian police took up their stations beside the machine guns. Fifteen of the stormtroops shot, and fifteen others loaded the guns. The Jews leapt naked into the graves. The bullets hit them while jumping.

Three graves had been dug there. The work of excavation had lasted for about a fortnight. It had been done by young Ukrainians who were members of the Petlura organisation. The Germans then explained to the Jewish Council that the Ukrainians were preparing stations for anti-aircraft against Bolshevik air attack. Nobody even imagined that six thousand Jews would meet with their deaths at this place.

The graves were deep, the naked people fell one on the other, whether dead or alive. The heap of bodies grew higher and higher. I stood and gazed. Early in the morning the murderers had stationed a group of Jews to watch the scene. This was far worse than death, and many people of our group, who could bear it no longer, burst out with shouts, 'Take us and murder us as well!' And the murderers satisfied them, and began dragging people from our ranks off to the graves as well.

My turn came. The only thing I had in mind was to reach the grave as soon as possible so that an end might be made of it all. 'Take off your clothes!' I was ordered, and quickly stood naked. Three of us approached the grave. There were shots. Two of us fell. Suddenly something strange happened. There came an order, 'Cease fire!' The stormtroopers standing ready stopped their shooting. I stood astonished and confused. One of the murderers approached me and said, 'Jew, you are lucky. You are not going to die. Dress again, quickly.'

The graves were filled to overflowing. All round lay the dead, strangled, trodden underfoot, wounded. Those of us who remained alive felt ourselves to be infinitely unfortunate. There were about one thousand seven hundred of us left in the cemetery grounds. We were afraid to move from the spot. One of those in command of the action announced that 'the action was completed', and that the survivors might return to their homes.[77]

More than two years had passed since the German invasion of Poland in 1939. In the East, more than a hundred days had passed since the German invasion of the Soviet Union. The victorious German war machine destroyed whatever it wished to destroy: Polish intellectuals, Soviet prisoners-of-war, Yugoslav partisans, French resistance fighters, each felt the full force of superior power. The Jews, scattered among many nations, few of them sympathetic, were singled out for murder and abuse. Reprisals, and the threat of reprisals, inhibited Jew and non-Jew alike, even the bravest. In Warsaw, on October 15, the Germans imposed 'punishment by death' on all Jews who left the ghetto without permission, and on any person 'who deliberately offers a hiding place to such Jews'.[78] These were not idle threats: later that same month, as a punitive measure and as a warning, German policemen drowned thirty Jewish children in the water-filled clay pits near Okopowa Street.[79]

14

'Write and record!'

WHAT GOERING HAD CALLED the 'final solution' in May 1941 was under active discussion five months later in Berlin, Cracow and Prague. 'As far as Jews are concerned,' Hans Frank told the ministers of the General Government in Cracow on 9 October 1941, 'I want to tell you quite frankly that they must be done away with one way or another.'[1] On the following day, at a meeting in Prague at which Adolf Eichmann was present, the notes of the discussion recorded that 'the Führer wants the Jews to leave the centre of Germany and this matter has to be dealt with immediately'. It was the transport problem, the meeting was told, that 'constitutes a difficulty'.[2]

That difficulty was being overcome. On October 16 the first of twenty trains left Germany 'for the East'. By November 4 they had all completed their journey, taking 19,837 Jews to the Lodz ghetto. One of these trains, with 512 Jews, came from Luxembourg. Five trains, with 5,000 Jews in all, came from Vienna, a similar number from Prague, and 4,187, in four trains, from Berlin. Other trains came from Cologne, Frankfurt, Hamburg and Dusseldorf.[3]

As in 1933 and again in 1938, many German Jews responded to the renewal of persecution by committing suicide. Hildegarde Henschel, who was among the deportees from Germany to Lodz in October 1941, later recalled not only the suicides, as many as 1,200, but also the efforts of the German authorities, often successful, to revive those who had attempted suicide. It was these Jews, she noted, whom the Germans deported first.[4]

The arrival of the 'Western European' Jews in the Lodz ghetto made a considerable impression: six months later, one of the ghetto chroniclers recalled how, as the deportees arrived:

We were struck by their elegant sports clothes, their exquisite footwear, their furs, the many variously coloured capes the women wore. They often gave the impression of being people on some sort of vacation or, rather, engaged in winter sports, for the majority of them wore ski clothes. You couldn't tell there was a war on from the way those people looked; and the fact that, during the bitter cold spells, they strolled about in front of the gates to their 'transports', and about the 'city' as well, demonstrated most eloquently that their layers of fat afforded them excellent protection from the cold.

Their attitude toward the extremely unsanitary conditions in which they were quartered was one of unusual disgust, though perhaps that was not without justification; they shouted, they were indignant, and beyond the reach of any argument.

The 'Western European' Jews protested to the ghetto dwellers that, 'somewhere along the line, they had been led astray'. They had been told they were going 'to some industrial centre, where each of them would find suitable employment'. Some of them even asked if they could not 'reside in a hotel of some sort'. Losing their bearings, they began to feel 'small and hopeless'.

The Ghetto Chronicle also recalled the arrival of the deportees from Hamburg. They had reached the Lodz ghetto on a Thursday evening, and were housed in a former cinema. On the Friday morning, Rumkowski called on them. 'They were spread out on the floor,' the Chronicle noted, 'sleeping on their bundles, the old people and the women sitting in chairs lining the walls.' That evening they arranged a Friday evening service, to welcome the Sabbath:

Dressed in their best clothes, with many candles lit, they said their first prayer to God with uncanny calm and in a mood of exaltation. Those who had left Judaism a long time before, even those whose fathers had broken any connection with their forefathers, stood there that day, festively attired, in a sort of grave and exalted mood, seeking consolation and salvation in prayer.

When their prayers were concluded, they went out into the lobby, the same words on all their lips: 'Now we see that we are all equal, all sons of the same people, all brothers.' This was either mere flattery or, perhaps, a genuine compliment to the old population – or perhaps a premonition of the not-too-distant future.

The chronicler added, in the retrospect of six months:

Events outpaced time, people changed visibly, at first outwardly, then physically, and finally, if they had not vanished altogether, they moved through the ghetto like ghosts. The turnips and beets they had at first disdained, they now bought at high prices, and the soups they had scorned became the height of their dreams. Once it had been others, but then it was they who prowled the 'city' with a cup or a canteen on a chain to beg a little soup.[5]

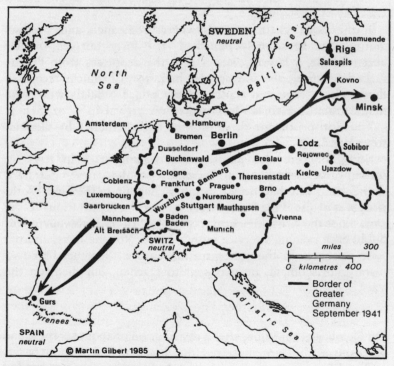

DEPORTATIONS FROM GERMANY

Among the Viennese deported to Lodz that October was Stephan Deutsch, the 'dean of Viennese journalists', who was to die in the ghetto six months later,[6] and Leopold Birkenfeld, a brilliant pianist, who from the moment of his arrival entertained the ghetto-dwellers to his music. Birkenfeld's performances, noted the Ghetto Chronicle for November 1941, 'deserve special mention'; each of his concerts 'is truly a feast for the ghetto's music lovers'. In all, more than thirty musicians, actors, singers and painters had arrived from Vienna, and were to contribute to the ghetto's cultural activities.[7] At a concert on December 3, Birkenfeld 'literally enchanted the audience', as the Ghetto Chronicle recorded, with his 'absolutely marvellous piano performance' of Schubert's *Unfinished Symphony*, Beethoven's *Moonlight Sonata*, Liszt's *Rhapsody No. 2*, and works by Mendelssohn.[8]

In the Lodz ghetto, as elsewhere, resistance and protests continued to be severely punished. The forty-four-year-old Dr Ulrich Schulz, a lawyer, was one of the deportees from Prague to Lodz. During the journey he had, the Chronicle recorded, 'flown into a rage and slandered the police officials who were on the train as escorts'. Imprisoned on arrival in Lodz, Schulz was held in prison for three months and then shot by German policemen.[9]

Non-Jews were also punished for seeking to help Jews: in Berlin, on October 23, a German Catholic priest, Bernhard Lichtenberg, who had been a military chaplain in the First World War, was arrested for his protests against the deportations to the East. Since the Kristallnacht in November 1938, Lichtenberg had closed each evening's service with a prayer 'for the Jews, and the poor prisoners in the concentration camps'. Sentenced to two years' imprisonment, he was sent to Dachau, but died 'on the way'.[10]

On October 24, in Vilna, after a distribution of about six thousand work passes, the Germans seized four thousand Jews without passes and took them to Ponar. In vain had the recently appointed head of the Jewish Council, Jacob Gens, appealed to the Germans for further passes.[11] Thousands of Jews hid in cellars, or in attics, but groups of Lithuanians went from house to house in search of them, often returning several times to the same house.[12] 'We feel like beasts surrounded by hunters,' noted one fifteen-year-old boy, who survived these October raids.[13]

In many of the cellars, Jews resisted the Lithuanian 'hunters', and refused to leave. They were shot dead on the spot.[14] In two days, more than 3,700 Jews were taken to Ponar and murdered, or killed in the cellars. Of those killed, according to the precise German statistics, 885 were children.[15]

To the distress of the Einsatzgruppen, the local population in White Russia, one commander reported, had 'not proposed to take part in any pogroms', a fact which made 'vigorous' action by the Germans themselves all the more imperative. It was experienced repeatedly, according to one Einsatzgruppen report, that 'Jewish women showed an especially obstinate behaviour'. For this reason, the report continued, '28 Jewesses had to be shot in Krugloje and 337 at Mogilev'. In Tatarsk, the Jews had left the ghetto to which they had been deported and had returned to their homes 'attempting', the report noted, 'to expel the Russians who had been quartered there in the meantime'. As a result of this 'act of defiance', all male Jews, as well as three Jewesses, were shot. In nearby Starodub, 'the Jews offered some resistance against the establishment of a ghetto, so all 272 Jews and Jewesses had to be shot'. In Mogilev also, the Einsatzgruppen reported, 'the Jews attempted to sabotage their removal to the ghetto. 113 Jews were liquidated.' This was in addition to four Jews 'shot on account of their refusal to work', and two more shot because they had allegedly ill-treated wounded German soldiers, and 'because they did not wear the prescribed markings'.

In Bobruisk, according to this same Einsatzgruppen report, which was sent to Berlin on October 25, those executed included 'rebellious Jews and persons who had shielded Red Army soldiers or who had acted as spies for the partisans.' Some fifty-two Jews who had fled from Gorodok to Vitebsk, and 'had made the population restive by spreading rumours'. They were given what the report of October 25 described as 'special treatment'.[16]

On October 16 Rumanian and German forces had occupied Odessa, after a two-month siege. Six days later, at 5.35 in the afternoon, an explosion blew up the Rumanian command headquarters in the city. Seventeen Rumanian and four German officers were killed, including General Glogojeanu, head of the Rumanian Occupation Command. 'I have taken steps', telegraphed Glogojeanu's deputy, General Trestioreanu, three hours later, 'to hang Jews and Communists in Odessa squares.'[17] By noon on the following day, October 23, as the reprisals gathered momentum, five thousand civilians had been seized and shot, most of them Jews, of whom at least eighty thousand had been unable to flee before the city was surrounded in August.

The campaign which now ensued against the Jews of Odessa was reported by the Germans who witnessed it. That same morning, October 23, nineteen thousand Jews were assembled into a square near the port, which was surrounded by a wooden fence; they were sprayed with gasoline and burnt alive. In the afternoon, the gendarmerie and the police rounded up over twenty thousand persons in the streets – again, most of them Jews – and squeezed them into the municipal gaol. The next day, October 24, they removed sixteen thousand Jews from the gaol and led them out of the city in long columns, in the direction of Dalnik, a nearby village.

When the first Jews reached Dalnik they were bound to one another's arms in groups of between forty and fifty, thrown into an anti-tank ditch and shot dead. When this method proved too slow, they were pressed into four large warehouses which had holes in the walls. Machine-gun nozzles were pushed into the holes, and in this manner mass murder was committed in one warehouse after another.

The soldiers who carried out the murders were under the command of Lieutenant-Colonel N. Deleanu and Lieutenant-Colonel C. D. Nicolescu. German soldiers also took part in the shooting. For fear that someone might escape nevertheless, three warehouses, which were filled mainly with women and children, were set on fire. Those who were not killed by the flames sought to escape through the holes in the roof, or through the windows; these were met with hand grenades or machine-gun fire. Many women went mad and threw their children out of the windows. The fourth warehouse, which was filled with men, was shelled the next afternoon, October 25, at 5.35, exactly three days after the bombing of command headquarters.

Following the massacres of October 23, 24 and 25, a further ten thousand Jews were deported from Odessa to three concentration camps established near Golta: Bogdanovka, Domanovka and Acmecetca. There, they were murdered two months later, together with tens of thousands of other Jews who had been brought to these camps from northern Transnistria and Bessarabia.[18]

Throughout the autumn of 1941, methods of mass murder were being devised which were intended to be more efficient, and more secret, than the shooting hitherto employed in the East. On October 25, as news of the previous day's slaughter in the streets of Vilna reached Berlin, Alfred Wetzel, an official in the Ministry for the Occupied Eastern Territories, noted that Dr Viktor Brack, a member of Hitler's Chancellery and an expert on euthanasia, had already 'coordinated the supply of instruments and apparatus for killing people through poison gas'. This was to be the new method. Wetzel noted that Brack 'is ready to collaborate in the installation of the necessary buildings and gas plants'. He was willing to send his own chemist, Kallmeyer, to Riga.

Wetzel added that Eichmann 'is in agreement with this procedure'. Eichmann had already informed the ministry, Wetzel noted, 'that the camps are intended for Riga and Minsk, where even Jews from the Old Reich may be sent'. To judge from the 'actual situation', Wetzel added, 'one need have no scruple in using Brack's method to liquidate Jews who are unsuitable for work'. In this way, it would be possible to avoid 'incidents' such as occurred 'during the shootings at Vilna – and these shootings were public, according to the report that I have before me'. Such public shootings 'will no longer be possible or tolerated'.[19]

In the western Polish town of Kalisz, the Jewish community was informed by the Germans on October 26 that, in order 'to reduce the danger of epidemics to a minimum', patients in the Jewish old people's home were to be transferred to convalescent homes in another town at ten in the morning on the following day. The patients were to be 'washed and dressed in fresh underwear'. Nothing else need be done for them, 'even bedding was unnecessary as everything had now been prepared'.

Jewish mechanics, returning to their homes in the ghetto later that day from their work at Gestapo headquarters, reported that 'a large number of strange Gestapo men had arrived with a mysterious large black lorry that was closed on every side and had no ventilation holes at all'.

Many inside the ghetto linked these facts with the order to evacuate the old people's home. As one of those persons later recalled: 'There were still many optimists, hoping for the best, but the majority were ill at ease and apprehensive.'

On the morning of October 27, precisely at ten in the morning, a large black lorry similar to the one described by the mechanics drove up in front of the old people's home. 'Its roof was as high as the first storey,' an eye-witness later recalled, adding that it looked 'like a great black coffin'. With the lorry came two shiny black cars filled with uniformed and unfamiliar Gestapo men. The eye-witness, Dr Gross, continued:

> We had to fetch out those who were called by name, for they were mostly chronic patients and cripples. The Germans ordered us to carry them, seat the patients or stretch them on the benches within the lorry.
>
> 'When you come down the steps, be careful nothing happens to the patient!' 'Take it easy, we're not in a hurry.' 'Please put the man down here in the corner till he feels better!' Meanwhile they saw to it that we should fill up the cold lorry. But they would not permit the younger folk to join their departing relatives.
>
> The metal doors were banged to, the heavy bars were dropped in place, the large lorry set off silently but swiftly, followed by the gleaming cars. Next day, October 28, two more trips were made and about one hundred and ten persons were removed. Everything was done swiftly, in order not to spoil the weekend. They must have grown tired of putting on a show and stopped being polite, calming the weepers with their whips and shooting at anybody who looked out of the windows. The only ones who did not feel the general apprehension and bitterness were the lucky insane.
>
> The two last groups left on Monday, 30 October, and included a few hospital patients. The chair of one of the old women was brought back on one of the trips. The Gestapo man who brought it explained, 'She doesn't need it any longer because she's received a new one.' That day the Council of Elders was required to pay the cost of transport at the rate of

four Reichsmarks a person, and to arrange all matters connected with the departure of 290 persons at the Economic Office.

In the days that followed, the Jewish community pressed the Germans for news of where the old and sick had been taken. 'At the moment they're in transit camps,' they were told by the Gestapo, 'and from there they'll be sent to the permanent convalescent homes. As we don't know in advance who's being sent where, you'll have to be patient for a few days, until everything is in order.'

Repeated enquiries could not locate those who had been deported. Then the Jewish community were informed that 'a few of the old people had died of heart failure, brain fever or pneumonia'. The rest of the deportees were said to be in a town called Padernice, 'and were in good health'. But, as Dr Gross later recalled, 'No map showed where Padernice might be, because it did not exist.' Dr Gross continued:

> Little by little we understood that we would never see the dead again, unless we followed in their footsteps. We lived in a state of constant dread, for we could see the sword hanging over our own heads and knew that we would go the same way sooner or later. The Germans were exploiting our working power, but would clearly exterminate us too. The hermetically sealed gas-wagons which were first tried out on our folk were about to commence the great action of 'purifying' Europe of the Jews, which was afterwards perfected in the large extermination camps.

The old people, who had been choked by exhaust fumes piped back into the lorry through a specially designed tube, had been taken to the neighbouring forest and buried or burnt. It was rumoured that they had been buried near Winiary. 'Nobody knew precisely,' Dr Gross later recalled, 'because the roads had been strictly blocked on that day, but it was clear that the action had taken place near Kalisz, for the lorries returned within three hours.'[20]

A new policy was emerging: to deport, and to gas, and to do so unobserved by passers-by or curious soldiers: to take the killings off the streets and away from the environs of the towns and cities. It was to take several months before this policy could be put into effect. But with the German army at the gates of Moscow, British forces on the defensive in Egypt, and the United States still neutral, the Germans had time enough. Meanwhile, further evidence of the unsatisfactory nature of visible execution reached Berlin in the form of a letter of protest from the Commissioner of the Territory of Slutsk, who reported, first by telephone and then by letter, the statements of German troops in Slutsk during a round-up on October 27. Jews and White Russians had been 'beaten with clubs and rifle butts' in the streets; rings were pulled off fingers 'in the most brutal manner'; and in different streets were 'the corpses of Jews who had been shot'. The action, he added, 'bordered already on sadism', the town itself being 'a picture of horror'.

The recipient of this letter, Wilhelm Kube, the Commissioner General of White Russia, sent this letter on to Berlin, to the Reich Minister for the Occupied Eastern Territories, Alfred Rosenberg. 'Peace and order cannot be maintained in White Russia with methods of that sort,' Kube wrote. And he added: 'To have buried alive seriously wounded people, who then worked their way out of their graves again, is such extreme beastliness that this incident as such must be reported to the Führer and the Reich Marshal.'[21]

The evolving plans for murder by gas would ensure that most future killings would be done behind a mask of secrecy, by methods which far fewer people would have to see, and in circumstances which would reduce to a minimum the chance of disgust or discovery. In anticipation of the new method, individual Jews were now refused permission to emigrate, even within regions under German influence. In refusing an application from a Jewish woman, Lily Satzkis, to move from Nazi Germany to Vichy France, Adolf Eichmann noted on October 28: 'in view of the approaching final solution of the European Jewry problem, one has to prevent the immigration of Jews into the unoccupied area of France.[22]

Meanwhile, the shootings in the East continued, despite the advancing plans for a less public method. At each 'selection' in the Eastern ghettos, as in Kovno, the Germans had imposed a system of work permits, whereby those who had a permit were exempt, together with their families, from the selection. As an added cruelty, the German authorities in each ghetto imposed upon the Jews themselves, through the Jewish Councils, the burden of saying who should receive the work permits and who should not.

One such incident took place in Kovno on October 26. On that day, when the Chairman of the Jewish Council was ordered to post a notice in the streets of the ghetto that two days later, October 28, all the inhabitants of the ghetto – men, women and children, including the aged and sick – were to gather in the Democracy Square, and that no Jew might remain at home at that time. Such work permits as existed were to be given out by the Council itself.

The head of the Council, Dr Elkes, immediately sent four people to the home of the Kovno rabbi, Rav Avrohom Dov Ber Kahana-Shapira, to ask whether they must obey the German order or not; how could the Council give out the passes, thus giving life to a few, but condemning many others to death?

It was late at night when the four emissaries came to the rabbi's house. The rabbi, seriously ailing, was already asleep. Despite this, his wife woke him and told him about the delegation. Upon hearing the gravity of the new decree, he began to tremble in anguish and almost passed out.

Recognizing the responsibility that lay upon him, Rabbi Shapira told the delegation that Jewish history was 'long and bloody and replete with such evil decrees'. Nevertheless he could not rule on the matter immediately. He needed time. That night he did not return to his bed, but searched through volumes dealing with the relevant aspects of Jewish law. After lengthy deliberation, he ruled as follows: 'If a decree is issued that a Jewish community be destroyed and a possibility exists to save some part of this community, the leaders of the community are obligated to gird themselves with the courage necessary to act with the fullest sense of the responsibility that lies upon them and to take every possible measure to save as many as can be saved.'

This meant that the Council should give out the work permits. Though many without these permits would die, the head of the Council had 'to take courage', the rabbi asserted, and distribute them in such a way as to save as many lives as possible: giving them, where possible, to those with the largest families, all the members of which would thus be exempted from the deportation.[23]

The round-up in Kovno took place on October 28. Dr Aharon Peretz, who was present in Democracy Square that morning, later recalled the events of the day:

. . . at six in the morning it was still dark. But from all alleys, from the ghetto, you could see people pouring to the place destined for them to gather. Mothers with prams, pushing children. There was snow falling. And they all gathered in that square – twenty-seven thousand people.

The Council was told that they want to select the working people to increase their rations. And the second part, those who do not work will be sent somewhere else, and will be given other food rations. After the previous actions, we did not believe. But it is the nature of a human being always to believe that he will remain alive, he will be spared. Some twenty-seven thousand people gathered, not knowing their fate.

All of a sudden a truck arrived and an SS man, Rauca, jumped off. In the ghetto he was known. He mounted a small hill, he was a tall man, he looked like a racehorse – and started to pass the Jews for inspection. We did not know what the game meant. But the place, the centre where he stood – we started grasping the game. He would separate with the movement of his finger – right or left. To the left, we saw the healthier, the younger, less the children. They were accompanied by Jewish policemen.

To the other side, there were people with many children, the older, in rags, tired, and so on. And when we realized that they were received by Germans and Lithuanians, beaten up and treated entirely differently, we understood that this was the side of death, and the other was the side for those to live. This was the power of this regime and rule. They would divide the people. And in this way, also break their resistance. Because everybody hoped to live.[24]

Rauca continued all day with the selection, clutching a leather whip with metal tips, drinking coffee, and munching sandwiches, his dog at his feet. One by one, as people stepped forward, his voice could be heard calling, 'You left, you right.' For Rauca, recalled Leon Bauminger, 'Right was death and left was life.' When Bauminger's turn came, Rauca stared, 'for what seemed like an eternity', at the blond hair of the twenty-eight-year-old Cracovian, then waved him to the left.[25]

No one who was sent to the left, to life, and who survived the torments of the next three and a half years, has forgotten that moment. Vera Elyashiv, then eleven years old, reached Democracy Square with her father and her grandparents as SS men, 'cursing, abusing and hitting about with the butts of their rifles', sorted the thousands of Jews into long narrow columns. 'Then a terrible and incomprehensible thing happened,' she later wrote. 'Grandfather and grandmother were thrown to the right and father and I to the left. Of all the terrible moments that were to follow, this was one of the worst for me. I don't think I'll ever forget their big helpless eyes. They kept turning to us with outstretched arms and their lips were moving but no words came out.'

Vera Elyashiv's account continued:

> Two Gestapo officers pushed them brutally away. Only when I saw them joining the other separated group I started to cry. Father told me not to move and he ran to the officer. He returned after a few minutes, his face bleeding. I shut my eyes and let myself be dragged on by him. The first snow started to come down. Large wet flakes covered our shoulders, heads and faces.
>
> That day ten thousand people were taken away by the SS.
>
> We, the remaining, were kept in the square until the evening. When eventually the orders were given to leave, many dead bodies remained behind on the snowy ground.
>
> Father and I returned 'home' to the tiny flatlet we had in the poor Jewish quarter of Kovno, which had become the ghetto. All the cupboards and drawers were open and turned out. Father undressed me and put me to bed – he didn't talk to me that night. I slept in grandmother's bed. There was no need any more to sleep two in a bed. I squeezed grandmother's pillow in my arms and cried myself into sleep.[26]

Those Kovno Jews who were sent by Rauca to the right could still not believe that they had really been marked out for death. 'That morning in Democracy Square,' a Lithuanian doctor, Helen Kutorgene, noted in her diary, 'nobody suspected that a bitter fate awaited them. They thought that they were being moved to other apartments.'[27] They were indeed taken, not to the Ninth Fort, but to the houses of the small ghetto. On the night of October 29, Dr Peretz has recalled, everyone sent to the small ghetto 'was trying to find a better place, there was better order, because they thought they would stay there'.[28] Then, at four in the morning, all those in the small ghetto were ordered to assemble again. It was still dark. But with the dawn a rumour began, that prisoners had been digging 'deep ditches' at the Ninth Fort, and by the time those who had been sent to the small ghetto were led away towards the fort, Helen Kutorgene noted in her diary, 'it was already clear to everybody that this was death'.

Dr Kutorgene added that once the Jews whom Rauca had sent to the right realized where they were being sent:

> They broke out crying, wailed, screamed. Some tried to escape on the way there but they were shot dead. Many bodies remained in the fields. At the fort the condemned were stripped of their clothes, and in groups of three hundred they were forced into the ditches. First they threw in the children. The women were shot at the edge of the ditch, after that it was the turn of the men. Many were covered while they were still alive. All the men doing the shooting were drunk. I was told all this by an acquaintance who heard it from a German soldier, an eye-witness, who wrote to his Catholic wife: 'Yesterday I became convinced that there is no God. If there were, He would not allow such things to happen.'[29]

The massacre had been carried out by German SS men and Lithuanian police. On return from the killing, one of the Lithuanians 'boasted' – as a Jew, Alter Galperin later recalled – 'that he had dragged small Jewish children by the hair, stabbing them with the edge of his bayonet, and throwing them half alive into pits'. The smallest children 'he just threw into the pit alive, because to kill all of them first is too much work'.[30]

One of the few survivors was a twelve-year-old boy. It was only when he managed to return to the main ghetto on October 30 that those in the ghetto realized the full horror. Avraham Golub, an assistant in the Jewish Council, later recalled how the boy, 'covered in dirt and smeared with blood', stumbled into the Council office. Golub's account continued:

> . . . he reported how everyone was forced to strip and made to march in groups of one hundred to the edge of freshly dug pits. The guards fired on each group as they stepped forward.

Some were only wounded but they too fell into the deep pits and were covered with a layer of earth.

The boy was with his mother, was covered by her, and so was not hit [by bullets]. The boy and his mother were destined to be the second layer of bodies from the top of the grave.

His mother had embraced him and covered him. She bent forward and fell into the pit with him, so that he was not suffocated by the layer of earth poured on top.

When it was dark, the boy slowly moved to the edge of the pit. With great effort he pushed away the bodies around him and crawled out.

There he was able to see that the earth which covered the pit was moving, meaning that many others were still alive in the pit but were unable to save themselves.

Under darkness he escaped back to the ghetto and was later smuggled out. No one knows if he is alive today.[31]

A few women also managed to survive the massacre. 'Some tried to escape from the transport,' Aharon Peretz later recalled. 'I was asked to go to a neighbouring house, where there were women with dum-dum bullets in their bodies.'[32]

The number of those murdered was recorded, once again, in the precise statistics of the Einsatzkommando: '2,007 Jewish men, 2,920 Jewish women, 4,273 Jewish children.' There was the added comment, 'cleaning the ghetto of superfluous Jews'. Of the total death toll of 9,200, nearly half were children.[33]

An SS officer, Captain Jordan, now promised the Jewish Council that the killing was over. 'You have nothing to be afraid of in the future; you will work and live; you will work for the German army, and we will take care of you!' With that, Dr Zalman Grinberg recalled, 'he throws 10,000 marks on the table and states that this was the first payment to the ghetto for the work they will do.' Nobody trusts the German promise. 'However,' Grinberg noted, 'the coming months and years proved him to be true. Life in the ghetto became hard, everyone being forced to fulfil extreme physical labour.'[34] Kovno had become a 'working ghetto'.

Kovno Jews began to work in the German shops and factories. In Vilna, the same prospect was in store, but not before one final

228 · THE HOLOCAUST   1941

'action', as the Germans described it. This particular 'action' began on November 3, and lasted for three days, during which more than a thousand Jews were killed. When the 'action' was over, a group of rabbis told the head of the Jewish Council, Jacob Gens, that he had no right to select Jews and hand them over to the Germans. Gens answered that by surrendering the few, he was rescuing the others from extinction. The rabbis replied, however, with a ruling of Maimonides, 'Better be all killed than one soul of Israel be surrendered.'[35]

Following the November killings, there were twelve thousand Jews in Vilna with valid work passes, and at least three thousand in hiding. Searches for those without passes continued until the end of the year, and those caught were killed at Ponar. But Vilna, like Kovno before it, had now become a 'working ghetto'. 'Days began which we called days of civilization,' Meir Dvorjetzky later recalled. 'The large actions stopped.'[36] As soon as they stopped, the Jews found help in an unexpected quarter: a German army sergeant, Anton Schmidt, who helped to smuggle Jews out of Vilna in military trucks. These Jews went to Bialystok, just inside the border of the Greater Germany, believing that this would enable them to escape destruction. Schmidt, who was from Austria, was later caught, and executed.[37]

Gens in Vilna, Dr Elkes in Kovno, and Ghetto Elders in a hundred scattered towns and villages throughout the Eastern Territories, sought, in their different ways, to preserve, amid the slaughter, the precarious balance between work and death. Each had to decide how best to serve the needs of his community. At Kleck, on October 31, two members of the Jewish Council, Elisser and Lipe Mishelevski, had been shot together with two hundred other Jews: the 'crime' of these Council members was to have tried to make contact with non-Jews outside the ghetto, in an attempt to obtain more food for the ghetto.[38] In Minsk, the Chairman of the Jewish Council, Eliyahu Myshkin, was active in helping hundreds of young Jews to escape to the forest. He was killed during an 'action' in Minsk on November 7, when twelve thousand Jews were slaughtered in pits outside the city.

The heads of several of the Jewish Council departments in Minsk – Rudicer of the economic section, Dulski of the housing section, Goldin of the workshop section, and Serebianski, the police commander – had all cooperated with resistance groups, providing clothing, shoes, hiding places and false documents. Serebianski went so far as to hire members of the resistance into the ghetto police. Also active in helping the resistance in Minsk were two of the secretaries in the labour department, Mira Strogin and Sara Levin.[39]

The massacre at Minsk on November 7 was followed within three days by the arrival in the city of the first German Jews, one thousand who had been deported from Hamburg. 'They felt themselves as pioneers who were brought to settle the East,' one eyewitness later recalled.[40] The deportees from Hamburg were followed within days by more than six thousand deportees from Frankfurt, Bremen, and the Rhineland. On November 18 a train arrived from Berlin. The twenty-two-year-old Haim Berendt was among the deportees from Berlin. On reaching Minsk, he later recalled, 'the carriages were opened and they started beating us up, driving us out of the carriages in a hurry and, within a moment, there was complete chaos. He who succeeded in getting out of the door was beaten up. Women, children and men.'

The Berlin deportees were taken beyond the ghetto of Minsk Jews to a special ghetto for the Jews of Germany, known as 'Ghetto Hamburg'. There, they became a part of the Jewish labour force in Minsk.[41]

German Jews were also deported to Riga and Kovno. On November 27 the first of nineteen trains left the Reich for Riga: it came from Berlin. Even as this train was on its way from Berlin, the Riga ghetto was the object of a massive raid, during which 10,600 Jews were seized, taken to pits in the nearby Rumbuli forest, and shot. When the train from Berlin arrived a few days later, most of the thousand German Jews were likewise taken out to Rumbuli, and killed.[42] Then, in a second, three-day raid on the Riga ghetto, from December 7 to December 9, a further twenty-five thousand Riga Jews were killed, among them the eighty-one-year-old doyen of Jewish historians, Simon Dubnov.

According to one account, Dubnov was murdered by a Gestapo officer who had formerly been one of his pupils.[43] Another account tells of how, sick and with a fever, with enfeebled legs, he could not move quickly enough out of the ghetto, and was shot in the back by a Latvian guard. According to this account, Dubnov's last words, as he fell, were, 'Schreibt un farschreibt!', 'Write and record!'[44] This exhortation in Yiddish was typical of Dubnov, the lover of historical record, and the firm believer in the Yiddish culture of Eastern European Jewry, a culture which was being swept away.

With this second Rumbuli massacre, eighty per cent of Riga Jewry had been murdered. The few survivors were put into a forced labour camp, 'the little ghetto', the women being imprisoned separately from the men.[45] The Riga ghetto was ready for any further deportees from Germany.

The subsequent deportees from Germany, beginning with 714 who left Nuremberg on November 29, and 1,200 sent from Stuttgart on December 1, were sent to labour camps, or to the Riga ghetto: in all, seventeen thousand more Jews were to reach Riga, and forced labour, that winter.[46]

A further fifteen thousand German Jews were sent to Kovno, principally from Berlin, Munich, Vienna, Breslau and Frankfurt. An eye-witness in Kovno, Dr Aharon Peretz, later recalled how, as the deportees were being led along the road which went past the ghetto, towards the Ninth Fort, they could be heard asking the guards, 'Is the camp still far?' They had been told they were being sent to a work camp. But, Peretz added, 'We know where that road led. It led to the Ninth Fort, to the prepared pits.' But first, the Jews from Germany were kept for three days in underground cellars, with ice-covered walls, and without food or drink.[47] Only then, frozen and starving, were they ordered to undress, taken to the pits, and shot.

In the suitcases of the murdered deportees were later found printed announcements, uring them to prepare for a difficult winter. For this reason, some had brought little heating stoves with them. Later, the Jews inside the Kovno ghetto heard of the resistance of these German Jews when they reached the Ninth Fort. 'They did not want to undress,' Peretz explained, 'and they struggled against the Germans.'[48] But it was a hopeless struggle and the killing of these deportees was recorded by the Einsatzkommando with its accustomed precision: on November 25, 1,159 Jews, 1,600 Jewesses and 175 Jewish children, 'settlers from Berlin, Munich and Frankfurt-on-Main'; and four days later, 693 Jewish men, 1,155 Jewesses and 152 Jewish children, 'settlers from Vienna and Breslau'.[49]

Amid this slaughter, a Lithuanian, Dr Petras Baublis, the head of the Infants' House in Kovno, risked his own life and the safety of his family by offering to smuggle Jewish children out of the ghetto and to hide them in his Infants' House. To ensure their safety, Dr Baublis, who had a number of close friends among the Lithuanian Catholic priesthood, obtained blank birth certificate forms, which the priests then agreed to authenticate with church seals and signatures, stating that this was a Christian child.

Among the Jewish children saved by Baublis was the two-year-old Ariela Abramovich, whose father later testified that he knew of at least another seven children similarly saved. Another Jewish child, Gitele Mylner, who had been born only a few months before the massacre, was also handed to Baublis by her parents: he gave her the name Berute Iovayshayte, and a certificate stamped by the church authorities stating that she was a Christian child.[50]

No Jewish community, however small, no Jewish family, however remote, was safe from the questing killers. In a small village east of Chernigov, only one Jewish couple lived. Yakov Gorodetsky and his wife Dvoira were peasants. Forty-three years later their grandson, also Yakov, spoke of how his grandparents, remembering as they did the German occupation of the Ukraine in 1918, could not envisage in 1941 the barbarism that was about to be unleashed. Fortunately, their three sons were in safer regions when invasion came.

In June 1941 Dvoira Gorodetsky was fifty-nine years old, her husband Yakov, sixty-two. Both were murdered on October 30. All three of their sons fought in the Red Army, and survived the war.[51]

Throughout the late autumn and early winter of 1941, details had filtered through to the West of many eastern executions. On November 14, in a message to the *Jewish Chronicle* on its centenary, Winston Churchill gave public recognition to the Jewish suffering. 'None has suffered more cruelly than the Jew', he wrote, 'the unspeakable evils wrought on the bodies and spirits of men by Hitler and his vile regime. The Jew bore the brunt of the Nazis' first onslaught upon the citadels of freedom and human dignity. He has borne and continues to bear a burden that might have seemed to be beyond endurance. He has not allowed it to break his spirit: he has never lost the will to resist.'

Churchill's message continued: 'Assuredly in the day of victory the Jews' sufferings and his part in the struggle will not be forgotten. Once again, at the appointed time, he will see vindicated those principles of righteousness which it was the glory of his fathers to proclaim to the world. Once again it will be shown that, though the mills of God grind slowly, yet they grind exceedingly small.'[52]

Inside the Warsaw ghetto, the deaths from starvation were accelerated by the winter cold. 'The most fearful sight is that of freezing children,' Ringelblum noted in mid-November. 'Little children with bare feet, bare knees and torn clothing stand dumbly in the street weeping. Tonight, the 14th, I heard a tot of three or four yammering. The child will probably be found frozen to death tomorrow morning, a few hours off.' Six weeks earlier, Ringelblum recalled, when the first snow had fallen, some seventy children were found frozen to death on the steps of ruined houses.'[53]

On the morning of November 17, Warsaw Jewry was shocked to learn of the death sentence carried out on eight Warsaw Jews, for leaving the ghetto 'without permission'. Six of those sentences were women. All had been caught after crossing into Aryan Warsaw in search of food. 'One of the victims,' Chaim Kaplan noted in his diary, 'a young girl not quite eighteen, asked the Jewish policeman who was present at the execution to tell her family that she had been sent to a concentration camp and would not be seeing them for some time. Another young girl cried out to God imploring Him to accept her as the expiatory sacrifice for her people and to let her be the final victim.'

Kaplan noted that it was the Jewish police who had been ordered to tie the hands and cover the eyes of those about to be executed. The two men among them refused, however, to be bound or blindfolded. Their wish was granted. 'The execution squad', Kaplan wrote, 'was composed of Polish policemen. After carrying out their orders, they wept bitterly.'[54]

'All past experience', Ringelblum noted, 'pales in the face of the fact that eight people were shot to death for crossing the threshold of the ghetto.' The execution 'has set all Warsaw trembling'. A few

SS officers had attended, 'calmly smoking cigarettes and behaving cynically all through the execution'. Three members of the Jewish police were also present; one of them, Jakub Lejkin, was said to have 'distinguished himself with his zeal in dragging the condemned from their cells'.

One of the six executed women was a beggar, another was a woman with three children. 'It is said', Ringelblum added, 'that the prisoners bore themselves calmly.'[55]

The deaths from cold continued: 'In the streets', Mary Berg noted on November 22, 'frozen human corpses are an increasingly frequent sight'. Sometimes a mother 'cuddles a child frozen to death, and tries to warm the inanimate little body. Sometimes a child huddles against his mother, thinking that she is asleep and trying to awaken her, while, in fact, she is dead'.[56]

Inside the Warsaw ghetto, news of a horrific kind arrived during November. Hearing it, the Chairman of the Jewish Council, Adam Czerniakow, summoned the leading members of the underground to hear the messenger. His name was Heniek Grabowski. 'I came to Czerniakow,' Zivia Lubetkin later recalled. 'It was in the evening, there was no electricity, and Heniek told his story.' Grabowski had been sent by the Jews of Warsaw to Vilna, and he had returned.

The story Grabowski told was about Ponar. 'For the first time,' Zivia Lubetkin recalled, 'we heard that Jews of Vilna are being deported by the thousands and tens of thousands, and being killed, children and women.'[57]

Yitzhak Zuckerman had also been summoned to hear Grabowski's report. 'I am from Vilna myself,' he later recalled. 'I was born in Vilna. In Vilna I left behind all my parents and relatives. And here he brought this tragic news from Vilna. While still a child, I had played among the trees in Ponar, and here he spoke about Ponar. My Vilna, the Jews of Vilna, were being killed in Ponar, my playground.'

Zuckerman and his friends realized at once the truth of Grabowski's report. They realized also that it was now a question of the 'total destruction' of the Jews of Europe.[58]

Forty miles north-east of Warsaw, a labour camp had been set up in the gravel pits near the tiny rural station of Treblinka. The Jewish and Polish prisoners living there were employed loading slag, cleaning drains and levelling the ground in and around the engine sheds at Malkinia junction, on the main Warsaw–Bialystok line. Later, they were put to work repairing and strengthening the embankment along the River Bug. The staff of the camp consisted of twenty SS men and a hundred Ukrainians. The commandant was Captain Theo von Euppen. Franciszek Zabecki, a Polish railway worker at Treblinka station, later recalled that von Euppen was 'a sadist who ill-treated the Poles and Jews working there, particularly the Jews, taking shots at them as if they were partridges'.[59]

The Eastern murders continued throughout November 1941. At Liepaja, however, all such shootings had been forbidden by direct orders of the Reich Commissar for the 'Ostland' region of the Baltic, Hinrich Lohse. Asked by his superiors in Berlin to explain why he had halted the executions, Lohse replied on November 15 that 'the manner in which they were performed could not be justified'. Not moral, but economic reasons, were his complaint: the destruction of much manpower that could be of use to the war economy. Was it intended, Lohse asked, that Jews were to be killed, 'irrespective of age, sex or economic factors'.[60]

A month later Lohse was informed, by the Ministry of Occupied Eastern Territories, that 'as a matter of principle, no economic factors are to be taken into consideration in the solution of the Jewish question'.[61] Only a fragment of Eastern Jewry had been kept alive for work purposes. On December 1, the chief of Einsatzkommando 3, SS Colonel Karl Jaeger, reported to Berlin that only fifteen per cent of Lithuanian Jewry remained alive. All of them, he explained, were *Arbeitsjuden*, working Jews. 'Today', Jaeger added, 'I can confirm that Einsatzkommando 3 has reached the goal of solving the Jewish problem in Lithuania.' The only 'remaining' Jews were labourers and their families: about four and a half thousand in Siauliai, fifteen thousand in Kovno and fifteen thousand in Vilna.

In his report of 1 December 1941, Jaeger set out what he called the 'Organizational problem' which had confronted his Einsatzkommando, a problem which had only been surmounted because SS First Lieutenant Hamann 'shared my views in full' and knew how to 'cooperate' with the Lithuanians. As Jaeger explained:

The decision to free each district of Jews necessitated thorough preparation of each action as well as acquisition of information about local conditions. The Jews had to be collected in one or more towns and a ditch had to be dug at the right site for the right number. The marching distance from collecting points to the ditches averaged about three miles. The Jews were brought in groups of five hundred, separated by at least 1.2 miles, to the place of execution. The sort of difficulties and nerve-scraping work involved in all this is shown by an arbitrarily chosen example:

In Rokiskis 3,208 people had to be transported three miles before they could be liquidated. To manage this job in a twenty-four-hour period, more than sixty of the eighty available Lithuanian partisans had to be detailed to the cordon. The Lithuanians who were left were frequently being relieved while doing the work together with my men.

Vehicles are seldom available. Escapes, which were attempted here and there, were frustrated solely by my men at the risk of their lives. For example, three men of the Commando at Mariampole shot thirty-eight escaping Jews and Communist functionaries on a path in the woods, so that no one got away. Distances to and from actions were never less than 90–120 miles. Only careful planning enabled the Commando to carry out up to five actions a week and at the same time continue the work in Kovno without interruption.

In Kovno itself, Jaeger reported, 'trained' Lithuanians were available 'in sufficient number'. As a result, the city was, as he expressed it, 'comparatively speaking a shooting paradise'.

Jaeger added that in his view 'the male work-Jews should be sterilized immediately to prevent any procreation'. A Jewess who, 'nevertheless', was pregnant 'is to be liquidated'.[62]

In Lithuania, Einsatzkommando 3 had succeeded, as Jaeger phrased it in his report of December 1, in 'solving the Jewish problem'. In the other eastern regions – in White Russia, the Volhynia and the Ukraine – that same solution continued to be the policy of the other Einsatzkommando units, inhibited only momentarily in December when the extreme cold made the ground too hard in many places to dig death pits in.[63] But no such inhibition prevented the 'action' in Nowogrodek which began on December 5, when seven thousand Jews were collected in the yard of the municipal courthouse. 'It was already very, very cold,' Idel Kagan later recalled, of the weather in a region which had long been known as 'the Polish Siberia'.

Throughout December 5, the seven thousand Jews of Nowogrodek were kept in the yard. In the evening, they were taken into the courthouse building. So crowded were they, that most had to remain standing all night. In the morning, the courthouse gates were opened, and German officers came in. They then proceeded to ask each Jew his profession, and how many children he had. On hearing the answer, the German indicated either to the right, or to the left.

No logic dictated who went in which direction. Moshe Kagan was a saddlemaker, and had two children: they were sent to the left. Moshe's brother Yankel, who was also a saddlemaker with two children, was sent to the right. 'And so', Idel Kagan later recalled, 'my father went to life, my uncle to death.'

Of the seven thousand Jews assembled, five thousand were taken away. The Jewish Council members were also sent to the left. 'The Germans didn't need any cooperation from anybody,' Idel Kagan reflected, and he added: 'We did not have any idea what happened to the five thousand. When people said, "They have been killed," we answered, "They took them away to work. Why should they kill them?" But they had been taken to Skridlewe, three miles away, and shot in the ravine. There were no survivors.'

The Jews who had been sent to the right were taken out of Nowogrodek to the tiny suburb of Pereshike, whose twenty-two houses had now to accommodate two thousand people. First, the Germans drove out the Polish and White Russian inhabitants of the houses. Then they built a fence around the area. More than eighteen Jewish families were forced into each room, and two labour groups created, one skilled and one unskilled. The skilled were put in workshops where they made gloves, boots and other items of clothing for the German army.[64]

In the General Government of Poland, and in Western Europe, it was not the massacres in a nearby ravine, as at Nowogrodek, but deportation to distant sites, as far as a thousand miles away, that was emerging as the plan: with gassing, not shooting, as the method of death.

The authorities in Berlin had begun the process needed to implement this 'final solution'. On November 19, when the German Foreign Ministry raised with Eichmann the request of Flora Bucher to leave Germany, in order to join her mother at Gurs camp in the French Pyrenees, Eichmann replied, as he had done in a similar case three weeks earlier, using the same words as before: 'In view of the forthcoming final solution of the problem of European Jewry, one

THE NOWOGRODEK REGION

has to prevent the immigration of this Jewess into the unoccupied zone of France.'[65]

On November 24, five days after Eichmann wrote this letter, a ghetto was set up in the eighteenth-century fortress of the Bohemian town of Theresienstadt, to which Jews were to be sent from throughout the Old Reich, and in particular from Vienna, Prague and Berlin. Uprooted from their homes, penniless, deprived of their belongings, ill-fed, overcrowded, thirty-two thousand were to die there of hunger and disease.[66] Many of the deportees to Theresienstadt were to be old people. But that November morning it was 342 young men who were brought, from Prague, to work at a construction camp, preparing Theresienstadt for its new occupants.[67]

The first deportees reached Theresienstadt on November 30, from Prague. They consisted mostly of women, children and old people. A second train arrived on December 2, from Brno.[68]

Neither deportation to the eastern ghettos nor deportation to Theresienstadt was the 'final solution'. That was still being prepared, brought one step nearer that October, at Buchenwald, when twelve hundred Jews had been medically examined by Dr Fritz Mennecke, a euthanasia expert, and then subjected to 'Action 14 f 13' in a clinic at Bernburg, one hundred miles away.[69] 'Action 14 f 13' was death by gassing: a method in use since 1939 in the mass murder of tens of thousands of mentally defective Germans in more than a dozen special institutions.

The origin of the euthanasia killings of 1939, as of these subsequent killings, was an order issued by Hitler, backdated to 1 September 1939, the day of the German invasion of Poland. In this order, Hitler empowered the chief of his Chancellery, as well as his own personal physician, 'to widen the authority of individual doctors with a view to enabling them, after the most critical examination, in the realm of human knowledge, to administer incurably sick persons to a mercy death'.[70] The qualifying phrases had quickly been abandoned. In Germany, the chief of the Criminal Police Office in Stuttgart, Christian Wirth, an expert in tracking down criminals – took charge of the technical side of a more 'humane' method of killing, constructing gas-chambers in which the victim was exposed to carbon monoxide gas, 'a device', one SS officer later explained, 'which overwhelmed its victims without their apprehension and which caused them no pain'.[71]

Between January 1940 and August 1941, more than seventy thousand Germans had been killed by gas in five separate euthanasia institutions, by what was called *sonderbehandlung*, 'special treatment'. The principal victims were the chronically sick, gypsies, people judged 'unworthy of life' because of mental disorders, and, after June 1941, Soviet prisoners-of-war.

On 3 September 1941, at Auschwitz Main Camp, hitherto used principally for the imprisonment and torture of Polish opponents of Nazism, an experiment had been carried out against six hundred Soviet prisoners-of-war, and three hundred Jews, brought specially to the camp. There, in the cellar of Block II, a gas called Cyclon B, prussic acid initially in crystal form, was used to murder the chosen victims. The experiment was judged a success.[72]

At Buchenwald, Dr Mennecke had continued with his own experiments. 'Our second batch', he wrote to his wife Mathilde on November 25 from the Zum Elefant hotel in nearby Weimar, 'consisted of 1,200 Jews who do not have to be "examined"; for them it was enough to pull from their files the reasons for their arrest and write them down on the questionnaires.'[73]

Five days after Dr Mennecke's second experimental selection at Buchenwald, Reinhard Heydrich decided that, considering 'the enormous importance which had to be given to these questions', and in the interest 'of achieving the same point of view by the central agencies concerned with the remaining work connected with the final solution', that a 'joint conversation' should be held by all concerned. Such a discussion was especially needed, he wrote on November 29, 'since Jews have been undergoing evacuation in continuous transports from the Reich territory, including Bohemia and Moravia, to the East, since 15 October 1941'.[74]

Heydrich's conference was called for 2 January 1942. Before it met, one further experiment was to be tried, near the remote Polish village of Chelmno. There, on the evening of 7 December 1941, seven hundred Jews arrived in lorries. They had come from the nearby town of Kolo, having been told that they were being taken to a railway station at Barlogi, ten kilometres from Kolo, and thence to work in 'the East'.

Michael Podklebnik, one of the Jews assembled by the SS at the Jewish Council building in Kolo, but himself registered as a resident of nearby Bugaj, later recalled how 'I brought to the lorry my own father, my mother, sister with five children, my brother and his wife and three children. I volunteered to go with them, but was not allowed.' Podklebnik also saw how a Jew by the name of Goldberg, the owner of a saw-mill, 'approached the Germans with a request to be appointed manager of a Jewish camp in the East. His application was accepted and he was promised the requested position.[75]

It was not to Barlogi railway station, however, but to a small villa known as the 'Palace' or the 'Mansion', on the road to Chelmno, that the seven hundred Kolo deportees were brought; and kept there overnight.

On the following morning, December 8, eighty of the Kolo Jews were transferred to a special van. The van set off towards a clearing in the Chelmno woods, a few miles away, on the River Ner. By the time the journey was over, the eighty Jews were dead, gassed by exhaust fumes channelled back into the van. Their bodies were thrown out of the back of the van, and it returned to the Mansion. After eight or nine journeys, all seven hundred Jews from this first day's deportation from Kolo had been gassed.[76]

For four more days, until December 11, the lorries came to Kolo. Each day up to a thousand Jews were deported, as they believed, to the 'East' to agricultural work, or to work in factories. Michael Podklebnik later recalled how, on the last day, when it was the turn of the sick Jews of Kolo to be deported, the drivers were advised 'to drive carefully and slowly'.[77] All went to Chelmno, the sick and the able-bodied alike, men and women; and all were gassed there on the morning after their arrival. The new scheme was now in being: the deportation of whole communities 'to work' in the so-called 'East', a deception which was followed by the immediate murder of the community by gas.

On 7 December 1941, as the first seven hundred Jews were being deported to the death camp at Chelmno, Japanese aircraft attacked the United States Fleet at Pearl Harbor. Unknown at the time either to the Allies or to the Jews of Europe, Roosevelt's day that would 'live in infamy' was also the first day of the 'final solution'.

15

The 'final solution'

THE NEWS OF PEARL HARBOR reached the Jews of German-occupied Europe within forty-eight hours. 'Most people believe that the war will not last long now,' Mary Berg noted in her Warsaw diary on 9 December 1941, 'and that the Allies' victory is certain.' America's entry into the war, she added, 'has inspired the hundreds of thousands of dejected Jews in the ghetto with a new breath of hope'.[1]

This hope was tragically misplaced, On December 10, just over one thousand Jews who had been deported from seven villages to the 'rural' ghetto at Kowale Panskie were deported yet again, to Chelmno, to be pushed into the vans which had carried the Jews of Kolo to their death.[2] Four days later, on December 14, all 975 Jews from the nearby riverside village of Dabie were likewise driven to Chelmno, kept overnight in the Palace, and gassed in the vans on the morning of December 15.

The Einsatzkommando killings also continued unabated: 14,300 Jews were murdered in the Crimean city of Simferopol on December 13, 14 and 15.

None of this was known in the Warsaw ghetto, beset by its own troubles, starvation, executions and random shootings. On December 14, Ringelblum recorded, at a Jewish funeral, a German policeman 'suddenly, without warning, began shooting at the funeral procession'. Two of the mourners, Ringelblum noted, 'fell dead on the spot', one of them 'Mrs Runda, the director of the old people's home'. Five Jews, including a child of ten, were wounded. 'Jews have no peace,' Ringelblum commented, 'even when accompanying their dead to eternal rest.'[3] In Paris, on the following day, more than forty Polish-born Jews were shot for resistance, among them Nysin Alterleib, Simon Nadel and Israel Bursztyn, each of whom had been born in Warsaw forty-five years before, and the twenty-five-year-old Albert Borenheim, also born in Warsaw.[4]

December 15, the day of these executions in Paris, marked the first day of the Jewish festival of Chanukkah, during the eight days of which Jews recall the triumph of the Maccabees more than two thousand years earlier. That same morning, in Warsaw, fifteen Jews were shot to death in the courtyard of the ghetto prison, 'within earshot', Chaim Kaplan noted, 'of thousands of people'. His account continued:

> The cries of the victims in the prison courtyard were heard by the throng outside. Rage and frustration turned into mass weeping. Other prisoners locked inside the prison began to shout and beat their heads against the walls. There is nothing more nerve-shattering than the concerted weeping of a great crowd. The wailing at this hour in history was an echo of the weeping and lamentation decreed upon the generations of the people of Israel. It was a protest against the loss of our human rights. The sentence was carried out by Polish policemen in the presence of rabbis and other representatives of the Jews. The Poles fired the shots – and they too wept. They had been given no choice either.[5]

In the East, the Einsatzkommando continued its work throughout December. After the Channukah festival, it was the Jews in one of the smallest ghettos, that in Radom, near Lida, who were its target. Avraham Aviel was a witness to what occurred:

> . . . suddenly a group of Germans arrived. They wore special uniforms and came from Lida. They were on motorcycles. They went from house to house and were searching for people who were not local residents. And they did find about forty Jewish refugees who had been living for quite some time in Radom. They took them outside of town, up on a hill about one and a half kilometers out of the town. We heard shots immediately. Thereupon a few moments later they returned and gave instructions that we had to go out and bury these men. I was among these people. We had been living at the edge of the ghetto near the hill. We were driven out there and we buried these bodies. That was the first time I had ever seen so

much Jewish blood spilled. It was very cold then. There was
frost. The ground was frozen. . . .[6]

In Riga, a forty-year-old Latvian, Yanis Lipke, who worked as a
loader in the German air force storehouse in the city, was charged
by the Germans to take a group of Jews from the ghetto each
morning to the storehouse, and to supervise their work. Outraged
by the massacres he had witnessed in the first weeks of the German
occupation, Lipke was determined to find ways of helping as many
Jews as possible. During his daily journey into the ghetto, he would
smuggle in food and medicine. He also befriended two Latvian
drivers, working for the German air force, Karl Yankovsky and
Janis Briedys, with whom he planned to rescue as many Jews as
possible from the ghetto.

On December 15, with the help of Briedys, Lipke smuggled ten
Jews out of the ghetto, finding them hiding places in the cellars of
houses belonging to his friends, and hiding four Jews in his own
house.

When a further six Jews were smuggled out of the ghetto, Lipke
took three of them to his home. It was then that he decided to build a
special hiding place underneath a shed near his house. Bringing logs
and cement, and building a henhouse above the entrance to the
hide-out, Lipke built a secure haven, helped in his task by his wife
Iohanna and their eldest son, Alfred.[7]

Each week, more Jews reached Riga from the Reich. One of the
arrivals in December was Joseph Carlebach, the Chief Rabbi of
Hamburg and Altona. Among the deportees on the same train was
Josef Katz, a twenty-three-year-old Jew from Lubeck, who later
recalled:

A tall, thin man with a long, flowing beard stands before SS
Major Lange and the other SS officers. With his furrowed face
and stooped back, he looks like one of the Jewish patriarchs of
old. It seems as if the whole burden of the past centuries were
resting on his shoulders.

'Stand up straight, buddy, when I'm talking to you,' the
Major tells him sharply. 'What's your occupation?'

'Chief Rabbi,' the Jew says clearly and proudly, eyeing the
Major from top to bottom.

'Ha, ha, ha! Chief Rabbi! Just see you don't open up shop
here again. You hear, Chief Rabbi?'

No reply comes from the lips of the Jew.

'Did you hear me, Judas?'

Still no reply.

Suddenly the SS Lieutenant-Colonel reaches out and strikes
the Chief Rabbi full in the face with his fist.[8]

In the Lodz ghetto, Jewish doctors worked in a special Gypsy
section which had been attached to the ghetto, and into which
several thousand German, Austrian and Czech Gypsies had been
deported. One of these doctors, Dr Dubski, himself a recent deportee from Prague, died on December 17 while performing a consultation in the Gypsy camp. Dubski died of the spotted typhus which
he was trying to treat.[9] A second Jewish doctor, Karol Boetim, also
from Prague, died on December 29 of spotted typhus, likewise
contracted while he was working in the Gypsy camp.[10] A third
doctor then drew his turn by lot to replace Dr Boetim. The third
doctor was the thirty-two-year-old Aron Nikelburg, a paediatrician, who had completed his studies in Berlin before returning to
Poland to practise in Warsaw. He was one of thirteen doctors
brought from Warsaw to Lodz in May 1941 by Chaim Rumkowski,
the Eldest of the Lodz ghetto. Dr Nikelburg died of typhus on 26
January 1942, 'the latest victim', the Chronicle noted, 'of his own
profession'.[11]

Among the German, Czech and Austrian Jews who had been
deported to the Lodz ghetto were 250 who were only Jews according to Nazi designation. Although of Jewish birth, all 250 were
baptized Christians. On Christmas Eve they held two services,
one for Catholics and the other for Protestants. The Catholic
service, attended by forty people, was conducted by Sister Maria
Regina Fuhrmann, a Carmelite nun from Vienna, and a Master of
Theology. Two Catholic priests, both Jews by birth, were among
those at the service.[12]

Since November 1941, the German authorities in Lodz had
instituted a Jewish postal service, for postcards to be sent out of the
ghetto. Hundreds of cards were written by the dwellers of the
ghetto, addressed to relatives and friends in Poland and Czechoslovakia. For seven months, until it was suspended on 5 June 1942, this

postal service gave those in the ghetto a sense of security, of a link with the outside world. Most of the cards which have survived never left the ghetto: on them are overprinted messages which indicate that the Germans did not want them to reach their destination. These overprints read: 'Write legibly!' 'dirty!' 'Not understandable', or 'Hebrew, Yiddish language not allowed'.[13]

Some cards, however, did reach their destination. Oskar and Paula Stein, who had been deported from Prague to Lodz in October 1941, wrote three cards to a relative in Prague. Each card reached its destination. 'Send us as often as possible', one message read, 'the maximum permitted amount, because we need money most urgently.' One of the cards sent to the Steins, however, was sent back to Prague with the rubber stamp notation: 'Return. At the moment there is no mail delivery on the addressee's street.'[14]

The discussion planned by Heydrich for January 2 had been post-poned because of the Japanese attack on Pearl Harbor, and Germany's declaration of war on the United States. One of those who would be sending a delegate to Heydrich's discussion was Hans Frank. On December 16, in Cracow, he explained to his Cabinet the reason for this Berlin meeting. 'I want to tell you quite frankly,' he began, 'the Jews must be done away with in one way or another.' The war would only be a 'partial success', he said, 'if the Jewish clan survived it', and he reminded his Cabinet of Hitler's words in January 1939: 'Should united Jewry again succeed in provoking a world war, not only will the nations forced into the war by them shed their blood, but the Jew will have found his end in Europe.'

Frank, who had recently visited Berlin, told his colleagues that a 'great discussion' would take place at the meeting in January, as a result of which 'a great Jewish migration will begin, in any case'. His remarks continued:

> But what should be done with the Jews? Do you think they will be settled in the Ostland, in villages? We were told in Berlin: 'Why all this bother? We can do nothing with them either in the Ostland or in the Reichskommissariat. So liquidate them yourselves'.

> Gentlemen, I must ask you to rid yourself of all feelings of pity. We must annihilate the Jews wherever we find them and wherever it is possible, in order to maintain here the integral structure of the Reich.[15]

The many German officials waiting throughout the Reich for instructions realized that a decision was imminent. Some even assumed that it had already been taken. 'Clarification of the Jewish question', Hinrich Lohse was informed from Berlin on December 18, 'has most likely been achieved by now through verbal discussion.'[16]

The killings in the East were not restricted to Jews. On the night of December 21, the bodies of several thousand Soviet prisoners-of-war were laid out by the Germans along a six-kilometre stretch of road in Minsk. On the previous day most of the Russians had been deliberately frozen to death in a march across the open fields. Some had been shot when, in desperation, they had sought some shelter from the fierce wind.[17] In Vilna, when thousands of Jews were driven from the ghetto to the railway junction after a heavy blizzard, to clear snow from the lines, they found hundreds of Soviet prisoners-of-war shovelling the snow, half-naked, many of them without boots. 'Among the Jews', Reuben Ainsztein has written, 'was my sister Mania Liff, who saw a Jewish woman give a piece of bread to a Russian. This was noticed by a German guard who at once shot dead both the Russian and the Jewess.'[18]

Like the Jews being gassed that week at Chelmno, the dead Jewess outside Vilna and the dead Russian prisoners-of-war at Minsk and Vilna were murdered without even their names being recorded. They had become, in Nazi eyes, vermin to be 'exterminated'. On 6 January 1942 Michael Podklebnik was among thirty young men brought to Chelmno to dig pits for the corpses of those who had been gassed. The previous group of diggers had all been shot. But on the wall of the cellar in which they were to live, Podklebnik and his fellow diggers found several scratched inscriptions: 'No one leaves this place alive'; 'Whoever can, should save himself'; 'Every day, two or three of us are being taken away and they do not return'; 'No one survives this place very long'; and 'When people are taken to work, they are being shot'.

On the following morning, January 7, Michael Podklebnik was

present when a truckload of deportees reached Chelmno from a nearby village. The deportees were told, over a loudspeaker: 'Now you are going to the bath-house; you will get new clothes and go to work. Some people applauded – they were happy that now they were to work.'

The deportees went through a corridor, and into a truck on the other side. Some of the Jews saw these trucks, Podklebnik recalled, 'and didn't want to board them, but the SS had big sticks and they beat people and forced them to get in'. His account continued:

> The next day we continued to work, and more people were brought in – we heard the screams from the trucks as the engine began working and the gas flowed in; then the screams died down, and we – five of us – were taken from a cellar and we had to take the clothes and shoes left behind and put them in a room which was already full of shoes and clothing.
>
> And in the evening people came back from working in the woods.
>
> They returned from work, but two or three were already missing – these people had grown weak and could no longer work: they were shot and left behind.
>
> The next day I didn't want to stay where I was. I was among the first five who were taken out to work in the forest. That's where they dug the trenches: there were twenty-five people there and they were all digging trenches.
>
> They were all completely dead. No one was alive any more. These people who were taken from the trucks were dead. But I remember that there was one in all that period, a man of my town, a healthy and strong man who still showed signs of life, and then someone approached him and shot him dead. But this was the only time. The man's name was Jakobowitz.
>
> When the trucks arrived we were still not permitted to go near them; we had to wait until they had stopped for two or three minutes and the fumes had dispersed. Then five or six people would open the doors and take out the corpses and place them right near the trenches.

The corpses would be placed carefully, side by side. Ukrainians and Germans, working in pairs, using pliers, would pull out the gold teeth and take off the rings of the murdered Jews. 'If the ring did not come off easily,' Podklebnik recalled, 'they would cut off the entire finger.'

After the gold teeth and the rings had been taken, the corpses were buried. This was the task of the thirty young men. On January 12, the corpses of the Jews from Podklebnik's own village, Bugaj, were brought to the woods. His wife, his seven-year-old son and five-year-old daughter were among them: 'I lay near my wife and two children and wanted them to shoot me,' he later recalled. 'One SS man told me, "You still have enough strength, you can work," and he pushed me away. That night I came home and wanted to hang myself but my friends would not let me. They said that as long as my eyes were open, there was some hope.'

Several days later, Podklebnik managed to jump out of the truck taking the grave diggers to the woods. 'By the time they turned round and started shooting,' he later recalled, 'I was already in the forest.[19]

No one in the ghettos of the General Government knew of the gassings at Chelmno. Jews waited and suffered, not knowing what lay ahead. In Warsaw, at the beginning of January, three Jews were killed in one day, while smuggling food. That in itself was an event which caused comment: three in a single day. One of those shot was the father of eight children. That too seemed cause for comment.[20] In Lodz, Ringelblum noted, 'hundreds of people are said to be dying daily from cold and hunger'.[21] In Warsaw, too, one Friday in January, ninety bodies were discovered, sixteen of them from refugee centres, while even in a centre for foundlings, 'a child froze to death'.[22] That same winter month, throughout the General Government, Jews were ordered to give up all furs and fur coats, 'a severe blow to the poorer people', Ringelblum noted, 'who sometimes had nothing but an old tattered fur coat to wear'.[23]

In the isolation of the ghetto, rumours abounded, not of death and slaughter, but of imminent rescue: of the advance of the Red Army virtually to the gates of Warsaw. Ringelblum described it in his notes:

> . . . ex-newspapermen are spreading reports of exaggerated communiqués. They're always far in advance of Russian army movements – a couple of hundred kilometres. After the break-through at Kholm, they advanced as far as Vilna; after the

victory at Mozhaisk, they sped past Smolensk, Vitebsk, Minsk, and the like. Stalin telegraphed them: 'God, not so fast. I can't keep up with you!' On the 2nd of January, Jews were talking about the Russian occupation of Vilna, the German evacuation from Kiev.[24]

In the Lodz ghetto, on December 16, the Germans demanded of Chaim Rumkowski that he provide Jews for 'work battalions'. Rumours of this demand prompted fears that those who were not chosen to work might be deported. Four days after the German demand, Rumkowski informed the ghetto representatives that his aim was 'to provide work for everybody' inside the ghetto. 'Everyone in the ghetto must have work as his passport. If new work battalions are prepared, I will report to the authorities that my reserves are mobilized and waiting to be employed.' The enemies of the ghetto were those who launched stories 'with the intention of disturbing society's peace'. Of these people Rumkowski declared, 'losing his temper', as the Ghetto Chronicle recorded: 'I would like to murder them.'

Rumkowski told the Jews of the Lodz ghetto, about the Germans: 'They respect us because we constitute a centre of productivity.' For this reason he would present them, Jews and Germans alike, with a plan for the New Year 1942. 'The plan is work, work, and more work! I will strive with an iron will so that work will be found for everyone in the ghetto.'[25] More than one hundred and sixty thousand Jews were living in the Lodz ghetto as Rumkowski spoke. These included citizens of Lodz, deportees from towns in western Poland and deportees from Greater Germany. Within a week of the Elder pledging work for all, and protection through work, the Germans demanded the ten thousand Jews be found for 'resettlement': a special 'Resettlement Commission' chose for deportation Jews who had reached Lodz from Wloclawek and its environs the previous October, the families of Jews who had already been sent out of the ghetto for forced labour in Germany, prostitutes, and other so-called 'undesirable elements'. Beginning on January 13, these ten thousand were ordered to report at the rate of seven hundred a day. Those not reporting would be 'forcibly conducted to the assembly point'.[26]

In Bialystok, the acting head of the Jewish Council, Ephraim

Barasz, felt a new security for the Jews of the ghetto when the German military authorities indicated a possible future order for the manufacture of boots for the German army. Summoning the Council department heads, he told them, as the protocol of the meeting recorded, that he was 'certain' that this order for boots 'will protect the ghetto from calamity'. He therefore 'demands that industry be assigned top priority in Jewish Council activities'.[27] Five months later, the order for boots arrived. 'This is sufficient', Barasz told his Council, 'to ensure our security and that of the ghetto.'[28]

Each ghetto was almost completely cut off from the outside world. News of the different fates of different ghettos was virtually non-existent. Only after the war was it possible to piece together the wider picture. Even as Rumkowski and Barasz spoke with confidence of security through productive work, more and more German, Austrian and Czech Jews were being deported to Riga: some to immediate death, others to labour camps, such as that at Salaspils, where prisoners were hanged 'on the flimsiest pretext, after having been tortured before their death', or died 'from sheer exhaustion'. A thousand deportees from Theresienstadt had been sent to Riga on January 9; four hundred of them being transferred to Salaspils on arrival.

Of the thousand deportees of January 9, only 102 survived the war.[29] Two days later, on January 11, more than fifteen hundred Viennese Jews were seized, and sent likewise by train to Riga. One of them, Liana Neumann, later recalled how 'there was no water. The coaches were sealed, and we could not leave them. It was very cold, and we chipped off some of the ice from the windows to have water.' Many froze to death on the journey. On reaching Riga, 'we were received by SS men, who made us run, and beat us up.' Old people, and children, were taken away by force. They were taken away, and killed.

Liana Neumann was sent to work in a hospital; her job was to disinfect the clothing of those Jews who had been killed, for despatch to the German clothes store. With her were a number of local Latvian Jews. 'There was a man from Latvia', she later recalled, 'who cried out all of a sudden, holding the coat of his little daughter, full of blood.'[30]

At Chelmno, the gassing of whole communities was continuing day by day. Gypsies, too, were among the first victims. On January

7, the first of five thousand Gypsies, who had earlier been deported to the Jewish ghetto in Lodz from their encampments in Germany, were taken from Lodz to Chelmno by truck. All were gassed. With them was a Jewish doctor, Dr Fickelburg, and a Jewish nurse, whose name is unknown. They had been working as a medical team in the Gypsy section of the ghetto. They too were gassed.[31]

On January 9, a thousand Jews from the nearby village of Klodawa were deported to Chelmno. Every one was gassed.[32]

The deportation of Gypsies from the Lodz ghetto having been completed, on January 13 the deportation began of ten thousand Jews from the Lodz ghetto, also to Chelmno, at the carefully controlled rate of seven hundred a day. To lull the deportees with a belief in 'resettlement', they had been made to exchange whatever Polish or other money they had into German marks. They were also told that they could either sell their furniture, or leave it 'for safekeeping' at the carpenters' shops in the ghetto. [33] Before leaving, each deportee was given a 'free distribution' of clothing: warm underwear, earmuffs, gloves, stockings, socks and clogs. They were also given 'half a loaf of bread and a sausage for the road'.[34]

The Chronicle of the Lodz ghetto recorded with precision the number of deportees: 5,353 men and 5,750 women.[35] The Chronicle only knew that they had been 'resettled', not that they had been deported to Chelmno, and gassed.[36]

16

Eye-witness to mass murder

ON 14 JANUARY 1942 the sixteen hundred Jews of Izbica Kujawska, in German-annexed western Poland, were ordered to assemble. Alarmed, the leaders of the Jewish Council warned the Jews of the order in advance. Several hundred managed to escape to nearby villages. Furious, the Germans took the members of the Jewish Council to a nearby wood, and shot them. The remaining Jews were then taken to Chelmno. All were gassed.[1]

One witness of the destruction of the Jews of Izbica Kujawska was Yakov Grojanowski, a young Jew from the same village. A week earlier, he had been among twenty-nine Jews assembled in Izbica for a special work detail, and driven off, with their shovels, to Chelmno. There, fifteen of them had been taken to join the 'grave-digger' squad, of which Michael Podklebnik from Bugaj had also just become a member.

Yakov Grojanowski escaped from Chelmno on January 19. Eventually, on reaching Warsaw, he told the story of what he had seen and done to a devastated Ringelblum, who urged him to record every detail of his fourteen days at the death camp.

Grojanowski's ordeal began in the cellar of an old castle in Chelmno village; a cellar in which the grave-diggers were kept overnight, its window bricked up to prevent their escape. His notes are published here in full:

Tuesday, 6 January 1942

We arrived at 12.30 noon. At both doors stood Gestapo men and gendarmes doing guard duty.

When we came into the second courtyard we were pushed out of the lorry. From here onwards we were in the hands of black-uniformed SS men, all of them high-ranking Reich Germans.

We were ordered to hand over all our money and valuables. After this fifteen men were selected, I among them, and taken down to the cellar rooms of the Schloss. We fifteen were confined in one room, the remaining fourteen in another. It was still bright daylight outside but down in the cellar it was pitch dark.

Some Ethnic Germans on the domestic staff provided us with straw. Later a lantern was also brought. At around eight in the evening we received unsweetened black coffee and nothing else. We were all in a depressed mood. One could only think of the worst, some were close to tears. We kissed each other and took leave. It was unimaginably cold and we lay down close together. In this manner we spent the whole night without shutting our eyes.

We only talked about the deportation of Jews, particularly from Kolo and Dabie. The way it looked, we had no prospect of ever getting out again.

Wednesday, 7 January 1942

Wednesday, 7 January, at seven in the morning, the gendarme on duty knocked and ordered us to get up. We hadn't slept anyway, because of the cold. It took half an hour till they brought us black coffee and bread from our provisions.

We drew some meagre consolation from this and told each other there was a God in heaven; we would, after all, be going to work.

At about 8.30 in the morning (it was already late, because the days were short) we were led into the courtyard.

Six of us had to go into the second cellar room to bring out two corpses. The dead were from Klodawa (Kladow), and had hanged themselves. (I don't know their names.) They were conscript grave-diggers. Their corpses were thrown on a lorry.

We met the other fourteen enforced grave-diggers from Izbica. As soon as we came out of the cellar we were surrounded by twelve gendarmes and Gestapo men with machine guns. We got on the lorry together with the twenty-nine enforced grave-diggers and the two corpses; our escort were six gendarmes with machine guns. Behind us came another vehicle with 10 gendarmes and two civilians. We drove in the direction of Kolo for about seven kilometres till turning left into the

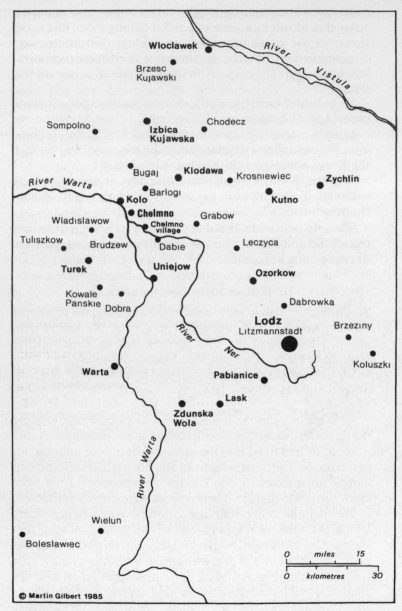

Włocławek

Brzesc
Kujawski

River Vistula

Sompolno

Izbica
Kujawska

Chodecz

River Warta

Bugaj

Barlogi

Klodawa

Krosniewiec

Zychlin

Kolo

Chelmno

Chelmno
village

Grabow

Kutno

Władysławow

Tuliszkow

Brudzew

Dabie

Leczyca

Turek

Uniejow

Ozorkow

Kowale
Panskie

Dobra

Dabrowka

Lodz
Litzmannstadt

Brzeziny

River Ner

Koluszki

Warta

Pabianice

Lask

Zdunska
Wola

River Warta

Wielun

Boleslawiec

0   miles   15

0   kilometres   30

© Martin Gilbert 1985

CHELMNO

forest; after half a kilometre we halted at a clear path. We were ordered to get down and line up in double file.

An SS man ordered us to fall in with our shovels, dressed, despite the frost, only in shoes, underwear, trousers and shirts. Our coats, hats, gloves, etc., had to remain in a pile on the ground. The two civilians took all the shovels and pick-axes down from the lorry. Eight of us who weren't handed any tools had to take down the two corpses.

Already on our way in to the forest we saw about fourteen men, enforced grave-diggers from Klodawa, who had arrived before us and were at work in their shirtsleeves.

The picture was as follows: twenty-one men in twos, behind them eight men with two corpses, ringed by armed Germans. The people from Klodawa were also guarded by 12 gendarmes.

All in all we were guarded by thirty gendarmes. As we approached the ditches the men from Klodawa asked us in whispers, 'Where are you from?' We answered, 'From Izbica.' They asked how many of us there were and we replied twenty-nine. This exchange took place while we worked.

The eight men without tools carried the two corpses to the ditch and threw them in. We didn't have to wait long before the next lorry arrived with fresh victims. It was specially constructed. It looked like a normal large lorry, in grey paint with two hermetically closed rear doors. The inner walls were of steel metal. There weren't any seats. The floor was covered by a wooden grating, as in public baths, with straw mats on top. Between the driver's cab and the rear part were two peepholes. With a torch one could observe through these peepholes if the victims were already dead.

Under the wooden grating were two tubes about fifteen centimetres thick which came out of the cab. The tubes had small openings from which gas poured out. The gas generator was in the cab, where the same driver sat all the time. He wore a uniform of the SS death's head units and was about forty years old. There were two such vans.

When the lorries approached we had to stand at a distance of five metres from the ditch. The leader of the guard detail was a high-ranking SS man, an absolute sadist and murderer.

He ordered that eight men were to open the doors of the lorry. The smell of gas that met us was overpowering. The victims were gypsies from Lodz. Strewn about the van were all their belongings: accordions, violins, bedding, watches and other valuables.

After the doors had been open for five minutes orders were screamed at us, 'Here! You Jews! Get in there and turn everything out!' The Jews scurried into the van and dragged the corpses away.

The work didn't progress quickly enough. The SS leader fetched his whip and screamed, 'The devil, I'll give you a hand straight away!' He hit out in all directions on people's heads, ears and so on, till they collapsed. Three of the eight who couldn't get up again were shot on the spot.

When the others saw this they clambered back on their feet and continued the work with their last reserves of energy. The corpses were thrown one on top of another, like rubbish on a heap. We got hold of them by the feet and the hair. At the edge of the ditch stood two men who threw in the bodies. In the ditch stood an additional two men who packed them in head to feet, facing downwards.

The orders were issued by an SS man who must have occupied a special rank. If any space was left, a child was pushed in. Everything was done very brutally. From up above the SS man indicated to us with a pine twig how to stack the bodies. He ordered where the head and the feet, where the children and the belongings were to be placed. All this was accompanied by malicious screams, blows and curses. Every batch comprised 180–200 corpses. For every three vanloads twenty men were used to cover up the corpses. At first this had to be done twice, later up to three times, because nine vans arrived (that is nine times sixty corpses).

At exactly twelve o'clock the SS leader with the whip ordered: 'Put your shovels down!' We had to line up in double file to be counted again. Then we had to climb out of the ditch.

We were surrounded by guards all the time. We even had to excrete on the spot. We went to the spot where our belongings were. We had to sit on them close together. The guards continued to surround us. We were given cold bitter coffee and a frozen piece of bread. That was our lunch. That's how we sat for half an hour. Afterwards we had to line up, were counted and led back to work.

What did the dead look like? They weren't burnt or black; their faces were unchanged. Nearly all the dead were soiled with excrement. At about five o'clock we stopped work. The eight men who had worked with the corpses had to lie on top of them face downwards. An SS man with a machine gun shot at their heads. The man with the whip screamed: 'The devil, get dressed quickly!'

We dressed quickly and took the shovels with us. We were counted and escorted to the lorry by gendarmes and SS men. We had to put the shovels away. Then we were counted again and pushed into the lorry.

The journey to the Schloss took about fifteen minutes. We travelled together with the men from Klodawa and talked very quietly together.

I said to my colleagues: 'My mother wanted to lead me to a white wedding canopy, she won't even have the experience of leading me to a black one.' We cried softly and spoke in whispers so the gendarmes sitting at the back shouldn't hear us.

On the first day the following happened: it was ten in the morning. A certain Giter from Bydgoszcz, a fat individual, resident in Izbica during the war, belonged to the group of 'eight' and was unable to keep up with the speed of the work. The SS man with the whip ordered him to undress. He flogged him and others till they lost consciousness. His body looked black as spleen. He had to lie down alone in the ditch where he was shot.

It turned out that there were many more rooms in the Schloss. We numbered twenty in our room, with fifteen more in the adjacent one. There weren't any other enforced grave diggers. As soon as we came into the cold and dark cellar we threw ourselves down on the straw and cried about everything that had befallen us. The fathers wept from pain at never seeing their little ones again. A fifteen-year-old boy by the name of Monik Halter embraced and kissed me. Weeping, he said to me, 'Ah, Schlomo, even if I die a victim, my mother and sister should at least stay alive.' Meir Pitrowski, forty years old from Izbica, my neighbour on the straw, kissed me and said, 'I have left my dear wife and eight children at home. Who knows if I'll ever see them again, and what is going to happen to them.'

Gershon Prashker, a fifty-five-year-old from Izbica, said, 'We

258 · THE HOLOCAUST

have a great God up in heaven and must pray to him. He won't desert us – that's why we must all now together say the prayer of confession and penitence before death.' Amid great pain and tears we recited the prayer. It was a very depressing sight. The sergeant-major knocked at the door, shouting, 'Quiet, you Jews or I shoot!' We continued the prayer softly with choking voices.

At 7.30 in the evening they brought us a pot of thin kohlrabi soup. We couldn't swallow anything for crying and pain.

It was very cold and we had no covers at all.

One of us exclaimed, 'Who knows who among us will be missing tomorrow.' We pressed close together and lapsed into exhausted fitful sleep haunted by terrible dreams. We slept for about four hours. Then we ran about the room freezing cold and debated the fate that was in store for us.

Thursday, 8 January 1942

On Thursday, 8 January, early in the morning, the gendarme knocked and asked maliciously: 'Ah, you Jews; did you sleep well?' We replied that we had been unable to sleep because of the cold.

At 7.30 the cook brought us hot but bitter coffee with dry bread. We got the coffee in a large cauldron, which we had to scoop out with our cups. Some of us drank it but most didn't want that breakfast. They said they were close to death anyway.

At 8 o'clock we heard the arrival of many people. They were high-ranking SS men. The gendarmes reported to one of them that the Jews had remained quiet throughout the night. The SS man ordered him to open our cellar door. (The door had three locks and a chain.)

The officer screamed, 'All Jews clear out!' and remained alone in the corridor. (We had assumed the SS would be afraid of a desperate reaction on our part.)

As we left the cellar, our numbers were checked. In the courtyard we had to line up in double file. The second SS man checked the number of grave-diggers once again. Then we had to board the lorry. (Two vehicles always conveyed us to our place of work and back, a tarpaulin-covered lorry and a low passenger car with panes at the side, in other words a limousine. There was, naturally, a further car with SS men.) We stood in the lorry, behind us were six gendarmes with machine guns, ready to shoot. The courtyard, into which we came out of the cellar, was strictly guarded by gendarmes with machine guns for as long as I remained in Chelmno.

When we drove to work we were followed by a carload of SS men. On arrival we got exactly the same treatment as the day before. After getting off the lorry we were counted. Eight of us who weren't strong enough for digging were selected. These eight stepped out of the ranks quite calmly, their heads lowered. Naturally we had to undress; then all of us had to go to the same place of work as on the day before. The only things we were allowed to keep on were shoes, shirt, trousers and underwear. (One man who wore two shirts was viciously beaten.) We placed our belongings on one spot. Half an hour later came the next transport, with the remaining grave-diggers, who had been in the other cellar room. They had to go through the identical procedure.

The place where we found ourselves was surrounded by armed gendarmes ready to shoot. The entire forest was patrolled by gendarmes. The tiniest false move on our part gave the gendarmes cause for the most dreadful and cruel behaviour. The 'eight' were working twenty paces from us. One of them, Mechel Wiltschinski from Izbica, nineteen years old, called over to me, 'Stay healthy. I hope you remain alive. We are leaving this world. I hope you'll get out of this hell.' The remainder of the 'eight' didn't utter a sound, they only sobbed dejectedly.

Two hours later the first lorry arrived full of Gypsies. I can state with one hundred per cent certainty that the executions had taken place in the forest. In the normal course of events the gas vans used to stop about one hundred metres from the mass graves. In two intances the gas vans, which were filled with Jews, stopped twenty metres from the ditch. This happened once on this Thursday, the other time on Wednesday the 14th.

Our comrades from among the 'eight' told us there was an apparatus with buttons in the driver's cab. From this apparatus two tubes led into the van. The driver (there were two execution gas vans, and two drivers – always the same) pressed a button and got out of the van. At the same moment frightful screaming, shouting and banging against the sides of the van could be heard. That lasted for about fifteen minutes. Then the driver reboarded the van and shone an electric torch into the back to see if the people were already dead. Then he drove the van to a distance of five metres from the ditch.

After five minutes 'Big Whip', the SS leader, ordered four of the work detail to open the doors. A strong smell of gas prevailed. Five minutes later he shouted, 'Hey, Jews, go and lay Tefillim (i.e. throw out the corpses)!' The dead bodies were heaped up higgledy-piggledy. They were still warm and looked asleep. Their cheeks weren't pale; they still had natural skin colour. The men who had to do this work told us they didn't feel cold, because they dealt with warm bodies.

After the 'eight' had finished their work with the dead and in the van they put on Gypsy clothes because of the cold and sat down on top of the corpses. It was a tragic-comic sight. The 'eight' were in any case forbidden to mix with the others. At lunchtime they used to be left in the ditch. They were given cold bitter coffee to drink and a piece of bread. It was done like this: one of the gendarmes poured coffee into a cup with a long ladle. After the first man had drained the cup it was refilled for the next one, and so on. The 'eight' were treated like lepers.

After half an hour the second van with Gypsies arrived. It did not halt at a distance of twenty metres from us, but a hundred metres further away this time, so we shouldn't hear anything. (The muffled screams had unsettled us.)

Until lunch we had 'processed' five vans, and another four in the afternoon. (We counted the vans.) Our lunch consisted of cold, bitter coffee and frozen dry bread. The working day ended at 5 p.m. Before we left the ditch the 'eight' were made to lie on top of the dead Gypsies, face downwards, and a gendarme shot them through the head with a machine gun. Immediately afterwards we returned to the Schloss, which was 100 metres from the highway, so that curious villagers shouldn't notice anything.

With us rode seven gendarmes in front, and three at the back. The seven who sat in front alighted first (in the courtyard of the Schloss). They surrounded the lorry with machine guns. Then the other three gendarmes alighted. Finally we had to get down

and line up in twos. We were counted and led into the same
dark cellar. It was cold and dim in the cellar. We told each
other, 'This is a veritable paradise (in comparison to the
dreadful graveyard).' At first we sat in the dark on the straw,
shivering with emotion at our terrible fate.

Fifteen-year-old Monik Halter from Izbica clung to me the
whole time. He embraced me, kissed me and said to me, 'We're
all lost,' and repeated his wish that his sacrifice should enable
his mother and sister to remain alive.

Others said, 'Once again eight innocent souls have left this
world.' The time passed amid sobs, wails and groans.

At about seven in the evening the chef brought a cauldron of
kohlrabi soup and filled our bowls. A few of us, who were
hungry, had some soup, but the majority didn't touch it. Bitter
tears flowed into the soup plate.

Together with the food a night-light was placed in our room.
Nearly all of us said we were prepared to spend our lives in this
terrible place, if we could thereby save our dear ones and
survive to see punishment meted out to the murderers.

Meanwhile the gendarme ordered us to sing. At first we
disobeyed. However when he threatened to shoot and opened
the door, my two neighbours Meir Pitrowski from Izbica, and
Jehuda Jakubowicz from Wloclawek, who had lately been
resident in Izbica, begged me to stand up and sing.

I myself don't know from where I drew the strength to get up
because I was very tired. I addressed my comrades in a feeble
voice: 'Friends and honourable people, get up and sing after
me; first we shall cover our heads.'

They stood up.

We covered the slop pail with a white shirt. Angrily the
impatient gendarme, who stood in the open door, ordered us to
sing at last. I therefore began to sing 'Hear! O Israel, the eternal
one is our God, the eternal one is unique'. Those assembled
repeated each verse in depressed tones.

Then I continued: 'Praised be his name and the splendour of
his realm for ever and ever', which the others repeated after me
three times. We felt as if we were at the end of our lives. Sadness
and fear gripped us. All were as sombre as if before the Last
Judgement. We were very much mistaken in thinking we had
now sung enough. The gendarme insisted that we go on.

262 · THE HOLOCAUST

I said: 'Friends and honourable people, we shall now sing the "Hatikvah".' And we sang the anthem with our heads covered. It sounded like a prayer. After this the gendarme left and bolted the door with three locks.

We couldn't stop crying and said that the world had never ever known such barbarism. To liquidate Jews and Gypsies in such murderous fashion, and to force us to sing on top of it. We hoped they would end up like 'Haman'. The Almighty should put an end to this terrible fate.

Mosche Asch, a worthy man from Izbica, said, 'We are a sacrifice, indicating that the time of the Messiah is at hand.'

The guard opened the door again and the German cook, a civilian, fetched a pail of black bitter coffee, which he poured into the bowl. (We had poured the remains of the kohlrabi soup into the slop bucket.)

Each of us took a piece of bread and some coffee.

After fifteen minutes the gendarme asked us to sing again. We tried to get out of it by pleading tiredness but to no avail. He ordered us to repeat after him: 'We thank Adolf Hitler for everything!' We did so. Then we had to repeat: 'We thank Adolf Hitler for our food.' Then he demanded that we sing again. We sang the 'Hatikvah', and afterwards the twenty-sixth Psalm. (That was our response to the torment in our souls.) Then he bolted the door again. We slept late into the night.

I woke in the middle of the night probably from cold or nightmares. I began thinking everything over again. I wanted to scream: 'Where is God in heaven? How can he see our torment and permit the slaughter of the innocent. Why doesn't he perform a miracle?'

Then it occurred to me that I had to escape from this prison. I carried a tiny flame to the walled-up window and tried loosening a brick with a knife. But my efforts were in vain. The frost which also penetrated the interior had frozen the bricks fast. After two hours of trying I lay down again disappointed.

By five in the morning everybody was awake because of the cold. We had a conversation. Getzel Chrzastowski, a member of the Bund, and Eisenstab, both from Klodawa (Eisenstab owned a furriers in Klodawa), had lost their belief in God because he didn't concern himself with injustice and suffering. In contrast others, myself included, remained firm in our belief and said, like Mosche Asch, that the time of the Messiah was at hand.

Friday the 9th in the morning we were again given bitter coffee. Asked if we had enough bread we said yes – we had some left over from before. At 8 a.m. the SS men appeared and were told that the Jews had spent an uneventful night. After the door was opened we had to go out and be counted.

The courtyard was already ringed round with gendarmes carrying machine guns. (It was the first time that the barrels of the guns were trained on us. We caught a terrible fright, thinking we were about to be shot.)

In the courtyard we saw two large carts full of gypsies with their wives, children and all their possessions. We were quickly loaded into a lorry in order to deny us the opportunity for communicating with the Gypsies. This, incidentally, was the only occasion on which we saw a transport with live victims.

We stood towards the front of the lorry, seven gendarmes with machine guns behind us. A car with eight SS men followed.

At our place of work we were surrounded by gendarmes. We undressed as before. We were counted, after which eight people were selected from out of our ranks.

We picked up the axes and shovels and started work. The bottom of the ditch was about 1.5 metres wide, the top five metres and its depth was five metres. The mass grave extended a long way. If a tree stood in the way it was felled.

Friday, 9 January 1942

On the third day of our tragic experiences the work was particularly difficult and harsh. Within an hour the first van with dead Gypsies arrived, twenty minutes later the second. 'Big Whip' raged without let-up. Whilst working we were able to get a little closer to the 'eight'. Among them were Abraham Zelinski from Izbica, thirty-two years old, Gawerman from Izbica, seventeen years old, Zalman Jakubowski from Izbica, fifty-five years old, and Gershon Praschker from Izbica. Around five o'clock there wasn't much to do, and they did not rush us as usual. Gershon Praschker who was down below in the pit got up, took his prayer book, and covering his head with his hand began to pray.

At about eleven in the morning they said to us: 'Our death is a tragic death, a sacrifice on behalf of our relatives and of the whole Jewish people. We shall be in this world no more.'

On this day we ate at 1.30 p.m.

The temperature was down to twenty degrees below freezing. The gendarmes lit a fire to thaw out our bread. The bread tasted smokey and burnt. Lunch was very brief because another van with Gypsy victims had arrived.

In the afternoon 'Big Whip' went deeper into the forest to drain a bottle of schnapps. When he returned he started to scream: 'Damn it; you don't want to work,' and began hitting out with the whip. He drew blood from the grave-diggers. Blood flowed from their heads, faces, brows and noses. Their eyes were swollen. On this day we buried seven to eight transports (batches) of Gypsies. We finished work at 5.30. The 'eight' were killed as usual.

We had to dress quickly and were chased back into the lorry. Then we were counted a number of times; this was obviously taken very seriously.

On arrival back at the courtyard of Schloss Kulmhof we were disagreeably surprised to see a new transport. They were probably a new batch of grave-diggers: sixteen men from Izbica and sixteen from Bugaj. Among those from Izbica were: 1. Moshe Lesek, forty years old, 2. Avigdor Palanski, twenty years old, 3. Steier, thirty-five years old, 4. Knoll, forty-five years old, 5. Izchak Preiss, forty-five years old, 6. Jehuda Lutzinski, fifty-one years old, 7. Kalman Radzewski, thirty-two years old, 8. Menachem Archijowski, forty years old. Among those from Bugaj was my friend and comrade Haim Reuben Izbizki, thirty-five years old.

Twenty of the old grave-diggers, together with five new ones (twenty-five in all), were driven into another room in the cellar. This room was somewhat smaller than the previous one. There we found bedding, underwear, trousers, suits as well as foodstuffs (bread, dripping, and sugar). These items belonged to the new grave-diggers.

Tired and broken in spirit, we sat down on the belongings. The first thing we questioned the new arrivals about was if any of our relatives were among them. Questions and answers mingled with our sobs. We heard voices from the adjacent room. I banged at the wall and shouted at a spot where a missing brick let the air through. I asked if H. R. Izbizki was in the room. He came to the wall. I asked if at least his mother and sister had escaped.

The guard interrupted our conversation.

During supper Steier shared out dripping among us, and said, 'May God not let me see so much suffering, hopefully I won't be in this world tomorrow.' (He was indeed killed the next day.)

Moshe Lesek shared out his sugar. After supper we covered the slop pail and recited the evening prayer.

Our prayer mingled with tears. Afterwards the new arrivals gave us some political news. They said that the Russians had already retaken Smolensk and Kiev, and were making their way towards us.

We wished they would with God's assistance come and destroy this terrible place. Some of us debated where we would shelter during bombing attacks. Others said they wouldn't remain alive, because it would take at least another month. Nobody believed that they would get out of this hell in the normal way.

The discussion about divine justice took place as follows: some of those present, also older people among them, had entirely lost their belief in God. They thought faith was nonsense and God didn't exist. Otherwise he couldn't simply watch our tortures without helping us. Those, myself included, whose faith had remained firm, asserted that it wasn't for us to understand God's actions. Everything, we said, was in the hands of God.

Then we at last covered ourselves with our clothes and fell asleep.

I want to add something important: on both Thursday and Friday the latest two transports comprised Jewish victims. They were younger and older people with suitcases and rucksacks. On their clothes a Jewish star was affixed front and back. We assumed they were diseased camp inmates whom the Nazis wanted to get rid of in this manner. They were buried with their belongings.

These events shook us to the core because up until then we had hoped that Jews in the camps would survive these terrible times.

Saturday, 10 January 1942

On Sabbath the 10th of January at 7 a.m. they brought us breakfast: bitter coffee and bread. After breakfast Moshe Lesek recited the prayer of penitence and confession, and we repeated it after him.

We had to endure the seven stations of hell until we had been counted several times. The guards pointed guns at us as we climbed into the lorry. We told the five newcomers they should stick closely to us.

Together with the new arrivals our group numbered fifty-three people. We were crushed together in the lorry. At the back stood ten gendarmes with machine guns at the ready. Behind us drove a limousine with ten SS men.

On arrival the old group was separated from the others and got ready for work. The newcomers still had to undergo all our tortures. This time the 'eight' weren't selected immediately.

At about eleven o'clock the first van loaded with victims arrived. Jewish victims were treated in this way: the Jewish men, women and children were in their underwear. After they had been tossed out of the van two Germans in plain clothes stepped up to them to make a thorough check if anything had been hidden. If they saw a necklace round a throat they tore it off. They wrenched rings from fingers, and pulled gold teeth out of mouths. They even examined anuses (and, in the case of women, genitals). This entire examination was done most brutally.

It was only after the arrival of the Jewish transport that the 'eight' were selected. All the victims were from Klodawa – as Getzel Chrzastowski (who himself hailed from Klodawa) reported to us.

After the first van had been dealt with the 'eight' returned to their previous work, i.e. digging.

At 1.30 p.m. the second van arrived. At a certain moment Eisenstab from Klodawa began to cry softly. He told us he had no further reason for living since his wife and fifteen-year-old only daughter had just been buried. He wanted to beg the Germans to kill him so he could lie together with his nearest in the grave. We restrained him under the pretext there would still be time for that later. In the meantime he might be able to survive and exact revenge.

At 1.45 p.m. we consumed our lunch (bitter cold coffee and smoky bread).

As the 'eight' were on the point of completing their work two carloads of high-ranking SS officers arrived.

They got out and viewed the charnel house with pleasure. They received a report from 'Big Whip', after which they shook his hand in token of their contentment and appreciation.

In the afternoon we very hurriedly buried a further five transports. At about 6 p.m. everybody was deployed to fill in the ditch right up to the edge.

We were taken back to the Schloss in the usual way. Haim Reuben Izbizki got accidentally included in our group. Back in the cellar we all cried a lot. It is a fact that I was so tired that I didn't recognise my best friend Izbizki. Today, as yesterday, we were so depressed that crying came quite naturally to us. Eisenstab wailed more than the others.

After the evening meal which consisted of a quarter litre of potato soup per person with black bitter coffee and bread, we carried the slop pail outside. Under a smoking lamp we said the evening prayer. Then Eisenstab recited 'Kaddish'.

We talked only of the terrible catastrophe that had befallen the Jewish people. We were obviously witnesses of the extermination of an entire Jewish community (Klodawa). None of us were able to sleep. Suddenly Eisenstab got up. He was overwrought and began to sob. He screamed he had no cause to live any more. All hope had been taken away from him. He beat his head against the wall. Above all he bemoaned the fact that he couldn't take his life. In the end he lay down exhausted and fell asleep.

I stayed awake all night. I embraced my two neighbours Meir Pietrowski and Jehuda Jakubowitcz and cried softly.

Sunday, 11 January 1942

Sunday the 11th of January at 7 a.m. they brought us breakfast. We were told we wouldn't have to work because it was Sunday.

After the morning prayer and the prayer for the dead we remained in our paradisical cellar. We didn't recite the prayer of penitence. We again talked about ourselves, politics and God. Everybody wanted to hold out until liberation. Our overwhelming worry was the fate of the Jewish people. All would gladly have forfeited their own lives if only the Jewish nation could survive.

At 11 a.m. ten men were called out to push a van which had stuck fast because of the cold. A huge gas-van stood in the courtyard. When I was in the courtyard I had a mind to run away but my courage failed me in the last minute.

When we had done the work we were chased back into the cellar. At one o'clock we got lunch: kohlrabi soup and bread. After lunch we sat down on top of our belongings. Some pulled their boots off. Finally we fell asleep for an hour. After the change of the watch at six o'clock the guard again ordered us to sing. This time we didn't sing, but shouted 'Hear! O Israel' and the 'Hatikvah' at the top of our voices like madmen. After we had finished a high-ranking SS man came in and rebuked the guard because Jews weren't allowed to sing.

At seven in the evening we ate. Then we carried the slop pail away; afterwards we recited the evening prayer and the prayer for the dead. Then we laid down, covered ourselves with our coats and dozed.

Monday, 12 January 1942

Monday, the 12th of January, at 5 a.m. six people got up and recited the Psalms amid crying and wailing. Some of the others made fun of us because of our piety. They said there was no God. This consolation struck them as youthful foolishness. We replied that our life was in the hands of God. If all this was his will then we accepted it with love, all the more so as the days of the Messiah were approaching. After the morning prayer and Kaddish, in which even Eisenstab took part, we recited the prayer of penitence.

At 7 a.m. they brought us coffee and bread. Some of the men from Izbica (who had lately lived in Kutno) drank up all the coffee. The others got very annoyed and said we were already facing death and had to behave with dignity. It was decided to share out a little coffee to everyone in future. At 8.30 we were all already at work. At 9.30 the first gas van appeared.

Among the 'eight' were Aharon Rosenthal, Schlomo Babiacki and Schmuel Bibedgal, all of them aged between fifty and sixty.

On this day we were absolutely slave-driven. They wouldn't

even wait till the gas smell had evaporated. You can imagine the screams of the tortured people. Immediately after the first van the second one arrived. By twelve o'clock noon the third had already come.

When we went to lunch the 'eight' remained behind to dispatch the last transport. Meanwhile a black limousine arrived and four officers got out. They heard a report from 'Big Whip' after which they shook his hand most appreciatively. 'Big Whip' then once again beat the 'eight' violently to his joy and satisfaction.

When the SS men left the 'eight' received their meagre lunch: bitter coffee and smoky bread. Around one o'clock the next van arrived already. That afternoon the work lasted till six. Nine transports, each of sixty Jews from Klodawa, were buried; five hundred people from Klodawa in all.

My friend Getzel Chrzastowski screamed terribly for a moment when he recognised his fourteen-year-old son, who had just been thrown into the ditch. We had to stop him, too, from begging the Germans to shoot him. We argued it was necessary to survive this suffering, so we might revenge ourselves later and pay the Germans back.

After work the five oldest men in the detail that handled the corpses were shot and we had to cover the grave as quickly as possible.

Because of the late hour – it was already very dark – the Germans feared there may be an uprising. We were hurriedly split into groups and chased into the lorries. Seven gendarmes travelled with us. In the evening at seven we returned to our place of refuge.

The sons of Rosenthal and Bibedgal, whose fathers had been killed that day, cried bitterly. We tried to console them and said it didn't matter whom fate struck down first; we would all die anyway. On this occasion those two also took part in the prayer of the mourners.

After supper which, as always, consisted of kohlrabi soup, black coffee and dry bread – all shared out justly, as agreed – Mosche Lesek said the prayer of penitence. He wanted to take his life, so he would not have to watch the sufferings of his nearest. He gave away all his belongings: bread, syrup and clothes.

In the meantime we heard a noise in the corridor. The other group in the adjacent room told us through the wall the Germans had captured an escaped Jew from Klodawa. Next morning they told us the following details: the captured escaper, Mahmens Goldmann, had told them in detail how the Jews were driven into the gas vans. When they arrived at the Schloss they were at first treated most politely. An elderly German, around sixty, with a long pipe in his mouth, helped the mothers to lift the children down from the lorry. He carried babies so that the mothers could alight more easily and helped dotards to reach the Schloss.

The unfortunate ones were deeply moved by his gentle and mild manner. They were led into a warm room which was heated by two stoves. The floor was covered with wooden gratings as in a bath-house. The elderly German and the SS officer spoke to them in this room. They assured them they would be taken to the Lodz Ghetto. There they were expected to work and be productive. The women would look after the household, the children would to go school, and so on. In order to get there, however, they had to undergo delousing. For that purpose they needed to undress down to their underwear. Their clothes would be passed through hot steam. Valuables and documents should be tied up in a bundle, and handed over for safe keeping.

Whoever had kept banknotes, or had sewn them into their clothes, should take them out without fail, otherwise they would get damaged in the steam oven. Moreover they would all have to take a bath. The elderly German politely requested those present to take a bath and opened a door from which 15–20 steps led down. It was terribly cold there. Asked about the cold, the German said gently they should walk a bit further: it would get warmer. They walked along a lengthy corridor to some steps leading to a ramp. The gas van had driven up to the ramp.

The polite behaviour ended abruptly and they were all driven into the van with malicious screams. The Jews realised immediately they were facing death. They screamed, crying the prayer 'Hear! O Israel'. At the exit of the warm room was a small chamber in which Goldmann hid. After he had spent 24 hours there in the icy cold and was already quite stiff, he decided to look for his clothes and to save himself.

He was caught and pushed in among the grave-diggers. There his comrades tried to cheer him up, gave him food and trousers and a jacket.

We then discussed his story excitedly. Everybody said if they had been in Goldmann's place they would have done better for themselves. At about three in the morning Mosche Lesek woke us all. He kissed and took leave of everybody. He had prepared a rope to hang himself. He already had the noose round his neck when his strength left him. He simply couldn't take his own life.

Tuesday, 13 January 1942

Tuesday morning, the 13th of January, we barely had time after breakfast to recite the prayer of penitence before we all, including Goldmann, were loaded on to the lorry. On arrival we got ready for work. Goldmann was meanwhile ordered to lie in the ditch and was shot.

The first van arrived already at eight. On this day the transports were brimful – roughly ninety corpses in each van. When we opened the van doors the corpses fell out of their own accord. Although we worked at murderous pace, each batch took longer than usual. On this day the Jewish community at Bugemin was liquidated. One van after another arrived.

At the fourth transport a small baby wrapped in a pillow was thrown out of the lorry. It began to cry. The SS men laughed. They machine-gunned the baby and tossed it into the ditch.

In the course of this Tuesday we buried approximately eight hundred Jews from Bugaj. In the icy cold we worked till six in the evening. We buried nine transports; after work, five of the men who had unloaded the corpses were shot. When in our cellar Michael Worbleznik burst into tears; he had lost his wife, two children and his parents.

After supper we emptied the slop pail and some of us said the evening prayer. Then we had a conversation about topical issues.

We kept returning to the question of how one could escape in order to warn the whole Jewish population. Nothing seemed more important than that. Some wanted to dig a 50-metre-long tunnel. The argument against that was the problem of how to dispose of the dug-up earth. Others suggested we should open the bricked-in window. But because of the frost we young, healthy men could not shift even one brick. Resigned we lay down to sleep.

Wednesday, 14 January 1942

Wednesday the 14th of January they brought us bitter coffee and bread. Immediately after breakfast Krzewacki from Klodawa, who had long contemplated suicide, put a noose round his neck. He begged Chrzatowski to remove the small packet from under his feet and shove it into his mouth, so that his breathing should stop sooner. Chrzatowski fulfilled his request and Krzewacki died an easy death. He committed suicide because he couldn't bear to watch the murderous deeds any longer. We cut him down and placed him against the wall.

Immediately after this Gershon Swietoplawski from Izbica also wanted to commit suicide. He had been Krzewacki's colleague in digging. He said he had dug together with Krzewacki and wanted to lie in the ditch with him. Because of the late hour nobody wanted to help him. The guard could turn up at any moment. He quickly took a rope and tied a noose round his neck. He stood with his feet on the ground and bent forward to throttle himself more quickly. While he tortured himself in this way there was a knock at the door.

Young Monik Halter quickly cut the rope. Swietoplawski fell to the ground choking. He began to gasp horribly as he got his breath back. When the guard had gone, on the one hand we didn't want to save him (whatever for?), but on the other hand we couldn't bear to watch his torments. We begged Getzel Chrzatowski to put an end to them. Chrzatowski tied a noose tightly round Swietoplawski's neck, pinned his body down with his feet, and tugged hard at the rope till he had throttled Swietoplawski.

We left both corpses lying uncovered in the cellar. They remained there for a few days.

At eight in the morning we were already at the ditches. Around ten o'clock there appeared the first van with Jewish victims from Izbica. By noon we had already dispatched five overloaded transports. Out of one of these transports the corpse of a German civilian had been pulled out. The person concerned was one of the cooks.

He had presumably strayed into the van in the following manner: he had probably noticed one of the Jews purloining some object and had run after him to reclaim it. At that very moment the doors had clanged shut. His shouting and knocking had been ignored; in this way he was gassed together with the others. Immediately after he had been lifted out of the van a special car with an ambulance man aboard arrived from the Schloss. The corpse was taken back there. Some of us thought he had been deliberately poisoned so that no witness of this killing should remain alive.

During the lunch break two carloads of SS men arrived who viewed our slaughterhouse with pleasure. In the afternoon a further five transports were buried.

From one of the vans a woman with a suckling at her breast was thrown out. The baby had perished while sucking its mother's milk.

In the light of headlamps we carried on working till seven in the evening. On this day one of the vans drove in error right up to the ditch. We heard the muted cries for help and knocking at the door of the tortured victims. At the end of the day six men of the 'eight' were shot.

Back in the cellar we all burst into tears. After supper we said the evening prayer and the prayer of mourning.

Thursday, 15 January 1942

Thursday the 15th of January we again drove to work very early. On this occasion we rode in a bus. At a certain moment Monik Halter called across to me the windows of the vehicle could easily be opened with a hook. The thought of escape had lodged in my brain all the time. With all my being I wanted to reach the Jews who were still alive, to tell them about the atrocities taking place in Chelmno.

At 8 a.m. we were already at the place of work.

At ten o'clock the first victims arrived – again from Izbica.

Till noon we dispatched four overloaded transports. One van waited in line after the next. I must describe again how barbarously the corpses were examined.

Imagine the following picture: one German drags one corpse

from the pile to one side, while another drags a corpse else-where.

They searched the women's necks for golden chains. If they found any, they immediately tore them off. Rings were pulled off fingers. They pulled out gold teeth with pliers. Then the corpses were stood up, legs apart so that a hand could be inserted into the posterior. In the case of the women an examination was also carried out in front. Although these examinations took place every day while we worked, our blood and brains boiled.

At midday I received the sad news that my brother and parents had just been buried.

At one o'clock we were already back at work. I tried to get closer to the corpses to take a last look at my nearest and dearest.

Once I had a clod of frozen earth tossed at me, thrown by the benign German with the pipe. The second time 'Big Whip' shot at me. I don't know if the shot missed me deliberately, or by accident. One thing is certain: I remained alive. I suppressed my anguish and concentrated on working fast so as to forget my dreadful situation for five minutes.

I remained lonely as a piece of stone. Out of my entire family, which comprised sixty people, I am the only one who survived. Towards evening, as we helped to cover the corpses, I put my shovel down. Michael Podklebnik followed my example and we said the prayer of the mourners together. Before leaving the ditch five of the 'eight' were shot. At seven in the evening we were taken back home. All those who hailed from Izbica were in absolute despair. We had realised that we should never see our relatives again. I was quite beside myself and indifferent to everything.

After the evening prayer all those from Izbica said the prayer of mourning together. In the next room, we had learnt, were eighteen grave-diggers from Lodz.

We heard through the wall that Rumkowski (the elder of the Jewish Council at Lodz) had ordered the deportation of 750 families from Lodz.

We spent a night filled with nightmares and images of horror. The strongest among us tried again to open the bricked-in window.

Friday, 16 January 1942

On Friday, 16 January, we woke at five in the morning. We once again debated our hopeless position. What was the use of living without relatives, friends or saviour – without anyone to talk to. At work the new grave-diggers from Lodz were beaten terribly by 'Big Whip', for it was he who gave the orders how they had to work.

At 10 a.m. the first gas vans arrived. By one o'clock we had already buried four transports. The victims came from Lodz. Some of them looked starved and showed signs of having been beaten and injured; one could gauge the degree of famine in Lodz. We felt great pity when we saw how they had hungered for a long time merely to perish in such a cruel manner. The corpses hardly weighed anything. Where previously three transports were put in layers one on top of the other now there was room for four.

In the afternoon 'Big Whip' again drank a bottle of schnapps; afterwards he began to deal murderous blows with his whip. In the afternoon we buried another four transports, and when we were near the end, seven of the 'eight' were shot. On Friday they started to pour chloride on the graves because of the stench caused by the many corpses.

In our room there were also three men from Lodz who told us more details about the fate of the 750 families from the Lodz ghetto. On Thursday they had arrived by train at Kolo. They were lodged in a synagogue. Eighteen healthy men from among them were selected and sent away as grave-diggers. The three in our room were so famished that they consumed our entire supper.

Saturday, 17 January 1942

On Sabbath, the 17th January, we again said the penitential prayer before leaving. On that day we buried seven overloaded transports. That afternoon five SS officers appeared to watch the goings-on. We had finished the work at five o'clock when a car suddenly appeared with the order to shoot sixteen men. This was obviously punishment for the escape of Abraham Rois. (He had run away at 10 o'clock on Friday night.)

Sixteen men were selected. They had to lie down in groups of eight, face downwards, on top of the corpses, and were shot through the head with machine guns. When we returned to the cellar we thought we wouldn't work on Sunday, as in the previous week. The men from Lodz told us that the price for a newspaper in that town was 10 marks. After supper we lapsed into a deep sleep.

Sunday, 18 January 1942

Sunday, the 18th January, we learnt at breakfast that we would have to go to work. At eight o'clock we were already at the place of work. Twenty new pick-axes and shovels were taken down from the lorry. We now realised that 'production', far from coming to an end, was on the increase.

We assumed it would soon be the turn of the Jews of Warsaw to be gassed. The turn of the Lodz Jews had already come.

Because it was Sunday not all the gendarmes were on duty. Because there were too many of us our things were thrown into the ditch. We consumed our lunch in the grave. They probably wanted to make sure that we didn't attack any of them. We didn't even attempt to hurl ourselves upon our executioners. The guns levelled at us filled us with too much fear. In the course of our night-time conversations we always reproached each other with cowardice.

I actually cannot understand till this day why strong healthy men who had nothing to lose didn't do anything. It could be that we didn't want to be mere heroes, but wanted to save ourselves so we could alert the Jewish population.

I would like to say a few more words about the gendarmes who guarded us; as a rule they were either hostile or indifferent. There was only one among them who always looked sad and never screamed at us. Nor did he ever slave-drive us at work. We told each other: 'Look, that's a human German; he himself cannot bear to watch how we are being murdered.'

In the afternoon we buried a further four transports. On this day no one was shot at the end of work. After the evening prayer we decided to run away, no matter what the cost.

I asked Kalman Radzewski to give me a few marks because I didn't have a single pfennig. He gave me 50 marks which he had sewn into his clothing. The escape by Rois was an example that had made a deep impression on me because he had got out through a cellar window. I had tried the day before, once again without success, to prise the brick loose.

Monday, 19 January 1942

On Monday the 19th January we again boarded the bus in the morning. I let all the others get on in front of me and was the last one aboard. The gendarme sat in front. On this day no SS men rode behind us. To my right was a window which could be opened easily. During the ride I opened the window. When fresh cold air streamed in I caught fright and quickly shut the window again. My comrades, among them Monik Halter in particular, encouraged me, however.

After I made a decision I softly asked my comrades to stand up so the draught of cold air shouldn't reach the gendarmes. I quickly pulled the window pane out of its frame, pushed my legs out and turned round. I held on to the door with my hand and pressed my feet against the hinges. I told my colleagues they should put the window pane back immediately after I had jumped. I then jumped at once.

When I hit the ground I rolled for a bit and scraped the skin off my hands. The only thing that mattered to me was not to break a leg. I would hardly have minded breaking an arm. The main thing was that I could walk in order to get to the next Jewish settlement. I turned round to see if they had noticed anything on the bus but it continued its journey.

I lost no time but ran as fast as I could across fields and woods. After an hour I stood before the farm of a Polish peasant. I went inside and greeted him in the Polish manner: 'Blessed be Jesus Christ.' While I warmed myself I asked cautiously about the distance to Chelmno. It was only 3 kilometres. I also received a piece of bread which I put in my pocket. As I was about to go the peasant asked me if I was a Jew – which I absolutely denied. I asked him why he suspected me, and he told me they were gassing Jews and Gypsies at Chelmno. I took my leave with the Polish greeting and went away.

An hour later I came to another Polish farm, where they gave me sweet white coffee and a piece of bread. The people there told me: they are gassing Jews and Gypsies at Chelmno, and when they have finished with them it will be our turn. I laughed about that. They explained to me what route I should take. I carried on walking till I reached a German village. (The German houses could be easily recognised because they were richly ornamented and had radio antennae on their roofs.)

I decided to walk on bravely through the whole village. Only at the end of the village did I find a house that belonged to a Pole. It transpired that I was 10 kilometres away from Grabow, which had a Jewish community. I introduced myself as a Polish miner on the way to Grabow in search of work. The householder sent me to the neighbouring town, where I was to ask for a certain Grabowski. Grabowski had a horse and cart and would surely take me to Grabow.

This time I could not make detours but had to walk along the open road part of the way. When I suddenly saw military vehicles my heart nearly stopped. I already had visions of being captured. At the last moment I took a peasant woman's arm and turned off into a footpath with her. I asked her if she had furs to sell. The vehicle drove past and I was saved. I appealed to God and my deceased parents they should help me to save the Jewish people.

At Grabowski's I introduced myself as a certain Witjowski who was looking for work in Grabow. It turned out that he, Grabowski, had gone to the market at Dabie. His neighbour to whom I was sent had likewise gone to the market at Dabie. I wandered a bit further and pondered my ill-luck. Now and then I asked passers-by for directions. All the time I was on the alert for gendarmes because I didn't have any documents on me. I finally reached a village seven kilometres away from Grabow. There I arranged with a Polish farmer he would drive me to Grabow for 15 marks. I put on his fur coat and cap.

On Monday at two o'clock we arrived at Grabow. The Jews took me for an Ethnic German because I didn't wear a star. I asked for the rabbi. I looked rough; in Chelmno we had had no opportunity to wash and shave.

I asked where the rabbi lived. 'Who are you?' he asked. 'Rabbi, I am a Jew from the nether world!' He looked at me as if I was mad. I told him: 'Rabbi, don't think I am crazed and have lost my reason. I am a Jew from the nether world. They are killing the whole nation Israel. I myself have buried a whole town of Jews, my parents, brothers and the entire family. I have remained lonely as a piece of stone.'

I cried during this conversation. The rabbi asked: 'Where are they being killed?' I said: 'Rabbi, in Chelmno. They are gassed in the forest, and buried in mass graves.' His domestic (the rabbi was a widower) brought me a bowl of water for my swollen eyes. I washed my hands. The injury on my right hand began to hurt. When my story made the rounds many Jews came, to whom I told all the details. They all wept.

We ate bread and butter; I was given tea to drink and said the blessing.[2]

The rabbi to whom Grojanowski told his story, Jakub Szulman, realized that Grojanowski was telling the truth. 'The place where everyone is being put to death is called Chelmno,' he wrote to relations in Lodz, adding some of the details which he had just heard. 'People are killed in one of two ways,' he reported, 'either by shooting or by poison gas,' and he then listed some of the communities that had been destroyed. 'Do not think that a madman's writing,' Rabbi Szulman added. 'It is the cruel and tragic truth (Good God!).'

The rabbi's letter ended: 'O Man, throw off your rags, sprinkle your head with ashes, or run through the streets and dance in madness. I am so wearied by the sufferings of Israel, my pen can write no more. My heart is breaking. But perhaps the Almighty will take pity and save the "last remnants of our People". Help us, O Creator of the World!'[3]

Rabbi Szulman sent his letter to the Lodz ghetto; but it did not arrive there, so it seems, until the summer, and even then, as Lucjan Dobroszycki has written, 'one cannot be sure who in the ghetto had read the letter or even knew of it, much less what influence that letter might have had on the attitudes of ghetto dwellers'.[4]

On Tuesday, 20 January 1942, having told his story to the Rabbi of Grabow, Yakov Grojanowski set off on a slow and dangerous journey to Warsaw, hoping to alert the half million Jews there to what was happening at Chelmno. That same day, at a villa on the shore of the Wannsee, near Berlin, Reinhard Heydrich held his high-level conference, postponed for nearly three weeks because of America's entry into the war.

17

20 January 1942:
the Wannsee Conference

THE WANNSEE CONFERENCE took place on 20 January 1942. The notes which were taken of its deliberations make no reference to the gassings which had taken place at Chelmno throughout the previous forty-four days; a period during which more than forty thousand Jews and Gypsies had been murdered. According to the notes of the Conference, Heydrich began telling the assembled senior civil servants of his appointment 'as Plenipotentiary for the Preparation of the Final Solution of the European Jewish Question'. As a result of this appointment, he told them, it was his aim 'to achieve clarity in essential matters'. Heydrich went on to tell the Conference that Goering had asked to see 'a draft project' of organizational, factual and material 'essentials' in consideration of this 'final solution'. Such a draft, he added, would require 'prior joint consultation' of all the ministries involved 'in view of the need for parallel procedure'.

The struggle waged against the Jews 'so far', said Heydrich, had first involved the expulsion of the Jews 'from various spheres of life of the German people' and then the expulsion of the Jews 'from the living space of the German people'. Now, following 'pertinent prior approval of the Führer', the 'evacuation of the Jews to the East' had emerged 'in place of emigration' as a 'further possible solution'. But both emigration and evacuation, he pointed out, were to be considered 'merely as a measure of expediency', from which experience could be gained which would be of importance 'in view of the approaching final solution of the Jewish question'.

Heydrich then explained that this 'final solution' concerned, not only those Jews who were already under German rule, but 'some eleven million Jews' throughout Europe. He then gave the meeting a list of the numbers involved, including 330,000 Jews in as yet unconquered Britain. All the Jews in the neutral countries of Europe were also listed: 55,500 in European Turkey, 18,000 in Switzerland, 10,000 Jews in Spain, 8,000 Jews in Sweden, 4,000 Jews in the Irish Republic and 3,000 in Portugal.

The figures presented by Heydrich included 34,000 for Lithuania. The other 200,000 Jews of pre-war Lithuania had, though he did not say so, been murdered between July and November 1941 by Einsatzgruppe A, their numbers meticulously listed town by town and village by village in Colonel Jaeger's report of 1 December 1941.

The largest number of Jews listed by Heydrich were those in the Ukraine: his figure was 2,994,684. The second largest was for the General Government, 2,284,000. The third largest was for Germany's ally, Hungary, 742,800, a figure which included the Jews in Ruthenia, Transylvania and those areas of Czechoslovakia annexed by Hungary in 1938 and 1939. The fourth highest figure was for unoccupied France, 700,000, a figure which included the Sephardi Jews in France's North African possessions, Morocco, Algeria and Tunisia. Next largest in the list was White Russia, 446,484, followed by the 400,000 Jews of the Bialystok region.

Hungary was Germany's ally. Jews living in five other countries which were allied to Germany were also listed: 342,000 in Rumania, 88,000 in Slovakia, 58,000 in Italy, including Sardinia, 40,000 in Croatia and 2,300 in Finland. The smallest number given was the 200 Jews of Italian-occupied Albania. Estonia was listed as 'without Jews'. This was true. Of Estonia's 2,000 Jews in June 1941, half had fled to safety inside the Soviet Union, while half had already been killed by the Einsatzkommando.

The senior officials present at the Wannsee Conference were from the Ministry for the Occupied Eastern Territories, the Ministry of the Interior, the Justice Ministry, the Foreign Office, the General Government of Poland, the Chancellery, and the Race and Resettlement Office. Also present was the Plenipotentiary for the Four Year Plan, responsible for disposing of Jewish property. All were asked by Heydrich to cooperate 'in the implementation of the solution'. His remarks continued:

In the course of the final solution, the Jews should be brought under appropriate direction in a suitable manner to the East for labour utilization. Separated by sex, the Jews capable of work will be led into these areas in large labour columns to build roads, whereby doubtless a large part will fall away through natural reduction.

The inevitable final remainder which doubtless constitutes the toughest element will have to be dealt with appropriately, since it represents a natural selection which upon liberation is to be regarded as a germ cell of a new Jewish development.

Heydrich then explained the European aspect of the plan:

In the course of the practical implementation of the final solution, Europe will be combed from West to East. If only because of the apartment shortage and other socio-political necessities, the Reich area – including the Protectorate of Bohemia and Moravia – will have to be placed ahead of the line.

For the moment, the evacuated Jews will be brought bit by bit to so-called transit ghettos from where they will be transported farther to the east.

It was intended, according to the statistics presented to the Wannsee Conference, that a total of eleven million European Jews should 'fall away', including those in the neutral and unconquered countries. The Conference discussed the various problems involved. 'In Slovakia and Croatia', they were told, 'the situation is no longer all that difficult, since the essential key questions there have already been resolved.' As for Hungary, 'it will be necessary before long', Heydrich told the Conference, 'to impose upon the Hungarian government an adviser on Jewish questions'. Rumania posed a problem, as 'even today a Jew in Rumania can buy for cash appropriate documents officially certifying him in a foreign nationality'. Speaking of the occupied and unoccupied zones of France, however, Heydrich commented that there 'the seizure of the Jews for evacuation should in all probability proceed without major difficulty'.

The representative of the General Government, Dr Joseph Buhler, stated that his administration 'would welcome the start of the final solution in its territory, since the transport problem was no overriding factor there and the course of the action would not be hindered by considerations of work utilization'. Buhler added:

Jews should be removed from the domain of the General Government as fast as possible, because it is precisely here that the Jew constitutes a substantial danger as carrier of epidemics and also because his continued black market activities create constant disorder in the economic structure of the country. Moreover, the majority of the two and a half million Jews involved were not capable of work.

Buhler had, he said, 'only one favour to ask', and that was 'that the Jewish question in this territory be solved as rapidly as possible'.

The meeting was drawing to its end. 'Finally,' the official notes recorded, 'there was a discussion of the various types of solution possibilities.'

What these 'possibilities' were, the notes of the Conference do not record.[1]

'I remember', Adolf Eichmann later recalled, 'that at the end of this Wannsee Conference, Heydrich, Muller and myself sat very cosily near the stove and then I saw Heydrich smoke for the first time, and I thought to myself, "Heydrich smoking today": I'd never seen him do that. "He is drinking brandy": I hadn't seen him do that for years.' After the Conference, Eichmann recalled, 'we all sat together like comrades. Not to talk shop, but to rest after long hours of effort.'[2]

The 'long hours of effort' were over. As Heydrich knew, the time was right for the deportation and destruction of millions of people. From many parts of Europe, there was evidence that only one more step had to be taken, and could be taken: the step already tried in the villages around Chelmno: the uprooting of whole communities, and their total disappearance. Few, if any, would care to enquire what had become of them. In hidden camps, a small band of sadists could then destroy them.

What had hitherto been tentative, fragmentary and spasmodic was to become formal, comprehensive and efficient. The technical services such as the railways, the bureaucracy and the diplomats would work in harmony, towards a single goal. Local populations would be cajoled or coerced into passivity. Some would even cooperate: that had been made clear already. On January 9 the Polish underground in Warsaw had warned the Polish Government in Exile of 'a blind and cruel anti-Semitism' among the Polish population, itself the victim of Nazi terror.[3]

By the end of January 1942, the Germans needed only to establish the apparatus of total destruction: death camps in remote areas, rolling stock, timetables, confiscation patterns, deportation schedules, and camps; and then to rely upon the tacit, unspoken, unrecorded connivance of thousands of people: administrators and bureaucrats who would do their duty, organize round-ups, supervise detention centres, coordinate schedules, and send local Jews on their way to a distant 'unknown destination', to 'work camps' in 'Poland', to 'resettlement' in 'the East'.

The officials present at the Wannsee Conference had agreed with Heydrich's suggestion that the 'final solution' should be carried out in coordination with Heydrich's own 'department head', Adolf Eichmann. The result of this decision was that Eichmann's representatives now travelled to all the friendly European capitals. Although they were attached to the German Embassies, they received their instructions direct from Eichmann's section in Berlin and reported back to Eichmann, by telegram, as each deportation was planned and carried out.

In addition to the technical arrangements involving thousands of trains and tens of thousands of miles, a complex system of subterfuge had to be created, whereby the idea of 'resettlement' could be made to appear a tolerable one.

All this was done by Eichmann's section, whose representatives were soon active in France, Belgium, Holland, Luxembourg, Norway, Rumania, Greece, Bulgaria, Hungary and Slovakia. Regular meetings were held in Berlin to coordinate the complex yet essential aspect of the impending deportations: the despatch of full trains and the return of empty trains. In a document dated 13 January 1943, and signed by Dr Jacobi of the General Management, Railway Directorate East, in Berlin, one sees the amount of work, and the number of people, involved in these deportation plans. The document took the form of a 'telegraphic letter' addressed to the General Directorate of East Railways in Cracow; the Prague Group of Railways; the General Traffic Directorate, Warsaw; the Traffic Directorate, Minsk; and the Railway Directorates in fourteen cities, including Breslau, Dresden, Königsberg, Linz, Mainz and Vienna. Copies were also sent to the General Management, Directorate

South, in Munich, and to the General Management, Directorate West, in Essen: a total distribution of twenty copies. The subject was: 'Special trains for resettlers' during the thirty-nine days from 20 January to 28 February 1943.[4]

By the time of this railway telegram, sent a year after Wannsee, the transport aspects of the 'final solution' were well tested, and well arranged. For anyone whose cooperation was needed, but who might be reluctant to cooperate, the full rigours of Nazi terror were readily available: perfected even at the time of Wannsee by nine years of Nazi rule and practice.

On January 30, nine years after coming to power in Germany, and only ten days after the Conference on the shore of Wannsee, Hitler spoke at the Sports Palace in Berlin of his confidence in victory. He also spoke of the Jews, telling his listeners, as reported by the Allied monitoring service on the following day: 'They are our old enemy as it is, they have experienced at our hands an upsetting of their ideas, and they rightfully hate us, just as much as we hate them.' The Germans, Hitler added, were 'well aware' that the war could only end when the Jews had been 'uprooted from Europe', or when 'they disappear'. Hitler then declared, as recorded by the Allied monitoring service:

. . . the war will not end as the Jews imagine it will, namely with the uprooting of the Aryans, but the result of this war will be the complete annihilation of the Jews.

Now for the first time they will not bleed other people to death, but for the first time the old Jewish law of an eye for an eye, a tooth for a tooth, will be applied.

And – world Jewry may as well know this – the further these battles [of the war] spread, the more anti-Semitism will spread. It will find nourishment in every prison camp and in every family when it discovers the ultimate reason for the sacrifices it has to make. And the hour will come when the most evil universal enemy of all time will be finished, at least for a thousand years.

Such was Hitler's message, as received in London and Washington: the war would end with 'the complete annihilation of the Jews'.[5]

Even as Hitler spoke, new death camps were being prepared. Three of the sites chosen were remote villages on the former German

—Polish border, just to the west of the River Bug. Although remote, each site was on a railway line linking it with hundreds of towns and villages whose Jewish communities were now trapped and starving. The first site, at Belzec, had been a labour camp in 1940: the railway there linked it with the whole of Galicia, from Cracow in the west to Lvov in the east, and beyond; and with the whole of the Lublin district. The second site, at Treblinka, also the site of an existing labour camp, was linked by rail, through both Malkinia junction and Siedlce, with Warsaw and the Warsaw region. The third site, at Sobibor, a woodland halt where Jewish prisoners-of-war had been murdered in 1940, linked by rail to many large Jewish communities, among them Wlodawa and Chelm.

Although a tiny handful of Jews, like Michael Podklebnik and Yakov Grojanowski, might be chosen in these camps as a small labour force to dispose of the corpses, or to sort out the clothes of the victims, most of the deportees were gassed within hours of their arrival, husbands with their wives, mothers with their children, the old, the sick, the infirm, pregnant women, babies; no exceptions were made and no mercy was shown.

Later, camps were to be set up at which as many as half of the deportees were 'selected' for forced labour, but at Chelmno, Belzec, Sobibor and Treblinka no such 'selections' were made. In these four camps, between the early months of 1942 and the first months of 1943, many hundreds of Jewish communities were to be wiped out in their entirety: more than fifty communities at Chelmno alone. Yet within a few months Chelmno was to prove the second smallest of the four death camps; a camp at which, nevertheless, at least 360,000 Jews were killed within a year.

A fifth camp was also set up in the spring of 1942, an extension of an existing camp, Auschwitz. Situated across the railway line from Auschwitz Main Camp, where Polish prisoners suffered cruel torments, the new camp was in a birch wood, known in German as Birkenau.

At the railway yard near Auschwitz station, a selection was to be made of each incoming train, and as many as half those brought to the camp were to be 'selected', not for gassing, but for forced labour. The labour was, first, in the camp itself, and subsequently in the surrounding factories of East Upper Silesia: coal mines, synthetic coal and rubber factories, and other military and industrial enterprises. From each train, however, of a thousand deportees, at least five hundred were to be gassed within a few hours of their arrival: all old people, all those who were sick, all cripples and all small children. The gassings took place, at first, in a gas-chamber in Auschwitz Main Camp, or in a specially constructed gas-chamber in the birch wood.

Auschwitz was not a remote village in eastern Poland, but a large town at a main railway junction, in a region annexed to the German Reich. The railway was part of a main line, with direct links to every capital of Europe: to the Old Reich, to Holland, France and Belgium, to Italy, and to the Polish railway network.

Fewer Jews were to be killed at Auschwitz–Birkenau than at the four death camps combined, but far more Jews were to survive Auschwitz–Birkenau, having been 'selected' for slave labour, than were to survive the four death camps.[6] Indeed, from Belzec there were to be no more than two survivors, from Chelmno only three, from Treblinka less than forty, and from Sobibor a total of sixty-four; while from Auschwitz–Birkenau, several thousand Jews were to survive. But in February 1942 all this was in the future: the special gas-chambers in these camps were still under construction, except at Chelmno, whose gas-vans had been working without interruption since 8 December 1941. By the time of the Wannsee Conference, three special gas-vans were in operation at Chelmno. 'At the beginning, Jews were brought to Chelmno daily,' recalled Andrzej Miszczak, a resident of Chelmno village. 'The gendarmes used to say, "Ein Tag – ein tausend," "One day – one thousand."'[7]

In the Eastern Territories, despite the frozen ground, the Einsatzkommando killings continued. On January 9, at Khmelnik in the Ukraine, all the Jews were assembled under the guns, not only of the Einsatzkommando, but also of all the regular German army officers in Khmelnik, of the local volunteer Ukrainian militia, and of volunteers from others towns. 'On that day,' the eighteen-year-old Maria Rubinstein recalled, 'my mother was killed, one of my brothers, and three of my sisters.'[8]

In Yugoslavia, in the last week of January, Hungarian soldiers ran amok, killing several thousand Jews and Serbs. On January 23, at Novi Sad, 550 Jews and 292 Serbs were driven on to the ice of the

Danube, which was then shelled. The ice broke, and the victims drowned. At Stari Becej, on January 26 and the two following days, a hundred Jews and a hundred Serbs were slaughtered. At Titel, thirty-five of the thirty-six Jews living in the village were killed.[9] These killings, seen and publicized, led the Hungarian government to charge the senior Hungarian officer responsible for the murder of six thousand Serbs and four thousand Jews: before he could be brought to trial, however, he fled to Germany.[10]

Six weeks after the Wannsee Conference, a second death camp was opened, at Belzec. In those six weeks, in addition to the continuing gassings at Chelmno, tens of thousands of Jews were to die elsewhere: the largest number, 5,123, died of starvation in Warsaw in January.[11] Thousands also died in each of the ghettos in the General Government, and, further east, in White Russia, the Ukraine and Volhynia, of starvation, typhus and shooting. On January 24, in the Volhynian town of Luck, the dead from typhus included the distinguished neurosurgeon, Dr Pawel Goldstein, born in Tsarist Poland in 1884, a graduate of Freiburg University, who between the wars had worked in the surgical department of the Jewish hospital in Warsaw. In 1939 Goldstein had been the Chief Surgeon of the Polish army hospital in Chelm.[12] In 1940 he had managed to cross the Soviet border and reached the safety of Luck.

On January 26, in the Volhynian village of Teofipol, three hundred Jews were assembled from the village itself and the neighbouring hamlets, stripped naked, 'and led down a stretch of three miles in zero weather and then were shot down': among them eight members of the Spivack family.[13]

January 1942 saw the final destruction of the Jewish community of Odessa. Following the mass murder and deportation of the Jews of Odessa in October 1941, the thirty thousand survivors had been driven into an enclosed area in the Slobodka suburb of the city. Because most of the houses in that area had been destroyed during the battle for the city, several thousand of the Jews had to lie in the open, in the rain and snow, and many perished. Some Jews committed suicide rather than go to Slobodka. A few were able to hand over their children to Christian families for conversion and adoption, the conversion ceremonies being performed by Russian Orthodox priests.

A beer mat with the inscription: 'Whoever buys from a Jew is a traitor to his people.'

Nazi youth watch as Viennese Jews are forced to scrub the streets, March 1938 (*pages 59–60*).

Jewish refugees at the Polish border town of Zbaszyn having been driven out of Germany at the end of October 1938 (*pages 66–8*).

The synagogue in Memel set on fire, 19 November 1938 (*page* 72).

A Jewish family leaves Memel watched by grinning Nazis, 19 November 1938.

German soldiers on a train leaving for the east, 1 September 1939. The inscription reads: 'We're off to Poland – to thrash the Jews' (*page 84*).

A German soldier kicks a Jew in a Polish street as the soldier's civilian prisoner is lined up against a wall. This photograph was taken on 10 November 1939.

In Lublin, in German-occupied Poland, an old Jew is forced to stand by the synagogue gates with the synagogue's ornamental Star of David around his neck.

German soldiers kicking a Jew in a street in Wloclawek, in German-occupied Poland.

Jews driven from their homes in Lodz, and forced to move into the specially designated 'ghetto' area (*page 116*).

Warsaw: the ghetto wall, built in November 1940 (*page 132*).

The Warsaw ghetto: Jewish children, driven from their homes in villages outside the city, find refuge and somewhere to live on the decorated balcony of a small synagogue.

The Warsaw ghetto: a queue for food.

On January 12 the deportations from the Slobodka 'ghetto' began. Within six weeks, a total of 19,582 Odessa Jews, the majority women, children and old people, had been taken by rail in sealed cattle trucks to Berezovka, and then on to two concentration camps in the Golta district. If someone died while the trucks were being loaded, the body would be put in the truck 'just the same', as Dora Litani, the historian of the fate of Odessa Jewry, has recorded, 'because the exact number that appeared on the list had to be handed over in Berezovka.' These bodies and those of persons who died on the way, she added, fifty to sixty in each shipment, were taken off the train and piled up near the Berezovka railway station platform, gasoline was poured on them, and they were burned before the eyes of their families and all those present. There were instances where those burned included dying persons, who still had breath in their bodies.

Once the deportees had reached the Golta district, Dora Litani has written, they were sent to two camps, one at Bogdanovka, the other at Domanovka. There they were packed into partly destroyed houses, without doors or windows, and into warehouses, stables and pigpens. 'Disease cut short the lives of hundreds of people, for they lay without food or medical care.' Those capable of working were sent to farms in the region, some nearby, others some distance away. 'They lived like work-animals, but unlike animals they received neither food nor care of any kind.'

Within a year and a half, almost none of these 19,582 deportees were alive. Most had died of starvation, severe cold, untreated disease, or in repeated mass executions in which several hundreds would be shot at a time.

In Odessa, many of the apartments in which the Jews had lived before the war were assigned, together with their furniture, to the 7,500 Ethnic Germans living in the city. Even the tombstones in the Jewish cemetery were made use of, being shipped to Rumania and sold to stonemasons. A year later, in Bucharest, 831 cubic metres of marble, all from the Odessa Jewish cemetery, were found in a stone-cutting plant. Among the marble slabs was the gravestone of the poet Simon Frug.[14]

Evidence survives of some non-Jewish attempts to help Jews during these Eastern slaughters. On January 16 the Einsatzkommando unit at Kremenchug reported that they had shot a Red Army officer, Major Senitsa Vershovsky, because he had 'tried to protect the Jews'.[15]

Throughout January the deportations of elderly Jews to Theresienstadt, and of whole communities from the Old Reich to Riga had continued. On January 28 Eichmann personally rejected a request from the Swedish explorer, Sven Hedin, to prevent the deportation of Alfred Phillipson, a Jew living in Bonn. 'It cannot be agreed that he stays in Bonn until he dies,' Eichmann noted, 'because when we deal with a final solution of the Jewish problem, the plan is that Jews above the age of sixty-five will be put in a special Ghetto for the aged.'[16] Three days later Eichmann's office, IV-D-4, sent a note to all its officials in the Reich, urging them to miss no 'opportunity' to forward more deportations from the Old Reich. 'For additional deportations', the note explained, 'it is necessary to draw up a list of the Jews still in the Reich. . . .'[17]

One of those who witnessed the deportations from the Reich was Gertrude Schneider, who was deported on February 6 from Vienna. The transport commander was Alois Brunner, one of whose charges during the long journey was the Viennese financier, Siegmund Bosel. During the second night of the train journey, Brunner chained Bosel, still in his pyjamas, to the floor of the first wagon and berated him for having been a 'profiteer'. The old man repeatedly asked for mercy; he was very ill, and it was bitterly cold. Finally, Brunner wearied of the game and shot him. Afterwards Brunner walked into the second wagon and asked whether anyone had heard anything. 'After being assured that no one had,' Gertrude Schneider later recalled, 'he seemed satisfied and left.'

This Viennese transport reached Riga on February 10. It was met at the station by Dr Rudolph Lange, one of the Nazi officials who had been present at the Wannsee Conference. Gertrude Schneider later recalled how Lange told these latest arrivals that those who were 'unwilling or unable' to walk the seven kilometres to the ghetto could make the journey on trucks which had been especially reserved for them. 'In this way,' he said, 'those of you who ride can prepare a place for those who walk.' Gertrude Schneider's account continued:

It was an extremely cold day — forty-two degrees below zero, to be exact — and so the majority of the hapless, unsuspecting Jews from Vienna took his advice and lined up to board the trucks. They did not know that those greyish-blue trucks had been manufactured by the Saurer Works in Austria especially for the implementation of the 'final solution'. These trucks were the famous gas-vans, which were used from time to time despite the fact that the SS did not especially like them because they always had mechanical problems.

At the time of the arrival of this train on February 10, more than five thousand of the twenty thousand Riga Jews who had come from the Reich had already been murdered. From Jungfernhof continual selections were made for 'resettlement'. The Jews were told that they were to go as a workforce to the city of Duenamuende where they would be working in fish-canning factories. 'To the Jews,' Gertrude Schneider later wrote, 'the plan sounded credible. The Baltic Sea was rich in fish, and everyone knew that workers were badly needed everywhere.' To the hungry old people who were ordered to go to Duenamuende, she added, 'the magic words "fish canneries" implied food as well as a certain security and reprieve from the cold. While most of those selected for this work were elderly or ailing or parents with small children, some of the ghetto functionaries were chosen as well. A number of physicians were also put on the lists, ostensibly to take care of workers who might get sick.'[18]

At Auschwitz, a further experiment had been carried out using Cyclon B to murder several hundred Jews who had been brought to the camp from several cities in Upper Silesia. This gassing took place, not in Auschwitz Main Camp, but across the railway line, in a cottage at the village of Birkenau. This cottage had been specially adapted for the purpose. Once more, the experiment was judged a success. The corpses were then buried in a number of mass graves in the adjoining meadow.[19]

On March 6, at a meeting of experts at the Head Office for Reich Security, Adolf Eichmann spoke of the forthcoming deportation of fifty thousand Jews from the Old Reich — Germany, Ostmark

—Austria and the Protectorate of Bohemia and Moravia. 'Among others,' Eichmann explained, 'we include herewith Prague with twenty thousand; Vienna with eighteen thousand Jews; all these have to be deported.' A representative from the Reich Security Office in Dusseldorf, Mann, told the meeting: 'One must never permit Jews to learn about preparations for deportation. Therefore strict secrecy is required.'[20]

Strict secrecy was indeed meticulously maintained: bureaucrats in Berlin, and construction experts in the 'East', worked under the protection of wartime censorship and silence.

Not only in Europe, but also in North Africa, Jews were murdered in remote, unknown camps. One such camp was at Hadjerat M'Guil, in the Sahara desert. There, on January 13, a Jew, Paul Levinstein, was murdered. Ten months earlier, on 22 March 1941, Marshal Petain had signed a law authorizing the construction of a railway across the Sahara. As a result of this law, several forced labour camps had been opened in the Sahara desert.

Of the fifteen hundred prisoners sent to these camps, two hundred and fifty were Jews. The rest were Spaniards who had been interned in Vichy France at the time of the Franco–German armistice in June 1940, most of them refugees from the Spanish civil war who had fled to France for safety in March 1939, with the defeat of the Republican forces. The Jews were mostly German and Austrian Jews who, like Paul Levinstein, on release from concentration camps in Germany early in 1939, had fled to France, and had then enlisted in the French Foreign Legion. This had enabled them, although not French nationals, to fight alongside French forces in May 1940. First German or Austrian citizens, then prisoners, then refugees, then soldiers, they were prisoners once more, in circumstances of considerable hardship.[21]

The camp at Hadjerat M'Guil was opened on 1 November 1941, as a punishment and isolation camp. It contained one hundred and seventy prisoners, nine of whom were tortured and murdered in conditions of the worst brutality. Two of those murdered were Jews.[22]

Paul Levinstein, murdered on January 13, was the son of Dr

Oswald Levinstein who, with his wife, had found refuge in Britain shortly before the outbreak of war. On learning of their son's murder, they committed suicide.[23]

18

'Journey into the unknown'

THROUGHOUT FEBRUARY 1942 the deportations to the death camp at Chelmno continued, systematically destroying the Jewish communities of western Poland. Also throughout February, gas-chambers were under construction at Belzec and Sobibor. But even as these preparations were being made, the Jews of German-occupied Poland and western Russia continued to suffer from the earlier German policies of spasmodic massacre and deliberate starvation. In the Warsaw ghetto, deaths from starvation in 1941 had approached the horrific total of fifty thousand.[1] As that figure was reached, during February 1942, thirty-three Jewish doctors living in the ghetto decided that, as they could not alleviate the hunger, they should at least study it scientifically, for whatever benefits could be accrued for post-war medicine.

To coordinate their researches, these thirty-three doctors met once a month, knowing that their work was likely to come to an abrupt end, for they were starving as were their patients. They decided to focus on two age groups, children between the ages of six and twelve, and adults between twenty and forty, hoping by this means to exclude from their investigations the chemical and biological imbalances created in the normal course of infancy, puberty and old age. During more than a year of research, the doctors carried out tens of thousands of examinations, and 3,658 autopsies.

Only eight of the thirty-three doctors were to survive the war, but their work, which did survive, was to serve as a basis for a fuller understanding of the process of starvation. In their book, which was published in Warsaw in 1946, the doctors made no mention either of Hitler's name or of the word 'Nazi'. Hugo Gryn, himself a survivor of the Holocaust, has written of how, through this book, the spirit of the doctors emerged 'not so much triumphant, but civilized and with human dignity intact'.[2]

As the doctors worked on their study of starvation, the Warsaw ghetto's torment continued. 'The Germans impose the death penalty on people who leave the ghetto,' Mary Berg noted in her diary at the end of February, 'and several people have recently been shot for this crime. But', she added, 'no one cares. It is better to die of a bullet than of hunger.'[3]

In the Minsk ghetto, on February 13, the Germans shot the leaders of those Jews deported from Hamburg the previous November.[4] That same month, somewhere behind the lines on the Russian front, a German soldier, Private Christian, noted in his diary: 'Since we have been in this town we have already shot more than thirteen thousand Jews. We are south of Kiev.'[5]

As the killing continued, there were disagreements among the German authorities. On February 10 the Commissar in Barano-wicze, Gentz, protested in writing to his superior in Minsk, Wilhelm Kube, that the German army authorities in Baranowicze wanted Jews to be spared as 'skilled workers'. But these Jews, Gentz insisted, were in fact 'no more than office cleaners, housekeepers etc.'. It was not merely a question of 'categories', for, as Gentz told Kube, 'even officers in responsible positions lack the instinct for the Jewish problem'.[6]

The Jewish Councils continued to face the dilemma of compliance or opposition. On February 12, when three thousand Jews were rounded up in the Ukrainian town of Brailov, to be marched away for execution, the Council Elder there, Josef Kulok, refused an offer to join the skilled workers who were to be spared, and chose to die with the community.[7]

In the ghetto at Dvinsk, now formally designated a concentration camp, a forty-eight-year-old Jewess, Chaya Mayerova, was arrested and shot on February 19 for giving a non-Jewish worker in the camp a piece of cloth in return for a two-kilogramme bag of flour. The Jews of Dvinsk were assembled in order to witness the execution. In reporting the episode to his superiors, the German commander of the concentration camp enclosed the bag of flour.[8]

Beyond the area of Nazi control, the precarious fate of those who had succeeded in escaping was cruelly demonstrated when a small cattle boat, the *Struma*, was torpedoed in the Black Sea. On board were 769 Jewish refugees, among them 70 children and 260 women. They had been on their way from the Rumanian port of Constanta to Palestine. But on reaching Istanbul their boat was halted for two months, while the British government tried to persuade the Turkish government not to let it proceed. Only a single person, Medea Salamovitz, who was in the last stages of pregnancy, was allowed to leave the ship. As the negotiations continued, the British prepared to allow the children to proceed to Palestine, but the Turks, impatient at the dragging on of the discussions, ordered the ship to turn back into the Black Sea. On the night of February 24 it was sunk.

All but a single refugee were drowned.[9] Thirty-six years later, a Soviet naval history disclosed that the 'unguarded' *Struma* had been sunk by a Soviet submarine. The history added: 'Sergeant Major V. D. Chernov, Unit Commander Sergeant G. G. Nosov, and the Torpedo Operator Red Navy man I. M. Filatov, demonstrated exemplary courage in the action.'[10]

There had been no halt during February to the deportations to Chelmno. As the deportations continued, so too did the deception. In a second deportation of ten thousand Jews from the Lodz ghetto between February 22 and February 28, all of whom were sent to Chelmno and gassed, it was rumoured in the ghetto 'that the deportees were set free in Koluszki' – a railway junction less than twenty miles from Lodz, on the main Warsaw–Cracow line, and in the opposite direction to Chelmno. Another rumour 'had it that the deportees were in Kolo county and also in the vicinity of Brzesc Kujawski': Chelmno was indeed in Kolo county, although it was situated twenty-five miles from Brzesc Kujawski, again in the opposite direction. 'We mention these stories', the Ghetto Chronicle recorded at the end of February, 'only for the sake of accuracy in chronicling events, for in reality the ghetto has not received any precise information on which to base an idea as to the fate or even the whereabouts of the deportees.'

The Chronicle added that the 'mystery' of the destination of the deportees was depriving all the ghetto dwellers of sleep. One thing was certain: the 'resettlement' in February had been 'significantly more severe' than the one in January. Most of the German guards, the Chronicle recorded, had ordered the deportees 'to throw away their knapsacks and often even the bundles they were carrying by hand, including the food supplies they had taken with them for their journey into the unknown'.[11]

The first week of March 1942 saw the Jewish festival of Purim, a time of rejoicing at the defeat of Haman the Amalekite. It was Haman who had tried, in ancient days, to destroy all the Jews of the Persian Empire, intending not to leave 'the least remains of them, nor preserve any of them, either for slaves or for captives'. Since the first days of the invasion of Poland in September 1939, the Germans had used the Jewish festivals for particular savagery: these days had become known to the Jews as the 'Goebbels calendar'.

In Minsk, on the eve of Purim, the Germans ordered the Jewish Council to hand over five thousand Jews for deportation 'to the west'. The Council did not know what to do. Some members suggested that small children, and the elderly, might be sent away. But those Jews who wanted no collaboration whatsoever with the Germans in these demands insisted on 'no trading in Jewish souls'. Hiding places had already been prepared in cellars and ruined buildings. Those who felt they were endangered hid.

On the morning of March 2 the Jewish labour battalions were sent out of the ghetto as usual. Then the Gestapo approached the Jewish Council for the five thousand, urging haste, 'because the trains were ready and waiting'. The Jewish Council refused. In fury, the Gestapo sent German and White Russian policemen to search the ghetto. Reaching a children's nursery, they ordered the woman in charge, Dr Chernis, and the supervisor, Fleysher, to take their children to the Jewish Council building.

The order was a trap. On reaching a specially dug pit on Ratomskaya Street, the children were seized by Germans and Ukrainians, and thrown alive into the deep sand. At that moment, several SS officers, among them Wilhelm Kube, arrived, whereupon Kube, immaculate in his uniform, threw handfuls of sweets to the shrieking children. All the children perished in the sand.[12]

That night, when the Jewish forced labourers returned to Minsk from their tasks outside the ghetto, they were ordered to lie down in the snow outside the ghetto gates. Any who tried to get up and run into the ghetto were shot. Others were taken to the pit in Ratomskaya Street and killed. Some were marched away from the city, to the Koidanovo forest, and murdered there. At least five thousand Jews were killed in Minsk during that Purim day.[13]

The Purim destructions were widespread; on March 1 the Jews of Krosniewice, in western Poland, after having been ordered to assemble, were told by the German mayor that, on the following day, they were to be resettled in the south, in distant Bessarabia. They should go home, he said, and have a good night's sleep in preparation for such a long journey. On the next morning they were all deported thirty miles westward, to Chelmno, and gassed.[14]

In the Baranowicze ghetto, in White Russia, the Chairman of the Jewish Council, Joshua Izykson, and his secretary, Mrs Genia Men, were ordered, that same Purim, to draw up a list of all old and sick Jews, and to deliver these Jews to the Gestapo. They refused to do so. Both were shot.[15] But first, they had been forced to watch the torture and execution of some of the three thousand Jews rounded up that day.

The system chosen by the Gestapo to 'select' Jews of Baranowicze for destruction was one which they were to repeat in different cities at different times. Cards were issued, in this instance marked with the letter 'O', as alleged evidence that the holder was employed by the German authorities as a labourer. But the holders of the cards feared a trap, and hid. Even while the cards were being distributed in the ghetto square, White Russian police, known as 'Ravens', would strike at random with their rifle butts at the stomachs of those being given their cards.

On the following day, March 5, the holders of the cards were ordered to assemble. German, Lithuanian and Ukrainian police, brought specially to Baranowicze, dragged hundreds from their homes and hiding places. The local 'Ravens' were equally active. Then, as an eye-witness later recalled, 'SS men made their selection, sending some people to the left and some to the right. Those on the left were beaten cruelly, while those on the right were compelled to look on at the spectacle. Those sentenced to death were carried away from the ghetto in lorries. Later it became known that these had been taken away to a grave near the railway line, some three kilometres from the town.'

Pits had been dug at this site by Russian prisoners-of-war. Ten Jewish policemen, led by their commander, Weltman, were then ordered to dig a further pit, for the Russians. Jews and Russians were then murdered. As for the Jewish policemen, 'not one of them returned'. In all, 3,300 Jews were murdered that Purim in Baranowicze.[16]

Also during the Purim festival, at Zdunska Wola, thirty miles west of Lodz, the Gestapo asked the Jewish Council for ten young, healthy Jews, 'for work'. Dora Rosenboim, an eye-witness of what followed, later recalled:

> The Gestapo ordered the Jewish police to bring the ten Jews to a place where a gallows had already been prepared and the Jewish police had to hang the ten Jews with their own hands. To add to this horrible, unheard-of crime, the Gestapo drove all the Jews out of the houses to the hanging-place, so that all the Jews should witness the great catastrophe. Many women fainted seeing the terrible and horrible sight, how ten of our brothers were writhing on the gallows. Our faces were ashamed and our hearts ached, but we could not help ourselves.[17]

According to another account, the Chairman of the Jewish Council at Zdunska Wola, Dr Jakub Lemberg, had been ordered by the Germans to deliver ten Jews to the Gestapo, as 'substitutes' for the ten hanged sons of Haman, the Jew-hater, in the biblical narrative. But Dr Lemberg replied that he would only deliver four Jews, himself, his wife and their two children. In revenge for this defiance, Dr Lemberg was taken out and shot by orders of Hans Biebow, the chief of the German Ghetto Administration in Lodz.[18]

The sadism of the murderers was in evidence throughout the lands of their occupation. In the Janowska labour camp at Lvov, on the first day of Purim, six Jews were forced to spend the night outside the barracks, on the grounds that they 'looked sick' and should not infect the others. The temperature was at freezing point. 'In the morning,' Leon Weliczker later recalled, 'all six people were frozen lying down where they were put out the night before; completely white like long balls of snow.'

Two days later, early on the morning of March 4, eight more labourers were picked out at Janowska because, according to Dibauer, the Gestapo chief, 'they didn't look too clean'. Dibauer ordered a barrel of water to be brought. The eight Jews were then forced to undress, and to stand in it. It was early morning. All day and all night they were not allowed to get out. 'Next morning', Weliczker recalled, 'we had to cut the ice away. Ice. It was frozen. The men were frozen to death.'

A week after this incident, Dibauer was joined at the camp by SS Second Lieutenant Bilhaus. The two men decided to compete in a shooting game. They would stand at their windows while Jews were being marched to and fro carrying stones, and would shoot, 'aiming at the tip of a nose or a finger'. In the evening, Weliczker recalled, these two 'sportsmen' would go round 'picking out what they called the *kaput* people, those who were injured, because as injured people they were no good any more, and finish them off with a shot'.

Dibauer also had a reputation for enjoying strangling people. 'In my group,' Weliczker later recalled, 'a man who was working alongside me happened to look away, didn't look so busy; Dibauer approached, took him, and strangled him with his own hands on the spot.'[19]

Confronted by such sadism, Jews everywhere sought some means of survival. But even in White Russia, where groups of Red Army partisan groups had begun fighting behind German lines, the path to resistance was perilous. After the Purim massacre in Minsk, many Jews had tried to escape from the ghetto to join the partisans. One group, led by Nahum Feldman, reached the forests just as a battle was being fought between the Germans and the partisans, and, unable to approach the battle zone, was forced to return to the ghetto. Others who escaped were caught by the Germans while on their way to the forests, and shot. One well-known Jewish Communist in Minsk, Hirsh Skovia, reached the partisans, but died when his feet froze during a German attack on the partisan base.[20]

News of one act of resistance, reaching the Jews of Warsaw in March, was published in one of the many underground newspapers which kept the ghetto population informed of whatever was known. This particular report came from the town of Nowogrodek, in eastern Poland, scene of the execution of five thousand Jews in December 1941. 'In the city of Nowogrodek,' the newspaper wrote, 'there were two hundred Jews who refused to go to the execution site like beasts driven to the slaughter. They found the courage to rise, weapon in hand, against Hitler's hangmen. Although they all fell in the unequal fight, before their own death they killed twenty of the murderers.' The newspaper added: 'In wonder and respect we bow our heads at the grave of the heroes of Nowogrodek. They are a symbol of the end to surrender and slavish obsequiousness. They are a symbol of the proud bearing of human beings who wish to die as free men.'[21]

Although this act of defiance at the massacre site in Nowogrodek has been shown by historical research to be a myth, the report of it certainly gave the Jews of Warsaw cause for pride. At the same time, south-east of Warsaw, in the forests near Wlodawa, a group of young Jews had begun to form a small resistance group. Their fate, however, showed in miniature the stupendous problems of all such resistance. In a remote wood, twenty-five Jews were in hiding, women and children as well as men. They lived in dug-outs in the forest. After some months, more than a hundred peasants, local Ukrainians, came to their hide-out and ordered them to leave it. There was a short fight, but the Jews were outnumbered and overwhelmed.

The peasants were armed; the Jews were not. The hundred peasants were all able-bodied men; the twenty-five Jews included women and children. The peasants had lived in their villages with food and freedom to move about; the Jews had been in hiding, hungry and alone, so fearful of being betrayed that, while the peasants had been searching for them, a couple had killed their own child so that its crying would not reveal their hiding place.

'When we were taken out of the hole', the twenty-four-year-old Hersh Werner later recalled, 'I said, "We must run, or we're done for." The father of the dead child said, "I'm not running." He hadn't got it in him any more.'

The peasants took the Jews to their village, Zamolodicze, and locked them in a barn. Then they took the Jews out one by one. Twenty-one of the Jews were killed. Four managed to escape. These four had then to begin again the search for a hide-out, the search for other Jews, the search for the means of survival. 'You were running from one place to another,' Werner later recalled. 'You had no possessions.'[22] Eventually this particular group acquired some rifles, and began to ambush German patrols. It also organized, as best it could, the escape of Jews from some of the nearby ghettos. It even succeeded in rescuing several Jewish girls from a farm at Adampol, girls kept there 'for the pleasure of the German officers'.

On one occasion the group, when twenty-five strong, killed ten German soldiers. As this battle was in progress, one of the German soldiers, and a German woman who was with him, surrendered. Both were shot. 'We had seen such brutality inflicted on the Jews,' Werner later wrote, 'we had no mercy for them. It was the first time that we saw dead Germans in this war, not only dead Jews.'[23]

In the second week of March 1942, deportations began from central Europe to the region of the new death camp at Belzec. The first deportees were 1,001 Jews from the ghetto at Theresienstadt. Their train, 'Transport Aa', left the ghetto on March 11, reaching the village of Izbica Lubelska, north of Belzec, two days later. At Izbica they were kept in the ghetto, made to clear rubble, and later sent to Belzec. Of the 1,001 Jews in this first deportation from Theresienstadt, only six survived the war.[24]

On March 12, while the 1,001 Jews in this Theresienstadt transport were crossing central Europe, eight thousand Jews from the southern Polish town of Mielec were ordered to be at the railway station on the following morning. Like the deportees from Theresienstadt, they were told that they were to be sent to 'work' further east. Loaded with heavy bundles containing the basic necessities for life in a new region, a few personal mementoes, and whatever small items of value they still possessed after two and a half years of privation, the Jews of Mielec assembled on the morning of March 13. There, without warning, nearly two thousand children and old people were shot down.[25] The others were deported, not to work in the east, nor to a labour camp, but to Belzec.

This deportation from Mielec was among the first of more than two hundred deportations from almost every Jewish community in the Lublin region and Galicia. On March 16 the first sixteen hundred Jews from the Lublin ghetto were deported to Belzec, followed in the next week by a further ten thousand.[26]

On reaching Belzec, a few hundred Jews were chosen as forced labourers within the camp. All others were gassed. Of the six hundred thousand Jews deported to this single death camp, only two are known to have survived, Rudolf Reder and Chaim Hirszman. In 1942, Hirszman was a twenty-nine-year-old metal worker. In his eye-witness account to the Jewish Historical District

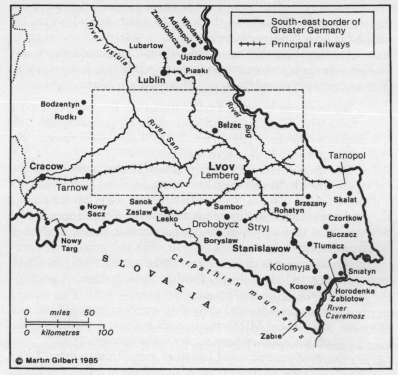

BELZEC

THE LVOV REGION

Commission in Lublin on 19 March 1946, he recalled how, in the deportation from Zaklikow, the town to which he and his family had earlier been deported from elsewhere, a 'selection' took place. 'I was sent to the side of those selected for work, but since my wife and my half-a-year-old son were sent to the opposite side, I asked to join them and was permitted to do so.' Hirszman's account continued:

We were entrained and taken to Belzec. The train entered a small forest. Then, the entire crew of the train was changed. SS men from the death camp replaced the railroad employees. We were not aware of this at that time.

The train entered the camp. Other SS men took us off the train. They led us all together – women, men, children – to a barrack. We were told to undress before we go to the bath. I understood immediately what that meant. After undressing we were told to form two groups, one of men and the other of women with children. An SS man, with the strike of a horse-whip, sent the men to the right or to the left, to death – to work.

I was selected to death, I didn't know it then. Anyway, I believed that both sides meant the same – death. But, when I jumped in the indicated direction, an SS man called me and said: 'Du bist ein Militarmensch, dich konnen wir brauchen.' ('You have a military bearing, we could use you.')

We, who were selected for work, were told to dress. I and some other men were appointed to take the people to the kiln. I was sent with the women. The Ukrainian Schmidt, an Ethnic German, was standing at the entrance to the gas-chamber and hitting with a knout every entering woman. Before the door was closed, he fired a few shots from his revolver and then the door closed automatically and forty minutes later we went in and carried the bodies out to a special ramp. We shaved the hair of the bodies, which were afterwards packed into sacks and taken away by Germans.

The children were thrown into the chamber simply on the women's heads. In one of the 'transports' taken out of the gas chamber, I found the body of my wife and I had to shave her hair.

The bodies were not buried on the spot, the Germans waited until more bodies were gathered. So, that day we did not bury. . . .[27]

Chaim Hirszman's experiences at Belzec were also set down in 1946 by his second wife, Pola, to whom he often retold them after the war. Among the incidents of which he told her was one, when a transport with children up to three years old arrived. 'The workers were told to dig one big hole into which the children were thrown and buried alive. My husband recollected this with horror. He couldn't forget how the earth had been rising until the children suffocated'.

Later, as Pola Hirszman recalled:

The Germans discovered that one of the prisoners, a Czechoslovak Jew, had been planning an escape. The SS men ordered the prisoners to build gallows. They gathered all the prisoners and ordered them to participate in the execution. My husband was told to fetch a rope and to tie the convict up. My husband managed somehow to get out of this, since there was one Jew there, an expert in tying up.

Before he was hanged, the condemned said: 'I am perishing, but Hitler will die and the Germans will lose the war.'

The prisoners were constantly beaten and every day many of the workers from the regular staff were killed.

Typhus was prevailing, but one had to avoid admitting the disease. The sick were murdered on the spot. Getting medical treatment or lying down was out of the question.

Sick with typhus and with a fever of 40°C, my husband worked and somehow managed to conceal his condition from the Germans. . . .

Transports arrived every day. Mainly from Poland, but also from other European countries, from Germany, Austria, Czechoslovakia and others. In one of the transports there was a Ukrainian woman. She possessed documents that proved she was a genuine Aryan and there was no doubt about it. And yet she went to the gas-chamber.

Once you crossed the gate to the camp, there was no chance to get out of there alive. Not even any Germans, except for the camp staff, had access to the camp. . . .

Two Czechoslovak Jewesses were working in the camp office. They, too, had never entered the camp. They even enjoyed a certain freedom of movement. They often went with the SS men to town to arrange different matters. One day they were told that they would visit the camp. The SS men showed them around the camp and in a certain moment they led the women to the gas-chamber and when they were inside, the door closed behind them. They finished with them in spite of the promise that they would live.

The Germans ordered the prisoners to set up a football team and on Sundays games were being played. Jews played with SS men, the same ones who tortured and murdered them. The SS men treated this as a matter of sport, and when they lost a game, they had no complaints.

There wasn't even one day without a transport. Mainly women and children were being conveyed. The Ukrainians employed in the camp treated people even more sadistically than the Germans. The Jews were planning a revolt and a general escape, but due to treason they had to abandon the plan. There were also women employed in the camp, but their number was much smaller than the number of men. There were no children at all.

Women worked. They were selected from the transports. One had always to look content, never to look sad, because if an SS man didn't like the look on someone's face, he would shoot him or send him to the chimney. At work they used to beat terribly. To turn around was forbidden, they shot for that.[28]

Trains travelled to Belzec from throughout the Lublin and Galician regions: a smooth pattern of deportation which had needed less than three months of bureaucratic preparation. The trains travelled mostly by night. Luba Krugman, a Jewish woman living in Chorbrzany, a small village near Lublin, later recalled:

At night the rumbling of the train woke me up. I rushed to the door and found it wide open, with father watching the dark monster, which had only one brightly illuminated car window behind the locomotive.

'It's a real Cyclops,' I said.

'I can't hear you,' replied father.

Our voices were drowned out by the clatter of the wheels and the penetrating whistle of the engine. I counted sixty-two cars. Father was breathing heavily, and his temples were moist with sweat. He wiped his forehead and opened his shirt.

'Please, close your shirt,' I implored. 'It's bitterly cold.' He did not hear; his eyes were fixed on the train.

A few windows opened. Our Gentile neighbours were awakened by the noise. The train passed, leaving behind a cloud of smoke. Windows were closing when one harsh voice came through loudly: 'Those damned Jews – they won't even let one sleep at night.'[29]

Determined to maintain the deception, the German authorities gave persuasive reasons for each deportation. In the Eastern Galician town of Drohobycz they declared that three thousand Jews were needed 'for the reclamation of the Pripet marshes'. To secure the necessary numbers, the Jewish Council compiled a list of three hundred poorer Jews, those who were particularly in need of some remunerative work, or at least of a roof over their heads, and fixed the date of their departure. An eye-witness later recalled how these three hundred Jews 'calmly made preparations for the journey'. Although it was rumoured 'that while getting into the train the Germans robbed the Jews of their belongings', nobody had been able to confirm even this rumour.[30] As for the destination of the three thousand, it was not the Pripet marshes, it was Belzec.[31]

The village-by-village massacres in German-occupied Russia had continued without respite throughout the early months of 1942. No village was too remote, no Jewish community too small, to be overlooked. On the night of March 16 it was upon the 1,816 Jews of the village of Pochep that the execution squads descended. All were 'brutally killed' in an anti-tank ditch just outside the village, as a memorial stone in the local cemetery records.[32]

On March 20, four days after the Pochep massacre, a train left the Rhineland for the ghetto of Piaski, near Belzec. At Piaski, as at Izbica Lubelska, new deportees were held only until a further deportation train arrived: sometimes for a few weeks, sometimes only for a few days. The train of March 20 included several Jews from Worms, among them Herta Mansbacher, the fifty-seven-year-old teacher who had so courageously sought to prevent the burning down of the synagogue in Worms in November 1938. Among those with whom she was deported were sixteen Jews who had been wounded and decorated in the First World War: three of these German army veterans were Julius Neumann, Manuel Katz and Moritz Mayer.

From the ghetto at Piaski, Moritz Mayer was allowed to send a postcard. Its message read: 'We hope and pray with unswerving faith in God that, in time, the Almighty will rectify all things.'[33] The historian of the destruction of the Jewry of Worms has commented on this message: 'There is no greater courage than the one required to sustain hope and faith in the presence of evil.'[34]

On March 26 it was the turn of more than two thousand of the Jews in the ghetto at Izbica Lubelska to be deported, to 'make room', they were told, for the recent deportees from Theresienstadt. These were the 1,001 Jews from 'Transport Aa' of March 11, and a further 1,000 on 'Transport Ab', which had left Theresienstadt on March 17. From this second group of 1,000, only three were to survive the war.[35] Deportations from the ghetto at Izbica Lubelska to Belzec were to take place each time a new deportation reached the ghetto from the west. None was spared. Nor was escape from Izbica Lubelska possible. 'The Jews of Izbica are completely disorientated,' the Polish doctor, Zygmunt Klukowski, of nearby Szczebrzeszyn, was to note in his diary on March 29, 'don't know what to do, whether to hide or sit still and wait. They are afraid to go beyond the town because the Germans kill them without question if discovered. We keep hearing of such incidents.'[36]

With the daily deportations from the west paralleled by daily deportation to 'the east', rumours abounded throughout the Lublin region. On March 26 Klukowski noted in his diary:

There is great unhappiness and fear among the Jews. From everywhere comes the news about the incredible violence against the Jews. They are bringing trainloads of Jews from Czechoslovakia, Germany, and even from Belgium. They are also resettling the Jews from various towns and villages and taking them somewhere towards Belzec. Today I heard a story about what they did to the Jews in Lublin. It is difficult to believe it's true. Today they deported the Jews from Izbica – they were also taken to Belzec where there is supposed to be some monstrous camp.[37]

At this 'monstrous camp' more than six hundred thousand Jews were murdered in less than a year.[38] No selection was made to keep alive those capable of work: only a few hundred were chosen

to be part of a *Sonderkommando*, or 'Special Commando', some
employed in taking the bodies of those who had been gassed to the
burial pits, others in sorting the clothes of the victims and in
preparing those clothes and other belongings for despatch to Germany. Eventually, the members of this Sonderkommando were also
murdered. 'The procedure is pretty barbaric,' Josef Goebbels noted
in his diary on March 27, 'one not to be described here most
definitely. Not much will remain of the Jews.'

'On the whole,' Goebbels added, 'about sixty per cent will have to
be liquidated, whereas only forty per cent can be used for forced
labour.' In fact, at Belzec, even the two or three per cent of arrivals
who were sent to join the Sonderkommando were then murdered.
The measures necessary, Goebbels noted, were being carried out by
the former Gauleiter of Vienna, General Odilo Globocnik, who was
acting 'with considerable circumspection and according to a
method that does not attract too much attention'. A judgement was
being visited upon the Jews, Goebbels concluded, that, 'while
barbaric, is fully deserved by them'.[39]

At Auschwitz, the gas-chambers and crematoria being built at
nearby Birkenau were not yet ready. The first deportees, 999 Slovak
Jewish women, were therefore kept in barracks after their arrival at
Auschwitz on March 26. In the following four weeks, Jews reached
the camp every few days, the majority, more than six thousand,
being men and women from Slovakia.[40] But there were also 1,112
Jews from Paris, most of them Polish-born, who had been seized in
Paris in the previous months, held in detention camp at Compiègne,
and who reached Auschwitz on March 30.[41] Here, they waited with
the Slovak Jews, not knowing what was in prospect.

This first deportation from France had left Paris three days
earlier, on March 27, as 'special train 767'. As with all the deportations of the coming two years, a precise timetable had been
devised for it:

27 March		
Bourget-Drancy	dep 17.00	
Compiegne	arr 18.40	
	dep 19.40	
Laon	arr 21.05	
	dep 21.23	
Reims	arr 22.25	

                              28 March
                                    dep 9.10
          Neuberg (frontier)   arr 13.59
                    30 March
          Auschwitz   arr 5.33

Of the 1,112 deportees on this train from Paris, one, Georges
Rueff, managed to jump from the train and escape. Of the rest, only
twenty-one were alive five months later. Among those on the train
who were to be gassed during the summer was the forty-four-year-
old Israel Chlebowski, who had been born in Przytyk, the village in
which the pogrom of 1936 had so shocked Polish Jewry. Others
murdered from this train of March 27 were the forty-year-old
Ignatz Baum, born in Haifa; Henry Eckstein, born in London in
1915; several Jews born in French North Africa, including Sadia
Sarfati from Oran and Maurice Behar from Tunis; a twenty-nine-
year-old Jew born in Constantinople, Abram Adjibel, and Moise
Schneider, aged forty-one, who had been born in the then Austro-
Hungarian frontier town of Auschwitz, to which he was now,
unsuspecting, to return.[42]

By the end of March 1942 the gassing of Jews was taking place daily
at Chelmno and Belzec. At the same time, gas-chambers were under
construction at Birkenau and Sobibor. To gain a first-hand report of
the effectiveness of the new system in action, Gestapo chief Heinrich
Muller sent Adolf Eichmann to Chelmno. Nineteen years later, in a
courtroom in Jerusalem, Eichmann recalled his visit:

> There was a room – if I remember correctly – perhaps five
> times as large as this one. Perhaps it was only four times as big
> as the one I am sitting in now. And Jews were inside. They were
> to strip and then a truck arrived where the doors open, and the
> van pulled up at a hut. The naked Jews were to enter. Then the
> doors were hermetically sealed and the car started.

Eichmann could not recall how many people were inside the van,
explaining to the court:

> I couldn't even look at it. All the time I was trying to avert my
> sight from what was going on. It was quite enough for me what

I saw. The screaming and shrieking – I was too excited to have a look at the van. I told Muller that in my report. He didn't derive much profit from my report and afterwards I followed the van. Some of them knew the way, of course. And then I saw the most breathtaking sight I have ever seen in my life.

The van was making for an open pit. The doors were flung open and corpses were cast out as if they were some animals – some beasts. They were hurled into the ditch. I also saw how the teeth were being extracted. And then I disappeared; I entered my car and I didn't want to look at this heinous act of turpitude. Then I took the car; for hours I was sitting at the side of the driver without exchanging a word with him. Then I knew I was washed up. It was quite enough for me. I only know that I remember a doctor in a white apron – there was a doctor in white uniform. He was looking at them. I couldn't say anything more. I had to leave because it was too much, as much as I could stand.

According to Eichmann, he had told Muller that the scene at Chelmno was 'horrible, it's an indescribable inferno'.[43]

At Belzec, the man in charge of the killings was Christian Wirth, who was also given the task of choosing someone to organize a third death camp, at Sobibor. Wirth chose Franz Stangl, who went to prepare the site at Sobibor, helped by Michel Hermann, formerly the head male nurse at the largest of the German euthanasia centres, Schloss Hartheim. Stangl later recalled his first visit to Belzec, by car from Sobibor. 'The smell,' he said, 'oh God, the smell. It was everywhere.' Stangl's account continued:

Wirth wasn't in his office; they said he was up in the camp. I asked whether I should go up there and they said, 'I wouldn't if I were you – he's mad with fury. It isn't healthy to be near him.' I asked what was the matter. The man I was talking to said that one of the pits had overflowed. They had put too many corpses in it and putrefaction had progressed too fast, so that the liquid underneath had pushed the bodies on top up and over and the corpses had rolled down the hill. I saw some of them – oh God, it was awful. A bit later Wirth came down. And that's when he told me. . . .

I said to Wirth that I couldn't do it, I simply wasn't up to such an assignment. There wasn't any argument or discussion.

Wirth just said my reply would be reported to HQ and I was to go back to Sobibor. In fact I went to Lublin, tried again to see Globocnik, again in vain; he wouldn't see me. When I got back to Sobibor, Michel and I talked and talked about it. We agreed that what they were doing was a crime. We considered deserting – we discussed it for a long time. But how? Where could we go? What about our families?

Stangl continued with the construction of the gas-chambers and crematoria at Sobibor. One afternoon, before the gas-chambers were finished, Wirth arrived unexpectedly. Stangl was at once summoned to the still unfinished gas-chamber. 'When I got there,' he later recalled, 'Wirth stood in front of the building wiping the sweat off his cap and fuming. Michel told me later that he'd suddenly appeared, looked around the gas-chambers on which they were still working and said, "Right, we'll try it out right now with those twenty-five work-Jews: get them up here." They marched our twenty-five Jews up there and just pushed them in, and gassed them. Michel said Wirth behaved like a lunatic, hit out at his own staff with his whip to drive them on. And then he was livid because the doors hadn't worked properly.'

Wirth ordered the gas-chamber doors to be changed, and left.[44]

At camp Jungfernhof in Riga, Gerda Rose-Wasserman was present on March 26 at a further selection of German Jews for work at the alleged 'fish factory' in Duenamuende. That day the Germans asked for fifteen hundred 'workers'. Many refused to be separated from their parents; others were tempted by the promise of easy indoor work and the likelihood of better food at such a location. 'But when some of the young people', Gerda Rose-Wasserman later recalled, 'wanted to go along with their parents,' SS Sergeant Seck, the commandant of Jungfernhof, refused to give them permission to do so. Gerda Rose-Wasserman went down on her knees, begging to be allowed to go along with her mother and little brother. 'Seck just smiled at her,' Gertrude Schneider, the historian of the Riga ghetto, later wrote, 'said something about how pretty she was, and refused her pleas. To many of the inmates, his behaviour seemed ominous, but for those already loaded upon the trucks, such second thoughts came much too late.'

As a result of the pressure of those who hoped for better conditions away from Riga, four hundred more Jews than the SS had asked for left the city that Sunday, March 26. They were taken, not to a distant labour camp, but to the nearby Bikernieker forest. On the following day several trucks entered the Riga ghetto, and were unloaded. 'Their cargo was an assortment of personal effects of the people who had been resettled. There were clothes that had been taken off hurriedly by their owners – still turned inside out – stockings attached to girdles and shoes encrusted with mud. The trucks also yielded nursing bottles, children's toys, eye-glasses, bags filled with food, and satchels containing photographs and documents.'

The women from the ghetto were ordered to sort out the clothes. The best items were to be sent to Germany, the rest to be distributed among the inmates of the ghetto. Gertrude Schneider later recalled how, as the women worked at the sorting, 'They recognized many of the clothes, some by the names that had been sewn into them, some by the identity cards still in the pockets, and there were of course, dresses, coats and suits which they had seen on their friends and neighbours when they had left the ghetto only a few days before.' Her account continued:

> Soon everyone in the ghetto knew about the cargo that the trucks had brought and about the conditions of the clothes. It did not take any great imagination to understand what had happened to their owners. No longer did anyone scoff at the tales of the Latvian Jews nor think that this could happen only to Ostjuden and never to the Jews from Germany. In many houses, in the ghetto, *Kaddish*, the Hebrew prayer for the dead, was recited. The German ghetto was plunged into despair.[45]

Among those murdered at the Bikernieker forest that day was Chief Rabbi Joseph Carlebach.[46]

Throughout Eastern Europe, rumours abounded as to some sinister fate for the growing number of Jews being deported 'to the East'. But the exact nature of that fate was still unknown. Also unknown was the reason: the 'final solution', worked out administratively at Wannsee, remained a tight secret. Even so, evidence that the killings were not to be limited to a single region, or to chance, began to be clear to the Jews in Warsaw towards the end of March 1942, with a second messenger with evil tidings. The first had been Heniek Grabowski, who had brought with him in November 1941 an account of the mass killings in Vilna that autumn. The second was Yakov Grojanowski, who now gave his eye-witness account of the disposal of the murdered Jews and Gypsies at Chelmno.

One of those who had heard both messengers tell their stories was Yitzhak Zuckerman. He and his friends had been trying for some months to organize at least the nucleus of an underground organization. 'We, after we heard the story about Vilna on the one hand and the story about Chelmno on the other, we believed that this was the system and this was the plan.' Until then, he recalled, 'we could not believe that a nation in the twentieth century can pronounce a sentence of death on a whole nation, and we used to ask ourselves: "They degrade us, they suppress us, do they plan to exterminate us all?" We did not believe that.'[47]

A small band of young men and women now came to understand that the killings were part of a wider, sinister plan. As Yitzhak Zuckerman recalled, 'In the East it burned and in the West it burned. Chelmno is in the Warthegau area and we were right in between, in the middle.' Of course, he added, 'the fire would reach us. We, the Jews of Warsaw, knew we were no better. We would not be spared.'

Looking back upon those years, Zuckerman later recalled the isolation of the Jews of Warsaw. 'We thought the entire world was being defeated,' he said. 'The undergrounds all over the world had not yet started operating.'[48]

In spite of what they felt to be their total isolation, a small group of Warsaw Jews decided to organize for resistance. 'There can be no doubt', one of their underground newspapers wrote on March 28, 'that Hitler, sensing that the downfall of his regime is approaching, intends to drown the Jews in a sea of blood.' The cultural and educational work that had continued in the ghetto would have to give way to preparation 'for such difficult days'. Despite the destruction, 'mobilization of the vital forces of the Jews' would have to begin. 'From generation to generation,' the article added, 'we are troubled by the burden of passivity and lack of faith in our own strength; but our history also contains glorious and shining pages of heroism and struggle. We are obliged to join these eras of heroism. . . .'[49]

The young Jews were able to build upon certain existing preparations. Three months earlier, Emanuel Ringelblum was invited, during a break in a lecture that he was giving on the history of the Jewish labour movement, by two of the organizers of resistance, Mordecai Anielewicz and Yosef Kaplan, to a room in which they showed him 'two revolvers'. These revolvers, they explained, 'were to be employed to train youth in the use of arms'.[50]

As these preparations continued, so did the deportations, gassings and random killings, without respite. On April 1 a further thousand Jews were deported from Theresienstadt to the ghetto at Piaski. Only four were to survive the war.[51] On April 2 a further 965 Slovak Jews were deported to Auschwitz, and held in the barracks at Birkenau; by the end of the month, eight more transports brought the number of Slovak Jews deported to Birkenau to eight thousand in a single month.[52]

April 2 was Passover, festival of the liberation of the Jews from their bondage in Egypt. In different towns it was remembered in different ways. The historian of the Jewish community in Jaworow, in Eastern Galicia, has recorded:

> During the Passover holidays of 1942, there came to Jaworow a high-ranking Nazi, a fellow by the name of Steuer. His ferocious deeds will never be erased from the memory of Jaworow Jews, and those of Grodek, Krakowice and Janow. Each time this Hitler satrap visited a town or village, he left a trail of tears, torture and sorrow. His appetite for loot was insatiable, and the Jewish Council had no choice but to supply him with whatever they could. . . .
>
> Steuer made surprise visits to the Council and lashed out at those present. Unexpectedly he forced his way into Jewish homes, swept the dishes from the table to the floor, smashed the furniture and obscenely humiliated the women. He flogged Ida Lipshitz. He grabbed Polka Cipper who was married to the Jew, Dolek Guttman, ordered her to undress, ground her bare toes with his boots, and whipped her unmercifully. He delighted in striking blows at women with bare fists until their blood flowed, and chasing them nude into the cold outdoors.[53]

The Jews of Jaworow were unaware of the deportations to Belzec: deportations of which they, too, would be the victims within a few months. But Jews escaping from Lublin did bring to Warsaw accounts of the killings in their city, and of the deportations from Lublin to Belzec between March 15 and March 26, when ten thousand Jews had been seized, deported and gassed. 'We tremble at the mention of Lublin,' Chaim Kaplan noted in his diary on April 7. 'Our blood turns to ice when we listen to tales told by refugees from the city. Even before they arrived in the Warsaw ghetto, the rumours reaching us were so frightful that we thought they came from totally unreliable sources.'

The refugees had not mentioned Belzec. 'When the great hunt began,' Kaplan noted, 'thousands of Jews were rounded up and led – where? Nobody knows.' Kaplan added: 'That is the Nazis' way. Forty thousand homeless and panic-stricken Jews were taken by the Nazi overlords and led to some unknown place to be massacred. According to one rumour they were taken to Rawa-Ruska and were electrocuted there.'

The trains from Lublin had indeed set off in the direction of Rawa-Ruska. But ten miles before that town their journey had ended, at Belzec. The shocking details brought by the refugees related, not to the fate of the deportees, but to the savagery of the Germans in Lublin itself, as the deportations began. As Kaplan recorded:

> As Jews tried to escape, the Nazis hunted them down. Heeding the advice of the prophet, 'Wait a little until the danger is past', some Jews tried to conceal themselves in obscure holes and corners. Perhaps God would have mercy and spare them? Perhaps the Keeper of Israel would take pity? But the killers discovered the hiding places and swiftly put to death anyone they found. Some of the Jews suffocated in these airless holes even before the Nazis discovered them, for the doors could not be opened from within and there was no one to open them from without because everyone above ground had been arrested.[54]

What was unknown in Warsaw was known at Szczebrzeszyn, one of the towns nearest to Belzec. On April 8 the Polish doctor, Zygmunt Klukowski, noted in his diary 'a great depression among the Jews', and he went on to explain: 'We know now for certain that one train every day from the direction of Lublin, and one from the direction of Lvov, of twenty-odd wagons, each are going to Belzec. Here, they are taking the Jews out of the trains, pushing them behind barbed-wire fences and killing them either by electrocution or poisoning with gas, and after that they burn the remains.' Klukowski added:

> On the way to Belzec people can see horrifying scenes – especially the railwaymen – because the Jews know very well why they are being taken there, and on the journey they are given neither food nor water. On the station in Szczebrzeszyn the railwaymen could see with their own eyes, and hear with their own ears Jews offering 150 zlotys for a kilo of bread (i.e. about a month's wages), and a Jewess took off a gold ring from her finger and offered it in exchange for a glass of water for her dying child. The inhabitants of Lublin told me of some incredible scenes which are happening there among the Jews, shooting the sick on the spot, and outside the town – shooting the healthy ones and transporting thousands of others to Belzec.[55]

Even for those Jews unaware of Belzec, the spring of 1942 had become a time of horror. 'When will this terrible bloodshed finally end?' Dawid Rubinowicz asked in his diary on April 10, after three Jews had been murdered in a village near his own Bodzentyn. 'If it goes on much longer then people will drop like flies out of sheer horror.'[56]

Neither in Jaworow, nor in Warsaw, nor in Bodzentyn, was the truth about Belzec known. Meanwhile, immediately following the Lublin deportations, thousands of Jews from Eastern Galicia had been deported to Belzec and gassed, among them six thousand from Stanislawov on March 31, a thousand from Kolomyja on April 2, twelve hundred from Tlumacz on April 3 and fifteen hundred from Horodenka on April 4.[57] Among the Jews deported to Belzec from the Lublin region on April 9 were eight hundred from Lubartow.[58]

No day passed without a deportation, the railway routings having been meticulously planned, and the pace of gassing devised to match the number of arrivals. At Chelmno, too, the killings continued throughout April, at least eleven thousand Jews being murdered there in the single month, from more than ten communities in the Warthegau.[59] From the Lodz ghetto, more than twenty-four thousand Jews had been deported to Chelmno in March. All had been gassed.[60]

To maintain the deception of deportations to labour camps, an SS officer visited the Lodz ghetto on April 12, ten days after this third major 'resettlement' had ended, to explain the whereabouts of the forty-four thousand Jews deported from the ghetto since January. All had been sent to Chelmno, and gassed: but the SS officer 'explained' to the 115,000 Jews who remained 'that the deportees had all been brought to a camp near Warthbrucken', where a total of one hundred thousand Jews were already 'located'. The SS man added that some thirty thousand Germans, settlers, he said, from Galicia, had earlier stayed in this camp, and had left behind 'well-equipped barracks and even furniture'. Provisions for the Jews, he assured their worried relatives and friends, 'were excellent, and deportees fit for work were repairing roads or engaged in agriculture'.[61]

Warthbrucken was the German name for Kolo, the town nearest the Chelmno death camp. Workshops were to be set up there 'in the very near future', the SS officer explained.[62] It was an explanation cleverly designed to put the ghetto dwellers even more at their ease. For in the Lodz ghetto, workshops and survival were synonymous, so that the 'large influx of new orders' during April for shoes and knitted goods, as well as for clothing for the German army, gave an even greater sense of security.[63]

To maintain the deception that the camp near Kolo was a work camp, the Germans arranged for postcards to be sent from the deportees to say that they were 'in good health'. One such postcard, sent from a family that had been deported in January to Chelmno, from Turek, reached the Lodz ghetto in mid-April. This single card, with its encouraging message, was of sufficient importance to merit a special mention in the Ghetto Chronicle. No mention was made of the lack of postcards from any of the forty-four thousand Lodz deportees. At the same time there was ominous news: the arrival in the ghetto of large numbers of sewing machines, in the drawers of which notes and printed matter had been found from which 'one may conclude that they were sent here from small towns in Kolo and Kutno counties'.[64] These were in fact the sewing machines of the

Jews of Kolo, Bugaj, Dabie, Izbica Kujawska, Klodawa, Sompolno, Kutno, Krosniewice and Zychlin, all of whom had been deported to Chelmno and gassed between mid-December 1941 and mid-April 1942.[65]

The Germans were determined to maintain total deception. 'The Reichsführer desires', wrote Himmler's personal secretary to the Inspector for Statistics on April 10, 'that no mention be made of the "special treatment of the Jews". It must be called "transportation of the Jews towards the Russian East".'[66] Even 'special treatment' – *sonderbehandlung* – was understood to be too explicit a term.

While seeking to maintain their deception, the Germans also denounced those Poles who tried to help Jews. 'It is unfortunate', declared a German proclamation issued in Lvov on April 11, 'that the rural population continues – nowadays furtively – to assist Jews, thus doing harm to the community, and hence to themselves, by this disloyal attitude.' Poles were entering Jewish homes, the proclamation warned, to sell the Jews, 'at inflated prices', bread, butter, poultry and potatoes. Together with the money which the peasants took from the Jews, they also 'carry away from these homes pests, and germs of diseases, and distribute them over the village'.[67]

From throughout the Lublin region, once so vibrant a centre of Jewish life, the deportations to Belzec continued. On April 11, Zygmunt Klukowski noted in his diary that the Jews of Szczebrzeszyn had heard 'that today there was a transport of Jews from Chelm'. After their train had reached Belzec, 'the empty train – the so-called *Judenzug* – went back to Zamosc. Towards evening came the news that Zamosc was surrounded. Everyone is sure that now the round-up and transportation of the Zamosc Jews to their deaths will begin. In our town, the fear is indescribable. Some are resigned, others are going around the town insanely looking for help. Everyone is convinced that any day now the same thing will happen in Szczebrzeszyn.'[68]

As feared, the round-up of Zamosc Jews took place. An eyewitness, David Mekler, later recalled:

> On 11 April 1942, the SS, SD and the mounted police fell like a pack of savages on the Zamosc Jewish quarter. It was a

complete surprise. The brutes on horseback in particular created a panic; they raced through the streets shouting insults, slashing out on all sides with their whips. Our community then numbered ten thousand people. In a twinkling, without even realizing what was happening, a crowd of three thousand men, women and children, picked up haphazardly in the streets and in the houses, were driven to the station and deported to an unknown destination.

The spectacle which the ghetto presented after the attack literally drove the survivors mad. Bodies everywhere, in the streets, in the courtyards, inside the houses; babies thrown from the third or fourth floors lay crushed on the pavements. The Jews themselves had to pick up and bury the dead.[69]

News of the Zamosc deportation reached Szczebrzeszyn on the following day, April 12. 'Several hundred were killed on the spot,' Klukowski noted, 'apparently some tried to resist. However, we don't have any details and we don't know anything for sure. Among our own Jews there is a great panic. Some old Jewish women were sleeping in the Jewish cemetery, they would rather die here in their own town – among the graves of their own people – than in Belzec, among horrifying tortures.'

Some Jews, Klukowski added, were taking the risk of 'running away' to other villages. Many others were 'preparing hide-outs on the spot'. Others were sending their children to Warsaw 'to be cared for by trusted Aryans'.[70]

On April 12 there was a rumour in the Warsaw ghetto that an 'extermination squad' had reached Warsaw itself. This squad, so rumour reported, had 'begged' the local Gestapo for permission 'to go on a rampage through the ghetto for just two hours'. Permission, Ringelblum noted, 'was not granted'. 'One is always hearing reports', he added, 'about extermination squads that are wiping complete Jewish settlements off the face of the earth.'

Ringelblum also made a note of the fate of 164 German Jews who had come to Warsaw in mid-April, 'the cream of the young people'. They had been sent to the 'penal camp' at Treblinka, 'where most of them were exterminated in a short time'. Also at Treblinka, 'out of 160 Jewish young people from Otwock only 38 were left', after only three weeks at the camp.[71]

Unknown to Ringelblum, or to the Jews of Warsaw, the labour

camp at Treblinka was in the process of being transformed into a death camp, for Warsaw Jewry. The rumours that month were of other places and plans, however. 'It is said that all the Jews will be settled in Arabia or somewhere,' Mary Berg noted in her diary on April 15. She added that because the hours of curfew had been reduced, it was said that 'regular workshops' were to be set up in the ghetto 'which would ensure steady jobs for the Jews'. This, Mary Berg added, 'seems to contradict the talk of mass deportation'.[72]

In those communities where Jews had not yet been deported, the random killings continued. Early in April, in the Mlawa ghetto, a number of Jews were seized, among them several who were sick. They were made to stand on boxes, their hands tied behind their backs, and ropes tied around their necks. Then, for more than an hour, they were kept waiting, while their families were made to stand opposite them. All the while, the German policemen were mocking the victims, laughing, and dancing in front of them.

As the men stood there, one of them, Leibl Rumaner, died of a heart attack. Another, Mordechai Volarsky, declared: 'I wish we were the last victims.'

Jews were then taken from the crowd and ordered to pull the boxes from under the feet of the surviving victims. All were killed. That same day, two Jewish women were shot because bread and cakes were found on them. The Jews could no longer control their feelings: they were crying and shouting, to the fury of the Germans, who announced, to calm them, that the punishment was over, that nothing bad would happen to them in the future.

Two weeks later a hundred more Jews were seized in Mlawa, divided into two groups of fifty, and lined up facing each other. An announcement was then read out, stating that because, during the hangings of two weeks earlier, the Jews of the ghetto 'have cried and shouted', so now a new punishment was necessary. A hundred men ought to be shot. But the Gestapo had been 'kind enough' to reduce the number to fifty. If any Jew were to weep, however, or if the smallest sound were heard, all hundred would be shot.

The new victims were surrounded by German policemen with machine guns. All those assembled stood 'as if blood had frozen in their veins'. No sigh could be heard. The Gestapo chief then addressed the policemen: 'This is your fate,' he said, 'but also your good honour, to annihilate so many Jews. You should be proud, and carry out your task energetically. Shoot straight in the head.'

Five Jews were taken to the pit. Only then did it become clear which of the two groups was to be shot. The men led to the pit were ordered to face the firing squad. They were not blindfolded. One of the first five moved his head at the moment of firing, and was unscathed. He was ordered to wait at the side.

As each group of five tumbled into the pit, the commander shook the hands of the firing squad. Finally, the man who had moved his head and avoided death in the first group was taken back to the pit and shot: the fiftieth victim.[73]

The fifty who had been spared were then ordered to cover the dead with earth. Shlomo Malevantshik, a deportee from the nearby village of Szrensk, was among the saved. His brother Leibel had been among those shot. As Shlomo began to shovel earth on the bodies he heard his brother's voice crying: 'Shlomo, what are you doing, I am still alive!' But the Gestapo ordered the shovelling to continue. This, noted the historian of Szrensk, was 'the most dreadful tragedy of those dreadful times'.

Two of the dead, Yehiel and Jacob Shchepkovski, were the sons of a shoemaker from Szrensk. Before the war, the historian of the village recalled, 'there was always the sound of singing from his workshop. His love of children was widely known in the town. He was prepared to fight the whole world for his children.' When his sons Yehiel and Jacob were shot, 'It is not surprising that he lost his reason.'[74]

As the Jews of Mlawa waited, numbed by the savagery of the two mass executions, one Einsatzkommando unit, working deep inside the Soviet Union, reported back to Berlin that the whole Crimea had been 'purged of Jews'. More than ninety thousand Jews, the Einsatzkommando unit reported, had been murdered in the Crimea in the previous four and a half months.[75]

On April 3, 580 Jews were seized in Berlin for deportation 'to Poland'. On the eve of the deportation, 57 committed suicide. Six months later, when more than nine hundred were seized and sent to Estonia, 208 committed suicide.[76] Suicide was the conscious decision to end the unendurable: to refuse to remain at the whim of tormentors whose cruelties were sadistically drawn out: to die at one's chosen moment.

On May 4, in Lodz, a deportee from Frankfurt, the sixty-year-old Julia Baum, hanged herself. 'The reason', noted the Ghetto Chronicle that same day, was 'fear of deportation'.[77] Within a week, five more German Jews committed suicide in Lodz, rather than face a second 'resettlement'.[78] Fear of the unknown had led to what Michael Etkind, a survivor of the Lodz ghetto, has called 'the courage to commit suicide'.[79]

Suicide was a recognition not just of helplessness but of hopelessness. For the better educated, even when thousands were still alive around them, it followed the realization that there was no escape. Rabbinical wisdom opposed suicide. Rabbi Oshry had laid down six months earlier, during one of the German raids on Kovno ghetto, that although a man knew that he would 'definitely be subjected to unbearable suffering by the abominable murderers, and so hoped to be buried among Jews, he still was not allowed to commit suicide.' Oshry had gone on to say that permitting suicide, even to avoid witnessing the suffering and death of loved ones, meant 'surrendering to the abominable enemy', and as such was not permitted.

Rabbi Oshry also noted that, in Kovno, the Germans often remarked to the Jews: 'Why don't you commit suicide as the Jews of Berlin did?' Suicide, he said, was viewed 'as a great desecration of God, for it showed that a person had no trust in God's capability to save him from the accursed hands of his defilers.' The murderers' goal, Oshry commented, 'was to bring confusion into the lives of the Jews and to cause them the greatest despondency in order to make annihilating them all the easier.'

Oshry later reflected: 'I say proudly that in the Kovno ghetto there were only three instances of suicide by people who grew greatly despondent. The rest of the ghetto dwellers trusted and hoped that God would not forsake His people.'[80]

On the evening of Friday, April 17, shortly after the coming of the Sabbath, the Gestapo entered the Warsaw ghetto. Going from building to building with a list of names, they ordered the caretakers to summon those on the list. Six caretakers who hesitated were shot. Alexander Donat has recalled how those on the lists 'were told to walk straight ahead, and were shot through the back of the head'.

Fifty-two corpses, he wrote, 'were left lying in their own blood that night'.[81]

'Only when morning came,' noted Chaim Kaplan, 'and we found the bodies at the house gates round the ghetto, did we discover the extent of the calamity.' Kaplan added:

> At 36 Nowolipki Street a man by the name of Goldberg was killed. He was a barber in peacetime, and when the war broke out he went to work in the quarantine house. His wife worked there too. When he was killed, his wife set up a terrible wailing and would not leave his side. To silence her, they killed her too. Both were left lying by the gate. In death as in life they remained inseparable.
>
> The baker, David Blajman, on Gesia Street, was murdered in the same way. They came to take the husband but the frantic wife ran after him. To rid themselves of this hindrance, the murderers killed her along with her husband. The morning light revealed both bodies at the gate.
>
> At 52 Leszno Street, Linder was killed. At number 27 on the same street a father and son were killed. So it went down to the last victim.[82]

In her diary on April 28, Mary Berg noted that on the night of April 17 'fifty-two prisoners were killed, mostly bakers and smugglers'. Her account continued:

> All the bakers are terrified. Epstein and Wagner, who own the bakery in our house, no longer sleep at home. The Germans come to various houses with a prepared list of names and addresses. If they do not find the persons they are looking for, they take another member of the same family instead. They lead him a few steps in front of the house, politely let him precede them, and then shoot him in the back. The next morning these people are found lying dead in the streets. If a janitor fails to open the door for the Germans as quickly as they want him to, he is shot on the spot. If a member of the janitor's family opens the door the same fate befalls him, and later the janitor is summoned to be killed, too.[83]

In mid-April a new death camp was ready to receive deportees. This was Sobibor camp, in a remote woodland area near the River Bug.

As at Chelmno and Belzec, there were to be almost no survivors: the aim of the camp was to kill, not to segregate and preserve for forced labour.

One of the sixty-four survivors of Sobibor, Moshe Shklarek, was not quite fifteen years old when, on April 17, he was deported in a train from Zamosc, with 2,500 other Jews. On its journey, the train was guarded by Ukrainians. No food or water was given to the deportees. Three days later, the train reached Sobibor: a journey in normal times of less than four hours. All the deportees were then taken, first to Camp No. 2, the barbers' huts, and then on to Camp No. 3, the gas-chamber: all except Shklarek. This one young man, out of 2,500 deportees, was chosen to work with the hundred or so Jews in the 'Corpse Commando', the 'Work Commando' and other camp duties. Shklarek later recalled the characteristics of some of the camp staff, among them SS Technical Sergeant Michel Hermann:

> He treated his servants decently, but his victims rudely and brutally. Because of the slippery-tongued speeches which he delivered to the arrivals at camp, we nicknamed him the 'Preacher'. When a new transport would arrive Hermann would deliver his lying speech, in which he assured the arrivals that this was a transit camp where they would only undergo classification and disinfection, and from here they would be taken to work in the Ukraine until the war was over.
>
> In his apartment in the camp there was concentrated the abundant property that the arrivals had brought with them — silver, gold, rings, watches, jewellery and various other valuables. Actually, he was the camp treasurer.
>
> All the transports passed into Hermann's hands; he classified the arrivals, ordered them to strip and instructed them how to arrange their clothing so they would get it back when they came out of the 'bath house'. He would escort the people on the special road that led from Lager No. 2 to the barbers' huts and from there — to the gas-chambers. With his tricks and his smooth tongue, Hermann was more dangerous than his comrades in crime.

Another of those whom Shklarek recalled was SS Staff Sergeant Paul Grot:

Grot was the leader of the Ukrainian 'columns', between the two rows of whom the camp prisoners were frequently ordered to pass, to be scourged with leaden whips, rubber clubs and all kinds of flagellation instruments with which the servants of the Nazis, who stood on both sides of the row, were equipped.

Grot carried out this task with zeal and pleasure. He had a trusted assistant in this work: his dog, Barry, a wild beast the size of a pony, well trained and obedient to the short, brutal orders of his master. When he heard Grot cry 'Jude!', the dog would attack his victim and bite him on his testicles. The bitten man was, of course, no longer able to continue his work, and then Grot would take him aside and ask him in a sympathetic voice, 'Poor fellow, what happened to you? Who did such a thing to you? It certainly must be hard for you to keep working, isn't it? Come with me; I'll go with you to the clinic!' And, sure enough, Grot accompanied him, as he accompanied scores of workers every day, to the Lazaret, to the giant grave behind the worn-out hut, where armed Ukrainian 'bandagers' greeted the sick and bitten men.

In most cases, these men would place buckets on the heads of the victims, after they made them get into the pit, and would practise shooting, along with Grot, who was, of course, always the most outstanding shot.

Grot would return from the clinic satisfied and gay – and look for more victims. His dog knew his master's temperament and helped him in his murderous pleasures. Sometimes Grot would have himself a joke; he would seize a Jew, give him a bottle of wine and sausage weighing at least a kilo and order him to devour it in a few minutes. When the 'lucky' man succeeded in carrying out this order and staggered from drunkenness, Grot would order him to open his mouth wide and would urinate into his mouth.

A third SS man at Sobibor, technical Sergeant Bauer, was noted for his perverse sense of humour. Shklarek, who was then working in the German soldier's casino at Sobibor, recalled:

One day he told a story about the 'stupid Jews': a transport of naked women was brought into the 'bath house'. One woman saw Bauer as he stood on the roof, waiting for the doors to be hermetically sealed so that he could order that the gas-taps be opened. The woman stopped the armed soldier who stood by the entrance door and asked him, 'What's the officer in uniform doing on the roof? Is something wrong? How can we wash ourselves here inside while they're fixing the roof?'

The guard pacified her, saying that in just a moment the roof would be fixed and, as for her, she need not hurry to push herself inside; there would be enough room for her, too.

This was Bauer's story about the naive Jewess. At the end of his story Bauer dissolved in laughter; he even succeeded in infecting the camp commander and the officers around the casino with his laughter.[84]

On April 18, as the deportees from Zamosc were still on their way to Sobibor, yet another train left Theresienstadt for Poland. Its immediate destination was the ghetto of the small village of Rejowiec. But within a few months, almost all the thousand deportees had been sent on to Sobibor. Only two survived the war.[85] A second Theresienstadt deportation that month went direct to Warsaw, where the thousand deportees were put in the main synagogue. Shortly after their arrival, thirty-seven young men were taken away, to Treblinka, where the fourth death camp, after Chelmno, Belzec and Sobibor, was still under construction.[86] That same day, April 25, 852 Jews from Wurzburg, and 103 from Bamberg, were sent eastwards from Germany in a special freight train 'in the direction of Lublin', as a telegram from the Wurzburg Gestapo informed Adolf Eichmann in Berlin and General Globocnik in Lublin.[87] Two days later, on April 27, a further thousand Jews were deported from Theresienstadt to Izbica Lubelska. The sole survivor was a woman who, after two weeks in Izbica, managed to escape to Warsaw, where she lived under a false name until the end of the war.[88] Belzec, or Sobibor, claimed all the other Theresienstadt deportees of April 27.

Inside the Warsaw ghetto, the executions continued. 'Last night sixty more persons were executed,' Mary Berg, who was shortly to be given her freedom as an American citizen, noted in her diary on April 28. 'They were members of the underground,' she added, 'most of them well-to-do people who financed the secret bulletins.

Many printers who were suspected of helping to publish the underground papers were also killed. Once again in the morning there were corpses in the street.'[89]

On April 29 a number of Jews working in the Ghetto Administration in Lodz were present when a large truck stopped to refuel on its way to the city. 'The truck was fully loaded with luggage of all sorts,' the Ghetto Chronicle recorded, 'but chiefly with knapsacks belonging to the people recently resettled from the ghetto.'

These belongings were being sent to Pabianice, a small town south of Lodz, where they were to be sorted and graded for despatch to Germany. Hundreds of Jews, many of them from the Lodz ghetto, were to be employed in this task. Unknown to the observers in the Administration, to the writers of the Chronicle, or to the sorters in Pabianice, the owners of these belongings were all Jews who had earlier been sent to Chelmno, and gassed.[90] It was already known in the Lodz ghetto that many of the deportees had been forced to throw down their belongings during the deportation. Once again, a logical explanation, and definite knowledge that the bundles had not gone on with the deportees to their destination, helped to hide the truth and to preserve the deception.

To those Jews still alive in the ghettos, the deception was also self-deception, strong because the will to survive was strong. One young Polish Jew, Ben Helfgott, then aged thirteen, later recalled how, as the deportation trains passed Piotrkow, Poles would say to the Jews who were watching: 'You too will soon be turned into soap.' 'The Jews knew that the deportees would not return,' Helfgott added, 'but would their own fate be the same? Might they not be spared?'[91]

Deception and illusion went hand in hand: both were accentuated by a sense of isolation and hopelessness.

19

'Another journey into the unknown'

WITH EACH MONTH, the surviving Jews of Europe hoped that the worst times were over. Those in the 'working' ghettos, such as Lodz, Bialystok or Dvinsk, lived a life of unremitting work, flickering hope, and recurrent fear. In the Dvinsk ghetto, following the slaughter of October 1941, the survivors had worked in the German soldiers' canteen, and in several factories outside the ghetto. The ration for these labourers was 100 grams of meat once a week, some margarine, and a tablespoon of sugar every second day, to supplement the cabbage soup on which the non-workers had to subsist.

Typhoid killed hundreds. Lice and boils affected hundreds more. That winter, on the road from the ghetto to the factories, the corpses of hundreds of Russian prisoners-of-war had been found, covered in a thin layer of snow where they had fallen on the march. Maja Zarch later recalled:

> One Sunday, when no one was going to work, an order was issued. Panic broke out once more. What now? We were all out in the yard when an announcement was made. We were terrified. The announcement was: 'You arc about to witness what happens to a woman who wants to hide her Jewishness.' A beautiful blond woman was brought in with a noose attached to her neck and publicly hanged. Her crime? She was found walking in the street with her shawl covering her yellow star.[1]

On the morning of 1 May 1942 the working Jews of the Dvinsk ghetto went to work as usual. During the day, someone ran into the factory to tell them that they had seen black canvas-covered vans with people inside leaving the ghetto. 'This meant only one thing,'

Maja Zarch recalled, 'another action. Each time Jews were taken to their deaths it was in one of these lorries.'

The workers returned along the road to Griva; Maja Zarch recalled the sequel:

> As we approached the gates, an oppressive silence enveloped the ghetto. At the gates a drunken guard met us. He was rejoicing as his job had been well done.
>
> Walking through the gates we saw puddles of blood, broken bottles and chairs strewn all over the place. This sight bore testimony to the fact that this last lot of people had put up a useless resistance.
>
> We walked on, only to see sights that defy any description. Children's bodies lay around, torn in half with the heads smashed in. We were stunned, speechless. Is it possible that such inhumanity to man by man can exist?
>
> We returned to our barracks. It was like a morgue. We were scared to move. A few of us went to the toilet. On entering we heard voices faintly calling. We looked at each other. We thought we were going mad. We looked around – there was no one there. Yet the voices persisted. Urgent, muffled, faint. We could not move. It was as though we were rooted to the ground.
>
> Then suddenly someone caught sight of faces, two teenage boys, deep in excrement with only their faces sticking out. They were on their last breath as they must have stood there most of the day. They had nothing to lose – this was their last chance for survival on this occasion. They had to be rescued immediately – but how?
>
> We women could not reach them by bending over. We had no rope necessary for this operation. We ran to find some men who by now had returned from work and who also were as stunned as we. They dragged them out. The rest of the night we spent huddled together waiting for someone to come for us. . . . [2]

Only five hundred Jews now lived in the Dvinsk ghetto, survivors of a population of sixteen thousand less than twelve months earlier. Maja Zarch, whose thirteenth birthday was on the day of the May Day action, was to be the youngest survivor.

Not only the killings in the East, as in Dvinsk, but also the deportations, from the Polish towns and villages, reached a new intensity in May 1942, with Chelmno, Belzec and Sobibor each the scene of daily mass murder of Polish Jews. Repeatedly, the Jewish Councils, on whom the Germans thrust the burden of selecting the deportees, refused to comply. Early in May, in Bilgoraj, when the Jewish Council was ordered to compile a list of candidates for deportation, the Vice-Chairman of the Council, Hillel Janover, and three other members of the Council, Szymon Bin, Shmuel Leib Olender and Ephrain Waksszul, refused to do so. All four were shot dead on May 3. On the following day, the deportations from Bilgoraj to Belzec began.[3]

Two days later, in the East Upper Silesian town of Dabrowa, the Chairman of the Jewish Council, Adolf Weinberg, refused to deliver a list of 'resettlement' candidates, or to reveal where those threatened with deportation were hiding. He and his entire family were deported.[4]

At Markuszow, on May 7, the Jewish Council warned the Jews of the village of an impending 'action' and advised the community that 'every Jew who is able to save himself should do so'.[5] At Szczebrze-szyn, a Council member, Hersh Getzel Hoichbaum, on learning that none of those sent away to be 'resettled' were ever heard of again, told his Council colleagues that he did not wish to be the despatcher of fellow Jews to their deaths, and hanged himself in his attic.[6] At Iwje, two Council members, Shalom Zak and Bezalel Milkowski, were among those selected to remain in the ghetto. They at once insisted on joining the deportees, and were killed, together with their families and 2,500 other Jews, on May 8. In a final gesture, Milkowski had taken off his Council member's armband, telling the Germans that he did not want their 'favour'.[7]

In the Warsaw ghetto, the teachers and educationalists had declared Tuesday, May 5, as Jewish Child's Day. In the Jewish calendar, it was Lag Ba'omer, marking the thirty-third day in the seven-week period between the festivals of Passover and Pentecost, a period also identified with a moment in the Roman siege of Jerusalem when there was a sudden and short-lived relief for the beleaguered Jews.

On that 'festive' day in Warsaw in 1942, all thirty orphanages and boarding houses in the ghetto, housing four thousand children, were the scenes of special games and entertainment. 'We gave, to children, more food on this occasion, some sweets,' Adolf Berman later recalled, 'and our slogan was to give the children at least some semblance of joy.' But at the same time, Berman added, the 'tragic race' was going on 'between the efforts of the Jewish public, and starvation'.[8] In March 1942, 4,951 Warsaw Jews had died of hunger; in April, 4,432: hunger, filth, and the diseases which followed so rapidly and savagely in their train, typhus and typhoid fever.[9]

The climax of Child's Day was a theatrical performance of children's plays. The children, Berman recalled, 'though depressed and weak, were still able to exhibit great beauty and charm'. In the audience, hundreds wept 'from sheer happiness'. So successful was this moment of pleasure that a new date was set, July 23, for the festive opening of a special children's house, intended for the entertainment and care of more than a thousand children.[10]

'People have become a little more optimistic,' Ringelblum noted on May 8. 'They've begun to believe that the war will be over in a few months and life will return to normal.' This 'good mood', Ringelblum explained, had been aided by a series of 'false communiqués' circulating in the ghetto, within a week of a confident speech by Hitler in Berlin:

> What is in these communiqués? Well, first we learn that Smolensk has been retaken through an airdrop of sixty thousand soldiers who joined forces with the Russian army camped west of Smolensk. The same communiqué has taken Kharkov. Another communiqué disembarked a whole army in Murmansk, borne by 160 ships, not one of which was sunk en route. Of course, when Hitler heard this news (this was after his May 1 speech), he collapsed. Then, the Allies won a great victory on Lake Ilmen, where the communiqué killed forty-three thousand Germans and took more than eighty thousand captive. This was the Nineteenth Army; the captives included two German generals. As though this were not enough, a communiqué has deposed Mussolini and made a revolution in Italy. Add to all this an ultimatum from Roosevelt to the German people giving them until May 15 to surrender.

'In a word,' Ringelblum reflected, 'the Jews in the Warsaw ghetto aren't content merely to recite Psalms and leave the rest in God's hands, they labour day and night to lay their enemy low and bring an early peace.' Those in the ghetto, he concluded, 'can't bear it any longer, that's why we try our utmost to see the war's end as imminent'.[11]

In his ironic reflection, Ringelblum was referring to the Yiddish saying: 'Don't rely on miracles, recite Psalms!' He saw clearly that when people were starved for news and had no idea what was going on in the outside world, they would thrive, and indeed survive, on rumours. These rumours were seldom destructive. They usually reflected optimistic thoughts of victory and the imminent downfall of the enemy. It was as if each Jew was looking beyond the torment and fear of the unknown, hoping to find some kind of reassurance in what was, in fact, fantasy.

Unable to conceive of his own death, a man, even when surrounded by the death of others, grasps at any hope or rumour that might distance him from the realisation that he himself might be marked out for death. Any rumour which confirms that death might not be in prospect is acceptable. It was this psychological mechanism, the impossibility of conceiving of one's own death, that gave the hopeful rumours their force, and laid the groundwork for the deceptions that were to come. One might fear the worst, one might dread it, one might be told of it in the starkest terms, but one could not believe it. Even harder to grasp was the pathology of those who were committing the murders.

Not only among the outside world of Allies and neutrals, but among the Jews themselves in the midst of these terrible events, it was impossible fully to conceive that a child could be butchered in the way that so many hundreds of thousands of Jewish children had already been butchered. Yet once it had proved impossible for the Jews who witnessed these horrors to enter into the pathology of their persecutors, then it was possible for hope also to survive, which the full realisation of what was taking place would long before have destroyed.

On the morning of May 8 the Jews who awoke in the White Russian village of Radun, near Lida, found that the ghetto had been sealed off by the Gestapo. 'No one could go out,' Avraham Aviel, who was then fourteen, later recalled. 'Neither could one go out to work.

Even those who had special passes could not leave.' For four days the ghetto remained sealed. Then a group of Jews were given long-handled spades, and marched out of the ghetto. These Jews were ordered to dig pits. Realizing that the pits were intended as the graves of those in the ghetto, a number of them 'took their spades and picked up rocks and some of them managed to flee', among them Aviel's father, who recounted the story to his son. The rest of the rebellious grave-diggers were killed; others, Aviel's father recalled, 'did not have the strength to run. They just stayed put.'

Aviel managed to escape from the ghetto, and to meet his father in a nearby wood. But those with his father feared that the boy was too small to join them as fugitives. So he returned to the ghetto, where, as he recalled:

I tried to hide my smaller brother and my mother and the people who were with us in the house. I tried to hide them in the attic. I covered them with rags and boxes, then I went down and I tried to find out what was happening. As soon as I went down from the attic, I heard a terrible noise. Motorcycles were coming in. There were shouts.

Germans came in from the direction of Lida in battle uniform equipped with automatic weapons as if they were marching out to the front. It was a different uniform from what we had seen before. They had about the same uniform as that very first group had when they killed those forty people. I left the house and I saw a great mass of Jews being pushed from the edge of the ghetto, being driven on in the direction of Grodno. The same direction in which these groups with the spades had been going. And we knew something awful would happen.

At that moment a number of Germans entered our house. One of them stood at the entrance blocking it and the others scattered in the rooms and began searching and driving out people who were not yet in hiding. Whoever would pass through the entrance would absorb a blow from a rubber baton on his head and he would fall down right there. When I saw that, I wanted to avoid being beaten this way. I ducked and I jumped out and I managed not to receive this blow.

I mixed with that multitude. I tried to stop along the way to see whether I could find out what happened to my family. Whether they had been found or not. I thought if I was on the edge perhaps I could see them coming and I could join them. Unfortunately, however, I saw my mother, my small brother, an uncle and other Jews included in the group of those people who were found and my little brother then told me later that they were beaten severely. Then we marched together in this direction in which we were driven.

In all, more than two thousand Jews were driven from the ghetto. As many as a thousand were refugees who had fled in the months earlier from the slaughter in Lithuania. As they were driven towards the pits, Aviel's mother said to him: 'Say "Shema Yisrael" – "Hear! O Israel" – die as Jews.' That, he recalled, 'is how they all walked, calling to their God, "Shema Yisrael",' the traditional last line of the Jew's deathbed confession. Aviel added:

I repeated the words after her but I had inner resistance. I did not do this willingly. We were brought to the market place in the middle of the town. We were told to kneel, heads down. We were not permitted to lift our heads. Whoever did so would either be shot right through the head or would be beaten. Of course we saw from the corner of our eyes the people who tried to run away were shot right there.

Then we sat there in the centre of town for an hour or more. I can't estimate this time. They lectured us. I didn't hear what was being said. My thoughts were all concentrated on the possibility of escape. How could one get out of here, I thought. Then later we were told to get up and we were led out of town in the direction of the cemetery. The distance was about one kilometre. When we got there approximately one hundred yards from the cemetery, we were told to get off the road.

Again we had to kneel heads down. We were not permitted to lift our heads or look aside. We only heard shots from the sides. I was small then. I was shorter than the others so I could raise my head without being discovered and I saw in front of me a long trench about twenty-five or thirty yards long. They began leading us row after row, group after group. We were led to that trench. People were undressed. They would have to go on that little hill which was near the trench. Machine-gun bursts were heard and they would fall into the trench.

I saw one case of a Jewish girl who struggled. She refused to undress. They hit her and then she was shot too.

Children, women, family after family. The families were in groups together. At that moment I noticed a group of Jews who were digging those graves and knowing that my brother was in that group. . . .

Aviel decided to try, at whatever cost, to join his brother. His thought, he later recalled, 'was always: 'One must survive – *uberleben* – and tell what happened.' His account continued:

I took leave of my mother and started jumping over the heads of these people who were sitting next to me. I fell down and got up again – I didn't give a thought to what would happen; and thus – I don't really know how – I was not noticed, I was not discovered – it was a miracle, really.

I managed to reach the edge of the road, near the ditch there; I lay down in the ditch and they apparently did not notice me.[12]

Also in Radun during the destruction of the community were several families who had escaped the previous September from Ejszyszki in Lithuania, crossing into what had then seemed the comparative safety of White Russia. Moshe Sonenson, in hiding with his two sons, one an infant, later recalled that day in Radun:

The Germans were downstairs, shouting: 'Where are the Juden?' Could there be Jews here? My child began to cry at that moment. They were downstairs and we were upstairs, fifteen Jews. The situation was terrible. They were downstairs, and we were unable to quiet the child. There was one old man with us named Mendel who said: 'Do we all have to end our lives here because of your child?' And the child began to cry. It was awful. So they took a coat and put it over his mouth and he suffocated.

The 3,400 Jews of Radun were taken to the Jewish cemetery and shot at specially prepared pits. More then sixteen hundred were women, more than eight hundred were children. 'It was terrible, terrible,' Sonenson recalled. 'I can't forget it . . . . That's all . . . .'[13]

On May 8 a train left Ryki ghetto for Sobibor. One young boy, Abram Rubinsztein, who had celebrated his fourteenth birthday five days earlier, managed to jump from the train. He survived, both

SOBIBOR

the jump, and the war. His father Haim, a tinsmith, his mother Malka, his three sisters, and his two brothers, reached Sobibor with 2,500 others Jews from Ryki, and were gassed.[14]

On May 9, as the round-up for Sobibor was about to reach the village of Markuszow, four young Jews organized a mass escape to the nearby forests.[15] The four were Shlomo Goldwasser, Mordechai Kirshenbaum and the brothers Yerucham and Yaakov Gothelf. For five months the escapees hid in the woods, but then a massive German manhunt tracked them down: men, women and children, all were killed.[16]

The perils after escape were as great as the perils of escape itself. On May 11 a member of the Jewish Council at Zdzieciol, Alter

Dworzecki, who had tried to organize resistance inside the ghetto but had been forced to flee, reached a Soviet partisan group in the Lipiczanska forest. The Soviet partisans had only one demand: give up your pistol. Dworzecki refused, and they shot him.[17]

In Warsaw, daily shootings had become a feature of ghetto life since that Bloody Friday, April 18. 'Many a man has been killed or wounded by one of these wild street shootings,' Ringelblum noted on May 12, as Gestapo agents, driving through the ghetto streets, opened fire at random. 'The shooting of people in the streets has become a deliberate tactic since April,' Ringelblum added. 'The aim: to terrify the populace, to terrorize them.' That very night, four Jews had been shot, Sklar, head of a food kitchen, Feist, Patt 'a sportsman', and Tenenbaum.[18]

Moshe Sklar had been a printer, 'taciturn, obstinate, sarcastic', as his friend S. Sheinkinder described him. As foreman in the printers' shop of a Warsaw newspaper, 'his word was his bond'. In the ghetto he had become manager of a food kitchen. On April 17 he had been taken to Pawiak, and held for three weeks. 'It is assumed', noted Sheinkinder on learning of Sklar's death, 'that he was tortured, that they wanted to get something out of him. They did not know the tough character, the obstinacy of Moshe Sklar. If he knew anything at all, it went down with him to the grave.'

Another of those killed on the night of May 12, Roman Patt, had been a popular Polish footballer between the wars. It had not been known that he was a Jew. He had risen to become an important member of the Polish Referees' Council. In 1941 he was brought into the ghetto, and on May 16, at the age of forty-two, he had been shot in the street. Like Sklar, he was being held in prison at the time when he was taken out into the street and killed. 'All sorts of things are reported,' wrote Sheinkinder in his diary, 'but Patt himself was taciturn and reserved, and he took his secret with him to the grave. There was only one secret that was revealed to me. He died a Jew.'[19]

'Apparently', Ringelblum noted, 'these men were associated with the liberation movement.'

The Jewish efforts at self-help were considerable. That same May 12 Ringelblum recorded, of two Jewesses:

> The heroic girls, Chajke and Frumke – they are a theme that calls for the pen of a great writer. Boldly they travel back and

forth through the cities and towns of Poland. They carry 'Aryan' papers identifying them as Poles or Ukrainians. One of them even wears a cross, which she never parts with except when in the ghetto.

They are in mortal danger every day. They rely entirely on their 'Aryan' faces and on the peasant kerchiefs that cover their heads. Without a murmur, without a second's hesitation, they accept and carry out the most dangerous missions. Is someone needed to travel to Vilna, Bialystok, Lvov, Kowel, Lublin, Czestochowa or Radom to smuggle in contraband such as illegal publications, goods, money? The girls volunteer as though it were the most natural thing in the world. Are there comrades who have to be rescued from Vilna, Lublin, or some other city? They undertake the mission.

Nothing stands in their way, nothing deters them. Is it necessary to become friendly with engineers of German trains, so as to be able to travel beyond the frontiers of the General Government of Poland, where people can move about with special papers? They are the ones to do it, simply, without fuss, as though it was their profession. They have travelled from city to city, to places no delegate or Jewish institution had ever reached, such as Volhynia, Lithuania.

They were the first to bring back the tidings about the tragedy of Vilna. They were the first to offer words of encouragement and moral support to the surviving remnant of that city. How many times have they looked death in the eyes? How many times have they been arrested and searched? Fortune has smiled on them. They are, in the classic idiom, 'emissaries of the community to whom no harm can come'.

With what simplicity and modesty have they reported what they accomplished on their journeys, on the trains bearing Polish Christians who have been pressed to work in Germany! The story of the Jewish woman will be a glorious page in the history of Jewry during the present war. And the Chajkes and Frumkes will be the leading figures in this story. For these girls are indefatigable.

Chajka Grossman and Frumka Plotnicka, whom Ringelblum had referred to by their affectionate nicknames 'Chajke' and 'Frumke', had just returned from a clandestine journey to Czestochowa, where they had taken money and messages to the Jews trapped there in the ghetto. In a few hours, Ringelblum noted, 'they'll be on the move again. And they're off without a moment's hesitation, without a minute of rest.'[20]

Chajka Grossman survived the war. Frumka Plotnicka, in hiding in a cellar in Bedzin, was discovered in August 1943. She died fighting in the cellar, armed only with a hand gun. Her sister Chana had been caught by the Germans while trying to escape from the Warsaw ghetto in April 1943, and beaten to death.[21]

On 12 May 1942 yet more Jewish deportees were gassed at Auschwitz, fifteen hundred men, women and children brought from the nearby town of Sosnowiec.[22] The old, the sick, and those without regular employment, they had been told that they were to be sent 'somewhere else'. 'The Germans spread rumours', Frieda Mazia later recalled, 'that they were on their way to Theresienstadt, where all the Jews were being gathered.'[23]

At Auschwitz, as at Chelmno, Belzec and Sobibor, the Germans set up one of the most hellish aspects of the death camp system, the Sonderkommando, selecting a small number of Jews for a special team, whose job was to dispose of the corpses of those who had been murdered. At the nearby village and birch wood of Birkenau, in the summer of 1942, the task of the Auschwitz Sonderkommando was to dig up the burial pits near the camp, then to drag the corpses from the pits to specially constructed crematoria, where they were burnt to ash. Anyone who refused this work was shot on the spot by one of the SS guards. The first Sonderkommando team at Birkenau consisted of two hundred young Slovak Jews who had been deported from Slovakia at the end of March.[24]

It was not at Auschwitz, however, at Belzec, or at Chelmno, but at Sobibor, that the largest number of Jews was gassed in May 1942. In that one month, more than thirty-six thousand Jews were brought to Sobibor from nineteen communities between the Vistula and the Bug.[25] One of those communities was Turobin, from which 2,750 Jews were deported on May 12. Among the deportees was Dov Freiberg, a fifteen-year-old boy from Lodz, whose mother had taken him first to the Warsaw ghetto, then sent him away to Turobin for safety. 'Most of the people didn't believe that there was extermination,' he later recalled. 'Of course, we knew there were

isolated cases of murder, but we didn't know about mass extermination. We didn't want to believe it.'

Shortly before the deportation, a Jew had come to Turobin and
told the Jews about the deportations from nearby towns. 'Do not
believe what you are told – they are not sent to the Ukraine at all,
they are being sent to Belzec and killed there.' Of course, Freiberg
later recalled, 'nobody gave credit to his words – we just thought
that he was spreading panic.'

On May 12 the Jews of Turobin were assembled in the market
place, told that they were to be resettled in the Ukraine, were then
marched to the nearest railway station, several miles away at
Krasnowka. There, joined by several thousand Jews from nearby
villages, they were driven into goods wagons. 'They piled us into the
carriages,' Freiberg recalled. 'We were jammed to such an extent
that there was no room to stand at all. Many people fainted. Also, in
my own carriage, two women died in the course of the journey.'

Just to the east of Lublin was a notorious concentration camp,
Majdanek, which was becoming known throughout the region as a
place of severe hard labour. As the train moved eastwards, through
Lublin and beyond, 'we were happy', Freiberg later recalled, 'not to
go in the direction of Majdanek, because we knew that Majdanek
was a hard labour camp. We were rather happy to see that we were
going eastward.'

As the train continued eastward, it seemed as if the story of
resettlement in the Ukraine was indeed true. After three or four
hours, the train reached Sobibor. At the entrance to the camp were
written the words: *SS Sonderkommando Umsiedlungslager*, 'SS
special unit resettlement camp'. As Freiberg later recalled:

> Everything was done at a lightning speed. We had no time to
> think. The SS people began shouting, 'Schneller, schneller!'
> 'Hurry up, hurry up!' – and they brought us to a particular
> point. It was some sort of a small gate, and then they would tell
> us, 'Links, rechts'.
>
> To the right or to the left. These were not selections. Any-
> body who came was actually exterminated, so this selection
> was temporary – let me say, for a few hours or a few seconds.
> 'Links, recht' meant men apart and women and children apart.
> The arrangement was simply different for men and for women.
> I was, of course, taken together with the men.

Women and children went the way I only came to know later, as during the first period that camp, compared with what it was later, was rather primitive. It didn't really operate in the night, only in the morning. So men stayed there on the spot during the night, while women and children went straight to the gas-chambers, since there was no arrangement for everybody at that time.

There was a band there in the place. This was in Lager Eins – Camp No. 1. There was a band which was playing. And on that night, when we arrived there, when we spent the night there, in spite of the fact we didn't know what was going on – of course, the rumour was afloat, but we didn't yet believe – still we had an uncanny feeling.

Then in the camp we were already a few hundred metres from gas-chambers and the Germans still managed to hoodwink; they still assured us that within a few weeks we would rejoin our families – but we saw their belongings piled up. They said: 'They are getting new clothes.' In Camp 3, they said, they were to be concentrated and then sent to the Ukraine.

Camps 1 and 2 were, in fact, one camp, but as far as the various tasks and functions were concerned, one was separated from the other. One camp was for the experts – that means to say professional people – joiners, shoemakers etc.; whilst Camp 2 was composed of people who dealt with transports – everything in that connection. Lager 3 was the gas-chambers. At first people were buried in big pits – layers of people – that's how it operated.

In the morning the Germans came and began to select people who had some trade – tailors, shoemakers, joiners and so on; and I had a feeling that something was going wrong. Then I remembered the Jew who had told me about the extermination – I began to think about my family.

I was not an artisan, so my situation didn't look too good. They were choosing young and able-bodied people, singling them out by saying: 'Du!' I was in the group. After about half an hour most of the transport had been taken to the gas-chambers and we were left behind, to be sent to work.

Of the 2,750 Jews deported from Turobin to Sobibor on May 12, only 150 were 'sent to work'. As Dov Freiberg later recalled:

We worked all that day in groups; I was working in the transfer of belongings – people were undressing and we had to take their various belongings and place them in piles. I worked there for about an hour, and wherever we went, we saw that people had disappeared.

There was a dog. That dog belonged to an SS man from Camp 3 – we called him Beddo. The SS man was responsible for the 'showers' – the gas-chambers. Later on this dog was passed to SS Sergeant Pavel; he called him 'Mensch' ('Man'), and when he set the dog on the prisoners he would say: 'Man, get that dog!' He said. 'You are my deputy.' That's what he would say to the dog.

Whoever was caught by the dog would be killed by the Germans, because the Germans didn't like seeing any wounded or sick people around. I was bitten twice by that dog – I still have the scars. It was a fluke that I remained alive in spite of it.[26]

Within a week of the Turobin deportation, trains had begun to reach Sobibor from Theresienstadt, a distance of more than five hundred miles. Of two thousand Jews deported from Theresienstadt to Sobibor on May 17, in two separate trains, there was not a single survivor.[27]

Dov Freiberg was one of the few surviving witnesses of the fate of these deportees from Czechoslovakia, Austria and Germany. As he later recalled:

They didn't know exactly what was going to happen to them. Even if they feared, they didn't believe. But the treatment was that they would leave the carriages in great speed. They would be concentrated in one place. There would be the separation between men and women and children. People would enter a closed yard with barbed-wire entanglements on both sides. In the yard there were also sheds for showers and there was a door in a building in the middle of it and people had the impression that they were entering a bath-shower. There was a man who would come and, as it were, preach to the people concentrated there.

This man, Dov Freiberg later recalled, was known as 'the Preacher'. His speeches were 'adapted to each transport'. But their import was the same:

He would say that people were being sent to the Ukraine. They would have to work.

They would have to work hard. Some people asked what was going to happen to women. He would answer and say that women were also supposed to work there. That was more or less the gist of his speech. Then he would say that here you must strip but do it quickly because we have very little time. Try to do it as fast as you possibly can.

People would invariably give credit to his words. They would undress and arrange their belongings and there was a special box office where valuables were surrendered. At that time people would surrender money and gold but sometimes they would also bury part of their belongings, particularly gold and money, hoping to come back to that place one day and retrieve their belongings. Then they would walk a distance of about three hundred metres.

That walk was to the gas-chamber. But almost invariably some Jews would be ordered by the SS and Ukrainian guards to stay behind. 'Sometimes they would leave people there just to play with,' Freiberg recalled. 'They would have all sorts of torture. They would leave some people out of the transport and we could see what was going on. The shrieking was bloodcurdling. And then we would see their belongings soaked with blood.'

Freiberg survived as part of the small group of labourers: sorting through the clothing of the victims, cleaning the residential quarters of the Ukrainians, and, for a short time, 'shearing women's hair before they entered the gas-chamber'.[28]

Another who survived at Sobibor was Itzhak Lichtman. He had been deported from Zolkiewka, near Lublin, to Sobibor on May 22. On reaching the camp, he became one of the five shoemakers, kept alive to make boots and slippers for the SS and their families. Later he recalled how, in a transport from Holland, a hospital nurse, Mrs Hejdi, who had arrived with her husband, was sobbing. 'Are you crying because your husband left you?' the SS laughed, knowing that her husband had just been gassed. Whereupon 'they brought a Czechoslovak middle-aged prisoner and told them, 'You are husband and wife.' Then they forced them to sleep together.[29]

Beginning on May 4, and continuing without pause for eleven days, more than ten thousand Jews were deported from the Lodz ghetto to Chelmno, and gassed. These were the Jews who had been brought to Lodz from Western Europe six months earlier. On May 4, one thousand had been deported. All those sent away, the Ghetto Chronicle recorded that same day, 'had their baggage, knapsacks, and even their hand-held parcels taken away from them'. News of this, the Chronicle added, 'has cast a chill over the ghetto'.[30]

On the following day it was noted that at least one Jewish doctor, also a former deportee, was being sent with each transport of a thousand Jews.[31] On May 6, with the third deportation, the ghetto learned that as the deportees were about to board the train, 'the guards ordered them to step back five paces from the train, and then to throw all their baggage to the ground, not only their knapsacks and suitcases, but their hand-held parcels, bags etc. as well'. They were only allowed to keep their bread. The sight of wagons returning to the ghetto, noted the Chronicle, loaded with the bedding and blankets of the deportees, 'caused a feeling of hopelessness among passers-by'.

The Jews were deported according to their place of origin: Berlin first, then Vienna, then Dusseldorf, followed by more from Berlin, then Hamburg, Vienna, Prague and Cologne. The final transport was from Luxembourg. Those Jews, some 260 in all, who had long before been converted to Christianity, asked to be kept together, and to be 'resettled' in a group. Their request was granted.[32] Baptism could not protect either those who had converted to Christianity to save their lives, or those whose conversion, often many years before the war, had been an act of faith.

To calm the fears of those who were ordered to leave their baggage at the station, the Germans announced 'that they would receive their baggage in the next train'. The trains themselves were ordinary passenger trains, made up of third-class carriages. 'Each person leaving the ghetto is given a seat,' the Chronicle recorded on May 6, the train 'returning the same day, at eight o'clock p.m.' It had left at seven o'clock in the morning 'on the dot'.[33]

The timetable, the third-class carriages, and the promise that the baggage would soon follow, were all deliberate devices of a deceptive normality. All the deportees were taken to Chelmno and gassed. On May 7, the fourth day of the 'resettlement' of the once proud, prosperous Western European Jews, the Ghetto Chronicle commented: 'Ghosts, skeletons with swollen faces and extremities, ragged and impoverished, they now left for a further journey on which they were not even allowed to take a knapsack. They had been stripped of all their European finery, and only the Eternal Jew was left.'[34]

During the first six days of the deportations, six of the deportees committed suicide, fearing the worst. But the meaning of the deportations was unclear. 'Tears of joy or of terrible despair,' the Chronicle noted on May 11, 'everyone reacts one way or the other upon hearing his name called.'[35] The death toll in the ghetto was so high that resettlement offered the illusion of a better chance for life. Every day, as Western European Jews died in the ghetto of starvation, it served as a reminder of the precariousness of life under duress. On May 5, the second day of the deportations, a sixty-three-year-old Jew from Frankfurt had died: Professor Jakob Edmund Speyer, who, as the Ghetto Chronicle recorded, 'ranked among the greatest inventors in the field of medical chemistry', one of the discoverers of Eukodal, 'a preparation that constitutes an improvement over morphine'. He was also a noted researcher into the use of vitamins.[36]

On May 12 a further nine hundred Western European Jews were deported from Lodz. Another seven Jews had committed suicide, among them the sixty-three-year-old Rosa Kaldo, originally from Hungary, who, the Chronicle reported, 'threw herself from a fifth-floor window,' dying immediately.[37] The deportations continued on May 13 and again on May 14, when among those deported, and gassed on arrival at Chelmno, was the Viennese pianist, Leopold Birkenfeld, who for the past six months had entranced the ghetto with his music.[38] The last of the deportations took place on May 15. 'On the final day,' the Chronicle noted, 'the German guards treated the deportees in relatively mild fashion, allowing them to take their possessions with them.' Even so, fears for his fate had led to another suicide attempt. 'The person making the attempt', recorded the Chronicle, 'cut the veins in his arms; however this did not help him avoid deportation. After bandages were applied and the bleeding stemmed, he was sent to the train station'. The Chronicle added that, 'on the whole it must be said that in these tragic moments before another journey into the unknown, the exiles from the West preserved their equanimity to a greater degree than have their brothers here in similar situations. Lamentation, screaming, and wailing at the final assembly points were characteristic features of the previous deportations, whereas during this deportation the Western European Jews made an outward display of considerably greater self-control. On the other hand, they lost that self-control at the train station and, by causing confusion, drew down repressive measures from the guards.'

As well as Western European Jews in the deportations of May 4 to May 15 were some three hundred Lodz Jews, 'volunteers' who hoped for a better life after resettlement, unable to see any way of avoiding starvation if they were to remain in the ghetto. On May 17 alone there were fifty-eight deaths, most of them as a result of hunger and exhaustion, one, the thirty-one-year-old Josek Zajtman, 'shot to death a few feet from the building where he lived, which is located right by the barbed wire'.[39]

On May 17, the day of the deportation from Pabianice, the Germans separated all children under the age of ten from the parents, then asked for volunteers to 'accompany' the children. A leading Zionist in the town, Mordecai Chmura, although his children were not in the transport, being older, left his family and went over to the group of small children 'in order to be of help to them'. As he was led away with them, 'this proud Jew', a witness later recalled, 'was singing the "Hatikvah", the anthem of hope'. All were taken to Chelmno, and gassed.[40]

During May 17 more than two thousand Jews from Pabianice, including the parents of those children who had been sent to Chelmno, reached the Lodz ghetto. There they told the Jews of Lodz the harrowing story of how, that morning, at a football field outside Pabianice, as the selection was made, 'infants were torn from mothers, children ran crying and screaming around the field looking for parents, while their parents, unable to regard these scenes with composure, beseeched the guards to allow them to take their children from there. In response, they were shoved back, their children were torn from their arms and thrown to the grass like balls, and even thrown over the fence.'

All the children under ten, as well as all adults judged by

the Gestapo as 'unfit for work', were then 'loaded into peasant wagons and taken away on a different direction, to parts', the Lodz Chronicle reported, 'that remain unknown.' A day later, the Chronicle noted, it was 'terrible to see these desperate, lamenting women and men, wringing their hands from which those nearest and dearest to them had been rudely torn'.[41]

On May 18, a further 1,420 Jews arrived in the Lodz ghetto from Brzeziny. Like the Jews from Pabianice, they reported how, that same morning, all children under the age of ten, 'even babies at the breast', were, 'to the despair of their parents – taken from there and sent off to parts unknown', together with many adults, 'the weak, the sick, the elderly', seventeen hundred people in all. Among the Jews who reached Lodz from Brzeziny was Michal Urbach, a doctor from Lodz who had gone to Brzeziny a few months earlier as a pharmacist; his only child, a boy of five, had been among the children taken away.[42] All the children of Brzeziny, like those of Pabianice, had been sent to Chelmno, and gassed.[43]

Inside the Lodz ghetto, the news of the deportations from Pabianice and Brzeziny had a devastating effect. 'The greatest optimists have lost hope,' Bernard Ostrowski, one of the ghetto chroniclers, recorded, and he went on to explain: 'Until now, people had thought that work would maintain the ghetto and the majority of its people without any break-up of families. Now it is clear that even this was an illusion. There were plenty of orders (for new work) in Pabianice and Brzeziny, but that did not protect the Jews against wholesale deportation. Fear for our ghetto's fate is keeping everyone up at night. Our last hope is our Chairman; people believe that he will succeed, if not totally, then at least in part, in averting the calamities that now loom ahead.'[44]

Chaim Rumkowski was convinced that he could keep the Lodz ghetto in productive work and thus preserve life, and that he could find work for all the surviving 100,000 inhabitants. Ironically, part of that work derived from the belongings of the Jews gassed at Chelmno, and sent to the Lodz ghetto for sorting. On May 20 the Chronicle noted the arrival in the ghetto of 'three hundred train cars of underclothes for cleaning', as well as orders placed in the woodwork factory, for a million pairs of clogs, requiring the work of eight hundred people in three shifts. The straw-shoe workshop was now making army boots, and the metal workshop 'is supposed to have work enough for two years'.[45] On June 1 the Chronicle recorded 'sewing machines by the hundreds' reaching Lodz, as well as the arrival on May 29 of four five-ton trucks bringing 'enormous quantities of civilian footwear'. The trucks had come 'from the direction of Brzeziny'. From each pair of shoes, the tops, or the entire heels, 'had been torn off'.[46]

Thousands of Jews from Lodz were working in labour camps throughout the region, and taken from their labour camps to factories and other forced labour sites in Germany. Among these slave labourers was Leo Laufer, one of the survivors of Ruchocki Mlyn, who had been sent to a labour camp at Schwenningen. Later he recalled how, at Schwenningen:

> A fellow went out from his barrack and he went to the toilet which was a separate barrack away from the camp. Evidently he couldn't make it, and one of the guards saw him doing it against the barrack on the side. I'm sure he must have been sick, or had diarrhoea or whatever happened. The next morning they caught him; the next morning again we had to stay outside, and they actually opened a grave, and put him in alive, all the way to about his shoulder, and all of us looked at him when they put him in, then we left for work, and we were gone at least ten hours. When we came back, the man was barely living, and he had to die, slowly, in his own grave.

Laufer also recalled several attempts to escape from Schwenningen, all of them unsuccessful: 'they hanged people who escaped.'[47]

In and around Berlin, on May 18, 27 Jews were shot for having organized a display of anti-Nazi posters, and for various acts of defiance, among them the setting fire to several exhibits at an anti-Soviet exhibition in the German capital. Led by Herbert Baum, a Communist, the group included twelve young women, among them Baum's sister Marianne, aged thirty, the sisters Alice and Hella Hirsch, aged nineteen and twenty-two respectively, and Edith Fraenkel, aged twenty-one. A memorial in the Berlin Jewish cemetery of Weissensee records their fate.[48]

Also in May 1942, a group of Communist Jews living in Paris, some of them Polish- and German-born, took part in the first French acts of collective armed resistance against the Germans. These Jews were members of Jewish units in the French Communist underground.[49]

In a further selection of children, on May 22, in the town of Ozorkow, the Secretary to the Jewish Council, Mania Rzepkowicz, rejected an offer by the German ghetto-leader that her child should be excluded from the 'resettlement', and, together with her child, voluntarily joined a group of some three hundred children being deported, she knew not where. They too were sent to Chelmno, and gassed.[50]

May 22 was the first day of Shavuot, the festival of Pentecost. In Mielec, the Gestapo organized a fictitious fight between Jews in the ghetto and themselves, pretending that the Jews were partisans, taking them to the forest, breaking their heads and arms, and then killing them. 'I was present when they were buried,' Eda Lichtmann later recalled, 'and saw their mutilated bodies.'

Eda Lichtmann was also a witness to another Nazi 'sport', when some twenty orthodox Jews were taken from their homes, dressed in their prayer shawls, with prayer books in hand, and ordered 'to chant religious hymns, to pray, to raise their hands in supplication to God – and then the officers went up to them and poured kerosene and petrol under those Jews and set fire to all the Jews, while they were in their prayer shawls, holding their prayer books in supplication to God. I saw it with my own eyes.'[51]

Also on this festival at Zdunska Wola, the Gestapo ordered the Jewish Council to 'provide' ten Jews. The Council members resisted, knowing that the last time ten men had been demanded, they had been hanged. The Gestapo then told the Council that if the men were not produced, a thousand Jews would be shot. 'Having no choice,' Dora Rosenboim later recalled, 'and fearing that the Gestapo would carry out their terrible plan of shooting a thousand Jews, the Jewish Council, with bitter and broken hearts, had to give them another ten Jews for the gallows and the Jewish policemen had to hang them with their own hands in the presence of all twelve hundred Jews, men, women, old people and children.' Among those hanged was Binyamin Pavel Radil and his son-in-law, Shlomo Zhelochovski. As Zhelochovski was brought to the gallows, 'he cried out, with his head uplifted and his arms to heaven, "Jehovah is God".'[52]

Courage in the face of death, and courageous actions, were a source of inspiration for those Jews who heard them, an illustration of *Kiddush Ha-Shem*, sanctification of the name of God, through martyrdom. One example of such innocent, and indeed unwitting martyrdom, was recorded in Ringelblum's collection of materials from all over Poland. It concerned a Jew, by the name of Ankerman, in the town of Wlodawa, and Ringelblum himself drew attention to it. On May 23, two thousand Jews were assembled in Wlodawa for deportation. The Gestapo then asked: 'Where is the rabbi?' Ankerman, thinking that the Gestapo wished to save the rabbi from deportation, pointed him out, in order to save him. The Gestapo at once shot Ankerman. The rabbi was then deported with the rest to Sobibor, where all were gassed.[53]

From Warsaw, no Jews had yet been deported. But each day, Jews were beaten or murdered. 'The Gestapo men in the Pawia Street prison', Ringelblum noted on May 23, 'have to have their daily victims. Just the way a pious Jew feels bad if he misses prayers one day, the Gestapo men have to pick up a few Jews every day and break a few arms and legs.'[54]

During May, 3,636 Warsaw Jews died of starvation.[55] 'Sometimes', Ringelblum noted on May 25, 'one comes across former students from the Institute of Judaic Studies, who ask for help in Hebrew.' Some of the beggars were well dressed. On one street, Ringelblum wrote, 'stands a beggar whose clothes are impeccable; he has a pretty child with him who is clean and spotless; he begs, not with outstretched hand, but with his eyes alone.'[56]

In Chelm, on May 28, four Jews were executed by a German firing squad, their last moments recorded by a German cameraman.[57] Their 'crime' is unknown.

May 1942 saw the opening of yet another death camp, on the outskirts of Minsk. The site chosen was a former collective farm near the village of Maly Trostenets. Russian prisoners-of-war and Jews had been forced to build the barracks for the six hundred slave labourers and their guards. Beginning on May 10, and continuing every Tuesday and Friday, Jews were brought to Minsk from Germany, Austria and Czechoslovakia, then driven by truck towards Maly Trostenets. The trucks were mobile gas-chambers; when they reached the camp all those inside them were dead. The corpses were taken out, as at Chelmno, by a special prisoners' commando, which threw them into deep pits.[58]

20

'If they have enough time, we are lost'

As THE DEPORTATIONS to Belzec, Chelmno and Sobibor continued, reports reached Ringelblum in Warsaw of the destruction of sixteen communities. At Konskowola, Ringelblum learned, the Germans had taken the Jews to the banks of the Vistula and then ordered the rabbi: 'Be Moses! Divide the waters of the Vistula!' The Jews were then forced, with their rabbi at their head, into the water. Then, amid a barrage of shooting, all were shot, or drowned.

Warsaw itself, Ringelblum noted on 30 May 1942, had passed a 'bloody week'. On the previous night, a Friday, eight or nine Jews had been killed. One of them was a man called Wilner, who lay sick in bed. 'He could barely crawl out of bed at the command of the hangman; he sat down on a chair, unable to move any further. So they threw him out of the second-floor window, together with the chair, shooting after him as he fell. In the same apartment three other men were shot (a brother-in-law of his called Rudnicki, his son, and another person). Reason unknown.'

Ringelblum also noted the particular sadism of a German policeman, who had been dubbed 'Frankenstein', 'a bloodthirsty dog who kills one or two smugglers every day. He just can't eat his breakfast until he has spilled the blood of a Jew.'[1]

In the areas of Einsatzkommando killings, east of the River Bug, spring and summer had brought an upsurge of killings, now the ground was once again soft enough, but not too waterlogged, for the digging of pits for mass graves. At Radziwillow, in Volhynia, three thousand Jews were rounded up for slaughter on May 29. But a group of young men, among them Asher Czerkaski, organized a break-out. Fifteen hundred Jews were shot; but a further fifteen hundred reached the temporary security of the nearby forests.[2]

Another area in which the killings continued was south Russia. In the Kherson region, more than seventy thousand Jews were murdered, many of them farmers. No hamlet, however remote, could escape the thoroughness of the search. On May 27, in the village of Chaplinka, three Jewish families were found and shot.

As the killings gained a new momentum, the urge to resist, and to escape, was visible in every region, and in every village. In the Kherson region, there was resistance by a Jewish partisan group, led by S. M. Khazanovich.[3]

On May 30, over Germany, the British launched their first bombing raid with a thousand bombers. Their target was Cologne. Thirty-nine of the bombers were shot down. But for Richard Lichtheim, one of a group of Jews in Geneva, who were piecing together the evidence reaching them from Nazi-occupied Poland, it seemed that the war could be 'finished this year by heavy bombardments from the air'.[4]

Even in the Warsaw ghetto, the news of Cologne had affected morale. The 'Jewish jubilation', Ringelblum noted, 'was quite different from the general one', and he went on to explain:

> Day in, day out, in hundreds of cities throughout Poland and Russia, thousands upon thousands of Jews are being systematically murdered according to a preconceived plan, and no one seems to take our part. The bombing of Cologne, the destruction of thousands of buildings, the thousands of civilian victims, have slaked our thirst for revenge somewhat. Cologne was an advance payment on the vengeance that must and shall be taken on Hitler's Germany for the millions of Jews they have killed. So the Jewish population of tortured Europe considered Cologne its personal act of vengeance. After the Cologne affair, I walked around in a good mood, feeling that, even if I should perish at their hands, my death is prepaid![5]

On the day after the Cologne raid, at Monowitz, just to the east of Auschwitz, the first of a series of forced labour camps was opened for the construction of a massive synthetic oil and rubber factory, the Buna works.[6] One of the labour camps was for Jews. Known as Auschwitz III, it drew off thousands of Jews from Birkenau, or Auschwitz II. If these Jews could survive the harsh conditions of work, the starvation and the brutality, they could hope to survive the war, and several thousand did so, unlike the hundreds of

GREATER GERMANY

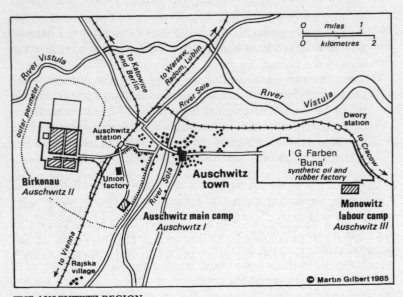

THE AUSCHWITZ REGION

thousands of adults sent to Chelmno, Sobibor and Belzec, where all, whether 'able-bodied' or not, were gassed.

On June 1, in Bodzentyn, Dawid Rubinowicz wrote his daily diary early. The entry ended:

> This morning two Jewish women, a mother and a daughter, had gone out into the country. Unfortunately the Germans were driving from Rudki to Bodzentyn to fetch potatoes and ran across them. When the two women caught sight of the Germans they began to flee, but were overtaken and arrested.
>
> They intended shooting them on the spot in the village, but the mayor wouldn't allow it. They then went into the woods and shot them there. The Jewish police immediately went there to bury them in the cemetery. When the cart returned it was full of blood. Who . . .[7]

Here Dawid's diary ended. He was not yet fifteen.

On 1 June 1942 in Warsaw, the underground newspaper *Liberty Barricade*, the bi-weekly publication of the Polish Socialist Party, published an extensive account of the gassing at Chelmno. They had received the information from Ringelblum, who had prepared it from Grojanowski's report. 'Bloodcurdling news', the report began, 'has reached us about the slaughter of the Jews. . . .' Six months and three weeks after it had begun its slaughter, Chelmno was identified by name, and Grojanowski's account of it given in detail.[8]

On June 2 there was a deportation of Jews from Vienna. They were taken by train to Minsk, and there, in the Minsk ghetto, shared the fate of tens of thousands of deportees to Minsk: starvation, sadistic cruelties, and mass executions. Among those deported on June 2 was a milliner, Elsa Speigel. It was three weeks before her thirty-third birthday. She was never heard of again. But in Vienna she left her tiny son, Jona Jakob Speigel, a baby of five and a half months.

Elsa Speigel's decision to leave her baby in Vienna saved his life. Three and a half months later he was deported from Vienna to Theresienstadt. By a miracle, he was still in Theresienstadt on the last day of the war, when the camp was liberated by the Red Army.[9]

On June 4 it was the Jews of Cracow who faced the perils and uncertainties of a round-up. A Polish Catholic, Tadeusz Pankiewicz, whose pharmacy was situated in Harmony Square, the very centre of the ghetto, later recalled how rumours spread that night 'that the Germans had disclosed secretly that the deportees will be taken to the Ukraine, where they will work on farms'. To add to the deception, German railway workmen spoke 'of large barracks that are awaiting the deportees'.

That night, Pankiewicz witnessed the round-up of thousands of Jews on Harmony Square. By the following morning, seven thousand had been assembled. There they were kept throughout that hot summer morning, then driven to the railway station, and sent off to an unknown destination. The round-up was repeated on the following day, June 6. 'The scorching sun is merciless,' Pankiewicz wrote, 'the heat makes for unbearable thirst, dries out the throats.' The crowd was standing and sitting: 'all wait, frozen with fright and uncertainty.' Armed Germans arrived, shooting at random into the crowd. Then the deportees were driven out of the square, amid 'constant screaming of the Germans, merciless beating, kicking and shooting'.

Pankiewicz's account continued:

Old people, women, and children pass by the pharmacy windows like ghosts. I see an old woman of around seventy years, her hair loose, walking alone, a few steps away from a larger group of deportees. Her eyes have a glazed look; immobile, wide open, filled with horror, they stare straight ahead. She walks slowly, quietly, only in her dress and slippers, without even a bundle, or handbag. She holds in her hands something small, something black, which she caresses fondly and keeps close to her old breast. It is a small puppy – her most precious possession, all that she saved and would not leave behind.

Laughing, inarticulately gesturing with her hands, walks a young deranged girl of about fourteen, so familiar to all inhabitants of the ghetto. She walks barefoot, in a crumpled nightgown. One shuddered watching the girl laughing, having a good time. Old and young pass by, some dressed, some only in their underwear, hauled out of their beds and driven out.

People after major operations and people with chronic diseases went by. . . .

Across the street from the pharmacy, out of the building at 2 Harmony Square, walks a blind old man, well known to the inhabitants of the ghetto; he is about seventy years old, wears dark goggles over his blind eyes, which he lost in the battles on the Italian front in 1915 fighting side by side with the Germans. He wears a yellow armband with three black circles on his left arm to signify his blindness. His head high, he walks erect, guided by his son on one side, by his wife on the other. 'He should be happy that he cannot see, it will be easier for him to die,' says a hospital nurse to us. Pinned on his chest is the medal he won during the war. It may, perhaps, have some significance for the Germans. Such were the illusions in the beginning.

Immediately after him, another elderly person appears, a cripple with one leg, on crutches. The Germans close in on them; slowly, in dance step, one of them runs toward the blind man and yells with all his power: 'Schnell!' 'Hurry!' This encourages the other Germans to start a peculiar game.

Two of the SS men approach the old man without the leg and shout the order for him to run. Another one comes from behind and with the butt of his rifle hits the crutch. The old man falls down. The German screams savagely, threatens to shoot. All this takes place right in the back of the blind man who is unable to see, but hears the beastly voices of the Germans, interspersed with cascades of their laughter. A German soldier approaches the cripple who is lying on the ground and helps him to rise. This help will show on the snapshot of a German officer who is eagerly taking pictures of all scenes that will prove 'German help in the humane resettlement of the Jews'.

For a moment we think that perhaps there will be at least one human being among them unable to stand torturing people one hour before their death. Alas, there was no such person in the annals of the Cracow ghetto. No sooner were they saturated with torturing the cripple than they decided to try the same with the blind war invalid. They chased away his son and wife, tripped him, and rejoiced at his falling to the ground. This time they even did not pretend to help him and he had to rise by himself, rushed on by horrifying screaming of the SS men hovering over him. They repeated this game several times, a truly shattering experience of cruelty. One could not tell from what they derived more pleasure, the physical pain of the fallen invalid or the despair of his wife and son standing aside watching helplessly. . . .

'The shots are echoing all over the ghetto,' Pankiewicz added.

Among those shot in Cracow that day was the Yiddish song writer and poet, Mordche Gebirtig. In one of his last songs, written a month before his death, he had expressed his hope that, 'from too much gorging, the invader's end would result, Amen. . . .'[10]

Dissatisfied by the number of Jews who had been assembled during the Cracow deportations, and critical of the 'technique of delivery' to Harmony Square, the Germans arrested the Chairman of the Jewish Council, Dr Artur Rosenzweig, and deported him together with his family.[11]

Unknown to Pankiewicz, or to the Jews left behind in Cracow, the seven thousand deportees of June 1 were sent to Belzec, and gassed. But to maintain the belief in 'resettlement', as Pankiewicz later recalled, German railway workers told those who begged them for news of the deportees that there were Jews from all over Europe in the resettlement camps in the Ukraine: 'They have a good life, work hard, but have everything they need, food and clothes. Naturally they are heavily guarded, barbed wire encircles the barracks, nobody is allowed to come near; they are not allowed to write letters, and this is the reason why no news is forthcoming from them.'

Such were the 'rumours': and the railwaymen offered, for money, to bring back 'news' of the deportees, or to take messages to them. They accepted the money, walked off, and were never seen again.[12]

One more death camp was now nearly ready to begin operation. On June 1 the Germans had begun to build a short branch-line off the existing side-line which ran from Treblinka station to the nearby gravel pits. This new track led to buildings which had been constructed during April and May on a site specially cleared in the forest: a site enclosed by barbed wire. A Polish railwayman, Franciszek Zabecki, later recalled that the capacity of this branch-line 'was estimated as twenty wagons and an engine'.[13]

Treblinka was being prepared for the Jews of central Poland, including the 350,000 surviving Jews of the Warsaw ghetto. Meanwhile, throughout June, the deportations to Belzec, Sobibor and Chelmno continued. On June 1, in an attempt to make contact with the Jews of Hrubieszow, two girls from the Warsaw ghetto, Frumka Plotnicka, of whom Ringelblum had written with such admiration, and Hava Follman, by removing their armbands, bribing the ghetto policeman, procuring forged travel papers, and with considerable personal courage, took the train eastwards. At some junctions it stopped for up to ten hours. Each time it stopped, their documents were examined, but without incident. Hava Follman's own account continues:

> On approaching Hrubieszow, we became aware of an unusual commotion; big crowds were gathered on the platform. Unsuspecting, we alighted at the station. But we soon learned that the thousands herded there were Jews: men and women, old and young, children pressed among bundles of household effects; cries and shouts of the Germans.
>
> Four stout, red-faced Germans, arms bare, gallop on horseback along the platform, ply their whips ceaselessly, tread on whomever they find in their way, vent their wrath on mothers holding babies in their arms.
>
> A huge German, with the face of a murderer, leads off four youths clad in kapotes. Their faces are frozen; a few metres from the window of the waiting-room, where Frumke and I took refuge, they are ordered to dig. They are urged along with the whip: 'Quickly, we have no time!' A few minutes later, four shots are heard, and again the whip is used on those who are bidden to fill in the open grave.
>
> Suddenly a horrible scream of a woman is heard, followed by a shot. A woman with a baby in her arms keels over. She wanted to throw the baby over the fence, in the hope that it would be spared. But a moment later she and the baby are trodden to death by the horses' hoofs. A deadly silence descends on the platform. I hold fast to the window-sill; I feel terribly dizzy.
>
> We start walking into town. The road is crowded with carts bearing old and sickly people who are unable to walk to their 'destination'. They are guarded by Ukrainian police.

We are allowed to look our fill. Only a 'trifle' is required of us: a smiling face! Are we not supposed to be true Goyim and is not spring in the air?

We go through well known lanes and streets, we reach the house of Aaron Frumer, where we used to meet frequently. The door to his flat is wide open, the floor is littered with all sorts of household objects, but not a living soul in sight.

Where to now?

In the centre of the town two Germans walk, preceded by a group of Gentile boys. The Germans carry axes, the boys are leading them to a house, where Jews are hiding.

In order not to draw attention to ourselves, we quicken our pace in the direction of the church. There Frumka stays behind and I make a short tour. In a shop I learn that the Jewish youth has been concentrated back of the town. They are intended for the labour camps, whilst the 'rubbish' will go elsewhere. This remark by my informant is accompanied by a sly smile, which I have to return in kind.

Despite my efforts, we could not reach our comrades, and, as there was no train to Warsaw until eight the following morning, we had to spend the night at the hotel. We pass the inspection of the hotel-keeper satisfactorily and are given a room.

Needless to say, we passed a sleepless night. Early in the morning, another inspection is thorough; the policemen are not quite convinced, and we are ordered to report later in the day at the police station.

We decide that we cannot risk another inspection. We check out and find our way to the station by devious ways. If we succeed in reaching Warsaw, we intend to return and try again to contact our friends.

A 'special' train stands on the platform, filled to overflowing with Jews. The platform is strewn with bundles, pillows, prams, pots and pans. A number of Gentile boys are waiting: as soon as the train steams out, they will appropriate the loot.[14]

Hava Follman and Frumka Plotnicka reached Warsaw safely, and made their report. Unknown to them, the Jews whom they had seen being deported that day were sent from Hrubieszow to Sobibor, 3,400 in all, followed a week later by a further two thousand.

Among these deportees was the fifteen-year-old Yaakov Biskowitz. From the transport of 3,400, only twelve were selected for work: Biskowitz and his father among them. They were put to work as carpenters. All the other Hrubieszow deportees were gassed in Camp 3.

One of Biskowitz's first tasks was to drag enormous branches of greenery from the nearby woods, to cover the barbed-wire fence on the path between the railway ramp and Camp 2, the undressing courtyard. He later recalled how those who were too sick or old to walk the length of the path were taken to the so-called *Lazarett*, or hospital, on a small rail spur used to carry coal. Men 'who could not run fast enough', and small children, would be thrown into the wagons and sent to the 'hospital'. There, they would be shot.

Eighty Jews were forced to work in Camp 3, burning the bodies which had been gassed. They had also to sort out the clothing of those who had been killed. Damaged clothing, and all personal documents, were burned. One day a young man who had known Biskowitz in Hrubieszow brought him some photographs. While burning the personal belongings of those who had been gassed, he had recognized the photographs of Biskowitz's family. 'He brought those pictures out of the fire,' Biskowitz recalled. His family had been killed. It was June 3.

Two months later, Biskowitz's father was taken ill. 'I tried to take him to work,' he recalled. 'I dragged him to work every morning. While he was down with typhoid, I worked at the casino of the Ukrainians. I would put him in the corner and work for two, but one day I could not drag him any longer. I tried, then all of a sudden, two SS men – Wagner and Frenschel – took him out of the barrack and he was taken to the "Lazarett", beaten all the way. He was shot in my presence. I wanted to run after him, but I was held back by the other workers.'[15]

In Warsaw, 110 Jews were shot on June 3 in the prison on Gesia Street, among them ten Jewish policemen. Mary Berg noted in her diary that Polish police were ordered to do the shooting, but refused. Both they, and Jewish policemen, were forced to watch the execution. 'One of the eye-witnesses told me that several Polish policemen wept,' Mary Berg noted. One of the Jewish Council members forced to be present had fainted. The Jewish policemen forced to watch 'were completely shattered'. The victims included several women, two of them pregnant. All had gone to their deaths 'in complete calm'. Some had even refused to be blindfolded.[16]

Ringelblum and his friends, known as the 'Joy of Sabbath' circle, worked continuously to record the fate of the Jews of Warsaw. 'Each Saturday', Ringelblum noted on June 6, 'we come together, a group of Jewish community activists, to discuss the writing of our diaries and journals. We want our suffering to remain on record for future generations and for the whole world.'[17]

Among those who were recording the events in the Warsaw ghetto was Abraham Levin, an historian whose books included a study of the 'Cantonists', the Jewish boys who, in the nineteenth century, had been forcibly conscripted in the Tsarist army for twenty-five years' military service. Levin gave his diary to Ringelblum's 'Joy of Sabbath' circle. 'On every Sabbath', Levin noted on June 6, 'we gather together, a group of Jewish public workers, in connection with our diaries and records. Our purpose is that our sufferings, "the pains before the coming of the Messiah", should be noted down for remembrance by future generations, for remembrance by the whole world.' Levin added: 'Sabbath by Sabbath we meet and discuss what we have to do in this connection, and in the course of this we cannot refrain from telling one another what the old-new Amalekites are doing to us Jews. The stories throw me into utter depression, my head begins to ache as if a heavy leaden weight were pressing on it. The same thing happened today. They told and they told, and I felt cold and impotent – and they went on telling.'

In his diary for June 6, Levin noted down several of these most recent stories. In Wlodawa, the rabbi of Radzyn had been killed. A young man, wanting to save him, told the Germans that he was the rabbi. But the Germans saw through the deception, found the rabbi, 'and killed both him and the young man'.[18]

On the following day, June 7, Levin recorded: 'Tonight once again a Jewish man and a woman fell into the hands of German murderers in uniform,' and he went on to explain:

At about one o'clock at night a Jew, thirty-five years of age, and two German officers, got out of a car at the corner of Karmelicka and Nowolipie Streets. They let him go a few paces then fired at him. The Jew was still alive, so they shot at him again until he died. They then rang at the gate of 22 Nowolipie Street and ordered the house porter to take the dead man inside. Early in the morning they removed the body. Who the Jew was, is not known. According to one source he was Rosen, of 24 Elektoralna Street.

'They brought a Jewish woman to Nowolipie and shot her,' Levin continued. 'It is believed that they had brought her from the Aryan side.'[19]

The Germans were still determined not to let a single Jew escape the widening deportations.

On 27 May 1942, SS General Reinhard Heydrich was fatally wounded in Prague by two Czech patriots parachuted into German-occupied Czechoslovakia from Britain. As Deputy Protector for Bohemia and Moravia, Heydrich's name had become a byword for repression. At the Wannsee Conference four months earlier, he had presided over the bureaucratic confirmation of the 'final solution'.

Following the attack on Heydrich, and even before his death eight days later, SS General Odilo Globocnik began preparations for what was called 'Operation Reinhard', the deportation of Jews to Treblinka, Belzec and Sobibor to their immediate deaths. Two weeks later, a thousand Jews were deported from Prague to death in the East. At the same time, in a reprisal action on Czech soil, 199 Czech men and boys were murdered in the mining village of Lidice. The village was then burned to the ground.[20]

On the day of the Lidice massacre, thirty Jews were driven from Theresienstadt to the smouldering ruins of the small mining community. There, at pistol point, they were forced to bury the 199 victims. For thirty-six hours they worked without a break at their grim task.[21]

As Operation Reinhard gathered momentum, the deportation of Jews was accelerated from the Reich itself. The background of Heydrich's assassination was not yet clear, wrote Josef Goebbels at the end of May, but 'in any event we are holding the Jews to account. I am ordering the arrest of 500 Berlin Jews which I had been planning, and I am informing the Jewish community leaders that for every Jewish assassination and for every attempt at revolt on the part of Jews, 100 or 150 Jews in our hands will be shot.' In the wake of the Heydrich assassination, several hundred Jews had already been shot in Sachsenhausen. 'The more of this filth that is eliminated,' Goebbels added, 'the better for the security of the Reich.'[22]

On June 6, Eichmann sent a telegram from Berlin to Gestapo officials in Coblenz, concerning the composition of a transport to Lublin. Among the 450 Jews in the Coblenz region to be deported, the inmates of a mental home in one small town were to be included. Later, in its constant efforts to maintain secrecy, Eichmann's office reiterated its instruction that even the words 'deportation to the East' should not be used, but, instead, 'people who emigrated elsewhere'.[23]

The fate of these deportees was the same for each deportation. Of the thousand Jews sent from Prague on June 10, as part of Operation Reinhard, the only survivor was a man who jumped from the train during the journey.[24] There were no survivors at all of the thousand deportees from Theresienstadt on June 12.[25] Nor was there a single survivor of a further thousand sent from Theresienstadt on June 13 'to an unknown destination in the East'. As no deportee returned, the historian of Theresienstadt has written, 'it must be assumed that all prisoners perished in death camps.'[26]

The only indication of the fate of the deportees from the first of the Operation Reinhard deportations, that of June 10, was in a letter smuggled from the Lublin district in September 1942, from one of the deportees to his son. According to this letter the transport had been taken to a camp at Ujazdow in the Lublin district, from where the prisoners continued their journey in sordid cattle trucks to a camp which the writer described as a 'selection camp on the River Bug'. There they were robbed of all their belongings, and those unfit for work were killed.

The letter gave no details as to how the murders had been carried out. The prisoners – Czech, Dutch, Polish, Austrian and German Jews – slept in barns on the bare floor without blankets. They had to walk many miles to their place of work, where men and women alike were forced to dig trenches in marshland. So debilitated did they become that they could scarcely hold their spades. They worked and slept in wet clothing. The camp doctor, himself a prisoner, had no medical supplies for those who fell ill. The camp commander recognized only typhus as a disease exempting from work. All typhus patients were taken to a special typhus camp, where they were left to die.

On the subject of the camp guards, the letter says: 'They shout but they do not beat.' The letter ended with a desperate appeal for food, clothing or money. Food, clothing and money were sent as asked. But there was no reply. Nor did any one of the Theresienstadt deportees on that transport of June 10 return after the war. The road from Ujazdow led only to Belzec.[27]

In German-occupied Poland, the Jewish Councils continued to try to give a lead: on June 8 the head of the Council at Pilica, Fogel, warned the community 'that every able Jew must flee to the forests'. Several hundred succeeded. Fogel later visited those in the forests, and helped to supply them with weapons.[28]

In Riga, the Einsatzkommando decided to use gas-vans to facilitate its killings. Two such vans, which could kill fifteen to twenty-five Jews at a time, had already been used in Belgrade. On June 9, after one of the vans had been returned to Berlin after completion of a 'special assignment' in Belgrade, it was sent on to Riga. Six days later, the Riga authorities requested a second van.[29] At his testimony before the Nuremberg Tribunal, General Ohlendorf told the court that the Einsatzkommando units had not liked to use the vans, because the burial of those gassed in them was 'unpleasant'.[30] The vans were, however, effective. On July 5 an official in Eichmann's department noted that, since December 1941, ninety-seven thousand people had been 'processed' in three vans, without any 'defect' being discovered in the vans; that the defects found at Chelmno were 'a solitary case'.[31]

In Warsaw, the diarists of the 'Joy of Sabbath' circle continued to record the news which reached them. 'During the deportation from Pabianice,' Chaim Kaplan noted in his diary on June 9, 'there was one mother who fought like a lioness and refused to turn her baby over to the murderers. They immediately grabbed the baby and hurled it out of the window.'[32] That month in Sosnowiec, Frieda Mazia later recalled, the Germans entered the Jewish hospitals, 'took women after childbirth, people after operations; they took all the babies from the children's ward and threw them from the second floor into large trucks in the street.' All those in the hospitals were supposed to be going 'to new settlements'.[33] They were sent, in fact, to Auschwitz, and gassed.[34]

Five young Sosnowiec Jews decided to try to steal weapons from an apartment lived in by a German officer. One of these Jews, Harry Blumenfrucht, was caught. He tried to shoot the German who seized him. This German was known throughout the district as 'Dog with Dog', because he was always with his dog. The dog sunk his teeth into Blumenfrucht's hand, making it impossible for him to shoot.

Under torture, Blumenfrucht refused to betray his four colleagues. As Frieda Mazia recalled:

> They put chips of wood under his fingernails and put fire to them. They put him on an iron net and held him there for forty-eight hours, without a stop. And when he screamed, all he said was, 'I will not speak. I am dead, in any case.'
>
> They brought his mother and she prayed and begged with him, 'Harry, to shorten your torture – you will not come out alive – but just to shorten your torture, admit something.' Harry said nothing. He told his mother, 'I am doomed. I will not speak.' The Germans kept him, I believe, two weeks. And they admired the boy.
>
> Usually people were hanged in public and Jews were ordered to come and watch. Harry they hanged before dawn, during curfew hours, because they were afraid. They saw there was something unusual in the man.[35]

The German reaction to all such defiance was savage. Writing from Lodz on June 9, the German criminal police reported to their superiors in Poznan: 'Thus far ninety-five Jews have been hung publicly here.' These hangings, they explained, 'have caused the Jew to understand the severe order here, and from now on he will obey all orders completely and peacefully'.

The Jews who had been hanged in the Lodz ghetto had been chosen at random, and killed in order to discourage others from resisting deportation by hiding or flight. On July 13, further such public executions were reported by the same police unit: nine Jews hanged in Warta, two in the county of Lask, and two more in the Lodz ghetto.[36]

Equally savage pressure against any hint of defiance was seen in the Janowska camp at Lvov, where Josef Buzhminski later recalled how his brother Isidore was killed 'by hanging by his feet and beating till he died'.[37] But even where successful physical resistance was impossible, acts of moral and spiritual resistance took place, to the fury of the murderers. At Dabrowa Tarnowska, in June, the Germans dragged Rabbi Isaac and his followers out of their underground hide-out, and drove them to the local Jewish cemetery. The Jews had waited in their prayer shawls for their inevitable discovery. They also had a bottle of vodka, which they managed to bring with them to the cemetery. There, facing their would-be murderers, they drank *lekhayim*, 'to life', held hands, began to dance, and were shot down as they danced. An eye-witness later recalled how the Germans 'were so enraged by the scene, which they had failed to prevent, that they slit their bellies and trampled on them until the bowels came out.'[38]

At Khmelnik, in the Ukraine, June 12 saw the third 'action' against the Jews. This time it was babies, children and old people who were ordered to assemble. Children were taken from their mothers. Mothers who begged to go with their babies were not allowed to do so. 'The children were taken to the forest,' the eighteen-year-old Maria Rubinstein later recalled. 'Nobody knew what really was there. There were rumours that the wives of the Ukrainian policemen were putting poison on their lips with their fingers.'

Among the children taken away was Maria Rubinstein's youngest sister Dina. She was not yet two years old. Following the murder of her mother six months earlier, Dina had been hidden with a peasant woman in a village some way from Khmelnik. But two days before this third 'action' she had been brought back to the ghetto because the Christian woman who was hiding her had 'had some family troubles with her husband'.

Dina was taken away, and, with hundreds of other babies and young children, was murdered in the nearby forest.[39]

On June 10 the Jews of Biala Podlaska had been deported to Sobibor. A week later, Ringelblum spoke in Warsaw to the head of the Jewish Social Relief Organization in Biala Podlaska, who asked in anger, 'How much longer will we go "as sheep to the slaughter"? Why do we keep quiet? Why is there no call to escape to the forests. No call to resist?' Ringelblum noted:

This question torments all of us, but there is no answer to it because everyone knows that resistance, and particularly if even one single German is killed, its outcome may lead to a slaughter of a whole community, or even of many communities.

The first who are sent to slaughter are the old, the sick, the children, those who are not able to resist. The strong ones, the workers, are left meanwhile to be, because they are needed for the time being.

The evacuations are carried out in such a way that it is not always and not to everyone clear that a massacre is taking place. So strong is the instinct of life of workers, of the fortunate owners of work permits, that it overcomes the will to fight, the urge to defend the whole community, with no thought of consequences. And we are left to be led as sheep to a slaughterhouse. This is partly due to the complete spiritual breakdown and disintegration, caused by unheard-of terror which has been inflicted upon the Jews for three years and which comes to its climax in times of such evacuations.

The effect of all this taken together is that when a moment for some resistance arrives, we are completely powerless and the enemy does to us whatever he pleases.

Ringelblum was critical of particular communities which had not done enough, he thought, to challenge their tormentors. 'One gendarme is sufficient to butcher a whole town,' he wrote bitterly, adding, of earlier reports of resistance which had been spread in Warsaw:

Of no use will be the lies that are being fabricated about Nowogrodek or the recent ones about Kowel; in no place did Jews resist the slaughter. They went passively to death and they did it, so that the remnants of the people would be left to live, because every Jew knew that lifting a hand against a German would endanger his brothers from a different town or maybe from a different country. That is the reason why three hundred prisoners of war let the Germans kill them on the way from Lublin to Biala; and these soldiers were known to have distinguished themselves in the fight for Poland's freedom.

Not to act, not to lift a hand against Germans, has since then become the quiet, passive heroism of the common Jew. This was perhaps the mute life instinct of the masses, which dictated to everybody, as if agreed upon, to behave thus and not otherwise. And it seems to me that no incitement, no persuasion, will be of any use here; it is impossible to fight a mass-instinct – you must submit to it.[40]

There were in fact many acts of resistance, even in Warsaw. But the subsequent reprisals were, as Ringelblum had written, a fierce deterrent. In Warsaw that June, the conflict between the will to resist and the horror of reprisals was seen when two Jewish porters, suspected of smuggling, were taken to be shot. A friend of theirs, a tailor named Izraelit, who had come by chance to spend the night with them, was taken with them to the execution site. These three 'candidates for death', Chaim Kaplan noted in his diary on July 6, 'were virile men with strength in their loins, and they did not want to die in spite of the Nazis'. Kaplan's account continued: ·

Thus in the dark of the night a terrible wrestling match began between those who were defending their lives and the killers. The porters fought with the strength of their bodies, without weapons; the killers were armed and confident of their superiority.

At such times there is no rational thought. Instinct comes in its stead. In time of danger the latent, hidden powers of a man burst out and are exposed; and in particular when one finds oneself in a condition of 'in any case we will die'. And therefore, before the killers had time to act, the condemned men pounced on them and tried to seize the pistols.

One of the pistols went off and wounded the tailor in the leg. Then the porters grabbed the Nazis by the throat and tried to strangle them. The two sides wrestled until their strength waned, and in the end the killers, who still had their weapons, were victorious. Izraelit the tailor saved himself by presenting the killers with a document showing that he was working in a factory for the German army. With the dawn, he was taken to the hospital.

On the morrow, the Nazis avenged the mutiny of the two porters with 110 Jews. They were put to death for the sins of men who had never laid eyes on them.[41]

At Mielnica, near Kowel, one of the two towns mentioned by Ringelblum in connection with 'lies' about resistance, an act of resistance had been recorded during the Einsatzkommando killings of July 1941, when Abraham Weintraub 'dashed out of a group drawn up for the massacre, pounced upon a German officer who was standing nearby, hit him and broke his teeth'. Weintraub was shot dead on the spot.[42] But in some of the larger ghettos, submission seemed a way to survival. Moses Merin in the Zaglebia region, Chaim Rumkowski in Lodz, Ephraim Barasz in Bialystok, each believed in the possibility of protecting tens of thousands of Jews by turning their respective ghettos into increasingly productive work centres for German needs.

In the Lodz ghetto, Rumkowski had always insisted that the ghetto's chances of survival lay in productive work. But on June 4 the Ghetto Chronicle had noted that 'fear of the possible resettlement of the unemployed, which would mean the break-up of families, runs deep in the ghetto dwellers' minds, weighs on them, and prevents them from working.' Were it not for that worry, the Chronicle added, 'it could all somehow be endured, for, on the whole, our people are greatly inclined to optimism and to believe in the power of the spirit in spite of physical exhaustion.'[43]

Work in the Lodz ghetto was, indeed, on the increase, particularly, as the Chronicle noted on June 10, in providing material for the German army. This increase in orders, it commented, had been observable 'since the time when the ghettos in the neighbouring small towns were eliminated'.[44]

Between the end of May and mid-July 1942, the Lodz ghetto workshops received nearly 800,000 kilogrammes of old clothing, nearly 70,000 kilogrammes of used shoes, and even 12 kilogrammes of old ties.[45] During the sorting of the old clothing, one woman worker found a gold necklace weighing 26 grammes.[46]

In his public address to the people of the ghetto on May 31, Rumkowski had stressed that work, and working papers, were the principal authorization 'for remaining in the ghetto'. Of the hundred thousand Jews in the ghetto, seventy thousand were employed. He would try to find employment for ten thousand more 'in the very near future', including 'easy work for children and old people'.[47] Nor was work lacking: German army representatives who inspected the ghetto in July expressed themselves 'entirely satisfied' by what they saw: including tailor workshops producing ten thousand pairs of pants and trousers in camouflage cloth, and jumpsuits for paratroops.[48]

During his speech on May 31, Rumkowski had told the Jews of the Lodz ghetto that 'considerable blame' for the 'resettlement' of fifty-five thousand Jews from Lodz in the previous six months was to be borne in Lodz itself by those Jews who had been 'reluctant to work'. He wished therefore to warn them again 'of the potential consequences of idleness'.[49]

Three weeks later, on June 21, Ephraim Barasz explained, at a mass meeting of Bialystok Jews:

> We have transformed all our inhabitants into useful elements. Our security is in direct proportion to our labour productivity. We already have twenty factories in operation. Any day now, there will be opened a weaving factory, a factory making wooden lasts, a woodwork and a wheel factory. . . .
>
> You are all aware of the visits we have recently had. It is hard to enumerate them all, and I shall only mention those most important ones, on which the fate of the ghetto depended. . . .
>
> All delegations have expressed their satisfaction with our work, and we received massive orders after the last visits. The visits brought about a continuously improving attitude toward us. The very person who, from the start, was totally against us, now has become friendly.
>
> Instead of contributions, evacuations etc., we are now given subsidies for our institutions, for the kitchens, training courses, hospitals, and also for industry. But the financial aspect is not as important as is the friendly attitude toward us.

Steps had to be taken, Barasz explained, so that the existence of thirty-five thousand Jews in the Bialystok ghetto would 'achieve justification, so that we may be tolerated'.[50]

Ringelblum had no illusions as to the Jewish fate under Nazi rule. 'The extermination', he wrote on June 25, 'is being executed according to a plan and schedule prepared in advance. Only a miracle can save us: the sudden end of the war. Otherwise, we are lost.'[51]

On June 26, using information collected by the 'Joy of Sabbath' circle and smuggled out of Poland, the British government broadcast details of the fate of Polish Jewry. 'Today,' Ringelblum noted, 'there was a broadcast summarizing the situation: seven hundred thousand, the number of Jews killed in Poland, was mentioned. At the same time, the broadcast vowed revenge, a final accounting for all these deeds of violence.' Ringelblum added, of his own circle's efforts:

> Our toils and tribulations, our devotion and constant terror, have not been in vain. We have struck the enemy a hard blow. It is not important whether or not the revelation of the incredible slaughter of Jews will have the desired effect – whether or not the methodical liquidation of entire Jewish communities will stop. One thing we know – we have fulfilled our duty. We have overcome every obstacle to achieve our end. Nor will our deaths be meaningless, like the deaths of tens of thousands of Jews. We have struck the enemy a hard blow. We have revealed his Satanic plan to annihilate Polish Jewry, a plan he wished to complete in silence. We have run a line through his calculations and have exposed his cards. And if England keeps its word and turns to the formidable massive attacks that it has threatened – then perhaps we shall be saved.

There were some people, Ringelblum noted, who believed that as a result of the broadcasts from London, the Germans would be afraid to perpetrate any new massacres. Some people cited 'evidence' of Jews 'supposed to have been deported from Ostrowiec being set free'. If this were confirmed, Ringelblum added, 'it is really the beginning of a new era'. But, he added, the 'more sober among us' warned against having any illusions: 'No compassion can be expected from the Germans. Whether we live or die depends on how much time they have. If they have enough time we are lost. If salvation comes soon, we are saved.'[52]

21

'Avenge our tormented people'

ON 7 JULY 1942 a meeting took place in Berlin, presided over by Himmler. Three other men were also present: the head of the Concentration Camp Inspectorate, SS General Richard Glueks; the hospital chief, SS Major-General, and also Professor, Gebhardt; and a leading German gynaecologist, Professor Clauberg. As a result of their discussion, it was decided to start medical experiments in 'major dimensions' on Jewish women at Auschwitz. The experiments would be done in such a way, the notes of the meeting recorded, that a woman would not become aware of what was being done to her. It was also decided to ask a leading X-ray specialist, Professor Hohlfelder, to find out if it were possible to castrate men by means of X-rays.

Himmler warned those present that these were 'most secret matters'. All who became involved in them, he said, would have to be pledged to secrecy.[1] Three days later, at Auschwitz, the first hundred Jewish women were taken from the barracks to the hospital block for sterilization and other experiments. One of those who survived such an experiment travelled, after the war, by ship to the Far East. She was then aged thirty-five years, but the ship's medical officer, Peter Mackay, reported that she 'looked at least twenty years older'.

During the voyage, Mackay also spoke to two Dutch doctors who had been prisoners in Auschwitz, and who described four experiments:

Experiment No. 1

These were performed by a Professor Samuel who was forced to do them. Three to four operations per day. The abdomen was opened and an incision made in the uterus, whereupon neoplastic cells were implanted. The origin of these neoplastic cells is unknown.

Three to six operations were performed after this at three to four weekly intervals and pieces of tissue from the uterus were taken and frozen sections made. The discharge which occurred through the cervix was clear and gave no indication of any change occurring. The women were unaffected by the actual operations.

Experiment No. 2

Fifteen girls aged seventeen to eighteen years old. The girls who survived the following operations are in German hands and little is known about them. The subjects were placed in an ultra-short-wave field. One electrode was placed on the abdomen and another on the vulva. The rays were focused on the ovaries. The ovaries were consequently burnt up.

Owing to faulty doses several had serious burns of the abdomen and vulva. One died as a result of these burns alone. The others were sent to another concentration camp where some were put in hospital and others made to work. After a month they returned to Auschwitz where control operations were performed. Sagittal and transverse sections of the ovaries were made.

The girls altered entirely owing to hormonal changes. They looked just like old women. Often they were laid up for months owing to the wounds of the operations becoming septic. Several died as a result of sepsis.

The third experiment, carried out by Dr Clauberg, was described by the Dutch doctors as the one 'most practised'.

The women were put on the table. With the assistance of an electrically driven pump a white cement-like fluid (possibly Barium) was driven into the uterus. As the fluid was pumped in, Rontgen photos were taken. The women were extremely ill under this experiment. They felt as though the abdomen was going to burst. After getting up from the table they rushed to the lavatory where the fluid came out again. The pains caused by this experiment were equivalent to labour pains. The fluid which was evacuated was often mixed with blood. The experiments were repeated several times. Those patients that could not be used owing to a small Os Uteri or those patients upon whom the experiments were completed, were sent to Birkenau, another camp, where they were killed. This was practised on practically all women at Auschwitz, about four hundred all told.

The aim of the experiment was not to affect sterility, nevertheless it is certain that many women owing to the inflammatory reaction set up did become sterile and many died from peritonitis due to a ruptured uterus.

A fourth experiment, carried out by SS First Lieutenants Weber and Munch, involved the reaction of the blood to various injections, among them malarial parasites, pure carbolic, and air. 'Many other cruelties were performed', Mackay added, 'which have not been set down.'[2]

Auschwitz was now ready to receive Jews from all over Europe: to gas the old, the sick, the infirm and the young, and to 'select' the able-bodied for forced labour, and for medical experiments. On July 15 the first two thousand deportees were sent from Holland to Auschwitz. Most of them were German Jews who had found refuge in Holland between 1933 and 1939. On the previous day the Germans had announced that they were going for 'labour service in Germany'.[3] Two weeks later, in Amsterdam, the Gestapo Commander assured the Jewish Council that 'all Jews taken to Germany are undoubtedly doing ordinary work.' In addition, he promised them that the Germans had made 'absolutely certain' that deported families would be kept together.[4]

The two thousand deportees from Holland had been sent east in two trains. Both trains reached Auschwitz on July 17. At Auschwitz, 1,251 men were sent to the barracks at Birkenau where they were tattooed on their forearm with the numbers 47088 to 47687 and 47843 to 48493. Of the women deportees, 300 were taken to the barracks and likewise tattooed, with the numbers 8801 to 8999 and 9027 to 9127. The remaining 449 deportees were gassed.[5] These included all the children, the elderly and the sick.

The 'numbering' of Jews at Birkenau was not only administratively tidy. It was also a method of depersonalising tens of thousands of men and women, who were being reduced to a cipher, a mere number. Once they had been tattooed, the only thing that was important about them was their number. Whatever productive work that was to be had of them was as if from a machine: a machine with a serial number by which alone it functioned. The tattoo on the forearm also inhibited escape: it was an indelible mark instantly recognisable. Unlike circumcision, which had become under German rule a tell-tale mark and curse only for Jewish men, the tattoo identified Jew and Jewess alike.

As the deportations from Holland gathered momentum, many Dutch Jews were given shelter by non-Jews. In the small town of Winterswijk, near the German frontier, hiding places were found for 35 of the 270 Jews. Eight miles away, at Aalten, of 85 Jews, 51 were hidden by non-Jews, and survived the war.[6]

On July 16, the day after the first Dutch deportation, seven thousand Jews were rounded up in Paris. They were taken, first, to an indoor stadium, the Velodrome d'Hiver, and then to an unfinished suburban building complex at Drancy. The original plan was for them to be deported on July 18, but the train was not ready. Adolf Eichmann was angered, pointing out, as SS First Lieutenant Heinz Rothke, his Paris representative, noted on July 19, 'that it was a matter of prestige: difficult negotiations had been successfully concluded with the Reich Transport Ministry for these convoys and now Paris was cancelling a train.' Such a thing 'had never happened to him before. The whole affair was "disgraceful".'[7]

Matters were soon rectified. On the very day of Eichmann's protest, July 19, the first thousand Jews, 879 men and 121 women, were deported from Paris to Auschwitz. These deportees from France included 386 Polish-born Jews, and many other Jews born in towns as far away as Odessa, Istanbul, Leningrad, Moscow and Jerusalem. On July 21 these thousand deportees reached Auschwitz. A selection was made, and 375, probably all those over forty-five, were gassed. The other men and women, 615 in all, received tattoo numbers and were sent to the barracks.[8] But only seventeen of the men sent to the barracks, and none of the women, survived the war.[9]

On their arrival at Auschwitz, the Jewish deportees were met with a combination of threats and deception. If there were several trains on a single day, haste was the predominant mood. Rudolf Vrba,

DEPORTATIONS TO AUSCHWITZ

THE WESTERN DEPORTATIONS

deported from Slovakia in July, recalled how, on arrival, the Jews in his carriage 'began to throw out all the corpses of the dead. But all of a sudden there were voices, "Juden, raus, raus, raus – schnell, schnell, schnell." "Jews, out, out, out – quick, quick, quick. . . ."'

Vrba was selected for the barracks, where he worked first as a clerk and later as one of those prisoners forced to sort out the belongings of the new arrivals. Later he recalled the days on which there was, perhaps, only a single train, and hence less hurry. On such occasions, Vrba noted, the SS 'might grant you the gentle technique, with humour'. This, he recalled, was the gist of the 'gentle' approach:

> Ladies and gentlemen, we are so sorry. Look just at this mess! How do they treat people! Would you please get out and please don't get in touch with those criminals – they are here only for taking your luggage and if you have got unmarked luggage and you are afraid that you might, it might get lost, just take it with you, but which you have got names on it, just don't worry. We are keeping a good eye that none of those criminals can take anything away. And our German honesty, about which I hope you have got no doubt, is a guarantee that all your property will be given to you. Now the whole thing is to make the whole procedure – please don't make us any trouble – so that we can give you water and allow you the basic sanitary conditions to be restored after this dismal journey.

In this way, Vrba added, the SS, while looking around at the 'excrement and urine and blood around the wagon', pretended it was all some terrible mistake. But the gentle or brutal techniques had only one objective, neither to be gentle nor to be brutal, but to ensure that the people who had arrived reached the gas-chamber 'as soon as possible and without a hitch'.[10]

The Jews who arrived at Auschwitz had been given many promises. Lilli Kopecky, who, like Vrba, was deported from Slovakia that summer, recalled a Dutch Jew asking, angrily, 'Where is my wife, where are my children?' The Jews in the barracks said to him, 'Look at the chimney. They are there. Up there.' But the Dutch Jew cursed them. 'There are so many camps around,' he said. 'They promised me we would be kept together.'

'This', Lilli Kopecky reflected, 'is the greatest strength of the whole crime, its unbelievability.' The explanations, and the warnings, were simply disbelieved. Lilli Kopecky herself recalled how, 'when we came to Auschwitz, we smelt the sweet smell. They said to us, "There the people are gassed, three kilometres over there." We didn't believe it.'[11]

In the East, the Einsatzkommando units had returned to the almost daily pattern of slaughter of the autumn of 1941. On 13 July 1942, two days after the first medical experiments had been performed at Auschwitz, a German engineer, Hermann Graebe, witnessed the round-up of several thousand Jews in the Rowne ghetto in the Volhynia. Graebe was present in order to prevent the deportation of a hundred Jews employed in the engineering works of which he was the manager. Immediately after the war he recalled, of the events of July 13:

> On the evening of this day, I drove to Rowne and posted myself with Fritz Einsporn in front of the house in the Bahnhofstrasse in which the Jewish workers of my firm slept. Shortly after 2200 the ghetto was encircled by a large SS detachment and about three times as many members of the Ukrainian militia. Then the electric arclights which had been erected in and around the ghetto were switched on. SS and militia squads of four to six men entered or at least tried to enter the houses. Where the doors and windows were closed and the inhabitants did not open at the knocking, the SS man and militia broke the windows, forced the doors with beams and crowbars, and entered the houses. The people living there were driven on to the street just as they were, regardless of whether they were dressed or in bed.
>
> Since the Jews in most cases refused to leave their houses and resisted, the SS and militia applied force. They finally succeeded, with strokes of the whip, kicks and blows, and rifle butts, in clearing the houses. The people were driven out of their houses in such haste that small children in bed had been left behind in several instances.
>
> In the streets women cried out for their children and children for their parents. That did not prevent the SS from driving the people along the road at running pace, and hitting them, until they reached a waiting freight train. Carriage after carriage was filled, and the screaming of women and children and the

cracking of whips and rifle shots resounded unceasingly. Since several families or groups had barricaded themselves in especially strong buildings and the doors could not be forced with crowbars or beams, the doors were now blown open with hand grenades.

Since the ghetto was near the railroad tracks in Rowne, the younger people tried to get across the tracks and over a small river to get away from the ghetto area. As this stretch of country was beyond the range of the electric lights, it was illuminated by small rockets. All through the night these beaten, hounded, and wounded people moved along the lighted streets. Women carried their dead children in their arms, children pulled and dragged their dead parents by their arms and legs down the road toward the train. Again and again the cries, 'Open the door! Open the door!' echoed through the ghetto.[12]

'Can there be a clearer picture than Graebe's', one historian has asked, 'of defenceless civilians resisting as best they could overwhelming odds?'[13] But the odds were overwhelming, and in the following two days, five thousand Rowne Jews were murdered.

In the Molczadz ghetto, in White Russia, the Chairman of the Jewish Council, Ehrlich, a refugee from Silesia, together with a locally born Council member, Leib Gilerowicz, urged the German authorities not to embark upon a 'resettlement' action. Both men were tortured and killed.[14] Another member of the Molczadz Jewish Council, Josef Korn, warned other Jews of the impending action, and urged young people not to sleep at home, but to make preparations 'in case anything happened'.[15]

A thousand Jews were seized in the Molczadz ghetto on July 15, driven to nearby woods, and shot. That same day, another thousand Jews were murdered in Bereza Kartuska, thirty miles to the south. At Horodzei, east of Molczadz, a further thousand Jews were murdered on July 16. Shalom Cholawski has recalled how, on July 17, when the news of these Horodzei killings reached the Nieswiez ghetto, eight miles away, it 'struck our ghetto like a bolt of lightning'. His account continued:

All delusions dissolved. What we did not know then was that this was no isolated incident. A wave of slaughter had already wiped out Jewish ghettos in White Russia and the Ukraine.

On that day, we, the Jews of the Nieswiez ghetto, gathered at the new synagogue. The congregation stood still as death. The Kaddish – the Jewish prayer for the dead – was spoken. Silent anguish gave way to moaning, to choked tears. Our grief was for those fallen Jews. Or did each person sense that the congregation was reciting Kaddish for itself?

At the memorial meeting, I rallied the mourners: 'Fellow Jews! We are isolated and cut off from the Jewish world, from the world at large. It may be that not a word of our plight has been heard. It may be that we are the last of the ghettos and the last of the Jews. We must fight for our lives! We shall defend the ghetto, the place of suffering. We will fight as would the last remaining Jews on the soil of their homeland. We will prepare, now, to strike. We will be on the alert. The right moment may come at any time!'

The entire population of the ghetto was with us. Last-minute arrangements were concluded. A plan of attack was finalized. As soon as the Germans advanced and surrounded the ghetto, a pile of straw would be ignited near the synagogue. The fighting groups would set fire to assigned houses, thereby directing the battle towards the forest, our cover. All would flee there.[16]

Two members of the Nieswiez Jewish Council supported the call to revolt: Jacob Klaczko and Yerechmiel Szklar. At the meeting in the synagogue, Szklar appealed to those present not to run away, not to leave behind the old, the sick and the children, but to remain in the ghetto to fight and die there, with dignity. The Council's Secretary, Miss Lachewicki, also supported those who wanted to resist.[17]

On July 18, while the Jews of Nieswiez prepared their act of resistance, an Einsatzkommando unit reached the nearby village of Szarkowszczyzna. There, the head of the Jewish Council, Hirsh Berkan, had already warned the community in advance that a mass execution was being prepared. As soon as the danger was imminent, an order was given 'for everyone to flee in order to save himself'. On the eve of the action, the village was set on fire and, by the light of the flames, nine hundred Jews escaped. When the Germans came they found six hundred, mostly the elderly and the sick.

The Einsatzkommando unit had been cheated of nine hundred

victims. But it murdered the six hundred, and in the woods, local farmers helped the Germans to track down some of those who had escaped. But even after the manhunt, more of Szarkowszczyzna's Jews were alive, hiding in the woods, than had been killed.[18]

On July 20, in the Warthegau, there was a further deportation from Kowale Panskie to Chelmno. Those who were sick, however, were shot in the hills just outside the village. A male nurse, Z. Stein, refused to leave his sick patients. He was killed with them.[19] Among those killed near Kowale Panskie that day were two Jews from Uniejow: Lenczycki, who was forced to dig his own grave and then shot, together with a young boy who had been brought back in a truck returning empty from Chelmno, having managed to hide in it when the other deportees had been ordered out of it. One Jew escaped: Yaakov Waldman, also from Uniejow.[20]

In Kleck, the Germans surrounded the ghetto on the night of July 20, intending to murder all fourteen hundred Jews in the morning. That night, one of the Jews, Moshe Fish, tried to organise a mass escape. While it was still dark the ghetto was set on fire. Led by Fish, four hundred Jews managed to break out before the Germans could open fire with their machine guns. Many of the four hundred were killed however, as they ran towards the forest. At dawn, the thousand Jews who remained in Kleck were slaughtered in the ghetto. Reaching the forest with Leva Gilchik, a Jew from the nearby ghetto of Kopyl, Fish and Gilchik formed a Jewish partisan detachment. Six months later, they were both to fall in battle against the Germans.[21]

The Jews of Nieswiez, like those of Kleck, were marked for destruction on July 21. On the previous evening they made their preparations. Gasoline and kerosene were their main weapons. They also had several gun parts and even parts of a machine gun smuggled out of the German gun repair shop by two Jewish girls working there, Rakhil Kagan and Liya Dukor. These girls were able to reassemble both the guns and machine gun and to teach the young men of the ghetto how to use them. At the same time, every Jew was ordered to provide himself with some means of defence, whether it was an axe, a hammer, or even a stout piece of wood. These preparations had been intensified when news reached Nieswiez of the massacre of the Jews in the nearby village of Gorodya.[22]

On the morning of July 21, Megalif, the head of the Jewish

Council, announced that the German commander had ordered an immediate selection. Only essential workers, first and foremost thirty textile workers, would not be taken. But even they would not be allowed to keep their families with them. Then, as Shalom Cholawski recalled:

> The members of the underground and the mass of Jews standing at the gate replied resolutely, 'No! There will be no selection! If some are to live, then all must; if not, we shall defend ourselves!'
>
> Megalif returned to the German commandant with our answer. The Germans opened fire. The fighting unit in the synagogue answered with a surprise volley of machine-gun fire. The Germans crashed through the ghetto gate. The Jews drew their knives and irons. They reached for their pile of stones. I saw a group of Jews attack a charging German and kill him. Klaczko, an older man, and Yisrael Shusterman battled with one of the policemen and knocked him dead. The Germans increased their firing. A battle began between Jews with steel weapons and Germans and police with guns. More skirmishes, hand-to-hand combat, shooting.
>
> Soon the ghetto was filled with dead and dying. Throughout the streets, bodies lay like discarded puppets. The Jews set fire to their houses. The flames spread quickly towards the centre of the town. A horde of local peasants from the outlying neighbourhood swarmed into the ghetto, plundering before all was devoured by the fire. The madness of their pillaging and the fury of the Germans to kill matched the frenzy of every Jew, man, woman, child, to flee from the burning ghetto.
>
> People were running, screaming, crying. I went to check the various fighting posts and then returned to my position. Siomka Farfel, Shmuel Nissenbaum and I were caught in a volley of gunfire at the post where I was stationed. We jumped into an underground bunker at Anuteshnik's house. After a few moments we escaped to the attic. There we lay on the floor with knives in hand, facing the ladder, the only access to the attic.
>
> A group of Germans entered the house. One of them took hold of the ladder, shook it, and began to go up. We held our breath, set to strike. Suddenly, another soldier called to the one climbing, 'We already looked the place over, let's go.' The soldier hesitated and then went down the ladder. They left.

From the attic we could see crowds of non-Jews with arms full of clothes and goods, wildly jumping and jeering whenever a Jew was shot. We remained in the attic until we were able to sneak out. We ran south through the alleys, circled the city, crossed the Nieswiez-Horodzei road, and entered the fields of grain.

Small groups of Jews like ours burst forth from the ghetto. Once outside, some were beaten by zealous peasants. Others were killed in flight. Small groups succeeded in reaching the forest. I saw Simcha Rozen carrying his small son wrapped in a pillow. As Simcha ran, he passed the bundle to a Christian woman standing near the gate and then continued running towards the woods.[23]

Among those killed in the battle were Yerechmiel Szklar and Jacob Klaczko.[24]

Megalif, a lawyer from Warsaw who had fled to Nieswiez in September 1939, did not seek safety in the woods. Realizing that his earlier reluctance to be associated with the resistance had led to his unpopularity, he took his place in the first line of those being deported. 'Brothers,' he said, 'I know you had no trust in me, you thought I was going to betray you. In this, my last minute, I am with you. I and my family – we are the first ones to go to our deaths.'[25]

Cholawski and his colleagues fled eastward. Reaching the forests, they met one group who had escaped from Kleck.[26] Another escapee from Nieswiez who succeeded in reaching the forests was the Nieswiez Council Secretary, Miss Lachewicki, who had managed to leave the ghetto, together with her father, on the day after the slaughter.[27] In the forests, Cholawski was joined by Simcha Rozen, as well as by Rachel Filler, a young mother who had escaped, with her son, from the ghetto of Timkowicze.[28] They also found, as Cholawski later recalled, the remnants of many murdered communities: 'Jewish families, some children, sometimes parents, even old men – they were there in the forest, and were afraid to leave their hiding places.'

Cholawski and his fellow escapees set up 'family camps' of Jews, whom they protected against German manhunts, against hostile peasants, and against starvation. They set up a Jewish fighting unit, and urged Jews in as yet untouched ghettos to join them.[29]

To another part of the forests of White Russia came 120 Jews who escaped from Dereczyn on July 24, the day of the destruction of the ghetto there, when three thousand Jews were killed. In the forest, these 120 met Jechiel Atlas, a twenty-eight-year-old doctor whose mother and sister had been murdered in the destruction of another of the White Russian ghettos, that of Kozlowszczyzna. Dr Atlas organized the escapees from Dereczyn into a small partisan band. 'We have not come here to live,' he told them. 'Our chances to survive are almost nil. Our sacred task is to avenge our dead, to fight and die if necessary.'

For four months Jechiel Atlas and his men attacked German troop trains and military convoys. Then, on December 5, when his unit was surrounded by the Germans, he was mortally wounded. As he lay dying, he told his men: 'Pay no attention to me. Go on fighting. Avenge our tormented people.'[30]

Vengeance was a much-heard cry, driving individual Jews to acts of hopeless heroism. On July 4, in the Odessa region, a Jewish girl, Riva Meierson, joined the Soviet partisans. Later she was caught and shot, her name recorded in the court-martial records at the time of her execution.[31]

In the East, in the areas occupied by Germany only after June 1941, there had been almost no deception. There had been no time to cog and lull and starve and coerce, no 'civilisation' in any form, just brutality without deception. The Jews in the East who saw what was happening did what they could to resist, to try to escape. They did so in almost every case without hope of success, but with defiance, barricading themselves in their ghettos, setting fire to their houses as the killers came for them, running to the woods through the barrage of the machine-gun and grenade attack. Wherever possible, those who reached the forests set up family camps to protect the women, the children, the old and the sick who could not fight or forage. They also formed partisan bands to attack any German military units or lines of communication which might be vulnerable. In the East, Jewish resistance was the main hope of those who had murder hurled at them, even though it rarely meant survival. It was a final act of desperation.

In the areas occupied by the Germans in Western Europe in 1939 and 1940, no immediate killings and no savage butchery in the streets had taken place. In these areas there had been a veneer of civilised, or at least rational, behaviour by the German occupying power. Rules and regulations had been imposed to restrict Jewish activities, but not to kill Jews. Even in the Polish ghettos, there seemed hope of survival through work, hope of being able to find enough to eat for some, if not all. Above all, especially in Western Europe, there was the deliberate mystery of deportation. There were no brief violent marches to a death-pit three or four miles away, but ordered assembly at railway stations for deportation to a distant, unknown and unidentified destination.

In Western Europe, the German rule was to create the maximum deception and to deny the Jews any knowledge of what was happening, either to their fellow Jews in the East, or to those local Jews who had been deported earlier. This policy of deception fitted in, and was designed to fit in, with the typical pattern of Jewish survival throughout the ages, the traditional dependence upon the utmost restraint, and the reliance for survival upon every type of ingenuity. The Jewish will to survive and the German policy of deception were linked in what for the Jews was a tragic magnetism. The German promise seemed clear: there was a means to save yourself if only you could find it. There was a chance to survive, even if the odds were not good. There was work at home or resettlement far away: fortifications to be dug or harvests to be brought in, a thousand miles to the east. All the evidence available seemed also to make it clear that Jews were surviving, some by submission, others by cunning, each one by using whatever resources he or she could muster.

The power of deception, and the power of self-deception, worked upon each other in fatal grasp.

22

From Warsaw to Treblinka:
'these disastrous and horrible days'

IN THE WARSAW GHETTO, tormented by hunger, and by the daily random shootings, cultural life had continued. Plans had gone ahead for the opening of a special Children's House in the ghetto on 23 July 1942. Meanwhile, on July 18, a performance of the play *The Dying Prince* was given by the students of Janusz Korczak's orphanage. The play had been written by Korczak himself. Among those present was the poet Yitzhak Katznelson.[1] That same day, the chairman of the Warsaw Jewish Council, Adam Czerniakow, informed the Council, and the Jewish police, that the Germans had given him assurances that they had no intention of resettling the population of the ghetto. Eye-witnesses reported, however, that a train, composed of several dozen goods wagons, was at that very moment being made up in the railway sidings adjoining the ghetto at its northern limit.[2]

On the following day, July 19, Heinrich Himmler sent a secret directive from Berlin to SS Lieutenant-General Friedrich Wilhelm Krüger, head of the German police forces in the General Government, which began: 'I herewith order that the resettlement of the entire Jewish population of the General Government be carried out and completed by December 31.' Himmler explained that these measures were required 'with a view to the necessary division of races and peoples for the New Order in Europe, and also in the interest of the security and cleanliness of the German Reich and its sphere of interest'. To avoid providing a 'point of application' for resistance, and in order to eliminate 'a source of moral and physical pestilence', a 'total cleansing is necessary, and therefore to be carried out'.[3]

On July 21 the Germans seized sixty Jews in the Warsaw ghetto, among them three members of the Jewish Council. At the same time, a number of Jews were shot in the streets, or in their homes.[4] On the following day, July 22, a telegram was received at Treblinka station 'informing us', as the Polish railwayman Franciszek Zabecki recalled, 'of the running of a shuttle service from Warsaw to Treblinka with settlers'. The trains would be made up of sixty covered goods wagons. After unloading, the trains were to be sent back to Warsaw. 'Our astonishment was immense. We wondered what sort of settlers they were, where they were going to live and what they were going to do? We connected this news with the mysterious buildings in the forest.'[5]

In Warsaw, an SS Major, Hermann Höfle, had been appointed Plenipotentiary in charge of deportations. On July 22 he went to see the Chairman of the Jewish Council, Adam Czerniakow, who noted in his diary Höfle's order 'that all Jews, irrespective of sex and age, with certain exceptions, will be deported to the East. By 4 p.m today a contingent of six thousand people must be provided. And this (at the minimum) will be the daily quota.'

In ordering Czerniakow to cooperate in the organization of this massive deportation, Höfle added, as Czerniakow noted, 'that for the time being my wife was free, but if the deportations were impeded in any way, she would be the first one to be shot as a hostage.'[6]

That same day, July 22, the ghetto walls were surrounded by Ukrainian and Latvian guards, in SS uniforms, armed, and at twenty-five-yard intervals.[7] The round-up and deportation of Jews from Warsaw now began. Adolf Berman, who was responsible for many of the orphanages in the ghetto, later recalled:

On that very day, the first victims were the Jewish children, and I shall never forget the harrowing scenes and the blood-curdling incidents when the SS men most cruelly attacked children – children roaming in the streets; took them by force to carts, and I remember, fully, those children were defending themselves. Even today the cries and shrieking of those children are clear in my mind. 'Mama, Mama,' this is what we heard. 'Save us, mothers.'[8]

The deportations from Warsaw continued, almost without pause, until September 12. In those seven weeks, a total of 265,000

Jews were sent by train for 'resettlement in the East'. Their actual destination was Treblinka, and its three gas-chambers. Death, not slave labour, was their fate. It was the largest slaughter of a single community, Jewish or non-Jewish, in the Second World War.

No one book, certainly no one chapter, can tell the story of those seven weeks, each day of which saw the murder of more than four thousand Jews. Merely to list the names of the murdered ones, a line for each name, would take nearly seven thousand printed pages. Among the many hundreds of Jewish doctors deported from Warsaw and gassed at Treblinka was Zofia Zamenhof, a graduate of the University of Lausanne, whose brother, shot by the Gestapo in January 1940, had been one of the first victims of Nazi terror in Warsaw.[9] Another of those who were gassed, Salomea Bau-Prussak, had been the first woman, Jewish or non-Jewish, to receive a doctor's degree from a Polish university. A leading neurologist, her clinical abilities and broad medical knowledge were widely known in Poland, and abroad. During the ghetto months, while active in distributing underground literature, she had sheltered and cared for a fellow doctor, a woman physician sick with typhus.[10]

Many Jews committed suicide, among them Leon Endelman, one of Poland's leading ophthalmologists.[11]

It was to Czerniakow, Chairman of the Jewish Council, that the Germans had looked for cooperation in the deportations: for a fixed number of Jews to be delivered daily to the railway sidings, the *Umschlagplatz*, at the northern edge of the ghetto. The Germans had assured Czerniakow that only unemployed Jews would be sent for 'resettlement'. As the overwhelming majority of the population of the ghetto was employed, Czerniakow had convinced himself that the 'resettlement' would therefore 'only' apply to some ten or twenty thousand people, mostly the recent arrivals from Germany and Czechoslovakia. But on July 22 the Germans had demanded six thousand Jews a day, and a day later increased their demand to seven thousand a day.[12]

'When I asked for the number of days per week in which the operation would be carried out,' Czerniakow noted in his diary on July 23, 'the number was seven days a week'. His diary entry continued: 'It is three o'clock. So far, four thousand are ready to go. The orders are that there must be nine thousand by four o'clock.'[13]

They demand from me to kill the children of my nation with my own hands, Czerniakow noted in his diary, later that day. 'There is nothing left for me but to die.'[14] That day, Czerniakow committed suicide.

Each day, several thousand Jews were taken from their homes or seized in the streets, and then marched on foot, or forced into trucks or horse-drawn carts and driven, to the Umschlagplatz. Those whom the Germans wished to keep in the ghetto, at productive work, were issued with a special employment card, or *Ausweis*. Sometimes even these cards proved insufficient protection, unless they were stamped 'Operation Reinhard', with a Nazi eagle and a swastika, and the inscription 'Not subject to resettlement'. Anyone without such a card was deported. Alexander Donat later recalled:

> I saw a young mother run downstairs into the street to get milk for her baby. Her husband, who worked at the Ostbahn, had as usual left earlier that morning. She had not bothered to dress, but was in bathrobe and slippers. An empty milk bottle in hand, she was headed for a shop where, she knew, they sold milk under the counter. She walked into Operation Reinhard. The executioners demanded her Ausweis. 'Upstairs ... Ostbahn ... work certificate. I'll bring it right away.'
>
> 'We've heard that one before. Have you got an Ausweis with you, or haven't you?'
>
> She was dragged protesting to the wagon, scarcely able to realize what was happening. 'But my baby is all alone. Milk ...' she protested. 'My Ausweis is upstairs'.
>
> Then, for the first time, she really looked at the men who were holding her and she saw where she was being dragged: to the gaping entrance at the back of a high-boarded wagon with victims already jammed into it. With all her young mother's strength she wrenched herself free, and then two, and four policemen fell on her, hitting her, smashing her to the ground, picking her up again, and tossing her into the wagon like a sack.
>
> I can still hear her screaming in a half-crazed voice some-where between a sob of utter human despair and the howl of an animal.[15]

Such scenes were repeated every day, in every street. Many Jews, resisting or fleeing, were killed on the spot, often by Ukrainian,

Latvian and Lithuanian volunteers, or their German SS officers. All who could not prove that they were employed by a German firm were seized and taken to the Umschlagplatz. The slightest hesitation in showing one's papers, Samuel Rajzman later recalled, 'a smile that the Germans did not find sufficiently pleasant, meant death on the spot. People were killed in their homes, in their courtyards, in the streets. In the end many preferred being deported to having their papers checked.'[16]

Even during the march to the Umschlagplatz, the guards did not hesitate to shoot, and to shoot to kill. 'The people had to march at a given tempo,' David Wdowinski later recalled. 'He who walked too quickly was shot. He who fell on the way was shot. He who strayed out of line was shot. He who turned his head was shot. He who bent down was shot. He who spoke too loudly was shot. A child who cried was shot.' Others were beaten by rifle butts as they marched. 'If a man, thus beaten, fell, he too was shot.'

There were acts of heroism even at the Umschlagplatz. As Wdowinski recalled, Nahum Remba, the Secretary of the Jewish Council, and his wife, 'used emergency ambulances and drove to the Umschlagplatz to rescue as many children as they could'. Even though, as an official of the Jewish Council, Remba had a certain immunity, he and his wife 'took their lives in their hands in this courageous act. In this way, they saved hundreds of Jewish children. . . .'[17]

For every one who was saved, if only for a day or two, thousands were taken. Yitzhak Katznelson was told of an incident at a round-up on Swietojerska Street, from one of the hundreds of small factories:

> At the shrill sickening commands of the SS, 'Herunter!' – 'Go downstairs' – all men and women had to descend into the yard of the factory. Amongst those that went down into the yard was the wife of the manager, Krieger. She was a young woman in her ninth month of pregnancy. The vile SS man pushed her over to the side where the queue condemned to go to Treblinka was standing. Thereupon the grey-headed Zuckerman approached the SS man and said, 'This woman is an outstanding worker, she is an artist at her job.' The SS man stared at the young woman and her abdomen. He then seized hold of his

whip and set about Zuckerman with murderous fury. He hit him on the head with the lead-weighted end until the blood poured from him. 'What! You want to save a pregnant woman?'

The pregnant woman was taken away. So too, in that round-up, was Katznelson's sister-in-law Dora, and her sister, Fania. Their mother, Esther Dombrowska, a leading philanthropist in pre-war Lodz, was shot dead in the street by a Ukrainian. 'The Ukrainians and the Germans are good companions,' Katznelson wrote bitterly a year later. 'May the very memory of these two nations be blotted from the world.'[18] Katznelson wrote these words in July 1943, a year after the start of the Warsaw deportations. Within another year, he himself had been deported to Auschwitz, and gassed. His diary, written on the eve of his deportation from Vittel, in France, is a testament to his Warsaw friends deported between July and September 1942, among them the fifty-seven-year-old writer and dramatist Shlomo Gilbert. 'You', he wrote, 'who are so inured to sickness, so scorched in God's own fire. Oh, where are you, and your gentle daughter, who though frail like you, was always alive to the word of God! Just like you!'[19]

Shlomo Gilbert and his daughter were among the 265,000 Warsaw Jews who were gassed at Treblinka. After Gilbert's deportation, Ringelblum searched his apartment for any hidden notes and diaries, but in vain.[20] Also deported was the diarist Chaim Kaplan. By chance, Mary Berg survived, her mother's American citizenship having enabled them both to be sent from Poland, and then to America. But there were few such exceptions. Orphan children especially had no means of protection, no chance of a work permit, no avenue of escape. During those seven weeks, a hundred orphanages and children's homes were emptied, and their children, more than four thousand sent to Treblinka. Outside Warsaw, at Otwock, the children in orphanages there, including one for the children of refugees from Germany, were murdered in the town itself, as were the two hundred children in nearby Miedzeszyn: both resort towns for the Jews of pre-war Warsaw.[21]

The children's guardians and teachers met their death together with their children. Among the guardians who chose this path was Janusz Korczak. Nineteen years later, Adolf Berman recalled the scene outside Korczak's orphanage:

I'll never forget the way the Germans were shouting at them – 'Alle Herunter!' 'All get off!' And his only concern, the only concern of Korczak, was that the children had not had time to dress properly, they were barefooted. Stephania Vicinska told the children that they were going on a trip, that this was a little outing, that at last they were going to see woods and fields and the flowers they had been yearning for and which they'd never seen in their lives; and one could see a smile flickering on the pale lips of those children.

After a few hours they were put into the death carriages and this was the last journey of the great educator.[22]

In his notes, which he tried to keep throughout the deportations, Ringelblum recorded many acts of heroism. But each act of resistance provoked savage reprisals. A Jew 'grabbed a German by the throat' and managed to wound him. The German 'went berserk and shot thirteen Jews in the courtyard'.[23] Feigele Peltel, watching Jews being forced into one of the waiting trucks, recalled how, after the initial shock, 'all the victims showed resistance; not one submitted willingly. They argued, they pleaded, and some even tried to force money into the hands of their captors – but all to no avail; no one was released from the van.'[24] On one occasion, walking towards her home:

Several vans went by, loaded with Jews, sitting and standing, hugging sacks that contained whatever pitiful belongings they had managed to gather at the last moment. Some stared straight ahead vacantly, others mourned and wailed, wringing their hands and entreating the Jewish police who rode with them. Women tore their hair or clung to their children, who sat bewildered among the scattered bundles, gazing at the adults in silent fear. Running behind the last van, a lone woman, arms outstretched, screamed:

'My child! Give back my child!'

In reply, a small voice called from the van.

'Mama! Mama!'

The people in the street watched as though hypnotized. Panting now with exhaustion, the mother continued to run after the van. One of the guards whispered something to the driver, who urged his horses into a gallop. The cries of the pursuing mother became more desperate as the horses pulled away. The procession turned into Karmelicka Street. The cries of the deportees faded and became inaudible, only the cry of the agonized mother still pierced the air.

'My child! Give back my child!'[25]

That child, with tens of thousands of other children, many of them separated from their parents, was deported to Treblinka. There, as at Chelmno, Belzec and Sobibor, death alone awaited them. As the trains reached Treblinka station, the Polish railway-man, Franciszek Zabecki, witnessed heart-rending scenes. The first train to arrive, on the morning of July 23, 'made its presence known from a long way off, not only', he later recalled, 'by the rumble of the wheels on the bridge over the River Bug, but by the frequent

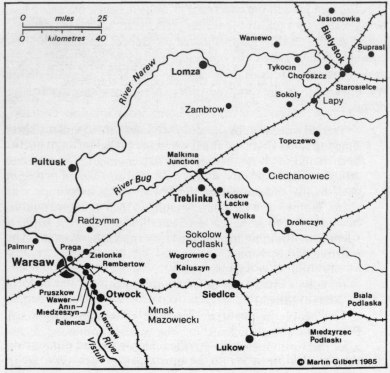

TREBLINKA

shots from the rifles and automatic weapons of the train guards'.[26] Zabecki's account continued:

The train was made up of sixty covered wagons, crammed with people. There were old people, young people, men, women, children and infants in quilts. The doors of the wagons were bolted, the air gaps had a grating of barbed wire. Several SS men, with automatic weapons ready to shoot, stood on the foot-boards of the wagons on both sides of the trains and even lay on the roofs.

It was a hot day; people in the wagons were fainting. The SS guards with rolled-up sleeves looked like butchers, who after murdering their victims washed their blood-stained hands and got ready for more killing. Without a word, we understood the tragedy, since 'settling' people coming to work would not have required such a strict guard, whereas these people were being transported like dangerous criminals.

After the transport arrived, some fiendish spirit got into the SS men; they drew their pistols, put them away, and took them out again, as if they wanted to shoot and kill straight away; they approached the wagons, silencing those who were shrieking and wailing, and again they swore and screamed.

Shouting, 'Tempo, schnell,' 'At the double, quickly,' to the German railwaymen who had come from Sokolow Podlaski, they went off to the camp, to take over their victims there 'properly'. On the wagons we could see chalk marks giving the number of people in the wagon, viz.: 120, 150, 180 and 200 people. We worked out later that the total number of people in the train must have been about eight to ten thousand.

The 'settlers' were strangely huddled together in the wagons. All of them had to stand, without sufficient air and without access to toilet facilities. It was like travelling in hot ovens. The high temperature, lack of air, and the hot weather created conditions that not even healthy, young, strong organisms could stand. Moans, shouts, weeping, calls for water or for a doctor issued from the wagons. And protests: 'How can people be treated so inhumanly?' 'When will they let us leave the wagons altogether?'

Through some air gaps terrified people looked out, asking hopefully: 'How far is it to the agricultural estates where we're going to work?'

Twenty wagons were uncoupled from the train, and a shunting engine began to push them along the spur-line into the camp. A short while later, it returned empty. This procedure was repeated twice more, until all sixty wagons had been shunted into the camp, and out again. Empty, they were returned to Warsaw for more 'settlers'.[27]

On July 28, six days after the deportations had begun, and when it was clear that they were to continue on a substantial scale, young Jews from the pioneer youth movements met to discuss the possibility of resistance. 'Various questions were raised at that meeting,' Zivia Lubetkin later recalled. ' "What can we do? We have no guns. . . ." ' One idea was to flee to somewhere safe, outside Warsaw. 'We rejected this idea. How many Jews can we save that way? Very few. Is there any point in trying to save those few when millions are dying? No, we all will share the same fate and it is our duty to stay with our people until the very end.'[28]

At this meeting of July 28, a Jewish Fighting Organization was set up, known by its Polish initials ZOB, *Zydowska Organizacja Bojowa*. The meeting decided: 'We, the youth, would take all the responsibility on our shoulders.' At that moment there were 'only two pistols in our entire arsenal'.[29] The Jewish Fighting Organization made one of its first tasks to try to link up the different ghettos, to prepare joint schemes, to smuggle arms and individuals, and to pass on messages and funds.

On July 29, to entice as many Jews as possible to the trains, notices were put up in the Warsaw ghetto offering a free issue of three kilogrammes of bread and one of jam for any families that would go voluntarily to 'resettlement'. The announcement added the reassurance that families would not be separated. For Jews who were starving, the offer was irresistible. Thousands volunteered. The Germans, exploiting the results of their starvation policy, allocated 180,000 kilogrammes of bread and 36,000 of jam for the new operation.[30]

Three months later Ringelblum estimated that a minimum of twenty thousand Jews had accepted the German offer. These were people, he wrote, 'driven by hunger, anguish, a sense of hopelessness of their situation', people who 'had not the strength to struggle any longer' or who 'simply had no place to live'.[31]

The posters set a short time limit for acceptance of the German offer: only two or three days. 'If the Germans are already giving out bread, it must be a sign that they need us. Otherwise why waste the flour?' people said to each other. For many, Feigele Peltel recalled, 'the possibility of assuaging their hunger just once, and the Germans' repeated promises of employment, were enough. . . .' Fears of deportation were set aside. 'After the resettlement,' a friend told Feigele Peltel, 'we might perhaps survive in another town.'[32] Reading the offer of bread and jam, many Warsaw Jews asked, as David Wdowinski recalled: 'If over there things were not so bad, and here we have to live in hiding and suffer hunger, and since we can be together with our families, why not go?' And so, Wdowinski added, 'entire families, bag and baggage gave themselves up. And, indeed, they were not separated. They were gassed all together.'[33]

Thousands of Jews sought safety by shutting themselves behind locked doors. One such was Baruch Zifferman, who told his story to Feigele Peltel when he met her a few days later:

> The Germans had sealed off Nowolipki Street, where he was hiding with his wife and young son in Birnbaum's house, whose massive iron door was very hard to open.
>
> As the Germans yelled, 'All Jews downstairs!' the residents had locked the door and stayed where they were. Then came the familiar loud banging to open the iron door. Crashing blows by iron bars came next, accompanied by barked commands in German to open the door at once. The five Jews within crouched petrified, not stirring, wondering whether the door would hold.
>
> The angry shouting of the Germans and the pounding on the door grew louder. At last, groaning and creaking on its hinges, the door gave way, and several scowling Ukrainians forced their way in, ordering everyone to put up his hands. After being searched and robbed of their valuables, the trembling victims were commanded to line up against the wall. Even with their carbines aimed at him, Zifferman did not dream that the invaders would actually fire; he supposed they were bent merely on intimidation. But the shots broke into his thoughts, and he toppled to the floor.

When he came to, everything was quiet. The Ukrainians had left. His wife, his son, and the Birnbaums lay dead.[34]

By August 2, the twelfth consecutive day of the deportations from Warsaw, more than seventy-six thousand Jews had been deported.[35] 'We have no information about the fate of those who have been expelled,' Chaim Kaplan noted in his diary on August 2, shortly before he himself was deported. 'When one falls into the hands of the Nazis one falls into the abyss. The very fact that the deportees make no contact with their families by letters bodes evil.'[36] That evil was later described by one of those who survived it, Samuel Rajzman:

> Immediately after their arrival, the people had to leave the trains in five minutes and line up on the platform. All those who were driven from the cars were divided into groups – men, children, and women, all separate. They were all forced to strip immediately, and this procedure continued under the lashes of the German guards' whips. Workers who were employed in this operation immediately picked up all the clothes and carried them away to barracks. Then the people were obliged to walk naked through the street to the gas-chambers.

The Germans had given this street to the gas-chambers a name, *Himmelfahrstrasse*, 'the street to heaven'. As Rajzman explained, 'The whole process of undressing and the walk down to the gas-chambers lasted, for the men eight or ten minutes, and for the women some fifteen minutes. The women took fifteen minutes because they had to have their hair shaved off before they went to the gas-chambers.'[37]

At Treblinka station, before the trains were uncoupled and sent into the death camp twenty coaches at a time, the Polish railwayman, Franciszek Zabecki, witnessed many scenes of savagery. Four of these concerned Jews who had tried to escape:

> I saw a policeman catch two young Jewish boys. He did not shut them in a wagon, since he was afraid to open the door in case others escaped. I was on the platform, letting a military transport go through. I asked him to let them go. The assassin did not even budge. He ordered the bigger boy to sit down on

the ground and take the smaller one on his knee, then he shot them both with one bullet.

Turning to me, he said: 'You're lucky, that was the last bullet.' Round the huge stomach of the murderer there was a belt with a clasp, on which I could see the inscription 'Gott mit uns', 'God is with us'.[38]

The second incident took place after a train, arriving late in the evening, had been kept overnight at Treblinka station. On the following morning a Ukrainian guard:

> . . . promised a Jewess that he would let her and her child go if she put a large bribe in his hand. The Jewess gave the Ukrainian the money and her four-year-old child through the air gap, and afterwards, with the Ukrainian's help, she also got out of the wagon through the air gap.
>
> The Jewess walked away from the train, holding her child by the hand; as soon as she walked down the railway embankment the Ukrainian shot her. The mother rolled down into a field, pulling the child after her. The child clutched the mother's neck. Jews looking out of the wagons called out and yelled, and the child turned back up the embankment again and under the wagons to the other side of the train.
>
> Another Ukrainian killed the child with one blow of a rifle butt on its head.[39]

A third incident witnessed by Zabecki also took place at Treblinka station:

> One mother threw a small child wrapped up in a pillow from the wagon, shouting: 'Take it, that's some money to look after it.' In no time an SS man ran up, unwrapped the pillow, seized the child by its feet and smashed its head against a wheel of the wagon. This took place in full view of the mother, who was howling with pain.[40]

A fourth incident involved Willi Klinzmann, from Wuppertal, one of the two German railwaymen who supervised the shunting work at the station:

> There was an SS man from the camp in Klinzmann's flat. A frightened, battered Jewess who had managed to get out of a wagon came into the station building. She probably thought

she would be safe here. Crossing the threshold of the dark corridor close by the door of the German railwaymen's quarters, she uttered a loud groan and a sigh.

Willi rushed out into the corridor, and seeing the woman he shouted: 'Bist du Judin?', 'Are you a Jewess?'. The SS man rushed out after Willi. The frightened Jewess exclaimed: 'Ach, mein Gott!' 'Oh, my God!', escaped to the waiting-room next to the traffic supervisor's office and fell down exhausted near the wall. Both the Germans grabbed the woman lying there; they wanted her to get up and go out with them. The Jewess lay motionless.

It was already late evening. As I went out to see to a military transport passing through the station, I shone my lamp on the woman lying there; I noticed that she was pregnant, and in the last months of pregnancy at that. The Jewess did not react to the German's calls, uttering groans as if in labour. Then Klinzmann and the SS man from the camp began to take turns at kicking the Jewess at random, and laughing.

After dispatching the train, I had to go into the office again through the waiting-room, but I could not do it. In the waiting-room a human being, helpless, defenceless – a sick, pregnant woman – had been murdered. The impact from the hobnailed boots was so relentless that one of the Germans, aiming at her head, had hit too high, right into the wall.

I had to go into the office and pass close to the murderers, since the departure of a train to Wolka Okraglik station had to be attended to. My entrance made the criminals stop. In their frenzy they had forgotten where they were, and somebody plucked up courage to break in and stop them in their 'duty' of liquidating 'an enemy of Hitlerism'.

They reached for their pistols. Willi, drunk, mumbled 'Fahrdienstleiter', 'Traffic supervisor'. I closed the door behind me. The butchers renewed the kicking. The Jewess was no longer groaning. She was no longer alive.[41]

In Warsaw, on August 3, the Ringelblum circle decided that the time had come to begin to bury their archive. The first set of documents was placed in ten tin boxes and milk cans, and buried by one of the circle, a schoolteacher, Izrael Lichtensztajn. Going to a school building where he had once taught, he buried the boxes deep in the ground. He was helped in his task by two of his former students, Dawid Graber and Nachum Grzybacz.

Graber was nineteen years old. 'The men who buried the archives', he wrote, 'know that they may not survive to see the moment when the treasure is dug up and the whole truth proclaimed.' 'Yesterday we sat up till late at night,' Grzybacz, who was eighteen, wrote. 'Now I am in the midst of writing, while in the streets the terrible shooting continues.' Grzybacz added: 'One thing I am proud of, namely, that in these disastrous and horrible days I had been chosen to help bury the treasure, in order that you may know of the tortures and murders of the Nazi tyrants.'[42]

Lichtensztajn, Graber and Grzybacz were not to survive the war: but their boxes and milk cans did. In them was preserved a formidable record of the destruction of Jewish Warsaw, and of Polish Jewry.[43]

23

Autumn 1942:
'at a faster pace'

As THE DEPORTATIONS from Warsaw to Treblinka continued, gathering in intensity during August, the pace of deportation and murder was accelerated throughout German-occupied Europe. On 23 July 1942, SS Colonel Viktor Brack, the euthanasia expert on Hitler's staff, informed Himmler that General Globocnik 'believes that we must carry out the entire operation against the Jews at a faster pace, for the difficulties that might turn up can freeze the entire operation, and then we will be stuck midway through'. Brack advised that all able-bodied Jews should be castrated, and the rest exterminated.[1]

The need for speed had become a driving force behind the daily measures. On July 24 the Under-Secretary of State at the German Foreign Ministry, Martin Luther, warned Ribbentrop of the Italian government's continued resistance to any deportation plans from the Italian-occupied zone of Croatia. The Italian Chief of Staff in Mostar, Luther reported, 'has declared that he cannot give his approval to the resettlement of the Jews, all inhabitants of Mostar having received assurance of equal treatment.'[2]

No such problems existed in either the General Government, or the Occupied Eastern Territories. On July 27, on the eve of the deportations from Przemysl to Belzec, a German proclamation warned that any Pole or Ukrainian 'who tries to hide a Jew, or to assist him in hiding, will be shot dead'.[3]

A part of this 'action' in Przemysl was seen by Josef Buzhminski, from his hiding place near the ghetto fence, bordering 'Aryan' Przemysl. It was from this hiding place that Buzhminski saw an SS man by the name of Kidash catch a Jewish woman who was holding a baby in her arms. The baby was about eighteen months old. 'She held the baby in her arms,' Buzhminski recalled, 'and began asking for mercy, that she be shot first, leaving the baby alive. From behind the fence there were Poles who raised their hands ready to catch the baby.' The woman was about to hand the baby over to the Poles, when Kidash 'took the baby from her arms and shot her twice' and then 'took the baby into his hands and tore him as one would tear a rag'.[4]

'The Occupied Eastern Territories are to become free of Jews,' Himmler wrote to one of his senior SS officials on July 28. 'The execution of this very grave order has been placed on my shoulders by the Führer. No one can deny me the responsibility anyway.'[5] In the Minsk region, General Commissar Kube reported to Gauleiter Lohse on July 31, 'Jewry has been completely eliminated without any danger to manpower requirements.' In the predominantly Polish area of Lida, 'sixteen thousand Jews were liquidated, in Slonim, eight thousand, etc.'. In the previous ten weeks, Kube reported, fifty-five thousand Jews had been 'liquidated'.[6]

To achieve the Nazi goal, mass executions, like the deportations, had to be carried out every day. On July 28, an Einsatzkommando unit in White Russia recorded a 'major action' in the Minsk ghetto, 'six thousand Jews are brought to pits'; and on July 29, 'three thousand Jews are brought to pits'. The following days, the report noted, 'were filled with cleaning weapons . . .'.[7] Among those who were shot in this action in Minsk were patients in the surgical ward of the Jewish hospital.[8] But there had been no quiet submission to the Nazi will. When the Jewish Council Chairman, now Moshe Yaffe, was ordered to address the Jews in Jubilee Square, in order to calm them down, he agreed to speak, then shouted to those assembled to run for their lives.[9]

Several examples also survive of non-Jews protecting Jews: in the Volhynian town of Hoszcza a Ukrainian farmer, Fiodor Kalenczuk, hid a Jewish grain merchant, Pessah Kranzberg, his wife, their ten-year-old daughter and their daughter's young friend, for seventeen months, refusing to deny them refuge even when his wife protested that their presence, in the stable, was endangering a Christian household.[10] In the last week of September, five hundred Jews were murdered in the town. The Kranzbergs survived. Their rescue, in the circumstances of the East, had been a rare act of courage. Less rare, if no less courageous, at the village of Le

Chambon-sur-Lignon, in France, where several dozen Jews had found refuge, when the police came in August to make a census of all Jews, the villagers hid them for three nights in a row, and the police could not find them.[11]

On July 28 it was the turn of the Jews of Tarnow to be ordered out of their houses. All had to remove their shoes, and, barefoot, were driven with rifle butts and whips into the market square. There, everyone was ordered to kneel down, after which, as one eye-witness recalled, 'Gestapo men walked among the kneeling people and took away the children. . . .'

The children were taken to a shed at the edge of the square, and shot. 'Indescribable lamentations, sobbing and weeping filled the market,' the eye-witness recalled. 'One could go mad,' and he added:

> In the corner of the square a thin, white-haired man was kneeling, and at his side his daughter, a slim brunette. A fat Gestapo man stopped near them, drew his revolver and killed the Jew. His daughter then leaped to her feet and cried to the Gestapo man in German: 'You scoundrel! What did my father do to you that you shot him?'
>
> The Gestapo man flew at her, hit her and threatened to kill her, too. The girl looked at him with a penetrating gaze. When he turned away, avoiding her eyes, she insulted him again, called him a mean coward who shot defenceless people, and shouted that he dared not look into her eyes.
>
> 'Look straight into my eyes, you coward,' she cried, 'and shoot! These eyes will pursue you and haunt you all your life!'
>
> The Gestapo man winced, turned away from the girl, as if to muster his courage, and after a moment aimed his revolver at her and shot her.[12]

A few Jews, the eye-witness among them, were taken off as forced labourers. The Jews of Tarnow were then deported: to Belzec, and to their death.[13]

Several hundred Tarnow Jews were given refuge by non-Jews. Among those who were saved in this way from deportation were the wife and daughter of Maximilian Rosenbusz, the head of the local Hebrew school in Tarnow, who had been taken to Auschwitz in June 1940 at the time of the camp's construction, and who had perished there. The man who gave shelter to the two women was Wladyslaw Horbacki, a former regional school inspector of the Polish Ministry of Education. Both women survived the war.[14]

All those who tried to escape from these deportations were hunted down, as were those who tried to run away from labour gangs taken outside the ghetto for work. On July 28 two Jews were hanged in the Lodz ghetto for having escaped from a work gang. One, the fifty-one-year-old Szymon Makowski, had been among the earlier deportees from Pabianice to Lodz. The other was Josek Grynbaum, a boy of sixteen. After Grynbaum's execution, a British certificate for Palestine was found in his clothing.[15]

Suicide also continued to be a means of escape from the whim and tyranny of deportation. On July 31, the nineteen-year-old Bluma Rozenfeld jumped to her death from the fifth floor of a building in the Lodz ghetto.[16] Two days later, Lota Hirszberg, a woman of fifty-six, and one of the surviving deportees from Berlin to Lodz, killed herself by an overdose of sleeping powders.[17]

On August 4, the first 998 Jews from Belgium were sent to Auschwitz, among them 394 women and 80 children under the age of sixteen. Less than a hundred of these deportees survived the war, and only two of the children. By the end of August, six trains had left for Auschwitz, with 5,669 deportees, of whom only 321 survived the war. Among the Belgian Jews murdered in this one month, 896 were children.[18] From Luxembourg, 723 Jews were deported; only 35 survived the war.[19]

On August 4, in the Polish city of Radom, ten thousand Jews were ordered to assemble on Graniczna Street. The SS began shooting. 'The defenceless Jews ran madly amidst flying bullets,' the historian of the destruction of Radom Jewry has written. 'The terror deprived men of their reason.' As in Warsaw, only a valid work permit enabled a man and his family to escape deportation. As the 'selection' proceeded, the shooting continued, until nightfall. 'On the pavement along the streets lay dead and wounded Jews. The reflectors threw a bright light on the bloodstained corpses.' That night, ten thousand Radom Jews were deported to Treblinka, and gassed.[20]

That same day, thirteen thousand Jews were rounded up in

Warsaw, 'among them', noted Chaim Kaplan, 'five thousand who came to the transfer of their own free will', and he added: 'They had had their fill of the ghetto life, which is a life of hunger and fear of death. They escaped from the trap. Would that I could allow myself to do as they did!'[21]

Near Minsk, the most eastern death camp had continued operation: in the Blagovshchina forest, three miles from the village of Maly Trostenets. On August 4 a train with a thousand Jews left Theresienstadt. Six days later it reached Maly Trostenets, where it stopped in open country. Forty 'experts' had already been taken off the train at Minsk. The remaining 960 deportees were ordered out of the train and into vans for the next stage of their journey, and driven off towards the forest. The vans were gas vans; once they reached the forest the doors were unlocked and the bodies of the deportees were thrown into open graves.[22] Of a thousand Jews sent from Theresienstadt to Maly Trostenets in a further deportation on August 25, only twenty-two of the younger men were taken to work at an SS farm. The rest were ordered into the gas vans and killed. Of the twenty-two men sent to the SS farm, two survived the hard labour and sadism of their overseers, and escaped in May 1943 to join the partisans. One was killed in action. One survived the war.[23]

At Zdzieciol, west of Minsk, where Jewish Council members had actively encouraged the acquisition of arms, eight hundred Jews managed to escape on August 6, the day of slaughter on which three thousand perished. Of those who were able to break out of the ghetto, about one hundred and fifty were strong enough to form a partisan unit, headed by Hirsh Kaplinsky. The unit went into action almost at once; four months later, Kaplinsky was killed in action.[24] At nearby Mir, on August 9, two hundred Jews managed to escape to the forests.[25] That same week, six thousand were killed at Nowogrodek.[26] These were the survivors of the 'action' of December 1941, as well as several thousand Jews who had been brought into the Nowogrodek ghetto from the surrounding villages of Naliboki, Lubcz and Karelicze. One of the survivors of this second Nowogrodek action was Idel Kagan. He has recalled how, on August 7, the workshop in which he was working outside the ghetto was surrounded by Germans with machine guns, while the Jews in the ghetto were taken away, to the ravine at nearby Skridlewe, and machine-gunned. 'Some people survived, three or four. They came back. Then we heard from them what had happened.'

The surviving Jews of Nowogrodek also heard that a group of Jewish partisans was in the area, between Nowojelna and Lida. 'To escape was easy,' Idel Kagan later recalled. 'But to escape – where *to*?' As Kagan explained, the local farmers 'used to take away the Jews' money, and hand over the Jews. They already had their money. So why to feed them for ever and a day? The Germans were winning the war.'

'We had the facilities to escape,' Kagan reiterated. 'But the weather was against us. If somebody didn't give you a hiding place, you'd freeze to death.' There were hazards, even in hiding. 'The little peasant boy used to give you away,' Kagan reflected. 'The population didn't want you.'

Kagan decided, nevertheless, to escape. He waited until the first snows, when the German guards would be preoccupied by the cold, and then escaped with fourteen others. The escapees walked through the snow for two to three hours. But crossing a river, Kagan fell through the ice. Regaining the bank, his body was so covered in ice that he could not keep up. When finally, and alone, he reached an isolated hut in the forest, he discovered that he had just missed the partisans. 'I felt I would freeze to death. I began to walk back to camp. I didn't want to freeze to death'.

Idel Kagan returned to Nowogrodek just in time. 'My toes were already going black.' Then, without iodine or bandages, his toes were cut off. His escape had failed, but he was still alive.[27]

The evidence of the fate of individuals is fragmentary, surviving only by chance. At the beginning of the second week of August, at Treblinka railway station, Franciszek Zabecki witnessed an incident otherwise unrecorded. A Polish partisan, Trzcinski, from a nearby village, had reached the station after being forced to flee across the River Bug. He was on his way south, armed, in search of another partisan group, and intended to travel south on the regular train to Sokolow. At an adjoining platform were carriages waiting to be shunted on to the death camp spur. Then, as Zabecki recalled, 'Trzcinski went up to a wagon, suddenly unfastened his coat, and gave a young Jew a grenade, asking him to throw it among the

Germans. The Jew took the grenade, and Trzcinski jumped into the moving passenger train and departed.'

Zabecki later learned that the Jew 'threw the grenade in the death camp at a group of Ukrainians standing beside the Germans on the unloading ramp'. One Ukrainian was seriously wounded. 'The revenge of the Germans and Ukrainians was terrible,' Zabecki added. 'The young men were beaten with sticks until they lost consciousness. All of them died.'[28]

Another Polish eye-witness of Jewish resistance in the second week of August was Dr Klukowski of Szczebrzeszyn. On August 8, he noted, two thousand of the Jews of Szczebrzeszyn were ordered to assemble in the market place. It was said that a train was waiting to take them 'to the Ukraine'. But, Klukowski commented in his diary, 'Not one Jew appeared of his own free will. They therefore started to seize them. . . .'

By nightfall, only a few Jews had been rounded up. Most of them 'hid in such a way that they could not be found'. Klukowski added: 'Many Poles, particularly youths, are enthusiastically assisting in the searches after the Jews.'[29]

Only four hundred Jews were found. Thirteen were shot in the streets. The rest were deported. Two days later Klukowski wrote in his dairy: 'We now know for certain that the train went towards Belzec. Everyone is convinced that those on it are dead already.' That same evening, in Szczebrzeszyn, 'three Jewesses who had come out of hiding were shot.'[30]

The deportees of August 8 from Szczebrzeszyn were only sixty kilometres by rail from Belzec, a line that passed through the nearby town of Zwierzyniec. On August 9 it was the Jews of Zwierzyniec who were ordered to assemble. But the Jewish Council, as a local Pole, Stanislaw Bohdanowicz, later recalled, 'bought itself out with gold', and only fifty-two Jews were taken, 'the poorest Jews who had nothing with which to buy themselves out – and newcomers from other towns'.

The number of trains passing through Zwierzyniec was increasing, Bohdanowicz later recalled:

> These trains looked terrible. The small windows were covered with planks or lots of barbed wire, and in some places planks were missing from the walls, which was proof of

desperate struggles taking place inside. Through the cracks in the planks and through the wired-up windows peered scared human faces.

Sometimes we could tell that a train was approaching, although it was still far off, because of the shooting by the guards; they were standing on the buffers of the wagons and shooting those who tried to escape.

When such a train stopped at Zwierzyniec station in order to allow another train to pass through, screams, laments and cries could be heard from all the wagons, 'Water, water!' The Jews were holding out bottles and money fastened to sticks or parts of broken planks – but no one was allowed to approach the wagons.

The Germans were shooting without warning all those who begged for water, as well as those who tried to give it to them. Soldiers were marching along the train breaking the bottles with sticks and pocketing the money. Women were throwing rings, ear-rings and jewellery through the windows and cracks, begging for a glass of water for their children who were dying of thirst. But it was forbidden to show even signs of sympathy or pity for the Jews; the punishment was instant death.

Bohdanowicz also recalled that the inhabitants of Belzec town 'were complaining about the stench which increased day by day. Everyone understood that in some way the Jews were being killed there. In the end, passengers travelling through Belzec by train also started to complain that the stench of rotting bodies was unbearable and was even penetrating to the interior of the carriages through tightly shut windows.[31]

On August 9, fifteen hundred Jews were taken out of the ghetto in the Volhynian town of Krzemieniec, to a camp five miles outside the town. Among those taken away were all the members of the Jewish Council and the Jewish police. According to a Jewish woman who returned to the region after liberation, the ghetto had been besieged immediately after these fifteen hundred had been taken out, but a young man in the ghetto opened fire, killing six Germans and Ukrainian policemen, and the 'liquidation squad' was withdrawn. On the second day, August 10, ten German and Ukrainian policemen were killed trying to enter the ghetto. On the third day, the Jews set the ghetto on fire: their last act of defiance before their destruction.[32]

During August 1942, Jews from more than twenty communities in Eastern Galicia, one of the heartlands of the Jewish diaspora, were deported to Belzec, among them more than forty thousand from Lvov. The round-ups in Lvov, beginning on August 10 and lasting until August 23, turned the city, as one of those present later recalled, 'into a city of nightmare and blood'. Among those murdered was Jakob Schall, an historian who, like Ringelblum in Warsaw, had collected material on the fate of Lvov Jewry. Schall's notes, hidden away by him, were all lost at his death.

Another historian to perish that August was Falik Hafner, who had been in charge of food distribution for the Jews of Lvov, and had used his position to organize secret assistance for writers and scholars in need.[33] Also killed in Lvov, on August 18, was Filip Eisenberg, a leading bacteriologist, who between the wars had been Director of the Hygiene Institute at Cracow: he was sixty-six years old.[34]

On August 14, the fourth day of the Lvov deportations, two rabbis employed in the religious department of the Jewish Council, David Kahane and Rabbi Chameides, formerly of Katowice, had visited the head of the Ukrainian Uniate Church in Galicia, the Metropolitan Andreas Sheptitsky. Aged seventy-seven, Sheptitsky was in poor health, and partly paralysed.

The two rabbis asked Sheptitsky if he would find a hiding place for several Jewish children. Sheptitsky agreed, and asked both his brother and his sister to help. His brother, Father Superior Clement Sheptitsky, was the spiritual head of the Uniate monasteries. His sister, Sister Josepha, was the Mother Superior of the Uniate nunneries. Both agreed to help, and 150 Jews, mostly small boys and girls, were found sanctuary. None was betrayed to the Germans. Sheptitsky himself hid fifteen Jews, including Rabbi Kahane, in his own residence in Lvov, a building frequently visited by German officials.[35]

During August 1942, 76,000 Jews were deported from Lvov, and from the other towns of Eastern Galicia. All were sent to Belzec. From Western Galicia, that same August, Jews from thirty communities were deported to Belzec, including 16,000 from the region of Nowy Sacz and 12,500 from Przemysl. In all, during that single month, from Eastern and Western Galicia, and from the Lublin region, more than 145,000 Jews were gassed at Belzec.[36]

Among those driven from their homes in the Eastern Galician town of Czortkow in the early hours of August 27 was Zonka Pollak. She later recalled that night, when several thousand Jews were assembled on the square near the Bristol Hotel, 'watching the scenes of children being shot to death in their mothers' hands and thrown from the balconies'.

Lined in formations of six, the Jews were then marched to the prison yard, where they were locked in until the following day. Zonka Pollak added:

> Our faces reflect silent despair. People ask each other about the circumstances of their arrest, and we are wondering what's going to happen next. Groups are formed, friends look for each other; there are many wounded people with bloody injuries from having been beaten, children without parents, separated families.
>
> It begins to dawn, and with the appearance of the sun, the heat grows. There is no water, and we quench our thirst with rain water in the nearby barrels. Hours are passing with the heat becoming unbearable. We are like animals destined for slaughter and kept in a a cage; but for those animals they spare neither water nor food. Everybody is hungry and forgets even the feeling of shame, making his ordure in public.

It was not until the early afternoon that the prison gates were unlocked and the Jews marched out. Zonka Pollak continued:

> We are sure we will be taken to the forest, where we can expect to be shot, but we are directed to the railway station. It seems to me that I never walked carefree and without fear through these streets. The feeling of thirst grows more intense. My lips are dry and the tongue sticks to the palate. It is a terrible feeling. People get rid of their belongings to ease their way.
>
> At the railway station, we are split up in groups of 120 and more, and packaged off into freight cars. The doors of the cars are shut. It is dark and tense, impossible to stretch out your arms, absolutely no air to breathe. Everybody strangles and chokes and you feel as if a rope were tied around your neck and

such a terrible heat, as if fire had been set under the car.

About ten people from our group are placed near the door; whoever has hairpins, nails, fasteners, starts to bore between the boards to get a little bit of air. People behind us are in much worse plight. They take off their clothes and look as if obsessed by bestiality and madness. They are choking and driven unto the utmost despair.

I cannot recall for how long we are waiting or after how many hours the train starts. But when, after a long waiting, the train is in motion, a sigh of relief emanates from the mouths of those who are still alive. They hope that now more air will find its way into the carriage, or it will start raining and a few drops will penetrate through the clefts. But none of these miracles happen.

It occurs to me that we are making our way towards Tarnopol. I notice that in our carriage there is more and more free space. People die and we are seated on their dead bodies. The remaining are raving and wild, mad from suffering, quarrel between themselves about water; mothers hand their children urine to still their thirst.

At night we are arriving at a station, where the train stops for some time. We can hear a conversation in Russian. We wonder what they will do to us next. A short ray of hope comes to our hearts; maybe we shall stay here to work. We hear many sounds, like that of a detachment of carriages, opening of doors, orders to undress, lamentations; we do not know from where, and whether there are more trains. Our train is driven back, and in our car there are still about twenty people alive. I remember, my mother with a very poor voice asking us to ease our suffering and to break open a small window, which if discovered, would not make any difference for us, being anyway condemned to death.

All of a sudden it becomes light in our car and from this moment I can hardly remember, how my mother insisted that I should jump out. I do not hesitate at all, because the motion of the train does not frighten me when I look on the dead bodies around me.

And then, I recall two countrymen leaning over me and insisting that I should run away, but all I wanted was to drink, drink, drink.

I throw myself in a nearby pond, and I can hardly quench my thirst which burns my stomach. I am pouring handfuls of water, with those hands which had lifted, a short while ago, dead bodies in the carriage.

Within a short distance from me, I notice a body of a woman from our car. She certainly has been shot to death by the Germans, who were on guard on the roof of the train.

Zonka Pollak survived, but those deported with her either died on the train during the journey to Belzec, or were murdered at Belzec within hours of their arrival.[37]

Among the deportees that August from Lvov to Belzec was Rudolf Reder, a soap manufacturer, and one of only two Jews to survive Belzec. His train was among the first to reach the death camp from Lvov, on August 11. As he later wrote:

About mid-day the train entered Belzec, a small station surrounded by small houses inhabited by the SS men. Here, the train was shunted off the main track on to a siding which ran for about another kilometre straight to the gates of the death camp. Ukrainian railwaymen also lived near the station and there was a post office nearby as well.

At Belzec station an old German with a thick, black moustache climbed into the locomotive cab. I don't know his name, but I would recognise him again, he looked like a hangman; he took over command of the train and drove it into the camp. The journey to the camp took two minutes. For months I always saw the same bandit.

The siding ran through fields, on both sides there was completely open country; not one building. The German who drove the train into the camp climbed out of the locomotive, he was 'helping us' by beating and shouting, throwing people out of the train. He personally entered each wagon and made sure that no one remained behind. He knew about everything. When the train was empty and had been checked, he signalled with a small flag and took the train out of the camp.

The whole area of Belzec was occupied by the SS – no one was allowed to approach; any individuals who stumbled accidentally into the area were immediately shot. The train entered a yard which measured about one kilometre by one kilometre and was surrounded by barbed wire and fencing about two metres high, which was not electrified. Entry to the yard was through a wooden gate covered with barbed wire. Next to the gate there was a guard house with a telephone and standing in front of the guard house were several SS men with dogs. When the train had entered the yard the SS men closed the gate and went into the guard house.

At that moment, dozens of SS men opened the doors of the wagons shouting 'Los!' They pushed people out with their whips and rifles. The doors of the wagons were about one metre above the ground. The people, hurried along with blows from whips, were forced to jump down, old and young alike, it made no difference. They broke arms and legs, but they had to obey the orders of the SS men. Children were injured, everyone was falling down, dirty, hungry, frightened.

Beside the SS men stood the so-called 'Zugsführers' – these were the guards in charge of the permanent Jewish death kommando in the camp, they were dressed in civilian clothes, without any insignia.

Reder's recollections continued:

The old, the sick and the babies, all those who could not walk, were placed on stretchers and taken to the edge of the huge mass graves. There, the SS man Irrman shot them and then pushed them into the graves with his rifle. Irrman was the camp expert at 'finishing off' old people and small children; a tall, dark, handsome Gestapo man, with a very normal-looking face, he lived like the other SS men in Belzec – not far from the railway station in a cottage, completely alone – and, like the others, without his family and without women.

He used to arrive at the camp early in the morning and meet the death transports. After the victims had been unloaded from the trains, they were gathered in the yard and surrounded by armed Ukrainian SS men, and then Irrman delivered a speech. The silence was deathly. He stood close to the crowd. Everyone wanted to hear, suddenly a feeling of hope came over them. 'If they are going to talk to us, perhaps they are going to let us live after all. Perhaps we will have work, perhaps. . . .'

Irrman spoke loudly and clearly, 'Ihr geht's jetzt baden, nachher werdet ihr zur Arbeit geschickt,' 'Now you're going to the bath house, afterwards you will be sent to work.' That's all.

Everyone was happy, glad that they were going to work. They even clapped.

I remember those words being repeated day after day, usually three times a day – repeated for the four months of my stay there. That was the one moment of hope and illusion. For a moment the people felt happy. There was complete calm. In that silence the crowd moved on, men straight into a building on which there was a sign in big letters: *Bade und Inhalationsraume*, 'Bath and inhalation room'.

The women went about twenty metres farther on – to a large barrack hut which measured about thirty metres by fifteen metres. There they had their heads shaved, both women and girls. They entered, not knowing what for. There was still silence and calm. Later, I knew that only a few minutes after entering, they were asked to sit on wooden stools across the barrack hut, and Jewish barbers, like automatons, as silent as the grave, came forward to shave their heads. Then they understood the whole truth, none of them could have any doubts any more.

All of them – everyone – except a few chosen craftsmen – were going to die.

The girls with long hair went to be shaved, those who had short hair went with the men – straight into the gas-chambers.

Suddenly there were cries and tears, a lot of women had hysterics. Many of them went cold-bloodedly to their deaths, especially the young girls.

There were thousands of intelligentsia, many young men and – as in all other transports – many women.

I was standing in the yard, together with a group left behind for digging graves, and was looking at my sisters, my brothers and friends being pushed to their deaths.

At the moment when the women were pushed naked, shorn and beaten, like cattle to the slaughter, the men were already dying in the gas-chambers. The shaving of the women lasted about two hours, the same time as the murder process in the chambers.

Several SS men pushed the women with whips and bayonets to the building housing the chambers; three steps led up to a hall, and Ukrainian SS men counted seven hundred and fifty people to each chamber. Those who did not want to enter were stabbed with bayonets and forced inside – there was blood everywhere.

I heard the doors being locked, the moaning, shouting and cries of despair in Polish and Jewish; the crying of the children and women which made the blood run cold in my veins. Then came one last terrible shout. All this lasted fifteen to twenty minutes, after which there was silence. The Ukrainian guards opened the doors on the outside of the building and I, together with all the others left over from the previous transports, began our work.

We pulled out the corpses of those who were alive only a short time ago, we pulled them using leather belts to the huge mass graves while the camp orchestra played; played from morning 'till night.[38]

Reder was a member of the 'Death Commando', consisting of five hundred able-bodied Jews 'selected' from the incoming transports. As he recounted it:

The 'craftsmen' numbered two hundred and fifty, but they did not do any work which required specialist knowledge – only digging the graves and dragging the corpses to them. We dug huge mass graves and dragged bodies. We used spades, but there was also a mechanical excavator which dug up the sand and piled it into mounds and later covered over the graves already full of bodies. About four hundred and fifty of us worked at the graves. It took a week to dig one pit.

The most horrible thing for me was that there was an order to pile the bodies up to a level one metre above the edge of the graves, and then cover them with a layer of sand, while thick, black blood flowed out and flooded the ground like a lake. We had to walk along the ledges from one pit to the next, and our feet were soaked with our brothers' blood. We walked over their bodies and that was even worse.

The brute Schmidt was our guard; he beat and kicked us if he thought we were not working fast enough. He ordered his victims to lie down and gave them twenty-five lashes with a whip, ordering them to count out loud. If the victim made a mistake, he was given fifty lashes. No one could withstand fifty lashes. Usually they managed somehow to reach the barrack-hut afterwards, but the following morning they were dead. This happened several times a week.

Thirty or forty of us were shot every day. A doctor usually prepared a daily list of the weakest men. During the lunch break they were taken to a nearby grave and shot. They were replaced the following morning by new arrivals from the first transport of the day. Our kommando always numbered five hundred – we knew, for example, that although Jews had built the camp and installed the death engine, not one of them now remained alive. It was a miracle if anyone survived for five or six months in Belzec.

When people who arrived on the transports begged for water, any of us who helped them was shot.

Besides digging graves, the death brigade had the task of dragging the bodies out of the chambers and piling them into a huge mound, after which they had to be dragged to the graves. The ground was sandy. One corpse was dragged by two men. We had leather belts which we tied around the wrists of the bodies. It often happened that the corpse's head dug into the sand while being dragged along. We carried the bodies of children two at a time, one over each shoulder – this was a German order. We worked either at grave digging or emptying the gas-chambers. We worked like this from early morning until night-fall. Only darkness halted our work.[39]

The 145,000 deaths at Belzec in August 1942 represented less than a half of the Jews murdered in that single month on the soil of German-occupied Poland. From Warsaw more than one hundred and forty thousand Jews were deported in August to Treblinka, and gassed, as were thirty thousand Jews from Radom, and more than sixty thousand from other towns in central Poland, including twenty thousand deported from Kielce.[40] 'It gave me great pleasure', SS Lieutenant-General Karl Wolff wrote to the manager of the Reich Transportation Ministry on August 13, 'to learn that already since fourteen days ago, one train goes daily with five thousand passengers of the Chosen People to Treblinka; and we are even in a position to complete this mass movement of people at an accelerated rate.' Wolff added: 'I have made personal contact with the participants so that an uninterrupted accomplishment of the total undertaking seems guaranteed.'[41]

At Auschwitz, thirteen thousand Jews were brought from the two nearby towns of Bedzin and Sosnowiec, as well as more than twenty-two thousand from Holland, Belgium, Luxembourg and France.[42] The French deportees of August 17 included twenty-seven children under the age of four, and 323 girls under the age of sixteen. All were gassed, among them Suzanne Perl, aged seven, and her three-year-old sister Micheline. Both girls had been deported without their parents. Some days earlier, the Germans had deported most of the parents of the children of this convoy to Auschwitz, where many of them had already been gassed. The children believed that they were to join their parents. But they were never to see them again. On arrival at Auschwitz, all the children were taken to the gas-chamber.[43]

24

'The most horrible of all horrors'

MORE THAN FOUR HUNDRED THOUSAND JEWS were murdered in German-occupied Europe in August 1942. Neither their suffering, nor their courage, can be adequately conveyed in words. So little is known of the fate and reaction of individuals. Statistics can dull the mind, and examples numb it. Nevertheless, the historian must try, through the records and stories that have survived, to give an insight into the many different ways in which individuals met their death. Those who remembered such stories, and who retold them, did so in order that the fate of individuals would not be forgotten. Rudolf Reder recalled an incident shortly after his arrival in Belzec on August 11:

> Soon after my arrival at Belzec, one very young boy was selected from each transport. (I don't know where he was from as we didn't know the origin of the transports.) He was a fine example of health, strength and youth. We were surprised by his cheerful manner. He looked around and said quite happily, 'Has anyone ever escaped from here?'
> It was enough. One of the guards overheard him and the boy was tortured to death. He was stripped naked and hung upside down from the gallows – he hung there for three hours. He was strong and still very much alive. They took him down and lay him on the ground and pushed sand down his throat with sticks until he died.[1]

On the evening of August 14, the first day of the Hebrew month of Ellul, a Friday, the SS surrounded the ghetto of the village of Zagrodski, near Pinsk, home of five hundred Jewish families. The 'commotion and noise on that night', recalled Rivka Yosselevska, 'was not customary, and we felt something in the air'. On Saturday morning, August 15, the Germans entered the ghetto, ordering the Jews to leave their houses for a roll call. All day, the Jews were kept standing, waiting. Towards sunset, the children screamed, demanding food and water. But the Germans would allow no one back into their homes.

That evening a truck arrived at the ghetto gates. The Jews were ordered on to it, and it drove out of the ghetto. Those for whom there had been no room on the truck were ordered to run after it. 'I had my daughter in my arms,' Rivka Yosselevska recalled, 'and ran after the truck. There were mothers who had two or three children and held them in their arms – running after the truck. We ran all the way. There were those who fell – we were not allowed to help them rise. They were shot – right there – wherever they fell.'

On reaching the destination, Rivka Yosselevska saw that the people from the truck had already been taken off, and were undressed, 'all lined up'. It was some three kilometres from the village, by 'a kind of hillock'. At the foot of the hillock was a ditch. The Jews were ordered to stand on the hillock, where four SS men stood, 'armed to the teeth'.

'We saw naked people lined up,' Rivka Yosselevska recalled. 'But we were still hoping that this was only torture. Maybe there is hope – hope of living.' Her account continued:

One could not leave the line, but I wished to see – what are they doing on the hillock? I turned my head and saw that some three or four rows were already killed – on the ground.

There were some twelve people amongst the dead. I also want to mention that my child said while we were lined up in the ghetto, she said, 'Mother, why did you make me wear the Shabbat dress; we are being taken to be shot;' and when we stood near the dug-out, near the grave, she said, 'Mother, why are we waiting, let us run!'

Some of the young people tried to run, but they were caught immediately, and they were shot right there. It was difficult to hold on to the children. We took all children, not ours, and we carried – we were anxious to get it all over – the suffering of the children was difficult – we all trudged along to come nearer to the place and to come nearer to the end of the torture of the children. The children were taking leave of their parents and parents of their elder people.

We were driven; we were already undressed; the clothes were removed and taken away; our father did not want to undress; he remained in his underwear. We were driven up to the grave. . . .

When it came to our turn, our father was beaten. We prayed, we begged with my father to undress, but he would not undress, he wanted to keep his underclothes. He did not want to stand naked.

Then they tore the clothing off the old man and he was shot. I saw it with my own eyes. And then they took my mother, and she said, let us go before her; but they caught mother and shot her too; and then there was my grandmother, my father's mother, standing there; she was eighty years old and she had two children in her arms. And then there was my father's sister. She also had children in her arms and she was shot on the spot with the babies in her arms.

And finally my turn came. There was my younger sister, and she wanted to leave; she pleaded with the German; she asked to run, naked; she went up to the Germans with one of her friends; they were embracing each other; and she asked to be spared, standing there naked. He looked into her eyes and shot the two of them. They fell together in their embrace, the two young girls, my sister and her young friend. Then my second sister was shot and then my turn came.

We turned towards the grave and then he turned around and asked, 'Whom shall I shoot first?' We were already facing the grave. The German asked, 'Whom do you want me to shoot first?' I did not answer. I felt him take the child from my arms. The child cried out and was shot immediately. And then he aimed at me. First he held on to my hair and turned my head around; I stayed standing; I heard a shot, but I continued to stand and then he turned my head again and he aimed the revolver at me, ordered me to watch, and then turned my head around and shot at me. Then I fell to the ground into the pit amongst the bodies; but I felt nothing.

The moment I did feel I felt a sort of heaviness and then I thought may be I am not alive any more, but I feel something after I died. I thought I was dead, that this was the feeling which comes after death. Then I felt that I was choking; people falling over me. I tried to move and felt that I was alive and that I could rise. I was strangling. I heard the shots and I was praying for another bullet to put an end to my suffering, but I continued to move about.

I felt that I was choking, strangling, but I tried to save myself, to find some air to breathe, and then I felt that I was climbing towards the top of the grave above the bodies. I rose, and I felt bodies pulling at me with their hands, biting at my legs, pulling me down, down. And yet with my last strength I came up on top of the grave, and when I did I did not know the place, so many bodies were lying all over, dead people; I wanted to see the end of this stretch of dead bodies, but I could not. It was impossible. They were lying, all dying; suffering; not all of them dead, but in their last sufferings; naked; shot, but not dead. Children crying, 'Mother', 'Father'; I could not stand on my feet.

The Germans had gone. There was nobody there, no one standing up. 'I was naked, covered with blood, dirty from the other bodies, with the excrement from other bodies which was poured on me.' Rivka Yosselevska had been wounded in the head. But she managed to crawl out of the grave. Then she recalled:

I was searching among the dead for my little girl, and I cried for her – Merkele was her name – Merkele! There were children crying, 'Mother!' 'Father!' – but they were all smeared with blood and one could not recognise the children. I cried for my daughter. From afar I saw two women standing. I went up to them. They did not know me, I did not know them, and then I said who I was, and then they said, 'So you survived.' And there was another woman crying, 'Pull me out from amongst the corpses, I am alive, help!' We were thinking how could we escape from the place. The cries of the woman, 'Help, pull me out from the corpses!' We pulled her out. Her name was Mikla Rosenberg. We removed the corpses and the dying people who held on to her and continued to bite. She asked us to take her out, to free her, but we did not have the strength.

And thus we were there all night, fighting for our lives, listening to the cries and the screams and all of a sudden we saw

Germans, mounted Germans. We did not notice them coming in because of the screamings and the shoutings from the bodies around us.

The Germans ordered that all the corpses be heaped together into one big heap and with shovels they were heaped together, all the corpses, amongst them many still alive, children running about the place. I saw them. I saw the children. They were running after me, hanging on to me. Then I sat down in the field and remained sitting with the children around me. The children who got up from the heap of corpses.

Then Germans came and were going around the place. We were ordered to collect all the children, but they did not approach me, and I sat there watching how they collected the children. They gave a few shots and the children were dead. They did not need many shots. The children were almost dead, and this Rosenberg woman pleaded with the Germans to be spared, but they shot her.

They all left – the Germans and the non-Jews from around the place. They removed the machine guns and they took the trucks. I saw that they all left, and the four of us, we went on to the grave, praying to fall into the grave, even alive, envying those who were dead already and thinking what to do now. I was praying for death to come. I was praying for the grave to be opened and to swallow me alive. Blood was spurting from the grave in many places, like a well of water, and whenever I pass a spring now, I remember the blood which spurted from the ground, from that grave.

I was digging with my fingernails, trying to join the dead in that grave. I dug with my fingernails, but the grave would not open. I did not have enough strength. I cried out to my mother, to my father, 'Why did they not kill me? What was my sin? I have no one to go to. I saw them all being killed. Why was I spared? Why was I not killed?'

And I remained there, stretched out on the grave, three days and three nights.

I saw no one. I heard no one. Not a farmer passed by. After three days, shepherds drove their herd on to the field, and they began throwing stones at me, but I did not move. At night, the herds were taken back and during the day they threw stones believing that either it was a dead woman or a mad woman.

They wanted me to rise, to answer. But I did not move. The shepherds were throwing stones at me until I had to leave the place.

A farmer took pity on Rivka Yosselevska, hid her, and fed her. Later, he helped her to join a group of Jews hiding in the forest. There, she survived until the Soviet forces came in the summer of 1944. Nineteen years after her escape from the pit, she told her story to a court in Jerusalem.[2]

In that same eastern region, one thousand Jews had been murdered at Lenino on the previous day, one thousand at Antopol and four hundred at Byten two weeks later. 'And where are the Jews today?' Hans Frank asked a Nazi Party meeting at Cracow on August 15. 'You hardly see them at all any more. If you see them, they are working. . . .'[3]

In Warsaw, the round-ups had continued each day. On August 15 they reached the street on which lived the thirty-nine-year-old Henryk Zylberberg, a member of the two-week-old Jewish Fighting Organization. Zylberberg had considerable hopes of acquiring arms from a German policeman, Corporal Kneibel, who had made it clear that 'he did not give a damn for the Führer and Vaterland and was prepared to sell food to Jews as long as he was paid in gold and diamonds'.

On August 15, Kneibel was on duty when Zylberberg, his wife, and his daughter Michaela were among those in the street. 'The Nazis drew up a line in the street,' Zylberberg recalled twenty-seven years later, 'separating the men from the women and children. Then a second cordon of Nazis separated the children from the women. Michaela gripped her mother's hand and screamed, "Mummy, mummy!" I saw Kneibel seize her by the arm and drag her away. She would not let go of her mother. In the end he dragged her behind the line, got hold of her waist and before my eyes smashed her little head against the wall of the house.'[4]

Five days after the murder of Zylberberg's daughter, the Jewish Fighting Organization carried out its first action: the attempted assassination of the commander of the Jewish Police in the Warsaw ghetto, Jozef Szerynski, a convert to Christianity. The man chosen to kill Szerynski was also a member of the Jewish police, Yisrael Kanal. On the evening of August 20 he shot Szerynski in the face, but, as another Jewish police officer later recalled, 'in a rare fluke, the bullet penetrated his left cheek, a bit high, and exited through his right cheek without touching the tongue, teeth or palate.'[5]

Szerynski survived. But the small, clandestine posters which appeared on walls in the ghetto, announcing 'Death to a Dog', were, as Alexander Donat recalled, 'a turning point in the history of the Warsaw ghetto, and perhaps a turning point in the history of the Jewish people'.[6]

That same night, other members of the Jewish Fighting Organization, among them Zivia Lubetkin, set on fire a warehouse filled with 'loot' collected by the Germans from Jewish houses. 'We collected mattresses and furniture,' she recalled, 'anything inflammable, piled them together and set them on fire. Success! the flames swept into a great blaze and crackled in the night, dancing and twisting in the air. We rejoiced as we saw the reflection of the revenge that was burning inside us, the symbol of the Jewish armed resistance that we had yearned for, for so long.'[7]

Near Auschwitz, a new slave labour camp was opened on August 15 at Jawiszowice.[8] In it, one hundred and fifty Jews, sent from the barracks at Birkenau, were used in the underground coal mines of the Hermann Goering Works. Later their number rose to two thousand five hundred. A month earlier, three hundred Jews had been sent from Birkenau to Goleszow, to work in the Portland Cement Factory.[9] Here, too, the numbers were to rise, to one thousand. On October 1, a third camp was opened at Chelmek, in which Jews from the barracks at Birkenau spent over two months clearing ponds needed to provide water to the Bata Shoe Factory in the town.[10] In these three camps, and eventually in more than twenty others in the Auschwitz region, tens of thousands of Jews died of the harsh conditions. Those who became too weak to work were often returned to Birkenau, and gassed.

At Auschwitz, gassing was carried out by a commercial pesticide, Cyclon B. At Belzec, Chelmno, Treblinka and Sobibor, the four death camps, Jews were killed by the exhaust from diesel engines: carbon monoxide poisoning. At Treblinka, it was the engines of captured Russian tanks and trucks which provided the exhaust. At his headquarters in Lublin, however, SS General Globocnik was anxious to find 'a more toxic and faster working gas', as he explained to the thirty-seven-year-old chief of the Waffen SS Technical Disinfection Services, Kurt Gerstein, who visited him in Lublin on August 17. Globocnik also sought Gerstein's help in disinfecting 'large piles of clothing coming from Jews, Poles, Czechs etc.'.

On August 18 Globocnik took Gerstein to Belzec. With them was SS Lieutenant-Colonel Dr Wilhelm Pfannenstiel, Professor of Hygiene at the University of Marburg. Two and a half years later Gerstein recalled:

> We saw no dead bodies that day, but a pestilential odour hung over the whole area. Alongside the station there was a 'dressing' hut with a window for 'valuables'. Farther on, a room designated as 'the barber'. Then a corridor 150 metres long in the open air, barbed wire on both sides, with signs: 'To the baths and inhalants.' In front of us a building like a bath-house; to the left and right, large concrete pots of geraniums or other flowers. On the roof, the Star of David. On the building, a sign: 'Heckenholt Foundation'.

Gerstein and Professor Pfannenstiel stayed at Belzec village overnight, the guests of the camp commandant, Christian Wirth. As Gerstein recalled:

> The following morning, a little before seven, there was an announcement: 'The first train will arrive in ten minutes!' A few minutes later a train arrives from Lemberg: forty-five cars arrive with more than six thousand people; two hundred Ukrainians assigned to this work flung open the doors and drove the Jews out of the cars with leather whips.
>
> A loudspeaker gave instructions: 'Strip, even artificial limbs and glasses. Hand all money and valuables in at the "valuables" window. Women and young girls are to have their hair cut in the "barber's hut".' (An SS Sergeant told me: 'From that they make something special for submarine crews.')
>
> Then the march began. Barbed wire on both sides, in the rear two dozen Ukrainians with rifles. They drew near. Wirth and I found ourselves in front of the death-chambers. Stark naked men, women, children and cripples passed by. A tall SS man in the corner called to the unfortunates in a loud minister's voice: 'Nothing is going to hurt you! Just breathe deep and it will

strengthen your lungs. It's a way to prevent contagious diseases. It's a good disinfectant!'

They asked him what was going to happen and he answered: 'The men will have to work, build houses and streets. The women won't have to do that. They will be busy with the housework and the kitchen.'

This was the last hope for some of these poor people, enough to make them march toward the death-chambers without resistance. The majority knew everything; the smell betrayed it! They climbed a little wooden stair and entered the death-chambers, most of them silently, pushed by those behind them.

A Jewess of about forty with eyes like fire cursed the murderers: she disappeared into the gas-chambers after being struck several times by Captain Wirth's whip. Many prayed; others asked: 'Who will give us the water before we die?'

SS men pushed the men into the chambers. 'Fill it up,' Wirth ordered. Seven to eight hundred people in ninety-three square metres. The doors closed. Then I understood the reason for the 'Heckenholt' sign. Heckenholt was the driver of the diesel, whose exhaust was to kill these poor unfortunates.

Heckenholt tried to start the motor. It wouldn't start! Captain Wirth came up. You could see he was afraid because I was there to see the disaster. Yes, I saw everything and waited. My stopwatch clocked it all: fifty minutes. Seventy minutes and the diesel still would not start! The men were waiting in the gas-chambers. You could hear them weeping, 'as though in a synagogue', said Professor Pfannenstiel, his eyes glued to the window in the wooden door.

Captain Wirth, furious, struck with his whip the Ukrainian who helped Heckenholt. The diesel engine started up after two hours and forty-nine minutes by my stopwatch. Twenty-five minutes passed. You could see through the window that many were already dead, for an electric light illuminated the interior of the room. All were dead after thirty-two minutes.

Jewish workers on the other side opened the wooden doors. They had been promised their lives in return for doing this horrible work, plus a small percentage of the money and valuables collected. The people were still standing like columns of stone, with no room to fall or lean. Even in death you could tell the families, all holding hands. It was difficult to separate them while emptying the room for the next batch. The bodies were tossed out, blue, wet with sweat and urine, the legs smeared with excrement and menstrual blood. Two dozen workers were busy checking mouths which they opened with iron hooks. . . . Dentists knocked out gold teeth, bridges and crowns with hammers.

Captain Wirth stood in the middle of them. He was in his element and, showing me a big jam box filled with teeth, said, 'See the weight of the gold! Just from yesterday and the day before! You can't imagine what we find every day, dollars, diamonds, gold! You'll see!' He took me over to a jeweller who was responsible for all the valuables. They also pointed out to me one of the heads of the big Berlin store Kaufhaus des Westens, and a little man whom they forced to play the violin, the chief of the Jewish workers' commandos. 'He is a captain of the Imperial Austrian Army. Chevalier of the German Iron Cross,' Wirth told me.

Then the bodies were thrown into big ditches near the gas-chambers, about 100 by 20 by 12 metres. After a few days, the bodies swelled. . . .

When the swelling went down again, the bodies matted down again. They told me later they poured diesel oil over the bodies and burned them on railway sleepers to make them disappear.[11]

Gerstein went on from Belzec to Treblinka, where, on August 21, he witnessed further gassings. Then, on August 22, he took the express train back to Berlin. Also travelling on the train was a Swedish diplomat, Baron von Otter. Less than an hour from Warsaw, the train stopped in open country. 'We both got down to get a breath of air,' Otter later recalled. 'I offered him a cigarette. He refused. There were beads of sweat on his forehead. There were tears in his eyes. And his voice was hoarse when he said, at once, "I saw something awful yesterday – can I come and see you at the Legation?"'

Otter suggested that they talk on the train. Gerstein agreed. 'Is it the Jews?' Otter asked. 'Yes, it is,' Gerstein replied. 'I saw more than ten thousand die yesterday.'[12]

Deception was an essential part of the German plan. At Treblinka it took many forms. In late August, as Soviet aircraft flew over the camp on their bombing raids deep into the General Government, the Germans were forced to turn off the powerful searchlights which normally lit up the main field in the camp, so that any Jews who had been brought to the camp during the day, but had not yet been gassed, would not be able to escape. Brightly lit, the field was under the ever-vigilant eyes of guards with machine guns.

Jakub Rabinowicz, who escaped from Treblinka two months later, told Emanuel Ringelblum how, one night, when the air-raid sirens sounded, and the searchlights were as usual about to be switched off, the camp commandant, 'afraid that the Jews would take advantage of the darkness and try to escape', decided to allay their fears of what might happen to them on the morrow. A roll call was ordered, and the commandant made a speech to the Jews in which he stated 'with the most serious air' that an agreement had been negotiated between Hitler and Roosevelt for the sending of Polish Jews to Madagascar, and that the first transports would be sent from Treblinka 'as early as tomorrow morning'.

The searchlights were then switched off, as was the diesel engine which operated the gas-chamber. Soviet aircraft then flew over the darkened camp. When the aircraft had passed, Rabinowicz added, 'everything reverted to its previous state, and the death-trap worked unremittingly.'[13]

The pace of deportations to Treblinka was relentless. On August 19 it was the turn of more than a thousand Jews, all those in the ghetto at Rembertow, to be ordered to an assembly point just outside the ghetto. A Polish eye witness later recalled: 'They were ushered like a herd, driven quicker and quicker. Those who fell behind or tripped or fell down were killed.'

At the assembly point, about three hundred were separated from the main group and ordered eastwards, along the road to Wesola. Whether they expected to be resettled in that town, or put to work there, is not known; they were murdered less than a mile along the way.

The remaining Jews were marched southwards. Rembertow was now 'free of Jews'. The eye-witness recalled how, on the following day, Poles from the town entered the ghetto 'looking for gold'. They left the ghetto 'loaded with whatever they could carry', furniture, bedding, pots and pans, returning on the following day for a final session of looting.

The deported Jews had been driven past the woods south of Rembertow, where another Polish eye-witness remembered how 'one big lament, weeping and shots, shook the sky.' After they had passed the Catholic cemetery, another witness noted that 'the rutted sand of the path was covered all over with rags, packets, bundles and, among them, corpses.' That afternoon, the corpses were loaded on horse-carts and taken to ditches nearby.

As the deportees passed the village church at Anin, a Jewish woman broke away from the march. She then managed to lose herself among the crowd of Poles who had gathered in front of the church. A German gendarme tried to follow her, but could not push his way through the crowd. Local Poles believe that the Jewess survived the war hidden in Anin.

As the march passed through Anin, reaching the main Warsaw –Otwock railway, other Jews tried to escape. A plaque in Anin records the fate of forty-five Jews, shot while trying to escape. Another eye-witness of their escape bid recalled how, before they could reach the forest, 'all of them were killed by machine-gun fire.'

The deportees were now driven southwards, along the railway line in the direction of Otwock. 'They were weak because of the heat, and the dust choked them,' another eye-witness recalled of this stage of the march, adding that the gendarmes 'repeated again and again, "Schnell! Schnell!" "Quick! Quick!" and beat them. A Polish traveller passing by the train recalled after the war, how, every few yards along the railway line he had seen 'the corpses of old men and women'.

After several hours, the Jews from Rembertow reached the outskirts of the ghetto of Falenica. That same day, throughout Falenica itself, the Germans had gathered the Jews near the railway station, searched for Jews in hiding outside the ghetto, and killed those whom they had found in hiding. Also during August 19, the children of the ghetto were taken out, as if to mark the start of the continuing march and deportation. They were, however, shot in the ghetto itself, and their bodies thrown into a ditch.

The time had come to send the Jews of Rembertow and Falenica to Treblinka. Two Jews, resisting the order to assemble, killed the first German to enter their apartment, striking him down with an axe. Both were shot. Then, as one of the Jews to survive the deportation, a young man by the name of Najwer, noted in his diary, 'Latvian auxiliaries sit around and watch. They play. They choose someone from the dense crowd and shoot at that living target. Hit or not? Sometimes someone asks to be killed. But he has to ask again and again. And when he *is* shot, it is done as an act of grace.' Najwer himself was later murdered.

From the railway station of Falenica, just outside the ghetto limits, a train was waiting. On it, that August 19, the Jews of Rembertow and Falenica were taken to Treblinka, the wagons 'sprinkled', as a Polish eye-witness later recalled, 'with undiluted lime and chlorine'.[14]

On August 23 the fifty-two-year-old Jankiel Wiernik was among several thousand Jews deported from Warsaw to Treblinka. One of less than a hundred survivors of the camp, Wiernik later set down his recollections of that first day, when he was among a few Jews separated from the mass of the deportees, and put with the small work squad. The squad's first task was to remove corpses from a train which arrived that afternoon from Miedzyrzec. 'Eighty per cent of its human cargo consisted of corpses,' he later recalled. 'We had to carry them out of the train, under the whip-lashes of the guards. At last we completed our gruesome chore. I asked one of my fellow workers what it meant. He merely replied that whoever you talk to today will not live to see tomorrow.'

Wiernik's account continued:

> We waited in fear and suspense. After a while we were ordered to form a semicircle. Then Sergeant Franz walked up to us, accompanied by his dog and a Ukrainian guard armed with a machine gun. We were about five hundred persons. We stood in mute suspense. About one hundred of us were picked from the group, lined up five abreast, marched away some distance and ordered to kneel. I was one of those picked out. All of a sudden there was a roar of machine guns and the air was rent with the moans and screams of the victims. I never saw any of these people again. Under a rain of blows from whips and rifle butts the rest of us were driven into the barracks,

which were dark and had no floors. I sat down on the sandy ground and dropped off to sleep.

The next morning we were awakened by loud shouts to get up. We jumped up at once and went out into the yard amid the yells of our Ukrainian guards. The Sergeant continued to beat us with whips and rifle butts at every step as we were being lined up. We stood for quite some time without receiving any orders, but the beatings continued. Day was just breaking and I thought that nature itself would come to our aid and send down streaks of lightning to strike our tormentors. But the sun merely obeyed the law of nature; it rose in shining splendour and its rays fell on our tortured bodies and aching hearts.

I was jolted from my thoughts by the command: 'Attention!' A group of sergeants and Ukrainian guards, headed by Franz with his dog Barry stood before us. Franz announced that he was about to give a command. At a signal from him, they began to torture us anew, blows falling thick and fast. Our faces and bodies were cruelly torn, but we all had to keep standing erect, because if one so much as stooped over but a little, he would be shot because he would be considered unfit for work.

When our tormentors had satisfied their thirst for blood, we were divided into groups. I was put with a group that was assigned to handle the corpses. The work was very hard, because we had to drag each corpse, in teams of two, for a distance of approximately three hundred metres. Sometimes we tied ropes around the dead bodies to pull them to their graves.

Suddenly, I saw a live woman in the distance. She was entirely nude; she was young and beautiful, but there was a demented look in her eyes. She was saying something to us, but we could not understand what she was saying and could not help her. She had wrapped herself in a bed sheet under which she was hiding a little child, and she was frantically looking for shelter. Just then one of the Germans saw her, ordered her to get into a ditch and shot her and the child. It was the first shooting I had ever seen.

I looked at the ditches around me. The dimensions of each ditch were 50 by 25 by 10 metres. I stood over one of them, intending to throw in one of the corpses, when suddenly a German came up from behind and wanted to shoot me. I turned around and asked him what I had done, whereupon he told me that I had attempted to climb into the ditch without having been told to do so. I explained that I had only wanted to throw the corpse in.

Next to nearly every one of us there was either a German with a whip or a Ukrainian armed with a gun. As we worked, we would be hit over the head. Some distance away there was an excavator which dug out the ditches.

We had to carry or drag the corpses on the run, since the slightest infraction of the rules meant a severe beating. The corpses had been lying around for quite some time and decomposition had already set in, making the air foul with the stench of decay. Already worms were crawling all over the bodies. It often happened that an arm or a leg fell off when we tied straps around them in order to drag the bodies away. Thus we worked from dawn to sunset, without food or water, on what some day would be our own graves. During the day it was very hot and we were tortured by thirst.

When we returned to our barracks at night, each of us looked for the men we had met the day before but, alas, we could not find them because they were no longer among the living. Those who worked at assorting the bundles fell victim far more frequently than the others. Because they were starved, they pilfered food from the packages taken from the trains, and when they were caught, they were marched to the nearest open ditch and their miserable existence was cut short by a quick bullet. The entire yard was littered with parcels, valises, clothing and knapsacks which had been discarded by the victims before they met their doom.[15]

Meanwhile, in the part of Poland which had been annexed to Greater Germany, the deportations spread, preceded by scenes of terror. At Lask, on August 24, the Jews were locked into a church. One woman gave birth to a baby. Both she and the newborn child were killed. Three Jews managed to escape. Of the rest, about eight hundred were sent to factories in the Lodz ghetto, more than two and a half thousand to Chelmno, where they were gassed.[16]

That same day, at Zdunska Wola, 1,100 Jews were driven to the Jewish cemetery. Dora Rosenboim was with her brother. 'Being ill with a lung inflammation and very weak and not able to run, he fell on the ground and the Germans shot him, and I could not even save him.' At the cemetery the slaughter began. 'They tore children from their mothers' arms and tore them to bits, shot and murdered mercilessly, so that a thousand victims fell in a single day. And those of us who remained alive had to bury the dead Jews.' Shortly afterwards, her thirteen-year-old son was seized. 'To this day we do not know what became of him,' she recalled in 1946, 'but we understand that we will never see him, our only child, our eyesight itself.'[17]

In the regions of the General Government where the deportations were to Treblinka, these too were continuing from day to day without interruption. 'I seem to lose my reason in this atmosphere of doom and idleness,' the fifty-three-year-old Gertrude Zeisler, a deportee from Vienna, had written from the Kielce ghetto on August 13.[18] Eleven days later, on August 24, she was almost certainly among the many thousand Jews deported from Kielce to Treblinka. At Kielce station they were loaded on the trains by Ukrainian and German SS, and by the Polish police. The journey, which normally would take little over three hours, took twenty-four: many fainted from the heat and thirst, and hundreds died of suffocation. Others, in desperation, drank their own urine to try to avoid dehydration. When the train reached Treblinka, Izak Helfing later recalled, 'nearly a third of us were dead'.

At Treblinka, the women were the first to be sent to the gas-chambers. Then, as Helfing recalled, 'a certain Friedman' cut a Ukrainian in his throat with a razor blade. The guards at once opened fire, and many were killed or wounded. The shooting went on for a long time. By the time it was finished, eighty per cent of the men and boys were dead. Helfing was fortunate to be able to hide among the corpses, and then to slip among the labourers. 'For an entire day I employed myself by dragging the corpses away from the train cars. When nightfall came, I hid myself straightaway among the dead. Thus did I evade the gas oven for four days on end.'[19]

In the Lodz ghetto, every patch of waste ground had been given over to cultivation of vegetables. Throughout the summer, the hundred thousand inhabitants of the ghetto waited for the moment when the main crop, the cabbages, would be ready to eat. Then, amid a heat wave in August, when the temperature reached 45 degrees centigrade, almost the whole cabbage crop was, as the ghetto chronicle recorded, 'devoured by an enormous mass of caterpillars'. In this way, the Chronicle added, 'the work of so many hands, so much energy, and the last ounce of people's strength were lost with them!' Those who suffered most were 'little people without resources', who had worked alone, or with their families, 'giving every free minute they had to that tedious back-breaking work'. Now they were helpless for, as the chronicler wrote:

They had thought that by Sisyphean labour they would be able to set a little something aside for the hard winter months to come, they believed in some better tomorrow, assured them by the labour done in the hours free from the demands of the ghetto, and now, suddenly, disillusionment and despair!

But a Jew is a fatalist. He believes that if something happened, it was meant to be.

And, besides, he consoles himself with the knowledge that he has already suffered greater losses and ordeals and somehow survived them too. He must only think of how to protect his remaining vegetables from this plague, since the caterpillars are already moving on to the beets (for lack of anything else to feed on), so those too will soon be under serious attack.

Perhaps a salt, or even a soda solution will be found so that we can somehow go on living and survive this grievous affliction while we wait for a better tomorrow. Such is our mentality![20]

Into the Lodz ghetto, at this very moment, were brought the remnants of the Jewish ghettos from a dozen small towns around Lodz, among them those from Lask and Zdunska Wola. 'Pale shadows trudge through the ghetto,' the ghetto chronicler noted on August 28, 'with endemic swellings on their legs and faces, people deformed and disfigured, whose only dream is to endure, survive – to live to see a better tomorrow without new disturbances, even if the price is a small and inadequate ration'.[21]

In the Volhynia, August 1942 saw the massacre of more than sixty thousand Jews. It also saw the escape of tens of thousands to the woods. At Kostopol, on August 24, a Jew, Gedalia Braier, called upon his fellow Jews to run. All seven hundred ran. But less than ten survived the war. At Rokitno, where sixteen hundred Jews were assembled on August 26, surrounded by armed Ukrainians, a Jewish woman called out, 'Jews! We are done for! Run! Save yourselves!' and more than seven hundred managed to reach the woods. At Sarny, where fourteen thousand Volhynian Jews were assembled on August 28, two Jews, one a carpenter with his axe, the other, Josef Gendelman, a tinsmith with his tin-cutters, broke through the fence surrounding the ghetto and led a mass escape. Three thousand Jews reached the gap in the fence, and sought to push their way through it. But the Ukrainians were armed with machine guns, and two and a half thousand Jews were shot down at the fence. Five hundred escaped, but many of these were killed on their way to the woods, and only a hundred survived the war and its two more years of privation, manhunts, and frequent local hostility.

On August 25, when a group of Jews was taken from the town of Zofjowka, under guard, to dig burial pits, one of their number, Moshe-Yossel Schwartz, realising what was intended, urged his fellow Jews to attack their guards. They did so, using their spades to crush the heads of one of the German policemen and two of the Ukrainians. They then fled. But on the way to the woods, Schwartz was shot and killed.

Elsewhere in the Volhynia, individual Jews sought to challenge the German power. In Szumsk, two young women attacked the chief of the police, 'choking him and biting him until they were shot to death'. In Turzysk, a young man, Berish Segal, stole a gun, hit a German policeman in the face with it, but was shot by other policemen.

The Jews who reached the Volhynian woods and formed small partisan bands did so six months before the arrival of Soviet partisans from White Russia. When the Soviet partisans came, Jews helped them, and were protected by them. But in the interval, the death toll was high. Of a group of a hundred Jewish partisans and escaped Soviet prisoners-of-war near Radziwillow, only one, the platoon commander, Yechiel Prochownik, survived. Another of the Jewish partisan leaders, Moshe Gildenmann, began his anti-

German activities with ten men and a single knife. A year later, in the marshes north of Zhitomir, Gildenmann's group was to guide to safety a Russian division surrounded by the Germans.[22]

The deportations from France had continued throughout August. Individual Catholics protested. At the same time, on August 28, the Germans ordered all Catholic priests who sheltered Jews to be arrested.[23] One priest, a Jesuit, had hidden eighty Jewish children destined for deportation. He too was arrested.[24]

On August 26 more than four hundred children under the age of twelve had been deported from Paris to Auschwitz and gassed.[25] On August 28 the deportees included 280 children of sixteen and younger, among them Michel Rozes, who was only one and a half years old, deported with his mother and his five-year-old sister Sarah.

The journey from Paris to Auschwitz took three days. Albert Hollender, one of only eight survivors of the convoy, later recalled:

> Piled up in freight cars, unable to bend or to budge, sticking one to the other, breathless, crushed by one's neighbour's every move, this was already hell. During the day, a torrid heat, with a pestilential smell. After several days and several nights, the doors were opened. We arrived worn out, dehydrated, with many ill. A newborn baby, snatched from its mother's arms, was thrown against a column. The mother, crazed from pain, began to scream. The SS man struck her violently with the butt end of his weapon over the head. Her eyes haggard, with fearful screams, her beautiful hair became tinted with her own blood. She was struck down by a bullet in her head.[26]

On the day of the arrival of this train at Auschwitz, a new German surgeon, Dr Johann Kremer, who had reached the camp on the previous evening, and was to live in the SS Officers' Home near Auschwitz station, noted in his dairy: 'Tropical climate with 28 degrees centigrade in the shade, dust and innumerable flies! Excellent food in the Home. This evening, for instance, we had sour duck livers for 0.40 mark, with stuffed tomatoes, tomato salad etc.' The water, Kremer added, was infected, 'so we drink seltzer water which is served free'.[27]

Two days later Kremer noted: 'Was present for the first time at a special action at 3 a.m. By comparison, Dante's inferno seems almost a comedy. Auschwitz is justly called an extermination camp!'[28]

The Jews whom Kremer saw being gassed on September 2 were from France, including seventy boys and seventy-eight girls under fifteen. Many of the children had been deported without their parents, among them Helene Goldenberg, aged nine, and her sister Lotty, aged five; also Henri Garnek, aged eleven, and his brother Jean, aged three.[29]

Asked after the war about what he had seen on September 2, Kremer told his questioners:

> These mass murders took place in small cottages situated outside the Birkenau camp in a wood. The cottages were called 'bunkers' in the SS men's slang. All SS physicians on duty in the camp took turns to participate in the gassing, which were called *Sonderaction*, 'special action'. My part as physician at the gassing consisted in remaining in readiness near the bunker.
>
> I was brought there by car. I sat in front with the driver, and an SS hospital orderly sat in the back of the car with oxygen apparatus to revive SS men employed in the gassing, in case any of them should succumb to the poisonous fumes.
>
> When the transport with people who were destined to be gassed arrived at the railway ramp, the SS officers selected, from among the new arrivals, persons fit to work, while the rest – old people, all children, women with children in their arms and other persons not deemed fit to work – were loaded on to lorries and driven to the gas-chambers.
>
> I used to follow behind the transport till we reached the bunker. There people were first driven into the barrack huts where the victims undressed and then went naked to the gas-chambers. Very often no incidents occurred, as the SS men kept people quiet, maintaining that they were to bathe and be deloused.
>
> After driving all of them into the gas-chamber, the door was closed and an SS man in a gas-mask threw contents of a Cyclon tin through an opening in the side wall. The shouting and screaming of the victims could be heard through the opening and it was clear that they were fighting for their lives.
>
> These shouts were heard for a very short while. I should say

for some minutes, but I am unable to give the exact length of time.[30]

Non-Jewish eye-witnesses, like the three Germans, Herman Graebe, Kurt Gerstein and Dr Kremer, or the two Poles, Dr Klukowski and railwayman Zabecki, saw and recorded every facet of the Jewish fate. So terrible were the scenes at Treblinka station, Zabecki noted, that from September 1942 no more passenger trains stopped there, as hitherto: only military trains, and deportation trains being divided up and shunted into the death camp.

Beyond the railway lines, Zabecki recalled, and parallel to them, ran a concrete road, beyond which was an excavation overgrown with bushes. Fugitives, seeing this thicket, often hid there before fleeing further away. But, 'more often than not', they died there from wounds received as they had jumped from the train: injuries from falling, or shots from the guards. The SS men knew about this, Zabecki wrote, and scoured the thicket with a dog.

As Zabecki's own allotment was not far away from the thicket, 'I saw quite a few tragedies.' One of them took place on September 1, as a train of deportees stood in the station, waiting to be shunted forward. Several had managed to break out of the trains and, being shot at all the while, had made for the thicket:

> One of the SS men who had arrived at the station that day – he was Kurt Franz, deputy commandant of the camp – came out with his dog along the road. The dog, scenting something, pulled the SS man after it into the thicket. A Jewess was lying there with a baby; probably she was already dead. The baby, a few months old, was crying, and nestling against its mother's bosom.
>
> The dog, let off the lead, tracked them down, but at a certain distance it crouched on the ground. It looked as if it was getting ready to jump, to bite them and tear them to pieces. However, after a time it began to cringe and whimper dolefully, and approached the people lying on the ground; crouching, it licked the baby on its hands, face and head.
>
> The SS man came up to the scene with his gun in his hand. He sensed the dog's weakness. The dog began to wag its tail, turning its head towards the boots of the SS man. The German swore violently and flogged the dog with his stick. The dog

looked up and fled. Several times the German kicked the dead woman, and then began to kick the baby and trample on its head. Later, he walked through the bushes, whistling for his dog.

The dog did not seem to hear, although it was not far away; it ran through the bushes whimpering softly; it appeared to be looking for the people. After a time the SS man came out on to the road, and the dog ran up to its 'master'. The German then began to beat it mercilessly with a whip. The dog howled, barked, even jumped up to the German's chest as if it were rabid, but the blows with the whip got the better of it. On the 'master's' command it lay down.

The German went a few paces away, and ordered the dog to stand. The dog obeyed the order perfectly. It carefully licked the boots, undoubtedly spattered with the baby's blood, under its muzzle. Satisfied, the SS man began to shoot and set the dog on other Jews who were still escaping from the wagons standing in the station.[31]

That same day, in Wlodzimierz Wolynski, the Germans ordered the Jewish Council to provide seven thousand Jews. A member of the Council, Jacob Kogen, realizing that these Jews would be taken outside the town and shot, committed suicide, together with his wife and thirteen-year-old son. He did not want to be the one 'to decide who was to be taken away'.[32]

The Germans searched for their victims unaided. In all, in four days, 13,500 Jews were found, and killed. Five hundred managed to escape. After the first day of the 'action' the Treasurer of the Jewish Council, David Halpern, came out of the cellar in which he had been hiding in order to make enquiries about offering the Germans a ransom for the surviving Jews. He was caught, and killed on the spot.[33]

In the Lodz ghetto, on September 1, the Gestapo went to the hospitals. 'Such despair was never seen in the ghetto,' wrote the photographer Mendel Grossman, 'even during the deportations.'[34] 'The Germans threw the patients from the staircases,' recalled Dr L. Szykier, director of the health section of the ghetto, 'tore them from operating tables.'[35] In one of the hospitals, Ben Edelbaum's sister Esther had just given birth to a baby girl. On September 1 the baby was seven days old, with 'a headful of jet black hair'. As no one at home could agree on a name, it was agreed to wait until mother and baby returned. That morning Ben Edelbaum and his parents learned that the hospital had been cordoned off. They hurried to it:

When we got there, the whole area had already been cordoned off. Hundreds of people gathered around and were being kept in place behind the ropes. Dawid made way for us and we were able to get close to the ropes where we had full view of the whole scene. Inside, within the cordoned area, we saw German soldiers and Sonder run about frantically giving commands and taking orders. Several shots were fired in the air and we saw doctors and nurses leaving the entrance of the hospital. They were escorted by a soldier and taken to a waiting truck. It then drove away, out of the area and out of the ghetto. Two more trucks drove up and the Germans, with the assistance of the Sonderkommando, began going from room to room evacuating every patient who was able to get out of bed and walk down with them.

The people who came to witness this brutal eviction of their loved ones cried and yelled and pleaded to the Almighty to send a lightning bolt down to strike every German. We stood there in a huddle, sobbing and wringing our hands and watching the helpless, sick men and women being herded into those trucks and carried away. Then, as the next group of patients was being escorted to a waiting truck, we saw Esther. She stood there on the truck, looking around to see if we were there, but she didn't see us. She was pale and frightened as she stood there in her pink nightgown.

Oh God, how we wanted to jump over the rope, pass the soldiers with their bayonets fixed, run over to her and tell her how much we loved her; but we were forcibly and physically restrained by the Sonder. The people kept shouting, 'Murderers, where are you taking our loved ones?' 'Murderers!' 'Murderers!' Esther and the rest of the patients in the truck stood there in shock, silent and terrified. Soon the truck drove off and we knew we would never see our beloved Esther again. There was now only one truck waiting. A German soldier got into the truck behind the wheel and drove it closer to the hospital-building wall. There was silence for a moment. No one could figure what was going to happen next.

There were now about six to eight soldiers standing around

the truck plus about eighteen more positioned around the rope. Some of the soldiers looked very young, especially one who looked as if he had just graduated from the Hitler Youth. Even the SS uniform he was wearing seemed large on him. Suddenly, two Germans appeared in an upper storey window and pushed it open. Seconds later a naked baby was pushed over the ledge and dropped to its death directly into the truck below. We were in such shock that at first few of us believed it was actually a live, newborn baby. We thought it was an object of some kind until we saw another and another being hurled out the window and into the waiting truck. We had no more tears left. Our eyes had dried out. We could no longer cry and shout and scream since our throats were hoarse and parched as we stood there looking up to the window and to the Almighty. 'Dear God! Why are you doing this to us? It we have sinned take us, but why are you permitting this to happen to innocent newborn babies? Why? Why? Why?'

The SS seemed to enjoy this bloody escapade. Just then the youngest of the bunch asked his superior if it was all right to catch one of those 'little Jews' on his bayonet as it was coming down. His superior gave him permission, and the young SS butcher rolled up his rifle sleeve and caught the very next infant on his bayonet. The blood of the infant flowed down the knife on to the murderer's arm and into his sleeve. He tried his talent once more, and again he was successful in catching the wailing child on his sharp bayonet. He tried a third time but missed and gave up the whole game, complaining it was getting too 'messy'.

Each time a baby was hurled out that window we were certain it was our first little niece and my parents' first grand-daughter. We knew that one of the babies was ours for sure. Questions kept whirling in my mind: 'Why this? Why did this have to happen? Why are human beings so cruel to other human beings?'

I hardly knew my little niece, but I realized I would miss her very much. It was all so useless and purposeless and so unneces-sary for that to have happened. It was thirty years before I could bring myself even to talk about it. Now, when I do, I can refer to her only as my niece or as Esther's infant girl, because, you see, we didn't even have time to give her a first name.[36]

More than two thousand hospital patients were deported from Lodz that day, including four hundred children and eighty pregnant women. Eighteen patients who tried to escape were shot. The deportees were sent to Chelmno and gassed.[37] But neither their destination nor the fate of these hospital patients was known in the ghetto, where one of the chroniclers, Josef Zelkowicz, commented: 'And how much effort and manoeuvring had been required to get them into the hospital in the first place! Pull was needed to obtain a bed, even one in a corridor, a passageway. How happy was the family that was able to place a loved one in the care of a hospital! Then, all of a sudden. . . .'[38]

On the following day Zelkowicz noted that two hundred Jews had managed to leave the hospital during the round-up, but had all been found and deported. Also deported, he wrote, were people 'who had applied for admittance to the hospital', but had not yet been admitted. Many of the children who had been deported were in hospital long after they need have been, because, while 'essentially cured and healthy', their parents had used 'special "pull"' to have them stay on at the hospital. 'Depression and sadness', he added, 'reign in the workshops. . . .'[39]

On September 2 it was the Jews of Dzialoszyce who were marked out for destruction. Here was a town where, in 1939, seven thousand of the ten thousand inhabitants were Jews. 'It was not a wealthy community,' Martin Rosenblum, then eleven years old, later recalled. 'Life was very hard. But people made a living. They were shopkeepers and craftsmen. And they lived a decent family life.' In 1941, some three thousand Jews had been deported into Dzialoszyce from Cracow, Warsaw, Lodz, Poznan and Lask. 'Hunger and starvation was the order of the day,' Rosenblum recalled. 'People risked their lives for a few potatoes or a piece of bread. The Jews sold their personal belongings in order to buy some food to survive, and were hoping for a miracle.' On September 1 the Gestapo, together with Polish police and Ukrainians, surrounded the town. Rosenblum's account continued:

I have no words to describe the Nazi terror and brutality of that day. They were shooting and burning! There was hell all around us! The horrible things that happened exceeded all imagination. Who could have imagined such brutality and cruelty by human beings. The barbarism of past centuries is pale against what happened on that day of deportation. People were shot in the houses, in the streets, in the market square. There were dead Jews all over the town!

Two of Rosenblum's schoolfriends persuaded him to try to run away with them to the nearby town of Wodzislaw, whose Jews had not yet been deported. He agreed to go with them:

I tried to tell my parents of this plan, but the words in my throat were choking me, paralysing my lips and not letting me say more. For the same reason, they could not say much either. It is impossible to describe the agony of those few moments before we parted. I will never forget the wise eyes of my father and the tears of my mother when we embraced for the last time. In my wildest dreams I would have never imagined that I was parting from my whole family forever, never to see them again.

Rosenblum was among some two hundred young men who managed to escape from Dzialoszyce on the day of the round-up. Soon, however, Wodzislaw itself was surrounded. Some of the young men from Dzialoszyce escaped again, into the nearby woods. Others, including Rosenblum, returned to Dzialoszyce, where they found a dozen Jews still alive. One of these survivors, Moshe Hersh Rosenfrucht, told those who returned what had happened on the day of the deportation itself. As Rosenblum recalled:

He told us that on September 2, that day after I had run away, the Jewish people were all summoned to the market place in the early hours of the morning, with only a minimum of their belongings.

There they were kept waiting for a whole day, men, women, children, the old, the sick, the invalids, the Gestapo savagely beating and shooting them indiscriminately for no reason. God could not have devised a worse torment in hell than that of standing and waiting there in the market place beneath a blazing sun. Death would have been preferable to that. At last there came the signal to leave and they were marched to the train station.

During the day the people were told by the Gestapo that

those who could not walk to the train station would be taken there in carts. Many horses and carts came into the square, driven by the Poles and Ukrainians. Those who found it hard to walk to the distant train station were told to get on to these carts. And while the other people walked to the railway station, the carts went in the direction of the Jewish cemetery in the Dolles, a valley.

There, in the valley, three large graves were already waiting for them. They had been dug out that same day. The old, the sick, pregnant women and small children, two thousand innocent Jewish souls, were shot and brutally thrown into those graves, one on top of the other. Many of them were still alive! For most of the children they didn't even waste a bullet. They were just thrown in alive. And together with those who were only wounded, finished their lives under the pressure of the human mass.

The next morning, a few of the wounded were able to crawl out of the graves and managed to walk a few metres, but died shortly thereafter. I listened in horror and disbelief!

The larger grave contained a thousand bodies, and the two smaller graves contained five hundred bodies each. We learned of this massacre from the Polish police themselves. They told Moshe Hersh about it in minute detail, because they themselves had taken part in that slaughter.

On the following Sunday, they went to church with their families, as if nothing had happened. They suffered no guilt feelings. After all, they were only murdering Jews, with the blessing of their priests, who inflamed them from their pulpits on Sundays.

One more act in the savage drama had yet to be performed:

Moshe Hersh then told us that the next day, at dawn, we must go up to the cemetery and dig ditches around those mass graves, otherwise the water from the hills would wash out the dead bodies, and they would be left exposed.

And so, in the morning, with shovels in hand, we went up to the cemetery. God, O God, what a sight! What we saw there! What a massacre! What a slaughter! I cannot begin to describe that sight. Hundreds of bodies lay exposed, rotting and decaying. The stench of those corpses was intolerable. We threw ourselves on to the graves. We did not want to go on living any more!

Of the ten thousand Jews in Dzialoszyce on September 2, two thousand had been slaughtered in the mass graves outside the town. The remaining eight thousand had been deported to Belzec and gassed. Among those who perished were Rosenblum's father Joel, his mother Mirelle – who had been born in Warsaw – and his five brothers, Avrum Ire who was in his early twenties, Kalman Yitzchak aged twenty, Leibish Wolf aged twelve, Shimon aged seven, and Ezriel Shaptai aged four.[40]

The horrors of the massacre at Dzialoszyce were repeated all over Europe, and with them, many incidents of heroism. On September 2, in Oslo, the Chief Rabbi of Norway, Julius Samuel, was ordered to report to the Gestapo. His wife urged him to go into hiding, or to flee, but he told her: 'As Rabbi, I cannot abandon my community in this perilous hour.' He was then arrested, together with 208 Norwegian Jewish men.[41] They were sent to an internment camp at Berg, just south of Oslo.[42]

On September 3, the day after Rabbi Samuel's act of courage in Oslo, a whole community in eastern Poland, that of the Jews of Lachwa, was faced with destruction, when the ghetto was unexpectedly surrounded by White Russian police. On the following morning, September 4, the Gestapo entered the Jewish Council building, and ordered a member of the Council, Yisrael Dubski, to give them a list of Jews in the ghetto. When Dubski refused, he was shot. The Chairman of the Council, Berl Lopatyn, then went from house to house, warning the inmates that, when he saw that the action was about to begin, he would set fire to the Council building, and that they should then do likewise to their homes.[43] As Chairman of the Jewish Council, Lopatyn was offered the chance of survival by the Germans. He refused. 'No Jew', he insisted, 'was willing in this case to benefit from any special rights.' He was not, he said, 'master of life and death over anyone'.[44]

On Lopatyn's advice, many of those in the ghetto armed themselves with knives and axes. When the Council building was seen to be on fire, the Jews then set fire to their own homes. One Jew, Yitzhak Rechstein, the leader of a clandestine youth group, split open the head of a German policeman with an axe. At this signal, the Jews surged forward to the ghetto gates. Rechstein was killed at once, but Lopatyn managed to seize an automatic gun from a German, and to open fire. Lopatyn was wounded. The Germans then opened fire on the Jews, one of whom, Chaim Hajfec, a former soldier in the Polish army, seized a gun from one of the Germans and began to fire back. The Jews attacked the ghetto sentries with their knives and axes, seeking to break out.

The ghetto was ablaze, the fire spreading beyond its narrow confines to the German army headquarters, the post office, and the store containing goods stolen from the Jews in the previous months. All were burned.[45]

More than a thousand Jews were killed in Lachwa that day, but six hundred escaped. Of these six hundred, scarcely one hundred survived the ensuing manhunt. Among the survivors was Lopatyn, who formed a small Jewish partisan group in the Pripet marshes, armed at first with only one rifle and one pistol. Later he joined a Soviet military brigade, and in April 1944 was killed in action while checking a minefield.[46]

Berl Lopatyn had led his small ghetto in a courageous act of resistance. In the Lodz ghetto, on September 4, Chaim Rumkowski took another path, defending the imminent deportation of all children under ten, and of all adults over sixty-five. He had been ordered to deport 'some twenty thousand Jews', he told a meeting of Jews in the ghetto. The Germans had told him that if he refused, 'we shall do it ourselves'. Rumkowski added: 'I have to perform this bloody operation myself; I simply must cut off the limbs in order to save the body. I have to take away children, because otherwise others will also be taken.' The days of those who were sick were also numbered. 'Deliver to me those sick ones,' Rumkowski asked, 'and it may be possible to save the healthy ones instead.'[47]

An eye-witness, Oscar Singer, recalled the sequel: 'Horror seizes the crowd. "Why do the Nazis want our children?" Pandemonium broke out in the ghetto. But Rumkowski knew he had to deliver. "I love children as much as you do," he cried hysterically; "still I fear we must surrender the children as a sacrificial offering in order to save the collective, because should the Germans take matters into their own hands...." '

Rumkowski spoke 'with a broken heart', Singer added, 'he who was a "Father" to thousands of orphans'.[48] Another observer, Josef

Zelkowicz, one of the ghetto chroniclers, wrote in a special note of the 'days of nightmare', and of the decision to allow the elderly and the children to be deported:

> The sorrow becomes greater, and the torture more senseless, when one tries to think rationally. Well, an old man is an old man. If he's lived his sixty-five years, he can convince himself, or others convince him, that he should utter something like: 'Well, thank God, I've had my share of living, in joy and sorrow, weal and woe. That's life. Probably that's fate. And anyway, you don't live forever. So what's the difference if it's a few days, you've got to die, sooner or later, everything's over. that's life.'
>
> Maybe they can talk the old man into telling himself these things, maybe they can talk his family into telling themselves. But what about children who have only just been hatched, children who have only seen God's world in the ghetto, for whom a cow or a chicken is just a legendary creature, who have never in their lives so much as inhaled the fragrance of a flower, laid eyes upon an orange, tasted an apple or a pear, and who are now doomed to die?[49]

As the round-ups began throughout the Lodz ghetto, Jews who tried to rejoin those who were not to be deported were shot. This took place, as Josef Zelkowicz recorded in the Ghetto Chronicle, 'right before the eyes of the assembled tenants of a building'. Zelkowicz added:

> Dramatic scenes were played out in the hospitals. Escape attempts came to a bloody end. Anyone who attempted to save himself by fleeing and was spotted by the authorities had to pay for that attempt with his life. Because the operation proceeded so rapidly, the authorities gave no thought to the motives or causes for any particular act. At 38 Zgierska Street, an elderly woman from Sieradz did not understand if she had been ordered to go to the left or the right and, instead of going to a wagon, she walked over to a group of 'remainers'. This the authorities interpreted as an escape attempt. The woman was shot to death on the spot. At 3 Zgierska Street, Rozenblum, a thirteen-year-old boy, attempted to hide in a dustbin; he was seen and shot dead. There were many such victims but even

more numerous were cases of people who were wounded when a crowd was fired on.

Sometimes the deportees were seized and taken away so quickly that they had no time to hand over any of their ration documents. In one case, Zelkowicz recorded, 'a wife who was resettled along with her three children took all their cards with her and her husband starved to death after five days of nothing whatever to eat.'[50]

More than seven hundred children were left in the ghetto without parents, the parents having been rounded up and sent away.[51] Often, it was the children who were seized and deported without their parents. On October 22 the Ghetto Chronicle recorded the suicide of the parents of two children who had been deported a month earlier. The forty-six-year-old Icek Dobrzynski jumped from the fifth floor of a building. His wife Fraidla, unable to find a sentry willing to shoot her at the ghetto wire, jumped from a bridge.[52] On November 1 a highly respected ghetto official, Salomon Malkes, head of the ghetto's information department, committed suicide by jumping from a fourth floor. 'Malkes had recently been in a severe depression', the Ghetto Chronicle noted, 'that dated from the deportation of his mother.'[53]

Despite the September deportations, in which 15,685 Jews were 'resettled', the ghetto's survival through productive work seemed assured. There were still 88,727 Jews in the ghetto.[54] Orders were continuous: in the month following the deportations they included 5,500 decorative lampshades, and 'several million' toys. All were to go to Germany. 'These products are so imaginative', the Ghetto Chronicle noted, 'that no one can tell that they are made largely of paper and refuse.'[55]

Throughout August, information had reached Jewish representatives in Geneva, telling of the deportations from Western Europe. It was certain that tens of thousands of Jews were being seized, interned and deported to the East, but where in the East was not known. Nor was the precise fate of the deportees, but when Richard Lichtheim learned that it was not only the able-bodied who were being deported, but women, children, the old and the sick, he wrote in a letter to London, New York and Jerusalem on September 3: 'the intention cannot be to get labour supply but simply to kill off the deportees.' Lichtheim added: 'All the relief organizations in Europe, Jewish and non-Jewish, constantly dealing with these horrors are in a state of despair, because no force on earth can stop them. Announcements lately made that the perpetrators would be punished after the war have of course no effect. Also there is no adequate punishment for those crimes.'[56]

On September 3 the World Jewish Congress in Geneva learned of eleven deportations in August from the main internment camps in southern France and the Pyrenees, including Gurs and Les Milles. Five days later, in a letter to Jerusalem, Lichtheim reported that 'at least ten thousand have already been deported, despite a strong protest by two leading clergymen in southern France, the Archbishop of Toulouse and the Bishop of Montauban.'[57]

Throughout the first two weeks of September, The Times in London published full reports of the deportation of Jews from France. It had received these reports from its own correspondent at the frontier between Vichy France and neutral Spain. Each report was published in London on the day after it was received in Spain.

On September 7 the main article on the imperial and foreign page of The Times was headed: 'Vichy's Jewish victims, children deported to Germany'. The article told of the unabated ruthlessness of the deportation campaign. Women and children, it stated, 'suddenly notified' that they could visit their relatives in various internment camps, were then 'forced to accompany the deportees without being given any opportunity to make preparations'. At Les Milles there had been eighty-six attempted suicides: 'some men had cut their veins with broken glass.' Recently 'a train containing four thousand Jewish children, unaccompanied, without identification papers or even distinguishing marks, left Lyons for Germany.' But where in Germany was not known.[58]

In the House of Commons on September 8, Winston Churchill referred to the deportations from France during the course of a comprehensive survey of the war situation. The 'brutal persecutions' in which the Germans had indulged, he said, 'in every land into which their armies have broken', had recently been augmented by 'the most bestial, the most squalid and the most senseless of all their offences, namely the mass deportation of Jews from France, with the pitiful horrors attendant upon the calculated and final scattering of families'. Churchill added: 'This tragedy fills me with astonishment as well as with indignation, and it illustrates as nothing else can the utter degradation of the Nazi nature and theme, and the degradation of all who lend themselves to its unnatural and perverted passions.'

Pausing for a moment, Churchill declared: 'When the hour of liberation strikes Europe, as strike it will, it will also be the hour of retribution.'[59]

In the days following Churchill's speech, *The Times* continued to report the deportation of Jews from France, and to stress the opposition of the French people to the collaboration of the Vichy government in these measures. On September 9, it published news of the dismissal by the Vichy authorities of General de St-Vincent, the military Governor of Lyons, who had 'refused to obey Vichy's order' on August 28 'to cooperate in the mass arrests of Jews in the unoccupied zone'. General de St-Vincent had, it appeared, refused to place his troops at the disposal of the authorities in order to round up Jews.

The news item of September 9 also told of a Vichy order for the arrest of all Roman Catholic priests who were sheltering Jews in the unoccupied zone. 'Some arrests', it added, 'had already been made. In reply to these arrests, Cardinal Gerlier, the Archbishop of Lyons, had already issued a 'defiant refusal' to surrender those Jewish children whose parents had already been deported, and who were being 'fed and sheltered' in Roman Catholic homes.[60]

A main news item in *The Times* on September 11 reported 'popular indignation' in Lyons following the arrest and imprisonment of eight Jesuit priests who had refused to surrender 'several hundred' children for deportation; children whom they had kept hidden 'in buildings belonging to the religious order'. *The Times* also reported that the Papal Secretary of State, Cardinal Maglione, had informed the French Ambassador to the Vatican 'that the conduct of the Vichy government towards Jews and foreign refugees was a gross infraction' of the Vichy government's own principles, and was 'irreconcilable with the religious feelings which Marshal Pétain had so often invoked in his speeches'.[61]

In Warsaw, on September 3, disaster struck the fledgling Jewish Fighting Organization. One of their leaders, Yisrael Zeltzer, had already been arrested with a group of youngsters. Then, on

September 3, Joseph Kaplan, another of its leaders, was arrested. His colleague Shmuel Braslaw, while trying to find out where Kaplan was being held, was stopped on the street by uniformed Germans. He tried to pull a jackknife out of his pocket but was shot on the spot. Alarmed, Yitzhak Zuckerman and the remaining leaders decided to transfer their 'treasure', the small cache of grenades and revolvers which they had been able to assemble, to a new hiding place. The 'treasure', hidden in a sack of vegetables, was being carried to its new hiding place by Reginka Justman when she was stopped by a sentry, the arms were seized, and Reginka shot.

A few days later, both Kaplan and Zeltzer were taken to the Umschiagplatz. On the way they were ordered out of the line, marched to the entrance of a building, and shot. Aryeh Wilner, the group's representative with the Polish underground, told his devastated colleagues: 'Our weapons have been taken from us. We should therefore vanish off the face of the earth, burrow down and hide, prepare and train there, and then re-emerge once we have become a force that can assault the enemy in a single attack.' Some suggested going out on the streets, to attack the Germans with their bare hands, and die. But Yitzhak Zuckerman and Zivia Lubetkin persuaded them to try to rebuild the broken force. 'Our remaining strength', Zuckerman later recalled, 'would be dedicated to that end. No effort would be spared.'[62]

Neither compliance, nor resistance, could stop the juggernaut of death. At Birkenau on September 5 about eight hundred Jewish women, too weak to work, almost too weak to walk, were gassed. The gassing was watched by Dr Kremer, who described it as 'the most horrible of all horrors'. Another SS doctor in the camp, Heinz Thilo, commented to Kremer that day: 'we are located here in "anus mundi"', the 'anus of the world'.[63]

Kremer was not to forget the gassing of those eight hundred women. 'When I came to the bunker,' he recalled five years later, 'they sat clothed on the ground. As the clothes were in fact worn out camp clothes, they were not led into the undressing barracks but undressed in the open. I could deduce from the behaviour of these women that they realized what was awaiting them. They begged the SS men to be allowed to live, they wept, but all of them were driven to the gas-chamber and gassed. Being an anatomist I had seen many horrors, had dealt with corpses, but what I then saw was not to be compared with anything ever seen before.'[64]

The gassing of the eight hundred women had taken place at noon. Eight hours later it was a train from Holland whose deportees were gassed. Of 714 Jews in that train, only 53 women were sent to the barracks. All the other occupants were gassed. 'Another special action with a draft from Holland,' Kremer noted. 'Men compete to take part on such actions as they get additional rations – 1/5 litre vodka, 5 cigarettes, 100 grammes of sausage and bread.'[65]

The relentless killing missed no day and took no rest. The Nazis had cut off each Jewish community from the outside world, and from all other Jewish life, and using this isolation they worked without respite to destroy. In Warsaw, during a massive round-up on September 6 and 7, more than a thousand Jews were killed in the streets, including hundreds who, as Ringelblum noted, were 'forced to kneel on the pavement' to be shot.[66] One death of these thousand was witnessed by Feigele Peltel, who later recalled:

> On Gesia-Zamenhof I suddenly caught sight of an old woman walking all alone. How had she gotten there? Probably she'd been left alone in the house, and was now seeking a hiding place. I anxiously watched her halting steps. She was conspicuous in the deserted street. Two German automobiles happened to pass by; a young German jumped out and called to the old woman. She was evidently deaf; the German easily caught up with her, pulled out his revolver and fired twice. She toppled, bleeding profusely. The German calmly returned to his car and drove away. The incident had passed like a flash. We were not permitted by the Ukrainians to approach the dead woman, we passed by the corpse with lowered heads.[67]

Those with work cards were permitted to remain in the Warsaw ghetto. 'Did this coveted card mean only that I would be among the last to perish?' Feigele Peltel asked herself, when she received her card but her friends did not. 'Unable to control myself any longer,' she recalled, 'I broke down and wept.'[68] But the work card was the sole guarantee of remaining in the ghetto. Every family, with its bundles, passed by a 'selection' point, hoping against hope that deportation could be avoided. 'Even the faintest glimmer of hope for survival', Feigele Peltel recalled, 'was more powerful than any fear of selection.'[69]

At the Umschlagplatz itself, Jews sought the magic work cards, and sent urgent messages back to the workshops. One such message, preserved by Ringelblum, was sent by Rabbi Jechiel Meir Blumenfeld, a member of the Warsaw rabbinate. His appeal to the director of the workshops in which he had hitherto been employed was successful. He was taken out of the line and back to the workshop. But two weeks later, in the workshop itself, he was shot.[70]

Survival had been offered to those with work cards. But their children were not intended to benefit. Samek, a father, decided to carry his two-year-old daughter Miriam past the selection point in a knapsack. First, he gave her a sedative. Then, with his wife, he joined the line. Alexander Donat has recorded the sequel, and the fate, first, of another father and child, as Samek waited his turn:

> The column advanced slowly while up ahead the SS officer grandly dispensed life and death, left and right, links und rechts. In the tense silence the wails of a baby suddenly rose. The SS officer froze and a thousand men and women held their breaths. A Ukrainian guard ran out, plunged his bayonet several times into the knapsack from which the criminal sounds had come. In seconds the knapsack was a blood-soaked rag. 'Du dreckiger Schweinehund!' 'You filthy pig-dog!' the SS officer shouted indignantly, bringing his riding crop down on the ashen face of the father who had dared to try smuggling his child past. Mercifully, the Ukrainian's bullet put an end to the father's ordeal then and there. Thereafter it became routine for guards to probe every bundle and knapsack with their bayonets.

At that moment, Samek and his wife were only three ranks away from the SS men:

> All the blood drained from Samek's face, but his wife was stronger at that moment – or was it weaker? – or did she merely have presence of mind? 'Take off the knapsack!' she hissed. As if in a trance, he did so and without losing his place in the ranks, he edged over to the end of the row of marchers and carefully deposited the knapsack on the curb. It took no more than a fraction of a minute. Then he went back to his original place, eyes vacant.[71]

Such, at a moment of supreme danger, was the instinct for survival, the desperate Will to live, numerous examples of which have come down to us: the decision of an instant, for which there could be neither precedent nor logic.

A similar incident was witnessed by Samuel Rajzman. A mother had chloroformed her eleven-month-old baby, he later recalled, in order to smuggle it through the selection in a sack, but, 'just as she was being directed to the right side, the baby awoke and suddenly began to wail in its sack.' One of the Ukrainian guards pierced the baby with his bayonet through the sack. 'Then he returned the sack to the mother and ordered her to go leftward. A few moments later a shot resounded and the mother with her sack collapsed on the pavement.'

Rajzman added that throughout the deportation, 'We tried in vain to find out where and for what purpose all these people were being sent away, but the German machine worked flawlessly; no one learned what happened to the victims.'[72]

The destination was Treblinka, and death. Between September 6 and September 9, more than thirty thousand Jews were deported from the Warsaw ghetto to Treblinka. On September 10 more than five thousand were deported, a further five thousand on September 11, and 4,806 on September 12. The deportations then ceased for nine days.[73]

September 11 had been the eve of Jewish New Year. Among those deported that day was the seventy-one-year-old Hillel Zeitlin, philosopher, journalist and author, whose *Alphabet of Judaism* had been published in 1922. Zeitlin was seized that day with other patients in the Jewish hospital; given, as all patients were, five minutes to 'pack' their belongings.

Zeitlin put on his prayer shawl, took with him a volume on Jewish mysticism, and walked towards the Umschlagplatz. 'His dignified figure,' Hillel Seidman later recalled, 'his flashing eyes and vigorous gait cast awe on all around. Even the murderous Ukrainian militia were impressed. They did not push him brutally and did not molest him. He walked immersed in his thoughts, his lips murmuring incessantly and his eyes staring afar.'[74]

Zeitlin was deported to Treblinka and gassed. That same day, on the ramp at Treblinka, Meir Berliner, a Jew from the Argentine who had been visiting relatives in Warsaw on the outbreak of war, and was now deported, stabbed an SS man with a knife.[75]

Whatever resistance was possible was also futile. Meir Berliner's gesture saved nobody. But it served as a signal of human dignity, and as a gesture of outrage. Inside Treblinka, however, a number of those chosen for the gruesome task of burning the bodies, sorting the clothing of those who had been gassed, and cleaning the trains, were trying to organize themselves into a resistance group, to plan a mass escape. One of the leaders of this plan was a Jew from Warsaw, Alfred Galewski, an engineer. Another Warsaw Jew, Samuel Rajzman, who was deported to Treblinka on September 17, recalled three years later:

> While undressing I saw Engineer Galewski, of Warsaw, a friend of mine, among the workers. Galewski asked one of the Ukrainian guards to assign me to the workers' brigade. I was told to dress and was placed in a group employed in carrying bundles of clothing from this square to the storehouses. I never saw my travelling companions again. After a few minutes I understood everything. I felt resentment against Galewski, due to whose intervention I was still alive.
>
> Carrying extremely heavy bundles, we had to run the gauntlet between lined-up overseers who beat anyone they could lay their hands on with heavy sticks. All those who carried bundles had swollen faces. By noon no one who knew me would have recognized me, for my face had become a bluish mass, my eyes were bloodshot.
>
> During the pause for lunch I complained to my friend and reproached him for having saved me. His answer was unexpected: 'I did not save you to keep you alive,' he whispered, 'but to sell your life at a higher price. You are now a member of a secret organization that is planning an uprising, and you must live.'

Rajzman did live, not only to participate in the revolt, but to give testimony at the Nuremberg Tribunal of what happened at Treblinka. Of the fate of those in the working groups, he recalled:

> There were thousands of pretexts for killing. If a piece of bread coming from an outside bakery was discovered on a worker the penalty was death. Death was meted out for not carefully removing the Jewish insignia from the clothes of the

murdered. Death for having kept a coin or a wedding ring, the last relic of the worker's murdered wife.

The methods of execution were the following: (1) lashing to death while cold water was constantly poured on the victim; (2) hanging on gallows by the feet; (3) tearing to pieces by dogs (Franze's favourite amusement); (4) the mildest form of death, yearned for by everyone – shooting.

For drinking water during work, smoking a cigarette, improper saluting, and similar offences, the penalties were from fifty to one hundred lashes on the bare body, but usually the worker was finished after fifty lashes, and if several pails of water did not bring him to, he was thrown on the fire.

Samuel Rajzman also gave testimony after the war of how the women, on arrival, were 'shaved to the skin', their hair being later packed up for despatch to Germany. His account continued:

Because little children at their mothers' breasts were a great nuisance during the shaving procedure, later the system was modified and babies were taken from their mothers as soon as they got off the train. The children were taken to an enormous ditch; when a large number of them were gathered together they were killed by firearms and thrown into the fire. Here, too, no one bothered to see whether all the children were really dead. Sometimes one could hear infants wailing in the fire.

When mothers succeeded in keeping their babies with them and this fact interfered with the shaving, a German guard took the baby by its legs and smashed it against the wall of the barracks until only a bloody mass remained in his hands. The unfortunate mother had to take this mass with her to the 'bath'. Only those who saw these things with their own eyes will believe with what delight the Germans performed these operations; how glad they were when they succeeded in killing a child with only three or four blows; with what satisfaction they pushed the baby's corpse into the mother's arms.

The invalids, cripples and aged who could not move fast were put to death in the same way as the children. The ditch in which the children and infirm were slaughtered and burned was called in German the 'Lazarett', 'infirmary', and the workers employed in it wore armbands with the Red Cross sign.[76]

Five days before Samuel Rajzman had reached Treblinka, another Jew had managed to escape from the camp. His name was Abraham Jacob Krzepicki and he had been at Treblinka for eighteen days, since August 26. A Jew in his early twenties, Krzepicki had fought in the Polish army in 1939. Deported from Warsaw in 1942, on the evening of August 25, he had worked in Treblinka until September 12, when he escaped and returned to Warsaw.

In Warsaw, Emanuel Ringelblum entrusted one of his colleagues, Rachel Auerbach, with the task of recording Krzepicki's testimony, the first eye-witness account of Treblinka, Written in Yiddish, the account was later buried with other documents collected by Ringelblum's 'Joy of Sabbath' circle. It was found by Polish building workers on 1 December 1950, under what had once been 68 Nowolipki Street.

In his account of his deportation to Treblinka, Krzepicki wrote of how, during a halt on the journey, with hundreds of Jews suffocating in the heat, a German soldier had told them that 'in Treblinka' everybody would be given work 'at his own occupation'. At this news, some of the deportees applauded. Others tried to work out what kind of work they would be given. As for water, for which the deportees were desperate, at Treblinka, the soldier assured them, 'everyone would get water'.

On reaching Treblinka, and being ordered out of the train, women and children were sent to the left, men to the right. Krzepicki's account continued:

> The women all went into the barracks on the left and, as we later learned, they were told at once to strip naked and were driven out of the barracks through another door. From there, they entered a narrow path lined on either side with barbed wire. This path led through a small grove to the building that housed the gas-chamber. Only a few minutes later we could hear their terrible screams, but we could not see anything, because the trees of the grove blocked our view.
>
> As we sat there, tired and resigned — some of us lying stretched out on the sand — we could see a heavy machine gun being set up on the roof of the barrack on the left side, with three Ukrainian servicemen stretched out around it. We figured that any minute they would turn the machine gun on us and kill us all. This fear put some new life into me, but then I again felt

the terrible thirst which had been torturing me for so many hours. The Ukrainians on the barracks roof had opened an umbrella over their heads to shield them from the sun. My sole thought at the moment was, 'A cup of water! Just one more cup of water before I die!'

Some of the people I had known from the factory were sitting near to me. Our book-keeper K., our warehouseman D., and several other young people. 'It's no good,' they said. 'They're going to shoot us! Let's try to get out of here!' We all thought that there was an open field beyond the fence which surrounded both barracks. We didn't know then that a second fence lay further on.

When I had revived a little, I followed some of the others through an open door to the barracks on the right. I planned to break down one of the boards in the wall and to run away. But when we got into the barracks, we were overcome by stark depression. There were many dead bodies lying in the barracks, and we could see that they had all been shot. Through a chink in the barracks' wall we could see a Ukrainian guard on the other side, holding a gun. There was nothing we could do. I went back outside.

As I later learned, the corpses were those of a transport of Jews from Kielce who had arrived in Treblinka that morning. Among them were a mother and her son. When it came time to separate them – women to the left and men to the right – the son wanted to say a last goodbye to his mother. When they tried to drive him away, he took out a pocket-knife and stuck it into the Ukrainian. As a punishment, they spent all that day shooting all the Jews from Kielce who were at the camp.

Krzepicki was chosen, with sixty other men, to throw bodies into a ditch. These were the bodies of Jews from earlier transports, most of whom had died on the journey. Krzepicki noted:

Countless dead bodies lay there, piled upon each other. I think that perhaps ten thousand bodies were there. A terrible stench hovered in the air. Most of the bodies had horribly bloated bellies; they were covered with brown and black spots, swollen, and the surfaces of their skin already crawling with worms.

The lips of most of the dead were strangely twisted and the

tips of their tongues could be seen protruding between the swollen lips. The mouths resembled those of dead fish. I later learned that most of these people had died of suffocation in the boxcar. Their mouths had remained open as if they were still struggling for a little air. Many of the dead still had their eyes open.

We, the new arrivals, were terror-stricken. We looked at each other to confirm that what we were seeing was real. But we were afraid to look around too much, because the guards could start shooting any minute.

Each day amid the murder of thousands of Jews, it was the killing of individuals that horrified Krzepicki most. As an SS man was talking to him, he caught sight of another prisoner:

He was standing in the ditch, receiving the bodies which others had been dragging over. It seemed to the German that he was not working fast enough.

'Halt! Turn around!' the SS man ordered the young man. He took his rifle from his shoulder and before the young man could have figured out what was expected from him, he lay dead among the bodies in the ditch. They dragged him farther along and soon additional corpses were piled on top of him.

The German returned the rifle to his shoulder and resumed our conversation, as if nothing had happened.

Later, Krzepicki was put to work cleaning out the railway wagons before they were sent away empty:

A Ukrainian and an SS man stationed themselves at either side of the exit gate and shone flashlights under the wheels to see whether anyone was hiding beneath the cars. A few cars pulled out in good order. But when he got to the third or fourth car, the German shouted, 'Halt!' He had discovered two boys lying hunched up between the wheels.

One of them got a bullet even before he could crawl out from under the car. The other was able to jump out and started running quick as lightning, trying to lose himself in the crowd of Jews. But the SS man stopped him right away. The young man immediately took his papers out of his pocket and tried to prove that he was a worker. He shouted and pleaded, but this did not impress the German. He started hitting him over the head as hard as he could with his rubber truncheon, until the boy collapsed. Then the Ukrainian came up, turned his rifle upside down and with great force, as if chopping wood, hit his victim over the head with the rifle butt. Finally, they put a bullet in him. Then, at last, they left him alone. The train rolled out.

On his second day at Treblinka, Krzepicki had been taken to an incoming train. 'I was stunned by what I saw there. The train contained only corpses. They had suffocated on the journey from lack of air: six thousand Jews, from the town of Miedrzyrzec, some seventy-five miles from Treblinka. As the Jewish prisoners worked, they discovered a few of the Miedrzyrzec deportees who had 'merely fainted, and were now regaining consciousness'. Among the living, Krzepicki found 'a little child, about a year or a year and a half old. The child had regained consciousness and was crying at the top of its voice. I put it down, too, apart from the others, next to the pile of rags. By the next morning the child was dead and it was thrown into the ditch.'

Krzepicki also recalled the last act of defiance of those who were driven to their deaths. 'All over Treblinka', he wrote, 'one would find scattered bits and pieces of money notes including dollar bills and other foreign currencies. These bills had been torn up and thrown away by Jews who finally understood what kind of place this was. This was their final protest and act of revenge before disappearing forever in the "bath house".'[77]

Eight days after Krzepicki had managed to escape from Treblinka, an underground newspaper in Warsaw published his story. The article ended:

> Today every Jew should know the fate of those resettled. The same fate awaits the remaining few left in Warsaw. The conclusion then is: Don't let yourself be caught! Hide, don't let yourself be taken away. Run away, don't be fooled by registrations, selections, numbers and roll calls! Jews, help one another! Take care of the children! Help the illegals!
>
> The dishonourable traitors and helpers – the Jewish police – should be boycotted! Don't believe them, beware of them. Stand up against them!
>
> We are all soldiers on a terrible front!

We must survive so that we can demand a reckoning for the tortured brothers and sisters, children and parents who were killed by the murderer's hand on the battlefield for freedom and humanity![78]

The following night, September 12, was the eve of the Day of Atonement. During the day, a further 2,196 Warsaw Jews, most of them women and children, were rounded up, sent to Treblinka, and gassed, bringing the total number of deportees in the previous seven weeks to 253,741. There were now, in the Warsaw ghetto, no more than fifty-five thousand Jews, most of them 'exempt workers', some, 'wildcats' in hiding. A further eight thousand Jews had managed to cross illegally from the ghetto to 'Aryan' Warsaw.[79]

In each deportation, whether to Treblinka, Belzec, Sobibor or Chelmno, Jews tried to jump from the trains. But armed guards shot most of them down. When yet more Jews from Jaworow were deported to Belzec at the beginning of September, 'Youthful Jadzia Beer got her skirt caught in the car window. She dangled in mid-air until a Nazi guard "helped" her with a bullet through the heart.'[80]

No corner of Nazi-controlled Europe, or of occupied Russia, was too distant for the murderers of Jews to reach it. On September 7, as the German army reached the Caucasus in their drive towards the Caspian Sea, the Jews of remote and isolated Kislovodsk were told that, 'for the purpose of colonizing sparsely populated districts of the Ukraine', all those with 'no permanent abode' were to present themselves at the railway station in two days' time, at six in the morning. Every Jew was to bring luggage 'not exceeding twenty kilogrammes in weight' and food 'for a minimum of two days'. Further food would be provided by the German authorities 'at the railway stations'. Also 'subject to transfer' were Jews who had been baptised.[81]

Two thousand Jews assembled at Kislovodsk railway station in the early hours of September 9. They boarded the train, and set off. Not to the distant Ukraine, however, but to the nearby spa of Mineralnye Vody, where they were taken out of the train, marched two and a half kilometres to an anti-tank ditch, and shot. Also brought to this spot, and killed, were Jews from the nearby towns of Essentuki and Piatigorsk.[82]

In the German-occupied Volhynia, the Jews of Krzemieniec awaited the moment when the SS would seek to destroy their ghetto, where an underground youth organisation had been able to procure arms and even German documents. These young men believed that by taking up arms outside the ghetto at the decisive moment, they would be able to prevent the SS entering the ghetto. They were mistaken: on September 9 the ghetto was unexpectedly surrounded by gendarmes and police, forestalling the youngsters' plan to draw them into battle outside the ghetto walls.

A stubborn struggle began within the ghetto itself. On the first day of battle six German soldiers and policemen were killed, and ten on the second day. Still surrounded on the third day, the fighters set fire to the ghetto, which burnt for a full week, during which time the battle continued until the last defender was killed.[83]

On September 19, the three thousand Jews of the Volhynian town of Tuczyn were ordered into a ghetto, in which there were only sixty buildings. Three days later, Jews from several nearby villages, and young men who worked on peasants' farms outside the ghetto, reported that Russian prisoners-of-war were digging pits in the nearby woods. That night, German and Ukrainian police surrounded the ghetto, and on the following morning the head of the Rowne Gestapo appeared and ordered the Chairman of the Jewish Council, now Getzel Schwartzman, and two of his assistants, Meir Himmelfarb and Tuwia Czuwak, to assemble all the Jews at the ghetto gate, ostensibly to select young workers for work elsewhere. Schwartzman, Himmelfarb and Czuwak at once gathered the Jews in the synagogue and urged them to set fire to the ghetto, rather than accept slaughter, unchallenged. Another Council member, Aharon Markish, distributed petrol and axes.

In the early hours of September 24, at 3.30 in the morning, German and Ukrainian policemen began shooting into the ghetto. Those Jews who possessed pistols shot back and, at the same time, set the ghetto on fire. As the German shooting intensified, some Jews threw themselves into the flames, or drowned themselves in wells. Others, armed with axes, ran towards the barbed-wire fences and escaped. Out of three thousand Jews in the ghetto, two thousand made their way to the forest. But in a three-day manhunt, German and Ukrainian police, helped by local Ukrainian peasants, rounded up a thousand of those who had escaped, brought them to the

Jewish cemetery, and shot them. Getzel Schwarztman, unable to break out of the German cordon, surrendered, asking to die in the Jewish cemetery. His request was granted; he was shot by the graves of his ancestors.[84]

On the fourth day after the escape from Tuczyn, three hundred woman and children came back to the ghetto. Lack of food and the cold nights had been too much for them to bear. To tempt them back, the Germans had promised to let them live. On their return all were shot. The remaining seven hundred escapees fended as best they could. But only fifteen survived the war. Six days later, on September 29, eight hundred and fifty Jews were killed during a similar break-out attempt at Serniki. Only one hundred and fifty reached the forest. Of these, only ten survived the war.[85]

The problem of survival in the woods was compounded by the frequent hostility of other partisan groups, and of bands of escaped Soviet prisoners-of-war. Shmuel Krakowski, the historian of the forest fugitives, has described how these hostile bands 'quickly learned to rob the unarmed Jews of their meagre possessions'. The Jews prepared bunkers for themselves in the forest, but the assaults on them became more and more frequent. In addition to these assaults, acts of fraud often took place. The Russians, wrote Krakowski, 'saw that what the Jews most wanted were arms, and promised to supply them. Deceptively, they took money from the Jews, and then disappeared.' There was also 'a plague of rape': armed groups of former Soviet soldiers, escaped prisoners-of-war, 'attacked Jewish bunkers in order to take defenceless Jewish women'. Zipora Koren, who survived in the Parczew forests near Lublin, 'tells of how Russian partisans bound an old woman, tied her to a tree, and tortured her, because she refused to reveal the hiding place of her daughter whom they schemed to rape'.

This was not an isolated incident. When a Jewish woman, Sarah, from the town of Parczew, resisted an attempt by a Soviet partisan, Alyosha Vasilevich, to rape her, Vasilevich killed her. Her murder was avenged by a Jewish partisan, who killed Vasilevich. Such incidents, coming as they did on top of frequent German searches through the forest, gave added danger to those who sought to survive in hiding and had no other place of refuge.[86]

A new Jewish Year, 5,703, had come into being. A new Day of Atonement had passed. The slaughter was unabated. At Stolpce, on

September 23, the ghetto was surrounded by German soldiers. Pits had been prepared outside a nearby village. Hundreds of Jews hid in cellars. The Germans entered the ghetto, shooting and searching. Eliezer Melamed later recalled how he and his girl friend found a room in which to hide behind some sacks of flour. A mother and her three children followed them into the house. The mother hid in one corner of the room, the three children in another.

The Germans entered the room and discovered the children. One of the children, a young boy, began to scream, 'Mama! Mama!' as the Germans dragged the children away. But another of them, aged four, shouted to his brother in Yiddish, 'Zog nit "Mameh". Men vet ir oich zunemen.' 'Don't say "Mama", they'll take her too.'

The boy stopped screaming. The mother remained silent. Her children were dragged away. The mother was saved. 'I will always hear that,' Melamed recalled, 'especially at night: "Zog nit Mameh." "Don't say Mama." And I will always remember the sight of the mother as she watched her children being dragged away by the Germans. She was hitting her head against the wall, as if to punish herself for remaining silent, for wanting to live.'[87]

25

September – November 1942:
the spread of resistance

BY THE END OF SEPTEMBER 1942 German troops stood victorious throughout Europe. The Soviet Union was still struggling to restrain the onward thrust of the German armies. Stalingrad was threatened, and with it Russia's river lifeline, the Volga. In the Caucasus, German troops stood poised to strike at the oil wells of Baku, on the shores of the Caspian. Britain, still battling in North Africa, was as yet without the means to launch a major invasion of Europe. Germany was supreme. And with her supremacy came the thirst for Jewish blood; for the completion of the 'final solution'.

The surviving Jews of Poland and western Russia had no means of escape. The Jews of Germany, Austria and Czechoslovakia were likewise trapped within the iron ring of Nazi rule. But in Denmark, Italy, Bulgaria and Hungary the Jews were as yet untouched, and on September 24 Martin Luther, of the German Foreign Ministry, passed on to those concerned von Ribbentrop's instructions 'to hurry as much as possible the evacuation of Jews from the various countries of Europe'. For a start, he wrote, negotiations should begin with the governments of Bulgaria, Hungary and Denmark 'with the object of starting the evacuation of the Jews of these countries'.[1]

Negotiations were also begun by Germany with the Italian authorities in Croatia. But within three weeks Siegfried Kasche, Hitler's envoy in Croatia, had reported that General Roatta, the Italian military commander, had 'flatly refused' to hand over Jews in his zone to the German army. Four days later Kasche reported that some of Mussolini's subordinates have 'apparently been influenced' by opposition in the Vatican to German-style anti-Semitism.[2]

No Jews were deported from Italy to the death camps until after the fall of Mussolini and the German occupation of northern Italy in the autumn of 1943. But from France, Belgium and Holland the deportations to Birkenau continued, despite several local protests. On September 24, in Brussels, Cardinal Van Roey and Queen Elizabeth both intervened with the German occupation authorities after the arrest of six leading members of the Jewish community. As a result of their intervention, five were released. The sixth, Edward Rotbel, Secretary of the Belgian Jewish Community, was a Hungarian citizen, and thus a citizen of an 'Allied country'. He was deported to Birkenau two days later.[3]

Among those gassed at Birkenau in the last week of September 1942 were several hundred from Slovakia and 806 from France on September 23; 481 from France on September 25, including René, the brother of Léon Blum, the former French Prime Minister; several hundred from Holland on September 26; 897 from France on September 27, several hundred from Belgium on September 28, among them Edward Rotbel; and a further 685 from France on September 29: at least four thousand in a single week.[4]

As the killing continued, resistance spread. On September 24, as pits were being dug outside the White Russian town of Korzec, Moshe Krasnostavski, a member of the Jewish Council, set himself and his house aflame. Other Jews helped to set the ghetto ablaze, and several dozen broke out of the German and Ukrainian cordon, among them Moshe Gildenmann, who then formed and led a Jewish partisan band. But in the break-out, two thousand Jews were killed. Such were the fearsome odds.[5] Five days later, at nearby Serniki, three hundred Jews escaped during the round-up, the chairman of the Jewish Council, Shlomo Turfkenitz, having given his house to the escapees. His Chief Assistant on the Council, Shimon Rosenzweig, later died fighting with the partisans.[6]

On September 25, in Kaluszyn, near Warsaw, the Chairman of the Jewish Council, Abraham Gamzu, had refused a Gestapo demand to deliver Jews for 'resettlement'. He was shot in his home.[7] Two thousand Jews were then deported to Treblinka, and killed.[8]

The death camps were working at fever pitch: and piling up in huts and yards was a mountain of belongings. On September 26 a senior SS officer, Lieutenant-General August Frank, sent the Auschwitz camp administration, as well as the head of administration in the Lublin region, a note of what was to be done with the 'property of the evacuated Jews'. Foreign currency, jewellery, precious stones, pearls, and 'gold from teeth' were to go to the SS for 'immediate delivery' to the German Reichsbank. Watches, clocks, alarm clocks, fountain pens, electric and hand razors, pocketknives, scissors, flashlights, wallets and purses were to be cleaned, 'evaluated' and 'delivered quickly' to front line troops.

The troops would be able to buy these items. No officer or soldier could buy more than one watch. The proceeds would go 'to the Reich'. Gold watches would be distributed to the SS. Underwear and footwear would be sorted, valued, and given, in the main, to Ethnic Germans. Women's clothing, including footwear, children's clothing and children's underwear was to be sold to Ethnic Germans. Underwear of pure silk was to be handed over to the Reich Ministry of Economics.

Quilts, woollen blankets, thermos flasks, earflaps, combs, table knives, forks, spoons and knapsacks; all were listed. So too were sheets, pillows, towels and table cloths. All were to go to Ethnic Germans. Spectacles and eye-glasses were to go to the Medical Office of the Army. Gold frames were to go to the SS. 'Valuable furs' were likewise to go to the SS. Prices were to be established for each item: 'for instance, one pair of used men's trousers, 3 Reichsmarks; one woollen blanket, 6 Reichsmarks etc.' It was to be 'strictly observed that the Jewish star is removed from all garments and outer garments which are to be delivered'. All items should be searched 'for hidden valuables sewn in'.[9] Within two weeks, fifty kilogrammes of the dental gold already accumulated were to be sent to the SS for its own dental needs, all additional amounts to be sent to the Reichsbank.[10]

From the first days of the war, the destruction of Jewish life in German-occupied Europe had been parallelled by the acquisition of Jewish property. Killing and looting had gone hand in hand. Nor was this the spontaneous looting of armies and soldiers, but the deliberate and systematic search for every type of wealth that could be seized or sequestered. Shops, businesses and factories had been taken first, transferred without recompense to local Ethnic Germans or to the German war machine. Furs, jewellery, radios, even pets had been taken next. Almost every week notices were posted up in cities and ghettos announcing some new confiscation.

At the end of the path of this deliberate impoverishment of a whole people came the looting of their last meagre possessions, their bundles, the clothes they were wearing, even their hair, at the edge of the death pit or on the final approach to the gas-chamber. Nor was that the very end: even from the corpses the last ounce of a gold tooth had to be extracted.

Under the Nazi system, murder had become as profitable as commerce; even more so, for there had been nothing to pay, no bargain to strike, only the point of a gun and the lash of a whip, and the wealth and possessions of many generations lay in the palm of the conqueror.

For nearly six weeks, the Swiss frontier police had been sending back hundreds of Jews who had crossed over the border into Switzerland from France. 'Under current practice', explained a Swiss Police Instruction of September 25, 'refugees on the grounds of race alone are not political refugees.' Since 1938, more than twenty-eight thousand Jews had been allowed into Switzerland. Now, more than nine thousand were to be refused entry, and sent back across the border.

One witness of the fate of these Jews was a Swiss woman, Madame Francken, who lived at the Swiss border village of Novel, near the town of Saint-Gingolph. Recalling two Czech Jews, a brother and a sister, who had managed to cross over to Swiss soil, Madam Francken wrote:

> We never found out what became of those two! The notorious Sergeant Arretaz of Saint-Gingolph turned people back like a sadist, whereas his confrère, the customs officer, ran and hid so as not to see the agonizing cortège of those sent back to the border, straight into the hands of the French militia.
>
> Two of these poor wretched creatures slit their wrists on the bridge on the same day, while a woman (whom we had seen being hunted down in l'Haut de Morge) threw herself from the fourth story of the hotel in Saint-Gingolph where she was staying.[11]

Another Jewish couple who had succeeded in crossing into Switzerland at Novel were Elli and Jan Friedländer, Czech Jews who had managed, while still in France, to find their son Saul a safe haven with Catholic nuns. Their son, who survived the war brought up as a Catholic, later received the copy of two letters and a telegram written by his parents. The first letter was dated September 30:

> We reached Switzerland after a very tiring journey and were turned back. We were misinformed. We are now awaiting our transfer to the camp at Rivesaltes, where our fate will be decided in the way that is already quite familiar to you.
>
> There are no words to describe our unhappiness and our despair. Moreover, we don't have our baggage. Can you imagine our physical and mental state?
>
> Perhaps if you could intervene at Vichy we would be spared the worst. It is not the camp that we are afraid of. You know that. If there is the slightest possibility of helping us, do not hesitate, we beg you. Act quickly. There must be a solution at Vichy that would be less catastrophic for us. Don't forget the little one!

On October 3, Elli and Jan Friedländer sent a telegram from the camp at Rivesaltes. It read: 'Without intervention Minister Interior, our imminent departure inevitable. Regards, Jan Friedländer, 3548 Rivesaltes, Block K.'

Two days later, the Friedländers were deported from Rivesaltes to Drancy. They believed that they were on their way to Germany. From the train, they threw out their second letter, the first few lines written in ink, the rest in pencil. The letter was addressed to the Director of the Catholic Boarding School to whom they had entrusted their son for baptism and for survival:

> Madame, I am writing you this in the train that is taking us to Germany. At the last moment, I sent you, through a representative of the Quakers, 6,000 francs, a charm bracelet, and, through a lady, a folder with stamps in it. Keep all of this for the little one, and accept, for the last time, our infinite thanks and our warmest wishes for you and your whole family. Don't abandon the little one! May God repay you and bless you and your whole family. Elli and Jan Friedländer.

Publishing this letter thirty-four years later, their son asked bitterly, 'What God was meant?'[12]

Jan and Ella Friedländer were taken to Drancy. From there, with a thousand other Jews, they were deported to Auschwitz. Of those thousand, only four men, and no women, survived. The Friedländers were among those who perished. Were they able to derive any comfort from the fact that their son had been spared, by their efforts, that terrible journey? Among those deported with them, and gassed on arrival at Auschwitz, were more than two hundred children, among them the three-year-old Solange Zajdenwerger and her four-year-old brother David.[13]

On September 23, 2,004 Jews were deported from Theresienstadt to Maly Trostenets, near Minsk. There were no survivors.[14] Three days later a further two thousand were deported from Theresienstadt, also to Maly Trostenets.[15] Three days after that, a further two thousand were deported from Theresienstadt, 'probably to Maly Trostenets'.[16] Once more, there were no survivors. Among the dead were Albert Lob from Worms, his wife Katherine, and their twenty-four-year-old son Ernst. Also killed was Sussel Spatz, born in the Austro-Hungarian town of Nowy Sacz in 1864, whose husband Peter, sent first to Buchenwald after the Kristallnacht in 1938, had died in Dachau two years later.[17]

A meeting of railway officials in Berlin on September 26, resumed on September 28, reflected the new pace and comprehensiveness of the deportation plans. It was decided that one train a day would go from the Radom district to Treblinka, one train a day from the Cracow area to Belzec, and one train a day from the Lvov district to Belzec. Each train was to consist of fifty freight cars and one passenger-car escort; and each train was to carry two thousand people. A new rail track was to be ready in November 1942 to link Lublin and Chelm with Sobibor.[18]

In October, deportees from Theresienstadt were sent by the improved railway services, not to the small gas-vans of distant Maly Trostinec, but to the gas-chambers of Treblinka. Of one thousand deportees on October 5, none survived.[19] Of a further thousand on October 8, about twenty-eight escaped. The rest were gassed. Of the twenty-eight escapees, only two survived the war.[20] The three remaining deportations from Theresienstadt to Treblinka in October were more crowded: six thousand Jews in all. Not one survived.[21]

In Warsaw, following the devastating deportations of August and September, the doctors in the ghetto who had been studying the medical effects of starvation realized that the time had come to end their work. 'Never have I experienced a feeling with such force', wrote Dr Izrael Milejkowski, 'as right now, writing a preface to this work. I hold my pen in my hand and into my room peers the spectacle of death from beneath black empty windows of abandoned, sullen buildings, standing on deserted streets that are strewn with the remains of plunder.' Milejkowski ended his preface with a tribute to his fellow physicians in the ghetto: 'You, my associates in misery, were part of the community. Slavery, famine, evacuation, you shared them all. Death hung constantly over your heads. But by your work you gave the assassins your reply. And this ringing answer will resound forever. "Non omnis moriar!", "Not all of me shall die!"'[22]

Dr Milejkowski organized the final meetings, to hasten the typing of the accumulated material. Three months later, when the deportations from Warsaw to Treblinka were renewed, he was caught and deported. On the short journey to Treblinka, he committed suicide.[23]

Medical experiments on defenceless prisoners had continued at Auschwitz without respite. 'Today I preserved fresh material from the human liver, spleen and pancreas,' Dr Kremer noted in his diary on October 3, 'also lice from persons infected with typhus, in pure alcohol.'[24] Five years later he explained how:

It was like this: I had been for an extensive period of time interested in investigating the changes developing in the human organism as a result of starvation. At Auschwitz I mentioned this to Wirth who said that I would be able to get completely fresh material for my researches from those prisoners who were killed by phenol injections. To choose suitable specimens I used to visit the last block on the right (Block 8), where sick prisoners from the camp came for medical examination.

During the examination the prisoners who acted as doctors presented the patients to the SS physician and described the illness of the patient. The SS physician decided then – taking into consideration the prisoner's chances of recovery – whether he should be treated in the hospital, perhaps as an out-patient, or be liquidated.

Those attributed by the SS physician to the latter group were led away by the SS orderlies. The SS physician set aside for liquidation above all those prisoners whose diagnosis was *Allgemeine Korperschwache*, 'general bodily exhaustion'.

I used to observe such prisoners and if one of them aroused my interest, owing to his advanced state of starvation, I asked the orderly to reserve the given patient for me and let me know when he would be killed with an injection. At the time fixed by the orderly the patients selected by me were again brought to the last block, were put into a room on the other side of the corridor opposite the room where the examinations, during which the patient had been selected, had taken place.

The patient was put upon the dissecting table while he was still alive. I then approached the table and put several questions to the man as to such details which pertained to my researches. For instance I asked what his weight had been before the arrest, how much weight he had lost since then, whether he took any medicines, etc.

When I had collected my information the orderly approached the patient and killed him with an injection in the vicinity of the heart. As far as I knew only phenol injections were used. Death was instantaneous after the injection. I myself never made any lethal injections.[25]

On October 10, Dr Kremer noted in his diary two items of interest to him: 'Fresh material from liver, spleen and pancreas taken and preserved. Had a stamp with facsimile of my signature made for me by prisoners. . . .'[26] Five days later he noted: 'First frost this night, the afternoon again sunny and warm. Fresh material of liver, spleen and pancreas taken from an abnormal individual.'[27]

Four kilometres from Birkenau, in the village of Budy, Jewish women were brought to the schoolhouse which, circled by barbed wire, served as the centre of a small labour camp whose prisoners worked in the surrounding fields. There, in the first days of October, an incident took place of unusual savagery even for that savage and tormented region. An account of it was set down after the war by an employee of the Political Section at Auschwitz, SS Corporal Pery Broad, who learned of it from his superior, SS Lieutenant Maximilian Grabner. Summoned urgently to Budy by the camp guards, Grabner, his assistant, an investigator and two clerks entered Budy with what Grabner described as 'a feeling of curiosity'. His account continued:

The guard saluted them. They heard a peculiar buzzing and humming in the air. Then they saw a sight so horrible that some minutes passed before they could take it in properly. The square behind and beside the school was covered with dozens of female corpses, mutilated and bloody, lying in complete chaos. All were covered only with threadbare prisoners' undergarments. Half-dead women were writhing among the corpses. Their groaning mixed with the buzzing of immense swarms of flies, which circled round the sticky pools of blood and the smashed skulls. That was the origin of the strange humming sound which the newcomers had found so peculiar on their arrival. Some corpses hung in a twisted position on the barbed-wire fence. Others had evidently been thrown out from an attic window which was still open.

Grabner at once sought from the few survivors an account of the incident which had led to this gruesome scene. He was told, as Pery Broad later recalled, that:

The SS men, who acted as guards in the camp, used to get the German women prisoners to maltreat the Jewish women. If the former did not comply, they were threatened with being driven through the chain of sentries and 'shot while escaping'. The bestial SS men regarded it as a pleasant pastime to look at the sufferings of the maltreated Jewesses. The result of this unbearable situation was that the German women always were in a state of fear lest the tormented Jewish women take vengeance on them for their terrible lot. But the Jewish women, who mostly belonged to intellectual circles (e.g. some had formerly been students of the Sorbonne, or artists), never even thought of stooping to the level of the vulgar German prostitutes and of planning revenge, though it would have been understandable if they had done.

The evening before, one Jewess was returning from the lavatory and was on her way upstairs to the sleeping quarters. A German woman thought she held a stone in her hand, but that, of course, was only her hysterical imagination. At the gate below, a sentry was standing guard. As everybody knew, he was that woman's lover. Leaning out from the window, she cried for help, saying she had been hit by the Jewess.

All guards on duty immediately ran upstairs and together

with the depraved German women prisoners they began to hit the Jewish women indiscriminately. They threw some women down the winding stairs, so that they fell in a heap, one upon the other. Some were thrown out of the window and fell to their deaths. The guards also drove the Jewish women from the barracks into the yard. The German woman, who had instigated the butchering, stayed behind in the bedroom with her lover. This may have been what she originally intended.

The 'rebellion' was meanwhile mastered with bludgeons, gun butts and shots. Even an axe had been used as a weapon by one of the female capos. In their mortal fear a few Jewish women tried to creep under the wire fence in order to escape the butchering. They got stuck and were soon killed. Even when all the women lay on the ground, the fiends, drunk with blood, kept hitting the helpless victims again and again. They wanted, above all, to kill everybody, so as to destroy all witnesses of their atrocities.

At five that morning, the commandant of Auschwitz, Rudolf Hoess, was told that there had been a 'rebellion' at Budy, but that it had been 'successfully overcome'. He at once drove to Budy, Pery Broad recalled, 'and inspected the traces of the bloody orgy. A few wounded women, who had hidden among the corpses, then rose and thought that they were saved.' But as soon as Hoess left Budy, 'the wounded women were shot.'[28]

As the killing of Jews continued, so too did the acts of resistance, bravery or defiance. In Lukow, near Lublin, the Chairman of the Jewish Council, David Liberman, had collected money from the Jews assembled in the main square on October 1, believing that he could use the money to ransom the Jews. On learning that the deportation was to continue, he shouted at the German supervisor of this action, 'Here is your payment for our trip, you bloody tyrant,' and, tearing the money into small shreds, slapped the German in the face. Ukrainian guards murdered him on the spot.[29] The assembled Jews, four thousand altogether, two thousand of whom were Slovak Jews deported to Lukow five months earlier, were sent to Treblinka, as planned, and gassed.[30]

The deceptions were continuous. An eye-witness has recorded

how, at Treblinka, after the arrival of a train from Vienna, Sigmund Freud's sister approached SS Second Lieutenant Kurt Hubert Franz, who that day was supervising the arrival of the victims, 'and asked to be given lighter work on account of her poor health'. Franz 'assured her that her arrival in Treblinka was a mistake, in view of her poor health, and that as soon as she had had her bath, she would be put on the first available train back to Vienna.'[31]

Which of Freud's sisters this was, is not known; two of his five sisters were murdered at Treblinka, the eighty-two-year-old Marie and the eighty-year-old Pauline. Two other of his sisters also perished, the eighty-four-year-old Rosa in Auschwitz, and the eighty-one-year-old Adolfine in Theresienstadt.[32]

Under heavy armed guard, amid scenes of savage violence intermingled with cunning deceptions, the deportations to Belzec had also continued throughout the autumn: more than one hundred and fifty-five thousand in August, at least ninety-six thousand in September, and a further fifty-eight thousand in October. The October deportees included a thousand Jews deported from Sambor, two thousand from Drohobycz and three thousand from Skalat.[33] At the station platform at Belzec the deportees were met by a poster which proclaimed: 'First a wash and breakfast – then to work'. All were gassed.[34]

In Drohobycz, those who were sick, or who actively resisted the round-up, were shot on the spot.[35] Among those killed on the streets in Drohobycz was the novelist and short story writer, Bruno Schulz. In his writings, he had transformed Drohobycz into a fantastic world of the imagination. His last novel, *The Messiah*, he left for safekeeping, while still in manuscript, to a friend. But the friend also perished in the holocaust, and of the novel, nothing survives.[36]

In the Eastern Territories, the mass executions in pits continued. In August they had accounted for more than one hundred thousand deaths, in September for more than thirty-two thousand, in October for more than eighty thousand. One of these Eastern executions took place in Dubno on October 5, where more than three thousand Jews were killed. It was witnessed by the German engineer, Hermann Graebe, who had earlier seen the killings in Rowne. As he later recalled:

On 5th October 1942, when I visited the building office at Dubno, my foreman told me that in the vicinity of the site Jews from Dubno had been shot in three large pits, each about thirty metres long and three metres deep. About fifteen hundred persons had been killed daily. All were to be liquidated. As the shooting had taken place in his presence he was still very upset.

Moennikes and I went straight to the pits. Nobody prevented us. I heard a quick succession of shots from behind one of the mounds of earth. The people who had got off the lorries – men, women and children of all ages – had to undress upon the order of an SS man, who carried a riding or dog whip. They had to put their clothes on separate piles of shoes, top clothing and underclothing. I saw a heap of shoes that must have contained eight hundred to one thousand pairs, great piles of clothes and undergarments.

Without screaming or weeping these people undressed, stood in family groups, kissed each other, said their farewells, and waited for a sign from another SS man, who stood near the pit, also with a whip in his hand. During the fifteen minutes that I stood near the pit, I did not hear anyone complain or beg for mercy.

I watched a family of about eight, a man and a woman, both about fifty, with their children, aged about one, eight and ten, and two grown-up daughters of about twenty to twenty-four. An old woman with snow-white hair was holding the one-year-old child in her arms, singing something to it and tickling it. The child was crowing with delight. The man and wife were looking on with tears in their eyes. The father was holding the hand of a boy of about ten, speaking to him softly. The boy was fighting back his tears. The father pointed to the sky, stroked the boy's head and seemed to explain something to him. At that moment the SS man at the pit shouted something to his comrade, who separated off about twenty persons and ordered them to go behind the mound of earth. Among them was the family that I have mentioned. I still clearly remember a dark-haired, slim girl who pointed to herself as she passed close to me and said, 'Twenty-three.'

I walked to the other side of the mound and found myself standing before an enormous grave. The people lay so closely packed, one on top of the other, that only their heads were visible. Nearly all had blood running over their shoulders from their heads. Some of them were still moving. Some lifted an arm and turned a head to show that they were still alive.

The pit was already two-thirds full. I estimated that it already contained about one thousand people. I looked round for the man who had shot them. He was an SS man, who was sitting on the edge of the narrow end of the pit, his legs dangling into it. He had a submachine gun across his knees and was smoking a cigarette. The people, completely naked, went down some steps which had been cut in the clay wall of the pit and climbed over the heads of those already lying there, to the place indicated by the SS man. They laid down in front of the dead or injured people. Some of them caressed those who were still alive and spoke to them softly.

Then I heard a series of shots. I looked into the pit and saw that the bodies were twitching or that the heads lay motionless on top of the bodies which lay before them. Blood was pouring from their necks. I was surprised that I was not ordered away, but saw that there were also two or three uniformed policemen standing nearby.

The next batch was already approaching. They climbed into the pit, lined up against the previous victims and were shot. When I walked back round the mound I noticed another lorry-load of people which had just arrived. This time it included sick and infirm people. A very thin old woman, with terribly thin legs, was undressed by others who were already naked, while two people supported her. The woman appeared to be paralysed. The naked people carried the woman around the mound. I left with Moennikes and drove back to Dubno in the car.[37]

Two weeks after Hermann Graebe witnessed this slaughter in Dubno, Dr Kremer was present at another 'special action' in Auschwitz. 'Terrible scenes', he noted in his diary on October 18, 'when three women begged to have their lives spared.'[38] The women were Jewesses from Holland, three of 1,710 deportees, of whom 116 were sent to the barracks, and 1,594 were gassed. 'They were young and healthy women,' Kremer later recalled, 'but their begging was to no avail. The SS men taking the action shot them on the spot.'[39]

On October 17 more than ten thousand Jews being held in the concentration camp at Buchenwald, and several thousand in Sachsenhausen, were deported to Auschwitz. Among them was Fritz Beda, the Viennese satirist, who had been held in Buchenwald since October 1938, and who, under another name, had submitted the prize-winning song to a competition he had organized himself. The song ended:

> Whatever our fate,
> We still say 'yes' to life.[40]

On October 21 it was the turn of the remaining Jews of Szczebrzeszyn to be rounded up. Dr Zygmunt Klukowski, a member of the Polish 'Home Army' underground movement, witnessed the scene as SS men, German policemen and Polish gendarmes 'wandered about the city, chasing after the Jews and following after their tracks'. Klukowski's account continued:

> They drove them out of various hideouts, broke down gates and doors, broke shutters, and threw hand grenades into a few cellars and apartments. They were shooting with pistols, submachine guns and machine guns that were positioned in various places. They beat them, kicked them and were generally cruel in an inhuman way.
>
> At three o'clock, they took nine hundred Jews – men, women and children – out of the town, forcing them to run by hitting them with sticks and rifle butts, and shooting the whole time. Only members of the Jewish Council and the Jewish police rode in wagons.
>
> The action did not stop with their departure. They continued to look for those still hiding. They announced that death awaits anyone hiding Jews or their belongings. Those who discover Jewish hide-outs were promised a prize. The Jews who were caught were shot on the spot without mercy. The Poles had to bury the dead. How many – it is hard to say. Their number is estimated at four to five hundred. I will try to get the exact number from the municipality. From the numbers mentioned, it is possible to estimate that about two thousand are still hiding. Those who were captured were brought to the station.

Where the Jews were taken, Klukowski added, 'I do not know.'[41]

It was in fact Belzec, where all were gassed. With them were sent the Jews of Zwierzyniec, deported on foot to Szczebrzeszyn on the afternoon of October 21. Another Pole, Stanislaw Bohdanowicz, who witnessed this deportation, later recalled:

> The police were armed with rifles and pistols and each one had in his left hand a walking stick. Their facial expression showed boredom and indifference. Some of them took the Jews to the town square, the others got into the car and drove off. The shooting in Zwierzyniec didn't stop.
>
> All the Jews, women and children, were first gathered in the town square and then taken along the road in the direction of Szczebrzeszyn. They walked fast. The older and weaker ones couldn't keep up. These were shot at once in the back of the head with a rifle or pistol.
>
> Only now did I understand the meaning of those walking sticks. If one of the Jews swayed, the Germans hooked the sticks around their thin necks, pulled them out of the line and shot them. The road to Szczebrzeszyn was covered with bodies.

At one point, Bohdanowicz recalled, a Jewish butcher threw himself at a German 'in an attempt to snatch his rifle. He would have succeeded, but at the same moment another German shot him dead with his pistol.'[42]

For two more days, in Szczebrzeszyn, the searches continued for every Jew in hiding. Those found, Dr Klukowski noted on October 22, 'were shot on the spot, or brought to the cemetery and killed here'.[43] To Klukowski's amazement, many fellow Poles 'helped enthusiastically' in dragging Jews from their hiding places. One Pole, a gatekeeper, 'cracked the skulls of Jews who had been taken out of their hide-outs without the use of a gun or a pistol'.[44]

Luba Krugman, a Jewess in hiding in nearby Chorbrzany, watched while the Jews of the region were driven through her village. 'Hundreds marched slowly,' she later recalled, 'in broken rows, supporting the old and sick.' Her account continued:

> An infant's shrill cry pierced the air. The mother, sensing danger, covered the child with her shawl, desperately trying to quiet him. Instantly, an impatient German grabbed the unruly bundle and dumped it in the nearest ditch. Then he forced the sobbing mother into a row of marchers, and when she pro·

Jews ordered on to the balcony of their courtyard before being taken away for execution.

Jewish women and children, having been forced to undress, are led to the pit in which they will be killed. This photograph was taken at Misocz, in the Volhynia (*page 178*).

Emanuel Ringelblum, historian of the Jewish fate in Poland and archivist of the Warsaw ghetto, with his son Uri, a photograph taken before the war. He and his son were killed in Warsaw in March 1944 (*pages 659–60*).

Jewish partisans in the woods of German-occupied Russia.

An *Einsatzgruppe* murder squad arrives at its place of work, the Eastern Galician town of Drohobycz, autumn 1941 (*pages 170–1 and 173–4*).

The Lodz ghetto: Jewish women at work in one of the ghetto sewing factories.

Children in the Warsaw ghetto.

Jews ordered on to the balcony of their courtyard before being taken away for execution.

Jewish women and children, having been forced to undress, are led to the pit in which they will be killed. This photograph was taken at Misocz, in the Volhynia (*page 178*).

Emanuel Ringelblum, historian of the Jewish fate in Poland and archivist of the Warsaw ghetto, with his son Uri, a photograph taken before the war. He and his son were killed in Warsaw in March 1944 (*pages 659–60*).

Jewish partisans in the woods of German-occupied Russia.

tested, he struck her with his rifle butt and threw her unconscious body into another ditch.

Excited voices in the crowd were silenced by Germans
shouting: 'Vorwaerts, vorwaerts, los, los!', 'Forward, forward,
move, move!'

Minutes later, the laments of an elderly Jew, beaten by a
husky SS man, brought the marchers to a second halt. The old
man, apparently stricken by a heart attack, was unable to
move; but the German continued to strike him. Trying to put
an end to the senseless beating, the victim's son sent a powerful
blow to the German's red face. Another SS man shot the young
Jew in the back. He fell to the ground, covering the body of his
dying father.[45]

Later, Luba Krugman was to learn that among the Jews deported
from Zwierzyniec to Szczebrzeszyn on October 21 had been her
parents, Anna and Tewja Krugman. 'They refused to obey the order
of a German who marched them to the collection centre,' she later
wrote. 'They were buried in a mass grave in Zwierzyniec.'[46]

In the East, when Jews who had escaped the ghetto slaughter sought
safety in the forests, guarded by their own feeble forces, the
Germans mounted a series of military operations. On October 21
the Commanding Officer of one Police Company reported that his
men had killed, in the Kobryn area, two peasant families 'who
maintained contacts' with the partisans, eight 'accomplices of
partisans', one 'bandit' and five Jews, while a neighbouring Police
Company had seized a Jewish family camp in the forests along the
Brest Litovsk–Kobryn highway 'and shot 461 Jews'.[47]

Among the largest of the Jewish communities destroyed in October 1942 was the community of Piotrkow, where fifteen thousand
Jews had lived on the eve of war. Of these, two thousand had
managed to escape eastwards to the Soviet Union in the first weeks
of war. Those who remained inside the cramped confines of their
ghetto were forced to take in a further eight thousand Jews from the
neighbouring towns and villages. At two in the morning of October
14 the Piotrkow 'action' began. It was to last for eight days. About a
thousand Jews, including many who were too sick to leave their
hospital beds, were shot. Also shot in his bed was the baker Yehuda

Leib Russak, who refused to abandon his paralysed wife. She too was shot.

More than twenty thousand Jews were deported from Piotrkow. All were sent to Treblinka, and gassed. The convert Dr Shanster, the Turkish subject Jacob Witorz and his family, and the Egyptian subject, Kem, and his family, those Jews who had originally been allowed to stay out of the ghetto, were deported with the rest. So too, in the last train, was Rabbi Lau, who, on the eve of his departure, gave a sermon on the theme of *Kiddush Ha-Shem*, the sanctification of God's name through martyrdom. A witness of the sermon later related that Rabbi Lau spoke 'with as much pathos and enthusiasm as he used to do in the good old days, from the pulpit of the synagogue'. Lau told the Jews around him: 'Better a living death than a dead life. Everyone who is killed as a Jew is a saint.'

Although Lau had earlier received an offer to escape back to his home town in Slovakia, he had declined, calling now upon the Jews of Piotrkow 'to fulfil the will of God with joy'. He was then deported to his death.

The Piotrkow deportation ended on October 21. More than twenty thousand Jews had been deported and killed. Less than two thousand succeeded in hiding. In the weeks ahead, these 'illegals' were to face the daily risk of discovery.[48]

On October 23, as part of the process of Allied counterattack, General Mark Clark met in Morocco with the leaders of the Algerian resistance, to plan for 'Operation Torch', the Allied landings in North Africa. Among those whom he met was a Jew, Jose Aboulker, one of the leaders of Algerian resistance. As a result of this meeting, the United States provided Aboulker and his colleagues with 800 sten guns, 800 grenades, 400 revolvers and 50 portable radios. These arms were landed on November 5, enabling the resistance groups to paralyse the main strategic points in Algiers, and to prevent any effective Vichy response to the American landings three days later.[49] With these landings, the 117,000 Jews of Algeria were freed from the danger of deportation to metropolitan France, to Drancy, and beyond. But at the same moment, with the German occupation of Tripoli, 2,600 Jews were seized and taken to forced labour at Giado. For fourteen months they worked, in severe conditions, building military roads. During those months, 562 died of starvation and of typhus.[50] In Tunis, on December 9, German soldiers rounded up 128 Jews and marched them to a labour camp. One young Jew, who was sick, fell down with exhaustion on the march. A German soldier shot him dead.[51]

In Nazi-occupied Europe, the deportations continued. On October 24 the Jews of Lichtenstein were deported. Eight months earlier there had been a complaint from Eichmann's office in Berlin that a number of Jews in Lichtenstein were still being allowed to visit a public café, to eat there, 'and to have a cup of coffee'.[52] On October 25, in the eastern Polish town of Oszmiana, the Germans demanded four hundred Jews. In order to save the remaining six hundred, Jacob Gens, head of the Vilna ghetto, agreed that all old people should be given up. Many were hiding in the thousands of 'malines', or secret hiding places, in basements, attics and cupboards.

Reporting on this decision two days later, Gens told his fellow Council members in the Vilna ghetto:

> Today I will say that it is my duty to soil my hands, because terrible times have come over the Jewish people. If five million people have already gone it is our duty to save the strong and the young, not in years only, but in spirit, and not to indulge in sentimentality. When the rabbi in Oszmiana was told that the number of persons required was not complete and that five elderly Jews were hiding in a 'maline', he said that the 'maline' should be opened. That is a man with a young and unshaken spirit.
>
> I don't know whether everybody will understand this and defend it, and whether they will defend it after we have left the ghetto, but the attitude of our police is this – rescue what you can, do not consider your own good name or what you must live through.
>
> All these things that I have told you do not sound sweetly to our souls nor yet for our lives. These are things one should not have to know. I have told you a shocking secret which must remain locked in our hearts.

Gens had only 'regret', he said, that there were no Jewish police present when the 'action' was carried out in the nearby villages of Kiemieliszki and Bystrzyca. 'Last week', he explained, 'all the Jews were shot there, without any distinction.'[53]

Jacob Gens believed that by helping to supervise the actions, he and the Jewish police could save a percentage of those who would otherwise be killed. But not all his Council members shared his confidence or moral convictions. Early in the following month, Zelig Kalmanovitch noted in his diary: 'We have bought our lives and our future with the death of tens of thousands.'[54]

On October 26 the first deportations from Theresienstadt to Birkenau took place: 1,866 Jews were deported. On arrival, 350 men under fifty were selected for the barracks, while all the other deportees, the old men, all the women, and all the children, were gassed. Of the 350 men 'selected' for forced labour, only 28 survived the war.[55] In the next two years, twenty-five trains were to leave Theresienstadt for Birkenau, with a total of more than forty-four thousand deportees, of whom less than four thousand were to survive.[56]

From Opoczno, on October 27, three thousand Jews were sent to Treblinka.[57] During the deportation, a few managed to escape to the nearby forests, where they established a partisan group, the 'Lions'. Led by Julian Ajzenman, this group succeeded in damaging German rail communication in the Opoczno region, but not enough to halt the pace of the deportations.[58] During October alone, eighty-two thousand Jews were deported to Treblinka and gassed, among them the twenty thousand Jews from Piotrkow deported between October 14 and October 21.[59] A further seventeen thousand Jews were deported to Sobibor, among them eight thousand from Wlodawa and the surrounding towns and villages. Aizik Rottenberg, a bricklayer from Wlodawa, who survived, later asked:

> You may also wonder why eight thousand people did not fight the Nazis. But a hundred men armed with machine guns are more powerful than an unarmed crowd. The young ones would have tried to escape, but refused to abandon their parents; they knew it would mean the death of the older people, and how was it possible to leave behind the helpless little brothers and sisters without support?[60]

That same October, sixty-four thousand Jews were deported to Belzec, among them, on October 28, two thousand children and six thousand adults from Cracow. Among the adults was Gizela Gut-man, a leading pediatrician.[61] On October 28 a 'top secret' SS directive ordered all children's stockings and children's mittens from the death camp stores to be sent to SS families.[62]

On October 28, a former Jewish soldier in the Polish army, Mie-czyslaw Gruber, who was being held with several hundred other Jewish prisoners-of-war in the Lipowa Street prison camp in Lublin, escaped together with seventeen other Jews held captive there. Under the code name 'Mietek', Gruber and his fellow escapees established a small partisan group in the woods north-west of Lublin, taking under their protection Jews who had escaped five months earlier from the village of Markuszow, on the eve of their deportation to Treblinka.[63]

News had begun to reach the West that the Jews deported 'to the East' were being murdered by gas. Most of this news reached neutral Switzerland from Germany, and was passed on at once to London, Washington and Jerusalem. These reports soon found an echo in the speeches and declarations of Allied statesmen. On October 29 a protest meeting was held in London, under the chairmanship of the Archbishop of Canterbury. Winston Churchill wrote to the Archbishop, for those at the meeting: 'The systematic cruelties to which the Jewish people – men, women, and children – have been exposed under the Nazi regime are amongst the most terrible events of history, and place an indelible stain upon all who perpetrate and instigate them. Free men and women denounce these vile crimes, and when this world struggle ends with the enthrone-ment of human rights, racial persecution will be ended.'[64]

Inside Warsaw, the Jewish Fighting Organization had continued to prepare itself for action. On October 29 Eliyahu Rozanski, a member of the Organization, killed Jakub Lejkin, Szerynski's replacement as commander of the Jewish police in the ghetto. Rozanski's accomplices were Mordechai Grobas and a seventeen-year-old girl, Margalit Landau. Their act was met, Ringelblum later noted, with the 'heartfelt acclamation of the Jewish population'.[65]

Thereafter, thirteen Jewish policemen, those who had been par-ticularly active in the August and September deportations, were killed. Also killed, on November 29, was the head of the economic section of the Jewish Council, a hated, active collaborator.[66] 'We wanted everyone to know', Zivia Lubetkin later wrote, 'that from now on there would be reprisals for every criminal act committed against Jews.'[67]

In the Bialystok ghetto, the Jews received two messengers from the Warsaw ghetto, Tamar Sznajderman and Lonka Koziebrodzka. 'They had faces radiant with cheerfulness,' Bronia Klibanski later recalled. 'They brought us new hope, news and regards from the other part of the movement which, for some time, had been without contact with us.'

Bronia Klibanski added that the two girls from Warsaw 'inspired all of us with plenty of courage and hope. We began to believe that Vilna's ghetto, too, would be there to stay'.

The leader of the Jewish Fighting Organization in Bialystok was Mordecai Tenenbaum. He would meet his fellow conspirators, Bronia Klibanski later recalled, to the whistled tune of the Hebrew song, 'There in the Plain of Jezreel'.[68]

In Bialystok, too, resistance was developing. The historian Reuben Ainsztein has pointed out, also, that in that city the number of Germans and Austrians who helped Jews was unique in the history of the Jewish resistance movement in Poland. One of these was Schade, a German Social Democrat, and the manager of a textile mill.

Through a group of Jewish girls, led by Maryla Rozycka, Schade maintained contact with the Jewish resistance organization inside the ghetto and with the Jewish partisans in the forests, supplying them with arms, clothes and valuable information. After the liquidation of the ghetto he hid twelve Jews in his factory. All twelve survived until the arrival of the Red Army.

Another German who helped Jews was a man by the name of Beneschek, a Sudeten German and a Communist. Beneschek was in Bialystok hiding from the Gestapo under a false identity. As manager of another textile mill situated on the border of the ghetto, he employed both Jews and Poles, and was instrumental in making it possible for Jews to smuggle arms into the ghetto. Beneschek also provided the Jews with false documents and money, and introduced another Sudeten German, Kudlatschek, to the Jewish resistance organization.

It was Kudlatschek who was in charge of the motor pool of all the textile mills in the city. A number of Jews left Bialystok in Kudlatschek's own car, travelling in it to partisan territory, and transporting arms back to the Jewish resistance organization in the ghetto from Grodno and other distant, and for Jews inaccessible, towns.

The Jews of the Bialystok ghetto were also helped by a number of German soldiers stationed in the city, from whom they obtained a few weapons, and several wireless sets. Arms also reached the ghetto from Walter, a Viennese, and Rischel, a German, who worked as storekeepers in the 'Beutenlager', or 'Booty Stores', in Kolejowa Street; until their posting to a front-line unit, they enabled the Jews working for them in the Stores to take arms back into the ghetto.

Another German, Otto Busse, who was in charge of a painting shop attached to the SS units in Bialystok, helped the Jews employed in his shop to smuggle pistols and several rifles into the ghetto. Two other Germans in Bialystok were sentenced to death for helping Jews.[69]

Some Jews were helped, others were betrayed. Near Cracow, at the end of October, six members of the Jewish Fighting Organization who set off for the forests near Rzeszow, armed with pistols and a knife, were betrayed by local peasants. They survived the first German manhunt, but later, in a second, unexpected clash, five of the six were killed.[70] Inside Cracow, in November and early December, the Jewish Fighting Organization sabotaged railway lines, raided a German clothing store, and killed, in separate attacks, a German soldier, a German policeman, an SS man, a German air force pilot, two Gestapo detectives and a senior clerk of the German administration.[71]

By the end of 1942 the once vibrant pre-war Jewish community of Yugoslavia had been destroyed: at four camps, Loborgrad, Jasenovac, Stara Gradiska and Djakovo, more than 30,000 men, women and children had been starved, tortured and shot.[72] More than 4,500 Jews, escaping from their homes, joined the Yugoslav partisans. Of those Jews who fought with the partisans, 1,318 were killed in battle.[73]

At Birkenau, the corpses of more than one hundred thousand Jews gassed during the autumn of 1942 had been dumped into deep pits behind the farmhouse which had been converted into Birkenau's gas-chamber. As more and more Jewish 'transports' reached the camp, the two hundred men of the Sonderkommando, who had since April been forced to drag the bodies from the pits to the crematoria ovens, were joined by two hundred more Jews and ordered, as their most urgent task, to dig up and burn the remaining corpses.

Enormous pyres were built out of stacks of wood. The wood was then drenched in petrol, the corpses dug up, placed on the pyres, and burned. To dig up and then to destroy so many corpses, the Sonderkommando worked by day and by night, pulling the corpses from the pits, laying them on the pyres, and, when the fire died down, covering the ash with earth.

During November, as this task drew to an end, the Sonderkommando realized that they too would be murdered, to ensure that no witnesses survived of what they had done. A plan was made to escape, but was discovered at the beginning of December. The escape bid was foiled. As a punishment, almost all members of the Sonderkommando who were still at work were taken from Birkenau to the gas-chamber at Auschwitz Main Camp, where they were killed.

A few days later, three hundred Jews were selected from the trains reaching Birkenau from ghettos in Poland, to form a new Sonderkommando. Their task was to take the corpses of those who had just been gassed, including often their own families, and to drag them to new pits where the fires were never allowed to die down. After six or seven weeks, five members of this new Sonderkommando managed to break out beyond the camp perimeter. All five were caught and shot. Their bodies were then exhibited in the camp as a deterrent to any further escape bid.[74]

During October, rumours of impending deportations spread through the Bialystok region. Ephraim Barasz, head of the Jewish Council in Bialystok itself, believed that the city could be spared if its factories worked to fulfil the German needs. 'It is imperative', he had told his fellow Council members and the heads of the various ghetto workshops, on October 11, 'that we find means to postpone the danger, or at least reduce its scope.'[75]

Barasz was not the only person in the Bialystok region who did not believe that they would be deported. The region had been annexed to Germany in June 1941, and was entirely separate, administratively, from the Eastern Territories. 'People came from Slonim,' a girl from Siemiatycze, Helen Bronsztejn, later recalled. 'They were running away from the horrors over there. We didn't believe it. "People, why don't you listen," one man cried out. "My wife was killed. My son was killed." People said: "This is the Third Reich. They won't do it to *us*." '76

On 2 November 1942, however, on the twenty-fifth anniversary of the Balfour Declaration in support of a Jewish National Home in Palestine, the deportations finally came to the Bialystok region, though not to the city. Once more, the pattern of terror, courage, deportations, revolt and destruction was repeated.

From Siemiatycze, 3,200 Jews were deported; Helen Bronsztejn was one of the very few who found shelter in a Polish home. Resistance, too, was widespread. In Lomza, a member of the Jewish Council, Dr Joseph Hepner, committed suicide 'rather than cooperate with the Nazis'.77 In Marcinkance, the Chairman of the Jewish Council, Aron Kobrowski, called out to the Jews who had been brought to the railway station: 'Fellow Jews, everybody run for his life. Everything is lost!' As the Jews ran towards the ghetto fence, attacking the guards with their bare fists, 105 were shot. Kobrowski, who had hid in a cellar, was discovered, and, with his brother and two other Jews, began shooting with revolvers at the Germans. The Germans replied with hand grenades, ending the revolt. Only a fragment of the Jews succeeded in reaching the forests, where they joined the growing number of partisans.78

From almost a hundred towns, villages and hamlets in the Bialystok region, mass escapes took place. Almost all six hundred Jews of Lapy fled. Of four hundred Jews at Suprasl, only 170 could be rounded up; of Zambrow's four thousand Jews, almost half escaped; of nearly six hundred Jews in Drohiczyn, almost half escaped. But the recapture rate was high. Of seven hundred who escaped from Ciechanowiec, only sixty succeeded in avoiding recapture.79

Many of the Jews who fled found shelter with Poles. Some were betrayed by Poles. A few survived. 'My parents suffered death for having kept Jews,' recalled Henryk Woloszynowicz of Waniewo;

'my father was murdered on the spot, my mother was taken and murdered at Tykocin.'[80]

As the trains tooks the Jews of the Bialystok region to Treblinka, some managed to jump from the wagons, and to survive: eleven of the deportees from Siemiatycze survived in this way. But J. Kohut, a teacher, remained with his students, singing with them as the train proceeded the Jewish national anthem, 'Hatikvah', 'Hope'. All but 152 of the 3,200 deportees from Siemiatycze were gassed. The 152 became slave labourers in Treblinka. One of the few survivors of the 152 later recalled how, on one occasion, they were driven naked out into the snow, where many were shot. One of the Siemiatycze Jews to die in Treblinka, Samuel Priss, was killed with a pick-axe in front of his father. Another Siemiatycze Jew, Kalman Kravitz, saw his two younger brothers 'savagely beaten to death with an iron bar'.[81]

Samuel Rajzman, from Warsaw, was in Treblinka when the Jews from the Bialystok region were brought there. 'The most heartrending scenes took place that winter', he later recalled, 'when women were compelled to strip their children at temperatures of twenty to thirty degrees below zero in the yard or in open barracks whose walls were of thin plywood. The unfortunate creatures had nervous shocks, cried and laughed alternately, then wept desperately while standing on line in the cold, their babies pressed close to their breasts. The hangman lashed their naked bodies to force them into silence.'[82]

So massive had been the round-ups on November 2 in the Bialystok region, involving as they did more than one hundred thousand Jews, that thousands were kept for several weeks in special camps elsewhere in the region, before being taken to Treblinka. In one such camp, just outside Bialystok, guarded by Ukrainians, a few Jews were able to escape when their guards, overcome by a bout of particularly heavy drinking, passed out. Two of those who escaped eventually came back: one caught, and one of his own accord. Their fate was horrible, as a young married man, Meir Peker, later recalled:

> I had contemplated escape, but because of my small child, could not see us succeeding, and so we remained. There were a few other families in the same position. It was my misfortune to

have to stay and see what befell those who were captured by the murderous Germans.

A girl who had fallen behind the escapees was caught, and in the course of the terrible tortures which followed, admitted that she had broken through a board in the toilet against the fence and escaped. They tore out her hair and poked out her eyes with their fingers, and when she had lost consciousness, they killed her.

There was also a young man who had returned of his own accord. It seems that he was frightened of going into the forest and believed that they would pardon him and allow him to go back to work in his trade.

He was, undoubtedly, afraid of the Gentiles in the area, as they had handed over the roving Jews to the Germans. With his capture, the beastly and vicious tortures began. The German in charge of the Ukrainian guards broke the boy's hands, first one, then the other, joint by joint. This done, two Ukrainians stretched him out on a chair, still half-conscious, and broke his back: they then laid out his lifeless body, like an empty sack, and emptied their rifles into it.

I saw these things with my own eyes, and curse the day on which I was forced to witness such bestial atrocities. For many days this picture would not leave me, the face of the bound youth, contorted with terror from the tortures, the eyes protruding from sockets as if they were two superfluous items detached from the face. It is hard to forget.

Meir Peker also recalled the next stage of his deportation:

At midday a train arrived and a German with a stick separated the prisoners, some to the left, some to the right. I was parted from my wife and child. A Russian guard, one of the POWs, a Gentile as good as any Gentile, was pleased to announce to us that those on the right were to be taken to a labour camp, and those on the left to Treblinka. He already knew our fate. I never saw my family again.[83]

The deportations continued through the winter, to Treblinka and also to Belzec. On November 2, in Zloczow, the Chairman of the Jewish Council, Dr Meiblum, refused to sign a document stating, in order to justify the deportation, that the ghetto had to be closed because of a typhus epidemic. He was shot.[84] Among the 2,500 deportees from Zloczow was the Yiddish poet S. J. Imber, nephew of the author of the 'Hatikvah'. Imber's wife and friends sought to guard his last manuscripts. But later they too were killed, and Imber's writings were lost with them.[85]

On November 3 the Jews of Zaklikow were deported to Belzec. Dana Szapira, then eight years old, later recalled how, at the time of the deportation, 'there was a Jewish woman dentist. Her leg was broken. A German came, not a bad sort, and took her out on a stretcher.' The 'good' German then went off to see what could be done to help the woman. While he was gone, a German soldier, known as 'Moustache', came up. ' "What are you doing here?" he said, and shot at her, not to kill her, but to see her writhe. Slowly, here and there, here and there, she was killed.'

Dana Szapira and her mother were hidden by a Polish farmer. They survived, living inside a cubby hole in his cowshed. One day the farmer heard a knock on the door: it was a Jew, holding in his arms his teenage son. 'I have been hiding in the woods for months,' the Jew told the farmer. 'My son has gangrene. Please get a doctor.'

The farmer went to the Gestapo and told them about the two Jews. 'He got two kilogrammes of sugar for reporting them,' Dana Szapira recalled. 'They were taken away and shot.'[86]

Here, the same man had both saved and betrayed: a bizarre example of the disjointing of moral values, in the unending atmosphere of fear and suspicion. Not only did individuals succumb, but throughout Europe the hitherto apparently natural conventions of human trust were undermined.

In a study of Polish–Jewish relations in the Second World War, Emanuel Ringelblum wrote of how in Lukow the Jews hid in the surrounding woods for some time after the 'resettlement action'. It was 'a frequent occurrence', Ringelblum wrote, 'for Polish children playing there to discover groups of these Jews in hiding: they had been taught to hate Jews, so they told the municipal authorities, who in turn handed the Jews over to the Germans to be killed.'[87]

Confirmation of the flight of numerous Lukow Jews to the surrounding forests, as well as the part played by the local population in tracking down the Jews and denouncing them, is to be found in the diary of a local Polish teacher from Lukow, S. Zeminski, who wrote in his diary on 8 November 1942:

On 5 November, I passed through the village of Siedliska. I went into the cooperative store. The peasants were buying scythes. The woman shopkeeper said, 'They'll be useful for you in the round-up today.' I asked, 'What round-up?' 'Of the Jews.' I asked, 'How much are they paying for every Jew caught?' An embarrassed silence fell. So I went on, 'They paid thirty pieces of silver for Christ, so you should also ask for the same amount.'

Nobody answered. What the answer was I heard a little later. Going through the forest, I heard volleys of machine-gun fire. It was the round-up of the Jews hiding there. Perhaps it is blasphemous to say that I clearly ought to be glad that I got out of the forest alive.

In Burzec, one go-ahead watchman proposed: 'If the village gives me a thousand zloty, I'll hand over these Jews.' Three days later I heard that six Jews in the Burzec forest had dug themselves an underground hide-out. They were denounced by a forester of the estate.[88]

Rescue and denunciation; the historian is overwhelmed by the conflicting currents of human nature.

26

'To save at least someone'

FROM BELGIUM, FRANCE AND HOLLAND, and from several Polish towns, the deportations to Birkenau continued throughout November and December 1942. A Jew from Ciechanow, Noah Zabludowicz, later described the round-up in his town on November 5: 'As we were standing in lines on the day of the deportation,' he recalled, 'there was this woman who was holding a baby of a few months old in her arms. The baby began crying and whimpering. One of the SS men said: "Give me that child, will you?" Of course, she resisted. But he said this rather courteously, so she eventually, tremblingly, she gave him the baby. He took the infant and threw it – with its head to the road. And, of course, the child died.' As for the mother, Zabludowicz added, 'She could not even cry.'[1]

On the evening of Friday, November 6, in preparation for the deportation from Drancy, one thousand Jews were locked into twenty cattle trucks on the railway siding. Among the deportees was the twenty-one-year-old Leo Bretholz, an Austrian Jew who had fled from Vienna to Luxembourg in 1938, then fled to Belgium, then, in May 1940, to France. In October 1942 he had managed to find safety by crossing into neutral Switzerland. But his safety was short-lived. Arrested on Swiss soil by the Swiss police, he was sent back to France, as were nearly ten thousand Jews who crossed to Switzerland in search of safety in September 1942, when the Swiss Police Instruction of September 25 had denied entry to refugees 'on the grounds of race alone', claiming that they could not be considered 'political' refugees.[2]

On being sent back across the border, Bretholz was interned by the French police in Rivesaltes, then sent to Drancy. In Drancy, he later recalled:

There was hardly enough space to sit or squat. The train stood all night on the railway siding in the station of Drancy–Le Bourget. In the middle of the car there was one bucket to be used by the occupants for their sanitary needs.

After a few hours, the bucket was full, and human waste overflowed. Thereafter, the people relieved themselves directly on the floor. The process of dehumanization had started in earnest. The putrid stench was unbearable, but it concerned us less than the thoughts of what was so ominously lying ahead of us.

At 8.55 in the morning of November 7, according to its precise schedule, the train moved eastward. Leo Bretholz had already discussed during the night, with two friends, the possibility of escape. Now, as the train began its eastward journey, they were determined at least to try. His account of the journey continued:

> The moans of the elderly, the screams of the children, the 'Sha! Sha!' 'Hush! Hush!' plea of a mother to her infant, were being drowned by the clatter of the death train as it moved through the French countryside of contrasting bucolic beauty and serenity.
>
> My thoughts flashed back to my childhood. Then, the sound of a train had that soothing, even romantic, quality – and it made me dream of faraway places I would have liked to visit. At this time, however, it was striking a note of fateful doom and finality. The gamut of emotions accompanying the rattle of the train ranged from hysterical cries of despair by many, to absolute silence of fatalistic resignation by others.
>
> The scenes were unbearable to the witness, who had all intentions to keep a clear mind and a cool grasp of the situation. We needed to keep our senses intact, as our decision was made to escape before the train would reach the devil's enclave, Nazi Germany itself.
>
> Two parallel iron bars in the rectangular opening in the corner of the cattle car represented the only obvious obstacle to our escape. We had to go to work immediately. The mood of the occupants provided the impetus, and set the stage. Many among them shouted words of encouragement. Our decision would give them some measure of hope, if only symbolically.
>
> We took off our sweaters, soaked them in human waste,

wrung them out, thereby giving the fabric greater tensile strength. We then wrapped them around the iron bars, tourniquet-style. Working feverishly, we applied that twisting method until the bars showed some inward bending. Relaxing the tourniquet, we tried with our hands to bend the bars in the other – outward – direction. The bars began to give.

We repeated that process for several hours, until the bars were loose enough in the frame, we were able to bend them at will. Having achieved this, we put the bars back into their normal position. All we had to do now was to wait for darkness to provide the cover for our escape. It was now early afternoon, and our attempt was only a matter of a few hours away.

By evening, the din which had emanated from the ghost-like forms in the car throughout the day had somewhat died down. We were now six or seven hours into our journey to oblivion, and many had dozed off, collapsed from exhauston or fainted. An old lady on crutches – one of her legs had been amputated below the knee – pointed a crutch toward us, faintly uttering the French words: 'Courrez, courrez et que Dieu vous garde!' 'Run and may God watch over you!' This woman's gesture of encouragement keeps flashing back to me through the veil of time. I shall never forget her words, or her face.

With nightfall, the train was scarcely two hours away from the German border. 'It was a dreary, raw and cold November evening,' Bretholz recalled. 'My body was shivering, my mouth was dry, my cheeks felt feverish.' He was also afraid. His account continued:

We chose the moment of escape very carefully. It had to come at a time when the train would slow down for a curve. It also had to be timed correctly to avoid the floodlights which the guards were aiming over the entire length of the concave curvature of the train during the period of reduced speed.

At the propitious moment we bent the bars into the spread-apart position. I lifted myself, rump first, out of the opening, holding on to the ledge above it on the outside. The rest of my body followed. My right leg, testingly, reached around the corner for the coupling which joined our car with the next. I found it and was safely standing on it holding on to one of the rungs of the iron steps leading to the roof of the car.

My friend followed, using the same method. The train, at

that point, was going full speed as the two of us were standing on the couplings between cars. Something had held up our friend who was part of the escape plan, for it took him some time to lift himself on to the opening. As he appeared to have reached the outside, the train went into a slight curve, slowing down as we had expected.

At this split second, we had to take our chances and leap before the beams of the floodlights would fall upon us. We jumped. We tumbled into a ravine and held our breath for what seemed like an eternity. Our friend never joined us. He must have been frightened or he had been caught in the glare of the lights and discovered.

The train continued on its way to Birkenau. On arrival, 145 men and 82 women were selected for the barracks and forced labour. The remaining 771 were gassed. Of those who had been selected to 'live', only four survived the war.[3]

On November 9 it was the turn of Greek-born Jews, arrested in Paris four days earlier, to be deported to Birkenau. Among them were several hundred Sephardi Jews from Salonica, and their children, most of them born in France. One of these children, Salvator Cabili, was eight months old.[4] A further 113 Greek-born Jews were among the 745 deportees on November 11, together with 35 patients from the Rothschild Old Age Home in Paris. Six of these patients were over eighty years old.[5]

On arrival at Birkenau, at night, the women, the children, the old and the sick, were lined up to be marched to the gas-chamber. The young Slovak Jew, Rudolf Vrba, who had already been in the barracks at Birkenau for several months, later recalled the arrival of this latest transport from France:

> For the SS this was an easy load. These people knew nothing of ghettos or pogroms. They had never had their senses toughened by real persecution. They were docile to the point of apathy, in fact, and they did precisely what they were told without a murmur of protest, an utterly amenable mass of human putty in the hands of experienced artists.
>
> Yet these were the people who nearly made the SS panic.
>
> It happened at midnight in the cold winter of 1942. Men, women and children were queuing obediently for selection when something went wrong.

Every night a truck, carrying a harvest of dead from Auschwitz to Birkenau, passed at right angles to the head of the ramp. Normally nobody saw what it held and it was gone before anyone could even think about it; but that night it was overloaded. That night it was swaying and heaving with the weight of dead flesh and, as it crawled over the railway lines, it began to bounce and buck on its tired, tortured springs.

The neatly packed bodies began to shift. A hundred, two hundred scrawny arms and legs flopped over the side, waving wildly, limply in a terrible, mocking farewell; and simultaneously from those three thousand men, women and children, rose a thin, hopeless wail that swept from one end of the orderly queue to the other, an almost inhuman cry of despair that neither threats, nor blows, nor bullets could silence.

With one, last desperate lurch, the lorry cleared the tracks, disappearing out of the arclights, into the darkness; and then there was silence, absolute and all-embracing. For three seconds, four at the most, those French people had glimpsed the true horror of Auschwitz; but now it was gone and they could not believe what their eyes had told them. Already their minds, untrained to mass murder, had rejected the existence of that lorry; and with that they marched quietly towards the gas-chambers which claimed them half an hour later.

Yet the SS realised well what could happen if mass hysteria of this nature had time to catch hold of their victims, if the lorry broke down, for instance. Every night after that, a secret signal was given when it was approaching and all arclights were switched off until it was safely out of sight.[6]

One more camp with selection and gas-chambers was about to begin operation: Majdanek, on the eastern outskirts of Lublin. As at Birkenau, a percentage of the able-bodied deportees were sent to the barracks, to toil, torture and tyranny. The young, the elderly and the sick were gassed. On November 9, four thousand Lublin Jews, who had already been deported, first in March to a camp at Majdan Tatarski, and then, in September, to another camp at Piaski, were brought to Majdanek.[7] Yet another name had entered the vocabulary of evil.

As at Chelmno, Treblinka, Sobibor and Belzec, and as in Birkenau, the scenes at Majdanek had few, if any, parallels in the catalogue of human crime. 'It was a Sunday,' Janina Latowicz later recalled. 'A lorry was brought into the camp. A woman guard and a young SS man went into the children's hut and began dragging them out. They had whips. The children were whipped towards the lorry. They were thrown into the air. Many were flung against the lorry and the side of the huts, their heads were smashed open. They were piled into the lorry like filth.' The mothers screamed. Callously, the woman guard asked the mothers why they were making such a fuss. 'The children are going to the rose garden,' she said.[8] The rose garden was the gas-chamber, five minutes' drive away.

In Oslo, on November 11, while the deportation of several hundred Jews was being prepared, the Norwegian Protestant bishops issued a public protest: 'God does not differentiate between peoples,' they declared, and went on to oppose all laws 'in conflict with the Christian faith'. That month, 531 Norwegian Jews, men, women and children, were deported to Birkenau.[9]

More Norwegian Jews were saved than were deported. Among those who were saved was Henriette Samuel, the wife of the already deported Chief Rabbi. Her children were saved with her. A twenty-five-year-old Norwegian girl, Inge Sletten, a member of the Norwegian resistance, not only warned Henriette Samuel of the impending deportation, but then took her and her children for safety to the home of a Christian friend, brought them food and clothing, and, a week later, arranged for them to be smuggled across the border into neutral Sweden, together with forty other Jews.[10] In all, 930 Norwegian Jews were saved in this way.[11]

One form of resistance which had begun in Nazi-occupied Poland concerned the protection of those in hiding. In the woods around the town of Siemiatycze in the Bialystok region, Jews who had managed to escape the November deportation to Treblinka organized a small group, five in number, found other fugitives to join them, and tried to protect those Jews who were in hiding. Under the leadership of Hershl Shabbes, and in its early days with a single rifle, the Siemiatycze group, as it became known, threatened to shoot any Poles who betrayed Jews to the Gestapo.

This was no idle threat. In December 1942 a Polish peasant captured three Jews, among them Motl Bluestein, tied them up, and handed them over to the Gestapo in Drohiczyn, where they were tortured and shot. As a warning to others, the Siemiatycze group murdered not only the peasant, but his family.[12]

In mid-November the remaining Jews of Zwierzyniec were deported to Belzec. They were forced to take off all their clothes before boarding the train, in order to make escapes more difficult. 'But they tried just the same,' Stanislaw Bohdanowicz later recalled. 'Along the railway line, everywhere one could see the naked corpses of shot people.' Once, at Zwierzyniec railway station, Bohdanowicz saw 'a young, nude Jewess who had only been wounded. The railway police caught her, and took her to the Jewish cemetery, where she was shot.'[13]

Inside Belzec, there was no escape: on November 15 Rudolf Reder was a witness to the arrival of a train from the city of Zamosc:

It was cold. The ground was covered with snow and mud. In such conditions and in the middle of a snow storm, a big transport arrived from Zamosc. The whole Judenrat was on the train. When they had all undressed and stood naked, as usual, the men were pushed towards the gas-chambers and the women to the barrack-hut to have their heads shaved. But the leader of the Judenrat was ordered to stay behind in the yard. The Ukrainian guards took the transport away and the complete Belzec SS detachment surrounded the Jewish leader. I don't know his name. I saw a middle-aged man, pale as death, but completely calm.

The SS men ordered the orchestra in the yard to await further orders. The orchestra – six musicians – was usually stationed in the area between the gas-chambers and the mass graves. They played all the time – day after day – using instruments taken from the dead.

I was working nearby on construction work, and saw everything that happened. The SS ordered the orchestra to play 'Es geht alles voruber, es geht alles vorbei' and 'Drei Lilien' on flutes, fiddles and harmonicas. This lasted for some time. Then they put the leader of the Judenrat against a wall and started to beat him about the head and face with whips. Those who tortured him were Irrmann – a fat Gestapo man – Schwartz, Schmidt and some of the Ukrainian guards.

Their victim was ordered to dance and jump around to the music while being beaten. After some hours he was given a quarter of a loaf of bread and made to eat it – while still being beaten.

He stood there, covered in blood, indifferent, very calm. I did not hear him even groan once. His torment lasted for seven hours. The SS men stood there and laughed, 'Das ist eine hohere Person, Prasident des Judenrates!' They shouted loudly and wickedly.

It was six o'clock in the evening when Gestapo man Schmidt pushed him towards a grave, shot him in the head and kicked the body on to the pile of gassed victims.[14]

On a subsequent train reaching Belzec, the SS had to leave a hundred people out of the gas-chamber, having calculated that even the able-bodied Jews of the Sonderkommando would not be able to handle such large numbers. The hundred not gassed were all young boys. Rudolf Reder later recalled:

All day long they were employed dragging corpses to the mass graves and were constantly beaten with whips. They were not given a drop of water to drink – and worked naked in the snow and mud. In the evening, Schmidt took them to the mass graves and shot them with his Browning automatic. As he was short of ammunition, he used his pistol butt to batter some of them to death. I didn't hear a sound from any of them. I only saw them jostling with each other to be the next in line in that death queue – the defenceless remnants of life and youth![15]

In Cracow, a Jewish couple who had not yet been deported, Moses and Helen Hiller, decided that whereas, as a young couple, they might possibly survive deportation to what they believed would be a labour camp, their two-year-old son Shachne would surely perish. They had already made contact with two Catholics, Josef Jachowicz and his wife, in nearby Dabrowa, and on November 15 Helen Hiller managed to leave the ghetto with her son, and to reach the Jachowicz home.

Helen Hiller gave her son to the Catholic couple. She also gave them two envelopes. One contained all the Hillers' precious valuables; the other, letters and a will. One of the letters entrusted Mr and Mrs Jachowicz with Shachne, and asked them to 'return him to his people' in the event of his parents' death. A second letter was addressed to Shachne himself, telling him how much his parents loved him, and that it was this love which had prompted them to leave him alone with strangers, 'good and noble people'.

This second letter told Shachne of his Jewishness and expressed the hope that he would grow up to be a man 'proud of his Jewish heritage'.

A third letter contained a will written by Helen Hiller's mother, addressed to her sister-in-law in the United States, in which she asked her sister-in-law to take the child to her home in Washington should none of the family in Poland survive, and to reward Josef Jachowicz and his wife – the 'good people', as she described them.

As Helen Hiller handed the three letters to Mrs Jachowicz, she pleaded: 'If I or my husband do not return when this madness is over, please post this letter to America to our relatives. They will surely respond and take the child. Regardless of the fate of my husband or myself, I want my son brought up as a Jew.'

Mrs Jachowicz promised that she would fulfil the requests. The two women embraced, and Helen Hiller returned to Cracow. She was never to see her son again.[16]

The deportations within German-occupied Poland were almost over: 600,000 Polish Jews had been gassed in Belzec, 360,000 in Chelmno, 250,000 in Sobibor. Treblinka, where 840,000 were gassed, still awaited the German decision about the surviving 50,000 Jews of Warsaw.

Now it was in the forests and labour camps that the killings began. Throughout the winter, Polish peasants took part in raids organized by the Germans to track down Jews in hiding. 'The peasants,' noted Zygmunt Klukowski in his diary on November 26, 'for fear of repressive measures, catch Jews in the villages and bring them into the town, or sometimes simply kill them on the spot.' Klukowski added: 'Generally, a strange brutalization has taken place regarding the Jews. People have fallen into a kind of psychosis: following the German example, they often do not see in the Jew a human being but instead consider him as a kind of obnoxious animal that must be annihilated with every possible means, like rabid dogs, rats, etc.'[17]

At Karczew, outside Warsaw, four hundred Jewish forced labourers were killed on December 1.[18] On December 3, three young girls who had escaped from a labour camp in Poznan were brought to the Lodz ghetto and shot. The oldest of the girls, Sure Jamniak, had been born in Lodz twenty-eight years earlier. Matla Rozensztajn had been born in Radom: she was shot twelve days before her twenty-first birthday. Gitla Hadasa Aronowicz was only seventeen.[19]

The news of the labour camp executions, reaching Warsaw, stimulated the plans for resistance. 'The community wants the enemy to pay dearly,' Ringelblum noted on December 5. 'They will attack them with knives, sticks, carbolic acid; they will not allow themselves to be seized in the streets, because now they know that labour camp these days mean death.'[20]

In the labour camp at Kruszyna, near Radom, the Jews were told of 'evacuation plans'. Suspecting the worst, they decided to resist with knives and fists. On December 17, when they were ordered to assemble, they attacked the guards. In the fight that ensued, six prisoners were killed, but four escaped. The Germans summoned reinforcements: four machine guns and twenty-five armed Ukrainians. The Jews were then, on the following day, forced into trucks. But still they resisted deportation, and more than a hundred were shot refusing to board the trucks.[21]

Three weeks later it was the turn of the four hundred Jews imprisoned in the Kopernik camp in Minsk Mazowiecki to be destroyed. But as the SS and police unit approached, they barricaded themselves into the building and resisted with whatever implements they could lay their hands on: sticks, stones and bricks. After three Germans had been wounded in the first clash, the Germans gave up the idea of forcing the Jews out of the building. Instead, they opened fire on it with machine guns, and then set it on fire. All four hundred Jews died in the flames.

According to the testimony of the Polish doctor, Stanislaw Eugeniusz Wisniewski, a resident of Minsk Mazowiecki, this rebellion was headed by a tailor named Greenberg, whose entire family had been killed during the liquidation of the ghetto.[22]

To cut off whatever chance of haven might exist for any Jews who did escape from labour camps, the Germans published reiterated warnings to Poles not to help Jews. In Debica, on November 19, a public announcement had stated that, as from December 1, any Pole 'helping to lodge, feed or hide a Jew will be punished by death'.[23] On December 6, at Stary Ciepielow, the SS locked twenty-three Poles – men, women and children into a barn and then burned them alive on suspicion of harbouring Jews.[24]

That same day, in the Parczew forest, the Germans launched a four-day manhunt against more than a thousand Jews in hiding. 'We fled round and round in terror,' Arieh Koren later recalled, as Germans with machine guns, four small cannon and armoured vehicles penetrated the forest. 'We thought we had run twenty kilometres, but actually we circled an area of half a kilometre.'[25]

In the nearby village of Bialka, Jews found refuge with the villagers. But on the second day of the hunt, December 7, the Germans entered the village and shot ninety-six men for helping Jews.[26] The hunt intensified. As it did so, the unarmed Jews lost control, running, Arieh Koren wrote, 'like a herd of rabbits from a hunter straight into the hands of the Germans. They died easily, and lost one another. Afterwards, children without parents, husbands without wives, and vice versa, wandered about the forest.'[27]

On December 24, in a second manhunt in the Parczew forest, several hundred more Jews were slaughtered. The survivors, unarmed, freezing, and without food, were fortunate: that winter they found a protector, the twenty-four-year-old Yekhiel Grynszpan. Their saviour was from a family of local horse-traders. He entered the Parczew forest at the end of 1942, built up a partisan unit of thirty or forty Jews, foraged for food, acquired arms from the peasants whom his family had known before the war, and when German raiders entered the forest, he fought them off.[28]

Another Jewish group had begun to operate in White Russia, led by Tobias Belsky. By the end of 1942 it numbered 150 men, with eighteen rifles, two machine guns and one automatic rifle between them. Belsky encouraged Jews still trapped in the ghettos to escape and to join him. Among those who did so was Chaim Joffe, who came with a group of eleven young Jews from Nowogrodek. The

Belsky group attacked German vehicles, and took revenge against the families of German policemen. In an ambush at the end of the year, nineteen members of the group, fifteen men and four women, were killed, including Belsky's wife and his nephew, Gershon, one of the machine-gunners. The second machine-gunner, Wolkin, was captured and tortured until he died. Belsky's brother Asael, who was also captured, managed to escape.[29]

On December 4, in Warsaw, a group of non-Jewish Poles set up a Council for Assistance to the Jews. The originators of this Council were two women, Zofia Kossak and Wanda Filipowicz.[30] They knew full well that any Pole who helped a Jew, and was caught, could expect no mercy. On December 10, a few miles west of the Parczew forest, at Wola Przybyslawska, seven Poles were shot for concealing Jews.[31] It was not only the Poles who helped Jews. On December 13 Goebbels wrote bitterly in his diary:

> The Italians are extremely lax in the treatment of the Jews. They protect the Italian Jews both in Tunis and in occupied France and will not permit their being drafted for work or compelled to wear the Star of David. This shows once again that Fascism does not really dare to get down to fundamentals but is very superficial regarding problems of vital importance. The Jewish question is causing us a lot of trouble. Everywhere, even among our allies, the Jews have friends to help them.[32]

In Cracow, the Jewish Fighting Organization, although much weakened by earlier arrests and executions, decided to act. On December 22 its members, led by Adolf Liebeskind, attacked a café frequented by the SS and the Gestapo. Yitzhak Zuckerman, who had come from Warsaw that day, took part in a second attack, in order, he later recalled, 'to save what could be saved, at least honour'.[33]

Wounded in the leg, Zuckerman succeeded in returning to Warsaw. The Germans moved rapidly against the other members of the group, tracking them down to their hiding place. Judah Tenenbaum, snatching a pistol from a German, killed one German before he was shot by bursts of machine-gun fire. Liebeskind was also killed. His sister-in-law, Miriam, managed to reach Radom, where she hoped to organize a ghetto uprising. But she was captured there, tortured, and shot.[34] 'We are fighting', Liebeskind had remarked bitterly a few weeks before his death, 'for three lines in the history books.'[35]

Decimated, Liebeskind's group nevertheless survived his death. Some of them managed to escape altogether from 'Aryan' Cracow, intending, as Liebeskind's wife Rivka later recalled, 'to set up hide-outs, to work in forests, and to enable Jews to hide – because they still hoped that the war would end'. Their aim, she added, 'was to save at least someone to relate our story'.[36]

By December 1942, Volhynia was almost totally cleared of Jews. But in the town of Luck, a labour camp had been established for some five hundred young Jews allocated tasks by the German civilian administration in the town. On December 11, a Christian woman informed the head of the Jewish workers, a man by the name of Sawicki, that she had heard from the son of the Ukrainian mayor that the camp was about to be liquidated. Sawicki immediately organized plans for revolt. The centre of these preparations was the carpentry shop where two carpenters, Guz and Shulman, and a tinsmith, Moshe, equipped with a single pistol, put together a small pile of knives, acid, iron bars and bricks which they removed from the walls of their building.

On the morning of Saturday, December 12, the Germans approached the camp. Another carpenter, Bronstein, opened fire with the pistol. Others scattered acid, burning the face of the German commander. The Germans withdrew from the camp and began to shoot.

Later that day, the Germans entered the camp once more, and the Jews gave battle. By evening the revolt was over. Some of the defenders had been killed and some were shot afterwards.[37]

Because of the growing Jewish resistance, many different deceptions were devised. On 15 December 1942 the Jews of Holland learned that eighty-three letters and eighteen postcards had been received from the deportees at Birkenau, and another thirty-seven from those deported to Theresienstadt and Monowitz. According to the information bulletin of the Jewish Council, in Birkenau work was said to be rather hard but supplies and living conditions not unsatisfactory. In Monowitz, the postcards reported, 'The food is good, with hot lunches, cheese and jam sandwiches in the evenings.

. . . We have central heating and sleep under two blankets. There are magnificent shower arrangements with hot and cold water.'

In the information bulletin of December 16 it was admitted that only two postcards had come from Theresienstadt. But on that same day a further twenty-nine letters and twenty-four postcards arrived, describing Theresienstadt as 'a friendly town with broad streets and lovely gardens, and single-storey houses. The women and children seem to be very well looked after.' The letters also suggested that it was possible to get help with rough work, 'and that those who wished could take a nap in the afternoon. . . .'[38]

Also on December 16, a Jewess with the first name Laja, who was in a train of deportees being taken from Plonsk to Auschwitz, managed to throw a postcard out of the train as it passed through the Warsaw suburb of Praga. The postcard was addressed to a friend of hers who lived in the Warsaw ghetto. 'Being at Praga station', she wrote, 'I am writing a couple of words to you. We are going nobody knows where. Be well! Laja.'[39]

On the following day, December 17, this same deportation train was passing through Czestochowa. There, another Jewess, her first name was Gitla, also managed to throw out a postcard, likewise addressed to a friend of hers in the Warsaw ghetto. 'We are going to work,' she wrote. 'Be of good heart. I don't give you our new address, because up to now I don't know what it will be.'[40]

The Jews deported from Plonsk on December 16 were taken to Birkenau, where, on December 17, 523 men and 247 women were sent to the barracks, and all the other deportees, including all children, and all mothers with children, were gassed.[41]

In the many slave labour camps through German-occupied Poland, selections and deportations were frequent. In one such camp, Zaslaw, as many as twenty-five thousand Jews were being held behind barbed wire; they came from the beautiful mountain towns of Sanok and Lesko, near Poland's southern frontier, and from more than a hundred surrounding villages. One Jewish couple, Jaffa and Norris Wallach, managed to escape from Zaslaw on December 17, leaving behind, as they later recalled, 'our parents and the major part of our families'.

Jaffa Wallach and her husband Norris found refuge in the house of a Polish mechanical engineer, Jozef Zwonarz, who lived in Lesko. 'He was the only link we had with the external world,' Norris

Wallach later wrote. 'His wife and their five children knew nothing about our hiding in that house.'

Zwonarz also hid Jaffa Wallach's brother Pinkas and her sister Anna. He had already, in September, taken their four-year-old daughter Rena out of Lesko, on the eve of the deportation to Zaslaw, and found the child a home with a Polish 'uncle', Jan Kakol, who lived in the forest. 'It is important to emphasise', Norris Wallach later wrote, 'that Zwonarz, and the Kakols as well, endangered their lives for pure human motives without any financial gain nor expectations.'

Those whom Zwonarz saved were to honour his memory for the rest of their lives; and to remember, too, how he would use his knowledge as a mechanical engineer, while 'repairing' German vehicles, to sabotage these vehicles, especially, Norris Wallach later recalled, before those vehicles set out 'for hunting Jews'.[42]

Since October 21, in Piotrkow, the Germans had carried out a series of systematic searches for the two thousand Jews who had escaped deportation. Group by group, those who were found in cellars and hiding places were brought to the synagogue, held under armed guard, and sent to nearby Tomaszow Mazowiecki, where they were deported to Treblinka together with the Jews of Tomaszow. On November 19, a further hundred Jews, most of them old people, were found in Piotrkow and brought to the synagogue. These were also led away, but not to Tomaszow. They were taken instead to the Rakow forest, just outside Piotrkow, and shot.

On November 25 the remaining 'illegals' in hiding in Piotrkow had been offered the chance of staying in the ghetto legally, provided they came out of their hiding places. Many did so. They too were taken to the synagogue. The building was then surrounded by Ukrainians, who shot into the building at random.

The Jews being held in the synagogue had no food, no water and no light. They had to relieve themselves where they could on the synagogue floor. From time to time, men with skills, such as carpenters or watchmakers, would be called for, and allowed to return 'legally' to the ghetto.

For three weeks the torment continued. In an act of selflessness remembered to this day by the surviving Jews of Piotrkow, a Jewish couple still in hiding, Yeshayahu and Tova Weinstock, gave themselves up and entered the synagogue to change places with their children, thus saving their children's lives at the expense of their own. Inside the synagogue, the wife of Moshe Niechcicki, who had the chance of being 'ransomed', refused to abandon her three children to their fate.

One young girl, the daughter of Benjamin Liebeskind, tried to escape by jumping out of a window. She fell into the hands of the waiting Ukrainians and was shot. Among those hiding in the ghetto was Moshe Wohlreich, who had earlier succeeded in escaping from one of the trains on its way to Treblinka. He too was caught, and brought to the synagogue.

On Saturday December 19, at 9.30 in the morning, forty-two men were taken out of the synagogue, and led along the road towards Rakow. The Gestapo was waiting for them there with a truck and tools. They were given spades and shovels, led into the Rakow forest and ordered to dig five long ditches. The Jews, who worked under the strict surveillance of two SS men, decided that if the Nazis tried to shoot them, they would kill them and run away. At 3.30 that afternoon, German and Ukrainian reinforcements arrived. The Jews refused to obey the command to take off their clothes. Some of them attacked the guards, and a few managed to escape. The rest were shot.

That night, the Jews in the synagogue were taken out in groups of fifty and led to the Rakow forest. As they left the synagogue, where the people already knew about the newly dug graves, some of them tried to escape. The Germans opened fire and many were killed and left lying near the synagogue.

The Jews marched to Rakow through the darkness, weeping, reciting Psalms and saying the 'Shema Israel', 'Hear! O Israel', as they went to their own funerals.

Forced to strip, 560 Jews were shot in the Rakow forest that night. Those who were only wounded were buried, together with the dead, in the mass grave. A tale is told of a certain Saneh, a former abattoir worker, who pulled himself out from among the corpses and, half naked, reached the home of a pre-war friend of his, the municipal dog-catcher, who was an Ethnic German. This dog-catcher, notwithstanding his previous friendship, gave Saneh over to the Germans.

A few other instances have been recorded of people who managed to get out of the mass graves. The Piotrkow historian, Tadeusz Nowakowski, relates that after one mass execution in the Rakow forest, a Jew managed to crawl out from under the mountain of corpses and ran wildly through the streets, 'bloody and half-naked'. When he reached the neighbourhood of the hospital, he was caught by the German police who shot him on the spot.[43]

Among those murdered in the Rakow forest that day was the thirty-seven-year-old Sara Helfgott, and her eight-year-old daughter Lusia. Among the survivors still in the ghetto was Lusia's elder brother Ben.[44]

Throughout German-occupied Poland, Jews searched for the whereabouts of their deported relatives. On December 21, M. Michner, a Jew who was working in the Schultz tailoring workshop in the Warsaw ghetto, sent a postcard to the Jewish Council at Turobin to ask about the fate of his son Izaak Michner. His card was returned by the German postal authorities with a derisive note: 'Your son Izaak Michner has gone to Abraham's bosom. He is dead.'[45]

In the Warsaw ghetto, three leading rabbis, Alexander Zysze Frydman, Klonimus-Kelmisz Szpiro and Szymszon Sztokhammer, wrote a prayer for those who had been deported: 'Almighty God, defender of all those who have been taken away, protect them against poverty and misery, give them the strength to survive and to withstand the torture inflicted by their persecutors. Provide them with food, and cause them to live in health, and to return to their families; and the smaller children, who have been torn out of the arms of their mothers and fathers, let them appear – according to the example of the Exodus from Egypt – and come back to their parents. . . .'[46]

Deception masked the unthinkable reality. At Treblinka that Christmas, signboards were put up at the station. Each of the station buildings was given a spurious name: 'Restaurant', 'Ticket office', 'Telegraph' and 'Telephone'. The main store containing the clothing of the victims was covered with train schedules announcing the departure and arrival of trains to and from Grodno, Suwalki, Vienna and Berlin. 'When persons descended from the trains,'

Samuel Rajzman later recalled, 'they really had the impression that they were at a very good station from where they could go to Suwalki, Vienna, Grodno and other cities.'[47] Rajzman also recalled 'huge signposts' with the inscription 'To Bialystok and Baranowicze', a station clock, and an 'enormous arrow' on which was printed: 'Change for Eastbound Trains'.[48]

As 1943 opened, a new German deception was sprung on the surviving inhabitants of the Polish ghettos. Jews were to be sent, it was said, not to 'work in the East', but to a neutral country, as part of a special exchange programme. Germans overseas would return to Germany. Jews from German-occupied Europe would be sent to Palestine.

At Opoczno, all Jews with 'relatives in Palestine' were asked to register. Many came out of hiding to do so. In all, five hundred registered. It was yet another trick. On 6 January 1943, all five hundred were deported, sent to Treblinka and gassed.[49] Aaron, a young man of twenty-two who was in this deportation, later recalled the journey. As the train set off, he and the other deportees hoped that they were travelling westward, to a neutral country. Then, the train stopped, and the engine was uncoupled. Soon, it joined up again at the other end of the train. 'Within a few moments the train began to move off,' the young man recalled. 'At first there was a terrifying silence. Everybody waited for a miracle to happen or an abyss to open.' His account continued:

> But the miracle did not happen, and within a few moments we knew definitely that the train had changed its direction and we were travelling eastwards.
>
> It was as though there was an explosion and a collapse in the carriage. People shrieked to the high heavens. The little children in the carriage could not understand what it all meant, but they also began to cry at the tops of their voices.
>
> I looked at my own family members and it seemed to me as though they had all grown old in a single moment. My little sister Malkale, who was nine years old, understood what it all meant and was weeping bitterly, 'Mother, but I never did anybody any harm.' My sister Rochele, who was twelve years old, clung to me and said, 'Aaron, I am terribly afraid. Look after me . . .' and she clung to me with all her strength.
>
> My sister Bracha, who was pregnant, wept in a loud voice.

She was about twenty-eight. 'But my baby hasn't even been born yet, and never sinned, why is he doomed?' Her husband stood stroking her hair. Looking at them I could no longer restrain myself, and also began weeping; but did my best to weep silently, so that my voice should not be heard.

It was now plain that the deportees were being taken to Treblinka:

I looked round at the people. They were images of dread and horror. Some tore their hair, some flung themselves about in despair, and some cursed with all their strength.

A woman clutched her baby to her breast with all her force. The child began to make strangled noises, while the woman whispered loving words to it and pressed it to her heart all the more.

'Look what she's doing, look what she's doing. She's gone mad,' came cries from all sides.

'It's my child, mine, and I want him to die a holy death. Let him die a holy death.' And by the time people succeeded in getting the child away, he was choked.

One Jew near us went mad. Round his neck was a white scarf. He took it off and tried to tie it to one of the iron hooks in the carriage wall in order to hang himself. People tried to stop him. He punched and kicked with tremendous force and cried: 'Let me hang myself!' They succeeded in dragging the scarf out of his hands and he collapsed in the corner.

A group of young men in the sealed carriage made plans to try to break out. But many parents argued against such a plan: 'Mother sat at a loss,' the young man recalled. 'What will happen to us?' his mother asked. 'Don't let us separate. Don't let us separate. Death is lying in wait everywhere. Let us die together, at least.'

After a few hours the train came to a halt. It was the middle of the night. The doors of the carriages were opened 'and the chill air burst into the carriage and beat down on the exhausted and fainting travellers'. The young man recalled:

Into the carriage climbed a group of Mongols and Ukrainians, submachine guns in their hands. The carriage was crowded from end to end, but still room was made for them. Everybody crowded and crushed together in fear, while they began to rob and pillage the passengers. Ample experience had taught them where such travellers hid their belongings. First they went to the women, tore off whatever clothes they were still wearing, thrust their hands into their bosoms and their private parts, and found money and jewellery. They pulled rings off fingers. Most of the travellers were exhausted and had no spirit of resistance. The few who refused or resisted were beaten with the rifle butts.

'Diengi davay!' 'Hand over the money,' they kept shouting and cursing and abusing. It had been clear enough that we were being taken to slaughter.

Among those in the carriage was the head of the Jewish Council of Opoczno, Przydlowski. It was clear, he told the deportees, that the end had come. 'Anyone who could run away should do so.'

Aaron and some other young men decided they would try to make a run for it. First, Aaron said goodbye to his parents. But, as he later recalled: 'When I came to my sister Bracha I almost changed my mind and wanted to go back on my resolution. "What has my unborn baby done? Why is he doomed never to see the light of the world?" she went on whispering in a tremulous voice.'

The young men made their plans, and jumped. The guards were shooting. Many were killed. But between bursts Bracha's brother managed to jump unharmed, falling into a ditch filled with snow. There, he sank in the snow out of sight. He was, he later recalled, 'in an alien and hostile world', but he had made his escape, and was to survive the war.[50]

In Radomsko, the German authorities assured members of the Zionist youth groups in the ghetto that they were to be sent to Palestine as part of a 'special exchange programme', whereby German nationals interned by the British in Palestine would be returned to Germany. But the chairman of the Jewish Council, Gutstadt, warned them that this was 'another Gestapo trick', and urged them to flee while they could. Hundreds did so.[51]

Acts of resistance continued, as did the reprisals which so deterred resistance. In Czestochowa, on January 4, several young men and women, members of the Jewish Fighting Organization, among them Mendel Fiszlewicz, were caught up in a 'selection'. They possessed only one pistol and one knife, but Fiszlewicz used his pistol to attack and wound the German commander of the 'action'. After the first shot, Fiszlewicz's pistol jammed, and he was killed by one of the guards.

As a reprisal, the Germans took twenty-five men out of the line-up, and shot them on the spot. Then, as a further reprisal, three hundred women and children were sent to nearby Radomsko, where the deportation to Treblinka was in progress.[52] All three hundred were gassed, together with four thousand five hundred Radomsko Jews.

From each death camp, the clothes of the murdered Jews were cleaned and sent to Germany. For those Jews murdered at Chelmno, the sorting of the clothes was done in Pabianice, south of the Lodz ghetto. The German administration of the Lodz ghetto then sent the clothes to the German People's Winter Aid Campaign, for distribution among needy Germans. On January 9 the Campaign complained to the administration that the jackets, dresses and underwear just received had not been properly cleaned. Many articles 'are badly stained and partly permeated with dirt and bloodstains'. On 51 of 200 jackets sent to Poznan, 'the Jewish stars had not been removed!' If those receiving the clothes were to become aware of their origin, the Winter Aid Campaign would become 'discredited'. A further complaint was that, despite promises, the Ghetto administration had supplied 'various assorted articles of clothing, but no whole suits'.[53]

In the forests and fields of the Volhynia, several Jewish resistance groups were actively engaged in sabotage of strategic railway lines, and the destruction of German storage depots. As soon as Soviet partisans entered the area, most of these units joined the Soviet partisan movement. Since May 1942, Moshe Gildenman had built up a unit of more than a hundred Jews north of Zhitomir. In January 1943, Gildenman's unit was accepted by one of the Soviet partisan brigades as the Special Jewish Fighting Company. Since August 1942, fifteen Jews who had escaped from Zhitomir formed a partisan group commanded by a former corporal of the Polish army, Haim Henryk Rozenson. They too joined the Soviet partisan brigade at the end of 1942.

Small, detached groups could not always survive the German manhunts long enough to find or to join a professionally trained

Red Army unit. A group of Jews who escaped from Olyka was almost entirely wiped out in January 1943. One of the groups that was organized in Dubno under the command of Yitshak Wasserman was completely destroyed in battle with the Germans. Of the members of the Radziwillow-Brody group, after several battles with the Germans and the subsequent manhunts, only one of their number, Yechiel Prochownik, survived to tell its story.

It is estimated that between fifteen and sixteen hundred Volhynian Jews managed to survive long enough in the woods to join Soviet partisan detachments; by the end of 1943 more than ten per cent of those in the Soviet partisan movement were Jews. In the Rowne Brigade, the commander of the reconaissance unit, Alexander Abugov, was a Jew, as was Dr Ehrlich, commander of the Brigade's medical services.[54]

In Minsk, on January 9, the twenty-year-old Jewish partisan Emma Radova was caught, tortured and killed. But she betrayed nobody.[55]

The deportations to Chelmno, Belzec and Sobibor had almost ended, the majority of Poland's pre-war Jewish communities having been deported and gassed during 1942. It was Birkenau that had become the focal point of mass murder of Jews from the rest of German-occupied Europe. On 2 November 1942 the head of the Ancestral Heritage Institute in Germany, Dr Sievers, wrote to Dr Karl Brandt, asking for 150 skeletons of Jews.[56] 'We have the opportunity', Dr Sievers had explained earlier, 'of obtaining real scientific evidence by obtaining the skulls of Jewish Bolshevik commissars, who are the exemplification of the sub-human type, the revolting but typical sub-human type.' Each head, Dr Sievers explained, must be detached from its body, dipped in preservative liquid, and put in a specially prepared hermetically sealed tin.[57]

The corpses were duly provided. Seven months later Eichmann was informed that 115 people had been killed for their skeletons: seventy-nine Jews, thirty Jewesses, four central Asians and two Poles.[58] In this way, mass murder was made to serve the cause of one of the most bizarre, and obscene, forms of 'science'.

Transports of Jews reached Birkenau every day, 'guiltless people,' Salmen Lewental noted, 'unaware of their fate.' As a member of the Sonderkommando from December 1942, Lewental was one of several hundred Jews whose task was to 'burn and smash their remains'. Other Jews, at the railway siding, gathered up 'all packages and suitcases'.[59]

These packages and suitcases were taken to a part of the camp known as 'Canada', the huts in which the Jews of a so-called 'Clearing Commando' would unpack them, sort them, and prepare them for dispatch to Germany. Hundreds more Jews, mostly women, were employed in the huts of 'Canada', assembly point of the remaining wealth and possessions of more than two million Jews. Rudolf Vrba later recalled how the camp Trusties, or Kapos, would give the order, 'Clearing Command, forward!'

> With that we marched into Canada, the commercial heart of Auschwitz, warehouse of the body-snatchers where hundreds of prisoners worked frantically to sort, segregate and classify the clothes and the food and the valuables of those whose bodies were still burning, whose ashes would soon be used as fertiliser.
>
> It was an incredible sight, an enormous rectangular yard with a watchtower at each corner and surrounded by barbed wire. There were several huge storerooms and a block of what seemed like offices with a square, open balcony at one corner. Yet what first struck me was a mountain of trunks, cases, rucksacks, kitbags and parcels stacked in the middle of the yard.
>
> Nearby was another mountain, of blankets this time, fifty thousand of them, maybe one hundred thousand. I was so staggered by the sight of these twin peaks of personal possessions that I never thought at that moment where their owners might be. In fact I did not have much time to think, for every step brought some new shock.
>
> Over to the left I saw hundreds of prams. Shiny prams, fit for a firstborn. Battered prams of character that had been handed down and down and down and had suffered gladly on the way. Opulent, ostentatious, status-symbol prams and modest, economy prams of those who knew no status and had no money. I looked at them in awe, but still I did not wonder where the babies were.
>
> Another mountain, this time of pots and pans from a

thousand kitchens in a dozen countries. Pathetic remnants of a
million meals, anonymous now, for their owners would never
eat again.

Then I saw women. Real women, not the terrible, sexless
skeletons whose bodies stank and whose hearts were dead.

These were young, well-dressed girls with firm, ripe figures
and faces made beautiful by health alone. They were bustling
everywhere, running to and fro with bundles of clothes and
parcels, watched by even healthier, even more elegant women
kapos.

It was all a crazy jigsaw that made no sense to me and seemed
sometimes to verge on lunacy. Beside one of the storerooms I
saw a row of girls sitting astride a bench with zinc buckets on
either side of them. One row of buckets was filled with tubes of
toothpaste which the girls were squeezing out on to the bench
and then throwing into the other, empty buckets. To me it
seemed thoroughly un-German, an appalling waste of labour
and material; for I had yet to learn that perhaps one tube in ten
thousand contained a diamond, a nest egg that some pathetic,
trusting family had felt might buy privilege or even freedom.[60]

The wealth collected in 'Canada' came from Jews who were alive
on arrival at Birkenau, but who were dead by the time their
belongings had been sorted. Just before being gassed, further
'wealth' was extracted from the women: their hair. On 4 January
1943 the head office of the SS administration wrote to all concentration camp commandants, including Hoess at Auschwitz, requesting them to forward human hair for processing at the firm of
Alex Zink, Filzfabrik A.G., at Roth near Nuremberg. For each
kilogramme of human hair, camp commandants would receive half
a mark.[61]

From January 7 to January 24, fifteen trains reached Auschwitz,
from Belgium, Holland, Berlin, Grodno and the Bialystok region.
From them, about four thousand Jews were selected for the
barracks, and more than twenty thousand gassed. To enable such
numbers to be 'processed' rapidly, and even to increase the scale and
pace of the killing, four new crematoria were under construction,
planned to come into operation in March. On the train from
Belgium which arrived on January 18, 387 men and 81 women were

sent to the barracks, while the remaining 1,558 deportees, including all the children and old people, were gassed.[62]

On the train which left Theresienstadt on January 20, 160 young women and 80 young men were taken to the barracks at Birkenau, and the remaining 1,760 Jews loaded into lorries and driven to the gas-chamber. Only 2 of the 160 women and 80 men survived the slave labour of the next six weeks. Taken to marshland four miles from Auschwitz, they were forced to stand knee-deep in the marsh, digging out sand and stones. They were barefoot, and dressed in rags. Many, as the historian of Theresienstadt has recorded, 'contracted frostbite and their festering fingers fell off'. But, crippled as they were, they had to carry on. SS women beat them with sticks and set Alsatian dogs on them. They had to rise at 3.30 a.m.; for breakfast they were given tea made of herbs; at 5 a.m. they marched to their place of work whence they returned between 6 and 7 p.m. to the strains of the camp band, carrying the bodies of their fellow prisoners murdered at work by the SS men. Their supper consisted of saltless hot water, with pieces of beetroot or bits of nettles swimming in it, and four ounces of bread.[63]

One of those who recorded some of the events at Birkenau was a member of the Sonderkommando whose twenty-nine-page notebook was found in 1952 buried near one of the crematoria. He recorded how, at the beginning of 1943:

> The gas-chamber was crowded with Jews and one Jewish boy remained outside. A certain sergeant came to him and wanted to kill him with a stick. He mangled him in a brutish manner, blood was dripping on all sides, when all of a sudden the maltreated boy, who had been lying motionless, jumped to his feet and began to regard, quietly and silently, his cruel murderer with his childish gaze. The sergeant burst into loud cynical laughter, took out his revolver and shot the boy.

The author of this notebook also recorded how another of the SS men at Birkenau, SS Staff Sergeant Forst, 'stood at the gate of the undressing room in the case of many transports and felt the sexual organ of each young woman that was passing naked to the gas-chamber. There were also cases when German SS men of all ranks put fingers into the sexual organs of pretty young girls.'

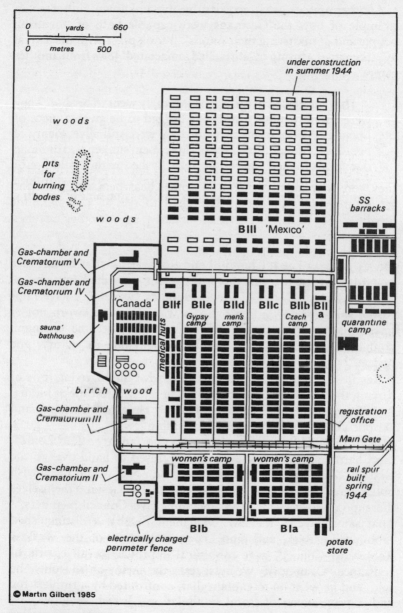

0   yards   660
0   metres   500

under construction in summer 1944

woods

pits for burning bodies

woods

SS barracks

BIII 'Mexico'

Gas-chamber and Crematorium V

Gas-chamber and Crematorium IV

'Canada'   BIIf   BIIe   BIId   BIIc   BIIb   BII a

Gypsy camp   men's camp   Czech camp

medical huts

sauna' bathhouse

quarantine camp

birch wood

Gas-chamber and Crematorium III

registration office

Main Gate

Gas-chamber and Crematorium II

women's camp   women's camp

rail spur built spring 1944

electrically charged perimeter fence

BIb   BIa

potato store

© Martin Gilbert 1985

AUSCHWITZ—BIRKENAU

Another episode was recorded by this unknown author as an example of how the Germans were capable both of 'torturing people and of mastering their minds'. It took place with the arrival at Birkenau of a group of 'shrivelled, emaciated' Jews from another camp:

> They undressed in the open and singly went to be shot. They were horribly hungry and they begged to be given a piece of bread at the last moment while they were still alive. Plenty of bread was brought; the eyes of those men, sunken and dimmed due to protracted starvation, now flashed with a wild fire of staggering joy, they snatched big chunks of bread with both hands and voraciously swallowed, at the same time descending the steps straight on to be shot.[64]

On 14 January 1943, Churchill and Roosevelt met at Casablanca in North Africa to plan the strategy for an Allied invasion of Western Europe. News of the Casablanca Conference gave hope to the surviving Jews. In Kovno, a wife who had sworn not to have children while disaster threatened now became pregnant, confident that Casablanca would be a prelude to victory, and rescue.[65]

Rescue was more than two years away for the surviving Jews of Kovno; there was little chance of finding safety by escape or hiding. At Pilica, in southern Poland, on January 15, a Polish woman and her one-year-old child were shot for hiding Jews.[66]

Jewish resistance continued to grow: on January 14, at Lomza, the Chairman of the Jewish Council refused to hand over to the Gestapo forty Jews 'of his own choosing'. Nor would the Jewish police agree to participate in the selection. The Gestapo themselves thereupon 'selected' the Jews, including two Council members.[67] That same day, in Warsaw, Menahem Zemba, a distinguished rabbinical scholar, and since 1935 a member of the Warsaw Rabbinical Council, gave rabbinical approval for all efforts of resistance. 'Of necessity we must resist the enemy on all fronts,' he said, and he went on to explain that, confronted by a ruthless foe and a programme of 'total annihilation', Jewish religious law 'demands that we fight and resist to the very end with unequalled determination and valour, for the sake of sanctification of the Divine Name.'[68]

From the deportation trains, Jews now jumped whenever they could, despite the risk of being crushed under the wheels, or shot by the guards. On January 15 a total of seventy-seven Jews managed to jump from a train on its way east from Belgium, and did so before it reached the German frontier. German SS men, and members of the Flemish SS, tracked most of them down.[69]

On January 15 the Germans decided to empty the camp at Zaslaw in which thousands of Jews from the towns and villages of the River San were being held. All the inmates were sent by train to Belzec, and gassed. The twenty-one-year-old Yaacov Gurfein was in one of the last deportation trains. For two days and three nights the deportees were locked into the train, while it stood stationary. They were given neither food nor water. Then the train set off. 'When we saw that the train was moving to Belzec,' Gurfein later recalled, 'one person jumped out. Then people again had this spark of hope. I don't think I would have jumped were it not for my mother. She pushed me out.'[70] When the last train left Zaslaw for Belzec, only one Jew managed to survive, Jaffa Wallach's younger brother, Emil Manaster, who succeeded in jumping from the train, and who found refuge, like his sister Jaffa, with the Polish engineer, Jozef Zwonarz.[71]

In Birkenau, a similar spark of hope survived. Rivka Liebeskind later recalled her first Friday night there, on January 22, crowded with hundreds of other women into one of the huts, or 'blocks', tier upon tier. Candles had been acquired and, 'on the top shelf of our block – we were at the time ten to twelve girls – we lit those candles. We lit the candles and quietly began singing the songs for the Sabbath. We did not know', she added, 'what was happening around us, but after a few minutes we heard stifled crying from all the shelves around us. First we were frightened, then moved. Then we saw that they could jump from one shelf to another. There were Jewish women who had already been there for years. They gathered around us and listened to our prayer and singing; soon there were those who came off their own shelves and asked to be allowed to bless the candles.'[72]

On 18 January 1943, after nearly four months without a single deportation, the Germans entered the Warsaw ghetto, intent upon a further deportation to Treblinka. 'We were in the ghetto and hid in an attic,' Bluma Shadur later recalled. 'They went from house to house and killed people, throwing them out of the windows and taking whatever they could.' Her own young brothers were among those taken, stripped naked, and deported to Treblinka.[73]

Among those deported on January 18 was Meir Alter, a well-known cantor of pre-war Warsaw. 'With him', Stanislaw Adler has recalled, 'they dragged out his father and his brother Mieczyslaw.' On the way to the Umschlagplatz, Alter supported his father, who was blind, and moving with difficulty. When asked by the SS escort why the old man did not walk by himself, Alter explained that his father was blind. The Nazi fired a shot, 'killing the blind man instantly . . .'.[74]

Another of those killed in the streets was the director of the American Jewish Joint Distribution Committee, Yitzhak Gitterman, who had been a 'moving spirit' behind self-help in the ghetto, and who was shot while talking to two friends on the stairs outside his apartment.

More than six hundred Jews were killed in the streets during that day of round-ups.[75] An eye-witness later recalled:

> The action proceeded at a rapid pace. It did not help to show a work card; all had to be taken to the Umschlagplatz. The 'life certificates', which had given their holders illusions, were torn up by SS men. There were no longer 'useful' and 'useless' Jews; all were condemned to death. The Jewish hospital was emptied out. The patients who could still walk were dragged to the Umschlagplatz; those who could not were killed on the spot.
>
> The cries of the victims were drowned by rifle and machine-gun fire. The road to the Umschlagplatz was strewn with bodies of the dead and the dying. Those still alive would lift their eyes to the passing Jews, hoping for help, but no one paid any attention.[76]

Within several hours the Germans succeeded in rounding up five thousand Jews. Their success sprang from the element of surprise. Thousands of Jews had no time to seek shelter, others were caught on their way to work.

Among the five thousand Jews deported to Treblinka on January 18 were 150 doctors, including Izrael Milejkowski, who had led the team of researchers studying starvation disease. During the train journey he committed suicide. News of Dr Milejkowski's suicide was brought to Warsaw by his nephew, who managed to jump from the train and to make his way back into the ghetto.[77] Another doctor who committed suicide on the journey was Zofia Binsztejn-Syrkin, chairman of the board of health of the Warsaw Jewish Council, and a former director of TOZ, the pre-war Organization for the Protection of the Health of the Jews of Poland.[78]

The Germans expected no resistance, but preparations to resist had been made in the ghetto throughout the autumn and winter. Tuvia Borzykowski's group hid three pistols and three grenades. Those who had no weapons, he recalled, 'armed themselves with lengths of iron pipe, sticks, bottles, whatever could serve to attack the enemy'.

A large number of Jews were being deported along the street as Tuvia Borzykowski watched. Suddenly, a small group of them, led by Mordechai Anielewicz, began to throw grenades at the German guards and at the special SS task force. Several of the Germans fell. Others ran away.[79] All but two of the group of fighters were killed, among them the seventeen-year-old Margalit Landau, who had helped carry out the death sentence on Jacob Lejkin two and a half weeks earlier.[80]

Nine Jewish fighters were killed. But the armed clash had taken place. Jews had raised the standard of revolt. Then, as Tuvia Borzykowski recalled:

> The fighters set up a barricade in a little house on Niska Street and held it against the German reinforcements which soon arrived. The Germans found it impossible to enter the house, so they set it afire. The fighters inside continued firing until the last bullet.
>
> I should like to mention here one of the fighters, Eliyahu Rozanski (Elik). When he was mortally wounded, he asked one of the comrades to take his rifle so that it should not fall into German hands. Of the entire unit only Mordechai Anielewicz survived; in the final stage of the battle he fought with a rifle which he forced out of the hands of a German.
>
> Though the unit was destroyed, the battle on Niska Street

encouraged us. For the first time since the occupation we saw Germans clinging to walls, crawling on the ground, running for cover, hesitating before making a step in the fear of being hit by a Jewish bullet. The cries of the wounded caused us joy, and increased our thirst for battle.[81]

On January 19 the Germans entered the ghetto once more. One of those in hiding that day was David Wdowinski. 'Again we went into our shelters,' he wrote. 'Again the familiar voices, the heavy treads, the alarming hammering.' The Germans were clearly nearby:

A child began to cry. Fright, alarm – we'll be betrayed. The mother closed her hand tightly over the child's mouth and nose. The crying stopped. The child was quiet, very quiet. The German went away. The quiet child was a little bluish in the face and from his mouth issued a small stream of bloody foam. It was never to cry again. So went a Jewish child into the other world.[82]

On January 21 the Germans began firing into windows, and hurling grenades. 'All through the day', Borzykowski recalled, 'the ghetto resounded to the explosions in which hundreds of Jews perished.' But the resistance continued, forty Jews going from house to house and rooftop to rooftop, not all of them armed, but taking arms from the Germans, and keeping up firing. Then, to the amazement of the fighters, the Germans withdrew from the ghetto. 'At the time', Borzykowski later wrote, 'we had only ten pistols.' Had the Germans known this, they would probably have continued the raids, and Jewish resistance 'would have been nipped in the bud as a minor, insignificant episode'.[83] 'We obtained faith', Yitzhak Zuckerman later recalled, 'that we can fight; we know how to fight.'[84]

Among the Jewish fighters killed was Tamara Sznajderman, one of the Jewish Fighting Organization couriers who had been on missions to Bialystok and elsewhere. She was the girlfriend of Mordecai Tenenbaum, leader of the growing resistance group in Bialystok.[85]

Twelve Germans were killed in the fighting. They died, Yitzhak Katznelson recalled a year later, 'in utter bewilderment', and he added:

SS agents who stood some distance away and many gendarmes who fled in confusion cried out: 'The Jews are shooting!' I, myself, heard these astonished cries from the lips of a
vile loathsome German as he ran down the stairs of the house
which he had entered for the deliberate purpose of killing us.
'The Jews are shooting!' he cried out in utter bewilderment.
Something unheard of! Jews firing! 'They have guns!'[86]

The Germans, Feigele Peltel later wrote, 'had received their first
blow at the hands of the contemptible Juden'.[87]

27

'Help me get more trains'

ON THE EASTERN FRONT, the German armies were in disarray: cheated of their objective – the city of Stalingrad – surrounded by the Red Army, and driven back over hundreds of miles. No military setback, however, could halt the deportation of Jews. Indeed, it seemed only to make the deportations more urgent. On 20 January 1943 Himmler sent the Reich Minister of Transport a special letter about 'the removal of Jews' from the General Government, the Eastern Territories, and 'the West'. For this, he wrote, 'I need your help and support. If I am to wind things up quickly, I must have more trains for transports.'

'I know very well', Himmler added, 'how taxing the situation is for the railways and what demands are constantly made of you. Just the same, I must make this request of you: help me get more trains.'[1] That same day, the deportations from Theresienstadt to Birkenau were renewed, with two thousand deportees sent 'to the East'. Of the two thousand, only 160 young men and 80 women were 'selected' for the barracks, and the rest were gassed.[2]

All the deportees from Theresienstadt to Birkenau were Jews who had already been uprooted from their homes in 1941, when they had been deported to Theresienstadt from Austria and Czechoslovakia. The new deportation seemed nothing more than another stage on their road; one more move at the whim of the conqueror.

In a train which left Holland on the day after Himmler wrote his letter on the need for 'more trains', the deportees were mental defectives from the Jewish mental hospital at Apeldoorn.

One historian of the destruction of Dutch Jewry, Dr Jacob Presser, has recorded, of the deportees:

> They were escorted into the lorries with pushes and blows, men, women and children, most of them inadequately clad for

the cold winter night. As one eye-witness put it: 'I saw them place a row of patients, many of them older women, on mattresses at the bottom of one lorry, and then load another load of human bodies on top of them. So crammed were these lorries that the Germans had a hard job to put up the tail-boards.'

More than one document mentions pitiable screams. From the very start, the patients were thrown together indiscriminately, children with dangerous lunatics, imbeciles with those who were not fit to be moved.

The lorries hurtled to the station. The matter-of-fact, unadorned report of the station-master at Apeldoorn, who stood by the train throughout, gives us a few more particulars. At first everything went smoothly. The earliest arrivals, mainly young men, went quietly into the front freight wagons, forty in each. When the station-master opened the ventilators, the Germans quickly closed them again.

At first, men and women were put into separate wagons, but later they were all mixed together. Although it was a very mild night, it was 'not nearly mild enough for old people in night-dresses to travel in open lorries'. As the night wore on, the more seriously ill were brought into the station. Some wore strait-jackets, 'staggered into the carriages and then leant helplessly against the wall'.

The report goes on to say: 'Of course, a person in a strait-jacket cannot protect himself if he slips between the platform and the train. I remember the case of a girl of twenty to twenty-five, whose arms were pinioned in this way, but who was otherwise stark naked. When I remarked on this to the guards, they told me that this patient had refused to put on clothes, so what could they do but take her along as she was. Blinded by the light that was flashed in her face, the girl ran, fell on her face and could not, of course, use her arms to break the fall. She crashed down with a thud, but luckily escaped without serious injury. In no time she was up again and unconcernedly entered the wagon.'

'In general,' the station-master went on, 'the loading was done without great violence. The ghastly thing was that when the wagons had to be closed, the patients refused to take their fingers away. They simply would not listen to us and in the end the Germans lost patience. The result was a brutal and inhuman spectacle.'

Early the next morning the commander of the German Security Police in Holland, F. H. Aus der Funten, called for volunteers among the nurses to accompany the train. Some twenty came forward; he himself chose a further thirty. The 'volunteers' travelled in a separate wagon, at the back of the train. All were offered the choice of returning home immediately after the journey, or working in a really modern mental home.[3]

The arrival at Birkenau of the mentally defective from Apeldoorn shocked even those Jewish inmates of the camp who had become used to the obscenities of deportation. One eye-witness of their arrival, Rudolf Vrba, recalled twenty years later the arrival of the Apeldoorn deportees after the twelve-day journey in the sealed cattle trucks:

> In some of the trucks nearly half the occupants were dead or dying, more than I had ever seen. Many obviously had been dead for several days, for the bodies were decomposing and the stench of disintegrating flesh gushed from the open doors.

> This, however, was no novelty to me. What appalled me was the state of the living. Some were drooling, imbecile, live people with dead minds. Some were raving, tearing at their neighbours, even at their own flesh. Some were naked, though the cold was petrifying; and above everything, above the moans of the dying or the despairing, the cries of pain, of fear, the sound of wild, frightening, lunatic laughter rose and fell.

> Yet amid all this bedlam, there was one spark of splendid, unselfish sanity. Moving among the insane were nurses, young girls, their uniforms torn and grimy, but their faces calm and their hands never idle. Their medicine bags were still over their shoulders and they had to fight sometimes to keep their feet; but all the time they were working, soothing, bandaging, giving an injection here, an aspirin there. Not one showed the slightest trace of panic.

> 'Get them out!' roared the SS men. 'Get them out, you bastards!'

> A naked girl of about twenty with red hair and a superb figure suddenly leaped from a wagon and lay, squirming, laughing at my feet. A nurse flung me a heavy Dutch blanket

and I tried to put it round her, but she would not get up. With another prisoner, a Slovak called Fogel, I managed to roll her into the blanket.

'Get them to the lorries!' roared the SS. 'Straight to the lorries! Get on with it for Christ's sake!'

Somehow Fogel and I broke into a lumbering run, for this beautiful girl was heavy. The motion pleased her and she began clapping her hands like a child. An SS club slashed across my shoulders and the blanket slipped from my numbed fingers.

'Get on, you swine! Drag her!'

I joined Fogel at the other end of the blanket and we dragged her, bumping her over the frozen earth for five hundred yards. Somehow she clung to the blanket, not laughing now, but crying, as the hard ground thumped her naked flesh through the thick wool.

'Pitch her in! Get her on the lorries!' The SS men were frantic for here was something they could not understand. Something that knew no order, no discipline, no obedience, no fear of violence or death.

We pitched her in somehow, then ran back for another crazy, pathetic bundle. Hundreds of them were out of the wagons now, herded by the prisoners who were herded by the SS; and everywhere the nurses. Still working.

One nurse walked slowly with an old, frail man, talking to him quietly, as if they were out in the hospital grounds. Another half-carried a screaming girl. They fought to bring order out of chaos, using medicines and blankets, gentleness and quiet heroism instead of guns or sticks or snarling dogs.

Then suddenly it was all over. The last abject victims had been slung into one of the overloaded lorries. We stood there, panting in the chill January air; and all our eyes were on those nurses. In unemotional groups they stood around the lorries, waiting for permission to join their patients.

Rudolf Vrba later recalled how the SS men were watching the nurses 'with a respect they seldom showed for anybody', hoping that the nurses would be 'selected' to remain in the barracks. 'God knows, we could use some decent medical help around here,' one of them commented. But the doctor making the selection – his name is not known – decided that the nurses must die. Vrba noted: 'One of the SS officers shrugged and shouted, "Get the girls aboard! It seems they've got to go, too." The nurses climbed up after their patients. The lorry engines roared and off they swayed to the gas-chambers.'

Not a single nurse, nor a single patient, survived.

Among the deportees who reached Auschwitz at this time was a Frenchwoman, Claude Vaillant Couturier, who had been deported from Paris in the last week of January 1943, with 230 French intellectuals, doctors and teachers. She reached Auschwitz on January 27. Three years later she recalled the fate of the deportees 'selected' for destruction:

> They were taken to a red-brick building, which bore the letters 'B-a-d', that is to say 'bath'. There, to begin with, they were made to undress and given a towel before they went into the so-called shower room. Later on, at the time of the large convoys, they had no more time left to play-act or to pretend; they were brutally undressed, and I know these details as I knew a little Jewess from France who lived with her family at the 'Republique' in Paris. She was called 'little Marie'.
>
> Little Marie was the sole survivor of a family of nine. Her mother and her seven brothers and sisters had been gassed on arrival. When I met her she was employed to undress the babies before they were taken into the gas-chamber. Once the people were undressed they took them into a room which was somewhat like a shower room, and gas capsules were thrown through an opening in the ceiling. An SS man would watch the effect produced, through a porthole. At the end of five or seven minutes, when the gas had completed its work, he gave the signal to open the doors, and men with gas masks – they too were internees – went into the room and removed the corpses. They told us that the internees must have suffered before dying, because they were closely clinging to each other and it was very difficult to separate them.[5]

On January 22 more than four thousand Jews were seized in Marseilles under 'Action Tiger'. Two years earlier the Germans had mocked Marseilles as 'the new Jerusalem of the Mediterranean', where the Jews 'reigned as lords of the cafés and restaurants, waiting for the victory of the Americans'. Now these Jews, many of them refugee children, were held in detention camps, awaiting deportation, among the orphan refugees and the women who looked after them. At La Rose, four miles east of Marseilles, thirty Jewish orphans were seized, together with their guardian Alice Salomon, who insisted on sharing their fate.[6] Two months later they were deported from Paris to Sobibor and gassed.[7]

The Germans also sought to round up all Jews living in the zone of France under Italian control. But on January 23 the Italians refused to 'cooperate'.[8] Five weeks later Italian troops prevented the Germans from deporting them.[9] From the region under direct German control there was however no pause. Of two thousand Jews deported from Theresienstadt to Birkenau on January 23, eighteen hundred were gassed on arrival, and of the two hundred 'spared', and sent to the Buna works at Monowitz, only three survived the war.[10]

For almost exactly a year, the mass deportation of Jews to an 'unknown destination', and their murder there by gas, had proceeded amid tight secrecy, and to the growing alarm of those in the yet untouched communities. Day by day, the inexorable round-up spread to every hamlet, however remote, of that vast population which had once been known, in its years of glory, as the 'Jewish Nation in Poland'. Nor was the truth about the final destination any longer easy to hide, especially from those remaining communities which were situated in the same regions as the death camps.

On January 24, all thousand Jews from Jasionowka, near Bialystok, were rounded up for deportation to Treblinka, and put on sledges for the journey to the nearest railway station. 'They knew what is "Treblinka",' Szymon Datner later recalled. 'They knew their fate,' and he added:

> There was one man, a very big man physically, a carter, who was accustomed to such terrible things as winter and cold and rain. He had lived outside in the winter, and he could have escaped. He could have run off into the woods.
> But he had in his arms a six-month-old baby – the youngest of his children. And he was together on the sledge with his wife and other children. His wife, who knew also all the truth, she

said, 'Get away, jump, you will survive. What is the use of
dying together?' But he said, 'No. I will not leave you.'

The carter's decision, Datner later reflected, 'was also an act of
heroism: *not* to escape. It was a passive act of heroism,' and he went
on: 'I have my full respect before such an act of a simple man. I bow
my head in respect before him.'[11]

Those who sheltered Jews were also taking a mortal risk. On
January 29, in the village of Wierzbica, the Germans executed
fifteen Poles: three families who were accused of sheltering three
Jews. Among the fifteen Poles executed that day was a two-year-old
girl.[12] Even independent states came under continual German
pressure. In February 1943 the German government pressed the
Hungarian government to send ten thousand Hungarian Jews as
forced labourers in the copper mines at Bor, in Yugoslavia. For
several months the Hungarian government refused; then it yielded.
While three quarters of a million Hungarian Jews remained unmolested, ten thousand were sent to a camp in whose harsh
conditions several thousand perished.[13]

Disobedience to German orders, difficult for an independent state
such as Hungary, was impossible for the Jews. On February 4, in
Lvov, the Germans summoned the surviving twelve members of the
Jewish Council to appear before them. Ten appeared. Refusing to
comply with the German wishes, they suffered the supreme penalty.
Four were murdered: Eberson, the Chairman, Marceli Buber,
Oswald Kimmelman and Jacob Chigier. The other six were sent
to the concentration camp at Janowska. The two Council
members who hid, Dr Schertzer and Leib Landau, were discovered by the Germans in their hiding place in 'Aryan' Lvov, and
shot.[14]

In Buczacz, most of the thirteen hundred surviving Jews not
deported to Belzec were murdered on February 1. One of the few
who survived, fourteen-year-old Netka Goldberg, lost her three
sisters, her two brothers and her mother on that day of killing. Her
father, who also survived the massacres, was killed seven months
later.[15]

At Birkenau, on February 5, a roll-call was held from three-thirty
in the early hours of the morning until five in the evening. All day the
Jews stood there, for nearly fourteen hours, in the snow, and

without any food. Three years later, Claude Vaillant Couturier recalled how, at five o'clock that evening:

> We had to go through the door one by one, and we were struck in the back with a cudgel, each one of us, in order to make us run. Those who could not run, either because they were too old or too ill, were caught by a hook and taken to Block 25, the 'waiting block', for the gas-chamber.
>
> On that day ten of the French women of our convoy were thus caught and taken to the waiting block.
>
> When all the internees were back in the camp, a party to which I belonged was organised to go and pick up the bodies of the dead which were scattered over the plain as on a battlefield. We carried to the yard of Block 25 the dead and the dying without distinction, and they remained there stacked in the courtyard.
>
> This Block 25, which was the ante-room of the gas-chamber, if one may so call it, is well known to me because at that time we had been transferred to Block 26 and our windows opened on the yard of Block 25. One saw stacks of corpses piled up in the courtyard, and from time to time a hand or a head would stir amongst the bodies, trying to free itself; it was a dying woman attempting to get free and live.
>
> The rate of mortality in that Block was even more terrible than elsewhere because, having been condemned to death, they received food or drink only if there was something left in the cans in the kitchen; which means that very often they went for several days without a drop of water.

Madame Vaillant Couturier added that in the courtyard of Block 25 'there were rats as big as cats running about and gnawing the corpses, and even attacking the dying, who had not enough strength left to chase them away.' Her account continued:

> One of our companions, Annette Epaux, a fine young woman of thirty, passing the Block one day, was overcome with pity for those women who moaned from morning till night in all languages, 'Drink, drink, water!' She came back to our Block to get a little herbal tea, but as she was passing it through the bars of the window she was seen by the Supervisor, who took her by the neck and threw her into Block 25.

All my life I will remember Annette Epaux. Two days later I saw her on the truck which was taking the internees to the gas-chamber. She had her arms round another French woman, old Celina Forcher, and when the truck started moving, she cried, 'Think of my little boy, if you ever get back to France,' then they started singing the 'Marseillaise'.[16]

During February, fifteen trains reached Birkenau: from Westerbork camp in Holland, from Drancy near Paris, from Berlin, and from Bialystok. At least five thousand of the deportees were gassed.[17] The deportees from Berlin were mostly Jewish factory workers, seized in the factories in which they were working, and not allowed to go home even to collect personal belongings.

Eight of the deportees from Berlin had been brought from Finland. They were the first of more than two thousand Finnish Jews, and Jews who had found refuge in Finland, whom the Germans wished to deport.

The only survivor of those deported from Finland was the Viennese-born Dr Georg Kollman. He, with the other seven, had been brought from Helsinki by boat across the Gulf of Finland to Reval, then by train to Berlin, and then on the Berlin train to Auschwitz, a journey of more than twelve hundred miles.

The seven Jews from Finland who were deported included the thirty-six-year-old Hans Eduard Szubilski, who had come to Finland as a refugee from Germany in 1938, and two children, Kurt Huppert, aged eleven, whose father Heinrich Huppert, an Austrian Jew who had reached Finland as a refugee in 1938, also perished, and George Kollman's son, the twenty-two-month-old Frans Olof Kollman, who was gassed together with his mother. Szubilski, taken to the barracks at Birkenau, was later 'shot while attempting to escape'.

No further Jews were deported from Finland after this first transport. Following protests by the minority Social Democratic Party, several Lutheran ministers, and the Archbishop, the Finnish Cabinet which in August 1942 had deferred to Himmler's pressure while on a 'private unofficial holiday visit' to deport the Jews from Finland to Germany, refused to agree to any further deportations.[18]

At Auschwitz, those not gassed immediately, but sent to the barracks, also died in considerable numbers. In February 1943 there were 3,049 deaths in the barracks at Birkenau, of whom 1,690 were men and women judged too weak to work, and gassed.[19] Some were so weak, from hunger or disease, that they died in the barracks, or on the parade ground. Many were killed by the guards.

The Bialystok deportation on February 5 was accompanied by an act of defiance. A dyer, the forty-year-old Yitzhak Malmed, whose wife, two children and parents had been murdered by the Germans in Slonim in June 1941, on finding his apartment block surrounded, threw sulphuric acid into the face of the first German to enter it, a police officer by the name of Muenter. Blinded and in pain, Muenter started shooting, and, by mistake, shot a Gestapo officer, Wilhelm Fritsch, in the head. Fritsch died instantly. As a reprisal, the Germans seized and shot a hundred Jews, most of them from the apartment block where Malmed lived. Malmed managed to escape, whereupon the Germans then announced that unless he were found, five thousand Jews would be shot. This threat was brought to Malmed, who, according to several Jewish survivors, gave himself up.[20] He was hanged by the Germans at the entrance to the ghetto, 'suspended', Abraham Karasick recalled, 'for three days at the gate'.[21]

A wall plaque, in Yiddish, records to this day Yitzhak Malmed's desperate act.[22]

After learning that the Jewish Council had prepared a list of candidates for deportation, Zvi Wider, a member of the Council, and former Chairman of one of the leading Jewish charitable organizations in Bialystok, committed suicide.[23] A ladies' tailor, the forty-three-year-old Nochum Babikier, was one of those deported, in a train escorted by Ukrainian guards, and surrounded at each station where it stopped by yet more Ukrainians. Three years later Babikier, who was deported with his father, his son, and his sister Niomke, recalled:

> The train left at about 3 p.m. The people were anxious, they hardly spoke, buried in their thoughts, waiting anxiously to see which direction the train will take. The train went past Starosielce. After a while those watching by the little window called out in despair: 'We are lost, we are going to Malkinia, that means to our deaths in Treblinka.'
> Panic broke out in the carriage, people wringing their hands.

The young decided to force open the door and jump from the train. With a piece of iron a hole was made in the door and a few people jumped. From Starosielce onwards the sound of gunfire filled the train. Young people from all the carriages were jumping, and the Ukrainians were shooting at them. Most of those who jumped were killed on the spot.

In my carriage people stopped jumping. In the carriage the thirty-year-old owner of a cosmetics shop on Gieldowa Street cut his throat with a razor. No one came to his assistance. Suddenly the train stopped in the middle of a field. The Germans walked from carriage to carriage and where they found the door had been opened, fired into the carriage. In my carriage the passengers themselves bolted the door.

The train started. A refugee doctor gave himself an injection. The injection did not work. There was a hook in the middle of the ceiling; he put his belt through it and then, not molested by anyone, hanged himself. But the belt did not hold him, he fell down, and remained alive. Another doctor gave his thirteen-year-old son poison, then took it himself. They talked: 'My child, what will your mother, in heaven, say about me, for killing you?' The child: 'I don't want to die, but I prefer death from you than from the Germans.'

After a while a bullet from a rifle went through the wall of the carriage and hit one person in the stomach. He suffered for half an hour, shouted for help, then died.

Babikier and his son had two bottles, which they decided to break over Germans' heads in Treblinka if and when it became certain that they were going to be killed. In the meantime the train went on, for quite some time; according to their calculations they should have reached Treblinka long ago. The train stopped. They asked the Ukrainian where they were going. He told them they were going to Lublin:

By now Malkinia was twenty kilometres behind us. Indescribable joy pervaded the carriage. People kissed and congratulated each other. Niomke said to my father: 'You'll see, we'll remain alive after all.'

The man who had cut his throat gestured for help. There were no means to help him and he died. Dr Gawze, who sat apathetically, keeping his own injection until the last moment, now rushed to the assistance of the other doctor and his son, ordered them to drink water with soap suds to make them vomit. I gave the rest of his water, but it did not work. The father put his arm round his son's waist, felt his pulse with his other hand, their faces were joyous, they were swaying like drunks. After a while they died. The man whose belt broke came round. They put all the four dead together in a corner of the carriage.

When the fear of death passed, came the worry about water. Their tongues were dry, they were calling for water, but no one gave it to them. At one stop one person gave the Ukrainian a gold watch, and he brought two bottles of water. Everyone reached for the bottles, they fell and broke and no one got any water. The shooting stopped, everyone thought they were going to a labour camp. No one had heard about Majdanek. After midnight they arrived at Lublin and stopped at a railway platform. All night they stayed in the carriage with their tongues hanging out with thirst like dogs. From the whole train came cries for help. Suddenly there was shooting.

In the morning it was discovered that the Germans were shooting people who could no longer stand the heat and the thirst and left carriages. Dawn came. They saw a group of Jewish women, marching in formation. They asked them by gestures – by pointing at their necks – whether they were brought here to be killed. The women shook their heads in denial. They began to curse them loudly, for they were certain that the Germans had put them up to it, wishing to deceive them.

At 7 a.m. they were unloaded. By the carriages stood SS men and Ukrainians with large dogs, and beat them as they came out. They put them in fives. Whenever anyone moved out of line the dogs attacked him and bit him. They breathed deeply the air of which they were so short for such a long time. They asked the Ukrainians for water and were told that they are going to a camp and will get everything here.

Before the carriages lay a few naked bodies. Those were the people shot in the night, who tried to get out of the carriages. They had undressed in the train, because they were so unbearably hot.

Dr Kaplan was told that his daughter is dead in a carriage of a train which arrived earlier. A cordon of SS men with dogs surrounded them and they moved off.[24]

During the Bialystok deportation, twelve young Jews managed to escape from the ghetto and find refuge in the nearby forests. Led by Eli Baumats, they obtained arms, and on February 13 struck at a German police unit at Lipowy Most. One of their number, Moshe Slapak, known to his fellow partisans as 'Maksym', was killed in this engagement. Two months later, on the night of May 24, a second group of young Jews, sixteen in all, organized by Judith Nowogrodzka, likewise managed to break out of the ghetto, led out by Szymon Datner.

Datner's destination was a nearby wood, but he and his group were forced to return that same night to the ghetto. When they did so, they discovered that three of the young men with them had disappeared in the darkness. 'I went out alone to find them,' Datner later recalled. 'Two German guards came across me. I shot first. The shooting continued. Both Germans were killed. One died on the spot. The second died of his wounds two days later, attended on his deathbed, on Gestapo orders, by a Jewish doctor, Tuviah Cytron.'

Datner returned to the Bialystok ghetto, and again, on June 3, set out for the woods, together with another would-be partisan, Chaim Chalef, and the group of sixteen. This time they managed to reach the woods, and were to fight, first alone and later with Red Army partisan units, until liberation.[25]

Jews were deported from Bialystok to Treblinka, to Majdanek and to Auschwitz. During the deportation to Auschwitz, several Jews had tried to jump out of the trains. Passing through Lodz, a husband, wife and daughter had managed to jump. The mother was shot dead. The father and daughter reached the ghetto. The father, Chaim Jankelewicz, distraught at his wife's death, hanged himself. The daughter, with a broken leg, was taken in by Rumkowski.[26]

Among the deportees from Bialystok to Auschwitz was Dr Aharon Beilin. During the 'selection', he later recalled, the SS doctor 'whistled the aria "La Donna e Mobile" from *Rigoletto*'. At this particular selection, 150 men and 150 women, including Dr Beilin, were selected for the barracks at Birkenau. The rest, more than four thousand seven hundred, were gassed, among them Dr Beilin's mother. As he later recalled, the four thousand seven hundred were sent 'the way which I later learned was the way to the crematorium'. Then, 'I saw these trucks, three or four hours later – that's how long we waited – through a barbed wire; we were standing on the other side of the fence – we had not yet entered the camp. I saw these trucks returning with coats and I saw my mother's coat. I then understood that she was no longer with us.'

Beilin was a physician for epidemic diseases. He had worked as such in the Bialystok city hospital, and later in the ghetto. During his first month in Birkenau, as he later recalled, a Dutch physician arrived:

> He asked me – he said: 'Tell me, colleague, when shall I see my wife and children?' I said: 'Why do you ask me this question?' He said to me: 'We were told on the ramp at Birkenau that those who were fit for labour were going to a separate camp, and the women and children would go to another camp in which they would get better treatment; and after two weeks there would be a reunion.' And he asked me: 'When will this reunion take place, and how?'
>
> I told him the truth, but then I was sorry. He told me: 'Small wonder that the Germans accuse the Jews of spreading atrocity stories – it is impossible what you are telling me now!' I showed him the crematoria, a hundred yards outside the camp, and I asked him: 'Do you see that building? What do you think it is?' He said: 'That is a bakery'.

Two weeks later, Dr Beilin saw the Dutch physician again:

> He called me. I wanted to evade this meeting. I saw him from afar and he came up to me. It was very embarrassing to me. He said, 'Colleague, you were right. It is murder.'
>
> I later learned from his Dutch colleagues that he had committed suicide by hanging himself. This was the most popular method of committing suicide in Birkenau. He hanged himself on the electrified barbed wire.[27]

On February 6, Himmler received a report on the 'quantity of old garments' collected from Birkenau and the camps in the Lublin region. The list included 97,000 sets of men's 'old clothing', 76,000

540 · THE HOLOCAUST

sets of women's 'old clothing', 132,000 men's shirts, 155,000 women's coats and 3,000 kilogrammes of women's hair. The women's hair filled a whole freight car.

Children's items on the list included 15,000 overcoats and 11,000 boys' jackets, as well as 9,000 girls' dresses, and 22,000 pairs of children's shoes. Also listed were 135,000 handkerchiefs and 100,000 hand towels. All were to be distributed, some of them to the Reich Youth Leadership.[28] The question had also been raised three weeks earlier, by Himmler personally, after a visit to Warsaw, as to what to do with watch glasses, 'of which hundreds of thousands – perhaps even millions' were lying in warehouses in Warsaw.[29]

The Jewish clothing sent to the Reich filled 825 freight cars. In addition, the amount of foreign currency, gold and silver listed was considerable, including half a million United States dollars, and 116,420 dollars in gold.[30]

Clothes, valuables, hair: these were among the spoils of the German war against the Jews. Children and their parents were equally stripped of their pathetic possessions at the entrance to the gas-chamber. On February 11, in a deportation from Paris to Birkenau, were 123 children under twelve, many deported without their parents. Also on that train, and also gassed, was the sixty-six-year-old rabbi, Ernest Ginsburger, awarded the Medaille Militaire in the First World War, while serving as Chaplain in the French Eighteenth Army Corps.[31]

At the German border, three Jews had managed to escape from this train. They were caught, and forced back on to the train. Of 998 Jews deported, 143 men and 53 women were sent to the barracks: the remaining 802 deportees, including all the children, were gassed.[32]

The belongings and clothes of the dead were sorted by prisoners in the 'Canada' section of Auschwitz for despatch to Germany. One of the destinations, for further sorting, was Dachau. Among those in Dachau when railway carriages full of clothes reached the camp from Birkenau was Pastor Heinrich Grüber. 'We were shaken to the depths of our soul', he later recalled, 'when the first transports of children's shoes arrived – we men who were inured to suffering and to shock had to fight back tears.' Later they saw yet more thousands of children's shoes: 'this was the most terrible thing for us, the most bitter thing, perhaps the worst thing that befell us.'[33]

Children and adults, artisans and artists, the unknown and the well known; Birkenau devoured them all. Among the Russian-born Jews who had been living in Paris when the Germans entered the city in June 1940 was the artist Aizik Feder. Born in Odessa in 1885, fleeing Russia at the age of nineteen to avoid being sent to Siberia, he had studied painting first in Berlin and then in Geneva, becoming a pupil of Matisse in Paris in 1910. Feder belonged to the group of Jewish artists of the 'Ecole de Paris', exhibiting for the first time in 1912. In 1926 he spent some time in Palestine, painting landscapes. Following the German occupation of Paris, he sought contact with the resistance, but was arrested, imprisoned, and then sent to Drancy, where he drew seventeen pastel and watercolour portraits of his fellow internees.[34]

On February 12, in Drancy, Aizik Feder managed to smuggle out a letter to his wife. 'Tomorrow I am leaving,' he wrote. 'My morale is good. Our separation will not be long. I beg you not to be desperate. We'll see each other again soon. Take care of my belongings. All that belongs to me belongs to you. Courage! Courage! Courage!'

On February 13, the fifty-eight-year-old Feder was one of the thousand Jews deported to Auschwitz. Only 311 were selected for tattooing and for the barracks. Less than twenty survived the war. Feder was not among them.[35]

The German government continued to press those states not under its direct control to deport its Jews. In an agreement signed on February 22, the Bulgarian government allowed the Germans to deport all eleven thousand Jews from two areas occupied by Bulgaria in 1941: the former Yugoslav region of Macedonia, and the former Greek region of Thrace.

The Germans allocated twenty special trains for these deportations, starting from six collecting points. At the railway stations of Demir-Hisar and Simitli, where there was a change of trains because of the wider gauge, the Germans gave priority in changing trains to 'invalids on stretchers' and women who were 'ready for childbirth'. Conditions inside the trains, and on the barges, in which some of the deportees were sent up the Danube, were horrific: terrible over-

THE BALKANS

crowding, no sanitary arrangements, virtually no food, and no water.

Each morning on their journey northward the trains would stop in the open countryside, and the bodies of those who had died during the night were thrown out. The Germans would not allow any form of burial. Several hundred sick and old people died during the six-day journey, which ended at Treblinka.[36]

Shortly after these Thracian and Macedonian deportations, all Jewish property and belongings in Thrace and Macedonia were confiscated and sold. The money raised had first to go towards the cost of the rail and boat 'fare' to Treblinka. The rest was then deposited in bank accounts, and, to give those still in Greece a sense of normality, the deposit statements sent to their Jewish owners. These statements reached Treblinka long after the Jews had been murdered.[37]

'The German Reich', so stated the Bulgarian agreement of February 22, 'is ready to accept these Jews in its eastern regions.' A month after the agreement was signed, 'these Jews' were dead.

In Italy Mussolini continued to reject all appeals for the deportation of Jews. On February 22, the day of the Thrace and Macedonia deportation agreement with Bulgaria, the German government learned that the Italian military authorities in Lyons had forced the French police chief in the city to annul an order for the arrest of several hundred Jews who were to have been sent to Auschwitz 'for labour service'. Three days later, Ribbentrop complained personally to Mussolini that 'Italian military circles, and sometimes the German army itself, lacked a proper understanding of the Jewish question.'[38]

Throughout February, a division of the Red Army, the Sixteenth (Lithuanian) Division, had been training for combat. Many of its twelve thousand men were Jews. On February 23 the Division attacked the Germans at Alexseyevka, in the Ukraine, Jewish riflemen and machine-gunners charging on foot across the snow-covered plain. For two days the Division struggled against superior German firepower until, its ammunition gone, it was ordered to withdraw. Several hundred Jews lay dead.

The Lithuanian Division fought for a further twenty-eight

months, until the last day of the war. During its advance, it was to take more than twelve thousand Germans prisoner. Its soldiers were to include twelve Heroes of the Soviet Union, and one Heroine, Roza Deweltow, who had been born in Vilna in 1919, and who was killed in action shortly after her twenty-fifth birthday.[39]

The Bialystok deportation was coming to an end. In the train which reached Birkenau on February 6, only 85 men and 47 women, from more than two thousand deportees, were sent to the barracks. The rest were gassed. In the train which reached Birkenau on February 7, only 123 men, and no women, were sent to the barracks.[40]

The Germans had promised Ephraim Barasz, the head of the Jewish Council in Bialystok, that only 'non-working' Jews would be deported. The survivors of the action were outraged and bewildered that so many able-bodied men and women had been taken. But at a meeting on February 27, those who wished to try to organize some form of resistance decided, after a long discussion, not to try to escape from the ghetto in anticipation of a further action, but to resist within the ghetto, and to resist 'to the last Jew'.[41]

In the Lodz ghetto, an increase in work orders gave a renewed sense of security. 'Sizeable orders have been confirmed,' the Ghetto Chronicle noted on February 27. Among the twenty-six largest workshops, orders had included the manufacture of 1,354,172 pairs of shoes.[42] Two weeks later, Chaim Rumkowski told the workshop delegates that 'young people must be given the production jobs', in place of people aged fifty and over who had been 'utterly exhausted by hard physical labour'. It was clear that this made the old people liable for 'resettlement'. But Rumkowski stressed, 'We will have to be firm, for everything is at stake here.'[43]

Two weeks after Rumkowski's speech, a further 'resettlement' was carried out. Among those deported were all those 'with active tuberculosis' and others who were 'hopelessly sick'. The deportees were mainly taken from among 850 Jews recently brought into the ghetto from Poznan. But, as the Chronicle noted, 'a small number of skilled workers from the Poznan contingent, primarily shoemakers, were spared resettlement'. Of the 850 Poznan deportees, 23 were 'assigned to the shoe factories'. Among those deported were some who, as they were taken in horse-drawn carts from the ghetto, sang the Zionist anthem 'Hatikvah' – Hope.[44] Their destination was unkown: their fate, death.

Few could escape the ghettos: even to approach the guards at the walls or wire was to risk death. But risks continued to be taken, and success was possible. In March 1943 a twelve-year-old boy, Matti Drobless, managed to escape from the Warsaw ghetto with his fourteen-year-old sister and his nine-year-old brother. In the ghetto, their mother had died of illness, and their father had been deported, together with their aunts and uncles, during one of the earlier round-ups. 'The three of us were weak,' Drobless later recalled, 'barely skin and bones'. His account continued:

> We left the ghetto via the sewers and first tried to stay with a Polish family – the head of the household had worked for my father. They took all the valuables we had managed to remove from our home – our mother's jewellery and other items – and after three days he told us we would have to leave. Otherwise, he said, he would inform on us. We cried and pleaded but to no avail.
>
> So we headed for the forests and swore that whatever happened we would stay together and never part.
>
> Our survival was based on our will to live and the talents we adopted. We stole food from the farms and removed articles of clothing from the washlines. We scrounged and when there was no alternative we sent our youngest brother into homes to beg. We taught him prayers and instructed him to pose as a Polish war orphan.
>
> I still bear the scars on my legs when I failed to outrun the dogs we encountered. I carry other types of scars, too.
>
> We thought we were the only Jews left in the world. We would survive, but I believed that we would be the sole survivors. We never met another Jew in our wanderings through the forests. I once asked my sister, perhaps out of despair, what would be our fate at the war's end. She replied: 'There is a place called Palestine. There, Jews are living and building a home, a state. When this is over we'll be going home to Palestine.'[45]

At Treblinka, following a visit by Himmler, orders were given for the digging up and burning of the hundreds of thousands of corpses that had been dumped in vast pits behind the gas-chambers. Yankel

Wiernik was among those prisoners who had to perform the task. 'Wherever a grave was opened,' he recalled two years later, 'a terrible stench polluted the air, as the bodies were in an advanced stage of putrefaction. It turned out that women burned easier than men. Accordingly, corpses of women were used for kindling fires.' Wiernik added: 'The sight was terrifying, the worst that human eyes have ever beheld. When corpses of pregnant women were cremated, the abdomen would burst open, and the burning of the fetus inside the mother's body would become visible.'[46]

Himmler also visited Sobibor at this time. According to an eye-witness, three hundred young Jewish women, the prettiest that could be found, had been selected on that occasion in Majdanek, and brought specially to Sobibor, where Himmler had watched them, naked, being gassed. Several survivors also recalled how SS Staff Sergeant Hubert Gomerski and another SS man used to amuse themselves by swinging Jewish children by their legs and then flinging them to their deaths. He who threw a Jewish child farthest won. Eye-witnesses also described how Gomerski would walk past the lines of Jews as they left the cattle trucks and kill those who appeared too weak to be able to walk to the gas-chambers by smashing their skulls with a heavy iron watering can.[47]

On March 2, in one of the almost daily deportations to Birkenau, the deportees, who came from Paris, included the thirty-five-year-old Yetta Flater, who had been born in New York, the fifty-six-year-old Helene Rosenberg, born in London, and Mazel Menace-Misrahi, born in Jerusalem seventy-two years before. On this same train were Jews who had been born in Kiev, Odessa, Vitebsk, Minsk and Moscow. More than three hundred of the deportees of March 2 were over seventy years old.

Of the thousand deportees of March 2, only a hundred men and nineteen women were selected for work.[48] Two of them, Joseph Dorebus and Jankiel Handelsman, were to be among the leaders of the revolt in Birkenau a year and a half later. Another of the deportees, Chaim Herman, who was later sent to work in the Sonderkommando, pulling the bodies out of the gas chamber and taking them to the crematorium, buried underground some letters in Flemish and Yiddish describing his experiences. But he did not survive.[49]

A further deportation train from Paris, on March 4, was sent, not to Birkenau, but to the Polish town of Chelm, east of Lublin, from where it is possible that the majority of the deportees were sent to Sobibor, and gassed. A minority, it is known, were sent to Majdanek, of whom several were to survive the war.[50] Among those who did not survive the deportation of March 4 was the Munich-born painter, Hermann Lismann. After studying painting in Lausanne, Rome and Paris before the First World War, Lismann had seen active service in the German army. When Hitler came to power in 1933 he had fled to France. There, in 1939, he was interned, escaped, was caught, and deported.[51]

In the Eastern Territories and in the Ukraine, the slaughter continued, as hitherto, without deportations. On March 5 more than a thousand Jews were murdered outside the Khmielnik ghetto. The Chairman of the Jewish Council, Shmuel Zalcman, who had maintained contact with the Jewish underground, and advised them on how to organize resistance in the ghetto, was betrayed, arrested, and dragged through the town tied behind a horse-drawn cart, until he died.[52] At Swieciany, on the night of March 6, twenty youngsters armed only with two revolvers and a single rifle, managed to escape from the ghetto to the forest. They were the lucky ones.[53]

Also lucky were forty-eight thousand Jews of Bulgaria: those living within the pre-war borders of the state. At first, it seemed that they too would be deported, as had those from the Bulgarian-occupied zones of Thrace and Macedonia. Following German insistence, the Bulgarian government had indeed ordered the deportation of all Jews from Bulgaria proper, some of whom had already been interned. But the deportation order led to such an outcry from the Bulgarian people, including many intellectuals and church leaders, that the government rescinded the order, and Jews already taken into custody were released.[54]

In the northern part of Bulgaria, farmers had threatened to lie down on the railway tracks to prevent passage of the deportation trains. It was also said that the King himself had intervened. Despite the fact that he was German, of the family of Coburg, he was known to be opposed to the anti-Semitic measures then in force in Bulgaria, helpless though he considered himself to be in the face of the German might. The release of the Jews, which took place on March 10, came to be known in Bulgaria as a 'miracle of the Jewish people'.[55]

The Bulgarian experience highlights the possibility that was open to certain states in Europe to refuse to allow their Jewish citizens to be deported. There were several other occasions on which this refusal was exercised. By March 1943, Finland, Italy and Hungary had each likewise chosen to refuse, and had refused successfully, the German government's demands to deport Jews to Germany. Slovakia and Vichy France, however, had complied with the German demands, and had done so with alacrity, as had Vidkun Quisling's government in Norway. Those countries whose governments agreed to deport Jews also put their local police forces at the disposal of the Germans in the work of rounding up Jews.

On the eastern front, the Red Army was about to attack the Germans at Sokolovo. Among the Soviet forces was a thousand-strong battalion of Czechoslovak troops, soldiers who had fled from Czechoslovakia to Poland in March 1939, and from Poland to Russia in September 1939: part of the survivors of five and a half thousand Czech Jews who had sought refuge on Soviet soil, and been deported by the Soviet authorities to labour camps, where three thousand of them had perished.

Of the thousand men in the Czech battalion at Sokolovo, six hundred were Jews. The battle began on March 8 and lasted for three days. By the end of it, 140 of the Jews had been killed and 160 severely wounded. Among the Jews in the battalion was an eighteen-year-old girl, Malvine Friedmann, one of eighteen Jewish nurses who served at Sokolovo. During the battle, she saved more than seven severely wounded men by carrying them out of the danger zone.[56]

The battle of Sokolovo ended on March 13. On the following morning, in Cracow, in German-occupied Poland, two thousand Jews were rounded up for deportation. Even before the trains could leave for Birkenau, several hundred small children were shot in the entrance to one of the houses, and several hundred old people were killed in the street. Also killed were those who were sick.[57] When the Gestapo entered the hospital, an officer ordered Dr Zygmunt Fischer to abandon his patients. He refused to do so, and was shot, together with his wife and child.[58] The patients were then killed in the wards.

One eye-witness of the events of March 14 in Cracow was Maria Hochberg-Marianska, a Jewish woman living on the 'Aryan' side who had given home and shelter to Jewish children. Three years later she described the fate of the Jewish children in the ghetto orphanage:

> At midday cars drove up before the institution. The Gestapo men flung themselves upon the children. Little ones, three years of age, were flung into baskets and placed on platforms or hoisted on to carts. The older children were driven off to the Plac Zgody, flanked by armed soldiers. There, they joined the grown-ups. The baskets with the little ones were emptied behind the city like so much rubbish. They were thrown into a ditch, most of them alive. Some were killed by a blow with a rifle butt before burial.[59]

Among those deported from Cracow were Moses and Helen Hiller, whose two-year-old son had been given refuge by Josef Jachowicz and his wife in nearby Dabrowa. Neither parent survived. When Shachne cried out for his father and mother, as he often did, Jachowicz and his wife feared that neighbours would betray them to the Gestapo. Mrs Jachowicz became very attached to the little boy, loved his bright inquiring eyes, took great pride in her 'son', and took him regularly to church. Soon, he knew by heart all the Sunday hymns.

A devout Catholic, Mrs Jachowicz decided to have Shachne Hiller baptised, and went to see a young parish priest, Karol Wojtyla, who had a reputation for wisdom and trustworthiness. Revealing the secret of the boy's identity, Mrs Jachowicz told the priest of her wish that Shachne should become a 'true Christian' and devout Catholic like herself.

Wojtyla listened intently to the woman's story. When she had finished, he asked: 'And what was the parents' wish, when they entrusted their only child to you and to your husband?' Mrs Jachowicz then told him that Helen Hiller's last request had been that the child should be told of his Jewish origins, and 'returned to his people' if his parents died. Hearing this, Wojtyla replied that he would not perform the baptismal ceremony. It would be unfair, he explained, to baptise Shachne while there was still hope that, once the war was over, his relatives might take him.

Shachne Hiller not only survived the war, but was eventually united with his relatives in the United States. Karol Wojtyla was later to become Pope, as John Paul II.[60]

Several thousand able-bodied Cracow Jews, Moses and Helen Hiller among them, were sent to a slave labour camp in the suburb of Plaszow. The conditions of work at Plaszow were later described by one of the Jews there, Moshe Bejski. There was a case, he later recalled, where a man who was whipped, and cried, had to go to the commandant's office 'and inform him that he thanked him for his punishment, and when he turned around he was shot in the back.' On another occasion, all fifteen thousand prisoners were called to witness a double hanging, of a boy named Halbenstock and an engineer, Krauwiert:

> The boy Halbenstock was hanged and something happened. The rope snapped. The boy was put up again on a high chair under the rope; he started begging for his life; he was ordered to be hanged again, and he did go up to the gallows once again and was hanged. And then he was shot at.
>
> The engineer was on the second chair and here the perfidy reached even further – the SS men came with their machine guns and ordered the man to gaze upon the hanging as it was being carried out, and the engineer, Krauwiert, cut his veins with a razor and thus he was hanged. Bleeding.[61]

The majority of the Cracow deportees had been sent to Birkenau, and gassed. Such was the scale of murder there that four new gas-chambers had been under construction for some months, to enable the Jews to be gassed and cremated in the quickest possible time. Built to the most modern design, each of the new brick buildings had a vast underground undressing room adjacent to the underground gas-chamber, with the crematorium ovens above reached by special electrically controlled lifts.

The gas-chamber and crematorium in Auschwitz Main Camp, or Auschwitz I, was known henceforth as Crematorium I. The four new gas-chambers and crematoria at Birkenau, or Auschwitz II, became known as Crematorium II, Crematorium III, Crematorium IV and Crematorium V. Crematorium IV was the first to be ready: it began operation on March 22. Crematorium II began operation nine days later, on March 31; Crematorium V four days after that, on April 4; and Crematorium III on June 25.[62]

On March 15, in the Theresienstadt ghetto, a fifty-two-year-old woman died of hunger. She was one of the many thousand Theresienstadt Jews to die in the ghetto, before deportation to Birkenau. Her name was Trude Neumann. From 1918 until 1942 she had been a mental patient in an institution near Vienna. In 1942 she had been sent to Theresienstadt together with all Jewish mental patients in the Vienna area.

Trude Neumann was the daughter of Theodor Herzl, founder of the Zionist movement. Her son Stephan, born in the year in which she had been taken ill, had been educated at a British public school, and was, in 1943, an officer in the British army.[63]

On the day of the death of Herzl's daughter in Theresienstadt, the deportations began of the Jews of Salonica: an ancient Sephardi community. Ten thousand had been deported by the end of March, a further twenty-five thousand in April, and another ten thousand in May. They had no idea of their destination, having been told that it was a 'resettlement' area in Poland.

Each deportee from Salonica was allowed to take a food parcel for the journey, and up to fifteen kilogrammes of clothing for the 'resettlement' area. It was in fact Birkenau.

For many generations the Jews of Salonica had serviced the port as stevedores and dockworkers: the smooth working of the port depended upon them. But the Nazi design would allow no exceptions, no logic, no special pleading. Jews from the villages around Salonica were also deported, except from Aicatherine, where the local Director of police gave the Jews three hours to flee after receipt of the deportation order. Thirty-three Jews fled, and were hidden by Greek villagers. Three, who were unable to leave, were shot.[64]

Each act of escape or resistance still led to immediate and massive reprisals. On March 16, in Lvov, a Jew, Engineer Kotnowski, killed an SS policeman who was noted for his cruelty. The next day, as a reprisal, the Germans burst into the ghetto and hanged eleven Jewish policemen from the balconies in the main street of the ghetto. That same day more than a thousand Jews were taken out of the working groups and shot, while in Janowska camp, nearly two hundred Jews were killed: a reprisal ratio of almost twelve hundred to one.[65]

Jews who had managed to hide were continually being betrayed. In the village of Topczewo, the thirty-year-old Dr Julian Charin, a Jew from nearby Lapy, had his hiding place betrayed. His Christian rescuers could save him no more. A graduate from Padua University just before the war, he had later worked at the Bialystok Jewish hospital. He was shot on March 18: one of tens of thousands of Jews betrayed for money, fear or sheer hatred.[66] That same day, in Auschwitz Main Camp, the Jewish underground fighter Lonka Kozibrodska, who had been captured in June 1942 while on a mission to Bialystok, and sent to Auschwitz as an 'Aryan' Pole, died of typhus.[67] She was twenty-six years old. Her 'Aryan' disguise had not failed her: her fate was that of millions of Poles, who, like the Jews, were marked out for labour camp, prison, ill-treatment, execution and death.

March 20 was the eve of the festival of Purim, day of rejoicing at the downfall of Haman the Jew-hater. That day, in Czestochowa, more than a hundred Jewish doctors and their families were taken to the cemetery and shot. Among those killed was the forty-four-year-old neurologist, Dr Bernard Epstein, whose postgraduate work had been done in Vienna and Paris. He was murdered with his wife and two sons.[68]

Another of those shot down in the cemetery at Czestochowa was a woman gynaecologist and obstetrician, Dr Kruza Gruenwald: she was fifty-six years old.[69] Another of the murdered doctors, Irena Horowicz, a former general practitioner in Lodz, was thirty years old. She was murdered with her three-year-old child.[70]

Lawyers and engineers were also murdered in the Czestochowa cemetery that day: that same Czestochowa which is revered by Polish Catholics for the shrine of the Madonna there. On the following day, March 21, the actual day of the Purim festival, there was another 'Purim massacre' in nearby Piotrkow. That day, Jews living legally in the ghetto were told that there was to be an exchange with German citizens living in the settlement of Sarona, in Palestine. Ten people were needed for this exchange, the Germans declared. All must possess university degrees: that was the only condition for emigration.

The Jews chosen for Palestine were driven out of Piotrkow in

Gestapo cars, and then driven round the city a few times, before being taken, as darkness fell, to the Jewish cemetery. A deep pit had been dug. The Gestapo lined up the 'chosen', made derisive speeches amid much drinking and laughter, and then ordered the Jews to undress.

Among the Jews shot that night at the Piotrkow cemetery was Dr Maurycy Brams, a paediatrician and popular figure among the poor Jews of pre-war Piotrkow, shot that day with his wife and sixteen-year-old daughter, Hannah – 'Ania'. The teenage girl had managed to run away from the cemetery at the last moment, but the Gestapo chased her among the tombstones until they caught her. Also shot that night was a young lawyer, Simon Stein, killed with his mother, and the psychiatrist Dr Leon Glatter.

Part of the Nazi 'Purim game' was to 'revenge' the ten sons of the Jew-hater Haman. These ten had been hanged in the biblical story. But only eight Jews had been brought from Piotrkow that night, so the Jewish watchman of the cemetery and his wife were included, at the last moment, in the execution.[71]

In Radom, all Jewish doctors were taken that Purim to nearby Szydlowiec, ostensibly to 'go to Palestine'. On arriving in Szydlowiec they found graves, newly dug, awaiting them. Among those killed were the neurologist Dr Wladyslaw Cung and the gynaecologist Dr Anatol Fryd.[72]

Tens of thousands of Jews were still in hiding throughout the General Government, the Eastern Territories and the Ukraine. But German searches for them were continuous. On March 22 Dr Klukowski noted in his diary, in Szczcbrzeszyn, where he had earlier witnessed the harrowing scenes of deportation:

> Yesterday they brought me a dangerously wounded peasant from Gruszka Zaporska. He had concealed six Jews from Radecznica in his cow barn. When the police appeared, he began to run and was shot at. He died last night. The gendarmes did not permit the family to carry away his body and ordered the Municipal Administration to bury him as a bandit. The Jews were shot by the Polish police of Radecznica and, shortly after the event, the gendarmes appeared in Gruszka and shot the peasant's wife and two children: a six-year-old girl and a three-year-old boy.[73]

On March 25 an anonymous letter, written by a German, was forwarded by Hans Frank from Cracow to Berlin, to Hitler's Chancellery. In the letter, the writer described with disgust the liquidation of an eastern ghetto, and told of how children were thrown to the ground, and then had their heads deliberately trampled on with boots.[74] On the same day that this letter was received in Berlin, *Der Sturmer* announced in triumph that 'the extermination of the Jews is in progress'.[75]

On April 5, the third and last train bringing Jews from Macedonia for 'resettlement' reached Treblinka. All were gassed.[76] That same day three hundred Jews from the ghettos of Sol and Smorgon were deported to Ponar. They had been told that they were to be 'resettled' in the Kovno ghetto. On reaching Ponar, they realized that they had been deceived. That night a fifteen-year-old Vilna schoolboy, Yitshok Rudashevski, noted in his diary the story that reached Vilna within a few hours: 'Like wild animals before dying, the people began in mortal despair to break the railway cars, they broke the little windows reinforced by strong wire. Hundreds were shot to death while running away. The railway line over a great distance is covered with corpses.'[77]

All those Jews from Sol and Smorgon who survived the rail-side massacre of April 5 were shot in the pits at Ponar by the German and Lithuanian SS men. A few hours later, five thousand more Jews reached Ponar, mostly young men from the ghettos of Swieciany and Oszmiana, whom the Gestapo feared might find a way of escaping from the ghettos in order to join the growing number of Jewish and Soviet partisans. These five thousand were sent first to the Vilna ghetto. Then, as with the Jews of Sol and Smorgon, they were sent on as if to the Kovno ghetto, 'where there was more room'. Just outside Vilna their train came to a halt. They too had been brought to Ponar. Sensing the danger, these young men tried to break out of the freight cars and fought, with revolvers, knives and fists. They were shot down in the cars themselves, and along the railway line. A few dozen managed to escape to Vilna. The rest were killed on the spot.[78]

The Polish journalist, W. Sakowicz, noted in his diary:

> Bonfires burn near the station. They were kindled by policemen. Again a train from Vilna. They have arrived. The people

were driven out from the carriages, and immediately a small batch was taken to the pit. The ones with poorer clothes on weren't even undressed. They were driven to the pit, and shooting began immediately.

Another batch of people were standing nearby and, on seeing what had happened to their nearest, began to yell. Some started running. A little lagging behind the others with her hair dishevelled, a woman is running pressing her child to her breast. The woman is chased after by a policeman, he smashes her head in with the rifle butt, the woman collapses. The policemen seizes the child by its leg, drags it to the pit.[79]

Among those participating in this Ponar massacre of April 5 was SS Sergeant Wille. 'While shooting,' noted a German Security Police report, Wille 'was attacked by a Jew' and wounded 'by two knife blows in the back and one blow in the head'. He was immediately taken to the military hospital in Vilna. 'His life is out of danger,' the report continued, and added: 'A Lithuanian policeman was fired at while some fifty Jews tried to escape, and he is badly wounded.'[80]

In Vilna, the poet Shmerl Kaczerginski was standing not far from the ghetto gate. 'I saw a young fellow sneaking in,' he later recalled, 'bloody, weary, disappearing quickly into a doorway.' In the security of someone's home, the young man then 'pulled off his clothes, washed away the blood, tied up his wounded shoulder', and whispered to those who had crowded around him: 'I come from Ponar!'

Kaczerginski added: 'We were petrified'. The young man told them: 'Everyone – everyone was shot!' The tears rolled down his face. 'Who?' he was asked. Did he mean the four thousand who were being sent to Kovno? 'Yes!'[81]

A month after the Germans had been humiliated by Bulgaria's refusal to allow Bulgarian Jews to be deported, Hitler personally urged the Hungarian Regent, Admiral Horthy, to allow the Jews of Hungary to be 'resettled'. The two men met at Klessheim Castle, near Salzburg, on April 17. Horthy, aware of what was intended, was adamant: 'The Jews cannot be exterminated or beaten to death,' he insisted. Hitler then set out his own reasoning, as recorded on the following day by his interpreter:

Where the Jews were left to themselves, as for instance in Poland, the most terrible misery and decay prevailed. They are just pure parasites. In Poland this state of affairs had been fundamentally cleared up. If the Jews there did not want to work, they were shot. If they could not work, they had to succumb. They had to be treated like tuberculosis bacilli, with which a healthy body may become infected. This was not cruel, if one remembered that even innocent creatures of nature, such as hares and deer, have to be killed, so that no harm is caused by them. Why should the beasts who wanted to bring us Bolshevism be spared more? Nations which did not rid themselves of Jews, perished. One of the most famous examples of this was the downfall of a people who were once so proud – the Persians, who now lead a pitiful existence as Armenians.[82]

Horthy refused to accept Hitler's arguments, or his pressure, and returned to Budapest; for the time being, the Jews of Hungary remained in Hungary.

28

Warsaw, April 1943: hopeless days of revolt

ON THE NIGHT OF 18 APRIL 1943 the Jews of Warsaw learned that plans were about to be put into effect for the final destruction of the Warsaw ghetto. 'Even though we were prepared,' Zivia Lubetkin later recalled, 'and had even prayed for this hour, we turned pale. A tremor of joy mixed with a shudder of fear passed through all of us. But we suppressed our emotions and reached for our guns.'[1]

The Germans had chosen yet another date in the 'Goebbels calendar', Passover 1943, for the destruction of what was left of the Warsaw ghetto. Driven out of the ghetto in ignominy in January, they were determined not to fail in April. The Jews were equally determined not to be destroyed without a struggle. 'He who has arms will fight,' the commander of the Jewish resistance groups, Mordechai Anielewicz, told his colleagues on the eve of the German attack, 'he who has no arms – women and children – will go down into the bunkers.' In the first 'chaos' of the fighting, he added, those in the bunkers should seek to cross into Aryan Warsaw. 'Go to the woods,' he advised. 'Some of them will be saved.'[2]

The Germans entered the Warsaw ghetto on the morning of April 19. Man for man and gun for gun, their forces were formidable: 2,100 German soldiers, including SS troops, against 1,200 Jewish fighters; 13 heavy machine guns, against which the Jews had no equivalent armament; 69 hand-held machine guns, against which the Jews had none; a total of 135 submachine guns, against which the Jews had 2; several howitzers and other artillery pieces, of which the Jews had none; a total of 1,358 rifles, as against only 17 rifles among the Jews. The Jews had acquired some pistols, about five hundred. But pistols were of little or no use in street fighting.

The main Jewish weapons were several thousand grenades and incendiary bottles.[3]

As the German forces entered the ghetto, the Jews opened fire. Zivia Lubetkin was with her group of fighters, looking out of an attic window at that precise moment, as thousands of German soldiers surrounded the ghetto with machine guns. Then, as she later recalled:

> ... all of a sudden they started entering the ghetto, thousands armed as if they were going to the front against Russia. And we, some twenty men and women, young. And what was our arms? The arms we had – we had a revolver, a grenade and a whole group had two guns, and some bombs, home-made, prepared in a very primitive way. We had to light it by matches and Molotov bottles. It was strange to see those twenty men and women, Jewish men and women, standing up against the armed great enemy glad and merry, because we knew that their end will come. We knew that they will conquer us first, but to know that for our lives they would pay a high price. . . .
>
> When the Germans came up to our posts and marched by and we threw those hand grenades and bombs, and saw German blood pouring over the streets of Warsaw, after we saw so much Jewish blood running in the streets of Warsaw before that, there was rejoicing. The tomorrow did not worry us. The rejoicing amongst Jewish fighters was great and, see the wonder and the miracle, those German heroes retreated, afraid and terrorized from the Jewish bombs and hand grenades, home-made.
>
> And after an hour we saw the officer hastening his soldiers to retreat, to collect their dead and their wounded. But they did not move, they did not collect their dead and their wounded. We took their arms later. And thus on the first day, we the few with our poor arms drove the Germans away from the ghetto.[4]

The first day's fighting was over. According to the German Commander, SS General Jurgen Stroop, the German losses had been six SS men and six Ukrainian auxiliaries.[5]

It was clear from Stroop's account that in every instance that day, it was the Jewish fighters who had opened fire, catching the Germans by surprise. It was also apparent that the Germans had met not only with the organized resistance of several hundred Jewish fighters, but with the resistance of tens of thousands of Jews in hiding in the cellars, bunkers and sewers of the ghetto.[6] That same first day of revolt, the Polish underground organization, the Home Army, presented the Jewish insurgents with twenty-two rifles.[7]

The first evening of the ghetto uprising was also the Seder night, the first night of Passover, the Jewish 'festival of liberty'. During the evening, one of the fighters, Tuvia Borzykowski, went in search of flashlights at 4 Kacza Street:

> Wandering about there, I unexpectedly came upon Rabbi Maisel. When I entered the room, I suddenly realized that this was the night of the first Seder.
>
> The room looked as if it had been hit by a hurricane. Bedding was everywhere, chairs lay overturned, the floor was strewn with household objects, the window panes were all gone. It had all happened during the day, before the inhabitants of the room returned from the bunker.
>
> Amidst this destruction, the table in the centre of the room looked incongruous with glasses filled with wine, with the family seated around, the rabbi reading the Haggadah. His reading was punctuated by explosions and the rattling of machine guns; the faces of the family around the table were lit by the red light from the burning buildings, nearby.

'I could not stay long,' Borzykowski added. 'As I was leaving, the Rabbi cordially bade me farewell and wished me success. He was old and broken, he told me, but we, the young people, must not give up, and God would help us.'[8]

In Vilna, the poet Shmerl Kaczerginski was among a group of Jews listening, on the morning of April 19, to a clandestine radio. 'Hello, hello!' they heard over the air waves. 'The survivors in the Warsaw ghetto have begun an armed resistance against the murderers of the Jewish people. The ghetto is aflame!'

'We knew of no other particulars yet,' Kaczerginski later recalled, but 'we suddenly saw clearly the flames of the Warsaw ghetto and Jews fighting with arms for their dignity and self-respect.'[9]

Leon Najberg, who was to survive the war, noted how, on April 20, 'things look more and more serious'. The Warsaw ghetto was being bombarded 'by mortars and machine guns of different calibre. Hopeless plight.' At noon the German industrialist, Walter Toebbens, ordered all those employed in his factories to assemble at the Umschlagplatz on the following morning. Their destination, Toebbens told them, truthfully, was to factories set up in two labour camps at the villages of Trawniki and Poniatow, near Lublin. But no one believed him. Najberg himself commented:

> So this is a new trick of murderers! They want to get us into a new mechanized factory of slaughter! The Treblinkas are too popular – they invented Trawniki and Poniatow. The news had spread over the whole factory. People have decided not to go to the Umschlagplatz. Everybody prefers to shut himself alive in tomb-shelters rather than to yield himself alive to the murderers.

During April 20 the Germans broke into the Czyste hospital on Gesia Street where, as Najberg noted, 'They shot all the sick lying in beds.' Among those killed was Michal Gluski, the editor, before the war, of the monthly *Foreign Languages Echo*. 'That talented man', Najberg wrote, 'found his tragic death on a hospital bed.'[10] Alexander Donat later recalled: 'German soldiers went through the wards shooting and killing all whom they found. Then they set the building on fire. Those patients and staff who had managed to reach the cellars, died in the fire.'[11]

The Germans moved through the ghetto, shelling the buildings from which shots were fired at them, and burning down the apartment blocks, building by building. Several hundred Jews were forced by the smoke and flames to jump from the blazing buildings, and to their deaths. Leon Najberg wrote in his diary:

> Our brave defenders are holding out at their posts. Germans – in spite of everything – have to fight for access to each house. Gates of houses are barricaded, each house in Ghetto is a defensive fortress, each flat is a citadel – Jewish defenders are showering missiles from flats' windows and throwing shells at bandits.
>
> The defenders are passing over from one street to another through garrets and recapturing places which are threatened by German bandits. The murderers have introduced flame-throwers into action. Houses in the ghetto are set on fire.

'From tomorrow', Najberg ended his notes for April 20, 'we will

have to lock ourselves up in terrible shelters until the end of the war
— perhaps for ever.'[12]

Despite being outnumbered and outarmed, the Jewish fighters
continued to engage the German forces. On April 23 Mordecai
Anielewicz wrote to Yitzhak Zuckerman, who was seeking help for
the uprising on the 'Aryan' side: 'You should know that the pistol is
of no use. We hardly made use of it. What we need is grenades, rifles,
machine guns and explosives.' Anielewicz wrote also of the 'victory'
that only a single man from his fighting units was missing. His letter
ended: 'Keep well. Perhaps we'll still see each other. What's most
important; the dream of my life has become a reality. I lived to see
Jewish defence in the ghetto in all its greatness and splendour.'[13]

On April 25 Leon Najberg witnessed the death of several Jews
during the fires started by the Germans in the buildings around
where he was hiding. In one cellar nearby lay a German Jew, Hoch,
of whom Najberg wrote:

> He had hidden in a hide-out on the fourth floor. He had started
> to be asphyxiated under the influence of the smell of burning
> carbon monoxide. When the first tongues of flame had reached
> Hoch's hide-out, the staircase was already destroyed. He had
> jumped from the fourth floor. He had his arms broken, his
> spine shattered, and coagulated blood on his face. Yesterday he
> was still conscious and crawled up to the cellar on his own.
> Today he is lying and dying.

In the courtyard of the next building, Najberg saw the bodies of
two children and a woman. 'They have burned hair,' he wrote,
'mangled faces and rifle-shot wounds. What yesterday was alive is a
heap of flesh and bones.'[14]

On April 26 the German commander, SS Brigadier General Stroop,
reported that the continuing resistance in the bunkers and underground shelters had been 'broken, either by returning fire or by
blowing up the bunkers'.[15] As the buildings of the ghetto were set on
fire, and thousands of unarmed Jews were rounded up and marched
to the Umschlagplatz, the battle in the bunkers continued; even the
roofs and upper floors of unburned houses gave shelter to Jews with
guns. On April 27 Alexander Donat was among those being
marched to the Umschlagplatz. As he later recalled:

When we passed Niska Street, the fighting was still going on; from roofs, from the windows of burning buildings, from doorways. Suddenly Lena clutched my hand and squeezed it with all her might. A blood-curdling scream rang out from an upper-storey window filled with flames where a woman appeared holding a child by the hand, and toppled down to the street. That was our last sight of the Warsaw ghetto.[16]

From a building on the 'Aryan' side of the ghetto wall, Feigele Peltel, in hiding, watched as the ghetto was set on fire. Later she recalled what she had seen as a Pole pointed out to her one of the burning buildings:

On the balcony of the second floor a woman stood wringing her hands. She disappeared into the building but returned a moment later, carrying a child and dragging a featherbed, which she flung to the pavement to break her fall. Clutching her child, she started to climb over the railing. A spray of bullets caught her midway – the child dropped to the street – the woman's body dangled lifeless from the railing.

By now the flames had enveloped the upper floor, their rise matched by the increased frequency and intensity of the explosions. Jews were jumping out of windows, some of them caught by bullets in mid-air, others shot on the ground. Two Jews opened fire from the third floor, then retreated. A knot of people stood crowded in a third-storey window, lowering a rope to the ground. One man, then another, climbed out of the window and slid down the rope. The Germans opened fire, and both fell to the pavement. The cough of the machine gun mixed with the screams of agony.

As the room in which Feigele Peltel was hiding filled with 'the acrid smoke and stench of the burning ghetto', she returned again and again to the window, watching through the night as the flames spread from building to building. Her account continued:

Dawn came quiet and ghastly to the ghetto, revealing the burnt shells of the buildings, the charred, blood-stained bodies of the victims. Suddenly one of those bodies began to move, slowly, painfully crawling on its belly until it disappeared into the smoking ruins. Others began to show signs of life. The enemy was on the alert, a spray of machine-gun fire – and all was lifeless again.[17]

Fighters and civilians were intermingled, drawn closer together by the street-by-street destruction of the ghetto. The fighters at 29 Mila Street were sheltering several hundred women and children. Then, as their building too was set on fire, the order was given to withdraw. Tuvia Borzykowski later recalled:

> The unit commander went from hole to hole dragging out those who were afraid to move, warned the tardy that the convoy would start without them. When we finally started to move, a thin, childish voice heard from a distance stopped us. Then we saw a girl of about ten come out of a passage connecting two courtyards. She pleaded with us to save her mother who was still in the bunker with her clothes on fire. The girl herself was in severe pain from several burns.
>
> Several comrades immediately ran to the passage, but they were too late. In the few minutes since the girl had left her, the woman had been buried under burning debris. The child could not understand that her mother was gone; she cried and screamed and refused to leave the place. We had to take her by force.[18]

Some civilians and fighters managed to get through the cellars and sewers of the ghetto to the relative safety of 'Aryan' Warsaw. But the aim of the insurgents, to fight the Germans house by house and cellar by cellar, was foiled by the German decision to bombard the ghetto from afar, and to set it ablaze, avoiding hand-to-hand combat. 'We had not expected this,' Zivia Lubetkin later recalled. 'All our plans had been for nothing,' and she added, recalling the scene on May 1:

> We sat in the dark, scores of Jewish fighters, still carrying our weapons, surrounded by thousands of eager and expectant Jews. Was it not May Day? The feeling of responsibility lay heavy on our hearts, on our conscience, and gave no respite.
>
> The crowded, cowering masses of Jews huddled around us waiting for a word of hope from the fighters' lips. We were bewildered and lost. What should we say to them? What could we say to ourselves? How terrible was this feeling of helplessness! How grave the responsibility we felt as the last desperate Hebrew warriors! We could not hold out against the Germans' consuming fire for long without water or food or weapons.[19]

Even those who had managed to escape to 'Aryan' Warsaw were not secure. On May 3 the Germans arrested twenty-one women of Jewish, or suspected Jewish, origin, in the streets. All were killed. 'Their names are not known,' records one of the historians of those years. Nine days later there was a second such round-up and execution.[20]

The Jewish fighters made attempts to contact their fellow fighters on the 'Aryan' side: but when, on May 7, Pawel Bruskin, a unit commander, led a group of fighters through the sewers to try to reach the 'Aryan' sector, he fell into a German ambush, was captured and killed.[21] Others were caught in the bunkers without any chance of escape. From Warsaw to London the message came: 'We fight like animals for naked life.'[22]

'When they took me out,' Hadassa Talmon later recalled, 'I was like a wounded animal. There were lots of stones there, and I started to throw stones at the Germans. They hit me with their rifle butts. I was beaten and injured all over. I was covered with blood'.[23]

Among those wounded by the German shelling was Abraham Krzepicki, the young man who had escaped from Treblinka the previous September, after eighteen days in the camp, and had brought his story to Warsaw. Wounded in the leg during the shelling, he could not move; nor were his colleagues able to drag him from the burning building in which he and other wounded men were trapped.[24]

Another of those who probably perished in the Warsaw ghetto uprising was Yakov Grojanowski, the man who, in January 1942, had brought the news of the Chelmno death camp to Warsaw.[25]

By the end of the first week of May the last main focus of Jewish resistance in the Warsaw ghetto was a bunker at 18 Mila Street, in which 120 fighters were gathered. This too was attacked by the Germans, on May 8. For two hours the entrance was bombarded, but in vain. Then the Germans began to send gas into the bunker. Four years later Zivia Lubetkin recalled:

Aryeh Wilner was the first to cry out: 'Come, let us destroy ourselves. Let's not fall into their hands alive.' The suicides began. Pistols jammed and the owners begged their friends to kill them. But no one dared to take the life of a comrade. Lutek Rotblatt fired four shots at his mother but, wounded and bleeding, she still moved. Then someone discovered a hidden exit, but only a few succeeded in getting out this way. The others slowly suffocated in the gas.

Among the hundred Jewish fighters who were killed in the battle for the bunker under 18 Mila Street was Mordechai Anielewicz, 'our handsome commander', Zivia Lubetkin wrote, 'whom we all loved'.[26] 'We fought back,' she later reflected, 'and it made our lot easier and made it easier to die.'[27] Also killed was Berl Broyde, a leading member of the Jewish Fighting Organization, who, deported to Treblinka in January 1943, had managed to jump from the train and return to the ghetto.[28]

The Germans combed the ghetto for any surviving Jews. In all, according to Jurgen Stroop's calculations, 7,000 Jews had been killed in the fighting, and 30,000 had been deported to Treblinka. Five to six hundred Jews, he added, 'were destroyed by being blown up or by perishing in the flames'. A total of 631 bunkers had been destroyed.[29]

Many Jews chose suicide rather than execution or deportation: among them the seventeen-year-old Frania Beatus, who had helped to smuggle Jewish fighters out of the ghetto through the sewers, and who, from the 'Aryan' side, was able to maintain a certain contact by telephone with the fighters inside the ghetto: she committed suicide on May 12.[30] Also on May 12, in London, a leading member of the pre-war Jewish Social Democrat Party, the Bund, Shmuel Zygielbojm, committed suicide. A member of the pre-war Municipal Council in Lodz, and briefly a member of the Jewish Council in Warsaw, he had been sent out of Poland in January 1940 at the request of the Bund. In London he had become a leading speaker and broadcaster on the fate of the Jews under Nazi rule.

In his suicide letter, Zygielbojm stated that he could not live 'when the remnant of the Jewish people in Poland, whom I represent, is being steadily annihilated'. He had not been 'fortunate' to die, as had his comrades in the Warsaw ghetto, 'with weapons in their hands', but he 'belonged' to them, and to their mass graves. 'By my death,' Zygielbojm's letter ended, 'I wish to express my vigorous protest against the apathy with which the world regards and resigns itself to the slaughter of the Jewish people.'[31]

On May 16 Jurgen Stroop reported to his superiors that the

Warsaw ghetto 'is no longer in existence'. The 'large-scale action' had ended at 8.15 that evening 'by blowing up the Warsaw synagogue'.[32] Systematically, street by street, the buildings of the ghetto were now destroyed. But small groups of Jews continued to live in the bunkers, and to fight. Leon Najberg was still in hiding on May 19: he and forty-four others, still undetected in what they called their 'den'. That Sunday he wrote in his diary:

We are on the third floor and we have done away with stairs. We go upstairs with the help of rope-ladder. We are in burnt rooms, i.e. the Lidzbarski brother and sister, the Szarmans, the Koplows and so-called group of Klonski – it is ours. One floor lower there is the apartment of Tojst, quite saved and with complete furnishings. I am looking at that apartment and see an analogy to present life of Jews. From among families there are – *for the present* – only individuals who saved their lives, from the whole streets which were occupied by Jews – individuals. From Jewish towns – individuals. From the whole Poland, from the millions – the thousands. And that life of ours is for the present saved by a miracle and overshadowed by the ruins of Polish Jewry. It is useless and incapable of anything and for ever unfit for normal life. Though our hearts are still beating, there will never be a joy of life in them. After months of darkness and stuffiness we can again bask in the sun, fresh air and light of day. We are once again people who see sky and sun though sun does not shine for everybody.

At 4 Walowa Street two bodies of new female victims lie and sun speeds up their decay and cats and crows eat up pieces of flesh from faces. There was a quiet at noon.

The murderers arrived only at 1 p.m. and uncovered the bunker at 38 Swietojerska Street. After having bored holes, the Huns have let in 'foreign', that is, poison gas, and smoked out people. Then, after preliminary work, searching the captives and robbery of the properties, they have been forcing victims to confess where are Jews still hidden.

From among sixty persons they found Moniek K. with a gangrenous leg who was rather like a dead man (eighteen years old). They demanded Moniek to tell them where the other bunkers with Jews are. Moniek categorically stated that he did not know. The murderers were waiting only for that. Riding-whips and lead cables were used. Moniek clenched his teeth so as not to betray his brothers. But the Germans contrived everything. One of the SS men shot down Moniek's arm threatening: 'Wenn du zeigst nicht juden-bunker schiese ich dich tot', 'If you don't show us the Jewish bunker, I'll shoot you dead.' Writhing with agony, brave brave Moniek was shouting: 'Murderers, I don't betray! You can kill me!'[33]

Moniek was killed. Two weeks later, on June 3, the Germans destroyed a bunker on Walowa Street containing 150 people. 'Those living in the shelters', Leon Najberg later recalled, 'became harrowingly thin and looked like skeletons. After six weeks in these graves, they looked like ghosts frightened of living.'

Najberg's group lived on among the ruins. But starvation, exhaustion and sickness took their toll. Only four of them were still alive by September 1943, when they managed to cross into 'Aryan' Warsaw.[34]

That September, the Germans sent a Polish labour battalion to the site of the ghetto, to demolish any walls and structures still undestroyed. 'Those who still remained in hiding', one of the ghetto's most recent historians has written, 'evidently met their deaths during these demolition activities, although a few individuals continued to live in dug-outs, totally cut off from nature, light and human company.'[35]

29

'The crashing fires of hell'

ON 1 MAY 1943, while the battle still raged in the Warsaw ghetto, a group of Jewish writers and poets had gathered in the Vilna ghetto for an evening on the theme, 'Spring in Yiddish literature'. Every speaker, and every poem, was permeated with the spirit of the fighting in the Warsaw ghetto. At the meeting, the poet Shmerl Kaczerginski saw his fellow poet, the twenty-three-year-old Hirsh Glik. 'Well, what's new with you, Hirsh?' he asked. 'I wrote a new poem,' Glik replied. 'Want to hear it?'

Glik brought the poem to Kaczerginski's room on the morning of May 2. 'Now listen carefully,' he told his friend. 'I'll sing it for you.' Then, as Kaczerginski later recalled: 'He began to sing it softly, but full of excitement. His eyes glowed with little sparks. "The hour for which we yearned will come anew." Where did he get his faith? His voice became firmer. He tapped out the rhythm with his foot, as if he were marching.'

The song which Hirsh Glik sang to his friend in Vilna on that May morning was to spread like wildfire in the ghettos and camps, and among the Jewish partisans, becoming the song of hope, and battle hymn of oppressed Jewry. Itself inspired by the struggle in the Warsaw ghetto, the song was to inspire tens of thousands of Jews to fight if they could, and if they could not fight, to survive:

> Never say that you have reached the
> very end,
> Though leaden skies a bitter future
> may portend;
> And the hour for which we've
> yearned will yet arrive,
> And our marching step will thunder:
> 'We survive!'

From green palm trees to the land
of distant snow,
We are here with our sorrow, our
woe,
And wherever our blood was shed
in pain,
Our fighting spirits now will
resurrect again.

The golden rays of morning sun will
dry our tears,
Dispelling bitter agony of
yesteryears,
But if the sun and dawn with us
will be delayed,
Then let this song ring out to you
the call, instead.

Not lead, but blood inscribed this
mighty song we sing,
It's not a carolling of birds upon the
wing
But a people midst the crashing fires
of hell,
Sang this song with guns in hands,
until it fell.[1]

Most of the Jews seized in the Warsaw ghetto as the revolt was crushed were deported to Treblinka and gassed. Others were sent to Majdanck, or to labour camps in the Lublin region, principally those at Trawniki and Poniatowa. Several thousand Jews found refuge in 'Aryan' Warsaw.

About seventy of the surviving ghetto fighters managed to reach the forests east of Warsaw. There, many were betrayed, among them Zygmunt Frydrych, who had been active during the revolt smuggling arms and men from 'Aryan' Warsaw into the ghetto, and who was betrayed while leading a group of fighters to shelter. He was thirty-two-years old. Others, seeking safety further afield, went towards the forests near Hrubieszow, among them the twenty-three-year-old Pesia Furmanowicz. She and her comrades were murdered before they reached their destination.[2]

The Jews who were deported from Warsaw to Majdanek went through torments which few survived. Lena Berg later recalled the repeated selections:

> Every roll call was a selection: women were sent to the gas-chamber because they had swollen legs, scratches on their bodies, because they wore eye-glasses or head kerchiefs, or because they stood roll call without head kerchiefs. Young SS men prowled among the inmates and took down their numbers and during the evening roll call the women were ordered to step forward, and we never saw them again. Maria Keiler, a childhood friend and schoolmate, died that way. She had a scratch on her leg and an SS man took her number. When they singled her out at roll call, she simply walked away without even nodding goodbye. She knew quite well where she was going, and I knew it, too; I was surprised at how little upset I was.[3]

Alexander Donat, who was also at Majdanek, recalled how SS Lieutenant Anton Thumann would ride his motorcycle into a group of prisoners, then single out two of them for 'punishment', roping their hands to the motorcycle and dragging them after him, 'gradually speeding up until they were no more than torn flesh and crumpled bones and the barrack square was crisscrossed with blood'.

One of the most 'notorious' of the murderers in Majdanek was an SS man by the name of Dziobaty, as Alexander Donat later recalled:

> One of the men working near me was a weak-looking individual who – while the more experienced prisoners picked out huge flat stones that looked impressive, but weighed little – picked up only small stones, ignoring his neighbours' advice. Eventually the foreman noticed him and made him pick up an enormous rock. The man bent under its weight and said apologetically, 'I can't carry anything heavy, I have a hernia.'
>
> 'What's he saying?' Dziobaty was suddenly next to the foreman.
>
> The foreman told him.
>
> 'Oh, a hernia, rupture,' the SS man said sympathetically. To the prisoner he said, 'Show me, I've never seen one.'
>
> Flattered by the SS man's interest, the prisoner complied and lowered his trousers. The SS man bent forward, then swung his

foot back and with all his might kicked the man in the genitals with his hobnailed boot. The animal shriek that resounded froze the whole column, and faces of curious camp officials appeared in front of every barrack. Blood poured from the body of the prisoner, who now lay writhing on the ground, howling like a dog.

Dziobaty, overcome with rage, began to kick him over and over again, roaring, 'Du dreckiges Arschloch, verfluchter Judenschmarotzer. . . . Ruptur hat er!' 'You shitty asshole, you goddam Jew parasite. . . . He's got a rupture!' The body finally lay still.[4]

Another of the Jews deported from Warsaw to Majdanek after the ghetto revolt was Israel Gutman, who had been wounded in the eye during the fighting. By good fortune, he was allowed to go to the camp hospital in Majdanek. While in the hospital, Gutman and the other patients heard a noise outside, and looked out of the window. 'All this took only a few seconds,' he later recalled, 'because all those who had got up to look at what was happening were quickly driven back from the windows.' But what he saw was to be engraved on Gutman's memory. 'I saw the march of naked people. I saw amongst them a boy – I do not know how old he was, about ten years of age – I saw that the boy had in his arms a smaller child. I saw two SS men, one pointing out this picture to the other, and laughing.'

In the few seconds available to him, Gutman tried to look in the eyes of the two SS men, 'stealthily, because a direct gaze was too dangerous. I wanted to see in their eyes if there is no expression of a self-struggle – a spark of humanity in those eyes. I always met the same gaze. When we were sad and grieving, they were happy. Whenever they could torture us, they laughed. They were drunk with blood.'[5]

Thirty-six years later, a survivor of Majdanek, Wanda Bialas, told a court in Düsseldorf of how Jewish children 'were enticed with sugar lumps by Nazi SS guards to mount the lorries to take them to their deaths in the gas-chambers'.[6]

Some Jews, sent from Warsaw to Majdanek, were sent away again after a few days to other camps in the Lublin region, among them Budzyn, a camp that provided labour for the Heinkel aircraft factory nearby. One of those sent to Budzyn was David

Wdowinski, who later recalled how the camp commandant ordered all the newcomers, 'exactly 807 men', to stand in two lines. He then went up to one of the Jews 'and told him to step out of line, and ordered him to undress'. As the Jew began to undress, the commandant 'began shouting at him, "Hurry up! Undress completely!" until he was stark naked. And then he took out a pistol and killed the Jew on the spot, and said to us, "This is what is going to happen to each one of you if you are not going to hand over everything you've got here with you and on you."' [7]

At Trawniki, the Jews deported from Warsaw included Emanuel Ringelblum, who was later smuggled out of the camp by the Jewish underground and returned to Warsaw, where he found refuge in a bunker in the 'Aryan' part of the city. At Poniatowa, the second of the two labour camps to which Jews had been deported from Warsaw, the Jews resisted. Hundreds were killed, and hundreds more committed suicide. In his Warsaw bunker, Ringelblum began work on a history of Trawniki, and also of the Jewish Fighting Organization. [8]

Thus, at the very moment of deepest depression, when the hopelessness of revolt had been made clear in all its cruelty, a man who had witnessed the worst torments of his people, and understood that many must go unavenged, settled down amid daily dangers to record what could be recorded; he, an historian in his mid-forties, convinced that the truth must survive, even if those who recorded it would not. [9]

Also in hiding in 'Aryan' Warsaw was Abrasha Blum, a friend of Ringelblum, one of the organizers of armed resistance in the ghetto, and a member, with Yitzhak Zuckerman, of the Coordinating Committee of Jewish Organizations. Blum, in hiding, retained his power to inspire others. But he was betrayed, arrested, and tortured by the Gestapo. Feigele Peltel, who saw him in prison, was the last of his friends to see him alive:

How horrible he looked! His face was livid and swollen on one side, his head bloody, his hands bruised, his mouth bleeding, he was barely able to walk. I appealed to the police to let him lie down. They permitted him to lie down but went on torturing him with their questions. Abrasha was weak and incoherent.

After a prolonged investigation, the police sent us out of the room. Abrasha did his best to walk, grimacing with pain. When I asked in a whisper how he was feeling, he was unable to utter a word.[10]

On May 10 or May 11, Abrasha Blum was shot.

News of the Warsaw ghetto uprising spread throughout German-occupied Europe, thrilling those Jews who heard it. But the pressure against Jews in hiding was relentless. Hundreds were killed in the Parczew forest when, that same Passover, the Germans launched a major military action against the partisans, and the refugees in the family camp which the partisans were protecting.[11] Zeew Jung-sztajn, one of the refugees in the forest, who had just reached his ninth birthday, later recalled how, after three hours of aerial bombardment, 'the forest began to burn. The Jews were in the bunkers. The Germans discovered many bunkers. They caught two young boys who betrayed a bunker in which there were many Jews and Russians, who were shot.'[12]

The refugees in the Parczew forest were soon to find a new protector who organized them under his command, Yekhiel Gryns-zpan, whose group grew from eighty fighters in mid-1943 to three hundred a year later. From the outset of Grynszpan's command, in April 1943, he led a number of successful attacks on German, Ukrainian and Polish police posts in the area, as well as setting fire to the German police headquarters in Parczew itself.[13]

At Treblinka, during the very first days of the Warsaw ghetto uprising, the small group of Jews employed there to sort the clothes of those who had been gassed, and to carry out menial tasks for the SS, were in the last stage of preparing for a break-out. Their target date was April 1, and three separate 'combat units' had been organized under the leadership of Dr Julian Chorazycki, a fifty-year-old ear, nose and throat specialist who had practised before the war in Warsaw.[14] In Treblinka, Chorazycki had been put in charge of a small infirmary.

A former captain in the Polish army, Chorazycki had managed to make contact with a Ukrainian guard at Treblinka who, in return for a substantial sum of money, was willing to buy arms for the rebel group. A few such purchases had already been smuggled in when, on April 19, the deputy commander of Treblinka, Kurt Franz, entered Chorazycki's medical office, and saw a packet of banknotes peeping out of the doctor's apron pocket.

'Give me that money,' screamed Franz. But Chorazycki attacked him with a surgical knife, wounding him in the neck.[15] Jumping out of the window, Franz called out that the doctor must be captured alive.

Chorazycki himself then jumped through the window, walked a few steps, stumbled, and fell. He had taken poison. An eye-witness of what followed, Kalman Feigman, later recalled:

> They lifted Chorazycki up. He still showed some signs of life. All the prisoners were assembled in the camp's courtyard. They lined us up in rows and ordered us to watch how they wash out the doctor's stomach. The cruellest of them all, the Ukrainian Rogoza, opened the doctor's mouth, pulled his tongue with some kind of sharp instrument and poured water in. After this Franz jumped on Chorazycki's stomach, and with his shoes on started to skip on his stomach. Two Jews were forced to pick the doctor up feet first, and so the water came out. They repeated this a few times. However, Chorazycki did not move. They put him nude on a bench and beat him. The doctor showed no signs of life. He was apparently dead.[16]

With Chorazycki's death, Samuel Rajzman later recalled, 'we had no qualified leader, and none of us wanted to take the moral responsibility for an unsuccessful coup.'[17] Two weeks later, on May 3, there was a second blow to the plans for an uprising when one of the underground commanders, Rakowski, was searched, and money found on him. For this crime, he was shot. The money had been intended for the purchase of arms.[18]

All over German-controlled Europe, deportations and attempted escapes continued. From Belgium, on April 19, fourteen hundred Jews had been deported 'to the East'. One of those deported, Suzanne Kaminsky, was only thirty-nine days old; she had been born on March 11. The oldest of the deportees, Jacob Blom, was ninety years old. Because of previous escapes on trains from Belgium, even the small windows of the cattle trucks were boarded up.

Escape was uppermost, however, in the minds of many of the deportees. Three Belgians who were then at liberty, a young Jewish doctor, Youra Livschitz, and his two non-Jewish friends, Jean Franklemon and Robert Maistriau, arranged to stop the train at a small station well inside the Belgian border. There, they were able to open three of the wagon doors. Five deportees managed to escape. Before reaching the frontier, a further 231 deportees jumped from the train: twenty-six bodies were later found alongside the railway.[19]

In Cracow, on April 29, the Jewish resistance fighters who had been captured during the December uprising, and held in prison, were driven by truck to Plaszow camp. During the short drive, they were able to break out of the truck, but most of them were machine-gunned by the guards. Among the few who escaped being shot was Abraham Leib Leibowicz, founder of the Jewish Fighting Organization in Cracow. He was recaptured, however, taken to Plaszow, and shot.[20]

Also on April 29, the Jewish women fighters held in prison in Cracow were being transferred, on foot, from one prison to another. As they reached the road in front of the second prison, two of them, Gusta Draenger and Gola Mira, attacked the nearest SS men with their hands. The other women at once joined in, among them Rose Jolles and Genia Maltzer. Mira and Jolles were killed by machine gun fire. Maltzer and Draenger escaped. Most of the others were killed.[21] Six months later Draenger, who had joined her husband Szymszon, gave herself up to the Gestapo after he had been captured.[22]

On April 30, two thousand Jews were deported from Wlodawa to Sobibor. On arrival at the unloading ramp, they attacked the SS guard with bare hands and pieces of wood torn from the wagons. All of them were killed by grenades and machine-gun fire.[23]

Preparations for revolt had also been made inside Sobibor, but they too were doomed to failure. Dov Freiberg, who had been taken to Sobibor in its first days, in May 1942, later recalled:

> . . . there was a captain from Holland, a Jew. He headed an organization, secret organization. It was a period when there were difficulties among the Ukrainians and we thought maybe we could get in touch with them. We heard stories about the

partisans from them and some contact was established between this Dutchman and the Ukrainians for a revolt.

They began plotting an uprising. And then one day in a roll call they took him out, this Dutchman, and began questioning him. 'Who were the ringleaders?'

This man withstood tortures and endless blows and he never said a word. The Germans told him that if he does not speak they would give orders that the Dutch block would be ordered to move to Camp III and they will be beheaded in front of his eyes. And he said, 'Anyway you are doing what you wish, you will not get a word out of me, not a whisper.' And they gave the orders to this Dutch block to move, all of them, about seventy people, and they were brought to Camp III. On the next day we learned that the Germans kept their word.

They beheaded the people. Yes, they cut off their heads.[24]

All ghetto and death camp inmates understood, and had to accept, that the price of revolt was torture and mass execution. The Germans were always able to call, as in the Parczew operation, on whatever weapons they judged necessary, including heavy artillery, and air power. Reprisals were continuous: in Riga, at the end of April, during a search for weapons, the Germans found a list of names. It was not at all clear what the list referred to. But three hundred of those on the list were seized, and shot.[25]

At Birkenau, throughout April, medical experiments had continued. Aaron Wald, from Poland, one of the few survivors of the castration experiments, later recalled:

In April 1943 the SS doctor Schumann arrived in our block, no. 27, in Birkenau, and took all the men between twenty and twenty-four years old to Auschwitz, Block 21. First they shaved us, bathed us, gave us an enema (two litres), and two intramuscular injections.

At first, I resisted, I wanted to run away. Professor Schumann said: 'We need it for an experiment.' After the operation I was in terrible pain for forty-eight hours. Ninety per cent of the patients died. After eight days, I had to go back to work.[26]

On April 28 an SS telegram instructed the camp commandant at

Auschwitz to place 120 women on the list of 'prisoners for various experimental purposes'.[27]

The young girls on whom the experiments were carried out quickly became old and decrepit in appearance, probably because of the damage done to their sex glands by the experiments. The victims' wounds healed badly, causing all of them prolonged suffering. Many of them died.

The medical experiments at Auschwitz were veiled in secrecy. Block 10 and its residents were isolated from the rest of the camp. The windows were shuttered, so that the women could see only through cracks in the shutters what was going on directly opposite their own block. There they saw the 'Death Square', the execution ground for Block 11, where the murder of Polish and other prisoners was constantly taking place. The daily sight of these executions only intensified the women's fears. When they heard that Professor Clauberg was coming on one of his regular visits, they would hide in corners and become hysterical, crying out: 'The obese butcher is coming! The revolting rooster is here!'

The first experiments, intended to provide evidence about the effects and consequences of sterilization, were carried out on a number of young Jewish girls between the ages of fifteen and eighteen. All were from Greece. First, they were sterilized by X-rays. Then their ovaries were removed. Or, three months after the sterilization, parts of their reproductive organs would be removed and sent to the Research Institute in Breslau. Such experiments were performed two to three times a week. Each experiment would 'use up' about thirty women. Hundreds of women, having been mutilated by these experiments, were then sent to Birkenau and to its gas-chambers.[28]

By the summer of 1943, the four new gas-chambers at Birkenau, as well as those at Majdanek and Sobibor, were in daily operation. In Sobibor, Eliezer Karstatt was a witness to the arrival of a transport of Jews from somewhere in the Lublin region:

> They were human skeletons really. On that day there was some kind of a malfunction apparently in the gas-chamber and they spent the night with us outside in the open courtyard. These people didn't care about anything. They were beaten, they just sighed. They could not even speak.

We were ordered to give them some food and we did. The last ounce of energy they spent in trying to get up. They were piled on top of each other and they stepped on each other in order to get that crumb of bread which we could give them. On the next morning they were taken to the gas-chambers and in the courtyard where they had been during the night were several hundred dead.

The SS ordered a group of twenty Jews, among them Eliezer Karstatt, to undress the corpses of the Jews in the courtyard, and to carry them to small wagons about 150 yards away:

It is difficult to describe what a feeling it was to be naked and carry these dead bodies on our shoulders. The Germans egged us on and beat us to run faster. We had to drag them along. Grab them by their feet and drag them along and it was a hot day.

I left a body for a moment and wanted to rest and this man whom I thought to be dead sighed and he sat up straight and he said, 'Is it far?' It was a very weak voice and must have been a supreme effort and I could not carry him any more. I raised him up and I put his hand around my shoulder. I was very weak myself and couldn't go very far but at a certain moment I felt whip lashes on my back and an SS man beat me and I let go of the body and I again dragged the man to the wagons.[29]

Enemies of the Jews were everywhere. On May 6 the Mufti of Jerusalem, Haj Amin al-Husseini, who was then in Europe, protested to the Bulgarian Foreign Minister about allowing Jewish children to leave Bulgaria for Palestine. They should be sent, he suggested, to Poland, 'under strong and energetic guard'.[30] In Tunisia, the German occupation on May 7 led to widespread plunder of Jewish homes, and confiscations of Jewish property, in Djerba, Sfax, Sousse and Tunis. These Jews were oriental Sephardi Jews who had been living under Arab and Muslim rule for many centuries, until the French conquest of 1881. From the moment of the German occupation in November 1942 their lives had been at risk, and in May 1943 more than four thousand were sent as forced labourers to construction sites near the front line. A considerable number were killed during Allied air bombardments of the airfields on which they were forced to work. Others died as a result of malnutrition and ill-treatment.[31]

The Gestapo chief of Tunis was Walter Rauff, who had supervised the construction and use of gas-vans in the Eastern Territories from October 1941 to July 1942. In Tunis, Rauff 'harassed, persecuted and killed Jews, winning rewards from Berlin, and condemnation to death in absentia after the German evacuation'.[32]

In German-occupied White Russia, the five hundred surviving Jews of the five thousand Jews of Nowogrodek remained alive in the ghetto labour camp, at the whim of their overseers. 'They didn't care if you didn't work,' Idel Kagan later recalled. 'If you didn't work, you will starve, and that's that.' But on May 7 there was a roll call. Kagan, having lost his toes after his unsuccessful escape bid four months earlier, watched the roll-call from his bed. 'Suddenly I saw German and White Russian police. My mother came to the window. "Don't fear. It's nothing." I couldn't bear the shouting of the people. I covered my ears with the pillow.'

During this unexpected 'action', half of the five hundred surviving Jews of Nowogrodek were killed, among them Idel Kagan's mother Dvora, and his sixteen-year-old sister Nehama. He and his father survived. 'You will remain until the end of the war,' the Germans told them. 'The Reich needs you.'

The Nowogrodek survivors formed an escape committee, and began to try to work out some means of escape from their labour camp.[33] In Eastern Galicia, likewise, the surviving Jews in the ghettos and labour camps were, despite hunger and isolation, still searching for means of survival. In Rohatyn, Jewish ghetto police in secret session decided on May 15 to acquire weapons and to despatch armed groups to the forest. The decision was acted upon. But the Germans, learning of it, executed many of the policemen. Three weeks later, all one thousand surviving Jews in Rohatyn were killed.[34]

At nearby Brody, once the Austro-Hungarian frontier town for Jews fleeing from Tsarist Russia, German and Ukrainian units, having killed thirty Jewish partisans in the nearby woods, and paraded six more captives through the streets of the town, entered the ghetto in the early hours of May 21. Almost all the two and a half thousand surviving Jews of Brody were driven to a waiting train. But in their attempts to resist deportation, the Jews killed four Ukrainians and several Germans. Even on the train, many tried to break out. The walls of several of the cattle trucks were broken, and several hundred escaped. But many more died under the wheels, or were machine-gunned by the Ukrainian guards travelling on top of the wagons.[35]

To the anger of the Germans, some of the Jews of Brody had acquired arms from Italian troops stationed in the town. So also had Jews in Lvov. Nor had they hesitated to use them. Reporting on these efforts by Lvov Jews to avoid deportation, SS General Katzmann told his superiors five weeks later:

> The Jews tried every means to evade evacuation. They not only attempted to escape from the ghetto, but hid in every imaginable corner, in pipes, in chimneys, in sewers, and canals. They built tunnels under the hallways, underground; they widened cellars and turned them into passageways; they dug trenches underground, and cunningly created hiding places in lofts, woodsheds, attics, and inside furniture, etc.

Special bunkers and dug-outs had been built, Katzmann wrote. 'We were compelled therefore to act brutally from the beginning in order to avoid sustaining greater casualties among our men. We had to blast and burn many houses.'[36]

In Riga, several dozen Jews had continued to find shelter in the cave which had been dug by Yanis Lipke underneath his henhouse. Lipke himself continued to smuggle bread and potatoes into the ghetto on his daily journey to collect Jewish workers for work in the German air force storehouse. Lipke also cast about for men to help him save the 'doomed' Jews of the nearby village of Dobele, asking three Lithuanian friends of his, Yanis Undulis and the brothers Fritz and Yan Rosenthal, to help him.

On May 10, the first two Jews of Dobele were driven to Yan Rosenthal's farmhouse ten kilometres away, in the hamlet of Annasnuizha. Both Jews were hidden in a haystack on the farm. A second shelter was already being prepared at a farm belonging to Fritz Rosenthal's aunt, Wilhelmina Putrinia, and within a short time, several more Jews from Dobele were hidden there as well.[37]

The killing and deportation of Jews had continued to enrich the German Reich. On May 13 Hans Frank sent Himmler a list of the 'utilization of Jewish concealed and stolen goods' in the General Government. Up to April 30, Frank reported, 94,000 men's watches, 33,000 women's watches, 25,000 fountain pens, and 14,000 propelling pencils had been delivered to Germany. So had 14,000 scissors, most of them sold to the German Equipment Works Limited 'for technical purposes'. Men's watches were being distributed to the combat troops, to the submarine service, and to concentration camp guards. The 5,000 watches 'of most expensive Swiss make', those in gold or platinum cases, or partly fitted with precious stones, were either to go to the Reichsbank 'for melting down', or were to be retained 'for special use'.[38]

The Germans were confident that even their enemies would one day share their hatred of the Jews. On May 19 Himmler had written to Ernst Kaltenbrunner, sending him copies of a special edition of the book *The Jewish Ritual Murder*, about the alleged Jewish use of Christian blood in the baking of Passover bread. Himmler suggested that all those 'dealing in the Jewish problem' should see the book, and that extracts from it should be broadcast to Britain and America to increase 'anti-Jewish feelings' in those two countries. The book should also be distributed, he wrote, in Rumania, Hungary and Bulgaria.[39] But still, von Thadden reported on June 3, the Hungarian government was unwilling to adopt anti-Jewish measures.[40]

On May 24 a new SS doctor reached Auschwitz. His name was Josef Mengele, and he had just celebrated his thirty-second birthday. His SS rank was that of Captain. Driven by the desire to advance his medical career by scientific publications, Dr Mengele began to conduct medical experiments on living Jews whom he took from the barracks, and brought to his hospital block. In many instances, amounting over a year and a half to several thousand, Mengele used the pretext of medical treatment to kill prisoners, personally injecting them with phenol, petrol, chloroform or air, or by ordering SS medical orderlies to do so.

From the moment of his arrival at Auschwitz, Mengele joined the other SS officers and SS doctors, among them Dr Clauberg, and later Dr Kremer, in the 'selection' of Jews reaching the railway junction from all over Europe, with a movement of the hand or the wave of a stick indicating as 'unfit for work', and thus destined for immediate death in the gas-chambers all children, old people, sick, crippled and weak Jews, and all pregnant women.

Between May 1943 and November 1944 Mengele took part in at least seventy-four such selections. He also took an equally decisive part in at least thirty-one selections in the camp infirmary, pointing out for death by shooting, injection or gassing Jews whose strength had been sapped by hunger, forced labour, untreated illness or ill-treatment by the guards.[41]

Azriel Ne'eman, a Jew who worked in the hospital block as a male nurse, later recalled how one of the men in his ward, a middle-aged Polish Jew with six fingers on each hand, was singled out for special attention by Mengele. Later, when Mengele made his rounds, and found that the man had died, he flew into a rage, his 'scientific' interest having been frustrated. Shortly thereafter he held a selection, in which every patient who was too weak to stand to attention at the foot of his bed was sent to the gas-chambers.[42]

One of the few people to speak to Mengele in Auschwitz about his attitude to the Jews was a Christian woman, Dr Ella Lingens. She had been deported to Auschwitz from Vienna three months before Mengele's own arrival in the camp, having been denounced for sheltering Jews, and for helping them escape across the Austrian border into Switzerland. She later recalled how, in Auschwitz, 'I was in a triply privileged position, as a German, as a non-Jew and as a doctor.' During one of his conversations with her, Mengele 'said that there were only two gifted nations in the world' – the Germans and the Jews.' 'The question is,' he asked her, 'which one will dominate?'

Ella Lingens later recalled an example of Mengele's 'ruthlessness'. After all efforts to contain spotted fever had failed, he ordered an entire block cleared by sending all its six or seven hundred inmates to the gas-chambers. Then he had the barracks disinfected and populated by the thoroughly deloused prisoners of another block. This process, delousing and gassing, was repeated many times, until the spotted fever was brought under control.[43]

The 'elimination of Jews', SS Lieutenant-General Krüger noted on May 31, at a meeting of General Government ministers in Cracow, was 'the most difficult and unpleasant task for the police'. Yet it 'had to be done', Kruger added, 'on the Führer's orders, because it is necessary from the standpoint of European interests.'[44] The reports of German administrators made clear what the methods of 'elimination' were. The prison administrator in Minsk reported on May 31 that '516 German and Russian Jews' had been 'finished off' in Minsk in the previous two weeks, but not before all of them had 'had their gold bridgework, crowns and fillings pulled or broken out'. This always took place, the administrator added, 'one to two hours before the respective action'.[45]

Poles also recorded the fate of Jews. On June 3, during a deportation from Michalowice, three Jews had hidden in a barn, opening fire as the Germans approached. Tadeusz Seweryn, a Pole, later recalled how one of the Jews was killed, one escaped, and the third fought to the end, being burnt to death when the barn was set on fire. Enraged at the resistance, the Germans then killed two Polish farmers, Stefan Kaczmarski and Stanislaw Stojka, for hiding the three Jews.[46] In 'Aryan' Warsaw, Feigele Peltel, in hiding, learned of the murder of an entire Polish family who had sheltered Jews: the family had been burnt alive in their house 'as a sort of object lesson'.[47]

For the Jews still alive in certain ghettos, among them the ghettos of Lodz, Vilna, Bialystok and Czestochowa, the future was a terrifying uncertainty. To the heads of these ghettos, the only hope of survival seemed to be if the ghetto could continued to serve as a productive one. 'The ghetto's food supply depends entirely on productivity here,' noted the Lodz Ghetto Chronicle on May 21. 'If the orders from the German authorities are not filled, on time and in the desired quantity, the ghetto faces enormous danger.'[48] In Vilna, the head of the Jewish Council, Jacob Gens, argued on June 6 that if the Jews continued to show that they were 'very useful and irreplaceable' as workers, especially for the German army, they would 'enhance the justification for our existence'.[49]

At Auschwitz, Dr Clauberg reported on June 7 a sterilization rate of a thousand women a day.[50] Many of these women were Jewesses from Greece. On June 8 a Greek Jewish doctor, Albert Menasche, reached Birkenau from Salonica in a transport of 880 Greek Jews. He was the only one of a family of more than thirty to survive, first as a member of the camp orchestra, then as a doctor. His daughter Lillian, aged eleven, had also been sent to play in the orchestra, as a drummer, but was later gassed.[51] These 'musicians of Auschwitz', as they have been called, had to amuse the Germans by playing when new arrivals reached the camp, and at special concerts for the SS.[52]

A week after Dr Menasche's arrival in Birkenau, the camp was visited by SS Major-General Richard Glueks, head of the Concentration Camp Inspectorate, who noted that the 'special buildings' were not well located, and ordered them to be relocated. They should be sited, he wrote, where it would not be possible for 'all kinds of people' to 'gaze' at them.[53] One result of this complaint was the planting of a 'green belt' of fast-growing trees around the two crematoria nearest the camp entrance.

On the day of Glueks's report, June 15, a new labour camp was opened in the Auschwitz region, at the coal mines of Jaworzno.[54] On the following day, Himmler's permission was given for eight Jews in Birkenau, condemned to death for resistance activities, to be sent to the concentration camp at Sachsenhausen, near Berlin, for experiments into jaundice.[55] Five days later, on Himmler's instructions, in what he called the interest of 'medical science', seventy-three Jews and thirty Jewesses were sent, alive, from Birkenau to the concentration camp of Natzweiler, in Alsace. On reaching Natzweiler, their 'vital statistics' were taken. They were then killed, and their skeletons sent as 'exhibits' to the Anatomical Museum in Strasbourg.[56] Within a year and a half, Himmler ordered the skeleton collection to be destroyed because of the 'deterioration of the military situation'.[57] Allied forces were then approaching Strasbourg.

Since early 1943, the advance of the Red Army on the eastern front had led to the decision to dig up the corpses of hundreds of thousands of murdered Jews, and to burn them. A former Einsatzkommando chief, SS Colonel Paul Blobel, was appointed to supervise this task. The units operating under Blobel's command were known as the 'Blobel Commando' or 'Special Commando 1005'.

One large-scale Blobel 'action' began on June 15, at the Janowska death pits in Lvov, when hundreds of Jewish forced labourers in Janowska were taken to the nearby mass murder site and forced to dig up the putrefying corpses. They were ordered to extract gold teeth and pull gold rings off the fingers of the dead. 'Every day', recalled Leon Weliczker, a survivor of the first of the Blobel 'actions', 'we collected about eight kilogrammes of gold.'

The corpses had then to be burned. Leon Weliczker recalled how, as the disinterred corpses were put on the pyre:

> The fire crackles and sizzles. Some of the bodies in the fire have their hands extended. It looks as if they are pleading to be taken out. Many bodies are lying around with open mouths. Could they be trying to say: 'We are your own mothers, fathers, who raised you and took care of you. Now you are burning us.' If they could have spoken, maybe they would have said this, but they are forbidden to talk too – they are guarded. Maybe they would forgive us. They know that we are being forced to do this by the same murderers that killed them. We are under their whips and machine guns. They would forgive us, they who are our fathers and mothers, who if they knew it would help their children. But what should we do?[58]

This question of what to do was asked by all surviving Jews: but none could know for certain the answer, or by what path life might be preserved. In mid-June the head of the Jewish Council of Sosnowiec, Moshe Merin, who for more than two years had sought the safety of his ghetto in compliance with German orders for labour gangs and deportees, was invited to a meeting with the head of the local SS, together with four other Council members. Neither Merin nor his companions was seen again. Those Jews who had believed in Merin, especially the 'simple folk', were in a panic, hoping that he might still find some way to lead them. His opponents were relieved that he, the 'despotic tyrant', had gone. It was later reported that Merin and the other four had been deported to Birkenau and gassed: the fate, six weeks later, of almost all the other Jews of Sosnowiec.[59]

Resistance, given so dramatic a manifestation in the Warsaw ghetto, continued elsewhere. Its most frequent manifestation was escape. But the Germans were persistent in their search for escapees. In Lodz, the thirty-one-year-old Abram Tandowski, who had earlier escaped from the ghetto, was executed on June 12, together with two other Jews, the twenty-three-year-old Hersch Fejgelis and the twenty-nine-year-old Mordecai Standarowicz, both of whom had escaped from a labour camp. The heads of the Jewish police in the Lodz ghetto were made to watch the execution.[60]

In Minsk, a well known local doctor, Niuta Jurezkaya, had escaped from the ghetto to the forests. But she too was caught, brought back to Minsk, and tortured. 'Who was with you?' she was asked. 'All of my people were with me,' she replied; and was then shot.

Niuta Jurezkaya was shot on June 16. That same day, in Berlin, two hundred patients in the Jewish hospital were deported to Theresienstadt, many of them on stretchers.[61] The same was the fate a week later of the residents of the Jewish old people's home in Moravska Ostrava.[62] For the old and the sick, revolt was impossible. For those who did revolt, the German power was impregnable. On June 19, Hillel Katz, held by the Gestapo in Paris, wrote to his baby girl of seven months, his 'dear little Annette', whom he had not seen since she was twelve days old:

> Your desire to appear in our lives was fierce. Nothing counted with you, neither the dangers of wartime, nor our desire that you wait until after the war. Obviously, you could not share our earthly point of view, you who were still in eternity.
> It was with love, joy and courage that we submitted to your imperious will. Your birth gave us such life as we have now.[63]

Hillel Katz was shot by the Gestapo: he helped to provide the Soviet Union with information about the German war effort. His daughter Annette survived. She is my cousin. Her grandfather, my great uncle, had been murdered in Czestochowa in the early months of the war.[64] Almost all her other cousins, my cousins also, were later deported from Czestochowa to Treblinka: something I did not know either on my own first visit to Treblinka in 1959, or on my second visit in 1981.

In Lvov, on June 21, the Germans hunted down and killed the remnant of the ghetto population. In search of a hiding place, and survival, 500 Jews entered the city's sewers; 350 were caught and killed. The remaining 150 hid in the sewers. After a week of starvation and stench, 130 had committed suicide.[65]

For escape and hiding to be effective, the help of non-Jews was almost always essential. In Lvov, it was a professional thief, Leopold Socha, and one of his pre-war companions in crime, Stefan Wrobleski, who made it possible for some Jews to survive the final round-up of June 21. One who was saved, seventeen-year-old Halina Wind, later recalled how, as the Gestapo surrounded the ghetto on June 1:

> We did not know what to do. We went down with a group into the basement through a pipe, steps, water, a tunnel, other pipes. Finally we were crawling in the sewers of Lvov. We heard a rush of water. Suddenly we were standing on a narrow ledge against a wall. In front of us flew the Peltew river. Along this ledge very slowly and carefully people were moving. Sometimes there was a splash, when someone slipped and fell in or couldn't stand the stress any more and deliberately jumped in.

At that moment, Halina Wind saw Leopold Socha, who, as a thief, had long been familiar with the sewers as a hiding place for his stolen goods. Socha took twenty-one of the Jews whom he found in the sewer to one of his subterranean hiding places, telling them to 'stay put' and promising to bring them food on the following day.

Halina Wind later recalled that among those hidden in the sewers by Socha was one whole family, Jerzy Chigier, his wife Peppa, their seven-year-old daughter Christine, and their four-year-old son Pawel. 'We were brought food every day,' she added, 'always by different manholes so as not to arouse suspicion.'

One of those whom Socha sheltered was a pregnant woman, Weinbergowa. Shortly after giving birth, her child died. Weinbergowa survived.

Halina Wind also recalled how several of the group decided to leave that particular hiding place for some other refuge elsewhere in the sewers. 'None ever returned. Three of them left one morning and we found their bodies the same evening.'

Each week Leopold Socha would take the dirty clothes of those in hiding and return them washed. He also brought them a Jewish prayer book which he had found in the now deserted ghetto. At Passover, knowing that Jews could not eat leavened bread, he brought a large load of potatoes which he pushed down through several manholes. 'We were careful of the potatoes,' Halina Wind later recalled, 'always eating the rotten ones first, until we realized that the rats were having a feast on the fresh ones.' On the day that the Red Army forced the German surrender at Stalingrad, Socha and Wrobleski brought those in hiding vodka to celebrate. Ten of the twenty-one Jews survived in that sewer hide-out, until liberation nearly a year later.[66]

Having completed the 'action' in Lvov, the SS turned to nearby Czortkow, where 534 Jews were living in the former Jewish religious school, and sent each day to work for the Germans. A normal day's work lasted twelve to fourteen hours. Their food consisted of a hundred grams of bread each day, a little black coffee, and, as Gerta Hollaender later recalled, 'a little sparse water, which was supposed to be soup'.

At five o'clock in the morning of June 23, the Jews woke up to find the school surrounded by Ukrainian policemen. The camp commandant, Thomanek, then appeared. 'Like a beast sneaking to its prey,' Gerta Hollaender wrote in her diary:

> . . . he approached the people who were doomed to death. His head was bent a little forward, the plump face red like a cray-fish and in his sparkling eyes lust for murder. He stopped a few paces in front of his victims and stood, his legs spread wide and both hands resting on his sides, examining the miserable creatures for a few minutes without uttering a word, while they all stared at him in silence, dumbfounded with horror, as if they were hypnotized.
>
> Then suddenly he screamed with his grating voice: 'Lie down! Whoever raises his head will be shot!' Obediently and without resistance almost five hundred people fell down and prostrated themselves in the dust. It was a pitiful sight, yet could they have done otherwise? Would resistance against this gang of murderers, armed from head to foot, be of any use?

Thomanek ordered some of the Jews to get up and wait at the

side. During the selection, Gerta Hollaender saw the man next to her, the camp barber, who had not been selected, raise his head and call out to Thomanek: 'Mr Camp Manager, surely you know me, let me live.' Then, she recorded in her diary:

> Thomanek lifted his automatic rifle, leveled it and aimed in my direction. It seemed that he was aiming at me. For a fleeting instant it occurred to me that it would be better to be shot here, so that an end might come to the agonies, and I asked myself whether the bullet would cause pain, and at once the shot was fired.
>
> Without knowing what had happened, I looked at my blood-stained right hand and my blood-spattered frock. As I raised myself a bit in order to look for my wound, I saw the barber lying crooked in a pool of blood. It was his blood spattered on my hand and frock.
>
> Thomanek shot several other people. One man whose lung was hit suffered terrible agonies: he was groaning and coughing up blood. Only later when the sorting out was finished, and the men were driven to the big gate on the other side of the camp, a German gendarme released the man from the suffering by shooting him in the head.
>
> The horrible dying of the man and the other gruesome sights made no impression on me any more. I was as if stupefied, and obeyed apathetically the Germans' orders when the women were led to the rear entrance of the camp and were ordered to sit down in front of the bath-house.

The horror of the selection continued for several hours. During a brief moment of confusion, Gerta Hollaender was able to break away from the entrance to the bath-house, hiding in a nearby building. 'Outside rose a tumult of wild crying,' she wrote, 'the begging voices of women, desperate cries, bawling commands, and cracking beatings. The pitiless bestial torturers were forcing the first miserable women on to the lorry.'

Gerta Hollaender survived, but the majority of those who had been held in the school were taken to Yagielnica and shot.[67]

All non-Jews who decided to hide and feed a Jew risked death, as did Jan Nakonieczny, who hid five Jews in a henhouse. The henhouse was only two feet high, four feet wide, and thirteen feet long. The five Jews were Henryk Sperber, his mother, his sister, his fiancée and his cousin. All five survived the war. So too did their saviour.[68]

Following the crushing of the Warsaw ghetto revolt, Zivia Lubetkin had managed to reach Czestochowa from Warsaw. There, she told Rivka Glanc, a fellow member of the Jewish Fighting Organization, that, since the Warsaw uprising ended as it did, 'it would be better for you to join the partisans. You will be able to kill more Germans and save more Jews.' But Rivka Glanc replied: 'We too want to stay with our own people until the very last.'[69]

On June 25 the Germans suddenly and unexpectedly began the final destruction of the Czestochowa ghetto. As best they could, the Jewish Fighting Organization, led by Mordechai Zylberberg and Lutek Glickstein, distributed their few weapons, and sent their members to their prearranged position in the bunkers. But the Germans stormed the bunkers, and most of the fighters were killed. The Jews had been poorly armed: the Germans captured thirty grenades, eighteen pistols and two rifles. Six fighters, commanded by Rivka Glanc, were cut off by the Germans. They had only two pistols and a single grenade. All six were killed.[70]

No mercy was shown to Jews who were captured, nor could those who escaped do so without leaving behind a tornado of reprisals. When six Jews at the Baltoji-Volke camp near Vilna fled into the woods while on a work detail cutting trees, sixty-seven of the camp's three hundred inmates were shot immediately.[71] South of Warsaw, that same day, June 29, five Poles were shot for hiding four Jews. One of the Poles was a child aged thirteen, another, a one-year-old baby. The four Jews were also shot.[72] But Poles could also turn against Jews: that summer, in the woods near Wyszkow, Poles of the underground Home Army murdered Mordechai Grobas and his small group of fellow survivors of the Warsaw ghetto uprising.[73]

As the killing of Jews continued, so too did rumours of these killings. On July 11 Martin Bormann, head of the Nazi Party secretariat, issued a special circular 'on instructions from the Führer'. Whenever the Jewish question was 'brought up in public', the circular warned, 'there may be no discussion of a future overall solution. It may however be mentioned that the Jews are taken in groups for appropriate labour purposes.'[74] Five days later, however, Theophil Wurm, Bishop of the Evangelical Church in Württemberg, wrote to the German government: 'In the name of God and for the sake of the German people, we urgently request the responsible leaders of the Reich to stem the persecution and extermination to which many men and women under German rule are being subjected without any indictment by jury.' The Bishop added: 'There must be an end to putting to death members of other nations and races who are not even accorded a trial by either civil or military courts. A day will come when we shall have to pay for this.'

Bishop Wurm avoided the dangerous term 'Jew'. But he did refer to 'other races'. He also mentioned the children of mixed marriages, and the plight of those married to Jewesses, demanding the Government 'not to do any further wrong to them'.[75]

Five months later, on 20 December 1943, Bishop Wurm directed another letter to Dr Hans Lammers, the State Secretary of the Reich Chancellery. This time he made explicit reference to the 'final solution'. 'We Christians', he wrote, 'consider the policy of exterminating the Jews as a grave injustice and of fatal consequences for the German people. Our people see the suffering imposed on us by the air raids as an act of punishment for what was done to the Jews.'[76]

30

'To perish, but with honour'

IN THE VILNA GHETTO, a resistance organization had been growing, led by Yitzhak Wittenberg. Among its actions was the sabotage of German troop trains in the area around Vilna, using explosives smuggled out of the ghetto to partisans in the neighbourhood. On 8 July 1943, a Jewess, Vitka Kempner, managed to leave the ghetto, together with two colleagues, carrying a landmine. Their objective was to blow up a German military train five miles south-east of the city. They planted the mine, and nobody noticed them.

On the following morning, at dawn, Vitka Kempner returned to the ghetto, her legs torn and bleeding. 'Her face', Hava Shurek later recalled, 'was radiant.' Hava Shurek's account continued:

> There was a strength in her eyes which gave them an unusual brightness, while her face had a different expression. When she was asked what she had thought during the long night, she answered: 'How to do the job without falling into their hands. I was sorry that I had no cyanide of potassium with me.'
>
> News of the explosion arrived at 3 p.m. The train was destroyed, both engines and ammunition wagons. The Germans were at a loss, for this was the first operation of its kind near Vilna where there were many garrison troops. They did not suspect the Jews, for they were sure that the Jews were already defeated and would not raise their heads. Such a deed could only be done by free men.

'It was a happy day for fighters in the ghetto,' Hava Shurek added. 'They laughed in the streets. Passers-by shrugged their shoulders thinking that the others had gone crazy.'[1]

Within a week of this 'triumph', one of the members of a Lithuanian Communist group captured by the Gestapo, revealed under torture the name of the resistance commander. On the night of 16

July 1943, Wittenberg and other members of the United Partisan Organization were at a meeting with the head of the Jewish Council, Jacob Gens, when armed Lithuanian policemen burst into the room, and Wittenberg, in fetters, was led away.

As Wittenberg and his escort were about to leave the ghetto, Jewish partisans attacked the escort, and rescued Wittenberg, still in fetters. The SS then announced that if Wittenberg was not handed back to them, they would burn the ghetto to the ground.

One of Wittenberg's partisan colleagues, Abba Kovner, who had been present when Wittenberg was seized and taken away, later recalled how, at two in the morning, Gens summoned the Jews of the ghetto, telling them 'that because of this one man, Wittenberg, the ghetto may be destroyed and annihilated'. There was chaos in the ghetto, with Jews attacking the partisans and demanding that they hand Wittenberg over. 'You cannot endanger the ghetto for one man,' they insisted.

Wittenberg's colleagues went to the attic where their commander was in hiding. 'Give an order and we shall fight,' they told him: Jew would fight Jew to prevent the partisan leader being handed over.[2]

Outside, a crowd of Jews, assembled by Gens, was shouting: 'We want to live.' Wittenberg agreed to be guided by his Communist colleagues, who urged him to surrender.[3] Appointing Abba Kovner as his successor, Wittenberg walked out of his hiding place and turned himself over to the Gestapo. An attempt was made to smuggle cyanide into his prison cell, but it failed. It is thought that he managed to kill himself before he could be tortured.

The surrender of Wittenberg, Abba Kovner later declared, was 'one of the greatest acts of heroism of the Jewish fighting underground in the ghetto': the avoiding of conflict between Jew and Jew.[4] It was followed, within six weeks, by the deportation of five thousand Vilna Jews to camp Vayvari, in Estonia. The deportation was supervised by Gens, while the Jewish police were brutal in enforcing the German order.[5]

Also deported to Vaivara were several thousand Kovno Jews. As they were being sent to a labour camp, they were told that families could apply to join their menfolk. Assurances were given that, once at the labour camp, families would be kept together. Leah Klompul was among those wives who decided to join her husband, together with her five-year-old son Michael, and her mother-in-law. Forty-one years later she recalled how 'We decided, for better or for worse, we will be together.'

The Jews who volunteered to join their menfolk were brought to the train siding. But there, the children and old people were separated from the rest. 'We were told, it's only for the train journey.' But when Vaivara was reached, Leah Klompul's little son, and her mother-in-law, were nowhere to be found. They had been deported to Birkenau, and to their deaths.[6]

At Vaivara, too, death came to many, among them an old lady, Mrs Ruttenberg, who had emigrated before the war to Canada, with her husband. The couple's son, a Hebrew actor, had remained in Kovno. It was while visiting him in 1939 that the couple had been caught in Europe by the outbreak of war, and were unable to return. Mrs Ruttenberg's husband, and her son, had been taken away during one of the Kovno 'actions' and were never seen again. She, in Vayvari, was protected by Leah Klompul, until Leah got sick and was taken to the camp hospital. 'As soon as I left', Leah later recalled, 'there was no one to look after her. She was taken out to work. She was old and sick. She was lying in the snow.' After a while, a male nurse, a Croat, came and took the sick away in a sledge, to the nearby wood. 'There, he shot them all.' But Mrs. Ruttenberg was not killed. 'Shoot me again,' she pleaded, 'I am still alive.' Later, telling the story to Leah Klompul, the male nurse boasted, with the tone of one who has done a great favour, 'I was sorry for her. So I did fire her another shot.'

While at Vaivara, Leah Klompul witnessed an unusual act of defiance. A girl from Kovno, Miriam Ksanskiewicz, aged sixteen or seventeen, had just received her ladle of soup. It had been ladled from the top of the cauldron, and was thin. Miriam decided to protest. 'She overturned the bowl. It was such a gesture. She was so annoyed. That soup, it could have been her life. But she survived.'

To turn over a bowl of soup; such, in the nightmare world of a Nazi labour camp, was an act of courage to be remembered by those who saw it for forty years.[7]

Even as some Jews from Kovno were being sent to Vaivara for slave labour, and others to Birkenau to be gassed, Jews already in the barracks at Birkenau were being sent away. The reason for their departure was that the Germans had decided to comb the deserted ruins of the Warsaw ghetto for anything of value, such as bricks, steel, iron and other metals, as well as any jewellery, gold, silver or currency that might have been hidden before the destruction of the ghetto. To carry out the search, 3,500 Jews were brought from Birkenau to the Gesiowka camp, on the ruins of the ghetto. These Jews were former deportees from France, Belgium, Holland, Slovakia, Greece and Poland, who had been sent to the barracks at the time of the selection, and were now brought north, the first group on July 19, for this massive task. A year later, they were still at work.[8] As the Jewish prisoners cleared and sifted the rubble, German soldiers watched and searched for any surviving Jews in hiding, shooting all whom they caught: the first sixteen were shot on July 27, as well as a seventeenth person 'suspected' of Jewish birth.[9]

On July 23, four days after the first deportation from Auschwitz to the new labour camp in Warsaw, a Jew who had been born in Auschwitz town forty years earlier, Mandel Langer, was executed in Toulouse. For more than seven months, he and a group of other Jews had blown up railway lines, bridges and electric pylons in the Toulouse region. Langer, a Communist, had migrated from Poland to Palestine as a young man. Imprisoned in Palestine by the British, he had left Palestine for France in 1933: and there, ten years later, he was shot.[10]

Escape and rescue continued, but the threat of reprisals was never an idle one. When twenty-one young Jews escaped from the Vilna ghetto on July 24, the Germans seized and shot thirty-two of their relations. It was then decreed that if even a single Jew were to escape from one of the ten-man labour gangs that worked outside the ghetto, the remaining nine in the gang would be shot.[11]

Also on July 24, the Spanish government acted, successfully, to save 367 Sephardi Jews in Salonica. More than 48,000 Greek Jews had already been deported from Salonica to Birkenau: the remnant, as Spanish subjects, were about to be deported when the Spanish government intervened. Instead of being sent to Birkenau, all 367 Spanish subjects were transferred by train to the concentration camp at Bergen-Belsen. There, they were exempted from forced labour, and six months later, were sent to Spain, and to safety.[12]

On July 25, Mussolini was deposed as ruler of Italy. Although he had not allowed Jews under Italian rule to be deported to Germany, his downfall was greeted by Jews under Nazi rule with rejoicing. The end had come for one of Hitler's allies. In Janowska camp, in Lvov, a Gestapo man accused a young Jew who crossed his path of greeting him with veiled mockery, in celebration of Mussolini's downfall. The youth was sentenced to death. Two SS men carried out the execution: 'They hung the youth upside down,' the historian Philip Friedman has recorded, 'cut off his male organ and placed it in his mouth, and kicked him ceaselessly in the stomach to make the blood flow to his head. The youth died in terrible agony.'[13]

At Treblinka, a group of forced labourers had continued to plan their revolt, despite the cruel killing of Dr Julian Chorazycki the previous April. New leaders had emerged, among them Israel Sudowicz, an agronomist, who before the war had been head of 'Toporol', an organization that had encouraged farming among Polish Jews. In the Warsaw ghetto, Sudowicz had organized the growing of vegetables on every vacant plot of land.[14] Other leaders of the Treblinka plotters included Engineer Alfred Galewski, Zelo Bloch and Dr Leichert, a Jewish physician from Wegrow, who had been an officer in the Polish army.

Shortly after Leichert's arrival, in May 1943, the number of labourers in Treblinka had grown to seven hundred, as the Germans not only continued to gas new arrivals, but to dig up and burn the tens of thousands of corpses which had earlier been buried, after gassing, in enormous ditches. A special machine or 'excavator', with an enormous metal grab, picked up these corpses and then dumped them on vast pyres.

One of the corpse-burning squad at Treblinka, Izak Helfing, later recalled how, as the old corpses were being burned, and the new ones also consigned to the flames, 'people began to think they would not be able to hold out any longer and they concluded that everyone would be exterminated. That thought created the strength to resist: to perish, but with honour, and to take revenge for our sufferings.' Another survivor later recalled how 'the days and nights dragged on in the most terrible vale of tears ever conceived by man. Death stalked Treblinka without respite. People fell like flies, from sickness, from bullets, from the axe,' and he added: 'Everyone knew that if not today then tomorrow would be his turn. A majority of the prisoners became so depressed that their will to escape became paralysed. But there were a few who maintained hope and made plans to save themselves.'[15]

One attempt at revolt had taken place in Treblinka in June 1943, when forty hand grenades had been stolen from the arsenal. But the grenades were without either explosives or pins, and could not be used.[16] Then, on August 2, the conspirators found their opportunity. Managing once more to break into the arsenal, they hid one of their members inside it. From the arsenal, this conspirator had pushed twenty primed hand grenades, twenty rifles and several revolvers with ammunition through a window, from which he had cut out a pane of glass. The weapons were then hidden, briefly, under a pile of debris; soon a cart was pulled to the debris, the arms taken away and distributed. Petrol was then put into the camp disinfector, operated by one of a group of Jews in the plot, and petrol instead of disinfectant was sprayed on buildings throughout the camp, as part of the daily disinfecting procedure.[17]

The signal for revolt was to have been given at 3.45 in the afternoon. But about half an hour earlier two of the conspirators, entering the living quarters, were searched and undressed. Money was found on them, and they were whipped. Fearing that they had been betrayed, the others in the plot decided to act at once. The SS man who was whipping the two prisoners was shot by another of the conspirators, and a hand grenade was thrown. This was understood to be the signal.[18]

The previously 'disinfected' buildings were ignited, and an enormous fire broke out. The arsenal exploded, and many of the camp buildings were set on fire, among them the storerooms for the shoes and clothes of the victims. The chief of the guards, SS Quartermaster Sergeant Kittner, was shot dead, and in the ensuing fighting fifteen other German and Ukrainian guards were killed. Of the seven hundred Jewish workers in the camp, more than one hundred and fifty succeeded in escaping. The rest were killed in the camp.[19]

Some of the escaped Jews were hunted down by German and Ukrainian units and shot. Others, reaching the River Bug, were helped by a Pole, Stanislaw Siwek.[20]

Acts of revolt and resistance continued throughout August 1943. In the labour camp at Konin the Jews, led by Rabbi Joshua Moshe Aaronson, burned down the huts in the camp, and tried to escape.

Almost all of them were killed.[21] At Bedzin, on August 3, Baruch Graftek was among the Jews who challenged the Nazis on the eve of the deportation. At the age of thirty, he had commanded the Jewish Fighting Organization in the ghetto. But he and his fellow fighters were all killed.[22] In Vilna, on August 6, dozens of Jews who attempted to resist deportation to Vaivara labour camp in Estonia were shot down.[23] In Warsaw, another twenty-seven Jews, all women, who had been seized in the 'Aryan' part of the city, were executed on August 10, followed at the end of the month by a further forty-seven women and fifty men, charged with 'non-Aryan descent'.[24]

Inside the labour camps, conditions were savage: on the night of August 15 nearly a thousand French Jews, most of them born in Poland, were taken to a camp on the Channel Island of Alderney. One of the survivors of Alderney camp, Albert Eblagon, later recalled how the Jews, on reaching the port, were forced to run the two kilometres to the camp, 'while the German guards continuously stabbed into our backs with their bayonets while also kicking us all the time'. Eblagon added:

> There were many men among us over seventy years of age but nobody was spared. Work, hard physical work for twelve and fourteen hours a day, every day, building the fortifications. Every day there were beatings and people's bones were broken, their arms or their legs. People died from overwork. We were starved and worked to death, so many died from total exhaustion.[25]

Hundreds of Jews died at Alderney, of exhaustion and ill-treatment: 384 were buried in the camp itself, and many others dumped at sea. Among the names recorded on the few marked graves are Chayim Goldin, Robert Perlestein and Leib Becker, each of whom died in December 1943.[26]

Throughout German-occupied France, Jews were active in the various underground groups which had begun to disrupt German communications, and to make plans to assist the Allies to prepare for the cross-Channel invasion. On August 6, a fifty-five-year-old French Jew, Albert Kohan, was smuggled out of France, to Britain. His mission was to make contact between the French underground forces in France and their representatives in London. Kohan remained in London for only a few weeks, before being parachuted back into France. There, he continued with his resistance activities, but on his second journey to Britain was killed in an air crash.[27]

In the Bialystok ghetto, thirty thousand Jews lived and worked unmolested since that black February six months earlier when ten thousand Jews had been deported to Treblinka, Majdanek and Auschwitz. In Bialystok itself, it was still thought that work for the German army would prove the ghetto's protection. A hundred and fifty young Jews, members of the Jewish Fighting Organization, prepared to resist, should deportation come, but they had no means of knowing when the day would arrive.

At four in the morning of August 16, German soldiers entered the ghetto, occupied the factories, and set up their headquarters in the Jewish Council building.

The twenty-one-year-old Bertha Sokolskaya later recalled how there had been an announcement in the ghetto that 'they will begin to deport us to work and that each of us will be allowed to take a five-kilogrammes parcel of belongings.' Her account continued:

> I went home. At that time I had with me my very sick mother whom I managed to hide with great difficulties during the first raid. I couldn't tell her anything. She began collecting some clothes and was terribly agitated because the hinge of the cupboard came off and she was worried how she could leave without closing it. The scale of the tragedy did not reach my mother's consciousness. It was still daytime and she said, 'Go to the Judenrat, maybe you'll be able to find out something,' and suddenly she added, 'My darling little girl, perhaps you will be saved.'
>
> I went to the Judenrat where the Sonderkommando already were bossing the whole show. Smart, elegant Barasz was trying to ingratiate himself, but I saw for myself that they were no longer speaking to him, they were just ordering him about and kicking him.
>
> I went into the building of the Judenrat where all its members were gathered. Everybody was in a great state of agitation. We all finally understood that the end had come. I left the Judenrat and went – no, it's more accurate to say – I joined the group of

young people, and we found a bunker where we hid for several days and where preparations were being made for an uprising. We had bottles filled with molten lead.

When we were discovered and turned out, we were put against the wall. We thought that we will be shot, but instead we were driven into the general stream of people on the road heading towards Boyary, the eastern railway station on the outskirts of the town, and to the goods trains. It was horrifying. The stream of people were shepherded by barking dogs and were kicked with rifles by the Germans and by the Ukrainian Gestapo dressed in black uniforms. The Ukrainians, ordered by their masters in white gloves, did all their dirty work.

People who had a right to live walked on the pavement, maybe I am wrong, but I think they were indifferent to us. Our march was long and tortuous. Finally we reached our destination, the large square. After having been sorted out, the goods trains were leaving. I know now that these trains were going towards Lublin-Majdanek, because Treblinka was already destroyed by the Jewish fighters. Panic-stricken, we hung on to each other. We were hit with rifles, we were pushed and shoved like cattle.

I saw my aunts and a cousin. They told me that my mother had already left and that she hoped I managed to hide somewhere. The Ukrainians were beating us and were stealing from us. We were lying on the ground, above us a star-studded sky on a warm August night. Every now and then cries of prayers and screams of 'Hear! O Israel' were heard.

In the morning they began to separate families. The Ukrainian women kept on laughing sadistically, saying: 'Kiss goodbye. You'll never see each other again.' The men separated from the women. I cannot describe the horrific heartrending screams of anguish and weeping.[28]

A group of Jewish fighters, led by Mordecai Tenenbaum and Daniel Moszkowicz, tried to break out of the ghetto. But the ghetto fence was surrounded by machine guns. For two hours they fought, their principal weapon being two light machine guns. They also had revolvers and hand grenades produced in the ghetto. The Germans attacked the Jews in the bunkers, and, with far superior fire power, drove them out. 'We were about sixty to seventy people at that time,' Abraham Karasick later recalled, 'and afterwards we could not resist any more'.

The captured fighters were sent to join the forty thousand Jews of the ghetto who were being assembled in a 'concentration field' near the city's railway junction. There, groups of armed Germans were beating any Jew who fell out of line, and from time to time shooting them. All day and all night the Jews were kept in the field. Then, at noon on the second day, August 17, the Germans asked for all children under thirteen 'under the pretext', as Abraham Karasick recalled, 'of giving them lunch'. Some parents hid their children, or tried to hide them. But more than twelve hundred children were rounded up and taken away. 'I do not know what happened to them,' Karasick recalled. 'None of them was ever seen afterwards.'[29]

The children deported from Bialystok were taken first to Theresienstadt, where their arrival was noted with concern by the tens of thousands of German, Austrian and Czech Jews being held there. 'A train arrives at the ghetto,' recalled Josef Polak, 'bringing nearly thirteen hundred children aged from six to fifteen years. Nobody is allowed out in the streets, nobody is allowed to talk to the children. Closely guarded by the sentries and the SS, the children walk in a straggling procession, barefoot or in old boots, clad in rags, dirty, nothing but bags of skin and bone, to the delousing station.' Polak added: 'They are terrified, none of them utters a word, none of them smiles, but when they see the noticeboard with the word "gas" before the delousing station, they cling to each other, begin to cry, and refuse to enter. They evidently have some experience with gas from the East. But finally they are all bathed and furtively and in secret they tell some of the members of the disinfection group of their fate. At Bialystok the SS 'Death Commando' has shot their mothers and fathers before their eyes.'

While in Theresienstadt, the Bialystok children were lodged in houses surrounded by barbed wire, and 'several score', as Polak noted, died of disease. Those who were taken ill, he added, were taken to the Small Fortress section of the ghetto by the SS men 'and beaten to death'.[30] Four weeks later, the surviving children were deported again, this time to Birkenau, where all of them were murdered, together with the fifty-three adults who had volunteered to accompany them.[31]

During the Bialystok ghetto deportations, several hundred Jews managed to hide from the German search parties, thirty of them in an underground bunker in which, among others, the young Samuel Pisar and his mother found refuge. Later Pisar recalled:

> By the glow of a candle I made out the features of my teacher of Latin and History; Professor Bergman, a fragile and kindly man, was rocking his infant son, trying to stop his coughing. On the other side of the trapdoor above us came the shouts of German search parties and the barking of their dogs.
>
> We all fell silent; only the baby's coughing continued. 'Shhh', hissed a burly man near the door. The coughing did not stop. The man crawled over and placed a hand over the baby's mouth. The coughing ceased. Minutes passed. The child sank limply to the ground.
>
> All the while, Professor Bergman sat petrified. I knew he was not a coward. Even then, I understood that if he could think or feel anything at all, he was weighing one life against thirty, even if that life was his own son's.

On the following day, Samuel Pisar and his mother found refuge in a hospital. 'Another night passed. At dawn, an announcement was made that the SS would evacuate the hospital compound. We were to be taken elsewhere. The men, we were told, would go separately from the women, the children, and the sick.'[32]

On the third day, August 18, the Jews still confined to the field outside Bialystok were deported to Treblinka. Their train was the last to be sent there. About seventy men were not sent to Treblinka, but kept in prison in Bialystok. Some were locksmiths, some carpenters. 'When we came to the gaol,' Karasick recalled, 'the Germans told us that we should take off the badge "because the Jews in Europe are no more", and we were marked with a cross on the back. . . .'

Each morning, the seventy Jews were taken from prison to work for the Germans. For several months they saw how the Germans continued to round up Jews who had managed to hide during the action of August 16, and deport them. 'At the beginning,' Karasick recalled, 'they were liquidating every three or four days.'[33]

The last Jews to reach Treblinka, on August 18, had been Jews from Bialystok. All were gassed. Four days later, a wagon laden with the clothing of the dead left Treblinka for Germany. The camp was ready to be closed down. Parts of demolished huts, large numbers of wooden planks, and quantities of chlorinated lime were taken away, followed by the excavator.

The Jews who were made to dismantle the camp realized that once their work was done they too would be killed. But within the camp, they were always outnumbered by the armed guards. On September 2, however, a group of thirteen Jews killed their Ukrainian SS guard with a crowbar while working just outside the camp wire. The leader, an eighteen-year-old Polish Jew, Seweryn Klajnman from Falenica, put on the dead guard's uniform, took his rifle, and 'marched off' his fellow prisoners as if to a new work detail further off, cursing and bellowing at them as they went, as befitted an SS guard. Guided by one of their number, Shlomo Mokka, a carter and horse-trader from Wegrow who knew the area well, they escaped their pursuers and evaded capture.[34]

Later in September the gas-chambers at Treblinka were demolished and the barbed-wire fencing was removed. Then the remaining Jews who had carried out these tasks were deported to Sobibor. The shunting-engines and the armoured cars were then sent elsewhere; and the SS men were transferred to other camps. In all, a hundred goods wagons full of equipment had been seen to leave. Treblinka was no more.

The last of the camp personnel to leave Treblinka for other camps were the Ukrainian guards. Then the site of the killings was ploughed up, a house and farm buildings were built, seed was sown, and Strebel, a German from the Ukraine, himself a former member of the camp staff, moved into the farm, bringing his family to join him from the Ukraine.[35] They were the first true 'settlers', in a camp where the overriding deception had been that it was for 'resettlement'.

Among the Jews deported from Bialystok was the twenty-one-year-old Bertha Sokolskaya. Later she recalled:

> We were forty in the cattle truck, the train started out and then after a while stopped. Shooting began. We discovered that some of the younger people managed to hide screwdrivers, and

opened the engine cabin. Many were killed, some managed to escape to the woods. One of them was Yosif Makovsky, a friend of mine, now living in Israel. Then the train stopped in Treblinka, it stopped for a long time. We felt the smell of burning. It hung all over Treblinka. We thought that we will be taken there. In desperation one of the girls in the cattle truck squeezed through the little window gap. The Germans caught her and led her into the camp.

Finally the train moved, leaving Treblinka. The heat was terrible, we had no water, our mouths were like dry wood. We were insane with thirst. Everyone tried to give the German guards all their valuable possessions for a drop of water. But we pushed each other to be near the little window, and only spilled and lost the precious drops. We went berserk, hitting each other. The train stopped many times. We finally arrived in Lublin. When we were still in Bialystok we were told that girls from previous transports will come to our window and will tell us that we were being sent to work. Indeed, that's what happened. But we could not stand it any longer, we decided to commit suicide.

There was amongst us a doctor from Lodz, Charnoleskaya, who had a razor and she began slashing our wrists. We were beside ourselves, pushing and shoving and stretching out our hands. She cut one of my wrists and a fountain of blood burst out and I fell. I remember distinctly, it reminded me of Sienkiewicz's *Quo Vadis*. I had no strength left in me to lift myself to have my other hand cut. We were lying on the floor losing blood. Next morning the Germans opened the door. I was alive.[36]

Bertha Sokolskaya was sent to a labour camp at Blizyn, in the Lublin region. Among the other Jews deported from Bialystok were several thousand who were taken by train to Majdanek. Among these was Samuel Pisar, then aged fourteen, who later recalled the journey to the camp:

No air, no water, no food. How long we were inside these cattle cars I don't really know. I remember someone saying seventy-two hours. We were horribly dehydrated. I saw people with faces that were literally blue, licking their own sweat;

there was urine and excrement all over the floor. It was like a sewer.

When we stopped and the doors were opened, blinding floodlights lit up the night. A long line of SS men, each holding a restive police dog on a short leash, stood along the ramp. A short order – Everything Out – and several of the great beasts leaped into our car. In the space of seconds, two or three of the half-conscious prisoners were torn to pieces. Horrified, the prostrate men dragged themselves up with their last ounce of strength and staggered out. Other bodies lying on the floor the dogs did not touch; they were dead. Of the hundred or so men in the car, more than a score had succumbed along the way.

On the railway platform there was panic – blows, screams, and the gruff barking of the dogs. I held my suitcase up against my chest for protection as I stumbled over corpses.[37]

The pace and pattern of murder was unchanging. On August 25, at Janowska camp, the SS had selected twenty-four of the prettiest Jewish girls in the camp, aged between seventeen and twenty. That night, they were the 'guests' of the SS at an all-night 'party', something strictly forbidden according to Nazi prohibitions against 'race defilement'. In the morning, there was a suggestion that the girls should be allowed to remain alive, to work henceforth as cleaners in the labour camp. But one of the girls jumped out of the truck carrying them back to the barracks. She was shot, and the other twenty-three taken to the execution site.[38]

These girls were murdered on August 26. On the following day, all the Jews employed in the cement factory at nearby Drohobycz were murdered, among them the thirty-six-year-old Dr Mojzesz Bay, a graduate of the Sorbonne.[39]

Behind the lines in German-occupied Russia, a Polish Jew, Zygmunt Grosbart, who had earlier been the interpreter of an SS officer, Lieutenant Bingel, succeeded, first in passing essential Intelligence information to the Soviet partisans in the nearby forests, and then in escaping to the partisans himself.[40] Forty Jews in hiding in the forests of Koniecpol, however, were attacked by Poles, and many of the fugitives were killed.[41]

Jews in hiding were rarely fortunate. In the autumn of 1943 a group of young Jews in the Wlodawa region attacked a former Jewish farming estate, the Turno Estate, then being used by the

Germans. In what had once been David Turno's barns, the crops were ready to be shipped to Germany. The Jewish raiders set the buildings on fire. One of those in the attack, Hersh Werner, later recalled:

> As we were pulling out of the burning estate, I noticed a bulky form crawling on all fours, like an animal, and making very strange noises. I showed it to Symcha who was near me, and we both decided that it might be a human being, perhaps a Jew. We both took him by the arms, and dragged him along with us.
>
> After we covered about five miles from Turno, we sat down to rest and looked at the human mess we were dragging. He was covered with hair like an animal, his clothes were torn, he couldn't stand up on his two feet, and he looked like a skeleton. He could hardly talk, but from his mumblings we learned that this man was Yankel, David Turno's relative, and my friend from Warsaw.
>
> From his mumblings, we understood that he had stayed buried in the barn, in a hole under the feed trough for the cows. No one knew that he was there and he lived there for over a year. He ate the food that was given to the animals and never stood up. The heat from the burning buildings had forced him out of his hole.
>
> We walked to our base, and tried to help Yankel. He couldn't hold any food, and the following day he died.

'We buried him in the woods', Harold Werner added, 'and I cried over what had happened to my friend'.[42]

On September 1 the Germans began the final deportations from Tarnow to Birkenau. For two days the Jews resisted with arms. But none of those who took up arms survived. As with the resistance in nearby Sandomierz, the only reports that survive of the resistance of the Jews came from Polish eye-witnesses.[43] In Tarnow, according to a Polish underground report, the Germans used grenades to break up the resistance, then loaded the surviving Jews into goods wagons, the insides of which were covered with carbide and lime. According to the Polish report, the wagons were then 'sealed, inundated with water, and sent off to extermination'.[44]

It was also on September 1, in Vilna, that the deportations to the

Estonian labour camps had begun. Among those who disappeared during the deportations was Hirsh Glik, the twenty-three-year-old author of the song of hope and defiance, 'Never say that you have reached the very end'. On the first day of the deportations, the Jewish resistance group in Vilna, the United Partisans Organization, issued a proclamation, 'Jews, prepare for armed resistance!' Death was certain. 'Who can still believe that he will survive when the murderers kill systematically? The hand of the hangman will reach out to each of us. Neither hiding nor cowardice will save lives.'[45]

On September 6, following the deportation of more than seven thousand Vilna Jews to the labour camps in Estonia, Jacob Gens urged the ten thousand Jews who had not been deported to register with the Jewish Council, in order 'to be able to return to normal life in the ghetto as soon as possible'.[46] The partisans now made for the forests. 'I send you an additional group of fighting Jews,' Abba Kovner wrote on September 10 to the commander of one of the Soviet partisan units in the region.

Most of the Jews in Vilna were, however, in despair, broken, starving and afraid. 'I saw desperate people commit suicide,' Kovner later recalled. Not the 'battle of an underground', Kovner added, but the 'very existence' of a fighting resistance organization, 'was the amazing and incredible achievement'.

Those who reached the forests fought as best they could. Vitka Kempner's exploit at the beginning of July had been a source of pride to the Jewish fighters. 'Lithuanians did not do it,' Kovner later recalled, 'nor Poles, nor Russians. A Jewish woman did it, a woman who, after she did this, had no base to return to. She had to walk three days and nights, with wounded legs and feet. She had to go back to the ghetto.' Were she to have been captured, Kovner added, the whole ghetto might have been held responsible.[47]

Two months after she returned to Vilna, Vitka Kemper blew up an electric transformer inside the city, and then made her escape from the scene of her sabotage. On the following day she managed to enter the labour camp at Keilis on the outskirts of Vilna, where she smuggled out several dozen prisoners, leading them from the camp to the forest. Later, with five other Jewish partisans, she entered the town of Olkiniki and set fire to the turpentine factory there.[48]

On September 14 the Gestapo summoned Jacob Gens, head of the Vilna Jewish Council, to their headquarters. A friend urged him to flee, but he replied that if he were to run away, 'thousands of Jews will pay for it with their lives'. Gens went to Gestapo headquarters, and did not return. He was shot, it was said, for maintaining contact with the United Partisans Organization, and for financing its activities.[49]

Nine days later, the Vilna ghetto was 'liquidated'. The pretext was a further deportation of all Jews to the labour camps in Estonia, but after eight thousand of the ten thousand surviving Jews had been taken to Rossa Square, beaten and robbed, there was a selection. More than sixteen hundred men were sent to the Estonian labour camps, but five thousand women and children were sent to Majdanek, and to its gas-chambers. Several hundred old and sick Jews were sent to Ponar, and shot. By September 25, only two thousand Jews remained in Vilna, in four small labour camps:[50] the remnant of fifty-seven thousand inhabitants of that once vibrant secular and spiritual Jewish centre, the Jerusalem of Lithuania.

The reality of extermination was so terrible that the civilised mind of man rebelled against it. 'Persistent rumours circulate', wrote Jakub Poznanski, in the Lodz ghetto, on 27 September 1943, 'about the liquidation of the ghettos in various Polish cities. In my opinion, people are exaggerating, as usual. Even if certain excesses have taken place in some cities, that still does not incline one to believe that Jews are being mass-murdered. At least I consider that out of the question.'[51]

Poznanski's doubts were a sign of the isolation of one ghetto from another. So little was known by the Jews in any one locality of the fate of the Jews elsewhere. In the labour camp at Nowogrodek, the two hundred and fifty survivors of the once flourishing Jewish population of five thousand had no idea of the events that had so recently taken place in Vilna, or in Bialystok. All they knew was that their destruction could be ordered at any moment; that urgent efforts were needed if they were to avoid being slaughtered.

With enormous difficulty, a tunnel was dug under the wire of the camp, out towards the surrounding woods. Some of the prisoners saw no point in making the escape bid, arguing, as Idel Kagan later recalled, 'If we are going to die why run for it?' But by September 22 the tunnel was ready, and the escape began.

'When I came out of the tunnel', Idel Kagan later recalled, 'there was a tremendous machine-gun fire. The guards did not know what was happening. Because we had light in the tunnel, people lost their sense of direction when they came out into the dark. Some ran back towards the camp by mistake.'

Of the two hundred who escaped, eighty were killed or captured. The others reached the woods, and survived as best they could, searching for food, and for partisans. Idel Kagan had no weapon, only a pistol cover. But with this, he was able to give sufficient impression of being armed, so as to demand food from a farmer. Finally, after hiding by day and walking by night for ten days, he reached the partisan group led by Tobias Belsky.

Belsky's three hundred partisans were not only an armed unit. They had also been, since their first days in the forest, the protectors of more than a thousand women, children and old people, who had managed to escape from the surrounding ghettos, or whom Belsky and his three brothers had succeeded in rescuing. In an area without any large forests, the Belsky brothers had still managed to fend off repeated German searching. One of the four brothers, Zusl, followed Soviet instructions and took a group of eighty fighters into the woods as an unencumbered unit, devoted solely to anti-German attacks. Tobias Belsky and his fighters remained with the 'family camp', as did his other brothers Asael and Achik. With them was Idel Kagan, who recalled how the brothers opened a bakery, a sausage workshop, a shoe repair workshop and, eventually, a munitions workshop, all of which were much used by the Soviet partisans in the neighbourhood. Tobias Belsky's fighters would also go out from time to time on an anti-German expedition, to cut telegraph wires. Later in the war, Asael Belsky was killed in action near Königsberg. His girlfriend, Haya Dzienciolski, whose escape from Nowogrodek in July 1941 had led to the establishment of the family camp, survived. One of her first acts, with the Belsky brothers, had been to try to rescue their parents from the village of Stankewicz. But the Germans had already taken them to their deaths.[52]

With the destruction of each ghetto, the Germans continued to gather the clothing and belongings of the dead. On September 6 the Lodz Ghetto Chronicle noted a further 'twelve freight cars' of used shoes reaching the ghetto. 'The old-shoe workshop', it added, 'will be busy for many months just sorting this vast quantity.' Leather shoes had to be sorted from other shoes. Men's, women's and children's shoes had to be separated. Right shoes had to be sorted from left shoes, 'whole shoes from half shoes', black shoes from brown shoes, and finally, 'and this is the hardest job of all', the matching pairs 'have to be ferreted out'.[53]

The penalty for any theft from this mass of shoe leather brought into the ghetto was execution. In each of the ghetto factories a notice stated: 'Every act of theft will be punishable by death'.[54] Icek Bekerman, a thirty-four-year-old shoeworker, had already been hanged in the Lodz ghetto in September 13, for taking a few scraps of leather in order to make himself a pair of shoe laces.[55] The ghetto carpentry shop had been ordered to build the gallows, and the entire personnel of the leather and saddlery workshop, and the shoe workshop, were ordered to be present at the execution, together with representatives of each of the other workshops in the ghetto.[56]

Bekerman's wife and two children were not allowed to the place of execution to witness the death sentence. Instead, forced to remain at home, their cries could be heard by all those on the way to the execution. Those cries, recalled the twelve-year-old Ben Edelbaum, 'were the most terrifying lamentations I had ever heard'.[57]

31

'A page of glory . . . never to be written'

ALMOST EVERYWHERE within their control, the Germans sought to destroy the remnants of long-since decimated Jewish communities. On 18 September 1943, two thousand Minsk Jews were deported to Sobibor, where all but a dozen, chosen for the labour camp, were gassed.[1] On September 20, at Szebnie camp in southern Poland, the thousand Jewish inmates were driven in trucks to a field outside the camp. The road to the field was cordoned off by German and Ukrainian police. An eye-witness, who escaped and reached England at the beginning of 1945, recalled how:

> Half-naked and without shoes, Jewish men, women and children were pushed along by Ukrainian guards with rifles to the place of execution near the woods. As soon as one party arrived, it was mowed down by SS men with tommy-guns. Thus party after party was slaughtered. First one heard a burst of shot, then later single shots killing those who had not fallen in the first instance.
>
> Most of the victims walked to death calm and resigned. The children were mostly unaware of what was to happen to them and waved their hands in goodbye. One beautiful girl begged the Ukrainian policeman to let her escape. He let her go but the next one shot her dead.
>
> Clothing was removed from the bodies which were left unburied until the next day when Jews brought from another camp were ordered to pile them and set fire to them. When they had done so, they themselves were shot and thrown on to the pyres.
>
> These bodies burned for forty eight hours. Later the bones were collected and thrown into the River Jasiolka.[2]

The destruction of the evidence of mass murder now followed in the wake of the murders themselves, or at the sites of earlier killings. To Ponar, the death pits near Vilna, was brought a group of seventy Jews, nine Russian prisoners-of-war, and a young Polish peasant who had given refuge to a Jewish child. All eighty had been held in prison in Vilna. For four months, from September 1943, they worked at Ponar, as another 'Special Commando 1005', under the direct orders of Blobel, building massive log pyres, digging up corpses, placing the corpses on the pyres, igniting them, and scattering the ashes. Each pyre could hold 3,500 bodies, and burnt for up to ten days.

The first grave opened by the 'Blobel Commando' at Ponar contained the corpses of eight thousand Jews, five hundred Soviet prisoners-of-war and several hundred Catholic priests and seminarists. Most of the corpses were blindfolded and had their hands tied behind their backs. The second grave contained the corpses of 9,500 Jewish children, women and men. In the third grave the prisoners counted 10,400 corpses. Hardly any of the children's remains showed marks of bullets, but their tongues were protruding. In the fourth pit the prisoners found twenty-four thousand corpses, among them many Soviet prisoners-of-war, a number of Poles, Catholic priests and nuns, and one German soldier. In the fifth grave they found 3,500 women, children and men, all naked, and all shot in the back of the head. In the sixth grave they counted five thousand naked corpses. In the seventh grave they found several hundred political prisoners, and in the eighth and ninth graves they found five thousand naked corpses of Jews from the rural ghettos in the Vilna region; these were the Jewish deportees who had earlier received assurances that they were being taken to the Kovno ghetto, and had found themselves, on 5 April 1943, at Ponar.[3]

Since August 18, a third 'Blobel Commando' had been at work at Babi Yar, in the suburbs of Kiev. Blobel himself had visited the site to see the work being done. After the earth on top of the grave had been removed, he later recalled, 'the bodies were covered with inflammable material and ignited. It took about two days until the grave burnt to the bottom.' Blobel added: 'I myself observed that the fire had glowed down to the bottom. After that the grave was filled in and the traces practically obliterated.'[4]

More than four hundred Jews and Soviet prisoners-of-war were working at this gruesome task, knowing that when their work was finished they would be killed. They worked with shackles around their ankles, guarded by sixty SS men armed with submachine guns, and accompanied by Alsatian dogs trained to kill. Within a month, seventy of the prisoners had been killed in random executions, staged each night by the guards for their amusement.

Throughout their work, the SS would address the Jews working in the pits at Babi Yar as *Leichen*, 'corpses'. But, as the historian Reuben Ainsztein has written, 'in those half-naked men who reeked of putrefying flesh, whose bodies were eaten by scabies and covered with a layer of mud and soot, and of whose physical strength so little remained, there survived a spirit that defied everything that the Nazis' New Order had done or could do to them. In the men whom the SS men saw only as walking corpses, there matured a determination that at least one of them must survive to tell the world about what they had seen in Babi Yar.'

Plans were made to break out. Among those who coordinated these plans was a Jewish soldier of the Red Army, Vladimir Davydov. Independent of these plans, a non-Jewish Red Army man, Fyodor Zavertanny, managed one day to loosen his shackles, and to escape. In retaliation, the Germans shot twelve of the prisoners. They also shot the SS man in charge of the guards who had been watching Zavertanny's group.

The scale of the reprisal seemed to rule out individual escapes, and make a mass break-out the only possible course. The method was to search for any keys that remained among the thousands of rotting corpses and decaying garments, in the hope that one of these keys might fit the padlock of the bunker in which the prisoners were locked at night.

Miraculously, on September 20, one of the prisoners, Jacob Kapler, discovered a key that fitted the padlock. Nine days later, on the third anniversary of the first mass slaughter at Babi Yar, the escape plans were put into effect. In all, 325 Jews and Soviet prisoners-of-war made the break-out. A total of 311 were shot down as they ran; 14 reached hiding places, 5 of whom hid for twenty days in the chimney of a disused factory. Two were hidden by the Ukrainian sisters Natalya and Antonina Petrenko, underneath their henhouse.

Five weeks after the escape, on November 6, the fourteen

survivors welcomed the victorious Red Army into Kiev, and then joined its ranks. Four of them, Filip Vilkis, Leonid Kharash, I. Brodskiy and Leonid Kadomskiy, all Jews, were later killed in action against the Germans. Two of them, David Budnik and Vladimir Davydov, also Jews, gave evidence about the mass murders of Babi Yar in 1946, when they were both witnesses at the Nuremberg Tribunal.[5]

The fourteen survivors of the Babi Yar revolt had found temporary safety in flight; ten of them were to survive the war. There was also a miraculous escape, at the end of September 1943, for more than seven thousand Danish Jews. During the previous three years, following the occupation of Denmark in the spring of 1940, the Germans had embarked on a policy of cooperation and negotiation with the Danish authorities. As a result, the Jews had been left unmolested. But growing Danish resistance to the German occupation had slowly undermined any chance of continued cooperation, and on 28 August 1943 the Germans had declared martial law.

The SS hoped to use the opportunity of martial law to deport all of Denmark's Jews and half-Jews. Forewarned of the planned deportation, however, Danes and Jews plotted to ensure that, on the eve of the deportation, Danish sea captains and fishermen ferried 5,919 Jews, 1,301 part-Jews – designated Jews by the Nazis – and 686 Christians married to Jews, to neutral Sweden.

On 1 October 1943, the second day of the Jewish New Year, the Germans found only 500 Jews still in Denmark. All were sent to Theresienstadt; 423 survived the war.[6] The Danish Jews who had been ferried to Sweden also survived, unmolested, as did a further 3,000 Jewish refugees who had reached Sweden before the outbreak of war, from Germany, Austria and Czechoslovakia.

The escape of more than seven thousand Danish Jews at the end of September 1943 was a setback for German plans. But those plans had continued without respite throughout September. From Holland, Belgium and France more than five thousand Jews had been deported to Birkenau and gassed during that same September. Even those sent to the barracks at Birkenau were in daily danger: on October 3 an SS doctor, as part of a regular inspection, selected 139 Jews from the barracks whom he judged too sick to work: they were taken away and gassed.[7]

At Poznan, on October 4, Heinrich Himmler addressed his senior SS officers. At one point in his remarks he said that he wished to speak 'quite frankly' on 'a very grave matter'. 'Among ourselves,' he added, 'it should be mentioned quite frankly, and yet we will never speak of it publicly'. Himmler went on to explain:

> I mean the evacuation of the Jews, the extermination of the Jewish race. It's one of those things it is easy to talk about. 'The Jewish race is being exterminated', says one Party member, 'that's quite clear, it's in our programme – elimination of the Jews and we're doing it, exterminating them.' And then they come, eighty million worthy Germans, and each one has his decent Jew. Of course the others are vermin, but this one is an A-1 Jew.
>
> Not one of all those who talk this way has watched it, not one of them has gone through it. Most of you must know what it means when one hundred corpses are lying side by side, or five hundred, or one thousand. To have stuck it out and at the same time – apart from exceptions caused by human weakness – to have remained decent fellows, that is what has made us hard. This is a page of glory in our history which has never to be written and is never to be written, for we know how difficult we should have made it for ourselves, if with the bombing raids, the burdens and the deprivations of war, we still had Jews today in every town as secret saboteurs, agitators, and trouble-mongers. We would now probably have reached the 1916–17 stage when the Jews were still in the German national body.

Himmler then spoke of the belongings of the murdered Jews, and of the penalties for individual looting:

> We have taken from them what wealth they had. I have issued a strict order, which SS Lieutenant-General Pohl has carried out, that this wealth should, as a matter of course, be handed over to the Reich without reserve. We have taken none of it for ourselves. Individual men who have lapsed will be punished in accordance with an order I issued at the beginning which gave this warning; whoever takes so much as a mark of it is a dead man. A number of SS men – there are not very many of them – have fallen short, and they will die without mercy.
>
> We had the moral right, we had the duty to our people, to destroy this people which wanted to destroy us. But we have not the right to enrich ourselves with so much as a fur, a watch, a mark, or a cigarette, or anything else.

Because we have exterminated a germ, we do not want in the end to be infected by the germ and die of it. I will not see so much as a small area of sepsis appear here or gain a hold. Wherever it may form, we will cauterize it. Altogether, however, we can say that we have fulfilled this most difficult duty for the love of our people. And our spirit, our soul, our character has not suffered injury from it.[8]

These proud boastings of 'spirit', 'soul' and 'character' reflected a state of mind which made possible unimaginable horrors. On the day after Himmler's speech in Poznan, the 1,260 children deported from the Bialystok ghetto in August, together with the 53 doctors and nurses who had accompanied them, left Theresienstadt for Birkenau. They had been told that their destination was Palestine, or Switzerland. There were no survivors.[9] Four days later, on October 9, during the opening evening hours of the Day of Atonement, the holiest moment in the Jewish year, a thousand men and women in the barracks at Birkenau, all of whom were judged too sick to work, were sent to the gas-chambers.[10]

Among those Jews in captivity who tried, despite adversity, to celebrate that night according to their faith, were several hundred Jews being held prisoner in Warsaw in the Pawiak prison. Most of them had been caught while in hiding, following the destruction of the ghetto and crushing of the uprising six months earlier.

One of those who was imprisoned in Pawiak that night was Julien Hirshaut, who later recalled:

> In a cell in the Pawiak prison, ruled by barbarians bent on exterminating world Jewry, stood a group of Jews deep in prayer.
> Atlasowicz was standing by the greenish-brown prison table which served as a makeshift lectern. His broad back swayed reverently in a constant motion as he recited the ancient prayer. Atlasowicz intoned the psalm in a muffled voice, not quite his own.
> 'Light will shine on the righteous.'
> 'And joy upon the upright of heart.'
> For a moment he was silent. Then he turned to the others, and in a hushed voice, as though talking to himself, he continued.

'Our Kol Nidre in this place is unique and symbolic. It is our continuation. Here we take up the golden tradition of sanctity handed down to us by generations of Jews before us. We are human beings and will not yield our souls to the barbarians; we defy our enemies by remaining true to our people and traditions. Therein lies the true meaning of our services here today. God will hear our prayers although I may not be the proper person to address Him in the name of this congregation. Some of you may not derive as much pleasure from my praying as you were accustomed to on these High Holy Days. . . .'

As the prayers continued Atlasowicz began to cry. His son too in prison with his father wept, repeating over and over again, 'Mother . . . mother . . . mother. . . .'

The boy's mother had been in hiding in Warsaw, wearing a gold crucifix in the hope that the authorities would believe that she was a Christian. When her son was taken away from her, she had hung this crucifix around his neck.[11]

In Riga, the Latvian Yanis Lipke had continued to devise methods of rescuing Jews from the ghetto. Isaak Dryzin later recalled how he and his brother, an engineer, were approached by Lipke while working in one of the work gangs outside the ghetto. Lipke told the two brothers to go to the ghetto gate on the Day of Atonement, October 10. That morning, Lipke approached the guards at the ghetto gate. 'Give me some Yids to work in my kitchen garden,' he said, in what Isaak Dryzin later recalled as 'drunken familiarity', adding: 'Here, take two packets of cigarettes.'

For these two packets of cigarettes, Lipke received the Dryzin brothers, as well as a third Jew, Sheyenson, all three of whom had been waiting at the gates. Lipke took them to the nearest doorway, tore off their yellow stars, gave them peasants' hats to put on, and drove them out of Riga, to a farm of another friend. There, like the Jews whom Lipke had earlier taken from the ghetto, they were hidden in barns and haystacks.

His mission accomplished, Yanis told the Dryzin brothers: 'tomorrow I will go to the ghetto again and will keep bringing people here every day.' That same night he began to plan a similar rescue, which he was able to carry out on the following day.[12]

For the 'Goebbels calendar', the Day of Atonement had always been a central date. On that day, at Plaszow camp outside Cracow, fifty Jews, mostly elderly people, were chosen for their 'final day of judgement', and killed.[13] At Sobibor, however, the Jewish prisoners in Camp No. 1, the labour camp, were allowed to pray. All six hundred gathered in a hut. A third of them were girls and boys of fifteen and sixteen. One of the young boys, Yaakov Biskowitz, noticed several older men among those who were praying. These were Jews, most of them Red Army prisoners-of-war, who had been brought from Russia; now they were 'whispering among themselves'.[14]

The slaves of Sobibor were preparing to revolt, led by these Red Army veterans. Among the Red Army men, now captives, was a Jew who took the lead in planning revolt, Alexander Pechersky. Aged thirty-four, Pechersky had been a student of music before the war, writing music for plays in his home town of Rostov-on-Don. He had gone to the front on the very first day of the war. On his second day at Sobibor, he had been invited to join the underground committee where it had been agreed, as he later wrote, 'to give me the leadership'.[15]

To make revolt possible, several of the Jewish girls who worked in the SS quarters, polishing shoes and cleaning floors, had managed to steal a few hand grenades, some pistols, a rifle, and a submachine gun.[16]

Meanwhile, the trains continued to arrive with new victims. On the morning of October 11, before the conspirators were ready with their plans, a group of new deportees, already undressed and on the way to the gas-chamber, tried to run in the direction of the barbed wire. The guards began to shoot, killing many of them instantly. The others were dragged naked to the gas-chambers. 'That day', Alexander Pechersky recalled, 'the crematorium burned longer than usual. Huge flames rose up in the grey autumn sky and the camp was lit with strange colours. Helpless and distressed, we looked at the bodies of our brothers and sisters.'

On the night of October 13, Pechersky, and his co-conspirator, Leon Feldhendler, a Polish Jew, distributed knives and hatchets, as well as warm clothing.[17] Then, in the early afternoon of October 14, their plan was put into action. As individual German and Ukrainian guards entered the huts on their regular tours of inspection, they were attacked. Nine SS men and two Ukrainians were killed, whereupon, as Yaakov Biskowitz later recalled, the signal was given for the revolt to begin, the password 'Hurrah'.[18]

Of the six hundred prisoners in Camp No. 1, three hundred escaped. Nearly two hundred were shot by the SS and Ukrainian guards while trying to break out; the rest were killed in the camp with the arrival of military and police reinforcements from nearby Chelm. Many of the escaped prisoners joined partisan units: one of them, Semyon Rozenfeld, a Russian Jew who later joined the Red Army, was in Berlin on the day of victory.[19]

Among the three hundred Jews killed in the revolt was Max Van Dam, a thirty-three-year-old Dutch painter, who before the war had travelled and painted in Italy, France and Spain. In July 1942, when the deportations from Holland had begun, Van Dam was hidden by a Dutch friend, Professor Hemmelrjik, in the village of Blaricum. Later that year he tried to reach Switzerland, was caught, sent to Drancy, and from there to Sobibor.[20]

On October 21, a week after the Sobibor revolt, all two thousand Jews in the Minsk labour camp, the last survivors of the Minsk ghetto, were rounded up and killed in pits outside the city. On the day of this massacre, twenty-six Jews hid in an underground bunker which had been built by two Jewish stonemasons. In the first month three died; the survivors buried them in the ground on which they themselves lay. Two girls left the hide-out in search of food; they were captured and killed. After eight months, only thirteen of the twenty-six remained alive. There was no more food. The children were in a coma and the adults were weak from hunger. It was then that a girl called Musya left the hide-out in search of food. She did not look like a Jewess, but she took the risk, nevertheless, of running into somebody who knew her and might denounce her to the Germans. During her search for help, Musya met Anna Dvach, a White Russian woman with whom she had worked in the same factory before the German invasion. Her friend took her home, gave her food and shelter, and then sent her back with food for the other survivors. From that day until the arrival of the Red Army six months later, Anna Dvach ensured the survival of the thirteen Jews.[21]

Between July 1941 and October 1943 more than five thousand

Jews had fled to the forests around Minsk. As many as five thousand of those who had fled had been killed on their way to the partisan areas, or in German manhunts. But others had survived to fight in the growing number of partisan units, or to be protected, as were some six hundred women and children, in another family camp, known as the 'Family Detachment', commanded by Shlomo Zorin.

Unknown to the Jews in hiding or in action, the head of the first small Minsk underground organization, an officer in the Red Army known as Isai Pavlovich Kazinets, had in fact been a Jew whose real first name was Joshua. In June 1941 two of his children had been shot during the mass flight eastward; his father, a Red Army soldier in 1919, had been killed by anti-Bolshevik forces in south Russia.[22] Kazinets himself had been caught and killed before the end of 1941. Nor did his underground group survive. Only the Jews in the ghetto sustained effective resistance in Minsk.

Jewish partisan units were indeed active throughout White Russia, Lithuania and the forests of Poland. One such unit began its operations in the Vilna region on October 7, when it destroyed more than fifty telegraph poles on the Vilna to Grodno road, cutting the wires and breaking the insulators. This group carried out five more operations in October; one of them, on October 17, under the command of Abba Kovner, destroyed two bridges and two railway engines. On October 23 telephone and telegraph lines were both destroyed on the Vilna to Lida railway.[23]

Also on October 23, an incident took place in Birkenau, symbolizing the courage of unarmed individuals. At the time of the Warsaw ghetto uprising six months earlier, three thousand Jews had been persuaded by the Germans to emerge from hiding on the grounds that, as owners of South American passports, visas, or promissory visas, they would be spared deportation. These Jews were not sent to Treblinka, Majdanek or the labour camps in the Lublin region, but to two camps, one at Bergen-Belsen, the other at Vittel, in France. There they had awaited their transfer to South America.

On October 23, 1,750 Polish Jews from the group held at Bergen-Belsen were deported to Birkenau. There, they were driven into the undressing chamber by SS Sergeant Major Josef Schillinger. A former roll-call leader in the men's camp at Birkenau, Schillinger had become feared and hated for his habit of choking Jews to death while they were eating their meagre meals.[24]

The women were ordered to undress. As they did so, the German guards, as usual, seized rings from fingers and watches from wrists.[25] During this activity, Schillinger himself ordered one of the women to undress completely. This woman, who according to some reports was a former Warsaw dancer by the name of Horowitz, threw her shoe in Schillinger's face, seized his revolver, and shot him in the stomach. She also wounded another SS man, Sergeant Emmerich.[26] The shooting of Schillinger served as a signal for the other women to attack the SS men at the entrance to the gaschamber. One SS man had his nose torn off, another was scalped.[27]

Schillinger died on the way to the camp hospital. The other SS man fled. Shortly afterwards the camp commandant, Rudolf Hoess, entered the chamber, accompanied by other SS men carrying machine guns and grenades. They then removed the women one by one, and shot them outside.[28]

The revolt of the Jewish women at Birkenau was recorded by two prisoners who worked in the camp. One of them, a Jew, Stanislaw Jankowski, remembered only one other such attempt, when a Soviet prisoner-of-war, who was about to be shot with four other comrades, snatched the gun of an SS man, 'but did not manage to make use of it and was overpowered'.[29] The second prisoner, Jerzy Tabau, who later escaped from Birkenau and passed news of the episode to the West, noted that, after October 23, 'the extermination of Jews continued relentlessly. . . .'[30]

One such gassing, recorded by Dr Albert Menasche, a deportee from Salonica, was of 2,500 girls, including his own eleven-year-old daughter Lillian. Locked in the notorious Block 25 for three days, with no food and almost no water, on October 25 the girls were all gassed. Menasche added: 'Eight hundred Jewish girls from Salonica were burned on that cursed day.'[31]

Lena Berg, from Warsaw, was an eye-witness of the death of the women and girls from Greece:

They had been brought to Auschwitz only weeks before, slender, black-eyed against the sleet and cold of the northern October. They sang a sentimental song called 'Mama', whose melody made one weep.

In a few weeks Auschwitz had withered those exotic flowers,

their fiery eyes had become dull in sunken sockets, empty and dead. Emaciated, dirty, repulsive, those Greek women could barely drag themselves around. Once so shapely, they now had legs like sticks and their breasts hung like bags. Their complexions, made velvet smooth by the southern sun, were now covered with horrible abscesses, vermin bites, and the marks of scabies incessantly scratched. They stank of gangrene, dysentery, unwashed sweat, and wretchedness.

When they went to their deaths they sang the 'Hatikvah', that song of undying hope, the song of an old people which has always carried the vision of Zion in its heart. Since then, every time I hear 'Hatikvah' I always see them, the dregs of human misery, and I know that through mankind flows a stream of eternity greater and more powerful than individual deaths.[32]

On 16 September 1943, less than seven weeks after the fall of Mussolini, as German forces occupied all but the southern tip of Italy, the first twenty-four Jews had been deported from Merano, in northern Italy, to Birkenau.[33] Even though Allied forces, fighting in the south of Italy, were forcing the Germans back towards Rome, the deportation of Jews was a high priority for the German occupying power. Of the thirty-seven thousand Jews who suddenly found themselves in danger, only a few hundred managed to escape over the mountain passes to Switzerland. In Italy itself, several thousand found refuge in Catholic homes and institutions.

The Pope also helped the Jewish community in Rome that September, offering whatever amount of gold might be needed towards the fifty kilogrammes of gold demanded by the Nazis, which the community could not raise in full on its own.[34] At the same time, at the Capuchin convent on the Via Siciliano, Father Benoit, under the name of Father Benedetti, saved large numbers of Jews by providing them with false identification papers. In this work he was helped by the staffs of the Swiss, Hungarian, Rumanian and French Embassies in Rome and also by a number of Italians – among them the 'marshal of Rome', Mario di Marco, a high official of the police, who was later tortured by the Gestapo but did not disclose what he knew.[35]

On October 16, the Germans combed the houses and streets of

Rome in search of Jews who, regardless of age, sex or health were taken to the Collegio Militare. A few days earlier, Pope Pius XII had personally ordered the Vatican clergy to open the sanctuaries of Vatican City to all 'non-Aryans' in need of refuge. By the morning of October 16, a total of 477 Jews had been given shelter in the Vatican and its enclaves, while another 4,238 had been given sanctuary in the many monasteries and convents in Rome. Only 1,015 of Rome's 6,730 Jews were seized that morning. Held for two days in the Collegio Militare, they were then deported to Auschwitz. 'The children were crying,' a non-Jewish eye-witness later recalled. 'Everywhere you could hear pleas for help and cries of distress.'[36]

Of the 1,015 Jews deported from Rome on October 18, only 16 survived the war. Within two months, a further 7,345 Jews had been seized throughout northern Italy. Of these, 6,746 were gassed on arrival at Auschwitz, or died soon afterwards.[37] Near Trieste, at a camp set up principally for Italian prisoners-of-war, and in which three thousand Italian soldiers were murdered by SS and Ukrainian guards, 620 Jews from Trieste were also murdered. The camp, La Risiera di San Sabba, was run by SS men transferred to Italy from the Polish death camps.[38]

Among the Jews in hiding in Poland was Helena Manaster. A survivor of several ghettos and 'actions', including the Petlura Day massacre in Lvov, she had found refuge in the Capuchin monastery in Cracow. There, posing as a Catholic, and as the wife of a Polish army officer, she was safe. At the same time, she was expecting a baby. On October 6, at two in the morning, as labour pains began, Helena Manaster was driven to the hospital. There, in the delivery room, as she later recalled:

> ... all of a sudden a nurse rushed in frightened, and told me, 'Get up quick! The Gestapo are waiting for you'.
>
> Forty years have passed and I am still not able to describe the shock I was in. Helped by two nurses, one on each side, shaking all over, probably more from fear than labour pains, I walked out to the lobby to face the Gestapo agents. They were young, very tall and strong-looking, and when I noticed their insignia, the skull with two crossed bones, insignia of death, I knew that this was my end.

I don't remember what thoughts went through my mind then, I only remember apologizing to my unborn child for having created him, when I would not be able to bring him up to see the light, to let him live.

At that moment a miracle happened: the two butchers looked at me – I kept calm – told me to go back to bed and turned away.

A few hours later, my oldest son, Arthur, was born. I learned later that the Gestapo were not exactly checking on me, but on the midwife who had been out after curfew on her way to assist me in labour. They just wanted to see her patient and didn't suspect that the patient was Jewish.[39]

A month later, Helena Manaster was given a second baby to care for, Krysia, a Polish orphan brought to the monastery from a rescue mission. 'What a paradox!' she later recalled. 'Jewish and in hiding, I was raising a Polish child. I hoped to survive in the monastery but it was not to be. Some refugees suspected my origins and denounced me. I was forced to flee, leaving Krysia behind. But before I left, I had another encounter with the Gestapo. I was confronted by two of them, while watching the children in the garden. Again I thought that the end had come, but miraculously they just had a look at us and then left. It was in June 1944 that I thus had to resume my struggle to survive, with an eight-month-old child.'[40]

At Janowska camp in Lvov, the killing of the surviving Jews of Eastern Galicia took place at 'the sands', a hilly, sandy area containing a deep pit, beyond which burned the huge pyres on which the newly shot corpses were placed. Here, too, any resistance by the unarmed and naked was without hope. 'The victims', Leon Weliczker noted in his diary on October 26, 'undress quickly, wanting to get it over with as fast as possible, to save themselves from prolonged torture.' Mothers undressed their children, he noted, and then 'the naked mother carries her child in her arms to the fire.' However, he ended:

Sometimes a mother will undress herself, but will fail to undress the child, or the child refuses to let itself be undressed out of panic. When this happens, we can hear the voices of the children. 'What for?' or 'Mother, mother, I'm scared! No! No!' In these cases, one of the German police takes the child by its small feet, swings it, crushing its head against the nearest tree, then carries it over to the fire and tosses it in. This is all done in front of the mother.

When the mother reacts to this, which happens a few times, even if only by saying something, she is beaten and afterward hung by her feet from a tree with her head down until she dies.[41]

At Koldyczewo camp in White Russia, where six hundred Jews, Poles and White Russians had been burned alive in the crematorium a year earlier, and twenty-two thousand prisoners murdered within eighteen months, the Jews still refused to lose their desire to live. One of the prisoners in the camp, a rabbi from Slonim, had managed to hold a form of service on the Sabbath. The camp's Jewish doctor, Dr Levinbok, himself a prisoner, not only succeeded in making contact with the partisans, but smuggled medicines to them from the SS store.

On October 30 Dr Levinbok decided to try to escape. Together with his wife and eight-year-old child, he ran away, reaching the partisans. Before escaping, he wrote a letter for the camp commandant. 'I apologize', he declared, 'for being such a swine as to leave. But nobody is guilty who runs away. Nor are we guilty, although we are Jews. We are still young, and ready to serve humanity. Forgive us that we want to live.'[42]

In Greece, the will to live had been given a focal point on September 25, when the Chief Rabbi of Athens, Ilia Barzilai, escaped from the capital disguised as a peasant, and reached the relative security of Thessaly. There, in a village near to the Greek partisan headquarters, Rabbi Barzilai encouraged Greek Jews who could do so to join the partisans, or to go into hiding. He also worked with the Greek partisans to arrange for more than six hundred Greek Jews to be smuggled by boat across the Aegean Sea to the safety of neutral Turkey. In return, the Jewish Labour Federation in Palestine smuggled boots and money by sea to the Greek resistance.

In the Volos region, another Greek rabbi, Rabbi Pessah, through his contact with the resistance, obtained shelter for more than 752 fellow Jews of Volos. When the Germans came to deport the Jews of

Volos, only 130 were found. In Trikkala, 470 Jews found refuge with Greek villagers in the mountains; only 50 were captured. In Patras, the German Consul wrote to his superiors that 'after the newspapers announced the obligatory registration of all Jews, they disappeared.'[43]

In Poland, where helping Jews meant certain death, if caught, individuals continued to defy the threat of execution. Indeed, the help given to Jews by non-Jews had led, in Cracow, to an increase in the number of special courts set up to try Poles accused of helping Jews. A report of the German Chief of Police in the Government General, dated October 7, recommended that cases of Poles helping Jews should be dealt with by the police 'without the necessary delay of court hearings'.[44]

Even in Berlin, there were Germans who helped Jews, among them a senior Intelligence officer, Hans von Dohnanyi, who saved fifteen Berlin Jews and their families from deportation by having them sent to Switzerland as 'counterespionage agents'.[45]

Courage could be shown in every conceivable circumstance of horror. Every day, Jewish girls who had been selected for the barracks at Birkenau were driven, starving, beaten and naked, to the bath-house. As they were pushed along, SS men and SS women, as a Jewish girl from Poland, Kitty Hart, has recalled, 'sniggering and idly flickering their whips', watched them pass. On one such occasion, Kitty Hart recalled, a Jewish girl 'deliberately scraped a handful of lice from her body and flung them in the face of a guard who had come too close. She died immediately; but after that the SS were even more careful to keep their distance.'[46]

'She died immediately.' We do not know her name, nor from what country she came; only that she was a Jewess whose spirit no surfeit of torment had been able to destroy.

32

'Do not think our spirit is broken'

THE BRITISH AND AMERICAN BOMBING of Germany, and especially of the industrial cities of the Ruhr, continued relentlessly throughout the autumn of 1943. The Western Allies, including Polish national forces and Palestinian Jews, were now in southern Italy. Plans were also well advanced for a landing in northern Europe in seven months' time. In the east, the Red Army advanced steadily, albeit with massive casualties. Four years after Hitler's first, confident onslaught on Poland, Germany had to face the prospect of setbacks, retaliation and even defeat.

The spectre of defeat, and the reality of daily losses of territory in the east, led to an intensification of the murder of Jews, in order to ensure the completion of the 'final solution'. In the Riga ghetto, on November 2, more than a thousand Jews, most of them old people, children and the sick, were sent by train to Birkenau, reaching the camp three days later. Only 120 men and 30 women were sent to the barracks. The rest were gassed.[1] In the Lublin region, on November 2, an operation, given by the Germans the code name 'Harvest Festival', was begun, its object being the murder of those survivors of the Warsaw ghetto uprising who had been held since April in labour camps at Poniatowa, Trawniki and elsewhere in the Lublin region. In a few days, fifty thousand Jews were shot in ditches behind the gas-chambers of Majdanek, among them more than five thousand former Jewish soldiers of the Polish army, who had been held prisoners for the previous four years in the Lipowa Street camp in Lublin.

Brought to Majdanek in small groups from Lipowa Street throughout November 2, for each two Jews in the group, one SS man stood guard. But even then, the instinct for survival could not be crushed. Led by a former Hebrew teacher, with the surname Szosznik, the Jews broke through the armed guards shouting, 'Long live freedom.' The SS opened fire. Most of the prisoners were killed. Ten were able to escape. Other Jews from the Lipowa Street camp, also former soldiers, taken to Majdanek, refused to the last moment to take off their army uniforms. They too were shot.[2]

Only one camp in the Lublin region escaped the 'Harvest Festival' slaughter, that at Budzyn, whose labour was needed to operate the Heinkl aircraft works. But even at Budzyn, all elderly people were 'selected' in November 1943 and taken to Majdanek. One of the Jewish cleaners in the camp, Jacob Katz, saved the lives of seven elderly Jews by hiding them under the mattresses during the selection, and later smuggling in bread to them.[3] The rest, taken to Majdanek, were shot.

The Jews deported from Warsaw in May had been offered the 'protection' of work in two industrial installations, one set up in Poniatowa by Walter Toebbens, a German merchant from Bremen, the other set up in Trawniki by Fritz Schultz. Both men had owned large factories in the Warsaw ghetto, employing thousands of Jews. Both had enriched themselves in Warsaw by the exploitation of Jewish labour and the confiscation of Jewish possessions.

Schultz and Toebbens had promised the Jews 'protection' at Trawniki and Poniatowa. But in the first week of November that protection came to an end. The 'Harvest Festival' began at Trawniki on November 2. 'That night all Jews were killed by machine-gun fire,' David Wdowinski has written. 'That night I lost my wife, my older brother, my brother-in-law, and two nephews.' A year earlier, in Warsaw, he had lost his mother, his two sisters, his younger brother, a brother-in-law, a sister-in-law and three nephews. Of five hundred thousand Warsaw Jews driven to Treblinka from July 1942, and to the camps in the Lublin region, in May 1943, Wdowinski added, 'only about three hundred survived. I am one of those few fortunates, or unfortunates.'[4]

One of the few survivors of the Poniatowa executions later recalled the moment when all fifteen thousand Jews had been assembled in the camp hall. It was rumoured that they were to be sent to a new camp elsewhere. The women, it was said, 'would go by train'. In groups of fifty, the men were led away. Then it was the women's turn. 'Together with my daughter I left the hall,' the eye-witness recalled. 'We looked around and heard shots, but were still unable to grasp what was going on.' Her account continued:

The Germans stopped us on the road near the new huts, and ordered us to pull off our shoes. I said loudly: 'It seems to me that we are being led to the grave.' With stockings for our only footwear, we reached the second hut. We heard the voice of an SS man, 'Gold, silver, jewels, watches! Those who fail to hand them over will be shot!'

I looked around and saw naked women in a circle with arms raised aloft as if they wanted to show their beauty. 'What's that?' I thought. 'Selecting naked women? I am young and my body is well-shaped, but I shall not pass the examination, for they would not let my child stay with me.'

One had to enter the hut and to undress quickly. I could see a naked woman calling to her mother-in-law, 'Mother, till we meet again in the next world!' In one of the rooms of the hut three women were sorting out the clothing. It occurred to me that I could join them and take part in the sorting, but I could not leave my child. I still had a few thousand zlotys in my possession. I put them into a handkerchief which I concealed. I told my acquaintance that I would take the money with me into my grave. My wedding ring as well as another ring I had to hand over. One ring I concealed in my hair.

We undressed quickly and, our arms uplifted, we went in the direction of the ditches we had dug ourselves. The graves which were two metres deep were full of naked bodies. My neighbour from the hut with her fourteen-year-old, fair-haired and inno-cent-looking daughter seemed to be looking for a comfortable place. While they were approaching the place an SS man charged his rifle and told them: 'Don't hurry.' Nevertheless we lay down quickly, in order to avoid looking at the dead. My little daughter was quaking with fear, and asked me to cover her eyes. I embraced her head; my left hand I put on her eyes while in my right I held her hands. In this way we lay down, our faces turned downwards.

Shots were fired; I felt a sharp pain in my hand, and the bullet pierced the skull of my daughter. Another shot was heard very close nearby. I was utterly shaken, turned giddy and lost consciousness. I heard the groaning of a woman nearby, but it came to an end after a few seconds.

I realized that I was still alive, and expected another bullet to hit me, but I did not move. After a few moments, an SS man brought a woman with a child. I heard her imploring him to permit her to kiss the boy, but the murderer did not permit it and so the unfortunate woman lay down close to myself, her head near my head. A shot was heard and blood splashed on my head and neck. Apparently I made the impression of being dead. More shots were heard for some while, and then silence descended.

An hour later I heard the voices of SS men. One of them put his foot on my body and went on shooting, remarking: 'This blonde, that brunette.' Apparently he had come to examine whether somebody was still alive. Many of the women were only wounded, and groaning was heard all the time. Following these shots there was complete silence. The SS men went away, but I still did not dare to raise my head. I shivered with cold. Ukrainians approached the place several times. They talked loudly to one another, spat at the bodies and went away.

Time passed very very slowly. When darkness fell the Ukrainians came back once more and covered the grave with spruce foliage. I was terribly frightened. I thought that they might burn the bodies. I wanted to shout that I was still alive, but the words stuck in my throat. When I perceived that they were going off I allowed myself to raise my head. I glanced at my daughter. Her face was usually oval, but now it was round and as pale as a sheet. With my lips I touched her back and hair, and her little hand slipped out of my hand. I looked at my own left arm, which ached very much and I saw two holes and blood trickling from them.

I put my head on the ground again for I felt terribly tired. Yet in spite of the tiredness and my sore head I racked my brains: What am I to do? I did not know the neighbourhood too well. I thought I might succeed in reaching the forest, but how could I do so while I was naked? The grave was near the road that led to the living quarters. Should I stealthily try to reach the living quarters and get some clothing there? In order to reach the living quarters it was necessary to pass the guards; and the gate was lit up. I realized that this was no way out. I kept gazing at the huts of the Ukrainians and the hotel.

It seemed to me that I was seeing a naked woman running in

the direction of the gate, and I thought that I would never succeed in passing it. I do not know whether she actually succeeded in passing it or not for suddenly I heard a woman screaming terribly: 'Help! Help!' I do not exactly know whether the voice came from the huts of the Ukrainians, or from the hotel. I thought that they would do better to die like myself. After a few minutes the screaming died away.

Suddenly I heard a voice from the grave: 'Mammy, mammy,' and a few more words which I did not understand because of the wind. I wanted time. It had grown even darker. It was surely seven o'clock already. Where the guards were standing a large fire suddenly broke out and spread to the huts where our clothing was kept. When I saw the fire I thought that they might burn the dead. I shivered at the thought of being burned alive. I caressed my daughter – I was afraid to kiss her because of the blood-stained bodies lying all around – and shook off the foliage. I passed by the heaps of bodies and started running in the direction of the forest.

After a few steps, while I was creeping on all fours, I noticed two naked women. Without realizing what I was doing I started passing my hands over them and asked them whether they were really alive. I did not believe my own eyes and caressed them again and again.

We had to hurry and get away from the place as quickly as possible. I made up my mind to go to Melnik, the nearest village. I recalled that I had concealed several thousand zlotys and told my companions in misfortune: 'Don't worry because you are naked. I have got money and we shall buy clothing.' They asked me how I had managed to conceal the money, and I showed them how I had concealed the banknotes.

We had not time to lose and entered the first hut, still creeping on all fours. In the hut an old peasant and his wife were living. At the sight of three naked women they appeared frightened to death, and started crossing themselves. The old peasant woman flung us a pair of worn-out trousers and a torn gown, and turned us out for fear of the Ukrainians. I wanted to go to the kitchen in order to get a bit warm, but the old woman insisted on her demand and forced us out of the house. One of us tore off a curtain and muffled herself in it. When we left the hut I did the same.

We went into another hut, and asked for some water to wash off the blood-stains from our faces and bodies. Our request was granted, and I was given a blouse for I was still naked. Each of us received a slice of bread and we were told to go away.

We entered a third house, where a young girl gave us a linen skirt and ordered us to get out quickly.[5]

Among the thirteen thousand Jews killed at Poniatowa on November 5 was Israel Feiwiszys, one of the leading Jewish composers and conductors in pre-war Poland. On the outbreak of the war he had gone from Lodz to Warsaw for safety, and in the Warsaw ghetto had become the conductor of the youth choir. He was fifty-five years old.[6]

According to Polish underground sources, Jews at Poniatowa who realized what was taking place had managed to set fire to the military storehouse and the barracks. But those who had carried out this act of defiance 'were shot at once by machine guns, and their bodies were thrown into the sewage canals'. One of the barracks, this report added, 'contained a squad of fighting Jews, who hid the group that had set fire to the buildings. But the struggle ended with the death of all the fighters in the burning buildings.'[7]

The survivors of such massacres were few, as were the survivors from the continuing deportations to Birkenau. Among those gassed at Birkenau in November was Riccardo Pacifici, Rabbi of Genoa, and historian of the Genoa Jewish community. This community could trace its origins to AD 511. On November 3 Rabbi Pacifici and two hundred of his congregation, as well as one hundred Jewish refugees from northern Europe who had found shelter in Genoa, were deported to Birkenau.[8] Not one of them survived.

On November 5 it was the turn of the children of the Siauliai ghetto in Lithuania to be deported to Birkenau. Two members of the Jewish Council in Siauliai, Aron Katz and Berl Kartun, had tried to save the children. They were deported with them, and gassed.[9] In the undressing chamber, Jews from the Sonderkommando were ordered to undress the children. A member of the Sonderkommando recorded what he saw in notes which were later buried near the gas-chamber, and were among several such fragments discovered after the war in the places where they had been hidden. This eye-witness in the inner sanctum of hell recorded:

And there a girl of five stood and undressed her brother who
was one year old. One from the Kommando came to take off
the boy's clothes. The girl shouted loudly, 'Be gone, you Jewish
murderer! Don't lay your hand, dripping with Jewish blood,
upon my lovely brother! I am his good mummy, he will die in
my arms, together with me.' A boy of seven or eight stood
beside her and spoke thus, 'Why, you are a Jew and you lead
such dear children to the gas – only in order to live? Is your life
among the band of murderers really dearer to you than the lives
of so many Jewish victims?'[10]

On November 9, four hundred Jews were deported to Birkenau
from Florence and Bologna. More than three hundred were sent to
the barracks, but eighty-five were gassed. Among those gassed was
the fifty-year-old Armando Bachi, an Italian army officer who had
won the Military Cross in the First World War. By 1938 Bachi had
risen to the rank of Lieutenant-General in the Italian army. He was
gassed with his family.[11] That same day, in Theresienstadt, the head
of the Council of Elders, Jacob Edelstein, was accused with three
other Jews of having falsified the daily reports concerning the
number of Jews in the ghetto, thus enabling fifty-five Jews to avoid
deportation.[12]

Edelstein and those accused with him were later deported to
Birkenau, together with their families.

Thursday, 11 November 1943, was the twenty-fifth anniversary
of Germany's defeat in 1918. On that same Armistice Day in 1943 a
punishment was devised for forty seven thousand Jews, many of
them elderly, who had not yet been deported from the Theresienstadt ghetto to Birkenau. The event chosen for Theresienstadt on
November 11 was a census. For this purpose, beginning at four
o'clock in the morning, all forty-seven thousand Jews were taken
outside the ghetto to a large square, formerly an army drill ground.
There they were forced to stand throughout the morning.

One of those present, Zdenek Lederer, later recalled how, shortly
after midday, three SS officers who had come from Prague by car
began the census. Inevitably, with such large numbers on the
square, their figures did not tally. They began again. Again the
numbers did not match:

By then it was five o'clock and the shivering multitude was becoming agitated and fearful of the approaching night. The old people sat on the damp ground, and children cried and it began to drizzle. Still the results did not tally. Gradually confusion expanded into chaos; symptoms of panic appeared. The weary ranks disintegrated. The SS men disappeared, nobody knew what would come next or what the Germans intended. Even the gendarmes lost their heads having been left without orders. Meanwhile the drizzle turned into rain.

It was night, and in the dark the freezing crowds walked aimlessly around in utter confusion. All attempts of the officials of the Jewish administration to restore order among this desperate and miserable mass of humanity proved futile.

While part of the crowds pressed from the drill ground towards the gate of Theresienstadt, other groups were already streaming back, shouting in the dark that a cordon of gendarmes was barring their return. It was now nine o'clock. Sobbing women tried to protect their children from being trampled on. Many of the aged collapsed by the roadside.

Yet no order came permitting the prisoners to leave the drill ground. It was an ironic situation – all these people pushing, pressing, longing to be allowed to return to the misery of the ghetto.

Finally, at ten o'clock, a few volunteers succeeded in organising the return of the prisoners to the ghetto. Women, children and elderly people were helped back and protected from the whirlpool of maddened humanity. But it took another two hours to empty the drill ground. A stretcher service was improvised and car lamps illuminated the drill ground, enabling the gendarmes to pick up aged people who had collapsed.

Several Jews died during that day of torment. Others, taken ill as a result of their exertions, died soon afterwards. The 'census' death toll was estimated at between two and three hundred.[13]

In 'Aryan' Warsaw, there had been an earlier tragedy, unconnected with any anniversary, revenge or plan. In the suburb of Praga, on the eastern side of the River Vistula, eight ghetto fighters were in hiding in a loft, filled with boxes of ammunition and explosives. One of the fighters was wounded, and it was while trying to heat a spoonful of ointment for her that a lighted match fell to the floor. A fire began, the crates exploded, and within minutes the loft was ablaze.

Five of the fighters were burned to death. Three were able to break a hole in the ceiling, and get out on to the roof. One of the three was Tosia Altman, whose dress had caught fire. She died on the roof. Another, Meir Schwartz, fled to a nearby block of flats, and was given sanctuary in a cupboard: but during a German search of the flats, although his hiding place was not discovered, he died of a heart attack. Only one of the eight, Eliezer Geller, survived. 'We were crushed by our misfortunes,' recalled Feigele Peltel, herself still in hiding in 'Aryan' Warsaw.[14]

To deter Poles from giving shelter to Jews, the Germans intensified their searches and arrests. 'As a sort of object lesson,' Feigele Peltel recalled, they set fire to a house on Kazimierz Place, in Warsaw, 'killing the entire Gentile family living there because they had given asylum to Jews.'[15] But still the will to survive animated those in hiding. 'Do not think our spirit is broken,' Yitzhak Zuckerman wrote on November 15 in a letter to Palestine.[16]

Whether broken or unbroken, the spirit could not always triumph, at least not in the temporal world, against superior force and evil intent. At the Skarzysko-Kamienna ammunition factory, one of the most ferocious of all the labour camps in German-occupied Poland, the morning of November 16 saw the camp surrounded by Ukrainians who, directed by SS men, approached the barrack in which had been dumped those who had collapsed from weakness and exhaustion during the night shift. The Ukrainians announced: 'Come out, all those who are weak will receive a double portion of soup.'

At first, the offer was successful, as many of these weak, sick and starving slaves staggered from the barrack in search of the life-giving soup. Suddenly, however, the danger became apparent, as they saw the armed Ukrainians and the lorries beyond. Those who could run began to run. All were shot down. The rest were loaded on the lorries, to be driven to an execution site in the camp itself.

As the trucks moved off, the Ukrainians threw in a few pieces of bread to the victims. Despite their weakness, those Jews who could now began to fight among themselves for the bread, and to fight with every ounce of strength and viciousness they could summon up. An eye-witness, Roza Bauminger, later recalled: 'It suddenly dawned on me what hunger really was, I who was so hungry myself. Inside the lorry, I saw scenes from Dante's Inferno. The sick people forgot about their illnesses, and, at that moment when they were being driven off to their deaths, they fought. For each of them, the piece of bread was more important than the thought that they were going to be killed.' The bread represented salvation, the salvation of that particular moment, the means to assuage, for a few brief moments, the terrible pangs and pain of hunger: salvation, even though, half an hour later, they would be killed.[17]

On November 17, of 995 Jews brought to Birkenau from Holland, 531 were taken to be gassed, among them 166 children.[18] At the same time, 164 Poles were brought to the gas-chamber, twelve of these being young women from a Polish underground group. The member of the Sonderkommando whose manuscript was among those discovered after the war, recorded:

A certain young Polish woman made a very short but fiery speech in the gas-chamber, addressing all who were present, stripped to their skins. She condemned the Nazi crimes and oppression and ended with the words, 'We shall not die now, the history of our nation shall immortalize us, our initiative and our spirit are alive and flourishing, the German nation shall as dearly pay for our blood as we possibly can imagine, down with savagery in the guise of Hitler's Germany! Long live Poland!'

Then she turned to the Jews from the Sonderkommando, 'Remember that it is incumbent on you to follow your sacred duty of revenging us, the guiltless. Tell our brothers, our nation, that we went to meet our death in full consciousness and with pride.'

Then the Poles knelt on the ground and solemnly said a certain prayer, in a posture that made an immense impression, then they arose and all together in chorus sang the Polish anthem, the Jews sang the 'Hatikvah'.

The cruel common fate in this accursed spot merged the lyric tones of these diverse anthems into one whole. They expressed in this way their last feelings with a deeply moving warmth and their hope for, and belief in, the future of their nation. Then they sang the 'Internationale'.

At that moment the vans arrived, marked deceptively and mockingly with the symbol of the Red Cross. The tins of gas pellets were taken from the van, and gas was thrown into the chamber. All perished, 'amidst singing and ecstasy, dreaming of uniting the world with bonds of brotherhood and of its betterment'.[19]

Although, despite the advance of the Red Army, the German killings of Jews continued unabated, Germany's allies hesitated, fearing retribution. On November 17 the Rumanian dictator, General Antonescu, warned his Cabinet against acceding to German plans to massacre those Jews who had been deported to the eastern Rumanian territory of Transnistria during the autumn of 1941. Hundreds of thousands had perished during those deportations, but hundreds of thousands more had survived in camps and ghettos.

'Regarding the Jews who are in danger of being murdered by the Germans,' Antonescu told his Cabinet, 'you have to take measures and warn the Germans that I don't tolerate this matter, because in the last analysis I will have a bad reputation for these terrible murders. Instead of letting this happen, we will take them away from there.'[20]

Antonescu moved quickly to win credit with the Western Allies. A month after his warning, the Jews of Transnistria began to be sent back to Rumania: first were 4,400 orphans who had lost both parents. More than fifteen thousand Jews were repatriated. Many of the orphans were subsequently allowed to proceed to Palestine, the first three hundred in March 1944, a further nine hundred in April 1944, allowed by the Rumanian authorities to leave Rumania, by the Turkish authorities to land at Istanbul, and by the British authorities to enter Palestine without obstacle, on collective passports.[21]

In German-occupied Poland, the destruction of labour camps had continued throughout November. At Szebnie, where the labourers tried to revolt, 3,898 men, women and children were deported to Birkenau on November 4. When the train reached the camp on the following day, 952 men and 396 women were sent to the barracks, 2,550 men, women and children to the gas-chambers.[22] At Janowska camp, the liquidation of the corpse-burning squad had begun on October 25. There were about one hundred and thirty men in the squad. But the deception was such that, as each group of inmates was selected, they believed they were being sent to a camp somewhere else. Before being marched out, each member of the squad was given warm clothing and a pair of good shoes: a clear sign that they were to be sent elsewhere. They were then marched out to 'the sands', and shot.

As soon as it became clear to the thirty or so Jews left in Janowska exactly what had happened to their colleagues, they decided to try to escape. Not all the surviving inmates joined the escape plan. One of them, Jehuda Goldberg, a man in his forties, had been a member of the First World War Polish underground, fighting for Polish independence against Germany, Austria-Hungary and Russia. Between the wars, Goldberg had been a schoolteacher in Lvov. When told, on the evening of November 18, that there was to be an escape attempt that night, he went to bed. Other prisoners approached him, asking if he was not aware of what was happening. Goldberg answered them:

> I know about everything, and let God be of such help to you that this escape is a success. I pray and hope that He will help you to survive and tell the world, as witnesses, how they murdered a people.
>
> But as for me, where will I go? To the city, to hide? Who will hide me? I have no friends among the Aryans who will take me in. I am not young enough to go to the woods with you. I will only be a hindrance to you, and you will be captured because of me. I cannot run like some of you, and if I go with you, you will not leave me behind on the road, and it will be your end, too.
>
> When you escape, the German police will shoot everyone left here, and I am better off dead than on the road, a hindrance to you. What have I to live for? My wife and seven children have been killed, and I, too, want to die.

Goldberg told the would-be escapees: 'Good night! Good luck! God help you to survive this war, and give me an easy death!' Then he closed his eyes, and turned his head away to sleep.[23]

The Janowska revolt took place on the morning of November 19. It is not known how many Germans were killed or how many Jews managed to escape. The eighteen-year-old Leon Weliczker, whose parents and six brothers and sisters had all been killed in Lvov or in Janowska, did get away, together with a Jew by the name of Korn. A Polish friend of Korn lived in one of the suburbs of Lvov, and through him the two escapees found a second Pole who was already hiding twenty-two Jews. They were allowed to join the others. All twenty-four Jews then remained in hiding until Lvov was liberated by the Red Army eight months later.[24]

Another unit of the 'Blobel Commando', had been sent to the Borki woods, near Chelm, thirty miles east of Lublin. These were Jews who had been taken out of Majdanek on the day of the 'Harvest Festival', among them Josef Reznik, one of the former Jewish soldiers in the Polish army who had been held as prisoners-of-war at the Lipowa Street camp in Lublin since November 1939.

Reznik later recalled how, on the evening of the 'Harvest Festival', an SS officer, Major Rollfinger, had entered their barrack 'filthy all over, covered with blood', to announce to the three hundred inmates that they were not to be killed. For two weeks they remained at Majdanek. Then another SS officer addressed them. 'You are not considered as prisoners-of-war from now on,' he told them. 'You are Jews, unworthy of life; you are now supposed to work.'

At Borki the three hundred Jews were ordered to dig. 'I was digging with my spade,' Reznik later recalled, 'and after removing two or three spadefuls of earth, I felt the spade hit something hard and then I saw it was the head of a human being.'[25]

More than thirty thousand bodies were dug up at Borki, in eight long trenches. All were burned. Then the bones were ground to a powder in a special machine, and taken away in sacks: thirty sacks a day. Most of the corpses were Red Army men, taken prisoner by the Germans in the autumn and winter of 1941; all had been murdered. Some were Italian soldiers, killed after Italy had abandoned the German cause, and they had become prisoners-of-war. Others were Jews, among them children from Hrubieszow.[26]

Even as the graves were being uncovered, new corpses were brought and thrown into them. 'One of the graves would remain open all the time for new corpses,' Josef Reznik recalled. 'The new corpses would be coming all the time, continuously. A truck would bring warm bodies, which would be thrown into the graves. They were naked like Adam and Eve.' Reznik also recalled how, when one of the mass graves was opened, 'we saw a boy of two or three, lying on his mother's body. He had little white shoes on, and a white little jacket. His face was pressed against his mother's, and we were touched and moved, because we ourselves had children of our own.'

After the graves had been emptied, disinfected, and filled with earth, grass was planted over them. The bodies had meanwhile been placed on massive pyres, a thousand on each pyre. 'There were two pyres of bodies going all the time,' Reznik recalled, 'and they burnt for two or three days, each heap of the dead.'[27] Today, a small memorial plaque marks the site.[28]

The mass executions continued, aimed at destroying the remnants of many Jewish communities. At Sandomierz, on November 19, a thousand Jews were taken from the ghetto to the Jewish cemetery. There, they were shot; a monument marks the site.[29] At Miechow, the Jews were taken to the nearby forest, and shot down. One of the victims managed to wound a German official with a knife. He was set upon by dogs and torn to pieces. The other Jews were shot. Here too, a stone memorial marks the site.[30]

As fragments of information reached the West, the Jews who read them were distraught. 'Half of the night I spent reading the last report, No. 9, from Poland,' Ignacy Schwarzbart noted in his diary, in London, on December 1. 'It is the end of Polish Jewry. The remaining Jews in hiding are hunted like beasts, picked up and killed.' The Poles denounced the Jews, he added. 'But there are some Poles who pay with their lives for hiding Jews.'[31]

A few Jews continued to believe that safety lay in work and compliance to the bitter end: such was the assurance given, on December 12, by the Chairman of the Jewish Council in Wlodzimierz Wolynski, to the remnant of the ghetto. But the assurance was in vain. By the end of December, all had been 'resettled'.[32]

The conflict between escape and reprisal could not be resolved. Following the escape of several Jews from Kovno early in December, an execution was ordered as a reprisal. On December 16, the day before the execution, the German authorities in the city agreed to a request for 7 litres of schnapps and 140 cigarettes, as a bonus for the seven executioners.[33]

Some Jews tried to escape even from Birkenau. On November 13, Fritz Lustig had tried, but been caught. He was shot ten days later.[34] On December 21, a Pole, Stanislaw Dorosiewicz, and a Jew, Hersh Kurcwajg, escaped from Auschwitz, after killing an SS guard.[35] They were not recaptured.[36] In Warsaw, on December 22, the Polish underground reported that the Gestapo had discovered a group of sixty-two Jews in hiding in the cellar of a building on Krolewska Street. All the Jews were killed.[37]

Despite the savage penalties, a few Poles continued to hide Jews. Feigele Peltel has recorded how Dankiewicz, a Pole living in Pruszkow, near Warsaw, hid a Jewish woman named Zucker in a large tile stove. The stove was hollow, and could be entered from the top, which 'masqueraded' as a metal flue. Despite frequent searches, the hiding place was never discovered.[38]

By the end of 1943, several Jewish resistance groups were active throughout France, among them the Organisation Juif de Combat, founded in 1942, and the Jewish Scout Movement, which had been in existence since 1923. Several thousand other Jews joined the various French underground groups, Communist, Socialist and Gaullist. One French resistance group, the National Liberation Movement, had been founded by a Jew, Maurice Löwenberg, who was killed by the Gestapo, under torture, at the end of July 1944. The leader of the Scouts, Captain Robert Gamzon, was among several Jews who rose to command specifically Jewish resistance units in the Toulouse-Lyons area. The work of these units included preparing hiding places and food for hundreds of Jewish women and children, smuggling Jews across the borders to Switzerland and Spain, and engaging the Germans in combat. A total of 124 members of the scouts resistance group were killed in 1943 and 1944, thirty of them in action, twenty-one shot by the Germans after capture, and seventy-three after being deported to the concentration camps, among them Birkenau, Natzweiler and Mauthausen.[39]

In the barracks at the concentration camp of Mauthausen, on the Danube, a British prisoner-of-war, known as Lieutenant-

Commander Pat O'Leary, in fact the British agent Albert Guérisse, a Belgian, found himself assigned as a cleaner of Block 5. The Kapo, or overseer, of the block was a German chosen for his brutality: a merchant seaman before the war, he had murdered his mother. He was, O'Leary later recalled, 'over six feet tall and the epitome of brute force'.

The only occupants of Block 5 were seven Jews. Fifteen years later, O'Leary told their story to Vincent Brome, who recorded it as follows:

> With no other purpose than brutal destruction the SS had said that all seven must die by Christmas. But the emaciated skeletons were still dragged out every morning to work in the stone quarries. Silent, drooping, they set off, some with tears in their eyes, some talking to themselves, some with the furtive look of hunted animals.
>
> The Kapo had put it to them bluntly: 'You must all die by Christmas. You had better choose amongst yourselves who goes first.'
>
> When no one volunteered for death in the first week, he addressed them again. 'If you don't choose, I will.'
>
> The following day, somewhere out in the stone quarries, while seven skeletons struggled to move stones weighing more than they themselves did, with heavy snow soaking their thin garments and tongues sucking the snow to quench their thirsts, the Kapo suddenly leapt on one man, dragged him down, and as his screams echoed round the quarry, beat out his brains with a pick-axe.
>
> That evening the remaining six crowded round Pat. News of a possible Allied invasion had swept across Europe and the mysterious drumming of intelligence had carried the message into the heart of Mauthausen. Was it possible that the invasion would begin soon, and once begun would break through swiftly? Was there, possibly, the hope that . . . or if not . . . ? Could they at least believe that the bombing raids might scare the SS or the Kapo into relaxing their sentence? Had they any hope if they hung on, tried to evade the death by pick-axe? Was there any point in struggling?
>
> Pat spoke very carefully. Many things were possible. Hope sprang indestructibly for those about to die, and he did not

wish to destroy a hope which might miraculously realize itself. They seemed to feel better after he had spoken.

In the second week there were still no volunteers for death. The ragged file of scarcely human men, who seemed tall because they were paper-thin, whose eyes were large in sunken faces, whose voices were sometimes whispers from weakness, staggered out into the ice-cold dawn, but no one volunteered to die.

Two amongst them were father and son, a boy of nineteen, frequently in tears, and the father aged forty-five, who looked seventy. He was a Jewish tailor who had deliberately withdrawn from political life of any kind to remain completely innocent, but he was a Jew and that was enough. The son had hardly begun adult life and if he possessed any coherent views of the world, they were scarcely worth exterminating.

They stayed together as much as possible, sleeping next to one another, and sometimes, far into the night, Pat heard the old Jew's slow, melancholy voice trying to soothe his son's fears. Or they talked to Pat and occasionally the great owl-like eyes enlarged in the thin faces, stared at Pat as though he had it in his power to save them, and would not save them. Always Pat encouraged them, helped them in their illnesses, tried to add scraps to their food; but what they needed even more than food was some re-affirmation of their right to live, and several times the old man turned away, tears in his eyes, and shambled back to his stinking bunk, while Pat cursed his powerlessness.

At the end of November the Kapo spoke to them again. 'You're not dying quick enough. It's easy to do it. You can walk out in front of the wire and get machine-gunned. Or – you can run into the wire. You frizzle quick then. But get a move on – time's getting short.'

No one died the next day; but on the following night when they returned from the quarry one of their number was again missing, and crowding round Pat, five Jews in terrible fear spoke of the cries they had heard. On the hundred steps which led down into the quarry, the berserk Kapo had torn another emaciated body to pieces with his pick-axe. There followed the same questions about the British, the Allies, the hope of an armistice before the year was out; but the Jewish tailor and his son were fatalistic now and the father said to Pat: 'We may walk into the wire tomorrow.' It was clean and simple. The flash which shrivelled life was better than a long death by mutilation and starvation.

Three days later there were still five Jews, each no longer interested in the fate of the others, and all fighting desperately with the cunning of despair to remain alive.

By the beginning of December the snow was very deep, the winds icy, and the five Jews could not sleep very much because of the cold. One day in the second week in December another man did not return from the quarry. And on the 15th, Pat heard the Jewish tailor say to his son, 'There's no hope. We had better die.' The boy burst into tears. The tailor said again to Pat the next day. 'We shall walk into the wire'. But they did not. December 18 came and still the four Jews remained in a state resembling life. Still Pat tried to help them. Encouragement seemed the last indignity when hope had so long died, but Pat talked to them and sometimes they seemed stronger afterwards.

Sometimes, too, he looked down at his own fast-wasting body and knew that he could not continue losing weight himself at such a rate without collapse. Originally he had weighed 160 lb. Now he was 90 lb and still losing weight. His face had yellowed, his absurd cotton clothes hung on bones, a sense of deep lethargy very easily overtook him, and hunger pains sometimes brought him awake in the night as though a knife had entered his bowels. He drank more and more water. Everyone drank and drank.

Still he wondered why he remained alive, why they had not shot him, why the fate reserved for the Jews was not his also. If espionage against the religion of Nazism was a crime too simple to redeem by sudden death, this expiation, this long-drawn-out death by hardship and starvation was the kind of penance paid only for the most mortal sin; but why should he still be allowed hope while the Jews had none?

In the early morning of December 23 he began to clean the bunks of Block 5. Suddenly he saw the Jewish tailor leading his son gently by the hand towards the door. The boy sobbed and there were tears in the old man's eyes. Outside, with clumsy, fumbling steps, the old man began running, his arm around the boy. They could not run properly. They had not the strength.

But they stumbled hopelessly towards the margin, and the shots which Pat expected did not come.

They did not run straight and clean into the electrified wire. They blundered into it, and Pat felt the great blue flash as if it had seared his own body. And there on the ground were the two twitching bodies, entwined with one another, and presently still.

It was very silent and empty in the block that evening. The two remaining Jews were cowering animals. One shivered continuously. Tomorrow was the 24th and one must die. Neither spoke, and when Pat went to them and used whatever words he could find to hold their broken minds together, they stared back mutely.

The dawn was cold, grey, and misty. They could hardly walk as they left for the stone quarry, but one distorted drive remained: nothing mattered but the will to survive for another single day. The man who came back was a ghost, with fixed eyes and twitching lips, who tried to talk to Pat but could not articulate clearly. The last glimmering of the human spirit had almost gone. An animal looked out from the prison of shrivelled flesh and made meaningless whimpers.

On Christmas morning the Kapo almost carried him from the block. That night, as the sound of a Christmas carol came across from one of the blocks, Block 5 was empty.[40]

At the Ninth Fort in Kovno, Christmas 1943 saw the end of their tether for the sixty-four men and women who had been formed into a unit of the 'Blobel Commando', to dig up and then to burn the corpses of more than seventy thousand Lithuanian, German and Czech Jews, murdered in the Ninth Fort in the autumn and winter of 1941. By December 1943 they had dug up and burned more than twelve thousand bodies, seven thousand of them Jews from Kovno. Examination of the bodies showed that many of the victims had been buried alive.

The members of 'Blobel Commando' in the Ninth Fort included twelve members of the Jewish Fighting Organization from the Kovno ghetto, several Russian–Jewish prisoners-of-war, among them a major in the Red Army, Mikhail Nemyonov, a few Jewish women, a Jewish convert to Catholicism, three non-Jews, and one of Lithuania's best known rabbis, Gabriel Shusterman.

An escape committee was formed, and security maintained by another of the Russian–Jewish prisoners-of-war, 'Mishka the Tramp', a former Soviet naval officer. A locksmith among the prisoners, Pinchas Krakinovsky, made keys to open the cells, and then, on the eve of the escape, drilled 314 holes, with primitive tools, in a long-forgotten iron door leading out of the fort near the cells.

On December 24 the escape plans were ready. That evening, as the guards celebrated Christmas Eve, all sixty-four prisoners made their way out of their cells, through the door, up a rope ladder, over the fortress wall, and, rolling like logs in prostrate bundles, across the deep snow of the surrounding fields. But despite the festive carousing of the guards, the escape was noticed, and thirty-two escapees were quickly rounded up. Another five were shot, trying to resist capture. Eight more were caught on their way to the ghetto. Nineteen reached the ghetto undetected. One of the nineteen, Rabbi Shusterman, died soon afterwards of frostbite, suffered during the escape.

The escape of members of 'Blobel Commando' from the Ninth Fort provided witnesses of the fate of tens of thousands of Jews. 'You are more important than I,' the head of the Jewish police in Kovno, Moshe Levin, told them. 'You must remain alive to tell the world what you saw with your own eyes in the Ninth Fort.' To ensure that the escapees did remain alive, Levin hid them in a secure bunker, equipped with lighting, heating and water.

While in hiding, the escapees were given weapon training by another Russian-Jewish prisoner-of-war, Captain Israel Veselnitsky, himself from an Orthodox Jewish farming family from the Ukraine. They were then smuggled out of the Kovno ghetto, to join the partisans in the Rudniki forest, ninety miles to the east. Six of them later fell in battle. One of the escapees, Major Nemyonov, committed suicide. He was too old, he said, to run, and 'happy to die by my own hand as a free man'.[41]

Also on December 24, the Jews in 'Blobel Commando' at Borki were ready to try to escape, although there were more German guards than prisoners. In frozen ground, without proper tools, they had dug a tunnel from under the barracks to the field beyond the camp fence. It took six weeks to dig. At dawn on December 24 all was ready.

All sixty prisoners entered the tunnel led by the escape organizer, Oscar Berger. One of the escapees, Josef Reznik, later recalled how a fellow escapee was so large that he had to be pushed through the opening at the end of the tunnel. As he was being pushed out into the field Reznik recalled, 'There was noise, and this alerted the Germans. It was impossible to wait for everyone.'

Of the sixty prisoners who tried to escape, only three survived the war. It is not known how many died in the camp, in the tunnel, at the tunnel exit, or on the way to the nearby woods. Several of those who escaped joined the Soviet partisans across the River Bug, and fought eventually in the ranks of the Red Army. One of them, Singer, fell in a partisan battle. Another, Aharonowicz, was wounded in battle in the Carpathians. A third, Josef Sterdyner, testified at the trial of the Borki guards in West Germany in 1962. A further survivor of the revolt at Borki, Josef Reznik, was a witness at the Eichmann Trial in Jerusalem in 1961. Reznik testified that after his escape he had been helped in hiding by a Polish priest.[42]

33

'One should like so much to live a little bit longer'

THE OPENING MONTHS OF 1944 saw no pause in the search for victims, or in the cruelties of the slaughter. At Birkenau, at Christmas 1943, Madame Vaillant Couturier, a non-Jew, had been opposite the notorious Block 25, the 'Waiting Block', when she had seen Jewish women brought naked from the barracks. These were women who had been judged too sick or too frail to work, or even chosen at random. From Block 25, after being kept for up to a week without food or water, they were all sent, invariably from that hut, to the gas-chamber. Of the fate of the women who had been brought to Block 25 that particular Christmas, Madame Vaillant Couturier recalled how uncovered trucks were driven up to the block, and then:

> . . . on them the naked women were piled, as many as the trucks could hold. Each time a truck started, the famous Hessler ran after the truck and with his bludgeon repeatedly struck the naked women going to their death.
>
> They knew they were going to the gas-chamber and tried to escape. They were massacred. They attempted to jump from the truck and we, from our own block, watched the trucks pass by and heard the grievous wailing of all those women who knew they were going to be gassed.[1]

Perhaps it was these same women whom Rudolf Vrba saw being put on open lorries to be taken to one of the gas-chambers. 'They were all prisoners already,' he later recalled, 'and they knew that they were going to the gas-chamber, and they were quiet. And somehow people were accustomed to live with the moment, with the knowledge that death will come.' But when the lorry motors started, the noise 'created a panic'. A terrible noise arose, Vrba recalled, 'the death cry of thousands of young women', who were already 'reduced to skeletons'. Many tried to jump out of the lorries, knowing 'that they can't succeed'. But still they tried.

As the women tried in vain to break out, a rabbi's son, Moshe Sonnenshein, called out, in Vrba's presence, 'God – show them your power – this is against You.'

'Nothing happened,' Vrba added. Then Sonnenshein cried out, 'There is no God.'[2]

Among the most remarkable documents to have survived the war is the manuscript written in Birkenau by one of the members of the Sonderkommando, Salmen Lewental. This particular manuscript was discovered in 1962 in a jar buried in the ground near Crematorium III, where Lewental worked. The gaps in it are words destroyed by dampness which seeped into the jar. Lewental, who did not survive his gruesome work, recalled in his note book what may have been the same episode witnessed in its opening stages by Madame Vaillant Couturier and Rudolf Vrba.

Lewental's account is headed '3,000 naked people'. It reads:

This was at the beginning of 1944. A cold, dry lashing wind was blowing. The soil was quite frozen. The first lorry, loaded brimful with naked women and girls, drove in front of Crematorium III. They were not standing close to one another, as usual, no; they did not stand on their feet at all, they were exhausted, they lay inertly one upon another in a state of utter exhaustion. They were sighing and groaning.

The lorry stopped, the tarpaulin was raised and they began to dump down the human mass in the way in which gravel is unloaded on to the road. Those that had lain at the edge, fell upon the hard ground, breaking their heads upon [. . .] so that they weakened completely and had no strength left to move. The remaining [women] fell upon them, pressing them down with their weight. One heard [. . .] groans.

Those that were dumped down later, began to extricate themselves from the pile of bodies, stood [. . .] on their feet and tried to walk [. . .] the ground, they trembled and jerked horribly with cold, they slowly dragged themselves to the bunker, which was called *Auskleidungsraum*, 'undressing room' and to which steps led down, like to a cellar.

The remainder [of the women] were taken down by men from the Kommando who swiftly ran upstairs, raised the fainted victims, left without help, extricated them carefully, crushed and barely breathing, from the heap [of bodies] and led them quickly downstairs. They were a long time in the camp and knew that the bunker (the gas-chamber) was the last step [leading] to death.

But still they were very grateful, with their eyes begging for mercy and with [the movements] of their trembling heads they expressed their thanks, at the same time giving signs with their hands that they were unable to speak. They found solace in seeing tears of compassion and [an expression] of depression [. . .] in the faces of those who were leading them downstairs. They were shaking with cold and [. . .].

The women, taken downstairs, were permitted to sit down, the rest of them were led into this [con]fined, cold room, they jerked horribly and trembled with cold, [so] a coke stove was brought. Only some of them drew near enough to be able to feel the warmth emanating from the small stove. The rest sat, plunged in pain and sadness. It was cold but they were so resigned and embittered with their lives that they thought with abhorrence of physical sensations of any kind. . . . They were sitting far in the background and were silent.

Lewental then set down the story of a girl from the ghetto of Bedzin, who had been brought to Birkenau 'towards the end of the summer', and who now talked as she lay 'helpless':

She was left the only one of a numerous family. All the time she had been working hard, was undernourished, suffered the cold. Still, she was in good health and was well. She thought she would survive. Eight days ago no Jewish child was allowed to go to work. The order came. 'Juden, antreten!' 'Jews, leave the ranks!' Then the blocks were filled with Jewish girls. During the selection nobody paid attention whether they looked well or not, whether they were sick or well.

They were lined outside the block and later they were led to Block 25, there they were ordered to strip naked; [allegedly] they were to be examined as to their health. When they had stripped, all were driven to three blocks; one thousand persons in a block and there they were shut for three days and three nights, without getting a drop of water or a crumb of bread, even.

So they had lived for three awful days and it was only the third night that bread was brought; one loaf of bread weighing, 1,40 kilogramme for sixteen persons, afterwards [. . .]

'If they had shot us then, gassed us, it would have been better. Many [women] lost consciousness and others were only semi-conscious. They lay crowded on bunks, motionless, helpless. Death would not have impressed us at all then.

'The fourth day we were led from the block, the weakest were led to the *Krankenstube* (infirmary), and the rest were again given the normal camp ration of food and were left [. . .] were taken [. . .] to [life].

'On the eighth day, that is five days later, we were again ordered to strip naked, *Blocksperre* (permission for prisoners to leave the blocks) was ordained. Our clothes were at once loaded and we, after many hours of waiting in the frost, were loaded into lorries and here we were dumped down on the ground. Such is the sad end of our last mistaken illusions. We have been, evidently, cursed even in our mothers' wombs, since such a sad end fell to our lot.'

The girl from Bedzin had finished her story. As Lewental noted:

She could no more pronounce the last words because her voice became stifled with flowing [tears] [. . .] from [. . .] some women still tried to wrench themselves away, they looked at our faces, seeking compassion in them.

One of us, standing aside and looking at the immensity of unhappiness of those defenceless, tormented souls, could not master his feelings and wept.

One young girl then cried, 'Look, what I have lived yet to see before my death: a look of compassion and tears shed because of our dreadful fate. Here, in the murderers' camp, where they torture and beat and where they torment, where one sees murders and falling victims, here where men have lost the consciousness of the greatest disasters, here, where a brother or sister falls down in your sight, you cannot even vouchsafe them a [farewell] sigh, a man is still found who took to heart our horrible disaster and who expressed his sympathy with tears. Ah, this is wonderful, not natural. The tears and sighs of a living [man] will accompany us to our death, there is still somebody who will weep for us. And I thought we shall pass away like deserted orphans. The young man has given me some solace. Amidst only bandits and murderers I have seen, before my death, a man who still feels.'

She turned to the wall, propped her head against it and sobbed quietly, pathetically. She was deeply moved. Many girls stood and sat around, their heads bowed, and preserved a stubborn silence, looked with deep revulsion at this base world and particularly at us.

One of them spoke, 'I am still so young, I have really not experienced anything in my life, why should death of this kind fall to my lot? Why?' She spoke very slowly in a faltering voice. She sighed heavily and proceeded, 'And one should like so much to live a little bit longer.'

Having finished, she fell into a state of melancholy reverie and fixed her gaze on some distant point; fear of death emanated from her wildly shining eyes. Her companion regarded her with a sarcastic smile, she said, 'This happy hour of which I dreamed so much has come at last. When the heart is full of pain and suffering, when it is oppressed by the criminal world, full of baseness and low corruption, [full of] limitless evil, then life becomes so troublesome, so hard and unbearable that one looks to death for rescue, for release. The nightmare, oppressing me, will vanish forever. My tormented thoughts will experience eternal rest. How dear, how sweet is the death of which one dreamed in the course of so many wakeful nights.'

She spoke with fervour, with pathos and with dignity. 'I am only sorry to sit here so naked, but to render death more sweet one must pass through that indignity, too.' A young emaciated girl lay aloof and was moaning softly, 'I am . . . dy . . . ing, I . . . am . . . dy . . . ing' [;] a film was covering her eyes which turned this way and that [. . .], they begged to live [. . .].

A mother was sitting with her daughter, they both spoke in Polish. She sat helplessly, spoke so softly that she could hardly be heard. She was clasping the head of her daughter with her hands and hugging her tightly. [She spoke] 'In an hour we both shall die. What tragedy. My dearest, my last hope will die with you.' She sat [. . .] immersed in thought, with wide open, dimmed eyes [. . .] threw [. . . around her so [. . .].

After some minutes she came to and continued to speak, 'On account of you my pain is so great that I am dying when I think of it.' She let down her stiff arms and her daughter's head sank down upon her mother's knees.

A shiver passed through the body of the young girl, she called desperately, 'Mamma!' And she spoke no more, those were her last words.

The order was then given, as Lewental noted, to conduct the women 'into the road leading to the crematorium'.[3]

In the Lodz ghetto, where eighty thousand Jews were still living in the hope that their productive work would ensure their survival, deaths from hunger were increasing. 'People are faced with the catastrophe of inevitable starvation,' the Ghetto Chronicle noted on 20 January 1944.[4] On the following day, Professor Wilhelm Caspari, one of the deportees from Berlin to Lodz, died in the ghetto, at the age of seventy-two. A specialist in cancer research, Caspari had been a professor in Frankfurt until 1933. He had also been a German delegate at the 1930 International Congress of Physicians in Madrid.[5]

A month later, the Ghetto Chronicle recorded the death of Adam Goetz, an engineer from Hamburg, and one of the pioneers of the rigid dirigible airship. In the ghetto, at the age of sixty-eight, Goetz had founded a research group to promote the cultivation of medicinal herbs.[6]

The workers in the Lodz ghetto continued to survive because, unknown to them, other ghettos were being destroyed. On February 9 the ghetto received machines from what the Chronicle called 'an evacuated buckle factory' at Poniatowa. With the arrival of these machines, yet another factory was to be established, thus ensuring further productive work for the ghetto.[7] Unknown to those who worked the new machines, they had been sent to the Lodz ghetto, together with hundreds of sewing machines from Poniatowa, only because the Jews held in Poniatowa, most of them deportees from Warsaw, had been murdered the previous November.[8]

The Germans continued to round up the remaining Jews from the smallest hamlets. Even in the remote French countryside, Jews were not safe, either from round-ups or from reprisals. On January 10, two German Jewish refugees, Professor Victor Basch and his wife, who had spent two years in the safety of the village of Saint-Claire-à-Caluire, in the Lyons region, were executed as a reprisal for the death of a French collaborator, killed by French partisans. On the corpse of Professor Basch the Germans placed a placard: 'Terror against terror. The Jew pays with his life for the death of a National'.[9]

On January 15, among the Jews deported from Belgium to Birkenau were the Polish-born Meir Tabakman and his wife Raizl. Tabakman had been deported some months earlier, but had jumped off the train. Later he had been caught. Now, branded as a 'flitzer', one who had tried to flee, he was locked into a special goods wagon with many other former escapees. At Birkenau, his wife later recalled, 'not one of them entered the camp'. All went straight to the gas-chamber.[10]

In the woods near Buczacz, more than three hundred Jews had been in hiding for more than nine months. On January 18 the whole area was surrounded by German tanks, and in a systematic military sweep and search all were found and killed.[11] In Warsaw, hundreds of Jews in hiding were suddenly at risk when one of the surviving liaison men of the Jewish Fighting Organization was caught and tortured. Under torture, he broke; many of those in hiding were then rounded up and killed.[12] Among those whose hiding place was not betrayed, was Emanuel Ringelblum. He was on a list of nineteen former Jewish underground leaders whom the Polish Government in London agreed to rescue, through the Home Army underground. By the time the list could be acted upon, however, only three of the nineteen were still alive. Ringelblum, who was one of the three, declined to leave, as did his two colleagues, 'because', they informed the Polish underground, 'we must fulfil our duty to society'.[13]

Ringelblum remained in hiding, but the German pressures to force Poles to betray and abandon Jews were relentless. On January 29, in Cracow, a special court sentenced five Poles to death for helping Jews. One, Kazimierz Jozefek, was hanged in a public square.[14] Four weeks later, on the night of February 23, in the remote Polish village of Zawadka, the Germans arrested a former primary school headmaster, Aleksander Sosnowski, and his seventeen-year-old daughter, together with two Jewish women whose father and daughter he had hidden and sheltered in an attic for a year and a half. All four were killed.[15]

In Lublin, a ten-year-old girl had managed to hide in a barn during the last of the deportations. Her hiding place was a hole under a beam, where she could only stay lying down. Eventually, her whole body was covered in sores. Only with difficulty could she crawl to a corner of the barn where there was some bags of grain.

The girl's name was Irena Szyldkraut. In 1938, at the age of six, she had starred in the Polish film *His Great Love*. Known as 'the Polish Shirley Temple', she gained fame on the screen. Her father, a pharmacist in Warsaw, served in the Polish army in 1939, and was among the hundreds of thousands of Polish soldiers who surrendered to the Russians. He spent the rest of the war years, first in Siberia, then with the Polish forces in Italy.

After many months hiding in the barn, Irena Szyldkraut was discovered by a Christian overseer who came to look for the bag of grain. Seeing 'a human foot' peeping out from under the beam, he discovered the girl, and brought her food and drink. Later she was discovered by the Gestapo. Then, as a post-war inquiry into her fate revealed:

> All German authorities, being very much astonished that the child could live in such conditions, considered her as a curiosity and, exceptionally, promised her to protect her life, and even guaranteed her life. The young Szyldkraut Irena was entrusted a special protection.
>
> The child had been under a careful special medical treatment and after a long time the girl again looked as a girl. One day she was very happy and overjoyed, receiving from the Germans a pair of new shoes and a dress. But alas, her happiness lasted not very long.
>
> Some days later Szyldkraut Irena has been called to appear in her new dress and shoes before the German officials. The child became trembling and tremulous. It occurs to her mind: 'for what destination?'
>
> But the guardian appeases her, saying, 'You have to receive today a new overcoat.' The child, quite calm, followed her guardian. They went downstairs and the poor child, pale as a corpse, had been pushed in – in a cell of death.

'Such', commented the inquiry, 'was the German's life-guarantee.'[16]

On February 3, yet another train left Drancy for Birkenau, the sixty-seventh in less than eighteen months. Among those on it was the thirty-nine-year-old Rabbi of Mulhouse, René Hirschler, who, as chaplain to all foreign-born Jews interned in France, had carried out considerable relief work on their behalf, as well as for hundreds of Jews in hiding.[17]

Of the 1,214 Drancy deportees that day, 985 were gassed on arrival at Birkenau, among them 14 people who were over eighty years old, and 184 children under eighteen. Neither Hirschler, nor his wife Simone who was deported with him, survived. Another of those who perished was the thirty-three-year-old Betty Zilberstein, who had been born in London. Before the war she had left England for France, to marry a Frenchman. They had three children. At the time of Betty Zilberstein's arrest, her husband was with the resistance. Her children, too, had a chance of hiding, and two of them were saved. But because her youngest son, Harvey, who was not yet five years old, had a bad earache, she decided not to send him away from her, but to take him with her into the unknown. After the war, her husband was told that the young boy's cries of pain from his earache were such that he was shot by one of the guards during the journey. Nor did Betty Zilberstein survive.[18]

On February 8, five days after this deportation from Drancy, a thousand Jews were deported from Holland to Birkenau. Among them were 268 of the camp's hospital patients, including children with scarlet fever and diphtheria. 'Of all these diabolical transports,' one eye-witness, Philip Mechanicus, later recalled, 'perhaps this was the most fiendish.' Many of the sick were brought to the train on stretchers. 'All the while,' Mechanicus recalled, 'wet snow was falling out of a dark sky, covering everything with slush.'[19]

This Westerbork train reached Birkenau two days later: 142 men and 73 women were taken to the barracks, the remaining eight hundred deportees, including all the children, were gassed.[20]

At Birkenau, the SS had learned of a second escape plan by members of the Sonderkommando. As a protection against such escapes, they decided to reduce the growing number of Sonderkommando members, and on February 24, two hundred of the eight hundred prisoners in the Sonderkommando were transported to Majdanek. There they were shot, their shooting reported by nineteen Soviet prisoners-of-war who were brought from Majdanek to Birkenau a year later.[21]

'The Jews are a race which must be wiped out,' Hans Frank told a meeting of Nazi Party speakers in Cracow on March 4. 'Whenever we catch one – he will be exterminated.'[22] That same day, in Warsaw, four Jewish women, caught in the city, were shot in the ruins of the ghetto, together with eighty non-Jews. The bodies of those who had been shot, some of whom had not been killed outright, were thrown into the basement of a ruined house. The basement was then doused with an inflammable liquid and set on fire. 'For four to six hours,' the historian of this episode had written, 'there could be heard the screams of the wounded as they burned alive.'[23]

The names of the four Jewish women killed in Warsaw on March 4 are unknown, like most of the millions who perished. Some of the victims, their names and careers, are a part of Jewish history. On March 5, at Drancy, while awaiting deportation, the sixty-year-old Max Jacob died of bronchial pneumonia. A poet of the Cubist and Surrealist movements, he had been baptised in the Catholic Church in his late thirties. Picasso had been his godfather. Despite his devout Catholicism of more than thirty years, Max Jacob was still forced to wear the yellow star, and sent to Drancy for deportation.[24]

Also at Drancy, and there on the day of Max Jacob's death, was another poet, David Vogel, who had been born in Tsarist Russia fifty-two years before. For one year, in 1929, he had lived in Palestine, before settling finally in France. On March 7 he too was deported to Birkenau in a transport with 1,501 other Jews, of whom only twenty survived the war. Vogel perished.[25] So too, among the children from that same transport, did Henriette Hess, aged eleven, and her brother Roger, aged nine, who had been deported without their parents.[26]

At Birkenau, one group of deportees had not only been kept alive, but whole families had been kept together in a special family camp. These were some 3,860 Czech Jews, survivors of the 5,000 Jews who had been brought to Birkenau from Theresienstadt six months earlier. At the beginning of March they were visited by a German Red Cross delegation, which was not allowed to see the rest of Birkenau. Then, on March 3, the inmates of the family camp were told to write postcards to their relatives who were still in Czechoslovakia, saying that they were alive, well, and working. They were also made to date the postcards March 25, 26, or 27, and to ask their relatives to send them food parcels.

Four days later, the 3,860 'Czech family camp' inmates were told that they were to be resettled at a nearby labour camp, Heydebreck. No such 'resettlement' was in fact planned. All 3,860 were to be sent to the gas-chambers only a few hundred yards away from their 'haven'.

On March 6 a Slovak Jewess, Katherina Singer, who worked as a secretary to the senior SS guard in the women's camp at Birkenau, overheard by chance an SS remark about 'special treatment' for the family camp inmates. Aware that in the SS language 'special treatment' meant gassing, she at once passed on the news to two young Jewish prisoners who were at that moment, as maintenance men, repairing cauldrons in the kitchen of the women's camp. These two, under the pretext of 'urgent repairs' needed elsewhere, managed to pass the news that same day to Freddy Hirsch, one of the leaders of the family camp, while urging Hirsch to act.

Hirsch was convinced that there was nothing whatsoever to be done to save the family camp. That night he took poison. It was not strong enough to kill him, however, and on the following day, March 7, while still in a state of unconsciousness, he was taken by truck, together with the 3,860 other survivors of the family camp, to the gas-chamber.[27]

Themselves deceived, these victims of a wider deception were driven into the undressing room of the gas-chamber. Realizing suddenly that they really were about to be gassed, they tried to resist, attacking the guards with their bare hands. The SS were quick to answer back, first with rifle butts and then, when the resistance spread, with flame-throwers. Filip Muller, a member of the Sonderkommando at Birkenau, and one of the few men to survive it, was then on duty in the undressing room. He later recalled how these Czech family camp victims, 'heads smashed and bleeding from their wounds', were driven across the threshold of the gas-chamber. As the gas pellets were released, they began to sing the Czech national anthem, 'Kde domov muj', 'Where Is My Home', and the Hebrew song 'Hatikvah', 'Hope'.[28]

Of this whole Jewish group of 3,860 men, women and children, only thirty-seven were spared, among them eleven pairs of twins, who were kept alive so that medical experiments could be performed on them by Dr Mengele.[29]

The destruction of the Czech family camp at Birkenau on March 7 was paralleled that same day, in 'Aryan' Warsaw, by the betrayal of thirty-eight Jews in hiding in a bunker. Among those caught when the bunker was raided was Emanuel Ringelblum.[30]

Ringelblum was taken, with the others who had been caught, to the Pawiak prison, together with his wife Yehudit, and their thirteen-year-old son Uri. Another Jewish prisoner in Pawiak, Julian Hirszhaut, was involved in an attempt to move Ringelblum out of the condemned cells, to those with prisoners who had every expectation of being sent to work for the Germans as shoemakers and tailors. Four years later Hirszhaut recalled how he managed, four days after Ringelblum's arrest, to enter the prison cell in which the historian was being held:

> The cell was jammed with people, apparently these were the Jews whom the Germans had seized with Ringelblum in his bunker. Ringelblum himself was sitting on a straw mattress close to the wall, on which hundreds of names had been scratched out by nails. These were the names of the persons who had made their final journey through this cell.
>
> On his lap Ringelblum was holding a handsome boy. This was his son Uri. When I approached Ringelblum, I told him, without losing any time, whose messenger I was. I remember how astonished Ringelblum was to learn that there were still Jews in the Pawiak.
>
> Then I told him that we were making attempts to take him in with us.
>
> 'And what will happen to him?' he asked, pointing his finger at his son. 'And what will happen to my wife who is in the women's section?'
>
> What could I answer him? We all knew well that even if we succeeded in taking Ringelblum out of there and bringing him to us as a shoemaker or tailor, his family would still be doomed. My silence conveyed the truth to him, and he added

right away: 'Then I prefer to go the way of *Kiddush Ha-Shem* ("Hallowing His Name") together with them.'

Later he told me how he had been tortured by the Gestapo. The bandits wanted to extort from him the addresses of the persons with whom he was in contact on the 'Aryan' side. They enquired about his recent activities. Ringelblum remained silent and did not reveal anything, therefore, they had beaten him murderously for three days. He showed me black and blue spots all over his body, the results of the savage beatings.

In the middle of our conversation he suddenly asked: 'Is death so hard to bear?' And then, a little later, he went on with a voice broken from despair: 'What is this little boy guilty of?' – and he again pointed his finger at his son – 'It breaks my heart to think of him.'

I stood helpless before Ringelblum, I did not know what to answer, and a wave of sorrow swept over my heart.[31]

Ringelblum was executed a few days later, as were his wife and their son. Thus perished the historian of the Warsaw ghetto; the humane chronicler of events too terrible to chronicle; the eye-witness, in words and documents, of the destruction of Polish Jewry.

To the last, Ringelblum had continued to work as an historian. At the time of his capture he was forty-three years old. Twelve years earlier, he had published his first book, a history of the Jews of Warsaw from the earliest times to their expulsion in 1527. His last two books, written while in hiding in 'Aryan' Warsaw, were a history of Trawniki camp, and a history of Polish–Jewish relations during the Second World War. When published after the war, this second book filled 248 printed pages. In it Ringelblum wrote of the individual Poles who had helped him, among them Teodor Pajewski, a railway worker who had helped to get him out of Trawniki, and Mieczyslaw Wolski, the gardener in whose hide-out he had lived in 'Aryan' Warsaw, and who was shot by the Germans after the hide-out had been discovered. After describing the dangers involved in helping Jews, Ringelblum wrote, of the Poles who accepted these dangers:

> Idealists from among both the educated and the working classes, who saved Jews at the risk of their lives and with

boundless self-sacrifice – there are thousands such in Warsaw and the whole country. The names of these people, on whom the Poland to come will bestow insignia for their human acts, will forever remain engraved in our memories, the names of heroes who saved thousands of human beings from destruction in the fight against the greatest enemy of the human race.[32]

Parts of Ringelblum's book dealt with those Poles who had betrayed Jews, and reflected on the fact that only a small percentage of Jews were given sanctuary by non-Jews in Poland compared with those who were given sanctuary by non-Jews in countries such as France or Holland. Ringelblum ascribed this difference to many generations of anti-Jewish feeling. As a result of this, he wrote, the Warsaw ghetto deportations of July 1942 had met with 'blank indifference' on the Aryan side of the city.[33] There were even Poles who remarked, as the ghetto went up in flames: 'The bugs are burning'.[34] In the whole of Poland, including Warsaw, noted Ringelblum in the early months of 1944, 'there are probably no more than thirty thousand Jews hiding', and he added,

Among the Polish families hiding Jews there are doubtless some anti-Semites. It is, however, the anti-Semites as a whole, infected with racialism and Nazism, who created conditions so unfavourable that it has been possible to save only a small percentage of the Polish Jews from the Teuton butchers. Polish Fascism and its ally, anti-Semitism, have conquered the majority of the Polish people. It is they whom we blame for the fact that Poland has not taken an equal place alongside Western European countries in rescuing Jews.

The blind folly of Poland's anti-Semites, who have learnt nothing, has been responsible for the death of hundreds of thousands of Jews who could have been saved despite the Germans. The guilt is theirs for not having saved tens of thousands of Jewish children who could have been taken in by Polish families or institutions. The fault is entirely theirs that Poland has given asylum at the most to one per cent of the Jewish victims of Hitler's persecutions.[35]

Such was Ringelblum's bitter conclusion.

34

From the occupation of Hungary
to the Normandy landings

ON 10 MARCH 1944 Adolf Eichmann and his principal subordinates met at Mauthausen concentration camp in order to work out a
deportation programme for the 750,000 Jews of Hungary.[1] Eight
days later, on March 18, Hitler again summoned the Hungarian
Regent, Admiral Horthy, to Klessheim Castle, near Salzburg.
Horthy agreed to deliver 100,000 'Jewish workers' for the German
war effort, but he was still reluctant to agree to a general deportation. At 9.30 that evening his train left Salzburg for Budapest.
Forty-five minutes later, German troops began to move into
Hungary.[2]

Early on the evening of the following day, March 19, the Germans took their first independent action in Hungary against Hungarian Jewry, arresting two hundred Jewish doctors and lawyers,
their names chosen at random from the Budapest telephone book.
All were deported to Mauthausen.[3] The Gestapo then moved into
hundreds of Hungarian towns and villages; prepared a list of all
Jewish wealth in each town; took the leaders of the local community
into custody; and then threatened to shoot the leaders if the money
and valuables were not forthcoming. The technique was devastat-
ingly successful. First, it drained the communities of their money, so
that they could not even buy railway tickets, or pay bribes. Second,
after the Gestapo released the community leaders on payment of the
ransom, it made their threats seem plausible and finite: they had
done what they had promised. Provided the Jews conformed, they
would keep their promises in future. As Hugo Gryn, a survivor of
the subsequent deportations from Hungary has recalled, 'When, in
the weeks after the ransomings, the Gestapo said, "All Jews are to
leave their homes, and assemble in brick factories and timber yards

and *no harm will come to you*," it could be believed. Then all they had to say was, "And now you will be sent by train to help with the harvest". . . .'[4]

Each German demand was accompanied by threats. But when the demand was met, the threats were withdrawn. Thus on March 21 the Germans made their first demand of the Jewish community in Budapest: 600 blankets, 300 mattresses, and 30 Jewish printers to print propaganda leaflets. The Jewish leaders asked for time. One of the Germans present then took out his revolver and said that if the request was not fulfilled in an hour and a half, the leaders would be shot. 'The Jews had to learn', one historian has written, 'that nothing was impossible.'[5] Nine days after the German occupation of Hungary, one of the leaders of Hungarian Jewry, Fulop Freudiger, who had already persuaded the Gestapo to release his brother from detention, wrote to the leader of the Orthodox Jewish Community in the Hungarian city of Nagyvarad: 'I do not believe that we shall suffer the same fate that befell Polish Jews. We shall have to give up our wealth, we must be prepared for many struggles and deprivations, but I am not worried for our lives.'[6]

Eichmann himself, speaking to a delegation from the Jewish Council at the end of the month, created a basis for the forthcoming deceptions. 'After the war,' he told them, 'the Jews would be free to do whatever they wanted.' Everything 'taking place on the Jewish question', Eichmann added, 'was in fact only for the wartime period'; with the end of the war, 'the Germans would again become good-natured and permit everything, as in the past.'

Eichmann added that he was 'no friend of force', and he 'hoped that things would go well without it'. Violence and executions had occurred 'only where the Jews had taken up opposition', as with the Jewish soldiers serving in partisan bands in Ruthenia and Yugoslavia, he explained. 'As in Greece,' Eichmann added, 'he would mow them down mercilessly, because there was war on.' But he would be equally severe, he promised, against any Hungarian citizen who harmed a Jew because he saw the yellow star. 'He would not tolerate the harming of Jews for wearing the yellow star,' Eichmann assured the Jewish leaders, and he asked them to report any incident of attacks on Jews to him 'and he would deal with the attackers'.[7]

While the Jews of Hungary were being caught for the first time in the Nazi net, those few who remained alive in German-occupied Poland, after four and a half years of war, still struggled to resist. At Koldyczewo camp, in White Russia, a mass revolt of the labourers took place on the night of March 22, led by a Jew, Shlomo Kushnir. Ten Nazi guards were killed, and hundreds of labourers reached the forests, and the partisans. Kushnir, and twenty-five others, were caught: Kushnir committed suicide before he could be tortured and shot.[8] On the following day, in the Bialystok region, a Soviet partisan group, led by a Jew, Sergeant Andrei Tsymbal, with a large number of Jewish fighters under him, destroyed a German military train carrying armoured cars to the eastern front.[9]

In Western Europe, as resistance activity grew, so too did reprisals against civilians unconnected with any underground action. On March 24, in Rome, the Germans drove 335 civilians into the Ardeatine caves, and then shot them: 253 were Catholics, and 70 were Jews.[10] The cave itself, in the vicinity of Rome's ancient catacombs, is now an Italian national monument. On March 26, at Limoges, three Jews were shot for being actively involved in resistance work, among them the sixty-five-year-old Victor Rubinstein, who had been born in New York.[11] On March 27, the eighteen-year-old Abraham Geleman, born in Lodz, was killed by the Germans in the Dordogne: he too had been active in the resistance.[12] In Belgium, three members of the Belgian resistance, 'Dolly', 'Sabor' and 'Nic', were arrested, sent to concentration camps, and were killed. Their real names were Jacques Gunzig, Isi Springer and Nic Spitz.[13]

The Red Army continued its westward advance, approaching to within three hundred miles of Riga, Kovno and Vilna. The Germans now accelerated their moves against the remnants in the ghetto and labour camps. In Zezmariai camp, near Kovno, all children were seized on March 27. 'Our eleven-year-old Hannah'le went too,' her seventeen-year-old sister Lea Svirsky, later recalled. 'My mother tried to hide her, not give her up, so they set a big dog on my mother, which attacked and began biting her. She fainted. When she woke up, Hannah'le was no more.'[14]

In Kovno, on March 27, all remaining children up to the age of thirteen were seized by the SS, thrown into trucks, and driven off to their deaths. Thirty-seven Jewish policemen, among them the commander of the Jewish police and his two deputies, refused to take part in this round-up of children. They were shot on the spot.[15]

The 'children's action' in Kovno took two days to complete. Several thousand children were rounded up, driven off in trucks, and shot. Only a tiny fragment survived, among them the five-year-old Zahar Kaplanas. This young boy was saved by a non-Jew, a Lithuanian, who smuggled him out of the ghetto in a sack. Later Kaplanas's parents were both killed in the ghetto. Zahar survived the war.[16]

In a desperate act, as the search intensified, some parents poisoned their children, and then committed suicide. Dr Aharon Peretz, who witnessed the events of March 27, later recalled:

> I saw shattering scenes. It was near the hospital. I saw automobiles which from time to time would approach mothers with children, or children who were on their own. In the back of them, two Germans with rifles would be going as if they were escorting criminals. They would toss the children into the automobile.
>
> I saw mothers screaming. A mother whose three children had been taken away – she went up to this automobile and shouted at the German, 'Give me the children,' and he said, 'How many?' and the German said, 'You may have one.' And he went up into that automobile, and all three children looked at her and stretched out their hands. Of course, all of them wanted to go with the mother, and the mother didn't know which child to select, and she went down alone, and she left the car.
>
> And a second mother just hung on to the car and didn't want to let go. And a dog bit her; they set a dog against her.
>
> Another mother with two children, a girl and a boy – I saw that from my window – went and pleaded, and begged that the Germans should return one child, so he took the girl by her shoulders and threw the girl down to her.

'Such scenes', Dr Peretz recalled, 'repeated themselves all day.'[17]

In the Lodz ghetto, a similar 'children's action' had been witnessed by a fifteen-year-old boy. Among those in the ghetto was a

mother, Rachel, and her little boy Hershl, who was so physically
handicapped from birth that he had to be carried everywhere in a
small handcart. Suddenly, the order went up in the street, 'All out.'
Then, as the young boy, Ben Edelbaum, later recalled:

> The silence was suddenly broken by screams from apartment
> 11. It was Hershl crying and saying, 'No, Mama! No! Mama,
> no!' We heard a thud, and Hershl cried no more.
>
> We ran in and saw Rachel standing over Hershl with a lead
> pipe in her hand. Hershl was lying on the bed in a pool of
> blood. His head was split wide open. Before we could reach
> Rachel, she ran to the window and threw herself out, shouting,
> 'They won't get him now!'
>
> Rachel fell to the sidewalk below and died instantly.
>
> 'May God forgive her for what she has done,' a woman said.
>
> 'Forgive her?' another asked. 'Why, it was His will, or else
> this would not have been allowed to happen.'[18]

On April 5, 835 Jews were deported from northern Italy to Birkenau. On arrival, 559 were gassed. The deportees included Jews who
had found refuge in Italy for more than four years: Jews from all
over Europe and North Africa, Ashkenazi and Sephardi Jews. Some
were from old Sephardi families expelled from Spain in 1492, like
the Alkalai family from Sarajevo. The seventy-one-year-old Sara
Klein had been born in Istanbul, the seventy-six-year-old Genia Levi
in Moscow, the five-year-old Rosetta Scaramella in Venice, the
three-year-old Roberto Zarfatti in Rome.[19]

On April 6, the day after this deportation from Italy, forty-three
Jewish children and ten nurses were arrested at a small centre for
children in Izieu, in the French province of Ain. All were sent first to
Lyons, then to Drancy, then to Birkenau. Their fate is recalled today
in a memorial opposite the village post office.[20] Among the children
deported from Izieu was the eleven-year-old Liliane Berenstein,
who before leaving wrote a letter to God. The letter read:

> God? How good You are, how kind, and if one had to count
> the number of goodnesses and kindnesses You have done us he
> would never finish. God? It is You Who command. It is You

Who are justice, it is You Who reward the good and punish the evil. God? It is thanks to You that I had a beautiful life before, that I was spoiled, that I had lovely things that others do not have. God? After that, I ask You one thing only: MAKE MY PARENTS COME BACK. MY POOR PARENTS, PROTECT THEM (even more than You protect me) SO THAT I SEE THEM AGAIN AS SOON AS POSSIBLE. MAKE THEM COME BACK AGAIN. Ah! I could say that I had such a good mother and such a good father! I have such faith in You that I thank You in advance.[21]

Two of the children from Izieu, and the man in charge of the centre, Miron Zlatin, were deported to Reval, in Estonia, and shot.[22] On the same day, in a raid on 'Aryan' Warsaw, three thousand Germans were deployed from four in the morning to nine in the evening in a search for Jews in hiding. In all, seventy 'non-Aryan' men and thirty-one 'non-Aryan' women were seized: all were executed five days later.[23]

There were other Polish Jews who believed they were on their way to safety; those who, with South American passports, often acquired at enormous cost, were being held in a camp at Vittel, in France. Negotiations to transfer them out of Europe altogether were making slow progress. But there was a precedent; on February 4 the 365 Spanish-protected Jews of Salonica had been sent, finally, from Bergen-Belsen camp to the safety of neutral Spain.[24]

Some of the Vittel Jews were fortunate, but not all. On April 8, the first night of Passover, a member of the Sonderkommando in Birkenau noted: 'a transport from Vittel in France arrived.' On it were 'worthy Jewish notables', among them Mosze Friedman, one of Polish Jewry's leading scholars, and in the immediate pre-war years, Rabbi of Bayonne. 'He undressed together with the others,' the eye-witness wrote. Then 'a certain SS Lieutenant came'. The Jews were about to be driven from the undressing room to the gas-chamber. Rabbi Friedman took hold of the SS man's lapels and said to him, in German:

You common, cruel murderers of mankind, do not think you will succeed in extinguishing our nation. The Jewish nation will live forever and will not disappear from the world's arena. And you, villainous murderers, will pay very dearly, for every innocent Jew you will pay with ten Germans, you will disappear not only as a power but even as a separate nation. The day of reckoning is approaching, the blood shed will cry for retribution. Our blood will not have peace until the flaming wrath of destruction does overflow upon your nation and does annihilate your beastly blood.

The eye-witness noted that the Rabbi spoke 'in a strong lion's voice and with great energy'. He then put on his hat and cried out, 'with immense fervour', 'Shema Israel!' – 'Hear! O Israel'. All those present then cried out with him, 'Hear! O Israel' – that prayer of all Jews in their moment of distress.

The young men of the Sonderkommando, so inured to suffering, so cauterized by the daily sight of death, were themselves overcome by this 'rapture of profound faith'. It was, added the eye-witness, 'an extraordinarily sublime moment, not to be equalled in the lives of men, and it confirmed the eternal spiritual power of Jewry.'[25]

Neither the squalor of death nor the debilitating force of fear could crush the spirit of hope. On April 11 Anne Frank, a fourteen-year-old Jewish girl who, as a pre-war refugee from Germany, was now in hiding in Holland, noted in her diary:

> Who has inflicted this upon us? Who has made us Jews different to all other people? Who has allowed us to suffer so terribly up till now? It is God that has made us as we are, but it will be God, too, who will raise us up again. If we bear all this suffering and if there are still Jews left, when it is over, then Jews, instead of being doomed, will be held up as an example. Who knows, it might even be our religion from which the world and all peoples learn good, and for that reason and that reason only do we have to suffer now. We can never become just Netherlanders, or just English, or representatives of any country for that matter, we will always remain Jews, but we want to, too.[26]

Literally in the depths of the pit, Jews still struggled to remain Jews, and to retain human dignity. At the Ponar execution site outside Vilna, Szloma Gol was among seventy Jews, and ten Russian prisoners-of-war suspected of being Jewish, who, as members of a 'Blobel Commando', had to dig up and then burn the bodies of those who had been murdered in 1941, 1942 and 1943. Each night the eighty prisoners were forced to sleep in a deep pit to which the only access was by a ladder drawn up each evening. Each morning, chained at the ankles and waist, they were put to work to dig up and burn tens of thousands of corpses. These eighty prisoners were supervised by thirty Lithuanian and German guards and fifty SS men. Their guards were armed with pistols, daggers and automatic guns: one armed guard for each chained prisoner.

Two and a half years later Szloma Gol recalled how, between the end of September 1943, when their work began, and April 1944:

> We dug up altogether 68,000 corpses. I know this because two of the Jews in the pit with us were ordered by the Germans to keep count of the bodies: that was their sole job. The bodies were mixed, Jews, Polish priests, Russian prisoners-of-war.
>
> Amongst those that I dug up I found my own brother. I found his identification papers on him. He had been dead two years when I dug him up: because I know that he was in a batch of 10,000 Jews from the Vilna ghetto who were shot in September 1941.

The Jews worked in chains. Anyone removing the chains, they were warned, would be hanged. As they worked, the guards beat and stabbed them. 'I was once knocked senseless on to the pile of bodies,' Szloma Gol recalled, 'and could not get up, but my companions took me off the pile. Then I went sick.' Prisoners were allowed to go sick for two days, staying in the pit while the others worked. On the third day, if they were still too sick to work, they would be shot. Szloma Gol managed to return to work.

As the digging up and burning of the bodies proceeded, eleven of the eighty Jews were shot by the guards: sadistic acts which gratified the killers, and were intended to terrorize and cow the prisoners. But inside the pit, a desperate plan of escape was being put into effect: the digging of a tunnel from the bottom of the pit to a point beyond the camp wire, at the edge of the Ponar woods.

While the tunnel was still being dug, a Czech SS man alerted the Jews to their imminent execution: 'They are going to shoot you soon', he told them, 'and they are going to shoot me too, and put us all on the pile. Get out if you can, but not while I'm on guard.'[27]

One of the sixty-nine surviving prisoners, Isaac Dogim, took the lead in helping to organize the escape. Dogim had been placing the corpses in layers on the pyre one day, when he recognized his wife, his three sisters and his three nieces. All the bodies were decomposed; he recognized his wife by the medallion which he had given her on their wedding day. Another prisoner, Yudi Farber, who had been a civil engineer before the war, joined in the preparations for escape.[28]

On April 15 the prisoners in the pit at Ponar made their bid for freedom. Forty of them managed to get through the tunnel, but a guard, alerted by the sound of footsteps on the pine branches, opened fire. In the ensuing chase, twenty-five Jews were shot, but fifteen managed to reach the woods; later, most of them joined the partisans in the distant Rudniki forest. Five days after the escape, the remaining twenty-nine prisoners were shot.[29]

Destruction and liberation travelled along parallel paths during the spring of 1944. Among the few Jews in hiding in Lubartow was Raya Weberman, who was a week short of her twenty-first birthday. Together with her father and her uncle, she had been in hiding since the final 'action' in Lubartow in November 1942. The three of them had hidden at first in a hole under the kitchen floor of a Polish farmer, Adam Butrin. Then, as the German searches began, they hid in a pit which Butrin dug under the floor of his stables.

After a further search, Raya and her father had to live for three weeks lying down in a field, and then in the nearby forest, drinking stagnant water. 'The water was green, bitter and full of insects,' she later recalled. Returning to the hole under the stable, Raya, her father and her uncle survived. 'For two years we wore the same clothes,' she recalled. 'I read bits of newspaper, dozens of times each.' When liberation came in late July, 'Butrin joyously told us the good news. Afterwards he returned and announced sadly: "The Russians hate Jews too." '[30]

In Hungary, the Germans were moving all Jews out of their homes and into specially designated 'ghetto' areas in each town. These 'ghettos' were often an abandoned barracks, a deserted brickworks, or a timber yard. The first deportation from Hungary to Birkenau took place on April 29, from the town of Kistarcsa. Only 'able-bodied' Jews between the ages of sixteen and fifty were deported.[31]

The Jewish leaders in Budapest were told that the Kistarcsa deportees had been sent to a labour camp at 'Waldsee'. But when one of those leaders, Rudolf Kastner, questioned Eichmann's deputy, SS Lieutenant-Colonel Hermann Krumey, about why not a single letter or postcard had been received from the deportees, the conversation was inconclusive, and disturbing:

Krumey: Haven't they written?
Kastner: Where should they have written from?
Krumey: From Waldsee.
Kastner: Where is Waldsee?
Krumey: Well, I can't say anything about it. It's not far from here. West of Hungary. And I took only professional workers.
Kastner: Professional workers? These deportees were bourgeois!
Krumey: Well – they'll learn a profession in the Reich. . . .[32]

On April 30 a second deportation, of two thousand 'able-bodied' Jews, left the Hungarian town of Topolya, also for Birkenau.[33]

To lull those who had stayed behind into a sense of false security, the SS arranged for some of those who had been deported to send postcards. The eighteen-year-old Moshe Sandberg later recalled how his father was one of a number of those who had sent such postcards to their home town, Kecskemet:

The contents were brief and all said the same thing: they were well, were working, and lacked for nothing. The cards came from the mysterious place Waldsee.

It is impossible to describe the effect these cards had on the Jews. One heard the exclamations, 'See! They're at work! Nothing has happened to them, and now nothing will happen to them for the war will soon be over! The Russians are closing in from the East, and the Americans and British are only waiting for the right moment to invade Europe and reoccupy it! The important thing is not to become nervous, but to suffer patiently, for we will outlast them!'

The postcards acted as a sleeping drug, coming just at the right time to tranquillize us, to dispel the accumulated misgivings of the past weeks and to remove any thought of revolt or escape.[34]

Even in the undressing rooms at Birkenau, some Jews were given postcards to write. Each had to contain the same brief message: 'Es geht mir gut', 'I am well'.[35]

Also sent to Birkenau at the end of April were a further 238 Polish Jews being held at Vittel, in France: among them the poet Yitzhak Katznelson and his eighteen-year-old son. Katznelson's wife and two youngest sons, Bension and Benjamin, had been murdered at Treblinka more than a year and a half before.[36] While at Vittel, shortly before his own deportation, Katznelson had written, in his poem, the 'Song of the Murdered Jewish People':

> I had a dream,
> A dream so terrible:
> My people were no more,
> No more!
>
> I wake up with a cry.
> What I dreamed was true:
> It had happened indeed,
> It had happened to me.[37]

Katznelson, who before the war had translated Heine's lyrics into Hebrew, had been best known in Poland for his light verses, songs and poems for children: songs reflecting youthful pleasures and the joys of life.[38]

On the night of April 30, Katznelson and his surviving son were gassed.

As the killings continued on Polish soil, Polish Jews were fighting with Polish units in the Allied armies in Italy. At Monte Cassino, many Jewish soldiers were among the Polish and Allied dead. Among the Jews who fought with the Polish army in Italy was Dr Adam Graber, a surgeon of the Jewish hospital in Warsaw between the wars. In 1932, and again in 1935, Graber had been a representative of the Polish Maccabi at their World Games, held in Palestine. In 1939, as head of a field hospital with the Polish forces, Dr Graber had been captured by the Russians, who later allowed tens of thousands of captured Poles, among them many Jews, to join the Polish forces who fought in North Africa and Italy. On May 11, Dr Graber was among those who fell at Monte Cassino.[39] That same day, in Warsaw, forty-three women were taken from the Pawiak

Four Jews executed at Chelm, in eastern Poland, 28 May 1942 (*page 351*).

A Jewish boy, deported to Theresienstadt.

After the Warsaw ghetto revolt, April 1943 (*pages 557–67*): OPPOSITE Jews being forced out of their homes; ABOVE Jews from the Toebbens workshops being led away to the railway sidings, to slave labour, and to death (*pages 628–32*);

BELOW German officers question a Jew captured during the fighting.

The start of a deportation: Thrace, February 1943 (*page 541*).

Deportees from Thrace boarding the trains to an 'unknown destination', in fact to the death camp at Treblinka.

Women at the barred window of a deportation train.

The 'ramp' at Birkenau: deportees from Hungary arrive in Auschwitz, summer 1944 (*pages 674–8*).

Hungarian Jews arrive in Auschwitz, summer 1944. This particular railway wagon had come from the Hannover depot of the German railways.

Hungarian Jews walking beside the barracks at Birkenau, on their way to the distant gas-chamber.

At Mauthausen, an inmate finds death on the electrified fence.

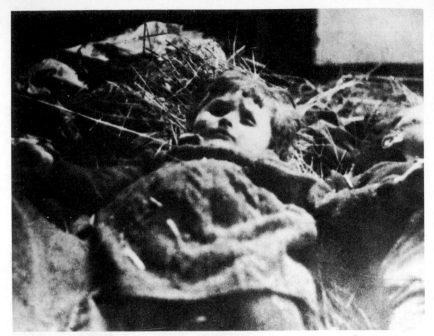

After the German troops had retreated, Jews continued to be killed. This picture shows a four-year-old orphan girl murdered, with six other Jews near Bialystok, by an anti-Semitic Pole (*pages 782–3*).

A survivor of the Transnistrian death marches, allowed to leave Rumania in the summer of 1944, reaches Palestine.

prison, and shot. Fifteen of these women were Jewish: one of them was shot with her four-year-old child.[40]

On May 18 it was the turn of a Jewish partisan leader in the Parczew region, Aleksander Skotnicki, to fall in action when his unit ran into a tank force of the heavily armoured SS Viking Division.[41]

In preparation for the imminent arrival of several hundred thousand Hungarian Jews, some of whom would be chosen for forced labour, the German industrial plants in the Auschwitz region began to expand. At Gleiwitz there were to be four such plants: one, for the production and packing of black smoke for smoke screens, was opened on May 3. The others were for repairing railway carriages and oil wagons, for making railway bogies and gun carriages, and for repairing and remodelling military motor vehicles.[42]

The factories in the Auschwitz region had expanded during the first five months of 1944, using both prisoners-of-war and Jews. Among the prisoners-of-war were Polish, Yugoslav, Soviet, French and British soldiers.

In the power station and coal mine at Neu Dachs, known also by its Polish name, Jaworzno, more than sixteen hundred prisoners were employed by May 1944.[43] At the synthetic petrol plant at Blechhammer, opened on April 1, four thousand prisoners were employed, among them almost two hundred women who were in the SS and prisoners' kitchens and laundry.[44] At Bobrek, from April 22, the two hundred and fifty prisoners in the Siemens Schuckert works had included fifty children: all were employed making electrical apparatus for aircraft and submarines.[45]

A further labour camp at Myslowice provided thirteen hundred slave labourers for the Furstengrube coal mines, working the old mine, and constructing a new one.[46] Another thousand prisoners were employed at the Laurahutte steel works, making anti-aircraft guns.[47] At the Gunthergrube coal mines there were six hundred prisoners, most of them Jews brought from Birkenau, working the old mine and constructing a new one.[48] In May 1944, on the eve of the mass deportation of Hungarian Jews to Birkenau, a new labour camp was opened at Sosnowiec, the second there, for nine hundred prisoners needed to work the gun-barrel foundry and shell production of the Ost-Maschinenbau Gesellschaft works.[49]

Between Birkenau and Auschwitz Main Camp, fuses for grenades were manufactured at the Union factory.[50] At Monowitz, the synthetic oil and rubber factory was already absorbing tens of thousands of Jewish workers, as well as some British prisoners-of-war, all non-Jews.[51] Hungarian Jews were also to be sent from Birkenau to the labour camp on the site of the Warsaw ghetto, to continue to clear the rubble, and to search for valuables.[52]

On May 15 the trains from Hungary began crossing Slovakia and southern Poland, on their way to Birkenau. Mel Mermelstein, who was among the earliest of the deportees from Hungary, later recalled the change in mood as the train crossed from Slovakia into Poland, and stopped at a town somewhere inside the German-occupied area:

> Tall buildings were in sight and the air was thick. I managed to get to the little barbed-wired window. Another train just like ours was in sight.
> I began to shout across, 'Who are you . . . ? Where are you coming from . . . ?'
> 'We are Dutch Jews . . . We are headed for Germany . . . to a labour camp . . .'
> The SS ran over to put a stop to our communication. From across I could hear a woman scream to the guard, 'You killed my child . . . my baby's dead . . . you killed it, you Nazi swine . . . I'll kill you!'
> He turned his head toward the noise, removed his automatic weapon and delivered a burst of fire into the boxcar. I heard another SS shout back derisively, 'With what will you kill me, you bitch?'
> 'With my bare hands.'
> Another burst, but this time in the air as he moved away to the other end of the transport.

On May 16 the tattoo numbers at Birkenau were given a new series, beginning with the letter A. The seventeen-year-old Mermelstein, arriving on May 21, was given the tattoo number A.4685. But only those chosen for work were given numbers.[53] A specially built railway spur now brought the trains to the very gates of two of the gas-chambers, only a few yards' walk away. 'When we arrived in Birkenau,' one eye-witness wrote four months later, 'such a smell of burning flesh wafted towards us that in the groups arriving at night, who not only smelt the stench but saw the flames rising from the crematoria, many committed suicide at once.'[54]

A Jewess from Hungary, Judith Sternberg, later recalled the moment of arrival at Birkenau:

> Corpses were strewn all over the road; bodies were hanging from the barbed-wire fence; the sound of shots rang in the air continuously. Blazing flames shot into the sky; a giant smoke cloud ascended above them. Starving, emaciated human skeletons stumbled toward us, uttering incoherent sounds. They fell down right in front of our eyes, and lay there gasping out their last breath.[55]

With each arriving train from Hungary, selections were made, and some men and women from each train were sent to the barracks. But within a few days, twelve thousand Jews were being gassed and cremated every twenty-four hours. Alter Feinsilber, one of the few survivors of the Sonderkommando at Birkenau, noted, of these Hungarian transports:

> If the number of persons to be gassed was not sufficiently large, they would be shot and burned in pits. It was a rule to use the gas-chamber for groups of more than two hundred persons, as it was not worth while to put the gas-chamber in action for a smaller number of persons. It happened that some prisoners offered resistance when about to be shot at the pit or that children would cry and then SS Quartermaster Sergeant Moll would throw them alive into the flames of the pits.
>
> I was eye-witness of the following incidents: Moll told a naked woman to sit down on the corpses near the pit, and while he himself shot prisoners and threw their bodies into the flaming pit he ordered her to jump about and sing. She did so, in the hope, of course, of thus saving her life, perhaps. When he had shot them all, he also shot this woman and her corpse was cremated.[56]

Two of the gas-chambers, numbered II and III, were at the end of the railway spur. But two more, IV and V, were some way across the

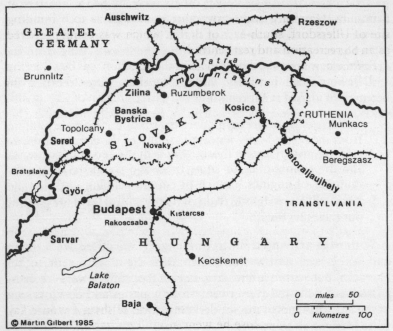

Auschwitz
Rzeszow
GREATER
GERMANY
Brunnlitz
Tatra
mountains
Zilina   Ruzumberok
Banska   Kosice
Bystrica   RUTHENIA
Topolcany   Munkacs
Sered   S L O V A K I A
Novaky
Beregszasz
Bratislava   Satoraljaujhely
Györ   TRANSYLVANIA
Budapest   Kistarcsa
Rakoscsaba
Sarvar   H U N G A R Y
Kecskemet
Lake
Balaton   0   miles   50
Baja   0   kilometres   100
© Martin Gilbert 1985

HUNGARY

camp, nearly three thousand yards, at the edge of the Birkenau
woods. To these two more distant gas-chambers, the Jews were
marched on foot. Those who were sick, as well as old men and
women who were too weak to walk, and sometimes children, were
taken from the railway ramp to these two distant gas-chambers by
truck. Ten months later, Alter Feinsilber recalled how, when those
brought by truck reached the gas-chamber: 'they were dumped into
the yard just as is done when refuse is dumped from lorries into pits,
expressly prepared for that purpose.' When it happened, Feinsilber
added, 'that after gassing we found a still moving body among the
corpses, we did not want to throw a still living person into the fire
and then one of the SS men finished him off with a revolver shot.'[57]

From the first days of their arrival in Birkenau, Hungarian Jews
were among those taken from the barracks for work, not only in
the factories of the Auschwitz region, but in many distant factories
and projects in the Reich. On May 15, a thousand Jews were sent

to a factory at Wustegiersdorf; others were to go to factories at Brünnlitz, Hamburg and Schwarzheide, as well as to a building site of Ullersdorf, south-east of Berlin, which was being prepared as an SS recreation and rest centre.[58]

For the new arrivals, the moment of the selection was bewildering and without meaning. Hugo Gryn, a fourteen-year-old boy from Beregszasz, in the Hungarian-annexed eastern region of Czechoslovakia, later recalled his arrival in Birkenau with his father, his mother and his younger brother:

> We were exhausted, thoroughly demoralised and frightened and the train stood for some time. We could only hear the shunting of engines, crunch of people walking outside, and eventually, well into daylight, the door pulled open and people being now herded out, and an amazing scene. It reminded me of what I imagined a lunatic asylum would be like, because in addition to the SS who were moving up and down and pushing people around towards the head of the platform, the other people there wore this striped uniform, with a very curious-shaped hat, and they were just moving up and down taking so-called luggage out of the train. One of them I would say saved my life, because he went around muttering in Yiddish, 'You're eighteen, you have a trade,' which I took to be the mutterings of a lunatic because it was such a curious thing to say – that's all he kept saying to people – particularly to young people.
>
> My father was there and took it seriously, and by the time we in fact came to the head of this platform where the selection was taking place I had already been rehearsed, so that when the SS man says: 'How old are you?' I said I was nineteen; and 'Do you have a trade?' 'Yes, I'm a carpenter and a joiner.' My brother who was there was younger, he couldn't say he was nineteen, and so he was sent with the old people the wrong way and my mother went after him. The SS man quite crudely and violently pulled my mother back. She said, 'Well, I want to be with my little boy, he's frightened.' 'Don't worry,' he said, 'you will meet him later.' Well that of course was in fact the last time I saw my brother. . . .[59]

Gabi Gryn was eleven years old.

The deceptions which alone made the murder of so many people possible were continued to the very door of the gas-chamber where, as Yehuda Bakon, a deportee from Hungary, was later told by the Sonderkommando, the word 'showers' was written 'in all languages'. Of the Jews who were about to be gassed, Yehuda Bakon was told:

> They were brought into the chambers for undressing. There were benches, and there were hangers with numbers. Sometimes women would be separated from the men, but when there was no time, they were put into those chambers together, and had to undress all together. The SS men would warn them, 'Please, remember the number of your hanger for the clothes. Tie both shoes well, and put your clothing in one pile, because they will be handed back to you at the end of the showers.'
>
> They would ask for water. They were very thirsty after the long journey in those sealed trucks. They were told, 'Hurry. Coffee is waiting. Coffee is ready in camp. The coffee will be cold.' And similar things to calm them, to mislead them.[60]

During the second half of May, tens of thousands of Jews were deported to Birkenau not only from Hungary, but from Theresienstadt, Italy, Belgium, Holland, France and the former Polish city of Sosnowiec: more than thirty trains in fifteen days.[61] Of the 575 Jews brought to Birkenau from Fossoli, in Italy, on May 16, 518 were gassed, among them the seventy-seven-year-old Daria Bauer, who had been born in Florence, the six-year-old Elena Calo, also from Florence, the three-year-old Alina di Consiglio from Rome, and Gigliola Finzi, born at Roccastrada in Italy less than three months before the deportation.[62]

There was also one deportation in May which did not go to Birkenau, but to Kovno. Leaving Paris on May 15, the train reached Kovno three days and three nights later. Of the 878 deportees, only 17 survived the war. On May 19, the day after these Paris deportees reached Kovno, the SS ordered the prisoners to undress. A Lithuanian eye-witness, Pavilas Tcherekas, later recalled how, 'understanding what that meant, the prisoners threw themselves at the SS and disarmed some of them. There was shooting. The prisoners fled, running in all directions, but they were in a concrete enclosure. Bullets poured from the guard towers.' None escaped.[63]

At Munkacs, in Hungarian Ruthenia, and at the Hungarian town of Satoraljaujhely, a number of Jews tried to resist being put on the train to Birkenau, but they were shot down by the SS. The remainder, cowed, entered the wagons.[64] During the five-day journey from Munkacs, which began on May 22, many went mad. Some died during the first three days inside the sealed wagons. At one town on the journey, all corpses were removed, and those who had gone mad were shot.[65]

On May 25 the German representative in Budapest, SS Brigadier General Edmund Veesenmayer, reported to the German Foreign Ministry that 138,870 Jews had been deported to their 'destination' in the past ten days.[66]

That same evening, May 25, as the group of Hungarian Jews were being led to one of the two more distant gas-chamber buildings in Birkenau, they sensed that something was wrong, and scattered into the nearby woods. Special searchlights, installed around the gas-chamber, were at once switched on by the SS, who opened fire on those seeking to flee. All were shot. A similar act of revolt, similarly suppressed, took place three days later, on May 28.[67]

On the following day, May 29, several thousand Jews who had been deported from the southern Hungarian city of Baja reached the German frontier. Only then, after three and a half days in the wagons, were the doors opened for the first time: fifty-five Jews were found dead, and two hundred had gone mad.[68]

One eye-witness of the arrival of Hungarian Jews at Birkenau was a German soldier whose account was eventually passed on to British military Intelligence. He was a member of a German anti-tank artillery unit, transferred from the Russian front to the west. During the journey, the train on which he and his unit were being transferred had to stop for a few days owing to 'jammed railways'. At the place where it stopped, it was shunted on to a side track. The side track was at Auschwitz junction, at the entrance to the spur line into Birkenau.

On the siding, alongside the soldiers' train, stood a goods train. Its tiny upper windows were covered in barbed wire. The train was guarded by the SS.

The soldier's account, as sent to London, read:

> This train was full of Hungarian Jews brought up for extermination. Nobody was allowed near the train, but some

of the soldiers managed to get near all the same, and caught glimpses of what was going on.

The Jews were packed together in the carriages, men, women, children, old people; they were not allowed out and had to obey the calls of nature inside. The carriages were full of excrements, and a putrid fluid was trickling from the carriages.

The captives cried out for water but it was forbidden to bring them any. Some of the soldiers did it all the same, in spite of the SS guards' threats. The Jews offered them valuables, rings, watches, etc., in return, but the soldiers refused. One Jew insisted on throwing his watch to a soldier, making the gesture of throat-cutting to indicate that he was going to his death anyhow, and the watch was no more use to him. One SS man accepted valuables from the captives in return for giving them half a loaf of bread.

This went on for two days when the death train was emptied and the inmates were driven into the camp. Meanwhile the soldiers had found out through interviews with the local locomotive driver who had to shunt the trains, and with SS guards, what was going on in this camp. The engine driver told them to watch out at nightfall; then they would see smoke coming out of twelve chimneys that were visible at some distance, and smell the burned flesh – that was the mass cremation of the people murdered during the afternoon hours in gas-chambers.

Indeed, when night fell after the emptying of the death train, the chimneys began to smoke and the smell of burned flesh filled the air. Also open fires were seen – the corpses being burned on pyres because the crematorium could not deal with the masses of victims. Another crematorium, bigger than the first, was seen under construction nearby. The soldiers – the whole unit witnessed the events – were aghast. They had heard of these things before but could not believe them. They stayed up all night and discussed what they had seen. Even the most diehard Nazis were silent and pale. No action was possible; the guns had been sent ahead, they had next to no arms, and the place was full of SS.

The following day, six carriages rolled out of the death camp and were put on the side track for the night. The soldiers crept into the carriages to inspect the contents. It consisted of the clothes of the Jews murdered on the previous day – all with labels of Hungarian firms – anything from shorts to shirts, men's and women's underwear, to babies' swaddling clothes, shoes, suits, dresses, etc., all addressed to Textilverwaltung, Litzmannstadt (the German Textile Administration in Lodz), which was to use them.

The engine driver said he could hardly hold out any longer at this place, but what could he do? He was scarcely able to eat his meals for disgust. He told the soldiers appalling stories from the camp, especially the treatment of women, which defy description.

There was also a real romantic drama. One SS man had fallen in love with a Jewish girl and became intimate with her. He protected her and managed for months to get her out of the death batches into some batch which was still to remain alive. But in the end he was found out. The SS man and the girl were killed immediately.[69]

Inside Birkenau, two Jews who had witnessed the first ten days of the Hungarian arrivals escaped on May 27. One, Arnost Rosin, was a Czech Jew, the other, Czeslaw Mordowicz, was Polish-born. They managed to reach Slovakia, and their report, combined with that of two earlier escapees who had fled before the Hungarian deportations, reached the West towards the end of June. The two earlier escapees were the young Slovak Jew, Rudolf Vrba, and an older Slovak Jew, Alfred Wetzler. In their report, Vrba set out the fate and the statistics of the deportations into Birkenau since the summer of 1942, when he himself had arrived from Slovakia.[70]

Even while Rosin and Mordowicz were struggling to cross the Tatra mountains, trekking southward, but only able to move by night, into Slovakia, Edmund Veesenmayer was again reporting to Berlin on the scale of the deportations from Hungary. On May 25 he gave 138,870 as the number of Jews already deported.[71] Six days later, on May 31, the figure had risen to 204,312.[72] That same day, from one of the trains reaching the German border, forty-two corpses were removed, one of them a child's, before the train proceeded to Birkenau.[73]

At Birkenau, the torments imposed upon those sent to the barracks reduced many of them to despair. Leon Szalet has recalled how, on one occasion, the prisoners were ordered to drink out of the unflushed toilet bowls. 'The men could not bring themselves to obey this devilish order,' he wrote. 'They only pretended to drink. But the block-führers had reckoned with that; they forced the men's heads deep into the bowls until their faces were covered with excrement. At this the victims almost went out of their minds – that was why their screams had sounded so demented.'[74]

A prisoner in the women's camp at Birkenau, Halina Birenbaum, has recalled how many women with diarrhea relieved themselves in soup bowls or in the pans provided for 'coffee'; then they hid the utensils under the mattress to avoid the punishment awaiting them for doing so. The punishment was twenty-five strokes on the bare buttocks, or kneeling all night long on sharp gravel, holding up bricks. These punishments, Halina Birenbaum added, 'often ended in the death of the "guilty".'[75]

At least twice after the arrival of the Hungarian Jews, blood was taken from Jewish girls in considerable quantities, almost certainly, as one Jewess recalled, 'for wounded German soldiers'. No medical help or additional food rations were given to those from whom normally excessive quantities were taken, 'and many of them died soon after'.[76]

On June 3, as the Hungarian deportations continued, Rudolf Kastner, summoned by Eichmann, urged Eichmann to allow six or eight hundred Jews from the provinces to travel to Budapest, in order to avert their deportation. 'Your nerves are too tense, Kastner,' Eichmann replied. 'I shall send you to Theresienstadt, or perhaps you prefer Auschwitz.' Eichmann added: 'You must understand me. I have to clean up the provincial towns of their Jewish garbage. I must take this Jewish muck out of the provinces. I cannot play the role of the saviour of the Jews.'[77]

Eichmann did eventually agree to a Jewish request that 1,686 Hungarian Jews be allowed to leave Hungary for Switzerland.[78] But he refused absolutely to increase that number, or to halt the provincial deportations to Birkenau, even though he had sent a Hungarian Zionist, Joel Brand, to negotiate the 'sale' of a million Hungarian Jews to the Allies. At the very moment that Brand was explaining Eichmann's proposals to British, American and Jewish leaders in Istanbul and Aleppo, the Jews who were meant to be the basis of the bargain were being gassed.[79]

On June 3, a further train arrived at Birkenau from France. Among those who had been deported on it was the nineteen-year-old Freda Silberberg, who later recalled with some bitterness how, in the village near Lyons where she had been living, 'it was not the Germans who arrested us, it was the French police.' Reaching Birkenau, Freda Silberberg watched as a Dutch woman handed her mother a baby for safety. At the selection, her mother was sent to the right with the baby. 'I wanted to go with her', Freda later recalled. Then Dr Mengele said, 'She is going with the baby to a place where there are special creches to look after them.'

Freda Silberberg was sent with fifty other girls to the left. Reaching the barracks, they asked those whom they found inside what had happened to the people who were sent to the right, their mothers, brothers, sisters. In the barracks was a nineteen-year-old Jewish girl from Belgium, Mala Zimetbaum. It was she who tried to comfort the new arrivals. 'They had to go into another camp,' she told them. But after a while, as Freda Silberberg later recalled, 'you realised something was wrong, you saw convoys arrive and then nobody came into the barracks at all.'

The impact of Mala Zimetbaum on the new arrivals was considerable. 'She was the one who tried to make it easier for us when we arrived,' Freda Silberberg later recalled. But even Mala Zimetbaum could not hide forever the truth that Freda's mother, and the baby she had taken for safety, were dead.[80]

On 6 June 1944 the Allied forces landed in Normandy. The long-awaited second front was in being. In the east, the Red Army was poised to renew its offensive. That same day, on the Greek island of Corfu, the Germans rounded up 1,795 Jews. All were deported to Birkenau, where 1,500 were gassed on arrival.[81] Also on June 6, 260 Jews living on the island of Crete, who had been seized on May 20, were taken, together with four hundred Greek hostages and three hundred Italian soldiers, Germany's former allies, a hundred miles out to sea, beyond the island of Santorini, where the boat was scuttled. All were drowned.[82]

On the Greek island of Zante, not far from Corfu, the Mayor, Lukos Karrer and the leading churchman, Archbishop Crysostomos, not only alerted the Jews to the danger, but sent 195 of them to remote villages in the hills. Unfortunately, 62 Jews, all of them elderly, who could not make the sudden journey into the rough terrain, were seized by the Gestapo in Zante and taken to the port. 'If the deportation order is carried out,' Crysostomos declared, 'I will join the Jews and share their fate.' But when the boat arrived from Corfu to collect them, it was already so packed with Jews that it did not stop.[83]

In the Lodz ghetto, news of the Normandy landings, heard on illegally owned radios, circulated throughout the ghetto. Hitherto, war news had been spread cautiously and slowly, in order to protect the owners of the radios. Such was the joy on this occasion, however, as Lucjan Dobroszycki, a survivor of the ghetto, has written, 'that for a moment people seemed to forget themselves', behaving as if Lodz would be liberated 'in a very short while'.[84] The German authorities realized that the news of the landing could only have reached the ghetto by illegal radios. Searches were mounted, and six Jews arrested.

One of the Jews who could not be found was Chaim Widawski, a young man who, the Chronicle noted on June 8, was well known in the ghetto and 'widely popular'. It was feared, the Chronicle added, 'that he will commit suicide rather than turn himself in to the German authorities'.[85]

On June 9, Chaim Widawski's body was found in the street. He had taken poison.[86]

One young boy in the Lodz ghetto, reflecting on the D-Day landings, wrote in his diary: 'It is true. The fact has been accomplished. But shall we survive? Is it possible to come out of such unimaginable depths, of such unfathomable abysses?'[87]

'Could we be granted victory this year, 1944?' asked Anne Frank, in hiding in Holland. 'We don't know yet, but hope is revived within me; it gives us fresh courage, and makes us strong again.'[88]

35

'May one cry now?'

WITH EVERY DAY of the Allied struggle on the Normandy beaches and across the fields of northern France, Jews were being gassed in Birkenau, or hunted down and shot throughout German-occupied Europe. On D-Day itself, Hanna Szenes, one of the Palestinian Jews parachuted behind German lines by the British to make contact with the Hungarian and Slovak resistance, was caught on the Hungarian border. 'Even if they catch me,' Hanna Szenes told Reuven Dafni, a fellow parachutist, on the eve of her mission, 'that will become known to the people in the concentration camps. They will know that someone was coming to try to help them.'[1]

On 10 June 1944, in the tiny French village of Oradour, on the River Glane, the SS massacred 642 villagers. Among the dead were several Jews who had found refuge in the village, and of whose presence the Germans were completely unaware. Like the other villagers, they were locked in the village church, and then killed, as a reprisal for the killing of an SS man by French partisans in a distant village, but one with the same name.

Of the Jews murdered at Oradour, the forty-five-year-old Maria Goldman had been born in Warsaw, and the eight-year-old Serge Bergman in Strasbourg.[2] Both were refugees. Elsewhere in France, Jews were shot for active participation in the partisan struggle: several, on June 12, near Lyons.[3] In Greece, in the wheat fields of Thessaly, where partisans were trying to deprive the Germans of the harvest, Leon Sakkis was among several Jewish resistance fighters in action against German military units. On the night of June 14 he was killed by machine-gun fire as he tried to help a wounded colleague.[4]

On June 16, in France, the historian Marc Bloch, leader of the Franc Tireur resistance group, was executed.[5] But it was still upon

Hungarian Jewry that the worst terror fell. On June 17 Veesen-mayer telegraphed to Berlin that 340,142 Hungarian Jews had now been deported.[6] A few were relatively fortunate to be selected for the barracks, or even moved out altogether to factories and camps in Germany. On June 19 some five hundred Jews, and on June 22 a further thousand, were sent from Birkenau to Dachau, to work in factories in the Munich area.[7] Since 1933 Dachau had been a camp for political prisoners; now it became a centre for Jewish deportees from the east being sent to labour camps in the Munich region.

Ten days later, the first Jews, 2,500 women, were deported from Birkenau to Stutthof concentration camp. From Stutthof they were sent to several hundred factories in the Baltic region.[8] But most Jews brought to Birkenau continued to be gassed. To 'greet' these deportees, yet another element of deception had been devised. Among those who witnessed it day after day was the Frenchwoman, Claude Vaillant Couturier. Less than two years later, she recalled how, from her block directly facing the special rail spur that came right into Birkenau, 'practically right up to the gas-chamber':

> . . . we saw the unsealing of the coaches and the soldiers ordering men, women and children out of them. We then witnessed heart-rending scenes, old couples forced to part from each other, mothers made to abandon their young daughters, since the latter were sent to the camp whereas mothers and children were sent to the gas-chambers.
>
> All these people were unaware of the fate awaiting them. They were merely upset at being separated but they did not know that they were going to their death. To render their welcome more pleasant at this time – June, July 1944 – an orchestra composed of internees – all young and pretty girls, dressed in little white blouses and navy blue skirts – played, during the selection on the arrival of the trains, gay tunes such as 'The Merry Widow', the 'Barcarolle' from *The Tales of Hoffmann*, etc. They were then informed that this was a labour camp, and since they were not brought into the camp they only saw the small platform surrounded by flowering plants. Natur-ally, they could not realise what was in store for them.

Those selected to be gassed, Claude Vaillant Couturier added, 'i.e., the old people, mothers and children', were 'escorted' to a red-brick building. They were not tattooed. 'They were not even counted.'⁹ They were all gassed.

The only children who were not gassed at Birkenau were twins. For more than a year, Mengele, who personally made so many of the selections at Birkenau, had sought to become an expert on the medical and genetic problems of twins. He therefore continued to take out all twins, both children and adults, to a special barracks, and for medical experiments.

Few aspects of the history of the Holocaust are as horrific as these experiments. More than fifteen hundred Jewish twins were experimented on by Mengele in the eighteen months after his arrival at Birkenau in May 1943. Less than two hundred survived.¹⁰ One of those survivors, Vera Kriegel, recalled, forty years later, the moment when she and her twin sister Olga reached Birkenau. Speaking to a shocked gathering in Jerusalem she described first her arrival at the spot where Mengele practised his selection process, sending people with a flick of his finger either in one direction, to instant death in the crematorium, or in the other, to the labour camp. 'Children were having their heads beaten in like poultry by SS men with their gun butts,' she recalled, 'and some were being thrown into a smoking pit. I was confused: I thought that this was some sort of animal kingdom or perhaps I was already in Hell.'

Vera Kriegel and her sister Olga were five years old at that moment of horror. Their father was among those sent to his death. The twins, and their mother, survived. They did so because, as Vera Kriegel explained to the court, Mengele 'wanted to know why our eyes were brown while our mother's were blue'.

Vera and Olga Kriegel were forced to live in a straw-covered cage for ten days, while Mengele performed his experiments. 'They injected our eyes with liquid that burnt,' she said. 'But we tried to remain strong, because we knew that in Auschwitz the weak went "up the chimney".'

Vera Kriegel also recalled in 1985 how, forty years earlier, she had entered an Auschwitz laboratory to find herself confronted by a collection of human eyes being used in experiments of which she, her twin sister Olga, and their mother were a part. She recalled: 'I was terrified.'¹¹

Among the Jews who died as a result of Mengele's experiments were two Hungarian twins on whom Mengele had performed head operations, a thirty-year-old Jewish woman from Szombathely whose twin sister was also killed by Mengele or on his orders to allow for a comparative autopsy, and a one-year-old triplet from Munkacs on whom Mengele was said to have conducted a 'post-mortem' under anaesthesis while the child was still alive.[12]

Although hundreds of young children died during these experiments, many in an agony of torment, others survived. To be selected for the 'twin' experiments in Birkenau was, by a grotesque irony, the only way in which a child under ten could avoid being sent to the gas-chambers on arrival. Two twins who survived were Ernest Spiegel, who was already twenty-nine years old when he was deported to Birkenau from Munkacs, and his twin sister Magda. Both survived the war, although Magda's own child perished. As the eldest twin in the male twins' barracks, Ernest Spiegel was given the duty of supervising and caring for about forty boys, aged from six to eighteen, and of washing and feeding the younger ones. Without any books, paper or writing material, Spiegel also strove to teach them the rudiments of history, geography and mathematics.

Mengele allowed Spiegel to take school books from among the mass of belongings taken from the Jewish children who had been gassed, and with these books Spiegel taught them what he could. He was also in charge of the filing cards in the twins' barracks. A fellow survivor later recalled how:

> One day two little boys arrived with a Hungarian Jewish family transport. They were dressed exactly alike and thus it was assumed that they were twins. When they were brought into this barracks and he made out the file cards, Ernest discovered that the brothers had different birth dates. He realized they were doomed if it were discovered they were not twins, so he immediately went to the Jewish doctor in charge of the barracks – with whom he had become very friendly – and together they decided to keep the little boys as twins. They had to make it very clear to the children that they had the same birthday from now on, and thus the lives of these two little boys were saved.[13]

These two boys survived not only Mengele's experiments on them, but also the war.

Not only Jews, but also Gypsies, were the victims of Mengele's perversion of medical sciences. Another survivor, Vera Alexander, recalled in the same courtroom how two Gypsy twins, one a hunchback, had been sewn together and their veins connected by Mengele who concentrated on blood transfusions in many experiments. 'Their wounds were infected,' she said, 'and they were screaming in pain. Their parents managed to get hold of some morphine and used it to kill them in order to end their suffering.'

Jews and Gypsies had both been chosen by Mengele for the ultimate senseless and barbaric suffering. As well as twins, he also selected Jews with physical deformities, hunchbacks and dwarfs in particular, in order to experiment on them as well. Among the Jews who reached Birkenau from Hungary in the summer of 1944 were seven dwarfs and three children of normal height, all members of the Ovitch family, who had been famous in the pre-war European music halls. Forty years later the eldest of the dwarfs, Elizabeth Moshkovitz, who was nineteen years old in 1944, explained how, when the family reached the selection at the railway ramp, Mengele did not believe that the 'little people' were Jewish. On discovering that they were, he became 'very excited' and was overheard to say: 'I now have work for the next twenty years.'

Later, as Elizabeth Moshkovitz recalled, Mengele personally rescued the dwarfs from inside a gas-chamber in order to keep them for his experiments. These included injecting into the womb, and the pulling out of their healthy teeth, to compare them with those of normal humans. The three members of the Ovitch family who were of normal height were allowed to live to serve their little brothers and sisters. All of them survived.

On one occasion, Mengele exhibited the entire Ovitch family naked at the SS hospital, in front of an audience of SS officers and camp guards, many of whom had been brought by bus and car from distant camps. The dwarfs were displayed on a pedestal, along with a detailed family tree drawn by Mengele.

Various experiments were carried out on the dwarfs' bodies, Elizabeth Moshkovitz added. The girls were forced to strip naked, and then to perform circus-type acts. Some were sexually abused.[14]

Among those murdered at Birkenau in June 1944 was the former

Elder of the Theresienstadt ghetto, Jacob Edelstein. SS Lieutenant Franz Hoessler was present during Edelstein's last moments. An eye-witness, Yossl Rosensaft, recalled a year later:

> Jacob was in the same barracks as I was – number 13 – on that Monday morning. It was about nine a.m. and he was saying his morning prayers, wrapped in his prayer shawl. Suddenly the door burst open and Hoessler strutted in, accompanied by three SS men. He called out Jacob's name. Jacob did not move. Hoessler screamed: 'I am waiting for you, hurry up.'
>
> Jacob turned round very slowly, faced Hoessler and said quietly: 'Of the last moments on this earth, allotted to me by the Almighty, I am the master, not you.' Whereupon he turned back to face the wall and finished his prayers. He then folded his prayer shawl unhurriedly, handed it to one of the inmates and said to Hoessler: 'I am now ready.'
>
> Hoessler stood there all the while without uttering a word, and marched out when Edelstein was ready. Edelstein followed him and the three SS men made up the rear. We have never seen Jacob Edelstein again.[15]

On June 16 the Jews of the Lodz ghetto were confronted by a proclamation appealing for 'voluntary registration for labour outside the ghetto'. According to the proclamation, parents whose children were 'old enough to work' could register their children for such labour. Those who volunteered could 'collect their rations immediately, without waiting their turn'.[16]

The destination of the volunteers was unknown in the ghetto. The Chronicle recorded that they had been told by the Gestapo Commissioner, Gunter Fuchs, that their task would be 'the clearing away of debris in cities that have been bombed'. This assurance, the Chronicle added, 'somewhat alleviates the terror occasioned by every previous resettlement'.

The Germans had asked for more than three thousand Jews a week, for three weeks. The first, it was said, were to go to Munich 'to clear away debris'. The proclamation calling for volunteers was signed by the Eldest of the Ghetto, Chaim Rumkowski. Two earlier registrations in the previous month had indeed been for labour. This one, however, was for Chelmno.

During June 16 the head of the German administration in Lodz, Hans Biebow, went to see Rumkowski. Biebow was seen entering Rumkowski's office 'in a highly excited state'. Once there, he had struck Rumkowski a savage blow to the face. The reason for this attack was, and remains, unknown. In the ghetto, it was believed that Rumkowski had insisted that he was 'unable to comply' with the new, large-scale demands for manpower.[17]

On June 22 the search for deportees intensified. That day, Oskar Rosenfeld recorded the arrival of the German police at an apartment in which they believed they could find all eleven members of a family named Szmulewicz. 'They knock at the door,' Rosenfeld wrote, 'shove it open, and question the occupant':

'Does the Szmulewicz family live here?'
'They used to. Now I do. Dawid Botwin. I took over their apartment.'
'What about Mordko Szmulewicz?'
'Dead.'
'Szaja?'
'Dead.'
'Lajzer and Sure Szmulewicz?'
'Resettled.'
'Jankel?'
'Jumped out the window. Dead.'
'Chawe Szmulewicz?'
'Resettled.'
'Mojsze Szmulewicz, the fifteen-year-old?'
'Shot to death near the barbed wire.'
'The two brothers, Boruch and Hersz?'
'Tried to escape to Warsaw. Didn't make it.'
'Boruch's son Josef?'
'No idea. Never came to the ghetto in the first place.'

'The two officers look around the apartment. A miserable scene. No trace of the Szmulewicz family. Eleven people snuffed out. Nothing to be done now.' The police had come 'too late'. Rosenfeld commented: 'Death has thumbed its nose at the authorities. Even the quickest hand is powerless against death.'[18]

The deportations from the Lodz ghetto began on June 23, and continued until July 14. All were sent to Chelmno, and to their deaths.[19] To deceive the deportees up to the last moment, Gunter Fuchs assured the first of them while they were at the railway station on June 23, waiting to board the train, 'that they would be working in the Reich and that decent food would be provided'. It was only the shortage of passenger carriages, he explained, that made it necessary to load them 'initially' on to goods wagons. But they would be transferred to passenger carriages en route: 'No one had anything to fear.' News of these assurances, the Ghetto Chronicle noted, 'spread through the ghetto like wildfire and had a somewhat calming effect'. In addition, it was noted that 'the travellers' of June 23 did not have to carry any of their luggage to the station; 'everything was brought to the station in wagons. Everyone collected his hand luggage at the station, while larger pieces were stowed in separate freight cars. Everything was properly numbered. People were treated correctly.'[20]

The train set off into the unknown. On the following day the ghetto was 'agitated', as the Chronicle noted, because the wagons were already back at the ghetto station. People recalled the 'frequent shuttle' of wagons during the 'great resettlement' of September 1942, and the 'alarming rumours' at that time. As a result, 'a wave of terror is spreading through the ghetto.'

A note was said to have been found in one of the goods wagons, indicating that the train had only gone as far as Kutno, thirty-three miles north of Lodz, when the 'travellers' had been transferred to passenger carriages. The Ghetto Chronicle commented: 'The information has not been confirmed. No one has actually seen this note: so no conclusions can be drawn about the quick return of the carriages. Perhaps further transportation is being staged in Kutno.'[21]

On the following day, June 25, it was announced that twenty-five transports would have to leave the ghetto. The Chronicler Oskar Rosenfeld noted that day: 'Reality has completely stemmed the tide of rumours. Ghetto dwellers are now being shipped out of the ghetto to perform manual labour,' but he added:

> Everyone knows that the situation is serious, that the existence of the ghetto is in jeopardy. No one can deny that such fears are justified. The argument that not even 'this resettlement' can imperil the survival of the ghetto now falls on deaf

ears. For nearly every ghetto dweller is affected this time. Everyone is losing a relative, a friend, a room-mate, a colleague.

And yet — *Jewish faith in a justice that will ultimately triumph does not permit extreme pessimism.* People try to console themselves, deceive themselves in some way. But nearly everyone says to himself, and to others: 'God only knows who will be better off: the person who stays here or the person who leaves!'[22]

Among those deported in this June 'resettlement' was Mordechai Zurawski. He later recalled how Hans Biebow told them that they would be sent to a labour camp near Leipzig. 'For you Jews who work diligently', he added, 'it will be good.'

Zurawski, who recalled Biebow using these words, also remembered, at the railway station, words written in Polish on the wagons: 'You are going in the carriages of death.' But no one believed it. A few hours later, the train reached Kolo, and from there the Jews were taken in trucks to Chelmno, and gassed. Zurawski, sent to the 'Forest Commando' to cut wood for the crematorium, recalled how, when the deportees reached Chelmno, they were confronted by signs saying 'To the bath-house' and 'To the physician'. Then, having been given a cake of soap and a towel, and told they were being taken to the shower room, they were put into special vans, and driven off. After three hundred metres, at the entrance to the crematorium, they were dead. 'But in some cases,' Zurawski recalled, 'people still showed signs of life.' When that happened, the van's driver, a man named Belaff, 'would pull out his pistol and shoot these people'. After the bodies had been burned, the bones were ground to a fine powder in a special 'grinding apparatus'.[23]

On one occasion, Zurawski witnessed an incident when one of the SS guards 'threw a living Jewish worker into the furnace'.[24]

Another survivor, Shimon Srebnik, was given the task of pulling gold teeth from the corpses before they were burned. One day, he later recalled, a boy who was working in the 'Forest Commando', taking corpses to the crematorium, saw his sister's body. He determined to escape, succeeded in slipping off one of the chains wound round his feet, and with the chain still hanging from the other foot, reached the River Ner. There he found a Polish peasant willing to ferry him across the river. But, as Srebnik recalled, the peasant:

> . . . saw the chain on his foot, so left him, went back to the bank, and ran to his house where there was a German. He said, 'There's a Jew escaping,' and the German went out and killed him.
>
> We didn't know that, but at eight o'clock in the evening the SS Regimental Sergeant-Major came and told us, 'Everybody out!' and he told us to take a count – one was missing, and he asked us, 'Where is one?' and then he said, 'Four people out!' and the four went out and they went to the place where the body had been brought; they brought the body into the hut and then the sergeant-major said, 'You see, he had escaped – this is his fate.'
>
> And then SS Captain Hans Bothmann arrived at nine o'clock and said, 'Fifteen people out!' and fifteen people were taken out. He took out his pistol and killed them. Then he said to us, 'You know why I did it?' and we said, 'No.' He said, 'Because a man had run away and if any of you try to run away, I will kill you all.'

Srebnik also recalled another SS man, Master-Sergeant Piller, who, on Saturdays, would take four men out of the forced labour squads, and say to them: 'You see this finger? If I move it this way you will stand up and if it moves that way you will lie down.' It was 'up and down and up and down until we were completely out of breath'. Finally, Piller 'would whip out his pistol and shoot all those who remained lying down'.[25]

The renewed killings at Chelmno, like those in 1942, brought profit to the Reich. A note of September 9, two months after the renewed Lodz deportations, recorded 775 wrist watches and 550 pocket watches sent to the ghetto administration in Lodz.[26]

On June 23 the Red Army opened its Great Offensive on the White Russian and Baltic fronts. As Soviet troops pressed forward in the region of the Pripet marshes, Jewish partisans played their part behind German lines, disrupting the arrival of reinforcements, and seizing vital bridges. As Red Army tanks reached the partisan bases, Jewish partisans met victorious Red Army soldiers. But, 'the tremendous wave of joy that flooded the heart', Shalom Cholawski recalled, 'could not remove the feeling of deep sadness; if only they had come two years earlier! Now that the day of liberation was here, there was no one left to free.'[27]

On June 24, a Pole, Edward Galinski, known as 'Edek', and the Jewish girl from Belgium, Mala Zimetbaum, escaped from Birkenau.[28] Earlier locked into the 'death hut', Block 25, where those who were to be gassed from the barracks were kept, often for many days, naked and without food, the nineteen-year-old Mala Zimetbaum had escaped through an air vent with several others. Returning to her barracks, she had been given administrative work as a messenger. Fluent in French, German and Polish, she soon became the chief interpreter at Birkenau. Whenever she could, she would leave names off the selection lists, an act of considerable courage. While serving as an interpreter, Mala had fallen in love with Galinski, and together, she and her 'Edek' planned their escape.[29]

Edward Galinski had managed to steal an SS uniform for himself, and the uniform of a woman member of the SS, a camp guard, for Mala Zimetbaum. With the uniforms were the necessary SS identity documents. Together, he and Mala walked out of the main gate, and travelled by train to Cracow. 'To all of us,' Lena Berg later recalled, 'this was an impossible dream come true and the prisoners' pinched, starved faces lit up with smiles. Mala's fate became our main concern. They had escaped, we told ourselves; they were free and happy.'[30]

It was rumoured among the prisoners that Mala had stolen a number of documents giving details about the gassing, and, as Raja Kagan later recalled, 'that her intention was to make the documents public all over the world'.

For two weeks, Mala and Edek remained at liberty. But, according to one account, on reaching the frontier into Slovakia they were caught by customs officers, so Raja Kagan learned, 'in a very silly way'. When they asked the officers the way, the officers became suspicious 'that a couple in SS uniforms would come to ask for the road'.[31]

According to another account, the couple had been caught in

Cracow, when Edek had called at some office for papers. 'Mala was waiting for him outside on the stairs,' Lena Berg was told, 'and when she saw the Germans leading him out, she went with him.'[32] According to a third account, it was in the village of Kozy, not far from Auschwitz, that Mala, alone briefly in a café, had been joined by a Gestapo officer. 'He stared at her. Did he find her beautiful, or odd, or both?' Mala, worried, had tried to leave. The officer had seized her. Edek, returning at that moment, could have left unnoticed in his SS uniform. Instead, 'despite her desperate glance', he joined Mala, and let himself be arrested with her.[33]

Mala and Edek were brought back to Auschwitz, where both of them were tortured. Raja Kagan was able to pass the hut in which Mala was held. 'I asked her, "How are you keeping, Mala?" She answered peacefully and heroically, "Es geht mir immer gut", "I am always calm". . . .'[34]

Several thousand Jewish women were witnesses of Mala Zimetbaum's fate. This is Lena Berg's account:

> We were standing roll-call when Mala was brought back to camp. She was to be publicly hanged as a warning to the other prisoners that no one could escape from Auschwitz, that the only way out was via the crematorium chimney.
>
> Mala stood in front of the SS men's barracks, pale and calm, and the hearts of the thousands of women who watched her pounded with hers. She had disappointed them when her audacious dream of happiness and freedom had collapsed, but she was not going to disappoint them now.
>
> No one knew how Mala got the razor blade; it was said that some charitable soul had slipped it to her earlier, when she was being questioned. Now she suddenly produced it and, before everyone, quickly slashed both wrists, severing the veins. An SS man ran up to seize the razor blade and she punched him in the face, screaming, 'Get away from me, you dirty dog!'
>
> The Oberkapo strode up to her and said, 'You stupid Jewish whore, you thought you'd outsmart us, did you, that you could escape? You swine, is that how you show gratitude for our kindness?'
>
> Mala had fallen to her knees, blood spurting from her wounds. Suddenly, she staggered to her feet and cried out in a terrible, loud voice, 'I know I'm dying, but it doesn't matter.

What matters is that you are dying, too, and your gangster Reich with you. Your hours are numbered and pretty soon you'll be paying for your crimes!'

The SS men knocked her down and shot her. Then they dumped her in a hand cart and several women were ordered to pull the cart around the camp so everyone could see it. Thousands of women stood there in the setting sun saying farewell to Mala. Later it was said that she was still alive when they threw her into the crematorium furnace.

'Mala's death shocked the camp to the core,' Lena Berg recalled. 'She had been our golden dream, a single ray of light in our dark lives.'[35]

The fate of Edward Galinski has also been recorded by several survivors. The twenty-six-year-old Fania Fenelon, who had been deported from Paris to Birkenau in January 1944, and was one of the few 'fortunate' ones chosen for the Birkenau orchestra, later recalled:

On the other side, in the men's camp, a gallows had been put up. Like us, the men prisoners were there, motionless, silent. Edek Galinski appeared, hands tied behind his back, unrecognizable. He who had been so handsome seemed no longer to have any face at all: it was a swollen bloody mass.

We saw him climb on to a bench. A snatch of the verdict in German, then in Polish, reached us; but before it was concluded I saw Edek move: he himself put his head in the noose and pushed back the bench. Jup, a camp Kapo, intervened, took his head out, made him get back on the bench. The speech was resumed, but Edek didn't wait for it to end to shout: 'Poland isn't yet –'

We would never know the end. With a kick, Jup, his friend, tipped over the bench. An order rang out in Polish and thousands of hands were lifted to raise their caps. In final homage, the inmates of the men's camp bared their heads before Edek, who had been their hope.[36]

On June 27, in the Lyons region of France, the Germans executed the Jewish resistance leader, David Donoff, known as 'Dodo'. He was twenty-four years old. Four months earlier, they had shot the twenty-year-old Moise Fingercwajg, another of the leaders of the Jewish resistance groups which were an integral but prominent part of the French underground struggle. Donoff and Fingercwajg were two of more than eleven hundred Jews executed in France for their resistance activities.[37]

Each day saw a new development in the Jewish tragedy; on June 28 the advancing Red Army approached Maly Trostenets camp near Minsk. Russian aircraft attacked the camp itself. That day, the camp guards, Latvian, Ukrainian, White Russian, Hungarian and Rumanian SS auxiliaries, were replaced by a special SS detachment, all German, under German SS officers. This detachment locked all the surviving prisoners, Russian civilians, Jews from the Minsk ghetto, and Viennese Jews who had been brought from Theresienstadt, into the barracks, and then set the barracks on fire.

All those who were able to flee from the blazing buildings were shot. About twenty Theresienstadt Jews managed to escape the blaze and the bullets, and to hide in the forest until the arrival of the Red Army six days later. Taken to Moscow by their liberators, they were kept for two years in a Siberian camp on the Chinese border, before being released, in 1946.[38]

On June 30, the 1,795 Jews deported from Corfu reached Birkenau. An eye-witness of their fate was a Hungarian Jewish doctor, Miklos Nyiszli, who was then employed in Birkenau as doctor to the Sonderkommando. After the war he recalled how, on the morning of July 1, he was making his 'morning rounds':

> All four crematoria were working at full blast. Last night they had burned the Greek Jews from the Mediterranean island of Corfu, one of the oldest communities of Europe. The victims were kept for twenty-seven days without food or water, first in launches, then in sealed boxcars.
>
> When they arrived at Auschwitz's unloading platform, the doors were unlocked, but no one got out and lined up for selection. Half of them were already dead, and the other half in a coma. The entire convoy, without exception, was sent to number two crematorium.
>
> Work was accelerated during the night, so that by morning all that remained of the convoy was a pile of dirty, dishevelled

clothes in the crematorium compound. I gazed sadly at the hill
of rags, which, little by little, grew wet and soggy beneath a fine
autumn rain.

Glancing upward, I noticed that the four lightning rods,
placed at the corners of the crematorium chimneys, were
twisted and bent, the result of the previous night's high
temperatures.[39]

In Vilna, on July 2 and 3, as the city awaited the arrival of the Red
Army, there were two thousand Jews working in the Kailis factory,
emaciated, but heartened by their imminent liberation. But more
than eighteen hundred of them were seized and taken to Ponar,
where they were shot. Less than two hundred workers managed to
hide, and to remain in hiding until the Red Army entered the city on
July 13. In the battle for Vilna, which had lasted five days, eight
thousand German soldiers were killed.[40]

From Birkenau, more and more Jews were now being sent to
factories inside the Reich. On July 1, one thousand Jewish men were
sent to the synthetic oil works at Schwarzheide, on the Berlin–
Dresden autobahn.[41] Among those deported was a young Czech
Jew, Alfred Kantor. 'You dirty rats!' the camp commandant at
Schwarzheide addressed the new arrivals. 'I'll show you what a
concentration camp really is! So you think you've been places?'[42]
Alfred Kantor noted, of one SS man at Schwarzheide: 'Jumping on a
man's intestines makes him feel merry.'[43]

On July 4, one thousand Jewish women were sent from Birkenau
to Hamburg, where they had to demolish houses bombed in Allied
air raids.[44] That same day, 250 prisoners from Alderney camp on
the Channel Islands were put on board ship to be sent back to the
mainland. The ship was attacked by British warships, and sank. All
the prisoners were drowned. Most of them were French Jews.[45]

The Theresienstadt deportations to Birkenau had ceased on May
18, and were not to begin again until September 28.[46] But two small
deportations in July, and one in September, ostensibly of Jews in
Theresienstadt who were to be exchanged for Germans in Palestine
or Switzerland, had no survivors.[47] One of those deported from
Theresienstadt in July 1944 was Dr Erich Salomon, a pioneer
photographer, whose photographs of pre-war statesmen had be-

come a feature of international conferences. Salomon, who fought in the German army in the First World War, had been taken prisoner on the Marne, and spent three and a half years in captivity. In 1933, with the rise of Hitler, he fled to Holland, and it was from Holland, in 1942, that he had been sent to Theresienstadt, then, in 1944, to an unknown destination, possibly Belsen. Whatever the destination, he did not survive it.[48]

In March 1944 the surviving Jews of Cracow had been seized and deported to a camp at Plaszow. Here, while working as slave labourers, and subjected to the sadistic whims of the camp commandant, Amnon Goeth, thousands had been murdered. Near Plaszow was a factory which manufactured kitchen utensils, run by a German Catholic, Oscar Schindler, a man who, like all the factory managers in the neighbourhood, was allowed to employ Jewish workers.

Schindler, whose relations with the Gestapo were outwardly cordial, had always done his utmost to protect the Jews who worked in his factory. When the Gestapo tried to transfer some of his workers to Plaszow, Schindler, by bribery and persuasion, was able to keep them. By the summer of 1944, more than five hundred Jews were under Schindler's protection.[49]

In Warsaw, the search continued for Jews in hiding. On July 10, thirty men and several women 'of Jewish origin' were shot in the Pawiak prison.[50]

In France, a German-born Jewess, Marianne Cohn, had been active in helping Jews to escape through France to Switzerland. Caught by the Germans while accompanying a convoy of Jewish children to Switzerland, she refused to be freed as an 'Aryan' according to her forged documents, and insisted upon remaining with the children. She was executed in the early hours of July 8, together with five non-Jewish resistance fighters, at Ville-La-Grande, between Paris and Lyons.[51] That week, the deportees from Hungary were being taken from the suburbs of Budapest. But the news smuggled out by the escapees Vrba and Wetzler in April, Mordowicz and Rosin in May, telegraphed from Switzerland to London and Washington on

June 24, led to demands from the King of Sweden, the Pope, and the Geneva-based International Red Cross, as well as from Britain and the United States, to the Hungarian Regent, urging him to halt the deportations. On July 7, Horthy agreed to do so. On July 8, the deportations stopped.[52]

By this time, a total of 437,000 Hungarian Jews had already been deported.[53] More than 170,000 remained in Budapest, from where Eichmann had intended to begin the deportations in the second week of July.

On July 9 a Swedish diplomat, Raoul Wallenberg, reached Budapest from Sweden with a list of 630 Hungarian Jews for whom Swedish visas were available. No longer in danger of deportation to Auschwitz, these Jews were desperate nevertheless for whatever protection they could receive.

Raoul Wallenberg, the man who now sought to protect the Jews of Budapest from further disasters, was the great-great-grandson of Michael Benedics, one of the first Jews to settle in Sweden, at the end of the eighteenth century, and a convert to Lutheranism. Wallenberg's father had died of cancer three months before his son's birth in August 1912. In his youth, Wallenberg had studied in the United States. In 1936 he spent six months studying management at the Midland Bank at Haifa: it was there that he had met many refugees from Hitler. In 1944 four American institutions, the American-based World Jewish Congress, the American Jewish Joint Distribution Committee, the State Department, and President Roosevelt's recently established War Refugee Board, had persuaded the Swedish Foreign Ministry to send Wallenberg to Budapest, with instructions to do whatever he could to help save the surviving Jews of Hungary.[54]

Wallenberg's first list of 'protected' Jews was given to the Hungarian government together with a Swiss list of seven hundred Jews whose emigration for Palestine had been approved by the British government. To guard these Jews against local hostility, a number of 'protected' houses were set aside for them.[55] The deportations had already stopped. The months of protection, and diplomatic rescue activity, had begun. Within three weeks, at the initiative of the Swiss representative in Budapest, Charles Lutz, a large department store, the Glass House, was declared to be the 'Swiss Legation Representation of Foreign Interests, Department of Immigration', and several hundred Budapest Jews were able to register as Swiss-protected persons.[56]

Anticipating every advance of the Red Army, the Germans continued to kill or move the surviving Jews of Eastern Europe. On July 12 the remaining eight thousand Jews of the Kovno ghetto were taken by train to Stutthof. But in those last hours, hundreds were killed in Kovno itself. 'When we left the ghetto,' Dr Aharon Peretz later recalled, 'the entire ghetto was in flames. We saw groups of people gathering in the cemetery where they had dug graves and the corpses were put in graves. The entire ghetto was in ruins. There were feathers flying out of pillows, there were pieces of furniture, and there was a desert.'[57]

At this moment of slaughter and deportation, a Lithuanian carpenter, Jan Pauvlavicius, who had already taken several Jews into hiding, including a four-year-old boy, built a hiding place next to his cellar for yet more Jews. This cellar he equipped with two bunks on which eight people could lie, and a small opening to the vegetable garden above, to provide the hide-out with air.

Pauvlavicius was able to carry out his act of rescue even as the Jews were being deported from Kovno. Dr Tania Ipp, one of those whom he saved, later recalled: 'He was like a father to us – a man only to be admired.' As well as hiding nine Jews in the hole which he had dug next to his cellar, Pauvlavicius also found refuge elsewhere for two Soviet prisoners-of-war who had escaped from Germany, and for another young Jewish boy.[58]

One of those whom Pauvlavicius saved at the moment of the final deportation was a Jewish woman, Miriam Krakinowski, who had managed to break away from the line of deportees in the confusion of the moment. On reaching Pauvlavicius's house, she had been taken into the cellar, where Pauvlavicius took a broom, swept aside the wood shavings covering a small trap door, and knocked on the floor. 'I saw a small door being pushed up,' Miriam Krakinowski later recalled. 'He told me to go down the steps. I couldn't see where I was going, but I didn't say anything. Gradually the room became lighter, and I found myself in a very small, hot room filled with half-naked Jews. I began to cry as they asked questions about the fate of the ghetto.'

The Jews hidden in Pauvlavicius's cellar remained there for three weeks, until the day of liberation. 'After liberation,' Miriam Krakinowski recalled, 'Pauvlavicius was killed by Lithuanians who hated him for saving Jews.'[59]

One of those deported from Kovno to Stutthof on July 12, Vera Elyashiv, has recalled the long train journey, in sealed wagons. 'There were some who got hysterical,' she wrote, 'and some screamed in a terrifying way. People started to hit the wagon walls with their fists.' Two men managed to break the small window and jump out. Through the cracks between the boards, Vera Elyashiv wrote, 'it seemed that one fell under the wheels of the train and a second was hit by a bullet when he got on his feet and started to run.' The train continued for two days. There was no food or drink, and 'a terrible stench'. On the third day the train reached Stutthof:

> The door was slid open, and framed in a blinding sky was the fat face of an SS officer. He seemed quite revolted by what he saw. Withdrawing a little, he announced that all the women and children must come out and that the men remain inside, so that they could be counted separately.
>
> Soldiers' hands and rifle butts got the reluctant, frightened and by now weakened women and children out of the wagons. I, as with most of the others, could hardly stand and hardly knew what was happening when suddenly the doors of the wagons were closed. I could hear father crying out my name, his cry almost drowned by the noise of the engine and the other cries. I must have tried to run, because I fell and when I got up I could see the back of the fast-disappearing train. This was the last I saw of my father.[60]

On July 12 Shalom Cholawski entered his home town, Lachowice, now liberated by the Red Army. Before the war Lachowice had been the home of about three thousand Jews. 'The streets were empty,' he later recalled, 'houses were entirely empty. The wind was blowing, but we were breathing the spirit of death. . . .'[61] On the following day, July 13, the first Soviet soldiers entered Vilna, among them many Jewish partisans who had joined in the final three-day battle for the city. One of those partisans, Abba Kovner, later recalled how he reached the quarter that had been the ghetto: 'I saw a desert of ruined walls.' The streets were empty. Then he saw a woman turn the corner of the deserted street, holding a girl in her arms:

In the first moment she stopped and shouted and screamed and wanted to hide. Some of us wore German uniforms; booty, captured uniforms which we had been wearing when we were partisans. Perhaps she thought that the Germans had returned. The German army perhaps had returned. But once she recognized us, she ran towards us and in an hysterical voice she started relating her story.

The girl whom she had been holding looked about three years old. Perhaps she may have been older, four and a half years, maybe. They had been hiding in a little cave in the wall more than eleven months. I don't know how they survived in this dark hole. She broke down. She cried bitterly and in that moment the girl who was in her arms who looked as though she had been dumb opened her mouth and said: 'Mommy, mother, may one cry now, mother?'

And I was told that for these eleven months, the mother, day in and day out, told the girl that one shouldn't and must not cry lest someone hear this outside and they be discovered. Now when the girl heard the mother crying, she asked her that question. I can speak of other scenes which I saw, but this matter of the girl, perhaps this speaks more eloquently than many other events.[62]

On July 13, at a pit near Bialystok, a group of Jews were at work, as part of the 'Blobel Commando' set up in Bialystok a year earlier, digging up and burning the bodies of those massacred in the autumn of 1941. Suddenly, German soldiers armed with automatic weapons surrounded them in a semi-circle. 'I was in the first row,' Abraham Karasick later recalled. 'I saw that near me they were coming.'

One of the Jews pulled out a small pistol, and fired a single shot. 'We heard a cry, "Comrades – run!"'

Karasick ran, jumped into the pit, fell, jumped again, and crossed a fence. The Germans opened fire. Karasick was wounded, but ran on. One friend was with him. They decided to go towards the Russian front. On the first night they saw a light, and crawled towards it. It was the place from which they had started. 'The bonfire was still burning.' All day they hid. The next night they crawled eastward. For nine days they continued crawling. Finally, they crossed the front line. 'My friend was killed, and I was taken to hospital.' Who had killed his friend, Karasick did not know: 'It was at night, the last night.' Karasick survived.[63]

With Bialystok under imminent attack, and even Warsaw vulnerable to a Red Army assault, the Germans decided to empty the Pawiak prison. On July 14, forty-two Jews employed in the prison workshops were murdered.[64]

On July 15, as the Red Army approached one of the few surviving ghettos, that of Siauliai, in Lithuania, four thousand local Jews, and a further three thousand from the nearby labour camps at Panevezys and Joniskis, were assembled in Siauliai and taken by train to Stutthof, and other camps in East Prussia. A hundred Jews who remained in Siauliai were killed on the spot. Twelve days later, the city was liberated.[65]

Such was the pattern of those July days in 1944: the Red Army approaching, the evacuation of the last thousands, the murder of the remnants. Those evacuated still had another ten months of war and terror in front of them. The handful who were able to hide, avoiding both evacuation and execution, welcomed their liberators and became survivors.

36

July–September 1944:
the last deportations

LIBERATION AND ENSLAVEMENT were taking place in the same days: on 18 July 1944 it was the turn of the 4,500 Jews of Rhodes and Kos to be caught up in the maelstrom. These new victims were descendants of Jews who had been expelled from Spain in 1492. Their language was Ladino, a form of medieval Spanish, spoken by the descendants of Jews who had been expelled from Spain and Portugal at the end of the fifteenth century. For the Jews of Rhodes, Ladino was the language in which their Jewish communal heritage was most diligently preserved. Together with Hebrew, the language of their Bible and their liturgy, it had given them 450 years of cohesion.

For many centuries, Rhodes and the islands around it had been a part of the Ottoman Empire, until conquered by Italy in 1912. Since 1936, under the Italian racial laws, Jews had been forbidden to be teachers, to employ non-Jewish servants, or to marry non-Jews. No Jew had been allowed to have a radio. But no Jews were killed, and none deported.

Following the fall of Mussolini in 1943, Rhodes and Kos had been occupied by German troops, as were each of the twelve Dodecanese Islands of which they formed a part. The Jewish quarter of Rhodes was near the port. On 2 February 1944, during an Allied air raid on German shipping in the port, bombs had fallen on the Jewish quarter, leaving eight Jews dead. In a second air raid, on April 8, the eve of Passover, in a second Allied air raid, twenty-six Jews were killed, among them the sweetmaker, Morenu Mayo.[1] These were the first victims of the war among two Jewish communities which had been unmolested for more than four and a half years of war: in 1944 there were 1,712 Jews in Rhodes, and 107 on Kos.

On 18 July 1944 all Jewish men in Rhodes, and in the nearby villages of Trianda, Cremasti and Villabova, to which many had fled to escape further air attacks, were ordered to assemble at the Aviation Palace in Rhodes, formerly the Italian air force headquarters, on the following morning. It was believed that this was a call for labourers to build fortifications on the island.[2] Once at the Palace, the Jews were made to give up their ties and their shoe laces. Two men were then sent back to the Jewish quarter to gather the women and children, the old and the sick. The women were told to bring all their jewels, money and rings, as they would need them 'once they were interned'. No one had any idea what this internment would involve.

The assembled Jews were kept in the Aviation Palace throughout the night of July 19. On the following morning a German officer came with a number of sacks to collect all valuables. One of those present, the twenty-two-year-old Violette Fintz, later recalled him as 'the one with the white shirt: we never knew his name. He had an interpreter who spoke Ladino.' The jewellery alone, she added, 'filled four sacks'.[3]

Among those who had been rounded up with the Jews of Rhodes, and was present during this looting session, was one non-Ladino-speaking Jewish family, the Fahns, from Czechoslovakia. In May 1940 they had escaped by boat from Europe; two brothers, Rudolf and Sidney, and Sidney's wife Regina. Travelling with many other refugees down the Danube, they had, after a veritable odyssey, become separated from the others, and eventually reached Rhodes. Once in Rhodes, there was no reason why the Fahns should have expected danger.

During the search for valuables, Sidney Fahn witnessed how, as he later recalled, 'despite the occasional meek protest, the looting proceeded in a quiet and orderly fashion until one teenage girl refused to part with a gold chain and with a Star of David pendant. Without a word, the SS major stepped forward, ripped the chain from around her neck, felled her with a blow and kicked her as she lay on the ground at his feet.'[4]

During the Jews' second day at the Aviation Palace, Bay Selahettin, the Turkish Consul General on Rhodes, came with documents for thirty-nine of the Jews, who had been born in Turkey. These thirty-nine were at once released, as were thirteen similarly Turkish-born Jews on Kos, protected by the representative of a neutral state.[5]

That night the mayor of Rhodes, Antonio Macchi, with a group of Italian volunteers searched the Jewish community to find the names of yet more Turkish-born Jews: among them Violette Fintz's mother Rachel. At least three hundred more of the internees were on the list, but the exercise was in vain: that day the Turkish Consul had a heart attack, and no further rescue documents could be drawn up.

On the second and third day of the internment, food was sent in to the Aviation Palace by local Italians. The Jews waited, 'hoping against hope', Violette Fintz has recalled, 'that a ship would come and take us off the island'.

On July 21 the air raid sirens sounded, and the people of Rhodes were ordered to stay indoors. Then the interned Jews were taken to the port. 'Everyone went with their bundles,' Violette Fintz later recalled, 'the aged and disabled who were not able to carry their possessions and were lashed by the Germans, cripples with their sticks, the children crying.' Three small petrol tankers were at the quayside. More than 550 Jews were put into each, like sardines, without food — no food at all.'

On the afternoon of July 23 the three boats set off across the eastern Aegean, within sight of the Turkish coast. On the first night a Jew died. On the following morning the boat stopped at a deserted little island, and two men were allowed off with the dead man to bury him. After a second night at sea the boats arrived at the island of Kos, where ninety-four Jews were brought on board.

The boats reached the Greek island of Leros. There, the captain, an Austrian, refused to continue the journey unless food was brought on board. Only after bread and water were produced did he agree to continue the voyage. For ten days, the boats continued on their way, without any further stops. Forty years later Violette Fintz recalled 'the very cold, very rough seas, all the water on top of us; we were soaking wet. Everyone was seasick.'[6] During the journey across the Aegean, five Jews died.[7]

On reaching Piraeus, the boats were met by SS officers who ordered the Jews to disembark, beating the men with sticks, and pulling the women by the hair. The women who struggled against the order were pulled by the breasts; the men were struck in the face, 'so hard they knocked out their teeth'. Others had their noses broken or their faces cut.

The Jews of Rhodes and Kos were ordered up into trucks. 'The moment you jumped in,' Violette Fintz recalled, 'you received a blow on the head.' Fourteen Jews were left at the quayside, the sick and the elderly. 'We never knew what happened to those people. We never, never found out.'

The trucks were driven to Athens, to the detention camp at Haidar. There the Jews were ordered to come down from the trucks, 'with whips and *schnell* and *schnell* and *raus*, as if the world was at an end. That was their principle, "Quick, quick, quick."' Once the Jews were off the trucks, the Germans demanded any hidden gold: 'If anyone is hiding any gold, they must give it, or they will be killed.' Thus was taken away the last remnants of such wealth as the Jews of Rhodes and Kos had acquired, most of them by a lifetime of hard toil.

For four days the Jews were held at Haidar, again without water, with no beds or bedding, 'sleeping on top of one another'. On the fourth day they were brought some soup. 'A man was dying of thirst,' Violette Fintz later recalled. His name was Michel Menache. 'They gave him urine to drink, to quench his thirst. He died that afternoon. He was a merchant, a good man.'

None of the assembled Jews knew what was in store for them. On August 3, after four days at Haidar, and two weeks after they had been taken off their beautiful island, they were lined up in rows of four, and driven with whips to Athens station. 'We entered the trucks. We found a little heap of bread in one corner and a little heap of onions, a barrel of water, and a barrel for sanitary purposes.'

Eighty Jews were pushed into each of the trucks, and the train set off northwards, travelling at night, and stationary during the day. Every two or three days 'they would open the doors and take out the dead people. Sometimes they would fill the barrel with water – not always.'

After more than a week the train reached Hungary. 'We saw when we arrived in Budapest white bread and butter sent by the community. But they would not let it in.' Next to Violette Fintz was a year-old baby, so thirsty 'that he was jumping on his mother's face to lick off her sweat'.

For fourteen days the train continued on its way. 'My father said prayers and sang. We thought they were taking us on a holiday. We didn't know what was happening in Europe.'[8] During that two-week journey, a further seventeen Jews perished.[9]

As the train continued northwards, Sidney Fahn, the Jew who had escaped with his family from Bratislava in 1940, realised that the train would shortly pass close to the town of Ruzomberok in the Tatra mountains, where his parents were still living. When the train stopped at Sered, Fahn saw through a crack in the carriage wall a man whom he had known before the war, and was able to call down to ask the man to telephone his father, to say that the train was heading his way. Receiving the message, Arnold Fahn, his father, went at once to the goods yard at Zilina where he learned that the train carrying his two sons, Sidney and Rudolf, his daughter-in-law Regina, and his nine-month-old grandson, Shani, whom he had never seen, would be passing through Zilina in a few hours.

The writer John Bierman has recorded how, a few hours later at Zilina, the last encounter took place between the Fahn brothers and their father. 'Through the cracks in their car, as the train stood at rest, they could see the old man searching frantically for them. They called out to him – "Here, Papa, here." The old man ran forward. "The child," he cried, "let me see the child!"' Then, 'an SS man jumped down on to the track. "Get back," he shouted. "Keep away from the train." Frantic to see his sons and grandson, the old man found the courage to ignore him. Pressed close to the car he had time – before the SS drove him off at gunpoint – to get his longed-for glimpse of Shani, held in the arms of his mother, and time to tell Sidney and Rudolf that he had bribed the relief engineer to slow down and give them a chance to jump from the train at a spot some miles up the track. 'But Arnold Fahn had wasted his money. The train did not slow down, and even if it had, there was no way the prisoners could have got out of the sealed cattle car.'[10]

On July 19, despite the halt in the deportations from Hungary, twelve hundred Jews were taken in trucks to Rakoscsaba and then locked into trains to be sent to Birkenau.[11] Elsewhere, the Germans were in retreat, but even the end of German occupation had its fatal hazards. On July 20, the day on which an attempt was made to murder Hitler, the Germans withdrew from Wlodzimierz

Wolynski, the principal town in western Volhynia. Hardly had German troops left than a Jewish doctor and partisan fighter, Hirsz Bubes, a laryngologist, was murdered by a Ukrainian.[12] In many towns, the killing of Jews continued long after the Germans had left, as local Ukrainians and Poles vented their own fury on Jews who sought to return to their homes and possessions.

When liberation came, it could be bitter-sweet: on the night of July 22 German forces withdrew westward from the Parczew forest, scene of their repeated hunts against Jews in hiding and Jews in partisan units. On the following morning, Red Army soldiers approached the forest from the east. A Jewish partisan, Avraham Lewenbaum, later recalled:

> I was sick and weak. I fell asleep exhausted under a tree. Someone from our group, Yankel Holender, woke me up saying that the Russians are already here. Soon Russian soldiers and artillery began streaming in here non-stop day and night. One major, a Jew, burst out crying when he met us. He said that he had been marching from Kiev and we were the first Jews he met.[13]

Even as the Red Army moved westward, driving the Germans from Polish soil, the deportations to Birkenau had continued. On July 24, from Sarvar, in Hungary, fifteen hundred Jews were deported to Birkenau.[14] This was the second deportation since the halt to all deportations had been ordered on July 8. After July 24 there were no further breaches of the order. A month later, his work incomplete, Eichmann left Budapest and returned to Germany, where he was awarded the Iron Cross, Second Class, for his services to the Reich.[15]

Also on July 24, Soviet forces entered Majdanek. War correspondents from all the Allied armies gazed in horror at gas-chambers, crematoria, and the charred remains of human beings. Photographs of these remains were published throughout the Allied world. Hitler, watching with growing disdain the collapse of his armies, was roused to an outburst of rage, fuming, as SS Brigadier Walther Hewel reported, against 'the slovenly and cowardly rabble in the Security Services who did not erase the traces' in time.[16]

The Western Allies were now pressing towards Paris. But among the last trains to leave France before the railway junctions were bombed beyond repair, was one, on July 31, with more than three hundred children and young people under eighteen, among the thirteen hundred deportees. Among the deportees was a baby only fifteen days old, deported in the wooden box that had served as his cradle.[17]

Also on July 31, from the labour camp at Blizyn, near Radom, three thousand Jews were deported to Birkenau, as the Red Army drew ever westward. Many of the deportees were Jews who had been brought to Blizyn after the crushing of the revolt in Bialystok a year earlier. Among the deportees was the twenty-two-year-old Bertha Sokolskaya. As a teenager in inter-war Poland, Bertha had studied at the State Commercial Lyceum in Bialystok. Of her best friends at the Lyceum, Lucy Albeck was later killed in her apartment by the Nazis, and Inna Galay died at Majdanek. Two of Bertha's cousins, Lena Fisher and Fannie Parasol, had left Poland for Palestine shortly before the outbreak of war. In 1939 her brother Menahem, who was living in Vilna, moved to Minsk. 'That is all I know about him,' she later recalled. 'Nor do I know about the fate of my sister Eva who left Bialystok in 1939.' In June 1941, with the German invasion of the Soviet Union, thousands of Jews had sought to escape eastward, among them Bertha and another of her brothers, Ovsey. During their flight, Ovsey was killed by a bomb fragment.

Of those deported to Birkenau, from Blizyn on July 31, more than five hundred were taken straight from the railway siding to the gas-chamber. Bertha was sent to the women's section of the camp, for slave labour. On reaching the women's camp she was tattooed on her forearm, her Auschwitz number: A.15772.

Still able to work, Bertha survived. From the women's camp at Birkenau she was sent to the labour camp at the nearby industrial town of Hindenburg. She was working at Hindenburg on her twenty-third birthday, a slave of the Reich.[18]

One large ghetto was still populated and working: the Lodz ghetto, where sixty-eight thousand Jews were still confined, following the

June deportations. 'All thoughts, considerations, hopes and fears,' the Ghetto Chronicle noted on July 22, 'ultimately culminate in one main question: "Will we be left in peace?"' The workshops were 'functioning normally'. Rumkowski had urged the ghetto workers 'not to allow discipline to slacken under any circumstances, in order to avert danger for the ghetto'.[19] As news of the Russian advance reached the ghetto, there was growing optimism. On July 22 the Red Army occupied Chelm, east of Lublin. 'The mood in the ghetto is rosy', the chronicler Oskar Rosenfeld noted. 'Everyone is hopeful of a speedy end to the war.'[20]

There was further cause for hope on July 25, when thirty-one postcards reached the ghetto, apparently from Leipzig, all postmarked 'July 19, 1944'. These were the first messages from a total of 6,496 deportees. They were either the result of coercion, or they were forgeries: for all the deportees had been sent, not to Leipzig but to Chelmno, where they had been gassed. The arrival of the postcards, however, gave the ghetto cause for optimism. As the Chronicle recorded:

> Fortunately, it is apparent from these cards that people are faring well and, what is more, that families have stayed together. Here and there, a card mentions good rations. One card addressed to a kitchen manager says in plain Yiddish: 'Mir lakhn fun ayre zupn!', 'We laugh at your soups!'
>
> The ghetto is elated and hopes that similar reports will soon be arriving from all the other resettled workers. It appears to be confirmed that labour brigades are truly required in the Old Reich. It should be recalled that before the departure of Transport I, there was mention of Munich as its destination. One group may well have gone there too.
>
> It is also worth noting that the postcards indicate that our people are housed in comfortable barracks.[21]

Each dweller of the Lodz ghetto surveyed the future with a mixture of hope and foreboding. On July 31 the boy who had commented in his diary on the hopes aroused by the Normandy landings noted: 'Although I write with a broken and hesitant Hebrew, I cannot but write Hebrew, for Hebrew is the language of the future, because I shall use Hebrew as a Jew standing proudly upright in the land of Israel.'[22]

Three days later, on August 3, the young diarist wrote again, in Yiddish: 'Oh God in heaven, why dids't Thou create Germans to destroy humanity? I don't even know if I shall be allowed to be together with my sister. I cannot write more. I am resigned terribly and black spirited.'[23]

The days of security in the Lodz ghetto were over. Deportations were to begin again, in order, so the Jews were told, to move both men and machines to safer places, inside Germany, far from the front. The new deportations were to begin on August 6, in three days' time.[24]

On July 27, the German army retreated from Lvov. Only a tiny remnant of this once flourishing Jewish community of one hundred thousand Jews had survived, among them ten of the Jews who had been hidden by Leopold Socha in the sewers underneath the city. This small group had heard the firing of the guns in the streets above. Suddenly they heard Socha shouting down to them, 'Get ready, you are free.' 'The manhole cover was opened, and one by one we climbed out,' Halina Wind later recalled, 'some reluctantly, since they were still afraid.' The manhole cover was in the courtyard of the house, inside which Socha's wife Magdalene had prepared a table with cake and vodka. Some months later, Leopold Socha was accidentally killed, run over by a truck in the streets of Lvov. 'As he lay on the pavement,' Halina Wind recalled, 'with the blood dripping into the sewers, the Poles crossed themselves and said that it was God's punishment for hiding Jews.'[25]

In 'Aryan' Warsaw, on 1 August 1944, sixteen months after the ghetto uprising, Polish resistance forces challenged the German occupation, taking up arms with equal proportions of hopelessness and courage. The Warsaw uprising began as Soviet forces approached the eastern bank of the Vistula. Its aim was both to accelerate the withdrawal of the Germans from Warsaw, and to establish Polish control in the city before the Soviets arrived. Three separate Jewish groups, about a thousand Jews altogether, took part in the fighting. The first group consisted of the surviving inmates of the Gesiowka labour camp, those former Birkenau and Majdanek inmates who had been sent to clear the ruins of the ghetto. The second group was made up of the surviving members of the Jewish Fighting Organization, those who had found hiding places in 'Aryan' Warsaw and who now formed a platoon of twenty-two Jews, commanded by Yitzhak Zuckerman. The third group was a Jewish 'battle unit', commanded by Shmuel Kenigswein, who, before the war, had been a boxer in Maccabi Warsaw. In 1939 Kenigswein had been a sergeant in the Polish army. His unit was made up of more than forty former concentration camp inmates, and fought until it was virtually destroyed.

On August 5 Polish forces liberated the Gesiowka camp, freeing 348 Jews, of whom 24 were women. These Jews included Greek, Belgian, French, Rumanian and Hungarian, as well as Polish Jews. One of the prisoners at Gesiowka, Hans Robert Martin Korn, was one of the eight Jews deported earlier from Finland to Auschwitz. German born, he had been a volunteer in the 'Winter War' between Finland and the Soviet Union in 1939. He did not survive the events of 1944.[26]

All of the Jews released from the Gesiowka camp joined the Warsaw uprising. Those who were technicians, like Korn, formed a special platoon for the repair of captured German tanks. The first to fall in battle was David Edelman, a deportee from France to Auschwitz.

One of the earliest actions in which the Jews from the Gesiowka camp were involved was recorded by a Pole, Second-Lieutenant Tadeusz Zuchowicz, who had taken part in the liberation of the camp. Three German 'Panther' tanks had approached his unit. One of them was hit by mortar fire and its crew killed. The other two tanks then retreated up the street, firing their machine guns. The third tank was immobile and abandoned. Then, as Zuchowicz recalled:

> The commander of the sector shouted: 'Who will succeed in entering the immobilized tank and turn the gun and hit the two retreating tanks?' One of the Jews jumped up like a cat and darted in the direction of the 'Panther' which was no longer a danger for us. Already he was at the entrance to the turret. We watched holding our breath as he slowly turned the cannon. The two retreating tanks were already two to three hundred metres away.
>
> Suddenly the air shook with a loud noise and a streak of fire

shot out of the barrel of the gun. As we looked on, the tank turned into a burning heap of metal. The second tank escaped. Our victorious Jew emerged with a glowing face while his lips were set in a stern rebellious expression. The commander of the sector, the major, ran towards him and kissed both of his cheeks and pinned the cross of 'Virtuti Militari' on the chest of the Jew. We all clapped for him and blessed him.

Many Jews who had survived the Warsaw ghetto revolt of April 1943 as fighters now fell in the Warsaw uprising of August 1944, either as part of the Jewish units, or in the various units of the Polish resistance forces. One of the three leaders at the political headquarters of the Polish resistance forces was a Jewess, Helena Kozlowska. One Polish unit was commanded by a Jew, Lieutenant Jan Szelubski. Another had a Jewish second-in-command, Lieutenant Rozlubirski; these two men were both awarded the Virtuti Militari, Poland's highest military decoration, for their part in the uprising.[27] Another Jew, Major Nastek, fell in defence of the Old City as a member of the Supreme Command of the uprising.[28]

Tragically, for the Jews who emerged from their hiding places to join the uprising and to fight for Polish independence, many anti-Semitic acts took place in those brief days of Warsaw's struggle. Some Jews were killed by Poles, including two Jews who were still in concentration camp clothes. A Jewish fighter, Chaim Goldstein, later recalled standing with the Lieutenant of his unit, a non-Jew, at the entrance to a large courtyard, when he heard shooting, 'and suddenly I saw a man on the ground in the last convulsions of death'. He then saw a second man 'calmly putting his gun back in his holster. He marched up to us with a confident step, like a hunter who has just killed a rabbit. On reaching us, he saluted the Lieutenant and said to him with a smile: "To hell with him, he was a Jew!" Then off he went.'[29]

In the centre of Warsaw, a Jewish doctor, Roman Bornstein, an officer in the Polish army, was in charge of the health services in the area won by the rebels. He has described the murder of thirty Jews in hiding in a house on Twarda Street. He also told of a Jewish engineer, who had visited the hospital to see his wounded brother, a Jew and soldier in the Home Army. On leaving hospital, this engineer was murdered by Poles.[30]

Feigele Peltel has recorded how another Jewish engineer named Golde, 'a splendid and jovial fellow', seeking refuge with Poles in their bunker after his own hide-out had been bombarded, was forced after several days of anti-Semitic insults to leave during a heavy German bombardment. He was killed by shrapnel.[31] Three other Jews, arrested by Polish partisans on suspicion of being German spies, were told that 'there would be no place for Jews in liberated Poland.' Two of them managed to escape, 'under a hail of bullets'. The third, Yeshieh Solomon, was murdered on the spot.[32]

Most Poles accepted Jewish help in the uprising, and Poles and Jews fought side by side as the German trap closed in upon them. But the murder, by Poles, of more than a hundred Jews during those same heroic weeks, gave a bitter twist to the Jewish fate.

As the Warsaw uprising was crushed, some Jews were also killed in Warsaw by those former Russian soldiers who were fighting in the German ranks as part of the anti-Soviet Kaminski Brigade. One such unfortunate was the forty-seven-year-old gynaecologist, Henryk Forbert. Co-opted on to the American Jewish Joint Distribution Committee in 1940, Forbert had worked that winter in the Jewish deportee camps in 'Lublinland'. Following the crushing of the Warsaw ghetto revolt, he had been in hiding in 'Aryan' Warsaw.[33] Other Jewish doctors who fought and died included Dr Fajgenblat, an opthalmologist, who had hidden in 'Aryan' Warsaw since the ghetto uprising; he was forty-four when he died of wounds received in action; and Dr Szymon Fajgenblat, one of the few surviving doctors who had worked in the ghetto on the study of starvation diseases.[34] The forty-four-year-old Warsaw neurologist, Maurycy Wolf, who had devoted much of his time and work before the war to the underprivileged, was killed on October 7, on one of the last days of the uprising.[35]

Of the thousand Jews who fought in the Warsaw uprising, at least five hundred were killed. The survivors, among them Yitzhak Zuckerman and Zivia Lubetkin, either escaped to the countryside, or hid once more in bunkers in the cellars of 'Aryan' Warsaw. At the outset of the revolt, on August 1, 'everybody', as Tuvia Borzykowski recalled, 'still thought that liberation was a matter of days or even hours'. In addition, for Jews like himself, the argument was strong that they should stay in hiding, so as to remain after the war as 'living' witnesses to the holocaust. But the desire to participate in battle against the Nazis overwhelmed all other arguments.[36]

While Jews joined the Polish uprising in Warsaw, elsewhere Jews in the labour camps were faced by the determination of the Germans either to evacuate them to Germany, or to kill them before the arrival of the Red Army.

At Strassenhof camp, near Riga, three thousand Jews were awaiting liberation. 'It was clear to everyone', the nineteen-year-old Ruth Chajet later recalled, 'that we were in a lion's mouth. Yet a spark of hope burned in everyone's heart that the Red Army might still succeed in taking Riga quickly and liberating us.' Then, on August 3, during roll call, the prisoners were surrounded by guards, and 2,400 Jews, all the youth under eighteen and all men and women over thirty, were marched away. They were never seen again. Later, the 600 survivors, most of them young women like Ruth Chajet, learned that those taken away 'had been gassed in a small, primitive crematorium set up on the River Dvina'. The event became known as 'the action of the thirty-year-olds'. Three days later, the survivors were evacuated by sea to Stutthof.[37]

The advance of the Western Allies towards Holland was likewise no deterrent to the continuing searches and deportations. In Amsterdam, on August 4, the Germans, ever vigilant in searching for hidden Jews, found several in hiding, among them Anne Frank. A month later, she and her family were deported to Birkenau.[38]

It was in the Lodz ghetto that the largest number of Jews still lived, 68,000 in all, of whom 67,000 were now to be deported. On August 7 both Chaim Rumkowski, the ghetto Elder, and Hans Biebow, the German administrator of the ghetto, urged them to accept resettlement. Its aim, Biebow told them, was to save lives, not to destroy them.[39]

More than 67,000 Jews were deported from the Lodz ghetto, not to safety, but to Birkenau. There, they faced the two-year-old selection procedure, the majority being sent, all unknowingly, to the gas-chambers, a minority being selected for the barracks. There was a third possibility, selection for medical experiments. Dr Miklos Nyiszli witnessed one such selection from among the Lodz ghetto Jews who reached Birkenau that August:

When the convoys arrived, Dr Mengele espied, among those lined up for selection, a hunchbacked man about fifty years old. He was not alone; standing beside him was a tall, handsome boy of fifteen or sixteen. The latter, however, had a deformed right foot, which had been corrected by an apparatus made of a metal plate and an orthopaedic, thick-soled shoe. They were father and son.

Dr Mengele thought he had discovered, in the person of the hunchback father and his lame son, a sovereign example to demonstrate his theory of the Jewish race's degeneracy. He had them fall out of ranks immediately. Taking his notebook, he inscribed something in it, and entrusted the two wretches to the care of an SS trooper, who took them to number one crematorium.

Dr Nyiszli's account continued:

Father and son – their faces wan from their miserable years in the Lodz ghetto – were filled with forebodings. They looked at me questioningly. I took them across the courtyard, which at this hour of the day was filled with sunlight. On our way to the dissecting room I reassured them with a few well-chosen words. Luckily there were no corpses on the dissecting table; it would have indeed been a horrible sight for them to come upon.

To spare them I decided not to conduct the examination in the austere dissecting room, which reeked with the odour of formaldehyde, but in the pleasant, well-lighted study hall. From our conversation, I learned that the father had been a respected citizen of Lodz, a wholesaler in cloth. During the years of peace between the wars he had often taken his son with him on his business trips to Vienna, to have him examined and treated by the most famous specialists.

I first examined the father in detail, omitting nothing. The deviation of his spinal column was the result of retarded rickets. In spite of a most thorough examination, I discovered no symptom of any other illness.

I tried to console him by saying that he would probably be sent to a work camp.

Before proceeding to the examination of the boy I conversed with him at some length. He had a pleasant face, and intelligent look, but his morale was badly shaken. Trembling with fear, he related in an expressionless voice the sad, painful, sometimes terrible events which had marked his five years in the ghetto. His mother, a frail and sensitive creature, had not been able long to endure the ordeals which had befallen her. She had become melancholic and depressed. For weeks on end she had eaten almost nothing, so that her son and husband might have a little more food. A true wife and Jewish mother, who had loved her own to the point of madness, she had died a martyr during the first year of her life in the ghetto.

So it was that they had lived in the ghetto, the father without his wife, the son without his mother.

Dr Nyiszli strove to overcome his personal emotions, sympathies and powerlessness. 'By whose will', he asked himself, 'had such evil, such a succession of horrors, been made to descend upon our wretched people?' His account continued:

By an immense effort of self-control I got hold of myself and examined the boy. On his right foot I noticed a congenital deformity: some of the muscles were lacking.

The medical term used to describe this deformity is hypomyelia. I could see that extremely expert hands had practised several operations on him, but as a result one foot was shorter than the other. With a bandage and orthopaedic socks, however, he could walk perfectly well. I saw no other deformity to be indicated.

I asked them if they wanted something to eat. 'We haven't had anything to eat for some time,' they told me.

I called a man from the Sonderkommando and had some food brought for them: a plate of stewed beef and macaroni, a dish not to be found outside the confines of the Sonderkommando. They began to eat ravenously, unaware that this was their 'Last Supper'.

Scarcely half an hour later SS Quartermaster Sergeant Mussfeld appeared with four Sonderkommando men. They took the two prisoners into the furnace room and had them undress. Then the Ober's revolver cracked twice. Father and son were stretched out on the concrete covered with blood, dead.

Late in the afternoon Dr Mengele arrived, 'already', as Dr Nyiszli noted, 'having sent at least ten thousand men to their death', and

ordered the bodies of the father and son boiled in water, so that the
flesh could be taken from the bones. The boiling finished, 'the lab
assistant very completely gathered up the bones of the skeletons and
placed them on the same work table, where, the evening before, I
had examined the still living men.' The skeletons were then sent to
the Anthropological Museum in Berlin.[40]

In the SS doctors at Birkenau, with their pre-war medical training
and qualifications, the transformation from good to evil was complete. The healer had become killer. The trained, professional saver
of life, dedicated to healing, had become the self-taught, enthusi-
astic taker of life, dedicated to killing.

For twenty-three consecutive days, the Jews from the Lodz ghetto
were brought to Birkenau. On the third day, the head of the Sonderkommando brought in to Quartermaster Sergeant Mussfeld a
woman and two children, 'drenched to the skin and shivering with
cold'. As Dr Nyiszli recalled:

> They had escaped when the last convoy had been sent to its
> death. Guessing what was in store for them, they had hidden
> behind the piles of wood that were used for heating and that,
> for lack of a better place, were stored in the courtyard. Their
> convoy had disappeared, swallowed by the earth before their
> very eyes. And no one had ever returned. Numb with fear and
> cold, they had waited there for some miraculous turn of fate to
> deliver them. But nothing had happened.
> For three days they had hidden in the rain and cold, with
> nothing to eat, their rags scant protection against the elements,
> till finally the Sonderkommando chief had found them, almost
> unconscious, while making his rounds. Unable to help them in
> any way, he had taken them to the quartermaster sergeant.
> The woman, who was about thirty but who looked closer to
> fifty, had gathered her waning forces and thrown herself at
> Mussfeld's feet, begging him to spare her life and those of her
> ten- and twelve-year-old children. She had worked for five
> years in a clothing factory in the ghetto, she said, making
> uniforms for the German army. She was still willing to work, to
> do anything, if only they would let her live.
> All this was quite useless. Here there was no salvation. They
> had to die.[41]

By the end of August, sixty-seven thousand Jews had been deported from the Lodz ghetto to Birkenau. Among them, Chaim Rumkowski, 'King of the Jews' of the Lodz ghetto, their protector and their mentor, was deported with his family, and perished in the gas-chamber together with more than sixty thousand other Jews from the ghetto over which he had exercised so much control, and, as he believed, protection.[42]

None of the ghettos and camps in which at least some Jews had been kept alive for their labour, whether in Riga, Vilna, Siauliai or Lodz, was able to avert the final deportation, on the eve of their potential liberation. On August 6 the Jews in Kaiserwald camp were taken to the Riga docks, and loaded into boats. For two days the boats sailed along the Baltic coast. 'There were no sanitary provisions,' Maja Zarch, a survivor of the Dvinsk ghetto, later recalled, 'and we were forbidden to go on deck.' After two days the boats reached Danzig, and the Jews were taken to Stutthof. Other Jews arrived at the same time from the Estonian camps. All were shocked by what they saw: 'Living corpses wandering aimlessly around, their eyes staring into nothingness, souls existing from hour to hour, with only the past as a crutch to lean on.' Such was Maja Zarch's description. 'For a bit of amusement,' she later recalled, 'the Germans would put a woman in a crouching position on a narrow bench and make her stay like that until she would faint, or drop dead.'[43]

While more and more Jews, and particularly Jewesses, were being brought to Stutthof from the camps in Estonia, Latvia and Lithuania, far to the south Jews were still reaching Birkenau. On August 16 a train from Athens arrived at Auschwitz with the 1,651 Jews from Rhodes and the 94 Jews from Kos who had been nearly a month on their deportation journey.[44] Through the tiny window at the top of one of the wagons, the twenty-two-year-old Violette Fintz from Rhodes 'saw some people without hair and walking like lunatics. I said to my mother, "I think we've come to a lunatic asylum." '

A voice was heard, through the carriage wall, calling out in Italian: 'The children to the old.' It meant nothing to those inside. Later they realized that it was a prisoner trying to save the young mothers, because if a mother was holding a child at the 'selection', she was automatically sent to the gas-chambers.

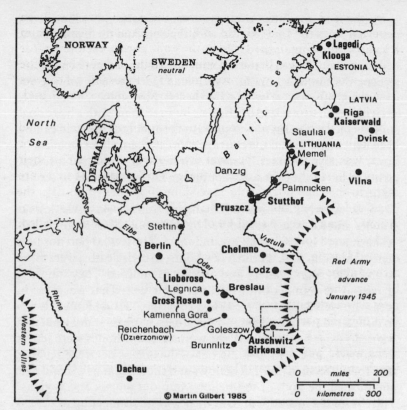

EVACUATIONS FROM EAST TO WEST

THE AUSCHWITZ REGION EVACUATIONS

A few moments after this mysterious message, the door of the carriage opened. 'They started with the dogs and the Germans and "Raus!"' Violette Fintz recalled.

It was about eleven in the morning. Amid the bedlam of noise and orders, the sun was shining. As Violette Fintz came down, she and one of her sisters were ordered to the left. Her mother, who tried to go with them, was seized by the hair by an SS man 'with a huge dog', and dragged to the right. She stood in the middle of the road calling, 'My daughters.' 'I had the courage', Violette Fintz later recalled, 'to say, "Goodbye, Mother." I never saw her again.' She had lost sight of her father in the chaos and confusion, nor was she ever to see him again.

Speaking only Ladino and Italian, and some Turkish, the Jews of Rhodes and Kos were bewildered by the babble of German, Polish, Yiddish and Hungarian all around them. Those who had not been sent to the right, and, within a few hours, to their deaths, were taken to an underground gallery and ordered to undress. 'They started to shave our hair, under our arms, our pubic hair. That was done by men who were laughing, mocking, shouting, "Raus! Raus!" It was so difficult for us to understand the orders, to understand what they wanted.' After being shaved, the women from Rhodes were sent to the showers, and then, coming out of the other side of the building they found 'SS men holding bellows and shouting at us to bend over and pushed the nose of the bellows into our anuses and vaginas'. This, Violette Fintz added, 'was their way of disinfecting us'.[45]

Among those who had survived the journey from Rhodes was the Czech-born Sidney Fahn. Later he was to recall how, on the platform at Birkenau, he saw the last of his wife Regina and their tiny son Shani. 'It happened so quickly,' John Bierman has written, 'that Sidney scarcely realized what had occurred. One moment they were side by side; the next they were forking off in different directions, he and Rudolf to the right, Regina and the baby to the left. He called out to her, and she turned eyes wide with uncomprehending fear on him before being swallowed up in the crowd of prisoners, kapos and SS guards.'

Like many of the prisoners in the barracks at Birkenau, it was to be several days before Sidney Fahn could really comprehend that he would never see his wife and child again; that they had already, in the jargon of the barracks, 'gone up the chimney'. Many years later

Sidney Fahn recalled how, on his second day at Birkenau, 'I happened to see a girl named Olga whom I had known in Bratislava and I gave her my wife and child's photographs and documents and asked her to look out for them. But she just shook her head and said, "They won't need these any more." She had been there two years and knew all there was to know about Auschwitz, but still I didn't realize what she meant. Then I was put into a barrack hut just one hundred metres from the crematorium in Block 4 and I could see the smoke rising all day and all night, and still I couldn't believe it. Finally, after two more days, I believed it.'[46]

Of the 1,673 Jews from Rhodes who reached Birkenau on August 16, only 151 survived the war. Of the 94 from Kos, 12 were to survive.[47]

The Red Army was now reaching town after town in which tens of thousands of Jews had lived before the war. But with the exception of a few dozen Jews who had managed in each town to survive in hiding, mostly in Christian homes, the Jews were dead, and with them the Jewish life of many centuries. In liberated Lvov, one of the survivors wrote on August 24, with her husband Mulik, to a friend in Palestine:

> We were rescued thanks to our neighbour, a nun of noble birth, who at the last moment prevented us from going to the ghetto and persuaded us to hide. She had had a presentiment of the imminent disaster, but we did not believe her.
>
> It is impossible to describe that period of our life while we remained in concealment under the permanent threat of search. We were living in the vicinity of Zloczow while all the other members of the family were in Lvov (with the exception of Jozio who was in Brzuchowice). We have lost all hope of seeing Jozio again. Max is no longer among the living and the same is true of Nathan, his wife and his sister-in-law. The same happened to Polek.
>
> The heart has turned into stone, the pain takes our very breath away; we cannot even weep any longer.
>
> We dreamt of dying a natural death. By day and by night we kept with us a dose of poison, and great was our grief when that poison was poured out. We were afraid that we might fall into

the hands of the Gestapo, where we would be unable to put an end to slow death under cruel torture.

What can you know, who are living over there, of the horrors of such a protracted, excruciating death!

We lived a life of that kind for over two long years, and the mark of Cain is engraved on our foreheads. You would not recognize us, so greatly have our faces changed. Mulik is beginning to regain his balance gradually, since he has succeeded in getting work. Instead of living the life of a criminal he is once more starting to live the life of a man who enjoys equal rights.

There is no greater sensation in town than the appearance of a Jew in the streets. Only three per cent of the Jewish population have survived.

The terrible events as well as the two long years of starvation have exhausted our strength. We have no clothing and no footwear. We had to sell part of our property in order to buy food. All the rest was pillaged by the murderers during the pogrom, when we fled from our home.

Yet I do hope that we shall succeed in rebuilding our lives in view of Mulik's diligence and talents, if we are treated in accordance with our natural gifts and not thrashed all the time with whips because we are Jews.[48]

Where they could, Jews fought in the battles for liberation. On August 25, large numbers of Jewish members of the French resistance, mostly Polish-born Jews, took part in the battle for the liberation of Lyons. Other Jewish units, led by Robert Gamzon, successfully blew up a German military train at Mazamet, and participated in the liberation of Castres.[49] In Slovakia, a special unit of Jews from the labour camp at Novaki fought in one of the main battles of the uprising, from August 31 to September 3, and later in the battle for Banska Bystrica.

More than fifteen hundred Jews joined the sixteen thousand Slovak soldiers and partisans who took part in the revolt. Of the 2,100 partisans who were killed in action, 269 were Jews.[50] One partisan battalion commander, Edita Katz, a Jewess, covered the retreat of her men with a machine gun, until her ammunition ran out. She then used hand grenades to hold off the Germans and the Hlinka Guard, until hit and killed.[51]

Within four weeks of the outbreak of the Slovak revolt, the Jewish units, and the Slovak fighters, were joined by Jewish parachutists sent from Palestine, among them a woman parachutist, Havivah Reik, who was captured during the battle at Kremnica at the end of October, and imprisoned.[52]

Among the Jews who were in Slovakia during the uprising, and survived, were two of the escapees from Birkenau, Rudolf Vrba and Czeslaw Mordowicz. During the uprising Mordowicz was captured and, together with several thousand surviving Slovak Jews, deported to Birkenau. The Auschwitz number tattooed on his forearm, if discovered by the camp authorities, would have meant the torture and execution always meted out to an escapee. But on reaching the tattoo barrack, Mordowicz had a magnificent multiscaled fish tattooed over and around the original number, and then a new number tattooed elsewhere.[53]

The Germans reacted savagely to the Slovak uprising. Tibor Cifea, a Jewish partisan, was shot, and left hanging for three days as a warning.[54] Pavel Ekstein was executed less than two months before his eighteenth birthday. In all, 722 Jews were 'specially handled' on the spot, mostly shot, or hanged. A Swiss Red Cross official, Georges Dunand, who was in Bratislava, tried as best he could to ameliorate the Jewish suffering. But Eichmann sent an emissary to Bratislava to ensure that the deportations were carried out, and a total of 8,975 Slovak Jews were deported to Birkenau.[55]

Trekking southward from Slovakia, one of the parachutists from Palestine, the twenty-four-year-old Abba Berdichev, hoped to bring some succour to the Jews of Rumania, his birthplace. 'I hope', he had written before leaving Palestine, 'that this time luck will be with me, because the desire and determination to fulfil my duty as a Jew is still strong.' Berdichev was captured while still in Slovakia, charged with spying and sabotage, and shot.[56]

At Birkenau, two separate policies were in effect. Simultaneously with the arrival of Jews from the Lodz ghetto, Rhodes, Kos, and from Slovakia, most of whom were gassed, other trains continued to take Jews from the barracks at Birkenau to the factories and labour camps of Germany. On August 29, while seventy-two sick Jewish adults and youths and several pregnant women from a labour camp at Leipzig, were brought to Birkenau and gassed, 807 Jews were sent from Birkenau to the concentration camp at Sachsenhausen, just north of Berlin, for work in a dozen nearby factories. On August 30, a further five hundred Hungarian Jews were sent by train from Birkenau to Buchenwald, to be sent on to a Junkers aircraft factory at Markkleeberg.[57] Others Jews were kept in Buchenwald, from where, as one young Jew from the Lodz ghetto, Michael Etkind, later recalled, 'no one escaped. No one was missing – except the dead.'[58]

Even as more and more Jews were being taken out of Birkenau to the factories and camps of western Germany, all four gas-chambers of Birkenau continued to be operated without respite. On August 30 there was a total of 874 prisoners employed in the Sonderkommando, burning the bodies in the crematoria. A day shift and a night shift ensured that the fires were always blazing. A further four hundred prisoners were employed burning bodies in trenches.[59]

However close Germany might be to defeat, the evil 'selections' went on. Among the new arrivals at Birkenau in early September were 1,019 Jews sent from Holland who reached Birkenau on September 5, of whom 549 were gassed.[60] Dr Gisella Perl, who watched these Dutch deportees arrive, later recalled 'a group of well-dressed, white-bearded gentlemen go by, fully dressed, with hats and gloves and well-cut overcoats. They carried fine plaid blankets and small overnight cases in their hands, like diplomats going to some important conference.' These were 'rich people', Gisella Perl was later told, 'who had been able to hide until now, thanks to their money and connections'. Most were gassed. 'Only a very few came out of the selection alive,' she recalled, 'dressed in rags like the rest of us.' Her account continued:

A few days later I spoke to one of these newcomers. He worked on the refuse heap near the crematorium. In that short time, the elegant, well-groomed man, who had looked like a diplomat, had become a dirty, lice-infected, human wreck, his spirits broken. He was a Dutchman and he spoke German.

I saw him go over to one of the camp foremen and whisper to him under his breath, anxiously, hurriedly. The foreman looked at him expectantly, and the new prisoner reached under his rags and brought out a small leather pouch, the kind which usually holds tobacco. He opened it with trembling hands and shook the contents into his palm.

Like a million little suns the diamonds shone and sparkled in his dirty, broken-nailed hands. Grinning broadly, the foreman nodded and held out three miserable uncooked potatoes, and the elderly man, shaking with impatience, tore them out of his hand and put them to his mouth, chewing, swallowing, as if every bite gave him a new lease of life. The little pouch full of diamonds already rested in the pocket of the foreman and he kept his hand on it, caressing the stones almost tenderly.

Here, in this Stock Exchange of Hell, the value of a bag of diamonds was three uncooked potatoes. And this value was the real one. Three potatoes had positive value, they prolonged life, gave strength to work and to withstand beatings, and strength meant life, even if for a short time only. The bag of diamonds itself was good for nothing. For a while, a short while, it might delight the eyes of a ruthless murderer, but when the day of reckoning came – it would not save his life.[61]

It was not only new arrivals who had to go through the selection procedure. Those who, like Lena Berg, had been in the barracks for many months, were also subjected to repeated selections. 'One after the other the women would be ordered to strip,' she later recalled. 'Sores to the right; abscesses to the right; rashes to the right; flabby breasts to the right. Eye-glasses to the right.' A chain formed by camp officials holding hands 'separated the rejected from the more fortunate inmates'. Lena Berg's account continued:

Half an hour later those selected to die would be marched slowly to Barrack 25. An hour before, they had all been fighting for a piece of bread, for an assignment to a Kommando, for a thousand and one other trivial things living people are concerned with. Now it was all over. The kapo would be very impatient: why did such carrion move so slowly? And she would urge them on with kicks and abuse.

Barrack 25 got no food. Prisoners sat there locked up for hours, sometimes for days, without food, without a swallow of water, without toilet facilities, dying before their deaths. For Auschwitz was governed by a strict rule: Berlin always had to confirm the gassing of those selected and, occasionally, confirmation was delayed. Berlin had plenty of other things to attend to.

From that death barrack came screaming and lamentation, 'Water, for God's sake, a little water.' But no one responded. No one walked over to that barrack, no one ever gave the dying water. Helplessly, hands stretched out between the bars, imploring, but in vain. Barrack 25 was taboo.

When it was dark the trucks came for them, headlights flashing, engines roaring up, then silenced. When the engines started again, there was the screaming, the last horrible cries of the women taken to the gas-chamber.[62]

On September 6, at Birkenau, Salmen Gradowski, a member of the Sonderkommando, who had been in Auschwitz since February 1943, collected together the notes which he had managed to write over the previous nineteen months, describing his deportation and first day at the camp, and buried them. He chose one of the pits of human ashes in which to bury them, explaining in a covering letter: 'I have buried this under the ashes, deeming it the safest place, where people will certainly dig to find the traces of millions of men who were exterminated.' Gradowski dedicated his notes to the members of his family 'burnt alive at Birkenau', his wife Sonia, his mother Sara, his sisters Estera-Rachel and Liba, his father-in-law Rafael and his brother-in-law Wolf. In his covering letter he wrote:

Dear finder, search everywhere, in every inch of soil. Tens of documents are buried under it, mine and those of other persons, which will throw light on everything that was happening here. Great quantities of teeth are also buried here. It was we, the Kommando workers, who expressly have strewn them all over the terrain, as many as we could, so that the world should find material traces of the millions of murdered people. We ourselves have lost hope of being able to live to see the moment of liberation.[63]

37

September 1944: the Days of Awe

BY THE FIRST WEEK OF SEPTEMBER 1944, the Slovak uprising was in its most desperate days. For the remnants of the Jewish communities of Slovakia, particularly those which were far from the centre of the revolt, fear of reprisals cast a dark shadow on many towns, among them Topolcany. Hardly had the German forces reimposed their authority in Topolcany than the Einsatzkommando unit of 150 men, commanded by an SS captain, Dr Hauser, entered the town.

Slovak Fascists who had 'disappeared' during the rebellion now re-emerged and reported for duty with the Einsatzkommando: thirty-seven of them were to join in the attempt to achieve what the Einsatzkommando described as the 'final solution of the Jewish question in Topolcany'. The first effort of the SS was to lull the Jews into a false sense of security. Their spiritual leader, Rabbi Haberfeld, was summoned by Captain Hauser and told that prayers could now be held in the Great Synagogue. Hauser gave the rabbi an assurance that nothing would happen to the Jewish community. Later that same day, Hauser summoned representatives of the community, telling them to go back to work and to normal life.

Even as these assurances were being given, the Germans arrested one of the leaders of the Jewish community, Karl Pollak, a former deputy mayor of the town, his wife, and one other Jewish family from a nearby village. After being held in the district prison for a few days, they were taken out and killed. On September 6, Moritz Hochberger was killed when he tried to escape the clutches of a number of SS men.

At noon on September 8 the 'action' began. Men of the Einsatz-kommando, together with their Slovak auxiliaries, broke into the homes of all Jews and dragged them to the SS headquarters. Few families, at most forty persons, managed to flee their homes and go into hiding. That afternoon the Jews of Topolcany were deported to the concentration camp at Sered.

Even as the deportation was in progress, Slovak peasants betrayed four Jews who were hiding in a farm outside the town. A detachment of the Einsatzkommando was sent down to the farm, where all four Jews were murdered.

For the next two days, peasants searched for Jews in hiding, and on September 10, fifty-two Jews who had been caught in hiding places were brought to an open field. There they were ordered to dig a deep pit, before being murdered by the Germans and their Slovak helpers. The corpses were then thrown into the pit. Among the dead were six children. The smallest was a three-month-old baby from the Linkenberg family.[1]

Rescue and slaughter marched hand in hand during the twilight days of the Reich. On September 3, as the result of a suggestion first put forward by Churchill's son Randolph, the evacuation began, by air, of 650 German, Austrian and Czech Jews from the partisan-held areas of Yugoslavia, to Allied-occupied Italy.[2] Also in Italy, in the German-held port of Fiume, now under German control, the Germans arrested a senior Italian police officer, Giovanni Palatucci, who had helped more than five hundred Jewish refugees who had reached Italy from Croatia, by giving them 'Aryan' papers and sending them to safety in southern Italy.[3] Palatucci was sent to Dachau, where he died.[4]

Jews were also active in their own defence: in Budapest, on September 7, the Hungarian authorities allowed Otto Komoly, a Jew who had been decorated for heroism in the Austro-Hungarian army during the First World War, to rent a number of buildings in the capital for the protection of Jewish children, under the aegis of the International Red Cross. Helped by two Polish Jews, Dr Osterweil and Sholem Offenbach, both of them refugees in Hungary, Komoly gave protection to five thousand children in more than thirty-five protected buildings. Like Palatucci in Fiume, however, Komoly did not escape the penalty for courage. Within four months of his scheme being put into effect, he was seized and murdered by Hungarian Fascists.[5]

Also in September 1944, shortly before the Red Army entered

Przemysl, Yosef Buzhminsky saw, in a courtyard, 'a little girl about six years old playing there. Gestapo and SS men arrived, surrounded the courtyard. It was a Polish family consisting of eight people. They began whipping the girl, and then they executed all of them right there in the courtyard.' The Polish family had hidden the Jewish girl. It was for that 'crime' that they, and the girl, were shot.[6]

On September 9, a group of thirty-nine Dutchmen, one American and seven Englishmen, all of them active in the anti-Nazi underground, were brought to Mauthausen. After spending the night inside the bunker they were driven, barefoot and in their underclothes, to the quarry, 'where' as the historian of Mauthausen has written, 'the 186 steps were lined on both sides by SS and Kapos swinging their cudgels and anticipating a spectacle.' The forty-seven prisoners were 'loaded with stone slabs of up to sixty pounds in weight, and then forced to run up the steps. The run was repeated again and again, and the blows fell faster and faster as the exhausted prisoners stumbled on the uneven steps.' One of the prisoners was a British Jew, Marcus Bloom, who had operated a clandestine radio in Nazi-occupied Europe. He, the historian noted, 'was the first to fall'.

Bloom was shot in the head at point-blank range.[7]

On September 17, as the Red Army drove through eastern Hungary, the Germans began to evacuate the labour camp at Bor, where thousands of Jews had worked, and many died, in the copper mines.

When the 'death march' from Bor reached Cervenka, the marchers were driven into the kiln of a brick works. There, six hundred were shot. That same day, about sixty more were shot on the march itself.[8] At Gyor, on November 4, hundreds of the exhausted survivors were either beaten to death or shot, their bodies being thrown into a mass grave which they themselves had been forced to dig. Among those whose bodies were found in this grave when it was uncovered in 1946 was Miklos Radnoti, a thirty-five-year-old poet, whose poems during the war years had graphically portrayed the impending disaster in Hungary.[9]

More than five thousand Jews had set off on this march to Belgrade, then to Austria, and finally to the concentration camps of Flossenburg and Buchenwald. Only nine survived the war.[10]

September 18 marked the eve of the Jewish New Year 5705. Three days earlier, at Birkenau, fourteen hundred Jewish boys in their early teens had been taken to the special Children's Block. They were kept there for three days, until the Jewish New Year. One of those who witnessed the 'action' that day was the fourteen-year-old Josef Zalman Kleinman. The SS 'began loading them into trucks', he later recalled, 'and the screams were terrible: "Hear! O Israel!" "Mother", "Father" – this took several hours. I had never heard anything like it. In Auschwitz usually, during summer, the people were taken to the gas-chambers by the hundreds of thousands, those people did not know where they were being led. But we, who had already become veterans of the camp – we knew. . . .'[11]

There were other 'veterans' in Birkenau who had no chance of survival. These were the 'mussulmen', Jews in the last stage of starvation. Dr Aharon Beilin, who had been sent to Birkenau from Bialystok in the autumn of 1943, has recalled their symptoms, and their fate:

> They began speaking about food. Usually this was a taboo. Two things were taboo – crematoria and food. Food – that was a reflex, a conditioned reflex; because whenever people spoke about food the secretion of digestive acids would increase, and people tried not to speak about food. As soon as a person lost that self-control and began remembering the good food which he used to have at home in the good old times, such a talk was called a 'mussulman conversation'.
>
> That was the first stage, and we knew that within a day or two, he would enter the second stage. There was not such a rigorous division, but he would stop taking an interest in his surroundings and would also cease reacting to orders, and his motions would become very slow, his face frozen like a mask. He would no longer have control over his bowels. He would relieve himself where he was. He was not even turning over when he lay down.
>
> And thus he entered the 'mussulmanship'. It was a skeleton with bloated legs. And these people, because they wanted to drag them from the blocks to the roll call, they were placed forcibly next to the wall with their hands above their heads, their face to the wall for support, and it was a skeleton with grey face that would lean against the wall, swaying back and

forth. They had no sense of balance. That was the typical mussulman, who would be taken afterwards by the 'skeleton' Kommando with the real bodies.[12]

On September 19, in the Baltic, Soviet troops approached Klooga camp, where more than three thousand Jews, Russians and Estonians were being used as forced labourers. The SS acted once more to prevent their victims, the witnesses of their crimes, from being rescued. Almost all the Klooga inmates were killed, among them fifteen hundred Jews who had been brought to the camp in 1943 from the Vilna ghetto, eight hundred Soviet prisoners-of-war, and seven hundred Estonian political prisoners. Only eighty-five survived. At nearby Lagedi camp, 426 Jews, among them many children and babies, were murdered only a few hours before the first Red Army soldiers entered the camp.[13]

At Birkenau, following the gassing of four hundred thousand Hungarian Jews in the summer of 1944, there was a substantial reduction in the number of trains reaching the camp, so much so that during September the SS decided to reduce the number of Sonderkommando prisoners. On September 24, two hundred men of the Sonderkommando were forced into freight cars at the ramp in Birkenau under the pretence of being sent to work at some distant camp. They were in fact taken to Auschwitz Main Camp, where they were gassed. That night their bodies were brought back to Birkenau, and burned.

The Sonderkommando was now reduced to 661 men. A hundred were housed in each of the attics of Crematoria II and III. The remaining 461, who worked in Crematoria IV and V, and at the cremation pits, slept in the large unused 'dressing room' of crematorium IV.[14] In the nightmare world that Nazism had created, one of the cruellest tasks of all was that imposed upon the Jews of the Sonderkommando.

The days between the Jewish New Year and the Day of Atonement mark the 'Days of Awe' in the Jewish calendar. Some Jewish sentiment maintains that only the virtuous die on the Day of Atonement. At Birkenau, many were to die that day, between the opening hours of the fast on the evening of September 26, and its ending twenty-four hours later.

Even before the fast began, there was a 'selection' of a thousand young boys, who had been told that, in preparation for the Day of Atonement, extra bread would be distributed: a third of a loaf instead of a fifth of a loaf, and also cheese. 'There had never been anything like it at Auschwitz,' Josef Kleinman later recalled. 'We were very happy that we could eat and then fast properly on the next day.' Then, at three o'clock in the afternoon, the boys were ordered back into Birkenau. Kleinman has recalled the sequel:

The preparations were very intensive. The chief clerk and other clerks were there. All the block seniors, they all gathered and arranged us in groups of a hundred. Somebody spread a rumour that we were to be taken to collect the potato harvest in the area so we were arranged in these groups of a hundred. There were two thousand of us altogether.

All of a sudden a tremble passed through the parade ground like an electric current. The angel of death appeared. Dr Mengele appeared on his bicycle. Somebody approached him, took his bicycle and leaned the bicycle near the barrack. I was in a group right near the road and I saw that. He put his hands behind his back, his lips as usual were tightly closed, he went to the centre of the parade ground, lifted his head so that he could survey the whole scene and then his eyes landed on a little boy about fifteen years old. Perhaps only fourteen years old or something like that. He was not far from me in the first row. He was a boy from the Lodz ghetto. I remember his face very well. He was blond, very thin and very sunburnt. His face had freckles. He was standing in the first line when Mengele approached him and asked him, 'How old are you?' The boy shook and said, 'I am eighteen years old.'

I saw immediately that Dr Mengele was very furious and started shouting, 'I'll show you. Bring me a hammer and nails and a little plank.' So somebody ran immediately and we were standing and looking at him completely silent. A deathly silence prevailed on the parade ground. He was standing in the middle and everyone was watching him. In the meantime, the man with the hammer and the nails arrived.

When the man with the tools was standing near Dr Mengele, Mengele approached another boy. He was a tall boy in the first row. His face was round and he looked quite well. Mengele approached him, grabbed him by the shoulder and led him to the goal post which was on that field. It was a regular football field. There were two goal posts. He led this boy by the shoulder and the man with the plank and the tools and the hammer also followed them. He put the boy near the goal post and gave orders to nail the plank above the boy's head so that it was like the letter L only in reverse. Then he ordered the first group to pass under the board. The first group of boys started going in single file.

We had no explanations. We understood that the little ones who did not reach the board, who were not tall enough, would be taken to their death.

It could have had no other meaning. It was one hundred per cent clear to everyone what the purpose of this game was. We all began stretching. Everyone wanted to get another half inch, another centimetre. I also stretched as much as I could but I despaired. I saw that even taller boys than myself did not attain the necessary height. Their heads did not touch the plank.

Single file they passed under the plank and whoever was too short would be set aside and taken with the little ones who were doomed to go to their death.

My brother was standing near me. I was so busy with myself that I didn't even have time to think about him. He was tall. This was his sixteenth birthday.

I was standing there quite desperately. I thought this was the end of my life and all of a sudden my brother whispered to me, 'You want to live. Do something.' As if I had awoken from a dream, I started looking for a way of rescue. My brain worked quickly. All of a sudden my eyes saw some stones near me. Perhaps this could be my rescue. We were all standing at attention in these lines and I bent down without being noticed, I picked up a few small rocks, I opened my shoe laces and started stuffing my shoes with little stones. I had shoes which were a little too big for me. I stuffed them with stones under my heel and this added about an inch to my height.

I thought this might be enough. Then I saw that I could not stand at attention with these stones in my shoes and I told my brother that I was going to throw away the stones. But my brother said not to throw them away that he would give me something. He gave me a hat which I tore in two and stuffed into the shoes. This made it a little softer so that I could stand.

I stood there for about ten minutes with these shoes full of stones and rags and I thought maybe I could make it. Then after about ten minutes all the boys would be passing under the board. Two would make it and two wouldn't. I stood there and finally my brother kept looking at me and said, 'No, it's not enough yet.' I was afraid that maybe out of excitement it would be difficult and they would notice that I have something in my shoes. My brother asked another boy in the third row to estimate my height. They all looked at me and said that I had no chance of making the proper height.

I started looking for another device to escape and hide among those tall boys who had already gone under the board and had passed the selection.

They were in groups of a hundred on the other side of football ground. And the little ones who were too short, they were on the extreme other side. And the little ones always tried to break away.

I tried to infiltrate into the groups of the big boys. I thought maybe I was safe. But then another boy tried to infiltrate and Dr Mengele noticed that and he started shouting at the guardsmen and Kapos, 'What are you doing? This is sabotage.' And he ordered the entire group to be taken and again passed under the board. When I heard this, when we were taken again to the board, I again escaped on the way into my old place, in my old group. It was a narrow passage and I managed to infiltrate this old group.

I thought that maybe I would live for another half hour with that illusion. Then after fifteen minutes I again fled into the group of the big boys. Nobody noticed this. And this is how the selection was ended. One thousand boys did not make the grade.

Those who did not make the grade were taken to barracks 25 and 26 and then darkness fell. They were kept locked in these two barracks until about two days after the Day of Atonement.

They were led to the gas-chambers. They were destroyed in the gas-chambers. Only a thousand boys survived.

'There was an impression', Joseph Kleinman concluded, 'as though Dr Mengele wanted to show, "It says in the Jewish prayers for Rosh Hashana and Yom Kippur that the Jews are like sheep who are led under the rod." And that he was the man who was leading us under the rod.'[15]

The selection of one thousand boys at Birkenau on Yom Kippur was part of the 'Goebbels calendar'. Dr Aharon Beilin, who was in Birkenau for more than a year, later recalled: 'A Goebbels calendar, that meant that every Saturday and every Jewish holiday, they would empty the sick infirmary, and the blocks of mussulmen who did not go to work – they were taken away. And we had forgotten, on the eve of the Day of Atonement 1944, that it was a day from the Goebbels calendar. So, that day also, the mussulmen's block was emptied, and the mussulmen taken to the gas-chamber.'[16]

Leon Szalet also recalled that Day of Atonement in Birkenau:

> The moon shone through the window. Its light was dazzling that night and gave the pale, wasted faces of the prisoners a ghostly appearance. It was as if all the life had ebbed out of them. I shuddered with dread, for it suddenly occurred to me that I was the only living man among corpses.
>
> All at once the oppressive silence was broken by a mournful tune. It was the plaintive tones of the ancient 'Kol Nidre' prayer. I raised myself up to see whence it came. There, close to the wall, the moonlight caught the uplifted face of an old man, who, in self-forgetful, pious absorption, was singing softly to himself. . . .
>
> His prayer brought the ghostly group of seemingly insensible human beings back to life. Little by little, they all roused themselves and all eyes were fixed on the moonlight-flooded face.
>
> We sat up very quietly, so as not to disturb the old man, and he did not notice that we were listening. . . .
>
> When at last he was silent, there was exaltation among us, an exaltation which men can experience only when they have fallen as low as we had fallen and then, through the mystic power of a deathless prayer, have awakened once more to the world of the spirit.[17]

'I remember one day when we were in Auschwitz,' Sala Kaye has recalled, 'my mother heard that it was Yom Kippur – the Day of Atonement. She took our pieces of bread in the morning and did not let us eat until sunset. I remember that it was a very hot day. At evening one of the Jewish girls, who was an overseer, gave us a candle and before our meal of bread we lit it. I believe that my mother's faith helped us to survive. And yet my father, who was so religious, did not survive.' Nor did Sala Kaye's sister Towa, killed in an air raid in the very first days of the war in 1939, nor her oldest brother, Joseph, in hiding near Radom, denounced to the Germans by Poles 'one day before the liberation', and killed.[18]

A sixteen-year-old Jewish boy from Transylvania, Nahum Hoch, recalled sixteen years later how, in Birkenau, at the end of that Day of Atonement in 1944 he tried, having fasted all day, to get some extra food. 'I did not get it,' he explained, 'I merely tried,' and he added:

> The upper part of my body was put in an oven – the type they had there in Auschwitz – and I was beaten on the lower part of my body, with a stick which was very thick, the sticks which they used to carry the lunch pails. At first they gave me ten strokes. I fainted; water was poured on me; then the second group of ten blows was delivered; I fainted again – again they poured water on me, until I received twenty-five blows.
>
> I could not move any more; they left me right there and, to this day, I can only sit on the left side and cannot sit on the right side because of these blows. The bones were not broken, but I have a piece of flesh completely mutilated – a red wound – to this very day.[19]

Among the Jews who were in labour camps in Germany on that Day of Atonement in 1944 was Levi Shalit. At the age of twenty-eight, he had survived the Shauliai ghetto and Stutthof. Now, near Dachau, he was forced to work, with thousands of other Jews, building a vast underground refuge for the bombed Messerschmidt aeroplane factory. Later he recalled how:

> Someone takes his stand near a tree, leans as if at the Holy Ark, and in the midst of fear and silence begins: 'By the Heavenly Court . . . Kol Nidrei. . . .'
> We gather closer to the cantor, a young Hungarian lad. Lips murmur after him – quiet, quiet, muffled words hardly manage to pass, remain sticking in the throat. Here stands Warsaw's last rabbi, his face yellow, hairless, wrinkled, his aged body bent; his hands are rocking like reeds in the wind; only the eyes,

sparkling stars, look out towards the cold sky above, and his lips, half open, murmur softly.

What does he say now, how does he pray, this last of the rabbis of Warsaw? Does he lovingly accept the pain and suffering, or does he, through the medium of his prayer, conduct a dispute with the Almighty, asking him the ancient question: is this the reward for faith?

Huddling to the cantor stands Alter der Klinger, the Kovno cab driver. His broad shoulders lean against a young tree and his mouth emits staccato sounds as if they were hummed out of his inside. No, he does not beg; he does not pray; he demands! He demands his rights, he calls for justice. Why were his children burnt by the Nazis, why was his wife reduced to ashes? He hums mutely, without words. He does not know the words, is not capable of saying the prayers by heart. Does the Lord require words? He requires the heart. Where, then, is His hearty, divine mercy? Since Alter, the cab driver, can't find this mercy, he hums in revolt against the Almighty.

Here stands Consul Naftel, his face drawn and worn. With his bowed head his figure reminds one of a bent thorn. Why does he cling so closely to the cantor? Why doesn't he want to miss a single word? Has he become so pious?

But, what difference does it make why Naftel called out to God near the crematorium of Dachau – he took poison on the day after Yom Kippur.[20]

The Day of Atonement passed, and the gassing at Birkenau continued. Of 2,499 Jews sent from Theresienstadt to Birkenau on September 28, more than a thousand were gassed.[21] Of a further 1,500 Jews sent from Theresienstadt on September 29, 750 were gassed.[22] Of 1,500 sent to Birkenau on October 1, more than a thousand were gassed.[23] From the transport sent from Theresienstadt on October 4, all women with children were sent to the gas-chambers.[24] From a further transport which left Theresienstadt two days later, on October 6, all those who were sick, all women with children, and everyone over forty-five, was gassed.[25]

One of those who reached Birkenau from Theresienstadt in the first week of October was Alfred Oppenheimer, a forty-three-year-old Jew who had lived in Luxembourg since 1926. Of the 723 Jews in Luxembourg who had not fled in 1940, only 35 survived.

Oppenheimer was one of them. His wife had died in Theresienstadt. At the 'selection' at Birkenau, a Jew who was with Oppenheimer on the journey, a former Czechoslovak ski champion, gave his current profession, lawyer. He was sent to join those about to be gassed. Oppenheimer, warned a few moments earlier by a veteran prisoner to whom he had given his watch, said he was 'a fine mechanic' by profession. He also, as advised, reduced his age, from forty-three to thirty-eight. He was sent to the barracks, and he survived, being sent shortly afterwards to one of the factories at Gleiwitz.[26]

In liberated Kiev, on September 29, Jews gathered to mark the third anniversary at Babi Yar. Among those who wished to commemorate their murdered relatives was Sara Tartakovskaya, whose father, mother and sisters had been among the murdered. 'We came to the place of execution, to Babi Yar', she later recalled, 'and descended there, to the bottom. We were gathering the burnt bones of arms, legs. I drew out from the slope, by its hair, which was not burnt, a girl's head with the remains of a scarf stuck to it. The head had two plaits, pins, and a hole in the temple. I was standing weeping: she could be my sister.'[27]

38

Revolt at Birkenau

AT BIRKENAU the Jews of the Sonderkommando were preparing to revolt. It was an enterprise of supreme hazard, and of supreme courage. Those men who dragged to the crematorium the bodies of their fellow Jews who had been gassed and were then forced to scatter their ashes on the barracks paths, and in the nearby ponds, were themselves murdered in strict rotation. 'I have wanted to live through it', one of them, a Greek Jew working at Crematorium II, wrote shortly before the revolt, 'to take a revenge for the death of my father, my mother, my beloved sister Nella.'[1] More than three hundred Greek Jews were among the Sonderkommando preparing for revolt, among them Errera de Larissa, a former lieutenant in the Greek army.[2]

In the nearby Union explosives factory, a group of Jewish girls had collected small amounts of explosives and smuggled them to the plotters. Among the girls were Giza Weissblum and Raizl Kibel, both of whom survived the war. The preparations, Raizl Kibel later recalled, 'were in connection with rumours that at the last moment, as the front approaches the camp, the SS may want to annihilate everybody by blowing up the camp'.[3]

Three girls in the Union factory, Ella Garnter, and two girls known only by their first names, Toszka and Regina, managed to smuggle explosives into Birkenau.[4] They handed them to a girl who was working inside Birkenau, Roza Robota, who passed them on to Wrobel, a member of the Sonderkommando. Two other Jewish prisoners were also privy to the plot, Israel Gutman and Jehuda Laufer.

Explosives were passed out of the Union factory hidden in a false bottom of a food tray. Israel Gutman has recalled how, on one such occasion:

When I was standing near my friend he told me that there was a search going on. He told me that he had not time to put the explosives in the saucers and that the explosives were on his body in a cigarette package. I knew quite well that not only we would be killed as retaliation, but all the underground of Auschwitz was jeopardized.

When they carried out the search they felt that I was trembling and they then searched me very thoroughly. When they didn't find anything then they didn't really look at my friend. Somehow or other they skipped him. Since I was a little excited they thought that I was the one who had explosives and not him.[5]

Inside the Sonderkommando, Salmen Lewental coordinated the plans for revolt. His record, written at the time in a small notebook and then buried in a jar under the earth, is the principal source for the events of 7 October 1944.

The Birkenau camp records show that four days earlier, on October 3, the number of Jews in the Sonderkommando at Crematorium II was 169, divided into a day shift and a night shift. At Crematorium III there were also 169 Sonderkommando on October 3, likewise divided, and at Crematorium IV a total of 154, also in two shifts. With the gassing at Birkenau coming to an end, the Sonderkommando were alert to any indication that their days too might be numbered, they who in their gruesome task were given the privilege of ample food and blankets, and such 'comforts' as they might need in their barracks.

On the morning of Saturday, October 7, the senior Sonderkommando man at Crematorium IV was ordered to draw up lists for 'evacuation' of three hundred men at noon that same day. Fearing that this was a prelude to destruction, he refused to do so. The SS ordered a roll-call for noon. The purpose of the roll-call, the Jews were told, was that they were to be sent away by train to work in another camp. As the SS Staff Sergeant called out their numbers, however, only a few men answered.

After repeated calls and threats, Chaim Neuhof, a Jew from Sosnowice who had worked in the Sonderkommando since 1942, stepped forward. He approached the SS Staff Sergeant, talked to him, and gesticulated. When the SS man reached for his gun, Neuhof, loudly yelling the password, 'Hurrah', struck the SS man on the head with his hammer. The SS man fell to the ground. The other prisoners then echoed Neuhof's 'Hurrah' and threw stones at the SS.[6]

Reporting these events at Crematorium IV, Salmen Lewental noted, of his fellow Sonderkommando:

> ... they showed an immense courage refusing to budge [from the spot]. They set up a loud shout, hurled themselves upon the guards with hammers and axes, wounded some of them, the rest they beat with what they could get at, they pelted them with stones without further ado. It is easy to imagine what was the upshot of this. Few moments had passed when a whole detachment of SS men drove in, armed with machine guns and grenades. There were so many of them that each had two machine guns for one prisoner. Even such an army was mobilized against them.

Some of the Sonderkommando at Crematorium IV attacked the SS so viciously with axes, picks and crowbars that several SS men fell wounded and bleeding to the ground. Other SS men sought cover behind the barbed-wire fence, shooting at the prisoners with their pistols.

Some of the prisoners then managed to run into their empty barracks, where there were hundreds of straw mattresses on the wooden bunks. They set the mattresses on fire. The fire spread at once to the wooden roof of Crematorium IV.

'Our men,' Lewental noted, 'seeing they were brought to destruction, wanted to set fire to Cre[matorium] IV at the last moment and perish in battle, fall on the spot under the hail of bullets. And in this way, the whole crematorium went up in flames.'

The arrival of SS reinforcements on motorcycles, from the SS barracks inside Birkenau, brought the revolt at Crematorium IV to an end. All those who had acquired implements, and all who had set fire to the crematorium roof, were machine-gunned.

The blazing roof of Crematorium IV was seen by the Sonderkommando of Crematorium II. They took the flames as a sign that the revolt, for which they too had been preparing, had begun. Before they could act as planned, however, their well-prepared scheme was foiled by an accident of fate. At that very moment, a group of Soviet prisoners-of-war who were working in Crematorium II saw armed

SS men coming towards the crematorium. The Russians, Lewental noted, thought that the SS were coming 'just to take them away'. It was 'impossible', he added, 'to restrain them in this last moment'.

In panic, the Russians seized the leading Kapo, a German, 'and in a flash threw him alive into the burning furnace'. The Jews of the Sonderkommando, 'seeing', Lewental wrote, 'that they were faced with an accomplished fact, and realizing that retreat was no longer possible, decided to begin their revolt. Distributing such tools as they had been able to assemble, they cut the wire near their crematorium, and fled into the nearby countryside.' During the escape, the Jews killed three SS corporals, Rudolf Erler, Willi Freese and Josef Purke.[7]

The men at Crematorium II had used neither arms nor grenades. Some of them hoped to find an escape route through the adjoining area in which the 'Cleaning Installations' Commando was living. They were joined there by Sol Schindel, a Jew from the southern Polish city of Rzeszow, who worked in the 'Cleaning Installations' squad. Schindel later recalled how 'as we ran past the watch tower, I saw the SS men shooting with machine guns. I saw many dead already lying on the ground. I threw myself to the ground and crept through a hole in the barbed-wire fence into the women's camp.' There, Schindel met a Kapo from the 'Canal Cleaning' Commando, with whom he was on friendly terms, joined the squad, and managed to get back to the barracks. The Sonderkommando men continued beyond the wire, in search of somewhere to hide in the fields and farmsteads between Birkenau and the River Sol.

Within minutes of the break-out through the wire near Crematorium II, the alarm siren had sounded. Almost immediately, SS men with dogs drove up in trucks and surrounded the whole area of the break-out. Catching up with those who had managed to get beyond the wire, the SS gave no quarter. Most of the escapees were shot. The rest found brief sanctuary in a barn. Not wishing to take risks, the SS set fire to the barn, then shot the escapees as they ran out.

Only twelve of those who had escaped were still outside the wire, and alive. About two hundred and fifty had been killed outside the wire, among them their leader, Jozef Dorebus, known in the camp as Jozef Warszawski. Later that day, a further two hundred men of the Sonderkommando were shot inside Birkenau.[8]

There had also been preparations for revolt among the Sonder-

kommando of Crematorium III, across the ramp from Crematorium II. There, explosives had also been hidden, thanks to the girls at
the Union factory. Most of the prisoners were in the attic of their
barracks when the break-out from Crematorium II took place.
Coming out as they heard the sirens, they saw that SS troops had
surrounded 'their' crematorium. A few moments before the SS
entered their barrack, they were able to move the explosives from
their hiding place and pour them down the latrine. The leader of the
SS troops ordered all prisoners locked up in one room and the
barracks searched, but the explosives were not discovered. The men
of Crematorium III were then marched across the ramp to Crematorium II and ordered to burn the six hundred corpses that were still
lying in the gas-chamber. Later that afternoon, the bodies of those
who had been shot trying to escape from Crematorium II were
brought to Crematorium III, stripped, and burned in ovens.[9]

Twelve men from Crematorium II had not yet been recaptured.
SS patrols with dogs found them, exhausted, in an empty building
on the other side of the river. They were killed, and their bodies
brought back to Birkenau.[10]

On October 9 the SS arrested three Jewesses in the Union factory,
Ella Gartner, Toszka and Regina. On October 10 they arrested two
other women, one of them Roza Robota. Fourteen men from the
Sonderkommando who worked in Crematoria III and V were also
arrested on October 10, among them another of the leaders of the
revolt, Jankiel Handelsman, who, with Jozef Dorebus, had been
deported from Paris to Birkenau in March 1943.[11] All the arrested
men and women were tortured, but none broke under torture. None
of the men survived the interrogation, but Roza Robota managed to
smuggle out a message from the cell in which she was being held:
'You have nothing to fear – I shall not talk.' The note went on, Israel
Gutman later recalled, to tell her fellow conspirators 'that we
should continue our work, that she knew quite well what was in
store for her, and that others would not be involved'.[12]

Roza Robota and three other Jewish girls were hanged in the
women's camp at Birkenau on 6 January 1945. All the women then
in the camp were ordered to watch the execution. 'They went calmly
to their death,' Raizl Kibel later recalled. 'Despite the torture, they
betrayed no one.'[13] The last words Roza uttered were 'that
vengeance would come'.[14]

On 9 October 1944, two days after the revolt of the Sonderkommando at Birkenau, the Jews celebrated the festival of Simhat
Torah, the Rejoicing of the Law. Since the day of the revolt, 650
boys, most of them between fourteen and sixteen, had been locked
into two of the barracks. Most were from Hungary, the remnant of
those who had been brought from Hungary in May, June and July.

A number of these boys planned to break out. But when, at
midnight on October 9, one boy managed to climb up the pole in the
centre of the barracks, to a window near the roof, the guard at the
front door of the barracks saw him. The escape bid was foiled. On
October 20, all 650 boys were then taken to the undressing room,
and ordered to undress. One of those 650, Nahum Hoch, later
recalled the cruel sequel:

> Some of us were frozen − we could not utter a word; like
> myself − I could not speak a syllable. Others began reciting a
> confessional prayer, and others sang. They took us through a
> little ante-chamber, opened a great door and put us into this
> hall. In the hall it was completely dark except for a small beam
> of light at the foot of the door by which we had entered.
>
> They shut the door behind us, and I heard the weeping for
> the first time. After some time − I don't know whether it was a
> matter of seconds or minutes − they opened the door and told
> us to come out again, back to the same camp we had come
> from. We were led into one part of the hall, and the SS
> commander, a tall man − I think maybe it was Hoess but I don't
> know for sure − it was the same officer who had first separated
> me from Dad when I arrived at the camp − he called out the first
> boy in the line, grabbed hold of him, felt his muscles and
> ordered him to do ten knee-bends and then run to the wall and
> back; then he turned him around. We were facing left and he
> was turned to the right.
>
> Then he called another boy − the one who had climbed that
> pole. He happened to be from my town − Salmanovitch was his
> name. He asked him how old he was (he was a short boy). The
> boy answered: 'Nearly one hundred.' He said: 'You pig! Is
> that the way to speak to me? You'll be sent right back in
> there.'
>
> I was the third boy. I was frozen. I looked at him. He ordered
> me to do knee-bends, then run to the wall and back, and he sent

me to the right, too, like the other boy. In this way he selected fifty boys. In the middle of this selection process the other boys realized that a selection was taking place, and they began to slip across to the right side. The SS man separated us and would not let them cross to the other side, over to us.

Of the 650 boys who had been put through this 'selection', only the fifty who had been sent to the right were ordered to get dressed. They were then taken away to the railway line, to unload potatoes. The remaining 600 were gassed, among them Salmanovitch, the boy who had climbed the pole.[15]

Salmen Lewental recorded that day, in his notes, the fate of the boys. 'In the middle of a bright day,' he wrote:

> Six hundred Jewish boys aged from twelve to eighteen, dressed in long striped clothes, very thin; their feet were shod in worn-out shoes or wooden clogs. The boys looked so handsome and were so well built that even these rags did not mar their beauty.
>
> They were brought by twenty-five SS men, heavily burdened [with grenades]. When they came to the square the Kommandoführer gave the order for them to un[dress] in the square. The boys noticed the smoke belching from the chimney and at once guessed that they were being led to death. They began running hither and thither in the square in wild terror, tearing their hair [not knowing] how to save themselves. Many burst into horrible tears, [there resounded] dreadful lamentation.
>
> The Kommandoführer and his helper beat the defenceless boys horribly to make them undress. His club broke, even, owing to that beating. So he brought another and continued the beating over the heads until violence became victorious.
>
> The boys undressed, instinctively afraid of death, naked and barefooted they herded together in order to avoid the blows and did not budge from the spot. One brave boy approached the Kommandoführer [standing] beside us [. . .] and begged him to spare his life, promising he would do even the hardest work. In reply he hit him several times over the head with the thick club.
>
> Many boys, in a wild hurry, ran towards those Jews from the Sonderkommando, threw their arms around the latter's necks, begging for help. Others scurried naked all over the big square

in order to escape from death. The Kommandoführer called the Sergeant with a rubber truncheon to his assistance.

The young, clear, boyish voices resounded louder and louder with every minute when at last they passed into bitter sobbing. This dreadful lamentation was heard from very far. We stood completely aghast and as if paralysed by this mournful weeping.

With a smile of satisfaction, without a trace of compassion, looking like proud victors, the SS men stood and, dealing terrible blows, drove them into the bunker. The sergeant stood on the steps and should anyone run too slowly to meet death he would deal a murderous blow with the rubber truncheon. Some boys, in spite of everything, still continued to scurry confusedly hither and thither in the square, seeking salvation. The SS men followed them, beat and belaboured them, until they had mastered the situation and at last drove them [into the bunker]. Their joy was indescribable. Did they not [have] any children ever?[16]

39

Protectors and persecutors

ON 13 OCTOBER 1944, Soviet forces entered Riga, where yet another Jewish community had been destroyed, a community which in 1935 had numbered more than thirty thousand Jews. Among the few survivors were those Jews who had been hidden in various farms in the region by Yanis Lipke. On the day of liberation, three Jews whom Lipke had hidden on a farm outside the town, Dr Shmulian, Yuter Shnayder, and the eighteen-year-old Girshman, were discovered by the retreating Germans and shot. During the battle for liberation of Riga, three Latvians who lived in the same farm, Yan Miller and his sisters Elza and Lyda, were killed, victims of the last bombardment; non-Jews who had risked their lives to help Jews. Now, both rescued and rescuers were dead.[1]

Not far from Verona in nothern Italy, an Italian partisan detachment was in action against the Germans. Known as the 'Eagle' group, it had already fought in several bitter battles. Its leader was a twenty-three-year-old Jewish girl, Rita Rosani, who had been with the partisans for nearly a year. During the battle she was killed.[2] In Verona, a street has been named in her memory.

In Hungary, on October 15, the Arrow Cross Hungarian Fascist Organization seized power in Budapest. On the previous day, Admiral Horthy's government had promised to release Hanna Szenes and the other imprisoned Palestinian parachutists. Now the parachutists, and all 170,000 Budapest Jews, were again at risk, three months after the halting of the deportations to Auschwitz.

On October 16 the Germans returned to Budapest. The Nyilas, a Fascist group whose members had been arrested by Horthy in July, were released and armed.[3] They at once began to drag Jews from their houses and made them walk the streets, as Arie Breslauer recalled, 'with their hands above their heads'.[4] Then, for ten days,

Jews were forbidden to leave their houses. Women in labour could receive no help. The dead could not be buried. No food could be bought and no doctor summoned to attend the sick. At the same time, Nyilas gangs seized a large number of Jewish forced labourers in the Obuda suburb, drove them across the Margit and Chain bridges linking Obuda with Pest, and, while they were still on the bridge, shot them and threw their bodies into the waters of the Danube.[5]

On October 17, Adolf Eichmann returned to Budapest. He at once demanded fifty thousand able-bodied Jews to be marched on foot to Germany, to serve as forced labourers there. All the remaining Jews of Budapest, he wanted to be assembled in ghetto-like camps near the capital.[6] 'You see,' Eichmann told the Hungarian Jewish leader, Rudolf Kastner, 'I am back again. You forgot Hungary is still in the shadow of the Reich. My arms are long and I can reach the Jews of Budapest as well.' The Jews of Budapest, Eichmann added, 'will be driven out on foot this time'.[7]

These deportations began on October 20. Even as Soviet troops approached Budapest from the south-east, Jews from Budapest were marched westward, away from the advancing Soviet forces, to dig anti-tank trenches. Beginning on October 22, twenty-five thousand men and boys and ten thousand women and girls were taken, in four days, for this task. As the Red Army drew even closer, thousands of the marchers were shot or died.[8]

On October 23 the Hungarian government agreed to allow twenty-five thousand Jews to be sent to Germany for forced labour.[9] That same day, a poster issued in Budapest announced that all Jews with foreign passports or foreign nationality would be exempt from forced labour. The Swiss Consul, Charles Lutz, at once began issuing further documents, similar to those which he had issued in July, stating that the holder was to be regarded as a Swiss citizen, and appeared in a collective passport held at the Swiss Consulate. The Swedish representative in Budapest, Raoul Wallenberg, likewise continued to issue protective documents, about four and a half thousand in all.

Lutz, who worked closely with Wallenberg, was a career diplomat in the Swiss consular service. Aged forty-nine in 1944, he had served before the war both in the United States and in Palestine. As the Swiss Vice-Consul in Budapest, in charge of the department for safeguarding the interests of foreign governments who were not represented in the Hungarian capital, Lutz was able to issue protective documents to Jews who held British, Rumanian and other citizenships. On one occasion he issued a collective passport listing 957 'protected' Jews on a single Swiss passport.[10]

As Nyilas bands seized Jews throughout Budapest and marched them through the streets, more than seven and a half thousand protective documents were issued in a few days. But hundreds of Jews, taken by the Nyilas to the brick factory, were robbed of all their valuables. Their Swiss and Swedish documents were also taken away, as were the protective passes issued by the International Red Cross.

Within a few weeks, Charles Lutz had seventy-six buildings under Swiss diplomatic protection. More than twenty-five thousand Jews, finding shelter in them, were saved.[11] But for tens of thousands of Jews, driven towards the old Austrian frontier, on November 6, no diplomatic protests or stratagems were of use. Hundreds died of exposure and exhaustion, or were shot down where they fell. At Issaszeg, seven men who had reported sick were shot, and their wives were compelled to dig the graves for them. The women were then also shot.[12] A Jewish woman who was told of this incident later set down her own recollections of the marches. She had been driven out of Budapest for many miles, then brought back to the city:

> In the morning a group of swastika-wearers appeared and took us off to the party building in Stephanie Street. There we were undressed and maltreated. Our clothes, shoes and documents were taken away, and we were told time and again: 'Where you are going to be taken you will not need any of this.'
>
> Half-naked I was brought to the brick kiln at Buda-Ujlak. I lost all my strength, fell ill and ran a temperature of forty degrees centigrade. A few days later I was again taken together with nine hundred people to the party building at 4 Stephanie Street, where we were put into a cellar.
>
> The swastika-wearers began to ill-treat us and threaten that they would kill us off with gas. Twenty people went mad as a result of the ill-treatment. A few days later several people were released.

In spite of the fact that I was in possession of a 'Schutzpass', 'protection pass', the swastika-wearers took me to the brick kiln. When I arrived there I found many detainees, including sick people, children and other people in possession of 'protection passes'. Part of them, including myself, were taken to the synagogue in Tabak Street. On the way the swastika-wearers shot and murdered the sick and weak.[13]

Watching the long line of marchers, one Hungarian gendarme said to his companion, Paul Gidaly, a Jew who was masquerading as a non-Jew: 'This is cruel. Why don't they shoot them and toss them into the Danube instead of making them drag themselves miserably like this?'[14]

As many as thirty thousand Jews were driven from Budapest towards the old Austrian border. Their task, they were told, would be to construct an 'East Wall' for the defence of Vienna. At least seven thousand died, or were shot, on the march. But several hundred were saved when Raoul Wallenberg and Charles Lutz, travelling along the line of the march, reclaimed their respective wards, and distributed Swedish and Swiss protective passes.[15]

On October 15 the Germans evacuated Plaszow camp, in the eastern suburbs of Cracow. Some seven hundred of the twelve hundred Jews who had been working in Oscar Schindler's factory at Plaszow were sent by train, not to Schindler's new factory in the Sudetenland, but to the concentration camp at Gross Rosen. The journey took three days. 'We arrived in the afternoon,' Moshe Bejski later recalled. 'We had to take off our clothes. It was cold. We remained naked from six in the afternoon until about noon the following day. There was nowhere to sleep.'

After two days in Gross Rosen, the Plaszow evacuees were sent on to Brünnlitz, in the Sudetenland. There, Oscar Schindler, their saviour in his factory near Plaszow, had opened a munitions factory, to which he had earlier evacuated five hundred of the Jews who had been working in his factory near Plaszow. Now he insisted that the seven hundred other Plaszow evacuees were also badly needed, if the armaments so essential for the German war effort were to be produced. He submitted a list of the seven hundred to the

SS, noting against each name some impressive, but purely fictional, skill, describing them as engravers, locksmiths and technicians.

The women from Schindler's factory at Plaszow, some three hundred, had been evacuated, not to Gross Rosen, but to Auschwitz. Schindler at once sought their release, going personally to Auschwitz and bribing the Nazi officials there to let him take the three hundred women to his Sudetenland factory. There, they were able to rejoin their menfolk. Thus wives, daughters and even mothers were saved.

'Every day from October 18 to May 8 at midnight', Moshe Bejski later recalled, Schindler helped. 'I will not leave you until the last SS man has left the camp,' he told the Jews. 'If a Jew lost his glasses,' Bejski added, 'Schindler went and bought glasses.' Above the ration of a hundred grammes of bread, a bowl of so-called soup, and two cups of ersatz coffee each day, he provided extra rations. When a young Jewess became pregnant, an 'offence' punishable by death, Schindler went into Brno 'and bought the necessary surgical equipment, and the doctor in the camp made an abortion.'[16]

Amid the murder of hundreds of thousands of children, often selected personally for death by Dr Mengele, there was one tiny group, the remnants of the twins who had been sent to Mengele's special children's barracks. By October 1944 there were about two hundred surviving children and in half-hell, half-haven, awaiting Mengele's whim. That month, a high-ranking SS officer, visiting Birkenau, chanced upon the barracks in which these 150 Jews, mostly children, were living, relatively well-fed, so near to the slaughter of so many other thousands of children every week.

Shocked that any Jewish children at all were still alive, the SS officer ordered the 150 to stand outside their barracks. Ernest Spiegel, the twenty-nine-year-old twin who had been the eldest in the barracks since his arrival from Hungary five months earlier, sensed that something was wrong. 'He ran to the gate', several of the twins later recalled, 'and announced that he had a most urgent message for Dr Mengele'. When Mengele heard what was happening, 'he immediately ordered that "his" twins be returned to their barracks.'

From time to time the twins would be taken away for experiments, and some would never return. There were also moments of sadism and sudden death. One of the surviving twins, Moshe

Bleyer, later recalled: 'The SS guard killed my father, and my twin brother Tibi died at my feet.'[17]

Despite these horrors, the twins were a small, privileged and protected band among the sea of horror and destruction; Ernest Spiegel himself, their guardian, was the only Jew in Auschwitz who received a ration card entitling him to purchase cigarettes from the non-Jewish prisoners' store. Spiegel later recalled how:

> The twins were looked after by Mengele. He needed them so he took great care of them. He would receive questions about the twins from the Kaiser Wilhelm Institute in Berlin, and he would send them the answers. He needed the twins alive, and they would receive white bread. When the rains came, he made sure that they worked in shelter, that is, in the washrooms. Every Saturday afternoon they would receive clean shirts.[18]

Mengele protected his twins. But all other children had to die. On October 17 yet another 'selection' took place at Birkenau. Among those at the selection was a thirteen-year-old Hungarian girl, Eva Heyman. Eva's mother, Agnes Zsolt, after speaking to many survivors of that selection, later described it, and the part taken in it by Mengele himself, at one of his 'last and largest selections':

> If until then he directed his helpless victims towards the left or the right with a conductor's elegant movements, now he was not satisfied with the rows of victims lined up in front of their executioners, but he himself searched for them in possible hiding places. And, in fact, a good-hearted female doctor was trying to hide my child, but Mengele found her without effort.
>
> Eva's feet were full of sore wounds. 'Now look at you,' Mengele shouted, 'you frog, your feet are foul, reeking with pus! Up with you on to the truck!' He transported his human material to the crematorium on yellow-coloured trucks. Eye-witnesses told me that he himself had pushed her on to the truck.[19]

Eva Heyman was gassed that day or the next. Also murdered at Birkenau on or about October 18 was Gisi Fleischmann, the head of the women's Zionist movement in pre-war Slovakia, and, until her deportation to Birkenau in July or August 1944, a leader of wartime rescue attempts, especially for children.[20]

On October 20 there was another 'selection', mainly of Jews from Theresienstadt. The women had to enter a room naked, in single file. An SS doctor standing in the door gripped each woman by her arm and pushed her either into the next room, or to the other side of the room where other naked women, already selected for gassing, sat on a kind of gallery.[21] The next train from Theresienstadt, with 1,715 deportees, was made up mostly of women with children, and orphans from the children's home in Theresienstadt. Only 200 men and 51 women were selected for the barracks. The remaining 1,464 deportees were gassed.[22]

The last deportation from Theresienstadt to Birkenau, 'Transport Ev', took place on October 28, with 2,038 Jews packed into the cattle trucks.[23] That same day, a train from Bolzano in northern Italy reached Birkenau. From it, 105 women and 59 men were sent to the barracks, and 137 men were gassed.[24] The train from Theresienstadt, 'Transport Ev', reached Birkenau on October 30, after a two-day journey. Only 217 men and 132 women were sent to the barracks. The remaining 1,689 Jews were gassed.[25]

There now began the systematic destruction of the evidence. Ten days before the gassings of October 30, two small taxis and a prison car had brought a mass of documents to Crematorium III. These were the files about individual prisoners, death certificates, and charge sheets. All were burned.[26] The destruction of evidence went in parallel with the last weeks of human killing.

The human evidence of Birkenau's horrendous barracks was also being removed. Throughout October 1944, thousands of Jews were marched away from Birkenau to other camps, and to factories, in central and western Germany. These marches became a new form of torture, in which tens of thousands were to perish.

For many days, the marchers would be without food. Anyone who fell would be shot. 'On the road as we were marching,' the twenty-five-year-old Maria Rebhun later recalled, 'we heard one, two shots, and a body fell. I remember there was a young girl, a fourteen-year-old, tall, very good-looking, with her mother. They liked the daughter very much. There came the moment the mother couldn't walk. The girl supported her, tried to make her keep up with us, but to no avail. The Germans finally killed the mother. Two days later they killed the girl because she was so grief-stricken that she couldn't take it any longer.'[27]

One of the camps to which thousands of Jews were sent from Birkenau was Dachau. The seventeen-year-old Mordechai Ansbacher later recalled how, on arrival in Dachau, they were met by a group of SS men singing:

> Jews, go through the Red Sea.
> The waves close in,
> And the world is happy –
> Jews are drowned.

From Dachau, the Jews evacuated from Birkenau were sent on various work details. While waiting to be allocated work, they received neither food nor water. 'Most of the people were extremely weak,' Ansbacher recalled, 'and found it extremely difficult to hold out.'[28]

Another camp to which several thousand Jews were evacuated from Birkenau was Stutthof, near Danzig. 'We hoped that we were going to Germany for work,' Gedalia Ben Zvi, who had been born in Bratislava, later recalled, so that 'again hope flickered in our minds that perhaps the situation would be better.' But this hope was yet another illusion. 'As soon as we alighted from the carriages,' he recalled, 'then we were received by a shower of blows and this was exactly like Auschwitz.' The guards were mostly Germans, former criminals. 'By them we were beaten as soon as we arrived.'

Gedalia Ben Zvi's account continued:

> This was a transport of about a thousand or fifteen hundred people and up to the registration, which was three days later, only five hundred people were left. These people were detailed for all kinds of work – very hard work, which can't even be defined because it defies description.
>
> We had to work at the port and we had to unload sacks of stones from the ship and we had to empty those sacks full of stones under a shower of blows, dealt to us by the SS.
>
> As soon as people would try to run away, they would be shot immediately. The Germans would come over to a man who was not able to lift such a heavy weight and they would say to him: 'Sit down, rest a little, relax,' and they would speak kindly to him, and of course, once he sat down he was no longer able to get up, and then of course they would finish him off.
>
> In that camp, there were awful sanitary conditions. People

died of dysentery, of typhoid fever, every day, and the mortality rate was staggering. There was a women's camp near us and there were also the barbed-wire fences charged with electricity. We could get near the women's camp and we could see that amidst cold and snow, women would be lying in the camp without even a blanket and there was no roof. This way they would freeze.[29]

By the end of October 1944 the Red Army had driven the Germans from eastern Poland and from most of Hungary. In the recently liberated areas, the surviving Jews emerged from their hiding places and returned to their homes. The thirteen-year-old Icchak Soneson had returned with his parents and his younger sister to the village of Ejszyszki. In 1941, Ejszyszki had been the home of two thousand Jews. Only thirty had survived the massacres of the war. 'We kept together,' Soneson later recalled, 'we took a few flats in neighbouring houses. We did our best to rebuild our lives.' But on October 20 disaster struck. Polish Home Army men, known as 'White Poles' attacked the Jewish houses. Soneson's mother and baby brother were killed, as well as two Soviet soldiers.

'The Jews wanted revenge,' Soneson recalled. 'They got hold of arms and attacked the Poles. But the Soviets arrested these Jews, among them my father, who wanted to avenge the death of his wife and child.' Soneson's father was imprisoned by the Soviets in Kazakhstan, for five years; the young boy left Ejszyszki for Vilna, where he had been born, and eventually reached Palestine, as did his father. His mother and her son were among several thousand Jews, survivors of the Nazi terror, who were murdered after 'liberation'.[30]

'Do not imagine', another survivor, Joseph Feigenbaum, wrote to a friend in the West from the recently liberated town of Biala Podlaska on October 30, 'that the handful of Polish Jews who survived the massacres have been spared thanks to their cleverness or material resources. No! Death simply did not like them and left them in this vale of woe, so that they may go on struggling with dark and gloomy life while they are bereft, and broken in body and spirit.'[31]

In Warsaw, still held by German forces, a bunker was discovered on October 27, in which seven Jews, among them three Hungarians, were in hiding. The seven Jews, survivors of the Warsaw uprising, were armed, and opened fire. They were all killed.[32] Other Jews were only saved when non-Jews, at grave risk, gave them shelter. In November 1944 a Polish doctor, Stanislaw Switala, took into his hospital and sheltered seven of the former leaders of the Jewish Fighting Organization, among them Tuvia Borzykowski, Itzhak Zuckerman, and his girlfriend, Zivia Lubetkin.[33]

At Birkenau, the gas-chambers had ceased their work on October 31, and were slowly being dismantled. Not only the documents, but also the buildings of destruction were to be destroyed. When a train with more than five hundred Jews reached Birkenau on November 3, from the Slovak labour camp at Sered, the Birkenau administration office telephoned to Mauthausen: 'We have a transport here; could you handle it in your gas-chambers?' The answer was, 'That would be a waste of coal burnt in the locomotive. You should be able to handle the load yourself.'[34]

But Birkenau no longer had the apparatus for mass murder, and on November 6 the men from Sered were given their tattoo numbers, followed on November 7 by the women and children. The men were then sent to the factory zone at Gleiwitz, the women and children to the barracks. A twelve-year-old girl who survived this Sered transport later recalled that there were about a hundred and fifty children in the transport.[35]

On November 25, at Birkenau, the demolition of Crematorium II was begun. 'It is interesting', a member of the Sonderkommando wrote, 'that first of all the ventilating motor and pipes were dismantled and sent to camps – some to Mauthausen, others to Gross Rosen.' The writer added, in a note dated 'Today, November 26, 1944': 'We are going to the zone, 170 remaining men. We are sure that we are being led to die. They selected thirty persons who will remain in Crematorium V.'[36]

On November 26 the last 204 members of the Sonderkommando were murdered. 'I am going away calmly,' one of them, Chaim Herman, had written on November 6 to his wife and daughter in France, 'knowing that you are alive and our enemy is broken.'[37]

Throughout December, the remaining crematoria at Birkenau were dismantled, men breaking down the walls and women clearing away the rubble. At the same time, the cremating pits and the pits filled with human ash were covered up and planted with grass. Those Jews still in the barracks were also sent to work on the banks of the Vistula. 'We would stand for hours on end', Louise S. from Cluj later recalled, 'in wooden clogs in the water, at a time when it was already very cold. Most of the women died at this work, which was beyond their powers.' Back in the barracks at Birkenau 'we would fall on our beds weary to death, and could only be roused with sticks and clubs in the morning to continue this terrible rigorous work.'[38]

In the dwindling areas under German control, the killings continued. During November 1944 several of the Palestinian Jews who had been parachuted behind German lines were executed, Hanna Szenes in Budapest on November 7, Enzo Sereni in Dachau on November 18, and Havivah Reik in Kremnica two days later, together with Raffi Reiss and Zvi Ben Ya'acov.[39] A sixth parachutist, Peretz Goldstein, perished in Sachsenhausen, one of the first concentration camps of the Nazi era, and now, north of Berlin, being filled again with Jews evacuated from the regions about to be overrun by the Red Army.

In Budapest, the Fascist Nyilas continued their random slaughter. On November 6 they entered and pillaged a building in which many Jews had found shelter, killing nineteen Jews.[40] On November 15, as the marches from Budapest to the frontier continued, yet more Jews were taken from their homes in Budapest. 'My mother was put on the march,' Aviva Fleischmann later recalled. 'She could not walk. She had unhealthy feet. She dragged along for five days. She could not carry on. So they shot her dead.'[41]

On November 15, as the deportations from Budapest continued, the Hungarian authorities agreed to the establishment of an 'international ghetto' in the city, consisting of the seventy-two buildings assigned to house Jews under Swiss protection.[42] A week later, on November 22, those engaged in trying to protect as many Jews as possible in Budapest met in the Swedish Legation. Raoul Wallenberg was their host. Also present was Miklos Krausz, a Jew who represented the Swiss Legation, and the representatives, also Jewish, of the Portuguese and Spanish Legations, Dr Koerner and Dr Farkas.[43] Arie Breslauer, who was also present, recalled that Koerner and Farkas were rescuing Jews who had been converted to Catholicism.[44]

The meeting heard that nearly eight thousand Jews had already crossed into Germany, with two thousand more about to cross; that thirteen thousand Jews were marching, and would reach the frontier in the next three days, and that ten thousand Jews had 'disappeared' on the march.[45]

It was agreed to try to help those whose 'immunity letters' had been taken away from them at the brick factory, on the eve of the march. Breslauer was given the official stamp of the Swiss Consulate, a typewriter, and blank protective letters, and on November 23, with an assistant, Ladislaus Kluger, and a driver, drove through the night to the former Austrian border. For four days, Breslauer and Kluger gave out as many protective documents as they could, about three hundred in all. On their return to Budapest on November 28 they prepared a report of what they had seen: hundreds of Jews, locked in a barn, with no medical care and no food. 'Those who had money could get a cup of water.' Many were dying. 'I saw people who could still scream.' In the barn, twenty Jews died 'that night alone'.

Hungarian gendarmes had driven Breslauer from the barn. On the return journey to Budapest he saw a group of several hundred people: 'Most of them were old, or pregnant women who were just not fit for work.' He tried to get permission for them to return with him to Budapest, but this was refused. Nor was he allowed to speak to them. In Budapest, he enquired about them, hoping still to be able to help them. 'I later learned from an authoritative source that these people were taken to the Danube, were shot and killed, and thrown into the Danube river.'[46]

In Budapest, where 120,000 Jews still lived, the Nyilas gangs ruled the streets. On December 28 they entered the Jewish hospital and took away twenty-eight patients. Two days later, all twenty-eight were murdered.[47] On the afternoon of December 31, a gang of forty to fifty Nyilas broke into the largest of the houses under Swiss protection, the 'Glass House' department store, blasting open the locked doors with grenades and opening fire with machine guns. Three Jews were killed, including the wife of Rabbi Lajos Scheiber. But when the Nyilas tried to attack the eight hundred Jews in hiding in the building, a Hungarian military unit intervened, and the Jews were saved. Only the building's patron, Otto Komoly, lured away for 'negotiations', was never seen again.[48]

At Monowitz, where twelve thousand Jews from Birkenau had been employed as slave labourers in the synthetic oil and rubber factory, two thousand had survived. 'That was a lot of survivors,' Shalom Lindenbaum later recalled. In this respect, Lindenbaum added, 'it was a "good" camp,' but he noted that during the several Allied bombing raids on the factory, 'we were apathetic because we did not believe that we would survive.'

On December 11, the festival of Chanukkah, when Jews celebrate the miracle of the lights at the time of the Maccabees, the surviving Jews in Monowitz found some candles and lit them in memory of that distant day of salvation. 'One of us', Lindenbaum recalled, 'said that in Palestine it is certain that they are celebrating; they are celebrating because the Germans are beaten.' Lindenbaum added: 'as for ourselves, we said a prayer for the dead. We wept. Our death was sure.'[49]

In the labour camps and factory zones of Upper Silesia, Jews had always dreaded the day when they would be judged too weak to work, and sent back to Birkenau, not to the barracks from which they had come, but to the gas-chambers. On December 25, at Gleiwitz, more than sixty men were picked out at a roll call as unfit for further work. 'Our numbers were recorded and we knew what to expect,' Alfred Oppenheimer later recalled. 'Had we not known, the commander of the hut told us that – informed us tactfully, and with feeling – that a few days later we would be taken to the chimney.' But 'the chimney', all the chimneys, had ceased working; they had, in fact, already been dismantled. 'We, as mussulmen, were already marked and chosen to be taken to our death. But there were no more freight trucks to collect the men. No one was taken to Auschwitz.'[50]

Among the camps to which Jews had been taken from Birkenau in September and October was Lieberose. There, under German and Ukrainian guards, they worked to build a holiday city for German officers, at nearby Ullersdorf. In December, as the Red Army drew ever nearer, Lieberose was closed down, and more than three and a half thousand Jews were marched out. They were being sent to Sachsenhausen.

Several hundred Jews were in the camp infirmary at Lieberose. On the eve of the march, they were shot, and the hut set on fire. The march then began. Each night, as darkness fell, the Jews were ordered into a field and told to lie down. At first light they would be marched off again. Some were too weak to rise. As the morning march continued, the marchers would hear the sound of firing.

Less than a thousand of the marchers survived their ordeal. One of the survivors, Hugo Gryn, who had been sent to Birkenau from Beregszasz during the Hungarian deportations, later recalled how, during a moment of rest, sitting on the slushy roadside with his father, Geza Gryn, a lorry passed them by:

> . . . by coincidence it had my father's name still painted on its side and back. He had been a timber merchant and somehow a part of his confiscated transport fleet and we were on the same road.
>
> It was a pathetic moment and to break the silence I said, 'Just you wait – one day you'll have it back again!' 'No,' he said, 'I think this was yours anyway!' And then he explained that whenever he acquired a forest or lorries or suchlike, he rotated the acquisitions: something for my brother, something for me, something for my mother and something for himself. It seemed that everything I thought he owned was already a quarter mine.
>
> Though it was academic, I was both touched and impressed. Finally, I asked him, 'Why did you do it that way?' 'Well,' he said, 'I made up my mind long ago that anything I have to give I want to give with a warm hand – and not wait until I have to give with a cold one.'

From Sachsenhausen, Hugo Gryn and his father were among thousands of Jews moved south to Mauthausen. And there, a victim of hunger and of typhoid, his father died. He was forty-five years old.[51]

In another labour camp that winter, at Neumark, were several thousand women, likewise brought from Birkenau. Hundreds of them, too weak to work, were put into a special tent, and told that they were to be deported to Stutthof. No such deportation was in prospect. All were later shot at Neumark. While being kept in the 'Stutthofers' tent', as it was called, their suffering became unendurable. Reska Weiss, who saw them, later recalled:

> No one was allowed into the Stutthofers' tent. If anyone was caught visiting a mother or a sister, she was never allowed to leave the tent again. The Stutthofers were seldom given food,

and on the rare occasions when it was supplied, it was placed on the ground in the dark in front of the tent. Then the strongest of them fetched it and distributed it.

Entering the tent from the blinding snow-whiteness, I could hardly distinguish anything in the semi-darkness, least of all the women lying on the ground. The stench was overpowering despite the airy tent. After a while my eyes became accustomed to the light, and I was completely overcome by what I saw.

I screamed in horror and shut my eyes to the sight. My knees trembled, my head began to swim, and I grasped the central tent-prop for support. It was hard to believe the women on the ground were still human beings. Their rigid bodies were skeletons, their eyes were glazed from long starvation. . . .

For two months the Stutthofers had lain on the ground, stark naked. The meagre bundles of straw on which they lay were putrid from their urine and excreta. Their frozen limbs were fetid and covered with wounds and bites to the points of bleeding, and countless lice nested in the pus. Their hair was very short indeed, but the armies of lice found a home in it. No stretch of the imagination, no power of the written word, can convey the horror of that tent. And yet . . . they were alive . . . they were hungry and they tore at their skeletal bodies with emaciated hands covered in pus and dirt. They were beyond help. The SS guards denied them the mercy of shooting them all at once. Only three or four were called out daily to be shot.

For days I couldn't swallow even a crumb of bread. The horror I lived through watching this agony will remain with me to the end of my days. Later I saw thousands of my fellow prisoners die from rifle shots, but even that could not compare with the terrible and unspeakable ordeal of the Stutthofers.[52]

East of Warsaw, Soviet troops had reached Treblinka, and began at once to examine what was left of the former death camp. One of those brought to the site was Dr Adolf Berman, a survivor of the Warsaw ghetto. 'I saw a sight which I shall never forget,' he later recalled, 'a tremendous area of many kilometres, and all over this area there were scattered skulls, bones – tens of thousands; and piles of shoes – among them tens of thousands of little shoes.'

Berman picked up a pair of children's shoes. 'I brought it as a very precious thing,' he told a court in Jerusalem sixteen years later, 'because I knew that over a million of such little shoes, scattered over all the fields of death, could easily be found.'[53]

40

The death marches

AT BIRKENAU, the gassing had ended at the end of October 1944. For two months, tens of thousands of Jews had remained in the barracks. Hunger and exposure took their toll. On 6 January 1945 Anne Frank's mother Edith died in the camp. Anne Frank, deported from Birkenau to Belsen the previous October with her elder sister, Margot, died there of typhus at about this same time, a few days after Margot, falling from the bunk above, had, in her weakened state, died from shock on hitting the barracks floor.[1]

In Budapest, as Soviet forces drew closer to the city, the deportations to the Austrian border came to an end. But in the city, the Nyilas continued to rob and torment Jews, and to threaten them with death. On January 6, as a result of negotiations between Raoul Wallenberg and the Hungarian authorities, it was agreed that five thousand Jews could be transferred to the 'international ghetto' under Swedish protective documents. A further five thousand Jews were moved under Swiss, Portuguese and Vatican protection.

For eleven days, the 120,000 Jews of Budapest waited for the arrival of the Red Army. On January 11 a gang of about eight men wearing German and Nyilas uniforms entered one of the protected houses: twenty-six women, fifteen men and a child were killed.[2] That same day a number of other Jewish protected buildings were attacked, and many Jews, taken to the bank of the Danube, were tied together in threes. The middle one was then shot, and the three thrown into the Danube, so that the weight of the dead man would pull down the other two.[3]

Also on January 11, the Nyilas surrounded the Jewish hospital, seizing ninety-two patients, doctors and nurses, torturing them, and then shooting them. Only a single nurse was able to escape. On January 14, in the Jewish Orthodox hospital, one hundred and fifty

Jews were killed, followed by the massacre of ninety Jews from an Orthodox almshouse, taken to the hospital and killed there.[4]

On January 17 Soviet forces entered the Hungarian capital: 120,000 Jews were safe from any further Nyilas attacks. Only Raoul Wallenberg, one of their protectors, came to grief. Summoned to Soviet military headquarters, he was seized, and disappeared.[5]

Soviet forces had also reached Warsaw on January 17. 'We have no need to go back down into the bunker,' Chaim Goldstein recalled. 'Our cries of "We are free" have reached the ears of our comrades, who now came out into the street one by one. We fall into each other's arms and kiss one another.'[6]

Goldstein rejoiced at the moment of liberation. But for the rest of his life he was to be haunted by the bitter personal reality of the war years: his mother, aged seventy-seven, killed during a transport to Treblinka, his brother shot while trying to help her, his sisters both dead, although 'time and place of death remain unknown'.[7]

No more than two hundred Jews had survived in Warsaw, the remnant of more than half a million. Most of the survivors had been in hiding in 'Aryan' Warsaw since the destruction of the ghetto more than a year and a half before. Among the survivors was an eight-year-old girl, Ania Goldman, my cousin.[8]

'I was like a walker between two walls,' Tuvia Borzykowski later recalled. 'One was the recollection of the past years, the life in the ghetto, the stacks of dead bodies, the destruction of my people, the other was the hope for the future, in a world free of the Nazi scourge.'[9] Feigele Peltel walked, on that day of Warsaw's liberation, through the rubble of the ghetto. 'Here a protruding length of pipe,' she recalled, 'there a bent iron rail, there a charred sapling – these are what is left of our devastated world.' There remained only the search for her father's grave in the Gesia cemetery:

> Wherever I turned, there was nothing but overturned tombstones, desecrated graves and scattered skulls – skulls, their dark sockets burning deep into me, their shattered jaws demanding, 'Why? Why has this befallen us?'
>
> Although I knew that these atrocities were the handiwork of the so-called 'dentists' – Polish ghouls who searched the mouths of the Jewish corpses to extract their gold-capped teeth, I nevertheless felt strangely guilty and ashamed. Yes, Jews were persecuted even in their graves.

Deliberately, in order not to trample the skulls and not to slip into an open grave, we made our way through this place of rest to the spot where my father's bones had lain. Though the location was well known to me, I could not find his grave. The spot was desolate, destroyed, the soil pitted and strewn with broken skulls and markers.

We stood there forlorn. Around our feet lay skull after skull. Was not one of them my own father? How would I ever recognize it?

Nothing. Nothing was left me of my past, of my life in the ghetto – not even the grave of my father.[10]

Zivia Lubetkin was hiding in the town of Grodzisk, outside Warsaw, when Soviet tanks entered on January 17. 'The people rejoiced and embraced their liberators,' she recalled. 'We stood by crushed and dejected, lone remnants of our people.'[11]

Those Jews who returned to what had once been the Warsaw ghetto saw at first glance the meaning of the Holocaust. Whereas the Poles had already begun the slow and painful process of rebuilding their shattered city, and re-establishing their interrupted lives and careers, the Jews could not do so. Firstly, there were far too few survivors. Secondly, the former Jewish buildings had been levelled to the ground. Polish Warsaw was able to return to life as the capital of modern Poland. Jewish Warsaw was destroyed forever, and with it the 'Jewish Nation in Poland' which had been so vibrant a feature of the pre-war Polish state.

The same was true of every city or town in what had once been German-occupied Poland. The Poles and the Jews both mourned their dead: but only the Poles had the numbers and the resources left to repopulate their cities. Unlike the Jews, many non-Jews had never even had to leave their homes. Whereas every non-Jewish family had suffered death and privation, few had been destroyed in their entirety. For the Jews, the vast majority of their families had been destroyed root and branch, so that for most families not a single individual remained alive, to return to claim a stake in the new world.

In the expectation of the imminent arrival of Soviet forces, the evacuations from areas still under German control were accelerated. So too were the killings. On January 15, in a labour camp at Brodnica, a branch of Stutthof, all Jewish women too sick or too weak to be moved were shot. A few, however, outwitting their guards, managed to escape.[12] In nearby Torun, a memorial tablet marks the common grave of 152 Jewish women, murdered by the SS in January 1945.[13]

On January 17, at Chelmno, the SS prepared to murder the surviving members of the special Commando which, for the previous two and a half months, had been forced to dismantle the crematoria. A hundred Jews had been put to this work. By mid-January only forty-one were still alive. There had been no work that final day, Mordechai Zurawski later recalled, 'and we were placed in a row; each man had a bottle on his head and they amused themselves shooting at the bottles. When the bottle was hit, the man survived, but if the bullet landed below the mark he had had it.'

On the night of January 17 the SS entered the barracks at Chelmno and one of them, waving his flashlight, demanded, 'Five men follow me!' Five people were taken out, Zurawski later recalled, 'and we heard five shots'. Then someone else came in and shouted, 'Five more – out!' More shots; then a third group of five was taken out. Further shots, then a fourth group was called, among them Zurawski. 'The SS man came in,' he recalled. 'I hid behind the door – I had a knife in my hand; I jumped on the SS man and stabbed him. I broke his flashlight and stabbed right and left, and I escaped.'

Running from the camp, Zurawski was shot in the foot. But he managed to reach the safety of the dense woods.[14]

A second Jew of the forty-one had also survived. Unknown to Zurawski, in the first group that had been taken out to be shot, one had been gravely wounded, but had not died. This was Shimon Srebnik, who later recalled being ordered out of the barracks:

> I was the youngest. I also ran. I didn't even put on my trousers. I just had my pants and singlet. And there was another boy from Czechoslovakia. He was a doctor. He got some sort of a shock. He began singing and dancing. And Lentz, our transport man, asked where to put us. And Bothmann said, 'A bit further from here,' and he told us that we should lie down. We lay down, the first five, and when we were thus lying, I heard some sort of a noise, and then I was hit.

The bullet had entered through the nape of Srebnik's neck, and came out through his mouth. At the Eichmann Trial in Jerusalem in 1961, the court was shown the scar. His account of the shooting continued:

> After a few minutes, I regained my consciousness, and when he passed by, I stopped breathing, so that he should think that I am dead. I was just lying there.
>
> And then there was another group of five. They shot them, and then the third group of five, in turn, and they were also shot. There was one soldier who was just guarding the groups of dead people and finishing off those who still showed signs of life.
>
> I was lying down and he would pass by, and when he heard some signs of life – there were all sorts of movements – so he would finish them off with a second shot.
>
> Then I ran away. I ran away when his gaze was not fixed on me, and I was hiding in the hut of a Gentile up to the liberation.
>
> When the Russians came, I was looking through a hole in a stable. I thought it was a dream. I didn't know what was going on. Somebody came in, opened the door, and said to me, 'You can now go out. The Russians have already arrived.'

A Russian physician gave Srebnik only twelve to twenty-four hours to survive: it was thought that the bullet had broken his spine.[15]

On January 17, as Soviet forces entered Budapest and Warsaw, Auschwitz lay finally exposed to imminent assault. A count was made of the number of Jews and other prisoners. At Birkenau, there remained 15,058, mostly Jews; at Auschwitz, 16,226, mostly Poles brought there after the Warsaw uprising the previous August; at Monowitz, 10,233, Jews, Poles, and forced labourers of a dozen nationalities, including British prisoners-of-war; and in the factories of the Auschwitz region, another 16,000 Jews and non-Jews.[16] On January 18 the order was given: immediate evacuation, on foot, often to a nearby railway junction from which they could be taken to a hundred different camps and sub-camps in western Germany, but sometimes by foot for hundreds of miles.

Learning of the order to evacuate, many Jews believed that it was a trap, a subterfuge for their mass-murder. Inside Auschwitz, a group of inmates decided therefore to resist: to die fighting rather than to be marched away to their deaths. But, as Israel Gutman later recalled, the camp underground told them that it really was 'evacuation and not execution', and through evacuation, there was a chance of survival.[17]

Thousands who were too weak to march away were shot in the camps themselves on the eve of evacuation. On the marches, tens of thousands were shot and killed wherever they chanced to stumble and fall: 'Anybody who was weak,' Gutman recalled, 'anybody who had to sit down for a few minutes, was shot at.'[18]

On the marches in the region of Blechhammer, fifteen hundred Jews were shot.[19] 'We heard shooting all the time,' Alfred Oppenheimer recalled, of his own march to Blechhammer from Gleiwitz. 'We were not allowed to turn our heads, but we knew what the shooting meant. All those lagging behind were shot dead.' On reaching Blechhammer the marchers were taken to a hut to sleep. Suddenly Oppenheimer was awoken by the sound of voices:

There was a call, 'Hurry! The SS men are back!' The excitement and the fear – I felt no pain any longer. I dragged my two friends, and crossed to a place across the ground. This was the public lavatories. We stood there and peeped through the cracks to what was going on in the camp. They started shooting from the towers, the watch-towers around the camp.

The SS men set fire to the huts where the people took shelter and where they were in hiding. They stood facing the doors with machine guns, and if anyone ran out of the burning huts, they were shot immediately by the SS men with those machine guns. Those who did not run were burned alive.

My friends and myself decided that they would be coming to the lavatories as well and set fire. Then we jumped through the seat into the pit, and this was the worst experience of my life.

When we entered those pits of the excrement, sinking, sinking slowly – and one does not know how deep we were sinking. The excrement reached up to my chest, and all of a sudden, I felt solid ground under my feet.

The smell of the burning of wood from the huts, the noise of the flames, and the half-burned people, those who were shot but not dead – they all formed this terrible experience, the worst I went through in those camps, far worse than the moment when a sentence of death was delivered against myself.

Dr Oppenheimer remained in the pit of excrement for several hours. Finally:

> We heard voices, people speaking and saying that the SS men had gone, that the gates were open. There were other prisoners-of-war, Jewish prisoners, also saved by some kind of miracle, because not all the huts were on fire. And then we cried out for help. A number of those Jewish prisoners came to help us, and pulled us out of this pit of excrement. We cleaned ourselves with snow. There was no water. We did what we could. Finally we were liberated by the Soviet army.[20]

As the death marches continued from the Auschwitz region, tens of thousands of Jews were shot, their bodies thrown into the nearest roadside ditches. At Miedzna, a memorial tablet records the killing of 42 prisoners by the SS, at Jejkowice 33, at Lyski 27, and at Rybnik 358. At Leszczyny a memorial records the murder of 250 prisoners who had been taken from the march to an evacuation train. They had been shot down as they jumped from the train and tried to flee to the neighbouring forests.[21]

Among the tens of thousands of Jews on the death marches was a Polish-born Jew, Moses Finkelstein. Under the name of Michael Fink, he had fought with the French resistance in the Vosges. Captured during an armed clash with the Germans, he had been deported to Birkenau. Now, within sound of the guns of the Red Army, he was killed.[22]

At Birkenau itself, with the arrival of the Red Army expected hourly, the SS set fire to twenty-nine stores, including all the clothing inside them. Even so, when Soviet troops entered Birkenau on January 27, they found, in the six remaining storehouses, 836,255 women's dresses, 348,000 sets of men's suits, and 38,000 pairs of men's shoes.[23]

In many of the camps which it liberated, the Red Army also found a few inmates still alive: the largest number being the eight hundred sick prisoners left behind at Monowicz. The four and a half thousand inmates who had been marched away from Monowicz were less fortunate: during an air raid alert they had scattered for protection in the forest, and then tried to remain there in hiding. But SS men surrounded them and opened fire, killing all but a hundred. The survivors were then marched on again, westward.[24]

Among those evacuated from Birkenau on the eve of 'liberation' were a group of boys aged fourteen and fifteen, who had been part of a special 'Cart Commando': twenty children harnessed to a cart that would normally be pulled by horses. Sometimes these boys had been used to pull wood needed for the crematorium ovens. Sometimes they had been made to spread human ash – the ashes of Jews burned in Crematorium III – on to the paths inside the camp. Yehuda Bakon, who was not quite fifteen years old, later recalled that this had been done 'so that people could walk on the road and not slip'.

On January 18 these boys were evacuated to Mauthausen. Yehuda Bakon later recalled how, on the march, 'The children said, "It is good that our parents were killed in the gas-chambers. They did not have to undergo all this torture and suffering." Because we saw they shot everyone who fell.'[25]

At the Furstengrube coal mine, the sick inmates too weak to leave the hospital hut were not left for the Red Army to liberate. Instead, all two hundred and fifty of them were killed with hand grenades and automatic-rifle fire, and the hut then set on fire.[26]

A few hundred Jews were able to escape from the marches, and hide in barns or ditches until the arrival of Soviet forces. Some found shelter with Polish families. On January 20 Louise S. from Cluj and several of her friends, marching from Birkenau, managed to escape in the thick mist, and although shot at, avoided capture. In the village of Brzezie a Polish farmer gave them hot coffee and bread, and let them sleep 'on warm straw' in his pig-sty. Whenever German soldiers entered the village, the farmer said the girls were Polish refugees. After three weeks, the Germans were gone.[27]

None of those who survived the 'death marches' of January 1945 can forget the horror. 'On the death march from Auschwitz,' one survivor later recalled, 'German women heard we were prisoners, and threw boiled potatoes. Those who picked up the potatoes died with a bullet – and a hot potato in their mouths.'[28]

Dr Aharon Beilin later recalled how, on the march from Birkenau to Kamienna Gora, 'We started counting the shots. It was a long column – five thousand people. We know every shot meant a human life. Sometimes the count reached five "hundred", in a single day. And the longer we marched, the more the number of shots increased. There was no strength, no food.' One night, the four thousand survivors were locked in a long concrete bunker, an air raid shelter. 'We felt that we had no air, that there was no air in this bunker, and those groups that were far from the door felt it much more than we did, and the screams, the tragic scenes, began, "Air, air!" . . .'

In the morning, a thousand corpses were found in the bunker. 'It was death by suffocation, Beilin recalled, 'horrible positions, naked, on their knees and with their mouths to the concrete floor. That's where the last pockets of air were. From the pores of the concrete, they got the last bit of air.'[29]

Not only for the fifty thousand from the Auschwitz region, but for a further six thousand or more from the labour camps around Czestochowa, and other labour camp regions in central Poland, the westward marches had begun. Some were lucky to be liberated at the last moment, before they could be evacuated, or shot. Others managed to run away at the last moment, and to hide. But for most, the marches were a time of agony for those who had already survived 'selections', camps and beatings. Raizl Kibel, on the march westward of girls from the Union factory, later recalled:

> In a frost, half-barefoot, or entirely barefoot, with light rags upon their emaciated and exhausted bodies, tens of thousands of human creatures drag themselves along in the snow. Only the great, strong striving for life, and the light of imminent liberation, keep them on their feet.
>
> But woe is to them whose physical strength abandons them. They are shot on the spot. In such a way were thousands who had endured camp life up to the last minute murdered, a moment before liberation.
>
> Even today I still cannot understand with what sort of strength and how I was able to endure the 'death march' and drag myself to Ravensbruck camp, and from there, after resting a week or two, to Neustadt, where I was liberated by the Red Army.[30]

Even on the death marches, the moment of liberation could come suddenly and unexpectedly. On January 22, Leilah Svirsky was with one group led into the forest to spend the night in an abandoned barracks. 'We did not sleep that night. The following morning we noticed that our guards were gone. A strange sensation: no one is watching us any more. . . .' And then the Russians arrived. 'The first Russian soldier we saw was a captain, a Jew named Weisbrot. He belonged to the first military Intelligence group of the army and rode a white horse. Our Messiah, we called him, and kissed the horse's feet.'

It was 23 January 1945. Leilah Svirsky was free. 'I am no longer one of a driven herd. I can decide my fate alone.'[31]

Further west, the death marches continued. On one, which began on January 24 from the River Oder, thirty-three men and seventy women were ill, walking, but desperately in need of keeping warm. The SS escort then took their blankets away, so that more than thirty of them died of cold. On this same march, however, another SS man, Meyer, acted with unexpected compassion, buying food with his own money for the women, while other guards also shared out their rations with the marchers.[32]

Among the Jews who managed to escape from a death march was Jakub Lichterman, the last cantor at the Noszik Synagogue in Warsaw, who had been deported to Majdanek in 1943, and to Birkenau in 1944. In Lichterman's group of marchers, about twenty Jews had managed to slip away. 'It was snowing. We ate snow. Many people died. I saw a little light in a hut. I decided to knock. The others said, "It is dangerous, it might be a German's hut". But I thought, "Must I die here? Maybe they will give me something."'

Lichterman knocked on the door of the hut. 'It was an Ethnic German. He gave me hot coffee in a bottle, and bread.' Then, as Lichterman left the hut, two other escapees came up to him, desperate for a drink. 'The bottle fell out of my hand. The coffee dropped in the snow. I went back. He had no more food. He gave me a box of matches and said, "There are lots of Germans around. If they catch you, they will kill you on the spot."'

The Jews wandered off, each to a different part of the wood. Lichterman knocked on another door, another small hut. 'Can you take me in?' 'How many are you?' 'Just one.'

Lichterman was taken in, hidden in a shack, and fed three times a day. Eight days later, with the arrival of Soviet troops, Lichterman was saved: saved because, during a week of risk and danger, he had been given sanctuary by a non-Jew.[33]

Other non-Jews risked their lives to save Jews. On January 29 the German Catholic, Oscar Schindler, who had earlier rescued several hundred Jews from Plaszow camp, was told of a locked goods wagon at the station nearest to his armament factory at Brünnlitz. The wagon was marked 'Property of the SS', and had been travelling on the railways for ten days, covered in ice. Inside were more than a hundred Jews, starving and freezing: Jews from Birkenau who had been at the labour camp at Golleschau, Jews who had once lived in Poland, Czechoslovakia, France, Holland and Hungary.

Schindler had no authority to take the wagon. But he asked a railway official to show him the bill of lading, and when the official was momentarily distracted, wrote on it: 'Final destination, Brünnlitz.' Schindler then pointed out to the official that the wagon was intended for his factory.[34] Schindler ordered the railway authorities to transfer the wagon to his factory siding. There he broke open the locks. Sixteen of the Jews had frozen to death. The survivors, not one of whom weighed more than thirty-five kilogrammes, he fed and guarded.[35] Schindler was helped by his wife Emilia, who provided beds on which they could be nursed back to life. 'She took care of these Golleschau Jews,' Moshe Bejski later recalled. 'She prepared food for them every day.'

In all, between 1943 and 1945, Schindler had saved more than fifteen hundred Jews by employing them in his factory, and treating them humanely. He died, in Germany, in October 1974. At his funeral in the Latin cemetery in Jerusalem, on the slopes of Mount Zion, more than four hundred of the Jews whom he had saved paid him their last respects.[36]

'The liberator is on the move, the knife is at the throat.'[37] With these words, written on January 17, Dov Levin, a young Jew then in liberated Vilna, decided to leave for Palestine, and, after nine months, reached his goal.[38]

On January 27, ten days after Levin set off from Kovno, units of the Red Army entered Birkenau. Among those still alive in the camp hospital was Otto Frank, father of Anne Frank. Otto Frank made his way across the Ukraine to Odessa, then by boat to Marseilles, and then to Amsterdam, where he found his daughter's diary.[39]

Survival was the dream of all who awaited the imminent arrival of the Allied armies. But the very act of hoping could lead to despair, with different dates being fixed in the mind for the moment of victory, the day of rescue. A Hungarian Jew, Moshe Sandberg, later recalled the mood in Muhldorf camp, near Dachau, where 1 January 1945 had originally been the date fixed in the inmates' minds for the end of the war:

> The first day passed, the second and the third and the fourth, on and on endlessly. We wondered how many had gone by and how many still remained until January 1, 1945, the date we decided would be the final one, by which time the war would surely end with the victory of the Allied powers, and whoever was lucky enough to see it would be able to leave this Hell. It was difficult to keep count of the days, the date we wanted approaching so infinitely slowly. Work hours seemed to get longer and the hours of sleep shorter.
>
> At last came the awaited day, but it did not bring deliverance. The disappointment was bitter. What would become of us? We could not endure much longer. Some of our comrades were already dead and most of the others looked shadows of themselves and it was a wonder that their legs could still carry them. The few who still kept up their spirits had set January 15 as the latest date for the war to end, then they extended it for a fortnight, and then later and so on, but the last date I no longer remember.
>
> With each new estimate the number of those who believed in it fell, while that of those who were apathetic about any guess rose. They stopped believing and hoping. Only two things remained in their thoughts: hunger and the beatings. How to get a little more food and how to get a little less beating. In a month of two we had turned into real camp denizens, indistinguishable from the veterans. The same way of thought, the same miserable appearance.
>
> Now we could understand why they had laughed at us when

we expressed our hopes and speculated about the 'last date'. The remark 'The war will never end' became clear to us. Death was the time of our deliverance.[40]

In East Prussia, where Soviet forces were driving toward the sea, the many labour camps in the Danzig and Königsberg regions were evacuated, many by sea. More than six thousand women and one thousand men, all of them Jews, were driven from these camps towards Palmnicken, a small fishing village beyond Königsberg, on the shore of the Baltic Sea. During the march to the sea, more than seven hundred were shot. Most of the marchers were women. 'Every time somebody bent down to scoop up a little snow to drink water,' Celina Manielewicz later recalled, 'the guard simply shot him dead.'

In Palmnicken the Jews were lodged in a deserted factory. The manager of the village, hearing of their arrival, ordered each of the marchers to be given a daily ration of three potatoes. 'We heard that he was a humane man who had objected to us prisoners remaining in his town under inhuman conditions. A few hours later a rumour circulated that the Nazis had shot him.'

One evening the Jews were ordered out of the factory building and lined up in rows of five. They were then marched in the direction of the Baltic Sea. During the march, some three hundred men hurled themselves at the SS guards with bare hands. They were all machine-gunned.

The surviving marchers continued towards the sea. Celina Manielewicz later recalled the sequel, as she marched with her three friends, Pela Lewkowicz, Genia Weinberg and Mania Gleimann:

> In addition to rumours of our embarkation for Hamburg and of the approach of the Russians, other rumours also reached us: people marching ahead of us in the front ranks were murdered along the shore and thrown into the sea.
>
> We were so starved, weak and demoralised that death seemed to us a merciful relief – and yet we lacked the courage to stoop down on the way, because of a glimmer of hope that at the last moment our life would be saved by a miracle. Yet in view of the approaching end we four friends said goodbye to each other.
>
> Finally, late at night we came to the coast. We found

ourselves on high ground beyond which cliffs descended steeply to the shore. A fearful vista presented itself. Machine-gunners posted on both sides fired blindly into the advancing columns. Those who had been hit lost their balance and hurtled down the cliffside. When we realized what was happening, we and people in front of us instinctively pushed to the back. The commanding SS man, Quartermaster Sergeant Stock, picked up his rifle and came cursing towards us, shouting, 'Why don't you want to go any further? You're going to be shot like dogs anyway!' He forced us forward to the precipice saying, 'A waste of ammunition,' and fetched each of us a terrible blow round the head with his rifle butt, so that we lost consciousness.

I don't know what happened to me; suddenly I felt something cold on my back and when I opened my eyes I beheld a mountain slope down which ever more blood-streaked bodies were rolling. I found myself in the foaming, roaring sea in a small, partly frozen bay on a pile of dead or injured, and therefore still living, people.

The whole coast, as far as I could see, was covered with corpses, and I, too, was lying on such a mountain of corpses which slowly sank deeper and deeper. Close beside me lay Genia Weinberg and Mania Gleimann and at my feet Pela Lewkowicz. Badly injured, she suddenly stood up and shouted to a sentry standing a few metres away from us on the shore, 'Herr Sentry, I'm still alive!'

The sentry aimed and shot her in the head — a few centi-metres away from my feet — so that she collapsed. Suddenly my friend Genia, who had also recovered consciousness in the ice-cold water, pinched me and whispered, 'Don't move.'

So we lay for some time, I don't know how long, almost completely frozen. Suddenly SS men appeared and shouted, 'Raise your heads!' Some of the injured who were still alive and capable of obeying this order were shot immediately. Then the SS men left. Thereupon Genia said, 'It is so quiet!', got up carefully and waded to the shore. She tore some clothes and blankets from the corpses that were lying around and tied them into a rope, with the aid of which she pulled us on shore.

We tried to move our limbs and began climbing the moun-tain slope with great difficulty. Genia was the one who hadn't lost courage yet. Half-way up she told us to wait, she wanted to go down again and see if there were any survivors. But after some time she came back alone. We felt very sick because we had swallowed a lot of sea water; in spite of this Genia kept driving us forward. At last we came to the top of the cliff which had been entirely deserted by the Germans. It was twenty-five degrees below zero. We were covered with a layer of ice and unable to go any further. Genia told us over and over again, 'We've got to go on!' Then, after an hour's staggering about in the snow, we suddenly saw smoke.

The three women found refuge with a farmer called Voss. Later, when Voss tried to turn them over to the Germans, they were saved by two other villagers, Albert Harder and his wife, who fed and clothed them, and pretended that they were three Polish girls. One day a German officer asked Frau Harder for permission to take them out. It would have roused too many suspicions to refuse. Celina, now known as Cecilia, later recalled her evening with the officer:

He led me to the spot along the seashore where I had endured the worst night of my life and said: 'In this place our people murdered ten thousand Jews. It is terrible that Germans were capable of such a thing. I can only tell you that if the Russians march in, which is only a question of days or weeks now, they will do the same to us as we have done to the Jews. A German will dangle from every tree. The forest will be full of German corpses!'

I felt faint and lost consciousness. When I had recovered we walked back to the Harders' in silence. On the way back the officer also told me that two hundred Jews had survived the night massacre, but had been handed over to the Gestapo by the population of the surrounding villages among whom they had sought asylum. They had all been killed.

He continued to pay court to me, assured me that I looked like his sister, and made a few attempts to go out with me. The night before the entry of the Russians, I remember him coming to Frau Harder with a suitcase at 11 p.m. in a state of great excitement. He had to speak to me at all costs – it could not wait till next morning. When I stood before him in my night-dress and dressing gown he opened the case and produced a mass of tinned preserves he had procured for family Harder from the officers' mess.

The German officer tried to persuade Celina to leave with him, 'for woe betide you if the barbaric Russians get hold of you here', but she persuaded him that she had to stay. Celina, for her part, urged the German to desert, and to throw away his uniform. 'I cannot do that,' he said. 'I've got to play out this bad game to the bitter end.'

The German left. The Russians arrived. Celina and her two friends were saved. But none of the Russians, even a Yiddish-speaking Red Army officer, a Jew, could believe that they were Jews. 'The Jews have all perished over there,' they said, pointing to the sea. Only the emergence from hiding of ten other survivors of the massacre gave credence to the story of their survival. Of nine thousand and more marchers brought to the sea at Palmnicken, only thirteen had survived.[41]

Freedom brought many hazards; among those who had set out from Auschwitz immediately after the liberation of the camp on January 27 was Ernest Spiegel, together with thirty-three of the surviving boy twins. Spiegel had been making plans to leave Auschwitz with another prisoner when the children had come to him and said: 'Uncle, you promised to take us home.' On the first stage of their journey, a Russian soldier driving a truck saw the children, and agreed to drive them to Cracow. During the journey, the truck was hit by another vehicle, and one of the twins was killed.

For seven weeks Spiegel led the twins southwards towards his home town, Munkacs. During the journey, Soviet officers asked him to take care of a further 120 survivors who had been found wandering in the Tatra mountains.[42]

For the liberated Jews, the dangers were far from over. On February 2 a woman from Russian-liberated Rokitno, in the Volhynia, wrote to her relatives in Palestine of the family's sufferings in the war. 'And now', she added, 'my Yechielke went off to take part in a committee meeting and fell victim to the Ukrainian nationalists.'[43]

On February 17, the Jewish Sabbath, Szymon Datner, head of the

Jewish regional committee which had been set up in Bialystok after the liberation, was summoned to the nearby village of Sokoly. There he found seven murdered Jews. The story he learned was as follows: earlier that day, all twenty survivors of the Jews of Sokoly had assembled in a room when a Pole had entered, and opened fire. Among the dead was a prominent local engineer, David Zholti, two brothers, Yankele Litwak, aged fifteen, and Shaikele, aged twelve, two other members of the Litwak family, Chaim and Shammai, a young woman, the twenty-year-old Batya Weinstein, and a man, David Kostshevski. Also murdered in that burst of fire was another woman, the twenty-two-year-old Shaine Olshak, and Tokele, the four-year-old orphan daughter of her sister.[44]

Not only the enmity of the local population, but the weakness brought about by such long privation, often gave the first days of freedom a bitter twist. Esther Epsztejn, from Lodz, whose parents and two brothers had both been murdered during the war, recalled how, in February 1945, after she and a large number of women had been liberated by the Red Army while being evacuated from Stutthof, 'Russian doctors did everything they could for us, but the mortality rate did not diminish. Eighty-five people died in five days, after we were liberated.'[45]

'For the time being I go on living,' a survivor wrote, from Kovno, on February 18. 'How hard it is to walk about on earth that is so saturated with Jewish blood.'[46]

41

The 'tainted luck' of survival

BY THE END OF FEBRUARY 1945, the factories to which the Jews from Birkenau had been evacuated in November and December 1944 were themselves within a few days of being overrun by the Red Army. On February 23 the Jews in Schwarzheide, on the Dresden to Berlin autobahn, were evacuated. The three hundred weakest were sent in open goods wagons to Belsen. There, all but one of them perished.[1]

A month earlier, from a camp at Neusalz, on the Oder, a thousand Jewish women, many of them survivors of Auschwitz, had been marched westward and south, away from the advancing Soviet forces. As with so many of the death marches, they passed through many German towns and villages: on February 28 they were at Bautzen. One of those on the march, Gisela Teumann, later recalled how, 'We passed through some German town. We asked for food. At first they thought that we were German refugees. The SS man who accompanied us shouted: "Don't give them anything to eat, it's Jews they are." And so I got no food. German children began to throw stones at us.'[2]

Of the thousand women who set off from Neusalz, only two hundred reached Flossenburg alive, forty-two days after they had been sent on their tragic way. From there, they too were sent on by train to Belsen.

Belsen and Dachau, Buchenwald and Mauthausen, Sachsen-hausen and Ravensbruck, and their many sub-camps, were now the destination of hundreds of evacuation trains and marches. Jews who had already survived the 'selections' in Birkenau, and work as slave labourers in factories, had now to survive the death marches. Throughout February and March columns of men, and crowded cattle trucks, converged on the long-existing concentration camps, now given a new task. These camps had been transformed into holding camps for the remnant of a destroyed people, men and women whose labour was still of some last-minute utility for a dying Reich, or whose emaciated bodies were to be left to languish in agony in one final camp.

It was in Dachau that Violette Fintz, the Jewess from Rhodes, found her brother Leon. 'I took him in my arms,' she later recalled. ' "You must have the courage to go on," I said. He said, "No." He showed me where hot soup had been spilled down his leg. It had gone gangrenous.' Violette Fintz was transferred to Belsen. Her brother remained in Dachau, and there, shortly after her own evacuation, he died.

Violette Fintz was moved to Belsen. Forty years later she recalled how, among the masses of earlier evacuees, she found her sister Miriam. 'She put her arms around me, saying, "Never will I be separated from you again." ' Violette Fintz's account continued:

> Belsen was in the beginning bearable and we had bunks to sleep on and a small ration of soup and bread. But as the camp got fuller, our group and many others were given a barracks to hold about seven hundred lying on the floor without blankets and without food or anything.
>
> It was a pitiful scene as the camp was attacked by lice and most of the people had typhus and cholera.
>
> Many girls died and we were all thinking that these were our last days. My sister Miriam had a very high temperature and she told me that if she did not get a little water she would die there and then.
>
> I took a tin and went out of the block to try and find some water. A woman pointed out to me that a block further away where there were children there was water.
>
> It is impossible for me to express the scene that was before me: piles of bodies already decomposing, in fact about a mile of bodies. Shivering at what I had seen, I still managed to go and find some water which I hid inside my dress so no one could see. This relieved my sister a bit.
>
> Many people talk about Auschwitz, it was a horrible camp; but Belsen, no words can describe it. There was no need to work as we were just put there with no food, no water, no anything, eaten by the lice.

From my experience and my suffering Belsen was the worst. I came to the point where everyone was saying, 'Violette is dying.'[3]

On March 3 a train of evacuees from Gross Rosen reached Ebensee, a sub-camp of Mauthausen. These 2,059 Jews had mostly been sent to Gross Rosen from Birkenau, or from the labour camps in central Poland. On the train journey to Ebensee, 49 had died. On the first day in Ebensee, 182 died during the disinfection procedure. They had become too weak to withstand any further effort.[4]

There was also a continual danger in the intensified Allied bombing raids. On March 20 many Jewish women in a camp at Tiefstack, near Hamburg, were killed when the camp was hit in an air raid, and burnt to the ground.[5] The accidents of bombing affected both the eastern and western fronts: on March 26 a Russian bomb hit the Jewish hospital in Stutthof. 'My sister was one of the victims of that bomb,' a Kovno Jewess wrote. 'All in all twenty-eight people were killed and thirty-five were wounded.' The Jewess added: 'It was fated that I should know where she was buried.'[6]

With liberation apparently so near, the Jews were still not safe. In Stutthof, as this same Jewess wrote two months later, 'If I had not seen with my own eyes how people were flung alive into the crematorium I would never have believed that any man could do anything like this to any other man. But that is the truth.'[7]

Stutthof, and Danzig, remained in German hands. But one by one the many branch camps around Stutthof were liberated by the Red Army. At one of these, Pruszcz, nine hundred prisoners had died, most of them Jewish women deported there in the summer and autumn of 1944 from Auschwitz and the Baltic States. Only two hundred women remained alive on March 21, when the Germans fled and Russian troops entered the camp. One of the Jewish women, Sonia Reznik Rosenfeld, later recalled:

As the horrible scene in the barracks met the eyes of the officer he stood transfixed and speechless. Then our 're-deemer', standing at a distance lest he be infected by our lice, asked us who we were. We told him we were Jews. To this he answered, 'You are free! Go where your hearts desire. Our Red Army has freed you from murderous hands.'

Everyone lay motionless, no one could utter a word. It is impossible to be freed when one already has one leg underground. As I could speak Russian better than anyone there, I told the officer that we were half-dead people, and I asked him where we would go, and how we would get there as none of us had a home any more for Hitler's hordes had shot everyone's family.

The officer sighed, and with eyes full of pity he said, 'Don't be disheartened, unhappy women, as long as your pulses throb within you, you will yet be people like everyone else. Remain in your places and we will take you to our military hospital. There you will convalesce and each one of you will be able to go on your way.'[8]

For many of those on the death marches, the distance they were from the Red Army could be calculated only by the sound of distant artillery fire, as their German guards drove them further and further away from the front line. When the Red Army drew too near, the marchers would be put in trains. Aliza Besser, one of the two hundred survivors of the thousand Jewish women who had marched on foot from the camp at Neusalz to Flossenberg, was among those who were sent on the next stage of their horrendous journey, by sealed cattle truck, they knew not where. On March 21, after three days and nights in the train, she noted:

It's almost a week already that we are in the trucks. No water. They die of thirst. Lips are parched. Every other day they give a few cups of water, occasionally they bring a bucket of water which is intended for seventy people. There's nothing with which to take the water. There are only a few cups in every truck, and everyone wants to drink. Commotion breaks out, and the German guards pour away the water in front of us all. Water that no one drank. . . .[9]

Three days later, the train reached Belsen. Of the thousand Jewish women who had set off two months earlier, less than two hundred reached Belsen alive.[10]

On March 30, at Ravensbruck, a number of women who were being led to their execution struggled with the SS guards. Nine managed to escape; but they were soon recaptured, and then executed.[11]

The Allied forces now stood on German soil both in the west and in the east, advancing steadily on both fronts. In southern Germany, French forces were on the edge of the Black Forest. In the forest, being marched towards Dachau, a group of eighty-three Jews agreed upon a plan to run away. Their password would be the Jewish greeting over a glass of wine, 'Lehayim!', 'To life!' Many of these Jews were survivors of a sequence of deportations and evacuations, from the Vilna ghetto to the Estonian labour camps, from the Estonian labour camps, by sea, to Stutthof, and from Stutthof to a camp in south-western Germany. One of them, Meir Dvorjetzky, later recalled, of the march towards Dachau:

> . . . we were walking along and we saw that orders were being given that people should get off the street, get into the forest, and we saw a big lake in front of us. It was near Baden-Baden. We understood that here we were being led to be drowned in the lake. We walked in single file and we decided – we shouted 'Lehayim' and all the Jews scattered in all directions, and in the evening we found ourselves in the forest – eighty-three people we were; others may have been scattered elsewhere in the other forests; others were lying dead, hit by German bullets.
>
> We went on, we lived in the forest, we had no arms – it was a German forest – it was near Baden-Baden, a forest in Germany; the date was the end of March 1945 – perhaps the middle of March; we had lost track of dates and days and hours – and we were there during the night. We would attack the foresters. They were even afraid of us – of the 'mussulman', of the prisoners; they would turn over bread to us – they had no choice. Then we would go elsewhere to avoid being caught and then one night we heard shots and we knew that we were in between the two fronts.
>
> We didn't know who was fighting whom. In the morning the fighting died down; it was the end of that battle. One boy climbed up a tree and saw tanks – tri-coloured tanks – we understood that this was the French army. We shouted, 'Liberté, Fraternité, Egalité,' and we were put into the tanks and we went in those tanks into the German town of Solgau and there, we, the eighty-three Jews, entered with the French army into the town. . . .[12]

Liberation did not always bring allies or safety: on 2 April 1945, on the liberated soil of Poland, Leon Feldhendler, one of the leaders of the Sobibor death camp revolt in 1943, was murdered by Poles.[13]

From the first days of April 1945 it became clear that the Russian and Western Allies would continue to advance until they met somewhere in the middle of Germany. But Hitler still hoped that the German army would be able to hold out in one of the mountainous areas that remained under his control, either the Sudeten mountains or the Austrian Alps, and from there to continue the war.

A new policy now drove the SS to prolong the agony of the death marches: the desire to preserve for as long as possible a mass of slave labour for all the needs which confronted the disintegrating German army: repairing roads and railway tracks, building up railway embankments, repairing bridges, excavating underground bunkers from which the battle could still be directed, preparing tank traps to check the Allied advance, and helping with the massive work involved in preparing mountain fortresses deep underground.

Sixty per cent of those on the death marches were non-Jews; for the Jews, there remained the all-pervading Nazi obsession that Jews were not human beings, that they must be made to suffer. 'This hatred of the Jews', Hugo Gryn, a survivor of the death marches, has commented, 'was the one fixed function of the Nazi ideology: all else could change, but the Jew must continue to suffer, and to die'. The death marches and death trains continued, despite the increasing chaos on the roads and railways following the collapse of both the western and eastern fronts.

At the beginning of April, as Soviet forces approached Vienna, a group of thirteen hundred Jews, who had been set to work repairing Vienna's badly bombed main railway station, were evacuated westward. Many of them were survivors of Theresienstadt, and of Birkenau. No food was issued on the march: the Jews ate whatever food they could find in the fields. Those who fell behind were shot. Only seven hundred reached Gusen camp, their destination, alive.[14]

On a march from a factory near Hanover to Belsen, Moshe Oster later recalled how prisoners had to pull three wagons full of SS men's property for more than forty miles. During the march, eighteen of the marchers were shot dead.[15] On April 4, near Gotha, Jews working in quarries were driven to Buchenwald. Before leaving, some were shot.[16]

On April 4, United States forces reached the village of Ohrdruf. Just outside the village they found a deserted labour camp: a camp in which four thousand inmates had died or been murdered in the previous three months. Hundreds had been shot on the eve of the American arrival. Some of the victims were Jews, others were Polish and Russian prisoners-of-war. All had been forced to build a vast underground radio and telephone centre, intended for the German army in the event of a retreat from Berlin.[17]

Among the Jews who had been held at Ohrdruf was Leo Laufer. Four days before liberation, Laufer had been fortunate to escape, as the evacuation of the camp began. Running off with three fellow prisoners, they had left their wooden shoes behind in order 'to run faster and not make any noise'. For four days they had hidden in the hills above Ohrdruf. When the American forces arrived, Laufer accompanied them into the camp. Many of the corpses which they found there were of prisoners who had been in the camp dispensary at the time of the evacuation of the camp four days earlier.[18]

The sight of the emaciated corpses at Ohrdruf created a wave of revulsion which spread back to Britain and the United States. General Eisenhower, who visited the camp, was so shocked that he at once telephoned Churchill to describe what he had seen, and then sent photographs of the dead prisoners to Churchill, who circulated them to each member of the British Cabinet.[19]

In Belsen, still under German control, thirty thousand prisoners watched in fear and agony as the SS prepared to leave the camp, but without knowing when liberation would come, or if it could possibly come in time. Fania Fenelon later recalled the first week of April:

> Hastily built to last a few months, our temporary barracks were half-collapsing; the planks were coming apart. Looking at the damage, a scornful SS man said, speaking of us, the Jews: 'They rot everything, even wood.'
> It was true, we were rotting, but it was hardly our fault — their presence alone would taint the healthiest beings.

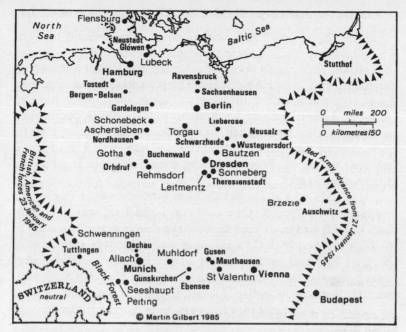

THE LIBERATION OF THE CAMPS

A few days later, I too had typhus. My last vision as a healthy person was of the women of the camp, like everyone else, outside naked, lining up to wash our dresses and underclothes in the thin trickle of water from the pierced pipe. On the other side of the barbed wire, the men were doing the same; we were like two troops of cattle at the half-empty trough of an abattoir.

Now the illness took me over entirely; my head was bursting, my body trembling, my intestines and stomach were agony, and I had the most abominable dysentery. I was just a sick animal lying in its own excrement.

From April 8 everything around me became nightmarish. I existed merely as a bursting head, an intestine, a perpetually active anus. One tier above, there was a French girl, I didn't know; in my moments of lucidity, I heard her saying in a clear, calm, even pleasant voice: 'I must shit, but I must shit on your head, it's more hygienic!' She had gone mad; others equally unhinged guffawed interminably or fought. No one came to see us anymore, not even the SS. They'd turned off the water. . . .[20]

On April 8, almost all the Jewish inmates at Buchenwald, many of whom had only reached there three months earlier, from Birkenau or Stutthof, were marched out, leaving the non-Jewish prisoners to await the arrival of the Americans. The Jews were driven east, then south, to the concentration camp at Flossenburg. Other Jews, in camps at Aschersleben and Schonebeck, were driven south, then north again, then back south, first on foot and in trucks, then by train, through the Sudeten mountains, to Leitmeritz. A third group was sent to nearby Theresienstadt, sixty being murdered at the village of Buchau.[21]

A few Jews had managed to hide in Buchenwald during the 'evacuation' of April 8. One of them, Israel Lau, was only eight years old. He had been kept alive by the devotion and ingenuity of his elder brother, Naftali, aged nineteen. Three days after most of the Jews had been marched out of the camp, American forces arrived. One of the American officers, Rabbi Herschel Schechter, later recalled how he pulled a small, frightened boy from a pile of corpses. The rabbi burst into tears and then, hoping to reassure the child, began to laugh.

'How old are you?' he asked Israel Lau, in Yiddish.

'Older than you.'

'How can you say that?' asked the rabbi, fearing the child was deranged.

'You cry and laugh like a little boy,' Lau replied, 'but I haven't laughed for years and I don't even cry any more. So tell me, who is older?'[22]

On April 10, Adolf Eichmann made his last visit to Theresienstadt. There, he was heard to say: 'I shall gladly jump into the pit, knowing that in the same pit there are five million enemies of the state.'[23] Three days later, one of the death marches, mostly of Auschwitz survivors, reached the area of Belsen. One of the survivors, Menachem Weinryb, later recalled:

> One night we stopped near the town of Gardelegen. We lay down in a field and several Germans went to consult about what they should do. They returned with a lot of young people

from the Hitler Youth and with members of the police force from the town.

They chased us all into a large barn. Since we were five to six thousand people, the wall of the barn collapsed from the pressure of the mass of people, and many of us fled. The Germans poured out petrol and set the barn on fire. Several thousand people were burned alive.

Those of us who had managed to escape lay down in the nearby wood and heard the heart-rending screams of the victims. This was on April 13.[24]

Trapped in the barn, the Jews had tried to escape by burrowing under the foundation walls. But as their heads appeared on the outside, they were shot by the Germans surrounding the barn.[25]

On April 13 the Red Army entered Vienna. One of the last trains to leave the city before the arrival of the Red Army reached Theresienstadt on April 15 with 109 Jews. This was the last deportation of the war organized by Eichmann's department.[26]

On April 14, United States troops reached Gardelegen itself. There, in yet another camp established for the death marchers, they found, in a huge open pit, the still burning logs on which the bodies of the dead had been cremated.[27]

On April 15, the first British tanks entered Belsen. By chance, three of the British soldiers in the tanks were Jews. But the survivors did not realize what had happened: 'We, the cowed and emaciated inmates of the camp, did not believe we were free,' one of the Jews there, Josef Rosensaft, later recalled. 'It seemed to us a dream which would soon turn again into cruel reality.'[28]

At Belsen, the 'cruel reality' came swiftly, as those first British tanks moved on, in pursuit of the German forces. For the next forty-eight hours the camp remained only nominally under British control, with the Hungarian SS guards in partial command. During that brief interval, seventy-two Jews and eleven non-Jews were shot by the Hungarians for such offences as taking potato peel from the kitchen.[29]

When, finally, British troops did enter Belsen in force, the evidence of mass murder on a vast scale became immediately apparent to them. Of ten thousand unburied bodies, most were victims of starvation. Even after liberation three hundred inmates died each day during the ensuing week from typhus and starvation. Even after the arrival of massive British medical aid, personnel and food, the death rate was still sixty a day after two weeks and more.[30]

Among those who died after liberation was Miriam Fintz, one of the deportees of July 1944 from Rhodes to Auschwitz.[31] 'Men and women, clad in rags,' Colonel Gerald Draper has recalled, 'and barely able to move from starvation and typhus, lay in their straw bunks in every state of filth and degradation. The dead and dying could not be distinguished.' Men and women 'collapsed as they walked and fell dead'. In order to cope with what they found in 'verminous and stinking barracks', Draper added, the British army doctors 'marked a red cross on the foreheads of those they thought had a chance of surviving'.[32]

Fania Fenelon has recalled, of those first days of liberation at Belsen:

> A new life breathed in the camp. Jeeps, command cars, and half tracks drove around among the barracks. Khaki uniforms abounded, the marvellously substantial material of their battle dress mingling with the rags of the deportees. Our liberators were well fed and bursting with health, and they moved among our skeletal, tenuous silhouettes like a surge of life. We felt an absurd desire to finger them, to let our hands trail in their eddies as in the Fountain of Youth. They called to one another, whistled cheerfully, then suddenly fell silent, faced with eyes too large, or too intense a gaze. How alive they were; they walked quickly, they ran, they leapt. All these movements were so easy for them, while a single one of them would have taken away our last breath of life! These men seemed not to know that one could live in slow motion, that energy was something you saved.[33]

Photographs, films and articles about Belsen circulated widely in Britain by the end of April, making so great an impact that the word 'Belsen' was to become synonymous with 'inhumanity'. For these were not reports of discoveries by the Red Army in the distant eastern regions of the Reich, but of horrors as seen by men from London and Manchester, from the Midlands and the north of England, battle-weary soldiers familiar enough with the horrors of war by April 1945, but shocked as they never thought they could be by the sights that confronted them. 'There had been no food nor water for five days preceding the British entry,' a British army review reported. 'Evidence of cannibalism was found. The inmates had lost all self-respect, were degraded morally to the level of beasts. Their clothes were in rags, teeming with lice, and both inside and outside the huts was an almost continuous carpet of dead bodies, human excreta, rags and filth.'

Soldiers and nurses set to work to save those who could be saved. But even the arrival of food was too much for hundreds of the inmates, who died as a result of the 'richness' of the British army rations: dried milk-powder, oatmeal, sugar, salt and tinned meat.[34]

Among the British soldiers who witnessed the first days of liberation at Belsen was Peter Coombs, who described in a letter to his wife the condition of the survivors:

> The sight of these affects one profoundly, for while there is still life and movement, we are interested in their salvation mentally and physically. The conditions in which these people live are appalling. One has to take a tour round and see their faces, their slow staggering gait and feeble movements. The state of their minds is plainly written on their faces, as starvation has reduced their bodies to skeletons. The fact is that all these were once clean-living and sane and certainly not the type to do harm to the Nazis. They are Jews and are dying now at the rate of three hundred a day. They must die and nothing can save them – their end is inescapable, they are too far gone now to be brought back to life.
>
> I saw their corpses lying near their hovels, for they crawl or totter out into the sunlight to die. I watched them make their last feeble journeys, and even as I watched they died.

'Every other day', Coombs added, 'the bodies were collected and buried and there is always an open grave.' Ninety-eight British medical students had arrived at Belsen, 'and will take a hut between two of them and see that the inmates get the right medical attention and food in the right quantities.' He added: 'I have never seen people looking so ill, so wretched and so near to death. Belsen is a living death, an example of Nazi methods, the best indictment of their government one could ever find, and if it is ever necessary, an undoubted answer to those who want to know what we have been

796 · THE HOLOCAUST

fighting for. One feeble movement of the hand in salutation to us from these people is also an answer, for our coming has saved thousands in this camp alone, but for many it is too late.'[35]

On the same day that British troops entered Belsen, American troops entered yet another camp at Nordhausen, where hundreds of slave labourers were found, 'in conditions', as the United States Signal Corps recorded, 'almost unrecognizable as human. All were little more than skeletons: the dead lay beside the sick and dying in the same beds: filth and human excrement covered the floors. No attempt had been made to alleviate the disease and gangrene that had spread unchecked among the prisoners.'

The Americans listened in horror, as did the British at Belsen, to the stories of past atrocities that every liberated prisoner could recount. 'I mention an example of greatest bestiality,' a United States investigator recorded. 'A woman in the last stages of pregnancy was thrown down by an SS man who then stepped on her with his boots until birth was forced. In blood and pain the woman died wretchedly.'[36]

The Germans realised that the war was nearly over, and that retribution was imminent. On April 14, a Swedish diplomat, Count Folke Bernadotte, negotiated the release of the 423 Danish Jews who had been held, unharmed, at Theresienstadt, and they were returned to Denmark.[37] But elsewhere, the cruel evacuations continued. On April 15, as the Western and Soviet armies drew together, seventeen thousand women and forty thousand men were marched westwards from Ravensbruck and Sachsenhausen. A Red Cross official who was present, by chance, as the marchers set off from Ravensbruck, wrote in his report: 'As I approached them, I could see that they had sunken cheeks, distended bellies and swollen ankles. Their complexion was sallow. All of a sudden, a whole column of those starving wretches appeared. In each row a sick woman was supported or dragged along by her fellow detainees. A young SS woman supervisor with a police dog on a leash led the column, followed by two girls who incessantly hurled abuse at the poor women.'[38]

Many hundreds of women died of exhaustion in the march from Ravensbruck. Hundreds more were shot by the wayside. Others

were killed by Allied bombs falling on German lines of communication; among these bomb victims was Mila Racine, a twenty-one-
year-old French girl who in October 1943 had been caught by the
Gestapo while on clandestine courier duty, escorting a group of
children to the Swiss border. Later she had been deported to
Auschwitz. Now she lay dead by a German roadside.[39]

In southern Germany it was the turn of French troops to stumble
across the evidence of mass murder, and of recent killings. Even
amid the beautiful spring fragrance of the Swabian Alps and
the upper Danube, it was the stench of death that assailed
them.

At four villages, the French troops found the mass graves of Jews
who had earlier been deported from camps and ghettos in the east.
With typical Gestapo thoroughness, the names, ages and birth-
places of the victims had all been recorded. The thirty-nine-year-old
Peisach Rudnicki had been born in distant Swieciany, where, in
September 1941, nearly four thousand Jews had been murdered,
but where several hundred had managed to escape, including his
own nephew, Yitzhak Rudnicki. The young Rudnicki survived the
war as a teenage partisan with the Red Army. Later, as Yitzhak
Arad, he was to become Chairman of Yad Vashem, the Holocaust
martyrs and heroes remembrance authority in Jerusalem.

Buchenwald, Belsen, Nordhausen, and more than a hundred
other camps and sub-camps had been liberated by the third week of
April. 'We are now reading', wrote Captain Foley, Britain's former
Passport Control Officer in Berlin, on April 19, 'about those places
the names of which were so well known to us in the years before the
war. Now the people here really and finally believe that the stories
of 1938–9 were not exaggerated.' Looking back, Foley added, 'I
feel grateful that our little office in Tiergartenstrasse was able to
assist some – far too few – to escape in time.'[40]

In Berlin, the day after Captain Foley wrote this letter, Heinrich
Himmler decided to win some credit with the approaching Allies. At
a meeting with Norbert Masur on April 20 he agreed to allow seven
thousand women, a half of them Jewish, to be taken from Ravensbruck to Sweden.[41]

In Croatia, Soviet forces were sweeping the German forces
northward to the Austrian border. One last camp remained to be
liberated, Jasenovac, where tens of thousands of Yugoslav Jews had

been murdered. By April 1945 there were only a thousand Jews and Serbs still alive in the camp. On April 22, six hundred of them rose in revolt. The guards had no hesitation in opening fire, and five hundred and twenty prisoners were shot down. But eighty managed to escape, among them twenty Jews.[42]

The Second World War was almost over. Yet no corner of the dwindling Reich was free from killing: on April 25, six Jews were taken by the Gestapo at Cuneo, in northern Italy, and shot. That same day, in the final evacuation from Stutthof, two hundred Jewish women were taken to the seashore and shot. The remaining four thousand prisoners, of whom fifteen hundred were Jews, were evacuated on five barges, across the Baltic to the Danish–German coastline. More than half of these evacuees were drowned, or shot by the Germans.[43]

For the Allied armies, April 25 was a day of historic importance: the meeting at Torgau of Russian and United States forces. Militarily, Germany had been cut in half. Three days later, the Red Cross arranged with the SS for the transport of 150 Jewesses from Ravensbruck, which was still under German control, to Sweden. These were to be the first of the 3,500 Jewish and 3,500 non-Jewish women whom Himmler had agreed should be transferred to safety. On their way out of Germany, five of the Jewesses were killed during an Allied air raid.[44] Many of those who did reach Sweden died, like tens of thousands of other survivors, after their rescue and after their liberation. They had been too much weakened by their experiences to be saved, even in surroundings of kindness and care. They had come, these survivors who could not survive, from all over Europe. Rozika Rosenbaum from Warsaw was thirty years old. Rosette Bas from Amsterdam, Helena Hausman from Dresden and Rozalia Katz from Beregszasz were each twenty. Bronislawa Dorfman from Czestochowa was sixteen. All died within a few months of liberation.[45]

On April 29, American troops entered Dachau. As at Buchenwald and at Belsen, the Allied journalists accompanying the troops were shattered by what they saw. Sam Goldsmith, a Jew from Lithuania who had come to Britain before the war, and who had earlier seen the horrors of Belsen, noted down his first sight of Dachau:

On a railway siding there is a train of fifty wagons – all full of terribly emaciated dead bodies, piled up like the twisted branches of cut-down trees. Near the crematorium – for the disposal of the dead – another huge pile of dead bodies, like a heap of crooked logs ready for some infernal fire. The stench is like that of Belsen; it follows you even when you are back in the Press camp.

There were 2,539 Jews among the 33,000 survivors, almost all of them Lithuanian Jews, the remnants of the ghetto Slobodka. I found some old friends, among them, people who went to school with me and others who used to be fellow members of Maccabi. And there was my doctor and friend of the Kovno days. He solemnly shook hands with me and enquired about my health.[46]

In the villages around Dachau, and in the lanes along which only days earlier they had been marched as prisoners southward into the mountains, hundreds of Jews wandered, free but bewildered, not knowing what they would encounter in liberated Europe. The twenty-eight-year-old Levi Shalit, a survivor of the Siauliai ghetto, Stutthof and Dachau, has recalled how he walked, a free man at last, into a small town in the Austrian Tyrol:

On the way into the town stood a German with a white band on his arm: an orderly. 'Where are you going, sir?'

Hm! So it was 'sir' now. But the Germans were still maintaining 'order'.

'To the town.'

'That's prohibited, sir. The Americans have prohibited it, sir; the refugees must remain in their camp, sir.'

So, the Americans have prohibited it, and you are carrying out their prohibition – as long as it's 'order', as long as it's a command.

There were many streets in that little town at the foot of the Tyrolean Alps. How lovely everything was. How quietly dreamed the little red-tiled houses with their little green gardens. There were the outlying houses.

Four days before, the inhabitants had rushed out at us with axes and blades. Now they were invisible. Now and again one of them slunk past with a band on his arm and wearing the short, greasy leather Tyrolean pants – slunk along with stealthy steps to take his turn at guard duty at the town entrance.

How quickly they had organized themselves! Not a sign of their defeat, of their world-destroying end.

In only one building, in the schoolhouse, there was hubbub. Food was being distributed to refugees, Germans who had fled from their homes and had been overtaken by the Americans.

I pushed my head into the open doorway. The smell of bread and milk met my nostrils.

'Please, sir, do you want something to eat?' One of them tried this approach carefully, fawning like a dog.

The main street of the town was quiet. No one was to be seen – as if they all had died out. They kept within their houses, which bore not the slightest trace of war damage.

Here and there American soldiers were on patrol. One came up to me, a short fellow with a cheeky face, little more than a child.

'A Jew?'

'A Jew!' I stuttered.

Our arms intertwined and we burbled crazily, 'A Jew, a Jew'.[47]

Joy and tragedy both came in unexpected forms. Sarah Friedmann, who had been deported to Birkenau from Hungary in June 1944, and had survived the death marches, reached Allach, near Munich in April 1945. Later she recalled the arrival of American forces on April 29. 'They distributed food and oil. Many of us perished that day as a result of overeating, because they were not used to such fat and nourishing food in their stomachs.' But the tins of food proved irresistible to the starving, emaciated survivors, and so they died. 'We called them "canned-goods victims".'[48]

Many survivors died because they were beyond the reaches of life. 'If their weight was thirty kilogrammes,' recalled Aharon Hoter-Yishai, 'they had no contact with life any more. They had no strength, no will to survive left in them, no resistance.' Hoter-Yishai, a member of the Jewish Brigade of the Eighth Army, visited Belsen, Dachau and other camps in the weeks and months following liberation.

In the camps, where Jews still lived in the huts which had once held them prisoner, as many as twenty-seven thousand died after liberation because they were too weak to respond to medical treatment. They looked, Hoter-Yishai recalled sixteen years later, 'like forests where only amputated trunks remained standing. A man with amputated limbs: his children had been taken, his wife had been taken, and what remained was a severed trunk, wounded and bleeding, and these wounds were only reopened after the liberation. He could not forget, and his inner life hardly made it possible to find any contact with others.'[49]

'We were in a daze,' Maria Rebhun later recalled, of the moment when the Red Army reached Lauenburg camp in Pomerania. 'Barely moving, supporting the ones that were not able to make a step, and pushing the ones that were already written off in a wheelbarrow, we went to face new reality. Our minds were like a vacuum, our hearts empty of any desires.' Maria Rebhun's parents had perished in the Warsaw ghetto uprising, each of her brothers and sisters had been killed. She was alone. 'On the streets', she recalled, 'ecstatic Russian soldiers offered us sweets and cigarettes amidst laughter and songs, but we were mute. Who are we? Where are we to go? Whom to turn to?'[50]

In hiding, in fields and ditches, barns and attics, Jews who had survived ghetto and deportation, Birkenau and the death marches, peeped out at the retreating Germans, and gazed into the distance to see the first Allied tanks and soldiers. Samuel Pisar has recalled how hiding with other teenage boys in a hayloft at Peiting in Bavaria:

> I suddenly became aware of a hum, like a swarm of bees, growing in volume. A machine gun opened fire alongside our barn and, when it stopped, there was that hum again, only louder, unearthly metallic.
>
> I peeped through a crack in the wooden slats. Straight ahead, on the other side of the field, a huge tank was coming toward the barn. It stopped, and the humming ceased. From somewhere to one side, machine guns crackled and the sounds of mortar explosions carried across the field. The tank's long cannon lifted its round head, as though peering at me, then turned slowly aside and let loose a tremendous belch. The firing stopped. The tank resumed its advance, lumbering cautiously toward me. I looked for the hateful swastika, but there wasn't one. On the tank's sides, instead, I made out an unfamiliar emblem. It was a five-pointed white star. In an instant, the

realization flooded me; I was looking at the insignia of the United States army.

My skull seemed to burst. With a wild roar, I broke through the thatched roof, leaped to the ground, and ran toward the tank. The German machine guns opened up again. The tank fired twice. Then all was quiet. I was still running. I was in front of the tank, waving my arms. The hatch opened. A big black man climbed out, swearing unintelligibly at me. Recalling the only English I knew, those words my mother had sighed while dreaming of our deliverance, I fell at the black man's feet, threw my arms around his legs and yelled at the top of my lungs:

'God bless America!'

With an unmistakable gesture, the American motioned me to get up and lifted me in through the hatch. In a few minutes, all of us were free.[51]

In another Bavarian village, Seeshaupt, in the railway station, the SS were guarding a train of men and boys brought from Dachau, on what had been intended as yet another journey away from the advancing Allies. Moshe Sandberg, who had survived deportation to Birkenau, and the death marches, later recalled the scene at the station:

A group of SS soldiers standing there pointed towards the village and said that the tanks parked there were American. I don't think that any of us believed them. It seemed a joke at our expense. Somebody asked if we could get out of the train and in a voice very different from the usual a soldier replied, 'Of course.'

Some of us got out, without any particular joy, unable to understand the meaning of that fateful moment. Some ran to the grass and began devouring it as if it was the most natural of foods. The Germans stood silent, only looking towards the tanks.

I and my friends decided to escape. We did not have strength enough to run or even to walk fast. Our movement was much more like that of two old men than of prisoners escaping from their cell.

We reckoned that we had nothing to lose. Either we would be killed by bullets or we would die of starvation. Slowly we crossed the railway line and left the station. At the first house we came to we asked for food. Apparently the German did not know that his village had been captured. He drove us away, saying that he had no food. We saw that his wife was peeling potatoes and carrots. We begged for the peelings, which we gobbled down with all the dirt on them. We then got to a second house, but the woman made us wait outside, no doubt because of our filthy condition and our terrible, unhuman appearance. She asked us to wait and then reappeared with two hard-boiled eggs. We tried to remove the shells, but our hands were palsied. It was months, perhaps a year, that we had not seen an egg! Finally, unable to wait longer, I swallowed the egg, shell and all.

We were free, but we did not know it, did not believe it, could not believe it. We had waited for this such long days and nights that now when the dream had come true it seemed still a dream. We wanted to go to a third house to beg something, but just then an American tank approached from which the soldiers motioned us to come nearer. Only then did we under-stand that it was not a dream. We were free! We were really free! We broke into weeping. We kissed the tank. A Negro soldier gave us a tin of meat, bread and chocolate, and pointed to us the way to the village centre. We sat down on the ground and ate up all the food together – bread, chocolate and meat. The Negro watched us, tears in his eyes.[52]

In the regions still under German control, Jews struggled to survive the final days and hours of incarceration. At Mauthausen, Rudolf Fahn, one of those who had escaped from Slovakia in May 1940, only to be caught again four years later in Rhodes, and sent to Auschwitz, found a scrap of clean cloth which he took into the wash-room in order to dry himself. To take the cloth was, in the rules of the camp, punishable by death; the guard, seeing Fahn commit this 'offence', beat him to death on the spot. Now, of the five Fahns deported from Rhodes to Birkenau nine months earlier, only Sidney Fahn was still alive.[53]

In Berlin, on April 29, Adolf Hitler dictated his political testament. The Second World War, he wrote, had been 'provoked exclusively' by those international statesmen 'who either were of Jewish origin or worked for Jewish interests'. The Jews were 'the real guilty party in this murderous struggle' and would be 'saddled' with the responsibility of it. Hitler added:

> I left no one in doubt that this time not only would millions of children of European Aryan races starve, not only would millions of grown men meet their death, and not only would hundreds of thousands of women and children be burned and bombed to death in cities, but this time the real culprits would have to pay for their guilt even though by more humane means than war.

The 'more humane means' had been the gas-chambers.

He had decided, Hitler declared, to die in Berlin so as not to 'fall into the hands of the enemy, who requires a new spectacle, presented by the Jews, to divert their hysterical masses'.[54]

On April 30 Hitler committed suicide in his bunker in Berlin. The news of his death, broadcast over Berlin radio, spread rapidly throughout the dwindling Reich. At a small farm in the Sudetenland, a column of Jews, from a labour camp at Sonnenberg, had been ordered to spend the night in a barn. One of the Jews, Michael Etkind, who had earlier been in the Lodz ghetto, recalled:

> Again, there was no food. We crowded in and lay down on the straw. The guards, posted at the open doorway, sat on stools with their guns resting on their knees. They were talking quietly in their alien, Germanic tongue when someone close by overheard the words: 'Hitler is dead.'
>
> Those three words were like a match thrown into the barn: in seconds the fire had spread from mouth to ear, from ear to mouth. And then there was a moment of silence. Suddenly, the 'Joker' – the man who'd kept the rest of us going with his humour and jokes – the man from my hut in Sonnenberg, jumped up. Like a man possessed, like a lunatic, he began to dance about waving his arms in the air; his high-pitched voice chanted with frenzy:
>
> > 'I have outlived the fiend,
> > my life-long wish fulfilled,
> > what more need I achieve –
> > my heart is full of joy'

he sang in a transport of ecstasy. We watched him in horror, speechless. His lanky frame was swirling round until it reached the open door. No one could move. He'd run into the field outside.

One of the German guards lifted his gun, took aim.

We saw the 'Joker' lift his arms again, stand up, turn around, surprised (didn't they understand, hadn't they heard, that the Monster was dead?) and, like a puppet when its strings are cut, collapse into a heap.[55]

On the day of Hitler's death, 2,775 Jews from Rehmsdorf, near Buchenwald, were being marched to Theresienstadt. A thousand of them, fleeing from the march during an Allied air raid, were caught and shot. The remaining fifteen hundred continued on the march. Only five hundred reached Theresienstadt alive.[56] That same day, April 30, the Red Army entered Ravensbruck, where twenty-three thousand women, Jews and non-Jews, were alive, and saved.[57] In that one camp alone ninety-two thousand Jews and non-Jews, most of them women and children, had been murdered in just over two years. As Soviet troops overtook the 'death marchers', who had been driven westward from Ravensbruck a few days earlier, several thousand were still alive.

Soviet and American forces had linked up in the middle of Germany, but in the dwindling pockets of territory still under German control, Jews still suffered for being Jews. At noon on May 1, Alfred Kantor, survivor of Birkenau and Schwarzheide, noted, as their death march continued: 'Last revenge of the guard's chief. Hanging for escape. Prisoners have to look on. Anybody turning face to the ground is whipped by SS fuhrer.'[58]

On May 2 Berlin surrendered to the Red Army. At the end of 1942 there had been thirty-three thousand Jews in the city. Following the round-ups and deportations of 1943, only 238 full Jews remained. By May 1945 this figure had been reduced to 162, all of them in hiding. There were also about 800 half-Jews and Jewish refugees, hiding in the cellars of the Jewish hospital. Also still in the city, undeported throughout the war, were 4,790 Jews married to non-Jews, 992 people of mixed parentage who admitted to being Jews by religion, and 46 Jews with citizenship of countries which were not at war with Germany.[59] In the previous three years, fifty thousand Jews had been deported from Berlin to the East, to

Auschwitz, and to Theresienstadt, of whom fewer than three and a half thousand survived.[60]

Among the first Soviet soldiers to enter Berlin on May 2 was Semyon Rozenfeld, one of the survivors of the Sobibor revolt. After nearly seven months in hiding he had been liberated by Soviet troops in July 1944, and despite a still-infected wound in his right leg, demanded to be sent to the front. Again wounded, and briefly in hospital in Lodz, he had returned to his unit for the final battles and final triumph, to witness the capture of the Reichstag. At the age of twenty-three his hair had already turned silver white, his brow deeply furrowed. On the Reichstag wall he carved the words: 'Baranowicze–Sobibor–Berlin'.[61] It was a paean to Jewish suffering, struggle, and survival.

On May 2, in Lübeck harbour, several hundred Jews who had been evacuated from Stutthof were taken out in small boats to be put on board two large ships in the harbour, the *Cap Arcona* and the *Thielbek*. The captains of these ships refused to take them, however; they already had 7,500 Jews on board. The small boats were ordered back to the shore. But, as they neared land in the early hours of May 3, and the starving Jews tried to clamber ashore, SS men, Hitler Youth and German Marines opened fire on them with machine guns. More than five hundred were killed. Only 351 survived.[62] That same day, May 3, the *Cap Arcona* was attacked by British aircraft in Lübeck Bay. Only a few of the prisoners managed to save their lives by jumping overboard.[63]

At another camp near Lübeck, Neustadt-Glowen, Jewish women, who had been brought from the Breslau area and from Ravensbruck, were made to dig trenches and anti-tank ditches: a futile gesture of continuing German defiance as the Allied armies prepared for their last assault. 'Everything was now a matter of physical endurance,' Lena Berg recalled: 'the food was wretched; we slept on the floor; and we were tormented by lice. Only by gritting our teeth could we go on.' An 'unusually warm spring', she recalled, 'helped us to hold out'. It helped those women who, like her, had survived so many separate torments, the Warsaw ghetto, Majdanek, Birkenau, Stutthof and the death marches.

Then, on May 2, the SS guards 'failed to appear at roll-call'. The Jewish women at Neustadt-Glowen were free. 'We walked out along the highway,' Lena Berg recalled. 'From the right a tank draped with an American flag was coming our way and behind it tall, slender boys in American uniform. They were terribly embarrassed when unappetizing creatures who bore only a remote resemblance to women suddenly threw themselves at them, kissing and hugging them.' Back in the camp, Lena Berg found wild enthusiasm. 'But I, who had unflinchingly believed that the moment would come, now for the first time felt bewildered and lost.'[64]

One of the last concentration camps under German control was Mauthausen, together with its satellite camps at Gusen, St Valentin, Gunskirchen and Ebensee. In just over four months, more than thirty thousand people had been murdered at Mauthausen, or had died from starvation and disease. Jews and Gypsies formed the largest groups of those killed, but other groups had also been singled out by the Nazis: homosexuals, Jehovah's Witnesses, Soviet prisoners-of-war, and tens of thousands of Spanish republicans. These Spaniards had been interned in France in September 1939, deported by the Germans to Mauthausen in 1940, and systematically worked to death in the stone quarry there, or shot at random. By January 1945 only three thousand of the Spaniards had remained alive. Of these, 2,163 had been killed in the next three months.[65]

Among those held prisoner in Mauthausen was the British agent, Albert Guérisse, known as Lieutenant-Commander Pat O'Leary. O'Leary's biographer, Vincent Brome, has recorded how O'Leary witnessed what happened when a prisoner who had managed to escape was recaptured. An SS guard, O'Leary recalled, 'launched a tremendous blow to the man's jaw. The prisoner's hand went up to ward off a second blow and the guard kicked him savagely in the stomach. As the man doubled up, another sledgehammer blow hit his jaw. He fell down. "Up! Up!" The SS man kicked him to attention again. Then alternately he slogged his jaw and kicked his stomach, eight, nine, ten, eleven times, until one tremendous kick in the pit of the stomach brought blood gushing from the man's mouth; he screamed and fell down. The guard continued kicking him in the face, head, groin and legs. The twitching form at last lay quite inert and the pavement was quickly thick with blood.'[66]

Hundreds of prisoners had been murdered each month in Mauthausen by similar savagery. By April 1945, there was no means of washing in the camp. 'At the time we were swarming with lice and filth,' the fifteen-year-old Yehuda Bakon later recalled. 'I remember that we would sometimes pull out some two hundred lice on each one of us. When I would sit down and try to rise I would go dizzy and see nothing for a couple of minutes. That is how weak we were.' During an Allied air raid, a bomb hit the prisoners' camp, 'and I saw, on the following morning,' Bakon recalled, 'people eating human flesh.' Some of the camp inmates were eating the flesh of those killed in the air raid.[67]

On May 1, as the American army approached Mauthausen, the last death marches of the war began, from Mauthausen itself, and from the nearby camps of Gusen and St Valentin, to Gunskirchen and Ebensee. Hundreds of marchers fell to the ground as they marched, dying in the mud from sheer exhaustion.[68]

Among those who reached Gunskirchen alive was the Hungarian writer and journalist, Geza Havas. But on May 5, only a few hours before the Americans arrived, he died.[69]

At Ebensee, as the American armies approached, all thirty thousand prisoners were ordered into a tunnel packed with explosives. As the historian of Mauthausen, Evelyn le Chêne, has written: 'The prisoners, to a man, blankly refused. The SS guards were paralysed with indecision. The hordes of humans swayed and murmured. For the first time since their arrest, the prisoners who were not already dying saw the possibility that they might just survive the war. Understandably, they neither wished to be blown up in the tunnel, nor mown down by SS machine guns for refusing. But they knew that in these last days, many of the SS had left and been replaced by Ethnic Germans.' A quick consultation with some of the officers under his command made it clear to the commandant 'that they too were reluctant either to force the men into the tunnel, or to shoot them down. With the war all but over, they were thinking of the future, and the punishment they would receive for the slaughter of so many human beings was something they still wished – even with their already stained hands – to avoid. And so the prisoners won the day.'[70]

Among those who had survived the last days at Ebensee was Meir Pesker, a Polish Jew from Bielsk Podlaski who had been deported to Majdanek, then to Plaszow, then to Mauthausen. 'We saw that the Americans were coming,' he wrote, 'and so did the Germans.' His account continued:

Suddenly a German Kapo appeared, a bloated primeval beast whose cruelty included the bare-handed murder of dozens of Jews. Suddenly he had become weak and emotional and he began to plead with us not to turn him in for he had 'done many favours for the Jews to whom that madman Hitler had sought to do evil'. As he finished his pleading three boys overpowered and killed him, there in the same camp where he had been sole ruler.

We killed every one of the German oppressors who fell into our hands, before the arrival of the Americans in the enclosure of the camp. This was our revenge for our loved ones whose blood had been spilled at the hands of these heathen German beasts.

It was only by a stroke of luck – even if tainted luck – that I had survived.[71]

Among those at Ebensee on May 5, as the Germans prepared to flee, was Dr Miklos Nyiszli, the eye-witness of Dr Mengele's brutality at Birkenau. Like all his fellow prisoners at Ebensee, he too had survived the death marches, including one from central Germany to Mauthausen on which three thousand had set off, and one thousand been killed on the march. 'On May 5th,' he later recalled, 'a white flag flew from the Ebensee watch-tower. It was finished. They had laid down their arms. The sun was shining brightly when, at nine o'clock, an American light tank, with three soldiers on board, arrived and took possession of the camp. We were free.'[72]

Once more the moment of freedom was one of deep shock for the liberators. When American troops reached Mauthausen, they found nearly ten thousand bodies in a huge communal grave. Of the 110,000 survivors, 28,000 were Jews. Among the survivors was Sidney Fahn, the last of the five Czech Jews whose odyssey, beginning in Bratislava, had taken them to the Aegean island of Rhodes and the 'selection' on the ramp at Birkenau. At liberation, Sidney Fahn weighed eighty pounds.

Confronted by so many starving skeletons, well-meaning American soldiers brought chocolate, jam and other rich foods which the camp survivors ate, but which many could not digest, and died. Fortunately for Sidney Fahn, he was too weak to stagger from the hospital bed in order to claim his share of these enticing foods, 'and so again', he later recalled, 'I survived: again my fate intervened.'[73]

Here, repeated in every liberated camp, was yet another insane version of reality for thousands of Jews: food, which had for so long been the life-giving substance, longed for with such desperation, was yet again the final blow. These emaciated men and women, here, as in other camps, were no longer used to such food, nor could their digestive systems cope with it. It was too rich, too fatty, too filling, and it killed, in the first hectic day of liberation, as surely as the bullets and the rifle butts of the day before.

More than three thousand of the 110,000 survivors at Mauthausen and its sub-camps died after liberation.[74] Among the dead was Andor Endre Gelleri, the thirty-eight-year-old Hungarian novelist. He died of typhus, two days after liberation.[75] When Geza Gryn died four days after liberation, his son Hugo was too weak even to follow his father's corpse.[76]

The last of the death marches and death trains were still under German control, in the dwindling areas not yet captured by the Allies. In Theresienstadt, on May 4, the International Red Cross took over the camp, and on the following day, the last of the SS men fled. Only in the Sudeten mountains were the last of the death trains and death marches still within the dwindling orbit of the disintegrating Reich. One such death march had left Schwarzheide on April 18, then continued in two open railway wagons towards Theresienstadt. On May 6 the wagons had reached Leitmeritz, only three miles from Theresienstadt. There, with its SS escort still in command, it came to a halt.

'Starving in open vans,' Alfred Kantor, a deportee on one of the two railway trucks, noted on May 6, and he added, 'Second van reports: sixteen more deaths and ten dying of cold and hunger.' No engine was available for the train. But the guard was 'still at his post'. When German railwaymen asked the SS chief if they could feed the prisoners with hot soup, the SS chief 'gives in to their request to help'. That night, the SS man 'yells "Everybody out!"' Many dead bodies are brought down by the living, to the side of the track.'[77]

On May 8 the German armies surrendered to the Allies. 'Our guards leave us to our fate and flee,' Alfred Kantor noted at eleven o'clock that evening. 'We can't believe it's over! 175 out of 1,000 are alive. Red Cross truck appears – but can't take 175 men. We spend the night on the road – but in a dream. It's over.'[78]

'I will tell the world'

THE WAR WAS OVER; the systematic murder of six million Jews was also at an end. But its reverberations continue to this day. Too many scars had been inflicted, too much blood had been spilled, for 8 May 1945 to mark the end of the story, or the end of tragedy for the two hundred thousand survivors of the ghettos, camps and death marches.[1] On May 10, in Flensburg naval hospital, SS General Richard Glueks, head of the concentration camp directorate, was found dead. It was not clear whether Glueks had committed suicide, or had been killed by 'Jewish avengers' who had already begun to track down and to kill a number of those who had carried out the policy of mass murder.[2]

A small amount of vengeance there undoubtedly was, but vengeance was the path of a minority. 'Sometimes', Israel Gutman, a survivor of Majdanek, Auschwitz and Gunskirchen has written, the 'desire and expectation of revenge' were the 'hope' that kept camp inmates alive 'during the final and most arduous stages of camp life', but, once the war was over, 'we find only a few cases of revenge, or organized vengeful activity on the part of the survivors.'[3] As Dr Zalman Grinberg, a survivor of the Kovno ghetto and the death marches, told those survivors who were still living in huts in Dachau on May 27, nearly a month after liberation, but a day nevertheless on which thirty-five Jews had died as a result of continuing illness and weakness:

> Hitler has lost every battle on every front except the battle against defenceless and unarmed men, women and children. He won the war against the Jews of Europe. He carried out this war with the help of the German nation.
> However, we do not want revenge. If we took this vengeance

it would mean we would fall to the depths of ethics and morals the German nation has been in these past ten years.

We are not able to slaughter women and children! We are not able to burn millions of people! We are not able to starve hundreds of thousands![4]

On May 20, Henry Slamovich, one of the Jews from Plaszow who had been saved by Oscar Schindler, returned with about twenty-five other young Jews, all of them survivors, to his home town of Dzialoszyce. 'We thought to ourselves,' he later recalled, 'we had survived. We are alive, we are going to enjoy freedom.' Even though his own home was now lived in by non-Jews, Slamovich was determined somehow to rebuild his life in his own town. But within a week, four of the twenty-five Jews who had returned were murdered by Polish anti-Semites. The rest of the young Jews realized they would have to leave. 'It was sad, very sad,' Slamovich recalled, thirty-five years later, in his home in San Francisco.[5]

In the aftermath of the war, there were many such personal tragedies. Returning to her home in Lodz, the former physician-in-chief of the ghetto hospital, Dr Maria Ginsberg-Rabinowicz, committed suicide on learning that her daughter had not survived.[6] Seeking to return to their village of Choroszcza, near Bialystok, on May 22, two brothers, Icchok and Mejer Sznajder, were in a train which was stopped by Polish thugs. Mejer was beaten, taken away, and never seen again. He and Icchok had survived the Bialystok ghetto and Birkenau. 'Icchok suffers depression as a result of his brother's death,' Dr Szymon Datner noted seventeen months later, 'his brother with whom he had lived through such terrible times.'[7]

Liberation and safety had proved inconstant partners. At Neustadt-Glowen, where Russian troops had taken over from the Americans within a few days of liberation, the Jewish women understood just how much Russian blood had been shed in nearly four years of fighting. 'They had paid dearly for their victory,' Lena Berg recalled, 'and they celebrated with all the forthrightness and lack of restraint characteristic of Slavs.' Those whom the Russians had liberated were recovering their health, their hair, even their looks. Lena Berg's account continued:

> The camp teemed with amorous couples, but the majority of the liberated women, despite their sympathy for their liber-

ators and admiration for the Red Army's heroism, were reluctant to express their gratitude with their bodies. The Russians were unable to understand that and the situation led to sharp, and occasionally tragic, conflicts. 'Aren't you our girls?' the Russians would say, surprised by the reluctance. 'We shed our blood for you. We liberated you, and you refuse us a mere trifle?'

Intoxicated by victory and often literally drunk, they felt they were entitled to anything and everything. Several times they took women by brute force, and I shall never forget the heart-rending screams and tears of a fifteen-year-old girl raped by a Soviet private in the barracks in front of hundreds of women. 'No! No! I don't want to!' the girl raved. We heard those words for a long time afterwards.[8]

Many survivors were to be haunted by memories of these immediate post-war months. Returning to Poland after their liberation in Theresienstadt, fifteen-year-old Ben Helfgott and his twelve-year-old cousin Gershon were still emaciated, as they worked their way northward. Ben Helfgott later recalled how, while passing through Czechoslovakia, they had been showered 'with food, warmth and sympathy'. This gave them a sense of well-being, as they reached Czestochowa, their first stop in Poland. The two boys waited at the railway station for the train to their home town of Piotrkow. In Ben Helfgott's words:

Hundreds of people were milling around talking and gesticulating excitedly when suddenly two Polish officers accosted us. 'Who are you? What are you doing here?' Somewhat taken aback and surprised, we replied, 'Can't you see? We are survivors from the concentration camps and we are returning to our home town.' To our amazement, they asked for some proof which we immediately produced in the form of an Identity Card which had been issued to us in Theresienstadt, the place of our liberation.

They were still not satisfied and ordered us to come with them to the police station for a routine check. It seemed rather strange to us, but we had nothing to fear. Fortified by our experience in Czechoslovakia and believing in a better world now that the monster that tried to destroy the people of Europe was vanquished, we walked along with the two officers chatting animatedly about the great future that was in store for the people of Poland.

The streets were deserted and darkness prevailed as there was still a curfew after midnight and street lighting was not yet restored. My cousin and I were tiring as we carried our cases which contained clothing we had received from the Red Cross.

Casually, I asked, 'Where is the police station? It seems so far.' The reply was devastating and shattering: 'Shut your f . . . mouth you f . . . Jew'!!!!!

I was stunned, hardly believing what I had just heard. How could I have been so naive; so gullible? The Nazi cancer was removed but its tentacles were widespread and deeply rooted. How had I lulled myself into a false sense of security?

I believed what I wanted to believe. I had experienced and witnessed so much cruelty and bestiality yet I refused to accept that man is wicked. I was grown up in so many ways, yet I was still a child dreaming of a beautiful world. I was suddenly brought back to reality and began to fear the worst. Here I was in the middle of nowhere, no one to turn to for help.

At last we stopped at a house where one of the officers knocked at the gate which was opened by a young Polish woman. We entered a room which was dimly lit by a paraffin lamp, and we were ordered to open our suitcases. They took most of the clothing and announced that they would now take us to the police station. It seemed inconceivable to me that this was their real intention, but we had no choice and we had to follow events as they unfolded.

As we walked in the dark and deserted streets, I tried desperately to renew conversation so as to restore the personal and human touch, but it was to no avail. I endeavoured to conceal and ignore my true feelings and innermost thoughts, pretending to believe that they were acting in the name of the law, but they became strangely uncommunicative.

After what seemed an eternity, we arrived at a place that looked fearfully foreboding. The buildings were derelict and abandoned; there was no sign of human habitation; all one could hear was the howling of the wind, the barking of the dogs and the mating calls of the cats.

The two officers menacingly extracted the pistols from their holsters, and ordered us to walk to the nearest wall.

Both my cousin and I felt rooted to the ground unable to move.

When, at last, I recovered my composure, I emitted a torrent of desperate appeals and entreaties. I pleaded with them, 'Haven't we suffered enough? Haven't the Nazis caused enough destruction and devastation to all of us? Our common enemy is destroyed and the future is ours. We have survived against all odds and why are you intent on promoting the heinous crimes that the Nazis have unleashed. Don't we speak the same language as you? Didn't we imbibe the same culture as you?'

I went on in the same vein speaking agitatedly for some time. Eventually, one of the officers succumbed to my pleas and said, 'Let's leave them. They are after all still boys.' As they put away their pistols, they made a remark which still rings loud in my ears. 'You can consider yourselves very lucky. We have killed many of your kind. You are the first ones we have left alive.' With this comment they disappeared into the dark of the night.[9]

Not every journey homeward was so brutal. In July 1945 David Shmueli, a Rumanian-born Jew who had served in the British army during the war, learned that his father, Yehiel Shmueli, was in Dachau, among the survivors. David's sister Rachel later recorded:

My brother immediately ran to his commander and received permission to go to Dachau. There he entered the office and found the list containing my father's name. He entered the shack and immediately noticed Father standing at the sink and washing dishes.

Father raised his head when he saw the door open, and looked back again at the dishes, for he didn't recognize my brother and thought him a British soldier. My brother ran to him and embraced him and said in a voice filled with emotion: 'Daddy, I'm your son David!'

Father raised his head in amazement and said: 'Pardon me, sir, there's some mistake here. My son is in Palestine and he's not a soldier.'

My brother, in order to convince him, took out of his pocket some family pictures from home, and thus he finally managed to convince him that he was his only son.

Then they burst out crying, not only they but everyone around them. Because Father had always told his friends in the camp that when he lay ill with typhus he had nightmares and also dreams of yearning, one of which was that his son came in an airplane, liberated the camp and said: 'Father, you can take ten people with you. Choose those who were most kind to you and take them.' And as if the dream came true, his son came to liberate him.[10]

The Jews who had survived understood that their experiences could not easily be conveyed, if at all. 'I realize', wrote Dow Lewi, a survivor of Birkenau, on 4 August 1945, to his sister in Palestine, 'that you, over there, cannot imagine even a hundredth part of the suffering, fear, humiliation and every kind of bullying that we lived through.' Lewi added: 'People who live and think as normal people cannot possibly understand.'[11]

The survivors did not expect to be understood. But they did expect to be allowed to live in peace. It was not to be: on August 20 anti-Jewish riots broke out in Cracow, followed by further riots in Sosnowiec on October 25 and in Lublin on November 19. Within seven months of the end of the war in Europe, and after a year in which no German soldier was on Polish soil, 350 Jews had been murdered in Poland.[12] Thousands more faced danger when they returned to their home towns and villages. On September 1, Yaakov Waldman, who had escaped the Chelmno deportation from Uniejow on 20 July 1942, was killed in nearby Turek.[13] In October 1945 eight Jews were killed in Boleslawiec by one of several Polish underground groups still engaged in killing Jews.[14] In December 1945 eleven Jews were killed by Poles in the village of Kosow-Lacki, less than six miles from the former death camp at Treblinka.[15] In February 1946, nine months after the Allied victory in Europe, four Jewish delegates to a Jewish communal convention in Cracow were murdered on the train from Lodz. The Polish government offered to give them a state funeral, as victims of anti-Communist forces, albeit Poles. Zerah Warhaftig, one of the main organizers of the convention, refused. 'I said they died as Jews, not in the fight for Communism.'[16]

On 1 February 1946 the *Manchester Guardian* published a full report of the situation of the Jews still in Poland. The four headlines to the report read:

JEWS STILL IN FLIGHT FROM POLAND
DRIVEN ABROAD BY FEAR
POLITICAL GANGS OUT TO TERRORIZE THEM
CAMPAIGN OF MURDER AND ROBBERY

Since the beginning of 1945, the newspaper reported, 353 Jews had been murdered by Polish thugs. 'Unfortunately,' it added, 'anti-Semitism is still prevalent in spite of the Government efforts to counteract it.' As a result of the war, this anti-Semitism, 'always present in Polish society', had been 'greatly aggravated by German propaganda'. Since the end of the war, ritual murder accusations had been made against Jews in Cracow and Rzeszow. In Radom, a hospital for Jewish orphans had been attacked. In Lublin, two Jews, already wounded by thugs while on a bus, had been tracked down to the local hospital and murdered there, in their hospital beds.[17]

On 5 February 1946, four Jews were killed in Parczew, the forests of which had been the scene of so much Jewish suffering and heroism scarcely two years earlier.[18] Six weeks later, on March 19, one of only two survivors of the death camp at Belzec, Chaim Hirszman, gave evidence in Lublin of what he had witnessed in the death camp. He was asked to return on the following day to complete his evidence. But on his way home he was murdered, because he was a Jew.[19]

Five days before Hirszman's murder, the British Ambassador in Poland, Victor Cavendish Bentinck, reported from Warsaw that food supplies belonging to the Chief Rabbi's Emergency Council had been allowed to proceed in a car flying the Union Jack. Yet even with this protection, the car had been stopped 'and four Polish Jews, one of whom was a woman, travelling in it, were taken out and shot by the roadside for being Jews'. The Ambassador added that anyone with a Jewish appearance was in 'danger', and on March 28 the Foreign Office learned that a group of Jewish leaders travelling from Cracow to Lodz had been seized, tortured and murdered.[20]

On Easter Sunday, April 21, five Jews were driving along the main road towards the southern Polish town of Nowy Targ. All five were survivors of Auschwitz, Buchenwald and Mauthausen. The oldest, Benjamin Rose, was thirty-five. Leon Lindenberger was twenty-five. Ludwig Hertz, Henrych Unterbruck, and the only girl among them, Ruth Joachimsman, were twenty-two.

As the five Jews approached the outskirts of Nowy Targ, their car was flagged down at what appeared to be a police check-point. The five Jews were ordered out of the car and shot. Their killers had been members of the former underground forces of the Polish Home Army. The five bodies were stripped of their clothing and left naked on the highway.

The Nowy Targ murders caused consternation among the Jews of Cracow, the nearest Jewish community of any size, a community of survivors. On April 24, at the public funeral organised by the Jewish community in Cracow, five thousand Jews were present, one of whom, Joseph Tenenbaum, later wrote: 'and there I witnessed something that lashed me with an iron rod. Windows opened, and guffaws poured out from the windows, balconies and porches. Gibes, scabrous and cynical, rained on the marching mourners. "Look, Jas, where did they come from, the Jews? The devil, I never knew so many of them were left alive."'

Six days after the funeral of the five who had been murdered at Nowy Targ, another seven Jews were murdered at almost the same spot. The oldest, Bela Gold, was forty-three. The youngest, Salomon Dornberg, was eighteen. Their funeral too was held in Cracow, on the evening of May 2, almost a year since the end of the war.[21]

That same May, Eliahu Lipszowicz, a former deputy to the partisan leader Dr Yehezkiel Atlas, and in 1944 an officer in the Red Army, was murdered by an anti-Semitic Pole at Legnica in Silesia.[22] At Biala Podlaska, in June, two Jews were murdered: of the six thousand Jews in the town in 1939, only three hundred had survived the war. After the killings, those who remained decided to leave Poland altogether.[23]

No Polish town was free from such incidents. In Piotrkow, a Jewess, Miss Usherowitz, sold her father's apartment to a Pole for six hundred zlotys, the equivalent of about five American dollars. That same day she was murdered, together with a friend Mrs Rolnik, and a young man, Mr Maltz, with whom she shared her apartment.[24]

Whether for money or out of hatred, the murder of Jews continued.

The climax of these post-war killings came on 4 July 1946. Three days earlier, an eight-year-old Polish boy from Kielce, Henryk Blaszczyk, disappeared from his home. Two days later he returned, claiming that he had been kept in a cellar by two Jews who had wanted to kill him, and that only a miracle had enabled him to escape. In fact, he had been to the home of a family friend in a nearby village. The friend had taught him what to say after his return.

On July 4 a crowd of Poles, aroused by rumours of Jews abducting Christian children for ritual purposes, attacked the building of the Jewish Committee in Kielce. Almost all the Jews who were inside the building, including the Chairman of the Committee, Dr Seweryn Kahane, were shot, stoned to death, or killed with axes and blunt instruments. Elsewhere in Kielce, Jews were murdered in their homes, or dragged into the streets and killed by the mob.[25]

Forty-two Jews were killed in Kielce that day. Two, Duczka and Adas Fisz, were children. Four, Bajla Gerntner, Rachel Zander, Fania Szumacher and Naftali Teitelbaum, were teenagers on their way to Palestine. Three, Izak Prajs, Abraham Wajntraub and Captain Wajnreb, were officers in the Polish army. Seven could not be named. One of those whose name was unknown was a survivor of Birkenau, a fact disclosed by the tattoo number on his arm, B 2969.

The Jews of Kielce published the names of the dead in the one surviving Polish–Jewish newspaper, in a black border.[26] The name of the Jew who had been in Birkenau was never found. The numbers B 2903 to B 3449 had been given to those Jews in a train from Radom on 2 August 1944 who had been 'selected' for the barracks.[27] Radom and Kielce are only fifty miles apart.

Following the Kielce 'pogrom', one hundred thousand Polish Jews, more than half the survivors, fled from Poland, seeking new homes in Palestine, Western Europe, Britain and the United States, Latin America and Australia.[28]

The facts of Jewish wartime suffering were only slowly coming to light, as letters, documents, diaries and fragments were discovered. Vast quantities of material, however, were lost forever, hidden in hiding places no one survived to identify, burned or destroyed by the Germans as they withdrew. On September 18 the first of the tin boxes and milk cans hidden by Emanuel Ringelblum's 'Joy of Sabbath' circle was dug up in the ruins of the Warsaw ghetto. The second was found four years later, in 1950.[29]

Among the Jews who remained in Poland were some who saw their task as recording the history of the war years. On 24 March 1947 the organization of Jewish writers and journalists in Poland wrote, from Lodz, to the American Jewish Joint Distribution Committee, in search of financial help for the forty Jewish writers in their organization:

> They are living under very difficult circumstances but are loath to forsake the ruined land that they might better absorb the atmosphere of the dreadful Jewish catastrophe and render it into literary and scientific work. We consider it a mission of particular importance that these Jewish writers provide, for the future generations, prose and poetry which will portray and document the recent experiences. Would that we now had such literary records from our forefathers of the Spanish era.[30]

Five manuscripts of the Sonderkommando at Birkenau, which are among the most vivid contemporary documents of the war, were discovered at different times between 1945 and 1962: that of Salmen Lewental on 17 October 1962. The notes of the Greek Jew were only found in the earth around one of the crematoria, in the late autumn of 1980, buried in a thermos flask. It was discovered there only by chance, by Polish schoolchildren planting a tree.

As the decades passed, many survivors, and the relatives of survivors, sought to return to the scenes of their youth, to the scenes of their family's suffering, even to the scenes of their own torment. The sites of the mass murder of Jews became places of solemn pilgrimage. For Jews in the Soviet Union, visiting these sites, such as Babi Yar in Kiev, and Rumbuli near Riga, Ponar outside Vilna or the Ratomskaya street pit in Minsk, became a means of renewing and asserting their sense of Jewish identity.

In the twenty years following the war, Babi Yar filled up with rubbish, mud and water, forming a deep lake. 'It was motionless,' Sara Kyron later recalled, 'and mixed up with silt, and it seemed from afar to be greenish, as if the tears of the people who had been killed there had come out of the soil.'

Above the Yar, a wall had been built to mark it off from an adjoining brickyard. One evening in 1961, the wall collapsed. Streams of clay and mud, mixed up with the remains of human bones, gushed out into the streets of Kiev below. In the wake of the rushing waters, a garage was completely destroyed, fires broke out, and the stream of liquid clay, reaching the nearby tram depot, overturned tram cars and buried alive in its onward rush both passengers and tramway workers. That night, as soldiers were busy digging out the dead, and searching for survivors in the mud, a second wave of liquid clay burst out from the Yar, wreaking further havoc, and death. In the two disasters, twenty-four citizens of Kiev were killed. A few days later, as a tram passed the site of the disaster, an old woman suddenly began to shout: 'It is the Jews who have done this. They are taking vengeance on us. They always will.'

Sara Tartakovskaya, going by taxi to work on the morning after the disaster, was told by the taxi driver: 'One could not fill up Babi Yar. Jewish blood is taking revenge.'[31]

Year by year, Jews throughout the world search for some echo of the past that is gone. In 1976 a Riga-born Jew, Jules Lippert, who had left Riga for the United States as a child in 1939, returned to the city of his birth. It was also the city in which his father had been murdered, his father whom he had not seen since he was eight years old. Lippert went to Rumbuli, where his father must have been murdered. 'I remembered he was tall, close to six feet,' Lippert later wrote. 'He was bald and the youngest of three brothers and he smoked cigars.' Lippert went on to ask:

How did you die, dear father? What thoughts crossed your mind as your brief thirty-eight years were extinguished here in Riga? Did the bullets find their mark quickly or did you suffer for interminable moments in agony? Where are your remains, where are they, where are they – I'll never know.[32]

In June 1981 a gathering of survivors was held in Jerusalem. More than six thousand survivors gathered there, from all over the world, to exchange recollections, to seek long-lost friends, and to

822 · THE HOLOCAUST

make one last desperate search for relatives who might, possibly, have survived. For many of those who gathered in Jerusalem, as for more than one hundred thousand survivors elsewhere, the passage of four decades had often brought with it new torments. Gone now were the years of struggling to adjust to new societies, of learning new languages, of earning a living, of bringing up a family, of being too busy for retrospection. Illness, old age, retirement, time for reflection, the questions asked by children and grandchildren, had revived memories and nightmares. Some survivors had never been able to drive out of their minds the evil associations: whether it was the barking of a dog, the cracks of a whip, or the smell of burning.

Others found the terrible images returning, or experienced a growing sense of guilt that they, alone perhaps of forty or fifty members of their family, had survived. The miracle of survival turned into an agony of personal self-recrimination.

For one survivor, Jona Jakob Speigel, the Jerusalem gathering of June 1981 had represented a different type of opportunity. When Theresienstadt had been liberated in May 1945 he had been only three and a half years old. He had been brought up in Britain by foster parents, knowing and being told nothing of his concentration camp past, nor of the deportation of his mother, Elsa Speigel, to the Minsk ghetto, when he, Jona, was only five and a half months old. He had first learned these facts in 1962, shortly before his marriage. For nearly twenty years he tried to find out more about himself, but other than the facts related here, he could find nothing.

Travelling to Jerusalem in 1981, Jona Speigel hoped to meet at least one person who had known his mother in Vienna, where she had been a milliner; or someone who had looked after him in Theresienstadt, between 1942 and 1945. But although hundreds of those at the gathering did find friends from their concentration camp days, and even relatives, Jona Speigel found no one.

On his return to London, Jona Speigel continued his search, but in vain. 'Deep down,' he wrote, 'I realized that it was a hopeless task.'[33] Perhaps someone reading these lines will recall Elsa Speigel, or her orphan son, and bring him some fragments of memory with which to link him to his lost past.

The pain of not knowing can never be assuaged. For those who survive, it mingles and sometimes overwhelms the feeling of personal guilt for survival. There was also gratitude for those who made survival possible. In February 1946, Rudolf Wessely, who had reached London from Prague on 1 July 1939, wrote to the people who had given him a new home in Britain:

> All efforts to trace my parents on the continent having failed, I must assume that they are amongst the victims of Nazism. I feel it to be my duty, to do what they would undoubtedly have done, had they been alive; I should like to thank you and express my deepest gratitude for having saved me, their son, in 1939, for having enabled me to live a full life and for the opportunity I thus gained to fight actively on the side of Britain.[34]

Eric Lucas, who had left Germany after the Kristallnacht in November 1938, and had seen his parents for the last time as the train taking him to Britain had pulled out of the frontier station, wrote, when the war was ended: 'We have waited, and hoped, for a sign or message from our parents. It will never come.' 'Overwhelming and crushing disaster', Lucas added, 'came upon millions of us. It leaves the wounded and sore human heart lonely. The disaster has spoken to each one directly.'

Lucas went on to ask: 'Can I ever grasp it? Can I fathom out why my father and my mother had to perish at the hands of insanely brutalised human beasts? Can I understand why the kind, help-seeking eyes of my father had to behold the slow, scientifically organized dying of himself and my mother, and the people with him in the death camp?'[35]

The survivors tell their story to their children, set it down in memoirs and testimonies, relive it in nightmares. They have so much to remember of parents, children, friends, communities, society and civilization, all destroyed: not only precious Jewish lives, but the rich, complex, vibrant fabric of Jewish life. Not all survivors wish the destruction to be commemorated, as it has been increasingly in recent years, by ceremonies, monuments, dedications, lectures, books and banquets. 'We do not want your commemorations!' David Wdowinski wrote in 1964. 'We, who do not even have graves to rest in peace – we do not need your easy tears, your empty words.' Too many people had forgotten. 'Leave us be. We do not need your prayers and your benedictions.' One day, perhaps, 'some new, clean generation will remember our agony', bestowing upon the dead, and upon the long dead survivors, the final Hebrew prayer for the dead, 'God, full of compassion'.[36]

Each survivor faces the past, and confronts the future, with a burden which those who did not go through the torment cannot measure. 'I may bear indelible scars in body and soul,' Cordelia Edvardson has written, 'but I don't intend to reveal them to the world – least of all to the Germans. That is the pride of the survivor. Hitler is dead – but I am alive.'[37]

Between 1939 and 1945 the Germans killed many millions of non-Jewish civilians in Germany itself, and in every occupied country, often in massive reprisal actions or after prolonged torture. The shooting down in cold blood of unarmed, defenceless Greeks, Poles, Yugoslavs, Czechs, Russians, and men, women and children of a dozen other nationalities, all of them civilians who had taken no part in military action, was a feature of Nazi rule throughout Europe. Among those murdered were as many as a quarter of a million Gypsies, tens of thousands of homosexuals, and tens of thousands of 'mental defectives'. Also murdered, often after the cruelties of tortures, were several million Soviet prisoners-of-war, shot or starved to death long after they had been captured and disarmed.

As well as the six million Jews who were murdered, more than ten million other non-combatants were killed by the Nazis. Under the Nazi scheme, Poles, Czechs, Serbs and Russians were to become subject peoples; slaves, the workers of the New Order. The Jews were to disappear altogether. It was the Jews alone who were marked out to be destroyed in their entirety: every Jewish man, woman and child, so that there would be no future Jewish life in Europe. Against the eight million Jews who lived in Europe in 1939, the Nazi bureaucracy assembled all the concerted skills and mechanics of a modern state: the police, the railways, the civil service, the industrial power of the Reich; poison gas, soldiers, mercenaries, criminals, machine guns, artillery; and over all, a massive apparatus of deception.

In the concentration camps, Jews were not people, but *figuren*, 'numbers' or 'figures'. But these 'figures', these 'men' who had become 'dogs', did not intend to die without there being a record of what had been done to them. The Jewish desire that the evidence of mass murder and inhuman torture should survive was an overwhelming one. Dr Aharon Beilin has recorded how, at Birkenau, he once saw a boy working, who told him that he had been castrated in a medical experiment in the camp. This boy asked Dr Beilin to examine him. 'I said I could not help him, but the boy said, "No, I want you to see what they are doing to us." '38

As soon after liberation as Yehuda Bakon was strong enough to 'hold a pencil in my hand', he made a series of drawings of everything he could remember of the gas-chambers, the undressing rooms and the crematoria at Birkenau: the things he had seen, and the things he had asked the Jews of the Sonderkommando to describe to him, so that if he survived, he could record it. 'I asked the Sonderkommando men to tell me,' he later explained, 'so that if one day I will come out, I will tell the world.'39

To see, and to record: this had been the self-imposed task of Emanuel Ringelblum and his 'Joy of Sabbath' circle in the Warsaw ghetto, from the ghetto's first days. It had been Simon Dubnov's last instruction as he was shot down in Riga in December 1941. In the concentration camps there had been a slogan, 'I am the victim! I am the witness!' Vitka Kempner, in hiding in the Vilna ghetto, and later in action with a group of partisans in the forests outside Vilna, later recalled how 'everyone in the ghetto thought that he was the last Jew in the world. People wanted us to leave one person outside the ghetto so that they can tell the world the story. We thought no one else was left in any other ghetto.'40

To survive was to give witness: a historic imperative. The Warsaw poet, Yitzhak Katznelson, in his last days at Vittel, before being deported to Auschwitz and his death, had also stressed the need to recall the acts of resistance: 'Sing a hymn to the hero of the remote hamlet! Sing loud his praise, see his radiant figure!'41

There was also a moral imperative: Zdenek Lederer, a survivor of the Theresienstadt ghetto and of Auschwitz, later reflected that, throughout the ages, 'it has been the lot of the Jews to deliver to men a warning'. This warning, seen so starkly in the years of the Holocaust, was a clear one: 'that violence is in the end self-destructive, power futile, and the human spirit unconquerable'.42

The stories told in these pages can convey only a fragment of the Jewish suffering, and courage, of those terrible years. With the Allied victory in 1945, the Holocaust became history, increasingly distant, remote, forgotten; a chapter, reduced to a page, shortened to a paragraph, relegated to a footnote. Yet it must still be remembered in each generation for what it was: an unprecedented explosion of evil over good. At Auschwitz, as Hugo Gryn, a survivor, has said, the ethical code which was part of his own Jewish tradition, and also 'part and parcel' of the Judaeo-Christian tradition, was 'denied and reversed':

> If you take the Ten Commandments, from the very first which starts: 'I am the Lord your God who brought you out of the land of Egypt'; here you had people who set *themselves* up to be Gods, to be masters of life and death, and who took you *into* Egypt: into an Egypt of the most bizarre and most obnoxious kind, and all the way to creating their own set of idols, to taking God's name in vain, to setting generations at each other so that children dishonoured parents.
>
> Certainly they murdered. Certainly they committed robbery. Certainly there was a great deal of coveting, of envy, involved in it. In other words, you had here an outbreak of the very opposite of everything that civilization was building towards.

'It was a denial of God,' Hugo Gryn added. 'It was a denial of man. It was the destruction of the world in miniature form.'[43]

In the face of so violent an upsurge of evil, the Jewish resistance that took place during the war years possessed a heroic dimension. Hardly a day passed without some act of defiance, as seen even in those records which have survived; records which are only a fragment of the whole story.

At every stage of the war, the Germans used insuperable deterrents: military superiority, a crushed and terrorized local population, sadistic helpers, and above all the threat and reality of massive reprisals. Hundreds were shot for the resistance of a single person. In Lvov, on 16 March 1943, when a Jew had killed a German policeman noted for his cruelty, the Germans murdered twelve hundred Jews as a reprisal: a far higher reprisal ratio than that used against the Czechs in Lidice in 1942, or against the French in Oradour in 1944. Yet despite the grotesque savagery of reprisals,

Jewish resistance was never crushed in its entirety, even in the death camps.

This was resistance not of people gathered together in a single town or region, but scattered in ten thousand different localities, divided by distance and frontier controls and language. It was resistance by those surrounded by captive populations which frequently collaborated with what should have been the common enemy, and often betrayed by those who were in essence their fellow victims. It was resistance by people for whom the possession even of an inadequate weapon was punishable by death. It was resistance by an army without arms, by an army of the old and sick, and the frail and the young, and by women for whom all forms of fighting were abhorrent. It was resistance above all by an army which did not have the right to surrender, which did not possess that basic right of the soldier to save his life by becoming a prisoner of war, by showing the white flag.

A Jew who sought safety in surrender was killed without mercy. A Jewish woman who ran away with her child and was caught was likewise murdered. For the Jews, resistance was almost invariably useless and helpless. It was carried out, as Rudolf Reder, a survivor of one of the death camps, has written, by 'the defenceless remnants of life and youth';[44] by Jews who had no strength or resources left, only the desire to remain human beings, yet even that desire could be, and was, sapped and destroyed by the deliberate intent of the conqueror.

The end was to be death: that was the German aim and plan. Yet there were many Jews who, sensing the plan, and having the ability to run away, to find at least a temporary haven in swamp or forest, decided not to run away, but, as Zivia Lubetkin had written, 'to share the same fate' as those who had no means of escape. 'It is our duty', she wrote amid the horrors of the Warsaw ghetto, 'to stay with our people until the very end.'[45]

A twenty-four-year-old Jewish girl in Cracow, Matilda Bandet, was approached one morning by her friends with news that the 'action' was imminent, that the time had come to try to escape from the ghetto and make for the woods. The girl hesitated. 'My place is with my parents,' she said. 'They need me. They are old. They have no means of defending themselves. If I leave them, they will be alone. I will stay here, with them.'

The girl's friends hurried off, to the cellars, the tunnels and the woods. Matilda Bandet remained, to be deported with her parents to Belzec, and to perish with them.[46] In her decision not to leave the ghetto, not to try to save herself, but to stay with her parents, Matilda Bandet showed that very human dignity which it was the German wish totally to destroy.

In every ghetto, in every deportation train, in every labour camp, even in the death camps, the will to resist was strong, and took many forms: fighting with those few weapons that could be found, fighting with sticks and knives, individual acts of defiance and protest, the courage of obtaining food under the threat of death, the nobility of refusing to allow the Germans their final wish to gloat over panic and despair. Even passivity was a form of courage. 'Not to act,' Emanuel Ringelblum wrote in the aftermath of one particularly savage reprisal, 'not to lift a hand against the Germans, has become the quiet passive heroism of the common Jew.'[47] To die with dignity was in itself courageous. To resist the dehumanizing, brutalizing force of evil, to refuse to be abased to the level of animals, to live through the torment, to outlive the tormentors, these too were courageous. Merely to give witness by one's own testimony was, in the end, to contribute to a moral victory. Simply to survive was a victory of the human spirit.

NOTES AND SOURCES
INDEX

NOTES AND SOURCES

Preface

1 Hugo Gryn, in conversation with the author, London.

1. FIRST STEPS TO INIQUITY

1 Martin Luther, *Von den Juden und ihren Lugen* ('On the Jews and their Lies'), Wittenburg 1543.

2 *Die Judischen Gefallenen des Deutschen Heeres, Der Deutschen Marine und der Deutschen Shutztruppen, 1914–1918* (The Jewish War Dead of the German Army, Navy and Defence Forces, 1914–1918), Berlin 1932.

3 For an eye-witness account of some of this violence, see Israel Cohen, *My Mission to Poland, 1918–1919*, London 1951.

4 Jehuda Reinharz (editor), *The Letters and Papers of Chaim Weizmann*, Jerusalem 1977, volume IX, series A, October 1918–July 1920, letter 44, page 48.

5 Report of 18 December 1919 from P. Wright to the Foreign Office, London: Rumbold papers, Bodleian Library, Oxford.

6 *The Times*, 14 August 1919.

7 For the full text of the Twenty-five points, as published shortly after Hitler came to power, see Konrad Heiden, *A History of National Socialism*, London 1934, pages 10–14.

8 Speech of 13 August 1920, quoted in Reginald H. Phelps, 'Hitler's "Grundlegende" Rede über den Antisemitismus', *Vierteljahrshefte für Zeitgeschichte*, volume 16, Stuttgart 1968, pages 400–20.

9 Heiden, *A History of National Socialism, op. cit.*, pages 73–4.

10 Norman H. Baynes (editor), *The Speeches of Adolf Hitler, April 1922–August 1939*, London 1942, volume 1, page 26.

11 Ruppin diary, 30 October 1923, quoted in Alex Bein (editor), *Arthur Ruppin: Memoirs, Diaries, Letters*, London 1971.

12 The edition cited here is the first English-language unexpurgated edition, two volumes in one, Adolf Hitler, *Mein Kampf*, London 1939, volume 1 'A Retrospect', volume 2 'The National Socialist Movement'. This edition was printed in February 1939.

13 Franz Jetzinger, *Hitler's Youth*, London 1958.

14 Hitler, *op. cit.*, page 31.

15 *Ibid.*, pages 61–2.

16 *Ibid.*, page 64.

17 *Ibid.*, page 273.

18 *Ibid.*, page 60.

19 *Ibid.*, page 176.

20 *Ibid.*, page 178.

21 *Ibid.*, page 66.

22 The full text of the Locarno Agreement is published in Lord D'Abernon, *An Ambassador of Peace*, London 1930, volume 3, appendix v.

23 Quoted in Ben-Zion Surdut, 'Sholem Schwartzbard' (Shalom Schwarzbard): *Board's-Eye View*, Bulletin of the South African Jewish Board of Deputies' Cape Council, Cape Town, December 1983. Acquitted at his trial in Paris, Schwarzbard later lived in South Africa, where he died in 1938, at the age of fifty-one.

24 Hitler, *op. cit.*, page 553.
25 Marvin Lowenthal, *The Jews of Germany: a History of Sixteen Centuries*, London 1939, page 375.
26 Voting figures were: Social Democratic Party, 8,575,343; National Socialist (Nazi) Party, 6,404,397; Communist Party, 4,590,178; Catholic Centre Party, 4,322,039.
27 'Guide and Instructional Letter for Functionaries', 15 March 1931, in Lord Marley, *The Brown Book of the Hitler Terror and the Burning of the Reichstag*, London 1933, page 234.
28 Quoted in Lowenthal, *op. cit.*, page 380.
29 *Idem.*
30 Leslie Frankel, in conversation with the author, Johannesburg.

2. 1933: THE SHADOW OF THE SWASTIKA

1 Lord Marley, *The Brown Book of the Hitler Terror and the Burning of the Reichstag, op. cit.*, page 196.
2 *Manchester Guardian*, 27 March 1933.
3 Shlomo Aronson, *The Beginnings of the Gestapo System: the Bavarian Model in 1933*, Jerusalem 1969, page 20.
4 *Manchester Guardian*, 27 March 1933.
5 Testimony of Benno Cohn: Eichmann Trial, 25 April 1961, session 14, verbatim transcript.
6 Lord Marley, *op. cit.*, page 238.
7 There were further mass protests at the Trocadero, Paris, on 20 May 1933, and at the Queen's Hall, London, on 27 June 1933.
8 Lord Marley, *op. cit.*, pages 262–3.
9 Lady Rumbold, letters of 2 April and 5 April 1933, Rumbold papers, quoted in Martin Gilbert, *Sir Horace Rumbold: Portrait of a Diplomat, 1869–1941*, London 1973, page 375.
10 Dr Joseph Goebbels, manuscript: 'From the Imperial House to the Reich Chancellary', International Military Tribunal, Nuremberg, document PS-2409.
11 Monday, 3 April 1933.
12 Speech reported in the *Völkischer Beobachter*, 7 April 1933, quoted in Baynes (editor), *The Speeches of Adolf Hitler, April 1922–August 1939, op. cit.*, page 729. The word used by Hitler was *gekrummpt*.
13 Testimony of Benno Cohn: Eichmann Trial, 25 April 1961, session 14.
14 *Judische Rundschau*, 4 April 1933: editorial reprinted in Ludwig Lewisohn, *Rebirth*, New York 1935, pages 336–41.
15 Law for the Restoration of the Professional Civil Service, 7 April 1933: text in full in Lucy S. Dawidowicz (editor), *A Holocaust Reader*, New York 1976, pages 38–40.
16 Speech reported in *Völkischer Beobachter*, 7 April 1933, quoted in Baynes, *op. cit.*, pages 728–9.
17 Letter of 11 April 1933, Rumbold papers, published in Martin Gilbert, *Britain and Germany Between the Wars*, London 1964, page 74.
18 Lord Marley, *op. cit.*, pages 309–10.
19 *Ibid.*, pages 189–90.
20 Law of 25 April 1933: text in full in Dawidowicz, *op. cit.*, pages 42–3.
21 *Deutsche Allgemeine Zeitung*, 22 April 1933.
22 Henry R. Huttenbach, *The Destruction of the Jewish Community of Worms, 1933–1945*, New York 1981, page 138.
23 *The Times*, 4 May 1933.
24 *Lokal Anzeiger*, 7 May 1933.
25 *Judische Rundschau*, 19 May 1933.
26 Lord Marley, *op. cit.*, page 347.

27 List, compiled from eye-witness and German newspaper reports, published in the *Manchester Guardian* on 27 September 1935.

28 Nathan Feinberg, 'Political Activities Against the Nazis', in *Jewish Resistance during the Holocaust: Proceedings of the Conference on Manifestations of Jewish Resistance, Jerusalem 7–11 April 1968*, Jerusalem 1971, page 78.

29 *Völkischer Beobachter*, 26 June 1933.

30 Letter of 2 June 1933: YIVO Institute for Jewish Research, New York, archive.

31 *Neier Morgen*, 14 July 1933.

32 Nachman Blumenthal, 'Sources for the Study of Jewish Resistance', in *Jewish Resistance during the Holocaust*, op. cit., page 57.

33 *Heil! A Picture Book Compiled from Authentic Material*, London 1934, page 112.

34 *Frankfurter Zeitung*, 2 August 1933.

35 *Ostjüdische Zeitung*, 20 August 1933.

36 Code of discipline, Dachau, 1 October 1933: International Military Tribunal, Nuremberg, document PS-778.

37 List of prisoners 'known to have been killed in Dachau': *Manchester Guardian*, 27 September 1935.

38 List enclosed by A. L. Easterman in a note to the Foreign Office, London, 12 April 1946: Foreign Office papers, 371/57545.

39 In 1932 only 353 German Jews had emigrated to Palestine; in 1931, only 122. The largest group of immigrants to Palestine in 1933 were Polish Jews, more than thirteen thousand of whom received Palestine certificates in that single year.

3. TOWARDS DISINHERITANCE

1 Report in the *Daily Express*, 25 May 1934.

2 Report in the *Manchester Guardian*, 3 April 1934.

3 *Heil! A Picture Book Compiled from Authentic Material*, op. cit.

4 *Frankische Tageszeitung*, 26 May 1934.

5 Huttenbach, *The Destruction of the Jewish Community of Worms, 1933–1945*, op. cit., page 16.

6 *The Yellow Spot. The Outlawing of Half a Million Human Beings: a Collection of Facts and Documents*, London 1936, page 85.

7 *Ibid.*, page 91.

8 Michel Abitbol, *Les Juifs d'Afrique du Nord sous Vichy*, Paris 1983, page 18.

9 *Memorandum on the Development of the Jewish National Home, 1934*, Geneva, June 1935, page 6. The number of Polish Jews admitted to Palestine in 1934 was 18,028. The third largest immigration, 2,031, was from Rumania, and the fourth largest, 1,964, was Jews from an Arab and Muslim land, the Yemen.

10 Arieh Tartakower and Kurt R. Grossman, *The Jewish Refugee*, New York 1944, page 29. On 29 September 1944, shortly before the publication of this book, Tartakower's son Jochanan, himself a refugee from Lodz in Poland, was killed in action in France while serving in the United States army.

11 Bella Fromm, *Blood and Banquets: a Berlin Social Diary*, London 1943, page 167. The diplomatic correspondent of the *Vossische Zeitung*, Bella Fromm reached the United States as a refugee in 1940.

12 List of prisoners 'known to have been killed in Dachau': *Manchester Guardian*, 27 September 1935.

13 These figures were given in the SS

newspaper, *Das Schwarze Korps*, on 1 July 1935.

14 See Naomi Shepherd, *Wilfrid Israel, German Jewry's Secret Ambassador*, London 1984, page 104.

15 Article 'Finish up with the Jews' in the book *The SA Man*, published on 27 July 1935: International Military Tribunal, Nuremberg, document PS-3050.

16 *Hakenkreuzbanner*, Mannheim, 1, 26 and 28 August 1935.

17 Leslie Frankel, in conversation with the author, Johannesburg.

18 Lowenthal, *The Jews of Germany: a History of Sixteen Centuries, op. cit.*, page 407, note 1.

19 *Das Schwarze Korps*, 5 September 1935.

20 Law respecting Reich Citizenship of 15 September 1935, *Reich Law Gazette*, 1935, part I, page 1146.

21 Law for the Protection of German Blood and German Honour of 15 September 1934, *Reich Law Gazette*, 1935, part I, page 1147. The German national flag was now the swastika.

22 Report by Ralph W. Barnes, Nuremberg, 15 September 1935: *New York Herald Tribune*, 16 September 1935.

23 *The Times*, 17 September 1935.

24 *Neue Züricher Zeitung*, 22 September 1935.

25 Report of 6 October 1935: Foreign Office papers, 371/18859.

26 Letter of 12 November 1935, to the Chief Secretary, Government of Palestine: Foreign Office papers, 371/19919.

4. AFTER THE NUREMBERG LAWS

1 *Kölnische Zeitung*, 13 October 1935.

2 Quoted in *The Yellow Spot*, page 117.

3 *New York Times*, 20 October 1935.

4 Bella Fromm, diary entry for 20 October 1935: Fromm, *Blood and Banquets: a Berlin Social Diary, op. cit.*, page 181.

5 Quoted in the *Manchester Guardian*, 28 March 1978, when Dr Hans Puvogel, then Minister of Justice in the State of Lower Saxony, was under pressure to resign, after the publication of excerpts from his thesis, which also argued in favour of castrating dangerous sex offenders as part of the plan to 'strengthen the valuable hereditary streams of our people while gradually drying out the inferior ones'.

6 Frankfurter was released in 1945, at the end of the war, and emigrated to Palestine. In February 1950 he wrote an account of the assassination of Gustloff in *Commentary* magazine. In 1976 a Swiss film was made of the killing, entitled *Konfrontation – Assassination in Davos*. Frankfurter died in Israel in 1982, aged 71.

7 Shalom Lindenbaum, in conversation with the author, Jerusalem.

8 David Shtokfish (editor), *Pshitik. A Memorial to the Jewish Community of Pshitik* (Przytyk), Tel Aviv 1973, page 157.

9 Yakov Lashtoshinsky, 'The Przytyk Pogrom' (Yiddish) in *Sefer Przytyk*, Tel Aviv 1973, pages 168–87.

10 *Memorandum on the Development of the Jewish National Home, 1936*, Geneva, June 1937, page 6.

11 Figures from the *Palestine Post*, individual issues from 15 April 1936 to 15 May 1936: see also Martin Gilbert, *The Arab–Israeli Conflict, Its History in Maps*, London 1974, map 20.

12 Telegram of 9 June 1936, Central Zionist Archive, S 73/193: in Shepherd, *Wilfrid Israel, German Jewry's Secret Ambassador, op. cit.*, page 122.

13 Arnold Hahn, *Vor den Augen der Welt! Warum starb Stefan Lux? Sein Leben – seine Tat – seine Briefe*, Prague 1936.

14 Celia S. Heller, *On the Edge of Destruction: Jews of Poland Between the Two Wars*, New York 1977, page 104.

15 World Federation of Polish Jews, 'The Migration of Polish Jewry in Recent Times', *Yearbook*, New York 1964, pages 7–27.

16 Ben Helfgott, in conversation with the author, London.

17 Lowenthal, *The Jews of Germany*, op. cit., page 424.

18 House of Commons, debate of 14 April 1937: *Hansard*.

19 William L. Shirer, diary entry for 4 June 1937: William L. Shirer, *Berlin Diary: the Journal of a Foreign Correspondent, 1934–1941*, London 1941, page 66.

20 'Law relating to measures to be taken in the former Upper Silesian Plebiscite area', 20 June 1937, published in the *Reichsgesetzblatt*, no. 76 of 2 July 1937.

21 *Memorandum on the Development of the Jewish National Home, 1937*, Geneva, June 1938, page 4.

22 The number of German Jews admitted to Palestine had dropped from 8,180 in 1936 to 3,601 in 1937, the number of Polish Jews from 11,596 in 1936 to 3,636 in 1937.

23 Figures of Jewish and Arab dead are taken from the daily issues of the *Palestine Post*.

24 Central Zionist Archive, 87/558: in Shepherd, op. cit., page 116.

25 Poster for 'The Eternal Jew' exhibition: facsimile in *The Judaica Collector*, October 1983.

26 Isaac Landman (editor), *The Universal Jewish Encyclopaedia*, New York 1943, volume 9, page 261.

27 Nathaniel Katzburg, *Hungary and the Jews: Policy and Legislation,*

1920–1943, Ramat Gan, Israel 1981, page 104.

5. 'HUNTED LIKE RATS'

1 According to statistics presented in a letter from A. L. Eastermann to the Foreign Office in London on 12 April 1946, between 200 and 225 Jews had been murdered in Germany between 30 January 1933 and 25 April 1938. Statistics compiled in 1938 by the Reich Representative of German Jews: Foreign Office papers, 371/57545.

2 *Germany Reports*, Paris 1938: quoted in G. E. R. Gedye, *Fallen Bastions: the Central European Tragedy*, London 1939, pages 341–2.

3 Oswald Dutch, *Thus Died Austria*, London 1938, page 246.

4 *Idem.*

5 Gedye, op. cit., pages 306–7.

6 Dutch, op. cit., page 250.

7 Testimony of Fleischmann: Eichmann Trial, 24 April 1961, session 17.

8 Lowenthal, *The Jews of Germany*, op. cit., epilogue, page 430.

9 Gedye, op. cit., page 310.

10 David Hindley Smith to Winston S. Churchill, 18 March 1938, Churchill papers, 2/328, published in Martin Gilbert, *Winston S. Churchill*, document volume 5, part 3, 'The Coming of War', London 1982, page 949.

11 Lowenthal, op. cit., page 430.

12 Dutch, op. cit., pages 246–7.

13 *Ibid.*, pages 247–8.

14 The Austrian census of 22 March 1934 listed 769 localities with Jewish inhabitants.

15 R. T. Smallbones, Despatch no. 48 of 5 May 1938: Foreign Office papers, 371/21635.

16 *Germany Reports*, Paris 1938: in Gedye, op. cit., page 342.

17 Beda died in Auschwitz in 1942, at the age of fifty-nine.

18 Getzel Kressel, 'Beda, Fritz

Loehner, 1883–1942':
Encyclopaedia Judaica, Jerusalem
1972, volume 4, column 368.

19 Report of 28 June 1938, smuggled
out of Berlin to Lord Samuel in
London, Samuel papers, House of
Lords Library: quoted in
Shepherd, *Wilfrid Israel, op. cit.*,
pages 126–7.

20 Bella Fromm diary, 28 June 1938:
Fromm, *Blood and Banquets, op.
cit.*, pages 235–6.

21 Report for June 1938, dated 16
July 1938: Foreign Office papers,
371/21635.

22 J. Hope Simpson, *The Refugee
Problem, Report of a Survey*,
London 1939, pages 323 (France),
340 (Britain), 350–1 and 353
(Belgium), 356 (Scandinavia), 397
(Switzerland), 473 note 1 (USA)
and Appendix VI, tables LXV and
LXVI.

23 Huttenbach, *The Destruction of
the Jewish Community at Worms,
1933–1945, op. cit.*, pages 142–3.

24 Sirkka Purkey, 'The Treatment of
Jewish Refugees in Finland during
the Hitler Era', letter to the author,
13 March 1984 (based upon Elina
Suominen, *Death Boat SS
Hohenhorn*, Helsinki).

6. 'THE SEEDS OF A
TERRIBLE VENGEANCE'

1 Letter of 25 October 1938, from
Sir George Ogilvie-Forbes to
Oliver Harvey, and comment:
Foreign Office papers, 371/22536.

2 Testimony of Zindel Grynszpan:
Eichmann Trial, 25 April 1961,
session 14.

3 Recollections of Rosalind
Herzfeld: *Jewish Chronicle*, 28
September 1979, page 80.

4 Nathan Eck, 'Ringelblum,
Emanuel, 1900–44':
Encyclopaedia Judaica, Jerusalem
1972, volume 14, column 189.

5 Testimony of Zindel Gryszpan:
Eichmann Trial, 25 April 1961,
session 14.

6 E. L. Woodward and Rohan Butler
(editors), *Documents on British
Foreign Policy, 1919–39*, London
1950, third series, volume 3,
telegram 294, page 262.

7 Paul Oestereicher, 'Terror, on
Berlin's Night of Broken Glass', in
The Times, 9 November 1978.

8 Wim van Leer, *Time of My Life*,
Jerusalem 1984, pages 166–8.

9 Lowenthal, *The Jews of Germany,
op. cit.*, page 436.

10 Letter dated Leipzig, 21 November
1938: submitted to the
International Military Tribunal,
Nuremberg, as document L-202.

11 Dr Arthur Flehinger, 'Flames of
Fury', *Jewish Chronicle*, 9
November 1979, page 27.

12 Eric Lucas, manuscript, 'The
Sovereigns', Kibbutz Kfar Blum
(Palestine) 1945, pages 169–71.

13 Huttenbach, *The Destruction of
the Jewish Community of Worms,
op. cit.*, pages 20–1.

14 A thousand million marks was the
equivalent in November 1938 of
£84,000 million in 1985.

15 H. D. Leuner, *When Compassion
was a Crime: Germany's Silent
Heroes*, London 1966, pages
113–14.

16 Sir George Ogilvie-Forbes,
Despatch no. 1224 of 16
November 1938: Foreign Office
papers, 371/21637.

17 *News Chronicle*, 23 November
1938.

18 Associated Press photographs,
50343a and 50343c, with
captions.

19 Testimony of Dr Ernest Abeles,
active in the Orthodox community
in Slovakia, and in the Slovak
office of the American Joint
Distribution Committee:
Eichmann Trial, 23 May 1961,
session 49.

20 Testimony of Benno Cohn:
Eichmann Trial, 25 April 1961,
session 15.

21 Wim van Leer, *op. cit.*, page 174.

22 *The Times*, 3 December 1938.

23 Hull Committee of the Council for German Jewry. Letter to potential supporters, 7 December 1938: archives of Hull Jewry, Jack Lennard papers.

24 'Plan for Assisting Emigration of Jews from Germany', note by Roger Makins, 8 December 1938: Foreign Office papers, 371/22539.

25 Cabinet no. 59 of 1938, London, 14 December 1938, Conclusion 6: Cabinet papers, 23/96; Captain Foley to Sir George Ogilvie-Forbes, 17 January 1939: Foreign Office papers, 371/24079.

26 Baynes (editor), *The Speeches of Adolf Hitler, April 1922–August 1939, op. cit.*, page 741.

27 Quoted by Goering in his letter to Heydrich of 31 July 1941: International Military Tribunal, Nuremberg, document PS-710.

28 Judith Tydor-Baumel, 'The Kitchener Transmigration Camp at Richborough', in Livia Rothkirchen (editor), *Yad Vashem Studies*, XIV, Jerusalem 1981, pages 233–46.

29 Lucas, 'The Sovereigns', *op. cit.*, pages 187–90.

30 *Ibid.*, page 190.

31 Ivone Kirkpatrick, Minute of 13 February 1939: Foreign Office papers, 371/24087.

32 Deputation of 18 May 1939: Foreign Office papers, 371/24983.

33 Inter-departmental conference, 26 May 1939, Minutes: Foreign Office papers, 371/24090.

34 Julius Lowenthal (now Yehuda Guy), in conversation with the author, Ramat Aviv, Israel.

35 Letters of 11 March 1939 and 13 May 1939: archives of the Hull Committee of the Council for German Jewry: Jack Lennard papers.

36 Note by Patrick Reilly, 24 July 1939: Foreign Office papers, 371/24100.

37 Letter of 30 July 1939: Neville Chamberlain papers.

38 Cabinet Committee Minutes, 7 August 1939: Cabinet papers, 27/651.

39 Report on Slovak Jewry, 17 August 1939: Foreign Office papers, 371/24085.

40 J. Rimon (editor), *The Jewish Community of Szrensk and the Vicinity: a Memorial Volume*, Jerusalem 1960, page 43.

41 Eva Michaelis, 'Youth Aliyah Report, August 25th – September 7th 1939': Central Zionist archives, S 75/746.

7. SEPTEMBER 1939: THE TRAPPING OF POLISH JEWRY

1 Yad Vashem archive, Photograph Collection.

2 Alexander Zvielli (Wojcikiewicz), 'The Day the Nazis Went to War', *Jerusalem Post*, 31 August 1979.

3 Joseph Kermish, *The Destruction of the Jewish Community of Piotrkow by the Nazis during World War II*, Tel Aviv 1965, column 5.

4 Jacob Apenszlak (editor), *The Black Book of Polish Jewry*, New York 1943.

5 Kermish, *op. cit.*

6 Czestochowa memorial book, Jerusalem 1967.

7 *Poland: the Communities of Lodz and its Region*, Jerusalem 1976, page 94, entry for Widawa.

8 Bedzin memorial book, Tel Aviv 1959.

9 *Scenes of Fighting and Martyrdom Guide, War Years in Poland, 1939–1945*, Warsaw 1968, page 161.

10 Quoted in Nora Levin, *The Holocaust: the Destruction of European Jewry 1933–1945*, New York 1968, page 153.

11 The fullest account of these events is in Szymon Datner, *55 Dni (1.ix – 15x 1939) Wehrmachtu w Polsce*, Warsaw 1967.

12 Testimony of Eda Lichtmann: Eichmann Trial, 28 April 1961, session 20.

13 Przemysl memorial book, Tel Aviv 1964.

14 *Poland: the Communities of Lodz*, *op. cit.*, entry for Sieradz.

15 Order No. 7, quoted in Louis Falstein (editor), *The Martyrdom of Jewish Physicians in Poland*, New York 1963, page 172.

16 Kermish, *op. cit.*, column 6.

17 Copies of this secret note of the discussion were sent to the Army High Command, the Ministry of the Interior, the Ministry of Food and the Economy, to the Commissioner for the Four Year Plan, as well as to chiefs of the Civilian Administration of the Occupied Territories. International Military Tribunal, Nuremberg, document PS-3363.

18 Eliezer Tash (Tur-Shalom), *The Community of Semiatych (Siemiatycze)*, Tel Aviv 1965.

19 Emanuel Ringelblum, notes, 26 April 1941: Jacob Sloan, (editor) *Notes from the Warsaw Ghetto: the Journal of Emanuel Ringelblum*, New York 1958, page 168.

20 Maria Feferman-Wasoff, typescript, 'The Processed', 1979, page 10.

21 Abraham Isaiah Altus, 'The Nazi Invasion of Raciaz' in *Gal-Ed Memorial Book to the Community of Raciaz*, Tel Aviv 1965.

22 Kermish, *op. cit.*, column 9.

23 S. L. Shneiderman (editor), *Warsaw Ghetto: a Diary by Mary Berg*, New York 1945, page 16.

24 Testimony of Joseph Berger-Ezrahi: Yad Vashem archive, 0–3/447, quoted in Shmuel Krakowski, 'The Fate of Jewish Prisoners of War in the September 1939 Campaign', *Yad Vashem Studies*, XII, Jerusalem 1977, page 303.

25 Ringelblum Archive: quoted in Krakowski, *op. cit.*, page 302.

26 Vitka Kempner, in conversation with the author, Jerusalem.

27 Pultusk memorial book, Tel Aviv 1971.

28 Tarnobrzeg memorial book, Tel Aviv 1973.

29 Apenszlak, *op. cit.*, page 143, quoting *Documents of Crime and Martyrdom*, Cracow 1945.

30 Testimony of Max Burger: Eichmann Trial, 27 April 1961, session 19.

31 Draft of an oral report, eventually given on 6 February 1940, criticizing atrocities committed by the SS and the police in the General Government in December 1939: International Military Tribunal, Nuremberg, document NO-3011.

32 Nachman Blumenthal (editor), *Obozy*, Lodz 1946, pages 127–8.

33 Eimann was found guilty of murder, and sentenced to four years' imprisonment, and three years' deprivation of citizen's rights: Tregenza collection, London.

34 David Wdowinski, *And We Are Not Saved*, London 1964, page 27.

35 Wladyslaw Bartoszewski, *Warsaw Death Ring, 1939–1944*, Warsaw 1968, page 21.

36 Ordinance of 26 October 1939: General Government Official Gazette, no. 1 of 1939, pages 6–7.

37 Yisrael Guttman, 'The Concept of Labour in Judenrat Policy', *Patterns of Jewish Leadership in Nazi Europe, 1933–1945*, Jerusalem 1979, pages 155–7.

38 Kermish, *op. cit.*, columns 9–10; information provided by Ben Helfgott.

39 The Radomsko ghetto was set up on 20 December 1939, the Lodz ghetto on 1 May 1940.

40 Mary Berg diary, 3 November 1939: Shneiderman, *op. cit.*, page 20.

41 *Contra-Komintern*, 2 November 1939.

42 Chaim Kaplan, diary entry for 17 November 1939, in Abraham I. Katsch (editor), *The Warsaw Diary of Chaim A. Kaplan*, New York 1973 (1965 edition entitled *Scroll of Agony*), pages 71–2.

43 Ordinance of 23 November 1939: General Government Official Gazette, no. 1 of 1939, page 61.

44 Lucas, 'The Sovereigns', *op. cit.*, page 191.

45 'Verzeichnis der deportierten Juden', *Heimatblatter des Kreises Aachen*, 1980, page 70.

8. 'BLOOD OF INNOCENTS'

1 Bartoszewski, *Warsaw Death Ring*, *op. cit.*, page 28.

2 *Poland: the Communities of Lodz*, *op. cit.*, entry for Zdunska Wola.

3 Circular of 12 November 1939, signed by Koppe, Higher SS and Police Chief, Warthegau: in Wladyslaw Bartoszewski and Zofia Lewin, *Righteous among Nations: How Poles Helped the Jews, 1939–45*, London, 1969, pages 622–3.

4 Wdowinski, *And We Are Not Saved*, *op. cit.*, page 24.

5 *Ibid.*, page 26.

6 *Ibid.*, pages 24–5.

7 Official notice, published in the *Nowy Kurier Warszawski* on 2 December 1939: Bartoszewski, *op. cit.*, page 23.

8 *Ibid.*, page 23.

9 *Litzmannstadter Zeitung*, 16 November 1939.

10 Quoted in the *Frankfurter Zeitung*, 28 March 1941.

11 Kaplan diary, 18 November 1939: Katsch, *op. cit.*, page 74.

12 *Nowy Kurier Warszawski*, 30 November 1939: Bartoszewski, *op. cit.*, page 24.

13 Bartoszewski, *op. cit.*, pages 24–5. Landau, arrested by the Germans in 1944, was never seen again. The German Security Police Commander in the Warsaw district, responsible for the execution, Joseph Meisinger, was sentenced to death in Warsaw on 3 March 1947.

14 Falstein, *The Martyrdom of Jewish Physicians in Poland*, *op. cit.*, page 493.

15 Wdowinski, *And We Are Not Saved*, *op. cit.*, page 28.

16 *Ibid.*, page 24.

17 Mary Berg diary, 1 December 1939: Shneiderman, *op. cit.*, page 22.

18 Kermish, *The Destruction of the Jewish Community of Piotrkow*, *op. cit.*, columns 14–15.

19 Testimony of Hirsch Pachter: Eichmann Trial, 1 May 1961, session 21.

20 Bartoszewski, *op. cit.*, pages 26–7. The Jews were all from Losice: Zygmunt Ochsenhorn, Mojse Marmelstein, Dawid Goldfarb, Stanislaw Mohsbock, Moses Gojnberg, and Dawid Rosenbind.

21 Kaplan diary, 13 December 1939: Katsch, *op. cit.*, pages 85–6.

22 Decree of 11 December 1939: quoted in full in Shirer, *Berlin Diary*, *op. cit.*, page 220, note 1.

23 SS Major Bischoff to the Mayor of Jarocin, 13 December 1939: Bartoszewski and Lewin, *op. cit.*, page 625.

24 Kaplan diary, 16 December 1939: Katsch, *op. cit.*, page 87.

25 Mary Berg diary, 18 December 1939: Shneiderman, *op. cit.*, page 24.

26 Hans Frank, diary entry for 19 December 1939: *Hans Frank Diary*, Warsaw 1961. The complete diary was submitted to the International Military Tribunal, Nuremberg, as document USSR-223.

27 The Jews included Elja Brajtman, Aron Fogelnest, Eliasz Nussenbaum, Jankiel and Uszer Rosenberg, Herszek and Lejbus Szajman and Mechel Tuchmacher.

28 Kaplan diary, 29 December 1939: Katsch, *op. cit.*, page 93.

29 Kaplan diary, 31 December 1939: *ibid.*, page 94.

30 Kaplan diary, 30 December 1939: *ibid.*, pages 93–4.

31 Immediately after seeing the boat off from Vienna, Ehud Uberall (later Ehud Avriel) had gone to Palestine, a legal Palestine visa in his valid German passport: Ehud Avriel, *Open the Gates! A Personal Story of 'Illegal' Immigration to Israel*, London 1975, page 104.

32 Communication from Professor Bauer, 1 October 1978: diplomatic protests were made by the British Ambassador in Belgrade, Sir Ronald Campbell, on 29 January and 5 February 1940.

33 Avriel, *op. cit.*, page 103.

34 Yitzhak Zuckerman, '25 Years after the Warsaw Ghetto Revolt': *Jewish Resistance during the Holocaust, op. cit.*, page 25.

9. 1940: 'A WAVE OF
    EVIL'

1 Ringelblum notes, January 1940: Sloan, *op. cit.*, pages 7–8.

2 Ringelblum notes, 2 January 1940: *ibid.*, page 11.

3 Ringelblum notes, 5 January 1940: *ibid.*, pages 11–12.

4 Ringelblum notes, 6 January 1940: *ibid.*, page 12.

5 Kaplan diary, 6 January 1940: Katsch, *op. cit.*, pages 97–8.

6 Mary Berg diary, 10 January 1940: Schneiderman, *op. cit.*, page 25.

7 Testimony of Avraham Buchman: Eichmann Trial, 2 June 1961, session 63.

8 Ringelblum notes, 6 March 1940: Sloan, *op. cit.*, page 25.

9 Testimonies of Arieh Helfgot, Nachum Perelman and Joseph Grosfeld, Yad Vashem archive: Krakowski, 'Jewish Prisoners of War in the 1939 Campaign', *op. cit.*, pages 316–17.

10 'The History of the Jews of Wlodawa in the Time of the Nazi Occupation', Yad Vashem archive: Krakowski, *op. cit.*, pages 315–16.

11 Kaplan diary, 14 January 1940: Katsch, *op. cit.*, page 102.

12 Kaplan diary, 16 January 1940: *ibid.*, page 103.

13 A list of the executed Jews, together with, where possible, their ages, professions and addresses, was put by Emanuel Ringelblum into his secret archive: it was discovered after the war, and published in full by Adam Rutkowski in the bulletin of the Jewish Historical Institute in Warsaw (henceforth referred to as *Biuletyn*, Warsaw), number 62, 1967, pages 68–75.

14 Kaplan diary, 24 January 1940: Katsch, *op. cit.*, page 107.

15 Zygmunt Klukowski, diary entry for 1 February 1940: *Dziennik z lat okupacji Zamojszczyzny*, Lublin 1959, page 99.

16 Kaplan diary, 4 February 1940: Katsch *op. cit.*, page 116.

17 Kaplan diary, 5 February 1940: *idem.*

18 Ringelblum notes, 7 February 1940: Sloan, *op. cit.*, page 16.

19 Ringelblum notes, 12 February 1940: *ibid.*, page 19.

20 Kermish, *The Destruction of the Jewish Community of Piotrkow, op. cit.*, column 16.

21 *Manchester Guardian*, 19 February 1940.

22 Ringelblum notes, 21 February 1940: Sloan, *op. cit.*, pages 21–2.

23 Ringelblum notes, 6 March 1940: *ibid.*, page 24.

24 Kaplan diary, 4 March 1940: Katsch, *op. cit.*, page 129.

25 There is a detailed report on the forced labour camps in the Ringelblum archive. Early in 1941 Ringelblum organized the despatch of Jews from Warsaw to collect material about these camps. Their report listed forty-one camps, employing seventeen thousand

Jews. At that time the largest of the camps was just to the south of the village of Belzec: YIVO journal, *Bleter far geshichte*, volume 2, New York, 1949, pages 242–72.

26 Kermish, *op. cit.*, column 17.

27 Ringelblum notes, 7 February 1940: Sloan, *op. cit.*, page 16.

28 Stefan Krakowski, 'Stutthof': *Encyclopaedia Judaica*, Jerusalem 1972, volume 15, column 464.

29 'The Sufferings of Jews in the Concentration Camp at Stutthof (near Danzig)': *Bulletin of the Rescue Committee of the Jewish Agency for Palestine*, March 1945, Foreign Office papers, 371/51116 (henceforth referred to as *Bulletin*, London).

30 Lucjan Dobroszycki (editor), *The Chronicle of the Lodz Ghetto 1941–1944*, New Haven 1984, page xxvii.

31 *Ibid.*, page xxxix.

32 Eichmann Trial, document T.383, submitted to the court on 27 March 1961, session 4. The villages were Piaski, Glusk and Belzyce.

33 Letter from the Joint Polish–Jewish Aid Commission to the Reich Chancellery, dated 28 March 1941: International Military Tribunal, Nuremberg, document NG-2490, quoted in Levin, *The Holocaust, op. cit.*, pages 182–3.

34 Testimony of Heinrich Grüber: Eichmann Trial, 16 May 1961, session 41. Grüber was later sent to Sachsenhausen.

35 Leon Pommers, conversation with the author, Jerusalem.

36 A. J. Sherman, *Island Refuge: Britain and Refugees from the Third Reich*, London 1973, pages 209–10.

37 Kurt Marcus, 'Japan and the Jews', *Jerusalem Post*, 2 April 1982 (Readers' Letters).

38 Kaplan diary, 7 March 1940: Katsch, *op. cit.*, page 129.

10. WAR IN THE WEST: TERROR IN THE EAST

1 Ringelblum notes, 4 May 1940: Sloan, *op. cit.*, page 37.

2 Ringelblum notes, 9 May 1940: *ibid.*, page 39.

3 Memorandum of 15 May 1940, submitted to Hitler on 20 May 1940: quoted in Philip Friedman, *Roads to Extinction: Essays on the Holocaust*, Philadelphia 1980, page 47.

4 Recollections of Rabbi Harry M. Jacobi, *Jewish Chronicle*, 29 September 1978; Harry Jacobi, in conversation with the author, London, 21 February 1985.

5 Kaplan diary, 18 May 1940: Katsch, *op. cit.*, page 154.

6 Sol Liptzin, 'Weiss, Ernst, 1884–1940': *Encyclopaedia Judaica*, volume 16, Jerusalem 1972, columns 412–13.

7 Kazimierz Smolen (editor), *From the History of KL Auschwitz*, Cracow 1967, volume 1, pages 2–3.

8 S. Krakowski, 'Tarnow': *Encyclopaedia Judaica*, Jerusalem 1972, volume 15, column 821.

9 Archive of the Panstwowe Muzeum w Oswiecimiu (henceforth cited as Auschwitz Museum Archive).

10 Maria Feferman-Wasoff, typescript, 'The Processed', *op. cit.*, page 26.

11 Klukowski diary, 17 July 1940: *Dziennik, op. cit.*, pages 138–9.

12 Klukowski diary, 23 July 1940: *ibid.*, pages 139–40.

13 S. Krakowski, 'Radom': *Encyclopaedia Judaica*, Jerusalem 1972, volume 13, column 1501.

14 S. Krakowski, 'Czestochowa': *Encyclopaedia Judaica*, Jerusalem 1972, volume 5, column 1212.

15 Ladislav Lipscher, *Die Juden im Slowakischen Staat 1939–1945*, Munich and Vienna 1980.

16 Cracow memorial books, Jerusalem 1959 and Haifa 1981.

17 Chaim Barlas, letter of 13 August 1940, from Ankara: Central Zionist Archive, Z.4/14,779.

18 Gershom Scholem, 'Benjamin, Walter, 1892–1940': *Encyclopaedia Judaica*, Jerusalem 1972, volume 4, columns 530–1.

19 Testimony of Chief Rabbi Cohen of Bordeaux: Leon Poliakov, *Harvest of Hate. The Nazi Programme for the Destruction of the Jews of Europe*, New York 1954, 1979 edition, page 243.

20 Abitbol, *Les Juifs d'Afrique du Nord sous Vichy*, *op. cit.*, page 44, note 49.

21 Emmanuel Bulz, Chief Rabbi of Luxembourg, 'Luxembourg': *Encyclopaedia Judaica*, Jerusalem 1972, volume 11, column 591.

22 'Japanese "Wallenberg" Honoured at 85': *Jewish Chronicle*, 25 January 1985. The occasion of this report was the award of a Righteous Gentile medal and certificate to Sugihara by Yad Vashem, Jerusalem. The ceremony was held in Tokyo.

23 Friedman, *op. cit.*, pages 74–5.

24 Ringelblum notes, 6–9 September 1940: Sloan, *op. cit.*, pages 46–8.

25 Ringelblum notes, 9 September 1940: Sloan, *op. cit.*, page 48.

26 Shirer diary, 24 September 1940: *Berlin Diary*, *op. cit.*, page 408.

27 Robert Edwin Herzstein, *The War that Hitler Won: the Most Infamous Propaganda Campaign in History*, London 1979, pages 310–12.

28 Ringelblum notes, 6–9 September 1940: Sloan, *op. cit.*, pages 47–48.

29 Klukowski diary, 1 October 1940: *Dziennik*, *op. cit.*

30 Klukowski diary, 17 October 1940: *ibid.*

31 Leo Laufer, recollections: Yad Vashem archive.

32 Ruth Rubin, *Voices of a People. The Story of Yiddish Folksong*, 2nd edition, New York 1973, page 429.

33 Ringelblum notes, 12 October

1940: Sloan, *op. cit.*, page 72.

34 Ringelblum notes, 13 October 1940: *ibid.*, page 73.

35 Toshia Bialer, recollections, in *Collier's*, New York, 20 February 1943, page 17: quoted in Levin, *The Holocaust*, *op. cit.*, pages 207–8.

36 Kaplan diary, 22 October 1940: Katsch, *op. cit.*, pages 212–13.

37 These camps were Gurs, Noé, Portet Saint Simon, Récébédou and Rivesaltes: Werner Nachman and Heinrich Freund, *Sie Sind Nicht Vergessen*, no date.

38 Gurs camp register, Gurs.

39 Testimony of Heinrich Grüber: Eichmann Trial, 16 May 1941, session 41.

40 Ringelblum notes, 23 October 1940: Sloan, *op. cit.*, pages 77–8, and 79.

41 Kaplan diary, 24 October 1940: Katsch, *op. cit.*, pages 213–14.

42 Kaplan diary, 8 November 1940 (Hebrew edition, Tel Aviv and Jerusalem, 1966): Leni Yahil, 'Jewish Resistance – an Examination of Active and Passive Forms of Jewish Survival in the Holocaust Period', *Jewish Resistance during the Holocaust*, Jerusalem 1971 (Yad Vashem conference proceedings, 7–11 April 1968), page 40.

43 Quoted in *Eksterminacja Zydow na Ziemiach Polskich podczas okupacji Hitlerowskiej* ('The Extermination of the Jews on Polish Soil at the Time of the German Occupation'), Warsaw 1957, page 55.

44 Isaac Kabeli, 'The Resistance of the Greek Jews', *YIVO Annual of Jewish Science*, volume 8, New York 1953, page 281. On 1 January 1941 the Governor-General of Salonica wrote to the President of the city's Jewish community: 'In the name of the Greek state, I congratulate you on the heroism displayed by the Jews on the field of battle.'

45 Mary Berg diary, 15 November 1940; Shneiderman, *op. cit.*, page 38.

46 Alexander Donat, *The Holocaust Kingdom*, New York 1965, page 27.

47 Ringelblum notes, 19 November 1940: Sloan, *op. cit.*, pages 86–9.

48 Mary Berg diary, 20 November 1940: Shneiderman, *op. cit.*, pages 38–9.

49 Kaplan diary, 21 December 1940: Katsch, *op. cit.*, page 234.

50 Mary Berg diary, 22 December 1940: Shneiderman, *op. cit.*, pages 41–2.

51 *Palestine Post*, 26 November 1940 and subsequent issues.

52 Hersztein, *op. cit.*, page 309.

53 Kaplan diary, 6 December 1940: Katsch, *op. cit.*, page 232.

54 Ringelblum notes, 10 December 1940: Sloan, *op. cit.*, page 108.

55 Richard Lichtheim, Geneva, to Joseph Linton, London, 11 December 1940: Central Zionist Archives, Z4/14,901.

56 Minutes of R. T. E. Latham and T. M. Snow, London, 17 December 1940: Foreign Office papers, 371/35242.

57 Testimony of Heinrich Grüber: Eichmann Trial, 16 May 1961, session 41.

58 Ringelblum notes, 24 December 1940: Sloan, *op. cit.*, page 115.

59 Donald Edgar, *The Stalag Men*, London 1982, page 55.

11. JANUARY–JUNE 1941: THE SPREADING NET

1 Mary Berg diary, 4 January 1941: Shneidermann, *op. cit.*, page 45.

2 Ringelblum notes, 5 January 1941: Sloan, *op. cit.*, page 120.

3 Mary Berg diary, 10 January 1941: Shneiderman, *op. cit.*, page 46.

4 Hans Frank diary, 22 January 1941: *op. cit.*, page 251.

5 Lodz Chronicle, 20 January 1941: Dobroszycki, *op. cit.*, pages 12–13.

6 Lodz Chronicle, 29 January 1941: *ibid.*, page 17.

7 J. Sandel, 'Maurycy Trebacz': *Biuletyn*, Warsaw, *op. cit.*, number 2, 1951, pages 236–7.

8 Kaplan diary, 31 January 1941: Katsch, *op. cit.*, page 239.

9 Testimony of Zivia Lubetkin: Eichmann Trial, 3 May 1961, session 25.

10 Photograph Album, *Le Pogromme Legionnaire de Bucharest*: Yad Vashem Photographic Collection, F.A. 37.

11 John Colville, diary entry for 2 February 1941: Martin Gilbert, *Winston S. Churchill*, volume 6, London 1983, pages 1004–5.

12 Theodor Lavi, 'Rumania': *Encyclopaedia Judaica*, Jerusalem 1972, volume 14, column 400.

13 Address of 1 February 1941: Yitzhak Arad, Yisrael Gutman and Abraham Margaliot (editors), *Documents on the Holocaust*, Jerusalem 1981, page 237.

14 Information provided by Dr Lucjan Dobroszycki.

15 Recollections of Moshe Shklarek (later Bahir), 'The Revolt' in Miriam Novitch, *Sobibor, Martyrdom and Revolt, Documents and Testimonies*, New York 1980, pages 140–1.

16 Josef Fraenkel (editor), *The Jews of Austria, Essays on their Life, History and Destruction*, London 1967, page 513.

17 Quoted in Jacob Presser, *The Destruction of the Dutch Jews*, New York 1969, page 51.

18 Paul Tillard, *Mauthausen*, Paris 1945, pages 20–1.

19 Presser, *op. cit.*, pages 50–4.

20 Ringelblum notes, 27 February 1941: Sloan, *op. cit.*, pages 127–8.

21 Ringelblum notes, 28 February 1941: *ibid.*, pages 130–2.

22 Recollections of a survivor of the Lodz ghetto, in conversation with the author, Montreal.

23 Testimony of Frieda Mazia:

Eichmann Trial, 4 May 1961, session 27.

24 Friedman, *Roads To Extinction*, *op. cit.*, pages 74–5.

25 Gertrude Zeisler, letter of 5 June 1941: Gerda Hoffer (editor), *I Did Not Survive: Letters from the Kielce Ghetto*, Jerusalem 1981, pages 4–5.

26 Ringelblum notes, 18 March 1941: Sloan, *op. cit.*, page 138.

27 *Kolnische Zeitung*, 5 April 1941.

28 Order dated 12 April 1941: A. Eisenbach (editor), *Dokumenty i Materialy, Getto Lodzkie*, Warsaw, Lodz, Cracow 1946, pages 86–7.

29 Lodz Chronicle, 10–24 March 1941: Dobroszycki, *op. cit.*, page 34.

30 Lodz Chronicle, 26 March 1941: *ibid.*, page 37.

31 Information from Miriam Novitch, Kibbutz Lohamei Hagettaot, Israel.

32 Charles W. Steckel, *Destruction and Survival*, Los Angeles 1973, page 14.

33 Steckel, *ibid.*, page 15.

34 *Yad Vashem News*, Jerusalem, June 1984, pages 11–12. On 29 January 1984 the state of Israel recognized Mustafa Hardaga as a 'righteous among the nations'.

35 Ringelblum notes, 17 April 1941: Sloan, *op. cit.*, pages 154–6.

36 Testimony of Yitzhak Zuckerman: Eichmann Trial, 3 May 1961, session 25.

37 After the war, Zuckerman married Zivia Lubetkin; they lived in Israel. The Polish spelling of his name was Cukierman.

38 Ringelblum notes, 11 May 1941: Sloan, *op. cit.*, page 170.

39 Ringelblum notes, 11 May 1941: Sloan, *op. cit.*, page 176.

40 Ringelblum notes, 11 May 1941: Sloan, *op. cit.*, page 174.

41 Lodz Chronicle, 21 April 1941: Dobroszycki, *op. cit.*, page 50.

42 Michael R. Marrus and Robert O. Paxton, *Vichy France and the*

Jews, New York 1981, pages 166–7.

43 'List of Jews Executed in France': Serge Klarsfeld, *Memorial to the Jews Deported from France, 1942–1944*, New York 1983, pages 642–54.

44 Document submitted to the Eichmann Trial, 11 July 1961, session 92. The phrase used was: 'Zweifellos kommende Endlösung'.

45 Marrus and Paxton, *op. cit.*, page 167.

46 Ringelblum notes, 11 May 1941: Sloan, *op. cit.*, page 173.

47 Donat, *The Holocaust Kingdom*, *op. cit.*, page 46.

48 Ringelblum notes, 11 May 1941: Sloan, *op. cit.*, page 177.

49 Krakowski, 'Jewish Prisoners of War in the 1939 Campaign', *op. cit.*, page 318.

50 Zalman Grinberg diary, 21 June 1941: quoted in Grinberg's speech of 27 May 1945, 'Address Delivered by Dr Zalman Grinberg on the Occasion of a Liberation Celebration', copy, Foreign Office papers, 371/55705.

51 Tash, *The Community of Semiatych*, *op. cit.*

12. 'IT CANNOT HAPPEN!'

1 Testimony of Zivia Lubetkin: Eichmann Trial, 3 May 1961, session 25.

2 Stanislaw Adler, *In the Warsaw Ghetto, 1940–1943, An Account of a Witness*, Jerusalem 1982, page 325.

3 Donat, *The Holocaust Kingdom*, *op. cit.*, page 46.

4 *Ibid.*, page 47.

5 Shalom Cholawski, *Soldiers from the Ghetto*, San Diego 1980, page 38.

6 Arieh Leon Bauminger, in conversation with the author, Jerusalem.

7 Interrogation report of a liberated

prisoner on Alderney Island, June 1944: Solomon H. Steckoll, *The Alderney Death Camp*, London 1982, page 33.

8 Testimony of J. Dawidowicz, 'Revenge – Recollections of a Partisan', *Folksshtime*, Warsaw, July–August 1958: Reuben Ainsztein, *Jewish Resistance in Nazi-occupied Eastern Europe*, London 1974, page 259.

9 Falstein, *The Martyrdom of Jewish Physicians in Poland*, op. cit., page 347.

10 'Sufferings of Kovno (Kaunas) Jewry', letter of 26 May 1945: *Bulletin*, London, November 1945, copy in Foreign Office papers, 371/57625.

11 Maja Abramowicz (Zarch), typescript, pages 24–5.

12 The story of the mass murder of Russian prisoners-of-war in German hands is one of the least known atrocity stories of the Second World War: on a visit to Poland in 1981, the author was overwhelmed by the number of sites at which Russian prisoners-of-war had perished. These sites are listed (for the area of post-1945 Poland) in *Obozy hitlerowskie na ziemiach polskich 1939–45: Informator encyclopedyczny*, Warsaw 1979.

13 Of a total of 5,700,000 Russian soldiers captured in the Second World War, 2,500,000 died in captivity. Of them, it is estimated that one million were shot by the Einsatzgruppen, and that the rest died from hunger, cold and disease, in camps where they were often denied even the rudiments of shelter and medical attention.

14 Cholawski, op. cit., page 39.

15 Szymon Datner, *Walka i Zaglada Bialystockiego Ghetta*, Lodz 1946, pages 10–14.

16 Jean Ancel, 'Faleshty' (Falesti), *Encyclopaedia Judaica*, Jerusalem 1971, volume 6, columns 1154–5.

17 Jean Ancel, 'Dombroveni',

Encyclopaedia Judaica, Jerusalem 1971, volume 6, columns 157–8.

18 Jean Ancel, 'The Rumanian Jewry between 23.8.1941 and 31.12.1947', doctoral thesis, Hebrew University of Jerusalem, submitted September 1979.

19 Zalman Grinberg diary, quoted in speech, op. cit.

20 *Le Massacre des Juifs de Jassy* (documents and photographs): Yad Vashem photographic archive, F.A.50.

21 Eye-witness account, first published in *Mantuirea*: 'Expulsion of the Remaining Jews of Jassy', *Bulletin*, London, op. cit., copy in Foreign Office papers, 371/51116.

22 Information provided by Jean Ancel.

23 Reports No. 1324 of 4 July 1941 (Roman), No. 4457 of 6 July 1941 (Prabova-Inotesti) and No. 10,252 of 6 July 1941 (Jassy): *Le Massacre des Juifs de Jassy*, op. cit.

24 Friedman, *Roads to Extinction*, op. cit., pages 246–8.

25 Testimony of Leon Weliczker Wells: Eichmann Trial, 1 May 1961, session 22.

26 Testimony of Joseph Melkman: Eichmann Trial, 10 May 1961, session 34; see also Presser, *The Destruction of the Dutch Jews*, op. cit., page 70.

27 Ainsztein, op. cit., pages 464–6.

28 Datner, *Walka*, op. cit., page 14.

29 Eichmann cross-examination: Eichmann Trial, 19 April 1961, session 10.

30 Testimony of Dr Aharon Peretz: Eichmann Trial, 4 May 1962, session 28.

31 'Recapitulation of Executions Carried Out in the Area of Strike Commando 3 until 1 December 1941', Kovno, 1 December 1941: Raul Hilberg (editor), *Documents of Destruction, Germany and Jewry 1933–1945*, London 1972, page 47.

32 Operational Situation Report,

USSR, no. 17, 9 July 1941: Yad Vashem archive.

33 Falstein, *op. cit.*, page 361.

34 N. M. Gelber (editor), *Lwow Volume*, Tel Aviv 1956, page 681.

35 Jack (Idel) Kagan, in conversation with the author, London, 21 May 1984.

36 Report of 1 December 1941: Hilberg, *op. cit.*, page 47.

37 Yitzhak Arad, *Ghetto in Flames: the Struggle and Destruction of the Jews in Vilna in the Holocaust*, Jerusalem 1980, pages 75–7.

38 *Scenes of Fighting and Martyrdom Guide, op. cit.*, page 62.

39 Landau diary, 14 July 1941: Yad Vashem archive, Photograph Collection.

40 Kishinev Memorial Book, Tel Aviv 1950; *The Jews of Bessarabia* (Memorial Book), Jerusalem 1971; Theodor Lavi, 'Kishinev', *Encyclopaedia Judaica*, Jerusalem 1972, volume 10, column 1068.

41 Itzhak Alfassi, 'Zirelson, Judah Leib, 1860–1941': *Encyclopaedia Judaica*, Jerusalem 1972, volume 16, column 1183.

42 F. H. Hinsley and others, *British Intelligence in the Second World War, Its Influence on Strategy and Operations*, volume 2, London 1981, appendix 5, page 671.

43 D. B. Levin, 'We Will Never Forget and Never Forgive the Fascist Criminals' (in Russian), Saratov 1942, page 34. I am grateful to Yigael Zafoni of Leningrad for this reference.

44 Operational Situation Report, USSR, no. 31, 23 July 1941: Yad Vashem archive.

45 Operational Situation Report, USSR, no. 32, 24 July 1941: Yad Vashem archive.

46 Friedman, *op. cit.*, page 249.

47 The five attacks were reported in Operational Situation Report, USSR, no. 37, 29 July 1941: Yad Vashem archive.

48 Steckel, *Destruction and Survival, op. cit.*, page 34.

49 Operational Situation Report,

50 Landau diary, 28 July 1941: Yad Vashem archive.

51 Friedman, *op. cit.*, page 199, note 30, and page 200, notes 31–33.

52 *Ibid.*, page 200, note 34.

53 *Ibid.*, page 291.

54 Melech Ravitch, 'Kacyzne, Alter, 1885–1941': *Encyclopaedia Judaica*, Jerusalem 1972, volume 10, columns 657–8.

55 Kishinev memorial book, Tel Aviv 1949.

56 *Einsatzgruppe 'C'*, reports for 17–31 July 1941: Yad Vashem archive.

57 Report entitled 'Attitude Towards the Civilian Population in the East', written in Kassel, Germany, on 3 January 1942: International Military Tribunal, Nuremberg, documents USSR-293. Quoted in Levin, *The Holocaust, op. cit.*, pages 260–1.

58 Letter of 31 July 1941: International Military Tribunal, Nuremberg, document PS-710.

59 Letter of 1 August 1941: Falstein, *op. cit.*, page 141.

60 Lodz Chronicle, 28 and 29–31 July 1941: Dobroszycki, *op. cit.*, pages 67, note 79, and 68.

61 Archive of YIVO, New York.

62 Diary of W. Sakowicz, 27 July–2 August 1941: *The Paneriai Museum*, Vilna 1966, pages 6–7. I am grateful to Boris Kelman of Leningrad for this reference.

63 Yad Vashem photographic archive.

64 Hilberg, *op. cit.*, page 49.

65 Operational Situation Report, USSR, no. 40, 3 August 1941: Yad Vashem archive.

66 Falstein, *op. cit.*, pages 337 and 340.

67 Hilberg, *op. cit.*, page 49.

68 Operational Situation Report, USSR, no. 43, 5 August 1941: Yad Vashem archive.

69 Yad Vashem archive, information provided by Dr Jean Ancel.

70 Maja Abramowicz (Zarch), *op. cit.*, page 27.

13. 'A CRIME WITHOUT A NAME'

1 Yitzhak Arad, 'The Lithuanian Ghettos of Kovno and Vilna', *Patterns of Jewish Leadership in Nazi Europe, 1933–1945*, Jerusalem 1979, pages 97–8.

2 Abraham Turi (Avraham Tory, formerly Golub), 'Debate', *Patterns of Jewish Leadership, op. cit.*, pages 181–2.

3 Sarah Neshamit, 'Debate', *Patterns of Jewish Leadership, op. cit.*, pages 183–4.

4 Isaiah Trunk, *Judenrat: the Jewish Councils in Eastern Europe under Nazi Occupation*, New York 1972 (paperback edition 1977), page 446.

5 Letter of Salomon Speiser, Warsaw 1945: *Hurben Gliniane* ('The Tragic End of Our Gliniany'), New York 1946.

6 Trunk, *op. cit.*, page 444.

7 *Idem.*

8 Operational Situation Report, USSR, no. 47, 9 August 1941: Yad Vashem archive.

9 Lohse directive, 15 August 1941: International Military Tribunal, Nuremberg, document NO-4539.

10 Dr Zalman Grinberg, diary, *op. cit.*

11 Testimony of Dr Aharon Peretz: Eichmann Trial, 4 May 1961, session 28.

12 *Scenes of Fighting and Martyrdom Guide, op. cit.*, page 61.

13 Report of 1 December 1941: Hilberg, *Documents of Destruction, op. cit.*, page 49.

14 Operational Situation Report, USSR, no. 54, 16 August 1941: Yad Vashem archive.

15 Maria Rubinstein, in conversation with the author, Beersheba.

16 Operational Situation Report, USSR, no. 51, 13 August 1941: Yad Vashem archive.

17 Operational Situation Report, USSR, no. 56, 18 August 1941: Yad Vashem archive.

18 Operational Situation Report, USSR, no. 58, 20 August 1941: Yad Vashem archive.

19 Operational Situation Report, USSR, no. 60, 22 August 1941: Yad Vashem archive.

20 Joseph Gottfarstein, 'Debate': *Jewish Resistance during the Holocaust, op. cit.*, pages 61–2.

21 Colonel Grigoriy Matveyevich Linkov, *War in the Enemy's Rear*: Ainsztein, *Jewish Resistance in Nazi-occupied Eastern Europe, op. cit.*, page 282.

22 Arad, *Ghetto in Flames, op. cit.*, page 98.

23 Broadcast of 24 August 1941: quoted in Martin Gilbert, *Winston S. Churchill*, volume 6, *op. cit.*, pages 1173–4.

24 Hinsley, *British Intelligence, op. cit.*, appendix 5, page 671.

25 Randolph L. Braham, 'The Kamenets Podolsk Massacres', *Yad Vashem Studies*, IX, Jerusalem 1973, pages 139–40.

26 Jaeckeln was later in charge of carrying out the 'final solution' in the Baltic states. He was given a one-day trial in Riga on 3 February 1946, and hanged that same afternoon (Gerald Reitlinger, *The Final Solution: the Attempt to Exterminate the Jews of Europe, 1939–1945*, London 1953, page 194, note 1).

27 Testimony of Leslie Gordon: Eichmann Trial, 6 June 1961, session 62.

28 Iosif Bregman, 'The Dubossary Ghetto': *Sovetish Geimland*, number 4, Moscow 1968, pages 48–9.

29 V. I. Bekesh, 'The Names of the Heroes are not Forgotten', *Folksshtime*, number 46, Moscow, 21 March 1968.

30 Ringelblum notes, 30 August 1941: Sloan, *op. cit.*, page 197.

31 Testimony of Dr Aharon Peretz: Eichmann Trial, 4 May 1961, session 28.

32 Hersh Smoliar, *Resistance in*

Minsk, Oakland, California, 1966, pages 9–16.

33 Recollection of former SS General Karl Wolff, *The World at War*, Thames Television documentary, London, 27 March 1974.

34 Testimony of Abba Kovner: Eichmann Trial, 4 May 1961, session 27.

35 Figures in the Jaeger report of 1 December 1941: Hilberg, *op. cit.*, page 53.

36 Avraham Sutzkever (Abram Suzkever), *Vilner Ghetto*: Azriel Eisenberg (editor), *Witness to the Holocaust*, New York 1981, pages 180–1. Sutzkever's wife, who was in the same prison, later escaped: Sutzkever reported what she had seen when he gave evidence to the International Military Tribunal, Nuremberg, on 27 February 1946.

37 Testimony of Abba Kovner: Eichmann Trial, 4 May 1961, session 27.

38 Testimony of Meir Mark Dvorjetsky: Eichmann Trial, 4 May 1961, session 27.

39 Ringelblum archive, YIVO, New York.

40 Report of 1 December 1941: Hilberg, *op. cit.*, page 54.

41 Evidence of Avraham Sutzkever (Abram Suzkever), International Military Tribunal, Nuremberg, 27 February 1946.

42 Directive of 12 September 1941 regarding 'Jews in the Newly Occupied Eastern Territories': International Military Tribunal, Nuremberg, document NOKW-3292.

43 Shmuel Spector, 'The Jews of Volhynia and their Reaction to Extermination', *Yad Vashem Studies*, XV, Jerusalem 1983, page 160.

44 Kermish, *The Destruction of the Jewish Community of Piotrkow*, *op. cit.*, columns 26–7.

45 Leah Leibowitz (Klompul), in conversation with the author, Johannesburg.

46 Mary Berg diary, 20 September 1941: Shneiderman, *op. cit.*, page 93.

47 'Testimony of a German Army Officer', Prisoner of War No. 2406004, 15 August 1945: Shaul Esh (editor), *Yad Washem Studies on the European Jewish Catastrophe and Resistance*, number 3, Jerusalem 1959, pages 303–20.

48 Information communicated by Professor Alexander Lerner. After the war, Judith Lerner had another daughter, Sonia, who was allowed to leave the Soviet Union for Israel. Lerner and his wife were refused permission to leave. After thirteen years in refusal, Judith Lerner died. Aged seventy-one, Professor Alexander Lerner remained in Moscow, an outcast in his own society, an inspiration to many younger Soviet Jews, but still denied the right to go to the homeland with which he, as a Jew, wished to be united. He was finally allowed to go to Israel in 1988.

49 Report of 1 December 1941, Hilberg, *op. cit.*, page 52.

50 Yitzhak Arad (Rudnicki), *The Partisan, from the Valley of Death to Mount Zion*, New York 1979, pages 39–42, and 100–1.

51 Shalom Ben-Shemesh Sonenson, the *Last Days of Ejszyszki* (in Hebrew) in the Eishyshok memorial book, Jerusalem 1950. Of the 4,000 Jews murdered in Ejszyszki 1,000 came from the nearby village of Olkenıkı and other hamlets. (*Olkenıkı in Flames*, Tel Aviv (1962).

52 Shalom Sonenson, *op. cıt.*

53 Idem.

54 'Jew, go back to the grave!': Yaffa Eliach, *Hasidic Tales of the Holocaust*, New York 1982, pages 53–5 (based on Yaffa Eliach's interviews with Zvi Michalowski).

55 Recollections of Konstantin Miroshnik: Babi Yar memorial volume, Tel Aviv 1978.

56 Recollections of Golda Glozman: *ibid*.

57 Report of 1 December 1941,
Hilberg, *op. cit.*, page 54.
58 Testimony of the Lukianov
cemetery watchman: Babı Yar
memorial volume, *op. cit.*
59 Testimony of David Rosen: *ibid.*
60 Testimony of Victoria Shyapeltoh:
ibid.
61 A. Anatoli (Kuznetsov), *Babi Yar*,
London 1970, pages 110–11 and
113.
62 Anatoli, *ibid.*, page 73.
63 Report of 2 October 1941:
International Military Tribunal,
Nuremberg, document NO-3137.
64 Recollections of Hadassah Rosen:
Eisenberg, *op. cit.*, pages 309–10.
65 Report of 1 December 1941,
Hilberg, *op. cit.*, page 52.
66 Information from the archive of
Moshe Jekutiel Lubetzky (whose
father Jekutiel, mother Polina and
sister Sarah were all murdered in
the action at Alytus, thirty-five
kilometres from Butrimonys).
67 'Number of Jewish Victims in the
Aktionen, June 24–December 23,
1941': Arad, *Ghetto in Flames, op.
cit.*, pages 210–11.
68 Evidence of Avraham Sutzkever,
International Military Tribunal,
Nuremberg, 27 February 1946.
69 Arad, *Ghetto in Flames, op. cit.*,
pages 175, 210–11.
70 Testimony of Abba Kovner:
Eichmann Trial, 4 May 1961,
session 27.
71 Arad, 'The Lithuanian Ghettos of
Kovno and Vilna', *op. cit.*, page
100.
72 Zalman Grinberg, *op. cit.*
73 Maja Abramowicz, typescript, *op.
cit.*, page 33.
74 Eye-witness account of Major A.
Zalcman, published in *Nasze
Slowo*, no. 7, Lodz 1947:
Ainsztein, *op. cit.*, page 258.
75 Directive of 10 October 1941:
International Military Tribunal,
Nuremberg, document D-411.
76 Order of the Day of the Eleventh
Army, 20 November 1941:
International Military Tribunal,

Nuremberg, document PS-4064.
The Crimean executions of
Einsatzkommando D were
reported in detail on 12 December
1941 (NO-2828), 19 January 1942
(NO-3338) and 8 April 1942
(NO-3359).
77 Account by 'MZ': *Bulletin*,
London, November 1945, *op.
cit.*
78 Order (signed by Hans Frank) of
15 October 1941: Law Gazette of
the General Government, no. 99,
25 October 1941, page 595:
Bartoszewski and Lewin,
Righteous among Nations, op. cit.,
page 632.
79 Report from Warsaw: *Poland
Fights*, 30 June 1942.

14. 'WRITE AND RECORD!'

1 *Hans Frank Diary, op. cit.*, speech
of 9 October 1941.
2 Eichmann Trial, 18 May 1961,
session 44, document T.264.
3 Report by Captain Künzel, 13
November 1941: B. Ajzensztajn
(editor), *Ruch podziemny w
ghettach i obozach*, Lodz 1946,
pages 203–6.
4 Testimony of Hildegarde
Henschel: Eichmann Trial, 11 May
1961, session 37.
5 Lodz Chronicle, 7 May 1942:
Dobroszycki, *op. cit.*, pages
165–6.
6 Lodz Chronicle, 29 June 1942:
ibid., page 216.
7 Lodz Chronicle, November 1941:
ibid., page 83.
8 Lodz Chronicle, 6 December 1941:
ibid., page 93.
9 Lodz Chronicle, 14–31 January
1942: *ibid.*, page 123.
10 Leuner, *When Compassion was a
Crime, op. cit.*, page 138.
11 Arad, 'The Lithuanian Ghettos of
Kovno and Vilna', *op. cit.*, page
102.
12 Arad, *Ghetto in Flames, op. cit.*,
pages 150–3.
13 Yitzhak Rudashevski, *The Diary*

of the Vilna Ghetto, June 1941–April 1943, Tel Aviv 1973, pages 38–9.

14 Arad, *Ghetto in Flames, op. cit.*, page 151.

15 Report of 1 December 1941, Hilberg, *op. cit.*, page 54.

16 'Activity and Situation Report No. 6': International Military Tribunal, Nuremberg, document R-102.

17 M. Carp, *Cartea Neagra*, Bucharest 1947, volume 3, page 208.

18 Dora Litani, 'The Destruction of the Jews of Odessa in the Light of Rumanian Documents': *Yad Vashem Studies*, VI, Jerusalem 1967, pages 135–41.

19 Letter of 25 October 1941: International Military Tribunal, Nuremberg, document NO-365.

20 Dr Moshe Gross (Henryk Zeligowski), 'The End of the Community': I. M. Lask (editor), *The Kalish Book*, Tel Aviv, 1968, pages 258–60.

21 Report of 30 October 1941, to the Commissioner General, Minsk: International Military Tribunal, Nuremberg, document PS-1104.

22 Letter dated 28 October 1941: Eichmann Trial, 17 May 1961, document 1559.

23 Rabbi Ephraim Oshry, *Reponsa from the Holocaust*, New York 1983, papers 14–16.

24 Testimony of Dr Aharon Peretz: Eichmann Trial, 4 May 1961, session 28.

25 Dr Leon Bauminger, recollection: *The Gazette*, Montreal, 13 November 1982 (in the article by Paul Dalby, 'How One Man Sent Thousands to Die').

26 Vera Elyashiv, 'After 25 Years', *Jewish Quarterly*, London, volume 18, 1970.

27 Helen Kutorgene, *Kaunaski dnievnik* (Kovno diary) 1941–1942, published in 1968: Arad, *Ghetto in Flames, op. cit.*, pages 405–6.

28 Testimony of Dr Aharon Peretz: Eichmann Trial, 4 May 1961, session 28.

29 Kutorgene, *op. cit.*, pages 405–6.

30 Letter of Alter Galperin, 3 December 1945: Yad Vashem archive MI/E, 128/56.

31 Recollection of Avraham Tory (Avraham Golub): *The Gazette*, Montreal, 13 November 1982.

32 Testimony of Dr Aharon Peretz: Eichmann Trial, 4 May 1961, session 28.

33 Report of 1 December 1941, Hilberg, *op. cit.*, page 52.

34 Zalman Grinberg, *op. cit.*

35 Arad, *Ghetto in Flames, op. cit.*, page 156.

36 Testimony of Meir Dvorjetzky: Eichmann Trial, 4 May 1961, session 27.

37 Abba Kovner, recollection of the 'Bialystok Operation': Eichmann Trial, 4 May 1961, session 27.

38 Trunk, *Judenrat, op. cit.*, page 438.

39 Trunk, *op. cit.*, page 466.

40 Testimony of Haim Berendt: Eichmann Trial, 5 May 1961, session 29.

41 Testimony of Haim Berendt: Eichmann Trial, 5 May 1961, session 29.

42 Gertrude Schneider, *Journey into Terror: the Story of the Riga Ghetto*, New York 1979, pages 21–46.

43 Letter from Dr Konstantin Bazarov to the author, 7 October 1978.

44 Koppel S. Pinson (editor), *Nationalism and History: Essays on Old and New Judaism by Simon Dubnow*, Philadelphia 1968, pages 3 and 39.

45 Joseph Gar, 'Riga, Holocaust Period', *Encyclopaedia Judaica*, Jerusalem 1972, volume 14, column 175.

46 Schneider, *op. cit.*, page 155. The trains reaching Riga left Berlin (27 November 1941), Nuremberg (29 November 1941), Stuttgart (1 December 1941),

Vienna (3 December 1941),
Hamburg (4 December 1941),
Cologne (7 December 1941),
Cassel (9 December 1941),
Düsseldorf (11 December 1941),
Bielefeld (12 December 1941),
Hanover (15 December 1941),
Theresienstadt (9 and 15 January
1942), Vienna (11 January 1942),
Berlin (13, 19 and 25 January
1942), Leipzig (21 January 1942),
Vienna (26 January 1942),
Dortmund (27 January 1942)
and Vienna (6 February
1942).

47 Testimony of Dr Aharon Peretz:
Eichmann Trial, 4 May 1961,
session 28.

48 Testimony of Dr Aharon Peretz:
Eichmann Trial, 4 May 1961,
session 28. The first group of
German Jews to reach Kovno, one
thousand in all, arrived on 25
November 1941.

49 Report of 1 December 1941,
Hilberg, *op. cit.*, pages 52–3.

50 Materials concerning Dr Petras
Baublis: Yad Vashem archive;
information provided by Eitan
Finkelstein.

51 Information provided by Yakov
Gorodetsky.

52 *Jewish Chronicle*, 14 November
1941.

53 Ringelblum notes, 14 November
1941: Sloan, *op. cit.*, page 233.

54 Kaplan diary, 19 November 1941:
Katsch, *op. cit.*, pages 279–80.

55 Ringelblum notes, 22 November
1941: Sloan, *op. cit.*, pages 236–7.
The names of the executed Jews
were Rywka Kligerman, Sala
Pasztejn, Josek Pajkus, Luba Gac,
Motek Fiszbaum, Fajga Margules,
Dwojra Rozenberg and Chana
Zajdenwach.

56 Mary Berg diary, 22 November
1941: Shneiderman, *op. cit.*, page
115.

57 Testimony of Zivia Lubetkin:
Eichmann Trial, 3 May 1961,
session 25.

58 Testimony of Yitzhak Zuckerman:
Eichmann Trial, 3 May 1961,
session 25.

59 Zabecki recollection, typescript,
op. cit., page 19.

60 Letter of 15 November 1941:
International Military Tribunal,
Nuremberg, document P5-3663.

61 Letter of 18 December 1941:
International Military Tribunal,
Nuremberg, document PS-3666.

62 Report of 1 December 1941,
Hilberg, *op. cit.*, pages 56–7.

63 During November 1941 the
following executions are known:
in Eastern Galicia, Boryslaw (800),
Kamionka (500), Kolomyja (800),
Przemyslany (400) and Lvov
(several thousand); in Eastern
Poland, Wolozyn (300), Mir
(1,500), Swierzen Nowy (500) and
Slonim (9,000, on November 14);
in Volhynia, at least 18,000 in
Rowne. Those murdered in
December included, in Eastern
Galicia, Horodenka (2,500),
Zablotow (1,000), Zabia (500),
Brezany (1,000); in the Vilna
region, Nowogrodek (5,000 on
December 6) and Jody (all 700 on
December 16).

64 Jack (Idel) Kagan, in conversation
with the author, London, 21 May
1984.

65 Letter of 19 November 1941:
Eichmann Trial, 17 May 1961,
session 43, document 1558.

66 Zdenek Lederer, *Ghetto
Theresienstadt*, London 1953,
pages 264–5.

67 Lederer, *op. cit.*, page 14.

68 *Ibid.*, page 15.

69 International Military Tribunal,
Nuremberg, documents NO-426
and NO-429.

70 International Military Tribunal,
Nuremberg, document PS-630.

71 International Military Tribunal,
Nuremberg, affidavit by Dr
Konrad Morgen, 19 July 1946
(Morgen was an SS officer who
had investigated SS corruption).
See Raul Hilberg, *The Destruction*

of the European Jews, New York
1961 (Harper Colophon edition,
1979, page 561).

72 Information provided by Dr
Kazimierz Smolen, Auschwitz
Museum and Archive.

73 Letter of 25 November 1941:
International Military Tribunal,
Nuremberg, document NO-3060.

74 Heydrich letter of 29 November
1941: International Military
Tribunal, Nuremberg, document
PS-709.

75 Testimony of Michael Podklebnik
(Michal Podchlebnik): Wladyslaw
Bednarz, *Das Vernichtungslager zu
Chelmno am Ner*, Warsaw 1946,
pages 39–45.

76 Testimony of Andrzej Miszczak,
Kolo, 26 June 1946: *ibid.*, pages
46–53.

77 Testimony of Michael Podklebnik:
ibid.

15. THE 'FINAL
SOLUTION'

1 Mary Berg diary, 9 December
1941: Shneiderman, *op. cit.*, page
117.

2 The four thousand Jews sent to
Chelmno on 13 December 1941
from Kowale Panskie came from
sixteen nearby villages, among
them Turek, Dobra, Uniejow,
Wladislawow, Brudzew and
Tuliszkow (for these locations, see
Martin Gilbert, *Atlas of the
Holocaust*, London 1982, map 95,
page 82).

3 Ringelblum notes, 14 December
1941: Sloan, *op. cit.*, pages
239–40.

4 Klarsfeld, *Memorial to the Jews
Deported from France*, *op. cit.*,
pages 642–54. The other
Warsaw-born Jews executed in
Paris on 15 December 1941 were
Szmuel Korenblum (born 1887),
Nathan Fuks (1889), Israel
Mardfeld (1898), Szama Knapajs
(1901) and Israel Eszenbaum
(1909).

5 Kaplan diary, 15 December 1941:
Katsch, *op. cit.*, page 283.

6 Testimony of Avraham Aviel:
Eichmann Trial, 5 May 1961,
session 29.

7 Material relating to Yanis Lipke:
Yad Vashem archive; information
provided by Aba Taratuta,
Leningrad.

8 Josef Katz, *One Who Came Back:
the Diary of a Jewish Survivor*,
New York 1973, page 19.

9 *Chronicle*, *op. cit.*, page 96, entry
for 17 December 1941.

10 *Chronicle*, *op. cit.*, page 101, entry
for 29–31 December 1941.

11 *Chronicle*, *op. cit.*, page 125, entry
for 14–30 January 1942.

12 *Chronicle*, *op. cit.*, page 100, entry
for 26–28 December 1941.

13 Dr Richard Bilski, 'Mail into and
out of the Lodz Ghetto': *The
Judaica Collector*, London,
summer 1984, pp. 24–5.

14 Information and material provided
by Ernest Stein, the son of
Oskar and Paula Stein (born 1874
and 1880 respectively).
Neither of them survived the war.

15 Governor Frank's speech of 16
December 1941: International
Military Tribunal, Nuremberg,
document PS-2233. (Excerpts from
the diary of Hans Frank, 25
October 1939–25 May 1945.)

16 Otto Bräutigam (Ostministerium)
to Hinrich Lohse, 18 December
1941: International Military
Tribunal, Nuremberg, document
PS-3666: quoted in Levin, *The
Holocaust*, *op. cit.*, pages 293–4.

17 Smoliar, *Resistance in Minsk*, *op.
cit.*, pages 26–7.

18 Ainsztein, *Jewish Resistance in
Nazi-occupied Eastern Europe*, *op.
cit.*, page 897, note 37.

19 Testimony of Michael Podklebnik:
Eichmann Trial, 5 June 1961,
session 65.

20 Ringelblum notes, January 1942:
Sloan, *op. cit.*, page 246.

21 Ringelblum notes, January 1942:
ibid., page 248.

22 Ringelblum notes, January 1942: *ibid.*, page 250.
23 Ringelblum notes, January 1942: *ibid.*, page 251.
24 Ringelblum notes, mid-January 1942: *ibid.*, page 254.
25 Chaim Rumkowski, speech delivered on Sunday, 4 January 1942: Lodz Chronicle, 1–5 January 1942, Dobroszycki, *op. cit.*, pages 111–15.
26 Lodz Chronicle, 10–13 January 1942: *ibid.*, pages 119–21.
27 Quoted in Yisrael Gutman, 'The Concept of Labour in Judenrat Policy', *Patterns of Jewish Leadership, op. cit.*, pages 161 and 169.
28 Gutman, *ibid.*, page 169
29 Lederer, *Ghetto Theresienstadt, op. cit.*, page 208
30 Testimony of Liana Neumann: Eichmann Trial, 8 May 1961, session 30.
31 Falstein, *The Martyrdom of Jewish Physicians in Poland, op. cit.*, page 211.
32 *Poland: the Communities of Lodz and its Region, op. cit.*, entry for Klodawa, pages 244–5.
33 Lodz Chronicle, 10–13 January 1942: Dobroszycki, *op. cit.*, page 121.
34 Lodz Chronicle, 14–31 January 1942: *ibid.*, page 125.
35 Lodz Chronicle, 14–31 January 1942: *ibid.*, page 127, and note 19.
36 Lodz Chronicle, 14–31 January 1942: *ibid.*, page 125, and note 15.

16. EYE-WITNESS TO MASS MURDER

1 *Poland, the Communities of Lodz and its Region, op. cit.*, entry for Izbica Kujawska, pages 53–4.
2 Testimony of Yakov Grojanowski: Jewish Historical Institute, Warsaw.
3 Lodz Chronicle: Dobroszycki, *op. cit.*, page xxi, note 32.
4 Lodz Chronicle: *ibid.*, Introduction, page xxi.

17. 20 JANUARY 1942: THE WANNSEE CONFERENCE

1 Protocol of the Wannsee Conference: International Military Tribunal, Nuremberg: document NG 2586 F (6).
2 Eichmann pre-trial interrogation, quoted in the Eichmann Trial, 20 June 1961, session 75.
3 Report of 9 January 1942: Archives of the Polish Government in Exile, London.
4 'A Railroad Timetable': Hilberg, *Documents of Destruction, op. cit.*, pages 106–11, document 16.
5 Franklin Watts (editor), *Voices of History 1942–43*, New York 1943, page 121; text as monitored by the Foreign Broadcast Monitoring Service, Federal Communications Commission, Washington D.C.
6 The figures for Jews murdered in those five camps would appear to be: Auschwitz-Birkenau, 1,000,000 up to May 1944 and 500,000 after May 1944 (total 1,500,000); Chelmno, 360,000, Sobibor, 250,000, Belzec, 600,000 and Treblinka, 840,000 (total 2,050,000).
7 Testimony of Andrzej Miszczak: Bednarz, *Das Vernichtungslager, op. cit*, pages 46–53.
8 Maria Rubinstein, in conversation with the author, Beersheba.
9 Affidavit of Dr Rudolf Kastner, 13 September 1945: International Military Tribunal, Nuremberg, document PS-2605.
10 Hilberg, *The Destruction of the European Jews, op. cit.*, pages 520–1.
11 Yisrael Gutman, *The Jews of Warsaw 1939–1943: Ghetto, Underground, Revolt*, Bloomington, Indiana, 1982, page 64.
12 Falstein, *The Martyrdom of Jewish Physicians in Poland, op. cit.*, page 359.

13 Letter received by Nochum
    Spivack from his brother in Russia:
    Shirley Resnick (editor), *Spivack
    Spirit*, January 1960. Of
    twenty-five members of the
    Spivack family in the Volhynia in
    1940, only seven survived the war.
    One of those killed, Yankel
    Spivack, a soldier in the Red Army,
    was killed in action at the battle
    of Stalingrad.

14 Dora Litani, 'The Destruction of
    the Jews of Odessa in the light of
    Rumanian Documents', *op. cit.*,
    pages 135–54. Simon Frug, who
    had died in 1916 at the age of
    fifty-six, described himself as 'a
    poet who wept all his life'. Among
    his best known poems was 'The
    Goblet', written in 1881 under the
    impact of the pogroms. Translated
    into Yiddish by I. L. Peretz as *Der
    Kos*, it was sung by Jews the world
    over. His Yiddish poem *Hot
    Rakhomones*, was written after the
    Kishinev pogrom of 1903. Recited
    and sung at mass meetings of
    protest, it bore the refrain: 'Have
    pity! Give shrouds for the dead,
    and for the living – bread.'

15 Operational Situation Report,
    USSR, no. 156, 16 January 1942:
    International Military Tribunal,
    Nuremberg, document NO-3405.

16 Letter of 28 January 1942, to the
    Foreign Ministry, Berlin:
    Eichmann Trial, 17 May 1961,
    session 43, exhibit T.728.

17 Letter dated 31 January 1942:
    Eichmann Trial, 17 May 1961,
    session 43, document 1278,
    exhibit T.730.

18 Schneider, *Journey into Terror*, *op.
    cit.*, pages 42–3 and 54.

19 Danuta Czech, 'Most Important
    Events in the History of the
    Concentration Camp
    Auschwitz-Birkenau', Kazimierz
    Smolen (editor), *From the History
    of KL Auschwitz*, Oswiecim, 1967,
    page 191.

20 Protocol of the meeting of 6 March
    1942: Eichmann Trial, 17 May

1961, session 43, document 119.

21 Letter and documents submitted
    16 April 1958 by Dr E. Schaefer:
    Wiener Library archives.

22 After United States forces captured
    Oran on 10 November 1942, the
    camp at Hadjerat M'Guil was
    liberated. In Algiers, on 3 March
    1944, four camp overseers,
    including two Germans, were
    sentenced to death for the murders.

23 Dr E. Shaefer, *op. cit.*

18. 'JOURNEY INTO
THE UNKNOWN'

1 48,662 from January 1941 to
    January 1942; 4,618 in February
    1942: Gutman, *The Jews of
    Warsaw*, *op. cit.*, page 64.

2 Hugo Gryn, reviewing *Maladie de
    Famine*, Warsaw 1946: *Journal of
    the '45 Aid Society*, no. 2, London,
    September 1976.

3 Mary Berg diary, 27 February
    1942: Shneiderman, *op. cit.*, page
    134.

4 Cholawski, 'The Judenrat in
    Minsk', *Patterns of Jewish
    Leadership*, *op. cit.*, page 129.

5 *New Soviet Documents on Nazi
    Atrocities*, Soviet Embassy,
    London, 1942.

6 Report of 10 February 1942:
    Trunk, *Judenrat*, *op. cit.*, pages
    407–8.

7 Trunk, *op. cit.*, page 442.

8 Report of 19 February 1942: Arad
    and others, *Documents on the
    Holocaust*, *op. cit.*, document 184,
    page 407.

9 The survivor was David Stoliar.

10 G. I. Vaneyev, *Black Sea Navy in
    the Great Patriotic War*, Moscow
    1978: Zeev Ben Shlomo,
    ' "Struma" was Torpedoed by
    Soviet Submarine', *Jewish
    Chronicle*, 3 September 1982.

11 Lodz Chronicle, February 1942:
    Dobroszycki, *op. cit.*, page 128.

12 Smoliar, *Resistance in Minsk*, *op.
    cit.*, page 42.

13 Ainsztein, *Jewish Resistance in*

Nazi-occupied Eastern Europe, op. cit., page 474.

14 Trunk, *Judenrat, op. cit.*, page 417.

15 *Ibid.*, page 440.

16 Account of the events of 4 and 5 March 1942 in Baranowicze; *Bulletin*, London, April 1945; Foreign Office papers, 371/51117.

17 Testimony of Dora Rosenboim: Yad Vashem archive.

18 Trunk, *op. cit.*, pages 439–40.

19 Testimony of Leon Weliczker Wells: Eichmann Trial, 1 May 1961, session 22.

20 Smoliar, *op. cit.*, page 43.

21 Article entitled 'Heroes of Nowogrodek' (in Polish): *Jutrznia*, 28 March 1942.

22 Harold (Hersh) Werner, in conversation with the author, Miami.

23 Harold Werner, typescript, 'Episodes of a Member of the Jewish Partisan Resistance Group in Poland During World War II', June 1981: Yad Vashem archive.

24 'Transport Aa': Lederer, *Ghetto Theresienstadt, op. cit.*, page 209.

25 Naftali Salsitz, 'The Holocaust in Kolbuszowa': I. M. Biderman (editor), *Kolbuszowa Memorial Book*, New York 1971.

26 Tatiana Berenstein, *Biuletyn, op. cit.*, Warsaw 1957, number 21.

27 Testimony of Chaim Hirszman, Lublin, 19 March 1946: archive of the Jewish Historical Institute, Warsaw.

28 Testimony of Pola Hirszman, Lublin, 20 March 1946: archive of the Jewish Historical Institute, Warsaw.

29 Luba Krugman Gurdus, *The Death Train: a Personal Account of a Holocaust Survivor*, New York 1978, pages 50–1.

30 Testimony of 'T': Baranowicze, *Bulletin*, London, April 1945, *op. cit.*

31 Berenstein, *Biuletyn*, Warsaw, *op. cit.*, number 61, 1967.

32 Pochep memorial stone,

photographed by Vladimir Lembrikov, photograph and transcription provided by Yigal Zafoni, letter No. 29, Leningrad, 18 March 1985.

33 Postcard dated 10 April 1942: Huttenbach, *The Destruction of the Jewish Community of Worms, op. cit.*, pages 175, 236.

34 Huttenbach, page 236.

35 'Transport Ab': Lederer, *op. cit.*, page 210.

36 Klukowski diary, 29 March 1942: *Dziennik, op. cit.*

37 Klukowski diary, 26 March 1942: *ibid.*

38 Belzec memorial stone, inscription photographed by the author, 7 August 1980.

39 Goebbels diary, 27 March 1942: Louis P. Lochner (editor), *The Goebbels Diaries*, New York 1948, pages 147–8.

40 Danuta Czech, 'Kalendarium der Ereignisse im Konzentrationslager Auschwitz-Birkenau', *Hefte von Auschwitz*: for 1942 (1960), for 1943 (1961, 1962) and for 1944 (1964); entry for 30 March 1942.

41 *Ibid*, entry for 30 March 1942.

42 Klarsfeld, *Memorial to the Jews, op. cit.*, pages 1–16.

43 Eichmann testimony: Eichmann Trial, 19 April 1961, session 10.

44 Conversations between Franz Stangl and Gitta Sereny, in Dusseldorf prison in 1971. Stangl died of a heart attack on 27 June 1971, the day after his last interview with Gitta Sereny: Gitta Sereny, *Into That Darkness: from Mercy Killing to Mass Murder*, London 1974.

45 Schneider, *Journey into Terror, op. cit.*, pages 56–8.

46 Katz, *op. cit.*, page 17, note 2. Carlebach's son and five of his nephews survived the war to become rabbis in their turn, his son in New York, his nephews in Jerusalem, London, Manchester, Montreal and New Jersey. In 1948

a sixth nephew, Ezriel Carlebach, founded the newspaper *Ma'ariv*, later the largest circulation Hebrew newspaper in Israel. A seventh nephew, Haim Cohn, became a Justice of the Supreme Court of Israel.

47 Testimony of Yitzhak Zuckerman: Eichmann Trial, 3 May 1961, session 25.

48 Testimony of Yitzhak Zuckerman: Eichmann Trial, 3 May 1961, session 25.

49 *Jutrznia*, 28 March 1942: Gutman, *The Jews of Warsaw*, *op. cit.*, page 166.

50 Ringelblum notes (recalling the end of December 1941, early January 1942): Gutman, *The Jews of Warsaw*, *op. cit.*, page 165.

51 'Transport Ag': Lederer, *op. cit.*, pages 210–11.

52 Czech, 'Kalendarium', *op. cit.*, entries for 2, 3, 13, 17, 19, 23, 24, and 29 (twice) April 1942.

53 'Swastika over Jaworow': Jaworow Memorial Book, page 12.

54 Kaplan diary, 7 April 1942: Katsch, *op. cit.*, pages 312–13.

55 Klukowski diary, 8 April 1942: *Dziennik*, *op. cit.*

56 Dawid Rubinowicz diary, 10 April 1942: Derek Bowman (translator and editor), *The Diary of Dawid Rubinowicz*, Edinburgh 1981, pages 55–6.

57 Tatiana Berenstein, 'Eksterminacja Zydow w Galicji, 1941–1943', *Biuletyn*, Warsaw, *op. cit.*, number 61, Warsaw 1967.

58 Tatiana Berenstein, 'Martyrologia, opor, i zaglada ludnosci zydowskiej', *Biuletyn*, Warsaw, *op. cit.*, number 21, 1957. ·

59 D. Dabrowska, 'Zaglada Skupisk Zydowskich w "Kraju Warty" w okresie Okupacji Hitlerowskiej', *Biuletyn*, Warsaw, *op. cit.*, number 13, 1955.

60 Lodz Chronicle: Dobroszycki, *op. cit.*, pages 140 and 143, note 29.

61 D. Dabrowska and L.

Dobroszycki, *Kronika ghetta Lodzkiego* (The Chronicle of the Lodz Ghetto), Lodz 1965, volume 1, pages 457–8.

62 Lodz Chronicle, 10–14 April 1942: Dobroszycki, *op. cit.*, page 145.

63 Lodz Chronicle, 18–20 April 1942: *ibid.*, pages 148–9.

64 Lodz Chronicle, 27 and 28 April 1942: *ibid.*, page 155.

65 Lodz Chronicle: *ibid.*, page 155, note 42.

66 Letter of 10 April 1942: International Military Tribunal, Nuremberg, document NO-5196.

67 *Gazeta Lwowska*, 11 April 1942: Bartoszewski and Lewin, *Righteous among Nations*, *op. cit.*, pages 638–9.

68 Klukowski diary, 11 April 1942: *Dziennik*, *op. cit.*

69 Testimony of David Mekler: Miriam Novitch collection, Kibbutz Lohamei Hagettaot, Israel.

70 Klukowski diary, 12 April 1942: *Dziennik*, *op. cit.*

71 Ringelblum notes, mid-April 1942: Sloan, *op. cit.*, page 257.

72 Mary Berg diary, 15 April 1942: Shneiderman, *op. cit.*, pages 140–1.

73 Mlawa memorial book, *Pinkas Mlawa*, New York 1950, pages 406–8.

74 J. Rimon (editor), *The Jewish Community of Szrensk and the Vicinity: a Memorial Volume*, Jerusalem 1960, page 67.

75 The *Einsatzkommando* figure was 91,678, in its report of 8 April 1942: International Military Tribunal, Nuremberg, documents NO-3338 and NO-3339.

76 Information provided by Konrad Kwiet. See also, Konrad Kwiet and Helmut E. Schwege, *Selbstbehauptung und Widerstand, Deutsche Juden im Kampf um Existenz and Menschwenwürde, 1933–1945*, Hamburg 1984.

77 Lodz Chronicle, 4 May 1942:

Dobroszycki, *op. cit.*, page 161.

78 Lodz Chronicle, 8 May 1942; *ibid.*, page 167.

79 Michael Etkind, ' "Youth" Remembered; Postman No. 102': *Journal of the '45 Aid Society*, no. 11, April 1984, page 3.

80 Oshry, *Responsa, op. cit.*, pages 34–5.

81 Donat, *The Holocaust Kingdom, op. cit.*, page 50.

82 Kaplan diary, 18 April 1942: *Katsch, op. cit.*, page 314.

83 Mary Berg diary, 28 April 1942: Shneiderman, *op. cit.*, pages 142–3.

84 Testimony of Moshe Shklarek: Miriam Novitch, *Sobibor, Martyrdom and Revolt, op. cit.*, pages 150–5.

85 'Transport Ap', 18 April 1942: Lederer, *op. cit.*, pages 211–12.

86 'Transport An', 25 April 1942: *ibid.*, page 212.

87 The train was number BA-49. The telegram, dated 25 April 1942, was cited in the Eichmann Trial, 17 May 1961, session 43.

88 'Transport Aq', 27 April 1942: Lederer, *op. cit.*, page 213.

89 Mary Berg diary, 28 April 1942: Shneiderman, *op. cit.*, page 144.

90 Lodz Chronicle, 29 and 30 April 1942: Dobroszycki, *op. cit.*, pages 155–6.

91 Ben Helfgott, in conversation with the author, London.

19. 'ANOTHER JOURNEY INTO THE UNKNOWN'

1 Maja Abramovicz (Zarch), typescript, *op. cit.*, page 34.

2 *Ibid.*, page 39.

3 Trunk, *Judenrat, op. cit.*, page 440.

4 *Ibid.*, page 441.

5 Dov Levin, 'The Small Communities', *Patterns of Jewish leadership, op. cit.*, page 136.

6 Trunk, *op. cit.*, page 444–5.

7 *Ibid.*, page 442.

8 Testimony of Adolf Berman: Eichmann Trial, 3 May 1961, session 26.

9 Gutman, *The Jews of Warsaw, op. cit.*, page 64.

10 Adolf Berman, 'The Fate of the Children in the Warsaw Ghetto': Yisrael Gutman and Livia Rothkirchen (editors), *The Catastrophe of European Jewry, Antecedents, History, Reflections*, Jerusalem 1976, pages 406–7.

11 Ringelblum notes, 8 May 1942: Sloan, *op. cit.*, pages 260–1.

12 Testimony of Avraham Aviel: Eichmann Trial, 5 May 1961, session 29.

13 Shalom Ben-Shemesh Sonenson, the *Last Days of Ejszyszki* (in Hebrew) in the Eishyshok memorial book, Jerusalem 1950.

14 'Supplementary Record – Face Sheet', 16 May 1946: Yad Vashem archive, PC 9170/344.

15 Falstein, *The Martyrdom of Jewish Physicians in Poland, op. cit.*, page 39.

16 Shmuel Krakowski, 'Jewish Armed Resistance in Poland, 1942–1944', typescript. See also his *The War of the Doomed: Jewish Armed Resistance in Poland, 1942–1944*, New York 1984, page 230.

17 Levin, 'The Small Communities', *op. cit.*, pages 142–4.

18 Ringelblum notes, 12 May 1942: Sloan, *op. cit.*, pages 266.

19 'The Diary of S. Sheinkinder': *Yad Vashem Studies*, V, Jerusalem 1963, pages 255–69.

20 Ringelblum notes, 12 May 1942: Sloan, *op. cit.*, pages 273–4.

21 Information from Shmuel Krakowski: letter to the author, 6 August 1984.

22 Kazimierz Smolen, Director, Auschwitz Museum: letter to the author, 16 March 1982.

23 Testimony of Frieda Mazia: Eichmann Trial, 4 May 1961, session 27.

24 Erich Kulka, 'Jewish Revolt in Auschwitz': *The Voice of Auschwitz survivors in Israel*,

Jerusalem and Tel Aviv, number 28, September 1984.

25 T. Berenstein, 'Martyrologia, Opor i Zaglada Ludnosci Żydowskiej w Dystrykcie Lubelskim', *Biuletyn*, *op. cit.*, Warsaw 1957, number 21.

26 Testimony of Dov Frieberg: Eichmann Trial, 5 June 1961, session 64.

27 'Transport Ax' and 'Transport Ay' of 17 May 1942: Lederer, *Ghetto Theresienstadt, op. cit.*, page 215.

28 Testimony of Dov Freiberg: Eichmann Trial, 5 June 1961, session 64.

29 Testimony of Itzhak Lichtman: Novitch, *Sobibor, Martyrdom and Revolt, op. cit.*, pages 80–5.

30 Lodz Chronicle, 4 May 1942: Dobroszycki, *op. cit.*, page 160.

31 Lodz Chronicle, 5 May 1942: *ibid.*, page 161.

32 Lodz Chronicle, 6 May 1942: *ibid.*, pages 161–2.

33 Lodz Chronicle, second entry for 6 May 1942: *ibid.*, page 163.

34 Lodz Chronicle, 7 May 1942: *ibid.*, pages 166–7.

35 Lodz Chronicle, 9–11 May 1942: *ibid.*, page 168.

36 Lodz Chronicle, 17 May 1942: *ibid.*, page 176.

37 Lodz Chronicle, 12 May 1942: *ibid.*, page 171.

38 Lodz Chronicle: Dobroszycki, *op. cit.*, page 83, note 97.

39 Lodz Chronicle, 17 May 1942: *ibid.*, pages 174–6.

40 Pabianice memorial book, Tel Aviv 1956, page 252. I am grateful to Mordecai Chmura's daughter, Helen Aronson, for drawing my attention to this reference to her late father (letter to the author, 12 February 1982).

41 Lodz Chronicle, 18 May 1942: Dobroszycki, *op. cit.*, pages 178–9.

42 Lodz Chronicle, 18 May 1942 and 20 May 1942: *ibid.*, pages 180 and 183.

43 *Poland: The Communities of Lodz and its Region, op. cit.*, entry for Brzeziny.

44 Lodz Chronicle, 20 and 21 May 1942: Dobroszycki, *op. cit.*, pages 181–2. Bernard Ostrowski was the only one of the fifteen Lodz chroniclers and archivists to survive the war.

45 Lodz Chronicle, 20–21 May 1942: *ibid.*, page 181.

46 Lodz Chronicle, 1 June 1942: *ibid.*, page 194.

47 Testimony of Leo Laufer.

48 Wiener Library photographic archive; Lucien Steinberg, *Not as a Lamb: the Jews against Hitler*, Glasgow 1974, pages 26–43 ('The Herbert Baum Campaign').

49 Jacques Ravine, *La Resistance organisée des Juifs en France*, Paris 1973; Professor Yehuda Bauer, letter to the author, 1 October 1978.

50 Trunk, *op. cit.*, page 443.

51 Testimony of Eda Lichtmann: Eichmann Trial, 28 April 1961, session 20.

52 Testimony of Dora Rosenboim: Yad Vashem archive.

53 Ringelblum archives: YIVO, New York.

54 Ringelblum notes, 23 May 1942: Sloan, *op. cit.*, page 275.

55 Gutman, *The Jews of Warsaw, op. cit.*, page 64.

56 Ringelblum notes, 25 May 1942: Sloan, *op. cit.*, pages 282–3.

57 Yad Vashem photographic archive.

58 Information from Yigal Zafoni, in conversation with the author, Leningrad, 23 August 1985.

20. 'IF THEY HAVE ENOUGH TIME, WE ARE LOST'

1 Ringelblum notes: Sloan, *op. cit.*, pages 283–4.

2 Information provided by Dr Shmuel Spector, from his doctoral thesis on the Jews of the Volhynia during the Holocaust; see also Spector, 'The Jews of Volhynia', *op. cit.*

3 *The Kherson Region during the Great Patriotic War, 1941–1945*:

documents and materials (in Russian), Odessa 1968. I am grateful to Yigal Zafoni for this reference.

4 Richard Lichtheim, letter: Central Zionist Archives.

5 Ringelblum notes, end of June 1942: Sloan, *op. cit.*, page 301.

6 Jozef Garlinski, *Fighting Auschwitz: the Resistance Movement in the Concentration Camp*, London 1975, page 14.

7 Rubinowicz diary, 1 June 1942: Bowman, *op. cit.*, pages 86–7.

8 Shmuel Krakowski, 'Holocaust in the Polish Underground Press': *Yad Vashem Studies*, XVI, Jerusalem 1984, pages 247–8.

9 Jack Young (Jona Jakob Speigel), typescript, 'Lost and Waiting to be Found', and conversation with the author, London, 30 May 1984.

10 Testimony of Tadeusz Pankiewicz: first published in book form in Cracow in 1947, reprinted in translation in Eisenberg, *Witness to the Holocaust*, *op. cit.*, pages 194–203.

11 Rubin, *Voice of a People*, *op. cit.*, pages 429–30 and page 458, note 15.

12 Pankiewicz, *op. cit.*

13 Franciszek Zabecki, *Wspomnienia dawne i nowe o tragedii Zydow w Treblince* ('Old and New Memories of the Tragedy of the Jews at Treblinka'), Warsaw 1977.

14 Hava Follman, 'The Liquidation of Hrubieszow Jewry': Baruch Kaplinsky (editor), *Pinkas Hrubieshov, Memorial to a Jewish Community in Poland*, Tel Aviv, 1962.

15 Testimony of Yaakov Biskowitz: Eichmann Trial, 5 June 1961, session 61.

16 Mary Berg diary, 3 June 1942: Shneiderman, *op. cit.*, page 154.

17 Ringelblum notes, 6 June 1942: Ringelblum archive, YIVO, New York. I am grateful to Lucjan Dobroszycki for this reference.

18 Abraham Levin diary, 6 June 1942: Joseph Kermish (editor), 'Extract from the Diary of Abraham Levin', *Yad Vashem Studies*, volume 6, Jerusalem 1967, pages 316–18.

19 Levin diary, 7 June 1942: Kermish, *op. cit.*, pages 318–19.

20 Günther Deschner, *Heydrich: the Pursuit of Total Power*, London 1981, pages 273–6.

21 Lederer, *Ghetto Theresienstadt*, *op. cit.*, page 32.

22 Deschner, *op. cit.*, page 276.

23 Documents submitted to the Eichmann Trial, 12 June 1961, session 74.

24 'Transport AAh', 10 June 1942: Lederer, *op. cit.*, pages 215–16.

25 'Transport AAk', 12 June 1942: *ibid.*, page 216.

26 'Transport AAi', 13 June 1942: *ibid.*, pages 216–17.

27 'Transport AAh', 10 June 1942: *ibid.*, pages 215–16.

28 Levin, 'The Small Communities', *op. cit.*, page 137.

29 Messages of 9 June 1942 and 15 June 1942: International Military Tribunal, Nuremberg, document PS-501.

30 Testimony of 3 January 1946: Record of Proceedings, International Military Tribunal, Nuremberg.

31 Letter of 5 July 1942: Eichmann Trial, document 1443. The verb 'processed' was rendered in the original German as 'verarbeitet'.

32 Kaplan diary, 9 June 1942: Katsch, *op. cit.*, page 350.

33 Testimony of Frieda Mazia: Eichmann Trial, 4 May 1961, session 27.

34 Czech, 'Kalendarium', *op. cit.*

35 Testimony of Frieda Mazia: Eichmann Trial, 4 May 1961, session 27.

36 Lodz Chronicle: Dobroszycki, *op. cit.*, page 208, note 69.

37 Testimony of Yosef Buzhminski: Eichmann Trial, 2 May 1961, session 24.

38 Testimony of B. Ajzensztajn:

Ainsztein, *Jewish Resistance in Nazi-occupied Eastern Europe, op. cit.*, page 876.

39 Recollections of Maria Rubinstein: in conversation with the author, Beersheba.

40 Ringelblum notes, 17 June 1942: Joseph Kermish, 'Emanuel Ringelblum's Notes Hitherto Unpublished': *Yad Vashem Studies*, VII, Jerusalem 1968, pages 178–80.

41 Kaplan diary, 3 July 1942: Katsch, *op. cit.*, pages 368–9.

42 Kermish, 'Emanuel Ringelblum', *op. cit.*, page 180, note 10.

43 Lodz Chronicle, 4 June 1942: Dobroszycki, *op. cit.*, page 199.

44 Lodz Chronicle, 8–10 June 1942: *ibid.*, page 203.

45 Lodz Chronicle, 21 July 1942: *ibid.*, page 227.

46 Lodz Chronicle, 21 October 1942: *ibid.*, page 274.

47 Lodz Chronicle, 1 June 1942: *ibid.*, pages 194–5.

48 Lodz Chronicle, 21 July 1942: *ibid.*, page 226.

49 Lodz Chronicle, 1 June 1942: *ibid.*, page 195.

50 Ephraim Barasz, speech of 21 June 1942: Trunk, *Judenrat, op. cit.*, page 402.

51 Ringelblum notes, 25 June 1942: Sloan, *op. cit.*, page 291.

52 Ringelblum notes, 26 June 1942: *ibid.*, pages 297–8.

21. 'AVENGE OUR TORMENTED PEOPLE'

1 Memorandum by Himmler's Secretary, Rudolf Brandt, 7 July 1942: International Military Tribunal, Nuremberg, document NO-216.

2 P. D. C. Mackay, member of the Royal College of Surgeons, to the *British Medical Journal*, 19 August 1945 (examined by censor, 22 August 1945): Foreign Office papers, 371/50989.

3 Announcement in the special edition of *Het Joodsche Weekblad* (the Jewish Weekly), Amsterdam, 14 July 1942, facsimile: Presser, *The Destruction of the Dutch Jews, op. cit.*, page 145.

4 Presser, *op. cit.*, page 150.

5 Czech, 'Kalendarium', *op. cit.*, entry for 17 July 1942.

6 Louis de Jong, 'Jews and Non-Jews in Nazi-occupied Holland': Max Beloff (editor), *On the Track of Tyranny*, London 1960, page 150.

7 Note of SS First Lieutenant Heinz Rothke, 19 July 1942, International Military Tribunal, Nuremberg, document RF-1226: Marrus and Paxton, *Vichy France and the Jews, op. cit.*, page 246.

8 Czech, 'Kalendarium', *op. cit.*, entry for 21 July 1942.

9 'Convoy 7, July 19, 1942': Klarsfeld, *Memorial to the Jews Deported from France, op. cit.*, pages 64–71.

10 Testimony of Rudolf Vrba: *The World at War*, documentary film, Thames Television, 1974.

11 Recollections of Lilli Kopecky: in conversation with the author, Jerusalem.

12 Testimony of Hermann Graebe, 10 and 13 November 1945: International Military Tribunal, Nuremberg, document PS-2992, quoted in Whitney R. Harris, *Tyranny on Trial, the Evidence at Nuremberg*, Dallas 1954, pages 356–7.

13 Ainsztein, *Jewish Resistance in Nazi-occupied Eastern Europe, op. cit.*, page 258.

14 Trunk, *Judenrat, op. cit.*, page 441.

15 *Ibid.*, pages 464–5.

16 Cholawski, *Soldiers from the Ghetto, op. cit.*, pages 67–8.

17 Trunk, *op. cit.*, page 472.

18 Levin, 'The Small Communities', *op. cit.*, pages 137–7.

19 *Poland: the Communities of Lodz and its Region, op. cit.*, entry for Kowale Panskie.

20 *Ibid*: entry for Uniejow.
21 Iosif Bregman, 'The Kletsk Ghetto': *Sovetish Geimland*, number 4, Moscow 1968, pages 50–51. See also Aharon Weiss, 'Kletsk-Kleck': *Encyclopaedia Judaica*, Jerusalem 1971, volume 10, columns 1107–8.
22 Iosif Bregman, 'The Nieswiez ghetto': *Sovetish Geimland*, number 4, Moscow 1968, pages 49–50.
23 Cholawski, *op. cit.*, pages 69–70.
24 Trunk, *op. cit.*, page 472.
25 *Ibid.*, pages 4170–1.
26 Cholawski, *op. cit.*, page 170.
27 Trunk, *op. cit.*, page 472.
28 Cholawski, *op. cit.*, page 170.
29 Testimony of Shalom Cholawski: Eichmann Trial, 12 June 1961, session 73.
30 Falstein, *The Martyrdom of Jewish Physicians in Poland*, *op. cit.*, page 309.
31 Information provided by Yigal Zafoni of Leningrad.

22. FROM WARSAW TO TREBLINKA: 'THESE DISASTROUS AND HORRIBLE DAYS'

1 Yitzhak Katznelson, *Vittel Diary* 22.5.43–16.9.43, Tel Aviv 1972, pages 158–9.
2 Donat, *Holocaust Kingdom*, *op. cit.*, page 53.
3 Himmler directive, 19 July 1942: International Military Tribunal, Nuremberg, document NO-5574.
4 'Liquidation of Jewish Warsaw', report prepared by Jewish underground organizations, and sent to London on 15 November 1942: *Biuletyn*, Warsaw, *op. cit.*, number 1, 1951, pages 59–126.
5 Zabecki, *Wspomnienia*, *op. cit.*, page 44.
6 Adam Czerniakow, diary entry for 22 July 1942: Raul Hilberg,

Stanislaw Staron and Josef Kermisz (editors), *The Warsaw Diary of Adam Czerniakow: Prelude to Doom*, New York 1979, page 384.
7 Stanislaw Adler, *In the Warsaw Ghetto 1940–1943: an Account of a Witness*, Jerusalem 1982, page 270.
8 Adolf Berman testimony: Eichmann Trial, 3 May 1961, Session 26.
9 Falstein, *The Martyrdom of Jewish Physicians*, *op. cit.*, page 493.
10 *Ibid.*, page 436.
11 *Ibid.*, page 335.
12 Adler, *op. cit.*, page 270.
13 Czerniakow diary, 23 July 1942: Hilberg *et al.*, *op. cit.*
14 *Biuletyn*, Warsaw, *op. cit.*, number 3–4, 1952, page 267.
15 Donat, *op. cit.*, pages 62–3.
16 Testimony of Samuel Rajzman: 'Punishment of War Criminals, Hearings before the Committee on Foreign Affairs, House of Representatives, Seventy-Ninth Congress, 22 March 1945'.
17 Wdowinski, *And We Are Not Saved*, *op. cit.*, pages 65–6.
18 Katznelson, *op. cit.*, page 110.
19 *Ibid.*, page 159.
20 Ruta Sakowska (editor), *Archiwum Ringelbluma Getto Warszawskie, lipiec 1942 – styczen 1943*, Warsaw 1980, page 317, note 39.
21 Berman, 'The Fate of the Children', *op. cit.*, pages 416–17.
22 Testimony of Adolf Berman: Eichmann Trial, 3 May 1961, session 26.
23 Ringelblum notes: *Sloan*, *op. cit.*, page 309.
24 Vladka Meed (Feigele Peltel-Miedzyrzecki), *On Both Sides of the Wall*, Tel Aviv 1972, page 41 (first published in Yiddish in 1948, in New York).
25 *Ibid.*, pages 29–30.
26 Zabecki, *op. cit.*, pae 45.
27 *Ibid.*, pages 45–8.
28 Zivia Lubetkin, *In the Days of*

Destruction and Revolt, Tel Aviv
1981, pages 111–12.

29 By the end of 1942 the Jewish
Fighting Organization had
established groups in eight ghettos:
Warsaw, Cracow, Czestochowa,
Bedzin, Bochnia, Pilica, Brody and
Bialystok: information provided
by Dr Shmuel Krakowski.

30 Gutman, *The Jews of Warsaw*, *op.
cit.*, pages 217–18.

31 Ringelblum diary, October 1942:
Sloan, *op. cit.*, page 329.

32 Meed, *op. cit.*, pages 43–5.

33 Wdowinski, *op. cit.*, pages 67–8.

34 Meed, *op. cit.*, pages 44–5.

35 The number of deportees from
Warsaw to Treblinka was 6,250
on July 22; 7,300 on July 23;
7,400 on July 24; 7,530 on July
25; 6,400 on July 26; 6,320 on
July 27; 5,020 on July 28; 5,480
on July 29; 6,430 on July 30 and
6,756 on July 31; 6,220 on August
1 and 6,276 on August 2: Gutman,
The Jews of Warsaw, *op. cit.*, page
212.

36 Kaplan diary, 2 August 1942:
Katsch, *op. cit.*, page 397.

37 Testimony of Samuel Rajzman, 27
February 1946: International
Military Tribunal, Nuremberg.

38 Zabecki, *op. cit.*, pages 58–9.

39 *Ibid.*, page 59.

40 *Ibid.*, page 60.

41 *Ibid.*, pages 99–100.

42 *Code Name 'Oyneg Shabes':
Emanuel Ringelblum's
Underground Archives in the
Warsaw Ghetto, 1940–1943*,
YIVO Institute for Jewish
Research, New York 1983, page
13.

43 Part of the Ringelblum archive was
published in Polish in Poland: Ruta
Sakowska (editor), *Archiwum
Ringelbluma, Getto Warszawskie,
lipiec 1942–styczen 1943*,
Warsaw 1980, documents no. 1 to
234.

23. AUTUMN 1942:
'AT A FASTER PACE'

1 SS Colonel Victor Brack to
Heinrich Himmler, 23 July 1942:
International Military Tribunal,
Nuremberg, document NO-205.

2 Memorandum by Martin Luther,
24 July 1942: Meir Michaelis,
*Mussolini and the Jews:
German–Italian Relations and the
Jewish Question in Italy,
1922–1945*, Oxford 1978, page
304.

3 Proclamation of 27 July 1942:
Bartoszewski and Lewin,
Righteous among Nations, *op. cit.*,
page 639.

4 Testimony of Yosef Buzhminski:
Eichmann Trial, 2 May 1961,
session 24.

5 Himmler to Gottlob Berger, 28
July 1942: International Military
Tribunal, Nuremberg, document
NO-626. Quoted in Dawidowicz,
Holocaust Reader, *op. cit.*, page
169.

6 Wilhelm Kube to Hinrich Lohse,
31 July 1942: International
Military Tribunal, Nuremberg,
document PS-3428. Quoted in
Arad, Gutman and Margaliot,
Documents on the Holocaust, *op.
cit.*, document 187, pages 411–13.

7 Report of 3 August 1942: Hilberg,
Documents of Destruction, *op.
cit.*, pages 57–8.

8 Smoliar, *Resistance in Minsk*, *op.
cit.*

9 Cholawski, 'The Judenrat in
Minsk', *Patterns of Jewish
Leadership*, *op. cit.*, page 126.

10 In 1967 Kalenczuk planted a tree
in the Avenue of the Righteous,
Yad Vashem, Jerusalem: Yad
Vashem archive. Arieh L.
Bauminger, *Roll of Honour*, Tel
Aviv 1971, pages 82–3.

11 Zosa Szajkowski, *Analytical
Franco-Jewish Gazetteer,
1939–1945*, New York 1966,
pages 213–14.

12 Eye-witness account in Eisenberg,

Witness to the Holocaust, op. cit., page 267.

13 Tatiana Berenstein, *Biuletyn*, op. cit., number 61, Warsaw 1967.

14 'Polish Couple Honoured': *Jerusalem Post International Edition*, week ending 26 January 1985. In January 1985 Horbacki's daughter Ludmila Waluszewska planted a tree in her parents' honour in the Avenue of Righteous, Yad Vashem, Jerusalem. Among those present at the ceremony was Rosenbusz's daughter, Mrs Zvia Shumert.

15 Lodz Chronicle, 29 July 1942: Dobroszycki, op. cit., page 231.

16 Lodz Chronicle, 31 July 1942: ibid., page 232.

17 Lodz Chronicle, 2 August 1942: ibid., page 235.

18 'Tableau recapitulatif des Israelites ed Tziganes Deportes du Camp de Malines vers Les Camps d'Extermination de Haute Silesie', Brussels, 28 November 1978, sheets 1 and 2.

19 Emmanuel Bulz, 'Luxembourg': *Encyclopaedia Judaica*, Jerusalem 1972, volume 11, column 591.

20 *Dos Yiddische Radom in Khorves*, 'Liquidation of the Glinice Ghetto', pages 218–42.

21 Kaplan diary, 4 August 1942: Katsch, op. cit., pages 398–400.

22 'Transport A Az', 4 August 1942: Lederer, *Ghetto Theresienstadt*, op. cit., pages 217–18.

23 'Transport Bc', 25 August 1942: ibid., page 219.

24 Levin, 'The Small Communities', op. cit., pages 142–4.

25 Aharon Weiss, 'Mir': *Encyclopaedia Judaica*, Jerusalem 1972, volume 12, columns 71–2.

26 Aharon Weiss, 'Novogrudok' ('Nowogrodek', 'Novaredok'): *Encyclopaedia Judaica*, Jerusalem 1972, volume 12, columns 1237–8.

27 Jack (Idel) Kagan, in conversation with the author, London, 21 May 1984.

28 Zabecki, *Wspomnienia*, op. cit., pages 67–8.

29 Klukowski diary, 8 August 1942: *Dziennik*, op. cit.

30 Klukowski diary, 10 August 1942 ibid.

31 'Testimony of Stanislaw Bohdanowicz of Zwierzyniec': Tregenza Collection.

32 Spector, 'The Jews of Volhynia', op. cit., pages 173–4.

33 Friedman, *Roads to Extinction*, op. cit., pages 276–7.

34 Falstein, op. cit., page 334.

35 Ibid., pages 190–2.

36 Tatiana Berenstein, *Biuletyn*, Warsaw, op. cit., number 21, 1957 (Lublin region) and number 61, 1967 (Galicia), 139–41.

37 Zonka Berkowicz (Pollak), 'The First "Action" in Czortkow': Yeshayahu Austri-Dunn (editor), *Memorial Book of Czortkow*, Haifa and Tel Aviv, 1967.

38 Rudolf Reder, 'Belzec' (typescript), pages 4–6: Tregenza Collection; translated by Maria Rozak from the Polish original, published in Cracow in 1946.

39 Ibid., pages 11–12.

40 T. Brustin-Berenstein, *Biuletyn*, Warsaw, op. cit., number 3, 1952 (Warsaw region), and A. Rutkowski, *Biuletyn*, Warsaw, op. cit., number 15, 1955 (Radom and Kielce region).

41 Letter from SS General Karl Wolff to Dr Albert Ganzenmuller, 13 August 1942: International Military Tribunal, Nuremberg, document NO-2207(2). Quoted in Konnilyn G. Feig, *Hitler's Death Camps: the Sanity of Madness*, New York 1981, page 36.

42 Czech, 'Kalendarium', op. cit., entries for August 1942.

43 'Convoy 20, August 17, 1942': Klarsfeld, *Memorial to the Jews Deported from France*, op. cit., pages 172–81.

24. 'THE MOST HORRIBLE OF ALL HORRORS'

1 Reder, 'Belzec', op. cit., page 16.
2 Testimony of Rivka Yosselevska: Eichmann Trial, 8 May 1961, session 30.
3 Hans Frank Diary, op. cit., 15 August 1942.
4 Artur Szarfer, 'Lekcja zycia' ('A Lesson of Life'), Folksshtime, Warsaw, 24 October 1970: Ainsztein, Jewish Resistance, op. cit., page 599.
5 Police officer's diary, Yad Vashem archive, 0-6/102, page 181: Gutman, The Jews of Warsaw, op. cit., page 239. Szerynski went into hiding. In January 1943, when the ghetto uprising began, he committed suicide.
6 Donat, Holocaust Kingdom, op. cit., pages 84–5.
7 Lubetkin, In the Days of Destruction and Revolt, op. cit., page 115. Among those who organized this first action was the twenty-two-year-old Shmuel Braslaw. He was killed two weeks later and buried by his colleagues in the sportsfield next to the Jewish cemetery on Gesia Street.
8 'Arbeitslager Jawischowitz', Obozy hitlerowskie na ziemlach polskich, op. cit., Camp Listing number 3295, page 371.
9 'Arbeitslager Golleschau', Obozy, op. cit., Camp Listing number 3292, page 370.
10 'Aussenkommando Chelmek', Obozy, op. cit., Camp Listing number 3284, page 370.
11 Kurt Gerstein, statement of 6 May 1945, Tubingen: International Military Tribunal, Nuremberg, document PS-2170. Held by the French, and interrogated in Paris by sceptical interrogators, Gerstein committed suicide on 23 July 1945.
12 Interview between Baron Guran von Otter and Gitta Sereny: Sunday Times, 7 June 1981.

13 Jakub Rabinowicz, Report of 25 October 1942: Sakowska, Archiwum Ringelbluma, op. cit., document no. 62, pages 122–3.
14 Wiktor Kulerski, Krytyka no. 15, Warsaw 1983; Szlak Rembertow-Falenica, Marsz Pamieci 19.08.1984, Warsaw 1984.
15 Jankiel (Yankel) Wiernik, 'One Year in Treblinka': Alexander Donat (editor), The Death Camp Treblinka, a Documentary, New York 1979, pages 152–3.
16 Poland, the Communities of Lodz and its Region, op. cit., entry for 'Lask'.
17 Testimony of Dora Rosenboim, op. cit.
18 Letter of 13 August 1942: Hoffer, I Did Not Survive, op. cit., page 26.
19 Testimony of Izak Helfing: Yad Vashem archive, M-1/518/460.
20 Lodz Chronicle, 25 August 1942: Dobroszycki, op. cit., page 244.
21 Lodz Chronicle, 28 August 1942: ibid., page 245.
22 Spector, 'The Jews of Volhynia . . .', op. cit.
23 International Military Tribunal, Nuremberg, document NG-4578(1) of 28 August 1942.
24 International Military Tribunal, Nuremberg, document NG-5127 of 2 September 1942.
25 'Convoy 24, August 26, 1942': Klarsfeld, Memorial to the Jews Deported from France, op. cit., pages 209–17.
26 'Convoy 25, August 28, 1942': ibid., pages 218–25.
27 'Diary of Johann Paul Kremer', entry for 31 August 1942: Kazimierz Smolen (editor), KL Auschwitz Seen by the SS, 2nd edition, Oswiecim 1978, pages 211–12.
28 Kremer diary, 2 September 1942: ibid., page 212.
29 'Convoy 26, August 31, 1942', Klarsfeld, op. cit., pages 226–35.

30 Smolen, *op. cit.*, page 212, note 50. Kremer was tried before the Supreme National Tribunal in Cracow from 24 November to 22 December 1947. He was sentenced to death, but subsequently released and returned to Germany.

31 *Zabecki, Wspomnienia, op. cit.*, entry for 1 September 1942.

32 Trunk, *Judenrat, op. cit.*, page 445.

33 *Ibid.*, page 441.

34 Note of 1 September 1942: Mendel Grossman, *With a Camera in the Ghetto*, Tel Aviv 1970, page 84.

35 *Ausrotung fun Lodzer Yiden*, Tel Aviv 1950.

36 Ben Edelbaum, *Growing Up in the Holocaust*, Kansas City 1980, pages 90–3.

37 Falstein, *The Martyrdom of Jewish Physicians in Poland, op. cit.*, page 211.

38 Lodz Chronicle, 1 September 1942: Dobroszycki, *op. cit.*, page 249.

39 Lodz Chronicle, 2 September 1942: *ibid.*, pages 249–50.

40 Martin Rosenblum, 'Holocaust Memorial Address', Toronto, 24 April 1983: enclosed in letter to the author, 25 February 1985.

41 Bauminger, *Roll of Honour, op. cit.*, page 65.

42 Tuvia Friedman (editor), *Dokumentensammlung über 'Die Deportierung der Juden aus Norwegen nach Auschwitz'*, Ramat Gan 1963; Katznelson, *Vittel Diary, op. cit.*, page 263.

43 Trunk, *op. cit.*, pages 471–2.

44 Levin, 'The Small Communities', *op. cit.*, pages 138–40 and 146.

45 Iosif Bregman, 'The Lakhva Ghetto': *Sovetish Geimland*, number 4, Moscow 1968, pages 51–52.

46 Trunk, *op. cit.*, pages 471–2. Lopatyn was killed by a mine on 1 April 1944.

47 Speech of 4 September 1942: Trunk, *op. cit.*, page 423.

48 Oscar Singer, *Destruction of Lodz Jewry*, Tel Aviv 1950, page 31. Quoted in Joseph Tenenbaum, *Underground: the Story of a People*, New York 1956, pages 173–4.

49 Josef Zelkowicz, 'Days of Nightmare': Dawidowicz, *Holocaust Reader, op. cit.*, pages 298–316.

50 Lodz Chronicle, 14 September 1942: Dobroszycki, *op. cit.*, pages 250–5.

51 'Caring for Orphans': Lodz Chronicle, 7 December 1942: *ibid.*, page 297.

52 Lodz Chronicle, 22 October 1942: *ibid.*, page 274.

53 Lodz Chronicle, 1 November 1942: *ibid.*, page 281.

54 'Population Changes in the Month of November, 1942': Lodz Chronicle, 27 November 1942: *ibid.*, page 294.

55 Lodz Chronicle, 31 October 1942: *ibid.*, page 280.

56 Lichtheim letter, 3 September 1942: Jewish Agency archives.

57 Lichtheim letter, 8 September 1942: Jewish Agency archives.

58 *The Times*, 7 September 1942.

59 Winston S. Churchill, speech of 8 September 1942: *Hansard* (Parliamentary Debates), 8 September 1942.

60 *The Times*, 9 September 1942.

61 *The Times*, 11 September 1942.

62 Yisrael Gutman, *The Jews of Warsaw, op. cit.*, pages 243–9.

63 Kremer diary, 5 September 1942: Smolen, *op. cit.*, page 214.

64 Kremer interrogation, 18 July 1947: *ibid.*, page 214, note 51.

65 Kremer diary, 5 September 1942: *ibid.*, page 214.

66 Ringelblum notes, 6 September 1942: Sloan, *op. cit.*, page 312.

67 Vladka Meed, *On Both Sides of the Wall, op. cit.*, page 88.

68 *Ibid.*, page 85.

69 *Ibid.*, page 92.

70 Sakowska, *op. cit.*, document number 86, page 162.

71 Donat, *The Holocaust Kingdom*, *op. cit.*, page 91.

72 Samuel Rajzman, 'Punishment of War Criminals', *op. cit.*, page 121.

73 Yisrael Gutman, *The Jews of Warsaw*, *op. cit.*, page 212.

74 Hillel Seidman's diary of the Warsaw Ghetto, published in 1947 in Buenos Aires (Yiddish) and Tel Aviv (Hebrew): Philip Friedman, *Martyrs and Fighters: the Epic of the Warsaw Ghetto*, New York 1954, pages 174–5.

75 Donat, *The Death Camp Treblinka*, *op. cit.*, pages 129–31.

76 Testimony of Samuel Rajzman: 'Punishment of War Criminals', *op. cit.*

77 Testimony of Abraham Krzepicki (first published in the original Yiddish in *Bleter far Geshikhte*, Warsaw 1956, volume XI, number 1–2): Donat, *The Death Camp Treblinka*, *op. cit.*

78 *Oyf der vakh* ('On Guard'), Warsaw, 20 September 1942: Lucy Dawidowicz, *The War against the Jews 1933–45*, London 1975, pages 374–5.

79 Gutman, *The Jews of Warsaw*, *op. cit.*, pages 212–13. A further 11,580 Jews had been sent from Warsaw to forced labour camps, after a 'selection' at the Umschlagplatz. More than ten thousand had been killed during the course of the deportations, and had died of hunger and disease during those seven weeks.

80 'Swastika over Jaworow', *op. cit.*, page 23.

81 Poster, 7 September 1942: International Military Tribunal, Nuremberg, document USSR-434.

82 Report of the Extraordinary State Commission of the Stavropol Region: International Military Tribunal, Nuremberg, document USSR-1.

83 Iosif Bregman, 'The Kremenets Ghetto': *Sovetish Geimland*, number 4, Moscow 1968, page 52.

84 Trunk, *op. cit.*, page 473; Levin,

'The Small Communities', *op. cit.*, pages 140–2; Spector, 'The Jews of Volhynia', *op. cit.*, pages 169–71; Iosif Bregman, 'The Tuczyn Ghetto', *Sovetish Geimland*, number 4, Moscow 1968, page 58.

85 Information provided by Dr Shmuel Spector.

86 Krakowski, *The War of the Doomed*, *op. cit.*, page 28.

87 Eliezer Melamed's recollections: Cholawski, *Soldiers from the Ghetto*, *op. cit.*, pages 119–20.

25. SEPTEMBER–
NOVEMBER 1942:
THE SPREAD OF
RESISTANCE

1 Letter of 24 September 1942: International Military Tribunal, Nuremberg, document NG-1517.

2 Reports of 16 October 1942 and 20 October 1942: Michaelis, *Mussolini and the Jews*, *op. cit.*, pages 304–5.

3 Maxime Steinberg, 'The Trap of Legality: the Association of the Jews of Belgium': *Patterns of Jewish Leadership*, *op. cit.*, page 369.

4 Czech, 'Kalendarium', *op. cit.*, entries from 23 to 30 September 1942.

5 Levin, 'The Small Communities', *op. cit.*, page 136.

6 *Ibid.*, pages 135–6.

7 Trunk, *Judenrat*, *op. cit.*, page 440.

8 T. Brustin-Berenstein, *Biuletyn*, Warsaw, *op. cit.*, number 3, 1952.

9 'Top Secret', 26 September 1942, 'Utilization of property on the occasion of settlement and evacuation of Jews': International Military Tribunal, Nuremberg, document NO-724.

10 Directive of 8 October 1942: International Military Tribunal, Nuremberg, document NO-2305.

11 Madam Francken, 'Novel-Memories, Reminiscences (1973)', 'A nightmare stay. From September 27 to October 6, 1942': Saul Friedländer, *When Memory Comes*, New York 1979, page 89.

12 *Ibid.*, page 90.

13 'Convoy 40, November 4, 1942': Klarsfeld, *Memorial to the Jews Deported from France, op. cit.*, pages 328–35.

14 'Transport Bq', 23 September 1942: Lederer, *Ghetto Theresienstadt, op. cit.*, page 222.

15 'Transport Br', 26 September 1942: *ibid.*, page 222.

16 'Transport Bs', 29 September 1942: *ibid.*, page 222.

17 Huttenbach, *The Destruction of the Jewish Community of Worms, op. cit.*, page 172.

18 Document submitted to the Eichmann Trial, 1 June 1961, session 63.

19 'Transport Bt', 5 October 1942: Lederer, *op. cit.*, pages 222.

20 'Transport Bu', 8 October 1942: *ibid.*, pages 222–3.

21 'Transport Bv', 15 October 1942, 'Transport Bw', 19 October 1942 and 'Transport Bx', 22 October 1942: *ibid.*, page 223.

22 *Maladie de Famine*, Warsaw, 1946.

23 Falstein, *The Martyrdom of Jewish Physicians in Poland, op. cit.*, page 419.

24 Kremer diary, 3 October 1942: Smolen, *op. cit.*, pages 219–20.

25 Kremer cross-examination, 30 July 1947: *ibid.*, page 219, note 71.

26 Kremer diary, 10 October 1942: *ibid.*, page 221.

27 Kremer diary, 15 October 1942: *ibid.*, page 222.

28 'Reminiscences of Pery Broad': Smolen, *KL Auschwitz, op. cit.*, pages 163–5. The son of a Brazilian merchant and a German woman, Broad was born in Rio de Janeiro but went to school in Germany. He was employed at Auschwitz from 1941 to 1945.

29 Trunk, *op. cit.*, page 443.

30 Stefan Krakowski, 'Lukow', *Encyclopaedia Judaica*, Jerusalem 1972, volume 11, column 561.

31 Ainsztein, *Jewish Resistance in Nazi-occupied Eastern Europe, op. cit.*, page 721.

32 Celia Hurst, archivist, Sigmund Freud Copyrights Ltd, letter to the author, 13 March 1985.

33 Tatiana Berenstein, 'Eksterminacja Zydow w Galicji, 1941–1943', *Biuletyn, op. cit.*, number 61, March 1967.

34 Tregenza Collection.

35 Testimony of 'T', *Bulletin*, London, April 1945: Foreign Office papers, 371/51117.

36 'Bruno Shultz, 1892–1940': Dr Konstantin Bazarov, letter to the author, 7 October 1978.

37 Hermann Graebe, testimony of 10 November and 13 November 1945: International Military Tribunal, Nuremberg, document PS-2992: Eisenberg, *Witness to the Holocaust, op. cit.*, pages 269–70.

38 Kremer diary, 18 October 1942: Smolen, *op. cit.*, page 223.

39 Kremer interrogation, 18 July 1947: *ibid.*, page 223, note 82.

40 Getzel Kressel, 'Beda, Fritz Loehner, 1883–1942': *Encyclopaedia Judaica*, Jerusalem 1972, volume 4, column 368.

41 Klukowski diary, 21 October 1942: *Dziennik, op. cit.*

42 Recollections of Stanislaw Bohdanowicz: Tregenza Collection.

43 Klukowski diary, 22 October 1942: *Dziennik, op. cit.*

44 Klukowski diary, 23 October 1942: *ibid.*

45 Gurdus, *The Death Train, op. cit.*, page 108.

46 *Ibid.*, page 163.

47 Ainsztein, *op. cit.*, page 265.

48 Kermish, *The Destruction of the Jewish Community of Piotrkow, op. cit.*, columns 36–8.

49 Abitbol, *Les Juifs, op. cit.*, pages 113–14.

50 *Jerusalem Post*, 14 March 1980.

51 Abitbol, *op. cit.*, page 131.

52 Documents dated 17 February 1942 and 24 October 1942; Eichmann Trial, 9 May 1961, session 33, documents 1188 and 509.

53 'Protocol of the Meeting on the "Aktion" in Oszmiana', 27 October 1942: Arad, Gutman and Margaliot, *Documents on the Holocaust, op. cit.*, pages 440–4, document 199.

54 Diary of Zelig Kalmanovitch, November 1942, first published in English in the *Yivo Annual of Jewish Social Science*, volume 3, New York 1953, page 34.

55 'Transport By', 26 October 1942: Lederer, *op. cit.*, page 223.

56 *Totenbuch Theresienstadt*, Vienna 1971, volume 1 ('Deportierte Aus Osterreich').

57 A. Rutkowski, *Zaglada Zydow w dystrykcie radomskim, Biuletyn, op. cit.*, number 16, Warsaw 1955, page 154.

58 Krakowski, *The War of the Doomed, op. cit.*, pages 106–8. (Ajzenman's name can also be spelt Eisenman.)

59 Arthur Cygielman, 'Piotrkow': *Encyclopaedia Judaica*, Jerusalem 1972, volume 13, column 557. See also, Rutkowski, *op. cit.*, page 141.

60 Testimony of Aizik Rottenberg: Novitch, *Sobibor, Martyrdom and Revolt, op. cit.*, page 104.

61 Falstein, *op. cit.*, page 365.

62 'Top secret' directive of 28 October 1942: International Military Tribunal, Nuremberg, document NO-2558.

63 Tennenbaum, *Underground, op. cit.*, pages 437–8.

64 Message of 29 October 1942: *Jewish Chronicle*, 6 November 1942.

65 Ringelblum, 'Polish–Jewish Relations during the Second World War', *Ktovim fun geto*, Warsaw 1961, volume 2, page 332: quoted in Gutman, *The Jews of Warsaw, op. cit.*, page 302.

66 Ainsztein, *op. cit.*, page 598.

67 Lubetkin, *In the Days of Destruction and Revolt, op. cit.*, pages 132–3.

68 Bronia Klibanski, 'The Underground Archives of the Bialystok Ghetto', *Yad Vashem Studies*, II, Jerusalem 1958, pages 310–11.

69 Ainsztein, *op. cit.*, pages 898–9.

70 Krakowski, *The War of the Doomed, op. cit.*, page 224.

71 *Ibid.*, page 225.

72 Yugoslavia, Memorial Book, Belgrade 1959.

73 Isaac Kowalski (editor), *Anthology on Jewish Armed Resistance 1939–1945*, volume 1, New York 1984, pages 89–90, 473–4 and 478–88.

74 Kulka, 'Jewish Revolt in Auschwitz', *op. cit.*

75 Speech of 11 October 1942: Trunk, *op. cit.*, page 402.

76 Recollection of Helen Shabbes (Helen Bronsztejn), in conversation with the author, Allentown, Pennsylvania.

77 Trunk, *op. cit.*, page 445.

78 *Ibid.*, page 473–4; see also Levin, 'The Small Communities', *op. cit.*, page 138.

79 Ainsztein, *op. cit.*, page 264.

80 Bartoszewski and Lewin, *Righteous among Nations, op. cit.*, page 600.

81 Siemiatycze memorial book, *op. cit.*

82 Testimony of Samuel Rajzman, 'Punishment of War Criminals', *op. cit.*, pages 121–2.

83 Meir Peker, 'In the Bielsk Ghetto and the Camps': Haim Rabin (editor), *Bielsk Poldliask*, Tel Aviv, 1975, pages 35–6.

84 Trunk, *op. cit.*, page 441.

85 Friedman, *Roads to Extinction, op. cit.*, page 291.

86 Recollections of Dana Schwartz (Dana Szapira) in conversation with the author, Los Angeles.

87 Joseph Kermish and Shmuel Krakowski (editors), *Emanuel Ringelblum: Polish–Jewish Relations during the Second World War*, Jerusalem 1974, page 138.

88 Ś. Zeminski, diary entry for 8 November 1942: *Biuletyn*,

Warsaw, *op. cit.*, number 27, 1958, pages 105–12, quoted in Kermish and Krakowski, *op. cit.*, page 138, note 25.

26. 'TO SAVE AT LEAST SOMEONE'

1 Testimony of Noah Zabludowicz: Eichmann Trial, 1 May 1961, session 21.
2 The Police Instruction was dated 25 September 1942. The deportations from Swiss soil back to France had begun on 13 August 1942.
3 Leo Bretholz, 'The Death Train Escape', *Evening Sun*, Baltimore, 5 November 1982; Leo Bretholz, in conversation with the author, Baltimore, 9 December 1984.
4 'Convoy 44, November 9, 1942': Klarsfeld, *op. cit.*, pages 344–53.
5 'Convoy 45, November 11, 1942': *ibid.*, pages 354–9.
6 Rudolf Vrba and Alan Bestic, *I Cannot Forgive*, London 1963, page 150.
7 Tatiana Berenstein, 'Martyrologia, opor i zaglada ludnosci zydowskiej', *Biuletyn*, Warsaw, *op. cit.*, number 21, 1967, page 56.
8 Testimony of Janina Latowicz, Dusseldorf, 28 February 1978: Patricia Clough, 'Recalling the Horrors of Majdanek', *The Times*, 1 March 1978 (report on the Dusseldorf trial of nine men and five women accused of murder at Majdanek).
9 Tuvia Friedman, *Dokumentensammlung, op. cit.*; Report of 19 April 1943, International Military Tribunal, Nuremberg, document NO-5193, published in full in Leon Poliakov, *Harvest of Hate, The Nazi Programme for the Destruction of the Jews of Europe*, New York 1979, appendix, pages 337–44.
10 Bauminger, *Roll of Honour, op. cit.*, page 64.
11 Hugo Valentin, 'Rescue and Relief Activities on Behalf of Jewish

Victims of Nazism in Scandinavia', *YIVO Annual of Jewish Social Science*, volume 3, New York 1953, page 232.
12 Siemiatycze memorial book, *op. cit.*
13 Bohdanowicz recollections: Tregenza Collection.
14 Rudolf Reder, recollections published in Cracow in 1946: Tregenza Collection, *op. cit.*
15 *Idem.*
16 Testimonies of Shachne Hiller (Stanley Berger) and Anne Wolozin, September 1977–October 1981: Yaffa Eliach, *Hasidic Tales of the Holocaust*, New York 1982, pages 142–7. Published as a news item, 'Pope and Jewish child' by Joseph Finkelstone, *Jewish Chronicle*, 28 May 1982.
17 Zygmunt Klukowski, *Dziennik z lat okupacji Zamojszczyzny*, Lublin 1959, page 299, quoted in Kermish and Krakowski, *Emanuel Ringelblum, op. cit.*, page 220, note 37.
18 Yad Vashem archive.
19 Grossman, *With a Camera in the Ghetto, op. cit.*, diary entry for 3 December 1942.
20 Ringelblum notes, 5 December 1942: Sloan, *op. cit.*, page 326.
21 Krakowski, *The War of the Doomed, op. cit.*, page 258.
22 *Ibid.*, pages 255–6.
23 Announcement of 19 November 1942, to come into effect on 1 December 1942: Bartoszewski and Lewin, *Righteous among Nations, op. cit.*, page 643.
24 *Ibid.*, page 607.
25 Arieh Koren, recollections: Krakowski, *The War of the Doomed, op. cit.*, page 31.
26 'Parczew District, Bialka': *Scenes of Fighting and Martyrdom Guide, op. cit.*, page 244.
27 Arieh Koren, recollections: Krakowski, *op. cit.*, page 31.
28 *Idem.*
29 The ambush took place on 29 December 1942, testimony of Chaim Joffe, born in Nowogrodek

on 22 November 1922: Yad Vashem archive, M-1/E, 950/794.

30 Bartoszewski and Lewin, *op. cit.*, page 362. Bartoszewski was a member of the Council.

31 *Ibid.*, page LXXXI.

32 Goebbels diary, 13 December 1942: Michaelis, *Mussolini and the Jews*, *op. cit.*, page 335.

33 Testimony of Yitzhak Zuckerman: Eichmann Trial, 3 May 1961, session 25.

34 Ainsztein, *Jewish Resistance in Nazi-occupied Eastern Europe*, *op. cit.*, page 843.

35 Diary of Gusta Draenger: Zeev Ben-Shlomo and David Sonin, 'The Unknown Jewish Freedom Fighters', *Jewish Chronicle, Colour Supplement*, 28 November 1980, page 27.

36 Testimony of Rivka Cooper (Liebeskind): Eichmann Trial, 3 May 1961, session 26.

37 Spector, 'The Jews of Volhynia . . .', *op. cit.*, pages 172–3.

38 Presser, *The Destruction of the Dutch Jews*, *op. cit.*, pages 176–7.

39 Postcard dated 16 December 1942: Sakowska, *Archiwum Ringelbluma*, *op. cit.*, page 197, document 148.

40 Postcard dated 17 December 1942: *ibid.*, page 198, document 149.

41 Czech, 'Kalendarium', *op. cit.*, entry for 17 December 1942.

42 Dr Norris N. Wallach, letter to the author, 29 May 1983 and 17 September 1984.

43 Kermish, *The Destruction of the Jewish Community of Piotrkow*, *op. cit.*, columns 39–42.

44 Information from Ben Helfgott, in conversation with the author, London.

45 Postcard dated 21 December 1942: Sakowska, *op. cit.*, page 200, document 152.

46 Prayer, December 1942: *ibid.*, pages 332–3, document 227.

47 Samuel Rajzman (cross-examined by Counsellor Smirnov): International Military Tribunal, Nuremberg.

48 Samuel Rajzman, affidavit: International Military Tribunal, Nuremberg.

49 *Poland: The Communities of Lodz and its Region*, *op. cit.*, entry for Opoczno.

50 'The Journey to Eretz Yisrael': Eisenberg, *Witness to the Holocaust*, *op. cit.*, pages 206–13.

51 Trunk, *Judenrat*, *op. cit.*, page 464.

52 Krakowski, *War of the Doomed*, *op. cit.*, pages 220–1.

53 Letter of 9 January 1943: Walter Bednarz, *The Extermination Camp at Chelmno (Kulmhof)*, Warsaw 1946, page 213.

54 Spector, 'The Jews of Volhynia . . .', *op. cit.*, pages 182–6.

55 Smoliar, *Resistance in Minsk*, *op. cit.*, 1966.

56 Letter dated 2 November 1942: Eichmann Trial, 9 June 1961, session 72, document T.1364.

57 Letter submitted to the Eichmann Trial, 9 June 1961, session 72, document T.1363.

58 Letter dated 21 June 1943: Eichmann Trial, 9 June 1961, session 72, document T.37 (95).

59 Manuscript of Salmen Lewental: Jadwige Bezwinska and Danuta Czech (editors), *Amidst a Nightmare of Crime: Manuscripts of Members of Sonderkommando*, Auschwitz-Oswiecim 1973, pages 135–6.

60 Vrba and Bestic, *I Cannot Forgive*, *op. cit.*, pages 127–8.

61 Letter of 4 January 1943: Auschwitz Museum archive.

62 Czech, 'Kalendarium', *op. cit.*, entries between 7 January 1943 and 23 January 1943.

63 'Transport Cz', 20 January 1943: Lederer, *Ghetto Theresienstadt*, *op. cit.*, pages 223–4.

64 Notebook of an unknown author: Bezwinska and Czech, *op. cit.*, pages 119–21.

65 Testimony of Dr Aharon Peretz: Eichmann Trial, 4 May 1961, session 28.
66 Bartoszewski and Lewin, *op. cit.*, page 608.
67 Trunk, *op. cit.*, page 440.
68 Arieh-Leib Kalish, 'Zemba, Menachem (1883–1943)': *Encyclopaedia Judaica*, Jerusalem 1972, volume 16, columns 986–7.
69 Serge Klarsfeld and Maxime Steinberg, *Memorial de la Deportation des Juifs de Belgique*, New York and Brussels, 1982.
70 Testimony of Yaacov Gurfein: Eichmann Trial, 1 May 1961, session 21.
71 Norris N. Wallach, letters to the author, 29 May 1983 and 17 September 1984.
72 Testimony of Rivka Cooper (Liebeskind): Eichmann Trial, 3 May 1961, session 26.
73 Testimony of Bluma Shadur: Yigal Lossin, *Pillars of Fire: the Rebirth of Israel, a Visual History*, Jerusalem 1983, page 359.
74 Adler, *In the Warsaw Ghetto*, *op. cit.*, page 325.
75 Yisrael Gutman, *The Jews of Warsaw*, *op. cit.*, page 309. The figure of 1,171 Jews 'summarily shot' in the streets of the ghetto between 18 and 21 January 1944 is given in Bartoszewski, *Warsaw Death Ring*, *op. cit.*, page 165.
76 Tuvia Borzykowski, *Between Tumbling Walls*, Tel Aviv 1972 (reprinted 1976), pages 22–3.
77 Wdowinski, *And We Are Not Saved*, *op. cit.*, page 87.
78 Falstein, *The Martyrdom of Jewish Physicians*, *op. cit.*, page 317.
79 Borszykowski, *op. cit.*, page 23.
80 Lubetkin, *In the Days of Destruction and Revolt*, *op. cit.*, page 316.
81 Borszykowski, *op. cit.*, page 24.
82 Wdowinski, *op. cit.*, page 87.
83 Borszykowski, *op. cit.*, page 29.
84 Testimony of Yitzhak Zuckerman: Eichmann Trial, 3 May 1961, session 25.

85 Meed, *On Both Sides of the Wall*, *op. cit.*, page 154.
86 Katznelson, *Vittel Diary*, *op. cit.*, page 177.
87 Meed, *op. cit.*, page 154.

27. 'HELP ME GET MORE TRAINS'

1 Letter of 20 January 1943, International Military Tribunal, Nuremberg, document NO-2405: Dawidowicz, *The War against the Jews, 1933–45*, *op. cit.*, page 183.
2 Lederer, *Ghetto Theresienstadt*, *op. cit.*, pages 104–5.
3 Presser, *The Destruction of the Dutch Jews*, *op. cit.*, pages 182–3.
4 Vrba and Bestic, *I Cannot Forgive*, *op. cit.*, pages 151–3.
5 Testimony of Madame Claude Vaillant Couturier: Nuremberg, 28 January 1946, *The Trial of German Major War Criminals: Proceedings of the International Military Tribunal Sitting at Nuremberg, Germany*, part 5, London 1946, pages 190–1.
6 Szajkowski, *Analytical Franco-Jewish Gazetteer*, *op. cit.*, entry for La Rose.
7 Klarsfeld, *Memorial to the Jews Deported from France*, *op. cit.* (deportation of 23 March 1943, to Drancy, thence to Sobibor), pages 410–11 and 414–19.
8 Report of 23 January 1943: International Military Tribunal, Nuremberg, document NG-4959.
9 Report of 3 March 1943: International Military Tribunal, Nuremberg, document NG-5087.
10 'Transport Cr', 23 January 1943: Lederer, *op. cit.*, page 244.
11 Szymon Datner: conversation with the author, Warsaw, 14 August 1980.
12 Bartoszewski and Lewin, *Righteous among Nations*, *op. cit.*, page 605.
13 Steckel, *Destruction and Survival*, *op. cit.*, page 38.

14 Friedman, *Roads to Extinction*, *op. cit.*, page 284.

15 'Goldberg Netka', Supplementary Record, Face Sheet, 16 May 1946: Yad Vashem archive.

16 Testimony of Madame Claude Vaillant Couturier: *The Trial of German Major War Criminals*, *op. cit.*, pages 185–6.

17 Czech, 'Kalendarium', *op. cit.* entries for 2 to 27 February 1943.

18 Sirkka Purkey, 'The Treatment of Jewish Refugees in Finland', *op. cit.*

19 Czech, 'Kalendarium', *op. cit.*, entry for 28 February 1943.

20 Ainsztein, *Jewish Resistance in Nazi-Occupied Eastern Europe*, *op. cit.*, page 531.

21 Testimony of Abraham Karasick: Eichmann Trial, 4 May 1961, session 28.

22 Author's personal photographic collection: Bialystok, 5 August 1980.

23 Trunk, *Judenrat*, *op. cit.*, page 444.

24 Nochem Babikier, evidence given to the Jewish Historical Commission in Bialystok, 24 November 1946: Yad Vashem archive M.11/143.

25 Szymon Datner, letter to the author, 10 October 1984; Tenenbaum, *Underground*, *op. cit.*, pages 437–8.

26 Lodz Chronicle, 11 February 1943: Dobroszycki, *op. cit.*, page 319 and note 7.

27 Testimony of Dr Aharon Beilin: Eichmann Trial, 7 June 1961, session 69.

28 'Report on the realization of textile salvage from the Jewish resettlement up to the present date', 6 February 1943: International Military Tribunal, Nuremberg, document NO-1257.

29 Report by Himmler of 15 January 1943: International Military Tribunal, Nuremberg, document NO-1257.

30 'Report by SS Sturmbannfuhrer Wippern, 27 February 1943, concerning values of money, precious metals, other valuables and textiles of Jews, delivered up to 3 February 1943': International Military Tribunal, Nuremberg, document NO-061.

31 'Ginsburger, Ernest, 1876–1943': *Encyclopaedia Judaica*, Jerusalem 1972, volume 7, column 583.

32 'Convoy 47, February 11, 1943': Klarsfeld, *op. cit.*, pages 361–70.

33 Testimony of Heinrich Grüber: Eichmann Trial, 16 May 1961, session 41.

34 Miriam Novitch, *Spiritual Resistance, 120 Drawings from Concentration Camps and Ghettos*, Milan 1979, page 54.

35 Klarsfeld, *op. cit.*, pages 377–83.

36 Arad, *Treblinka*, *op. cit.*

37 Michael Molho, *In Memoriam: Hommage aux Victimes Juives des Nazis en Grece*, Salonica 1973.

38 Michaelis, *Mussolini and the Jews*, *op. cit.*, page 307.

39 David Sonin and Zeev Ben Shlomo, 'For Our Fathers and Mothers': *Jewish Chronicle Colour Supplement*, London, 28 September 1979, pages 8–9.

40 Czech, 'Kalendarium', *op. cit.*, entries for 6 and 8 February 1943.

41 Discussion of 27 February 1943: Dawidowicz, *A Holocaust Reader*, *op. cit.*, pages 347–54.

42 Lodz Chronicle, 27 February 1943: Dobroszycki, *op. cit.*, page 321.

43 Lodz Chronicle, 13 March 1943: *ibid.*, page 323.

44 Lodz Chronicle, 30 March 1943: *ibid.*, pages 331–2.

45 Yisrael Medad, 'Flight through the Forest': *Israel Scene*, June 1981, pages 18–20. After the war, Drobless went first to Argentina, then to Israel. He later became a member of the Knesset (the Israeli Parliament), and in 1978 head of the settlement division of the World Zionist Organization.

46 Yankel (Jankiel) Wiernik, *A Year*

in Treblinka, New York 1945, page 28.

47 Trial of Hubert Gomerski, Frankfurt, 1950, document GB 06.08: Ainsztein, *op. cit.*, page 919, note 45.

48 'Convoy 49, March 2, 1943': Klarsfeld, *op. cit.*, pages 384–91.

49 Bezwinska and Czech, *Amidst a Nightmare of Crime, op. cit.*, pages 181–90.

50 'Convoy 50, March 4, 1943': Klarsfeld, *op. cit.*, pages 395–403.

51 Alfred Werner, 'Lismann, Hermann (1878–1943)': *Encyclopaedia Judaica*, Jerusalem 1972, volume 11, column 305.

52 Trunk, *op. cit.*, page 467.

53 Yitzhak Arad, *The Partisans: From the Valley of Death to Mount Zion*, New York 1979, pages 93–101.

54 Nissan Oren, 'The Bulgarian Exception: a Reassessment of the Salvation of the Jewish Community', *Yad Vashem Studies*, volume 7, Jerusalem 1968, pages 83–106.

55 Dr Rivka Kauli: letter to the author, 15 February 1979.

56 Erich Kulka (editor), *Collection of Testimonies and Documents on the Participation of Czechoslovak Jews in the War against the Nazi-Germany*, Jerusalem 1976, page 20; Erich Kulka, in conversation with the author, Jerusalem.

57 *The Third Anniversary of the Liquidation of the Ghetto in Cracow*, Cracow 1946, page 150.

58 Falstein, *The Martyrdom of Jewish Physicians in Poland, op. cit.*, page 342.

59 *The Third Anniversary, op. cit.*, page 150.

60 Yaffa Eliach, *Hasidic Tales of the Holocaust, op. cit.*

61 Testimony of Moshe Bejski: Eichmann Trial, 1 May 1961, session 21.

62 Bezwinska and Czech, *op. cit.*, page 7.

63 Trude Neumann's son committed suicide in 1946.

64 Molho, *op. cit.*; Danuta Czech, 'Deportation und Vernichtung der griechischen Juden': *Hefte von Auschwitz*, 11, 1970; 'Report from Salonica', *Bulletin*, London, *op. cit.*, February 1945: Foreign Office papers, 371/51115.

65 Friedman, *Roads to Extinction, op. cit.*, page 297.

66 Falstein, *op. cit.*, page 327.

67 Lubetkin, *In the Days of Destruction and Revolt, op. cit.*, pages 314–15.

68 Falstein, *op. cit.*, page 336.

69 *Ibid.*, page 363.

70 *Ibid.*, page 374.

71 Kermish, *The Destruction of the Jewish Community of Piotrkow, op. cit.*, columns 41–2.

72 Falstein, *op. cit.*, page 329 (Dr Cung) and page 347 (Dr Fryd).

73 Bartoszewski and Lewin, *op. cit.*, pages 599–600.

74 Letter received in the Reich Chancellery on 25 March 1943: International Military Tribunal, Nuremberg, document NG-1903.

75 *Der Sturmer*, 25 March 1943: International Military Tribunal, Nuremberg, exhibit M-138.

76 From Skopje, 2,338 Jews reached Treblinka on March 28 (after six days on the journey), 2,405 on March 31 (after six days) and 2,404 on April 5 (after seven days): Arad, *Treblinka, op. cit.*

77 Rudashevski, *Diary of the Vilna Ghetto, op. cit.*

78 Isaac Kowalski, *A Secret Press in Nazi Europe: the Story of the Jewish United Partisan Organization in Vilna*, New York 1969, page 394.

79 Diary of W. Sakowicz, 5 April 1943: *The Paneriai Museum, op. cit.*, pages 8–9.

80 Report of 1 May 1943: *ibid.*, page 9.

81 Kaczerginski's memoirs, first published in the magazine *Tsukunft* ('Future') in New York,

April 1949, pages 234–6: Rubin, *Voices of a People, op. cit.*, page 459, note 41.

82 Notes of a discussion held on the morning of 17 April 1943: International Military Tribunal, Nuremberg, document D-736.

28. WARSAW, APRIL 1943: HOPELESS DAYS OF REVOLT

1 Lubetkin, *In the Days of Destruction and Revolt, op. cit.*, page 178.

2 Recalled by Zivia Lubetkin: Eichmann Trial, 2 May 1961, session 25.

3 Stefan Krakowski, *Biuletyn*, Warsaw, *op. cit.*, number 62, 1967.

4 Testimony of Zivia Lubetkin: Eichmann Trial, 2 May 1961, session 25.

5 These were Brigadier Jurgen Stroop's figures: Gutman, *Jews of Warsaw, op. cit.*, page 375.

6 Gutman, *Jews of Warsaw, op. cit.*, pages 375–6. Stroop reports 380 Jews caught in the bunkers on the first day.

7 Testimony of Yitzhak Zuckerman: Eichmann Trial, 3 May 1961, session 25.

8 Borzykowski, *Between Tumbling Walls, op. cit.*, pages 57–8.

9 Rubin, *op. cit.*, page 453.

10 Leon Najberg, diary entry for 20 April 1943: YIVO Institute for Jewish Research, Archive (New York), document provided by Dr Lucjan Dobroszycki, translated by Mira Marody.

11 Alexander Donat, *The Holocaust Kingdom, op. cit.*, page 146.

12 Leon Najberg, *op. cit.*

13 Anielewicz letter: Meed, *On Both Sides of the Wall, op. cit.*, pages 194–5.

14 Najberg diary, 25 April 1943, *op. cit.*

15 B. Mark (editor), *The Report of Jurgen Stroop*, Warsaw 1958, page 55, teletype message of 26 April 1943.

16 Donat, *Holocaust Kingdom*, page 159.

17 Meed, *op. cit.*, pages 180–1.

18 Borzykowski, *op. cit.*, page 66.

19 Lubetkin, *op. cit.*, pages 202–3.

20 Bartoszewski, *Warsaw Death Ring, op. cit.*, page 179.

21 Lubetkin, *op. cit.*, page 293.

22 Ignacy Schwarzbart, diary, 19 May 1943, London: Schwarzbart papers, Yad Vashem archive.

23 Hadassa Talmon, testimony: Lossin, *op. cit.*, page 377.

24 Donat, *The Death Camp Treblinka, op. cit.*, page 77.

25 Information from Dr Krakowski of Yad Vashem.

26 Zivia Lubetkin, 'Last Days of the Warsaw Ghetto', *Commentary*, New York, May 1947.

27 Testimony of Zivia Lubetkin: Eichmann Trial, 2 May 1961, session 25.

28 Lubetkin, *In the Days of Destruction and Revolt, op. cit.*, pages 292–3.

29 Mark, *op. cit.*, pages 105–7, teletype message of 24 May 1943.

30 Lubetkin, *In the Days of Destruction and Revolt, op. cit.*, page 288.

31 Zygielbojm letter: Gutman, *The Jews of Warsaw, op. cit.*, page 363.

32 Mark, *op. cit.*, page 104, teletype message of 16 May 1943.

33 Najberg diary, 19 May 1943, *op. cit.*

34 Arie (Leon) Najberg, *The Last Ones* (in Hebrew), Tel Aviv 1958: Gutman, *The Jews of Warsaw, op. cit.*, page 399.

35 Gutman, *The Jews of Warsaw, op. cit.*, page 400.

29. 'THE CRASHING FIRES OF HELL'

1 Hirsh Glik, discussion and poem: Rubin, *op. cit.*, pages 453–5.

2 Lubetkin, *In the Days of Destruction and Revolt*, op. cit., page 300.

3 Recollections of Lena Berg: Donat, *The Holocaust Kingdom*, op. cit., page 299.

4 Donat, *The Holocaust Kingdom*, op. cit., pages 208–9.

5 Testimony of Yisrael Gutman: Eichmann Trial, 2 June 1961, session 63.

6 'Children lured to death with sugar': *Jewish Chronicle*, 9 November 1979.

7 Testimony of David Wdowinski: Eichmann Trial, 6 June 1961, session 67.

8 Sloan, op. cit., pages 345–6.

9 It was at Trawniki that the Germans trained the Ukrainian S.S. guards for Treblinka, Sobibor and Belzec.

10 Meed, *On Both Sides of the Wall*, op. cit., pages 210–11.

11 Krakowski, *The War of the Doomed*, op. cit., page 33.

12 Testimony of Zeew Jungsztajn (Ze'ev Yungstein), born in March 1934 in Zelechow, south-east of Warsaw: Yad Vashem archive, M-1/E, 1251/1209.

13 Ainsztein, *Jewish Resistance in Nazi-Occupied Eastern Europe*, op. cit., pages 422–3.

14 Falstein, *Martyrdom of Jewish Physicians in Poland*, op. cit., pages 327–8.

15 Shalom Kohn (Stanislaw Kon), 'The Treblinka Revolt': Donat, *The Death Camp Treblinka*, op. cit., pages 225–6.

16 Testimony of Kalman Feigman: Krakowski, *The War of the Doomed*, op. cit., page 240.

17 Testimony of Samuel Rajzman, 'Punishment of War Criminals', op. cit.

18 Krakowski, *The War of the Doomed*, op. cit., page 240.

19 'Convoi XX du 19 avril 1943': Klarsfeld and Steinberg, *Memorial de la Deportation*, op. cit.

20 Lubetkin, *In the Days of Destruction*, op. cit., pages 316–17.

21 Ainsztein, op. cit., page 848.

22 Gusta Draenger's diary, *Pamietnik Justyny*, was published in Cracow in 1945. An important extract was published in Dawidowicz, *A Holocaust Reader*, op. cit., pages 340–7.

23 Account taken down by Dr Olga Bamicz from six survivors of Sobibor: Yad Vashem archive, O3/2952, page 62.

24 Testimony of Dov Freiberg: Eichmann Trial, 5 June 1961, session 64.

25 Material on the Riga Ghetto: Yad Vashem archive.

26 Testimony of Aaron Wald: Friedman, *Roads to Extinction*, op. cit., page 327.

27 Telegram No. 2678, 28 April 1943: ibid., page 328.

28 Ibid., pages 327–8.

29 Testimony of Eliezer Karstatt, Eichmann Trial, 5 May 1961, session 29.

30 International Military Tribunal, Nuremberg, document NG-2757.

31 Robert Attal, 'Tunis, Tunisia': *Encyclopaedia Judaica*, Jerusalem 1972, volume 15, columns 1447–1448.

32 Tom Bower, 'Rauff: the Great Escape': *The Times*, 16 May 1984.

33 Jack (Idel) Kagan recollections: in conversation with the author, London,

34 Levin, 'The Small Communities', op. cit., page 137.

35 'Report on the Extermination of Jews in the Galicia District', 20 June 1943: International Military Tribunal, Nuremberg, document L-018.

36 Ainsztein, op. cit., pages 444–5.

37 Testimony of Colonel D. S. Zilberman: Yad Vashem archive.

38 Letter of 13 May 1943: International Military Tribunal, Nuremberg, document NO-2003.

39 Letter of 19 May 1943: International Military Tribunal,

Nuremberg, document NO-5789.

40 Randolph L. Braham, *The Politics of Genocide: the Holocaust in Hungary*, New York 1981, volume 1, page 252, note 70.

41 'The Mengele Case – a Summary', document no. 50/4, JS 340/68, Office of the Public Prosecutor, Regional Court of Frankfurt-on-Main, in connection with the Regional Court's Order of Arrest dated 19 January 1981. See Ernie Mayer, 'The Case against Josef Mengele', *Jerusalem Post International Edition*, week ending 9 February 1985, page 11.

42 Testimony of Dr Azriel Ne'eman, reported in the *Jerusalem Post International Edition*, week ending 16 February 1985.

43 Testimony of Dr Ella Lingens: *Jerusalem Post International Edition*, week ending 16 February 1985.

44 General Government, 'Working Session, 31st May 1943': *Hans Frank Diary, op. cit.*, entry for 31 May 1943.

45 Harris, *Tyranny on Trial, op. cit.*, pages 362–3.

46 Testimony of Tadeusz Seweryn: Bartoszewski and Lewin, *Righteous among Nations, op. cit.*, page 607.

47 Meed, *op. cit.*, page 205.

48 Lodz Chronicle, 21 May 1943: Dobroszycki, *op. cit.*, page 340.

49 Trunk, *Judenrat, op. cit.*, page 403.

50 International Military Tribunal, Nuremberg: document NO-065.

51 Doctor Albert Menasche, number 124,454, *Birkenau (Auschwitz II), Memoirs of an Eye-Witness: How 72,000 Greek Jews Perished*, New York 1947.

52 See Fania Fenelon (with Marcelle Routier), *The Musicians of Auschwitz*, London 1977.

53 Letter of 15 June 1943: International Military Tribunal, Nuremberg, document NO-1242.

54 'Jaworzno': *Obozy hitlerowskie,*

op. cit., page 371, Camp Listing number 3296.

55 Letter of 16 June 1943 (in reply to a request of 1 June 1943): International Military Tribunal, Nuremberg, document NO-011 (the request being document NO-010).

56 Letter of 21 June 1943: International Military Tribunal, Nuremberg, document NO-087.

57 Notes of 15 and 26 October 1944: International Military Tribunal, Nuremberg, document NO-091.

58 Leon Weliczker Wells, *The Janowska Road*, New York 1970, pages 141–2.

59 Friedman, *Roads to Extinction, op. cit.*, page 363.

60 Lodz Chronicle, 12 June 1943: Dobroszycki, *op. cit.*, page 345.

61 Cholawski, 'The Judenrat in Minsk', *op. cit.*, page 128.

62 Henry Wasserman, 'Ostrava' ('Moravska Ostrava', 'Maehrisch-Ostrau'): *Encyclopaedia Judaica*, Jerusalem 1972, volume 12, column 1512.

63 Leopold Trepper, *The Great Game: the Story of the Red Orchestra*, London 1977, Appendix 1, pages 419–21, with facsimile.

64 Ania Goldman, in conversation with the author, Czestochowa.

65 Leon Weliczker Wells, *op. cit.*, page 253, note 1.

66 Testimony of Halina Preston (née Wind): Yad Vashem archives.

67 Gerta Hollaender, 'Marvellously I Escaped Death: a Chapter of a Diary': Czortkow memorial book, *op. cit.*

68 Bartoszewski and Lewin, *op. cit.*, page 470.

69 Lubetkin, *In the Days of Destruction and Revolt, op. cit.*, pages 278–9.

70 Krakowski, *The War of the Doomed, op. cit.*, page 222.

71 Yitzhak Arad, 'The "Final Solution" in Lithuania in the Light of German Documentation', *Yad*

Vashem Studies, XI, Jerusalem
1976, page 261.

72 Bartoszewski and Lewin, *op. cit.*,
page 609.

73 Lubetkin, *In the Days of
Destruction and Revolt, op. cit.*,
page 305.

74 Circular No. 33/43g, 'Treatment
of the Jewish Question', Führer
Headquarters, 11 July 1943:
International Military Tribunal,
Nuremberg, document NO-2710.
The phrase 'future overall solution'
was rendered in German as
Gesamtlösung.

75 Letters of 16 July 1943 and 20
December 1943: Leuner, *When
Compassion Was a Crime, op. cit.*,
page 107.

76 Letter of 20 December 1943: *ibid.*,
page 107.

30. 'TO PERISH,
BUT WITH HONOUR'

1 *The Kalish Book, op. cit.*, pages
315–16.

2 Testimony of Abba Kovner:
Eichmann Trial, 4 May 1961,
session 27.

3 Friedman, *Roads to Extinction,
op. cit.*, page 376.

4 Testimony of Abba Kovner:
Eichmann Trial, 4 May 1961,
session 27.

5 Friedman, *Roads to Extinction,
op. cit.*, page 377.

6 Recollection of Leah Leibowitz
(Klompul), in conversation with
the author, Johannesburg.

7 Recollection of Leah Leibowitz,
ibid.

8 Tatiana Berenstein and Adam
Rutkowski, 'The Concentration
Camp for Jews in Warsaw',
Biuletyn, Warsaw, *op. cit.*, number
62, 1967, pages 3–22.

9 Bartoszewski, *Warsaw Death
Ring, op. cit.*, page 190.

10 Klarsfeld, *Memorial to the Jews
Deported from France, op. cit.*,
page 648.

11 Arad, *Ghetto in Flames, op. cit.*,
pages 397–9.

12 'Report from Salonica', *Bulletin*,
London, *op. cit.*, February 1945.

13 Friedmann, *Roads to Extinction,
op. cit.*, page 311.

14 Lubetkin, *Days of Destruction and
Revolt, op. cit.*, page 331.

15 'An Escape from Treblinka':
Eliezer Task, *The Community of
Semiatych*.

16 Testimony of Izak Helfing,
recorded in 1945: Yad Vashem
archive, M-1/518/460.

17 Testimony of Samuel Rajzman:
International Military Tribunal,
Nuremberg, *op. cit.*, pages 124–5.

18 Testimony of Kalman Teigmann:
Eichmann Trial, 6 June 1961,
session 66.

19 Testimony of Samuel Rajzman, *op.
cit.*

20 Zabecki, *Wspomnienia, op. cit.*,
page 126.

21 *Poland: the Communities of Lodz
and its Region, op. cit.*, entry for
Konin.

22 Lubetkin, *In the Days of
Destruction and Revolt, op. cit.*,
page 300.

23 Arad, *Ghetto in Flames, op. cit.*,
pages 404–5.

24 Bartoszewski, *op. cit.*, page 191.
The women were executed on 26
August 1943, the men on 27
August 1943.

25 Solomon H. Steckoll, *The
Alderney Death Camp*, London
1982, pages 72, 93.

26 Goldin, 7 December 1943;
Perlestein, 22 December 1943;
Becker, 30 December 1943: Alfred
Herzka, letter to the author, 14
August 1980.

27 Information in the diary of Oliver
Harvey, entry for 6 August 1943:
John Harvey (editor), *The War
Diaries of Oliver Harvey*, London
1978.

28 Bertha Shachovsky
(Sokolskaya): letter to the
author, Moscow, 14 April 1984.

29 Testimony of Abraham Karasick:

Eichmann Trial, 4 May 1961, session 28.

30 Josef Polak, 'The camp': *Terezin*, Prague 1965, pages 33–4.

31 On 7 October 1943: Czech, 'Kalendarium', *op. cit.*, entry for 7 October 1943.

32 Samuel Pisar, *Of Blood and Hope*, London 1980, pages 40–1.

33 Testimony of Abraham Karasick: Eichmann Trial, 4 May 1961, session 28.

34 Mieczyslaw Chodzko, 'Wspomnienia treblinkarza' ('Reminiscences of a Treblinka prisoner'), *Biuletyn*, Warsaw, *op. cit.*, number 27, 1958, pages 122–4: Ainsztein, *Jewish Resistance in Nazi-Occupied Eastern Europe*, *op. cit.*, pages 741–2.

35 Zabecki, typescript, *op. cit.*, pages 134–5.

36 Bertha Shachovsky (Sokolskaya): letter to the author, Moscow, 15 April 1984.

37 Pisar, *op. cit.*, page 55.

38 Weliczker Wells, *The Janowska Road*, *op. cit.*, pages 189–90.

39 Falstein, *Martyrdom of Jewish Physicians*, *op. cit.*, page 311.

40 Stefan Krakowski, 'Partyzancki oficer wywiadu' ('The Partisan Intelligence Officer'), *Nasz Glos*, number 30 (220), Warsaw, 8 October 1966.

41 Meed, *On Both Sides*, *op. cit.*, pages 294–303.

42 Harold Werner, testimony: Yad Vashem archive. After the war, Harold Werner settled in the United States.

43 Krakowski, *The War of the Doomed*, *op. cit.*, page 233.

44 *Glos Warszawy*, No. 67 (76), 26 October 1943: Ber Mark, *Uprising in the Warsaw Ghetto*, New York 1975, document 77, page 182. The five thousand Jews deported from Tarnow in the first week of September 1943 were sent to Birkenau together with three and a half thousand Jews from Przemysl

and three thousand from Bochnia: all three towns being on the Auschwitz–Tarnow–Lvov railway.

45 Proclamation of 1 September 1943: Arad, Gutman and Margaliot, *Documents on the Holocaust*, *op. cit.*, document number 209, pages 459–60.

46 Trunk, *Judenrat*, *op. cit.*, page 403.

47 Abba Kovner, *op. cit.*: after the war, Kovner married Vitka Kempner. They live in Israel.

48 *The Kalish Book*, *op. cit.*, pages 315–16.

49 Friedman, *Roads to Extinction*, *op. cit.*, pages 377–8: Trunk, *op. cit.*, page 470.

50 Arad, *Ghetto in Flames*, *op. cit.*, pages 429–35 and 470.

51 Jakub Poznanski, *Pamietnik z getta lodzkiego* (Memoirs from the Lodz Ghetto), Lodz 1960, page 102: Lodz Chronicle, Dobroszycki, *op. cit.*, page xxi, note 34.

52 Jack (Idel) Kagan: conversation with the author, London, 21 May 1984.

53 Lodz Chronicle, 6 September 1943: Dobroszycki, *op. cit.*, page 379.

54 Edelbaum, *Growing Up in the Holocaust*, *op. cit.*, page 65.

55 *Ibid.*, page 66.

56 Lodz Chronicle, 13 September 1943: Dobroszycki, *op. cit.*, page 381.

57 Edelbaum, *op. cit.*, page 67.

31. 'A PAGE OF GLORY ... NEVER TO BE WRITTEN'

1 Ainsztein, *Jewish Resistance in Nazi-occupied Eastern Europe*, *op. cit.*, page 482.

2 Report of an eye-witness: *Bulletin*, London, *op. cit.*, February 1945.

3 Ainsztein, *op. cit.*, pages 704–6.

4 Affidavit of Paul Blobel, 18 June 1947: International Military Tribunal, Nuremberg, document NO-3947.

5 Ainsztein, *op. cit.*, pages 691–6.
6 Leni Yahil, *The Rescue of Danish Jewry*, Philadelphia 1969.
7 Czech, 'Kalendarium', *op. cit.*, entry for 3 October 1943.
8 Himmler speech, 4 October 1943: International Military Tribunal, Nuremberg, document PS-1919.
9 'Transport Dn/a', 5 October 1943: Lederer, *Ghetto Theresienstadt*, *op. cit.*, page 228.
10 Czech, 'Kalendarium', *op. cit.*, entry for 8 October 1943.
11 Julien Hirshaut, *Jewish Martyrs of Pawiak*, New York 1982, pages 164–5.
12 Testimony of Colonel D. S. Zilberman: Yad Vashem archive.
13 Testimony of Moshe Bejsky: Eichmann Trial, 1 May 1961, session 21.
14 Testimony of Yaakov Biskowitz: Eichmann Trial, 5 June 1961, session 65.
15 Alexander Aronovitch Pechersky, letter to the author, Rostov-on-Don, 16 December 1980.
16 Adam Rutkowski, 'Ruch oporu w hitlerowskim obozie stracen Sobibor' ('The Resistance Movement in the Hitlerite Extermination Camp of Sobibor'), *Biuletyn*, Warsaw, *op. cit.*, numbers 65–6, 1968; Ainsztein, *op. cit.*, page 761.
17 Testimony of Alexander Pechersky: Novitch, *Sobibor, Martyrdom and Revolt*, *op. cit.*, pages 93–5.
18 Testimony of Biskowitz: Eichmann Trial, 5 June 1961, session 65.
19 Adam Rutkowski, 'Resistance Movement in the Death Camp of Sobibor', *Biuletyn*, Warsaw, *op. cit.*, numbers 65–66, 1968.
20 Novitch, *Spiritual Resistance*, *op. cit.*, page 146.
21 Ainsztein, *op. cit.*, page 483.
22 *Idem.*
23 'Operations Diary of a Jewish Partisan Unit in Rudniki Forest, 1943–1944': Arad, Gutman and Margaliot, *Documents on the Holocaust*, *op. cit.*, document 211, pages 463–70.
24 Ainsztein, *op. cit.*, page 795.
25 Report of Jerzy Tabau ('The Polish Major's Report'): International Military Tribunal, Nuremberg, document L-022.
26 Ainsztein, *op. cit.*, page 795.
27 Report of Jerzy Tabau, *op. cit.*
28 Ainsztein, *op. cit.*, page 796.
29 Deposition of Stanislaw Jankowski: Bezwinska and Czech, *Amidst a Nightmare of Crime*, *op. cit.*, pages 55–6.
30 Report of Jerzy Tabau, *op. cit.*
31 Menasche, *Birkenau (Auschwitz II), Memoirs of an Eye-witness*, *op. cit.*
32 Lena Berg, recollections: Donat, *The Holocaust Kingdom*, *op. cit.*, page 306.
33 Giuliana Donati, 'Deportazione degli Ebrei dall'Italia', *Elenco cronologico dei convogli*, Milan, March 1975.
34 Friedman, *Road to Extinction*, *op. cit.*, pages 415–16.
35 *Ibid.*, page 418.
36 Michaelis, *Mussolini and the Jews*, *op. cit.*, pages 364–5 and 369.
37 Donati, *op. cit.*
38 Information provided by Miriam Novitch.
39 Helena Manaster, 'An episode from the story of a survivor of the Jewish Holocaust', letter to Marianne Sachs, November 1983.
40 Helena Manaster, letter to Elie Wiesel, May 1983.
41 Diary entry for 26 October 1943: Leon Weliczker Wells, *The Janowska Road*, *op. cit.*, page 206.
42 Documents and materials collected by Dr Shalom Cholawski (Jerusalem).
43 Joseph Matsas, *The Participation of the Greek Jews in the National Resistance (1940–1944)*, Janina, Greece, 1982 (a lecture delivered in Athens on 2 October 1982 and in Salonica on 6 December 1982), text from Moshe Sakkis.
44 Report of 7 October 1943, Cracow: Bartoszewski and Lewin,

Righteous among Nations, op. cit.,
page 602.

45 Ger van Roon, *Widerstand im
Dritten Reich: Ein Ueberblick,*
Munich 1980; cited by Egon
Larsen, 'Resistance in Nazi
Germany', Association of Jewish
Refugees from Germany,
Information, January 1981,
volume 36, number 1.

46 Kitty Hart, *Return to Auschwitz,*
London 1981, page 101.

32. 'DO NOT THINK
OUR SPIRIT IS BROKEN'

1 Czech, 'Kalendarium', *op. cit.,*
entry for 5 November 1943.

2 Krakowski, *War of the Doomed,
op. cit.,* page 270.

3 Wdowinski, *And We Are Not
Saved, op. cit.,* page 66, note 1.

4 *Ibid.,* page 99.

5 'Liquidation of the Concentration
Camp at Poniatov: Report by a
Woman who Fled from the Grave',
Bulletin, London, *op. cit.*: Foreign
Office papers, 371/51112, folios
79–89. Sometimes also spelt
Poniatow, the correct spelling of
the camp, and village, is Poniatowa.

6 Lubetkin, *In the Days of
Destruction and Revolt, op. cit.,*
page 296.

7 'The Mass Slaughter at the
Poniatow Camp', *Bulletin,*
London, *op. cit.*

8 Sergio Della Pergola, 'Genoa':
Encyclopaedia Judaica, Jerusalem
1972, volume 7, columns 408–9.

9 Trunk, *Judenrat, op. cit.,* page 441.

10 'The Manuscript': Bezwinska and
Czech, *Amidst a Nightmare of
Crime, op. cit.,* pages 118–19.
This manuscript, written in
Yiddish, in black ink, on
twenty-one pages, was discovered
in 1952 on the site of Crematorium
III. The last entry in the text is
dated 26 November 1944. The
name of the author is unknown.

11 Mordechai Kaplan, 'Bachi,
Armando (1883–1943)':

Encyclopaedia Judaica, Jerusalem
1972, volume 4, columns 52–3.

12 Council of Jewish Communities in
the Czech Lands, *Terezin,* Prague
1965, page 34; Lederer, *Ghetto
Theresienstadt, op. cit.,* pages 101–2.

13 Lederer, *op. cit.,* page 104–5.

14 Meed, *On Both Sides of the Wall,
op. cit.,* pages 201–2.

15 *Ibid.,* page 205.

16 Yitzhak Zuckerman, 'Twenty-Five
Years After the Warsaw Ghetto
Revolt': *Jewish Resistance During
the Holocaust* (Proceedings of the
Conference on Manifestations of
Jewish Resistance, Jerusalem, April
7–11, 1968), Jerusalem 1971,
page 33.

17 Roza Bauminger, *Przy Pikrynie i
Trotylu,* Cracow 1946.
Translation by Ben Helfgott.

18 Czech, 'Kalendarium', *op. cit.,*
entry for 17 November 1943.

19 'The Manuscript': Bezwinska and
Czech, *op. cit.,* page 114–15.

20 Hilberg, *The Destruction of the
European Jews, op. cit.,* pages 505–7.

21 Central Zionist Archives,
Jerusalem: L 15/117.

22 Czech, 'Kalendarium', *op. cit.,*
entry for 5 November 1943.

23 Weliczker Wells, *The Janowska
Road, op. cit.,* page 217.

24 Ainsztein, *Jewish Resistance in
Nazi-occupied Eastern Europe, op.
cit.,* page 713.

25 Testimony of Josef Reznik:
Eichmann Trial, 5 June 1961,
session 64.

26 Krakowski, *The War of the
Doomed, op. cit.,* page 271.

27 Testimony of Josef Reznik:
Eichmann Trial, 5 June 1961,
session 64.

28 Author's photographic record,
Borki, 7 August 1980.

29 Sandomierz: *Scenes of Fighting
and Martyrdom Guide, op. cit.,*
page 209.

30 Miechow: *ibid.,* page 120.

31 Schwarzbart diary, 1 December
1943: Yad Vashem archive.

32 Trunk, *op. cit.,* page 418.

33 Document dated 16 December 1943: Lubetsky archive.
34 Czech, 'Kalendarium', *op. cit.*, entry for 13 November 1943.
35 *Ibid.*, entry for 21 December.
36 Ainsztein, *op. cit.*, page 922, note 57.
37 Report Number 238, 22 December 1943: Mark, *Uprising in the Warsaw Ghetto, op. cit.*, document 69, page 175.
38 Meed, *op. cit.*, page 290.
39 Joseph Ariel (Joseph Fischer), 'Jewish Self-Defence and Resistance in France during World War II': *Yad Vashem Studies*, VI, Jerusalem 1967, page 221–50.
40 Vincent Brome, *The Way Back: the Story of Lieutenant-Commander Pat O'Leary, GC, DSO, RN*, London 1958, pages 230–4.
41 Zvie A. Brown and Dov Levin, *The Story of an Underground: the Resistance of the Jews of Kovno (Lithuania) in the Second World War*, Jerusalem 1962.
42 Krakowski, *War of the Doomed, op. cit.*, pages 271–3; testimony of Josef Reznik, Eichmann Trial, 5 June 1961, session 64.

33. 'ONE SHOULD LIKE SO MUCH TO LIVE A LITTLE BIT LONGER'

1 Testimony of Madame Claude Vaillant Couturier, 28 January 1946: *The Trial of German Major War Criminals, op. cit.*, pages 191–2.
2 Rudolf Vrba recollections, *The World at War*, film documentary, Thames Television, 1974.
3 Salmen Lewental notebook: Bezwinska and Czech, *Amidst a Nightmare of Crime, op. cit.*, pages 142–5.
4 Lodz Chronicle, 20 January 1944: Dobroszycki, *op. cit.*, page 435.
5 Lodz Chronicle, 21 January 1944: *ibid.*, page 435.
6 Lodz Chronicle, 18 February 1944: *ibid.*, page 456.
7 Lodz Chronicle, 9 February 1944: *ibid.*, page 448.
8 Lodz Chronicle: *ibid.*, page 448, note 6.
9 Szajkowski, *Analytical Franco-Jewish Gazetteer, op. cit.*, page 150.
10 Testimony of Raizl Tabakman Kibel (born in Warsaw, 7 December 1915, emigrated to France with her parents in 1929): Yad Vashem archive, 03/882.
11 Stanislaw Wanshik, letters of 25 February 1947 and 29 January 1948: *The Diary of Adam's Father*, Tel Aviv 1973, pages 87 and 97–8.
12 Tuvia Borzykowski, diary entry for 28 January 1944: *Between Tumbling Walls, op. cit.*, pages 136–7.
13 Sloan, *op. cit.*, page 346.
14 Bartoszewski and Lewin, *Righteous Among Nations, op. cit.*, page 603.
15 *Ibid.*, pages 598–9.
16 David Guzik (American Jewish Joint Distribution Committee), Warsaw, 23 February 1946: copy sent to the author by Gustav Szyldkraut of Toronto, Irena Szyldkraut's father.
17 Z.S. 'Hirschler, René, 1905–1944', *Encyclopaedia Judaica*, Jerusalem 1972, volume 8, column 528.
18 Klarsfeld, *Memorial to the Jews Deported from France, op. cit.*, pages 498–507; private information.
19 Testimony of Philip Mechanicus: Presser, *The Destruction of the Dutch Jews, op. cit.*, pages 414–15.
20 Czech, 'Kalendarium', *op. cit.*, entry for 10 February 1944.
21 Erich Kulka, 'Jewish Revolt in Auschwitz', *op. cit.*
22 *Hans Frank Diary, op. cit.*, entry for 4 March 1944 (Loose-Leaf File).

23 Bartoszewski, *Warsaw Death Ring, op. cit.*, page 298.

24 Dr Konstantin, Bazarov, letter to the author, 7 October 1978.

25 Dan Pagis, 'Vogel, David, 1891–1944', *Encyclopaedia Judaica*, Jerusalem 1972, volume 16, columns 202–3.

26 'List of Deportees, Convoy 69': Klarsfeld, *Memorial to the Jews, op. cit.*, pages 508, 518 and 526.

27 For an account of the destruction of the 'family camp', written in Prague by the two maintenance men themselves, see Ota Kraus and Erich Kulka, *The Death Factory*, Oxford 1966, pages 172–4.

28 Erich Kulka, 'Five Escapees from Auschwitz': Yuri Suhl (editor), *They Fought Back: the Story of Jewish Resistance in Nazi Europe*, London 1968, page 224.

29 Lederer, *Ghetto Theresienstadt, op. cit.*, page 227.

30 Meed, *On Both Sides, op. cit.*, pages 264–5; Friedman, *Martyrs and Fighters, op. cit.*, pages 304–6.

31 Julian Hirszhaut, 'Dark Nights in the Pawiak' (Yiddish), Buenos Aires 1948, pages 196–200: Friedman, *Martyrs and Fighters, op. cit.*, pages 304–6; Julien Hirshaut, *Jewish Martyrs of Pawiak, op. cit.*, pages 175–6.

32 Kermish and Krakowski, *Emanuel Ringelblum, Polish–Jewish Relations during the Second World War, op. cit.*, page xxx. Among the Poles specifically mentioned by Ringelblum, with details of how they saved Jews, were Julian Kudasiewicz, Gerhard Gadejski, Professor Tadeusz Kotarbinski, Pawel Harmuszko, Witold Benedyktowicz and Ignacy Kasprzykowski.

33 *Ibid.*, page 8.

34 *Ibid.*, page 183.

35 *Ibid.*, pages 247–9.

34. FROM THE OCCUPATION OF HUNGARY TO THE NORMANDY LANDINGS

1 Affidavit of SS Captain Dieter Wisliceny, 7 October 1947, International Military Tribunal, Nuremberg: document NG-2867. See also Braham, *The Politics of Genocide, op. cit.*, volume 2, page 396.

2 Braham, *op. cit.*, volume 2, page 597.

3 Affidavit of SS Major-General Otto Winkelmann, 3 June 1947, International Military Tribunal, Nuremberg: document NO-4139.

4 Recollections of Hugo Gryn, in conversation with the author, London.

5 Braham, *op. cit.*, volume 2, pages 484–5.

6 Letter of 28 March 1944 to Alexander Leitner: *ibid.*, page 436.

7 *Ibid.*, page 485.

8 Material collected by Shalom Cholawski, for his doctoral thesis at the Hebrew University of Jerusalem (December 1977).

9 Ainsztein, *Jewish Resistance in Nazi-occupied Eastern Europe, op. cit.*, pages 386–7.

10 Robert Katz, *Death in Rome*, London 1967.

11 Klarsfeld, *Memorial to the Jews Deported from France, op. cit.*, page 650.

12 Yad Vashem photographic collection; Klarsfeld, *op. cit.*, page 645 (where his name is given as Gelchman).

13 Information from Solidarité Juive, Brussels.

14 Testimony of Lea Svirsky (born in Swieciany on 27 April 1926): Yad Vashem archive.

15 Zalman Grinberg, speech of 27 May 1945, *op. cit.*

16 Information provided by Eitan Finkelstein. In 1984, Zahar

Kaplanas was among more than 10,000 Soviet Jews who had been refused permission to emigrate to Israel.

17 Testimony of Dr Aharon Peretz: Eichmann Trial, 4 May 1961, session 28.

18 Edelbaum, *Growing Up in the Holocaust*, op. cit., pages 172–3.

19 'Transportliste', 5 April 1944: Archivio Centro di Documentazione Ebraica Contemporanea, Milan.

20 Szajkowski, *Analytical Franco-Jewish Gazetteer*, op. cit., page 150.

21 Klarsfeld, op. cit., page 534.

22 Tom Bower, *Klaus Barbie, Butcher of Lyons*, London 1984, page 93.

23 Bartoszewski, *Warsaw Death Ring*, op. cit., page 305.

24 They reached camp Fedallah in Casablanca on 21 June 1944, Port Said on 13 November 1944, and Palestine on 27 November 1944.

25 Notes of an 'Unknown author': Bezwinska and Czech, *Amidst a Nightmare of Crime*, op. cit., pages 117–18.

26 *The Diary of Anne Frank*, London 1954, pages 174–5. Anne Frank was fifteen years old on 12 June 1944.

27 Testimony of Szloma Gol, sworn at Nuremberg, 9 August 1946: International Military Tribunal, Nuremberg, document D-964.

28 Ainsztein, op. cit., pages 706–7.

29 Arad, *Ghetto in Flames*, op. cit., page 445.

30 Testimony of Raya Barnea (Weberman): written at Hadera, Israel, on 10 January 1982.

31 Braham, op. cit., volume 2, page 598.

32 Report by Rudolf Kastner (Rezo Kasztner): Eichmann Trial, 1 June 1961, session 62 (document 900).

33 Braham, op. cit., volume 2, page 599.

34 Moshe Sandberg, *My Longest Year: in the Hungarian Labour Service and in the Nazi Camps*, Jerusalem 1968, page 18.

35 International Military Tribunal, Nuremberg, document PS-2605.

36 On 8 August 1942: Klarsfeld, op. cit., page 552.

37 Yitzhak Katznelson, 'Song of the Murdered Jewish People': Hebrew text provided, and translated, by Miriam Novitch.

38 Dr Konstantin Bazarov, letter to the author, op. cit.

39 Falstein, *The Martyrdom of Jewish Physicians in Poland*, op. cit., page 361.

40 Bartoszewski, op. cit., page 312.

41 Ainsztein, op. cit., page 425.

42 'Gliwice' (Gleiwitz): *Obozy hitlerowskie*, op. cit., page 370, Camp Listing numbers 3288, 3289, 3290 and 3291.

43 'Jaworzno' (Neu Dachs): *ibid.*, page 371, Camp Listing number 3296.

44 'Kedzierzyn-Kozle' (Blechhammer): *ibid.*, page 371, Camp Listing number 3297.

45 'Bobrek': *ibid.*, page 369, Camp Listing number 3279.

46 'Myslowice' (Furstengrübe): *ibid.*, page 372, Camp Listing number 3301.

47 'Siemianowice Slaskie' (Laurahutte): *ibid.*, page 372, Camp Listing number 3307.

48 'Tychy' (Gunthergrübe): *ibid.*, page 373, Camp Listing number 3313.

49 'Sosnowiec (Sosnowice): *ibid.*, page 372, Camp Listing number 3309.

50 'Oswiecim' (Auschwitz-Birkenau): *ibid.*, page 365, Camp Listing number 3276.

51 'Monowice (Monowitz): *ibid.*, page 371–2, Camp Listing number 3300.

52 'Report drawn up on 12 October 1944' (by a Jew from Hungary): Pazner papers, Yad Vashem archive.

53 Mel Mermelstein, *By Bread Alone:*

the Story of A.4685, Los Angeles 1979, page 101.

54 'Report drawn up on 12 October 1944' (by a Jew from Hungary): Pazner papers, Yad Vashem archive.

55 Judith Sternberg Newman, *In the Hell of Auschwitz*, New York 1964, page 18: quoted in Terence Des Pres, *The Survivor: an Anatomy of Life in the Death Camps*, London 1976, page 86.

56 Alter Feinsilber, testimony given on 16 April 1945, Cracow: Bezwinska and Czech, *Amidst a Nightmare of Crime*, op. cit., page 56.

57 Alter Feinsilber: Bezwinska and Czech, op. cit., page 65.

58 *Deutsche faschistische Konzentrationslager auf dem Gebiet des heutige Polen 1939–1945* (single-sheet map, undated); recollection of Hugo Gryn, one of the deportees to the Ullersdorf site, in conversation with the author, London.

59 Recollection of Hugo Gryn, in conversation with the author, London.

60 Testimony of Yehuda Bakon: Eichmann Trial, 7 June 1961, session 68.

61 Czech, 'Kalendarium', op. cit.: entries from 15 May to 31 May 1944.

62 'Transportliste', 16 May 1944: Archivio, Centro di Documentazione Ebraica Contemporanea, Milan.

63 Testimony of Pavilas Tcherekas: Klarsfeld, op. cit., page 546.

64 Braham, op. cit., page 993.

65 *Ibid.*, pages 605–6.

66 Report of 25 May 1944: International Military Tribunal, Nuremberg, document NG-5608.

67 Garlinski, *Fighting Auschwitz*, op. cit., page 323.

68 Braham, op. cit., page 608.

69 'Secret' Report No. 18, 'Horrors of Oswiecim': Foreign Office papers, 898/423.

70 'The Vrba–Wetzler' and 'Mordowicz–Rosin' reports: International Military Tribunal, Nuremberg, document L-022.

71 Report of 25 May 1944: International Military Tribunal, Nuremberg, document NG-5608.

72 Report of 31 May 1944: International Military Tribunal, Nuremberg, document NG-5624.

73 Report of Dr Loewenherz (of Vienna): Eichmann Trial, 31 May 1961, document 1125.

74 Leon Szalet, *Experiment 'E'*, New York, 1945, page 42: quoted in Des Pres, op. cit., page 73.

75 Halina Birenbaum, *Hope is the Last to Die*, New York 1971, page 134: quoted in Des Pres, op. cit., page 60.

76 Louise S., 'The Camp at Birkenau': *Bulletin*, op. cit., November 1945. Louise S. had reached Birkenau from Cluj on 27 May 1944.

77 Testimony of Rudolf Kastner (Reszo Kasztner): Eichmann Trial, 30 May 1961, session 56.

78 The train with the 1,686 Hungarian Jews left Hungary for Belsen and then Switzerland on 29 June 1944. On 22 August 1944, 318 of the Hungarian Jews reached the Swiss city of Basle from Belsen. The second group, of 1,368 Jews, reached Switzerland on 7 December 1944: Braham, op. cit., pages 956–7.

79 For a full account of these negotiations, see Martin Gilbert, *Auschwitz and the Allies*, London 1981, pages 212–61.

80 Recollections of Freda Silberberg (Wineman), in conversation with the author, London.

81 Czech, 'Kalendarium', op. cit., entry for 30 June 1944.

82 Molho, *In Memoriam*, op. cit. According to a recent account by Shlomo Karmiel, the 260 Jews from Canea who were seized on 20 May 1944 were executed on Crete, and their bodies put on board the ship, which was sunk to destroy

the evidence. They were shot, he believes, 'because they were involved in helping British Intelligence in plans to abduct General Kreipe, who commanded the Nazi forces in Crete.' (Marcel M. Yoel, 'Canea Jews – the truth', *Jewish Chronicle*, 19 November 1984.)

83 Sam Modiano, 'Island's Jews Saved by Greek Archbishop': *Jewish Chronicle*, 3 November 1978. See also Molho, *op. cit.*

84 Lodz Chronicle: Dobroszycki, *op. cit.*, page 498, note 20.

85 Lodz Chronicle, 8 June 1944: *ibid.*, pages 499–500.

86 Lodz Chronicle, 9 June 1944: *ibid.*, page 500.

87 Diary entry for 6 June 1944: Eisenberg, *Witness to the Holocaust*, *op. cit.*, page 323. The boy's name and fate are unknown.

88 Anne Frank, letter of 6 June 1944: *The Diary of Anne Frank*, *op. cit.*, pages 203–4.

35. 'MAY ONE CRY NOW?'

1 Reuven Dafni, in conversation with the author, Jerusalem.

2 Klarsfeld, *Memorial to the Jews Deported from France*, *op. cit.*, pages 642 and 645.

3 Szajkowski, *Analytical Franco-Jewish Gazetteer*, *op. cit.*, page 150.

4 'Leon Yitshak Sakkis (1925–44)': letter from Moshe Sakkis to the author, Athens, 26 September 1983.

5 Szajkowski, *op. cit.*, page 150; Klarsfeld, *op. cit.*, page 643. On 29 June 1944 Isaac Ben Zimra, aged twenty-three, was shot for resistance: he had been born in French North Africa, in Oran.

6 Report of 13 June 1944: International Military Tribunal, Nuremberg, document NG-5617.

7 'Transports come to Dachau camp (of new interned and from other camps) for the time

22.3.1933–29.4.1945': KZ-Gedenkenstatte Dachau, Museum-Archiv-Bibliothek.

8 Krzystof Dunin-Wasowicz, 'Zydowscy wiezniowie KL Stuffhof', *Biuletyn*, Warsaw, *op. cit.*, number 63, 1967, pages 11–17.

9 Testimony of Madame Claude Vaillant Couturier, 28 January 1946: *The Trial of German Major War Criminals*, *op. cit.*, page 190.

10 David Horovitz, '40 Years of Despair': *Jerusalem Post*, 23 November 1984.

11 Testimony of Vera Kriegel: Horovitz, *op. cit.*; *Jerusalem Post International Edition*, week ending 16 February 1985.

12 'The Mengele Case – a Summary', document no. 50/4, JS 340/68, 19 January 1981: Ernie Mayer, 'The Case against Josef Mengele', *op. cit.*

13 'The Story of an Unsung Hero': *The Voice of Auschwitz Survivors in Israel*, number 27, June 1984.

14 Report from a Tribunal held at Yad Vashem, Jerusalem, in February 1985; *Jewish Chronicle*, 8 February 1985; *Jerusalem Post International Edition*, 16 February 1985.

15 Testimony of Yossl Rosensaft (Chairman of the Belsen Committee after the liberation of Belsen in 1945), talking (in Yiddish) to Sam Goldsmith, a war correspondent: Goldsmith papers (first published in Hebrew in *Haboker*, Tel Aviv, 9 May 1945; reprinted in English in S. J. Goldsmith, *Jews in Transition*, New York 1969).

16 Proclamation No. 416, 16 June 1944: Lodz Chronicle, 16 June 1944: Dobroszycki, *op. cit.*, pages 503–4.

17 Lodz Chronicle, 16 June 1944: *ibid.*, pages 503–5.

18 Lodz Chronicle, 22 June 1944: *ibid.*, page 513.

19 Lodz Chronicle, *ibid.*, page 503, note 21.

20 Lodz Chronicle, 23 June 1944: *ibid.*, pages 513–14.

21 Lodz Chronicle, 24 June 1944: *ibid.*, pages 514–15.

22 Lodz Chronicle, 25 June 1944: *ibid.*, page 515.

23 Testimony of Mordechai Zurawski: Eichmann Trial, 5 June 1961, session 65.

24 Testimony of Mordka (Mordechai, Mieczyslaw) Zurawski, of Wloclawek: Lodz, 29 October 1945: Bednarz, *Das Vernichtungslager zu Chelmno am Ner, op. cit.*, page 210.

25 Testimony of Shimon Srebnik: Eichmann Trial, 6 June 1961, session 66.

26 Note of 9 September 1944: Bednarz, *op. cit.*

27 Cholawski, *Soldiers from the Ghetto, op. cit.*, pages 176–7.

28 Czech, 'Kalendarium', *op. cit.*, entry for 24 June 1944. Galinski's camp number was 531; Mala Zimetbaum's, 19880.

29 Fenelon, *The Musicians of Auschwitz, op. cit.*, pages 160–1.

30 Recollections of Lena Berg: Donat, *The Holocaust Kingdom, op. cit.* pages 309–10.

31 Testimony of Raja Kagan: Eichmann Trial, 8 June 1961, session 70.

32 Recollections of Lena Berg: Donat, *The Holocaust Kingdom, op. cit.*, page 310.

33 Fenelon, *op. cit.*, page 167.

34 Testimony of Raja Kagan: Eichmann Trial, 8 June 1961, session 70.

35 Recollections of Lena Berg: Donat, *The Holocaust Kingdom, op. cit.*

36 Fenelon, *op. cit.*, pages 166–7.

37 'List of Jews Executed in France': Klarsfeld, *op. cit.*, pages 641–54.

38 Lederer, *Ghetto Theresienstadt, op. cit.*, page 218. More than two hundred thousand unarmed people, Jews and Soviet prisoners-of-war, had been murdered at Maly Trostenets between the autumn of 1941 and the summer of 1944. The murders had been carried out in two hamlets near the villages of Blagovshchina and Shashkovka. Soviet research after the war estimated that about one hundred and fifty thousand people had been murdered in Blagovshchina and a further fifty thousand in Shashkovka, where the Germans had built a special 'incinerator-pit': *Byelorussian Soviet Encyclopaedia, short encyclopaedia*, volume 1, Minsk 1979, page 699. I am grateful to Yigael Zafoni for this reference.

39 Miklos Nyiszli, *Auschwitz, a Doctor's Eye-Witness Account*, London 1962.

40 Arad, *Ghetto in Flames, op. cit.*, pages 446 and 460.

41 Lederer, *op. cit.*, page 228.

42 *The Book of Alfred Kantor*, New York 1971, plate 78. I am grateful to Roland Gant for a copy of this book.

43 *Ibid.*, page 80.

44 Lederer, *op. cit.*, page 229.

45 Steckoll, *The Alderney Death Camp, op. cit.*, page 92.

46 'Transport Eb' of 18 May 1944 and 'Transport Ek' of 28 September 1944: Lederer, *op. cit.*, pages 231–2.

47 'Transport Eh', 1 July 1944 (ten prisoners), 'Transport Eg', 4 July 1944 (fifteen prisoners) and 'Transport Ej', 27 September 1944 (twenty prisoners): *ibid.*, page 232.

48 Meir Ronnen, 'The Legacy of Herr Doktor Candid', *Jerusalem Post*, 20 January 1984.

49 Documents concerning Oscar Schindler: Yad Vashem archive.

50 Bartoszewski, *Warsaw Death Ring, op. cit.*, page 326.

51 Szajkowski, *Analytical Franco-Jewish Gazetteer, op. cit.*, page 81.

52 Jeno Levai (editor), *Eichmann in*

Hungary, Budapest 1961, page
126.

53 Report of 11 July 1944:
International Military Tribunal,
Nuremberg, document NG-5616.

54 Elenore Lester, *Wallenberg: the
Man in the Iron Web*, New Jersey
1983; Alexander Zvielli, 'Doomed
Saviour', *Jerusalem Post*, 15 July
1983.

55 Braham, *The Politics of Genocide*,
op. cit., volume 2, pages 788–9.

56 Lutz papers: Yad Vashem archive.

57 Testimony of Dr Aharon Peretz:
Eichmann Trial, 4 May 1961,
session 28.

58 Testimony of Dr Tania Ipp: Yad
Vashem archive.

59 Testimony of Miriam
Krakinowski: Yad Vashem
archive.

60 Vera Elyashiv, recollections, *op.
cit.*

61 Testimony of Shalom Cholawski:
Eichmann Trial, 12 June 1961,
session 73.

62 Testimony of Abba Kovner:
Eichmann Trial, 4 May 1961,
session 27.

63 Testimony of Abraham Karasick:
Eichmann Trial, 4 May 1961,
session 27. Karasick joined the Red
Army. He was demobilized in
1945 and went to Palestine.
Interned in Cyprus by the British in
1947, he finally settled in Israel in
1949.

64 Hirshaut, *Jewish Martyrs of
Pawiak*, *op. cit.*, page 228.

65 Eliezer Yerushalmi, *Pinkas Shavli*
(memorial book of
Siauliai–Shavli–Schaulen),
Jerusalem 1958.

36. JULY–SEPTEMBER
1944: THE LAST
DEPORTATIONS

1 Hizkia M. Franco, *Les Martyrs
Juifs de Rhodes et de Cos*,
Elizabethville (Katanga) 1952,
page 91.

2 *Ibid.*, pages 97–8.

3 Violette Fintz, in conversation with
the author, Cape Town.

4 John Bierman, *Odyssey 1940*,
New York 1984, pages 218–19.

5 Franco, *op. cit.*, page 99.

6 Violette Fintz, in conversation with
the author, Cape Town.

7 Franco, *op. cit.*, page 101.

8 Violette Fintz, in conversation with
the author, Cape Town.

9 Franco, *op. cit.*, page 104. (In the
journey by sea, five Jews had died;
at Haidar camp, and in the
combined, sea and rail journey,
twenty-two died.)

10 Bierman, *op. cit.*, pages 222–3.

11 Levai, *Eichmann in Hungary*, *op.
cit.*, pages 127–9.

12 Falstein, *The Martyrdom of Jewish
Physicians in Poland*, *op. cit.*, page
324.

13 Krakowski, *The War of the
Doomed*, *op. cit.*, page 59.

14 Braham, *The Politics of Genocide*,
op. cit., volume 2, page 1073.

15 Levai, *op. cit.*, pages 142, 144, and
facsimile of Iron Cross award,
page 143.

16 Fritz Hesse, *Das Spiel um
Deutschland*, Munich 1953
(Hewel was Ribbentrop's liaison
with Hitler, with the rank of
Ambassador.)

17 'Convoy 77, July 31, 1944':
Klarsfeld, *Memorial to the Jews*,
op. cit., pages 582–94.

18 Martin Gilbert, *The Jews of Hope*,
London 1984, pages 157–61.

19 Lodz Chronicle, 22 July 1944:
Dobroszycki, *op. cit.*, page 532.

20 Lodz Chronicle, 23 July 1944:
ibid., page 532.

21 Lodz Chronicle, 25 July 1944:
ibid., page 534.

22 Diary entry, 31 July 1944:
Eisenberg, *Witness to the
Holocaust*, *op. cit.*, page 324.

23 Diary entry, 3 August 1944: *idem.*

24 Friedman, *Roads to Extinction*,
op. cit., page 348.

25 Testimony of Halina Zipora
Preston (née Wind), *op. cit.*

26 Sirkka Purkey, 'The Treatment of Jewish Refugees in Finland', *op. cit.*

27 Krakowski, *The War of the Doomed, op. cit.*, pages 277–8.

28 Meed, *On Both Sides of the Wall, op. cit.*, page 323.

29 Charles (Chaim) Goldstein, *The Bunker*, New York 1973, page 105.

30 Krakowski, *The War of the Doomed, op. cit.*, page 287.

31 Meed, *op. cit.*, page 327.

32 *Ibid.*, pages 327–8.

33 Falstein, *op. cit.*, page 344.

34 *Ibid.*, page 338.

35 *Ibid.*, page 489.

36 Borzykowski, *Between Tumbling Walls, op. cit.*, pages 168–9.

37 Testimony of Ruth Chajet (born in Vilna on 20 July 1925), given to the Historical Commission in Feldafing, 2 January 1948: Yad Vashem archive.

38 *The Diary of Anne Frank, op. cit.*, page 223.

39 Friedman, *Roads to Extinction, op. cit.*, page 348.

40 Nyiszli, *Auschwitz, op. cit.*, pages 128–30.

41 *Ibid.*, page 133.

42 Friedman, *Roads to Extinction, op. cit.*, page 348.

43 Maja Abramowicz (Zarch), typescript, *op. cit.*, page 56.

44 Franco, *op. cit.*, page 103.

45 Violette Fintz, in conversation with the author, Cape Town.

46 Bierman, *op. cit.*, pages 223–4.

47 Franco, *op. cit.*, page 103. Of the 1,673 Jews deported from Rhodes on July 23, 22 had died on the sea and rail journey.

48 'Letter from Lwow to a Palestine Resident', Lvov, 24 August 1944: *Bulletin*, London, *op. cit.*, April 1945.

49 Joseph Ariel, 'Jewish Resistance and Self-Defence in France during World War II: *Yad Vashem Studies*, VI, Jerusalem 1967, pages 242–3. See also Anny Latour, *The Jewish Resistance in France 1940–1944*, New York 1981, pages 233–48.

50 Ladislav Lipscher, *Die Juden im Slowakischen Staat, 1939–1945*, Munich and Vienna 1980, pages 167–76.

51 Ainsztein, *Jewish Resistance in Nazi-occupied Eastern Europe, op. cit.*, page xxii.

52 Dorothy and Pesach Bar-Adon, *Seven Who Fell*, Tel Aviv 1947, pages 173–85. Havivah Reik was captured on 28 October 1944 and shot on 20 November 1944.

53 Czeslaw Mordowicz, in conversation with the author, Tel Aviv.

54 Yad Vashem photographic collection.

55 Georges Dunand, *Ne perdez pas leur trace!*, Neuchâtel 1951.

56 Bar-Adon, *op. cit.*, pages 184–5.

57 Czech, 'Kalendarium', *op. cit.*, entry for 30 August 1944.

58 Michael Etkind, in conversation with the author, London, 1 June 1982.

59 Czech, 'Kalendarium', *op. cit.*, entry for 30 August 1944.

60 *Ibid.*, entry for 5 September 1944.

61 Gisella Perl, *I was a Doctor in Auschwitz*, New York 1948, pages 114–15.

62 Lena Berg's recollections: Donat, *The Holocaust Kingdom, op. cit.*, pages 313–14.

63 Letter dated 6 September 1944: Bezwinska and Czech, *Amidst a Nightmare of Crime, op. cit.*, pages 76–7. The editors (Jadwiga Bezwinska and Danuta Czech) write: 'The manuscript of Salmen Gradowski was dug out on the site of crematorium II at Birkenau by Szlama Dragon, prisoner No 80359, former member of Sonderkommando. Dragon was one of the several members of Sonderkommando who had managed to survive the camp. He was lucky to have been able to escape from the evacuation transport (in the vicinity of

Pszczyna), which had left Birkenau on January 18, 1945. After liberation he returned to the site of the camp where he was present when the Extraordinary Soviet State Commission investigated Nazi crimes, committed in the camp. He handed over the disinterred manuscript to the Commission.'

37. SEPTEMBER 1944: THE DAYS OF AWE

1 Yehoshua Robert Büchler, *The Story and Source of the Jewish Community of Topoltchany*, Jerusalem 1976, pages 79–83.

2 List of Jews to be evacuated from Topusko (Yugoslavia) to Bari (Italy), 3 September 1944: War Office papers, 202/293. The first twenty-nine Jews were airlifted out on 18 September 1944.

3 'Rijeka' (Italian 'Fiume'): *Encyclopaedia Judaica*, Jerusalem 1972, volume 14, column 185.

4 Liliana Picciotto Fargion, 'Note biografiche dei decorati con medaglia d'oro': Giuliana Donati, *Persecuzione e Deportazione degli Ebrei dall'Italia durante la Dominazione Nazifascista*, Milan 1975, pages 52–3.

5 Braham, *The Politics of Genocide*, *op. cit.*, volume 2, pages 982–5.

6 Testimony of Yosef Buzhminsky: Eichmann Trial, 2 May 1961, session 24.

7 Evelyn Le Chêne, *Mauthausen: the History of a Death Camp*, London 1971, page 75.

8 Testimony of a former prisoner at Bor: Pazner papers, Yad Vashem archive. The Cervenka massacre took place on 8 October 1944.

9 Dr Konstantin Bazarov: letter to the author, 7 October 1978.

10 Steckel, *Destruction and Survival*, *op. cit.*, page 38.

11 Testimony of Josef Zalman

Kleinman: Eichmann Trial, 7 June 1961, session 68.

12 Testimony of Dr Aharon Beilin: Eichmann Trial, 7 June 1961, session 69.

13 M. Dworzecki, *The Camps for Jews in Estonia* (Hebrew, English summary), Tel Aviv, 1970.

14 Kulka, 'Jewish Revolt in Auschwitz', *op. cit.*

15 Testimony of Josef Zalman Kleinmann: Eichmann Trial, 7 June 1961, session 68.

16 Testimony of Dr Aharon Beilin: Eichmann Trial, 7 June 1961, session 69.

17 Leon Szalet, *Experiment 'E'*, New York 1945, pages 70–1: Des Pres, *The Survivor, op. cit.*, pages 104–5.

18 Sala Kaye, *Holocaust Testimony 1*, London 1983.

19 Testimony of Nahum Hoch: Eichmann Trial, 8 June 1961, session 71.

20 Levi Shalit, *Beyond Dachau*, Johannesburg 1980, pages 50–52.

21 'Transport Ek', 28 September 1944: Lederer, *Ghetto Theresienstadt, op. cit.*, pages 232–4.

22 'Transport El', 29 September 1944: *ibid.*, pages 234–5.

23 'Transport Em', 1 October 1944: *ibid.*, page 236.

24 'Transport En', 4 October 1944: *idem.*

25 'Transport Eo', 6 October 1944: *ibid.*, page 237.

26 Testimony of Alfred Oppenheimer: Eichmann Trial, 7 June 1961, session 68.

27 Testimony of Sara Tartakovskaya: Babi Yar memorial volume, *op. cit.*

38. REVOLT AT BIRKENAU

1 Manuscript, written in Greek, found in late autumn of 1980 in a thermos flask buried near Crematorium II, by Polish schoolchildren planting a tree: text

890 · THE HOLOCAUST

sent to the author by the
Auschwitz Museum.

2 Menasche, *Birkenau (Auschwitz
II), Memoirs of an Eye-Witness,
op. cit.*

3 Testimony of Raizl
Kibel-Tabakman: Yad Vashem
archive, 03/882.

4 Bezwinska and Czech, *Amidst a
Nightmare of Crime, op. cit.*, page
155, note 61.

5 Testimony of Israel Gutman:
Eichmann Trial, 2 June 1961,
session 63.

6 Kulka, 'Jewish Revolt in
Auschwitz', *op. cit.*

7 Bezwinska and Czech, *op. cit.*,
page 65, note 91.

8 Garlinski, *Fighting Auschwitz, op.
cit.*, page 238 and page 239, note
1.

9 Kulka, *op. cit.*

10 Garlinski, *op. cit.*, pages 239–40.

11 Dorebus was born in the Polish
town of Zyrardow on 27 July
1906. He was deported to
Birkenau with his Warsaw-born
wife, Pesa. Handelsman was born
in the Polish town of Lipsko on 30
August 1908. He was deported
with his wife Chana, born in
Sosnowiec. Pesa Dorebus and
Chana Handelsman were both
thirty-six years old at the time of
their deportation: both are
believed to have perished at
Birkenau.

12 Testimony of Israel Gutman:
Eichmann Trial, 2 June 1961,
session 63.

13 Testimony of Raizl Kibel, Yad
Vashem archive, 03/882.

14 Testimony of Israel Gutman:
Eichmann Trial, 2 June 1961,
session 63.

15 Testimony of Nahum Hoch:
Eichmann Trial, 8 June 1961,
session 71.

16 Salmen Lewental, manuscript:
Bezwinska and Czech, *op. cit.*,
pages 177–8.

39. PROTECTORS AND PERSECUTORS

1 Testimony of Colonel D. S.
Zilberman: Yad Vashem archive.

2 Levin, *The Holocaust, op. cit.*,
page 743, note 18.

3 Braham, *The Politics of Genocide,
op. cit.*, volume 2, pages 827–32.

4 Testimony of Arie Breslauer:
Eichmann Trial, 1 June 1961,
session 61. In Hungarian his name
was spelt Leopold Breszlauer.

5 Braham, *op. cit.*, volume 2, page
830.

6 *Ibid.*, page 834.

7 Report by Rudolf Kastner (Rezso
Kasztner): Eichmann Trial, 1 June
1961, session 62 (document 900).

8 Braham, *op. cit.*, volume 2, pages
836–8.

9 *Ibid.*, pages 838–9.

10 Bronia Klibanski, 'The Archives of
the Swiss Consul General Charles
Lutz', *Yad Vashem Studies*, XV,
Jerusalem 1983, pages 357–65.

11 Testimony of Arie Breslauer:
Eichmann Trial, 1 June 1961,
session 61.

12 Report by a Jewish woman from
Budapest: *Bulletin, op. cit.*, April
1945.

13 *Ibid.*

14 Paul Gidaly, 'Search for a Sister':
Jerusalem Post, 14 December
1979. Gidaly, who had escaped
from a forced labour battalion,
was using the identity of Ferdinand
Hetzey, first-year medical student
and ensign in the Hungarian army.

15 Braham, *op. cit.*, volume 2, pages
839–40.

16 Judge Moshe Bejski, in
conversation with the author,
Jerusalem.

17 'The Story of an Unsung Hero':
*The Voice of Auschwitz Survivors
in Israel*, number 27, June 1984.
The surviving twins met at a
reunion at Kfar Maccabia, Ramat
Gan, Israel, on 29 February 1984.

18 Ernest Spiegel's recollections, in
conversation with the author,
Jerusalem.

19 Agnes Zsolt, Budapest 1947: Dr Judah Marton, *The Diary of Eva Heyman*, Jerusalem 1974, page 20.

20 Letter from Joan Campion to the *Jerusalem Post*, 8 August 1979.

21 'Transport Ep', 9 October 1944: Lederer, *Ghetto Theresienstadt*, *op. cit.*, page 238.

22 'Transport Et', 23 October 1944: *ibid.*, page 241.

23 'Transport Ev', 28 October 1944: *ibid.*, page 242.

24 Czech, 'Kalendarium', *op. cit.*, entry for 28 October 1944.

25 *Ibid.*, entry for 30 October 1944.

26 Notes of the unknown author: Bezwinska and Czech, *Amidst a Nightmare of Crime*, *op. cit.*, page 120.

27 Recollection of Maria Rebhun, 12 January 1965: Oral History Program, Claremont Graduate School, Claremont, California, Maria Rebhun was born in Warsaw in 1919.

28 Testimony of Mordechai Ansbacher: Eichmann Trial, 12 May 1961, session 38. Ansbacher was born in Wurzburg on 11 January 1927.

29 Testimony of Gedalia Ben Zvi: Eichmann Trial, 8 June 1961, session 71.

30 Testimony of Icchak Sohnenson (born in Vilna on 7 January 1931), testimony taken on 2 February 1965: Yad Vashem archive, 03/2743.

31 'Letter from the town of Biala Podlaska', 30 October 1944: *Bulletin*, April 1945.

32 Krakowski, *The War of the Doomed*, *op. cit.*, page 291.

33 'The Seven from Promyka Street', a reminiscence of Dr Stanislaw Switala: *Biuletyn*, *op. cit.*, numbers 65–66, Warsaw 1968, pages 207–8.

34 Czech, *op. cit.*, entry for 3 November 1944.

35 Letter to the author.

36 Manuscript of the unknown author: Bezwinska and Czech, *op. cit.*, pages 121–2.

37 Chaim Herman, letter of 6 November 1944: *ibid.*, page 190, and note II. Herman had been brought to Birkenau from Paris on 4 March 1943. He had been born in Warsaw on 3 May 1901. His camp number was 106113. The letter was discovered in a bottle, hidden under the human ash near one of the crematoria, in February 1946.

38 Testimony of Louise S. from Cluj: *Bulletin*, London, *op. cit.*, November 1945.

39 Bar-Adon, *op. cit.*

40 *Bulletin*, London, *op. cit.*, April 1945.

41 Testimony of Aviva Fleischmann: Eichmann Trial, 1 June 1961, session 61.

42 Braham, *op. cit.*, volume 2, page 1129.

43 *Ibid.*, page 840.

44 Testimony of Arie Breslauer: Eichmann Trial, 1 June 1961, session 61.

45 Protocol of a meeting held on 22 November 1944: Chaim Barlas papers.

46 Testimony of Arie Breslauer: Eichmann Trial, 1 June 1961, session 61.

47 Braham, *op. cit.*, volume 2, page 870.

48 *Ibid.*, pages 870–71 and 985.

49 Shalom Lindenbaum recollections, in conversation with the author.

50 Testimony of Alfred Oppenheimer: Eichmann Trial, 7 June 1961, session 68.

51 Hugo Gryn, 'Thought for the Day', BBC broadcast, London, 18 May 1972 (pre-recorded 11 May 1972).

52 Reska Weiss, *Journey Through Hell*, London 1961, pages 188–9.

53 Testimony of Dr Adolf Berman: Eichmann Trial, 3 May 1961, session 26. A young child's shoe is now in a special display case, as the final exhibit in the holocaust

exhibition at Yad Vashem, in Jerusalem.

40. THE DEATH MARCHES

1 *The Diary of Anne Frank, op. cit.*, Epilogue, by Storm Jameson, pages 223–4.
2 Braham, *The Politics of Genocide, op. cit.*, volume 2, page 870.
3 *Ibid.*, page 883.
4 *Ibid.*, page 872.
5 *Ibid.*, pages 873–4.
6 Goldstein, *The Bunker, op. cit.*, page 257.
7 *Ibid.*
8 Living today in Czestochowa, Poland.
9 Borzykowski, *Between Tumbling Walls, op. cit.*, pages 224–5.
10 Meed, *On Both Sides of the Wall, op. cit.*, page 274.
11 Lubetkin, *In the Days of Destruction and Revolt, op. cit.*, page 274.
12 Lederer, *Ghetto Theresienstadt, op. cit.*, page 227.
13 'Torun, Grudziacka Street': *Scenes of Fighting and Martyrdom Guide, op. cit.*, page 96.
14 Testimony of Mordechai Zurawski: Eichmann Trial, 5 June 1961, session 65.
15 Testimony of Shimon Srebnik: Eichmann Trial, 6 June 1961, session 66.
16 Czech, 'Kalendarium', *op. cit.*, entry for 17 January 1945.
17 Testimony of Israel Gutman: Eichmann Trial, 2 June 1961, session 63.
18 Testimony of Israel Gutman: Eichmann Trial, 2 June 1961, session 63.
19 'Slawiecice' (Ehrenforst), 'Woods between Blachownia (Blechhammer) and Slawiecice': *Scenes of Fighting and Martyrdom Guide, op. cit.*, page 286.
20 Testimony of Dr Alfred Oppenheimer: Eichmann Trial, 7 June 1961, session 68.
21 'Miedzna', 'Leszczyny', 'Lyski', 'Rybnik': *Scenes of Fighting and Martyrdom Guide, op. cit.*, pages 171, 173 and 174.
22 Archive of the Centre de Documentation Juive Contemporaine, Paris.
23 Document T/1329: Eichmann Trial, 9 June 1961, session 72.
24 Lederer, *op. cit.*, page 235.
25 Testimony of Yehuda Bakon, Eichmann Trial, 7 June 1961, session 68.
26 Lederer, *op. cit.*, page 240.
27 Testimony of Louise S. from Cluj, *Bulletin*, London, *op. cit.*, November 1945.
28 A survivor, in conversation with the author, January 1981.
29 Testimony of Dr Aharon Beilin: Eichmann Trial, 7 June 1961, session 69.
30 Testimony of Raizl Kibel: Yad Vashem archive, 03/882.
31 Testimony of Leilah Svirsky-Holtzman, Tel Aviv, 7 September 1967: Yad Vashem archive.
32 Dr Robert Collis, *Straight On*, London 1947; H. D. Leuner, *When Compassion was a Crime, op. cit.*, pages 93–4.
33 Testimony of Jakub Lichterman: in conversation with the author, Cape Town.
34 Information based upon the official Bill of Lading (Yad Vashem archives, 0-1/164), and provided by Dr J. Kermisz, Director of Archives, Yad Vashem: letter of 19 October 1977.
35 Schindler files, Yad Vashem archive.
36 Information provided by Judge Moshe Bejski.
37 Don Levin diary, 17 January 1945: Don Levin papers.
38 For Levin's journeyings, see Gilbert, *Atlas of the Holocaust, op. cit.*, map 313, page 240.
39 *The Diary of Anne Frank*, Epilogue, *op. cit.*, page 223.
40 Moshe Sandberg, *My Longest Year, op. cit.*, page 75.

41 Testimony of Celina Manielewicz, Jerusalem, 7 November 1958: Yad Vashem archive, 03/1108. Celina Manielewicz was born in the Polish town of Ozorkow, near Lodz, on 21 July 1921.

42 Ernest Spiegel, in conversation with the author, Jerusalem.

43 'From a letter from Rokitno': Bulletin, London, op. cit.

44 Datner papers: consulted by the author in Warsaw, 14 August 1980.

45 Testimony of Ester Epsztejn: Yad Vashem archive, o-16/204.

46 'Extract from a letter from Lithuania', 18 February 1945: Bulletin, London, op. cit., April 1945.

41. THE 'TAINTED LUCK' OF SURVIVAL

1 Lederer, Ghetto Theresienstadt, op. cit., page 228 (tracing the fate of Theresienstadt Transport Dr of 15 December 1943).

2 Testimony of Gisela Teumann, Yad Vashem archive D-3/2737: Krakowski, 'The Death Marches in the Period of the Evacuation of the Camps': The Nazi Concentration Camps (Proceedings of the Fourth Yad Vashem International Historical Conference, January 1980), Jerusalem 1984, page 488.

3 Violette Fintz, conversation with the author, Cape Town.

4 François Wetterwald, Les morts inutiles, Paris 1946.

5 Lederer, op. cit., pages 229–30.

6 'Suffering of Kovno (Kaunas) Jewry', letter of 26 May 1945: Bulletin, London, op. cit., November 1945.

7 Letter of 26 May 1945, Bulletin, London, op. cit.

8 Sonia Reznik Rosenfeld, 'The Day of My Freedom': D. Wolpe (editor), She'erith Hapleta, Extermination and Survival, Johannesburg, April 1965, volume 1, number 1, page 19.

9 Testimony of Aliza Besser: Yad Vashem archive, o-3/3394; Krakowski, 'The Death Marches', op. cit., page 483.

10 See Gilbert, Atlas of the Holocaust, op. cit., maps 285 and 286, page 218.

11 Germaine Tillion, Ravensbrück, Garden City, New Jersey 1975, page 107.

12 Testimony of Meir Dvorjetzky (M. Dworzecki): Eichmann Trial, 4 May 1961, session 27.

13 Yitzhak Arad, 'Jewish Prisoner Uprisings in Treblinka and Sobibor': The Nazi Concentration Camps, Jerusalem 1984, page 398.

14 Lederer, op. cit., page 226 (tracing the fate of Theresienstadt Transport Cu of 1 February 1943).

15 Ya'acov Friedler, ' "Death March" Survivor Testifies': Jerusalem Post, 6 March 1980.

16 Lederer, op. cit., page 242 (tracing the fate of Theresienstadt Transport Et of 23 October 1944).

17 Alben W. Barkley, Atrocities and Other Conditions in Concentration Camps in Germany, Washington 1945; Hansard, 19 April 1945.

18 Leo Laufer recollections, op. cit.

19 Public Record Office, London: Premier papers, 4/100/11.

20 Fenelon, The Musicians of Auschwitz, op. cit., page 254.

21 'Johanngeorgenstadt–Theresienstadt': Death Marches (Marches de la mort), Routes and Distances, United Nations Relief and Rehabilitation Association, Central Tracing Bureau, 28 May 1946.

22 Bonnie Boxer, 'The High Holidays': Israel El Al, Tel Aviv, summer–autumn 1983, page 11. Israel Lau became Chief Rabbi of the Israeli coastal town of Netanya in 1979. His brother Naftali, as Naftali Lavie, was, in 1984, Israeli Consul-General in New York, and the editor of the memorial book for his birthplace, Piotrkow.

23 Remarks quoted in the Eichmann Trial, 7 July 1961, session 88.

24 Testimony of Menachem Weinryb, Yad Vashem archive o-3/3343: Krakowski, 'The Death Marches', *op. cit.*, page 484.

25 Jean Levin, letter to the author, 24 July 1983.

26 Lederer, *op. cit.*, page 172.

27 Recollections of Pershing G. Rolfe, Florrissant, Missouri, USA: Yad Vashem archive.

28 Josef Rosensaft, 'Our Belsen': *Belsen*, Tel Aviv 1957, page 25.

29 *Idem.*

30 W. R. F. Collis, 'Belsen Camp: a Preliminary Report': *British Medical Journal*, 9 June 1945, page 814.

31 Violette Fintz, conversation with the author, Cape Town.

32 G. I. A. Draper, recollection: *The Nazi Concentration Camps, op. cit.*, pages 348–9.

33 Fenelon, *op. cit.*, page 255.

34 Collis, *op. cit.*, page 814.

35 Peter Coombs, letter of 4 May 1945: I am grateful to Peter Coombs for letting me see, and use, this letter. Among the British soldiers who entered Belsen was a young Palestinian officer, Vivian Herzog, who in 1983 was elected President of the State of Israel.

36 Report of 12th US Army Group Investigation Teams, 25 May 1945: International Military Tribunal, Nuremberg, document PS-2222.

37 Nora Levin, *The Holocaust, op. cit.*, page 706.

38 International Committee of the Red Cross, *Documents relating to the work of the International Committee of the Red Cross for the benefit of civilian detainees in German Concentration Camps between 1939 and 1945*, Geneva 1965 (contains an eye-witness account of the evacuations from Ravensbrück and Sachsenhausen in April 1945).

39 Latour, *The Jewish Resistance in France, op. cit.*, pages 161–2.

40 Letter of 19 April 1945 (to Werner Senator): Central Zionist Archive, Jerusalem, 57/915.

41 *Jewish Chronicle*, 20 January 1981.

42 Dusan Sindik (editor), *Secanja Jevreja na Logor Jasenovac*, Belgrade 1972 (memoirs of Jews in Jasenovac camp).

43 Krakowski, 'The Death Marches', *op. cit.*, page 485 (based upon the researches of Professor Krzysztof Dunin-Wasowicz, published in Warsaw in 1966).

44 Germaine Tillion, *op. cit.*

45 *Liberated Jews Arrived in Sweden in 1945*, 2 volumes, Malmo 1946.

46 Sam Goldsmith, *Haboker*, Tel Aviv, May 1945 (translated by Sam Goldsmith).

47 Levi Shalit, *The Road from Dachau: 30 Years after the Liberation*, Johannesburg 1975, pages 22–3.

48 Testimony of Sarah Friedmann (born in Rachovo on 24 July 1923), given in Jerusalem on 18 August 1959: Yad Vashem archives, 03/1403.

49 Testimony of Dr Aharon Hoter-Yishai: Eichmann Trial, 12 June 1961, session 73.

50 Recollections of Maria Rebhun (born in 1919): Claremont Oral History Program, California.

51 Pisar, *Of Blood and Hope, op. cit.*, pages 93–4.

52 Sandberg, *My Longest Year, op. cit.*, pages 113–14.

53 Bierman, *Odyssey 1940, op. cit.*, page 228.

54 Harris, *Tyranny on Trial, op. cit.*, page 461.

55 Michael Etkind, ' "Youth" Remembered': *Journal of the '45 Aid Society*, no. 12, London, March 1985, page 7.

56 Affidavits by Pieter Langhort (8 January 1946) and Baron van Lamsweerde (18 March 1946): International Military Tribunal, Nuremberg, document D-924.

57 Ernst Schafer (editor), *Ravensbruck*, Berlin 1960.

58 *The Book of Alfred Kantor, op. cit.*, 1 May 1945, plate 119.

59 K. J. Ball-Kaduri, 'Berlin is "Purged" of Jews: the Jews in Berlin in 1943': *Yad Vashem Studies*, Jerusalem 1963, pages 271–316.

60 K. J. Ball-Kaduri, 'Berlin': *Encyclopaedia Judaica*, Jerusalem 1972, volume 4, columns 648–50.

61 Misha Lev, 'Almost a Legend': *Sovetish Geimland*, Moscow, January–February 1964, pages 78–93.

62 'Poles and *Cap Arcona*': *AJR Information*, London, January 1985, page 5.

63 Lederer, *op. cit.*, page 241.

64 Lena Berg recollections: Donat, *The Holocaust Kingdom, op. cit.*, page 316.

65 Le Chêne, *Mauthausen, op. cit.*

66 Brome, *The Way Back, op. cit.*, page 237.

67 Testimony of Yehuda Bakon: Eichmann Trial, 7 June 1961, session 68.

68 *Weg des Todesmarsches Mauthausen-Gunskirchen*: Yad Vashem archives.

69 Kalman Seigel, 'Havas, Geza, 1905–45': *Encyclopaedia Judaica*, Jerusalem 1972, volume 10, column 311.

70 Le Chêne, *op. cit.*

71 Recollections of Meir Pesker: *Bielsk Podliask* (memorial book), Tel Aviv 1975.

72 Nyiszli, *Auschwitz, op. cit.*

73 Bierman, *op. cit.*, pages 228–9.

74 Le Chêne, *op. cit.*

75 Baruch Yaron, 'Gelleri, Andor Endre, 1907–1945', *Encyclopaedia Judaica*, Jerusalem 1972, volume 7, column 366.

76 Recollections of Hugo Gryn, in conversation with the author, London, 20 May 1985.

77 *The Book of Alfred Kantor, op. cit.*, plate 120.

78 *Ibid.*, plates 122 and 123.

EPILOGUE

1 Yehuda Bauer, 'Jewish Survivors in DP Camps . . .': *The Nazi Concentration Camps, op. cit.*, pages 491–3.

2 'Nazi War Criminals: the Search and the Legal Process Continue', Institute of Jewish Affairs, *Research Report*, number 4, March 1983, page 3.

3 Israel Gutman, discussion in *The Nazi Concentration Camps, op. cit.*, page 521.

4 'Address Delivered by Dr Zalman Grinberg on the Occasion of a Liberation Celebration', Dachau, 27 May 1945.

5 Henry Slamovich, in conversation with the author, San Francisco.

6 Falstein, *The Martyrdom of Jewish Physicians in Poland, op. cit.*, page 352.

7 Testimony of Icchok Sznajder (born in Choroszcza in 1917), taken down by the Jewish Historical Commission, Bialystok, 30 October 1946, number 176/46: Yad Vashem archive, M 11/B, 244.

8 Lena Berg's recollections: Donat, *The Holocaust Kingdom, op. cit.*, page 317.

9 Ben Helfgott, manuscript: 'Welcome to Poland after the War', pages 2–5.

10 Testimony of Rachel Hirsch, recorded in Tel Aviv in January 1964: Yad Vashem archive, 03/2440.

11 Letter of 4 August 1945: Yad Vashem archive, 03/743. Lewi had been deported to Birkenau on 15 August 1942, from Belgium.

12 Testimony of Shmuel Lerer, Archives of the YIVO Institute for Jewish Research, New York, Testimony No. 343: Trunk, *Judenrat, op. cit.*, page 474.

13 *Poland: The Communities of Lodz and its Region, op. cit.*, entry for 'Uniejow', pages 46–7.

14 *Ibid.*, entry for 'Boleslawiec', pages 60–1.

15 Rachel Auerbach, *op. cit.*, page 66.

16 Zerah Warhaftig: in conversation with the author, Jerusalem.

17 *Manchester Guardian*, 1 February 1946.

18 Lucjan Dobroszycki, 'Restoring Jewish Life in Post-War Poland', *Soviet-Jewish Affairs*, volume 3, number 2, London 1973.

19 Archives of the Jewish Historical Institute, Warsaw.

20 Foreign Office papers, 371/57689: Martin Gilbert, *Exile and Return: the Emergence of Jewish Statehood*, London 1978, pages 281–2.

21 Tenenbaum, *Underground*, *op. cit.*, pages 469–70.

22 Falstein, *op. cit.*

23 Biala Podlaska Memorial Book, Tel Aviv 1961.

24 Kermish, *The Destruction of the Jewish Community of Piotrkow*, *op. cit.*, column 46.

25 Dobroszycki, *op. cit.*

26 *Opinia*, Warsaw and Lodz, 25 July 1946.

27 Czech, 'Kalendarium', *op. cit.*, entry for 2 August 1944.

28 On 14 June 1947 an American Jewish Joint Distribution Committee Report listed 88,735 Jews living in 158 towns. The Jewish community in Lodz was 13,860, followed by Wroclaw (9,102) and Dzierzoniow (6,750) in Silesia, Cracow (5,908) and Warsaw (4,973). Lublin, with 40,000 pre-war, had 774, and Bialystok, also with 40,000 pre-war, 586: American Jewish Joint Distribution Committee archive, Jerusalem, report by William Bein.

29 Sakowska, *Archiwum Ringelbluma*, *op. cit.*, page 19.

30 Letter 24 March 1947: American Jewish Joint Distribution Committee archives, Jerusalem, C-61.020.

31 Babi Yar memorial volume, *op. cit.*

32 Jules R. Lippert, 'The Return: Riga 1976': *Friday Forum*, Delaware 1977.

33 Jack Young (Jona Speigel), typescript, *Lost and Waiting to be Found*; and conversation with the author, London, 30 May 1984.

34 Letter of February 1946: Jack Lennard papers, *op. cit.*

35 Eric Lucas, *'Die Herrschaft': Geschichte einer jüdischen Grossfamilie in Kreis Aachen von der Mitte des 19 Jahrhunderts bis zum 2 Weltkrieg*, Aachen 1980 (translation from the English manuscript, by Eric Lucas).

36 Wdowinski, *And We Are Not Saved*, *op. cit.*, page 123.

37 Cordelia Edvardson, 'Am Yisrael Hai' ('The People of Israel Lives'): *Jerusalem Post*, 29 January 1984.

38 Testimony of Dr Aharon Beilin: Eichmann Trial, 7 June 1961, session 69.

39 Testimony of Yehuda Bakon: Eichmann Trial, 7 June 1961, session 68.

40 Vitka Kempner, in conversation with the author, Jerusalem.

41 Katznelson, 'Song of the Murdered Jewish People', *op. cit.*

42 Lederer, *Ghetto Theresienstadt*, *op. cit.*, page vii.

43 Recollections of Hugo Gryn, in conversation with Rex Bloomstein, London, 16 July 1981; first shown on the BBC television documentary, *Auschwitz and the Allies* (producer: Rex Bloomstein), 16 September 1982.

44 Reder, 'Belzec', *op. cit.*

45 Lubetkin, *In the Days of Destruction and Revolt*, *op. cit.*

46 Information provided by Matilda Bandet's brother, Baruch Bandet, in conversation with the author, Lod airport.

47 Ringelblum notes, 17 June 1942: see page 368 of this volume.

INDEX

compiled by the author

Emmerich, SS Sergeant: wounded, 621

Endelman, Leon: commits suicide (1942), 389

Endlösung (Final Solution): 'doubtless imminent' (20 May 1941), 152

Epaux, Annette: on the way to death (1943), 533

Epstein (a baker): 'terrified', 324

Epstein, Dr Bernard: killed with his wife and two sons (1943), 552

Epsztejn, Esther: recalls deaths from weakness, after liberation, 783

Erler, SS Corporal: killed (1944), 746

Esperanto: fate of children of inventor of, 99

Essen: 67, 284

Essentuki: Jews of, killed (1942), 462

Esterwegen concentration camp: established (1933), 36

Estonia: 155; anti-Jewish decree in (1941), 182; 'without Jews' (1942), 281; a deportation to, from Berlin (1942), 322; Jews deported to a camp in (1942), from Vilna and Kovno, 593–4; deportations from (1944), 722; survivors from the labour camps in, escape in the Black Forest (1945), 788

Eszenbaum, Israel: executed (1941), 241–2, 852 n.4

'Eternal Jew, The': exhibition, 55

'Eternal Jew, The': an anti-Semitic film (1940), 134

Ethnic Germans: 20–21; in Lodz (1941), 141–2; during a deportation, 142; and the German invasion of Russia, 154; at Chelmno (1942), 253; a Jew mistaken for, 278; and the Jews of Odessa, 289; at Belzec, 304; in Piotrkow, 509; a Jew helped by, 776; at Mauthausen, 808

Etkind, Michael: and 'the courage to commit suicide', 323; at Buchenwald, 728; and the news of Hitler's death, 804–5

Eukodal: death of the discoverer of, 346

Euppen, SS Captain Theo: 'a sadist', 234

Evian Conference (1938): 64–5

Fach, Ernestyna: shot (1941), 178

Fach, Dr Klara: shot (1941), 178

Fahn, Arnold: glimpses his family as they are deported, 710

Fahn, Regina: deported from Rhodes, 707; 'It happened so quickly', 724

Fahn, Rudolf: deported from Rhodes (1944), 707; killed at Mauthausen (1945), 803

Fahn, Shani (Alexander): glimpses his grandfather, 710; 'swallowed up in the crowd', 724

Fahn, Sidney: deported from Rhodes, 707; passes through his home town, 710; reaches Auschwitz, 724; and the death of his wife and son, 724–5; survives, 803; liberated, 809

Fain, Dr: hanged (1941), 188

Fajgenblat, Dr: dies of wounds (1944), 717

Falenica: Jewish children shot in (1942), 430

Falesti: deportation from (1941), 161

Family camps: discovered (near Brest-Litovsk), 481; established (north-west of Lublin), 485; finds a protector, 504; bombardment of, 573; defence of (in White Russia), 609; near Minsk, 620

Farber, Yudi: joins in preparations for escape, 670

Farfel, Siomka: escapes, 383

Farkas, Dr: attempts to save Jews, 761

Feder, Aizik: deported to Auschwitz, 541; does not survive, 541

Feferman-Wasoff, Mania: recalls indignities (1939), 90; recalls impact of fall of France on Jews of Poland (1940), 122

Feigenbaum, Joseph: a survivor, 759

Feigman, Kalman: recalls an episode at Treblinka, 574

Feinberg, Nathan: cited, 39

Feinsilber, Alter: *see his alias* Jankowski, Stanislaw

Feiwiszys, Israel: killed (1943), 632

Fejgelis, Hersch: executed (1943), 586

Feldhendler, Leon: helps lead a revolt, 618; murdered after liberation, 789

Feldman, Nahum: a would-be partisan, 300

Fell, Dr Boleslaw: shot (1941), 178

Fenelon, Fania: recalls an execution at Auschwitz (1944), 697; recalls torments at Belsen (1945), 790–2; and the liberation of Belsen, 794

Fichtencwajg, Annette: her birth gives life, 586

Fickelburg, Dr: gassed (1942), 251

Filatov, Torpedo Operator I.M.: his 'courage' (1942), 296

Filipowicz, Wanda: helps Jews, 505

Filler, Rachel: escapes to the forest, with her son, 384

Final solution: 'doubtless imminent' (20 May 1941), 152; envisaged (31 July 1941), 176; 'approaching' (28 October 1941), 222; and a 'discussion' of in prospect, 245–6; and the Wannsee Conference (20 January 1942), 280–5; and an appeal to Eichmann, 290; and

928 · THE HOLOCAUST

Lederer, Zdenek: witnesses a 'census', 633–4; and the 'lot of the Jews', 825

Leer, Wim van: recalls *Kristallnacht* (1938), 69; recalls a friend of the Jews, 74–5

Leftkowitz, Abraham: shot (1939), 85

Legnica (Leignitz): a Jew murdered in, after liberation, 818

'Lehayim' ('to life'): password for a break-out, 788

Lehburger, Karl: murdered (1933), 38

Leibowicz, Abraham Leib: escapes, captured, shot (1943), 575

Leichert, Dr: and plans for revolt, 596

Leipzig: 67; *Kristallnacht* in (1938), 69, 70; a deception concerning (1944), 693, 713; Jews deported from a labour camp near, to their deaths, 728

Leitmeritz: Jews evacuated to (1945), 792, 810

Lejkin, Jakub: his 'zeal', 233; killed as an act of vengeance (1942), 485; the fate of one of his assassins (1943), 523

Lemberg, Dr Jakub: shot (1942), 299

Lenczycki (from Uniejow): killed, together with his son (1942), 382

Leningrad: a Jew born in, deported from Paris to Auschwitz, 376

Lenino: mass murder at (1942), 424

Lentz (a 'transport man'): at Chelmno, 770

Lerner, Alexander: sends his daughters to safety, 199; not allowed to go to Israel (since 1971), 848 n.48

Lerner, Ingar: killed (1941), 199

Lerner, Judith: sends her daughters to safety, 199

Lerner, Sonia: allowed to leave Russia for Israel (1972), 848 n.48

Lerner, Victoria: killed (1941), 199

Leros: Jew deportees reach, 708

Lesek, Moshe: at Chelmno, 264, 265, 266, 269, 271

Lesko: Jews from, at Sanok camp, 507

Leszczyny: Jews murdered at (1945), 773

Leszno Street (Warsaw): starvation on, 137; a smuggler on, 144–5; three Jews killed on, 324

Levi, Genia: deported (1944), 666

Levin, Abraham: records events in Warsaw and outside it, 362–3

Levin, Dov: sets off for Palestine (1945), 777

Levin, Moshe: helps escapees, 646

Levin, Sara: helps resistance, 229

Levinbok, Dr: 'Nor are we guilty, although we are Jews', 625

Levinstein, Dr Oswald: death of his son (1942); his own suicide (1942), 293

Levinstein, Paul: murdered (1942), 292

Leviticus, Book of: its commandments broken, 829

Lewenbaum, Avraham: liberated, 711

Lewental, Salmen (Zalmen): an eye-witness of mass murder, 515–16, 649–53; an eye-witness of the revolt at Auschwitz-Birkenau, 744–6; an eye-witness of the fate of six hundred Jewish boys, 749–50; his notes discovered (1962), 820

Lewi, Dow: normal people 'cannot possibly understand', 816

Lewi, Israel: executed (1939), 85

Lewi, Liebe: shot (1939), 85

Lewin, Rabbi Aaron: murdered (1941), 164

Lewin, Yechezkel: seeks help, 163; murdered (1941), 164

Lewkowicz, Chana: shot (1941), 147

Lewkowicz, Pela: and the Palmnicken massacre, 779–80

Lezajsk: Jews driven from (1939), 93

Liberman, David: his act of defiance, 475

Liberty Barricade (Warsaw): gives details of gassings at Chelmno, 355

Lichtenberg, Bernhard: his prayers for the Jews, and his death (1941), 216

Lichtenstein: deportation of Jews of, 483

Lichtenstein, Awigdor: shot (1941), 147

Lichtensztajn, Bluma: commits suicide (1941), 138

Lichtensztajn, Izrael: hides archives (1942), 400–1

Lichtheim, Richard: reports on Jewish fate (1940), 134–5; forecasts end of the war 'this year' (1942), 353; reports on the German intention to 'kill off' the deportees, 449–50

Lichtmann, Eda: and the killing of Jews in Pilica (1939), 87–8; and the killing of Jews in Mielec (1942), 350

Lichterman, Jakub: escapes from a death march (1945), 776–7

Lichtman, Itzhak: recalls an incident at Sobibor (1942), 344

Lida: an act of defiance at (1941), 184; mass murder near (1941), 242–3; further mass murder near (1942), 333–6; mass murder at (1942), 403; Jewish partisans in region of, 407, 620

Lidice: massacre at (1942), 363

Lidzbarski brothers and sisters: in hiding, 566

Lieberose: a death march from, 763–4

Liebeskind, Adolf: killed during an act of resistance (1942), 505–6

Liebeskind, Benjamin: his daughter shot (1942), 509

Liebeskind, Miriam: shot (1943), 505

Liebeskind, Rivka: 'to save at least someone to relate our story', 506; recalls a Sabbath in Birkenau, 521

Sletten, Inge: helps Jews to safety, 499
Slobodka (Kovno): ghetto established in (1941), 155; survivors from, liberated at Dachau (1945), 799
Slobodka (Odessa): deportations from ghetto in (1942), 288–9
Slonim: mass murder at (1941), 235, 851 n.63; mass murder at (1942), 403; an alarming message from, 489; revenge for murder at, 534–5; a rabbi from, celebrates the Sabbath in a labour camp, 625
Slovakia: Jews attacked in (1938), 74; declares independence (1939), 78; 'Jew-baiting' in (1939), 82; deportations from (1940), 112; fate of Poles seeking to escape to (1940), 122; Jewish forced labourers from (1940), 123; Jews seek safety through (1940–1), 133–4, 149; Jews of, listed (1942), 281; the 'key questions . . . already resolved', 282; and the 'final solution', 284; deportations to Auschwitz from, 309, 315, 548; Jews from, at Auschwitz, 340; recollections of Jews deported to Auschwitz from, 376, 378, 378–9; renewed deportations to Auschwitz from, 467; Jews from, deported from Lukow to Auschwitz, 475; Jews from, in a Warsaw labour camp, 595; a Jewess from, warns of an imminent massacre in Birkenau, 658; trains from Hungary pass through, 674; Jews in uprising in, 726–7, 730; Jews deported to Auschwitz from (August 1944), 727; the fate of Jews in a town in, 730–1; death of a leading Zionist from, 756; a Jew from, killed at Mauthausen, 803
Slutsk: a protest about 'horror' in (1941), 222
Smallbones, R. T.: a witness (1938), 61–2
Smorgon (Smorgonie): deportation of Jews from, 554
Sobibor: Jewish prisoners-of-war executed near (1940), 111; a death camp set up near (1942), 286, 294, 310, 311, 312; the first gassings at (April 1942), 324–7; further deportations to, 336–7, 340–4, 351, 359–60, 484; and 'Operation Reinhard', 363; a new rail link planned for, 471; death toll in, 502; Jewish orphans gassed in, 531; Himmler visits, 546; a deportation from Paris to, 546; resistance of Jews reaching, 575; a deportation to, witnessed, 577–8; Jews from Minsk deported to, 611; Day of Atonement at (1943), 618; revolt at, 618–19; death of a leader of the revolt in, after liberation, 789; a survivor of the

revolt in, enters Berlin (May 1945), 806
Socha, Leopold: helps Jews, 587–8; his death, 714
Socha, Magdalena: on liberation day, 714
Sokolovo: Jews in battle of (March 1943), 548
Sokolow Podlaski: railwaymen from, at Treblinka, 395; a train to, 407
Sokolskaya, Bertha: recalls the Bialystok ghetto revolt, 599–600; recalls a deportation from Bialystok, 603–4; deported to Auschwitz, 712
Sokolskaya, Eva: her fate unknown, 712
Sokolskaya, Menachem: his fate unknown, 712
Sokolskaya, Ovsey: killed (1941), 712
Sokoly: murder of Jews at, after liberation (1945), 782–3
Sol river: Jews seek to escape to, 746
Sol (Soly): deportation of Jews from, 554
Solgau: liberated Jews enter, 788
Solomon, Yeshieh: killed by Poles (1944), 717
Sompolno: sewing machines of Jews deported from 318–19
Sonderkommando ('Special Commando'): set up from among Jewish deportees, at Belzec, 308–9, 414, 416–17, 501; at Sobibor (where it was known as the 'Corpse Commando'), 325, 605; at Auschwitz-Birkenau, 340, 488, 515–16, 518, 546, 632–3, 636–7, 649–53, 656–7, 658, 667–8, 675, 678, 720, 721, 728, 730, 733; at Treblinka, 431, 456, 596; revolt of, at Birkenau (1944), 743–50; fate of the remnant of, at Birkenau, 760; at Chelmno, 7170–1; discovery of the hidden manuscripts of, 820, 886 n.63; 'I will tell the world', 865
Soneson, Icchak: survives, 336; his mother and brother killed after liberation, 759
Soneson, Moshe: an eye-witness to mass murder, 336
Sonia (in Vilna): an eye-witness to mass murder at Ponary (1941), 193–4
Sonnenshein, Moshe: 'There is no God', 649
Sonneberg: Jews near, learn of Hitler's death, 804–5
Sonnonfeld, Dr Kurt: commits suicide (1938), 59
Sorbonne, the: murder of former students of, 474, 605
Sosnkowski, Aleksander: killed, with his family, for hiding Jews (1944), 654–5
Sosnowiec: a public execution in (1941), 146; Jews resettled in, 148; and Moses

The Sacred Chain

A History of the Jews

Norman Cantor

'I am not a Jew but Jew-ish. Professor Cantor's history is written for people like me, and for general students of the same mysterious topic . . . this is a serious work which will introduce any literate reader to the fascinating way in which Jewry occupies a position midway between religion and philosophy, and between history and myth.'
CHRISTOPHER HITCHENS, *Mail on Sunday*

Norman Cantor's extraordinary and highly controversial book focuses on the creation and perpetuation of a unique Jewish identity through three thousand years of dramatic, often catastrophic, change. Aimed squarely at the secular reader, it addresses itself vigorously to the defining moments of Jewish history – from the authenticity of the Old Testament stories to how and why Jews have played such a prominent role in every major Western intellectual movement, the formation of the state of Israel and the central question of the future of the Jewish people.

'Courageous . . . Cantor has insights which surprise, shock or even delight . . . All this makes for stimulating reading and there are very few pages of Cantor's long book which did not intrigue, enlighten or infuriate me.'
PAUL JOHNSON, *Sunday Telegraph*

'Fierce and readable history.'   JULIA NEUBERGER, *Evening Standard*

'Energetic and provocative – an opinionated history but a stimulating one.'
GERALD JACOBS, *Independent on Sunday*

'Nearly always an absorbing read . . . nobody could accuse Norman Cantor of telling Jews only what they want to hear.'   *Economist*

ISBN 0 00 686345 0

FontanaPress
An Imprint of HarperCollins*Publishers*